The SAGE Handbook of
Qualitative Data Analysis

International Advisory Editorial Board

Marcus Banks, Professor of Visual Anthropology, University of Oxford, United Kingdom

Rosaline S. Barbour, Professor in Health & Social Care, The Open University, United Kingdom

Marie Buscatto, Professor of Sociology at University of Paris (Sorbonne), France

Kathy Charmaz, Professor of Sociology and Director of the Faculty Writing Program at Sonoma State University, United States

Jan K. Coetzee, Senior Professor of Sociology at the University of the Free State, Bloemfontein, South Africa

Amanda Coffey, Professor at Cardiff School of Social Sciences, Cardiff University, United Kingdom

John Creswell, Professor of Educational Psychology at Teachers College, University of Nebraska–Lincoln, United States

Norman Denzin, Professor of Sociology at University of Illinois, Urbana–Champaign, United States

Thomas S. Eberle, Professor of Sociology at University of St Gallen, Switzerland

Nigel Fielding, Professor of Sociology at the University of Surrey, United Kingdom

Peter Freebody, Professor at the Faculty of Education and Social Work, University of Sydney, Australia

Giampietro Gobo, Professor of Sociology at Milan University, Italy

Hubert Knoblauch, Professor of Sociology at Technical University Berlin, Germany

Sonia Livingstone, Professor of Media Research, London School of Economics and Political Science, United Kingdom

Joseph Maxwell, Professor in the Graduate School of Education at George Mason University, United States

Donna Mertens, Professor in the Department of Education at Gallaudet University, United States

Janice Morse, Professor at the College of Nursing, Salt Lake City, United States

Anssi Peräkylä, Professor of Sociology at University of Helsinki, Finland

Jin Sun, Professor at the Institute for International & Comparative Education, Beijing Normal University, China

Wivian Weller, Professor at Universidade de Brasília – UnB, Faculdade de Educação, Brazil

Endorsements

Uwe Flick's handbook of qualitative data analysis is an illuminating new resource for qualitative and mixed methods scholars. What these authors do in exploring how we think when we do analysis will be invaluable for practicing researchers, novices and experienced hands alike. These essays will also provoke further investigation, discussion, and theorizing about what was once the most neglected area of qualitative research practice. The handbook represents the breadth and depth of what we do when we make sense of information we have gathered about our world. It is an exciting contribution to the methodological literature, and I congratulate Dr. Flick and his colleagues for their achievement here. *Judith Preissle, Professor Emeritus, University of Georgia*

This is an essential resource for the rapidly expanding ranks of researchers employing qualitative practices of inquiry. It represents the most sophisticated, broad-ranging, and multi-vocal array of contributions to the analysis of qualitative data yet available. There are now many texts on qualitative methods, but this is one is unique. It covers ground largely untouched by others, and with responsible attention to multiple points of view. My enthusiastic congratulations to the editor and authors. *Kenneth J. Gergen, President, The Taos Institute*

Qualitative data analysis frequently appears to be a mysterious process to students and often experienced researchers alike. This excellent handbook removes the mystery and unveils invaluable insights into all facets of this crucial phase of the research process. I can't think of a single aspect of analysis that is left without coverage, so that it will become a 'must read' for qualitative researchers for many years to come. Uwe Flick is to be congratulated for putting together such an exceptional collection. *Alan Bryman, School of Management, University of Leicester*

This is a comprehensive account of a large variety of approaches to qualitative data analysis, written by leading international experts in the relevant methodological fields. For those who are confused about different analytic methods in qualitative research this book will clarify overlaps and differences, inform readers about the key features of each approach and will in general be an important resource for students and practitioners of social research. *Clive Seale, Professor of Sociology, Brunel University*

1

The SAGE Handbook of Qualitative Data Analysis

Uwe Flick

Los Angeles | London | New Delhi
Singapore | Washington DC

Los Angeles | London | New Delhi
Singapore | Washington DC

SAGE Publications Ltd
1 Oliver's Yard
55 City Road
London EC1Y 1SP

SAGE Publications Inc.
2455 Teller Road
Thousand Oaks, California 91320

SAGE Publications India Pvt Ltd
B 1/I 1 Mohan Cooperative Industrial Area
Mathura Road
New Delhi 110 044

SAGE Publications Asia-Pacific Pte Ltd
3 Church Street
#10-04 Samsung Hub
Singapore 049483

Editor: Katie Metzler
Production editor: Ian Antcliff
Copyeditor: Neville Hankins
Proofreader: Anna Gilding
Indexer: Avril Ehrlich
Marketing manager: Ben Griffin-Sherwood
Cover design: Wendy Scott
Typeset by: C&M Digitals (P) Ltd, Chennai, India
Printed in Great Britain by Henry Ling Limited at
The Dorset Press, Dorchester, DT1 1HD
Printed on paper from sustainable resources

Editorial arrangement © Uwe Flick 2014
Parts I, II, III, IV and V introductions © Uwe Flick 2014
Chapter 1 © Uwe Flick 2014
Chapter 2 © Joseph A. Maxwell and Margaret Chmiel 2014
Chapter 3 © Jaber F. Gubrium and James A. Holstein 2014
Chapter 4 © Tim Rapley
Chapter 5 © Sabine Kowal and Daniel C. O'Connell 2014
Chapter 6 © Flora Cornish, Alex Gillespie and Tania Zittoun 2014
Chapter 7 © Monika Palmberger and Andre Gingrich 2014
Chapter 8 © Tim May and Beth Perry
Chapter 9 © Jo Reichertz 2014
Chapter 10 © Carla Willig 2014
Chapter 11 © Robert Thornberg and Kathy Charmaz 2014
Chapter 12 © Margrit Schreier 2014
Chapter 13 © Thomas S. Eberle 2014
Chapter 14 © Cigdem Esin, Mastoureh Fathi and Corinne Squire 2014
Chapter 15 © Ralf Bohnsack 2014
Chapter 16 © Andreas Wernet 2014
Chapter 17 © Rainer Winter 2014
Chapter 18 © Robert V. Kozinets, Pierre-Yann Dolbec and Amanda Earley 2014
Chapter 19 © Graham R. Gibbs 2014
Chapter 20 © Kathryn Roulston 2014
Chapter 21 © Rosaline S. Barbour 2014
Chapter 22 © Merran Toerien 2014
Chapter 23 © Carla Willig 2014
Chapter 24 © Amir B. Marvasti 2014
Chapter 25 © Amanda Coffey 2014
Chapter 26 © Darrin Hodgetts and Kerry Chamberlain 2014
Chapter 27 © Marcus Banks 2014
Chapter 28 © Lothar Mikos 2014
Chapter 29 © Christoph Maeder 2014
Chapter 30 © Hubert Knoblauch, René Tuma and Bernt Schnettler 2014
Chapter 31 © Winfried Marotzki, Jens Holze and Dan Verständig 2014
Chapter 32 © David Wästerfors, Malin Åkerström and Katarina Jacobsson 2014
Chapter 33 © Ladislav Timulak 2014
Chapter 34 © Rosaline S. Barbour 2014
Chapter 35 © Donna M. Mertens 2014
Chapter 36 © Janice M. Morse and Lory J. Maddox 2014
Chapter 37 © Joseph A. Maxwell and Margaret Chmiel 2014
Chapter 38 © Udo Kelle 2014
Chapter 39 © Norman K. Denzin 2014
Chapter 40 © Michael Murray 2014

Apart from any fair dealing for the purposes of research or private study, or criticism or review, as permitted under the Copyright, Designs and Patents Act, 1988, this publication may be reproduced, stored or transmitted in any form, or by any means, only with the prior permission in writing of the publishers, or in the case of reprographic reproduction, in accordance with the terms of licences issued by the Copyright Licensing Agency. Enquiries concerning reproduction outside those terms should be sent to the publishers.

Library of Congress Control Number: 2013934589

British Library Cataloguing in Publication data

A catalogue record for this book is available from the British Library

ISBN 978-1-4462-0898-4

Contents

List of Tables and Figures — xi
About the Editor — xii
Notes on Contributors — xiii
Acknowledgements — xxiv

PART I: MAPPING THE FIELD — 1

1 Mapping the Field — 3
  Uwe Flick

PART II: CONCEPTS, CONTEXTS, BASICS — 19

2 Notes Toward a Theory of Qualitative Data Analysis — 21
  Joseph A. Maxwell and Margaret Chmiel

3 Analytic Inspiration in Ethnographic Fieldwork — 35
  Jaber F. Gubrium and James A. Holstein

4 Sampling Strategies in Qualitative Research — 49
  Tim Rapley

5 Transcription as a Crucial Step of Data Analysis — 64
  Sabine Kowal and Daniel C. O'Connell

6 Collaborative Analysis of Qualitative Data — 79
  Flora Cornish, Alex Gillespie and Tania Zittoun

7 Qualitative Comparative Practices: Dimensions, Cases and Strategies — 94
  Monika Palmberger and Andre Gingrich

8 Reflexivity and the Practice of Qualitative Research — 109
  Tim May and Beth Perry

9 Induction, Deduction, Abduction — 123
  Jo Reichertz

10 Interpretation and Analysis — 136
   Carla Willig

PART III: ANALYTIC STRATEGIES — 151

11 Grounded Theory and Theoretical Coding — 153
    Robert Thornberg and Kathy Charmaz

12 Qualitative Content Analysis — 170
    Margrit Schreier

13 Phenomenology as a Research Method — 184
    Thomas S. Eberle

14 Narrative Analysis: The Constructionist Approach — 203
    Cigdem Esin, Mastoureh Fathi and Corinne Squire

15 Documentary Method — 217
    Ralf Bohnsack

16 Hermeneutics and Objective Hermeneutics — 234
    Andreas Wernet

17 Cultural Studies — 247
    Rainer Winter

18 Netnographic Analysis: Understanding Culture through Social Media Data — 262
    Robert V. Kozinets, Pierre-Yann Dolbec, and Amanda Earley

19 Using Software in Qualitative Analysis — 277
    Graham R. Gibbs

PART IV: TYPES OF DATA AND THEIR ANALYSIS — 295

20 Analysing Interviews — 297
    Kathryn Roulston

21 Analysing Focus Groups — 313
    Rosaline S. Barbour

22 Conversations and Conversation Analysis — 327
    Merran Toerien

23 Discourses and Discourse Analysis — 341
    Carla Willig

24	Analysing Observations *Amir B. Marvasti*	354
25	Analysing Documents *Amanda Coffey*	367
26	Analysing News Media *Darrin Hodgetts and Kerry Chamberlain*	380
27	Analysing Images *Marcus Banks*	394
28	Analysis of Film *Lothar Mikos*	409
29	Analysing Sounds *Christoph Maeder*	424
30	Video Analysis and Videography *Hubert Knoblauch, René Tuma and Bernt Schnettler*	435
31	Analysing Virtual Data *Winfried Marotzki, Jens Holze and Dan Verständig*	450

PART V: USING AND ASSESSING QUALITATIVE DATA ANALYSIS — 465

32	Reanalysis of Qualitative Data *David Wästerfors, Malin Åkerström and Katarina Jacobsson*	467
33	Qualitative Meta-analysis *Ladislav Timulak*	481
34	Quality of Data Analysis *Rosaline S. Barbour*	496
35	Ethical Use of Qualitative Data and Findings *Donna M. Mertens*	510
36	Analytic Integration in Qualitatively Driven (QUAL) Mixed and Multiple Methods Designs *Janice M. Morse and Lory J. Maddox*	524

37 Generalization in and from Qualitative Analysis   540
    Joseph A. Maxwell and Margaret Chmiel

38 Theorization from Data   554
    Udo Kelle

39 Writing and/as Analysis or Performing the World   569
    Norman K. Denzin

40 Implementation: Putting Analyses into Practice   585
    Michael Murray

Author Index   600
Subject Index   613

List of Tables and Figures

Table 1.1	Phases in the history of qualitative research	8
Table 6.1	Hall et al.'s (2005) iterative collaborative analysis process	85
Table 11.1	Initial coding	157
Table 11.2	Focused coding	158
Table 11.3	Examples of Glaser's coding families	160
Figure 13.1	Major perspectives of phenomenological sociology	199
Figure 15.1	Example of a typology	230
Figure 18.1	Search using search term "netnography"	271
Figure 18.2	Wikipedia.com entry on "netnography"	272
Figure 19.1	The number of refereed papers published using qualitative methods that used CAQDAS, 1983–2011	279
Figure 19.2	Document showing coding brackets in MAXQDA	284
Table 20.1	Transcription conventions drawn from conversation analysis	300
Table 26.1	Example of a media analysis grid	388
Table 26.2	Example of a homeless participant grid	388
Figure 27.1	No caption (Courtesy of Museum of Archaeology and Anthropology, University of Cambridge)	401
Figure 30.1	Audio-visual moves in auctioneer-audience interaction	441
Figure 30.2	Process of analysis (from Knoblauch and Tuma, 2011)	445
Figure 36.1	Hypothetical mixed methods project QUAL + *quan* + *quan* + *qual*. (QUAL grounded theory of *x*. Supplementary component: *quan* chart demographic data about population, *quan* psychological test, and *qual* focus groups adding data from the supplementary component)	530
Figure 36.2	Sequential qualitatively driven mixed methods design planned reflexively during the project (QUAL → *quan* or *qual*)	532
Figure 36.3	Simultaneous qualitatively driven mixed methods design (QUAL → *quan*)	533
Figure 36.4	Example of a complex mixed methods project	537
Figure 39.1	Two Interpretive Communities	580

About the Editor

Uwe Flick is Professor of Qualitative Research in Social Science and Education at the Free University of Berlin, Germany. He was trained as a psychologist and sociologist and received his PhD from the Free University of Berlin in 1988 and his Habilitation from the Technical University of Berlin in 1994. He has been Professor of Qualitative Research at Alice Salomon University of Applied Sciences in Berlin, Germany and at the University of Vienna, Austria, where he continues to work as Guest-Professor. Previously, he was Adjunct Professor at the Memorial University of Newfoundland in St. John's, Canada; a Lecturer in research methodology at the Free University of Berlin; a Reader and Assistant Professor in qualitative methods and evaluation at the Technical University of Berlin; and Associate Professor and Head of the Department of Medical Sociology at the Hannover Medical School. He has held visiting appointments at the London School of Economics, the Ecole des Hautes Etudes en Sciences Sociales in Paris, at Cambridge University (UK), Memorial University of St. John's (Canada), University of Lisbon (Portugal), Institute of Advanced Studies, Vienna (Austria) at the University of Padova (Italy), and at the School of Psychology at Massey University, Auckland (NZ). His main research interests are qualitative methods, social representations in the fields of individual and public health, homelessness and health, health and ageing, migration and health, and technological change in everyday life. He is author of *Introducing Research Methodology – A Beginner's Guide to Doing a Research Project* (London: Sage, 2011), *An Introduction to Qualitative Research*, 5th edition (London: Sage, 2014), *Designing Qualitative Research* (London: Sage, 2007) and *Managing Quality in Qualitative Research* (London: Sage, 2007). He is also editor or co-editor of *The SAGE Qualitative Research Kit* (London: Sage, 2007, 8 volumes), *A Companion to Qualitative Research* (London: Sage, 2004), *Psychology of the Social* (Cambridge: Cambridge University Press, 1998), *Quality of Life and Health: Concepts, Methods and Applications* (Berlin: Blackwell Science, 1995), *La perception quotidienne de la Santé et la Maladie: Théories subjectives et Représentations sociales* (Paris: L'Harmattan, 1993) and *Handbuch Qualitative Sozialforschung* (Munich: PVU, 1991). Most of his books have been translated into several languages throughout Asia, Latin America and Europe.

Notes on Contributors

Malin Åkerström is Professor of Sociology at Lund University in Sweden. Her research focuses on ethnographic studies of deviance. She has published several books, including *Betrayers and Betrayers* and *Crooks and Squares*, and articles such as 'Slaps, Punches, Pinches – But not Violence: Boundary Work in Nursing Homes for Elderly' (in *Symbolic Interaction*) and 'Doing Ambivalence: Embracing Policy Innovation – At Arm's Length' (in *Social Problems*), 'Balancing Contradictory Identities – Performing Masculinity in Victim Narratives' (with V. Burcar and D. Wästerfors in *Sociological Perspective*).

Marcus Banks trained as a social anthropologist at the University of Cambridge and studied documentary film at the UK National Film and Television School; he is currently Professor of Visual Anthropology at the University of Oxford. He has published widely on visual anthropology, ethnographic film, and visual methodologies in the social sciences, including *Visual Methods in Social Research* (2001) and *Using Visual Data in Qualitative Research* (2007). His last major research project was on the use of film in colonial India; he is currently commencing research on image use in forensic contexts.

Rosaline (Rose) Barbour has a particular interest in rigour in qualitative research and has published widely on this topic in a range of academic journals. She is currently Professor of Health Care at the Open University (UK). A medical sociologist, her research career has covered a wide variety of topics located at the intersection of the clinical and the social, for example HIV/AIDS; reproductive health and fertility; and psychosocial health and obesity. Reflecting her conviction that qualitative research is a craft skill, Rose has developed an innovative series of 'hands-on' qualitative methods workshops. She has been invited to present these workshops throughout the UK, in Sweden, Finland, Denmark, Switzerland, France, Austria, the United States and Canada. She co-edited (with Jenny Kitzinger) *Developing Focus Group Research: Politics, Theory and Practice* (Sage, 1999). Her most recent books, *Doing Focus Groups* (Sage, 2007–8, Book 4 of the Sage Qualitative Methods Kit) and *Introducing Qualitative Research: A Student Guide to the Craft of Doing Qualitative Research* (Sage, 2008; 2nd edition in preparation), bring together and share the expertise she has developed through running workshops for a variety of audiences over the past 20 years.

Ralf Bohnsack is a sociologist. After working as Assistant Professor in Sociology at the University of Erlangen-Nürnberg from 1977 and obtaining his Habilitation (Second Doctoral Degree) there in 1987, he has been Professor for Qualitative Methods at the Free University of Berlin since 1990 and, since 2001, Director of the Department of Qualitative Research on Human Development and Confidential Professor for the DFG (Deutsche Forschungsgemeinschaft – German Research Council) at the Free University, President of the ces (Centre for Qualitative Social Research and Evaluation) and from 2008 to 2012 elected member of the advisory committee (Fachkollegium) in Educational Science of the DFG. His main areas of research are: reconstructive social research; sociology of knowledge; analysis of talk, pictures, films and videos; qualitative evaluation research; and research on milieu, generation and human development. He is author of *Rekonstruktive*

Sozialforschung, 9th edition in preparation (UTB Publishers), and co-editor of *Qualitative Analysis and Documentary Method in International Educational Research* (Budrich Publishers) and of the book series Qualitative Sozialforschung.

Kerry Chamberlain is Professor of Social and Health Psychology at Massey University in Auckland, New Zealand. He is a critical health psychologist whose research interests focus broadly on health in everyday life, with a particular interest in projects that advance understandings and assistance to disadvantaged peoples. More specifically, his research interests include: media and health and the mediation of health issues in contemporary society; the meanings of medications and social practices in their use; food and health, and social practices around food and eating, dieting, and dietary supplementation; and everyday mundane illness and its embodiment. He utilizes a variety of qualitative methodologies in his research to examine the materiality and social practices of everyday life.

Kathy Charmaz is Professor of Sociology and Director of the Faculty Writing Program at Sonoma State University. She has written, co-authored or co-edited nine books including *Good Days, Bad Days: The Self in Chronic Illness and Time*, which received awards from the Pacific Sociological Association and the Society for the Study of Symbolic Interaction, and *Constructing Grounded Theory: A Practical Guide through Qualitative Analysis*, which received a Critics' Choice award from the American Educational Studies Association and has been translated into Chinese, Japanese, Korean, Polish and Portuguese. The expanded second edition of *Constructing Grounded Theory* and a four-volume co-edited set, *Grounded Theory and Situational Analysis,* with Adele Clarke are due to appear this year. Her recent multi-authored books are *Five Ways of Doing Qualitative Analysis* and *Developing Grounded Theory*. She offers intensive courses and presents professional development workshops on qualitative methods and writing for publication across the globe.

Margaret (Marjee) Chmiel is a doctoral candidate at George Mason University's College of Education and Human Development. She is interested in mixed methods approaches to studying science communication via new and emerging media technologies. With a background in physical sciences and an interest in science communication, she is interested in creating dialogues across research paradigms. Her dissertation research focuses on science education communication on user-generated video websites. She is currently the educational technology specialist for the Smithsonian Science Education Center at the Smithsonian Institution in Washington, DC.

Amanda Coffey is a Professor in the School of Social Sciences and Dean for Education and Students in the College of Arts, Humanities and Social Sciences, Cardiff University, UK. She has published widely on qualitative research methods and in the sociology of education. Her publications include *Making Sense of Qualitative Data* (Sage, with Paul Atkinson), *The Ethnographic Self* (Sage), *Education and Social Change* (Open University) and *Reconceptualising Social Policy* (Open University). She was elected an Academician of the Academy of Social Sciences in 2011.

Flora Cornish is a Lecturer in the Department of Methodology, London School of Economics and Political Science. She has particular interests in the critical and public significance of qualitative methods as means of creating better societies. She researches community mobilization as a means of improving public health, with increasing focus on the tensions and possibilities in the interface between global health organizations and local community action. She is Editor of the *Journal of Community & Applied Social Psychology*.

Norman K. Denzin is Distinguished Professor of Communications, College of Communications Scholar, and Research Professor of Communications, Sociology, and Humanities at the University of Illinois, Urbana–Champaign. He is the author of *The Qualitative Manifesto*; *Qualitative Inquiry Under Fire*; and *Interpretive Ethnography*; and co-editor (with Yvonna S. Lincoln) of four editions of the *Handbook of Qualitative Research*.

Pierre-Yann Dolbec is a Vanier Canada Graduate scholar completing his PhD in marketing at the Schulich School of Business, York University, Toronto. He holds an MSc in marketing from HEC Montreal. His research focuses on market system dynamics, looking at consumers' influence on the evolution of markets as well as on the dialectic between space and markets. His research also looks at consumers' accumulation of cultural and social capital. He has a virtual home at www.pydolbec.com.

Amanda Earley is a PhD candidate at the Schulich School of Business at York University in Toronto. Her work concerns the politics of marketing and consumer culture. She is particularly interested in how markets are constituted, and in turn constitute consumer subjects, and primarily conducts this work within the contexts of economic activism, food culture, social media, sustainable strategy, and art consumption. She is currently working on an ethnography of the original Occupy Wall Street encampment in New York City.

Thomas S. Eberle is Professor of Sociology and Co-director of the Research Institute of Sociology at the University of St Gallen, Switzerland. He served as President of the Swiss Sociological Association from 1998 to 2005 and as Vice-president of the European Sociological Association (2007–11). He was Chair of the ESA-Research Network 'Qualitative Methods' (2001–3) and of the ESA-RN 'Sociology of Culture' (2007–9) and still is a board member of both. His major research areas are sociology of culture and of communication, of knowledge and of organization, as well as interpretive sociology, methodology, phenomenological sociology and qualitative methods. In these areas, he published two books, edited nine and wrote more than 80 articles.

Cigdem Esin is a narrative researcher. Her research interests are in interconnections between individual stories and grand socio-political narratives in gendered contexts. She has been doing research on gender and employment, women's movements and organizations, and sexuality since the mid-1990s. She is a Lecturer and Research Fellow of the Centre for Narrative Research, University of East London. Her current research focuses on visual narratives and self-narratives of academic immigrants living in London.

Mastoureh Fathi is currently a Research Assistant in the Department of Psychosocial Studies, Birkbeck College, University of London, on a project called 'Mediated Humanitarian Knowledge: Audiences' responses and moral actions'. Her research interests include migrants' narratives, class and belonging stories, and women's social and political engagements in Iran. She was awarded her PhD, entitled 'Classed Pathways of Iranian Women Migrants', in 2011. Since then she has been writing on the publication of a series of papers on narratives of class and migration, classed identity, translation, narrative research, and the British public's involvement with NGOs on humanitarian causes.

Graham R Gibbs is a Reader in Social Research Methods at the University of Huddersfield, UK. His research interests include the use of software in qualitative data analysis and the use of technology in teaching and learning in higher education. He is the author of two books on qualitative data analysis and has led and participated in several funded projects related to the use of technology in the social sciences and their teaching. He is currently working on the EU-funded COPING project, which is examining the experience of children who have a parent in prison. He was made a UK Higher Education Academy National Teaching Fellow in 2006.

Alex Gillespie is a Lecturer in Psychology at the London School of Economics and Political Science, and Editor of *Journal for the Theory of Social Behaviour*. He is fascinated by social interaction, specifically how it produces novelty, distributes cognitive processes, creates our sense of self, and enables society to reproduce itself. He has published a monograph entitled *Becoming Other: From Social Interaction to Self-Reflection* (Information Age, 2006), and is co-editor, with Ivana Marková, of a 2012 volume entitled *Trust and Conflict: Representation, Culture and Dialogue* published by Routledge.

Andre Gingrich directs the Austrian Academy of Sciences' Institute for Social Anthropology (ISA) and is a member of the Royal Swedish Academy of Sciences. Based on his ethnographic fieldwork and his publications on time reckoning in south western Arabia, and on neo-nationalism in Europe, his current work concerns qualitative methodologies in anthropology. In this realm his recent publications include 'Comparative Methods in Socio-cultural Anthropology Today' in the *Handbook of Social Anthropology* (Sage, vol. 2), and 'Alliances and Avoidance: British Interactions with German-speaking Anthropologists, 1933–1953' in *Culture Wars: Context, Models, and Anthropologists' Accounts* (Berghahn).

Jaber F. Gubrium is Professor and Chair of Sociology at the University of Missouri. He has had a long-standing programme of research on the social organization of care in human service institutions and pioneered the reconceptualization of qualitative methods and the development of narrative analysis. A pragmatist in orientation, his publications include numerous books and articles on ageing, long-term care, the life course, medicalization, and representational practice in the therapeutic context. Collaborating for over 25 years with James Holstein, they have authored and edited dozens of books, including *Analyzing Narrative Reality*, *Varieties of Narrative Analysis*, *The New Language of Qualitative Method*, *The Active Interview*, *Handbook of Constructionist Research*, *Handbook of Interview Research*, *The Self We Live By*, *Constructing the Life Course* and *What is Family?*

Darrin Hodgetts is a Professor of Societal Psychology at the University of Waikato, New Zealand. He is an interdisciplinary social scientist who works within the interlinked domains of everyday life, media, community, culture, urban poverty, health inequalities and symbolic power. His research underlies efforts to improve the everyday lives of marginalized groups in society.

James A. Holstein is Professor of Sociology in the Department of Social and Cultural Sciences at Marquette University in Milwaukee. His research and writing projects deal with social problems, deviance and social control, family, and the self, all approached from an ethnomethodologically informed, constructionist perspective. His publications include numerous books and articles on qualitative inquiry and research methods. Collaborating with Jaber Gubrium for over 25 years, they have authored and edited dozens of books, including *Analyzing Narrative Reality*, *Varieties of Narrative Analysis*, *The New Language of Qualitative*

Method, *The Active Interview*, *Handbook of Constructionist Research*, *Handbook of Interview Research*, *The Self We Live By*, *Constructing the Life Course* and *What is Family?*

Jens Holze is Research Assistant and Lecturer at the Department of Educational Sciences, Otto-von-Guericke University of Magdeburg. His research interests in the general field of media literacy and education include Internet and Web studies as well as digital game studies.

Katarina Jacobsson is Associate Professor in Sociology at the School of Social Work, Lund University. Her major research areas are qualitative studies of deviance, social control and medical sociology. Recent publications include 'Accounts of Honesty' (2012) in *Deviant Behavior*, 'Moving from "gut-feeling" to "pure facts"' (2012) in *Nordic Social Work Research* (with E. Martinell-Barfoed) and 'Interviewees with an Agenda' (2013) in *Qualitative Research* (with M. Åkerström). Currently she is examining documenting practices and knowledge production within health care and social services.

Udo Kelle is a psychologist and sociologist. He has taught qualitative and quantitative methods of social research at various universities in Germany and, as a visiting researcher, in Austria and the UK. Currently he is a Professor for Social Research Methods and Statistics at the Helmut-Schmidt-University/University of the Armed Forces in Hamburg. His research interests cover the fields of the methodology of social sciences, especially qualitative methods and their epistemological underpinnings and the integration of qualitative and quantitative methods, the sociology of the life course and the sociology of ageing. At present he works on the use of qualitative methods in evaluation research and in research about prejudice. He has written a variety of books and articles (in both German and English) about the relation between theory and data in qualitative research, about the methodological foundations of grounded theory methodology, and about the methodology of category building.

Hubert Knoblauch has studied (1978–84) sociology, philosophy and history at the Universities of Konstanz and Brighton (1980–1). He received a DFG 'Heisenberg Scholarship' in 1995 and the 'Christa-Hofmann-Riem Award for Qualitative Research' in 1996. In 1997 he was a Senior Researcher at King's College in London, and a Guest Professor at the University of Vienna, and in 2000 a Professor for Sociology of Religion at the University in Zurich. Since 2002 he has been Chair for General Sociology/Theories of Modern Societies at the Institute of Sociology (Technical University of Berlin) and is currently Chair of the ESA RN Sociology of Culture. His recent publications include *PowerPoint, Communication, and the Knowledge Society* (Cambridge University Press, 2013).

Sabine Kowal received her PhD in experimental psychology from St. Louis University. Her Habilitation in General Linguistics/Psycholinguistics was at the Technical University of Berlin where she held an Extraordinary Professorship until her retirement. She has been engaged in research with Dan O'Connell for more than 40 years. The last decade of the twentieth century involved a shift in their orientation from mainstream psycholinguistic research to an emphasis on spoken dialogue and empractical speech under field observational conditions, and to empirical research on transcription and rhetorical language use. More recently, radio and TV interviews as well as American feature films have provided their empirical database, and the emphasis on spoken discourse has led to the investigation of neglected phenomena: fillers, pauses, interjections, laughter, and empractical speech in English and German.

Robert V. Kozinets is a globally recognized expert on social media, marketing research, innovation, and marketing strategy. He has extensive speaking, training and consulting experience with a range of global companies and organizations. An anthropologist by training, he is Professor of Marketing at York University's Schulich School of Business (Toronto), where he is also Chair of the Marketing Department. His research investigates the dynamic cultural interface of technology, consumption and media. It has been published in over 90 chapters, proceedings and articles in some of the world's top-tier marketing journals, including the *Journal of Marketing*, *Journal of Marketing Research*, *Journal of Retailing* and *Journal of Consumer Research*. His co-edited volume *Consumer Tribes* was published in 2007 by Elsevier. His 2010 book was published by Sage, entitled *Netnography: Doing Ethnographic Research Online*. *Qualitative Consumer and Marketing Research*, co-authored with Russel Belk and Eileen Fischer, was published in 2013.

Lory J. Maddox is a Senior Clinical Consultant, Intermountain Healthcare, in the State of Utah and a doctoral student at the University of Utah College of Nursing. She is responsible for Care Coordination project implementation with the Patient Flow Project team at 11 of Intermountain's largest hospitals. Previously, she was a Lieutenant in the US Navy, working in adult medical–surgical and pain services. From 2002 to 2007 she worked as an Assistant Professor of Nursing at Colorado Mesa University where she continues to teach part time. After completing informatics studies at the University of Colorado, she moved to Salt Lake City to work in the area of health care software design and delivery. Her doctoral studies concentrate on the design and delivery of health care systems in the provision of health care services to patients.

Christoph Maeder is Professor of Sociology at Thurgau University of Teacher Education, Switzerland. He is a former President of the Swiss Sociological Association and has conducted ethnographic research in a prison, hospitals, public welfare agencies and schools. Currently he is doing a discourse analysis of the public schools in Switzerland and undertaking fieldwork in classrooms on the use of information and computer technology. In his latest research he is trying to integrate the non-musical and non-linguistic acoustic environment into ethnography.

Winfried Marotzki is Professor of Education at the Otto-von-Guericke University of Magdeburg, where he has taught for more than 20 years on educational problems. His research and writing projects have addressed social problems, biographical work, mostly approached from an ethnomethodologically informed, constructionist perspective. His publications include numerous books and articles on education, qualitative research methods, media literacy and new media phenomena in the context of education.

Amir Marvasti is an Associate Professor of Sociology at Penn State Altoona. His areas of interest include race and ethnicity, deviance, and social theory. He is the author of *Being Homeless: Textual and Narrative Constructions* (2003), *Qualitative Research in Sociology* (2004), *Middle Eastern Lives in America* (with Karyn McKinney, 2004). His research focuses on social construction and management of deviant identities in everyday life.

Joseph A. Maxwell is a Professor in the College of Education and Human Development at George Mason University (Virginia), where he teaches courses on qualitative and mixed methods research design and methodology. He is the author of *Qualitative Research Design: An Interactive Approach* (3rd edition, 2012) and *A Realist Approach for Qualitative Research* (2011). His research and writing include work on integrating qualitative and quantitative approaches, the connections between research methodology and philosophy, qualitative methods for programme evaluation, Native American societies, and medical education. He has a PhD in anthropology from the University of Chicago.

Tim May is Professor and Director of the Centre for Sustainable Urban and Regional Futures, University of Salford, Manchester. He is the author and editor of books on social research, organizational change, reflexivity, social theory and philosophy of social science, which have been translated into 15 languages. He has also written many articles on knowledge, cities, universities, and urban policies and practices. He is currently working on projects funded by the Engineering and Physical Sciences and Arts and Humanities Research Councils, as well as Mistra (Swedish Environmental Research Foundation), where he is seconded part-time to the Mistra Urban Futures Centre, based in Gothenburg, Sweden.

Donna M. Mertens is a Professor in International Development at Gallaudet University in Washington, DC. She is author of *Program Evaluation Theory and Practice* (Guilford Press, 2012) and editor of the *Journal of Mixed Methods Research*. Her work focuses on expanding understandings of the role of research in addressing issues of social justice and human rights.

Lothar Mikos is Professor of Television Studies in the Department of Media Studies at the University of Film and Television 'Konrad Wolf' in Potsdam–Babelsberg, Germany, and Managing Director of the Erich Pommer Institute for Media Law, Media Economy and Media Research. The Erich Pommer Institute is one of Europe's leading centres of research and advanced training programmes following the process of media convergence. As a Visiting Professor at universities in Barcelona, Glasgow, Gothenburg, Klagenfurt, London and Tarragona he lectured on communication and media studies, film and television analysis, film and television history, and audience research. His main research interests are audience studies, film and television history, film and television analysis, international television format trade, popular film genres and television formats, convergence culture, global media market, and qualitative methodology. He has published several books in German, for example *Film- und Fernsehanalyse* (*Film and Television Analysis*) (UVK, 2nd edition). His latest publications in English are 'Travelling Style: Aesthetic Differences and Similarities in National Adaptations of *Yo Soy Betty, La Fea*' in *International Journal of Cultural Studies* (with Marta Perrotta, 2012); and 'National Heroes on the Global Stage: The 2002 Olympic Games and Football World Cup' in *Bodies of Discourse: Sport Stars, Media, and the Global Public* (Peter Lang, 2012).

Janice M. Morse has PhDs in nursing and anthropology, is a Fellow of the American Academy of Nursing, and as a Professor holds a Presidential Endowed Chair at the University of Utah College of Nursing, as well as being Professor Emeritus, University of Alberta. She was the founding Director and Scientific Director of the International Institute for Qualitative Methodology, University of Alberta, founding editor for the *International Journal of Qualitative Methods*, and presently serves as the founding editor for *Qualitative Health Research* (Sage). From 1998 to 2007 she was the editor for the Qual Press, and is currently editor for the series Developing Qualitative Inquiry: The Basics of Qualitative Inquiry (Left Coast Press). She is a recipient of the Lifetime Achievement in Qualitative Inquiry, from the International Center for Qualitative Inquiry (2011), in the International's Nurse Researcher Hall of Fame, of the Episteme Award (Sigma Theta Tau), and has honorary doctorates from the University of Newcastle (Australia) and Athabasca University (Canada). She is the author of 370 articles and 18 books on qualitative research methods, suffering, comforting and patient falls.

Michael Murray is Professor of Social and Health Psychology at Keele University, UK. Previously he worked in Northern Ireland and Canada. He is particulary interested in developing innovative change-oriented qualitative research designed to enhance community capacity and wellbeing. He has conducted research on various topics including smoking among young people, cancer screening practices and attitudes, occupational health and safety, baby-boomers, and older people and arts. He has published extensively, including *Smoking Among Young Adults* (1988, with L. Jarrett, A.V. Swan and R. Rumun), *Qualitative Health Psychology: Theories and Methods* (1999, with K. Chamberlain) and *Critical Health Psychology* (2014).

Daniel C. O'Connell received his doctorate in experimental psychology at the University of Illinois (Urbana–Champaign), and did postdoctoral work at Harvard. Until his retirement, he served as Professor of Psychology successively at St. Louis, Loyola (Chicago) and Georgetown Universities. His research with Sabine Kowal has spanned more than 40 years. In the last decade of the twentieth century, their orientation shifted from mainstream psycholinguistic research on speech production to an emphasis on spoken dialogue and empractical speech under field observational conditions, and to empirical research on transcription and rhetorical language use. More recently, radio and TV interviews as well as American feature films have provided their empirical database, and the emphasis on spoken discourse has led to neglected phenomena: fillers, pauses, interjections, laughter, and empractical speech in both English- and German-language corpora.

Monika Palmberger is a Research Fellow at the Max Planck Institute for the Study of Religious and Ethnic Diversity in Göttingen, Germany. In her doctoral research project, which she completed at the University of Oxford in 2010, she concentrated on the comparison of memory discourses among different generations in post-war and post-socialist Bosnia-Herzegovina. She has published the results of her research in various journals and currently is finishing her book *How Generations Remember: Contested Memories in Post-War Bosnia and Herzegovina*. Presently she is focusing her work on older first-generation migrants in a diverse Viennese neighbourhood. Her research is based on extensive ethnographic fieldwork including a mix of qualitative methods.

Beth Perry is Senior Research Fellow and Associate Director of the Centre for Sustainable Urban and Regional Futures, University of Salford, Manchester. Her interests are in urban and regional policy and governance and the role of universities in regional development and the knowledge economy. She is currently Director of the Greater Manchester Local Interaction Platform and undertaking work with support from the Arts and Humanities Research Council (AHRC). Among her recent publications are a book on social research and reflexivity (with Tim May); chapters on case study methods and comparative research; and a special edition of the *Built Environment* journal, with Tim May, on 'The Roles of Universities in Building Knowledge Cities'.

Tim Rapley is a Lecturer in Medical Sociology at the Institute of Health and Society, Newcastle University, UK. When not conducting research on a range of topics in medical settings, he is interested in thinking, talking and teaching about the practical, taken-for-granted ways that qualitative research gets done. He has written about the (extra)ordinary work undertaken in relation to qualitative interviews and analysis. He has also written a book, *Analysing Conversations, Discourse and Documents* (Sage).

Jo Reichertz, is a Professor of Communication Science. He has studied mathematics, sociology and communication science at the Universities of Bonn, Essen and Hagen; gained his doctorate in 1986 (University of Hagen); and his Habilitation in 1991 (University of Hagen). Since 1992 he has held a professorship at the University of Essen. His focus of research covers the sociology of communication, sociology of science, sociology of knowledge, sociology of culture, qualitative research, and hermeneutics. His publications include the methodology of social-scientific hermeneutics, manifestations of religiosity in the modern era, social forms of self-representation, sociology of the media, logic of research, pragmatism and abduction. He has held several guest professorships in Austria at the University of Vienna (Sociology) and at the Institute for Advanced Studies (Vienna) and in Switzerland at the University of St Gallen (Sociology).

Kathryn Roulston is a Professor in the Qualitative Research Program at the University of Georgia, Athens. Her research interests include qualitative research methodology, qualitative interviewing, teaching qualitative research, ethnomethodology and conversation analysis, doctoral education and topics in music education. She has published in a range of journals, including *Applied Linguistics*, *International Journal of Music Education*, *Music Education Research*, *Oxford Review of Education*, *Text*, *Qualitative Inquiry* and *Qualitative Research*. In addition to her book on qualitative interviewing, *Reflective Interviewing: A Guide to Theory and Practice* (Sage, 2010), she was a contributor to *The SAGE Handbook of Interview Research: The Complexity of the Craft* (2nd edition, 2012).

Bernt Schnettler is Chair for Sociology of Culture and Religion at the University of Bayreuth. He has undertaken studies on communicative genres including computer-supported visual presentations, extraordinary experiences and commemoration ceremonies. Recently he has become especially interested in combining hermeneutical and ethnomethodological approaches to sequential analysis for analysing video data. He is working in several national and international scientific associations, including the ESA Research Network 'Qualitative Methods' and the German Sociological Association's Section 'Sociology of Knowledge'. Among his recent publications are *Video-Analysis: Methodology and Methods: Qualitative Audiovisual Data Analysis in Sociology*, published by Lang (3rd edition, 2012).

Margrit Schreier has been Professor of Empirical Research Methods at Jacobs University Bremen, Germany, since 2003. She received her PhD in psychology from Heidelberg University and completed her Habilitation at Cologne University. Her research interests include qualitative research methods and methodology, mixed methods, media psychology, empirical study of literature, and health research. She has been a principal investigator in several DFG-funded research projects on these topics, and has authored and co-authored more than 90 book chapters and articles. She is co-editor of the issue 'Qualitative and quantitative research: Conjunctions and divergences' of Forum: Qualitative Social Research (2001, with Nigel Fielding) and author of *Qualitative Content Analysis in Practice* (Sage, 2012).

Corinne Squire is Professor of Social Sciences and Co-director of the Centre for Narrative Research, University of East London. Her research interests are in narrative theory and methods, popular cultures and subjectivity, and HIV and citizenship. Her publications include *Doing Narrative Research* (with M. Andrews and M. Tamboukou; Sage, 2008 and 2013); *HIV in International Perspective* (with M. Davis; Palgrave, 2010), *HIV in South Africa* (Routledge, 2007) and *Public Emotions* (with Perri 6, S. Radstone and A. Treacher; Palgrave, 2006).

Robert Thornberg is an Associate Professor in Education in the Department of Behavioural Sciences and Learning at Linköping University in Sweden as well as an international research faculty member of the Center for Research on School Safety, School Climate and Classroom Management at Georgia State University in Atlanta, GA. His current research is on school bullying as moral and social processes. His second line of research is on school rules, student participation, and moral practices in everyday school life. He uses a range of research methods such as qualitative interviews, focus groups and ethnographic fieldwork, but has particular expertise in grounded theory. He is also a board member of the Nordic Educational Research Association (NERA), and on the Editorial Board for the peer-reviewed journal *Nordic Studies in Education*. He has published in a range of journals, including *Teaching and Teacher Education, International Journal of Educational Research, Research Papers in Education, Children and Society, Ethnography and Education,* and *Journal of Adolescence*.

Ladislav Timulak is Associate Professor and Course Director of the Doctorate in Counselling Psychology at Trinity College Dublin, Ireland. His main research interest is psychotherapy research, particularly the development of emotion-focused therapy. He has written four books, over 50 peer-reviewed papers and various chapters in both his native language, Slovak, and English. His most recent books include *Research in Psychotherapy and Counselling* (Sage, 2008) and *Developing Your Counselling and Psychotherapy Skills and Practice* (Sage, 2011).

Merran Toerien's primary research interest is the application of conversation analysis (CA) to the study of talk in institutional settings. This has included nurse–patient interaction during recruitment appointments for a cancer trial; adviser–claimant interaction during 'work-focused interviews' in the UK's Jobcentre Plus; and beauty therapist–client interaction during salon hair removal sessions. Her current, collaborative research (funded by the UK's National Institute for Health Research) is examining how neurologists facilitate patient involvement in decision-making. She teaches CA at undergraduate and postgraduate level and has contributed to a range of CA short courses in the UK, China and South Africa.

René Tuma studied sociology at the TU Berlin and at King's College London. He served as a Research Assistant to a DFG Project on PowerPoint presentation and was a Fellow of the Studienstiftung. In 2008, he finished his MSc Dissertation in Medicine, Science & Society ('Learning to See – The Role of the Visual in Dermatology') at King's College London where he also collaborated with the Work, Interaction & Technology Research Team on the research project on Pervasive Computing for Markets (UTIFORO). Since 2009, he has been working and teaching as a full-time researcher at the Chair of General Sociology and Theory of Modern Societies, TU Berlin. He is currently finishing his PhD on vernacular video analysis.

Dan Verständig is a Research Assistant and Lecturer in the Department of Educational Sciences, Otto-von-Guericke University of Magdeburg, Germany. In his current research project, he is exploring the relation of participation and social formations with a focus on digital activism.

David Wästerfors is Associate Professor in Sociology in the Department of Sociology, Lund University, Sweden. His recent publications include 'Disputes and Going Concerns in an Institution for "Troublesome" Boys' in the *Journal of Contemporary Ethnography* (2011), and 'Analyzing Social Ties in Total Institutions' in *Qualitative Sociology Review* (2012). Apart from his interests in institutional youth care, he has also been engaged in studies of corruption, scandals, disabilities and masculinities, often from interactionist, ethnomethodological, narrative and constructionist standpoints.

Andreas Wernet is Professor of Science Education in the Department of Education at the Leibniz University of Hannover. His main research fields are theory of professionalization, classroom interaction, student biographies, and hermeneutic methodology and methods.

Carla Willig is Professor of Psychology at City University London, UK. She has a long-standing interest in qualitative research methodology in general, and discourse analysis in particular. She has published books and papers concerned with both methodological and epistemological issues. Her most recent book *Qualitative Interpretation and Analysis in Psychology* (McGraw-Hill, 2012) is concerned with the practical, conceptual and ethical challenges that qualitative researchers face when embarking upon qualitative data analysis.

Rainer Winter is Chair of Media and Cultural Theory and Head of the Institute of Media and Communications at Alpen Adria Universität Klagenfurt in Austria. He is Chair of the Section 'Sociology of Media and Communications' of the German Society of Sociology as well. In 2010 he taught as a Visiting Professor at Capital Normal University in Beijing and at Shanghai International Studies University. Since 2012 he has been Adjunct Professor at Charles Sturt University in Sydney (Australia). He is the author and editor of more than 50 books on Cultural Studies, including *Die Kunst des Eigensinns: Cultural Studies als Kritik der Macht* (2001), *Global America? The Cultural Consequences of Globalization* (2003; German Translation 2003; Chinese translation 2012), *Widerstand im Netz* (2010), *Die Zukunft der Cultural Studies* (2011, Chinese translation 2013) and *Transnationale Serienkultur (2013)*.

Tania Zittoun is a Professor of Psychology and Education at the University of Neuchâtel, Switzerland. She is interested in the dynamics by which, through their interactions with others and things, people create their life courses. For this she explores methodologies capturing people's changing experience in a complex cultural world. She is Associate Editor of *Culture & Psychology*; with Sergio Salvatore she recently co-edited *Cultural Psychology and Psychoanalysis: Pathways to Synthesis* (Information Age, 2011); and is co-author of the *Human Development in the Life Course: Melodies of Living* (Cambridge University Press, 2013).

Acknowledgements

The idea for this handbook goes back to some conversations with Patrick Brindle at Sage. Despite the central role of data analysis in qualitative research, we both had the feeling, that this step was not sufficiently covered in the varieties of its practices in the existing literature. Thus we started to think about a line-up for a handbook in this area. Patrick and then Katie Metzler and Anna Horvai at Sage supported the process of developing the outline of the handbook, the contact with contributors and the writing process patiently but also with very helpful ideas. To them and to all the other people at Sage involved in this process, I want to say "thank you".

A major role in supporting the development of the book from proposal to manuscript was played by the members of the International Advisory Board. They also helped to extend the vision on qualitative data analysis with an international perspective covering not only Europe and the United States, but also African, Asian and Latin American backgrounds. The Board members were also very helpful in reviewing the chapters of the book in the writing process. A big "thank you" to all of them!

The most important role in such a handbook in the end is that of the authors. Without their readiness to write their chapters, to deliver them in time and format and to revise them after the reviews, the book would not have come up like it looks now. Also, the authors were ready to engage in the peer reviewing process for other chapters. Both, writing their own and reviewing other chapters, is most appreciated!

Uwe Flick

PART I
Mapping the Field

Part I is a *general introduction* to the handbook and the content it covers. The aim of this part is to give a brief and concise overview of the state of the art of qualitative research, in particular with a focus on data analysis. The main purpose is to give an orientation for the handbook and its chapters and to make the background, structure and rationale of the book explicit.

Mapping the Field

Uwe Flick

Data analysis is the central step in qualitative research. Whatever the data are, it is their analysis that, in a decisive way, forms the outcomes of the research. Sometimes, data collection is limited to recording and documenting naturally occurring phenomena, for example by recording interactions. Then qualitative research is concentrated on analysing such recordings. Given the centrality of the analysis in qualitative research, in general, a kind of stocktaking of the various approaches to qualitative analysis and of the challenges it faces seems necessary. Anyone interested in the current state and development of qualitative data analysis will find a field which is constantly growing and becoming less structured. There are many changes which have evolved in parallel, making the field even more complex than it used to be. This introductory chapter aims to map the field of qualitative data analysis by discussing its extension and by drawing a number of axes through the field that the handbook will cover in its chapters. We will look at the current variety of traditional and new methods for analysing qualitative data before we consider the expansion of the phenomena and data available for analysis. The dimensions demarcating the proliferation of qualitative research and, especially, qualitative data analysis will be discussed here and unfolded in more detail in the individual chapters. After a definition of qualitative data analysis the major aims of qualitative data analysis will be outlined – such as reducing big data sets to core elements or expanding small pieces of data by adding extensive interpretations. Discussing some theoretical backgrounds and basic methodological approaches will complement this sketch of the field.

As the first axis, a historical line will be drawn, which intersects a second axis concerning geographical diversity, which is sometimes ignored. In the next step, we will look at the role of data analysis in the research process. Another axis is linked to the difference between producing new data and taking existing, naturally occurring data for a research project. A further distinction is related to the major approaches to analysing data – either to reduce the volume or the complexity of the data, or to expand the existing material by writing new texts consisting of interpretations about it. The rather simple relation of one kind of data to be analysed with one methodological approach has become more complex at both ends when triangulation is part of the methodology of a project. What are the consequences for the analysis if multiple types of data are employed? What becomes 'visible' if several forms of analysis are applied to the same set of data? Another axis through the field is linked to the tension between formalization and intuition in the analysis. At the end of this chapter, some new trends and developments in the field will be outlined. Here, new types of data, a trend to visualization and developments on the level of technological support for doing the analysis will be discussed. Qualitative research is more and more confronted with some new challenges – how to make data available for re- and meta-analysis; what do the calls for relevance and implementation mean in this context; and what are the ethical issues around qualitative data analysis? After briefly discussing these issues, an overview of the handbook and its parts and chapters will complete this introduction.

PROLIFERATION OF QUALITATIVE RESEARCH

Over the past few decades, qualitative research has undergone a proliferation on at least three levels. First, it has established itself in a wide range of disciplines beyond such disciplines as sociology, anthropology and education. We find qualitative research now in such varied fields as nursing, medicine, social work, psychology, information science, political science, and the like. Even if in many of these disciplines qualitative research is not in the mainstream of research and not at the core of methods training or teaching in general, ongoing research increasingly includes qualitative studies.

These developments have led to an interesting gap, which forms a second level of proliferation: a variety of methods and approaches for data analysis have been developed and spelled out in the methodology literature mainly in the original disciplines. The range stretches from content analysis to conversation analysis, from grounded theory to phenomenological analysis, from narrative to film analysis, from visual data analysis to electronic data analysis, etc. (see the respective chapters in this volume). However, experience with reviewing articles and PhD and other theses from different disciplines shows how often the *analysis* of qualitative data is done in more or less a 'hands-on' way in both the original and the other disciplines. Researchers sometimes 'just do it' (to use a phrase of Barney Glaser, 1998) or they look for certain topics in their materials and construct an account of their findings by illustrating these topics with 'interesting' quotations from interviews, for example. These quotes are often not really analysed in the article (or PhD dissertation) but treated as illustrations. Another way of describing (and doing) qualitative data analysis is to mix up tools with methods. Articles in which the method of data analysis is described by only referring to the Qualitative Data Analysis (QDA) program (see Gibbs, Chapter 19, this volume) that was applied are still quite common. All in all, this means that there is a gap between methodological developments on one side and research practice on the other. This gap results from the lack of a systematic and comparative overview and stocktaking of the variety of analytic procedures that are available for doing qualitative data analysis. This handbook intends to bridge this gap by giving an overview of methodological approaches with a strong focus on research practice in applying them to data and emphasizes the practical application of methods rather than their conceptual development.

Qualitative research has undergone a third major proliferation over the past few decades, which concerns the types of data that are used. Interviews, focus group transcripts and observation protocols are traditional types of data, which are now complemented with visual, virtual, textual, acoustic and other data. These forms of data represent the diversification of ways of communication and documentation of individual and social experiences. At the same time, methods for *producing* these data have proliferated as well and new devices for recording activities and processes in their complexity have been developed. Videotaping, acoustic recording devices, Internet formats like Facebook, etc., are adopted to catch relevant aspects of the life worlds in the twenty-first century. However, this proliferation of issues to be analysed and of data produced and available has not always been accompanied by a systematic and adequate proliferation of approaches for *analysing* such qualitative data. The methods that are used are often traditional ones (e.g. grounded theory, coding, content analysis) or are developed but mostly applied hands-on for the single project. The handbook intends to cover the variety of approaches starting from the diversity of types of data that are used in qualitative research.

WHAT IS QUALITATIVE DATA ANALYSIS?

The central focus of this book is the variety and diversity of the ways of doing qualitative data analysis. Therefore it might be helpful first to outline the common core of this practice by (1) giving a working definition, followed by (2) discussing the aims of qualitative data analysis and finally by (3) looking at theoretical backgrounds and basic methodological approaches.

Definition

In Box 1.1 a rather general definition of qualitative data analysis is outlined which emphasizes the move from data to meanings or representations.

Box 1.1   What Is Qualitative Data Analysis?

Qualitative data analysis is the classification and interpretation of linguistic (or visual) material to make statements about implicit and explicit dimensions and structures of meaning-making in the material and what is represented in it. Meaning-making can refer to subjective or social meanings. Qualitative data analysis also is applied to discover and describe issues in the field or structures and processes in routines and practices. Often, qualitative data analysis combines approaches of a rough analysis of the material (overviews, condensation, summaries) with approaches of a detailed analysis (elaboration of categories, hermeneutic interpretations or identified structures). The final aim is often to arrive at generalizable statements by comparing various materials or various texts or several cases.

Aims of Qualitative Data Analysis

The analysis of qualitative data can have several aims. The first aim may be to *describe* a phenomenon in some or greater detail. The phenomenon can be the subjective experiences of a specific individual or group (e.g. the way people continue to live after a fatal diagnosis). This can focus on the case (individual or group) and its special features and the links between them. The analysis can also focus on *comparing* several cases (individuals or groups) and on what they have in common or on the differences between them. The second aim may be to identify the conditions on which such differences are based. This means to look for *explanations* for such differences (e.g. circumstances which make it more likely that the coping with a specific illness situation is more successful than in other cases). The third aim may be to *develop a theory* of the phenomenon under study from the analysis of empirical material (e.g. a theory of illness trajectories).

The aims above are three general aims of qualitative data analysis. In addition we can distinguish the analysis of (1) *content* from that of (2) *formal aspects* and from approaches that (3) *combine both*. For example, we can look at what participants report about their illness experiences and compare the contents of such reports with statements made by other participants. Or we can look at formal aspects of an interaction about these experiences (with a family member or a professional), when the language becomes unclear, pauses become longer, and the like. Or we can look at the content *and* formal aspects in a public discourse about chronic illness. The handbook provides chapters on methods for pursuing each of these aims in qualitative analysis.

Theoretical Backgrounds and Basic Methodological Approaches

Qualitative data analysis – as qualitative research in general – can take three approaches to analysing social phenomena. A first approach puts subjective experiences as the focus: what are patients' experiences of being chronically ill from a specific disease; how do they describe living with it; what are their explanations for being in this situation? For this approach data often come from interviews with the patients – or from documents such as the diaries that patients have written. A second approach focuses on describing the making of a social situation: how does the family of the patient interact about the illness and its consequences for their family and public life? For this approach, data, for example, result from participant observation or from recording family interactions with or about the patient and the illness. A third approach is to go beyond the first two approaches and into spheres of implicit and even unconscious aspects of a social phenomenon. Data again come from recording interactions but also from analysing phenomena beyond individual awareness. Here the interpretation of phenomena, interaction and discourses comes to the fore. The backgrounds of these approaches are in the first case knowledge and meaning that can be reported by the participants. This can be linked back theoretically to social theories such as symbolic interactionism (Blumer, 1969). In the second approach, the practices and routines that make everyday life possible and work are in the background of the concrete methodological procedures. The theoretical roots of this approach are ethnomethodology (e.g. Garfinkel, 1967). Participants are not necessarily aware of these routines or reflecting on them. In the third approach, knowledge beyond the individuals' accessibility is to the fore. The theoretical roots are structuralist models and psychoanalysis and its concept of the unconscious. Although the focus of the handbook is on research practice rather than on theories, it covers methods that make all of these approaches work in qualitative data analysis.

HISTORICAL DEVELOPMENTS

When the history of qualitative research is considered, reference is often made to Denzin and Lincoln's (2005: 14–20; 2011: 3) stage model (see also Flick, 2014: ch. 2, for the following discussion). They present 'eight moments of qualitative research'. These stages can also be taken as a starting point for a developmental perspective on qualitative data analysis. The *traditional period* is located between the early twentieth century and the Second World War. The Chicago School in sociology or the research of Malinowski in ethnography are used as examples. During this period, qualitative data analysis aimed at a more or less objective description of social phenomena in society or in other cultures. The second stage is called the *modernist phase*, which extends from the 1950s to the 1970s. It is marked by publications such as Glaser and Strauss's (1967) textbook on how to do qualitative analysis with the aim of theory development. In that period, data analysis was driven by various ways of coding for materials often obtained from participant observation. Ethnomethodology (Garfinkel, 1967) at the same time turned the focus on more and more formal analysis of everyday practices and mainly of conversations. The attitudes of both kinds of research are still alive in current qualitative research (see Thornberg and Charmaz, Chapter 11, Eberle, Chapter 13, and Toerien, Chapter 22, this volume).

Denzin and Lincoln use a term introduced by Geertz (1983) to characterize the developments up to the mid-1980s: *blurred genres*. Various theoretical models and understandings of the objects and methods stand side by side, from which researchers can choose and compare 'alternative paradigms', such as symbolic interactionism, ethnomethodology, phenomenology, and others. Data analysis turned more to interpretation of phenomena (narratives, ethnographic descriptions) and writing essays rather than coding and categorizing (which continued to be used, however). In this period, the first software programs and packages for computer-supported data analysis were developed (see Gibbs, Chapter 19, this volume).

In the mid-1980s, the *crisis of representation*, the presentation and, in particular, the process of writing in research became central topics. The focus on analysing data was much more on interpretation than on identifying linear models. For example, the paradigm model suggested by Strauss and Corbin (1990) as an orientation for coding data assumes that causes lead to phenomena and they, in turn, lead to consequences, and proposes to look for such chains of concepts. In this period, qualitative research and data analysis are understood as a continuous process of constructing versions of reality. After all, the version of themselves that people present in an interview does not necessarily correspond to the version they would have given to a different researcher with a different research question. Researchers, who interpret the interview and present it as part of their findings, produce a new version of the whole. In this context, the evaluation of research and findings becomes a central topic in methodological discussions. This raises the question as to whether traditional criteria are still valid and, if not, which other standards should be applied in assessing qualitative research (see Barbour, Chapter 34, this volume). At the same time, the technical devices for analysing data proliferated and all sorts of programs were developed that could be selected if they matched the questions and type of research at stake.

For the *fifth moment* (in the 1990s) Denzin and Lincoln mention that narratives have replaced theories, or theories are read as narratives. Here (as in postmodernism, in general) the end of grand narratives is proclaimed; the accent is shifted towards (local) theories and narratives that fit specific, delimited, local, historical situations, and problems. Data analysis adapted to this turn. In the next stage (*sixth moment*) post-experimental writing, linking issues of qualitative research to democratic policies, became more prominent. The *seventh moment* is characterized by further establishing qualitative research through various new journals. Denzin and Lincoln's *eighth moment* in the development of qualitative research focused on the rise of evidence-based practice as the new criterion of relevance for social science and to the new conservatism in the United States.

Denzin and Lincoln's outline of its history is often taken as a general reference for the development of qualitative research. However, as authors like Alasuutari (2004) suggest, this general 'progress narrative' (2004: 599) is mainly focused on the development in the Anglo-Saxon area. Instead, he proposes a spatial, rather than a temporal, view of the development of qualitative research. In this way Denzin and Lincoln's history of qualitative research can be complemented with the various ways qualitative research has developed in other regions.

German-Speaking Areas

Qualitative research in German-speaking areas can be traced back to the works of Max Weber and Alfred Schütz, for example, but had become less influential after the Second World War here as well. They were rediscovered in the 1960s, when a series of anthologies imported and translated relevant articles from the American literature. Thus the basic texts on ethnomethodology or symbolic interactionism became available for German discussion. The model of the research process created by Glaser and Strauss (1967) attracted much attention and promoted the idea that it could do more justice to the objects of research than was possible in quantitative research.

At the end of the 1970s, a broader and more original discussion began in Germany, which no longer relied exclusively on the translation of American literature. This discussion dealt with interviews, how to apply and how to analyse them, and with methodological questions that have stimulated extensive research (see Flick et al., 2004, for an overview).

In the 1980s, two original methods were developed that became crucial to the establishment of qualitative research in Germany: the narrative interview by Schütze (1977; see Esin et al., Chapter 14, this volume) and objective hermeneutics (see Reichertz, 2004, and Wernet, Chapter 16, this volume). Both methods no longer were imports of American developments and stimulated extensive research practice, mainly in biographical research. Most important was their influence on the general discussion of qualitative methods in German-speaking areas.

In the mid-1980s, questions about the validity and the generalizability of findings obtained with qualitative methods attracted broader attention. Related questions of presentation and the transparency of results were also discussed. The quantity and, above all, the unstructured nature of the data also promoted the use of computers in qualitative research. One result was the development of software programs in Germany such as ATLAS.ti and MAXQDA (see Gibbs, Chapter 19, this volume). Finally, the first original textbooks or introductions on the background of the discussions in the German-speaking area were published (see Table 1.1).

This juxtaposition of American and German developments is relevant here for two reasons. First, the latter German developments – the theoretical and methodological discussions, the methods resulting from them and the research practice with them – are almost not represented in Denzin and Lincoln's stage model or in the methodological discussions around it – except for the two software programs. Thus, this development can be seen as an example of spatial differentiation

Table 1.1 Phases in the history of qualitative research

United States	Germany
Traditional period (1900 to 1945)	Early studies (end of nineteenth and early twentieth centuries)
Modernist phase (1945 to the 1970s)	Phase of import (early 1970s)
Blurred genres (until the mid-1980s)	Beginning of original discussions (late 1970s)
Crisis of representation (since the mid-1980s)	Developing original methods (1970s and 1980s)
Fifth moment (the 1990s)	Consolidation and procedural questions (late 1980s and 1990s)
Sixth moment (post-experimental writing)	Research practice (since the 1980s)
Seventh moment (establishing qualitative research through successful journals, 2000 to 2004)	Methodological proliferation and technological developments (since the 1990s)
Eighth moment (the future and new challenges – since 2005)	Establishing qualitative research (journals, book series, scientific societies – since the 1990s)

(Alasuutari, 2004) that is neglected in the general progress narrative recognized in the Anglo-Saxon literature.

Second, some of the methodological outcomes of this development will be taken up in this handbook in extra chapters on such topics as phenomenology (see Eberle, Chapter 13), (objective) hermeneutics (see Wernet, Chapter 16) and the further elaborations of content analysis (see Schreier, Chapter 12).

Several authors now argue for more openness to local and cultural diversity regarding the development and progress of qualitative research. In this context, several overviews of the internationalization of qualitative research, in particular in Europe and across the cultural, linguistic, and methodological diversities, can widen the perspective on what qualitative research in various geographical areas is like in times of globalization (see Knoblauch et al., 2005; Ryan and Gobo, 2011; Schnettler and Rebstein 2012; and Flick, forthcoming). Hsiung (2012), for example, discusses a core–periphery divide in this context. Anglo-American (core) methods and texts are translated and exported to Asian countries currently and define what qualitative research is about and push local methodologies aside. Alasuutari (2004) discusses this problem by juxtaposing a temporal development approach (the eight phases of qualitative research) with a spatial approach that focuses more on local traditions of qualitative research, in general.

At the same time, discussions started and are recognized as necessary about the Western-culture-based tacit assumptions of some of the major qualitative methods. This can only be illustrated here briefly for interview and observational methods. In Western European societies it is quite normal for people to be interviewed and it is also normal to talk about one's own personal history and individual experiences to a professional stranger. It is not uncommon to have such a conversation recorded if some rules are defined (anonymization, data protection, etc.). It may be an irritating idea, but it is still quite normal for your statements to be later analysed and interpreted. Gobo (2012) discusses a number of necessary and taken-for-granted preconditions of using this approach in qualitative research. These include the ability on the part of the interviewee to speak for him or herself, and an awareness of him or herself as an autonomous and independent individual; an extended concept of public opinion, necessary for communicating opinions and attitudes and describing behaviours considered private in a pre-industrial society, etc. As we experience in our own research with migrants from Russian-speaking countries, being interviewed (and recorded) has different connotations and is much less a normal routine (Flick and Röhnsch, forthcoming). Instead, we found that many interviews are connected with being investigated by the state and the expected self-disclosure is anything but normal, but conflicting with some cultural values. The same criticism applies to research involving observation where a researcher takes notes about everyday routines and interaction and writes reports about field contacts. Again this is linked to practices of control by the state and of breaching privacy. These cultural differences in the meanings linked to practices that are basic for prominent qualitative methods become relevant in applying these methods in intercultural contexts, in recruiting participants and in negotiating informed consent with them (see Mertens, Chapter 35, this volume), and has an impact on what we can analyse as data in the process. These issues cannot be discussed here extensively but illustrate the need for reflecting on our research approaches for their underlying and sometimes implicit cultural assumptions.

THE ROLE OF DATA ANALYSIS IN THE RESEARCH PROCESS

The analysis of qualitative data is often one step in a series of steps throughout the research process. It comes after field access has been found, sampling decisions have been taken, data have been collected, recorded and elaborated (e.g. transcribed). In such a model of the research process, an intensive data analysis only starts when all data have been collected and prepared. In other cases, the analysis begins with the collection of the data and both steps are applied in a parallel, sometimes entangled way. Qualitative data analysis can also be the central step in qualitative research to which all other steps are subordinated. Data collection then is only a means for advancing the analysis of the phenomenon and what is available so far as empirical material referring to it. Other decisions in the research process are driven by the state of the data analysis and the questions still unanswered. A prominent example for this approach to data analysis is grounded theory, where sampling decisions, sometimes the decisions about which methods to use for further collection of data etc., are driven by the state of the data analysis. Most prominent is the concept of 'theoretical sampling' (see Rapley, Chapter 4, and Thornberg and Charmaz, Chapter 11, this volume), which means that sampling decisions are taken with the focus on further elaborating or substantiating the categories developed in the analysis so far. The linear model of the research process then is replaced by a more modular model, in which the analysis of data has become the central node in the organization of the other elements of the researchers' work. This means it is not so much the specific features of the data that drives the analysis, but the analysis drives the search for data in different formats. A similar centrality of the analysis of phenomena and the search for appropriate types of data can be found in ethnographic research (see Gubrium and Holstein, Chapter 3, this volume), although here the writing about the phenomenon and the field becomes a major element in the data analysis (see Denzin, Chapter 39, this volume). These brief examples show that there are different approaches to the role of data analysis in the qualitative research process.

USING ELICITED DATA OR ANALYSING EXISTING PHENOMENA

Another axis through the field of qualitative data analysis is linked to the question of where the data come from or, in other words, what is used or accepted as data. On one side of this axis, we find data that result from employing specific methods to produce them for the purpose of the actual research: interviews (see Roulston, Chapter 20, this volume) are a prominent way of producing such data as are focus groups (see Barbour, Chapter 21, this volume). Data coming from participant observation (see Marvasti, Chapter 24, this volume) or ethnography (see Gubrium and Holstein, Chapter 3, this volume) and the field notes written for the research also fall into this category. On the other side of this divide, we find approaches based on the idea of using naturally occurring data instead of producing them specifically for the research. The act of data collection in such cases is limited to recording, for example, everyday interactions or routine practices in professional work. The analytic approaches such as conversation analysis (see Toerien, Chapter 22, this volume) and discourse analysis (see Willig, Chapter 23, this volume) but also hermeneutics (see Wernet, Chapter 16, this volume) not only use naturally occurring data, but also link their analyses closely to the data and their (temporal) structure. Researchers do not navigate through the data every which way in looking for excerpts for filling categories, but apply the principle of sequentiality (see Wernet, Chapter 16, but also Toerien, Chapter 22, this volume). This means the material is analysed from beginning to end and following its temporal development. Coming back to the line between produced and naturally occurring data, we again find approaches in which both forms are used. The analysis of documents (see Coffey, Chapter 25, this volume) is based either on existing documents (e.g. diaries written in everyday life) or on documents which are produced for the purpose of the research (diaries written as part of a project and stimulated by the researchers). In discourse analysis, interviews are frequently used (see the examples in Willig, Chapter 23, this volume) and the strong rejections of such data, which could be found in the beginning, have become less dominant. As recent developments demonstrate, conversation analysis (see Toerien, Chapter 22, this volume) is now also used for analysing the interaction and dynamics in focus groups (see Barbour, Chapter 21, this volume). Ethnography also makes the distinction between analysing 'natural' data – like observing everyday routines – instead of asking participants to talk about these routines in extra research situations like interviews, although much of the data in ethnography also come from talking with members in the field ('ethnographic interviews'). Again, the handbook will cover both alternatives discussed in this paragraph.

MAJOR APPROACHES TO ANALYSING DATA

In the range of approaches to analysing qualitative data, we can find two major strategies. The first one is oriented to reducing big sets of data or the complexity in the data. The major methodological step is to code the data. This basically means to find a label that allows the grouping of several elements (statements or observation) under one concept, so that we have a more or less limited number of codes (or categories) rather than a large variety of diverse phenomena. The most prominent way of pursuing this aim is qualitative content analysis (see Schreier, Chapter 12, this volume). However, grounded theory coding, also, in the end aims at reducing the diversity in the field and in the data by identifying a core category or a basic social process (see Thornberg and Charmaz, Chapter 11, this volume). The second strategy aims rather at expanding the material by producing one or more interpretations (see Willig, Chapter 10, this volume). Here, a second level of text is written in addition to or about the original material. This second level describes, analyses and explains the meaning of the original text (e.g. interview statements, focus group discussions, documents or images). Such interpretations often are longer and more substantial than the original text. Examples of making this strategy work in a methodological procedure are the phenomenological approaches (see Eberle, Chapter 13, this volume), the documentary method (see Bohnsack, Chapter 15, this volume) or hermeneutic approaches (see Wernet, Chapter 16, this volume). Maybe this juxtaposition of two alternative approaches overemphasizes the differences, as any process of coding includes interpretation at one point or another – for example, in the step of memo writing in grounded theory (see Thornberg and Charmaz, Chapter 11, this volume). At the same time, any sort of interpretation at some point turns to identifying some kind of structure – like types or patterns – for organizing the diversity in the material in a clear and orienting way. Thus, we often find combinations of both strategies when it comes to analysing specific types of data. The handbook is not confined to one sort of analysis, but intends to cover the range of the major approaches.

TRIANGULATION OF PERSPECTIVES

Multiple Types of Data

As the number of research projects which apply triangulation (see Flick, 2007) or mixed methods approaches (see Morse and Maddox, Chapter 36, this volume) has grown, there are also more and more projects that involve the analysis of multiple types of data. In our own research, we often have interviews and observations or interviews and routine statistical data (see Flick et al., 2012) in a single project. We also have various types of interviews applied in one study – for example, episodic interviews (Flick, 2007) with homeless adolescents and expert interviews with service providers. In all of these examples and in such multiple methods projects in general, the question arises as to whether we can use one and the same analytic method for all the types of data, or should we use different approaches to the data of each type? On a closer look, these multiple types of data not only vary in the way they were collected (which method was applied), but also vary in the form of sampling (see Rapley, Chapter 4, this volume) that was applied and this may have implications for any attempts at generalizing the findings (see Maxwell and Chmiel, Chapter 37, this volume). Finally, they vary in the degree of exactness in their documentation. Interviews, for example, are mostly available on two levels of documentation: the acoustic or audio-visual recording and the transcription (see Kowal and O'Connell, Chapter 5, this volume). Observations and ethnographic data, in general, are in most cases only documented on the level of the researcher's field notes.

Triangulation means to take several methodological perspectives or theoretical perspectives on an issue under study (see Denzin, 1970; Flick, 2007). In general, triangulation is not really a new trend as there has been a long discussion about combining methods in qualitative research or combining qualitative and quantitative research. But, mainly, triangulation is located in the phase of data collection. Recently, such a combination of perspectives has been applied to one set of data. In their book, similar to what Heinze et al. (1980) did much earlier with a biographical interview, Wertz et al. (2011) take one interview and analyse it with five different methods, among them grounded theory (see Thornberg and Charmaz, Chapter 11, this volume), discourse analysis (see Willig, Chapter 23, this volume) and narrative research (see Esin et al., Chapter 14, this volume). The book also provides some detailed comparisons of what pairs of methods produced as differences and similarities in analysing the text. It also becomes evident that not only the way the text is analysed, but also which aspects are put in the foreground, vary across the five approaches. Thus we find 'Constructing a grounded theory of loss and regaining a valued self' (Charmaz, 2011) as the approach and result of the grounded theory approach. The analysis of the same material focuses on 'Enhancing oneself, diminishing others' (McMullen, 2011). Thus this book provides an interesting insight into the differences and commonalities of various empirical approaches to the same transcript.

THE TENSION BETWEEN FORMALIZATION AND INTUITION

This example raises an issue that has been an implicit topic in the history of qualitative research as well and also plays a role in some of the points we will turn to later. How far can we expect and should we wish to formalize qualitative data analysis? There are two endpoints of this dimension. One is to set up more or less exact rules for how to apply a specific method formally correct (Mayring, 2000, in his version of qualitative content analysis is an example for this – see Schreier, Chapter 12, this volume). The other one is what Glaser (1998) has formulated for his version of grounded theory (see Thornberg and Charmaz, Chapter 11, this volume) as 'just do it' – go into the data (or the field) and find out what is interesting about them. The general dimension here is how far qualitative data analysis should be formalized by (methodological) rules or by a close and exclusive link of a specific sort of data to a particular method of analysis (and vice versa). Between these two endpoints we find the more realistic stance that a good qualitative analysis finds a combination of rules that are applied and make the analysis transparent on the one hand and the necessary degree of intuition on the other (and abduction – see Reichertz, Chapter 9, and Thornberg and Charmaz, Chapter 11, this volume) that make the analysis creative and fruitful. But the tension comes from the question of the right balance between formalization and intuition. How to avoid methods that bring too much of a formalization or are too much of an intuitive art? How to avoid certain aspects of the research process – for example, the use of software – having an unwanted impact on what counts as data and their analysis? This general tension has been relevant throughout the history of qualitative data analysis and becomes relevant again and again and is important for many of the approaches presented in the following chapters.

QUALITATIVE DATA ANALYSIS 2.0: NEW TRENDS AND DEVELOPMENTS

The field of qualitative data analysis has always been in movement as new methods or new formalizations of existing methods have been developed. One challenge for a handbook trying to cover this field could be just to cover what has been established and accepted as the most relevant methods in several fields of application. However, qualitative data analysis in the twenty-first century faces new challenges on several levels. These include new types of data, which call for adequate ways for analysing them. Progress in the areas of methodology and technology comes with new possibilities and new risks. The various contexts of utilization of qualitative analysis in the field of social science and beyond extend the expected and possible activities of the researchers. All these developments raise new ethical issues or existing ethical questions in a new way. Some of these challenges might have stronger impacts on the traditions and practices of qualitative data analysis than we might expect and at the same time open new areas and potentials for our analyses, so that it might be justified to use 'qualitative data analysis 2.0' as a label for its future development.

New Types of Data/Phenomena as Challenges

The range of types of data in qualitative research continues to expand. A major part of qualitative research is still based on interviews (see Roulston, Chapter 20, this volume) or focus groups (see Barbour, Chapter 21, this volume), in particular in those disciplines now just discovering qualitative research. However, in more cutting-edge discussions and research contexts of qualitative research, we can notice a diversification of phenomena of interest and of data used for analysing them. First we find a permanently growing interest in visual data – from photos (see Banks, Chapter 27, this volume) to videos (see Knoblauch et al., Chapter 30, this volume) and films (see Mikos, Chapter 28, this volume). This is complemented by the interest in analysing acoustic data such as sounds in general or music in particular (see Maeder, Chapter 29, this volume). Another trend, sometimes overlapping with the first two, is the interest in all kinds of documents (see Coffey, Chapter 25, this volume) from routine records to diaries and the like. At the same time, conversations (see Toerien, Chapter 22, this volume) and discourses (see Willig, Chapter 23, this volume) continue to play a major role in various research contexts. The changing ways of communicating in new media and channels and through new technological devices produce new forms of data, which can be used for analysing these phenomena. Here, virtual and mobile data play a central role (see Marotzki et al., Chapter 31, this volume). The transfer of the approach of cultural studies (see Winter, Chapter 17, this volume) to analysing culture through social media (see Kozinets et al., Chapter 18, this volume) calls for adequate strategies of analysing the resulting data.

Visualization of a Textualized Field

What is the more general result of these trends beyond the diversification in the field? In earlier days of qualitative research, texts (statements, transcripts, descriptions of fields and images) were the dominant medium for phenomena to become data in qualitative analysis. Compared with that we face a more or less fundamental change. More and more of the participants and contexts become visible in the data, in what is processed in the analysis and what is represented in the reports and publications. Images in general provide a much fuller 'picture' than spoken-word transcripts did. Quotes from images or videos used as evidence in writing about qualitative analyses often not only include participants' faces and furniture from rooms, for example, but a more or less comprehensive background information (e.g. other people in the scene, details of the setting). Virtual and mobile data provide their specific image of the participant in the study. These extensions can be described as a visualization of a field (qualitative data analysis) that was mainly built on texts (and their limits). It produces new demands for managing the richer (and bigger, more complex) data technically, but also in ethically sound ways. For the first demand, the rapid development of technologies for supporting analysis can become more and more attractive.

Technological Developments: CAQDAS

Since the mid 1980s there has been far-reaching technological change in the analysis of data, which is linked to the use of computers in qualitative research (see also Flick, 2014: ch. 28, for the following discussion). Here, we can note the general changes in working patterns in the social sciences brought about by the personal computer, word processing, cloud computing and mobile devices. However, it is also important to see the specific developments in and for qualitative research. A wide range of computer programs is available, mostly focused on the area of qualitative data analysis. The programs are sometimes referred to as QDA (Qualitative Data Analysis) software or as CAQDAS (Computer-Aided Qualitative Data Analysis Software – see Gibbs, Chapter 19, this volume). The introduction of computer programs in the field of qualitative data analysis has produced mixed feelings. Some researchers have high hopes about the advantages of using them, while others have concerns and fears about how the use of software will change or even distort qualitative research practice. Some of these hopes may be right, some of these fears may have a kernel of truth, but some parts of both are more fantasy than anything else. For both parts it should be emphasized that there is a crucial difference between this kind of software and programs for statistical analysis (e.g., SPSS). QDA software does not *do* qualitative analysis itself or in an *automatic* way as SPSS can do a statistical operation or a factor analysis: 'ATLAS.ti – like any other CAQDAS program – does not actually analyze data; it is simply a tool for supporting the process of qualitative data analysis' (Friese, 2011: 1).

The discussion about the impact of software on qualitative research began with development of the very first programs. In this discussion one finds various concerns. First of all, some of the leading programs were developed on the back of a specific approach – coding according to grounded theory – and are more difficult to apply to other approaches. Another concern is that software implicitly forces its logical and display structure upon the data and the researcher's analysis. Finally, there is a fear that the attention attracted by the computer and the software will distract the researcher from the real analytic work – reading, understanding and contemplating the texts, and so on. In the KWALON experiment (see Evers et al., 2011, and Gibbs, Chapter 19, this volume), this impact of software on qualitative analysis was studied by giving the same material to researchers using different software programs in their analysis. But, in the end, it depends on the users and their ways of making the computer and the software useful for the ongoing research and how they reflect on what they are doing.

However, in their account of the history and future of technology in qualitative research, Davidson and di Gregorio (2011) see us 'in the midst of a revolution'. These authors have linked developments in the field of QDA software to developments in the field of Web 2.0 applications such as YouTube, Twitter, Facebook, etc. Their basic idea for the future of using technologies in qualitative analysis is that the software so far discussed in the field of qualitative data analysis (see Gibbs, Chapter 19, this volume) will be challenged or replaced by apps developed by interested users again. The tools developed in such contexts are focusing much on collaborative analysis (of video data, for example), collaborative writing (see Cornish et al., Chapter 6, this volume) and developments (in wikis or cloud computing, for example) on blogging with hyperlinks as ways of collaborating and the like.

Reanalysis of Data and Meta-analysis of Results

Another challenge for qualitative data analysis is the trend to reuse the data and findings of studies – to make them available for reanalysis by other researchers (see Wästersfors et al., Chapter 32, this volume) and to do meta-analyses based on several qualitative studies in a field (see Timulak, Chapter 33, this volume). These approaches are new methodological tools for answering research questions. However, the question is whether the need of producing studies ready to be re- or meta-analysed has an impact on the way original studies can or should be done in the future.

The Call for Implementation and Relevance and Evidence

The call for relevance of qualitative analyses has been expressed in different contexts: funding agencies often have the expectation that research leads to results that can be implemented in specific areas (see Murray, Chapter 40, this volume). Researchers often have the aspiration to arrive at some change for the participants in their research. As the discussion about 'evidence' in qualitative research shows, this whole issue can become important for demonstrating the need for qualitative research and for facing the challenge of impact.

Ethical Issues in Qualitative Analysis

Finally, all the developments and discussions in the field of qualitative data analysis mentioned so far have implications on the level of research ethics. The new forms of data raise issues of data protection and more generally of keeping the privacy of research participants. They also raise questions of how comprehensive the knowledge about the participants and the circumstances has to be for answering the specific research question of a project. How can the analysis do justice to the participants and their perspective? How does the presentation of the research and its findings maintain their privacy as much as possible? How can feedback on insights from the analysis take the participants' perspective into account and do justice to their expectations and feelings (see Mertens, Chapter 35, this volume)?

QUALITATIVE ANALYSIS BETWEEN METHODS AND DATA – OVERVIEW OF THE HANDBOOK

The topics mentioned in this brief mapping of the field of qualitative data analysis will be addressed in the major parts and single chapters of the handbook in more detail.

Part II takes a perspective on issues prior to the work with data in qualitative analysis and addresses *concepts, contexts and frameworks* of qualitative data analysis. The epistemological framework will be outlined in the form of a theory of qualitative data analysis (see Maxwell and Chmiel, Chapter 2). Inspiration in fieldwork is what makes methodological approaches work (see Gubrium and Holstein, Chapter 3). Sampling (see Rapley, Chapter 4) and transcription (see Kowal and O'Connell, Chapter 5) are practical steps with a strong impact on the data that are finally available for analysis. Concepts of how to do the analysis are issues of the next three chapters: What are the benefits and challenges of working collaboratively on data (see Cornish et al., Chapter 6)? Which are the concepts of comparison (see Palmberger and Gingrich, Chapter 7) in a qualitative analysis? How to give reflexivity in the practice of qualitative analysis adequate space (see May and Perry, Chapter 8)? The remaining chapters in Part II address epistemological issues again. Inferences (see Reichertz, Chapter 9) can be drawn using induction, deduction and abduction. Interpretation is a basic operation in qualitative data analysis (see Willig, Chapter 10).

Part III takes a stronger focus on the available methods of qualitative data analysis and presents a range of *analytic strategies* on various levels and in greater detail. Variants of coding are the first strategy that is unfolded in chapters on grounded theory coding (see Thornberg and Charmaz, Chapter 11), on content analysis (see Schreier, Chapter 12) and on tools based on these methods (such as computer programs, see Gibbs, Chapter 19). These approaches can be applied to all kinds of data. Different analytic strategies are the issues of the following chapters. Phenomenology (see Eberle, Chapter 13) and narrative analysis (see Esin et al., Chapter 14) refrain from using codes and categories but emphasize the interpretation in their analysis. The same applies to the documentary method in the tradition of Karl Mannheim (see Bohnsack, Chapter 15) and hermeneutic approaches (see Wernet, Chapter 16), which both embed data analysis in an elaborated methodological framework. In the remaining chapters in this part, phenomena under study are analysed in the framework of culture. The analysis of culture as an approach to study specific issues has been pursued by cultural studies (see Winter, Chapter 17) and transferred to virtual forms of culture, mainly social media (see Kozinets et al., Chapter 18). The analytic strategies covered by the chapters in this part refer to a broad range of methods that can be applied to all sorts of data.

In Part IV, a different perspective is taken: here, specific *types of data* are the starting points for discussing the specific challenges they produce for qualitative data analysis. Distinctions made earlier in this chapter determine the structure of this part. The first three chapters address data elicited in applying specific methods of data collection: interviews (see Roulston, Chapter 20), focus groups (see Barbour, Chapter 21) and observations (see Marvasti, Chapter 24). The second group of chapters is about analysing data based on documenting existing phenomena such as specific practices. On the level of words and interactions, these phenomena include conversations (see Toerien, Chapter 22), discourses (see Willig, Chapter 23) and documents (see Coffey, Chapter 25). Visual data, for example pictures (see Banks, Chapter 27), films (see Mikos, Chapter 28) and videos (see Knoblauch et al., Chapter 30) also refer to documentations of existing phenomena on the level of still and moving images. Beyond and including these two levels, newly identified forms of data such as sounds (see Maeder, Chapter 29) and virtual and mobile data (see Marotzki et al., Chapter 31) complement the approaches to social worlds.

Part V extends the perspective beyond the actual work with data in qualitative analysis again as it focuses on *using and assessing qualitative data analysis* and its *results* on several levels. Reusing data and existing analysis for research purposes is quite common in quantitative research, but raises some new questions for qualitative research. The practical steps and problems of reanalysing qualitative data (see Wästersfors et al., Chapter 32) and the potential of qualitative meta-analysis (see Timulak, Chapter 33) are outlined. However, what will be the impact of such strategies on what counts as data and what as analysis in such contexts? Qualities of qualitative analysis are discussed in the next block of chapters: How to assess the quality of qualitative data analysis (see Barbour, Chapter 34)? What does an ethical use of qualitative data and findings (see

Mertens, Chapter 35) mean? What about integrating quantitative data (see Morse and Maddox, Chapter 36)? The final chapters go beyond the actual data analysis and discuss the transfer of its results into various contexts. Generalization (see Maxwell and Chmiel, Chapter 37) has been an unanswered question for a long time – how can findings be transferred to other situations beyond the one in which they were found? Theorization in and from qualitative analysis (see Kelle, Chapter 38) has been relevant for several approaches discussed in earlier chapters. Writing is in most cases much more than summarizing the facts and findings of the analysis but has an impact on the analysis itself and on what arrives at potential readers (see Denzin, Chapter 39). Finally, and in particular in qualitative research, the call for making our analyses relevant and for thinking about their implementation in political and social practices is becoming louder as more qualitative research is used in applied fields (see Murray, Chapter 40).

In all, this handbook is designed to provide those involved in qualitative data analysis with an awareness of many of the contemporary debates in the field. It is not designed to provide definitive answers to what is the best approach, but to introduce the variety of ways in which scholars are addressing qualitative data analysis from different disciplinary, conceptual, epistemological and methodological standpoints. It will provide practical tips on implementing the analytic methods as well as conceptual discussions of the major intellectual challenges of each method. It is designed to increase sensitiveness to the strengths and limits of the various methodological alternatives and also for the specific challenges coming from various – traditional and new – types of data for their analysis.

ACKNOWLEDGEMENTS

I want to thank Flora Cornish, Michael Murray and Bernt Schnettler for their helpful comments on an earlier draft of this chapter.

FURTHER READING

Denzin, Norman K. and Lincoln, Yvonna S. (eds) (2011) *The SAGE Handbook of Qualitative Research*, 4th edition. London: Sage.

Flick, Uwe (ed.) (2007) *The SAGE Qualitative Research Kit*. London: Sage.

Flick, Uwe (2014) *An Introduction to Qualitative Research*, 5th edition. London: Sage.

REFERENCES

Alasuutari, Pertti (2004) 'The globalization of qualitative research', in Clive Seale et al. (eds), *Qualitative Research Practice*. London: Sage. pp. 595–608.

Blumer, Herbert (1969) *Symbolic Interactionism: Perspective and Method*. Berkeley, CA: University of California Press.

Davidson, Judith and di Gregorio, Silvana (2011) 'Qualitative research and technology: In the midst of a revolution', in Norman K. Denzin and Yvonna S. Lincoln (eds), *Handbook of Qualitative Research*, 4th edition. Thousand Oaks, CA: Sage. pp. 627–43.

Denzin, Norman K. (1970) *The Research Act*. Englewood Cliffs, NJ: Prentice Hall.

Denzin, Norman K. and Lincoln, Yvonna S. (2005) 'Introduction: The discipline and practice of qualitative research', in Norman K. Denzin, and Yvonna S. Lincoln, (eds) *The SAGE Handbook of Qualitative Research*, 3rd edition. Thousand Oaks, CA: Sage. pp. 1-32.

Denzin, Norman K. and Lincoln, Yvonna S. (eds) (2011) *The SAGE Handbook of Qualitative Research*. London: Sage.

Evers, Jeanine C., Silver, Christina, Mruck, Katja and Peeters, Bart (2011) 'Introduction to the KWALON experiment: Discussions on qualitative data analysis software by developers and users' [28 paragraphs]. *Forum Qualitative Sozialforschung/Forum: Qualitative Social Research*, 12 (1), Art. 40, http://nbn-resolving. de/urn:nbn:de:0114-fqs1101405 (accessed 17 April 2013).

Flick, Uwe (2007) *Managing Quality in Qualitative Research*. London: Sage.

Flick, Uwe (2014) *An Introduction to Qualitative Research*, 5th edition. London: Sage.

Flick, Uwe (ed.) (forthcoming) 'Qualitative research as global endeavour', *Qualitative Inquiry*, Special issue.

Flick, U., Garms-Homolová, Vjenka, Herrmann, Wolfram, Kuck, Joachim and Röhnsch, Gundula (2012) '"I can't prescribe something just because someone asks for it . . .": Using mixed methods in the framework of triangulation', *Journal of Mixed Methods Research*, 6: 97–110.

Flick, Uwe, Kardorff, Ernst v. and Steinke, Ines (eds) (2004) *A Companion to Qualitative Research*. London: Sage.

Flick, Uwe and Röhnsch, Gundula (forthcoming) 'Migrating diseases – triangulating approaches: Challenges for qualitative inquiry as a global endeavor', *Qualitative Inquiry.*

Friese, Susanne (2011) *Qualitative Data Analysis with ATLAS.ti*. London: Sage.

Garfinkel, Harold (1967) *Studies in Ethnomethodology*. Englewood Cliffs, NJ: Prentice Hall.

Geertz, Clifford (1983) *Local Knowledge: Further Essays in Interpretative Anthropology*. New York: Basic Books.

Glaser, Barney G. (1998) *Doing Grounded Theory. Issues and Discussions*. Mill Valley, CA.: Sociology Press.

Glaser, Barney G. and Strauss, Anselm L. (1967) *The Discovery of Grounded Theory: Strategies for Qualitative Research*. New York: Aldine.

Gobo, Giampietro (2012) 'Glocalizing methodology? The encounter between local methodologies', *International Journal of Social Research Methodology*, 14 (6): 417–37.

Heinze, Thomas, Klusemann, Hans-Werner and Soeffner, Hans-Georg (eds) (1980) *Interpretationen einer Bildungsgeschichte*. Bensheim: päd.-extra-Buchverlag.

Hsiung, Ping-Chun (2012) 'The globalization of qualitative research: Challenging Anglo-American domination and local hegemonic discourse' [27 paragraphs]. *Forum Qualitative Sozialforschung / Forum: Qualitative Social Research*, 13 (1), Art. 21, http://nbn-resolving.de/urn:nbn:de:0114-fqs1201216 (accessed 17 April 2013).

Knoblauch, Hubert, Flick, Uwe and Maeder, Christoph (eds) (2005) 'Special issue "The state of the art of qualitative research in Europe"', *Forum Qualitative Social Research*, 6 (3): September. http://www.qualitative-research.net/fqs/fqs-e/inhalt3-05-e.htm (accessed 17 April 2013).

Mayring, Phillip (2000) 'Qualitative content analysis', [28 paragraphs]. *Forum Qualitative Sozialforschung / Forum: Qualitative Social Research*, 1(2), Art. 20, http://nbn-resolving.de/urn:nbn:de:0114-fqs0002204 (accessed 13 June 2013).

McMullen, Linda M. (2011) 'A discursive analysis of Teresa's protocol: Enhancing oneself, diminishing others', in Frederick J. Wertz, et al., *Five Ways of Doing Qualitative Analysis: Phenomenological Psychology, Grounded Theory, Discourse Analysis, Narrative Research, and Intuitive Inquiry* New York: Guilford. pp. 205–23.

Reichertz, Jo (2004) 'Objective hermeneutics and hermeneutic sociology of knowledge,' in Uwe Flick et al. (eds), *A Companion to Qualitative Research*. London: Sage. pp. 290–5.

Ryan, Ann and Gobo, Giampietro (eds) (2011) 'Special issue on "Perspectives on decolonising methodologies"', *International Journal of Social Research Methodology*, 14 (6).

Schnettler, Bernt and Rebstein, Bernd (eds) (2012) 'Special issue "International perspectives on the future of qualitative research in Europe"', *Qualitative Sociology Review*, 8 (2): http://www.qualitativesociologyreview.org/ENG/Volume22/QSR_8_2.pdf (accessed 17 April 2013).

Schütze, Fritz (1977) 'Die Technik des narrativen Interviews in Interaktionsfeldstudien, dargestellt an einem Projekt zur Erforschung von kommunalen Machtstrukturen', Manuskript der Universität Bielefeld, Fakultät für Soziologie.

Strauss, Anselm L. and Corbin, Juliet (1990) *Basics of Qualitative Research* (2nd edition 1998; 3rd edition 2008). London: Sage.

Wertz, Frederick J., Charmaz, Kathy, McMullen, Linda M., Josselson, Ruthellen, Anderson, Rosemarie and McSpadden, Emalinda (2011) *Five Ways of Doing Qualitative Analysis*. New York: Guilford Press.

PART II
Concepts, Contexts, Basics

Part II outlines the *concepts and contexts and basics* of qualitative data analysis. It includes nine chapters. Concepts that are discussed here include: What are the implications of specific topics and frameworks, like theory (see Maxwell and Chmiel, Chapter 2) and inspiration in the field (see Gubrium and Holstein, Chapter 3), for qualitative data analysis? How are issues of inference (induction, deduction and abduction – see Reichertz, Chapter 9) currently reflected, discussed and solved in qualitative data analysis? What is the role of interpretation in qualitative data analysis (see Willig, Chapter 10)?

Contexts to be discussed will be questions of selecting materials that become relevant for analysis (see Rapley, Chapter 4) or the reflexivity of the research (see May and Perry, Chapter 8). Technical aspects like transcription (see Kowal and O'Connell, Chapter 5) and comparison (see Palmberger and Gingrich, Chapter 7) are complemented by more general issues like working collaboratively in data analysis (see Cornish et al., Chapter 6).

Guideline questions as an orientation for writing chapters were the following: How has this issue become relevant for analysis of qualitative data? What are the basic assumptions of this concept? What are differing ways to deal with this issue in analysing qualitative data? What is the impact of these alternatives on the data analysis? What are new developments and perspectives in this context? What is the contribution of the concept/discussion to the analysis of qualitative data and critical reflection of it?

Reading the chapters in Part II should help to answer questions like the following ones for a study and its method(s): What is the impact on working with qualitative data coming from context matters like selecting materials or integration? How can subjective experience and culture be interpreted in qualitative data analysis? How can one draw inferences in qualitative data analysis? What is a theory of qualitative data analysis? How do the aims and strategies of comparison, or of collaboration, influence the process of qualitative data analysis? What is the role of interpretation in the actual analysis of qualitative data?

In answering questions like these, the chapters in this part are meant to contribute to the contextualization of the specific approaches to analysing qualitative data and highlight the impact of the ways in which the data were produced and processed in the analysis.

Notes Toward a Theory of Qualitative Data Analysis

Joseph A. Maxwell and Margaret Chmiel

'Theory of qualitative data analysis' can be interpreted in a number of ways. There has been a great deal written about using substantive theory – theories about the *phenomena* being investigated – in doing qualitative research (e.g., Anyon, 2009; Dressman, 2008; Flinders and Mills, 1994), and such theory has important implications for analysis. Instances of this use of theory include Manning (2004), on semiotics and data analysis, and Potter (2004: 609–11), on the theoretical principles of discourse analysis (see Willig, Chapter 23, this volume). For example, Potter argued that discourse analysis is based on three fundamental features of discourse: that it is action-oriented, situated, and constructed. These three principles shape the questions that discourse analysis is designed to answer: what is this discourse doing, how is it constructed to make this happen, and what resources are available to perform this? Potter stated that this focus is quite different from that of cognitive psychology, which attempts to relate discourse organization to cognitive organization.

For qualitative data analysis in general, substantive theories obviously have important implications for analysis, including the coding categories that the researcher creates and the identification of segments of data to which analytic procedures will be applied. Here, however, we want to focus on how qualitative analysis itself has been theorized – how we have understood, theoretically, what we do when we analyse data. The way in which qualitative data analysis is theoretically understood has important implications for how we analyse our data, and these implications have not been systematically developed.

Before we do this, we want to explain what we mean by 'theory.' A theory, in our view, is a conceptual model or understanding of some phenomenon, one that not only describes, but explains, that phenomenon – that clarifies *why* the phenomenon is the way it is (Anyon, 2009: 3; Hechter and Horne, 2009: 8; Maxwell and Mittapalli, 2008). We also hold that every theory is partial and incomplete, a simplification of the complexity of that phenomenon, and thus that there can be more than one valid theory of any phenomenon (Maxwell, 2011). What we present here is one way of theorizing qualitative data analysis, one that we think reveals some important, and largely undiscussed, aspects of analysis. We believe that this can help us to better understand what we are doing when we analyse data, and allow us to produce better and more insightful analyses.

Although there are many prescriptive accounts of how qualitative data *should* be analysed, very little has been done to develop an explicit, general theory of what qualitative researchers *actually* do when they analyse their data, and why: the 'theory-in-use' (Argyris and Schoen, 1992) or 'logic-in-use' (Kaplan, 1964) of qualitative data analysis, rather than its espoused theory or reconstructed logic. Anselm Strauss's statement that 'we have a very long way to go yet in understanding how we do qualitative analysis and how to improve our analysis' (1988: 99) still seems accurate.

In the remainder of this chapter, we present an outline of such a theory (for a more detailed presentation of this theory, see Maxwell and Miller, 2008, and Maxwell, 2011) and use this theory in discussing some prominent approaches to qualitative data analysis. A key component of this theory is the distinction between two types of relationships: those based on similarity, and those based on contiguity (Jakobson, 1956; Lyons, 1968: 70–81; Saussure, 1986 [1916]); we begin by explicating this distinction. We then apply the distinction to qualitative data analysis, arguing that two major types of strategies for analysis, which we call categorizing and connecting strategies, are respectively based on the identification of similarity relations and contiguity relations. We describe each of these two strategies in more detail, presenting the strengths and limitations of each strategy, and discuss ways of integrating these. We conclude with some observations on the use of computers in qualitative data analysis.

SIMILARITY AND CONTIGUITY

Similarity and contiguity refer to two fundamentally different kinds of relationships between things, neither of which can be assimilated to the other. Similarity-based relations involve resemblances or common features; their identification is based on comparison, which can be independent of time and place. In qualitative data analysis, similarities and differences are generally used to define categories and to group and compare data by category. Maxwell and Miller (2008) referred to analytical strategies that focus on relationships of similarity as *categorizing* strategies.[1] Coding is a typical categorizing strategy in qualitative research.

Contiguity-based relations, in contrast, involve juxtaposition in time and space, the influence of one thing on another, or relations among parts of a text; their identification involves seeing actual *connections* between things, rather than similarities and differences. In qualitative data analysis, contiguity relationships are identified among data in an actual context (such as an interview transcript or observational field notes). Contiguity relationships may also be identified among abstract concepts and categories, as a subsequent step to a categorizing analysis of the data. Maxwell and Miller referred to strategies that focus on relationships of contiguity as *connecting* strategies. Some narrative approaches to interview analysis primarily involve connecting strategies, as do microethnographic approaches (Erickson, 1992) to observational data.

The distinction between similarity and contiguity, generally credited to Saussure, was first explicitly stated by David Hume in his *A Treatise of Human Nature* (1978 [1739]). Hume defined three ways in which ideas may be associated: by resemblance (similarity), by contiguity in time or place, and by cause and effect. He then argued that causation is a complex relation based on the other two, leaving resemblance and contiguity as the two primary modes of association.

This distinction has been most extensively developed in structuralist linguistics, where it was explicitly introduced by Saussure (1986 [1916]). Saussure distinguished between associative (similarity-based) and syntagmatic (contiguity-based) relations, and grounded his theory of language in this distinction. Jakobson (1956) later developed this distinction, establishing the currently prevalent terms paradigmatic and syntagmatic, and explicitly basing these on similarity and contiguity, respectively. Jakobson's ideas were picked up and further developed by numerous other writers, including Barthes (1968), Levi-Strauss (1963; 1966), and Bruner (1986). However, with the decline in structuralist approaches to language, the distinction has received little recent attention.

The credibility of this distinction is supported by recent research on memory. Tulving (1983; Tulving and Craik, 2000) distinguished two distinct, though interacting, systems of memory, which he called semantic memory and episodic memory. Semantic memory is memory of facts, concepts, principles, and other sorts of information, organized conceptually rather than in terms of the context in which they were learned. Episodic memory, in contrast, is memory of events and episodes, organized temporally in terms of the context of their occurrence. Extensive experimental research (Dere et al., 2008; Tulving and Craik, 2000) has led to the general acceptance of this distinction as an important aspect of memory and information processing, in non-human animals as well as humans (Shettleworth, 2010: 249–56). Flick (2000; 2007: 53–64) applied this distinction to qualitative interviewing, developing a specific procedure for accessing episodic memory that he called episodic interviewing, but to our knowledge no one has explicitly connected this research to data analysis.

SIMILARITY AND CONTIGUITY RELATIONS IN QUALITATIVE DATA ANALYSIS

Although the role of similarity in categorizing is often recognized, the importance of contiguity relations in other types of analysis is rarely stated, and the similarity/contiguity distinction itself, though often implicitly accepted, is not linked to existing theoretical work on this distinction.

A particularly clear presentation (although not explicitly framed in terms of the similarity/contiguity distinction) of how this distinction is involved in the actual processes of data analysis is that of Smith:

> I usually start ... at the beginning of the notes. I read along and seem to engage in two kinds of processes – comparing and contrasting, and looking for antecedents and consequences ...
>
> The essence of concept formation [the first process] is ... 'How are they alike, and how are they different?' The similar things are grouped and given a label that highlights their similarity. ... In time, these similarities and differences come to represent clusters of concepts, which then organize themselves into more abstract categories and eventually into hierarchical taxonomies.
>
> Concurrently, a related but different process is occurring. ... The conscious search for the consequences of social items ... seemed to flesh out a complex systemic view and a concern for process, the flow of events over time. In addition it seemed to argue for a more holistic, systemic, interdependent network of events at the concrete level and concepts and propositions at an abstract level. ... At a practical level, while in the field, the thinking, searching, and note recording reflected not only a consciousness of similarities and differences but also an attempt to look for unexpected relationships, antecedents, and consequences within the flow of items. (1979: 338)

A similar distinction is found in many accounts of qualitative data analysis. For example, Seidman (2006: 119ff.) described two main strategies in his analysis of interviews (see Roulston, Chapter 20, this volume): the categorization of interview material through coding and thematic analysis, and the creation of what he called 'profiles,' a type of narrative condensation of the interview that largely retains the sequential order of the participant's statements. Coffey and Atkinson (1996) likewise distinguished 'concepts and coding' from 'narratives and stories,' and Dey (1993: 94, 153ff.) described the difference between creating categories and making comparisons (see Palmberger and Gingrich, Chapter 7, this volume), on the one hand, and 'linking data,' on the other. He described qualitative data analysis as an iterative process of describing, classifying (categorizing), and connecting data, and stated that 'linking data involves recognizing substantive rather than formal connections between things. Formal relations are concerned with how things relate in terms of similarity and difference. … Substantive relations are concerned with how things interact' (Dey, 1993: 152).[2]

However, none of these authors other than Dey examined the principles on which these distinctions are based, and the similarity/contiguity distinction has frequently been confounded with others. For example, Ezzy (2002: 95) distinguished narrative analysis from coding primarily in terms of its being more holistic, interpretive, and 'in process,' and as employing a constructivist approach and 'situated relativity.'

Both of these strategies depend on the identification of units of data that will be addressed by subsequent analytic procedures. This step has been called 'unitizing' by Labov and Fanshel (1977: 38–40) and Lincoln and Guba (1985: 344), and 'segmenting' by Coffey and Atkinson (1996: 26) and Tesch (1990: 91); Charmaz (2006: 43ff.) defined coding as 'categorizing segments of data.' This process has been extensively discussed in linguistics, but has not usually been recognized as a distinct step in qualitative analysis, instead being subsumed in subsequent categorizing steps (e.g., Charmaz, 2006; see Thornberg and Charmaz, Chapter 11, this volume).

Segmenting the data is obviously involved in categorizing analyses, but it is an implicit (and sometimes explicit) process in most narrative and other connecting approaches. For example, Gee (2010: 118–28), in his approach to discourse analysis, segments speech into units that he calls 'lines' and 'stanzas,' based on both linguistic cues and the content of the utterance. This step is as necessary to narrative and other connecting strategies as it is to categorizing ones (Linde, 1993: 61–7; Riessman, 1993: 58), although the particular way it is done, and the length of the segments, will depend on the type of analysis used (see Esin et al., Chapter 14, this volume).

Once segments of data have been identified, there are a number of analytic options available to the researcher. We see these as falling into three main groups: memos, categorizing strategies (such as coding and thematic analysis), and connecting strategies (typically involved in narratives, case studies, and ethnographic microanalysis). Memos are an important technique for analysing qualitative data (Miles and Huberman, 1994; Strauss and Corbin, 1990), but can be used for either categorizing or connecting purposes, or to perform other functions not related to data analysis, such as reflection on methods.

CATEGORIZING STRATEGIES

The most widely used categorizing strategy in qualitative data analysis is coding. In coding, the data segments are labeled and grouped by category; they are then examined and compared, both within and between categories. Many qualitative researchers have treated coding as the fundamental activity in analysis (e.g., Bogdan and Biklen, 2003; Ryan and Bernard, 2000; van den Hoonaard and van den Hoonaard, 2008: 187), and the only one that involves manipulation of actual data.

Coding categories 'are a means of sorting the descriptive data you have collected … so that the material bearing on a given topic can be physically separated from other data' (Bogdan and Biklen, 2003: 161). Coding and sorting by code creates a similarity-based ordering of data that replaces the original contiguity-based ordering. Tesch (1990: 115–23) referred to this replacement of an original contextual structure by a different, categorical structure as 'decontextualizing and recontextualizing.'

However, this new set of relationships is based on similarity rather than contiguity, and is thus not a 'recontextualization' in the usual sense of 'context,' that is, a set of phenomena or data that are connected in time and space. This new set of relationships is quite different from a contiguity-based context, and confusing the two can lead to the neglect of actual contextual relationships. Other researchers (e.g., Mishler, 1984; 1986) have also seen the neglect of context as a major defect of coding and other categorizing strategies.

TYPES OF CODING CATEGORIES

An important distinction among types of categories is that between organizational, substantive, and theoretical categories (Maxwell, 2012b: 107–8). These are not absolute distinctions; many actual coding categories can be seen as involving aspects of more than one type, or as being intermediate between two types. However, we believe that the conceptual typology is valuable.

Organizational categories are broad areas or issues that are often established prior to data collection. McMillan and Schumacher (2001: 469) referred to these as *topics* rather than categories, stating that 'a topic is the descriptive name for the subject matter of the segment. You are not, at this time, asking "What is said?" which identifies the meaning of the segment.' In a study of elementary school principals' practices of retaining children in a grade, examples of such categories are 'retention,' 'policy,' 'goals,' 'alternatives,' and 'consequences' (McMillan and Schumacher, 2001: 470). Organizational categories function primarily as abstract 'bins' for sorting the data for further analysis; they do not specifically address what is actually happening or what meaning these topics have for participants. They are often useful as organizational tools in your analysis, but they do not by themselves provide much insight into what is actually going on (Coffey and Atkinson, 1996: 34–5).

This latter task requires substantive and/or theoretical categories, ones that address what is actually taking place, or the actual understandings of this that participants have. These latter categories can often be seen as subcategories of the organizational ones, but they are generally *not* subcategories that, in advance, you could have known would be significant, unless you are already fairly familiar with the kind of participants or setting you are studying or are using a well-developed theory. They implicitly make some sort of claim about the phenomena being studied – that is, they could be *wrong*, rather than simply being conceptual boxes for holding data.

Substantive categories are primarily *descriptive*, in a broad sense that includes descriptions of participants' concepts and beliefs; they stay close to the data categorized, and do not inherently imply a more abstract theory. In the study of grade retention mentioned earlier, examples of substantive categories derived from interviews with principals would be 'retention as failure,' 'retention as a last resort,' 'self-confidence as a goal,' 'parent's willingness to try alternatives,' and 'not being in control (of the decision)' (McMillan and Schumacher, 2001: 472). Categories taken from participants' own words and concepts, what are generally called 'emic' categories (Fetterman, 2008), are usually substantive, but many substantive categories are not emic, being based on the *researcher's* understanding of what is going on. Substantive categories are often inductively generated through a close 'open coding' of the data (Strauss and Corbin, 1990). They can be used in *developing* a more general theory of what is going on, but they do not *depend on* this theory (see Thornberg and Charmaz, Chapter 11, this volume).

Theoretical categories, in contrast, place the coded data into an explicit theoretical framework. These categories may be derived either from prior theory, or from an inductively developed theory (in which case the concepts and the theory are usually developed concurrently). They often represent the *researcher's* concepts (what are called 'etic' categories), rather than denoting participants' own concepts. For example, the categories 'nativist,' 'remediationist,' and 'interactionist,' used to classify teachers' beliefs about grade retention in terms of prior theoretical distinctions (Smith and Shepard, 1988), would be theoretical.

WORKING WITH CATEGORIES

The categories generated though coding are typically linked into larger patterns; this subsequent step can be seen as contiguity-based, but the connections are made between the categories themselves, rather than between segments of actual data. In addition, using connecting techniques only on the categories, rather than the data, results in an *aggregate* account of contiguity relationships, and can never reconstitute the specific contextual connections that were lost during the original categorizing analysis. This strategy imposes a uniform account on the actual diversity of relationships in the data, obscuring the complexity of such relationships in order to emphasize the most prevalent connections (Maxwell, 1996; 2011: 49–51, 64–6).

Thematic analysis is also a categorizing strategy; Ayres (2008: 867) stated that 'thematic analysis is a data reduction and analysis strategy by which data are segmented, categorized, summarized, and reconstructed in a way that captures the important concepts within a data set.' While the term 'theme' thus refers to a kind of coding category, it is often one with a broader or more abstract scope than those involved in the initial coding of data. For example, a theme often has an internal connected structure: a relationship between two concepts or actions, a proposition or belief, a narrative or argument, or other more complex sets of relations. However, its identification and establishment *as* a theme – showing that it is more than an idiosyncratic occurrence – is inherently a categorizing process (Ayres, 2008).

Ayres argued that thematic analysis (which for her is broader than simply thematic coding) incorporates connecting as well as categorizing strategies. Thus, 'as identification of themes progresses, the investigator also considers the relationship among categories. In this way, data that have been decontextualized through coding retain their connection to their sources' (2008: 868). She argues that thematic analysis thus retains the connection of the data to their original context. However, as argued above, the relationships among thematic *categories* are *generic* relationships, not ones between actual data, and thus substitute a single understanding for the original variation in relationships that existed in the data (Maxwell, 2011: 64–6).

Most qualitative researchers are aware of the dangers of decontextualization in using categorizing techniques. Works on qualitative methods often warn about context stripping and the need to retain the connection of coded data with their original context. However, attention to context is often seen only as a *check* or *control* on the use of categorizing analytic strategies, and most works say little about how one might *analyze* contextual relationships.

Perhaps the most common strategy for retaining contextual information in qualitative research is the 'case study.' In this approach, the data are interpreted within the unique context of each case in order to provide an account of a particular instance, setting, person, or event. However, case studies often employ primarily categorizing analysis strategies (e.g., Merriam, 1988; Weiss, 1994; Yin, 2003: 101–11), and their main advantage is that the categorizing (coding, thematic analysis, etc.) occurs within a particular case rather than across cases, so that the contextual relationships are harder to lose sight of. Qualitative case studies *can* be highly contextual or connected in their analysis (e.g., clinical case description), but are not inherently so.

Narratives, portraits, and case studies are often included in qualitative research reports as an accompaniment to categorizing analysis, and Barone (1990: 358) argued that most qualitative texts are a mixture of narrative and paradigmatic (categorizing) design features. However, such uses of narrative are often largely presentational rather than analytic; even Patton, who clearly used case studies as an analytic strategy, confounded this claim by describing case studies as 'presenting a holistic portrayal' (1990: 388). Such presentational techniques partially compensate for the loss of contextual ties that results from a primarily categorizing approach, but they rarely are integrated with what is seen as the 'real' analysis, or go beyond what is apparent in the raw data.

Coffey and Atkinson (1996: 52) stated that:

> Our interview informants may tell us long and complicated accounts and reminiscences. When we chop them up into separate coded segments, we are in danger of losing the sense that they are accounts. ... Segmenting and coding may be an important, even an indispensable, part of the research process, but it is not the whole story.

We now turn to ways of analysing the connections within an account or event, what *makes* it an account, rather than a set of disconnected statements or actions.

CONNECTING STRATEGIES

What we call connecting strategies for analysis are designed not just to retain, but to analyse, connections among segments of data within a specific context. This is generally done by identifying key relationships that tie the data together into a narrative or sequence. For example, ten Have (1999: 105) described the first analytical step in conversation analysis (see Toerien, Chapter 22, this volume) as characterizing the actions in a sequence, and Seidman (2006: 120) stated that he creates what he called "profiles" from interviews as 'a way to find and display coherence in the constitutive events of a participant's experience.'

However, the process of doing connecting analysis has received less attention than categorizing analysis. Narrative analysis is the most prevalent approach that has emphasized alternatives to categorizing analysis, but much of narrative research, broadly defined, involves categorizing as well as connecting analysis, and the distinction has not been clearly defined in this approach (see Esin et al., Chapter 14, this volume).

For example, Lieblich et al. (1998) described two dimensions of narrative analysis: holistic vs. categorical approaches, and a focus on content vs. form. The first dimension was described as 'very similar to the distinction between "categorization" and "contextualization" as proposed by Maxwell.' However, their characterization of holistic analysis focused mainly on the holism rather than the connecting nature of the analysis: 'in the holistic approach, the life story of the person is taken as a whole, and sections of the text are interpreted in the context of other parts of the narrative' (Lieblich et al., 1998: 12). Their examples of the holistic approach emphasized a thematic analysis of the material and the use of these themes 'to create a rich picture of a unique individual' (15), and, in multiple case studies, a focus on similarities and differences among the cases. It is only in the discussion of the actual process of reading holistically that specifically connecting strategies, such as following each theme throughout the story and noting the context of each transition between themes, were described (63).

Detailed, concrete descriptions of connecting analysis are much less common than for categorizing analysis. Seidman's (2006: 120–2) strategy for creating what he calls 'profiles' from interview transcripts involves marking passages of interest in the interview (i.e., segmenting), and crafting these into a narrative, but he does not provide guidelines for the latter process. Similarly, Dey (1993) explicitly identified 'linking data' as a strategy for qualitative data analysis, providing several diagrams of links between text segments and suggesting hyperlinks as one way of creating these (153–67). Despite this, he focused mainly on using specific links between data segments to create links between categories, rather than on developing a more extensive connecting analysis of actual data.

The most detailed description that we have found of a connecting approach to analysis is that of Gee (2011: 126–35), who provided a 'toolkit' of 27 analytic strategies for doing discourse analysis (see Willig, Chapter 23, this volume). Many of these strategies involve identifying relationships among segments of data in a text; here, we will describe one particular strategy that Gee called the 'connections building tool.' He stated that this tool leads the analyst to 'ask how the words or grammar being used in the communication connect or disconnect things or ignore connections between things' (2011: 126). Gee analysed a number of texts to demonstrate the connections within these, showing how different linguistic forms (pronouns, conjunctions, determiners, substitution, etc.) create cohesion among phrases and sentences, and provided several exercises for the reader to analyse connections within a text.

Contiguity-based analytic strategies are not limited to linguistic or textual materials. What Erickson (1992: 204) called 'ethnographic microanalysis of interaction' involves the detailed description of local interaction processes, and analysis of how these processes are organized. The analytic process 'begins by considering whole events, continues by analytically decomposing them into smaller fragments, and then concludes by *recomposing* them into wholes. ... [This process] returns them to a level of sequentially connected social action' (1992: 217). Thus, instead of segmenting events and then *categorizing* these segments to create a structure of similarities and differences across situations or individuals, this approach segments the data and then *connects* these segments into a relational order within an actual context (see Gubrium and Holstein, Chapter 3, this volume).

Narrative strategies, as well as most other connecting strategies, do not rely exclusively on contiguity. As described above, they also tend to utilize categorization, to a greater or lesser extent, to discern the narrative structure of the data (Linde, 1993: 65–6). For example, identifying elements of plot, scene, conflict, or resolution in a narrative, as in structural or formal approaches (Lieblich et al., 1998), inherently involves classification. However, such classification is used to identify the elements of a narrative in terms of how they relate to other elements, rather than to create a similarity-based ordering of the data in terms of their *content*. Thus, Mishler (1986: 82) described some forms of narrative analysis that employ coding and categorization, but the categories he presented are *functional* rather than substantive categories. Such categories 'provide a set of codes for classifying the "narrative functions" of different parts of the account,' rather than constituting the basis for a reorganization of the data. Such categorization can be a necessary complement to a connecting analysis, rather than a separate analytic process.

Narrative and contextual analyses, as strategies based primarily on contiguity rather than similarity, have disadvantages of their own. In particular, they can lead to an inability to make comparisons and to gain insights from the similarity or difference of two things in separate contexts. An exclusive emphasis on connecting strategies can also lead to an imprisonment in the story of a particular narrative – a failure to see alternative ways of framing and interpreting the text or situation in question (see Esin et al., Chapter 14, this volume).

DISPLAYS AS CATEGORIZING AND CONNECTING STRATEGIES

Displays (Miles and Huberman, 1994), as techniques for data analysis, can also be divided into similarity-based and contiguity-based forms. Miles and Huberman described a wide variety of displays, but most of these fall into two basic types: matrices (tables), and networks (figures); Maxwell (2012b: 54ff.) referred to the latter as 'maps,' and provided additional examples of both types. Matrices are formed by the intersection of two or more lists of items; the cells in the table are filled with data, either raw or summarized, allowing for comparison of the similarities and differences among the cells. The lists forming the matrix can be of individuals, roles, sites, topics, or properties of these, and can be organized in numerous ways, creating a large number of different types of matrices. Networks, in contrast, are visual maps of the relationships (for Miles and Huberman, usually temporal or causal relationships) among individuals, events, social units, or properties of these.

We see matrices and networks as, respectively, similarity-based and contiguity-based displays. Matrices are a logical extension of coding; they are created by constructing lists of mutually exclusive categories and then crossing these to create cells. Such displays may then be used to make connections across items in a row or column, but these connections are based on, and limited by, the original categorization that was used to create the matrix. Networks, on the other hand, are a logical extension of narrative or causal analysis, organizing events or concepts by time and by spatial or causal connection; they capture the contiguity-based relationships that are lost in creating matrices. Miles and Huberman provided examples of networks that link specific events, as well as those linking more abstract categories, although none were included that link actual data segments. They also presented a substantial number of hybrid forms that involve both categorizing and connecting analysis, such as time-ordered matrices and segmented causal networks.[3]

There are striking similarities between Miles and Huberman's notions of data displays and emerging ideas in literary approaches to the analysis of texts. In *Graphs, Maps, and Trees: Abstract Models for Literary History* (Moretti and Piazza, 2007: 1), the authors discuss a series of analytical tactics through which 'the reality of the text undergoes a process of deliberate reduction and abstraction.' Studies of literature have traditionally focused on close reading, that is, careful analysis of individual texts. Moretti proposes a 'distant reading,' where distance is not an obstacle but a specific form of knowledge which allows for 'a sharper sense of ... overall interconnection.' As an example, he would take something like the narrative location of a story, that is, where events happen over the course of the story, and organize them on a map. After mapping out facets from a series of stories he compares how components of their narrative arcs reveal similarities and differences between how locations work in the stories. In this idea of distant reading, Moretti shows us how text can be analysed by bringing one particular feature of text across data sets into high relief in order to draw connections among the texts. These connections and the subsequent understanding they bring to the material would be missed during the course of the more standard close readings.

INTEGRATING CATEGORIZING AND CONNECTING STRATEGIES

We have alluded to some of the advantages of combining categorizing and connecting strategies for analysing qualitative data. However, even authors who explicitly discuss both types of strategies, such as Atkinson (1992; Coffey and Atkinson, 1996), Dey (1993), and Seidman (2006), rarely address how to integrate these.

While the separate use of the two approaches is legitimate and often productive, there are other possibilities as well. The most common is the sequential use of the two types of strategies, beginning with one and then moving to the other. For example, most qualitative researchers who employ coding strategies eventually develop a model of the causal connections or relational patterns among the categories, as discussed above. However, this final step rarely involves direct analysis of data, and usually receives little explicit discussion (prominent exceptions are the work of Strauss, discussed below, and Miles and Huberman).

Researchers who employ initial connecting or narrative strategies, on the other hand, often conclude by discussing similarities and differences among the cases or individuals analysed (this is the reverse of the previous strategy of connecting categories into a relational sequence or network.) For example, Erickson described the final step in ethnographic microanalysis as the 'comparative analysis of instances across the research corpus,' to determine how typical these analysed units of interaction are (1992: 220).

Maxwell and Miller (2008) suggested that it may be useful to think of this integration in terms of categorizing and connecting 'moves' (Abbott, 2004: 162ff.) in an analysis, rather than in terms of alternative or sequential overall strategies.[4] At each point in the analysis, one can make either a categorizing move, looking for similarities and differences, or a connecting move, looking for actual (contiguity-based) connections between things. In fact, it is often productive to alternate between categorizing and connecting moves, as each move can respond to limitations in the results of the previous move.

A widely used approach to qualitative analysis that seems to us to employ this strategy is the 'grounded theory' strategy (Strauss, 1987; Strauss and Corbin, 1990; see Thornberg and Charmaz, Chapter 11, this volume). The initial step in analysis, which Strauss called 'open coding,' involves segmenting the data, attaching conceptual labels to these segments, and making comparisons among the segments. However, many of the subsequent steps in analysis are predominantly connecting, despite being described as forms of coding; Strauss and Corbin used 'coding' to mean simply 'the process of analyzing data' (1990: 61). Thus, Strauss's next step, 'axial coding,'[5] consists of:

> specifying a category (*phenomenon*) in terms of the *conditions* that give rise to it; the *context* ... in which it is embedded; the action/interactional *strategies* by which it is handled, managed, carried out; and the *consequences* of these strategies. (Strauss and Corbin, 1990: 97)

This is almost a definition of what we mean by connecting analysis; Benaquisto (2008: 51) described axial coding as 'where the data [broken down by open coding] are reassembled so that the researcher may identify relationships more readily.' The main difference is that Strauss and Corbin described these relationships as between *categories*, rather than between specific statements or events. The analytical steps subsequent to open coding involve making connections among categories, developing a 'story line' about the central phenomena of the study, and identifying 'conditional paths' that link actions with conditions and consequences. Confusingly, Strauss and Corbin referred to these connections as 'subcategories,' stating that 'they too are categories, but because we relate them to a category in some form of relationship, we add the prefix "sub"' (1990: 97).

Strauss continually integrated categorizing steps into these later stages: 'Having identified the differences in context, the researcher can begin systematically to group the categories. ... This grouping again is done by asking questions and making comparisons' (Strauss and Corbin, 1990: 132). However, Strauss said very little about the grouping of *data* by category. Categorization, in the grounded theory approach, is manifested primarily in the development and comparison of concepts and categories. Nor does he deal with the analysis of specific contextual relations in the data, operating mostly in terms of relations among concepts.

Like Atkinson (1992; Coffey and Atkinson, 1996), we see categorizing and connecting approaches as inherently complementary strategies for data analysis. The complementarity of similarity and contiguity relations in language is generally recognized, and is a central theme in the article by Jakobson (1956) cited above. However, what seems distinctive about the approach that we advocate is that it involves an explicit, finer-grained integration of the two strategies, rather than seeing these as separate, independent analyses.

COMPUTERS AND QUALITATIVE DATA ANALYSIS

Computer programs for analysing qualitative data (see Gibbs, Chapter 19, this volume) have had a major influence on how analysis is done (Bazeley and Jackson, 2013), and will undoubtedly have even greater impact in the future. However, so far computers have been used primarily for categorizing rather than connecting types of initial data analysis, due to the ease and power with which computers can perform similarity-based functions such as sorting and comparison.

Connecting uses of computer software do exist. So-called 'theory-building' programs (Weitzman and Miles, 1995) can use connections between categories to assist in testing hypotheses about relationships and establishing typical sequences. Padilla (1991: 267) described the use of the program HyperQual to develop 'concept models,' networks of concepts that are 'assembled inductively from individual and small groups of concepts developed during the analysis.' However, these uses are based on a prior categorizing analysis, and the connecting functions focus on conceptual linkages rather than on linking actual data, as discussed above under categorizing strategies.

More recently, Richards (2005) described a number of ways of using computers to establish links among data and data files. However, she focused mainly on links between different *types* of data, such as between field notes and memos, and on links between *different* interviews or observations, as well as links between data *categories*. Her emphasis was almost entirely on categorizing analysis, and she did not discuss linking data *within* a specific context, or of identifying relationships of contiguity rather than similarity/difference.

Despite this, there are ways that computers can be used to assist in the direct connecting analysis of qualitative data. One way is to mark, extract, and compile selected data from a longer text, simplifying the task of data reduction in producing case studies, profiles, and narratives. Another is to use graphics programs (such as Inspiration) to develop network displays of specific events and processes, rather than only relations among abstract or generalized concepts. So-called 'hypertext' programs (Coffey and Atkinson, 1996: 181–6; Dey, 1993: 180–91) allow the user to create electronic links among any segments, within or between contexts. Software that is designed to facilitate such strategies could move case-oriented, connecting analysis beyond what Miles and Huberman (1994) called 'handicraft production.'

In summary, we have argued that the distinction between similarity-based (categorizing) and contiguity-based (connecting) analytic strategies is a useful theoretical tool, both for understanding how qualitative researchers analyse data and for seeing how to improve our analyses. The two strategies are best seen as complementary and mutually supporting, rather than being antagonistic and mutually exclusive alternatives, for each have their own strengths and limitations. We hope that our argument will lead to more explicit theorizing of what qualitative researchers do when they analyse data.

NOTES

1. Categorization in qualitative analysis is almost always based on similarity, despite the existence of theories of categorization (e.g., Lakoff, 1987) that include contiguity-based relationships (e.g., metonymy) as well as similarity-based ones.
2. Dey cited Sayer (1992: 88–9) for the distinction between 'substantial' relations of connection and interaction, and 'formal' relations of similarity and difference.
3. The reference to causality may seem inconsistent with qualitative analysis, since the investigation of causality is often taken to be the exclusive property of quantitative methods. We disagree with this claim, and see causal explanation as relying primarily on the analysis of contiguity relationships, rather than similarity or regularity (Huberman and Miles, 1985; Maxwell, 2011; 2012a).
4. This approach draws on Caracelli and Greene's distinction (1997) between 'component' and 'integrated' designs for combining qualitative and quantitative methods.
5. The concept of axial coding has been controversial within the grounded theory community. Glaser (1992) vehemently rejected Strauss and Corbin's incorporation of this strategy, claiming that it was too structured, and incompatible with the inductive nature of grounded theory as he and Strauss originally presented it. Axial coding has not generally been incorporated in constructivist approaches to grounded theory analysis (Charmaz and Bryant, 2008). In using this as an example of connecting analysis, we do not see it as dependent on prestructuring of the analysis, and believe that it is entirely compatible with an inductive approach.

FURTHER READING

Bazeley, Patricia (2013) *Qualitative Data Analysis: Practical Strategies*. London: Sage.
Coffey, Amanda and Paul Atkinson (1996) *Making Sense of Qualitative Data: Complementary Research Strategies*. Thousand Oaks, CA: Sage.
Erickson, Frederick (1992) "Ethnographic microanalysis of interaction," in Margaret D. LeCompte, Wendy L. Millroy, and Judith Preissle (eds.), *The Handbook of Qualitative Research in Education*. San Diego, CA: Academic Press. pp. 201–225.

REFERENCES

Abbott, Andrew D. (2004) *Methods of Discovery: Heuristics for the Social Sciences*. New York: W.W. Norton.
Anyon, Jean (2009) *Theory and Educational Research: Toward Critical Social Explanation*. New York: Routledge.
Argyris, Chris and Schoen, Donald A. (1992) *Theory in Practice: Increasing Professional Effectiveness*. San Francisco: Jossey-Bass.
Atkinson, Paul (1992) 'The ethnography of a medical setting: Reading, writing, and rhetoric,' *Qualitative Health Research*, 2 (4): 451–74.
Ayres, Lioness (2008) 'Thematic coding and analysis,' in Lisa M. Given (ed.), *The SAGE Encyclopedia of Qualitative Research Methods*. Thousand Oaks, CA: Sage. pp. 867–8.
Barone, Thomas (1990) 'Using the narrative text as an occasion for conspiracy,' in Elliot Eisner and Alan Peshkin (eds.), *Qualitative Inquiry in Education: The Continuing Debate*. New York: Teachers College Press. pp. 305–26.
Barthes, Roland (1968) *Elements of Semiology*, trans. from the French by Annette Lavers and Colin Smith. New York: Hill and Wang.
Bazeley, Patricia (2013) *Qualitative Data Analysis: Practical Strategies*. London: Sage.
Bazeley, Patricia and Jackson, Kristi (2013) *Qualitative Data Analysis with NVivo*, 2nd edition. London: Sage.
Benaquisto, Lucia (2008) 'Axial coding,' in Lisa Given (ed.), *The SAGE Encyclopedia of Qualitative Research Methods*. Thousand Oaks, CA: Sage. pp. 51–2.
Bogdan, Robert and Biklen, Sari K. (2003) *Qualitative Research for Education: An Introduction to Theory and Methods*, 4th edition. Boston, MA: Allyn and Bacon.
Bruner, Jerome (1986) 'Two modes of thought,' in Jerome Bruner, *Actual Minds, Possible Worlds*. Cambridge, MA: Harvard University Press.
Caracelli, Valerie J. and Greene, Jennifer C. (1997) 'Crafting mixed-method evaluation designs,' in Valerie J. Caracelli, and Jennifer C. Greene, *Advances in Mixed-Method Evaluation: The Challenges and Benefits of Integrating Diverse Paradigms*. New Directions for Evaluation, no. 74 (Summer 1997). San Francisco: Jossey-Bass. pp. 19–32.
Charmaz, Kathy (2006) *Constructing Grounded Theory: A Practical Guide Through Qualitative Analysis*. Thousand Oaks, CA: Sage.
Charmaz, Kathy and Bryant, Antony (2008) 'Grounded theory,' in Lisa M. Given (ed.), *The SAGE Encyclopedia of Qualitative Research Methods*. Thousand Oaks, CA: Sage. pp. 374–7.
Coffey, Amanda and Atkinson, Paul (1996) *Making Sense of Qualitative Data: Complementary Research Strategies*. Thousand Oaks, CA: Sage.
Dere, Ekrem, Easton, Alexander, Nadel, Lynn, and Huston, Joe P. (2008) *Handbook of Episodic Memory*. Oxford: Elsevier.
Dey, Ian (1993) *Qualitative Data Analysis: A User-Friendly Guide for Social Scientists*. London: Routledge.
Dressman, Mark (2008) *Using Social Theory in Educational Research: A Practical Guide*. London: Routledge.
Erickson, Frederick (1992) 'Ethnographic microanalysis of interaction,' in Margaret D. LeCompte et al. (eds.), *The Handbook of Qualitative Research in Education*. San Diego, CA: Academic Press. pp. 201–25.
Ezzy, Douglas (2002) *Qualitative Analysis: Practice and Innovation*. London: Routledge.
Fetterman, David M. (2008) 'Emic/etic distinction,' in Lisa Given (ed.), *The SAGE Encyclopedia of Qualitative Research Methods*. Thousand Oaks, CA: Sage. p. 249.
Flick, Uwe (2000) 'Episodic interviewing,' in Martin W. Bauer and George Gaskell (eds.), *Qualitative Researching with Text, Image and Sound*. London: Sage. pp. 75–92.
Flick, Uwe (2007) *Managing Quality in Qualitative Research*. London: Sage.
Flinders, David J. and Mills, Geoffrey E. (eds.) (1994) *Theory and Concepts in Qualitative Research: Perspectives from the Field*. New York: Teachers College Press.
Gee, James P. (2010) *An Introduction to Discourse Analysis: Theory and Method*. New York: Routledge.
Gee, James P. (2011) *How to Do Discourse Analysis: A Toolkit*. New York: Routledge.
Glaser, Barney G. (1992) *Basics of Grounded Theory Analysis*. Mill Valley, CA: Sociology Press.

Hechter, Michael and Horne, Christine (2009) *Theories of Social Order*. Stanford, CA: Stanford University Press.

Huberman, A. Michael and Miles, Matthew B. (1985) 'Assessing local causality in qualitative research,' in David N. Berg and Kenwyn K. Smith (eds.), *The Self in Social Inquiry: Researching methods*. Thousand Oaks, CA: Sage. pp. 351–81.

Hume, David (1978 [1739]) *A Treatise of Human Nature*, 2nd edition, ed., with an analytical index, by L. A. Selby-Bigge. Oxford: Oxford University Press.

Jakobson, Roman (1956) 'Two aspects of language and two types of aphasic disturbances,' in Roman Jakobson and Morris Halle, *Fundamentals of Language*. The Hague: Mouton. pp. 55–82.

Kaplan, Abraham (1964) *The Conduct of Inquiry*. San Francisco: Chandler.

Labov, William and Fanshel, David (1977) *Therapeutic Discourse: Psychotherapy as Conversation*. New York: Academic Press.

Lakoff, George (1987) *Women, Fire, and Dangerous Things: What Categories Reveal About the Mind*. Chicago: University of Chicago Press.

Levi-Strauss, Claude (1963) *Structural Anthropology*, trans. by C. Jacobson and B. G. Schoepf. New York: Basic Books.

Levi-Strauss, Claude (1966) *The Savage Mind*. Chicago: University of Chicago Press.

Lieblich, Amia, Tuval-Mashiach, Rivka, and Zilber, Tamar (1998) *Narrative Research: Reading, Analysis, and Interpretation*. Thousand Oaks, CA: Sage.

Lincoln, Yvonna S. and Guba, Egon G. (1985) *Naturalistic Inquiry*. Thousand Oaks, CA: Sage.

Linde, Charlotte (1993) *Life Stories: The Creation of Coherence*. Oxford: Oxford University Press.

Lyons, John (1968) *Introduction to Theoretical Linguistics*. Cambridge: Cambridge University Press.

Manning, Peter K. (2004) 'Semiotics and data analysis,' in M. Hardy and A. Bryman, *Handbook of Data Analysis*. Thousand Oaks, CA: Sage. pp. 567–87.

Maxwell, Joseph A. (1996) 'Diversity and methodology in a changing world,' *Pedagogía*, 30: 32–40.

Maxwell, Joseph A. (2011) *A Realist Approach for Qualitative Research*. Thousand Oaks, CA: Sage.

Maxwell, Joseph A. (2012a) 'The importance of qualitative research for causal explanation in education,' *Qualitative Inquiry*, 18 (8): 649–55.

Maxwell, Joseph A. (2012b) *Qualitative Research Design: An Interactive Approach*, 3rd edition. Thousand Oaks, CA: Sage.

Maxwell, Joseph A. and Miller, Barbara A. (2008) 'Categorizing and connecting strategies in qualitative data analysis,' in Patricia Leavy and Sharlene Hesse-Biber (eds.), *Handbook of Emergent Methods*. New York: Guilford Press. pp. 461–77.

Maxwell, Joseph A. and Mittapalli, Kavita (2008) 'Theory,' in Lisa M. Given (ed.), *The SAGE Encyclopedia of Qualitative Research Methods*. Thousand Oaks, CA: Sage. pp. 876–80.

McMillan, James H. and Schumacher, Sally (2001) *Research in Education: A Conceptual Introduction*. New York: Longman.

Merriam, Sharan (1988) *Case Study Research in Education: A Qualitative Approach*. San Francisco: Jossey-Bass.

Miles, Matthew B. and Huberman, A. Michael (1994) *Qualitative Data Analysis: An Expanded Sourcebook*, 2nd edition. Thousand Oaks, CA: Sage.

Mishler, Eliot (1984) *The Discourse of Medicine: Dialectics of Medical Interviews*. Norwood, NJ: Ablex.

Mishler, Eliot (1986) *Research Interviewing: Context and Narrative*. Cambridge, MA: Harvard University Press.

Moretti, Franco and Alberto Piazza (2007) *Graphs, Maps, Trees: Abstract Models for Literary History*. London: Verso.

Padilla, Raymond V. (1991) 'Using computers to develop concept models of social situations,' *Qualitative Sociology*, 14: 263–74.

Patton, Michael Quinn (1990) *Qualitative Evaluation and Research Methods*, 2nd edition. Thousand Oaks, CA: Sage.

Potter, Jonathan (2004) 'Discourse analysis,' in Melissa Hardy and Alan Bryman, *Handbook of Data Analysis*. Thousand Oaks, CA: Sage. pp. 607–24.

Richards, Lyn (2005) *Handling Qualitative Data: A Practical Guide*. London: Sage.

Riessman, Catherine K. (1993) *Narrative Analysis*. Thousand Oaks, CA: Sage.

Ryan, Gery W. and Bernard, H. Russell (2000) 'Data management and analysis methods,' in Norman K. Denzin and Yvonna S. Lincoln (eds.), *Handbook of Qualitative Research*, 2nd edition. Thousand Oaks, CA: Sage. pp. 769–802.

Saussure, Ferdinand de (1986 [1916]) *Course in General Linguistics*. La Salle, IL: Open Court.

Sayer, Andrew (1992) *Method in Social Science: A Realist Approach*, 2nd edition. London: Routledge.

Seidman, Irving E. (2006) *Interviewing as Qualitative Research: A Guide for Researchers in Education and the Social Sciences*, 3rd edition. New York: Teachers College Press.

Shettleworth, Sara (2010) *Cognition, Evolution, and Behavior*, 2nd edition. New York: Oxford University Press.

Smith, Louis (1979) 'An evolving logic of participant observation, educational ethnography, and other case studies,' *Review of Research in Education*, 6: 316–77.

Smith, Mary Lee and Shepard, Lorrie A. (1988) 'Kindergarten readiness and retention: A qualitative study of teachers' beliefs and practices,' *American Educational Research Journal*, 25: 307–33.

Strauss, Anselm (1987) *Qualitative Analysis for Social Scientists*. Cambridge: Cambridge University Press.

Strauss, Anselm (1988) 'Teaching qualitative research methods courses: A conversation with Anselm Strauss,' *International Journal of Qualitative Studies in Education*, 1: 91–9.

Strauss, Anselm and Corbin, Juliet (1990) *Basics of Qualitative Research: Grounded Theory Procedures and Techniques*. Thousand Oaks, CA: Sage.

ten Have, Paul (1999) *Doing Conversation Analysis: A Practical Guide*. London: Sage.

Tesch, Renata (1990) *Qualitative Research: Analysis Types and Software Tools*. New York: Falmer Press.

Tulving, Endel (1983) *Elements of Episodic Memory*. Oxford: Oxford University Press.

Tulving, Endel and Craik, Fergus I.M. (eds.) (2000) *The Oxford Handbook of Memory*. Oxford: Oxford University Press.

van den Hoonaard, Deborah K. and van den Hoonaard, Will C. (2008) 'Data analysis,' in Lisa M. Given (ed.), *The SAGE Encyclopedia of Qualitative Research Methods*. Thousand Oaks, CA: Sage. pp. 186–8.

Weiss, Robert S. (1994) *Learning from Strangers: The Art and Method of Qualitative Interview Studies*. New York: Free Press.

Weitzman, Eben A. and Miles, Matthew B. (1995) *Computer Programs for Qualitative Data Analysis*. Thousand Oaks, CA: Sage.

Yin, Robert K. (2003) *Case Study Research: Design and Methods*, 3rd edition. Thousand Oaks, CA: Sage.

3

Analytic Inspiration in Ethnographic Fieldwork

Jaber F. Gubrium and James A. Holstein

Debate over the place of methods and analysis in ethnographic fieldwork comes and goes. Some, such as Barney Glaser and Anselm Strauss (1967), have advocated rigorous and systematic coding, the method entailed becoming the analytic process (see Thornberg and Charmaz, Chapter 11, this volume). Earlier, Herbert Blumer (1969), Everett Hughes (1971), and others championed sensitizing concept formation, which amounted to working analytically in close proximity to empirical material and not straying into grand theorizing. More recently, some have questioned the ultimate empirical grounding of ethnographic methods and analysis, the extreme view being that these are literary projects (e.g., see Clifford and Marcus, 1986).

This chapter describes a perspective that places conceptual imagination at the center of the research process, featuring its transformational qualities for both methods of procedure and analysis. In part, the perspective follows in the footsteps of Blumer's, Hughes's, and others' theoretically minimalist proclivities. But it is more attuned to the epistemological dimensions of ethnographic engagement, continually tracking the reflexivity of the enterprise (see May and Perry, Chapter 8, this volume). The chapter starts by drawing a stereotypic distinction between quantitative and qualitative methods and analytic procedures. The aim is, by way of contrast, to champion the exceptional theme that researchers need to move beyond such divisions and their related methodological strictures. Slavish attention to procedure shackles the imagination. Highlighted instead is a kind of explanatory excitement not usually addressed in methodological discussions, which we call 'analytic inspiration.'

Some may claim analytic inspiration is more evident in qualitative than in quantitative research, a view we do not share. Some have flagged it themselves by other names, such as finding analytic 'hooks' or applying explanatory 'punch.' Some would resist considering it methodological because it has no procedural rules. But it is palpable, describable, and holds the keys to understanding. It can change everything, even while none of what it changes can be adjusted to readily bring it about.

We present three illustrations of how analytic inspiration develops in ethnographic fieldwork, leaving it to others to illustrate it for other research traditions. We take the liberty of using Harry Wolcott's (1999) apt phrase 'a way of seeing' as a working synonym for analytic inspiration. If Wolcott applied the term specifically to ethnographic understanding, it can refer more generally to imaginings of how the empirical world works in other research contexts. Analytic inspiration is a way of seeing across the board. It brings into view what methods of procedure cannot do on their own.

The first illustration is taken from our reading of Lila Abu-Lughod's (1993) feminist interpretation of Egyptian Bedouin life. Her empirical work is inspired by a storied sense of culture, which 'works against' a widely accepted alternative. The other two illustrations come from our own organizational fieldwork, so they will be more personal. Analytic inspiration in these cases works against formal organizational understandings of everyday life, bringing into view the way organization is socially situated and interactionally constructed.

MOVING BEYOND PROCEDURE

It is a time-honored saying that qualitative researchers analyse their data as they collect it. This may be contrasted with the quantitative proclivity to proceed stepwise; data collection and data analysis, among other activities, are undertaken sequentially. The common view is that, first, one conceptualizes and hypothesizes something about the phenomenon in question, such as defining one's concepts, formulating an argument about an empirical relationship, and hypothesizing how one expects the relationship to appear in the data. The hypothesis is not an educated guess, but results from careful conceptualization and concise definition. (That is the ideal anyway.) When this is complete, data collection proceeds. This second step does not unravel the concepts, definitions, or hypotheses. Rather, in quantitative research this step is taken to provide empirical evidence for 'testing' hypotheses and, by implication, their conceptualizations. The third step is to consider how the evidence – 'findings' – accords with what was hypothesized.

Qualitative research, in contrast, is not sequential. (At least, that is the claim.) While concepts, definitions, and hypotheses are evident, they are viewed as 'working' matters – conditional until further notice. The common view that qualitative researchers proceed by the seats of their pants without concepts, definitions, or hypotheses is farfetched, a perspective that Blumer (1969) rebuked decades ago. While qualitative researchers also conceptualize, define, and hypothesize, they do so in ongoing relationship with data collection. They entertain particular concepts, but they do so provisionally until data collection suggests something different. The same holds for definitions and hypotheses. Regardless of how this process transpires, there is a cultivated tentativeness about the steps, which is the reason why qualitative researchers habitually refer to *working* concepts, *working* definitions, and *working* hypotheses.

It is possible, however, to combine elements of both traditions in ethnographic research. To the extent procedure is sequential in fieldwork, it approximates the common view of quantitative research. Linda Mitteness and Judith Barker (1994), veterans of many large-scale field projects, suggest that a sequential process may be the only realistic choice when it comes to managing large data collection teams and navigating huge data sets. Ethnographers conceptualize, define, and hypothesize – tentatively or not – as a way of moving ahead with their work. The idea that one can proceed without concepts, from the ground up, and derive understandings of how things operate that way, was not Glaser and Strauss's (1967) sense of the craft, even if their 'grounded theory' approach has been formulated this way (see Thornberg and Charmaz, Chapter 11, this volume). Allaine Cerwonka and Liisa Malkki's (2007) portrayal of process and temporality in ethnographic fieldwork is closer to practice on this front.[1]

As a way of moving beyond such methodological distinctions, we take our point of departure from the need for analytic inspiration, something that would best be continually present during, not just before or after, the research process. Analytic inspiration not only provides insight, tentative or otherwise, but also supplies a roadmap for how to move along in the research. Inspiration also provides empirical excitement. How exciting, indeed, it is to see one's empirical material coalesce in an unexpected or new way, which is palpable in our illustrations. If representation of this coalescence may have rhetorical elements, it is not rhetorical in the research process; it is a constant and eminently useful ingredient of the craft. Research guided purely by procedural rules, sequential or not, misses the point, which is to provide understanding.[2] Above all, analytic inspiration should not be confined to a separate domain called 'theory.'

SEEING CULTURE AS NARRATIVE

Our first illustration, taken from Abu-Lughod's (1993) discussion of fieldwork in an Egyptian Bedouin settlement, relates to the adage that life comes to us in the form of stories. If it is a common expression, it also has been taken to heart by narrative ethnographers for analytic inspiration. Conceptualization, definition, and hypothesis formation remain in the mix, but analytic inspiration serves as a leitmotif in the research process. It is a strong partner indeed, as Abu-Lughod suggests. That life comes to us in the form of stories made the difference in how she 'unsettled' common themes of Arab life in Bedouin society, especially as they relate to women, patriarchy, and patrilinearity.

To attend narratively (see Esin et al., Chapter 14, this volume) while observing carefully is to pay concerted attention to the things people say about their inner lives and social worlds, something that will resonate in our second and third illustrations. Ethnographic fieldwork is traditionally participatory and observational, but it also has been something else – concerned with how people themselves account for experience. People say things about their lives, about others, to others, if not about them, about their thoughts, feelings, and actions. They recount their pasts, describe their presents, and muse over their futures. They comment on groups, some as small as families and marriages, some as large as communities and nations, whether already part of their lives, in formation, or imagined in the distant past or foreseeable future.

Much of this talk is story-like, extended commentary that describes, explains, or dismisses what is thought or figured about matters in question. If what is said comes in the form of mere yeses, noes, uh-huhs, nods of the head, or other brevities, these can nonetheless be story-like when embedded in collaboratively designed networks of exchanges. In the extended interactions observable in ethnographic fieldwork, the 'small' stories of mere yeses and uh-huhs located in chains of interactions can carry the same narrative weight as the 'bigger' stories told in life history interviews (see Bamberg, 2012; Gubrium and Holstein, 2009). As Abu-Lughod suggests about her initially ill-fated pursuit of Bedouin life stories, to think of stories as extended accounts of individual lives is to shortchange the social complexity and agency of accounts.

Reframed as culturally constructive (see Winter, Chapter 17, this volume), Abu-Lughod's interviews offer apt illustration of how a narrative approach inspired her view of culture in general and specifically of the place of women in Bedouin society. As she describes her conceptualization of culture, she brings narrative understanding to the forefront, appreciating cultural nuance. Analytic inspiration may be drawn from the opposite as well – the museum view of culture – in which indigenous meaning is 'fixed' in material and symbolic systems of shared meaning. But Abu-Lughod's aim is to unsettle cultural generalizations marked by expressions such as 'the' culture of 'the' Bedouins, which in her view takes understanding away from the ordinary production of culture evident in storytelling. She puts it this way:

> a serious problem with generalization is that by producing the effects of homogeneity, coherence, and timelessness, it contributes to the creation of 'cultures.' In the process of generalizing from experiences and conversations with a number of specific people in a community, the anthropologist may flatten out their differences and homogenize them. ... The appearance of a lack of internal differentiation makes it easier to conceive of groups of people as discrete, bounded entities, like the 'cultures' of 'the Nuer,' 'the Balinese,' or 'the Awlad "Ali Bedouin,"' populated by generic cultural beings who do this or that and believe such-and-such. ... [There] are good reasons to consider such entities dangerous fictions and to argue for what I have called writing *against* culture. (1993: 9)

Explanatory punch is evident in Abu-Lughod's eye-opening extended interviews with women. Of her book *Writing Women's Worlds: Bedouin Stories*, Abu-Lughod explains:

> This book is intended to present, in the form of a narrative ethnography made up of these women's stories and conversations, a general critique of ethnographic typification. ... I decided to explore how the wonderfully complex stories of the individuals I had come to know in this community in Egypt might challenge the capacity of anthropological generalizations to render lives, theirs and others', adequately. (1993: xvi)

As Abu-Lughod presents the women's stories, she is a listener, now procedurally poised to particularize and unsettle 'five anthropological themes associated with the study of women in the Arab world: patrilineality, polygyny, reproduction, patrilateral parallel-cousin marriage, and honor and shame' (1993: xvi–xvii). Referring to the book's chapters titled the same way, she adds, 'Rather than the chapter titles explaining the stories, the stories are meant to undo the titles' (1993: xvii). Themes such as patrilineality are not 'just there,' ready data to be carefully recorded in field notes and later systematically described in ethnographic writing as 'the' kinship system of Bedouin society.

The thematic unsettling of patrilineality is especially evident in the stories told by an old Bedouin woman named Migdim. They suggest that patrilineal decision-making does not so much rule the roost, so to speak, as much as the roost plays an important role in making that happen. If patrilineality is a theme of Arab society, it is one articulated and animated as much by women as it is instituted by men. The analytic inspiration of narrative understanding brings this into focus for Abu-Lughod, unsettling the theme as women's stories are taken into consideration. Listen to how Abu-Lughod describes a story Migdim tells of her 'arranged' marriage to a gathering of younger women relatives:

> One of the most vivid I heard from Migdim was the tale of how she had resisted marriages her father had tried to arrange for her. I even heard more than once, nearly word for word, the same tale of how she had ended up marrying Jawwad, the father of her children. I heard it for the first time one evening that winter; she told it for the benefit of her sons' wives, Gateefa and Fayga, and some of her granddaughters.
>
> She explained that the first person whom she was to have married was a paternal first cousin. His relatives came to her household and conducted the negotiations and even went as far as to slaughter some sheep, the practice that seals the marriage agreement. But things did not work out. The time was over fifty years ago, just after the death of her mother.
>
> 'He was a first cousin, and I didn't want him. He was old and he lived with us. We ate out of the one bowl. His relatives came and slaughtered a sheep and I started screaming, I started crying. My father had bought a new gun, a cartridge gun. He said, "If you don't shut up I'll send you flying with this gun."' (1993: 46–7)

As Migdim continues, she describes the strategies she used to escape the marriage. Patrilineality notwithstanding, Migdim recounts a tale of personal artifice and resistance, which transpires in the face of a sealed marriage agreement. Her father and relatives eventually come to an agreement based on another arrangement ostensibly made between them, not between them and Migdim. The story thematizes Migdim's active participation in the process. The account also is a vivid lesson for her listeners, the episodes of which highlight Migdim – a woman – as a determining force behind events. The telling is an unsettling cultural narrative for the women listening, who stand to share it again with their own daughters and others. If their own tellings do not reflect or produce the same results, the tellings nonetheless open their actions to what is possible in the circumstances.

DISCOVERING SOCIAL WORLDS

The second illustration of analytic inspiration takes us to an urban nursing home called 'Murray Manor.' Here, especially, we emphasize how analytic inspiration and methodology go hand in hand. As the illustration unfolds, the idea that expertly planned and deployed research technique leads to excellent data is unsettled. The illustration shows that analytic inspiration can make a difference in everything, from understanding, to procedure, to results – to the very meaning of 'excellent data.' Accenting what people do with words shows the analytic way forward.

One of the authors (Gubrium) conducted extensive fieldwork at Murray Manor in the 1970s, leading to the publication of the first book-length ethnography of its kind (Gubrium, 1997 [1975]). We will write in the first person in this section, from Gubrium's viewpoint. We will do the same for the third illustration in the section following, from James Holstein's viewpoint on fieldwork in civil commitment hearings (Holstein, 1993).

Because I was trained as a survey researcher, it wouldn't be obvious how my ethnographic fieldwork at Murray Manor came about. Along with other nursing homes in the metropolitan area where the Manor was located, it was originally one of several research sites where I'd planned to conduct a survey of residents' quality of life. At the time, a person–environment fit model was a popular analytic scaffold. The idea was that the fit between resident needs, on the one hand, and available institutional characteristics and resources, on the other, affected residents' quality of life. My hypothesis was that the better the fit, the better the quality of life. I wrote a federal grant proposal, but it wasn't funded. Disappointed, but undaunted, and using local funds and my own time, I decided to conduct the survey on a smaller scale in fewer nursing homes, considerably reducing the sample size. The Manor was included in the smaller survey.

I want to emphasize that Murray Manor at this point in my thinking was a survey research location, not an ethnographic field site. The difference is important, because the methodologies put into place and, as it turned out, the kind of analytic inspiration available for understanding the research topic – which eventually would be transformed – would dramatically alter my view of data and the utility of the research findings. I eventually would learn that a change in or new analytic inspiration can change everything.

The explanatory advantage of the person–environment fit model seemed obvious at the time. It moved beyond a simple bivariate model, in which the characteristics of institutions (one variable) related to the quality of life (the other variable). The better the nursing home, it was commonly argued, the higher the residents' quality of life. Instead, I was inspired by the more complex person–environment model, in which the fit between personal and institutional characteristics (two variables) related to the quality of life (the third variable). In this model, it was possible, for example, that low resident expectations might not lead some to demand as much in quality as would high resident expectations. As such, homes that were reasonably adequate could provide a high quality of life for some residents. (Never mind the unsavory policy potential of this model.)

My plan was to conduct interviews with diverse residents in two or three different nursing homes, code the personal and residential data for the target variables, and see how they co-related.

Ironically enough, now on my own and unhindered by the commitments of grant funding, I decided to 'hang around' in a facility, as I unwittingly referred to it then, to get a first-hand feel for life in a nursing home. If my gerontological interests kept nursing homes in view, amazingly I'd never spent much time in a nursing home nor knew anyone who lived there. (This can be par for the course among quantitative researchers.) Several facility administrators had originally expressed interest in participating in my proposed survey, but now I wanted to get a sense of life and work in a nursing home to get my bearings, something more intense than a survey proffered. The problem was that there was a great deal of bad press for nursing homes at the time and administrators were wary of that sort of thing. Only one of them welcomed me to 'look around to my heart's content,' and that happened to be the administrator of Murray Manor, my eventual field site.

I accepted the opportunity and was introduced to members of what I later called 'top staff' – the medical director, the director of nursing, charge nurses on the floors, the dietitian, the social worker, and the activity director. All talked with pride about the quality of care in the home. Top staff introduced me to employees I later called 'floor staff' – registered nurses or RNs, licensed practical nurses or LPNs, and NAs or nurses' aides. Soon enough, members of the floor staff introduced me to the patients and residents. The first floor of the facility was designated as residential care and those who lived there were called 'residents.' The other floors of the Manor were designated for various levels of skilled care and its residents were called 'patients.' This has changed since then; now all care receivers are called "residents" and that's what I'll do here.

So I was all set to hang around, but not mentally prepared to do ethnographic fieldwork.

I was ensconced in what eventually would become my field site, but with old analytic lenses. I figured that the administrator's welcome and the staff's follow-through were points of departure for what eventually would be expanded into a quality-of-life survey. In anticipation of that, I would get to know about the nursing home as a living environment and those who worked there as people. I expected to formulate better survey questions as a result.

An interesting facet of what lay ahead is the gradual change in the ordinary terms I used to refer to aspects of my work. The analytic lesson wasn't apparent at first, and couldn't have been, because I needed a different source of inspiration to recognize it. The terms with which I began, of course, were part of the language of variables, measurement, indicators, and correlates. When the Murray Manor research started to become ethnographic, this gradually turned into the language of social interaction, meaning, and representation. The retrospective lesson in this would be that the working vocabulary and procedural rules we apply in research relate to one's form of analytic inspiration (Gubrium and Holstein, 1997). Terms of reference in research are only as general as the analytic framework in place.

This was evident in the preceding illustration from Abu-Lughod's work. She found herself working against the language of culture commonplace at the time – one bereft of narrativity, member agency, and meaning-making. Instead, she was attracted to a language built from terms such as social construction, difference, contention, and resistance. This altered her method of procedure – from collecting cultural data to witnessing its storied production – and changed the way she chose to represent her empirical material in publications (see Gubrium and Holstein, 2009).

But this is getting ahead of the story. Murray Manor wasn't yet a field site and I didn't refer to it as such. I spoke of it as a 'pilot study' and source of background information for survey research. I wasn't doing fieldwork. I was familiarizing myself with things before the real research took off. I wasn't yet using ethnographic language to describe my activities, even while I was located in a kind of field and conducting a form of empirical work within it. Systematic participant observation (see Marvasti, Chapter 24, this volume) was far from my mind. Social interaction on the premises and the contexts of meaning-making were, as yet, incidental to my interests and were, consequently, undocumented.

In the months ahead I spent listening to, and speaking with, residents and staff, I don't recall having had a grand conversion to an ethnographic view. If anything, I slowly eased into what initially was only a whiff of fieldwork, done for ancillary purposes. A new analytic framework emerged only as I started to take notice of, and to take field notes about, the particular words and associated meanings that various groups used to refer to caregiving and the quality in life. I couldn't glibly leave my initial terms of reference behind because I needed them in order to relate to an informing person–environment literature. But I did start to catalog ordinary accounts of the quality of life and their situated points of reference.

These started to become proper field notes when I began to think seriously about the everyday connotations of what I had been unwittingly treating as background data. I grew serious about the possibility that there might be different worlds of meanings apparent in what was said about living and dying at the Manor. Still, I hesitated to take this fully on board. My sense was that if my survey-oriented definitions didn't quite fit the residents' definitions, for example, that could be corrected in time. If I found myself saying to myself and others that 'there are different worlds of meaning there' that don't jibe with person–environment fit, I still clung to the model. Seriousness didn't immediately prompt a leap in imagination, only troubled curiosity about empirical complexity.

Here's an example of what I found troubling. One of the ostensible characteristics of a good nursing home is the quality of the staff, especially the floor or front-line staff. Well-trained and considerate staff members were viewed as important ingredients of the quality of care, and presumably affected the residents' quality of life. The criterion could serve to categorize staff members into good and bad workers, or so I figured at first, and could be used as one indicator of the environmental part of the person–environment fit model. What I began to realize as I gathered preliminary ethnographic data – now in the field – was that good and bad couldn't be figured in terms of fixed criteria such as the background or personal characteristics of the staff. Time and again, I noticed instead that good and bad grew out of resident–staff interactions and was a matter of perspective. If, for some, the bad worker was inefficient and didn't conform to established standards of quality care, the same characteristics could signal good work to a resident who wanted a familiar face to 'stay and sit for a spell.'

Here's another troubling example. I coined a catchy term for the activities involved in keeping the premises neat and orderly and the residents dressed and tidy. This was the immediate responsibility of the floor staff. I called it 'bed-and-body work.' If, to the residents, 'staying a spell' and otherwise being attuned to personal needs signaled good care, bed-and-body work was equally significant. Keeping the premises clean and odor-free, keeping beds made and the surroundings otherwise attractive, keeping residents' skins and clothing free of bodily waste were important ingredients of good care for everyone. According to the top and floor staffs, families, and those residents who could care about it, follow-through on this front surely improved the quality of residential life.

But, here again, leaving it at that proved to be too simple; it failed to take account of the interactions and sentiments involved. It wasn't bed-and-body work as such that differentiated staff, family, and residents' understanding of quality. Rather, the associated sense of *for whom* bed-and-body work was undertaken made an important difference. When residents perceived bed-and-body work such as keeping them clean to be a matter of 'just getting it done' as opposed to actually 'caring,' it was viewed negatively. It mattered that all the standard quality-of-care criteria in this area were perceived as being done *for* the residents as opposed to 'just getting it done.'

This perspectival stance was the analytic hook needed to understand the complexity, which eventually led me to think the previously unthinkable: No set of quality criteria worked in all circumstances and from all perspectives. Generalizations (see Maxwell and Chmiel, Chapter 37, this volume) such as this helped to move me beyond thinking of what I was recording as background information and into proper field notes about meaning-making. Taken together, the notes gathered from staff, residents, and family interactions were becoming ethnographic data about diversity in meaning.

The shift to concerted ethnographic fieldwork required a more complex, dynamic form of analytic punch. What I was observing and dutifully recording as field notes needed the kind of analytic inspiration that would bring things together into a transportable argument about the quality of life in human service organizations. It's one thing to refer to empirical material as reflecting 'different worlds of meaning,' it's another matter altogether to start thinking that 'an' organization such as a nursing home could house different social worlds constructed out of the ordinary members' interactions, which could also transform from one occasion to another.

It was as much a turn away from the homogeneity assumption underlying the language and idea of 'an' organization, as it was the plural 'worlds' I was documenting, that made the difference. Working against the concept of 'the' organization ostensibly in place was my way of unsettling the desire to measure the quality of care. Thinking in terms of possible worlds, socially organized together within one facility (or scattered about the landscape of everyday life, as it otherwise might be), eventually did the analytic trick. The possible social worlds of the nursing home (of any organization really) opened my eyes to an entirely different way of proceeding. It put into bold relief the idea that formal organization was something different from social organization, that one couldn't be readily discerned from the other. The idea that the logic of one was different than the logic of the other framed my ethnography of Murray Manor. I now understand this as a matter of analytic narrativity, in which a new way of storying empirical material changes everything.

DOCUMENTING COLLABORATIVE CONSTRUCTION

Our third illustration highlights the way analytic inspiration can transform one's research question. Here again, we write in the first person, this time in Holstein's voice as he recounts how an altered perspective not only alters the research direction, but in this case also challenges leading views of the labeling process.

Like many sociologists and graduate students in the 1970s, I was fascinated by animated discussions of the labeling theory of deviance (see Kitsuse, 1962). The gist of the labeling argument was that 'residual deviance' such as mental illness was identified and stabilized by societal reaction (Scheff, 1966); mental illness was as much a matter of labeling as it was an intrinsic condition. Some argued that non-psychiatric factors – social contingencies and structural variables such as race, gender, social class – were more important in determining the likelihood of being identified and treated as mentally ill than were psychiatric factors. (See Holstein, 1993, for a synopsis of the controversy.) Involuntary mental hospitalization became central to the debate because it involved formal procedures whereby mental illness was determined and reactions to it were explicitly specified.

When I found myself in a postdoctoral position at UCLA, Robert Emerson pointed me to a courtroom in Los Angeles (which I'll call Metropolitan Court) that handled only mental health-related cases, including involuntary commitment hearings. My first visit to the courtroom revealed a striking display of the process about which I'd read so much. Florid psychiatric conditions were on full display, as were the side-effects of their remedies. So were the social processes of labeling and responding to troubles – both psychiatric and social.

Reading Erving Goffman (1961), Harold Garfinkel (1956, 1967), and Robert Emerson (1969) primed me to see the courtroom as a stage for the ceremonial moral degradation and denunciation to which candidate mental patients were subjected in order to account for and justify their involuntary commitment. Sitting in Metropolitan Court, it was hard not to see 'social forces' operating 'behind the backs' (and beyond the vision) of courtroom actors. I was captivated by two questions: *What* is going on here? *Why* do decisions turn out the way they do? On one hand, the answers seemed obvious: the social contingencies of troubled and disadvantaged persons appeared to account for their involuntary commitment. On the other hand, it wasn't clear how this actually transpired, given the extraordinary range of factors and troubles that seemed to characterize each case.

A new analytic inspiration eventually helped me sort through these matters and clarified my research focus, ultimately changing my fundamental research questions. As I watched court proceedings, it dawned on me that there was an important (perhaps even prior) question that I was not asking as I watched courtroom proceedings: *How* were involuntary commitment proceedings and decisions socially organized? It's not surprising that I should eventually ask this question, given that I was working in the sociology department at UCLA, ethnomethodology's hallowed ground. From the beginning, ethnomethodology has been preoccupied with the *hows* of social organization (see Heritage, 1984). As such, the inspiration to concentrate on the *hows*, rather than on the *whats* and *whys*, of court proceedings was close at hand.

Examples from my field notes and subsequent analysis reveal the difference this would make. As I began to study Metropolitan Court in earnest, I carefully recorded notes – brief narratives that Emerson et al. (1995) call 'jottings' – about what was going on in the hearings. I also recorded jottings of casual conversations or informal interviews I had with court personnel. At the end of each day, I would clean up my jottings and write analytic memos regarding what I observed. The jottings and memos were fairly substantive at the time, concerned with what I observed and with the larger patterns of labeling going on in the courtroom. These *whats* initially took precedence over the *hows* of the matters in view.

Early on, I came across an intriguing aspect of the hearings that District Attorneys (DAs) – whose job it was to seek involuntary commitment – called 'letting them hang themselves.' Several times in brief conversations, DAs indicated that their job was relatively straightforward. They said that candidate patients would reveal symptoms of mental disorder and interactional dysfunction if they were simply allowed to speak without constraint. Candidate patients would say something incriminating if they were allowed to speak their own minds. According to one DA, this amounted to 'getting them up there [on the witness stand] and just let them talk.' The implication was that if candidate patients were allowed to talk freely, they would almost invariably 'hang themselves,' or 'do themselves in.' As one DA stated, 'You let them talk and they hospitalize themselves.' The operational sentiment was candidate patients did this on their own; this was apparent in their actions if given a chance to reveal itself.

There did seem to be quite a few instances of candidate patients 'doing themselves in,' but was it as simple as that? Drawing from my field notes and a related analytic memo, I can reconstruct how I initially viewed one particular case involving a candidate patient I called 'PG,' a white female, perhaps 25–35 years old, with a long history of psychiatric treatment. My notes indicate that the DA began to cross-examine PG with a series of questions that appeared to explore PG's 'reality orientation' (Do you know where we are today? Do you know today's date?). Eventually, PG said that if she were released, she would go to see people who would help her 'recharge,' as she put it. The DA asked her to elaborate, and PG soon made an apparently delusional claim that she received rejuvenating 'power from the life force.' Soon thereafter, in summarizing his case to the judge, the DA argued that PG was 'delusional' and she 'lacked the ability to carry out the most basic tasks of everyday life.' He explained that PG was unable to focus on the important matters at hand even though she knew it was urgent for her to be on her best behavior. The hearing ended with the judge declaring that PG was 'gravely disabled' and 'unable to provide for her own upkeep due to her severe delusions and inability to focus properly on the important matters at hand.'

One of my analytic memos reads that 'PG seemed to hang herself.' My summary jottings indicated that the DA patiently allowed PG to talk about mundane matters until PG's delusions emerged. Other notes indicated that 'PG was under a lot of stress.' She was 'out of her element.' She didn't seem completely in touch with what was going on. The notes indicated that this may have been due to the side-effects of medication. I also noted that everyone else in the hearing was a professional (and male) and they looked the various parts. PG was dressed in institutional pajamas. She had been brought directly from (the State Hospital) to the hearing and wasn't given the opportunity to make herself 'presentable.' My notes read, 'See Garfinkel, Goffman on degradation.' These were some of my *what* questions.

Summary jottings also suggested that PG really didn't know her lawyer (a public defender) and 'was not adequately prepped' for her testimony. Additional notes indicated that she did not have access to the full range of legal safeguards or resources that might have been used to prevent her commitment. The notes suggested that while PG was delusional, multiple 'social contingencies' were at work, indicating that psychiatric factors were not the only determinant in the hearing outcome. These were *why* concerns.

Clearly, in tracing *what* was going on in this hearing, I was sensitized to the non-psychiatric (*why*) factors that could have influenced the hearing's outcome. The concerns of prior labeling studies were apparent in the ways I was prepared to account for this and other hearing outcomes. PG had, indeed, contributed to her own 'hanging,' and it was easy to speculate about the myriad social contingencies that were working against her. There was a great deal going on here, sociologically, but the complexity of the proceedings made a rigorous empirical explanation difficult since many possibly influential variables (e.g., social class) were not proximally apparent. In other instances, key variables seemed to operate in multiple ways.

My inability to get a grip on this opened the door to new analytic inspiration, changing the focus from *what* and *why* questions to how the moment-to-moment activities and realities of the court were interactionally organized. This would sharpen and narrow the research focus to what would be immediately visible. As simple as this shift sounds, its procedural and explanatory implications were profound. The concrete upshot of the change was apparent in the very way I conceived of and recorded happenings in the field. In order to grasp how interactional matters transpired, I began to pay much closer attention to social interaction, the turn-by-turn dynamics of courtroom talk. This was not a doctrinaire shift to a conversation analytic agenda, but it did involve greater appreciation of the sequential environment of courtroom talk.

Jottings and summary field notes were insufficient for this type of analysis. Instead, I began to produce close-to-verbatim 'do-it-yourself' transcripts of the commitment hearings (see Gubrium and Holstein, 2009; West, 1996). The procedural shift is evident from a before-and-after glance at my field notes. Jottings and detailed summaries were replaced by imperfect utterance-by-utterance records of courtroom talk. The initial drafts of my notes contained no summary, commentary, or analysis (although I would try to add summary comments afterwards). They were merely transcripts to be closely scrutinized and analysed later for their socially organized and socially organizing components.

Consider, for example, the following transcript and subsequent analysis inspired by the question of *how* candidate patients ended up 'hanging themselves.' This is a slightly revised version of the actual do-it-yourself transcript I captured in my notes. It was chosen because it parallels the case described above and clearly illustrates some of the ways in which the shift from *what* and *why* to *how* questions affects the ethnographic enterprise, in this case shaping what actually was put down on paper and the related sense of what constituted relevant field data. Formerly descriptive notes of happenings and personal characteristics (*whats*) turned into displays of collaborative construction (*hows*) of the matters formerly being documented.

Lisa Sellers (LS), an apparently poor black woman, perhaps 25–35 years old, illustrates how what the DAs called 'letting them hang themselves' was collaboratively accomplished, not just personally emergent (see Holstein, 1993). The do-it-yourself transcript of the DA's cross-examination in this case includes a series of 14 direct questions (not shown here) to which Sellers responded with brief answers (What's your name? Where are we right now? Where do you live? What day of the week is it?). This series comprised 14 straightforward question–answer pairs. There were no notable pauses at the end of questions and answers (i.e., possible speakership transition points), nor were there any intrusions or interruptions of one party by the other. At the end of this sequence, the DA began to pursue a different questioning tack:

1. DA: How do you like summer out here, Lisa?
2. LS: It's OK.
3. DA: How long have you lived here?
4. LS: Since I moved from Houston
5. ((Silence)) [Note: if unspecified, time is one to three seconds]
6. LS: About three years ago
7. DA: Tell me about why you came here.
8. LS: I just came
9. ((Silence))
10. LS: You know, I wanted to see the stars, Hollywood.
11. ((Silence))
12. DA: Uh huh
13. LS: I didn't have no money.
14. ((Silence))
15. LS: I'd like to get a good place to live.
16. ((Silence 5 seconds))
17. DA: Go on. ((spoken simultaneously with onset of the next utterance))
18. LS: There was some nice things I brought
19. ((Silence))
20. DA: Uh huh
21. LS: Brought them from the rocketship.
22. DA: Oh really?
23. LS: They was just some things I had.
24. DA: From the rocketship?
25. LS: Right.
26. DA: Were you on it?
27. LS: Yeah.
28. DA: Tell me about this rocketship, Lisa.

The sequence culminates in Sellers' seemingly delusional rocketship reference, with the DA avidly following up.

The detailed transcript and central question of *how* Sellers came to 'hang herself' yielded a significantly different analysis from that of PG's hearing above. Differently inspired, one can make the case that Sellers did not simply or inevitably blurt out the apparently 'delusional' rocketship reference as evidence of some troubled inner state or mental incompetence. Rather, I was able to view how the rocketship utterance came into play as a matter of conversational collaboration and Sellers' related interactional *competence* (see Holstein, 1993).

In examining how this exchange was organized, note that the DA significantly changed the question and answer pattern that had emerged as the normative expectation for the interrogation. After the previous series of questions that were answerable with short, factual replies, in line 1, the DA now asked an open-ended question. In his next turn (line 3), he returned to a more straightforward question, but when Sellers produced a candidate answer (line 4), the DA declined to take the next turn at talk. A silence emerged following line 4, where a question from the DA had previously been forthcoming. The gap in talk was eventually terminated (line 6) by Sellers' elaboration of her prior utterance.

In line 7, the DA solicited further talk, but this time it was not in the form of a question. Instead, it was a very general prompt for Sellers to provide more information. The adequacy of a response to this kind of request, however, is more indeterminate than for a direct question. In a sense, the DA put himself in the position to decide when his request for information was adequately fulfilled. The adequacy and completeness of Sellers' response thus depended, in part, on how the DA acknowledged it.

At line 9, the DA did not respond to Sellers candidate answer at the first possible opportunity. When silence developed, Sellers elaborated her previous answer (line 10). The DA did not respond to this utterance either, and another noteworthy silence ensued. Such silences signal conversational difficulties, troubles that implicate the prior speaker, who typically attempts remedial action. Sellers did just that by reclaiming speakership and embellishing a prior utterance on several occasions (lines 6, 10, 15, and 17). In each instance, she filled silences with her own talk, all competently accomplished.

Several times, then, in the course of this conversation, the DA's refusal to take a turn at talk provoked Sellers to continue her own turns. At line 12, the DA encouraged this practice by offering a minimal acknowledgement (Uh huh), which implied that an extended turn at talk was in progress but was not yet complete. He used this brief turn to subtly prompt Sellers to continue, which she did (lines 13 and 15). Her responses, however, met only with silence. At line 17, the DA explicitly encouraged Sellers to 'Go on,' which she did by changing the line of talk to focus on 'some nice things (she) brought' (line 18). The DA again declined speakership (line 19), then offered a minimal prompt (line 20), to which Sellers finally replied with 'Brought them from the rocketship' (line 21). This utterance elicited a strong display of interest from the DA ('Oh really?' – line 22), who then actively resumed questioning Sellers about the rocketship.

The DA's 'Oh really?' was a compelling display of interest. In the difficult conversational environment that had emerged, it provided a landmark toward which Sellers might orient her talk. Put differently, it signaled that the prior utterance was noteworthy, even newsworthy. Responding to this, Sellers launched a new, more successful line of talk, 'success' being defined in terms of the ability to re-establish and sustain a viable and dynamic question–answer sequence. In vernacular terms, the rocketship statement and its aftermath helped Sellers keep up her end of the conversation. But it also helped her 'do herself in.' In a sense, Lisa Sellers engaged in practices commonly followed in similar conversational circumstances. She *used* the rocketship reference to deal with conversational difficulties and elaborated it to sustain a thriving line of talk. She competently fulfilled her conversational responsibilities, but, in the process, displayed her mental incompetence. Only close examination of the sequential context of conversation makes this evident.

To summarize, in my initial observations of Metropolitan Court, I typically looked past conversational structure (see Toerien, Chapter 22, this volume) and dynamics, which were heard but not noticed. This was the case both procedurally – in the way I took field notes – and conceptually – in the way I formulated summaries of the proceedings with little mention of the interactional dynamics themselves. Initially, the field included constructs or variables not actually evident in the hearing talk but arguably operating at some other level to shape hearing outcomes. But this field did not – as a practical, procedural, or conceptual matter – include the turn-by-turn conversational practices and structures comprising the hearings themselves. New analytic inspiration transformed the field at least partially into the sequential environment of conversational turn-taking and adjacency pairs. The analytic mandate now was to describe in close detail and explain how the recognizable, orderly, observable interactional regularities of the courtroom proceedings were collaboratively accomplished, in situ, not analytically imported.

This transformation of perspectives resembles Abu-Lughod's shift in focus from merely describing culture (writ large) to analysing its narrative production. Hers was also a shift in emphasis to *how* questions, inspiring her to imagine culture in the local telling of stories. Exploring *how* questions clearly yields different sorts of reports and analyses than those emerging when questions of *what* or *why* focus research attention. Sources of inspiration are key to what can be seen, heard, described, and reported.

INSPIRATION AND METHOD

We hope these illustrations have shown how new ways of seeing can be analytically inspiring and bring punch to ethnographic fieldwork. At we noted, while there is no rule of thumb for inspiration – it is in the nature of the beast – it is palpable and describable. Inspiration is not procedural in that regard, because it is not derived methodically. Rather, it is closer to imagination; it is a leap in perspective that produces a new way of seeing things otherwise on display before our very own eyes.

Yes, the punch of analytic inspiration is rhetorical. It persuades as it inspires. But what it persuades us of is not derived from rhetorical tropes, but rather from the persuasiveness of insightful understanding, something centered in what comes into view in analytically satisfying ways. Like jokes told without an apparent punch line, empirical material and analysis without punch fall flat. We come away saying, 'Yes, I heard it, but what was that about?'

In her ethnographic fieldwork, Abu-Lughod sought cultural understanding. What opened her eyes to what she had been viewing was imagining herself observing cultural construction. The same was the case for Gubrium's pilot survey of the quality of life in a nursing home. Seeing the quality of life as a matter of perspective and social sentiments was inspirational in transforming a study of assessment into documenting sectors of meaning. Holstein's analytic impatience with labeling theory raised critical questions about the empirical status of labels, providing a route to seeing labels in the courtroom as a matter of collaboratively doing things with words, not simply being a victim of them.

If analytic inspiration is not straightforwardly procedural, neither is it simply empirical. None of the three ethnographers whose work we illustrated could have been closer to what they were studying. Abu-Lughod lived in the settlement where she conducted her observations. Gubrium spent months in various locations in the nursing home he observed. Holstein was a daily eyewitness to court proceedings. Their respective viewings were intense and extensive. While concertedly empirical, it was new ways of seeing that made a difference. What developed from the ground up for them was embedded in new imaginings, not simply discovered in data.

We stated earlier that analytic inspiration changes everything. A new way of seeing makes a difference on several levels. The very nature of what is being observed can change, the method of data collection is altered, the relevance of empirical observations is transformed, and the manner of reporting findings is altered. If analytic inspiration changes research practice, this is not to say that being methodical in data collection, systematic in thinking about empirical material, and accurate in reporting the results no longer matter. Analytic inspiration is not license for procedural recklessness. The aim still is systematic, empirically centered understanding. The key question is: Which way of seeing things provides an inspiring way of viewing those things? This is not a matter of doing away with methods, but making analytic inspiration an integral part of them.

NOTES

1. Glaser and Strauss's (1967) original idea of grounded theory, presented in their book *The Discovery of Grounded Theory*, was a reaction to what at the time was called 'grand theory,' especially the emphasis on the verification of theory. While not dismissing verification, Glaser and Strauss argued for a more balanced view of the place of theory in social research. They underscored the need to view theory as a form of abduction, in which theory formation goes hand in hand with data collection, which Cerwonka and Malkki (2007) describe as 'tacking' back and forth between the two in practice. It was not a particular kind of theory that Glaser and Strauss had in mind, but rather a perspective on how theory of any kind should develop and be used in social research.
2. While Glaser and Strauss's (1967) perspective on the place of theory in social research rewarranted the value of qualitative research at a time when quantification was dominant, the perspective was linked with a recipe-like view of analysis, especially coding, which served to formularize 'discovery' and work against analytic inspiration.

FURTHER READING

Cerwonka, Allaine and Malkki, Liisa H. (2007) *Improvising Theory: Process and Temporality in Ethnographic Fieldwork*. Chicago: University of Chicago Press.
Gubrium, Jaber F. and Holstein, James A. (2009) *Analyzing Narrative Reality*. Thousand Oaks, CA: Sage.

REFERENCES

Abu-Lughod, Lila (1993) *Writing Women's Worlds: Bedouin Stories*. Berkeley, CA: University of California Press.
Bamberg, Michael (2012) 'Narrative practice and identity navigation,' in James A. Holstein and Jaber F. Gubrium (eds.), *Varieties of Narrative Analysis*. Thousand Oaks, CA: Sage. pp. 99–124.
Blumer, Herbert (1969) *Symbolic Interactionism*. Englewood Cliffs, NJ: Prentice Hall.
Cerwonka, Allaine and Malkki, Liisa H. (2007) *Improvising Theory: Process and Temporality in Ethnographic Fieldwork*. Chicago: University of Chicago Press.
Clifford, James and Marcus, George E. (eds.) (1986) *Writing Culture*. Berkeley, CA: University of California Press.
Emerson, Robert M. (1969) *Judging Delinquents*. Chicago: Aldine.
Emerson, Robert M., Fretz, Rachel I., and Shaw, Linda L. (1995) *Writing Ethnographic Fieldnotes*. Chicago: University of Chicago Press.
Garfinkel, Harold (1956) 'Conditions of successful degradation ceremonies,' *American Journal of Sociology*, 61: 420–4.
Garfinkel, Harold (1967) *Studies in Ethnomethodology*. Englewood Cliffs, NJ: Prentice Hall.
Glaser, Barney G. and Strauss, Anselm L. (1967) *The Discovery of Grounded Theory*. Chicago: Aldine.
Goffman, Erving (1961) *Asylums*. Garden City, NY: Anchor Books.
Gubrium, Jaber F. (1997 [1975]) *Living and Dying at Murray Manor*. Charlottesville, VA: University of Virginia Press.
Gubrium, Jaber F. and Holstein, James A. (1997) *The New Language of Qualitative Method*. New York: Oxford University Press.
Gubrium, Jaber F. and Holstein, James A. (2009) *Analyzing Narrative Reality*. Thousand Oaks, CA: Sage.
Heritage, John C. (1984) *Garfinkel and Ethnomethodology*. Cambridge: Cambridge University Press.
Holstein, James A. (1993) *Court-Ordered Insanity: Interpretive Practice and Involuntary Commitment*. Hawthorne, NY: Aldine.
Hughes, Everett C. (1971) *The Sociological Eye*. Chicago: Aldine.
Kitsuse, John I. (1962) 'Societal reactions to deviant behavior: Problems of theory and method,' *Social Problems*, 9: 247–56.
Mitteness, Linda S. and Barker, Judith C. (1994) 'Managing large projects,' in Jaber F. Gubrium and Andrea Sankar (eds.), *Qualitative Methods in Aging Research*. Thousand Oaks, CA: Sage. pp. 82–104.
Scheff, Thomas J. (1966) *Being Mentally Ill*. Chicago: Aldine.
West, Candace (1996) 'Ethnography and orthography: A (modest) methodological proposal,' *Journal of Contemporary Ethnography*, 25: 327–52.
Wolcott, Harry F. (1999) *Ethnography: A Way of Seeing*. Lanham, MD: AltaMira.

4

Sampling Strategies in Qualitative Research

Tim Rapley

Put simply, sampling really matters. It matters in relation to an array of issues, for the whole trajectory of the analytic process, from initial questions asked about a phenomenon to the presentation of your work. Given that the claims that qualitative researchers want to make are routinely based on working closely with relatively small numbers of people, interactions, situations or spaces, it is central that these are chosen for good analytic reasons. Above all, sampling should never be the product of ad hoc decisions or left solely to chance. It needs to be thoughtful and rigorous.

There are some good discussions of the range of key conceptual issues about sampling (see e.g. Guba, 1981; Mitchell, 1983; Ward Schofield, 1993; Sandelowski, 1995; Williams, 2002; Gobo, 2004) alongside some useful, user-friendly, introductions to more practical considerations (see e.g. Patton, 2002; Charmaz, 2006). In this chapter, I want to explore sampling through a different narrative, one which uses a single case to demonstrate a range of issues researchers face in relation to sampling. I am going to offer a reasonably detailed account – although sadly far too brief – of a research project I undertook, in order to explore some of the pragmatic and theoretical issues you can face. Initially, I will explore issues of sampling prior to entering the field, both in relation to proposal writing alongside the forms of knowledge that can inform your ideas. I will then explore the evolution of the sampling practices over the life of the project – from exploratory rounds of sampling to those more focused on conceptual development – always outlining the iterative relationship between sampling and analysis. Finally, I will turn to sampling in relation to the presentation of data. Interwoven throughout this account will be some traditional overviews of the key debates and procedural issues that you need to consider. However, first, I will introduce the research project.

THE CONTEXT OF THE CASE

The case I want to explore focuses on delay in diagnosis for children with juvenile idiopathic arthritis (JIA). JIA is a form of arthritis that affects both children and adolescents. As soon as the diagnosis is suspected, these patients need to be referred to a paediatric rheumatology team, to get confirmation of the diagnosis and to get access to the effective treatments now available. The research team included a consultant in paediatric rheumatology, with whom I had worked closely on other projects. I need to stress that this was an extremely practically orientated project, funded by a research charity, Arthritis Research UK [1], that was seeking practically orientated findings.

Note: Genres of sampling and the generalizability question

Sampling can be divided in a number of different ways. At a basic level, with the exception of total population sampling you will often see the divide between random sampling of a representative population and non-random sampling. Clearly, for many more quantitative-minded researchers, non-random sampling is the second-choice approach as it creates potential issues of 'bias'. However, in qualitative research the central resource through which sampling decisions are made is a focus on specific people, situations or sites because they offer a specific – 'biased' or 'information-rich' – perspective (Patton, 2002). Irrespective of the approach, sampling requires prior knowledge of the phenomenon. Knowledge is essential in order to establish how 'typical' your sample is of the phenomenon alongside understanding the potential diversity, or variance, within the phenomenon. The higher the variance, the larger the sample required.

Within more quantitative work, when working with a random sample you need to be able to classify the population in order to generate a representative random or quota sample. That assumes various things. In survey work, you need to have enough a priori information to inform the design of the sample. Routinely, you would work with some kind of proxy for the issues that you are interested in, often based on socio-demographic data. In more experimental work, like randomized controlled trials, you conduct some prior research in order to establish the variance in the phenomenon, as documented by some outcome measure, in order to undertake sample size calculations to detect significant differences. However, routinely within research, especially social science, the focus is on issues – like actions, interactions, identities, events – where we do not have sufficient knowledge of the distribution of phenomena in order adequately to inform sampling issues.

When not sampling the total population, random sampling relies on large samples and attempts to minimize sample errors. You can then begin to claim statistical representatives. As Gobo notes:

> There is no evidence that the sampling assumptions underlying the natural sciences (i.e. that cases are interchangeable because they are *equal* and *distributed at random* in the population) work well in the social sciences. On the contrary, in society almost nothing is random, there are social inequalities affecting people's position in the population. (2004: 441; italics in original).

So, notwithstanding the problems of adequately understanding the distribution of a phenomenon to inform sample design and size, you cannot assume a random distribution.

Now, the logic behind this is that a representative, and ideally random, sample will mean that the findings are generalizable (in a statistical sense). As Gobo (2004) highlights, too often these two terms are used interchangeably, without reflection on what separates them.

> Representativeness connects to the questions about the sample whereas generalizability connects to questions related to the findings. Working with a representative sample does not automatically lead to generalizable findings; between these two issues are potential 'measurement errors', connected to a wide array of practical problems. Relatedly, working with a non-representative sample does not mean you can automatically assume that generalizability is not possible. For example, work within the tradition of conversation analysis has repeatedly demonstrated interactional practices, such as preference organization, that are routinely used across a wide variety of domains of everyday and institutional talk. In this way, the findings have theoretical generalizability (see Maxwell and Chmiel, Chapter 37, this volume).

PUBLIC ACCOUNTS OF SAMPLING STRATEGIES

Prior to undertaking the research, we had to offer the funding agency and the medical ethics committee an outline of our sampling strategies. Given that these audiences expect a reasonable degree of certainty and structure, the approach to sampling was simply introduced as 'purposive sampling' and later described as 'maximum variation sampling', with the variation defined by:

- duration of delay from onset of symptoms to first assessment by paediatric rheumatology;
- observed complexity of referral pathways (assessed by the known number of contacts with health and social care professionals).

Note that, even at this stage, the sampling strategy is not defined in terms of sociodemographic solutions; rather the strategy is led by the phenomena of delay and complexity. Given the focus of the research, this makes practical sense. Also, terms like 'maximum variation strategy' can have a currency with these types of mixed audiences. Certain key phrases have become part of the grammar of applications, in much the same way that terms like 'grounded theory' are found in data analysis sections.

We also outlined that we would focus on two patient groups. We proposed to sample new referrals to the paediatric rheumatology team, recruiting between 10 and 15 patients diagnosed within the prior nine months to minimize problems of recall. We also aimed to recruit between 10 and 15 more established patients, those who had been with the team for over nine months, in order test the emerging ideas. As we were working with children and adolescents, each 'case' would be understood through talking to families – so parents, guardians and, if they wanted to take part, the patients themselves. We would also interview the health and social care professionals either responsible for or involved in the referral to the paediatric rheumatology team – so our understanding of each case could be expanded to include these actors. We offered some sense of certainty around the numbers we would recruit, albeit offering the numbers within a range. This had practical value, in terms of offering the readers a sense of the work that the project would involve – so they could establish how plausible the project appeared given the time frame and resources requested.

MAKING SENSE OF THE PHENOMENA

Centrally, I already had access to four forms of data, which could assist in understanding the potential variation in the phenomenon:

- A review of 152 patients' case notes had already been conducted and published (Foster et al., 2007). This outlined that over 75% of patients exceeded 10 weeks from onset of symptoms to first paediatric rheumatology assessment. The median interval was 20 weeks and ranged from less than 1 week to 416 weeks (eight years!).

- I also had access to a Masters student's data set that updated the previous published review, and covered over 200 patients. Again, this outlined a similar range of delay.
- I had read some of the (limited number of) papers on delay in diagnosis, which outline some of the factors tied to delay. So, for example, in rheumatoid arthritis in adults, the central issue was family doctors not recognizing the patient's problems as disease related.
- Finally, as I had already worked with members of the paediatric rheumatology team, I had access to them. I was able to discuss their impressions of the range of issues faced. I was often confronted by one type of narrative, an atrocity story, where a child had been subjected to extensive delay through the incompetence of a range of medical practitioners who were, for whatever reason, unable to see the child's problem as arthritis related.

In this way, I could begin to gain a sense of some of the issues I *might* want to focus on over the life of the project. None of this offered a firm direction as to where to go next. And, over the life of the project, during rounds of sampling, I would return to these sources of information to inform my analysis.

Note: Qualitative approaches to generalizability

Qualitative research has recently grown in popularity and shifted in focus beyond documenting the unique and particular, in part due to funding from evaluation and policy-orientated sources. In this context, considerations about sampling, alongside considerable debate and discussion, have become more central (Ward Schofield, 1993). As Dingwall notes:

> The one-off case study, conceived and executed in magnificent isolation, has no place in modern social science and little more than anecdotal value to a policy maker trying to understand how an organisation works. (1992: 171)

In this context, in part as a reaction against the positioning of qualitative research as less vital and relevant given its refusal to undertake random sampling with large numbers – due to a fundamental asymmetry in goals (e.g. Lincoln and Guba, 1985) and inability in practical terms, given time, resources and funding (e.g. Hammersley, 1992) – alternative understandings have emerged. Various authors have argued, to various degrees of success, that qualitative research is bounded by different epistemological and ontological orders. As such, alternatives have emerged, for example:

> For the naturalist, then, the concept analogous to generalizability (or external validity) is transferability, which is itself dependent upon the degree of similarity (fittingness) between two contexts. The naturalist does not attempt to form generalizations that will hold in all times and in all places, but to form working hypotheses that may be transferred from one context to another depending upon the degree of "fit" between the contexts. (Guba, 1981: 81)

And in this situation, given adequate information about the context, it is for the reader to make the connections to other similar contexts, to judge the 'degree of "fit"'.

Alongside Guba's 'transferability', we have such concepts as 'analytical generalization' (Yin, 1994) 'moderate generalization' (Williams, 2002) and 'empirical generalizations' (Hammersley, 1992), among others. Hammersley (1992) argues that you need to establish that the people or settings are in some way 'typical' of the population to which you want to generalize. He suggests establishing this through reference to published statistics, embedding

> qualitative research within or alongside survey research, or working with multiple cases, in terms of either people or sites, and exploring the variance. In this way, empirical generalization is possible when the case, or cases, are in some way demonstrated as representative of the population. The case can only be generalized to defined settings over a defined period of time and, for Hammersley, it is for the author to define these other similar contexts. He contrasts this with what he refers to as 'theoretical inference', inference to a class of people, situations or sites in any setting or time. In this way, a case's adequacy is its ability to generate formal theories – with hypotheses, theoretical propositions, logical inferences or casual connections – that can be tested and verified in further empirical work in the same class of people, situations or sites (see Mitchell, 1983, and Silverman's, 1985, discussion of these ideas). As such, atypical or particularly interesting single cases would be ideal places to sample, as they would offer a rich space to generate and test theoretical principles (see Maxwell and Chmiel, Chapter 37, this volume).

AN INITIAL ROUND OF SAMPLING (*n* = 3)

I then engaged in a very exploratory round of sampling. I asked the team to suggest three different families of patients. I wanted to speak to people from three areas of referral: one that was fairly rapid, so under 10 weeks; one that was typical, so about 20 weeks; and one that was over a year. Following Patton, I saw this sample as 'illustrative not definitive' (2002: 236) – as a way to begin to explore the phenomenon. He notes that, 'It is important, when using this strategy, to attempt to get broad consensus about which cases are typical – and what criteria are being used to define typicality' (2002: 236). As I discovered, this was not a simple process. Below are extracts from an edited field note I wrote after meeting with some members of the team:

> The role of the team secretary, as part of distributed knowledge/memory of the team, is key. The secretary and one of the nurses looked through a list to offer a selection of about 10 patients.
>
> ...
>
> They had a key question – what is quick, routine and long? 24 weeks of history is 'long' for them, but 'routine' as far as prior research shows. Is 'quick' a fast diagnosis, via Accident & Emergency, or within the official target of ten weeks? Also, the nurse's caseload was tied to her vision. She deals with more complicated cases. They both thought about route to diagnosis and where interested in finding referral from an unusual source (like Plastic surgery or ophthalmology) – so they were thinking in terms of 'untypical' cases?
>
> ...
>
> This was NOT an easy or smooth process. Original list was questioned and modified by consultant and then we returned to some of those on the original list!

They finally agreed on six names of patients and three families agreed to be interviewed. Although the process was illustrative of a range of issues, I just want to focus on a few. Generating consensus on something that is a 'typical' case involved extensive discussion. The discussion itself was illuminating, highlighting taken-for-granted aspects of individual and team reasoning about how they categorize cases. Through this process, my understanding of 'typicality' was questioned and extended. So, rather than just focusing on issues of typical delay in relation to time, typicality should also include the route the patient took.

In conducting and then analysing these interviews, I discovered something interesting. In talking to these parents I got slightly different accounts from that presented in the patient's notes. For example, what the team categorized as a typical case of a 'quick' referral emerged as a more complicated process that lasted about 11 months. This might stem from parents' re-evaluation of prior symptoms. At the time of diagnosis they may not have told staff about the onset of some symptoms as they felt they had little to do with the illness, but, with growing knowledge about the disease, they now understood them as first signs of onset.

Also, the case that was typical of 'long delay', over one year, was, at this point in the project, an 'atypical' or 'deviant case'. The child had received a diagnosis of JIA at about 3 years old and the parents were told he was too young for further tests and he was given a short course of physiotherapy. After this, they where told he was fine and discharged. He did not complain of any problem for another five years and then was referred straight to the team. In this way, he received a rapid diagnosis but inappropriate care.

Note: Purposive sampling strategies

If you look at the literature on sampling, you can soon be overwhelmed by the diversity of approaches people write about. So, for example, Sandelowski (1995) refers to three approaches – maximum variation, phenomenal variation and theoretical variation – all described as purposeful.[2] Gobo (2004) refers to four: purposive, quota, emblematic and snowball. Patton (2002) refers to 16 different types – including critical case, stratified purposeful, snowball and convenience – all again described under the label purposeful.

Personally, I find Patton's list very useful to think with. He presents you with 16 different labels to work with, to think about, and this is incredibly useful as a way to sensitize your sampling strategy. It enables you to realize that you have choices, that you should be making choices and that those choices can have an impact. However, the issue is not that you have been able initially to sample five 'typical cases' of rapid referral, but rather that you have got five cases and you have thought through issues of how typical are they, what connects them, what divides them. As Sandelowski notes:

> These determinations are never absolute; depending on the purpose, analytic frame, and phase of an analysis, any one case can be a case of and about more than one thing and can, therefore, be analytically (re)located among other cases. (1996: 527)

So being able to call a case 'typical' is useful. Initially, you might know from some other source, say statistical data, the funder, colleagues or even other respondents, that a specific site is 'typical'. However, you need to question such a position – it might be 'typical' in the way that others have understood the issue, but your research might render the phenomenon in a different way.

Thinking about and categorizing your sampling strategies does not always occur prospectively or over different rounds of sampling. For example, Draucker et al. (2007), after an initial recruitment flyer, discovered they had 110 calls from people interested in taking part in their study. Given the nature of the focus of the study, people's experiences of sexual violence, they felt they had to interview those 43 who met the criteria sooner rather than later. They undertook an initial round of coding of 43 interviews, and developed initial codes and concepts. Rather than conduct more interviews, they re-explored their own data set, searching within this, initially for 'intense' cases, so undertaking a form of intensity sampling. Intensity sampling refers to 'excellent or rich examples of the phenomenon of interest, but not highly unusual cases' (Patton, 2002: 234). They looked again at their data set through various sampling approaches, and in one area, when conducting 'extreme or deviant case sampling', re-interviewed one of the participants.

> In some senses, the reality is a lot simpler than thinking about which of Patton's 16 labels fit. It is enough to make good, analytically driven, thoughtful, decisions. Poor sampling decisions, those driven by lack of access, response, knowledge, time or resources can lead to sampling driven by opportunism or convenience. Pragmatic considerations, especially in relation to access to institutional sites, situations or hard-to-reach people, do have their place (see Hammersley and Atkinson, 1995). However, as Murphy et al. note, 'opportunistic sampling will be seen as the method of last resort in anything other than the most exploratory research' (1998: 93). Centrally, being able to describe your sampling as in some way strategic offers increased confidence in your work. There is a rhetoric of expertise that is embedded in such work. But this is beyond sheer rhetoric. It is about doing good analysis.

EXPLORING THE PHENOMENON IN NO PARTICULAR ORDER: (*n* = 14)

After conducting the three interviews with three types of 'typical case', I decided to interview the families of recently diagnosed patients. I had no particular logic about whom I approached, the only criterion they had to fit was that they had had a diagnosis in the last six months. Despite wanting to interview families with fresh memories of the experience, families were contacted at least one month post-diagnosis so as to avoid burdening the parents.

In sampling strategy terms, I undertook the least analytically strong option. I undertook something similar to what Patton refers to as convenience sampling:

> doing what is fast and convenient. This is possibly the most common sampling strategy and the least desirable. ... Convenience sampling is neither purposeful or strategic. (2002: 241–2)

If my whole sample had been achieved by recruiting those who were easiest to hand, I would agree with Patton. For me, projects that *only* undertake such desperation sampling are generally problematic. However, as I was still in the initial stages, I wanted to explore the phenomenon, to get a generic sense of the potential issues and, with luck, to get a sense of the potential variance in the phenomenon.

I ended up conducting eight interviews with newly diagnosed families. As the unit of the analysis was paediatrics patients' route to diagnosis, I was interviewing parents, sometimes mothers or fathers on their own, sometimes both parents and, in one case, an adolescent child took part. The focus was on the very practical issues of what happened, in what order, alongside their emotional trajectory. For some of these patients, I also conducted parallel interviews with a health practitioner involved in their referral. I was still conducting very fine-grained coding, documenting the broad (and ever-growing) array of issues that were emerging in each new interview and constantly comparing the application of my codes with those that had gone before. However, at this stage, a potential key analytic issue was emerging, centred around the initial diagnosis the patients received from health professionals and how that impacted on delay. I kept returning to the same issue, within and across cases, and felt I might be getting somewhere.

EXPLORING THE PHENOMENON THROUGH SOMEBODY ELSE'S ORDER: (*n* = 11)

So far I had conducted 11 interviews with families and 6 interviews with health professionals involved in the referral pathway. I felt I had begun to make some sense of the issues. Family resemblances were starting to emerge – especially around issues of initial decisions to seek lay and medical help. Fewer new patients were coming through the service. I discussed some of the recruitment issues with the team and we decided also to recruit more established patients. In clinics, the team were seeing new patients as well as those returning for regular three- or six-month check-ups and then thinking, 'this would be an interesting case for Tim'. Their version of 'interesting' was often tied to specific issues of the case: for example, that the family had sought help from a private medical practice (a relatively uncommon thing in paediatric care in the UK) or that referral was 'fast' (i.e. under 10 weeks).

In this phase I interviewed another six families and a further five health professionals. The clinic staff felt they were offering interesting cases. For me, I was working with really quite 'information-rich cases', cases that, for whatever reason, could offer a new insight into the phenomenon. In technical terms I was using a mixture involving 'deviant or atypical sampling' (e.g. the parents who went private), 'intensity sampling' (e.g. the parents with relatively fast referrals) and 'critical sampling'.

One case did turn out to be a 'critical case'. Patton describes this as a case that makes a point dramatically: '[i]dentification of critical cases depends on the recognition of the key dimensions that make for a critical case' (2002: 237). This was another account where, after an initial visit to a family practitioner, the parents were told the child had JIA, but there was nothing that could be done. After a period of time, the child no longer complained and the symptoms did not flare. Only five years later, when the mother noticed the child's restricted movement, did they return to seek advice. The child was then referred to the team and given the necessary medication and physiotherapy routines. This case was key, and critical for me in rethinking the analysis. For example, rather than understand the phenomenon under study as 'delay in diagnosis', we realized we needed to focus on delay in diagnosis *and* in receiving appropriate care. So a previous case from the initial round of sampling where the parents were told there was little medicine could do (discussed above) was no longer to be understood as atypical or deviant. The phenomenon of 'inappropriate care' with a diagnosis of JIA was now central to our understanding. In Emmerson's (2004) terms, it was a 'key incident' in the trajectory of the analysis that enabled me to re-conceptualize the focus.

As noted above, our conceptualization of a 'case' included accounts from the patients' family members, patients, and health and social care professionals. So far, we had 10 cases, which included the health professionals' accounts and one teacher's account. Although they provided an additional layer of context, I felt that, analytically, they were often of relatively limited value. Also, it was proving very hard to contact practitioners, although once contacted they all agreed to take part, and then trying to arrange interviews was difficult, given their work schedules. I interviewed some of them on the phone, but found this less effective in generating a sufficient level of detail. Rather than spend more time on this, I decided to focus solely on families' accounts.

Note: Information-Rich Cases

Central to the success of purposive sampling is a focus on working with what Patton describes as 'information-rich cases' (2002: 230). These are the cases:

> from which one can learn a great deal about issues of central importance to the purpose of the inquiry, thus the term *purposeful* sampling. (Ibid.; italics in original)

> Now, a case can range from an individual, a group, to an organization (and beyond). However, a case is not a naturally occurring object, it is a researcher's construct, a product of what Ragin (1992) refers to as 'casing'. Centrally, through casing you are attempting to get information about some aspect of a particular phenomenon. As Miles and Huberman note, albeit it in relation to complex cases:
>
>> you are sampling people to get at characteristics of settings, events, and processes. Conceptually, the people themselves are secondary. (1994: 33)
>
> This might sound quite harsh, and beyond the limits of calls for qualitative research to do things like give others access to people's 'voices' or 'lived experience'. But we are always only giving access to some aspect of that lived experience or organizational context. And if we take it that exploring a specific phenomenon is central to our research, we need to think about what makes up the focus of our casing.
>
> What are the sampling units (or combination of units) that should guide your sampling? Rather than solely focus on the classic socio-demographic units, like age, ethnicity, etc., we need to think about more social, relational and conceptual units. For example, we could consider structuring our sampling to focus on other issues:
>
> - Actions – specific acts, processes, behaviours, intentions and motivations.
> - Interactions – activities, formats, consequences and outcomes.
> - Identities – roles, types, categories.
> - Events – situations, rituals, ceremonies, temporal orders or trajectories.
> - Settings and spaces – spatial (or conceptual) locations, organizations, milieu.
> - Objects – devices, artefacts, electronic and paper texts.
>
> Exploring the phenomenon is key, not being able to say 'I observed X number of men and X number of women'. Relatedly, within-case sampling can also be important, especially in relation to more ethnographic studies. So, for example, in exploring a children's ward in a hospital, you may initially choose to focus on junior doctors. Over time, you may switch your focus to other actors in the setting, say parents. You may sample a related setting, those spaces where discussions about referring children to the ward first happen, such as the accident and emergency department or the children's day clinic. Or you might sample discussions about changing a child's medication and want to observe similar discussions across a range of contexts (e.g. with and without parents present, on the ward and in clinics) or a range of times (e.g. day, night, weekend). In this way, sampling is driven by emergent analytic issues.

BUILDING IDEAS, CHALLENGING ASSUMPTIONS (*n* = 17)

The fourth round of sampling shifted towards more conceptual development as well as focusing on some specific criteria. Analytically, I felt I had some sense of the key issues. I was becoming interested in exploring these further. So, for example, in trying to make sense of how people navigate through the system, I was interested in exploring the impact of people's prior knowledge and experience. I asked the staff to help me find cases containing one of the following three dimensions:

- Child diagnosed with JIA who had another significant illness that had been diagnosed prior to JIA emerging and for which the child received ongoing care.

- Family member who, through illness, had led the family to have significant contacts with the NHS (National Health Service).
- Family member who worked in the NHS in some capacity.

I conducted six interviews, covering six different families, two per dimension. Put very simply, I found that irrespective of how much prior knowledge the families had, the key facets of the trajectories echoed those of the other children without access to such potential 'expertise'. This additional knowledge, in some cases, did impact on aspects of the trajectory, enabling the families to manage the problems they faced differently, but the same problems existed. The addition of a previously diagnosed illness added to delay, in that practitioners' diagnostic focus was confined to explaining the new emerging symptoms through that particular lens. Rather than seeing these cases as somehow 'atypical', they echoed a broader issue throughout the data set: that the practitioners' search for a new diagnosis was routinely constrained by prior diagnostic expectations. All these accounts not only enabled me to develop these hunches, but confirmed my understanding of other issues alongside raising new issues.

One of the tensions I had to contend with was that between the conceptual development of my ideas and the possibility that the staff knew enough about a patient's trajectory to tell me who to interview. So, I was interested in exploring what can be best described as the role of 'chance', 'luck' or 'timeliness' in the patient's trajectory, as I had seen how central this had been. For example, in one case, the mother met a nurse, whom knew the family, in a hospital corridor. The nurse could see that the mother was distressed. This led the nurse to get her colleague, an adult practitioner, to 'glance' at the patient's x-ray results over their lunch. Her colleague was the first to suspect a diagnosis of JIA. I did not sample for this explicitly, due to the rather ephemeral nature of the issue, but rather expected (or maybe hoped) it would emerge in interviews. It did. It helped me conceptualize the work parents sometimes undertook to engineer these 'chance' encounters, to increase the possibility of encountering someone who might offer a diagnosis or treatment that made sense.

In this phase, my coding and analysis were becoming a lot more focused. I was selecting within the material, selecting specific stretches of talk for more in-depth analysis. Such coding work has strong family resemblances to the practices of sampling, especially theoretical and within-case sampling, in that strategic choices are made about what issues to focus coding on in order further to explore, challenge and confirm emergent ideas.

Note: Theory and Sampling

Despite the range of things written about the relationship between theory and sampling, there appear to be two main approaches to using theory to inform sampling.

First, following the tradition of theoretical sampling in grounded theory (in whatever version, see e.g. Glaser and Strauss, 1967; Glaser, 1978; Strauss and Corbin, 1990), after an initial round of sampling (driven by a priori ideas) to generate ideas, your next choice of person, site or situation is driven by the need to develop and elaborate on your emerging conceptual ideas. In grounded theory terms, you undertake theoretical sampling to help develop codes and categories, to understand variation in a process, to saturate properties of categories and to integrate them. In this way, your sampling decisions are emergent, progressive and inductive. Your task is artfully to choose a next case in order to progress the development of your emergent conceptual ideas. The focus here is not to demonstrate empirical generalizability, in terms of choosing cases that might show others that you have sought variation to represent the population in some way. The focus is on developing the shape – the robustness – of your emergent categories and substantive theory. In this way, the demonstration of adequacy is understood in the transportability of the theoretical ideas.

Second, another tradition exists – one that receives less attention, but is potentially equally useful to consider. This is where the initial and often subsequent sampling decisions are driven by a priori theoretical ideas. This can take multiple forms. In such circumstances you may be exploring, testing and refining the ideas of an existing theory. Silverman notes that:

> in a case-study, the analyst selects cases only because he [sic] believes they exhibit some general theoretical principle. His account's claim to validity depends entirely on demonstrating that the features he portrays in the case are representative not of the population but of this general principle. (1985: 113)

So, for example, Silverman (1984) undertook some observations in a private medical clinic. He wanted to test Strong's (1983) theoretical ideas about the rituals of interaction between doctors and patients. Strong's work was based on extensive observations in public medical clinics, mainly in the NHS in the UK, so a private clinic offered an excellent space to test and refine Strong's theory. You will note that, in this example, as with others (see Murphy et al., 1998), this is often focused on ethnographic research where the choice of site is key. Given a lack of resources, use of more than a few sites is rare. So very good theoretical reasons for sampling a particular case can be central in claims-making. Of course, you need to choose a theory that is reasonably well recognized. Such a priori theory can also help support the selection of specific people, situations, times or places within a case.

FINDING A GOOD PRACTICAL SOLUTION TO THE PUZZLE

It was during the fourth phase of sampling, when I sampled for specific theoretically driven issues alongside some typical cases, that I had my 'eureka moment'. I met one of the team in the corridor and she asked me how it was going. I explained to her what I felt were the key issues emerging from my analysis. As I walked away, something in my account of the work kept coming back to me. I had used the analogy of the game 'snakes and ladders'. Then, over a three-hour period, I wrote a conceptual memo. The title, albeit rather elaborate, offered up the main issues I wanted to explore through writing it:

> MEMO – Snakes and Ladders – Persistence, Luck and Knowledge – Or how persistence (in symptoms and seeking a solution) combined with good and bad luck connect you with people with the relevant knowledge

In the memo, I conceptualized the main issues that were central to the phenomenon of delay in diagnosis. In writing it, I moved between a large number of different documents, including coded and uncoded interview transcripts, summaries of interviews and codes, field notes from interviews and a range of types of memos. In and through this process I checked my ideas, sought out disconfirming moments from the cases, and brought together the hunches and leads I had tried to explore.

I knew my conceptualization worked – it made sense of the data, it offered up a coherent account of the phenomenon. Given that I had now developed a conceptual model that I felt made good sense of all the 'variance' of the phenomenon, I went on to carry out a more structured review of my data set, to explore whether I had any deviant or atypical moments or features in my cases that did not fit. I did not find anything that meant I needed to re-evaluate my ideas.

With prior conceptualizations of the data, I had found exceptions that made me reconfigure my ideas.

Also, prior to writing the memo, I felt that, at least in terms of the accounts I was listening to, I had reached something like repetition. I was seeing the accounts as having very clear family resemblances. Some of the ideas were key; they were emerging again and again. More data would not help me understand or expand on my ideas any further. What was missing was some kind of conceptual model that linked the various ideas I was working with. All my attempts to offer something like a coherent account of the phenomenon either were far too unwieldy, or had too many exceptions, with many aspects of cases as atypical. However, repetition is not sufficient justification for stopping sampling. As Glaser notes:

> Saturation is not seeing the same pattern over and over again. It is the conceptualization of comparisons of these incidents which yield different properties of the pattern, until no new properties of the pattern emerge. (2001: 191, cited in Charmaz, 2006)

My eureka moment had enabled me to reach something like what grounded theorists call *theoretical* saturation. And in re-reviewing the already-collected data set, field notes and memos and engaging with the new data I was gathering, 'no new properties of the pattern' were emerging. However, I did not stop sampling at this point, as I wanted to test and refine this conceptual model. It still held over the next five interviews during this phase of sampling, albeit with some minor tinkering.

A FEW MORE FOR LUCK ($n = 2$)

By this stage, I now had a very good sense of my data; the issues and concepts were well developed; I had had my 'eureka moment'; and I had what I felt was a good analytic narrative. I had undertaken 34 interviews with families and 11 interviews with health and social care practitioners. The final stage emerged in part through pure opportunity and in part due to the 'doubts' many researchers feel. Two new patients had just been seen in the clinic and were now on the ward. I was told that these were both 'really interesting' cases. I did both interviews. Both cases were very interesting, and could be classified as 'intensity' cases. Conceptually, I did not need to do them. I felt I had a coherent account – that I had reached saturation. However, I decided to do them for two reasons: first, the clinical team felt they would be useful; second, irrespective of how beautiful your conceptual ideas are, you always have a nagging doubt that you might have missed something. I do not feel we should ever be overly confident. We should always be open to having our ideas challenged. At this point, after working with these two cases, we decided that we should close recruitment. Clearly, I could have gone on, but in terms of time, money and resources, as well as imposing on people's lives, this would have been overly intrusive.

THE PUBLIC FACES OF RESEARCH

Over the life of the project, I conducted 36 interviews with families. I had spoken to mothers ($n = 34$), fathers ($n = 9$), teenage patients ($n = 5$), grandmothers ($n = 2$) and an aunt ($n = 1$). I had also undertaken 11 interviews with professionals involved in the care pathway of these JIA patients: orthopaedic surgeons ($n = 4$), paediatricians ($n = 3$), a paediatric immunologist ($n = 1$), a GP ($n = 1$), a nurse ($n = 1$) and one non-health professional ($n = 1$), a primary school teacher.

The sampling strategy was purposive; it was designed to explore, test and refine our emerging ideas. It was not designed to replicate the pattern of delay shown in cohort studies but rather to explore and map the diversity of factors that impact on that. However – and this was not planned – the sample closely matched prior quantitative research. You may remember that I noted that a prior study of 152 patients' case notes found that over 75% of patients exceeded 10 weeks from onset of symptoms to first paediatric rheumatology assessment (median 20, range 1–416 weeks). In our purposive sample ($n = 36$), over 73% of patients exceeded 10 weeks from onset of symptoms to first paediatric rheumatology assessment (median 22, range 1–362 weeks).

Now, this happened purely by chance. I had never sat down and tried to work out which patients we would need to recruit to get something that mirrored the prior quantitative work. This was excellent news as it added another layer of confidence that the sample was not somehow atypical of the population as conceptualized through statistical means. This was also excellent news when presenting the data to audiences that demanded a specific version of representativeness. However, throughout the life of the project I had attempted to recruit a range of 'typical' cases. My sampling was driven by both theoretical and what Sandelowski (1995) refers to as phenomenal variation. I had tried to explore the range of cases the clinic sees, to explore the variance in the phenomenon in terms of both the substantive issues (like length of delay) and the emergent theoretical issues (like knowledge of navigating health systems).

I want to focus on one last issue: the sampling we undertake when we present our data to others (see also Barbour, 1998). At the time of writing this chapter, I have only presented the data at three time points, namely two posters and one conference presentation. The posters were presented prior to my 'eureka moment'. With these, in part, given the limited space on a poster, the posters focused on demonstrating the key ideas I was working with. They simply reported on specific concepts, with very few quotes of what I was thinking about. For example, in relation to how parents conceptualize initial physical signs, the poster text reports:

As parents notice 'low grade' and often subtle physical and behavioural changes they rationalise observations as normal (e.g. 'drama queen'), adopt a 'wait and see' approach, and/or provide modifications to compensate (e.g. getting child new shoes). When symptoms are severe, escalate or continue, they then seek a medical opinion.

Sampling specific accounts to demonstrate the phenomenon was offset by generic descriptions of process across the data set. The only direct quote in this section is 'drama queen', which I could have got from any number of transcripts.

Later in the analytic process, I offered a different presentational style. In drafting my conference presentation, I was unsure about how best to present the data. I tried various options, searching through my transcripts and memos to discover good exemplars. By 'good' exemplars I mean those that demonstrate specific aspects of an idea through concise and clear language. However, this became rather messy, as too much contextual detail was needed to place each issue in context and shifting between accounts of a large number of cases meant that the message was diluted.

In the end, I went for a different solution, simply comparing two cases, one 'intense' and one 'extreme'. So, for example, in relation to how parents conceptualize initial physical signs, the text on the slide for the conference presentation read:

Bella – aged 3

Started walking early, 8 months,

'... we'd occasionally see certain days that she'd be a little bit stiff and we'd think, "well is that because she's young and a bit too young to walk?" so you kind of pass that off as something else'

'... at first I was thinking, "well she's new to walking, her muscles are developing, is she stiff because them muscles are developing, how long do we let this go on?"'

And this discussion of the initial signs continued to another slide. After presenting the two cases, I directly compared their key features. As Sandelowski notes, in relation to more case-based research approaches:

cases [are] conceived as singular combinations of elements constituting each case that are compared to singular combinations of elements constituting other cases. (2011: 157)

The intense case was typical, in terms of delay in diagnosis, and the extreme case was atypical in terms of a very rapid diagnosis and appropriate care. Irrespective of time from onset of symptoms to diagnosis and care, both cases represented all the key aspects of the conceptual model. I was interested in demonstrating how a specific configuration of the same elements led to a different outcome. Now, I could have presented any of the 36 cases, as each demonstrates a particular configuration. However, these two were chosen, in part for their rhetorical impact, as they both presented well, given the relatively short time I had.

CLOSING COMMENTS

The aim of this chapter was to offer you, the reader, 'technical access' to the lived practices of sampling. I hope you can begin to make sense of some of the issues that can weave through sampling. Ideally, your sampling strategy should be something that evolves over time, that emerges through a mutual relationship with desk, field and analytic work.

The obvious question, given the subject of the chapter, is to ask: why choose this specific research project as my single case? It was chosen for a range of reasons. In part, for opportunistic and pragmatic reasons – I am still working trying to write up the findings, and so it is still fresh in my mind. I also chose it because, given the widespread use of interviews, it was potentially a 'typical' case in terms of the methods. However, in terms of the phenomenon of applying sampling strategies to qualitative research in a strategic way, I am not sure how I would classify it. Hopefully it is a typical or intense case. Hopefully, it reflects elements of the lived practices of researchers using a wide array of methods and methodologies. Maybe trying to undertake sampling, in what I hope is a reasoned and thoughtful way, might mean it is a relatively 'atypical' case. However, exploring deviant cases can be an extremely useful thing in itself.

We should also ask: how generalizable (see Maxwell and Chmiel, Chapter 37, this volume) or transferable (see Murray, Chapter 40, this volume) is this case? Sadly, I have not got enough data on other people's approaches to sampling-in-action, in order to understand how empirically generalizable it is. This is a product of the relative paucity of accounts that describe the lived practices of sampling. However, it does relate to the more theoretical accounts about sampling. It also shares similarities with some of the practical issues that fellow researchers have discussed with me. So, despite an underlying argument running through the chapter about the utility of exploring and documenting the variance in the phenomenon, I can do little to demonstrate this case's empirical generalizability. It is for you, the reader, to decide. Hopefully, you can see this case as an ensemble of the very practical, contingent, analytic and theoretical issues that researchers are faced with. Perhaps you can think with some of these ideas in order to inform your thinking about your own sampling practices.

NOTES

1. The research project was 'Exploring the pathways of referral for children with incident juvenile arthritis' Arthritis Research UK (Grant No: 17738).
2. For me, 'purposive sampling' and 'purposeful sampling' are synonyms.

FURTHER READING

Charmaz, Kathy (2006) 'Theoretical sampling, saturation, and sorting', Chapter 5 in *Constructing Grounded Theory: A Practical Guide through Qualitative Analysis*. London: Sage. pp. 96–122.

Gobo, Giampietro (2004) 'Sampling, representativeness and generalizability', in Clive Seale et al. (eds), *Qualitative Research Practice*. London: Sage. pp. 435–56.

Patton, Michael Q. (2002) *Qualitative Research & Evaluation Methods*, 3rd edition. Thousand Oaks, CA: Sage (1st edition 1990). See the section entitled 'Purposeful sampling', pp. 230–47.

REFERENCES

Barbour, Rose, S. (1998) 'Engagement, presentation and representation in research practice', in Rose S. Barbour and Guro Huby (eds), *Meddling with Mythology: AIDS and the Social Construction of Knowledge*. London: Routledge. pp. 183–200.

Charmaz, Kathy (2006) *Constructing Grounded Theory: A Practical Guide through Qualitative Analysis*. London: Sage.

Dingwall, Robert (1992) '"Don't mind him – he's from Barcelona": Qualitative methods in health studies', in Jeanne Daly et al. (eds), *Researching Health Care*. London: Tavistock/Routledge. pp. 161–75.

Draucker, Claire B., Martsolf, Donna S., Ross, Ratchneewan and Rusk, Thomas B. (2007) 'Theoretical sampling and category development in Grounded Theory'. *Qualitative Health Research*, 17: 1137–48.

Emmerson, Robert M. (2004) 'Working with "key incidents"', in Clive Seale et al. (eds), *Qualitative Research Practice*. London: Sage. pp. 457–72.

Foster, Helen E., Eltringham, Michal S., Kay, Lesley J., Friswell, Mark, Abinun, Mario. and Myers, Andrea. (2007) 'Delay in access to appropriate care for children presenting with musculoskeletal symptoms and ultimately diagnosed with juvenile idiopathic arthritis', *Arthritis Care and Research*, 57: 921–7.

Glaser, Barney G. (1978) *Theoretical Sensitivity*. Mill Valley, CA: Sociology Press.

Glaser, Barney G. (2001) *The Grounded Theory Perspective I: Conceptualization Contrasted with Description*. Mill Valley, CA: Sociology Press.

Glaser, Barney G. and Strauss, Anselm (1967) *The Discovery of Grounded Theory*. New York: Aldine de Gruyter.

Gobo, Giampietro (2004) 'Sampling, representativeness and generalizability', in Clive Seale et al. (eds), *Qualitative Research Practice*. London: Sage. pp. 435–56.

Guba, Egon G. (1981) 'Criteria for assessing the trustworthiness of naturalistic inquiries', *Education, Communication and Technology Journal*, 29: 75–91.

Hammersley, Martyn (1992) *What's Wrong With Ethnography? Methodological Explorations*. London: Routledge.

Hammersley, Martyn and Atkinson, Paul (1995) *Ethnography: Principles in Practice*, 2nd edition. London: Routledge (1st edition, 1983).

Lincoln, Yvonne S. and Guba, Egon G. (1985) *Naturalistic Inquiry*. Newbury Park, CA: Sage.

Miles, Matthew B. and Huberman, A. Michael (1994) *Qualitative Data Analysis: An Expanded Sourcebook*, 2nd edition. Thousand Oaks, CA: Sage (1st edition 1984).

Mitchell, J. Clyde (1983) 'Case and situation analysis', *Sociological Review*, 31: 187–211.

Murphy, Elizabeth, Dingwall, Robert, Greatbatch, David, Parker, Susan and Watson, Pamela. (1998) 'Qualitative research methods in health technology assessment: A review of the literature'. *Health Technology Assessment*, 2 (16).

Patton, Michael Q. (2002) *Qualitative Research & Evaluation Methods*, 3rd edition. Thousand Oaks, CA: Sage (1st edition 1990).

Ragin, Charles C. (1992) '"Casing" and the process of social inquiry', in Charles C. Ragin and Howard S. Becker (eds), *What Is a case? Exploring the Foundations of Social Inquiry*. Cambridge: Cambridge University Press, pp. 217–26.

Sandelowski, Margarete (1995) 'Focus on qualitative methods: Sample size in qualitative research', *Research in Nursing and Health*, 18: 179–83.

Sandelowski, Margarete (1996) 'One is the Liveliest Number: The Case Orientation of Qualitative Research', *Research in Nursing & Health*, 19: 525–9.

Sandelowski, Margarete (2011) '"Casing" the research case study', *Research in Nursing & Health*, 34: 153–9.

Silverman, David (1984) 'Going private: Ceremonial forms in a private oncology clinic', *Sociology*, 18: 191–204.

Silverman, David (1985) *Qualitative Methodology and Sociology*. Aldershot: Gower.

Strauss, Anselm and Corbin, Juliet (1990) *Basics of Qualitative Research: Grounded Theory, Procedures and Techniques*. Newbury Park, CA: Sage.

Strong, Phil (1983) *The Ceremonial Order of the Clinic*. London: Routledge & Kegan Paul.

Ward Schofield, Janet (1993) 'Increasing the generalisability of qualitative research', in Martyn Hammersley (ed.), *Social Research: Philosophy, Politics & Practice*. London: Open University/Sage. pp. 200–25.

Williams, Malcolm (2002) 'Generalization in interpretive research', in Tim May (ed.), *Qualitative Research in Action*. London: Sage.

Yin, Robert. K. (1994). *Case Study Research: Design and Methods*, 2nd edition. Thousand Oaks, CA: Sage (1st edition 1984).

Transcription as a Crucial Step of Data Analysis

Sabine Kowal and Daniel C. O'Connell

For the first decade of the twenty-first century, the Google Ngram viewer (Michel et al., 2011) shows a sudden increment in books and articles in both English and German on the topic of *qualitative research methods*. This development is clearly related to the large number of scientific disciplines – including communication, economics, education, health care services, linguistics, marketing, psychology and social work – which involve qualitative research. One upshot of this surge has been that the use of transcripts for such research can now be 'taken for granted' (Dresing and Pehl, 2010: 731; our translation); hence, the necessity to engage the complexity of transcripts as 'artefacts in need of thoughtful consideration' becomes all the more urgent. At the same time, Harris (2010: 4) has warned against a certain methodological 'incoherence' on the part of contemporary linguistics consequent upon 'a failure to recognize the nature of the disparity between oral and written communication'. His comment assumes a special importance with regard to the faithful representation of oral communication in written transcripts.

A large portion of this complexity – and incoherence – is traceable to the heterogeneity of purposes served by transcription and the consequent variable standards across disciplines. For example, Langer (2010: 520; our translation) has set the bar fairly low: 'In educational research projects, detailed notation systems are for the most part bypassed by reason of the specific *status quaestionis* and in order to foster simplicity and readability.' Frost (2011: 101) has emphasized a more detailed approach to the transcription of interviews (see Roulston, Chapter 20, this volume) used in psychology: 'The transcription of interviews is carried out in multiple rounds.' These rounds might begin with a rough transcript, including the words uttered and other features such as pauses or laughing, followed by another round wherein shorter pauses, fillers and false starts are added. An even more exacting and detailed approach to transcription in the linguistic field of pragmatic research is to be found in Schmidt and

Wörner's EXMARaLDA, 'a system for the computer-assisted creation and analysis of spoken language corpora'. According to the authors, such corpora focus on

> linguistic behaviour on *different linguistic levels*. It is usually not sufficient to simply record the syntactic and lexical properties of speech, because para-linguistic phenomena (like laughing or pauses) and suprasegmental characteristics (like intonation or voice quality) may play an equally important role in the analysis. The data structure must therefore also be able to accommodate and distinguish descriptions on different linguistic levels. (2009: 567)

An explicit concern about various levels of detail in transcribing is built into the German *Gesprächsanalytisches Transkriptionssystem 2 (GAT 2)* developed by a group of linguists (Selting et al., 2009) and into the English-language adaptation of *GAT 2* by Couper-Kuhlen and Barth-Weingarten (2011). These authors have themselves translated the acronym GAT as 'discourse and conversation-analytic transcription system' (2). It distinguishes 'three levels of delicacy: minimal, basic and refined transcript versions' (353).

In view of such diversity of research purposes and the concomitant transcription requirements, we wish to limit ourselves in the following to a consideration of what we think of as basic assumptions and principles needed for an informed use of transcription, with an emphasis on qualitative research in the social sciences and, more specifically, on dialogical interaction. Such an approach is in accord with Aufenanger's (2006: 111) recommendation that the choice of transcription methods be *appropriate for the specific purposes of a given research project*. Such adaptation also serves the purpose of avoiding superfluous and/or unanalysable transcripts.

The appropriate use of transcription entails an awareness of problems related to the tasks of both the transcriber and the reader of the transcript – conceptualized as *language users* who bring their own habits, competencies and limitations to these tasks. In addition, the relevance of transcription for both qualitative and quantitative data analyses should be noted, especially in view of an increasing interest in bridging the gap between qualitative and quantitative methods (e.g. Flick et al., 2004; Kelle and Erzberger, 2004).

In the following, examples are, unless otherwise noted, taken from our own psychological research on dialogical interaction in a variety of settings. These corpora include transcripts of audio recordings of English-language TV interviews (O'Connell and Kowal, 2005) and feature movies (O'Connell and Kowal, 2012).

TRANSCRIPTION – A UNIVERSALLY INDISPENSABLE STEP IN RESEARCH

According to Peez (2002: 24; our translation), 'all social scientists doing qualitative research must ... carefully attend to the phase of setting down the verbal research material in writing by means of transcription'. In addition, there are applied contexts such as courtrooms and medical offices where records of spoken data are important. In order to deal with these otherwise ephemeral and elusive materials in an orderly manner, transcripts must be derived. And yet, the research community must face the vast complexity involved in this transfer to the written mode, especially when multimedia dialogical interaction is involved. The putative close correspondence between the spoken discourse and the written record thereof must be examined. Presently it is widely acknowledged that the written record cannot be accepted uncritically as a reliable source of analyses accurately reflecting the mental, social, affective and cultural components of both individual and group performance. For example, Chafe (1995: 61) has commented in the very last sentence of his chapter on transcribing, 'Perhaps the spoken corpora of the future ... should be packaged with a legal requirement that users listen as well as look' (see also Harris, 2010).

In other words, transcription is both an inevitable and problematic step in the qualitative (and quantitative) analysis of data consisting of spoken discourse. There is in fact no transcription notation system capable of providing to the researcher a completely accurate and comprehensive narrative of the original performance: all transcription is in principle *selective* and entails the inevitable risk of systematic *bias* of one kind or another. Nonetheless, this risk can be countered by making decisions on the basis of reasoned choices rather than arbitrary, non-reflective ones. Consequently, both basic and applied researchers in the social sciences must approach transcription with a very critical eye (and ear).

Our critical remarks should therefore be understood as a sort of consciousness raising regarding the intrinsic methodological limitations of transcription and the consequent cautiousness that should be exerted in interpreting transcripts. Such cautiousness would also demand, quite in accord with Chafe's (1995) recommendation mentioned above, that the interpretation of transcripts should always be verified by a return to the audio and video recordings.

In light of the complex behaviours and contexts of dialogical interaction, we have chosen in this chapter to limit our more detailed discussion of transcription to the words spoken (the *verbal* component), to the way in which they are spoken (the *prosodic* component), and to whatever non-verbal vocal behaviour accompanies the words (the *paralinguistic* component). These three components are clearly the most frequently relied upon in qualitative analyses of spoken discourse. In addition, we have included a section on the transcription of turn-taking in the transcription systems presented below. Readers interested in the transcription of extralinguistic behaviour may turn to the readings we recommend below (Jenks, 2011; Kreuz and Riordan, 2011).

BASIC TERMINOLOGY FOR TRANSCRIPTION

Transcription

The generic term *transcription* here refers to any graphic representation of selective aspects of verbal, prosodic and paralinguistic behaviour; in other words, we limit our overview of transcription to vocal behaviour. Such representation presupposes a unique performance and is typically not meant as a script for a further performance. The selected aspects are by necessity represented sequentially because real time is involved. There is in principle a wide range of detail involved in the transcription of these various aspects. This range has been illustrated by Chafe (1995: 56ff.) by means of a short utterance which he has transcribed in seven steps, by adding more prosodic detail at each step, starting with the verbal utterance presented in step 1, transcribed in standard orthography:

(1)   the other thing you can do is (56)

and ending with step 7:

(7)   ...   (0.3)   the   **óther**   thing   you   can   **dò=**   **i=s:** (58)

The additional steps have added the following prosodic notations:

- acute (*óther*) and grave (*dò*) accents for pitch prominence;
- boldface type (**other**, **do** and **is**) for greater loudness;
- equal signs (=) for the lengthening of the preceding vowel;
- spacing between *do=* and *i=s* for an even stronger accentuation;
- measured pause duration (0.3) in seconds in parentheses;
- a colon for level pitch (*i=s:*)

It has become a commonplace now to emphasize that the choice among the behavioural aspects to be included in transcription of verbal interaction cannot be determined independently of the purposes of transcription; but the choice is also dependent upon the competencies of the transcriber. The most basic part of any transcript always remains the verbal component. Chafe's prosodic transcription of step 7 above demands a large measure of linguistic competency on the part of the transcriber; it is also appropriate only when a given research project calls for the representation of details regarding *how* a verbal utterance has been produced.

Description

Transcription is to be distinguished from *description*. The latter is useful as a supplement to denote paralinguistic or extralinguistic behaviours as well as non-linguistic activities observed in dialogical interaction.

Thus, a given instance of the paralinguistic behaviour of laughter may be transcribed, as shown in *Example 1* from a TV interview of Bill Clinton (BC; O'Connell and Kowal, 2005: 289):

Example 1

    BC   HE HA HA HA HE

Or it may be simply described as *laughter*. The description eliminates the notions of sequentiality, temporality, numerosity and the specificity of phonemes which are represented in the transcribed version of the laughter. More specifically, in *Example 1*, the sequential priority of the first occurrence of HE is to be noted along with the implication that the sequence occurs in measurable real time, involves five separable segments, and designates the phonemes specifically as HE and HA. As a simple notation of an event, the description of laughter is devoid of all these details.

Extralinguistic communicative behaviour includes *non-vocal* bodily movements (e.g. hand gestures and gaze) occurring during a verbal interaction. Both speakers and listeners may engage in extralinguistic behaviours. They are typically described rather than transcribed in qualitative research.

In some dialogical interactions, talking is not the primary activity of *all* the participants. A participant may initiate a verbal response or react to a verbal request with a *non-linguistic* activity. *Example 2* of a dialogical interaction where non-linguistic activities initiate brief verbal responses is taken from the movie *Bonnie and Clyde* (Beatty and Penn, 1967) as presented in O'Connell and Kowal (2012: 115). A police officer is silently presenting to a witness photographs of potential suspects in a grocery robbery, while the injured witness is lying in a hospital bed. The non-linguistic activity of the police officer is described in brackets:

Example 2

Police Officer	[presentation of photo]
Witness	no
Police Officer	[presentation of photo]
Witness	huh-uh [as negation]
Police Officer	[presentation of photo]
Witness	no ...

Coding

Transcription is also to be distinguished from *coding*, which refers to the classification of events in discrete categories and the labelling of these categories. An example can be found in Bull and Mayer (1993: 655) who have classified the reactions of British politicians in response to interviewer questions into three categories: *replies*, *non-replies* and *answers by implication*. Note that coding is logically dependent on previous transcription and entails a further theoretical orientation as foundation for its categorizations.

Transcript

A *transcript* is the result of the activity of *transcribing* performed by a single person or by several persons, sometimes by the researchers themselves, sometimes by personnel not otherwise involved in the research. Some researchers have emphasized that transcribing and the analysis of transcripts should be done by the same persons (see, e.g., Dittmar, 2009: 59f.; ten Have, 2007: 95; Lapadat and Linsay, 1999, as cited in Tilley, 2003: 751). In fact, Chafe (1995: 61) has bluntly stated, 'One cannot fully understand data unless one has been in on it from the beginning.'

Notations

The set of signs used to represent selective aspects of the behaviour of participants involved in a verbal communication, that is the tools for transcribing, are referred to as *notations*. A *transcription system* is the sum of all the notation signs plus the conventions for arranging the signs sequentially on paper or screen and the methods used to assess the various behavioural aspects. With respect to the assessment of prosodic parameters, namely duration, pitch and loudness, basically two methods may be distinguished: with reliance upon the perceptual reliability of the transcriber(s) and with supplementation by instrumental measurement.

Transcribers and Transcript Users

In addition, there are two personal roles involved in transcription: that of the *transcriber* and that of the *transcript user*. From a psychological perspective, both roles demand extremely complex processing. Riessman (1993; cited in Frost, 2011: 101) has emphasized the importance of the transcript user when choices have to be made about how to design transcripts: these choices 'have serious implications for how a reader will understand the narrative'. In fact, Du Bois (1991: 77ff.) has even made 'transcription design principles' a basis for his *Discourse Transcription (DT)* system in an effort to accommodate the needs of a large variety of users.

In the following section, we will discuss some common problems that have been shown in empirical research to have an impact specifically on the transcriber's job of faithfully representing selective aspects of spoken discourse and that should be considered when training novice transcribers.

THE TRANSCRIBER, AS A LANGUAGE USER, IS 'OFTEN QUITE UNRELIABLE' (MACWHINNEY AND SNOW, 1990: 457)

Results of Transcription Research

A number of psycholinguistic studies have indicated that the production of transcripts from audio and video recordings by use of various notation systems is a quite demanding task. This fact has to be taken into account, especially in applied contexts where a transcript can have important consequences. For example, Walker (1986: 209) has reported the case from a court transcript in which the spoken phrase 'male in extremis' had been changed in transcription to 'male, an extremist'.

O'Connell and Kowal (1994) have analysed four types of changes in the verbal component of transcripts in German corpora of spoken discourse (including parliamentary speeches, interviews and an informal conversation): deletions, additions, substitutions and relocations, including linguistic units ranging in size from phonemes to sentences. They found that changes were quite common, occurring on average every 13 syllables. Deletions were most frequent (42%), followed by additions (34.3%), substitutions (18.1%) and relocations (5.6%). Among the most frequent deletions were the function words *und, auch, also* (and, also, well) and the filler *äh* (uh); among the most frequent additions were corrections of elisions typical for spoken discourse, for example *is* was changed to *ist* and *n* was changed to *ein* or *eine* (a, masculine or feminine) indicating that transcribers were either deliberately or inadvertently 'introducing alterations from characteristically spoken discourse to properly written discourse' (132). These deletions and additions may be disregarded for some transcription purposes, but in other cases they may even constitute an open violation of the explicitly formulated transcription rules.

Dresing and Pehl (2011: 14; our translation), in their second transcription rule, have stipulated: 'Word contractions are not transcribed but instead are moved in the direction of standard German orthography.' Their motivation in this regard is to simplify transcription rules. *Example 3* provides an English-language transcript from the movie *Bonnie and Clyde* (Beatty and Penn, 1967) in standard English orthography and, for comparative purposes, in our own transcript notation (adapted from O'Connell and Kowal, 2012). The reader may note that our transcript notation coincides with what will be described below as *literary* transcription:

Example 3

Standard English	Clyde	since it does not look like you are going to invite me inside
	Bonnie	ah you would steal the dining room table if I did
Our Notation	Clyde	since it don't look like you're goin' to invite me inside
	Bonnie	ah you'd steal the dinin' room table if I did

In the present instance, the difference made by using our own notation amounts to three syllables (*does not → don't*; *you are → you're*; *you would → you'd*); our version is also more faithful to the acoustic realization as articulated by the actors and reflects familiar spoken English usage.

More recent data from Chiari's (2007) Italian corpora are couched in a similar set of four categories of changes as in O'Connell and Kowal (1994). Of interest is Chiari's 'most striking finding' regarding:

> the amount of repair that does not rely of [*sic*] linguistic form but on creative unconscious reconstruction made by the transcriber, that generally tends to preserve utterance meaning. The transcriber attributes intentions and beliefs to the voice heard, and tends to filter inevitably the spoken sounds re-interpreting them in a way that is always both grammatical and meaningful. (2007: 10)

An example of such a 'repair' is provided by Chiari herself in the following substitution: '*rendere flessibile il patto* ("make an agreement flexible") > *rendere possibile il patto* ("make an agreement possible")' (5). In this case, it is easy for the transcriber thus to pass over the import of the semantic difference by reason of the sound similarity of the two words *flessibile* and *possibile*. Chiari has concluded that the uncovering of changes (*errors* in her terminology) made by transcribers in research reports should be used as a teaching tool in the training of transcribers. We too consider this an important pedagogical device.

It should be emphasized that the changes (or errors) observed in transcripts are not primarily due to careless transcription but to the fact that transcribing is a highly unusual way of using language, often quite conflictual with respect to both one's everyday habits of spoken language use and one's schooling regarding proper written usage. More specifically, in everyday spoken discourse, listeners must seek out the *gist* of a message for their own purposes rather than attending carefully to the individual words, whereas in transcription the sequencing of sounds articulated by a speaker must be assessed as objectively and as accurately as possible. But what finds its way into a written transcript is not simply a matter of careful listening; it also involves decision processes which derive from implicit theories, goals and convictions. For example, Tilley (2003) has dedicated an entire article to the problems one inexperienced transcriber has had with the task of transcribing focus group interviews including five participants and two interviewers; in this instance, the source of the difficulty was clearly the quality of the recording and in particular the simultaneous speaking of participants.

In *Example 4*, taken from the movie *A Month at the Lake* (Fox and Irvin, 1995), a combination of rapid articulation and poor acoustic quality in the original recording led the transcribers (ourselves: Transcriber's Best Guess) to an absurdly irrelevant guess which could be disambiguated only by persistent repeated listening sessions on the part of both transcribers together (Original Recording):

Example 4

| Transcriber's Best Guess | Miss Bentley | I've always some (?)cakes and cheese |
| Original Recording | Miss Bentley | Miss Beaumont is hardly antique |

The task of transcribing may contradict over-learned habits regarding the use of well-formed structure in written language. Our own transcription research has shown that untrained transcribers frequently use self-instruction which contradicts the experimental instructions in order to produce correct written language use (O'Connell and Kowal, 1994: 129).

The Need to Train Transcribers

The consequence of all of this is that the task of producing even transcripts limited to the words spoken necessitates some training in order to avoid the transcripts becoming more a self-revelation of the transcriber than a record of the interlocutors' spoken discourse. In addition, such training should involve reliability checks by way of having several transcribers work independently on the same excerpt of spoken discourse and then comparing their transcripts so as to verify both their validity and reliability.

VARIOUS COMPONENTS OF VOCAL BEHAVIOUR

The Verbal Component

Typically, in transcripts of spoken dialogue, the words spoken constitute the core units of a transcript. Although this sounds like a straightforward task, in fact it is not. Before even turning to the different ways of putting spoken words on paper or on the screen, the question arises: *What is considered by the transcriber to be a word?*

Our own research mentioned above (O'Connell and Kowal, 1994) as well as Chiari's (2007) has shown that transcribers tend to delete parts of utterances which they may either fail to hear or hear but not consider as words to be noted in a transcript. These would include primarily fillers such as *um* and *uh*, repetitions of words which are not syntactically integrated (e.g. *the the child*), other varieties of haltingly produced spontaneous speech (e.g. *after he uh because he*), and also a variety of interjections of both the conventional (e.g. *gee*) and the non-conventional type (e.g. *oosh*). In recent linguistic, psycholinguistic and sociolinguistic research on dialogical interaction, the functional importance of such segments is typically acknowledged and consequently they are carefully noted in transcripts. But for the transcriber him- or herself, these elements may constitute a source of confusion for several reasons, among them the following:

- They typically do not occur in well-formed written text.
- They may be considered flaws in 'good rhetoric' and therefore not worthy to be written down.
- In spontaneous, casual dialogue, they are often articulated rapidly and at a lower pitch than the surrounding speech and are therefore difficult to hear.
- Their sequential occurrence in a chain of words may not be easy to ascertain perceptually.
- Orthographic representation may be difficult.

In other words, the inexperienced transcriber may either use his or her everyday habits of filtering them out without noticing that he or she is doing so, or consider them 'bad speech' and therefore deliberately exclude them from a transcript. Such exclusion, however, may lead to the loss of information crucial for purposes of interpretation. The various ways of transcribing the verbal component are sequenced in the following four paragraphs incrementally according to their approximation of phonetic accuracy.

Standard Orthography

The words can be represented in *standard orthography*, that is in the spelling given to them in a standard dictionary of the language. Deviations from standard pronunciation by a speaker are thereby lost. Optional variations in orthography, for example British -*our* and American -*or*, should be used appropriately and consistently. *Example 5*, taken from the movie *African Queen* (Spiegel, Woolf and Huston, 1951), is presented here in both standard orthography and in our own notation (adapted from O'Connell and Kowal, 2012):

Example 5

| Standard Orthography | Charlie | oh Miss it is not your property |
| Our Notation | Charlie | oh miss it ain't your proputy |

In *Example 5*, the standardization includes a replacement of the contraction *ain't* by *is not*, the spelling of *proputy* changed to *property*, and the initial capitalization of the address term *Miss*.

Literary Transcription

Another mode of transcribing the verbal component is by way of *literary transcription*. It constitutes part of Ehlich's (1993) originally German transcription system referred to by the acronym *HIAT* (*Halb interpretative Arbeitstranskriptionen*). A literary transcription of the words spoken takes account of deviations in pronunciation whereas *standard orthography* does not. According to Ehlich (1993: 126), this method allows for 'systematic departures from the standard orthography rendering of an item but in a manner that is meaningful to someone familiar with the orthographic system as a whole'. *Example 6*, from the movie *African Queen* (Spiegel, Woolf and Huston, 1951), provides a literary transcription of Charlie Allnut's response to Rose Sayer's comment that her brother, the reverend, has been killed by soldiers (adapted from O'Connell and Kowal, 2012). For comparative purposes, we have also included a version notated in standard orthography:

Example 6

| Literary Transcription | Charlie | oh well now ain't that awful if they'd up 'n shoot a reverend couldn't do 'em a bit of harm then |
| Standard Orthography | Charlie | oh well now is that not awful if they would up and shoot a reverend could not do them a bit of harm then |

Eye Dialect

The method of transcribing words in *eye dialect* is used especially in conversation analysis. It entails an even greater amount of deviation from standard orthography in the attempt to represent in a pseudo-phonetic way how words have actually been pronounced. In the following example of eye dialect, taken from Schegloff (1984: 288), only the words spoken are included; underlining and punctuation are deliberately left out. We have added a version notated in standard orthography for comparative purposes:

Example 7

| Eye Dialect | Curt: | I heard Little wz makin um was makin frames'n sendin 'm t'California |
| Standard Orthography | Curt: | I heard Little was making um was making frames and sending them to California |

The difference between literary transcription and eye dialect is a matter of degree; *Examples 6* and *7* illustrate this relativity quite well. But the difference between eye dialect and standard orthography is considerable. It is of interest that the *eye dialect* method has been criticized for its poor readability, inconsistency and wrong phonetics (Edwards, 1992: 368). In addition, Gumperz and Berenz (1993: 96f.) have argued that 'eye dialect tends to trivialize participants' utterances by conjuring up pejorative stereotypes'. Our readers may wish to ask themselves whether they themselves experience the eye dialect in *Example 7* as trivializing Curt's utterance.

Phonetic Transcription

Phonetic transcriptions by means of the International Phonetic Alphabet (IPA) entail a written representation of phonetic categories sequentially realized in a corpus of spoken discourse. According to Ehlich (1993: 125), 'phonetic transcriptions aim at one-to-one relationships between (a) graphemes and (b) phonetic units and other characteristics of the spoken language'. Although the IPA is well suited for detailed transcripts used by linguists, it is seldom used by social scientists in qualitative research. The reason for this unpopularity of the IPA is partly the onerous training required for transcribing and reading it. Its complexity also makes its use subject to frequent errors.

The Prosodic Component

This component specifies *how* the words are spoken in terms of the characteristics of pitch, loudness and duration. But it should be noted that the terms *emphasis* and *stress* both subsume one or more of these characteristics indiscriminately. The characteristics are also referred to as suprasegmentals insofar as the sequential segments are supplemented by the additional notation of diacritical marks. This is typically done by adding discrete graphic units (e.g. the question mark in *Example 8* below), by super- or subimposing diacritical marks (e.g. the acute and grave accents in Chafe (1995: 58) given above and the underlining in *Example 12* below), or by changing the sequential segments themselves (e.g. RACHEL ROBERTS in *Example 9* below). While the verbal component is typically assessed by listening to an audio recording repeatedly, the various suprasegmental characteristics are more difficult to assess perceptually due to the limitations of the human auditory system. Some researchers have insisted on the perceptual assessment of these characteristics on the ground that they aim at transcribing what the participants themselves perceive in a dialogical interaction. Others have pointed to the necessity of using instrumental measurement precisely because of the unreliability of the human ear and the correlative difficulty of transcribing from the perspective of the participants in a conversation.

Pitch

In basic transcripts, notation of the prosodic component may be relevant to disambiguate syntactic features of an utterance. *Example 8*, from the movie *Houseboat* (Rose and Shavelson, 1958), occurs in a scene where the father is talking to his young son, who is fishing. A question mark is used here as a prosodic notation of raised pitch in order to identify the utterance as a question rather than as an imperative (adapted from O'Connell and Kowal, 2012):

Example 8

Father   catch anything?

As Kowal and O'Connell (2003: 100) have shown in an analysis of five German-language and three English-language transcription systems, rising intonation has been notated in these systems in several different ways: as +, as ´, as ↑, or as ?. We have chosen the question mark because it is the common notation sign for written text and therefore is the easiest for inexperienced transcribers and transcript readers to use.

Loudness

Another prosodic notation is related to variations in loudness. Unfortunately, the concept of *stress* is frequently made synonymous in the archival literature with the concept of loudness; but there are many ways of accomplishing stress other than loudness, for example the very opposite of loudness, namely whispering. *Example 9*, taken from Atkinson and Heritage (1984: xii), uses capital letters to indicate 'an utterance, or part thereof, that is spoken much louder than the surrounding talk':

Example 9

Announcer:	an the winner: ↓iz:s (1.4) RACHEL ROBERTS for Y↑ANKS

Duration

Still another basic prosodic characteristic that is included in all current transcription systems is the temporal organization of utterances. It includes both *ontime*, that is the duration of utterances uninterrupted by pauses, and *offtime*, the duration of pauses. Whereas *pause duration* is consistently considered in current transcription systems, variation in ontime is only occasionally included. The following example is taken from the movie *Unforgiven* (Eastwood, 1992). It is part of a conversation between Delilah, a prostitute, and Bill Munny, a gunman. In order to emphasize the importance of pause durations, in *Examples 10a* and *10b* we provide our own transcription without and with pause notation (see O'Connell and Kowal, 2012: 125). All pauses were measured instrumentally to a cut-off point of 0.10 seconds by use of the PRAAT software, because the research of O'Connell and Kowal (2008: 105f., for a summary) has shown that the perceptual assessment of pauses may lack both reliability and validity. Pause duration in *Example 10b* is given in parentheses:

Example 10a

Delilah	... your friends they been takin' advances on the payment
Bill	advances
Delilah	free ones
Bill	free ones
Delilah	Alice and Silky been givin' them free ones
Bill	oo I see
Delilah	would you like a free one
Bill	no I I guess not ...

Example 10b

Delilah	... your friends (1.40) they been takin' advances on the payment (1.78)
Bill	advances (2.64)
Delilah	free ones (1.46)
Bill	free ones (1.31)
Delilah	Alice and Silky been givin' them free ones (2.12)
Bill	oo I see (4.33)
Delilah	would you like a free one (8.77)
Bill	no I (1.38) I guess not ...

Notation of pauses in *Example 10b* discloses the unusually slow pace of this conversational interaction as well as the thoughtful reflections identified by the long pauses. Note that turn-taking pauses between speakers are on a separate line, whereas pauses within the turn of a speaker are on the same line as his or her words. The assumption is that the former are shared by both participants, whereas the latter may be ascribed to the current speaker. In addition, these conventions facilitate the separate analyses of the two types of pauses.

The Paralinguistic Component

Vocal features occurring during speaking but not as part of the linguistic system are referred to as paralinguistic. They include audible breathing, crying, aspiration and laughter. Paralinguistic features may entail separate segments, or they may occur as suprasegmental additions to verbal segments. In both cases, they are not easy to transcribe and are therefore typically described in or omitted from transcripts in qualitative research.

In our own studies of laughter in TV interviews with Hillary and Bill Clinton, respectively (O'Connell and Kowal, 2004; 2005), and in the film *The Third Man* (O'Connell and Kowal, 2006), we have developed the following notation conventions: so-called *ha-ha laughter* was transcribed by an approximation to the number and phonetic constitution of laughter syllables; so-called *overlaid laughter*, that is laughter that occurs as overlay on spoken-word syllables, was transcribed by underlining those parts of an utterance which were produced laughingly and with occasional alteration and/or addition of syllables. *Example 11* is taken from an interview of Bill Clinton (BC) by Charlie Rose (CR) on the occasion of the publication of Clinton's memoir *My Life* (O'Connell and Kowal, 2005: 286):

Example 11

> CR well there was also this you were gettin' beat up so bad at home that you were anxious to get to the office
>
> BC that's right I said that uh yeah that's ri-hi-hi-hight HU HU HU HU I probably was more attentive to my work for several mo-honths just because I didn't want to have to attend to anything else

NOTATION SYSTEMS FOR TRANSCRIPTION

In the spirit of the critical approach to transcription in this chapter, Chafe (1995: 55) has stated 'that any transcription system is a theory of what is significant about language' (see also Ochs, 1979), and we might add: about paralinguistic, extralinguistic and non-linguistic components of communicative behaviour. With this basic fact in mind, we will briefly present a selection of transcription systems.

Among the most common transcription systems in use today are the Jeffersonian *Transcript Notation*, developed in the context of conversation analysis (CA) (Atkinson and Heritage, 1984; see Toerien, Chapter 22, this volume); the *Gesprächsanalytisches Transkriptionssystem 2 (GAT 2)*, developed by Selting et al. (2009) and translated and adapted for English by Couper-Kuhlen and Barth-Weingarten (2011); *Discourse Transcription (DT)*, developed by DuBois et al. (1993); and *HIAT* (Ehlich, 1993), an acronym for the German *Halbinterpretative Arbeitstranskriptionen*. For a more detailed summary of the Jeffersonian *Transcript Notation*, *DT* and *HIAT* see O'Connell and Kowal (2009).

The Jeffersonian Transcript Notation

According to ten Have (2007: 95), 'the basic system was devised by Gail Jefferson', but 'there is not *one* clearly defined, canonical way of making and formatting CA transcriptions'. The canonical reference to the system is Atkinson and Heritage (1984: ix–xvi). The main purpose of Transcript Notation is to represent the sequential characteristics of spoken interaction. It allows for the notation of the words spoken, the sounds uttered, overlaps in speaking of two or more participants, and various prosodic features (e.g. pauses, tempo, stress and volume). In addition, it may be used to transcribe laughter (e.g. Jefferson, 1979), applause and a variety of extralinguistic behaviours (e.g. gaze direction). The following example from Schegloff (1984: 288) is identical with *Example 7* above but includes suprasegmental notation signs (underlining):

Example 12

> Curt: I heard Little wz makin um, was makin frames 'n sendin 'm t' California.

According to CA transcript notation (Atkinson and Heritage, 1984: xif.), underlining of segments indicates emphasis, a comma indicates continuing intonation and a period (full stop) indicates a stopping fall in tone.

Gesprächsanalytisches Transkriptionssystem 2 (GAT 2)

GAT 2 has been developed over a period of more than 10 years, originally for the analysis of German-language data, to be used in particular in the context of conversation- and discourse-analytic research (see Toerien, Chapter 22, and Willig Chapter 23, this volume). Its emphasis is on the notation of 'the wording and prosody of natural everyday talk-in-interaction' and it is of interest for both 'the compilation of working transcripts … for research purposes and for transcripts in linguistic publications' (Couper-Kuhlen and Barth-Weingarten, 2011: 2). Its main asset for qualitative research is the fact that it is 'easily accessible for novices to transcription' (3) because it offers rules for the production of a minimal transcript 'sufficient for a range of purposes in the social sciences (such as content analysis in interviews)' (7). Couper-Kuhlen and Barth-Weingarten have provided a detailed account for notating the following characteristics in a *minimal* transcript: segments and wording, sequential structure (e.g. overlaps and simultaneous speech, pausing), other segmental transcription conventions (e.g. hesitation markers, laughter), non-verbal vocal actions and events (e.g. sniffs, sighs), and intelligibility (e.g. assumed or uncertain wording). All characteristics are documented with numerous examples. In case more detailed notation is necessary, the researcher may turn to the *basic* (see 18ff.) or to the *fine* transcript (see 25ff.).

Discourse Transcription (DT)

Du Bois et al. (1993: 45) have defined DT 'as the process of creating a written representation of a speech event so as to make it accessible to discourse research'. They have developed DT in a top-down manner on the basis of transcription design principles with the goal of developing a system that consists of good, accessible, robust, economical and adaptable notation conventions. The system uses standard orthography for the verbal component and most of the notations represent suprasegmental characteristics. For the sake of notation adaptable to different research purposes, Du Bois et al.'s goal of adaptability implies: '*Allow for seamless transition between degrees of delicacy*' (94). An example of a rather narrow transcript is given below (Du Bois, 1991: 77):

Example 13

    L: . . But `they never `figured ^out what he had?

The double period represents a short pause, the grave (`) and caret (^) accents represent the secondary and primary accent, and the question mark represents appeal.

HIAT

The acronym *HIAT* may be translated into English as *semi-interpretative working transcription*. The term *interpretative* is meant to emphasize the transcriber's role in structuring the spoken corpus by way of both segmentation and commentary. Peculiar to Ehlich's (1993: 125) notation system is the arrangement of speakers' contributions in '*score notation*' analogous to musical score: 'Semiotic events arrayed horizontally on a line follow each other in time, whereas events on the same vertical axis represent simultaneous acoustic events' (129). *Example 14* provides part of Ehlich's (1993: 130) longer example of score notation:

Example 14

  Mi: ... bottom.   Pardon? Hewers.

  In: Uh/hewers – did you use that term, too? Hewers.

TRANSCRIBING TURN-TAKING

All four transcription systems presented above include notations for the sequential organization of successive turns in dialogical interaction. In order to emphasize the similarities and differences among the systems, we present below a brief fictitious example of turn-taking between two participants (A and B), notated in standard orthography and without prosodic notation, but transcribed according to the different systems. Basically, there are three different modalities of turn-taking that might be noted: (1) with a measurable pause between two turns, (2) without a pause between turns (referred to as latching), and (3) with overlapping speech. *Examples 15a–d* include all three varieties in the sequential order indicated by the numbers above:

Example 15a (Jeffersonian Transcript Notation)

A	was it good
	(0.5)
B	I don't know=
A	=come on [tell me] more
B	[that's all]

Example 15b (GAT 2)

A	was it good
B	(0.5) I don't know=
A	=come on [tell me] more
B	[that's all]

Example 15c (DT)

A	was it good
B	.. I don't know
A	(0) come on [tell me] more
B	[that's all]

Example 15d (HIAT)

A	was it good come on tell me more
B	I don't know that's all

Turn-taking serves well to exemplify the complexity of spoken dialogue and the urgent importance of transcription appropriate for the specific purposes of a given research project. The omission of any explicit preference in *Example 15* for *a*, *b*, *c* or *d* can be considered our vote against standardization without reference to purpose.

NEW TECHNOLOGIES AND PERSPECTIVES

In their presentation of EXMARaLDA, Schmidt and Wörner (2009) have counted the following among the 'main objectives' of this computer-assisted system for research in corpus-based pragmatics : 'to pave the way for long term archiving and reuse of costly and valuable language resources (e.g. to ensure the compatibility of corpora with existing or emerging standards for digital archiving' (566). But Hartung (2006), in the context of qualitative methods in media research, has pointed out potential problems with digitalization of data in view of the formidable changes that continue to characterize this development of technology: 'It is precisely the enormous rapidity of technical progress which makes it difficult to say anything about the future and the further development of digital data formats and the corresponding hardware. For long-term archivization it is therefore not at all simple to make the right decisions' (476; our translation). At the same time, Hartung has emphasized that empirical data in the social sciences are typically analysed only within a given project and not kept in long-term archives.

With regard to future technological perspectives of transcription, it is our position that software remains a research *tool*; the finality of a research project is antecedent to and independent of the software itself. Transcribing 'accurately and unambiguously' (MacWhinney and Wagner, 2010: 156) still remains a property of the human transcriber, not of software of any kind. However, knowledge of the various capacities of available software may indeed determine for researchers what projects can prudently be engaged.

FURTHER READING

The rationale for our selection of recommended readings is as follows. Recency in such a rapidly developing field is obviously important; the earliest of our recommendations appeared within the last two decades. But breadth of treatment is another requirement. Edwards and Lampert (1993) have engaged the field of transcription quite generally, but provide further details by the authors of the transcription systems DT and *HIAT* mentioned above. Jenks (2011) has deliberately truncated his reference list for the sake of inexperienced students, has provided examples, and has referred to the Jeffersonian Transcript Notation, to DT and to *GAT 2*. Finally, Kreuz and Riordan (2011) have provided a concise and critical treatment of various transcription systems and have also included brief references to the transcription of child language, signed language and the language of cognitively impaired individuals.

Edwards, Jane A. and Lampert, Martin D. (eds) (1993) *Talking Data: Transcription and Coding in Discourse Research*. Hillsdale, NJ: Lawrence Erlbaum.

Jenks, Christopher J. (2011) *Transcribing Talk and Interaction*. Amsterdam: John Benjamins.

Kreuz, Roger J. and Riordan, Monica A. (2011) 'The transcription of face-to-face interaction', in Wolfgang Bublitz and Neal R. Norrick (eds), *Foundations of Pragmatics*. Berlin: De Gruyter Mouton. pp. 657–79.

REFERENCES

Atkinson, J. Maxwell and Heritage, John (1984) 'Transcript notation', in J. Maxwell Atkinson and John Heritage (eds), *Structures of Social Action: Studies in Conversation Analysis*. Cambridge: Cambridge University Press. pp. ix–xvi.

Aufenanger, Stefan (2006) 'Interview', in Ruth Ayaß and Jörg Bergmann (eds), *Qualitative Methoden in der Medienforschung*. Reinbek bei Hamburg: Rowohlt. pp. 97–114.

Beatty, Warren (Producer) and Penn, Arthur (Director) (1967) *Bonnie and Clyde*. USA: Warner Bros.

Bull, Peter and Mayer, Kate (1993) 'How not to answer questions in political interviews', *Political Psychology*, 14 (4): 651–66.

Chafe, Wallace (1995) 'Adequacy, user-friendliness, and practicality in transcribing', in Geoffrey Leech et al. (eds), *Spoken English on Computer: Transcription, Mark-up and Application*. Harlow: Longman. pp. 54–61.

Chiari, Isabella (2007) 'Transcribing speech: Errors in corpora and experimental settings', in Matthew Davies et al. (eds), *Proceedings of Corpus Linguistics 2007*: http://ucrel.lancs.ac.uk/publications/CL2007/ (retrieved 10 October 2011).

Couper-Kuhlen, Elizabeth and Barth-Weingarten, Dagmar (2011) 'A system for transcribing talk-in-interaction: GAT 2'. *Gesprächsforschung – Online – Zeitschrift zur verbalen Interaktion*, 12: 1–51: www.gespraechs-forschung-ozs.de (retrieved 31 October 2011).

Dittmar, Norbert (2009) *Transkription: Ein Leitfaden mit Aufgaben für Studenten, Forscher und Laien*, 3rd edition. Wiesbaden: VS Verlag für Sozialwissenschaften (1st edition, 2002).

Dresing, Thorsten and Pehl, Thorsten (2010) 'Transkription', in Günter Mey and Katja Mruck (eds), *Handbuch Qualitative Forschung in der Psychologie*. Wiesbaden: VS Verlag für Sozialwissenschaften. pp. 723–33.

Dresing, Thorsten and Pehl, Thorsten (2011) *Praxisbuch Transkription: Regelsysteme, Software und praktische Anleitungen für qualitative ForscherInnen*, 2nd edition. Marburg: www.audiotranskription.de/praxisbuch (retrieved 13 October 2011).

Du Bois, John W. (1991) 'Transcription design principles for spoken discourse research', *Pragmatics*, 1 (1): 71–106.

Du Bois, John W., Schuetze-Coburn, Stephan, Cumming, Susanna and Paolino, Danae (1993) 'Outline of discourse transcription', in Jane A. Edwards and Martin D. Lampert (eds), *Talking Data: Transcription and Coding in Discourse Research*. Hillsdale, NJ: Lawrence Erlbaum. pp. 45–89.

Eastwood, Clint (Producer and Director) (1992) *Unforgiven*. USA: Warner Bros.

Edwards, Jane A. (1992) 'Transcription of discourse', in W. Bright (ed.), *International Encyclopedia of Linguistics*, 4 vols. Oxford: Oxford University Press. pp. 367–70.

Edwards, Jane A. and Lampert, Martin D. (eds) (1993) *Talking Data: Transcription and Coding in Discourse Research*. Hillsdale, NJ: Lawrence Erlbaum.

Ehlich, Konrad (1993) 'HIAT: A transcription system for discourse data', in Jane A. Edwards and Martin D. Lampert (eds), *Talking Data: Transcription and Coding in Discourse Research*. Hillsdale, NJ: Lawrence Erlbaum. pp. 123–48.

Flick, Uwe, von Kardoff, Ernst and Steinke, Ines (2004) 'What is qualitative research? An introduction to the field', in Uwe Flick et al. (eds), *A Companion to Qualitative Research*. London: Sage. pp. 3–11.

Fox, Robert (Producer) and Irvin, John (Director) (1995) *A Month by the Lake*. UK/USA: Miramax.

Frost, Nollaig (2011) *Qualitative Research Methods in Psychology: Combining Core Approaches*. Maidenhead: Open University Press.

Gumperz, John J. and Berenz, Norine (1993) 'Transcribing conversational exchanges', in Jane A. Edwards and Martin D. Lampert (eds), *Talking Data: Transcription and Coding in Discourse Research*. Hillsdale, NJ: Lawrence Erlbaum. pp. 91–121.

Harris, Roy (2010) *Integrationism: A Very Brief Introduction*: www.royharrisonline.com/integrational_linguistics (retrieved 13 October 2011).

Hartung, Martin (2006) 'Datenaufbereitung, Transkription, Präsentation', in Ruth Ayaß and Jörg R. Bergmann (eds), *Qualitative Methoden der Medienforschung*. Reinbek bei Hamburg: Rowohlt. pp. 475–88.

Jefferson, Gail (1979) 'A technique for inviting laughter and its subsequent acceptance declination', in George Psathas (ed.), *Everyday Language: Studies in Ethnomethodology*. New York: Irvington. pp. 79–96.

Jenks, Christopher J. (2011) *Transcribing Talk and Interaction*. Amsterdam: John Benjamins.

Kelle, Udo and Erzberger, Christian (2004) 'Qualitative and quantitative methods: Not in opposition', in Uwe Flick et al. (eds), *A Companion to Qualitative Research*. London: Sage. pp. 172–7.

Kowal, Sabine and O'Connell, Daniel C. (2003) 'Datenerhebung und Transkription', in Gert Rickheit et al. (eds), *Psycholinguistik/Psycholinguistics: Ein internationales Handbuch/An International Handbook*. Berlin: Walter de Gruyter. pp. 92–106.

Kreuz, Roger J. and Riordan, Monica A. (2011) 'The transcription of face-to-face interaction', in Wolfgang Bublitz and Neal R. Norrick (eds), *Foundations of Pragmatics*. Berlin: De Gruyter Mouton. pp. 657–79.

Langer, Antje (2010) 'Transkribieren – Grundlagen und Regeln', in Barbara Friebertshäuser et al. (eds), *Handbuch Qualitative Forschungsmethoden in der Erziehungswissenschaft*. Weinheim: Juventa. pp. 515–26.

MacWhinney, Brian and Snow, Catherine (1990) 'The Child Language Data Exchange System: An update', *Journal of Child Language*, 19: 457–72.

MacWhinney, Brian and Wagner, Johannes (2010) 'Transcribing, searching and data sharing: The CLAN software and the TalkBank data repository'. *Gesprächsforschung – Online-Zeitschrift zur verbalen Interaktion*, 11: 154–73: www.gespraechsforschung-ozs.de (retrieved 12 October 2011).

Michel, Jean-Baptiste et al. (2011) 'Quantitative analysis of culture using millions of digitized books', *Science*, 331: 176–82.

Ochs, Elinor (1979) 'Transcription as theory', in Elinor Ochs and Bambi B. Schieffelin (eds), *Developmental Pragmatics*. New York: Academic Press. pp. 43–72.

O'Connell, Daniel C. and Kowal, Sabine (1994) 'The transcriber as language user', in Guillermo Bartelt (ed.), *The Dynamics of Language Processes: Essays in Honor of Hans W. Dechert*. Tübingen: Gunter Narr. pp. 119–42.

O'Connell, Daniel C. and Kowal, Sabine (2004) 'Hillary Clinton's laughter in media interviews'. *Pragmatics*, 14 (4): 463–78.

O'Connell, Daniel C. and Kowal, Sabine (2005) 'Laughter in Bill Clinton's *My Life (2004)* interviews'. *Pragmatics*, 15 (2/3): 275–99.

O'Connell, Daniel C. and Kowal, Sabine (2006) 'Laughter in the film *The Third Man*'. *Pragmatics*, 16, 2/3: 305-27.

O'Connell, Daniel C. and Kowal, Sabine (2008) *Communicating with One Another: Toward a Psychology of Spontaneous Spoken Discourse*. New York: Springer.

O'Connell, Daniel C. and Kowal, Sabine (2009) 'Transcription systems for spoken discourse', in Sigurd D'hondt et al. (eds), *The Pragmatics of Interaction*. Amsterdam: John Benjamins. pp. 240–54.

O'Connell, Daniel C. and Kowal, Sabine (2012) *Dialogical Genres: Empractical and Conversational Listening and Speaking*. New York: Springer.

Peez, Georg (2002) 'Rezension zu: Norbert Dittmar, Transkription. Ein Leitfaden mit Aufgaben für Studenten, Forscher und Laien. Opladen: Leske + Budrich 2002. *Gesprächsforschung – Online-Zeitschrift zur verbalen Interaktion*, 3: 24–8: www.gespraechsforschung-ozs.de (retrieved 20 October 2011).

Rose, Jack (Producer) and Shavelson, Melville (Director) (1958) *Houseboat*. USA: Paramount.

Schegloff, Emanuel A. (1984) 'On some gestures' relation to talk', in J. Maxwell Atkinson and John Heritage (eds), *Structures of Social Action: Studies in Conversation Analysis*. Cambridge: Cambridge University Press. pp. 266–96.

Schmidt, Thomas and Wörner, Kai (2009) 'EXMARaLDA – Creating, analysing and sharing spoken language corpora for pragmatic research', *Pragmatics*, 19 (4): 565–82.

Selting, Margret et al. (2009) 'Gesprächsanalytisches Transkriptionssystem 2 (GAT 2)', *Gesprächsforschung – Online-Zeitschrift zur verbalen Interaktion*, 10: 353–402: www.gespraechsforschung-ozs.de (retrieved 31 October 2011).

Spiegel, Sam and Woolf, John (Producers) and Huston, John (Director) (1951) *African Queen*. UK: Shepperton Studios.

ten Have, Paul (2007) *Doing Conversation Analysis*, 2nd edition. Los Angeles: Sage.

Tilley, Susan A. (2003) '"Challenging" research practices: Turning a critical lens on the work of transcription', *Qualitative Inquiry*, 9 (5): 750–73.

Walker, Anne D. (1986) 'The verbatim record: The myth and the reality', in Sue Fisher and Alexandra D. Todd (eds), *Discourse and Institutional Authority: Medicine, Education, and Law*. Norwood, NJ: Ablex. pp. 205–22.

6

Collaborative Analysis of Qualitative Data

Flora Cornish, Alex Gillespie and Tania Zittoun

While multi-researcher projects are an increasing feature of the research landscape, collaborative analyses, which integrate multiple points of view, remain the exception rather than the rule. A typical lament in a multidisciplinary project is that the researchers work in parallel, contributing separately to their original disciplines, rather than producing an integrated result which benefits from their diverse perspectives (Moran-Ellis et al., 2006). Given that contemporary research policies incentivize large-scale, multidisciplinary research projects, on the assumption that solutions to complex social problems require the contributions of multiple disciplines and the engagement of non-academic 'research users', qualitative researchers are increasingly likely to find themselves involved in research collaborations. The purpose of this chapter is to help qualitative researchers to capitalize on the potential benefits of collaborative data analysis, when appropriate, by presenting what has been learnt in the literature to date about this process.

By 'collaborative data analysis' we refer to processes in which there is joint focus and dialogue among two or more researchers regarding a shared body of data, to produce an agreed interpretation. Such dialogues may take place in a face-to-face workshop, or over the Internet, and may encompass a variety of dimensions of difference. (Box 6.1 summarizes some of these dimensions, with references to exemplary accounts, for reference.) They may pair researchers from different disciplines, countries or theoretical traditions; they can include both senior and junior researchers; and they may bring together academic researchers with professional experts or lay people. The key point is that different perspectives are brought to bear on the analysis and interpretation of the data, with the eventual interpretation being a result of that combination.

> **Box 6.1 Dimensions of Difference in Collaboration, with Exemplary Accounts**
>
> - Insider/outsider (Bartunek and Louis, 1996)
> - Interdisciplinary (Tartas and Muller Mirza, 2007; Lingard et al., 2007)
> - Different methodological approaches (Frost et al., 2010)
> - Academic–practitioner (Hartley and Benington, 2000)
> - Academic–lay person (Enosh and Ben-Ari, 2010; Lamerichs et al., 2009)
> - International (Akkerman et al., 2006; Arcidiacono, 2007; Bender et al., 2011; Marková and Plichtová, 2007; Tartas and Muller Mirza, 2007)
> - Senior–junior (Hall et al., 2005; Pontecorvo, 2007; Rogers-Dillon, 2005)

In what follows, we first introduce why collaborative data analysis is interesting from a methodological point of view, informed by the epistemological stance of perspectivism. Expanding this discussion, we then explore five potential methodological benefits of collaborative data analysis. These benefits primarily derive from juxtaposing diverse perspectives. Becoming more concrete, we then present an exemplar of a collaborative analysis process, and outline three different models of team organisation for collaborative analysis (in Box 6.2). The final section seeks to derive further practical lessons from others' experience, presenting typical challenges to successful collaborative analysis, along with proposed solutions.

EPISTEMOLOGICAL FRAME: PERSPECTIVISM

The epistemological position of *perspectivism* provides an intellectual rationale for the collaborative analysis of qualitative data. According to perspectivism, all knowledge is relative to a point of view and an interest in the world (James, 1907; Rorty, 1981). Knowledge, instead of being a 'mirror of nature', is more like a tool, something which either works or does not for a given interest (Cornish and Gillespie, 2009). This does not imply that all knowledge is equal. Far from it: the bottom line is always whether or not the knowledge is effective relative to an interest. A sociologist has a different perspective on the problem of domestic violence to that of a counselling psychologist because they are trying to do different things. A Foucauldian discourse analyst (see Willig, Chapter 23, this volume) has a different perspective on human resource management to that of a human resources manager, again, because they are trying to do different things. To ask who is right, the Foucauldian or the human resources manager, is akin to asking whether a saw is more 'true' than a hammer – the real issue is how effective the given tool is for the problem at hand. Collaborative analysis becomes useful when the interests of a research project seem not to be served by a single perspective, but require the engagement of multiple perspectives.

From a perspectivist point of view, the attraction of collaborative data analysis is that it brings a diversity of perspectives to the analysis. Our own perspectives are compelling: it is not easy to escape our social position and see the world from a different point of view (Gillespie, 2005). Researchers are embodied, socially located humans with investments and preoccupations, like anyone else. Yet the research role asks us to step back from our investment in the research topic, and take a critical attitude (Bauer and Gaskell, 1999). Being critical often means adopting more than one perspective, so that we can apprehend both positive and negative aspects of a phenomenon, or both insider and outsider perspectives (Bartunek and Louis, 1996). Combining perspectives gives externality to each perspective, enabling distanciation and critical reflection (Gillespie, 2012). Given the difficulty of stepping out of our perspectives, a collaborative analysis brings a diversity of perspectives to the project, embodied in different people.

Let us take as an example the fundamental perspectival distinction in the analysis of qualitative data, between description and interpretation of our participants' perspectives – that is, between aiming to elucidate participants' point of view and aiming to provide a critical explanation or problematization of that point of view. Ricoeur (1970) distinguishes between a 'hermeneutics of faith' and a 'hermeneutics of suspicion' (see also Josselson, 2004; Frost et al., 2010; see also Willig, Chapter 10, and Wernet, Chapter 16, this volume). When adopting a hermeneutics of faith, we treat the speaker's voice as an authentic representation of their point of view (as, for instance, in typical examples of thematic analysis seeking to present a summary of interviewees' beliefs). Adopting a hermeneutics of suspicion, we engage more critically with a text, treating the speaker's voice as a result of social or psychological processes which call for explanation. Smith (2004), exponent of interpretive phenomenological analysis, makes the case that analyses should reflect *both* of these perspectives, producing both an empathic reading of a person's experience and a 'more critical and speculative reflection'. To realize both the hermeneutic of faith and the hermeneutic of suspicion in a research project, it may be helpful to embody those different perspectives in different collaborators. Insiders to a field may often be more empathic to the local actors, given that they share assumptions and identifications, while outsider–researchers may take up a more suspicious/critical stance (Lingard et al., 2007). However, there is not a fixed relation between insider/outsider status and an attitude of empathy or critique; rather, it will vary according to the context (see the discussion of Cornish and Ghosh's differences below for a counter-example). The perspectivist stance informs our following discussion of the methodological benefits of collaborative analysis.

METHODOLOGICAL BENEFITS OF COLLABORATIVE ANALYSIS

Benefits claimed for collaborative analysis range from the goal of researchers confirming one another's analyses (i.e. affirming a single perspective) to more complex aspirations of constructing new ideas through the diversity of perspectives. The following subsections work through five potential benefits. Collaborative analysis is not the only way to achieve these benefits. Indeed, academic practices such as peer review, critical reflection, or participant observation research have long been means of bringing multiple perspectives to bear upon one's object. The argument is, however, that, by embodying different perspectives in different analysts, collaborative analysis is particularly well poised to capitalize on multiple perspectives.

Inter-coder Reliability

A second analyst in the role of coder, auditor, sounding-board or overseer is suggested as a safeguard against an interpretation representing the subjectivity of the observer more than the object of study (Gaskell and Bauer, 2000). If coding (see Thornberg and Charmaz, Chapter 11, this volume) and analysing are private activities, there is a risk, or at least a suspicion, that the resulting analysis may be unconstrained or unsystematic (Ryan, 1999). Collaborating on the coding process is said to enforce systematicity, clarity and transparency (Hall et al., 2005). Similarly, having a second researcher as 'auditor' is a form of accountability, preventing researchers from making unjustifiable leaps of the imagination (Akkerman et al., 2008).

Multiple coders also enable the assessment of inter-coder reliability statistics, where agreement between two or more coders is taken as evidence of the rigour of an analysis. (Ryan, 1999; Lu and Schulman, 2008). In research projects working with relatively small bodies of data, the second coder usually codes a subset of the data coded by the primary coder, checking for reliability. In research projects dealing with such large corpuses that multiple coders are needed to cover the material, inter-coder reliability is an important check on the consistency of coding. For example, when US government agencies seek public comment upon proposed legal changes, they may receive hundreds of thousands of email or Web-based submissions from members of the public, and they have a duty to digest all of these responses. Shulman (2003; 2006) and colleagues devised a process and a software package (CAT) to enable a team of multiple coders to code the submissions swiftly and consistently, producing a rigorous content analysis with multiple checks on inter-coder reliability.

Despite the popularity of inter-coder reliability in some fields, there are two important caveats. First, this form of collaborative data analysis is suited to content or thematic analysis, where representativeness is an aim. It is less suited to analyses, such as conversation analysis, discourse analysis or dialogical analysis, which do not make claims to representativeness, but instead claim transparency on the basis of publishing sufficiently long textual extracts to allow the reader to check the plausibility of the interpretations. Second, agreement between coders does not guarantee against collective idiosyncrasies, nor does it necessarily increase validity (Gaskell and Bauer, 2000). Two or more coders may agree because they share the same peculiar or limiting assumptions (see Barbour, Chapter 34, this volume).

Incorporating Rich Local Understandings

The complex phenomena of interest to qualitative researchers may require years of socialization to be understood 'from the inside', as a local expert, and through the local language. Local experts, as collaborators, may provide the role of a 'guide' or 'educator', explaining to the rest of the team the local context and customs – knowledge which is needed in order to produce a sensitive analysis (Hartley and Benington, 2000; Lingard et al., 2007). In the case of complex organizations, the insider can be an invaluable guide to the informal and unofficial processes adopted by the organization, which might otherwise be difficult for the outsider researcher to discern (Hartley and Benington, 2000; Lingard et al., 2007). Using collaboration in this way is similar to the function of the 'key informant' in ethnographic research (see e.g. DeWalt and DeWalt, 2010), a well-versed member of the community who can speed up the outsider–researcher's development of familiarity with an area.

In a series of collaborative studies of lay understandings of democracy in Eastern and Western European countries following the fall of the Iron Curtain, the researchers came to appreciate the necessity of rich local understandings of history, politics and linguistic nuance (Marková and Plichtová, 2007). Whereas political, economic or macro-sociological studies showed change to social institutions, and sought to compare countries on their degree of 'democratization', Marková and Plichtová (2007) argue that lay definitions of 'democracy' were more nuanced than large-scale comparisons could reveal. Not only did 'democracy' mean different things in different countries, but even where institutions were democratizing, lay beliefs, values and practices were slower to change. These authors argue that their team could not have understood this local diversity without team members fluent in the national languages and familiar with the national histories.

Incorporating local voices in the analysis, cutting across the social boundary between the researchers and participants in the field, prevents hasty interpretations being made by outsiders based on incomplete knowledge. It may also lead team members to problematize their own taken-for-granted assumptions. More ambitiously, collaboration may also produce a *transformation* of knowledge, as our following three subsections elaborate.

Perspective-Transcending Knowledge

If the narrowness of our individual perspectives is a rationale for collaborative research, one of the goals of collaborating may be to achieve 'perspective-transcending knowledge' (Gillespie and Richardson, 2011). Perspective-transcending knowledge is an understanding of the situation that goes beyond the limited individual perspectives to the 'emergence' (Zittoun et al., 2007) of a higher-level, more synthetic knowledge.

In the participant observation literature, the perspectives of 'insider' and 'outsider' or 'participant' and 'observer' are hailed as a productive dimension of difference, whose juxtaposition or integration is the source of the special insight of the participant observer (DeWalt and DeWalt, 2010; Atkinson and Hammersley, 2007; see Marvasti, Chapter 24, this volume). The combination of the embodied, practical understanding of the participant, and the reflective, distant understanding of the observer, are argued to yield the fullest understanding of social phenomena (Becker and Geer, 1957). Traditionally, the anthropologist or sociologist participant observer has sought to embody both participant and observer perspectives, by both undertaking the routine activities of the community being studied, and stepping back to observe and theorize those activities (e.g. Wacquant, 2004). Collaborative analysis can bring together these perspectives in two different persons in the research team. In the literature on collaborative data analysis, insider/outsider collaborations have attracted particular attention (e.g. Bartunek and Louis, 1996; Lingard et al., 2007).

In some of our own research on community mobilization of sex workers for HIV prevention in India, Flora Cornish, a European researcher, has worked with Indian colleagues Riddhi Banerji and Anuprita Shukla to understand the creation of successful projects (Cornish and Ghosh, 2007; Cornish et al., 2010). Contrasting socio-cultural and intellectual heritages led each of us to differing interpretations of our complex data. Cornish, conscious of the post-colonial politics of her outsider position, has generally begun with a sympathetic view of the sex worker projects, assuming that community mobilization is difficult to achieve, and that the projects studied are successful, against the odds. Indian colleagues, with more practical experience of the constraints of working in red-light districts and awareness of NGOs' self-publicizing as well as local controversies about the projects, have often been more sceptical and critical. Long debates have led us to interpretations that acknowledge both the achievements and the compromises of the projects. Rather than seeking to make singular interpretations of the projects, we have come to see them as workable, contradictory responses to contradictory pressures (e.g. Cornish and Ghosh, 2007). Our eventual interpretations, we suggest, bear the traces of each of our original starting points, in a novel synthesis. Not only does the collaborative analysis enhance the subtlety of the eventual interpretation, but it also is a learning process for each of us, so that our individual perspectives become extended as we incorporate something of each other's points of view.

Reflexivity

Assuming, as do many qualitative researchers, that the interpretation we produce is partially a function of our particular perspectives, reflexivity about our ideological, theoretical and methodological predispositions is advocated as a step towards transparency, if not emancipation from our constraints (see May and Perry, Chapter 8, this volume). A collaborator, bringing an alternative perspective, and questioning our own, might help us to step back from our taken-for-granted assumptions (Cornish et al., 2007). The particular dimension of difference of the collaboration is significant. While an international collaborator might help us to reflect upon our own national situation or practices, a collaboration with a practitioner might help us to reflect upon the potential practical usefulness of our conclusions.

In a collaboration between medical and sociological colleagues regarding doctor–patient communication, Barry et al. (1999) describe the stark differences that were revealed in their definitions of 'good' and 'bad' communication. In 'the seaweed incident', a doctor sought to reassure a patient that an anti-indigestion medication was 'actually just made from seaweed' (39). The pharmacist interpreted this as helpful framing in terms of lay knowledge, while the sociologist viewed it as paternalistic and persuasive. The confrontation of such diverse interpretations led each to reflect on their definition of 'good communication'. It also led the team to seek more objective measures of 'good communication', and to work much harder on developing analyses that would fit with doctors' models of medicine – given their goals of educating doctors.

Conducting collaborative analysis with lay people, academic researchers may seek to promote local critical thinking (Kagan et al., 2011; see Murray, Chapter 40, this volume). For instance, Lamerichs et al. (2009) describe using the 'Discursive Action Method' in a collaborative process with young people to promote their critical thinking about how they speak and act in relation to bullying. Learning some of the tools of discursive psychology, the young people analysed examples of their talk, in collaboration with the academics, leading both to a heightened awareness of their own interactional strategies and to the initiation of participatory anti-bullying activities.

Useful Knowledge

'Applied' research seeks to create useful knowledge, which answers to human interests, improving practice in some way. If researchers want to make knowledge that is useful beyond academia, either to practitioners or to the public at large, then it might be helpful to include these potential beneficiaries in conducting the analysis.

Academic communities develop their own peculiar languages, infused with assumptions, and embedded in historical traditions. What seems significant to a socio-cultural developmental psychologist might appear meaningless to a sociologist of education, or indeed to a teacher. An analysis that is endorsed by different collaborators (e.g. medical doctor and social worker; IT specialist and educator) is likely to address a wider audience than an analysis developed and articulated in the language of a single community.

Communication gaps between communities have been particularly evident in efforts to derive 'applied' benefit from 'academic' research (see Murray, Chapter 40, this volume), exemplified in debates about the problem of a 'theory–practice gap' and a consequent effort to initiate 'evidence-based practice'. Part of the problem may be that analyses developed in an academic language and context do not speak to the language and concerns of practice. For example, in a research project on young people's relationship to literary and philosophical texts in secondary school (Grossen et al., 2012; Zittoun and Grossen, 2012), we were surprised to discover the importance of teachers' often accidental recognition of students' out-of-school life for the students' commitment to learning. Eager to 'bring back' those discoveries to the teachers who took part in the project, we were surprised to be met with a total lack of interest. For one reason or another, the teachers did not consider this knowledge as useful-knowledge-for-teachers. Had the teachers been more involved in the construction of the knowledge, they might have had more commitment to it. Hartley and Benington (2000; see Box 6.2) suggest that the involvement of their co-researchers leads not only to useful knowledge being generated, but also to its being put into practice. Developing useful knowledge is not simply about discovering truths, or indeed useful truths, it is also about making 'ergonomic' knowledge that 'fits' with the aims and identities of the potential beneficiaries.

The following sections turn to presenting some practical steps to enable such methodological benefits to be realized.

AN EXEMPLAR: HALL ET AL.'S (2005) ITERATIVE COLLABORATIVE ANALYSIS PROCESS

Hall et al.'s (2005) account of their collaborative grounded theory study (see Thornberg and Charmaz, Chapter 11, this volume) of clerical workers' workplace distress serves as a useful exemplar to make the process of collaborative analysis more concrete. For alternative models of team organization, see Box 6.2. Hall and colleagues are differentiated on seniority (including two faculty members, graduate and undergraduate students, and volunteers, some with no prior research experience), discipline (including sociology, counselling, journalism, occupational health and safety, nursing), and amount of time committed to the project. Their grounded theory study aimed to develop a middle-range substantive theory of how workers manage their workplace distress, incorporating both contextual and person-level concepts. The grounded theory techniques of the constant comparative method and theoretical sampling – in which analysis of early data inform subsequent data collection – lend themselves well to an iterative model of individual and group stages of analysis. Table 6.1 presents a condensed account of the steps used by Hall and colleagues in their collaborative analysis.

Table 6.1 Hall et al.'s (2005) iterative collaborative analysis process

Steps	Description	Guiding principle
Preparation stage		
1. Team building	Understanding individual and group goals	Towards a shared understanding: coordination through mutual adjustment
2. Reflexivity exercises	Surfacing individual presuppositions and preferences	
3. Contracts	Formal agreements regarding data ownership, roles and responsibilities, timelines, etc.	
Analysis stage		
1. Individual analysis	Interviewing and preliminary open coding	Creating an atmosphere of critique and questioning
2. Pairs compare	Pairs compare/contrast their individual codes for the same data	
3. Full team analysis	Develop higher-level categories	
	Identify gaps, informing further sampling	
4. Individual synthesis	Draft tentative explanatory frameworks	
5. Full team debate	Critique and develop the proposed frameworks	
6. Individual writing	Co-authors write, varying responsibilities defined	
7. Individual feedback	Circulate drafts for all authors to review	

The guiding collaborative principle employed in this study was the aspiration to achieve 'coordination through mutual adjustment' rather than 'coordination through centralised decision-making' (Hall et al., 2005: 396). To enable the former model of coordination, in which each team member would have a sense of ownership of the common goals and understanding of the goals of others, the team placed great emphasis on activities to build a shared understanding, particularly in the preparation stage. Early team-building work was focused on constructing a shared understanding of grounded theory and the project goals, with a later activity creating space for reflections on experiences of teamwork. Part-way through the data collection, the team employed two 'reflexivity exercises' (detailed in Barry et al., 1999), designed to surface individual team members' presuppositions, biases and preferences. Finally, formal, signed, publication agreements clarified mutual expectations.

The analysis stage was also built around developing a shared perspective, with iterative moves between individual, pairs or three-person groups, and large-group work. In this phase, the importance of an atmosphere allowing critique and questioning came to the fore. Each team member serves as lead researcher for particular participants, interviewing them and beginning to code their data. To develop a shared perspective, subgroups of 2–3 participants analyse the same transcripts, comparing and contrasting their coding. At full team meetings, code lists are discussed, codes defined and categories developed, with a particular focus on codes that require further clarification or development. Gaps are identified, to inform the next round of theoretical sampling, with a return to individually conducted interviews and preliminary coding.

The process of discussion enables a coordinated and cumulative approach, so that the early collective experience of the team can inform the subsequent actions of each member. Once group meetings had produced agreement on higher-level categories, the task of drafting a tentative explanatory framework was undertaken by an individual, and brought back to the group for critical discussion. Finally, the writing phase was again a primarily individual task, with drafts circulated for individual-level feedback. Thus, the collaborative analysis consisted of numerous moves between individual and collective work, according to the benefits of each.

Box 6.2 Three Models of Team Organization for Collaborative Analysis

1. Insider/outsider pairs

Lingard et al. (2007) conducted an interdisciplinary study of health care novices learning their profession's discourse, bringing together experts in rhetoric, paediatric medicine, optometry and social work. They used 'insider/outsider pairs' to analyse their data, finding that this was the best way of unearthing tacit knowledge. Both the insider and the outsider conduct independent analyses and present them to the team for discussion, which benefits from the insider's local expertise and the outsider's relative lack of taken-for-granted assumptions about the topic. They report noticing that critical findings often derived from the discussion prompted by the insider and outsider encountering a discrepancy that could not be resolved.

2. Co-research (three perspectives)

In a collaboration between a university business school and 35 local authority organizations in the UK, three-person research teams are constituted (Hartley and Benington, 2000), comprising an academic, a 'host manager' from the case study organization and a 'co-researcher' from an equivalent organization. The academic is an outsider. The 'host manager' is an insider to the organization. The 'co-researcher' is an insider to the professional domain of the case study organization, but is an outsider to that particular organization. Similarities and differences between 'host' and 'co-researcher' organizations prompt the emergence of analytical insights.

3. Loose team research

Since the 1990s, Ana Cecilia de Sousa Bastos and her group of colleagues, including peers, Masters and PhD students, have worked on the general theme 'Developmental contexts and trajectories'. For eight years they have focused on the transition to motherhood, using a framework combining three theoretical models and a general methodological orientation.

> Each participant interprets the task in his or her own way (e.g. studying trajectories of mothers who have lost a child, of women who do not want to become mothers, of mothers from three generations), combining models as required. Collective analytical work is done through weekly seminars, one-to-one supervisions, and commenting on each other's papers). In addition, the group regularly organizes workshops, where each researcher presents his or her current work, and external 'experts' help to systematize the analysis, creating links between the perspectives, and supporting the development of a more comprehensive view of the problem and the theories (Cabell et al., forthcoming.). Following this model, the loose team previously produced a compelling account of poverty in a Brazilian *favela* (Bastos and Rabinovich, 2009).

CHALLENGES AND SOLUTIONS

The methodological gains of collaborative analysis are not easily won. It is typically more comfortable to work within a familiar disciplinary and methodological frame than to work across communities and disciplines. Some collaborations produce results that are hardly different to the lead researcher's starting assumptions (Akkerman et al., 2006). In other cases, teams have been unable to agree or to commit to writing up the findings of collaborative studies (Riesman and Watson, 1964; Erickson and Stull, 1998). In this section, based on a review of the literature reporting experiences of collaboration, we outline three sets of challenges and indicate possible constructive responses.

Practical Challenges

To coordinate a diverse, geographically dispersed team represents a significant management challenge. It requires the establishment of agreement (to varying degrees) on the goals, means, time frames, division of labour and valued outcomes of the collaboration. Establishing such coordination, itself, has a significant cost, in terms of time (to build a shared frame of reference) and money (to cover travel, host meetings, and pay for research managers to administer the relationships between different institutions, and between a large team and their funding body). In the literature there is an impression that collaborations are rarely well supported or rewarded by academic institutions (Lingard et al., 2007). Hall et al. (2005) report an impression that there was never enough time given to analysis, but instead their limited time was devoted to the urgent practical task of conducting the next set of interviews. Erickson and Stull (1998), seeking to account for the failures of a large team to write up fully their collaborative ethnographies, describe how individuals' competing commitments undermined their commitment to collaborative writing. A key hurdle, then, for collaborative analysis, is to arrange for sufficient time and resources.

To avoid misunderstandings, projects using collaborative analysis have a particular requirement to be clear and explicit in their formulation. To work together, each colleague needs to have a clear understanding of their particular role and how their work is going to be valued. To work with others on data, the organization of the data must be meticulous. Labelling of primary data files with key information must follow agreed formats. The definition of codes, categories, inclusion and exclusion criteria for individual codes, and other conventions needs to be clear and agreed upon. Clarity about the division of labour is important, whichever of the diverse possible forms of organization is chosen (see Box 6.2). For some teams, explicit written, signed agreements were found to be useful means of achieving clarity of understanding. Hall et al. (2005) wrote a 'publication agreement' outlining the rights and responsibilities of all team members in relation to the data, authorship and publication. Arcidiacono (2007) describes a 'collaborative contract' which served primarily to clarify questions of 'ownership' of data among a large international team, and secondarily to establish collaboration etiquette regarding timelines and communication. Both reprint the agreements in their papers' appendices, for reference.

Overall, the potential administrative burden of coordination is not to be underestimated. Insightful qualitative analyses require focused engagement with data, and administration should not overshadow this. For this reason multi-country EU research projects, for example, often employ research managers to take charge of the significant administrative tasks.

Recent developments in CAQDAS software (see Gibbs, Chapter 19, this volume), particularly the advent of Internet-based programs and servers hosting the data, should facilitate coordination. Early CAQDAS programs could not allow for simultaneous coding, and required one researcher to keep a 'master copy' of the analysis. Keeping track of multiple versions and iterations presented a significant management problem. When programs and data are hosted on servers, the 'master copy' is on the server, and so coders are working on the same material rather than on various versions.

It is not only due to lack of clarity of procedures that teams may fail to reach a consensus. Each collaborator works within particular social, institutional and national contexts which exert constraints on the collaborator's action. Collaborators have responsibilities to their 'home' discipline, institution or country, as well as to the 'collective' interest of the collaboration. Different institutions may have different goals, creating contradictory pressures on boundary-crossing collaborators.

Akkerman et al. (2006) describe a project in which a five-country team of educators sought to create a European syllabus for 'pioneer teachers' of information and communication technology. As their project developed, however, it became clear that differing national constraints made it impossible for them to agree on a common syllabus. They first settled on the production of a more vague 'curriculum framework' which would allow each country to create a syllabus suited to local needs. This solution, in acknowledging the diversity among the countries, suggests that collaborations sometimes cannot produce a single definitive outcome, but need some flexibility in the degree of sharedness of their product (see also Tartas and Muller Mirza, 2007).

However, in this instance, the project leader of the team was nervous that they had promised their funder (the European Commission) a European syllabus, something that would add 'European value' to the project, legitimating their five-country composition. In the interest of meeting their funder's expectations, the project leader created a syllabus, which was almost the same as the one he had suggested at the start of the project, and which thus did not reflect any of the learning that had taken place. Here, an institutional requirement (to meet the objective of producing a single syllabus), which was ostensibly directed at producing 'European added value', in fact effaced the diversity of the team in the end product.

Sometimes institutional diversity can be a source of advantages for collaborative teams. Lingard et al. (2007) described how different conventions for recognizing authorship in different disciplines led them to extract extra benefit from their publications. In the humanities, proximity to the first name on a paper signals author importance, whereas in health care sciences, the last name on a list of authors gains important recognition. By putting humanities scholars at the start and health scholars at the end, each gains significant recognition in their academic communities.

Identity Challenges

As scholars of inter-group relations have established, the simple act of defining people by virtue of their membership of a particular group runs the risk of creating a situation of inter-group tension. When people are labelled as 'academics' vs 'practitioners', or as 'medics' vs 'social scientists', they may become sensitive to their identity and to challenges to their group's status. In a project bringing together education researchers and IT specialists to create pedagogical software, each side developed nicknames for the other: the pedagogical teams were called 'dreamers', the technical teams were labelled 'technocrats' (Tartas and Muller Mirza, 2007).

As we have argued above, part of the value of interdisciplinary analysis comes from the problematization of assumptions, leading to questions of why practices are one way in one discipline and another way in another discipline. But, as Becker (1998) points out, the question 'why?' is often interpreted as a challenge, as calling the person to account for their unusual behaviour. An optometrist working in an interdisciplinary team (Spafford, in Lingard et al., 2007) reported that having her own discipline under the critical gaze of interdisciplinary colleagues was difficult. She writes: 'in the process of peeling back our words to their bones – feelings of exposure and exhaustion were my frequent companions' (2007: 505). In particular, she felt uncomfortable about exposing weaknesses of her discipline in front of the more powerful discipline of medicine.

Not only is our group identity an issue, but also our personal commitments and interests are at stake. In Hartley and Benington's (2000) co-research model, managers from one organization visit another organization in the role of a co-researcher. They describe the risk that the co-researchers interpret their findings in terms of a judgement or evaluation of their own organization or of the organization they are visiting. They write:

> a co-interviewer may deplore a particular set of organizational processes and believe and feel that their own organization manages better. (Alternatively, they may lionize a particular leading figure in the case-study organization, and feel that their own organization would work 'if only' they had someone of the same calibre in their own organization). (2000: 474)

For these authors, productive research generates knowledge about organizational processes – not evaluations of individual case study sites. Sometimes, they report, they have needed to guard against interpretations of case study data becoming judgemental evaluations. The human, interested, perspectives that we occupy, of course, lead us to interpret data in the light of our own experience and our own aspirations for ourselves and our organizations, but to make this interpretation into research is to make it more than a personal comment, to become an analytical understanding about processes that transcend individual cases.

Challenges to Open Debate

To capitalize on the diversity in a team, collaborators need to listen to each other's perspectives, not to ignore or silence difference (Akkerman et al., 2006). Social status is often cited as a factor undermining an atmosphere of open debate and critique (Cooper et al., 2013). If some team members are of a higher status on many of the dimensions of difference among the collaborators (e.g. discipline, seniority, length of time associated with the project), and others are consistently of a lower status, this poses a real risk that the lower-status members are unlikely to voice challenges, and the higher-status members are unlikely to listen to such challenges (Psaltis, 2007).

Lingard et al. (2007) report that their study suffered from the alignment of multiple dimensions of status. Their core team comprised specialists in English, paediatric medicine, optometry and social work, in a study of the socialization of novices to make 'case presentations'. Unintentionally, the social work team member was disadvantaged on several dimensions, leading to her perception of being a 'second stringer' throughout the project. Not only did she join the team later than the others, but an apparently arbitrary decision to analyse the data from medical students first meant that medicine became the 'authoritative first case' – a reference point in the process of analysis – so that social work data was always compared with the medical data. The authors describe how this situated social work 'outside' the core, and seemed to demand that the social worker continually account for the difference of her discipline.

The value of different dimensions of social status not being aligned is evident in Hall et al.'s (2005) account of a turning point in the group dynamics of their team, following which team members were able to challenge each other's interpretations respectfully. Their team included senior and junior members, with the junior members initially expressing a feeling of being inexpert, uncertain and unlikely to challenge interpretations. The turning point came when the faculty members engaged in a critical dialogue regarding the tentative analysis offered by one of them. There was an interesting social dimension to the development of this atmosphere of critique, which was that the faculty member presenting the interpretation was in a minority in her discipline. As a sociologist, she offered a social–structural interpretation. The other faculty members, like the majority of the junior team members, shared a background in counselling psychology, which led them to argue against an overly structural account which neglected individual agency. Again, the group dynamics needed to be managed to avoid inter-group alliances, but the numerical advantage of the students' theoretical perspective appeared to support them in raising challenges to the academically higher-status faculty member.

With a similar interest, Pontecorvo (2007) describes the distribution of expertise and status in her Italian team of students and faculty members working on video recordings of family dinners. While Pontecorvo was the project leader, she reports that the methodological expertise in conversation analysis required for the project was held by two other, more junior researchers. Moreover, the expertise in the content of the data was widely distributed, with pairs of students and their tutors being the experts in the sub-topics for which they had taken responsibility (Pontecorvo, 2007).

From this point of view, the social positioning of team members would ideally be ambiguous, so that those from more traditionally respected disciplines might be less central to the project planning, or the more junior researchers might have richest expertise in the details of the data, for instance. If this is not practical, teams ought to be aware of problems of social status, and work to compensate for them. In the family dinner study mentioned above, Pontecorvo and Arcidiacono describe an informal rule for their team analysis meetings, namely that it is not only the professor who offers interpretations, but all present should make a contribution (Cornish et al., 2007). More formally, in Hartley and Benington's (2000) work with local authorities in the UK, an institutionally recognized rule was invoked to enable free and critical exchange on sensitive matters. The 'Chatham House' rule is familiar to UK government bodies, and establishes that participants are allowed to use the information generated in a meeting, but not allowed to report speakers' identity or affiliation beyond the meeting.

CONCLUSION

From a perspectivist outlook, collaborative analysis of qualitative data seems to hold the potential for a variety of valuable gains, from producing a more informed, nuanced, complex or useful analysis, to creating new, perspective-transcending knowledge, or, indeed, to individual learning on the part of researchers. Such potential benefits are not risk- or cost-free. Risks and costs, like the benefits, derive from the confrontation of diverse perspectives. Institutional support and flexibility, explicit working procedures, and social relations, which promote debate without threatening identities, may all help to alleviate the risks of collaboration.

In reviewing the literature on collaborative analysis, for this chapter, we sought especially to understand the methodological significance of collaborative analysis. By 'methodological significance' we mean the consequences of collaboration for the substance of the resultant analysis. So, asking: what is different about the interpretation that results from a collaborative analysis compared with one produced by a single researcher? While the literature richly documents practical and inter-personal challenges of collaboration, and makes positive theoretical claims for the value of collaboration, we found few concrete examples unravelling how that value emerged as a result of the particular composition of the team. Social studies of science show us that the social conditions of knowledge production shape the content of the knowledge produced. This should be of concern to methodologists. An expansion of methodological discussions to include the social relations in which research is produced would aid qualitative researchers in designing, conducting, capitalizing on and understanding their collaborative research projects.

FURTHER READING

Akkerman, Sanne, Admiraal, Wilfried, Simons, Robert Jan and Niessen, Theo (2006) 'Considering diversity: Multivoicedness in international academic collaboration', *Culture and Psychology*, 12 (4): 461–85.

Lingard, Lorelei, Schryer, Catherine F., Spafford, Marlee M. and Campbell, Sandra L. (2007) 'Negotiating the politics of identity in an interdisciplinary research team', *Qualitative Research*, 7 (4): 501–19.

Zittoun, Tania, Cornish, Flora, Gillespie, Alex and Baucal, Aleksandar (eds) (2007) 'Collaborative research, knowledge and emergence', Special issue of *Integrative Psychological and Behavioral Science*, 41 (2): 208–17.

REFERENCES

Akkerman, Sanne, Admiraal, Wilfried, Brekelmans, Mieke and Oost, Heinze (2008) 'Auditing quality of research in social sciences', *Quality and Quantity*, 42 (2): 257–74.

Akkerman, Sanne, Admiraal, Wilfried, Simons, Robert Jan and Niessen, Theo (2006) 'Considering diversity: Multivoicedness in international academic collaboration', *Culture and Psychology*, 12 (4): 461–85.

Arcidiacono, Francesco (2007) 'Studying the practice of cooperation and collaboration within an international research project on the everyday lives of families', *Integrative Psychological and Behavioral Science*, 41 (2): 139–53.

Atkinson, Paul and Hammersley, Martyn (2007) *Ethnography: Principles in Practice*, 3rd edition. E-library: Taylor & Francis.

Barry, Christine A., Britten, Nicky, Barber, Nick, Bradley, Colin and Stevenson, Fiona (1999) 'Using reflexivity to optimize teamwork in qualitative research', *Qualitative Health Research*, 9 (1), 26–44.

Bartunek, Jean M. and Louis, Meryl Reis (1996) *Insider/Outsider Team Research*. London: Sage.

Bastos, Ana Cecilia S. and Rabinovich, Elaine P. (2009) *Living in Poverty: Developmental Poetics of Cultural Realities*. Charlotte, NC: Information Age Publishing.

Bauer, Martin W. and Gaskell, George (1999) 'Towards a paradigm for research on social representations', *Journal for the Theory of Social Behaviour*, 29 (2): 163–86.

Becker, Howard S. (1998) *Tricks of the Trade: How to Think about your Research while you are Doing it*. London: University of Chicago Press.

Becker, Howard S. and Geer, Blanche (1957) 'Participant observation and interviewing: A comparison', *Human Organization*, 16 (3): 28–32.

Bender, Amy, Guruge, Sepali, Aga, Ffekadu, Hailemariam, Damen, Hyman, Ilene and Tamiru, Melesse (2011) 'International research collaboration as social relation: An Ethiopian-Canadian example', *Canadian Journal of Nursing Research*, 43 (2): 62–75.

Cabell, Kenneth, Marsico, Giuseppina, Cornejo, Carlos and Valsiner, Jaan (forthcoming) *Making Meaning, Making Motherhood*, Annals of Cultural Psychology. Charlotte, NC: Information Age Publishing.

Cooper, Mick, Chak, Amy, Cornish, Flora and Gillespie, Alex (2013) 'Dialogue: Bridging personal, social and community transformation', *Journal of Humanistic Psychology*, 53 (1), 70–93.

Cornish, Flora and Ghosh, Riddhi (2007) 'The necessary contradictions of "community-led" health promotion: A case study of HIV prevention in an Indian red light district', *Social Science and Medicine*, 64 (2): 496–507.

Cornish, Flora and Gillespie, Alex (2009) 'A pragmatist approach to the problem of knowledge in health psychology', *Journal of Health Psychology*, 14 (6): 800–9.

Cornish, Flora, Zittoun, Tania and Gillespie, Alex (2007) 'A cultural psychological reflection on collaborative research', *Forum: Qualitative Social Research*, 8, Art. 21. Available: www.qualitative-research.net/fqs-texte/3-07/07-3-21-e.htm (accessed 18 April 2013).

Cornish, Flora, Shukla, Anuprita and Banerji, Riddhi (2010) 'Persuading, protesting and exchanging favours: Strategies used by Indian sex workers to win local support for their HIV prevention programmes', *AIDS Care*, 22 (2): 1670–8.

DeWalt, Kathleen Musante and DeWalt, Billie R. (2010) *Participant Observation: A Guide for Fieldworkers*, 2nd edition. Walnut Creek, CA: AltaMira Press.

Enosh, Guy and Ben-Ari, Adital (2010) 'Cooperation and conflict in qualitative research: A dialectical approach to knowledge production', *Qualitative Health Research*, 20 (1):125–30.

Erickson, Ken and Stull, Donald (1998) *Doing Team Ethnography: Warnings and Advice*. London: Sage.

Frost, Nollaig, Nolas, Sevasti-Melissa, Brooks-Gordon, Belinda, Esin, Cigdem, Holt, Amanda, Medizahdeh, Leila and Shinebourne, Pnina (2010) 'Pluralism in qualitative research: The impact of different researchers and qualitative approaches on the analysis of qualitative data', *Qualitative Research*, 10 (4): 441–60.

Gaskell, George and Bauer, Martin W. (2000) 'Towards public accountability: Beyond sampling, reliability and validity', in Martin W. Bauer and George Gaskell (eds), *Qualitative Researching with Text, Image and Sound: A Practical Handbook*. London: Sage. pp. 336–50.

Gillespie, Alex (2005) 'G.H. Mead: Theorist of the social act', *Journal for the Theory of Social Behaviour*, 35 (1): 19–39.

Gillespie, Alex (2012) 'Position exchange: The social development of agency', *New Ideas in Psychology*, 30 (1): 32–46.

Gillespie, Alex and Richardson, Beth (2011) 'Exchanging social positions: Enhancing perspective taking within a cooperative problem solving task', *European Journal of Social Psychology*, 41 (5): 608–16.

Grossen, Michele, Zittoun, Tania and Ros, J. (2012) 'Boundary crossing events and potential appropriation space in philosophy, literature and general knowledge', in Eva Hjörneet al. (eds), *Learning, Social Interaction and Diversity – Exploring School Practices*. Rotterdam: Sense Publishers. pp. 15–33.

Hall, Wend A., Long, Bonita, Bermback, Nicole, Jordan, Sharalyn and Patterson, Kathryn (2005) 'Qualitative teamwork issues and strategies: Coordination through mutual adjustment', *Qualitative Health Research*, 15 (3): 394–410.

Hartley, Jean and Benington, John (2000) 'Co-research: A new methodology for new times', *European Journal of Work and Organizational Psychology*, 9 (4): 463–76.

James, William (1907) *Pragmatism*. New York: Dover.

Josselson, Ruthellen (2004) 'The hermeneutics of faith and the hermeneutics of suspicion', *Narrative Inquiry*, 14 (1): 1–29.

Kagan, Carolyn, Burton, Mark, Duckett, Paul, Lawthom, Rebecca and Siddiquee, Asiya (2011) *Critical Community Psychology*. Oxford: Wiley-Blackwell.

Lamerichs, Joyce, Koelen, Maria and te Molder, Hedwig (2009) 'Turning adolescents into analysts of their own discourse: Raising reflexive awareness of every-day talk to develop peer-based health activities', *Qualitative Health Research*, 19 (8): 1162–75.

Lingard, Lorelei, Schryer, Catherine F., Spafford, Marlee M. and Campbell, Sandra L. (2007) 'Negotiating the politics of identity in an interdisciplinary research team', *Qualitative Research*, 7 (4): 501–19.

Lu, Chi-Jung and Schulman, Stuart W. (2008) 'Rigor and flexibility in computer-based qualitative research: Introducing the Coding Analysis Toolkit', *International Journal of Multiple Research Approaches*, 2: 105–17.

Marková, Ivana and Plichtová, Jana (2007) 'East-West European project: Transforming and shaping research through collaboration', *Integrative Psychological and Behavioral Science*, 41 (2): 124–38.

Moran-Ellis, Jo, Alexander, Victoria D., Cronin, Ann, Dickinson, Mary, Fielding, Jane, Sleney, Judith and Thomas, Hilary (2006) 'Triangulation and integration: Processes, claims and implications', *Qualitative Research*, 6 (1), 45–59.

Pontecorvo, Clotilde (2007) 'On the conditions for generative collaboration: Learning through collaborative research', *Integrative Psychological and Behavioral Science*, 41 (2): 178–86.

Psaltis, Charis (2007) 'International collaboration as construction of knowledge and its constraints', *Integrative Psychological and Behavioral Science*, 41 (2): 187–97.

Ricoeur, Paul (1970) *Freud and Philosophy: An essay on Interpretation*. New Haven, CT: Yale University Press.

Riesman, David and Watson, Jean (1964) 'The Sociability Project: A chronicle of frustration and achievement', in Philip E. Hammond (ed.), *Sociologists at Work: Essays on the Craft of Social Research*. New York: Basic Books. pp. 235–321.

Rogers-Dillon, Robin H. (2005) 'Hierarchical qualitative research teams: Refining the methodology', *Qualitative Research*, 5 (4): 437–54.

Rorty, Richard (1981) *Philosophy and the Mirror of Nature*. Princeton, NJ: Princeton University Press.

Ryan, Gery W. (1999) 'Measuring the typicality of text: Using multiple coders for more than just reliability and validity checks', *Human Organization*, 58 (3): 313–22.

Shulman, Stuart W. (2003) 'An experiment in digital government at the United States National Organic Program', *Agriculture and Human Values*, 20 (3): 253–65.

Shulman, Stuart W. (2006) 'Whither Deliberation? Mass e-Mail Campaigns and U.S. Regulatory Rulemaking', UMassAmherst: eRulemaking Research Group. Paper 2: http://scholarworks.umass.edu/erulemaking/2 (accessed 18 April 2013).

Smith, Jonathan A. (2004) 'Reflecting on the development of interpretative phenomenological analysis and its contribution to qualitative research in psychology', *Qualitative Research in Psychology*, 1 (1): 39–54.

Tartas, Valerie and Muller Mirza, Nathalie (2007) 'Rethinking collaborative learning through participation in an interdisciplinary research project: Tensions and negotiations as key points in knowledge production', *Integrative Psychological and Behavioral Science*, 41 (2): 154–68.

Wacquant, Loïc (2004) *Body and Soul: Ethnographic Notebooks of An Apprentice-Boxer*. New York: Oxford University Press.

Zittoun, Tania and Grossen, Michele (2012) 'Cultural elements as means of constructing the continuity of the self across various spheres of experience', in M. Beatrice Ligorio and Magarida César (eds), *The interplays between dialogical learning and dialogical self*. Charlotte, NC: InfoAge. pp. 99–126.

Zittoun, Tania, Baucal, Aleksandar, Cornish, Flora and Gillespie, Alex (2007) 'Collaborative research, knowledge and emergence', *Integrative Journal for Psychological and Behavioral Science*, 41 (2): 208–17.

Qualitative Comparative Practices: Dimensions, Cases and Strategies

Monika Palmberger and Andre Gingrich

Our reasoning is always guided by comparison, whether we intend it to be or not (Strauss and Quinn, 1997). Thus, scientific research is penetrated by comparison, even if in an implicit manner. Comparing is an elementary cognitive activity. It occurs in simple and routinized ways in everyday lives by comparing aspects between phenomena, and it regularly occurs in more complex ways as a set of standard practices focusing on the relations between phenomena (Schriewer, 1992).

MAIN DIMENSIONS

By its basic cognitive foundations as well as by it its central academic dimensions, comparison always enables us to identify similarities and differences:

> Depending on the theme or experience under scrutiny, one of comparison's main two component elements [similarities and differences] at times may become much more significant than the other. Yet essentially, comparison always entails at least some elements of both: it thus can be defined as the mental activity of simultaneously identifying similarities as well as differences. (Gingrich, 2012)

This insight is important, since it helps us to keep in mind that comparison is always an essential component of (scientific) reasoning, not just in explicitly comparative studies (see Boeije, 2010).

Qualitative empirical research such as ethnographic fieldwork is guided by comparison in its own ways. In order to come to more general conclusions, ethnographic fieldworkers constantly compare throughout their empirical activities similar events, situations and contexts in everyday life, or rituals, with those they have observed in an earlier phase (Gingrich, 2012). Only by repeatedly participating in these practices, by observing them and by comparing one with the other will the researcher be able to distinguish what is particular or accidental from what is regular and standard.

Parallel to the above-mentioned forms of implicit comparison that are part of any research, comparison is also an explicit research tool. Explicit comparison differs from implicit comparison in that it offers a higher level of abstraction. Lewis identifies five areas of contributions by a qualitative comparative approach:

- identifying the absence or presence of particular phenomena in the accounts of different groups
- exploring how the manifestations of phenomena vary between groups
- exploring how the reasons for, or explanations of, phenomena, or their different impacts and consequences, vary between groups
- exploring the interaction between phenomena in different settings
- exploring more broadly differences in the contexts in which phenomena arise or the research issue is experienced. (2003: 50)

The line between implicit and explicit comparison, however, is not always as clear as it may seem, and there are many different types of intermediate comparisons between the two ends. Moreover, there is no single method or theory of qualitative comparison but rather a plurality of approaches. Comparison has been an integral part of social sciences. Marx, Durkheim and Weber all tackled questions concerning differences between various countries and societies in history, although they did not necessarily declare their work to be comparative. Their comparisons were first and foremost concerned with macro-developments and historical change (Teune, 1990: 40).

This chapter first of all is concerned with explicit qualitative comparison and discusses a range of different approaches. Qualitative comparison is characterized by comparing whole cases with each other. While cases may be analysed in terms of variables (e.g. the presence or absence of a certain institution might be an important variable), cases are viewed as configurations – as combinations of characteristics. 'Comparison in the qualitative tradition thus involves comparing configurations' (Ragin, 1987: 3). Qualitative comparative methods are well equipped to tackle questions that require complex and combinatorial explanations. Since the cases are compared in their complexity, the number of cases has to be kept low. And although it may be tempting to compare larger samples and include more variables, it would not necessarily lead to finer comparison: 'It would be an error because with the multiplication of cases and the standardization of categories for comparison the theoretical return declines more rapidly than the empirical return rises' (Tilly, 1984: 144). As Lewis rightly reminds us, the value of a qualitative comparative approach is in 'understanding rather than measuring difference' (2003: 50).

Comparison in qualitative analysis aims to achieve abstraction by doing justice to the context in which the different cases are embedded: 'In keeping with their concern for context, they particularly dismiss the universalist methodologies that promised to find laws, regularities or states of development that would be applicable to all cultures or to humanity at large' (Fox and Gingrich, 2002: 12). As Scheffer argues along a similar line of reasoning with his concept of 'thick comparison', the context should not be perceived as some type of container loosely connected to the compared items but 'thick comparison approaches context as both, address and reason for differences' (2010: 34). With this argument Scheffer substantiates the case for theorizing contexts.

Qualitative comparison seeks to draw attention to both, to the differences and similarities, to consider endogenous as well as exogenous factors, and to carve out diversity as well as similarity (May, 1997: 187). We cannot, however, speak in the singular of 'the' comparative method in qualitative analysis. The remainder of the chapter will demonstrate the basic plurality of qualitative comparative methods. Although qualitative comparative research may differ greatly between the disciplines and even within a discipline, the different approaches have in common that they all seek a middle ground between a universalistic and a particularistic research agenda – sometimes tending more to the former, sometimes more to the latter. Although this chapter addresses a wide field of humanities and social sciences without restricting the discussion to a single discipline, examples from anthropology prevail because of the authors' disciplinary background.

> **Box 7.1 The Constant Comparative Method**
>
> Even if, as has been suggested above, all scientific reasoning possesses an element of comparison, it may play a stronger or weaker role in the process of the analysis. Glaser and Strauss developed a method that is strongly built on comparison, the so-called 'constant comparative method', which represents an integral part of the 'grounded theory' approach (see Glaser, 1965). In the constant comparative method 'sections of the data are continually compared with each other to allow categories to emerge and for relationships between these categories to become apparent' (Harding, 2006: 131). This method represents a tool for inductive theory building: 'The constant comparative method raises the probability of achieving a complex theory which corresponds closely to the data, since the constant comparisons force consideration of much diversity in the data' (Glaser, 1965: 444). The constant comparative method achieves abstraction of individual cases and is a valuable method for developing typologies (Flick, 2006).

COMPARISON AND ITS LEGACY IN ANTHROPOLOGY AND BEYOND

Social sciences and the humanities have their roots in the eighteenth and nineteenth centuries in the emerging comparative sciences of humans. They compared languages, religions, political systems and other aspects of society in ways that were similar to the natural sciences. Indeed, the evolving new social sciences gained their legitimacy through this 'scientific' comparative method (Kaelble and Schriewer, 2003). Comparison remained crucial in the early days of many social science disciplines, often under the influence of evolutionist paradigms derived from biology. This also was the case for anthropology: 'The whole comparative endeavor was part of the anthropologists' emulation of what they understood to be the scientific method' (Holy, 1987: 3). Decades later, the gradual abandonment of evolutionism and the simultaneous rise of statistical methods led to a preference for quantitative comparison. In anthropology, particularly in the United States with Murdock's Human Relations Area Files (HRAF), a holo-cultural approach was pursued that strongly relied on quantitative comparison. The HRAF were based on statistical sampling and aimed at worldwide comparison. With the HRAF, Murdock strove to reveal functional correlations between cultural traits. Together with neo-evolutionist and structuralist approaches, the holo-cultural approach dominated anthropology in the post-war period until the 1970s when the 'grand theories' and 'meta-narratives' of many fields in the humanities and the social sciences increasingly came under heavy criticism (Fox and Gingrich, 2002: 3–4).

One consequence of breaking with most grand theories was the fact that anthropologists for a while distanced themselves from comparison per se. This said, anthropologists continued to practise comparison, although often in a more implicit than explicit manner and mostly engaging in regional comparison (see Eggan, 1953). The main argument brought forward against comparison was that it could not do justice to analytical concepts that are bound to their native context (Niewöhner and Scheffer, 2010: 6). In its extreme form, cultural relativism indeed does not allow for any form of comparison whatsoever, because cultures are presented as unique (Yengoyan, 2006). In view of this particularist and empiricist impasse, anthropologists during the last couple of decades thus have carefully re-entered the field of comparison (see Holy, 1987; Gingrich and Fox, 2002). Much of comparative research today aims at revealing the cultural logic and culturally specific meaning of phenomena (see Urban, 1999), thus transcending the dichotomy between particularism and universalism.

Comparative research for these reasons always is confronted with the problem of translation. Translation transforms insights from the empirical 'context of discovery' into the publicized 'context of academic communication', to paraphrase (and, in fact, to translate) Reichenbach's well-known concepts for our purposes. In the end, this also includes an indispensable element of comparison since researchers have to compare the results of their translational activity, in order to ensure and maintain an essential and adequate correspondence between both ends. Although translation is always a crucial part of any empirical research – when concrete empirical observations are translated into abstract qualitative data, and in a second step are translated into a text for the respective readership – cross-cultural and cross-national comparison is confronted with an additional level of translation. It faces the task of translating different meanings that specific phenomena assume in different socio-cultural settings (see Ember et al., 2009).

As this chapter will show, comparison in qualitative research may assume very different forms. While anthropological comparison often is dominated by an interpretative and culturally sensitive approach, a more 'variable-oriented' approach is pursued in other disciplines such as political science (see Box 7.4). Sceptical voices concerning comparison, however, have maintained a presence in various disciplines. The main argument brought forward concerns the risk of decontextualization, the risk of losing the complexity and uniqueness of the cases under investigation (see Bryman, 2012). Meanwhile, many qualitative comparative studies have proven that if comparison is handled carefully and if the number of cases is kept low, decontextualization can be prevented or at least minimized. Qualitative case-oriented studies tend to restrict the number of cases to numbers between two and four. Thereby the case-oriented approach allows the researcher comprehensively to examine the context of each case. At this point it has to be said that the criterion of how many cases are enough and still manageable varies between disciplines and also depends on the choice of method. When, for example, ethnographic fieldwork is conducted, the number of cases has to be kept particularly low (especially in a one-person research design).

Box 7.2 Key Points

- All scientific research is in some way comparative. Still, we can distinguish between implicit and explicit comparison.
- Explicit comparison enables us to go beyond the particularities of an individual case and to reach higher levels of identifying similarities, commonalities and differences through careful abstraction.
- Qualitative comparison aims to understand certain aspects of society in its socio-cultural specific context. In order to do so, qualitative comparison concentrates on a comparably small number of cases.
- Qualitative comparison is based on purposefully selected cases. This means that generalizations in qualitative comparison are of a theoretical rather than a numerical kind.
- Comparative research designs may differ greatly in respect to the research question, the research aim and the units of analysis.
- Comparison in qualitative research most often means 'small-*n*'/controlled comparison. But the quality of the cases compared differs greatly. Cases may be closely related (e.g. in regional comparison) but they may also show great variety.

NEW INTEREST IN COMPARISON IN THE CONTEXT OF GLOBALIZATION

The gradual re-emergence of qualitative comparative methods before and since the turn of the century in the humanities and social sciences has had its internal academic reasons, as briefly described above: if many 'grand theories' obviously have failed, and if the description and interpretation of particular case examples rarely are sufficient for creating enduring academic substance, then that alone creates very fertile intellectual environments for all methodological procedures that move beyond the particular without necessarily reaching out for universals. By definition, comparative procedures precisely met these challenges. A second set of conditions favouring the re-emergence of comparative methodological inventories was more closely connected to changes in the real world, and to their recognition inside academia. This concerns the end of the Cold War in Europe, and the ensuing phases of current globalization.

Time–space compression has been identified as a key property of these current phases. The ensuing media-communicated simultaneity is resulting in an increasing local awareness of what is going on elsewhere, and about elsewhere being present inside the local (Beck, 1999; Harvey, 2006; Kreff et al., 2011). In addition to all existing continuities between current and earlier phases of globalization, this self-reflexive awareness about 'ourselves' being part of, and interacting with, wider worlds has led to an additional boost for comparative investigations about the intellectual and practical sides resulting from that explicitly growing awareness. If more and more groups of people are interacting with transnational and global conditions in ways that are similar and different, then it becomes increasingly important to compare how they do this, and to which ends. In addition, if in a post-colonial world more and more people find that this also applies to people in various parts of, say, Asia and Africa, then local researchers in, for instance, South Africa, India and Singapore will feel encouraged also to compare their research insights with each other, and not only with those in the UK, the United States and Australia (Chen, 2010). In addition to intra-academic developments in the social sciences and humanities, changing global conditions thus are providing excellent encouragement for the re-emergence of comparative procedures in all fields of global academia.

Box 7.3 Case Study: Migration and New Diversities in Global Cities

A question researchers have to face in an increasingly transnational and globalized world is whether nations are still legitimate units of analysis. In the field of comparative research this raises the issue of whether we should continue with the tradition of comparing nations or whether it is more fruitful to search for other units of analysis (e.g. regions, cities) in order to do justice to transnational processes and the increasing diversity we face today. The recently launched *Globaldivercities* research project led by Steven Vertovec at the Max Planck Institute for the Study of Religious and Ethnic Diversity faces these challenges when asking 'How can people with ever more diverse characteristics live together in the world's rapidly changing cities?' (Vertovec, 2011: 5). Of particular interest are conditions of diversification that are shaped when new diversity meets old diversity.

Within this comparative research project, several distinct methods are applied, which concentrate on conceiving, observing and visualizing diversity in public space and social encounters. The aim of the project is twofold: first, to gain theoretical insights in the fields of migration, diversity and urban change; and, second, to gain knowledge applicable to

> urban policies, for example to identify common patterns of social adjustment and ways to foster them. This is achieved through comparison.
>
> Comparison in this project can be described as controlled, strategic comparison of key cases. The units of analysis are not nations but three cities. Comparison is conducted across New York, Johannesburg and Singapore, whereby ethnographic fieldwork is conducted in selected neighbourhoods of each city. The main focus is on public space and its social and spatial patterns that arise under conditions of diversification when new forms of diversity meet pre-existing forms of diversity. Through comparison, typologies and models are developed. The models, however, are not presented as the 'Asian', 'African' or 'North American' model and not even as the 'New York', 'Singapore' or 'Johannesburg' model, 'but rather a variety of differences and commonalities of conditions and processes that cross-cut each case' (Vertovec, 2011: 27). This means that comparison achieves generalization but in a more moderate, middle-range way. As will be argued later in the chapter, a complex comparative project is better suited for a group of researchers than a single researcher. Moreover, it requires sufficient time and financial resources. In the case of the *Globaldivercities* project these prerequisites are met.

METHODOLOGICAL CHOICES

A legitimate question to be raised is whether comparative research requires different practices than other forms of research (see May, 1997; Øyen, 1990). Although different viewpoints exist on this subject, most researchers agree that it does not require other forms of research and that comparison and comparative inquiry does not present a relatively independent method per se (Yengoyan, 2006: 4; see Box 7.3). As is the case for any research, methodological choices depend on the primary research question and on its conceptual and theoretical formulation (see Flick, 2007; Gingrich, 2012). Since comparison in qualitative analysis is not restricted to a specific methodological approach, Parts III (Analytical Strategies) and IV (Types of Data and Their Analysis) of this handbook will be of particular interest to readers seeking practical advice for data analysis. What we can offer in the remainder of this chapter, however, is a discussion of the particular challenges one is likely to face when choosing and applying a comparative research design and how best to meet these challenges. For a better understanding, we shall provide examples to illustrate how comparative research can be designed.

When we think of comparison in qualitative analysis we first and foremost think of comparison between nations, or between diverse forms of cultural settings. The majority of qualitative comparisons indeed are of the cross-national or cross-cultural kind, as Teune states:

> Social science disciplines compare countries: sociologists, for example, compare the relationship between societies and political systems; social psychologists, for instance, patterns of national values and political behavior; anthropologists, culture (especially when it appears coterminous with national boundaries) and institutional change; psychologists, perceptions and language; and economists, national economies (market and non-market ones). (1990: 38)

Political sciences even include the specialized subfield of 'comparative politics' devoted to cross-national comparison. The 'comparative method' in political science is understood as a method in which specific phenomena among a small number of nations are investigated by comparison. Some scholars, however, have characterized the comparative method as inferior to statistical comparison. In their view 'small-*n*' comparison at best represents a tool for formulating hypotheses, which then should be tested by a large statistical sample (Lijphart, 1971). Regardless of these critical voices, 'the' comparative method in this subfield has become well established, convincing by its ability to grasp cases in their complexity in ways that are impossible if confronted with a high-number sample (see Bowen et al., 1999; Collier, 1993).

'The' comparative method in political sciences uses two modes of inductive enquiry based on John Stuart Mill: the method of agreement and the indirect method of difference (see Mill and Robson, 1996; Etzioni and DuBow, 1969). Since countries cannot be similar in all respects but one, the investigator selects countries that are similar in the relevant respects. The shortcomings of this method are that it cannot compare every possible characteristic and that it seeks for only one cause and dismisses the possibility of multiple or alternative causes (Vauss, 2008: 253). Moreover, the classification of countries into similar or different samples has a great impact on the conclusions drawn. This is problematic if we consider that agreement and difference in real life resemble a continuum or a sliding scale, rather than a dichotomy. Moreover, when using the method of similarity and difference it is crucial to consider the meaning of concepts within their socio-cultural context. Religiousness, for example, may have very different meanings in different countries (Vauss, 2008). From a wider epistemological perspective, it could thus be argued that approaches based on Mills' reasoning may be too tightly caught up in binary (and Aristotelian) reasoning: a Wittgenstein-inspired approach to 'family resemblances' (Needham, 1975) or alternative forms of philosophical reasoning might be more helpful in this regard, particularly so in a globalizing world.

Box 7.4   Case Study: National Revivals and Violence

The following case is an example of controlled comparison or of a 'small-*n*' approach, which investigates two sets of contrasting pairs, Catalonia and the Basque Country, and the Ukraine and Georgia. In his study, Laitin (1999) provides an explanatory model to show why in some cases of national revival violence breaks out, while in other cases it does not.

Laitin's comparative study is grounded in a phenomenon that can be observed in different places around the world. The question of why in some cases violence breaks out while in other cases it does not is the puzzle Laitin tries to solve with the help of comparison. First, he analyses the two Spanish cases and asks why the nationalist revival movement in Catalonia has been relatively peaceful while the nationalist revival movement in the Basque Country has been bloody. In order to answer this question, Laitin identifies the crucial differences and isolates conditions (variables) that led to violence. He is aware that in qualitative social sciences the identification of 'controlled' variables may be problematic. Still, he encourages researchers to do their best to isolate variables they see as important (Laitin, 1999: 57).

Since macro-factors have not been suited to explain sufficiently why some national revival movements are more violent than others, Laitin draws our attention to what he refers to as 'micro factors', such as social networks and language histories. Laitin argues that the tipping point in how national revivals develop is whether enough followers can be recruited or not. If the latter is the case, violence such as terrorist activities may be seen as a possibility to facilitate recruitment.

In order to test this hypothesis, Laitin in a second step then applies the variables identified in the Spanish cases to two cases of post-Soviet nationalism. The four cases he examines allow him to do justice to the social reality of each case and still to reach some degree of generality that goes beyond the individual case. Moreover, the historical dimension that Laitin integrates in his analysis ensures that none of the societies studied are presented as inherently violent or peaceful.

Although, as we have learned, the majority of comparative research projects are cross-national or cross-cultural in character, we should acknowledge that qualitative comparison is, by far, a much larger field. The units of analysis may be regions, sections of society identified by gender, ethnicity, religion, age, by socio-economic criteria, urban–rural background, as well as by family status or other elements of social differentiation. We may, for example, compare piousness and religiousness among men and women or among one ethnic group with another. We may also compare the medical choices people make in rural areas compared with urban settings or the medical choices of migrants and non-migrants. Comparison may also be of an explicit historical character as discussed in Box 7.5 in the case of 'dethroned' ethnic majorities in the collapse process of two empires. Historical comparison can again have many different faces (see Mahoney and Rueschemeyer, 2003). The subject of comparison may be a certain practice (e.g. warfare, distribution of social benefits or multi-ethnic co-existence) and its past and present manifestation. For this endeavour we may compare the chosen subject in only one place (past and present) or compare several places, which again will depend on the research question.

Box 7.5 Case Study: Distant Comparison

Perhaps binary comparison and regional comparison represent the most popular and best established among the more conventional forms of qualitative comparative procedures in the humanities and social sciences at large. Binary comparison would contrast one set of cases against another, as in comparative literature ('the trope of a hero in novels X and Y') or in comparative legal studies ('indigenous rights in late twentieth-century Australia and Canada'). Regional comparison, on the other hand, would compare a whole set of corresponding cases from one area within similar time horizons, as in archaeology ('Palaeolithic cave drawings in Saharan Africa') or art studies ('Temple sculptures in thirteenth-century Southeast Asia'). Both orientations have their advantages, but they also entail the possibility of ignoring an inherent bias. Binary comparison might tempt the researcher to pay too much attention to differences (up to the point of producing or re-producing stereotypes), while regional comparison might lead to the invention of closed 'cultural circles', 'style provinces' and similar constructs that may turn out to be more misleading than helpful. In some cases, such a bias might be minimized through the introduction, as an additional or as an independent device, of 'distant comparison', also called 'self-reflexive controlled macro-comparison' (Gingrich, 2002).

The comparative examples assessed and analysed by Gingrich for the elaboration of this method were historical, and focused on the emergence of mass violence in the disintegration processes of multi-ethnic state configurations. In a first step, sequences and key events of anti-Christian massacres during and after the First World War in the decaying Ottoman Empire were scrutinized. This was contrasted against the anti-Jewish mob violence in Nazi-ruled Vienna during November 1938, interpreted also as a protracted aftermath to the fall of the Habsburg Empire, in 1918. The comparison revealed dominant contrasts and differences, and minor parallels. These subordinate parallels were then compiled into a flow diagram, leading from the loss of legitimacy for previous rulers to a sense of humiliation for the 'dethroned' ethnic majority, ensuing pan-nationalism, the identification of minority groups as the enemy's 'fifth column', and a rapid transition from hate speech to the creation of 'virile militancy', mob violence and persecution.

The resulting flow diagram was then carefully applied to key sequences of the civil war in the former Yugoslavia during the 1990s, featuring surprising parallels. This led to a

(Continued)

> *(Continued)*
>
> number of conceptual conclusions and to the formulation of a theoretical hypothesis about the dangerous aftermath to the dethronement of ethnic majorities.
>
> This procedure implies a scope of comparison that is kept 'controlled' through a small choice of three samples connected by a conceptual constellation of 'disintegrating multi-ethnic societies' as a main selection criterion. In addition, the range of comparison is 'macro-' and 'distant' in time and space: processual developments inside the three units of comparison are related to each other merely in indirect ways if at all.

The groups to be compared may already be manifested in the research design but they may as well be identified in a later stage and may emerge from the collected data only during the analysing process (Lewis, 2003: 50, 51). The latter was, for example, the case in Palmberger's research project on Bosnia and Herzegovina (see Palmberger, 2010; Palmberger, 2013). In this research, which investigates narratives of the local past after the 1992–5 war, discursive patterns of different generations are compared. The units of analysis, the three generations, were first inductively drawn from ethnographic fieldwork. This means that each case (narrative) was first analysed and only at a later stage were the different cases compared with each other and the generational distinctions identified. The research design was comparative in nature but the units to be compared were not determined up front.

The research aims differ as much as the units of analysis differ. While one comparative project may aim for deep theorization, another project may be of a more applied character while aiming at solving a sociopolitical problem. Comparative education, for example, often is of an applied character, particularly when it assists in the development of educational institutions (see Steiner-Khamsi, 2009; Phillips and Schweisfurth, 2007). In a similar way, comparisons of public policies are conducted mainly to learn lessons rather than to develop theory (Teune, 1990: 58). Common to all comparative research, however, is the fact that it requires more time and resources and most likely a bigger budget than a non-comparative project. This is particularly true if the project relies on primary rather than on secondary data (see Box 7.3). As is the case with any qualitative research, we are likely to collect great amounts of data of very different kinds (oral, visual, written) but in comparative research we collect these kinds of data for even more than one place/group of people. This means that the researcher at some point (better sooner than later) has to identify key themes, concepts and categories. We have to choose a few cases as well as comparative dimensions based on the research question or a theory-inspired problem:

> Comparison can deal with either questions of larger processes *or* particular patterns that can be elicited from limited historical processes, but neither ever exhausts what might be possible, nor can we ever account for the full spectrum of cases. (Yengoyan, 2006: 11)

The number of comparative dimensions needs to be kept low in view of ensuring that the amount of data remains manageable. In this selection process it is also important to decide which of the demographic characteristics (e.g. age, gender, town or country etc.) needs to be considered and which one does not (Flick, 2009: 150).

Due to the above-mentioned particularities of comparative qualitative analysis, studies with a particular emphasis on comparison will usually also require more structure, since it is necessary to cover broadly the same issues with each of the cases compared. This is even more important when working in a team. In this case a structured approach is needed to ensure some consistency (Arthur and Nazroo, 2003: 111). In the last few decades computer-assisted qualitative analysis programs have become popular among some scholars. Although no computer program by itself is able to do qualitative analysis, it may be helpful to sort the data and to draw the researcher's attention to some patterns and correlations in an extensive data set. Since there are various computer programs available for qualitative analysis and they are constantly changing, this is not the place to discuss the pros and cons of various types and items of software (but see Gibbs, Chapter 19, this volume). Consulting the existing literature on this topic, however, is appropriate.

So far we have only dealt with a priori comparative research design, which means research that was designed comparatively from its very beginning. There is, however, also the possibility to bring in a comparative perspective a posteriori, once the research has been completed. Since, as we have stated above, comparative research is generally more time consuming and budget intensive, it is often better suited for larger individual or group projects than for smaller ones. This is particularly true if empirical research is required, such as in-depth interviews and/or participant observation. When resources are scarce, one can still consider an a posteriori comparison to highlight the wider relevance of a given analysis, to address a wider readership, or both. Often enough, such an a posteriori comparison merely concerns particular phenomena discussed within a wider research range. Units of comparison may then be drawn from different regions and sources (Gingrich, 2012).

UNITS AND PROCEDURES OF ANALYSIS

It has been argued that comparison is no independent methodological procedure: its creative employment presupposes that data already have been yielded previously through other procedures (a posteriori), or that it is applied together with other, independent methodological strategies (a priori). In both cases, comparative strategies seek to generate additional constellations of data that may then provide *additional* insights. Comparative research procedures thus may be characterized as *dependent* methodologies, because they usually depend on the primary procurement of data through other methods.

As in other methodological procedures of qualitative research, comparison at first is informed by the key research question and by the given empirical evidence to pursue it, or by the likelihood of such empirical evidence to emerge in the course of the research process. These issues become even more important when the choice of units to be compared has to be made.

These units, as we have said, usually are in one way or another configurations, which should suggest a relative likelihood of providing sufficient results by way of analysis – without, however, giving way to self-fulfilling prophecies. It depends on the research question whether the choice of these units does or does not make sense: if I am interested in their respective contents of water, sugar and vitamins, then I may very well compare 'apples and oranges', quite to the contrary of what folk wisdom believes to be self-evident.

Early on during the comparative process, it is important at least to try out what kind of *limits* might best be chosen for the potential units of comparison. This definitional question is not a matter of methodological principle: in some instances, it is highly appropriate to be as precise as possible in defining those limits. By contrast, there are many other cases where the opposite is more appropriate – that is, to define those limits in as fluid, loose and processual a manner as possible. During the actual comparative procedures, it may then become necessary to readjust and redefine those limits several times for reasons of inner consistency, or for reasons of more rewarding results. These major changes should be made accessible and transparent to the research communities among readers.

Defining the units of comparison and their limits is the first precondition for the decisive step in developing a comparative strategy of analysis. This decisive step is the identification of the *criteria of comparison* and, eventually, of their *empirical features* among the respective units of comparison. The criteria of comparison have to be formulated on a somewhat more abstract level, in the form of markers that basically raise the same set of questions to the empirical contexts that are being compared. The criteria of comparison thus have to convey and communicate the main research question towards the empirical issues under scrutiny. This implies that the criteria of comparison at the same time are developed in a dialogical relationship with the empirical evidence at hand. In this sense, the criteria of comparison correspond to what Aristotelian traditions have called the *tertium comparationis*. The empirical features to be compared, finally, are analogous to what quantitative procedures would refer to as their 'variables' – yet in qualitative comparative analyses, these features explicitly are subjected to transparent phases of reinterpretation, contextualization and translation.

For instance, if one's units of comparison are Southwest Arabian star calendars, as once was the case with one of us (Gingrich, 1994), then it becomes important to clarify by which cross-cutting criteria they can be compared among each other. Some of these criteria may then address the question of socio-economic contexts, such as fields of practical application and social carriers of stellar knowledge. Other cross-cutting criteria will refer to the contents of those calendars of oral traditions, such as linguistic contents and contents of observation. At the latest, during the actual process of comparative analysis, it then becomes important to examine which actual empirical features correspond in each unit of comparison to the cross-cutting criterion of comparison, and how to qualify the outcome. For instance, applying the criterion of linguistic contents then led to the possibility of qualifying the outcome according to a qualitative tripartite scale for the star terminology's linguistic background. The tripartite scale differentiated between 'standard Arabic terminology', 'predominantly South Arabian terminology' and 'mixed terminology'. In other forms of comparison, it might be useful for data analysis to work not with qualifiers, but with (loosely defined) indeterminate quantifiers, such as 'intense', 'average' and 'low'.

Comparative data analysis therefore requires a simultaneous affinity to empirical results as well as to possible avenues of interpretation and theorizing. For these reasons, the appropriate choice of cross-cutting criteria of comparison and of their empirical features in individual examples is the most decisive step in comparative data analysis. A transnational comparison of neo-nationalist movements and parties in Western Europe (and beyond) during the early years after the turn of the century (Gingrich and Banks, 2006) illustrates this point (see Box 7.6). Five main criteria of comparison could then be applied to detailed case studies from Australia, Austria, Belgium, Denmark, France, India, Italy, the Netherlands, Sweden and the UK, since these case studies did provide the empirical features to actually answer the questions raised through the criteria of comparison: this in fact is the crucial point – the criterion of comparison has to be designed in ways that raise a few relevant questions, and the results of empirical research have to be rich enough to answer these questions in a meaningful way that at the same time can be simplified to some extent. Whether these empirically derived simplified answers are then formalized by means of indeterminate quantifiers and/or qualifiers, or whether they are better formulated in a non-formal, narrative manner as in Box 7.6 is a pragmatic and communicative choice rather than a matter of principle.

Box 7.6 Case Study: Qualitative Comparison in Data Analysis on Neo-nationalism

Contributors to the Brussels Conference on Neo-nationalism in Europe and Beyond had elaborated their case examples on the basis of a set of common propositions and hypotheses regarding the development and manifestations of 'neo-nationalism', that is the parliamentary and basically legal versions of extreme right-wing populism during the 1990s and early 2000s in what was then the European Union and the European Economic Area. On the basis of the conference presentations and their discussion, as well as of the contributions to the resulting edited book (Gingrich and Banks, 2006), the editors elaborated a number of cross-cutting criteria of comparison:

(a) *Historical backgrounds and origins of neo-nationalist parties and movements in Western Europe*: This first criterion led to useful distinctions between those groups (or their respective predecessors) that had emerged during the first two decades after 1945, with somewhat stronger and more explicit continuities to post-fascist or post-Nazi groups of supporters during their formative periods (Italy, Austria, Flemish parts of Belgium), and most other neo-nationalist groups and parties (in Western Europe and elsewhere) that had been founded somewhat more recently, often emerging at least in part out of breakaway movements from established mainstream parties.

(b) *Relation to existing state and its territorial and regional/ethnic dimensions*: This second criterion led to the important differentiation between those movements/parties that were primarily oriented towards an enhancement of ethnic or regional self-determination (northern Italy, Flemish parts of Belgium, to a lesser extent also (then) the German-speaking parts of Switzerland) and most other neo-nationalist parties in Western Europe. The first group displayed interesting transitional forms to some among the more conventional forms of breakaway nationalism or regional secessionism elsewhere in Europe (e.g. UK/Scottish nationalism; Spain/Catalonia, the Basque region; France/Corsica).

(c) *Instances of neo-nationalism's most striking advances up to 2005*: For the main criterion for 'most striking advances' defined by national election results of 10% or more for distinctly neo-nationalist parties, it turned out that, until 2005, in Western Europe these were mostly cases of small affluent countries (e.g. Austria, Belgium, Denmark, the Netherlands, Norway, Switzerland). With the exception of Italy, none of the EU's then four other big countries (i.e. France, Germany, Spain, UK) had allowed for similar advances by neo-nationalists into their national parliaments. Since then, the situation has changed to some extent (e.g. British votes for the EU Parliament, or French votes during the first course of the 2012 presidential elections), and also through the ascension of Poland (with the different legacy of post-communism) as a sixth big EU country – while also displaying some continuities (e.g. through subsequent Swedish and Finnish national election results).

(d) *Common ideological features among most successful neo-nationalist parties*: Despite their obvious diversity, over-communicated by their own propaganda's emphasis on 'authenticity' and national specificity, this fourth cross-cutting criterion of comparison yielded several important results. Key among them was the finding that a basic tripartite ideological and programmatic hierarchy was common to most of these movements. In essence, this ideological and cognitive hierarchy featured – and continues to feature – at its lower level other ethnic and/or regional groups, potential or resident immigrant groups, and (among EU member countries) certain non-EU member countries (e.g. Turkey, as the most important case in point). The same hierarchy's uppermost level presents 'Brussels' and its respective local/national allies and mysterious supporters, as well as to some extent 'Washington'. Sandwiched between these two dangerous and powerful levels are 'us', that is the redefined nation, with neo-nationalism as its best and faithful representative.

(Continued)

(Continued)

(e) *Main tools of mass mobilization*: Unsurprisingly, the 'politics of emotionalizing' turned out to be a main result of applying this fifth criterion of comparison, aiming at reinforcing state security while promoting economic deregulation and downsizing the welfare state at the same time. A second main result was permanent campaigning by addressing (or creating) scandals that served as the mediatized environment in which neo-nationalist leaders could be presented as quasi-pop-culture icons, bringing justice and redistributing wealth to those who deserve it.

Identifying and defining one's units of comparison and their size, and, even more importantly, one's cross-cutting criteria of comparison and their corresponding empirical features, and then adjusting and readjusting them throughout the comparative project until it actually is consistent, plausible, transparent and insightful, are the central elements of qualitative comparison. Compared with these central elements, it is a rather pragmatic and flexible process to choose between the different available options of comparative *ranges*. In its simpler versions, the range of comparison can be binary, regional or distant (see Box 7.5). Systematic historical (or 'temporal') comparison usually works along a central timeline, while keeping the regional or spatial dimensions fairly stable. More complex versions of comparative ranges are 'fluid' forms of comparison, which follow phenomena through time and space that consequently change together with the comparative analysis that follows them. This applies when we explore, for instance, a new instrument and method of electronic communication emanating from a few centres, and then compare the similarities and differences of how it is used in different communities across the globe. 'Fluid' forms of comparison thus are especially useful for the comparative analysis of border-crossing phenomena and processes. In the contexts of today's phases of globalization, fluid and distant forms of comparison thus may represent a growth sector of qualitative comparison in today's and tomorrow's humanities and social sciences.

Box 7.7 Key Points

- Comparative research does not present an independent method per se. Methodological choices depend on the primary research problem.
- Comparison in qualitative research may be designed a priori or a posteriori.
- A priori comparative research is generally more time consuming and budget intensive. Particularly group projects (and the great amounts of data that come with them) require a structured approach, for example the comparative criteria markers need to be defined carefully.
- The definition of the units of analysis and their limits is a decisive step in the early stage of any comparative research. In a second step, the criteria of comparison need to be identified as well as their corresponding empirical features.
- Our exposure to and interaction with increasing transnational and global conditions opens up the possibility for comparative research that investigates how different people in different parts of the world position and adapt themselves to these conditions.

FURTHER READING

Bowen, John Richard, Petersen, Roger Dale and ebrary Inc. (1999) *Critical Comparisons in Politics and Culture*. Cambridge: Cambridge University Press.
Gingrich, Andre and Fox, Richard Gabriel (eds) (2002) *Anthropology, by Comparison*. London: Routledge.
Øyen, Else (1990) *Comparative Methodology: Theory and Practice in International Social Research*, Sage Studies in International Sociology. London: Sage.

REFERENCES

Arthur, Sue and Nazroo, James (2003) 'Designing fieldwork strategies and materials', in Jane Ritchie and Jane Lewis (eds), *Qualitative Research Practice: A Guide for Social Science Students and Researchers*. London: Sage. pp. 109–37.
Beck, Ulrich (1999) *What Is Globalization?* Cambridge: Polity Press.
Boeije, Hennie (2010) *Analysis in Qualitative Research*. Los Angeles: Sage.
Bowen, John Richard, Petersen, Roger Dale and ebrary Inc. (1999) *Critical Comparisons in Politics and Culture*. Cambridge: Cambridge University Press.
Bryman, Alan (2012) *Social Research Methods*, 4th edition. Oxford: Oxford University Press.
Chen, Kuang-Hsing (2010) *Asia as Method: Toward Deimperialization*. Durham, NC: Duke University Press.
Collier, David (1993) 'The comparative method', in Ada W. Finifter (ed.), *Political Science: The State of the Discipline II*. Washington, DC: American Political Science Association.
Eggan, Fred (1953) 'Social anthropology and the method of controlled comparison', *American Anthropologist*, 56 (5): 743–63.
Ember, Carol R., Ember, Melvin and ebrary Inc. (2009) *Cross-Cultural Research Methods*. Lanham, MD: Altamira Press.
Etzioni, Amitai and DuBow, Fred (1969) *Comparative Perspectives: Theories and Methods*. Boston, MA: Little.
Flick, Uwe (2006) 'Constant comparative method', in Victor Jupp (ed.), *The SAGE Dictionary of Social Research Methods*. London: Sage. pp. 37–8.
Flick, Uwe (2007) *Designing Qualitative Research*. Los Angeles: Sage.
Flick, Uwe (2009) *An Introduction to Qualitative Research*, 4th edition. London: Sage.
Fox, Richard G. and Gingrich, Andre (2002) 'Introduction', in Andre Gingrich and Richard G. Fox, (eds), *Anthropology, by Comparison*, London: Routledge. pp. 1–24.
Gingrich, Andre (1994) *Südwestarabische Sternenkalender: Eine ethnologische Studie zu Struktur, Kontext und regionalem Vergleich des tribalen Agrarkalenders der Munebbih im Jemen*. Wiener Beiträge zur Ethnologie und Anthropologie vol. 7, Vienna: WUV.
Gingrich, Andre (2002) 'When ethnic majorities are "dethroned": Towards a methodology of self-reflexive, controlled macrocomparison', in Andre Gingrich and Richard G. Fox (eds), *Anthropology, by Comparison*. London: Routledge. pp. 225–48.
Gingrich, Andre (2012) 'Comparative methods in sociocultural anthropology today', in Richard Fardon et al. (eds), *Handbook of Social Anthropology*, vol. 2. London: Sage. pp. 211–22.
Gingrich, Andre and Banks, Marcus (eds) (2006) *Neo-nationalism in Western Europe and Beyond: Perspectives from Social Anthropology*. Oxford: Berghahn.
Gingrich, Andre and Fox, Richard G. (eds) (2002) *Anthropology, by Comparison*. London: Routledge.
Glaser, Barney (1965) 'The constant comparative method of qualitative analysis', *Social Problems*, 12 (4): 436–45.
Harding, Jamie (2006) 'Grounded theory', in Victor Jupp (ed.), *The SAGE Dictionary of Social Research Methods*. London: Sage. pp. 131–2.
Harvey, David (2006) *A Critical Reader*, ed. Noel Castree and Derek Gregory. Oxford: Blackwell.
Holy, Ladislav (1987) *Comparative Anthropology*. Oxford: Blackwell.
Kaelble, Hartmut and Schriewer, Jürgen (2003) *Vergleich und Transfer: Komparatistik in den Sozial-, Geschichts- und Kulturwissenschaften*. Frankfurt/Main: Campus.
Kreff, Fernand, Knoll, Eva-Maria and Gingrich, Andre (eds) (2011) *Lexikon der Globalisierung*. Bielefeld: Transcript.
Laitin, David D. (ed.) (1999) *National Revivals and Violence*, ed. John Richard Bowen et al., Critical Comparisons in Politics and Culture. Cambridge: Cambridge University Press.
Laitin, David D. (2007) *Nations, States, and Violence*. Oxford: Oxford University Press.
Lewis, Jane (2003) 'Design issues', in Jane Ritchie and Jane Lewis (eds), *Qualitative Research Practice: A Guide for Social Science Students and Researchers*. London: Sage. pp. 47–76.
Lijphart, Arend (1971) 'Comparative politics and the comparative method', *American Political Science Review*, 65 (3): 682–93.

Mahoney, James and Rueschemeyer, Dietrich (2003) *Comparative Historical Analysis in the Social Sciences*. Cambridge: Cambridge University Press.

May, Tim (1997) *Social Research: Issues, Methods and Process*, 2nd edition. Buckingham: Open University Press.

Mill, John Stuart and Robson, J. M. (1996) *A System of Logic, Ratiocinative and Inductive: Being a Connected View of the Principles of Evidence and the Methods of Scientific Investigation*, Collected Works of John Stuart Mill. London: Routledge.

Needham, Rodney (1975) 'Polythetic classification: Convergence and consequences', *Man*, 10: 347–69.

Niewöhner, Jörg and Scheffer, Thomas (2010) 'Introduction. Thickening comparison: On the multiple facets of comparability', in Thomas Scheffer and Jörg Niewöhner (eds), *Thick Comparison: Reviving the Ethnographic Aspiration*. Leiden: Brill. pp. 1–16.

Øyen, Else (1990) *Comparative Methodology: Theory and Practice in International Social Research*, Sage Studies in International Sociology. London: Sage.

Palmberger, Monika (2010) 'Distancing personal experiences from the collective – Discursive tactics among youth in post-War Mostar', *L'Europe en formation*, 357: 107–24.

Palmberger, Monika (2013) 'Ruptured pasts and captured futures: Life narratives in post-War Mostar', *Focaal – Journal of Global and Historical Anthropology*, 66: 14–24.

Phillips, David and Schweisfurth, Michele (2007) *Comparative and International Education: An Introduction to Theory, Method and Practice*. London: Continuum.

Ragin, Charles C. (1987) *The Comparative Method: Moving Beyond Qualitative and Quantitative Strategies*. Berkeley, CA: University of California Press.

Scheffer, Thomas (2010) 'Comparability on shifting grounds: How legal ethnography differs from comparative law', in Thomas Scheffer and Jörg Niewöhner (eds), *Thick Comparison: Reviving the Ethnographic Aspiration*. Leiden: Brill. pp. 17–42.

Schriewer, Jürgen (1992) 'The method of comparison and the need for externalization: methodological criteria and sociological concepts', in Jürgen Schriewer and Brian Holmes (eds), *Theories and Methods in Comparative Education*. Frankfurt/Main: Peter Lang. pp. 25–83.

Steiner-Khamsi, Gita (2009) 'Transferring education, displacing reforms', in Jürgen Schriewer (ed.), *Discourse Formation in Comparative Education*. Frankfurt/Main: Lang. pp. 155–88.

Strauss, Claudia and Quinn, Naomi (1997) *A Cognitive Theory of Cultural Meaning*. Cambridge: Cambridge University Press.

Teune, Henry (1990) 'Comparing countries: Lessons learned', in Else Øyen (ed.), *Comparative Methodology: Theory and Practice in International Social Research*. London: Sage. pp. 38–62.

Tilly, Charles and Russell Sage Foundation (1984) *Big Structures, Large Processes, Huge Comparisons*, Russell Sage Foundation 75th Anniversary Series. New York: Russell Sage Foundation.

Urban, Greg (1999) 'The role of comparison in the light of the theory of culture', in John R. Bowen and Roger Petersen (eds), *Critical Comparison in Politics and Culture*. Cambridge: Cambridge University Press. pp. 90–109.

Vauss, David de (2008) 'Comparative and cross-national designs', in Pertti Alasuutari et al. (eds), *The SAGE Handbook of Social Research Methods*. Los Angeles: Sage. pp. 249–64.

Vertovec, Steven (2011) 'Migration and new diversities in global cities: comparatively conceiving, observing and visualizing diversification in urban public spaces', Working Paper, Max Planck Institute for the Study of Religious and Ethnic Diversity. pp. 1–32.

Yengoyan, Aram A. (ed.) (2006) *Modes of Comparison: Theory and Practice*, The Comparative Studies in Society and History Book Series. Ann Arbor, MI: University of Michigan Press.

Reflexivity and the Practice of Qualitative Research

Tim May and Beth Perry

Introducing a reflexive practice into qualitative research enables both an examination of the grounds upon which claims to know the social world are based and an exploration of the strengths and limitations of forms of knowledge. This allows researchers to sharpen subsequent research practices and correct an instrumental approach to knowledge that is informed by a desire to control, rather than understand, the social world.

To understand how this occurs, we first examine different social scientific approaches to reflexivity. We then look at the implications of this discussion for the process of conducting research. That, in turn, leads us into a discussion of reflexive spaces which we illuminate through the different forms of qualitative work we have conducted over the past few years.

CALLS TO REFLEXIVITY: HISTORY AND CONTENT

Reflexivity has a long history in social inquiry (see May, with Perry, 2011). Calls to reflexive social inquiry do not maintain a simple separation between subject and object or between the knower and the known. Reflexivity involves turning back on oneself in order that processes of knowledge production become the subject of investigation. It thus recognizes that: 'Inquiry is practice of a deeply cultural sort, which can become reflexive only by investigating these relationships through inquiry itself' (Hall, 1999: 255). This same impulse is apparent at an individual level in terms of the dynamic between self and society: 'Inner consciousness is socially organized by the importation of the social organization of the outer world' (Mead, 1964: 141).

For Max Weber (1949), the practice of social inquiry could not simply be about the collection of social facts, but 'idea of ideas' (Albrow, 1990: 149). His 'ideal type' thereby served as an analytic instrument for the ordering of empirical reality within an approach which supported a view that we cannot know the social world, but only our representations of that world. As researchers, there is no view we can derive that is free from social position given our participation in the social world. Instead, we should take our participation as a good starting point and learn from mediating between different cultures of inquiry.

Critics argued that Weber failed to recognize the episodic nature of human conduct and hence his call for causal adequacy was bound by sociological and historical understanding (Schutz, 1973). For Alfred Schutz, meaning is the event, or an act is a meaningful process. From this point of view *verstehen* (see Outhwaite, 1986) is not a method for doing social research, but what social scientists should study as it represents the 'experiential form in which common sense thinking takes cognisance of the social cultural world' (Schutz, 1979: 29).

Through such writings the mediation of first- (everyday meanings) and second-order (representation of those meanings) constructs became a topic of reflexive concern. Authors argued that a commonsense stock of knowledge orientates people to apply meaning to their own actions, those of others and the events that they encounter. The life world exhibits the basis for a primary experience that enables people to orientate their actions through taking its self-evidence, or pre-reflexive constitution, for granted. Through the study of 'lay' reflexivity, the analytic focus of research therefore moved towards a representation of everyday life and meaning production, providing a spur to qualitative inquiry (Moustakas, 1994).

A difference between the knower and known was apparent in the work of Schutz through the mediation of first- and second-order constructs. Harold Garfinkel took these insights, yet refused to differentiate between everyday theorizing and social science (Garfinkel, 1967). By attending to the ways in which everyday life was being produced through the work of interpretation by lay actors as both a starting *and* finishing point of social analysis, the context dependence of action and meaning became the focal point. Reflexivity thereby was seen to contribute to social order, displayed through situated and public activities that are open to various forms of qualitative analysis (ten Have 2007; Heath and Hindmarsh, 2002 – see also Eberle, Chapter 13, Toerien, Chapter 22, and Knoblauch et al., Chapter 30, this volume).

Alvin Gouldner took aim at ethnomethodology for attracting those who wished to engage in a 'non-violent revolt' against the status quo because they could not, or would not, challenge dominant social structures (Gouldner, 1971: 394–5). His reflexive aim was more concerned with social change and the 'background assumptions' of social inquiry. He argued that normalizing 'unpermitted worlds' that threaten stability reproduces the status quo while allusions to value neutrality enable an existential distance to be maintained from the consequences of research work and the subjects of investigation. An overemphasis upon technical approaches to research also denies the significance of practice in social contexts (Gouldner, 1971: 484–8).

Reflexive understanding in social inquiry was now directed towards how the researchers' praxis and their role and social position related to the product and process of their work. Reflexive processes were seen to deepen self-awareness of the production of valid and reliable 'bits of information', strengthen a commitment to the value of this awareness and generate a willingness to be open to 'hostile information' (Gouldner, 1971: 494).

Authors, writing from a feminist perspective, have argued that a critical and insightful gaze does not come from a position of disinterest from which the researcher works, but that interest itself comes from the advantage of 'being engaged' (Hartsock, 1987). What are immediately placed in question are unsustainable ideas of bias being constituted in terms of possessing 'interests'. Here we find an 'abstract masculinity' being compared with the 'connectedness and continuities' between women living in everyday life exemplified through the exercise of empathy and an 'ethic of care' (Larrabee, 1993). The absence of women's experiences in scientific accounts – symptomatic of 'relations of ruling' (Smith, 2002) – can then be deployed productively because an analytic focus upon the differences in men's and women's situations gives: 'a scientific advantage to those who can make use of the differences' (Harding, 1991: 120). The result is a 'standpoint' that, unlike a perspective, is socially mediated and requires *both* science and politics to achieve (Harding 1991: 276n). In Dorothy Smith's work this has led to an approach called 'institutional ethnography' (Smith 2002; 2005 – see also Gubrium and Holstein, Chapter 3, this volume).

To understand how mediating processes work between social inquiry and social life, authors have turned to hermeneutics (see Wernet, Chapter 16, this volume) in order to focus upon a two-way relationship between the knower and the known and lay and technical languages. Here we find what has been termed a 'double hermeneutic', which refers to the ways in which lay and professional concepts become implicated in slippages between frames of meaning (Giddens, 1984: 374). The 'revelatory' nature of expertise is seen to have given way to an 'interpretive' mode between the production and reception of social research. Set against the backdrop of 'reflexive modernization' (Beck et al., 1994) it follows that: 'No one can become an expert, in the sense of the possession either of full expert knowledge or of the appropriate formal credentials, in more than a few small sectors of the immensely complicated knowledge systems that now exist' (Giddens, 1990: 144).

The relations between social research and social life are now open to interpretive flexibility and incorporation without necessarily recognizing the origins of the insights. However, positioning in social relations has effects on what we see, how it is seen and with what consequences. This opens the path towards more complex understanding of the relations between the social scientific and life world in order to understand better the mediated nature of social inquiry and social life (Wynne, 1996).

One way forward is to understand better how both dispositions and positions enable particular views on social life to emerge. Here we find calls for what may be termed a 'genuine epistemology' that is based on knowledge of the social conditions under which scientific schemata actually function (Bourdieu, 2004). This moves us beyond 'the experiencing subject to encompass the organizational and cognitive structure of the discipline' (Wacquant, 1992: 40). The aim is not to 'discourage scientific ambition but to help make it more realistic ... *reflexivity makes possible a more responsible politics*, both inside and outside of academia' (Bourdieu, in Bourdieu and Wacquant, 1992: 194; original italics). For Bourdieu, this ethos was taken into the empirical investigation of many domains, including everyday life, the social structures of the economy and self-analysis (Bourdieu, 2007; 2008).

CONSEQUENCES AND ISSUES

Each of the authors and schools of thought examined so far have their own perspective on the dimensions of reflexivity that need to be incorporated into the research process. Yet we can find one feature which is important to take on board: reflexivity is not a method, but a way of thinking or critical ethos, the role of which is to aid interpretation (see Willig, Chapter 10, this volume), translation and representation. It does not legislate or seek closure and cannot be confined to one element of the research process, bracketed or appended; it is an iterative and continuous characteristic of good research practice.

Running through the above approaches are two different yet interrelated dimensions of reflexive practice: endogenous and referential reflexivity (May, with Perry, 2011). Endogenous reflexivity refers to the ways in which the actions and understandings of researchers contribute to the modes in which research practices are constituted. There are specific expectations, often latent and unarticulated, that are made of the practices and forms of knowledge that are deployed in particular disciplines. Endogenous reflexive practice refers to how we think and act in our social and cultural milieus, particularly within academic disciplines and communities. Referential reflexivity, on the other hand, takes place where the production of accounts meets contexts of reception that seek to render events, conditions and experiences intelligible via a meeting of points of view. The power to ignore or act upon these is variable among and between different groups, and that also informs the extent to which production and reception are differentiated, conjoined in various ways or collapsed into the same domain of activity.

To consider endogenous reflexivity alone would not allow us to see how it is that the social sciences are constitutive of social relations. What would then be replicated is a one-way hermeneutic whereby social research is simply separated from social life. Referential reflexivity is not just a reflection of everyday life, but must begin with that experience. The movement from endogenous to referential reflexivity may be characterized as one from reflexivity *within* actions to reflexivity *upon* actions, enabling connections to be made between individuals and the social conditions of which they are a part.

Both dimensions are informed by varying degrees of epistemic permeability. This refers to the boundaries between knowing communities within and outside academia and varies not only according to discipline, but also according to institutional position, disposition and research culture (see May, with Perry, 2011). Changeable dynamics between justification (for research within a bounded community of scholars) and application (of research in terms of its dissemination and interpretation by different groups – see Barbour, Chapter 34, this volume) inform these dynamics. We see both demands for a more socially accountable science, and an increased detachment from socially excluded communities through the clamour for an institutional elitism that concentrates resources in a principle site of research production: the university.

The 'contextualization' thesis holds that the traditional monopoly of the university, questioned by many, is being undermined in the twenty-first century as massification has led to new 'knowledge workers' leaving the university to set up alternative sites of knowledge production (Gibbons et al., 1994). Alongside those who embrace the new mantra of universities as 'engines of growth' or 'knowledge factories' (Castells and Hall, 1994), accounts also emphasize how universities are being irrevocably redefined by the myriad expectations placed upon them and increasingly managerialist approaches to playing the 'knowledge capitalism' game (May and Perry, 2006). The consequence is that spaces for critical reflection are being squeezed, squashed and diminished. Without care, and under pressure to meet these different expectations, the case study becomes no more than an exemplary vignette; comparison transmutes into the transplantation of models with no concern for context sensitivity and the quality and rigour of social scientific work is diminished.

A reflexive approach to analysis thereby requires navigation between the paths of scientism and relativism and deconstruction and reconstruction. This concerns how to acknowledge different viewpoints, ways of knowing and knowledge (lay/expert), without undermining the sites of knowledge production that enables a scientific gaze without giving over to 'scholastic slumbers' (Bourdieu, 2000). That brings the position of the researcher within the remit of reflexivity in social inquiry. In addition, how researchers define themselves, in particular through their difference from and distance to others with whom they compete in the academic field, are key elements that bring together the disposition *and* position of the individual. This is a continual process of seeking to understand what social inquiry sees, the manner in which it is constructed and its place within social relations more generally.

During the process of social investigation it is necessary to take these insights on board and translate them into research practice. The process of research itself is not regarded as valid by virtue of being constituted by the reflexive attitude of the investigator's point of view. Research becomes a dialogic process whereby the views of research participants are incorporated into the findings (Cook and Fonow, 1990). Rooting actual experiences within institutional relations not only brings to light similarities in experiences, but also demonstrates disjunctures between character and culture that demand analytic attention, as opposed to being glossed over in favour of formulaic neatness as determined by models of the isolated researcher.

The task is twofold: first, to be much smarter in arguments regarding the distinctiveness of knowledge produced through qualitative research, without collapsing into overstretched claims that such knowledge is 'truth' in terms of understanding the worlds we inhabit; second, to consider not only how knowledge relates to action, but what actions we must take to permit knowing. Active and practical efforts are needed to create spaces for reflection to enable research to improve and refine its insights and hence understandings of the world. In order to illustrate these issues in practice, we now turn to examples within our own work.

EXPERIENCES AND INSIGHTS FROM PRACTICE

The limits and possibilities for reflexive practice in our own work have been shaped by the different issues outlined above. Not only our characters and commitments, but also the contexts and cultures in which we have worked have shaped the 'multiple reflexivities' we have practised (see Mruck and Mey, 2007; Lynch, 2000). The Centre for Sustainable Urban and Regional Futures (SURF) was established in 2000 as an interdisciplinary research centre at the University of Salford. With an ethos of producing academically excellent research with high societal relevance, SURF has occupied different positions in its history on the continuum between research centre, think tank and consultancy. Over the last 12 years we have worked on a number of research projects, funded by academic research councils, European framework programmes, governmental organizations, charitable or research foundations and business organizations. This mixed economy of research was facilitated in the first years of SURF by our status as a cross-faculty centre with staff located within different university schools.

The history of SURF – in relation to the university, our urban and regional environment, funding regimes and policy frameworks for research – has shaped the 'degrees of reflexivity' we have been able to exhibit over the passage of time (Mauthner and Doucet, 2003). SURF has moved from a cross-faculty research centre to one 'normalized' within a single school, at the same time as notions of relevance, impact, interdisciplinarity, collaborative working and the need to be outward facing have collided with systemic organizational turbulence and restructuring, the latter brought about as a result of changes in the UK higher-education landscape.

Our common predispositions to be reflexive have been mediated through our variable positions and career trajectories, through shared and individual relationships to SURF, the institution and each other. Through our upbringings, histories and biographies, we each brought with us multiple 'ghosts' (Doucet, 2008). Collectively manifesting and exploring these was a critical element in creating a culture in which reflexivity could be a relational and collaborative, rather than self-referential and individualized, exercise. At Tim's instigation, all members of SURF – from the directors to the administrative staff – were asked to present and discuss their motivations, interests and passions to the team, reflecting the desire to create the possibility for 'intensive intellectual and affective fusion' (Bourdieu, 2007: 19–20). Such efforts were variably received and acted upon across the team. Yet for those with a disposition to do so, these initial explorations – continued through away-days and supervisions and a concern with a supportive culture – provided a basis upon which collaborations could be built and the uncertainties and insecurities of academic life shared and navigated.

How we approached research topics, the nature of the work, the methods deployed, the outputs desired and expected from varying groups have differed over time, according to a complex set of relationships between context, culture and content. We now draw on three specific examples of these in qualitative research practice and the iterative and embedded nature of data analysis, particularly in relation to writing, dissemination and representation.

Academic Research Projects, 2002–7

In 2002 we successfully applied for funding, with our colleague Simon Marvin, to the UK Economic and Social Research Council's (ESRC) Science in Society programme for a one-year pilot study. The research aimed to build an understanding of the dynamic interaction between existing scientific practice and regional needs, in particular to assess how far the articulation of regional needs in the UK had reshaped the governance, processes and outcomes of national science policy.

According to the criteria deployed by referees, the project was graded 'Outstanding' by the ESRC and led to a successful large grant under the second round of the programme (2004–7). By expanding the scale and scope of the project to include case studies in France, Germany and Spain, the work took the study of regional science policy into a comparative context and focused on different approaches for building science regions in the European Research Area. That project also gained an 'Outstanding' grading.

Neither project was conceived to embody an iterative or reflexive approach. A linear methodology was envisaged from research question and hypothesis through to fieldwork, followed by a discrete period of data analysis and representation. Within the terms of the project, reflexivity was neither planned, nor anticipated as a prerequisite of funding or assessment. Nonetheless, given the context and culture of SURF, research practices emerged which facilitated reflexivity within the project and a move from endogenous to more referential concerns.

Project meetings and supervisions provided critical spaces for reflexive practice (see also Elliott et al., 2011). These facilitated reflection on the design, conduct and results of the interviewing process as it unfolded, as well as constituted spaces for collective discussion of emerging themes and issues of validity, representativeness and authenticity (see Barbour, Chapter 34, and Mertens, Chapter 35, this volume). While we did not follow a single method, such as listening guides or multiple voice analysis (Gilligan et al., 2005; Mauthner and Doucet, 1998; 2003), project spaces enabled the data to be re-evaluated continuously through listening from different points of view, multiple readings or comparing field notes and observations with transcriptions of key interviews (see Roulston, Chapter 20, this volume).

That process enabled us to analyse the dynamics and asymmetries of power; not, as is often the case, through giving over power to research subjects as equals or co-constructors, but through acknowledging the inherent interests at play in presenting particular versions of events (England, 1994). These were not people from disadvantaged communities or marginalized groups; these were decision-makers; they were elites. Furthermore, the vast majority of interviewees were older, male and in positions of seniority in higher education with much to lose from an unfavourable account of their actions and decisions. A reflexive approach to data analysis was critical in highlighting the limitations of the data and the basis upon which claims could be made. While we had some privileged access to key decision-makers and documents, it became apparent that we could not expect our study, given the resources available, to penetrate the political spheres of influence shaping decision-making processes.

These reflections strongly influenced the aims and objectives of the second round project, which took us beyond a one-year time frame. The emphasis here was more deliberately on illuminating the construction and mobilization of discourses around scientific excellence and territorial relevance, rather than to reconstruct events and processes. Prior intellectual interests were critical in reshaping and refining the research to examine not only regulative and structural accounts, but also the normative and cognitive frames, which created particular conditions in which contemporary developments around the innovative region or city were being formed. At this time Tim had taken on the role of Lead Director within SURF and sought systematically to embed a supportive and reflexive culture – not only despite but because of external challenges of the changing policy, funding and governance of research within the UK, the content in the city of Manchester and Salford in particular.

In seeking to create a 'safe space' for critical reflection and engagement within SURF, we were able to submit the relationship between the Science in Society project and our own institutional position to scrutiny. While the methodology for the project remained relatively traditional and linear, the culture of SURF forged a context for us to examine how our roles as academics informed the analysis of our data. Our research was increasingly focusing on the mechanisms through which universities were engaging with 'their' localities, the hierarchies which emerged and the values attributed to and assumed by different organizations and forms of knowledge. This, combined with other projects which we were undertaking for the Greater Manchester Universities and Manchester: Knowledge Capital, forced us to examine how our position, within a marginalized university in regional/subregional terms, informed our critique of research-excellent universities and the capturing of the regional development agendas by a narrow and elitist search for global excellence.

The role of academics and university managers, often known to us, was subject to internal critique through the project and broader context. Collective and iterative discussions of interview material, encompassing discussions of the dynamics, body language, content and space of the interview, enabled us to see how our own positions were being invoked and used in particular ways to legitimize existing justifications, or constitute alternative discourses. With such statements as 'you know how it is, as academics, we all play these games', uncomfortable questions were often dismissed as naive, while interviewees simultaneously sought to co-opt us and invite us into the collective idea of regional relevance, while practices often carried on regardless.

These sets of reflections created an ambivalence and hesitancy about forms of writing, the prioritization of different narratives, modes and forums of representation and audiences (see Perry, 2006; Perry and May, 2006; May and Perry, 2006; Perry and May, 2007; May, 2011). The process of writing as an act of analysis (see Denzin, Chapter 39, this volume) was critical in this respect. Faced with complex sets of circumstances, we developed different forms of representation – to funders, participants, stakeholders, policy-makers, academics, etc. We produced versions of final reports for different groups, along with policy briefings and academic articles, and collectively discussed presentations and key messages for audiences (see Murray, Chapter 40, this volume). Anticipation and a desire to protect the integrity of our work were key facets of a reflexive approach. In this respect we were bolstered by having continuously 'tested' the validity of our analysis (see Barbour, Chapter 34, this volume) and the reception of work through presentations to those involved, informal workshops and formal seminars.

In these projects a reflexive approach to data analysis enabled not only checks on bias through a self-centred reflexive approach, but also the movement from endogenous to referential concerns. This took place through the culture of SURF rather than planned in-project methods. Data analysis could not be seen as clearly bounded within a single phase, as ongoing project meetings, workshops, presentations and forms of representation over time created different spaces for reflexive analysis.

Formative Project Evaluation, 2008–10

Our second example concerns a formative evaluation of the Manchester Innovation Investment Fund (IIF). The work itself was supported by the National Endowment for Science, Technology and the Arts, the North West Development Agency and Manchester City Council. The aim of the IIF was to bring about a step change in the innovation capacity in the city region through the injection of about £9,000,000. Our role, alongside the University of Manchester's Institute of Innovation Research, was not to act as consultants, but as 'critical friends', providing real-time feedback and lessons that could inform subsequent actions, rather than produce an end-of-project summative evaluation.

The mode of working was developed at our instigation – indeed, we wrote the brief – drawing on our critique of academic engagement and linear models of knowledge transfer as against those concerning 'exchange'. Our aspiration, shared by one of the key organizations involved, was to bring endogenous and referential concerns, excellence and relevance together in a novel approach to inform practice not as a by-product or end product, but as an intended, collaborative outcome. This can be seen as embodying a frustration with existing academic practices and desire for a more critical, emancipatory form of research (see McCabe and Holmes, 2009).

These concerns were reflected in the terms of reference for the research with the emphasis upon learning, evaluation and representation at a programmatic level. The intention was for direct access to materials and the methods deployed were observation of meetings and events, documentary analysis (see Coffey, Chapter 25, this volume), interviews (see Roulston, Chapter 20, this volume) with funders, participants and stakeholders, as well as questionnaires and focus groups (see Barbour, Chapter 21, this volume). We produced work package reports designed to inform the process with the intention that these might 'red-kite' any issues unfolding and thus provide the possibility of realignment or adjustment of priorities, processes and the trajectory of the IIF. The work was planned over three years, to run alongside a summative evaluation of funded activities, with the intention that we would then synthesize the formative learning into a summative report.

Reflexive spaces for participants were actively planned as part of the data collection and analysis process. Having explored the motivations, desires and perspectives of the funders and managers privately through interviews, they were then brought into a collective forum in which they could reflect on and within actions. Through analysing and comparing the transcriptions (see Kowal and O'Connell, Chapter 5, this volume) of the interviews and the focus groups, alongside a self-completion, open-ended questionnaire, we were able to see how individuals performed different roles publicly and privately and the extent of capacities to reflect and share their assumptions, uncertainties and concerns as a precursor to effective learning. At the time, these forums were credited by participants as being extremely helpful in generating a common understanding and exploring the purpose of organizational and individual motivations and contexts that otherwise would not have been gained. A temporary sense of belonging together in a collective endeavour then emerged.

As the political and governance context for the IIF altered over time, the degrees of reflexivity that the funders and managers were able to exhibit – in the spirit of real-time learning and evaluation – hit a limit. Our interview data revealed a mix of positive and negative messages for the managers in terms of structures, experiences, processes and impacts. These were met with variable reactions – from acknowledgement and legitimation through to dismissal and refutation – not only according to the nature of the statement (informally; through verbal asides; through interview spaces or in public forums), but also according to the point of time in the process. It was particularly noticeable how the dispositions of funders/managers to engage in reflexive learning changed in line with their positions and organizational expectations in the context of the financial recession.

What this highlights is the relational nature of reflexivity in qualitative research and the interactive nature of endogenous and referential dimensions. Reflexive spaces were planned as the basis for learning within in-project spaces – yet the limits to the reflexivity of others increased the need for reflexivity on our part at the very time when our own organizational culture was under pressure and not due to financial issues. We were working on different projects while trying to defend our governance model – which has worked well for 10 years – and responding to the needs of funders and clients. We were struggling with our own motivations and sense of belonging in a changing academic context and with meeting the expectations placed upon us in different spheres. The result of these contexts and cultures, despite our proclivities, was to reduce systematic reflexive spaces to ad hoc 'reflexive snatches', grabbed when servers failed and email was blissfully suspended, or on the telephone in the odd moments when we needed a break from discussions on the survival of a positive organizational culture.

The emphasis was on the representation of the work, given the sensitivities of the funders, our own involvement in the research and our commitments to those we had interviewed to ensure that their voices were clearly heard. Again, the process of report writing was essential to the process of analysis as we sought to navigate the thin and uncomfortable line between academic credibility and capitulation to the need for easily digestible and positive stories of success that would justify the investments made. To establish the legitimacy of the reports according to our concerns with accurate representation and the ethics surrounding data collection, we sought to give space to the voices of others to allow for the material to speak for itself, through including interview quotes alongside extracts from public meetings, minutes and workshops. We sought not just to deconstruct but reconstruct ways forward for the IIF to enable different perspectives to be recognized and reconciled within practices.

For the funders, representation took priority over learning; reputations were on the line for all involved. The feedback and review process on the final submitted report was extremely revealing (see Murray, Chapter 40, this volume). At the point of representation and with the prospect of the report being made publicly available, our work took centre stage. The report became a lens through which the funders saw themselves and simultaneously acted as a mechanism through which differences were seen. We received four different, contradictory word, line, paragraph and page amendments with no guidance on how to mediate between them. Our position became untenable and unwinnable. Ultimately, our report was described as 'so accurate it would never see the light of day'. At the same time, we were informed that we needed to provide solutions, as if differences of opinion between those involved were irrelevant. The contract came to an end with a consultant being employed to undertake the work of representation and produce 'best practice' case studies for other cities.

We were left with a series of ethical dilemmas and choices relating to the spirit in which we had undertaken the work and our responsibilities to the funder, our commitments to participants and our standing with academic and policy/practitioner circles. Distance and time away from the project were needed before we could systematically consider these issues, particularly as there were multiple battles to secure the boundaries and reproduction of the SURF, while Beth was completing her PhD by publication. It took 18 months before we had the space and time and felt able to return to the work. Acknowledging how painful we had found the process, we then created new spaces to reflect on the work, in part through removing ourselves from our environment and presenting at conferences, not on the work itself, but on the process (Knoblauch, 2004: 357). This ongoing reflexive reanalysis of our roles and the relationship between creativity and critique in urban governance and policy processes not only acted as 'confession, catharsis and cure' (Pillow, 2003), but informs our current practices.

The project illustrated multiple reflexivities in data analysis. Reflexivity was employed as a deliberate tool to produce transformative outcomes and learning among fund managers; to enhance the validity and integrity of the work; to inform choices about representation/analysis; as a mechanism of support and understanding; and as a rescue package for the work in an ironic retreat into endogenous circles. It also highlighted how the relationship between academic research and engaged work was not straightforward nor linear and the complexities of seeking to work in partnership with multiple organizations in the urban space (May and Perry, 2011a; 2011b).

Designing Reflexive Processes and Projects, 2009–

Taking these experiences forward, both positive and negative, we have retained a belief that the effort required to create, maintain and draw value from reflexive spaces for different participants in the research process is worthwhile. This is in a context where reflexivity is often invoked as a demand from those who exhibit a disjuncture between their expectations and the actual efforts needed to make it happen. Informed by our experiences and writings, we have increasingly sought to embed a reflexive methodology within all stages of the research process from conceptualization through to analysis, representation and evaluation (Knoblauch, 2004).

The history and development of SURF itself and the relationship between the content, culture and contexts for innovative, excellent and relevant work have increasingly formed the substantive subject matter for work. Drawing on our analysis of tensions placed upon universities and the 'devilish dichotomies' that shape research (Perry and May, 2010; Perry, 2011), alongside debates over the legitimacy of different knowledge claims and the fragmentation of authority and expertise, we have developed a systematic framework in which reflexivity can be subject to analysis. Within our projects, we are seeking proactively to deploy reflexivity in the formation of interdisciplinary epistemic communities and communities of practice, through the creation of spaces where endogenous and referential concerns meet and where all participants can be encouraged to think about their dispositions, positions and sense of belonging. The following examples illustrate this approach.

The first relates to the process of interdisciplinary knowledge production within large-scale collaborative projects. At a UK level, an increasing emphasis has been seen on funding mechanisms which encourage multidisciplinary, cross-institutional and multi-annual projects for the receipt of larger sums of research money. Mirroring developments elsewhere around the concentration of resources, linked to expectations of excellent academic work with high impact, groups of academics have increasingly needed to form alliances in order to apply successfully for Research Council funding. While this may happen independently of Research Councils, processes – such as research 'sandpits' – have been designed with the intention of forging new collaborations between academics who have never previously met but may work together for up to five years based on a single moment of contact.

Taking insights about the importance of context and culture, disposition, position and belonging in shaping the content of research in terms of its legitimacy, quality and potential impact, we sought to develop a reflexive process within such projects as a precursor for effective teamworking. From within the Retrofitting the City project, funded by the UK's Engineering and Physical Sciences Research Council (EPSRC), we instigated a process of bilateral exchanges to facilitate the sharing of orientations, motivations and expectations between team members as a foundation for interdisciplinary knowledge production (see also Mruck and Mey, 2007: 521). In 2011, we took a reflexive approach to team building in a development grant for a four-year £1.5 million project under the Arts and Humanities Research Council (AHRC) Connected Communities programme. Here we carried out individual interviews with team members, shared examples of previous work, had bilateral exchanges with a write-up of issues and developed a process of embedding reflexive analysis within the final project.

The results of both processes were variable: we were able to build a sense of orientation and history into new collaborations – the AHRC project was ultimately funded – and we have a commitment to collaborative reflexive analysis as a mechanism for integrated knowledge production in the project through the creation of the CIRCUS (Collaborative Interdisciplinary Research Connecting Urban

Society). Limits were also readily apparent, in terms of differential positions and dispositions to engage; disciplinary norms; levels of epistemic permeability; and the gap between intention and reality as the speed and urgency of different application deadlines and commitments took precedence. Both processes also raised the question of whether differences in institutional and disciplinary cultures towards knowledge production and exchange and reflexive dispositions can be addressed through creating spaces away from what are everyday cultures of inquiry.

In our work for Mistra – Urban Futures (2010–15) we are now seeking to bring all our experiences and knowledge to bear in analysing the role of reflexivity in the co-production of knowledge. Mistra – Urban Futures (M-UF) is an international centre funded by the Swedish Foundation for Strategic Environmental Research (MISTRA), the Swedish International Development Cooperation Agency (SIDA) and seven regional and local consortium partners. This operates through five Local Interaction Platforms in Sweden, Kenya, South Africa, China and the UK. Hosted by Chalmers University in Gothenburg, M-UF is based on the belief that the 'co-production of knowledge is a winning concept for achieving sustainable urban futures and creating fair, green and dense cities', through an innovative structure which brings local partners together in consortia to develop shared approaches to sustainability in city regions with local relevance and global applicability, the latter achieved through an international learning and collaboration mechanism: the Urban Futures Arena.

SURF is responsible for the development of a Local Interaction Platform in Greater Manchester, 2010–15. The complexities of mapping the funding and governance model of M-UF at an international level onto the contemporary urban context in the UK, with its own changing governance structures, funding regimes and redefinition of the roles of different agencies within the city, were immediately clear. As such, we are seeking to embed reflexivity through the research process as a prerequisite for building lasting and meaningful collaborations. Multiple aspects are at play in terms of the dynamics between individuals, the work and the broader contexts and cultures in the urban sphere which influence how joint knowledge production, exchange and learning might take place in cities. In so doing we are drawing on emerging work such as Gilbert and Sliep's (2009: 468) call for 'inter-relational reflexivity' which includes 'a concern for moral agency and the negotiation of accountability and responsibility for action, as social action requires a joint deconstruction of power in the voices and relationships operating between the stakeholders within a performative space'. Hosking and Pluut's (2010: 59) relational approach is also promising and highlights the need for 'regular reflexive dialogues as part of, and directed at, the research process [to] heighten the local use value of research for all participants and ... facilitate new possible realities and relations'.

In the development of the Greater Manchester Local Interaction Platform, reflexivity is an explicit and planned element to guard against bias, ensure legitimacy, improve quality and rigour, but also to increase the chances that knowledge collaboratively produced has an impact on the learning capacities of the city region over time. Multiple methods are planned and being deployed – from reflexive walking interviews with participants, entry/exit interviews, to diary keeping, writing reflections in between meetings and creating 'integrated actions' to allow others to reflect collectively on their experiences. An alternative approach to interviewing is being trialled, in which participants first write their own perspective on sustainable futures in the city and we subsequently discuss and examine their reasons and motivations and the choices they made. Systematized spaces – bilateral, internal and external – are being consolidated into a process through which those from different communities within the city region can examine the relationship between values and learning in urban environments. Learning, emancipation and transformation are facilitated through reflexive spaces in which individuals and groups can come to see themselves and their actions in different ways (Fay, 1987).

A number of issues are already emerging in taking our reflexive practices forward. The work requires a recasting of our role into facilitators or 'active intermediaries' (May et al., 2009) of different knowledge claims raising questions not only about our own interests, academic reputations and careers, but also about how we can resist being positioned as legislators, rather as illuminators of contemporary dynamics. The commitment to engage in reflexive thinking has been clearly communicated to participants at the outset and partners within Greater Manchester have already started writing reflexive diaries as well as ourselves; meetings are increasingly reflexive spaces for decision-makers to consider the challenges they are facing and as safe spaces to think through current practice and preconceptions. This raises clear ethical issues as well as highlights limits (Guillemin and Gillam, 2004). At the same time, as the demands of project management, the realpolitik of international collaborations and institutional turmoil in the UK increase, the potential gap between a reflexive design and its practical realization widens. While our experiences provide ample opportunity to remain sceptical as to the success of such a strategy, the aspiration is to contribute to the possibility of knowledge having transformative outcomes in society through collaborative reflexivity that improves collective capacities to act in order to create more just and sustainable futures.

SUMMARY

In this chapter we have examined core elements of a reflexive practice. Through examples from our practice, the movement from endogenous and self-referential to more 'inter-subjective' concerns has been traced as contexts, cultures and conditions for knowledge production transform under contemporary pressures (Beck, in Beck and Beck-Gernsheim, 2002: 212). The environments from which Bourdieu launched his critiques are different from many which the twenty-first-century researcher encounters. A common theme within teleological accounts of the twentieth century relates to how knowledge itself is implicated in redefining the societies and economies in which we live and work.

As modes of knowledge production are changing with researchers involved in collaborative knowledge generation, it is not only the multi-dimensional reflexivity of the researcher that comes into play, but that of all knowledge producers in the process – and of how they interrelate. In our fragmented, fast-speed, time-poor, high-pressured societies, where policy proceeds at a startling pace in the absence of collective learning, collective spaces for reflection are needed even more. As epistemic permeability questions the boundaries between and within disciplines and the social world, the challenge is to design mechanisms for collectively producing knowledge in a reflexive ethos, without collapsing into group therapy, while maintaining concern to contribute to the possibilities of transformation of the world to which we belong.

ACKNOWLEDGEMENTS

We would like to acknowledge our colleagues in SURF as co-participants in the above processes, though the interpretation is our own. We acknowledge the financial support of Mistra (Swedish Environmental Research Foundation) through Mistra Urban Futures, based in Gothenburg, Sweden, the UK Cross-Council Connected Communities programme (Arts and Humanities Research Council (AHRC) and the EPSRC (Engineering and Physical Sciences Research Council)) for funding current programmes of work within SURF. We also acknowledge the support of the ESRC (Economic and Social Research Council) in a number of projects we have conducted over an eight-year period. For further information, please see: www.surf.salford.ac.uk.

FURTHER READING

Mauthner, Natasha S. and Doucet, Andrea (2003) 'Reflexive accounts and accounts of reflexivity in qualitative data analysis', *Sociology*, 37 (3): 413–31.

May, Tim, with Perry, Beth (2011) *Social Research and Reflexivity: Content, Consequences and Context*. London: Sage.

Mruck, Katja and Mey, Günter (2007) 'Grounded theory and reflexivity', in Antony Bryant and Kathy Charmaz (eds), *The SAGE Handbook of Grounded Theory*. London: Sage. pp. 515–38.

REFERENCES

Albrow, Martin (1990) *Max Weber's Construction of Social Theory*. London: Macmillan.

Beck, Ulrich and Beck-Gernsheim, Elisabeth (2002) *Individualization: Institutionalized Individualism and its Social and Political Consequences*. London: Sage.

Beck, Ulrich, Giddens, Anthony and Lash, Scott (1994) *Reflexive Modernization: Politics, Tradition and Aesthetics in the Modern Social Order*. Cambridge: Polity Press.

Bourdieu, Pierre (2000) *Pascalian Meditations*, trans. R. Nice. Cambridge: Polity Press.

Bourdieu, Pierre (2004) *Science of Science and Reflexivity*, trans. R. Nice. Cambridge: Polity Press.

Bourdieu, Pierre (2007) *Sketch for a Self Analysis*, trans. R. Nice (originally published in 2004 as *Esquisse pour une auto-analyse*). Cambridge: Polity Press.

Bourdieu, Pierre (2008) *Political Interventions: Social Science and Political Action*, texts selected and introduced by F. Poupeau and T. Discepolo, trans. D. Fernbach. London: Verso.

Bourdieu, Pierre and Wacquant, Loïc J. (1992) *An Invitation to Reflexive Sociology*. Cambridge: Polity Press.

Castells, Manuel and Hall, Peter (1994) *Technopoles of the World*. London: Routledge.

Cook, Judith and Fonow, Mary (1990) 'Knowledge and women's interests: Issues of epistemology and methodology in sociological research', in Joyce McCarl Nielsen (ed.), *Feminist Research Methods: Exemplary Readings in the Social Sciences*. London: Westview Press. pp. 69–93.

Doucet, Andrea (2008) 'From her side of the Gossamer Wall(s): Reflexivity and relational knowing', *Qualitative Sociology*, 31: 73–87.

Elliott, Heather, Ryan, Joanna and Hollway, Wendy (2011) 'Research encounters, reflexivity and supervision', *International Journal of Social Research Methodology*, (iFirst available), DOI:10.1080/13645579.2011.610157.

England, Kim (1994) 'Getting personal: Reflexivity, positionality and feminist research', *The Professional Geographer*, 46 (1): 80–9.

Fay, Brian (1987) *Critical Social Science: Liberation and its Limits*. Ithaca, NY: Cornell University Press.

Garfinkel, Harold (1967) *Studies in Ethnomethodology*. Englewood Cliffs, New Jersey: Prentice Hall.

Gibbons, Michael, Limoges, Camille, Nowotny, Helga, Schwartzmann, Simon, Scott, Peter and Trow, Martin (1994) *The New Production of Knowledge: The Dynamics of Science and Research in Contemporary Societies*. London: Sage.

Giddens, Anthony (1984) *The Constitution of Society: Outline of the Theory of Structuration*. Cambridge: Polity Press.

Giddens, Anthony (1990) *The Consequences of Modernity*. Cambridge: Polity Press.

Gilbert, Andrew and Sliep, Yvonne (2009) 'Reflexivity in the practice of social action: From self- to inter-relational reflexivity', *South African Journal of Psychology*, 39 (4): 468–79.

Gilligan, Carol, Spencer, Renee, Weinberg, Katherine M. and Bertsch, Tatiana (2005) 'On the listening guide: A voice-centered relational method', in Sharlene N. Hesse-Biber and Patricia Leavy (eds), *Emergent Methods in Social Research*. Thousand Oaks, CA: Sage. pp. 253–60.

Gouldner, Alvin. W. (1971) *The Coming Crisis of Western Sociology*. London: Heinemann.

Guillemin, Marilys and Gillam, Lynn (2004) 'Ethics, reflexivity and ethically important moments in research', *Qualitative Inquiry*, 10 (2): 261–80.

Hall, John R. (1999) *Cultures of Inquiry: From Epistemology to Discourse in Sociohistorical Research*. Cambridge: Cambridge University Press.

Harding, Sandra (1991) *Whose Science? Whose Knowledge? Thinking from Women's Lives*. Milton Keynes: Open University Press.

Hartsock, Nancy C.M. (1987) 'The feminist standpoint: Developing the ground for a specifically feminist historical materialism', in Sandra Harding (ed.), *Feminism and Methodology*. Milton Keynes: Open University Press. pp. 279–301.

ten Have, Paul (2007) *Doing Conversation Analysis: A Practical Guide*, 2nd edition. London: Sage.

Heath, Christian and Hindmarsh, Jon (2002) 'Analysing social interaction: Talk, bodily conduct and the local environment', in Tim May (ed.), *Qualitative Research: An International Guide to Issues in Practice*. London: Sage. pp. 99–121.

Hosking, Diane M. and Pluut, Bettine (2010) '(Re)Constructing reflexivity: A relational constructivist approach', *The Qualitative Report*, 15 (1): 59–75.

Knoblauch, Hubert (2004) 'The future prospects of qualitative research', in Uwe Flick et al. (eds), *A*

Companion to Qualitative Research. London: Sage. pp. 354–8.

Larrabee, Mary. J. (ed.) (1993) An Ethic of Care: Feminist and Interdisciplinary Perspectives. London: Routledge.

Lynch, Michael (2000) 'Against reflexivity as an academic virtue and source of privileged knowledge', Theory, Culture and Society, 17 (3): 26–54.

Mauthner, Natasha S. and Doucet, Andrea (1998) 'Reflections on a voice centered relational method of data analysis: Analysing maternal and domestic voices', in Jane Ribbens and Rosalind Edwards (eds), Feminist Dilemmas in Qualitative Research: Private Lives and Public Texts. London: Sage. pp. 119–44.

Mauthner, Natasha S. and Doucet, Andrea (2003) 'Reflexive accounts and accounts of reflexivity in qualitative data analysis', Sociology, 37 (3): 413–31.

May, Tim (2011) Social Research: Issues, Methods and Process, 4th edition. Maidenhead: Open University Press/McGraw-Hill.

May, Tim, with Perry, Beth (2011) Social Research and Reflexivity: Content, Consequences and Context. London: Sage.

May, Tim and Perry, Beth (eds) (2006) 'Universities in the knowledge economy: Places of expectation/spaces for reflection?', Social Epistemology, 20 (3–4).

May, Tim and Perry, Beth (2011a) 'Urban research in the knowledge economy: Content, context and outlook', Built Environment, 37 (3): 352–68.

May, Tim and Perry, Beth (2011b) 'Contours and conflicts in scale: Science, knowledge and urban development', Local Economy, 26 (8): 715–20.

May, Tim, Perry, Beth, Hodson, Mike and Marvin, Simon (2009) 'Active Intermediaries for Knowledge Exchange: Populating the Missing Middle'. Available at www.surf.salford.ac.uk (accessed 19 April 2013).

McCabe, Janet and Holmes, Dave (2009) 'Reflexivity, critical qualitative research & emancipation: A Foucauldian perspective', Journal of Advanced Nursing, 65 (7): 1518–26.

Mead, George H. (1964) Selected Writings: George Herbert Mead, ed. A.J. Reck. Chicago: University of Chicago Press.

Moustakas, Clark E. (1994) Phenomenological Research Methods. London: Sage.

Mruck, Katja and Mey, Günter (2007) 'Grounded theory and reflexivity', in Antony Bryant and Kathy Charmaz (eds), The SAGE Handbook of Grounded Theory. London: Sage. pp. 515–38.

Outhwaite, William (1986) Understanding Social Life: The Method Called Verstehen, 2nd edition. Lewes: Jean Stroud.

Perry, Beth (ed.) (2006) 'Building science regions and cities', Regions Newsletter, 263.

Perry, Beth (2011) 'Universities and cities: Governance, institutions and mediation', Built Environment, 37 (3): 245–60.

Perry, Beth and May, Tim (2006) 'Round pegs, round holes: The English Science Cities', Parliamentary Brief, December: 43–4.

Perry, Beth and May, Tim (eds) (2007) 'Governance, science policy and regions: Special edition', Regional Studies, 41 (8).

Perry, Beth and May, Tim (2010) 'Taking urban knowledge exchange seriously: Devilish dichotomies and active intermediation', International Journal of Knowledge-Based Development, 1 (1–2): 6–24.

Pillow, Wanda S. (2003) 'Confession, catharsis or cure? Rethinking the uses of reflexivity as methodological power in qualitative research', Qualitative Studies in Education, 16 (2): 175–96.

Schutz, Alfred (1973) 'Problems of interpretative sociology', in Alan Ryan (ed.), The Philosophy of Social Explanation. Oxford: Oxford University Press. pp. 203–19.

Schutz, Alfred (1979) 'Concept and theory formation in the social sciences', in John Bynner and Keith Stribley (eds), Social Research: Principles and Procedures. Milton Keynes: Open University Press. pp. 25–36.

Smith, Dorothy E. (2002) 'Institutional ethnography', in Tim May (ed.), Qualitative Research in Action. London: Sage. pp. 150–61.

Smith, Dorothy E. (2005). Institutional Ethnography: A Sociology for People. Oxford: AltaMira Press.

Wacquant, Loïc, J. (1992) An Invitation to Reflexive Sociology. Cambridge: Polity Press.

Weber, Max (1949) The Methodology of the Social Sciences, ed. E. Shils and H. Finch. Glencoe, IL: Free Press.

Wynne, Brian (1996) 'May the sheep safely graze? A reflexive view of the expert-lay knowledge divide', in Scott Lash et al. (eds), Risk, Environment and Modernity: Towards a New Ecology. London: Sage. pp. 44–83.

Induction, Deduction, Abduction

Jo Reichertz

I have built and rebuilt upon
what is waitin' for the sand on the
*beaches carves many castles on
what has been opened before my time*
Bob Dylan: 11 Outlined Epitaphs

Induction, deduction and also abduction are forms of *logical reasoning* that are used in every type of research (qualitative and quantitative alike). Together with observation, they create the basis of all research. These forms of thinking are not concepts, nor are they methods or tools of data analysis, but means of connecting and generating ideas. Because they represent the intellectual building blocks of research, they are method neutral. Researchers are therefore compelled to take a close look at the logic of the logic of their thought processes – if they are to avoid falling victim to their own scientific common sense.

Contrary to a widely held belief, logic and logical conclusions do not simply fall from the sky. Syllogisms neither apply universally, to every being in the Universe, nor have all humans on Earth always reasoned the same way. What today is known as logical reasoning is, in one respect, the outcome of historical debate, the most important milestones of which are the work of Aristotle, the Port Royal School, Gottlob Frege, and finally the writings of Charles Sanders Peirce. The latter in particular showed logic and logical thinking to be deeply human, rooted in the human constitution, and ultimately arising from human needs.

That being so, this chapter begins by describing the anthropological conditions and historical development of 'good' and creative reasoning and goes on to introduce the different forms of thinking in detail and consider their usefulness to research. It then concludes by showing how induction, deduction and abduction are not separate, unconnected entities, but actually three stages of research.

ANTHROPOLOGICAL PREMISES

It was in the nature of evolution that in the human species instincts either disappeared altogether or relaxed considerably. If animals generally know *what* to do in *which* situation and *how* to do it, when humans find themselves in a particular situation they initially have a wide range of possibilities for action. They face the problem of having to choose which path to take – some also say 'to make a decision' – within this realm of possibility. This therefore initially hinders their action, causing them to pause and mobilize inner physical and mental resources with which to solve their problem of action. The human species has always been the species without inborn solutions, without inborn certainties. Humans have always had to manage more or less without the assistance of nature and its tried and tested solutions. *That is why humans by their very nature are problem-solvers.*

Of course, they never did and still do not manage entirely without some help from nature. Nature has given humans (luckily enough) a series of tools with which to solve, or more appropriately deal with, the problem of the constant 'pressure to make a decision'.

Nature's greatest gift is an inborn ability to *evaluate* existing knowledge in relation to a given problem. Human beings have a 'natural' feeling for the knowledge they possess. This feeling 'tells' them what their knowledge is worth. Humans have a kind of *feeling for knowledge*. Although they may 'feel' what a piece of knowledge is worth, the knowledge feeling (= a feeling of rightness or logicality) is not a feeling like disgust or shame, yet it is just as basal. It tells them whether they only sense something, whether they know something or are certain of something, or whether they find something completely obscure. Without this knowledge feeling, their entire knowledge would mean nothing.

These statements constitute the premises of European anthropology and sociology of knowledge (Gehlen, 1988; Berger and Luckmann, 1991), and they are represented very heavily in American pragmatism. They can also be found in the classical works on the development of communication and the ontogenesis of cognition (see Vygotsky, 1978; Tomasello, 2008).

Above all, these premises are found in the anthropology of Charles Sanders Peirce (Peirce, 1931–1935; see also Paavola, 2005 and Zeman, 1994). It was primarily he who defined the ways and means with which human beings solve or deal with the constant problem of 'What do I do next?' Peirce's main focus is on the forms (which emerge in the course of evolution and are inscribed on the brain) of cognitive thinking, also known as *reasoning habits*, which include: deducing, generalizing, conveying, inferring, inducing, sensing, guessing, recognizing, discovering, etc.

These reasoning habits help humans, in managing their everyday life, to make connections and continue with the tried and tested, or if necessary also to discover something new. When forms of cognitive reasoning stand the test, they turn into habits, becoming established as forms – as formats – of reasoning that can be used to build logical syllogisms. For Peirce, the forms of logical reasoning such as induction, deduction and abduction are not unhistorical inferences valid for their own sake, but rather different and more or less good forms of cognitive thinking, each of which is suited to a specific cognitive situation and specific groups.

FROM INDUCTION TO DEDUCTION AND TO THE ABDUCTIVE TURN

Humanity has developed and explored many ways of acquiring (reliable) knowledge. Particularly for scientists, observing reality is an especially valuable way of doing this, as it offers the best and safest way of arriving at valid statements and theories. For the proponents of empirical research, reason without sense data appears to be blind, and only systematic investigation of the inner and outer world with the aid of the human senses can (so it is believed) shed light on the dark: 'And as for the first, that all general elements are given in perception' (Peirce CP[1] 5.186–, 1905). From perception, if recurring reliably, a rule is then derived to which 'probability' or even 'validity' is ascribed. The manner of reasoning behind it is usually called *induction*, and for a long time it was considered to be the central form of inference for discovering new ideas.

In terms of the history of science, this claim (and hope) of inductionism was rejected very early on. Instead, many researchers (e.g. Popper, 2002; Reichenbach, 1983) relied on empirically based intuition in discovery (logic of discovery) and a strictly empirical–logical process of justification (logic of justification). This 'solution' went hand in hand with a strict division between the logic, or more appropriately the art, of discovery and the logic of justification. Since, by this account, discoveries result from psychological rather than logical factors, the unscientific discovery must be separated from the scientific justification of theories.

From the beginning, qualitative social research vehemently rejected separation of the context of discovery and the context of justification and, in some cases explicitly referring to the work of Peirce, regarded the operation of discovery, namely abduction, as *logic*: 'It must be remembered that abduction, although it is very little hampered by logical rules, nevertheless is logical inference, asserting its conclusion only problematically or conjecturally, it is true, but nevertheless having a perfectly definite logical form' (Peirce CP 5.188–, 1905).

Clearly in reference to Peirce's work on abduction, qualitative social researchers have, in the course of the last four decades, developed, tested and in some cases already canonized new plausibilities for socio-scientific research (methodologies and methods). These new plausibilities have themselves emerged out of the critique of classical standards (see the critique of a purely inductive approach in Gubrium and Holstein, 1997: 34, and Silverman, 2010: 85), and it is also through this criticism that qualitative research found its shape and its self-conception. This type of research, variously referred to as 'qualitative research', 'interpretative paradigm' and 'interpretive social research', claimed as its own the ability to shed (more) light on issues that previously attracted little attention from science or are socially enshrouded (subjective perspectives, latent patterns, or behind the scenes of organizations, for instance) and above all to discover new ideas in a systematic and 'logical' way, in other words by abduction. That is why, for proponents of qualitative social research, the logic of social research is made up of three stages: abduction, deduction and induction.

If there was long a belief within qualitative social research, in part due to formulations to that effect from early grounded theory circles, that induction was *the* fundamental logical operation for finding new theories, since the 1990s hopes have been pinned on abduction alone. Since then, almost all newer textbooks on qualitative social research have come to include a somewhat lengthy chapter on the form and strategic significance of abduction (Flick et al., 2004; Bryant and Charmaz, 2007). Proponents of virtually all qualitative methods are unusually unanimous in claiming abduction as the fundamental operation of their own research programmes (Reichertz, 2003, 2004 and 2010; Schröer and Bidlo, 2011; Eberle, 2011). According to them, only abduction can promise the discovery of truly new knowledge and theories.

DEDUCTION, INDUCTION AND ABDUCTION

If we are now to make a serious attempt, in (qualitative and quantitative) research, to analyse collected data, in other words to typologize them according to particular features and orders of features, the question very soon arises of how we may bring a little order to the chaos of the data. This is only to a very small extent a matter of work organization (sorting of data) and much more a question of how the unmanageable variety of the data may be related to theories: either pre existing or still to be discovered. In this undertaking (following the ideas of Peirce), we may, in ideal terms, distinguish between three procedures, and in what follows I subdivide the second procedure into two subgroups; not because there are fundamental differences between the two, but rather because in this way the difference we have already spoken of between abduction and hypothesis or qualitative induction can be made clearer (for a fuller discussion of this, see Reichertz, 2003, 2010).

Abduction as a Reasoning Habit

Research begins with an unpleasant feeling: the feeling of genuine surprise (see also Nubiola, 2003; 2005; Kruijff, 2005). *Surprise, doubt and anxiety are what make the beginnings of, or more accurately the reasons for, research*: 'Each branch of science begins with a new phenomenon which violates a sort of negative subconscious expectation' (Peirce CP 7.188–, 1901). Other authors also stress how doubt and anxiety drive the search for the new: 'Doubt, accordingly, is the initiator of inquiry. Doubt is not just the absence of belief; rather, it is that state of uncertainty as to what to do next that characterizes the existential situation that we sometimes call "anxiety", at other times simply "frustration"' (Strauss, 1988: 3). Genuine doubt drives research. And *very rarely* scientific research begins with pure *curiosity*.

Research thus does not begin with theories or suppositions we wish to test. Both qualitative and quantitative research rather begin when we are genuinely surprised to find that something is significantly different from what we expect. First comes the surprise that it is not what we expected, then the doubt about whether our old beliefs are still appropriate, and then the anxiety of not knowing what comes and what to do next. This generates the desire for research, the need to investigate reality, so that we can regain a sense of security for our actions.

Research is necessary, then, when old beliefs continually lead to surprises and therefore are of no help – in short, they obstruct rather than permit action. This is when new (socially) created beliefs must be brought into the world. The kind of reasoning that can bring about new beliefs (if we are to follow Peirce) is 'abduction'.[2] Abduction begins when the human actor is taken by surprise, and it ends when the surprise is replaced by understanding and the ability to make predictions (see also Aliseda, 2005).

The starting point for any abduction is empirical data. Scientists interpret the empirical data by de- and recontextualizing it, and in so doing arrive at *new* ideas: 'We turn over our recollections of observed facts; we endeavour so to rearrange them, to a few of them in such new perspective that the unexpected experience shall no longer appear surprising' (Peirce CP 7.36–, 1907). What is really 'new', however, it is only vaguely possible to say (see also Eberle, 2011): whether it is a new combination of old and partly familiar ideas, or the discovery of an idea that has never before existed, initially plays a secondary role for Peirce. The decisive point is that this idea, which in this form is new, explains or explains better something that was previously unexplained or unclear.

In terms of theoretical predisposition, abduction attempts as far as possible to begin its observations without presuppositions and, above all, without theories: 'Abduction makes its start from the facts, without, at the outset, having any particular theory in view, though it is motivated by the feeling that a theory is needed to explain the surprising facts. ... Abduction seeks a theory' (Peirce CP 7.218–, 1903). That is not to say that researchers embark on their work in ignorance or with no knowledge of the specialist literature, but it does mean that they put their knowledge of the world to one side for a moment and do not use it to help them in their observation of the world.

In the course of research, abduction occurs, if it occurs at all, in a kind of 'flash', spontaneously and completely, and it has a lot to do (as Peirce formulates in an often misinterpreted passage of text) with 'guessing': 'Abduction is that kind of operation which suggests a statement in no wise contained in the data from which it sets out. There is a more familiar name for it than abduction; for it is neither more nor less than guessing' (Peirce MS 692. 23–, 1901; see also Peirce, 1929: 268).

Yet abduction is not the product of uninformed guessing or a god-given ability to recognize what is right, *but is rather a matter of absorbing (the greatest possible amount of) environmental data*, which are then (albeit subconsciously) interpreted and used to arrive at a meaningful conclusion. The brain (and William James in particular referred to this repeatedly in his work – see Pape, 2002) stores, metaphorically speaking, all manner of worldly knowledge, its typifications and its extent in the course of human action. These also include the *'petites perceptions'* to which Alfred Schütz, following Leibniz, ascribes a central role for decisions between possible actions. These are the perceptions humans are not aware of, partly because they make such a minor impression and partly because they are so unified that it is no longer possible to tell them apart (see Schütz, 1972). These 'minor perceptions' correspond to Peirce's unconscious perceptions, interpretation of which is the basis of abduction. The 'spirit' or, more moderate, the 'brain' or the consciousness (in the sense of Schütz) then adds a unifying idea to the data. It does this 'by introducing an idea not contained in the data, which gives connections which they would not otherwise have had' (Peirce CP 1.383–, 1890). Only the human 'mind' creates connections in certain (logical) forms, believes it can see similarities and differences, and supposes it can distinguish between cause and effect.

From this perspective, it takes two things to make good research: observation *and* reason. Without the data acquired through observation, the mind is idle. And the mind can and should be prepared to work 'well': 'The clue lies with the relevance of control to the operation of its lumen naturale. We can control the flashes of insight involved in retroduction in so far as we can prepare our minds to receive them through research and discussion' (Ayim, 1974: 41). Or to put it another way: 'Abduction takes place in medias res and is influenced by previous thoughts' (Anderson, 1986: 161). That is why abduction is always *informed* guessing.

The objective of every form of cognitive reasoning is to create firm *beliefs* which help to make us (more) secure in our actions. The quality of the knowledge is measured by its future viability. If abduction helps us to act, then it is good (see also Houser, 2005).

The logical form of creating new ideas is that of *abduction*. Here one has decided (with whatever degree of awareness and for whatever reason) no longer to adhere to the conventional view of things. This way of creating a new 'type' (the relationship of a typical new combination of features) is a creative outcome which engenders a new idea. This kind of association is not obligatory, and is indeed rather risky. Abduction 'proceeds', therefore, from a known quantity (= result) to two unknowns (= rule and case). Abduction is therefore a cerebral process, an intellectual act, a mental leap, that brings together things which one had never associated with one another: *a cognitive logic of discovery*.

Deduction

A second type of data analysis consists in the procedure of *subsumption*. Subsumption proceeds from an already known context of features, that is from a familiar rule (e.g. 'all horses make a clattering noise with their hooves when they run') and seeks to find this general context in the data (e.g. the case in question is a horse), in order to obtain knowledge about the individual case (e.g. the horse in question makes a clattering noise with its hooves). The logical form of this intellectual operation is that of deduction: the single case in question is subordinated to an already known rule. Here a tried and trusted order is applied to the new case. New facts (concerning the ordering of the world) are not experienced in this way. Deductions are therefore tautological, they tell us nothing new. But deductions are not only tautological, they are also truth conveying: if the rule offered for application is valid, then the result of application of the rule is also valid.

Deductions nevertheless only convey the 'truth' contained in the original premise, which ultimately is always a general rule. The 'truth' of deductive reasoning in three steps (i.e. (1) All humans are mortal. (2) Socrates is human. (3) Therefore Socrates is mortal.) is based solely on the truth of the rule that all humans in the real world are mortal.

To what extent the truth of such deductions is dependent on the truth of the premise is shown very clearly in the following, as far as the logical steps are concerned similar, for example: (1) All men are pigs. (2) Peter is a man. (3) Therefore Peter is a pig. The truth of this inference does not ensue from logical reasoning (i.e. by deduction), but purely from the observable fact if Peter actually is a pig.

The general logical form of the deduction (i.e. (1) Y is true for all X. (2) Z is a proper subset of X. (3) Therefore Y is also true for Z.) is the formal description of a truth-conveying inference operation, yet it is essentially made up of tautological transformations of the original premise. This characteristic of deduction can be demonstrated particularly clearly using a deduction from geometry as an example of all forms of mathematical deduction. The example is as follows: (1) Any space having three and only three corners is called a triangle. (2) Space X has three and only three corners. (3) Therefore we call space X a triangle. It is important to stress here that deductions of this kind are nothing more than tautological transformations of definitions that are turned into new statements with the aid of formal logic; these new statements are 'true' if the transformations are made deductively.

It is only in this area of mathematical axiomatics that deduction reliably conveys a truth. *However, deduction only conveys the old, familiar truth; it does not produce a new one.*

By contrast, in the case of empirical premises, that is statements about reality, deductions only convey truths to a very limited extent; and the attempt at the beginning of the twentieth century to apply the propositional logic of mathematics in socio-scientific research is seen as having failed entirely: in the real world, logical deductions put no bread on the table, since empirical data are not logical, but diverse. To what extent formal deductive logic can produce nonsense has been demonstrated many times – but to particularly entertaining effect by Eugène Ionesco and more specifically in his play *Rhinoceros* (Ionesco, 2000).

Quantitative and Qualitative Induction

A third form of data analysis consists of extending, or generalizing, into an order or rule the combinations of features that are found in the data material. *Generalization* (see Maxwell and Chmiel, Chapter 37, this volume) takes the characteristics of a small selection of elements of a specific group to be representative of the characteristics of all elements of that group. The implication inherent in this manner of reasoning is that all the elements of a group have the same features.

To take again an example for illustrating this: I have seen a lot of horses when they are running, and they all make a clattering noise with their hooves. The generic group is 'horses', the subgroup contained within it is 'the horses I have seen running', and the 'same features' are 'the clatter of their hooves'. The generalization is: 'All horses make a clattering noise with their hooves when they run.' This statement is based on many observations of many horses, leading to the conclusion that all horses make a clattering noise with their hooves when they run. Yet that is not necessarily true, since observation was only of many, and not all, horses.

The logical form of this intellectual operation is that of *quantitative induction*. It transfers the quantitative properties of a sample to a totality; it 'extends' the single case into a rule. Quantitative inductions therefore are equally tautological, but not truth conveying. The results of this form of inferencing are merely probable. This example illustrates, in addition to the procedure of quantitative induction, also its shortcomings, since it can lead, as Russell's chicken shows (below), to grave errors and action that, by dint of being dangerous, is wrong.

One particular variant of the inductive processing of data consists of assembling certain qualitative features of the investigated sample in such a way that this combination of features resembles another (that is already available in the repertoire of knowledge of the interacting community) in essential points. In this case one can use the term that already exists for this combination to characterize one's 'own' form. The logical form of this operation is that of qualitative induction. The existence of certain qualitative features in a sample implies the presence of other features. (For example, I can hear a clatter that in many ways sounds like the clatter of hooves. Conclusion: the clatter of hooves comes from horses, so there must be horses nearby.)

The observed case (token) is an instance of a known order (type). To summarize: if quantitative induction makes inferences about a totality from the quantitative properties of a sample, qualitative induction (by contrast) supplements the observed features of a sample with others that are not perceived. It is only in this sense that this form of induction transcends the borders of experience; that is, only the experience of the sample in question. This inference only extends knowledge to the extent that it proceeds from a limited selection to a larger totality. Qualitative induction is not a valid but only a probable form of inference, although it does have the advantage of being possible to operationalize (albeit with difficulty). Qualitative induction is the basis of all scientific procedures that find, in collected data, only new versions of what is already known.

The selected example that reproduces the American saying, 'If you hear the clatter of hooves in Helsinki, think horse not zebra', was deliberately chosen because it makes clear the difficulties with the different forms of induction and abduction and their embeddedness in a situation. When is the conclusion 'horse' justified for the clatter of hooves, and when 'zebra'? Both are qualitative inductions, but they differ in terms of their probability in a particular situation (depending on whether I am in Cape Town or in Helsinki, at the zoo or in a street). This conclusion is nevertheless not an abduction, since it is not necessary to create a new idea to answer the question (who is making the clattering noise?), but to draw on an old one.

However, let us take a closer look at this example and find out something about induction as a reasoning habit: before a person can ask whether the clattering of hooves they are hearing is made by a horse or a zebra, their brain (or they themselves or their consciousness?) must decide or, better, discern what it is they are hearing – in other words, what the rhythmical, hollow sound actually means. Is someone banging two coconut halves together (as in *Monty Python and the Holy Grail*) or is someone hammering, or is it the sound of a hoofed animal running? This decision, which is the product of subconsciously registering and evaluating the features of the acoustic trace of the event (which in difficult cases can be raised into the consciousness), is in logical terms a cognitive improvement, a logical inference from the qualities of an event (certain noises) of a certain, familiar type (clattering of hooves). This induction is qualitative, as recognizing always has the structure of qualitative induction.

It is only when the brain (or the consciousness?) has become aware that the noise is the clatter of hooves that the person asks the next question (usually without experiencing the two as separate processes), namely whether the clatter of hooves is coming from a horse, a donkey, a pony, a foal or a zebra. In this case it is crucially important where the hearer is in the world and in what situation. Are they at the zoo, in a stable, or on a journey through the highlands of Tibet? Do they hear the sound in Helsinki or on the South African steppe or at a research station on the pack ice? In the first case (presuming they are not at the zoo), they will conclude that a horse, in the second a zebra and in the third a radio is responsible for the clattering of hooves.

The first inference, that it is the clatter of hooves, is probably the more complex and difficult, and it can only take place if the person has learned through socialization to recognize the special features of clattering hooves and can distinguish between them and other, similar noises. Once that has been learned, the inference takes place subconsciously, albeit not without reasons. The second inference is likewise of a social nature and requires the reasoner to reflect on the situation and the conditions surrounding it.

Inductive inferences are tenuous, since they are not truth conveying but only more or less probable. A good example of the logical form of an inductive inference and the problems associated with it was provided by Bertrand Russell:

> We know that all these rather crude expectations of uniformity are liable to be misleading. The man who has fed the chicken every day throughout its life at last wrings its neck instead, showing that more refined views as to the uniformity of nature would have been useful to the chicken. ... The mere fact that something has happened a certain number of times causes animals and men to expect that it will happen again. Thus our instincts certainly cause us to believe the sun will rise tomorrow, but we may be in no better a position than the chicken which unexpectedly has its neck wrung. (Russell, 1912: 54ff.)

Russell's chicken, which by inductive inference from its perception (= being fed by the man) derives a rule (the man is good, he will always feed me), has the ultimate certainty for its life, up until shortly before it comes to a bitter end, that the hand that feeds him is well meaning, because this hypothesis has been confirmed day in, day out and without exception.

To sum up: *deduction begins with a valid law and asserts that something will behave in a certain way. Induction observes individual parts of the unique diversity of the world and attempts to determine rules and laws to order its infinite manifestations.* Induction can only hope that the rules ascertained in one limited situation also apply in other contexts. Deduction interprets the world 'from above', from within a system of rules. Induction interprets the world 'from below', still searching for the rules. While deduction has the unresolved problem of the as yet still unproven rule, inductions have the handicap of not being able to consider all the data in their infinite diversity. *Both share the impossibility of creating new knowledge.* The one generalizes what is already known, the other subsumes everything to it. Only abduction, which creates hypotheses and conjectures from the interpretation of perception and ideas, is capable of bringing a new idea to life (for the application of abduction to the process of grounded theory analysis see Thornberg and Charmaz, Chapter 11, this volume).

THE THREE-STAGE LOGIC OF RESEARCH

The three aforementioned reasoning processes do not exist in isolation, each with its own value, they also make sense together – if they take place in a certain order. This practice of employing the three types of reasoning one after the other has proven itself in scientific research, which is why it is possible to talk of a research 'habit' here. Together, the three stages of reasoning form the basic framework of any scientific research – qualitative as well as quantitative (Santaella, 2005: 183; Chauviré, 2005). However, in quantitative research, less attention is paid to the first step, abduction. In an idealized way of speaking the three stages happen in a subsequent order. In the actual research processes they are sometimes mixed (see also Magnani, 2005).

As the first stage of scientific research, abduction searches for a *meaningful rule*, a possibly valid or fitting explanation for some surprising fact, which takes away the surprise by making us understand. The search culminates in a (linguistic) hypothesis. *Once a hypothesis has been found, it is generally followed (both in quantitative and in qualitative research) by several stages of testing.*

Abduction (according to Peirce) needs no justification, but that is not the case for the product of abduction, hypothesis. It can and must be tested, and with the hypothesis so too stands or falls the abduction. Hypotheses bear linguistic witness to non-linguistic logical processes. These hypotheses can be criticized because they can be tested. And they can be tested because they are propositions which are stated, supposed, feared or hoped for.

How can and should such testing be designed? Hypotheses are full of implications which can be derived from them. Attempting to do this and test them as fully as possible marks the beginning of the second major stage of research, the testing phase.

The hypothesis is the link between the discovery phase and the testing phase. The hypothesis says that something will be in the future with a certain probability. It supplies no justification of this statement, but it does offer possibilities for testing it. Systematic testing of the hypothesis takes place in three steps: *first comes the abductively derived hypothesis*, the formulation of a rule in a proposition; *then a prediction is deduced from this rule* and 'verified' or 'falsified' *by means of observation and induction*. Every induction, whether quantitative or qualitative, is thus preceded by a rule, in the broad sense: a theory. From this theory predictions are deduced, and the third stage looks for the facts to confirm the supposition. *Abduction searches for theories, deduction for predictions, induction for facts.*

If the facts prove elusive, the process starts again from the beginning and repeats itself until the facts that 'fit' are found. On these terms, it is possible (following on from Peirce) to develop a *three-stage* research logic of abduction, deduction and induction. If discovery is largely not open to conscious and systematic access, testing takes place according to operationalizable and rule-driven, reason-controlled standards.

Yet, however extensively an abductively derived hypothesis is tested, that is by deducing consequences from it and confirming them by induction, and then repeating the three stages ad infinitum, it is still not possible to achieve certainty as to its validity:

> It must then find confirmation or else shift its footing. Even if it does find confirmations, they are all partial. It still is not standing upon the bedrock of fact. It is walking upon a bog, and can only say, this ground seems to hold for the present. Here I will stay till it begins to give away. Moreover, in all its progress, science vaguely feels that it is only learning a lesson. (Peirce CP 5.589–, 1898)

A single stage on its own, abduction or induction in itself, can provide little certainty. It is for this reason that abduction is only the first part of an empirical research strategy – research must not under any circumstances restrict itself to the separate forms of reasoning. Abduction without testing is meaningless. Abductively derived hypotheses, however, which stubbornly continue to stand the test are much more valid – not because they are 'more true', but because they have proven useful in more situations. Nevertheless, 'I am not standing upon a bedrock, but I am walking upon a bog'. Such research logic intriguingly enough resembles the fallibilism explicitly developed later by Popper (2002) in the knowledge of Peirce's argumentation (see also Chauviré, 2005).

However, there is one error that 'abductionists' are prone to make in their research: they often believe that only true abductions are worth the research effort. This, however, is to confuse an ordinary day in research with a red-letter day. Researchers should not make the mistake of only chasing after abductive 'flashes'. *Everyday scientific research is not always about making new discoveries.* Often (or even usually), researchers will come across an already known order and a theory to explain it. That is why both qualitative induction and abduction are part of entirely routine scientific work. Both complement each other. New research data must constantly be tested to find out if their characteristics correspond adequately to those of existing types (= known theories and concepts). If this is the case, they are ascribed to a theory by qualitative induction – that is everyday research routine. It is only when this assessment concludes that none of the previously known concepts or theories adequately matches the data that abduction comes in. Then it is time to discover something new – and it is a red-letter day for research.

HOW TO RECOGNIZE THE OFFSIDE RULE IN SOCCER

A detailed example can help to explain the peculiarities, capabilities and limitations of all the forms of reasoning addressed here. For this purpose it would have been best to take an example from the concrete work of a social researcher. However, this would have involved presenting the case, its context and data in detail. As the space to do this is not available here, I have taken an example in which the circumstances, context and data are more or less familiar to everyone: soccer.

People virtually everywhere in the world are moved by soccer, and everywhere the game is the subject of sometimes very heated debate. Often, that debate centres on whether a referee's decision was right or wrong. *Offside decisions* are one particularly frequent point of contention – not only because they concern situations that can decide the outcome of a match, but because the rule is not an open book, even to soccer fans. Part of the reason why the offside rule is special is that soccer has rules about behaviour during a challenge for the ball and rules about the position of the players on the pitch.

The thought experiment begins here, and it is every bit *comparable with the everyday practice of social researchers* in that they too are constantly confronted with the problem of (re)-constructing rules in their field of observation. Anyone with *no* or only a *vague knowledge* of the rules of the game who watches a soccer match, either willingly or unwillingly, will see that the man in black, whom they have heard referred to as the referee, frequently blows his whistle loudly during the game. When he blows his whistle, the players stop playing.

If this person is a careful and accurate observer, they will notice after a certain amount of time that the referee always blows his whistle if a particularly rough challenge is made for the ball, a player is down and possibly injured. After the whistle, the ball is given to the team whose player suffered the rough challenge, and the match resumes. That (for anyone with any knowledge of other sports) is still possible to follow.

However, the observer will have difficulty with one particular type of whistle blowing, which occurs when one team is in front of the opponent's goal and play is suddenly interrupted by the whistle, without any rough challenge for the ball taking place beforehand. The observer is surprised and no longer knows what is happening.

If this problem is approached *deductively*, there are various possibilities anyone with a knowledge of other games could attempt in three steps. For example: (1) All players are governed by rules. (2) Soccer is a game. (3) Soccer is also governed by rules. It is also possible to deduce that: (1) All actors in a football match act according to rules. (2) The referee is an actor in the football match. (3) The referee acts according to rules. The chain can then be continued: (1) The referee blows his whistle when a rule is broken. (2) The referee has blown his whistle. (3) A rule has been broken. The deductive reasoner will *not get much further than this*. They will conclude that, on the basis of their deductions, a rule was, or rather must have been, broken during the game, otherwise the referee would not have blown his whistle.

Using *induction*, the observer would take a different approach: they would observe *in exactly which situations* the referee blows his whistle and would see that, when the referee whistles with no rough challenge for the ball preceding it, the referee's assistant raised his flag shortly before the whistle. Once the idea occurs to the observer that the unexpected whistle has something to do with the linesman's flag and they take a closer look, keeping track of the times it happens, they will find that the linesman raised his flag before the referee blew his whistle on each of the observed occasions. And the observer inductively comes to the realization that, whenever the linesman raises his flag, the referee blows his whistle, and, further, the referee always blows his whistle when the linesman raises his flag.

An observer using *abductive* inference would also watch the events on the pitch *very closely*. However, they would also be *looking for a rule* to *explain* the behaviour of the linesman and the referee. If the observer is able to take note of the players' positions at the moment the ball is passed, and realize that the referee blows his whistle whenever a player from the team in possession of the ball is closer to the opponents' goal line than the ball and the second-last opponent when the pass takes place, then the observer has reached this conclusion abductively. *As soon as this rule comes* to mind, *the observer also understands what is happening on the pitch*. This rule is by no means easy to find and can only be understood at second glance, when the observer has understood the point of the game.

Once the observer has arrived at this rule abductively, *they can predict when and why the referee will blow his whistle in future*. And if they too want to play football at some time, they will know how to avoid offside positions. If an observer already knows the offside rule and therefore concludes that a player must be offside if the whistle is blown unexpectedly, they reach that conclusion by qualitative induction. The observer 'recognizes' a case for the rule being applied and, rather than producing anything new, merely recognizes what they have seen as a token of a type.

When the observer has (re)constructed the offside rule, they can predict by deduction the situations in which the referee will whistle again (the referee always whistles when …). This rule can then be operationalized and tested in a small study. The observer watches the match with this rule in mind and checks whether the situation in the game corresponds to the rule every time it occurs. They will quickly find that the first rule applies often, but not always. Sometimes the situation is different – for example, for a throw-in or a goal-kick – and it is different again if the player with the ball takes a direct shot at the goal. All these tests add new information to the initial offside rule and thereby improve it. This continues until such time as observing the game reveals no new surprises. The rule is then complete and could sound like this:

> A player is offside if he is closer to the opponents' goal line than the ball and the second-last defence player. Being in an offside position does not constitute an offence. Similarly, it is not an offence if the offside player receives the ball directly from a goal-kick, throw-in or corner-kick. Players are penalized for being offside if the player is actively involved in play and his team-mate touches or plays the ball. Actively involved means that the player is in active play, interferes with his opponent or gains an advantage from his position. (Official rules of the German Soccer Association)

WHAT IS A GOOD THEORY?

What is a good theory (see Kelle, Chapter 38, this volume)? Before it is possible to answer this question, we have to ask what a good abduction is. Peirce's answer:

> What is a good abduction? … Of course, it must explain the facts. … The question of the goodness of anything is whether that thing fulfils its ends. What, then, is the end of an explanatory hypothesis? Its end is, through subjection to the test of experiment, to lead to the avoidance of all surprise and to the establishment of a habit of positive expectation that shall not be disappointed. (Peirce CP 5.198–, 1905)

From this it follows that a good theory is a theory *that keeps us safe from surprises*, in other words one that explains everything it is important to know for people and their actions. Such a theory is only possible, however, and this is the crux of the matter, if *all* members of a community are safe from surprises. Because 'all' also always refers to those who are born after us, the research process can never come to an end.

Some problems (according to Peirce) are easy to solve, others possibly never. Many questions have already been answered definitively and thus correctly, but it is also the case 'that some finite number of questions, we can never know which ones, will escape getting answered forever' (Peirce CP 8.43–, 1885). Since there is 'nothing to distinguish the answerable questions from the unanswerable ones' (ibid.), researchers have no choice but to test every answer over and over again. Truth is thus not definitive, but provisional. *The attitude of researchers, therefore, must be one of internalized scepticism.*

Just how important Peirce considered 'internalized' systematic doubt to be can be seen from the following anecdote in his writing. In a piece from 1897, Peirce remarks that he has largely been overlooked by scientific critique. Only once had he received praise, albeit originally intended as a reproach: 'It was that a critic said to me that I did not seem to be absolutely sure of my own conclusions' (Peirce CP 1.10–, 1897). A little more doubt in the certainty of its findings would also suit contemporary science.

NOTES

1. As is usual in the Peirce literature, the abbreviation CP refers to the Collected Papers of Peirce (1931–1935). The first figure names the volume. The figures following the full stop refer to the chapter number. I have additionally added the year of origin.
2. In the early days (of the reception) of the notion of 'abduction' there was a widespread misunderstanding of Peirce's position, namely that there are no differences between 'hypothesis' and 'abduction' as forms of inference. From the modern point of view it is beyond question that, up to about 1898, Peirce combined two very different forms of inference under the name of 'hypothesis'. When he became aware of this unclear use of the term, he elaborated a clear distinction between the two procedures in his later philosophy, calling the one operation 'qualitative induction' and the other 'abduction' – later also 'retroduction' (for more details see Reichertz, 2003, 2004 and 2010; also Eco, 1985 and the contributions to Semiotica, 2005, vol. 153).

FURTHER READING

Chauviré, Christiane (2005) 'Peirce, Popper, abduction, and the idea of a logic of discovery', Semiotica, 153: 209–22.
Nubiola, Jaime (2005) 'Abduction or the logic of Surprise', Semiotica, 153: 117–30.
Reichertz, Jo (2010) 'Abduction: The logic of discovery of Grounded Theory', in Antony Bryant and Kathy Charmaz (eds), The SAGE Handbook of Grounded Theory. London: Sage. pp. 214–29.

REFERENCES

Aliseda, Atocha (2005) 'The logic of abduction in the light of Peirce's pragmatism', Semiotica, 153: 363–74.
Anderson, Douglas (1986) 'The evolution of Peirce's concept of abduction', Transactions of the Charles S. Peirce Society, 22: 145–64.
Ayim, Maryann (1974) 'Retroduction: The rational instinct', Transactions of the Charles S. Peirce Society, 10: 34–43.
Berger, Peter and Luckmann, Thomas (1991) The Social Construction of Reality: A Treatise in the Sociology of Knowledge. London: Penguin.
Bryant, Anthony and Charmaz, Kathy (eds) (2007) The SAGE Handbook of Grounded Theory. London: Sage.
Chauviré, Christiane (2005) 'Peirce, Popper, abduction, and the idea of a logic of discovery', Semiotica, 153: 209–22.
Eberle, Thomas S. (2011) 'Abduktion in phänomenologischer Perspektive', in Norbert Schröer and Oliver Bidlo (eds), Die Entdeckung des Neuen. Wiesbaden: VS-Verlag. pp. 21–44.
Eco, Umberto (1985) 'Horns, hooves, insteps', in Umberto Eco and Thomas Sebeok (eds), The Sign of Three. Bloomington, IN: Indiana University Press. pp. 198–220.
Flick, Uwe, Kardorff, Ernst von and Steinke, Ines (eds) (2004) A Companion to Qualitative Research. London: Sage.
Gehlen, Arnold (1988) Man: His Nature and his Place in the World. New York: Columbia University Press.
Gubrium, Jaber and Holstein, James (1997) The New Language of Qualitative Method. New York: Oxford University Press.
Houser, Nathan (2005) 'The scent of truth', Semiotica, 153: 455–66.
Ionesco, Eugene (2000) Rhinoceros. Penguin: London.
Kruijff, Geert-Jan (2005) 'Peirce's late theory of abduction', Semiotica, 153: 431–54.
Magnani, Lorenzo (2005) 'An abductive theory of scientific reasoning', Semiotica, 153: 261–86.
Nubiola, Jaime (2003) 'The abduction of god', in Charles Pearson (ed.), Progress in Peirce Studies: Religious Writings: www.unav.es/users/LumeNaturale.html (accessed 14 June 2013).
Nubiola, Jaime (2005) 'Abduction or the logic of surprise', Semiotica, 153: 117–30.
Paavola, Sami (2005) 'Peircean abduction: Instinct or inference', Semiotica, 153: 131–54.
Pape, Helmut (2002) Der dramatische Reichtum der konkreten Welt. Weilerswist: Velbrück.
Peirce, Charles Sanders (1929) Guessing. The Hound and Horn, 2: 267–82.
Peirce, Charles Sanders (1931–1935) The Collected Papers of Charles S. Peirce, 8 vols. Cambridge, MA: Harvard University Press.
Popper, Karl R. (2002) The Logic of Scientific Discovery. London: Routledge (1st edition 1934).
Reichenbach, Hans (1983) Erfahrung und Prognose. Braunschweig/Wiesbaden: Vieweg (1st edition 1938).
Reichertz, Jo (2003) Die Abduktion in der qualitativen Sozialforschung. Opladen: Leske + Budrich.
Reichertz, Jo (2004) 'Abduction, deduction and induction in qualitative research', in Uwe Flick et al. (eds), A Companion to Qualitative Research. London: Sage. pp. 159–65.
Reichertz, Jo (2010) 'Abduction: The logic of discovery of grounded theory', in Antony Bryant and Kathy Charmaz (eds), The SAGE Handbook of Grounded Theory. London: Sage. pp. 214–29.

Russell, Bertrand (1912) *The Problems of Philosophy*. London: Williams and Norgate.

Santaella, Lucia (2005) 'Abduction: The logic of guessing', *Semiotica*, 153: 175–98.

Schröer, Norbert and Bidlo, Oliver (eds) (2011) *Die Entdeckung des Neuen*. Wiesbaden: VS-Verlag.

Schütz, Alfred (1972) 'Choice and the social science', in Lester Embree (ed.), *Life World and Consciousness*. Evanston, IL: Northwestern University Press. pp. 565–90.

Silverman, David (2010) *Doing Qualitative Research*. London: Sage.

Strauss, Anselm (1988) *Qualitative Analysis in Social Research: Grounded Theory Methodology*. Hagen: Studienbrief der Fernuniversität Hagen.

Tomasello, Michael (2008) *Origins of Human Communication*. Cambridge, MA: MIT Press.

Vygotsky, Lev (1978) *Mind in Society: Development of Higher Psychological Processes*. Cambridge, MA: Harvard University Press.

Zeman, Jay J. (1994) 'Das kreative Objekt in Peirce' Semiotik', in Helmut Pape (ed.), *Kreativität und Logik. Charles S. Peirce und das philosophische Problem des Neuen*. Frankfurt am Main: Suhrkamp. pp. 63–76.

Interpretation and Analysis[1]

Carla Willig

Interpretation is the challenge at the heart of qualitative research. Without interpretation, we cannot make sense of our data. As qualitative researchers, we aim to find out more about people's experiences, their thoughts, feelings and social practices. To achieve this aim, we need to ask questions about their meaning and significance; we need to make connections between different components and aspects of the data in order to increase our understanding. In other words, we need to make the data meaningful through a process of interpretation. This chapter aims to reflect on the process of meaning-making in qualitative research and to offer guidance in relation to the conceptual, practical and ethical dimensions of interpretative practice in qualitative research.

ORIGINS OF INTERPRETATION

Interpretation as a formal, purposeful and self-conscious activity first emerged in the culture of late classical antiquity. Originally, interpretation was concerned with making sense of difficult and/or obscure documents, usually mythical or religious writings such as biblical texts. Sontag (1964/1994: 6) describes this early approach to interpretation as 'respectful' in that it was motivated by a desire to 'reconcile the ancient texts to "modern" demands'. Here, interpretation was about making sure that ancient texts which had been revered and held sacred for a long time continued to play their traditional role within a culture despite the fact that their literal meaning did not make any obvious sense to a contemporary audience. Post-mythic consciousness and the emergence of scientific enlightenment meant that these texts did not speak for themselves anymore; instead, they needed to be interpreted to reveal their deeper, often symbolic, meaning in order to stay relevant. Schmidt (2006: 4) points out that the act of interpretation is based on 'the principle of charity or good will' because any interpretation is based on the assumption that, however nonsensical or obscure a text may appear to be, on some level 'what is written does make sense'. Since ancient times, the art of interpretation, or 'hermeneutics' (see Schmidt, 2006, for an excellent introduction), was practised in a range of disciplines including the interpretation of the law (legal hermeneutics), interpretation of the bible (biblical hermeneutics) and interpretation of the classics (philological hermeneutics). Later on, with the writings of Friedrich Schleiermacher (1768–1834) and Wilhelm Dilthey (1833–1911), interpretation as a generalized human endeavour ('universal hermeneutics') emerged as a concern, suggesting that interpretation happens whenever we try to understand spoken or written language or, indeed, any human acts (see Wernet, Chapter 16, this volume).

APPROACHES TO INTERPRETATION

Although interpretation happens wherever and whenever meaning is made, within the context of this chapter, we are particularly concerned with meaning-making in qualitative research. Most of the data qualitative researchers work with takes the form of written or spoken accounts and even though there are important exceptions to this, here we are primarily concerned with the interpretation of various types of texts. Interpretation is a response to the question 'what does this mean?' and it is concerned with generating a deeper and/or fuller understanding of the meaning(s) contained within an account. Depending on what we are looking for and depending on which aspects of the data we choose to focus our attention on, an interpretation could generate any of the following:

- A better understanding of the author's intended meaning (i.e. a clearer sense of what he or she was trying to express).
- A better understanding of the author's unconscious (i.e. unintended) communication (i.e. an understanding of what may have motivated the author to say what he or she said or did even though he or she may not be aware of this motivation him- or herself).
- A better understanding of the social, political, historical, cultural and/or economic context which made it possible (or indeed necessary) for the author to express what he or she expressed.
- A better understanding of the social and/or psychological functions of what is being expressed (i.e. an insight into what is being achieved, in relation to other people or the self, by what is being expressed).
- A better understanding of what the account may tell us about the nature and quality of a more general concept such as 'human existence', 'social progress' or 'human psychology'.

The fact that very different interpretations of the same material can be generated as a result of asking different questions of and about it suggests that every interpretation is underpinned by assumptions which the interpreter makes about what is important and what is worth paying attention to, as well as what can be known about and through the data. In other words, the type of interpretation we generate depends upon the ontological and epistemological positions we adopt before we start the process of interpretation. It is also shaped by the interpreter's ethical and perhaps also political commitments in that the questions we ask tend to be informed by our wider projects, be they personal, intellectual, social or political in nature (see Willig, 2012, for a fuller discussion of the epistemological bases of qualitative research in psychology).

The process of interpretation can generate quite different types of knowledge, ranging from (apparently) straightforward 'translations' of a surface meaning into a deeper, 'true' meaning, to an elaboration of meanings which adds texture to the original account without replacing it with something more 'true'. Broadly speaking, there are two rather different orientations to the interpretative task. These have been characterized as interpretation driven by 'suspicion' and interpretation driven by 'empathy', respectively (Ricoeur, 1970; see also Langdridge, 2007, for a clear account of the difference between these two).

'SUSPICIOUS' INTERPRETATION

'Suspicious' interpretation aims to reveal hidden truths. It is akin to detective work where clues are interpreted to find out what 'really happened'. Appearances are not taken at face value (hence the reference to 'suspicion') and instead are used as clues which point to a more significant, latent meaning. 'Suspicious' interpretation aims to unmask that which presents itself, to bring out latent meaning which is contained within but not immediately obvious or which is actually obscured by appearances. Psychoanalysis (in its original 'classical' Freudian form) is a good example of the use of 'suspicious' interpretation. The power of this approach to interpretation is that it can render apparently trivial or irrational phenomena (such as acts of forgetting or slips of the tongue) meaningful by going beneath the surface, following their traces right back to their origin and, therefore, discovering their 'true' meaning (see Wernet, Chapter 16, this volume).

'Suspicious' interpretations are theory driven in the sense that to extract deeper meaning from an account, it is necessary to have access to theoretical concepts with which to interrogate the text. Theory provides the lens though which the text is read. A theory-driven interpretation offers a reading which is informed by a set of given concepts whose usefulness and validity are being presupposed. One criticism of 'suspicious' interpretations is that they make the data fit the theory and this means that they can never constitute a genuine test of the theory (e.g. Popper, 1945). However, it could be argued that testing the validity of theories is not the aim of interpretation.

A 'suspicious' approach to interpretation presupposes that the phenomena we encounter (be they accounts, behaviours, symptoms, social practices, historical events or whatever) are merely the surface-level manifestations of underlying processes and structures which generate them. What we encounter, that is to say what appears before us, is not the whole story. In fact, it is only the tip of the iceberg; real understanding can only be gained by looking underneath to find out 'what is really going on'. According to Ricoeur (1983/1996: 152) this approach to interpretation aims 'at demystifying a symbolism by unmasking the unavowed forces that are concealed within it'.

One consequence of this approach to interpretation is that the interpreter occupies the role of the expert who is capable of generating a superior understanding of the phenomenon under investigation. The interpreter who has access to the theories required to decode what presents itself is in a position to gain a better understanding of the account, behaviour or experience than the person who is actually at the centre of it (e.g. the analytic patient, the research participant, the social actor). From this point of view, to experience something or to enact something is not the same as understanding it. That is to say, the patient who experiences a neurotic symptom does not necessarily understand its meaning and origin, the worker who goes on strike does not necessarily understand his or her role in the class struggle, the disaffected teenager does not necessarily understand his or her rebelliousness as a manifestation of a moment of life stage transition, and so on.

'EMPATHIC' INTERPRETATION

This approach to interpretation seeks to elaborate and amplify the meaning which is contained within the material. The interpreter stays with (rather than digs below) what presents itself and focuses on what is manifest (as opposed to that which is hidden). The interpreter attempts to illuminate that which presents itself by paying special attention to its features and qualities, by making connections between them and by noticing patterns and relationships. Looking at the material from different angles, zooming in and out, foregrounding different parts of the whole as well as moving between a focus on parts and a focus on the whole, are all ways in which this type of interpretation seeks to increase understanding.

'Empathic' interpretation requires the interpreter to enter the phenomenon, to get inside it and to try to understand it 'from within' (hence the reference to 'empathy'). This type of interpretation refrains (as much as possible) from importing ideas and concepts from the outside.

'Empathic' interpretations are very much grounded in the data. The aim is to amplify meaning rather than to explain what something 'is really about'. 'Empathic' interpretations do not set out to explain why something occurs or to identify a causal mechanism underpinning the phenomenon.

All this does not mean, though, that 'empathic' interpretation only works with what is explicit in the material that is being interpreted. In other words, there is a difference between conducting an 'empathic' interpretation and simply describing or summarizing what presents itself. One consequence of this is that there can be conflicting empathic interpretations of the same text. After all, interpretation is concerned with clarification, elucidation and understanding. It does seek to add something to the material that is being interpreted, even if that something is implicit in the material itself rather than being brought to bear on it from the outside. For example, an 'empathic' interpretation may involve the elucidation of an absence. Take the example of an account which emphasizes that 'every cloud has a silver lining' and which revolves around the various coping strategies the narrator is using in order to 'stay positive'. Although the narrator has not actually mentioned, explicitly, why she feels the need to 'stay positive' and, by implication, that she is struggling with feeling low, her distress shows itself indirectly through her account's preoccupation with trying to 'stay positive'. Interpretation as amplification of meaning requires that attention is paid to the absent term (the low mood) to which the coping strategies are a response. As such, it does require that we move beyond that which is foregrounded by the narrator, the manifest content which in this case is the positivity. However, interpretation as amplification of meaning does not replace the manifest content with another, more 'real' or 'true', meaning; rather it sheds further light on that which is foregrounded by illuminating the background against which this is set. It is a question of pointing to parts of the picture (perhaps less obvious, somewhat obscured ones) as opposed to introducing entirely new ideas or concepts into it.

This means that although 'empathic' interpretation is not easy and is a skill which needs to be developed and practised, it does not require familiarity with existing theories. In fact, 'empathic' interpretation benefits from being carried out collaboratively, for example when a client and a psychotherapist work together in order to gain a better understanding of the client's thoughts, feelings and actions. This approach to interpretation does not construct an opposition between the one who interprets (the expert) and that which is being interpreted (e.g. the research participants or the client's words); rather, 'empathic' interpretation seeks to generate shared understanding by helping the interpreter to enter the world of the other (e.g. the research participant, the client) and, by doing so, helping the other to notice aspects of their experience which they have not noticed before. It follows that this approach to interpretation 'aims at a re-collection of meaning in its richest, most elevated, most spiritual diversity' (Ricoeur, 1983/1996: 152).

THE RELATIONSHIP BETWEEN 'SUSPICION' AND 'EMPATHY'

The characterizations of the two approaches to interpretation provided above suggest that they are distinct, even opposing, approaches which have little in common. However, this is not necessarily the case. According to Ricoeur, the two approaches to interpretation produce different kinds of knowledge concerned with understanding (generated through 'empathy') and explanation (generated through 'suspicion'), respectively. However, Ricoeur (1983/1996) is quick to point out that neither of the two interpretative positions on its own can generate satisfactory insight and that a combination of the two is required. This is because neither 'a reduction of understanding to empathy' nor 'a reduction of explanation to an abstract combinatory system' will do as the former is based upon the 'romantic illusion of a direct link of congeniality between ... the author and the reader' while the latter presupposes the 'positivist illusion of a textual objectivity closed in upon itself'; instead, Ricoeur argues, what is required is 'a dialectic of understanding and explanation' (1983/1996: 153–4). Indeed, Ricoeur goes as far as 'to define interpretation by this very dialectic of understanding and explanation' (154).

Ricoeur's position is the product of his intensive engagement with the extensive literature in philosophical hermeneutics which has been grappling with the question of what constitutes a 'good interpretation' for a very long time. Philosophers such as Schleiermacher, Dilthey, Husserl, Heidegger and Gadamer, among others, have sought to clarify the meaning and nature of interpretation, and its relationship with and place within the human condition. The challenge which all of these philosophers have faced is to find a way of accepting the subjective nature of the process of attributing meaning to something while acknowledging that interpretations are more than idiosyncratic flights of fancy on the part of the interpreter – that they generate a kind of knowledge which is meaningful and which has some validity in its own right and not just by virtue of its relationship with the interpreter. Solutions offered to this problem range from Husserl's attempt to develop a method which would allow the meaning of things to show themselves uncontaminated by the interpreter's presuppositions and expectations, to Heidegger's turn to ontology whereby what is of interest is the role of meaning-making in human existence rather than the truth value of the products of this activity. In between these two positions, others have tried to specify just how much distance, how much of a reflexive gap, there can (or indeed needs) to be between the subject (i.e. the interpreter) and the object (i.e. the material to be interpreted) of the interpretation to allow some kind of understanding, some actual knowledge, to be generated. The challenge at the heart of interpretation is that to make sense of something, to understand something, we need to adopt a perspective from which to view it and we need to have a relationship with it and ask questions about it. However, this standpoint inevitably shapes how something is seen and, therefore, what can be known about it, thus removing the possibility of an 'objective' or 'neutral' view. This paradoxical dynamic is reflected in the 'hermeneutic circle', which describes how parts of a whole can only be understood on the basis of an understanding of the whole, while the whole itself can only be grasped on the basis of an understanding of the parts. For example, when we read or hear a sentence, we make sense of the meaning of individual words in the light of the meaning of the entire sentence (e.g. there is no way of knowing which meaning to attribute to the word 'blind' without having access to the context in which it is used, e.g. 'Please, draw the blind' versus 'She has been blind from birth'). At the same time, however, if we did not know the meaning of individual words in the first place, we would not be able to develop an understanding of the meaning of the whole sentence. Thus, the hermeneutic circle points to an interdependence between the parts and the whole, with neither of them taking precedence.

Prior knowledge and what we bring with us to the interpretative event play an important role in the process of making sense of something. Indeed, it could be argued that an interpretation tells us more about the interpreter than it does about the material that has been interpreted. However, Gadamer (1991; see also Schmidt, 2006: ch. five) proposes that for any understanding to take place, there needs to be a fusion of the interpreter's and the text's 'horizons' so that in the encounter between the interpreter and the text new insight can be generated. It is the combination of the old (in the form of the interpreter's presuppositions and assumptions which are informed by tradition and received wisdom) and the new (in the form of the text) which makes understanding possible. Ricoeur makes a related point when he says that 'the text … belongs neither to its author nor to its reader' (1983/1991: 74; see also Schmidt, 2006: ch. seven). Rather, the appropriation of the text by the interpreter requires that the interpreter enters the world of the text and makes it his or her own by taking up possibilities inherent within it. However, it is one thing to say that interpretation requires that the interpreter and the text adapt to one another and that both of them are changed by the encounter, but it is quite another thing to claim that the product of this assimilation is valid knowledge. This raises the question of how we evaluate an interpretation. As one would expect, hermeneutic philosophers' views on this question diverge radically, ranging from the position that the application of a correct methodology can generate valid interpretations (Ricoeur) to the view that interpretative truth is an experiential event which occurs when an interpretation's (always partial) truth shines forth and convinces those who encounter it, suggesting that agreement indicates the validity (or truth) of the interpretation (Gadamer). Other views include the position that there is no interpretative 'truth', since meaning itself is the product of a process of discursive construction which relies upon a decentred system of signifiers which only acquire meaning in relation to one another but which do not signify anything 'real' which may exist outside of the system of signifiers (Derrida).

It is clear, then, that how we go about generating interpretations and how we evaluate other people's interpretations depends to a large extent on our views about the nature and purpose of the act of interpretation. Anyone who engages with interpretation as a conscious and purposeful activity needs to think about the epistemological (and, after Heidegger, also the ontological) status of interpretation and to adopt a position in relation to the questions raised above. This is important because it helps us to clarify our relationship with the insights generated by our (and others') interpretations and to use them responsibly and ethically.

ETHICAL CHALLENGES

To interpret another person's experience means claiming to have access to (some of) its underlying meaning. During the act of interpretation the interpreter moves beyond the surface meaning of a description or representation and asks: 'What does it mean?' As a result, the act of interpretation always involves a degree of appropriation; the interpreter processes what he or she sees, hears and/or reads, digests it, metabolizes it and generates something new. Whether this happens in collaboration with the person whose experience is being interpreted (as would be expected in a more 'empathic' reading) or whether it is done from the top down (as would occur during a 'suspicious' reading), something is added to the original material and (part of) that something comes from the interpreter. This means that the interpreter has the power to shape what comes to be known about somebody's experience (see Mertens, Chapter 35, this volume). However, power always carries the risk of being abused and there are circumstances in which the experiences of some (usually less powerful) people are misrepresented by other (usually more powerful) people. For example, much has been written about the power issues raised by psychoanalytic practice where the analyst's expert status together with the patient's distressed and often vulnerable condition can lead to the imposition of meanings upon the patient's experience, meanings which can be unhelpful, inaccurate or even damaging (see Frosh, 1997, and Lomas, 1987, for reviews). At a more overtly political level, the imposition of meanings by ruling elites with the aim of silencing those who challenge their power is another example. Political protest can be interpreted as an expression of mental disturbance leading to the incarceration of political dissidents in asylums, as happened in Soviet Russia and as still happens in some parts of the world today. Similarly, socially undesirable behaviours or behaviours which challenge social norms can, through interpretation, be converted into symptoms of mental ill health and then treated accordingly. Historical examples of this include pathologizing interpretations of female sexuality leading to medical interventions such as clitoridectomy, still widely practised in the United States at the beginning of the twentieth century, and of homosexual desire leading to electroshock treatment and reconditioning schedules for gay men, still widely used in the second half of the twentieth century. It is clear that interpretation can be (ab)used in order to control, oppress or manipulate others. This means that interpretation raises ethical questions including questions about ownership: Does the interpretation belong to those who have generated it or to those whose words and actions have been interpreted? We also need to think about the status of the interpretation – what does it tell us about? Does it tell us something about the nature of the experience that has been interpreted or does it tell us something about those who have produced the interpretation, or perhaps both? We also need to think about the effects of the interpretation – what are its consequences for those who have produced it and for those at the receiving end of it? Once in circulation, does the interpretation change the lives of the people involved in them, and, if so, does it improve or undermine them? Does it change power relations between people or does it reinforce existing relations?

It could be argued that the ethical challenges associated with interpretation in qualitative research are particularly acute where researchers are seeking to generate 'suspicious' interpretations, particularly those which participants themselves would not recognize or agree with. Here, the risk of misrepresenting participants' experiences by imposing theory-driven meanings upon the data is great, and to avoid this risk some would counsel against the application of a 'suspicious' approach to interpretation, preferring a purely 'empathic' approach instead (e.g. Flowers and Langdridge, 2007). However, those who are willing to risk generating 'suspicious' interpretations argue that there is value in digging beneath participants' accounts of their experiences and that to refuse to do so would mean giving up the opportunity to gain a deeper understanding of what motivates people, especially at an unconscious level because taking people's accounts at face value means assuming that people are transparent to themselves and others, and that there is no depth and no mystery to their experiences (Hollway and Jefferson, 2005).

In the remainder of this chapter, we shall review a range of orientations to the use of interpretation which underpin different qualitative research methods, and reflect on their theoretical and ethical implications for the kind of insights these methods can generate. Methods covered in this discussion have been selected in order to capture a wide range of data collection techniques (ranging from the use of written texts to forms of participant observation) and epistemological positions so as to demonstrate the relevance of interpretation across quite different methods.

THE PSYCHOANALYTIC CASE STUDY

The psychoanalytic case study is probably the most obviously interpretative method of analysis in that it offers a reading of a client's clinical material and presentation which aims to make sense of something (a symptom, an unexplained behaviour, an irrational preference or dislike) which has failed to make sense before. A psychoanalytic case study applies concepts and perspectives informed by psychoanalytic theory in order to solve what appears to be a riddle, to unravel a mystery. It translates surface-level manifestations such as unreflected descriptions of experience and non-verbal expressions of emotions into their underlying, deeper meaning and, as a result, transforms a collection of puzzling phenomena into a meaningful account of a person's psychological dynamic, including their developmental history, unconscious desires and defence mechanisms. Through the case study, psychological mechanisms such as distortions, substitutions, condensation and displacements of meaning are identified and exposed as the psyche's ways of disguising the true significance of the person's experience, a significance which is not normally accessible to their own conscious mind. A successful psychoanalytic case study is, therefore, a tribute to the analyst's interpretative skills and ability.

In terms of its approach to interpretation, therefore, the psychoanalytic case study is committed to 'suspicious' interpretation. A psychoanalytic approach to qualitative data analysis presupposes that research participants 'may not know why they experience or feel things in the way that they do' and 'are motivated, largely unconsciously, to disguise the meaning of at least some of their feelings and actions' (Hollway and Jefferson, 2000: 26). Here, participants are unaware of the theoretical orientation of the researchers, their underlying research question(s) and their hypotheses. In the analysis of the data, the participants' words are not taken at face value and attention is paid also to what is not said and to what participants appear to want (or do not want) to come across as saying. The psychoanalytic case study researcher is alert to any evidence, both verbal and non-verbal, which points to unconscious defences and motivations which may be at work in the participant. This means that the psychoanalytic case study's approach to interpretation positions the analyst as the expert who (potentially) has superior skills in accessing the 'true' meaning of the participants' experience. Another important feature of this type of research is the use of the relationship between the researcher and the participant whereby the researcher's own experience of the participant's material and style of presentation provide further data to be interpreted as evidence of transference and counter-transference (see Grant and Crawley, 2002: 4).

PHENOMENOLOGICAL RESEARCH

There are important differences between a variety of phenomenological approaches (see Eberle, Chapter 13, this volume) to qualitative analysis, most particularly in relation to their stance regarding the desirability (and, indeed, the possibility) of producing accurate 'descriptions' of experiential phenomena (see Lopez and Willis, 2004, and Finlay, 2009, for further information about the differences between 'descriptive' and 'interpretative', or 'hermeneutic', phenomenology). However, all forms of phenomenological research are committed to staying very close to the text that is being analysed, ensuring that it is the participant's account (rather than the researcher's theoretical framework or hypotheses) which drives the interpretation. The participant's account is not just the point of departure but also the foundation of the interpretation, and it is constantly revisited throughout the analysis. In phenomenological research, it is the participant's account which 'is privileged as the source for the interpretative activity which occurs' (Eatough and Smith, 2008: 190). Even hermeneutic phenomenological analyses do not import a particular theoretical framework into the data and read the data through its lens. Instead, a hermeneutic approach merely argues that it is impossible to enter a text without adopting some provisional perspective on it, without posing some initial questions about it, and without making some preliminary assumptions about its possible meaning(s). A phenomenological analysis (even a hermeneutically inspired one), however, will always subject its initial understanding of the material to sustained questioning and review, allowing the emerging understanding of the text itself to challenge the researcher's own preliminary assumptions about it. Thus, while the phenomenological researcher accepts that it may have been necessary to adopt a provisional perspective on the text to find a 'way in' to the data, he or she also accepts that once the text has been entered, this initial perspective may prove to be inadequate to making sense of the account and it will then be the account itself which will continue to challenge and shape the researcher's interpretation of it. As such, phenomenological analysis is committed to an 'empathic' approach to interpretation.

DISCOURSE ANALYSIS

Again, there are important differences between versions of discourse analysis (see Willig, Chapter 23, this volume). The most well-known varieties of discourse analysis are probably discursive psychology (e.g. Edwards, 2004; Wiggins and Potter, 2008), Foucauldian discourse analysis (e.g. Parker,

1992; Kendall and Wickham, 1999) and critical discourse analysis (e.g. Wodak and Meyer, 2001; Fairclough, 2010). However, all varieties of discourse analysis share a conceptualization of language as constructive and performative. Here, language does not simply reflect what happens elsewhere (e.g. thoughts and feelings inside a person or objective events that take place in the social world). Instead, language is seen as the medium which actually brings particular versions of events and experiences into being by constructing them in a particular way, for particular purposes, in particular social contexts. From this point of view, language is not a means to an end and it is not a way of accessing what is 'really' of interest to the researcher (such as participants' subjective experiences and their inner worlds, or the social processes they are involved in); instead, it is language itself which is of interest to the researcher. Discourse analytic research is driven by research questions about the capacities and characteristics of language rather than by questions about the participants and their experiences. For example, discourse analysts might want to know what kinds of discourses are used in the construction of illness talk or what kinds of subject positions participants take up when they talk about their attempts to give up smoking. Some versions of discourse analysis (e.g. Foucauldian discourse analysis, or critical discourse analysis) are more concerned with the availability of discursive repertoires and the social, cultural and historical contexts within which particular ways of talking emerge. Other approaches (e.g. discursive psychology) focus on the specific ways in which discursive resources are actually deployed by participants within particular conversations. All forms of discourse analysis, however, are interested in the effects of discourse and in how particular ways of constructing meaning through language enable or prevent, empower or constrain, action.

Discourse analysts do not tend to describe their work as 'interpretation'. They are not interested in any hidden meanings which may be discovered within a text and they are not concerned with foregrounding and amplifying unacknowledged aspects of a text's meaning and significance. Rather, discourse analysts are concerned with how meaning is produced through language in the first place. This means that the analytic work focuses on the deconstruction rather than amplification of meaning. Meaning is removed, stripped away, if you will, rather than added through the process of analysis. And yet, there is interpretation in discourse analysis. This is because discourse analysis is based on a particular understanding of the role of language. It presupposes a particular interpretation of the meaning of language itself, of its function and its position in human experience and action. In discourse analytic research, therefore, interpretation enters the picture at a very early stage, before any actual analysis of data has been conducted. Interpretation sets the scene for the analysis, it shapes the choice of methodology and it informs the questions which the researcher asks of the text. It determines the 'status of the text' in that it dictates what the text is taken to represent and what it can tell us about; namely, the way in which language is used to construct a particular version of reality within a particular context. Discourse analysts, therefore, do not take participants' accounts at face value; instead, they subject them to an analysis driven by a particular theory of language and they generate insights about the function of discourse which those who produced the accounts are unlikely to be aware of or indeed to recognize. In this sense, it could be argued that far from refraining from interpretative activity, discourse analysis could be described as adopting a 'suspicious' approach to interpretation.

GROUNDED THEORY

Grounded theory methodology (see Thornberg and Charmaz, Chapter 11, this volume) seeks to facilitate a process whereby new theories can emerge from data. There are marked differences between grounded theorists in terms of the strategies which they recommend in support of the process of theory generation;

for example, while Glaser (1992) advises against approaching the data with anything other than an open mind, Strauss and Corbin (1990/1998) are much more prescriptive in that they recommend the use of a coding paradigm which directs the researcher's attention to particular features of the data (such as interactional strategies and their consequences). Despite these differences, grounded theorists share an understanding that theory is the goal of research rather than the starting point. To facilitate theory development, grounded theorists attempt to refrain from theory-driven interpretations of their data, preferring instead to take evidence at face value in so far as participants' accounts are not subjected to a 'suspicious' reading. It is assumed that participants mean what they say and say what they mean. In other words, they are treated as witnesses whose accounts provide useful information about social and psychological processes.

Grounded theorists tend to approach their data as a form of evidence of what goes on, either in participants' minds or in their social encounters and practices. Grounded theory methodology does not require the researcher to use a particular theoretical lens through which to read this evidence. The approach to interpretation which informs grounded theory research is, therefore, mainly 'empathic'. However, it is important to acknowledge that an inductively developed grounded theory can inform an increasingly 'suspicious' reading as the research progresses; in addition, constructionist versions of grounded theory (e.g. Charmaz, 2006) also acknowledge the importance of the researcher's subjectivity in shaping the analysis of the data.

ETHNOGRAPHY

Ethnography takes a similar approach in that the ethnographic researcher enters the field with an open mind regarding the nature of the events he or she will encounter there (see Gubrium and Holstein, Chapter 3, this volume). Like the grounded theorist, the ethnographer does have a research question in mind; however, this question is really little more than an acknowledgement of what motivates the researcher to commence the research in the first place rather than a theoretically derived problem statement. The aim of ethnographic research is to obtain an insider view of a particular dimension of people's everyday lives by participating, overtly or covertly, in it for a sustained period of time. There is a theoretical basis to such research in that ethnographic researchers tend to be interested in specific cultural practices and their meanings rather than, for example, being concerned with the quality of individuals' subjective experiences as a phenomenologist might be. As Griffin and Bengry-Howell explain, '[E]thnography focuses on cultural interpretation, and aims to understand the cultural and symbolic aspects of people's actions and the contexts in which those actions occur' (2008: 16). This means that ethnographic research, while being very open as to the precise nature and content of people's actions, does presume that people's actions are not devoid of cultural and symbolic meaning and that such meanings are significant.

Ethnography's theoretical base directs the researcher's attention to certain aspects of the data and it supplies the researcher with sensitizing concepts such as the notion of 'cultural practice' or 'cultural meaning'. However, within these broad assumptions and conceptual tools, the ethnographic researcher is encouraged to approach the data with humility and an attitude of not knowing as he or she is seeking to understand what is going on from the point of view of those who are involved in the action. The ethnographer rejects the role of expert and this means that, although theoretically grounded, ethnographic research aspires to maintain a flexible and reflexive stance (see May and Perry, Chapter 8, this volume), remaining explorative and open to changes in perspective throughout the research. However, there are also more theory-driven approaches to ethnographic research, such as those which seek to test out existing theories in the field (see Maxwell, 2011, for an example and Maxwell and Chmiel, Chapter 2, this volume). Ethnographic research is, therefore, perhaps best placed mid-way between a 'suspicious' and an 'empathic' interpretative position.

ACTION RESEARCH

Action research shares ethnography's respect for the perspectives of its research participants and its rejection of an expert role (see Murray, Chapter 40, this volume). Here, the researcher engages in collaboration with the research participants with the explicit aim of bringing about change in some parts of the latter's everyday lives. The precise nature and direction of this change is not predetermined by the researcher; instead it emerges from consultation with those who will be affected by it. The researcher contributes time and skills, and it is hoped that the researcher's involvement in the process of collectively identifying goals and implementing strategies to reach these goals will allow him or her to develop a better understanding of how social change comes about. Ideally, the action researcher develops a theoretical understanding of (some aspects of) social change as a result of being involved in an action research project. Again, as with grounded theory, it seems that theory generation is the goal of the research rather than its point of departure. However, at the same time we need to acknowledge that action research does rely upon a theoretical base. This can be more or less developed, depending on the researcher's background and theoretical and political commitments. At its most basic level, action research presupposes that the most effective way of bringing about an improvement in people's quality of life is through forms of collective action. It assumes that social practices inform how people experience aspects of their life world, and that these practices need to be modified in order to enhance individuals' well-being. Most action research also presupposes that empowerment of research participants (and, indeed, of people in general) is desirable. It has been acknowledged that action research is 'a value-based practice, underpinned by a commitment to positive social change' (Kagan et al., 2008). Action researchers' definition of what constitutes 'positive social change' tends to involve the redistribution of power in one way or another through empowering those who traditionally have little control over the conditions in which they live and work. At the more theoretical end of the spectrum of action research, there are action researchers who are committed to a sophisticated theoretical framework which equips them with an understanding of the structure of contemporary societies and the place of various social groups within this. For example, feminist or Marxist action researchers will bring with them a fully developed theoretical toolkit which informs the ways in which they understand the people and events they encounter during the action research process. There are, therefore, more and less prescriptive versions of action research, with the former being committed to a 'suspicious' approach to interpretation and the latter adopting a more 'empathic' stance.

NARRATIVE ANALYSIS

Narrative researchers share an interest in the stories people tell about their experiences, and they share a commitment to the idea that people organize and bring meaning to their experiences through constructing narratives (see Esin et al., Chapter 14, this volume). As Murray puts it, narrative allows us 'to define ourselves, to clarify the continuity in our lives and to convey this to others' (2003: 116). Narrative research concerns itself with the content, structure and form of the stories people tell. However, while some narrative research is primarily concerned with the content of the story, other styles of narrative research are particularly interested in the story's structure and form, its internal organization and use of linguistic features (see Smith and Sparkes, 2006, for a review of differences in approach and tensions within the field of narrative inquiry). The former approach is perhaps more psychological in orientation as it seeks to advance the researcher's understanding of the relationship between the stories that are told and the storytellers' subjective experience (e.g. Crossley, 2000; Smith and Sparkes, 2002). This approach to narrative research can be said to be underpinned by a phenomenological curiosity. Other styles of narrative analysis, however, have a more discourse analytic flavour whereby the researcher is interested in the narrative strategies through which particular versions of human experience, and indeed of social reality more generally, are constructed. This type of narrative analysis makes use of similar kinds of theoretically derived conceptual tools as discourse analytic research in its search for evidence of the various discursive strategies which are used in constructing a story and its characters. It could be argued, therefore, that the phenomenologically inflected version of narrative research is less theory driven and, therefore, would need to be placed closer to the 'empathic' interpretative position than the discursive version. However, it is important to acknowledge that all narrative research is based on the theoretical premise that telling stories is fundamental to human experience, and that it is through constructing narratives that people make connections between events and interpret them in a way that creates something that is meaningful (at least to them). This means that all narrative researchers will look for (and find) stories in their data.

THEMATIC ANALYSIS

Thematic analysis refers to the process of identifying themes in the data which capture meaning that is relevant to the research question, and perhaps also to making links between such themes. In this way thematic analysis helps the researcher identify patterns in the data (see Braun and Clarke, 2006). It has been argued (e.g. Boyatzis, 1998; Ryan and Bernard, 2000) that thematic analysis does not, in fact, constitute a method of analysis in itself because the systematic process of extracting themes from data can form a part of a wide range of qualitative approaches to data analysis which differ significantly in terms of their epistemological orientations. This means that, having extracted themes, the researcher still needs to decide what these themes represent; for example, does a theme represent a discursive construction, a thought, a feeling, a psychological mechanism? Does the researcher take the theme at face value, as something that directly reflects the research participant's experience, or does the researcher approach the theme as something which needs to be explained in its own right? Answers to these types of questions will reveal the epistemological and theoretical positions adopted by the researcher, and it is those positions that have implications for the approach to interpretation which is adopted in the study. Thematic analysis can, therefore, underpin both 'empathic' and 'suspicious' interpretations.

CONCLUSION

Every study makes assumptions about the type of knowledge it seeks to produce and it is given direction by the types of questions which it asks of the data. Every study needs to be clear about what 'status' it attributes to the data, that is to say, what it wants the data to tell the researcher about. In this sense, every qualitative study, irrespective of which specific method is used, interprets its data because the data never speaks for itself. It is always processed and interrogated in order to obtain answers to particular questions, to shed light on a particular dimension of human experience and/or to clarify a particular aspect of an experience or a situation. Indeed, Emerson and Frosh (2004) remind us that even apparently practical decisions about which transcription method to use contain theoretical assumptions about which features of discourse are significant and meaningful and will shape the type of reading that can be produced. A study's theoretical orientation, its focus and its procedures in themselves are interpretative. This is why it is so important for researchers to be explicit about their frame of reference and their (personal, theoretical, emotional, conceptual) investments in the research; after all, in one way or another, these will be used to interpret the data.

NOTE

1. Some of this discussion was originally formulated in Carla Willig, *Qualitative Interpretation and Analysis in Psychology* © 2012. Reproduced with the kind permission of Open University Press. All rights reserved.

FURTHER READING

Frosh, Stephen (2007) 'Disintegrating qualitative research', *Theory and Psychology*, 17 (5): 635–53.
Schmidt, Lawrence K. (2006) *Understanding Hermeneutics*. Stocksfield: Acumen.
Willig, Carla (2012) *Qualitative Interpretation and Analysis in Psychology*. Maidenhead: Open University Press/McGraw-Hill.

REFERENCES

Boyatzis, Richard E. (1998) *Transforming Qualitative Information: Thematic Analysis and Code Development*. London: Sage.
Braun, Virginia and Clarke, Victoria (2006) 'Using thematic analysis in psychology', *Qualitative Research in Psychology*, 3: 77–101.
Charmaz, Kathy (2006) *Constructing Grounded Theory*. London: Sage.
Crossley, Michelle (2000) *Introducing Narrative Psychology*. Buckingham: Open University Press.
Eatough, Virginia and Smith, Jonathan A. (2008) 'Interpretative phenomenological analysis', in Carla Willig and Wendy Stainton Rogers (eds), *The SAGE Handbook of Qualitative Research in Psychology*. London: Sage. pp. 179–94.
Edwards, Derek (2004) 'Discursive psychology', in Kristine L. Fitch and Robert F. Sanders (eds), *Handbook of Language and Social Interaction*. Mahwah, NJ: Lawrence Erlbaum. pp. 257–73.
Emerson, Peter and Frosh, Stephen (2004) *Critical Narrative Analysis in Psychology*. London: Palgrave.
Fairclough, Norman (2010) *Critical Discourse Analysis*. Harlow: Pearson.
Finlay, Linda (2009) 'Debating phenomenological research methods', *Phenomenology and Practice*, 3 (1): 6–25.
Flowers, Paul and Langdridge, Darren (2007) 'Offending the other: Deconstructing narratives of deviance and pathology', *British Journal of Social Psychology*, 46: 679–90.
Frosh, Stephen (1997) *For and Against Psychoanalysis*. London: Routledge.
Gadamer, Hans-Georg (1991) *Truth and Method*, 2nd edition, trans. Joel Weinsheimer and Donald G. Marshall. New York: Crossroad.
Glaser, Barney G. (1992) *Emergence vs. Forcing: Basics of Grounded Theory Analysis*. Mill Valley, CA: Sociology Press.
Grant, Jan and Crawley, Jim (2002) *Transference and Projection*. Buckingham: Open University Press.
Griffin, Christine and Bengry-Howell, Andrew (2008) 'Ethnography', in Carla Willig and Wendy Stainton-Rogers (eds), *The SAGE Handbook of Qualitative Research in Psychology*. London: Sage. pp. 15–31.
Hollway, Wendy and Jefferson, Tony (2000) *Doing Qualitative Research Differently. Free Association, Narrative and the Interview Method*. London: Sage.
Hollway, Wendy and Jefferson, Tony (2005) 'Panic and perjury: A psychosocial exploration of agency', *British Journal of Social Psychology*, 44 (2): 147–63.
Kagan, Carolyn, Burton, Mark and Siddiquee, Asiya (2008) 'Action research', in Carla Willig and Wendy Stainton-Rogers (eds), *The SAGE Handbook of Qualitative Research in Psychology*. London: Sage. pp 32–53.
Kendall, Gavin and Wickham, Gary (1999) *Using Foucault's Method*. London: Sage.
Langdridge, Darren (2007) *Phenomenological Psychology: Theory, Research and Method*. Harlow: Pearson.
Lomas, Peter (1987) *The Limits of Interpretation. What's Wrong With Psychoanalysis?* London: Penguin.
Lopez, Kay A. and Willis, Danny G. (2004) 'Descriptive versus interpretive phenomenology: Their contributions to nursing knowledge', *Qualitative Health Research*, 14 (5): 726–35.
Maxwell, Joseph A. (2011) *A Realist Approach for Qualitative Research*. London: Sage.
Murray, Michael (2003) 'Narrative psychology', in Jonathan A. Smith (ed.), *Qualitative Psychology: A Practical Guide to Research*. London: Sage. pp. 257–73.
Parker, Ian (1992) *Discourse Dynamics: Critical Analysis for Social and Individual Psychology*. London: Routledge.

Popper, Karl (1945) *The Open Society and Its Enemies*. London: Routledge & Kegan Paul.

Ricoeur, Paul (1970) *Freud and Philosophy. An Essay on Interpretation*, trans. Denise Savage. New Haven, CT: Yale University Press.

Ricoeur, Paul (1983/1996) 'On interpretation', in Richard Kearney and Mara Rainwater (eds), *The Continental Philosophy Reader*. London: Routledge. pp. 138–55.

Ryan, Gery W. and Bernard, H. Russell (2000) 'Data management and analysis methods', in Norman K. Denzin and Yvonne S. Lincoln (eds), *Handbook of Qualitative Research*, 2nd edition. London: Sage. pp 769–802.

Schmidt, Lawrence K. (2006) *Understanding Hermeneutics*. Stocksfield: Acumen.

Smith, Brett and Sparkes, Andrew C. (2002) 'Men, sport, spinal cord injury, and the construction of coherence: Narrative practice in action', *Qualitative Research*, 2: 143–71.

Smith, Brett and Sparkes, Andrew C. (2006) 'Narrative inquiry in psychology: Exploring the tensions within', *Qualitative Research in Psychology*, 3: 169–92.

Sontag, Susan (1964/1994) 'Against interpretation', in *Against Interpretation*. London: Vintage/Random House.

Strauss, Anselm L. and Corbin, Juliet (1990/1998) *Basics of Qualitative Research: Grounded Theory Procedures and Techniques*, 1st/2nd editions. London: Sage.

Wiggins, Sally and Potter, Jonathan (2008) 'Discursive psychology', in Carla Willig and Wendy Stainton Rogers (eds), *The SAGE Handbook of Qualitative Research in Psychology*. London: Sage. pp 73–90.

Willig, Carla. (2012) 'Perspectives on the epistemological bases for qualitative research', in Harris Cooper (ed.), *The Handbook of Research Methods in Psychology*. Washington, DC: American Psychological Association. pp. 5–21.

Wodak, Ruth and Meyer, Michael (2001) *Methods of Critical Discourse Analysis*. London: Sage.

PART III

Analytic Strategies

Part III turns to issues of how to do analysis of qualitative data. It discusses a range of *analytic strategies* in greater detail in nine chapters. Methods like grounded theory (see Thornberg and Charmaz, Chapter 11) or qualitative content analysis (see Schreier, Chapter 12) and tools (like computer programs – see Gibbs, Chapter 19) that are applied to all sorts of data are presented as approaches. Strategies relevant for specific types of analysis like narrative analysis (see Esin et al., Chapter 14) are discussed. But we also find descriptions of how to analyse culture (see Winter, Chapter 17) or virtual cultures (see Kozinets et al., Chapter 18). Again less specific in their objects of analysis are analytic strategies like phenomenology (see Eberle, Chapter 13), documentary analysis (see Bohnsack, Chapter 15) and hermeneutics (see Wernet, Chapter 16).

Guideline questions as an orientation for writing chapters were the following: What characterizes the approach and what is intended to reach with it? What is the developmental background of the approach? What is an outstanding example of using it? What are the major theoretical background assumptions of the approach? How does one proceed in applying the approach and what are its major practical procedures? What is a recent example of using it? What are the main areas of using the approach? What are the limits and outrange of the approach? What are the new developments and perspectives in this context?

Reading the chapters in Part III should help to answer questions like the following for a study and its method(s): What is the epistemological background of analysing qualitative data with this specific approach? How can data analysis in qualitative research be planned with this specific approach? How can data be prepared for this specific approach – for example, how to transcribe interview data, how to elaborate field notes? What are the steps in applying the selected approach for analysing the data? What characterizes good (and bad) examples of using the approach? What are the main stumbling blocks in using this approach? What are criteria of good practice with this approach of analysing qualitative data? What are the specific ethical issues in analysing qualitative data with this specific approach?

In answering questions like the ones just mentioned, the chapters in this part are meant to contribute to the development of a methodological toolkit for qualitative data analysis so that it becomes clearer how to use which method in a data-sensitive way of analysing empirical material in qualitative studies.

11

Grounded Theory and Theoretical Coding

Robert Thornberg and Kathy Charmaz

BACKGROUND

Grounded theory (GT) is a research approach in which data collection and analysis take place simultaneously. Each part informs the other, in order to construct theories of the phenomenon under study. GT provides rigorous yet flexible guidelines that begin with openly exploring and analysing inductive data and leads to developing a theory grounded in data. Induction starts with 'study of a range of individual cases and extrapolates patterns from them to form a conceptual category' (Charmaz, 2006: 188). Nevertheless, instead of pure induction, the underlying logic of GT actually moves between induction and abduction. Abduction means selecting or constructing a hypothesis that explains a particular empirical case or set of data better than any other candidate hypotheses, as a provisional hypothesis and a worthy candidate for further investigation.

GT was originally developed by sociologists Barney Glaser and Anselm Strauss (1967), and has since then been further developed in different versions, such as Glaserian GT (e.g., Glaser, 1978; 1998; 2005), Straussian GT (Strauss, 1987; later developed in collaboration with and furthered by Corbin, see Corbin and Strauss, 2008; Strauss and Corbin, 1990; 1998), constructivist GT (Bryant, 2002; Charmaz, 2000; 2003; 2006; 2009; Thornberg, 2012; Thornberg and Charmaz, 2012), Clarke's (2003; 2005) postmodern version called situational analysis, and Multi-GT (Goldkuhl and Cronholm, 2010). This chapter emphasizes constructivist GT.

Glaser's intellectual background had focused on rigorous training in quantitative methodology and middle-range theories at Columbia University in New York. He also had studied literature for a year at the University of Paris, and became familiar with the literary analysis method called *explication de text* – a method of careful reading and line-by-line comparisons of text. After his academic training, Glaser continued working at Columbia University under the guidance of Paul F. Lazarsfeld and Robert

K. Merton. In contrast, Strauss studied at the University of Chicago (within the so-called 'Chicago School') where he continued his undergraduate interest in pragmatism and further developed his interests in symbolic interactionism, ethnographic field studies and comparative analysis. At Chicago, the works of John Dewey, Charles S. Peirce, Robert Park, Herbert Blumer and Everett Hughes influenced his thinking (for further reading on Glaser and Strauss's backgrounds, see Morse et al., 2009).

From the beginning, GT had mixed epistemological roots in positivism, pragmatism and symbolic interactionism. Although Glaser and Strauss's GT took a critical stance towards the positivistic mainstream social research of the 1960s, at the same time they incorporated a taken-for-granted vocabulary and discourse of positivism when arguing for the scientific legitimacy of GT. Hence, the original GT as well as Glaserian GT later on have both been challenged for their unproblematic and rather naive realist view of data, that data 'could speak for itself', and the possibility of obtaining objective data 'by looking at many cases on the same phenomenon, when joint collecting and coding data, to correct for bias and make the data objective' (Glaser, 2003: 173; for examples of the critical voices, see Bryant and Charmaz, 2007a; Charmaz, 2000; 2006; Clarke, 2005; Corbin and Strauss, 2008; Olesen, 2007; Thornberg, 2012).

In contrast, Charmaz (1995; 2000; 2003; 2006; 2009) and others (e.g. Bryant, 2002; Mills et al., 2006) have developed and argued for a constructivist version of GT, rooted in pragmatism and relativist epistemology. This position assumes that neither data nor theories are discovered, but researchers construct them as a result of their interactions with their participants and emerging analyses (Charmaz, 2006; 2009; Thornberg and Charmaz, 2012). Researchers and participants co-construct data, and the researchers' socio-cultural settings, academic training and personal worldviews inevitably influence these data (Charmaz, 2009; Mills et al., 2006). This position takes a middle ground between realist and postmodernist positions (Charmaz, 1995) by assuming an 'obdurate reality' while also assuming multiple realities and multiple perspectives on these realities (Bryant and Charmaz, 2007a; Charmaz, 1995; 2009). Social realities are mutually constructed through interaction and may be redefined, and, thus, are somewhat indeterminate.

AIMS OF DOING GT RESEARCH

When doing a GT study, researchers aim to investigate individual and collective actions and social and social psychological processes, such as everyday life in a particular social setting, organizational changes, establishing and maintaining workplace practices, identity transformations, problem-solving processes in social groups, and responding to and coping with life changes. In GT, researchers concentrate on what people do and the meanings they make of their actions and on the situations in which they are involved.

Numerous manuals provide different and more or less rigid guidelines for conducting GT research (e.g. Charmaz, 2003; 2006; Clarke, 2005; Corbin and Strauss, 2008; Glaser, 1978; 1998; Glaser and Strauss, 1967; Strauss and Corbin, 1990; 1998). As constructivist grounded theorists, we view our methodological strategies as flexible guidelines rather than rigid prescriptions (Charmaz, 2006; Thornberg and Charmaz, 2012). Over the decades GT has spawned several related versions and some differ a lot from the original. Bryant and Charmaz (2007b) view GT as a family of methods, in accordance with Ludwig Wittgenstein's concept of *family resemblances*. Thus they view various approaches to GT as including numerous resemblances and similarities between the 'members' of the family, as well as differences and disputes. Charmaz (2010: 11) clarifies the points of convergence between versions of GT as follows:

1. Conduct data collection and analysis simultaneously in an iterative process.
2. Analyse actions and processes rather than themes and structure.
3. Use comparative methods.
4. Draw on data (e.g. narratives and descriptions) in service of developing new conceptual categories.
5. Develop inductive categories through systematic data analysis.
6. Emphasize theory construction rather than description or application of current theories.
7. Engage in theoretical sampling.
8. Search for variation in the studied categories or process.
9. Pursue developing a category rather than covering a specific empirical topic.

DATA GATHERING AND THEORETICAL SAMPLING

Whereas researchers from other traditions first collect all data and then analyse them, grounded theorists gather data and conduct analysis in parallel throughout the entire project (Charmaz, 2000; 2006; Glaser, 1978; 1998; Glaser and Strauss, 1967; Strauss and Corbin, 1990; 1998). GT is not limited to any particular method for gathering data but uses data collection methods that best fit the actual research problem and the ongoing analysis of the data. Thus GT remains open to a range of data collection methods, such as field observations (see Marvasti, Chapter 24, this volume), informal conversations (see Toerien, Chapter 22, this volume), qualitative interviews (see Roulston, Chapter 20, this volume), focus groups (see Barbour, Chapter 21, this volume), documents (see Coffey, Chapter 25, this volume), questionnaires and diaries. In addition to qualitative data, Glaser (1992; 1998; 2008) argues that even quantitative data can be used in GT. Although methods are just tools, the choices of methods have consequences: 'How you collect data affect *which* phenomena you will see, *how, where,* and *when* you will view them, and *what* sense you will make of them' (Charmaz, 2006: 15). Hence, reflexivity (see May and Perry, Chapter 8, this volume), flexibility, focus and the openness for shifting, adding or combining methods during the research project comprise essential aspects of data gathering.

At the outset, the initial choice of method or a combination of methods of data collection depends on the research problem. If, for example, a research team aims to explore a particular social group of high school students' resistance to school rules, they might start with identifying, gaining access to and doing field observations in one or more schools in which disciplinary problems, vandalism and violence occur and students show disinterest in and resistance to school. Nevertheless, questions, clues and incomplete insights might emerge during the research that lead the researchers to choose or construct new data collection methods and to revise earlier ones. In the example above, researchers' analysis of their field notes might lead them to begin conducting qualitative interviews with a particular focus and with a particular subset of students. Thus, the analysis of data evokes insights, hunches, 'Aha!' experiences, or questions that might lead researchers to change or add a new data collection method. Once they have a tentative theoretical category to develop, they focus this interplay between data collection and analysis on obtaining the data to illuminate this category, fill out its properties and define its implications. This process, called *theoretical sampling*, has distinguished GT as an analytic approach in qualitative inquiry.

According to Glaser and Strauss's (1967: 45) original definition, theoretical sampling refers to 'the process of data collection for generating theory whereby the analyst jointly collects, codes, and analyzes his data and decides what data to collect next and where to find them'. It keeps the researchers focused on checking and refining their constructed codes and categories, while simultaneously they avoid becoming overwhelmed and unfocused in data collection and analysis. Theoretical sampling should not be confused with sampling strategies used in other kinds of research, in which sampling decisions occur at the planning phase about who, when, what and where to sample (see Rapley, Chapter 4, this volume). Even in a GT study, researchers have to make such initial sampling decisions (e.g. convenience sampling or purposeful sampling) during the planning phase. For example, if researchers aim to investigate the experiences of living with chronic pain, they might plan to interview about 30 patients with chronic pain. Nevertheless, once researchers begin collecting data, moving between data and analysis 'takes over'. Early leads and ideas from their nascent analyses direct them as to where to go, whom to ask or observe, and what kind of data to collect next. For example, theoretical sampling might lead researchers to revise or add new questions in their interview protocol after constructing a tentative theoretical category, to conduct more interviews with the same or new participants, asking participants to make diary notes, to investigate medical journals, or to conduct field observations in some participants' everyday life.

CODING

Coding is about 'naming segments of data with a label that simultaneously categorizes, summarizes, and accounts for each piece of data' (Charmaz, 2006: 43). Coding begins directly as researchers first gather data for a GT study. Throughout the research project, they engage in this interplay between data collection and coding. By coding, researchers scrutinize and interact with the data as well as ask analytical questions of the data. They create their codes by defining what the data are about. According to constructivist GT (Charmaz, 2000; 2003; 2006), coding consists of at least two phases: *initial coding* and *focused coding*. However, coding is not a linear process, but in order to be sensitive to theoretical possibilities, researchers move back and forth between the different phases of coding, although they do more initial coding at the beginning than at the end of the study.

Initial Coding

When researchers conduct initial coding (also known as *open coding*), they compare data with data; stay close to and remain open to exploring what they interpret is happening in the data; construct and keep their codes short, simple, precise and active; and move quickly but carefully through the data (Charmaz, 2006). To scrutinize and code the data, grounded theorists ask questions: 'What is this data a study of?', 'What category does this incident indicate?', 'What is actually happening in the data?' (Glaser, 1978: 57), 'What is the participant's main concern?' (Glaser, 1998: 140), 'What do the actions and statements in the data take for granted?', 'What process(es) is at issue here? How can I define it?', 'How does this process develop?', 'How does the research participant(s) act and profess to think and feel while involved in this process?', 'What might his or her observed behavior indicate?', 'When, why, and how does the process change and what are its consequences?' (Charmaz, 2006: 51). These analytical questions serve as flexible ways of seeing, not as mechanical applications to search for and define what is happening in the data and to look at the data critically and analytically.

The researcher reads and analyses the data word by word, line by line, paragraph by paragraph, or incident by incident, and might use more than one of these strategies. For example, in her study of suffering, Charmaz (1999) engaged in both line-by-line coding of interviews with her research participants and incident-by-incident coding of interview stories about obtaining medical help during crises. Every code the researcher generates has to fit the data (instead of forcing the data to fit the code), and hence should earn its way into the analysis (Glaser, 1978). Coding helps researchers to see the familiar in a new light; gain distance from their own as well as their participants' taken-for-granted assumptions; avoid forcing data into preconceptions; and to focus further data collection, including the potential of leading the researchers in unforeseen directions.

This careful reading and coding encourages grounded theorists to confirm and saturate their 'emerged' codes and minimize missing important codes or significant details in data (Glaser, 1978). Coding with gerunds (noun forms of verbs) helps the researchers to detect and remain focused on process and action (Charmaz, 2006). Hence, a good rule of thumb to use in a flexible and sensitive way is to seek to label codes with gerunds such as 'avoiding attention', 'becoming sad' and 'giving up future orientation'.

Table 11.1 illustrates an example of line-by-line coding (Thornberg et al., 2013). The excerpt is from an interview with a 17-year-old upper secondary school student who had experienced being bullied as a younger child in school. Note that the authors kept initial codes close to the relevant data and focused on process and action.

Table 11.1 Initial coding

Initial coding	Interview data	
Becoming insecure; self-doubting; loss of self-confidence; thinking bullying depends on wrongness with self; believing bullies' negative image of you; getting bad self-confidence from being bullied; becoming passive out of social fear	Interviewer:	How did the bullying affect you during this period?
	Eric:	I started to feel very insecure. In other words, I started to doubt myself more and more. I lost my self-confidence. I thought there has to be something wrong with me, because otherwise they wouldn't have picked me as a victim. I believed all the stupid things they said about me. So, I really got very bad self-confidence from all the bullying. I really didn't dare to do things I wanted to do when other people were nearby.
Believing of the wrongness with self as a result of being bullied; feeling self-worthlessness; being globally disliked	Interviewer:	The bullying gave you bad self-confidence?
	Eric:	Yes, and it made me believe there was something wrong with me, that I was stupid. I felt worthless, that no one would like to be with me.
	Interviewer:	You said before that you thought they bullied you because there was something wrong with you. Can you tell me more about that?
Being bullied because of being different	Eric:	Because I was a different or a bit odd, I wasn't like them.
The constant message of being nerdish; a sense of not fitting in as a result of being bullied; inferring social deviance of self from the experiences of peer victimization; a lingering sense of being different	Interviewer:	You became bullied because you were different?
	Eric:	Yeah, that was what I was told all the time, that I was a nerd, I wore ugly clothes and stuff like that. But it was only when the bullying started that I began to feel different, that I didn't fit in. I didn't think like that before. But when they started to tease me, push me around, and when I was frozen out all the time, I began to understand that I was different. I can still remember that feeling.
Avoiding bullying	Interviewer:	What did you do when you got bullied at school?
	Eric:	I tried to avoid it.
	Interviewer:	How?
Inhibiting the social presence of self; believing social invisibility prevents bullying; inaction protects self from embarrassment and teasing	Eric:	For example, by not putting my hand up during the lessons, being quiet and not standing out. I thought if I didn't stand out, if they wouldn't notice me, then they wouldn't bully me. If I didn't say or do things when other people were around, nothing embarrassing would happen, no one would tease me.
	Interviewer:	What do you mean?
Standing out leads to more bullying; becoming silent; avoiding attention	Eric:	Well, if I said something, if I tried to take some space, then they would just say, 'We have to put him down! We have to bully him even more!' So, the best thing was to be quiet and not be noticed.

As grounded theorists, we treat our constructed codes as provisional and open to modification and refinement to improve their fit with the data. While coding, we use the *constant comparative method*, which means that we compare data with data, data with code, and code with code, to find similarities and differences (Glaser and Strauss, 1967). Initial coding and constant comparative practices lead to sorting and clustering of initial codes. In turn, sorting and clustering codes might result in revising codes as well as constructions of new, more elaborated codes by merging or combining identical or similar initial codes.

Focused Coding

As a result of doing initial coding, the researcher will eventually 'discover' the most significant or frequent initial codes that make the most analytical sense. In focused coding (also known as *selective coding*), the researcher uses these codes, identified or constructed as focused codes, to sift through large amounts of data (Charmaz, 2000; 2003; 2006). According to Glaser (1978; 1998; 2005), the researcher has to look for, identify and select *one* core category, which refers to the most significant and frequent code that is also related to as many other codes as possible and more than other candidates for the core category. The identified and chosen core category guides further data gathering and coding.

However, seeking one core category can limit the analytic rendering of the data and the theoretical usefulness of the completed report. We have argued earlier that Charmaz (2003; 2006) offers a more sensitive and flexible approach in her guidelines for focused coding: 'The constructivist position of grounded theory is more flexible by being open for more than one significant or frequent initial code in order to conduct this further work. Such openness also means that the researcher continues to determine the adequacy of those codes during the focused coding' (Thornberg and Charmaz, 2012: 48). Researchers still remain sensitive and open to modifying their focused codes and to being surprised by the data.

The study of upper secondary students and university students who had a previous history of being bullied in school (Thornberg et al., 2013) demonstrates this point. During the focused coding, the authors established a limited set of focused codes – codes that had previously been identified and elaborated by carefully comparing and sorting many initial codes. These codes subsequently guided their work. Charmaz (2006) states that focused codes are more directed, selective and conceptual than initial codes. The example in Table 11.2 illustrates a focused coding

Table 11.2 Focused coding

Focused coding	Interview data	
Self-inhibiting	Eric:	For example, by not putting my hand up during the lessons, being quiet and not standing out. I thought if I didn't stand out, if they wouldn't notice me, then they wouldn't bully me. If I didn't say or do things when other people were around, nothing embarrassing would happen, no one would tease me.
	Interviewer:	What do you mean?
	Eric:	Well, if I said something, if I tried to take some space, then they would just say, 'We have to put him down! We have to bully him even more!' So, the best thing was to be quiet and not be noticed.
Self-doubting	Ann:	I felt that there had to be something very wrong with me because everyone picked on me. I felt that I was worthless. I felt that I really must be a boring–, a very boring person because everyone avoided me and because they teased me and because of all things they did to me. I never thought that I didn't want to live anymore. I didn't think that way. I don't think I did. At least I can't recall I did. I just felt that I must be messed up in my head, and that I was much more inferior to the others.

of two interview transcription pieces – the first from the interview with Eric that was exemplified in Table 11.1 and the second from an interview with Ann, a 26-year-old university student.

As can be seen in Table 11.2, focused codes capture and synthesize the main themes in the students' statements. Thornberg et al. (2013) constructed the focused code 'self-inhibiting' through the constant comparison of initial codes like 'becoming passive out of social fear', 'inhibiting the social presence of self', 'believing social invisibility prevents bullying', 'becoming silent', and so on. The focused code 'self-doubting' was first selected among the initial codes as it captured many other initial codes, such as 'becoming insecure' and 'loss of self-confidence', and then merged with another focused code, 'developing self-worthlessness', which captured another set of initial codes, like 'feeling self-worthlessness' and 'getting bad self-confidence from being bullied'. The authors merged these two focused codes as a result of constantly comparing these two codes and the initial codes they captured. Subsequently Thornberg et al. chose the label 'self-doubting' over the label 'developing self-worthlessness', because it incorporated all the initial codes that constituted the new and more elaborated focused code.

When conducting focused coding, grounded theorists explore and decide which codes best capture what they see happening in the data, and raise these codes up to tentative conceptual *categories*. This process means giving these categories conceptual definitions and assessing relationships between them (Charmaz, 2003; 2006). For example, the authors later conceptualized the focused code 'self-inhibition' in Table 11.2 as a category defined as a self-protecting strategy in which bullied students held themselves back in social situations in order to avoid being noticed in hope of avoiding being picked on (Thornberg et al., 2013). To generate and refine categories, researchers have to make many constant comparisons such as: (1) comparing and grouping codes, and comparing codes with emerging categories; (2) comparing different incidents (e.g. social situations, actions, social processes, or interaction patterns); (3) comparing data from the same or similar phenomenon, action or process in different situations and contexts (Thornberg and Charmaz, 2012: 50); (4) comparing different people (their beliefs, situations, actions, accounts or experiences); (5) comparing data from the same individuals at different points in time; (6) comparing specific data with the criteria for the category; and (7) comparing categories in the analysis with other categories (Charmaz, 2003: 101).

Theoretical Coding

According to Glaser (1978), when employing *theoretical coding* researchers analyse how categories and codes constructed from data might relate to each other as hypotheses to be integrated into a theory. To achieve this integration, researchers have to inspect, choose and use *theoretical codes* as analytical tools to organize and conceptualize their own codes and categories with each other to develop a coherent GT (see Glaser, 1978; 1998; 2005). Holton (2007: 283) defines theoretical coding as 'the identification and use of appropriate theoretical codes to achieve an integrated theoretical framework for the overall grounded theory'. What are theoretical codes and how can these be distinguished from the codes and categories that the researchers generate during initial and focused coding?

Initial and focused coding generate data-driven and empirical codes and categories by building on constant comparisons of data, data and codes, and codes and codes. In contrast, theoretical codes consist of ideas and perspectives that researchers import to the research process as analytic tools and lenses from outside, from a range of theories. Theoretical codes refer to underlying logics that could be found in pre-existing theories. They include ideas, terms or abstract models that 'specify

Table 11.3 Examples of Glaser's coding families

Coding families	Theoretical codes
The 'Six C's'	Causes, contexts, contingencies, consequences, covariances and conditions
Process	Phases, progressions, passages, transitions, careers, trajectories, cycling, etc.
Basic family	Basic social process, basic social psychological process, basic social structural condition, etc.
Cultural family	Social norms, social values, social beliefs, etc.
Strategy family	Strategies, tactics, manipulation, dealing with, positioning, dominating, etc.
Degree family	Limit, range, grades, continuum, level, etc.
Type family	Type, kinds, styles, classes, genre, etc.
Dimension family	Dimensions, sector, segment, part, aspect, section, etc.
Identity-self family	Self-image, self-concept, self-worth, self-evaluation, identity, transformations of self, self-realization, etc.
Consensus family	Agreements, contracts, conformity, homogeneity–heterogeneity, conflict, discensus, etc.
Paired opposite family	Ingroup–outgroup, in–out, manifest–latent, explicit–implicit, overt–covert, informal–formal, etc.
Cutting point family	Boundary, cutting point, turning point, breaking point, deviance, etc.

Source: Adapted from Glaser (1978; 1998)

possible relationships between categories you have developed in your focused coding ... [and] may help you tell an analytic story that has coherence' (Charmaz, 2006: 63). Glaser (1998; 2005) argues that studying many theories across different disciplines enables researchers to identify theoretical codes embedded in them, and thus develop and enhance their knowledge base of theoretical codes: 'One reads theories in any field and tries to figure out the theoretical models being used. ... It makes the researcher sensitive to many codes and how they are used' (Glaser, 1998: 164). According to Glaser (2005: 11), the more theoretical codes the researchers learn, the more they have 'the variability of seeing them emerge and fitting them to the theory'. As a guide for researchers, Glaser (1978: 72–82) compiled a list of theoretical codes organized in a typology of *coding families*, to which he then made some later additions (Glaser, 1998: 170–5; 2005: 21–30). In Table 11.3 we present a sample of his coding families.

Whereas Glaser includes many more coding families in his list (1978; 1998; 2005), he acknowledges that his list is not exhaustive. His set of coding families also reveals considerable overlapping (e.g. compare the process family with the basic family or the cutting point family). Furthermore, Charmaz (2006) points out that several coding families are absent from Glaser's list and other coding families appear rather arbitrary and vague. As we have argued elsewhere, instead of being hypnotized by Glaser's list of coding families, researchers should investigate all kinds of extant theories that they encounter in different research disciplines or domains to figure out for themselves their embedded theoretical codes (Thornberg and Charmaz, 2012). Glaser's depiction of theoretical coding amounts to importing theoretical codes consciously. Hence, adopting and applying theoretical codes poses similar risks of preconceiving the analysis that Glaser (1992) accused Strauss and Corbin (1990) of doing. We see the implications of Karen Henwood and

Nick Pidgeon's concept, 'theoretical agnosticism' (2003: 138), as an advance and antidote to applying theoretical codes. They argue that researchers must remain critical of applying theories throughout the research process.

Glaser (1978; 1998; 2005) warns researchers not to get blinded by one theoretical code or forcing a personally preferred theoretical code onto the analysis as an insensitive 'pet code'. A combination of many theoretical codes most often captures the relationships between categories and is therefore typically used when relating and organizing categories and integrating them into a GT. Glaser (1978) argues that theoretical codes must earn their way into the analysis by the work of careful and constant comparisons between theoretical codes, data, empirically generated codes and categories, and memos (see below). Theoretical codes must work, have relevance, and fit the data and generated and refined categories. In their study of former victims' experiences of school bullying, Thornberg et al. (2013) took advantage of many theoretical codes to develop their categories further and to investigate their relations to each other to integrate them into a GT of victimizing of school bullying. Examples of the theoretical codes that Thornberg et al. used during coding that preceded the findings were basic social psychological processes, phases, deviance, strategies, self-transformation and social norms (see also the later memo excerpt and our discussion below). Abduction supplies the main underlying logic in theoretical coding. Researchers explore their knowledge base of theoretical codes and compare them with their data and their own constructed codes and categories. Then they choose (or construct) and use the 'best' theoretical codes as analytical tools to relate categories to each other and integrate them into a GT. Hence, theoretical coding is about abduction, not deduction.

ABDUCTION IN GT

The American pragmatist philosopher Charles S. Peirce first introduced and further developed the concept of abduction (e.g. Peirce 1960; 1979). In order to differentiate between induction, deduction and abduction (see Reichertz, Chapter 9, this volume), Peirce (1960) gave illustrative examples of how to reason and make inferences using beans. We start with his examples of beans but also made some changes and elaborations in order to capture the complexity of abduction as it has been further developed by Peirce and others (e.g., Anderson, 1987; Reichertz, 2007; Schurz, 2008; Walton, 2004). Suppose we enter a backyard and find a sealed bag on the ground. It has a label that says, 'Beans'. As we approach the bag, we detect a very small tear on the left side. Curious about what kind of beans might be in the bag, we lift up the bag and begin to shake it. As a result, a white bean falls from the tear in the bag. Encouraged by this first outcome of our 'data collection', we continue shaking the bag. Every new bean falling out of the bag is white. After a while – 10 beans have now dropped out and all of them are white – we conclude that because every bean we find from the bag is white, it seems to be plausible that all the beans in the bag are white. This is a simple example of induction: from a series of empirical and individual cases, we identify a pattern from which we make a general statement, which of course is probable and provisional. Now, suppose we enter another backyard and find a bag with a label that says, 'Only White Beans'. We know that every bean in this bag is white. A woman suddenly arrives, puts her hand into the bag and then pulls it out without showing us what she is holding. She turns to us and says, 'I have three beans in my hand. As you saw, I took them from this bag. What color are these beans?' Although we cannot see the beans in her hand, we can easily conclude that the three beans are white. This conclusion is a simple example of deduction: we predict what will be or happen in a particular case by applying a general statement or rule.

In order to understand the complexity of abduction, suppose we enter a third backyard. Here we find five bags in a line next to a wall. Bag A only contains white beans, Bag B only contains green beans, Bag C only contains red beans, Bag D only contains brown beans, and Bag E only contains black beans. Four metres in front of the line of bags, we discover three white beans on the ground. Based on these data and our accessible knowledge of Bag A, Bag B, Bag C, Bag D, and Bag E, we infer at once as a probability, or as a fair guess, that the three beans on the ground come from Bag A. On further investigation we discover footsteps on the ground parallel to the lines of bags but four metres in front them. The three white beans are just a few centimetres next to one of these footsteps. In addition, from our further investigations we see that there are no footsteps near the bags, and all the five bags are sealed. Thus, we come up with a new, more plausible hypothesis: the three white beans come from a person who has passed by and accidentally or deliberately dropped the three beans. Fortunately, we know that there are three people in the neighbourhood who happen to love white beans, usually have some in their pocket and eat them like candy. Two of them are children – an 8-year-old girl, and a 10-year-old boy. The third is a very old man, and he happens to have the very same shoe size that you have. We therefore investigate the shoeprints closer, and you put your foot next to one of the shoeprints. It is the same size! We can therefore dismiss the two children and choose the very old man as a reasonable hypothesis: as he was passing by, three white beans happened to fall out of his pocket when he pulled his hand from his pocket during his bean snack. But then we detect a 'surprising fact'. There are no imprints from a stick at the side of the footsteps. This is very puzzling because we know that the old man has a severe knee injury on the left side and always walks with a stick. In the light if this new surprising data, we no longer hold the old-man-who-loves-white-beans hypothesis as plausible (well, if we do not consider the possibility that he recently had undergone a new miracle treatment with an extremely fast-healing process). It is more reasonable that another person (perhaps someone we do not know) passed by and dropped the three white beans. We decide to follow the footsteps in a search for more data.

All these lines of reasoning in order to gain a better understanding of why there are three white beans on the ground are examples of abduction, and, as the example clearly illustrates, their outcomes are always provisional, open for revision in the light of new data as well as better hypotheses or explanations. Abduction means selecting or inventing a hypothesis that explains a particular empirical case or set of data better than any other candidate hypotheses, as a provisional hypothesis and a worthy candidate for further investigation. According to Atkinson et al. (2003: 149), abduction is 'a way of capturing the dialectical shuttling between the domain of observations and the domains of ideas'. Like the fictional detective Sherlock Holmes, a researcher who uses abductive reasoning constantly moves back and forth between data and pre-existing as well as developing knowledge or theories, and makes comparisons and interpretations in the search for patterns and the best possible explanations (Thornberg, 2012):

> Different from the situation of induction, in abduction problems we are confronted with thousands of possible explanatory conjectures (or conclusions) – everyone in the village might be the murderer. The essential function of abduction is their role as *search strategies* which tell us which explanatory conjecture we would set out *first* to further inquiry ... through the explosive *search space* of possible explanatory reasons. (Schurz, 2008: 203–4)

Furthermore, constructivist grounded theorists admit and use the analytical power of the constant interplay between induction (in which they are never *tabula rasa*) and abduction during the whole research process. In contrast to Glaserian GT (Glaser, 1978; 1998) which argues for delaying the literature review in the substantive area of the actual GT study until the analysis is nearly completed, constructivist grounded theorists (e.g. Charmaz, 2006; Thornberg, 2012) as well as many other grounded theorists (e.g. Clarke, 2005; Corbin and Strauss, 2008; Dunne, 2011; Goldkuhl and Cronholm, 2010; Kelle,

2005) take advantage of knowing and using the literature, not for forcing the research into preconceived categories but as multiple possible lenses. As Dey (1993: 63) puts it, 'There is a difference between an open mind and empty head.' Ignoring established theories and research findings in the substantive area implies a loss of knowledge. Instead of running the risk of reinventing the wheel, missing well-known aspects, and coming up with trivial products or repeating others' mistakes, researchers should take advantage of the pre-existing body of related literature to see further (Thornberg, 2012), as 'a dwarf standing on the shoulders of a giant may see further than the giant himself' (Burton, [1638] 2007: 27). The ability to draw good abductive inferences is dependent on the researchers' previous knowledge, rejection of dogmatic beliefs and development of open-mindedness (Kelle, 1995; for a discussion on how to use literature in a non-forcing and data-sensitive way, see Thornberg, 2012).

MEMO WRITING AND SORTING

During their gathering, coding or analysing of data, researchers will raise new questions for which they seek answers as well as having ideas and thoughts about their codes and relationships between codes. Researchers write down these questions and ideas to remember them. Such analytic, conceptual or theoretical notes are called *memos*. According to Glaser (1978: 83), memos are 'the theorizing write-up of ideas about codes and their relationships as they strike the analyst while coding'. Other definitions of memos are: 'the narrated records of a theorist's analytical conversations with him/herself about the research data' (Lempert, 2007: 247); and 'documentation of the researcher's thinking process and theorizing from data' (Thornberg, 2012: 254). By *memo writing*, grounded theorists step back and ask, 'What is going on here?' and 'How can I make sense of it?'

Writing successive memos throughout the research process helps researchers to investigate their codes and categories as well as possible relationships between them, to gain an analytic distance from data and generated codes, to increase the level of abstraction of their ideas, and to build up and maintain 'a storehouse of analytical ideas that can be sorted, ordered and reordered' (Corbin and Strauss, 2008: 120). Memo writing means putting things down on paper, which makes codes, categories, thoughts, reflections and ideas manageable and stimulates further theorizing. It leads the researchers to explore and scrutinize their codes, categories and emerging GT. Thus, memo writing is a prerequisite for theoretical sampling. Memos are about creating an intellectual workplace for the researcher and therefore must be written with complete freedom without worrying about language and grammar. The important thing is 'to record ideas, *get them out*, and the analyst should do so in any kind of language – good, bad or indifferent' (Glaser, 1978: 85). According to Pidgeon and Henwood (1997), the contents of memos are not constrained in any way. Memos can for example include:

- working definitions of codes or categories;
- comparisons between data and between codes and categories;
- identified gaps or vagueness in categories;
- hunches, questions, or conjectures to be checked out and further investigated in the empirical research;
- fresh ideas and newly created concepts;
- comparisons between categories and a range of theoretical codes, and the use of theoretical codes to suggest and investigate possible relations between categories and how categories might be integrated into a modifiable GT;
- comparisons with and links to relevant literature.

As with codes and categories, grounded theorists treats each memo as partial, preliminary and modifiable, open for correction and revision (Charmaz, 2006). Because grounded theorists work with data collection and analysis in parallel, they write memos from the beginning of the research process. Their early memos are often shorter, less conceptualized and filled with analytical questions and hunches. Box 11.1 illustrates an early memo from Thornberg et al.'s (2013) study on former victims' bullying experiences.

Box 11.1   Early Memo Example

Internal Victimizing

There are lots of initial codes from the first interview transcriptions that seem to indicate what could be labelled as *internal victimizing*. As a response to the bullying situation, the targeting students appeared to incorporate the victim-image produced by their classmates in conversations and behaviour directed towards them, and they started to think, feel and act upon this negative image. Examples of initial codes:

- believing bullies' negative image of you;
- feeling self-worthlessness;
- becoming insecure;
- loss of self-confidence;
- blaming oneself for being bullied;
- avoiding attention;
- becoming silent;
- avoiding others;
- inhibiting the social presence of self.

In order to gain a deeper understanding of bullying as a social psychological process as well as the victims' main concerns in these processes, we have to investigate this more complex code, internal victimizing, and the growing set of initial codes that could be associated with internal victimizing:

- What is going on in internal victimizing?
- How can internal victimizing be defined? What are its properties?
- How can internal victimizing be related to bullying and other social situations?
- How can the initial codes that seem to be indicators of initial victimizing be sorted and clustered? Similarities and differences? What is the variation or dimension of internal victimizing?
- What are the victims' main concerns in internal victimizing?
- What are the consequences?

We have to explore this further and search for more examples of internal victimizing by adding more questions about it in the interview guide as well as focusing on it when continuing coding.

As can be seen in Box 11.1, Thornberg et al. took an active, open and critical stance by constructing analytic questions about internal victimizing that they identified in many data segments in the first interview transcriptions. All the questions in the memo above were expressions of the basic question in initial coding: 'What is happening or actually going on here?' By asking these questions, Thornberg et al. formulated hunches and strategies for further data gathering and coding.

Because these codes appeared frequently and significantly in their coding of interview transcriptions, Thornberg et al. identified and constructed internal victimizing and a limited set of clustered and elaborated initial codes (e.g. a sense of not fitting in, self-protecting and self-blaming) from which internal victimizing 'emerged' as focused codes. Thus, the memo above as well as other memos helped Thornberg et al. to shift from initial coding to focused coding. Later on in the GT analytic process, memos become longer, more conceptualized, and more and more like written findings. Box 11.2 is one of the memos that Thornberg et al. (2013) wrote towards the end of their study. The memo begins with a title, 'Self-Protecting', which is the tentative name of the main category in the memo, and provides a definition of this category. Moreover, in the memo the category is explored by relating it to subcategories, represented with their tentative names as subheadings as well as working definitions. Thornberg et al. also conceptualize how self-protecting is an integrated part of internal victimizing and related to the basic social process of victimizing, which consists of an interplay or cycling process between external victimizing and internal victimizing.

During focused coding, researchers use memos to raise focused codes into tentative conceptual categories. They begin a memo with a title, usually the tentative name of the category. Then they devise a working definition for it by comparing this category with data, codes, subcategories and other categories, and by comparing the memo with other memos. During theoretical coding, researchers further compare, sort and integrate their memos. Through *memo sorting*, they explore, create and refine theoretical relationships. They compare categories, search for relationships between categories, and consider how their sorting of memos and integrating of categories into a GT reflect the studied phenomenon. Hence, memo sorting is the key to constructing a GT and writing drafts of papers.

Box 11.2   Example of Memo in the Later Stages of the Research Process

Self-Protecting

Whereas there is a set of subprocesses of internal victimizing that express thinking and feeling responses of bullying (e.g. a sense of not fitting in, self-doubting and self-blaming), there is also an action component of internal victimizing, which is about attempts to protect oneself from bullying or its harmful effects. Even if they could be seen as coping strategies, these self-protecting strategies have to be defined as a component of the internal victimizing because these strategies most often – and in contrast to the victims' intentions or hopes – supported the bullies' agenda and confirmed the socially constructed victim-image of them. These strategies became a part of the social psychological process that manifested and maintained the victims in the victim role. Five different self-protecting strategies were identified in the coding and analysis of the former victims' narratives of their prior bullying experiences.

Self-isolating

The victims actively began to isolate themselves by socially withdrawing and avoiding others in the hope of creating a zone where they were left alone, felt safe and avoided harassment (e.g. 'You were like a loner ... you kind of isolated yourself from the rest of the world ... to avoid meeting the people who bullied you. It was like a safe zone', My, 18 years old). Nevertheless,

(Continued)

(Continued)

this strategy socially confirmed and co-constructed a low-status loner and deviant position and hindered the opportunities of making and maintaining friendship alliances.

Introverting

The victims passed their time wrapped up in their own thoughts and lived in their own inner world, as a way of dealing with and protecting themselves from the suffering of the loneliness and alienation created by social exclusion (other classmates began to avoid and ignore them as a result of bullying) and their own self-isolating strategy (e.g. 'I lived very much in a sort of fantasy world that I had created, not necessarily by choice but more because I had a need, a need for relationships. If I didn't have any relationships outwardly, I had to create an inner world that I could relate to', Daniel, 28 years old).

Social shielding

The victims tried to appear emotionally unconcerned or unaffected in front of the bullies and other peers in order to hide how hurt, sad or upset they had actually become by the bullying (e.g. 'I became cold and hard on the outside, because if you don't show the bullies that you were in fact sad and upset, then they didn't think it was fun anymore, but you were actually terribly sad', John, 21 years old). Nevertheless, social shielding made the harming consequences more or less diffuse or invisible for others, which in turn made it easier for the bullying process to continue.

Turning off emotions

The victims tried to turn off their emotions or feelings in bullying situations ('Every time someone hurt me with their words, I somehow turned myself off. I kind of made myself faraway. I wasn't there. I can't really describe how that feels because I never felt it so much since I turned off those feelings', Daniel, 28 years old). Turning off emotions was a way of protecting self from hurting and negative feelings, but at the same time, it socially diffused the harming consequences of bullying, and hence made it easier for the bullies to continue, in the same way as in the case of social shielding.

Self-inhibiting

The victims held themselves back in social situations. They tried not to stand out or be detected by their peers in social situations in the classroom as well as in other school settings (e.g. 'It was better to be quiet and withdraw than to say or do something wrong so that others might laugh at me', Maria, 26 years old). The main idea behind self-inhibiting was the attempt to be more socially invisible, which they assumed reduced the risk of bullying. At the same time, this strategy made them look like weak, insecure and 'odd' students, and hence confirmed their social role as easy targets of bullying.

These self-protecting strategies of internal victimizing played a significant role in the interplay or cycling process between external victimizing (bullying) and internal victimizing. The findings of self-protecting deepen our understanding of what the interaction patterns of bullying might look like, and about the victims' main concerns in bullying. The presence of self-protecting indicates that victims are not passive receivers but active agents who try to cope with the bullying events as well as the harming effects and negative feelings these evoke.

QUALITY IN GT RESEARCH

A significant question to ask is when to stop collecting and analysing data. The answer is when the study has reached *theoretical saturation*, meaning that gathering fresh data no longer sparks new theoretical insights, nor reveals new properties of the generated GT and its categories or concepts. Questions to ask in order to evaluate theoretical saturation might for example be: Are there any gaps in the GT or in its categories? Are there any vague or underdeveloped definitions? Are we missing some data? Are the findings coherent? Glaser (2001: 191) talks about 'conceptual density' and 'theoretical completeness'. At the same time, a constructed GT is never a fixed endpoint nor an exact portrayal of the reality, but always remains provisional and open to later modification.

To judge the quality (see Barbour, Chapter 34, this volume) of a GT study, researchers as well as readers might use Glaser's (1998: 17) four criteria (workability, relevance, fit and modifiability) and his questions in relation to them: (1) Does the theory *work* to explain relevant behaviour in the substantive area of the research? (2) Does it have *relevance* to the people in the substantive field? (3) Does the theory *fit* the substantive area? (4) Is it readily *modifiable* as new data emerge? In addition, Corbin (Corbin and Strauss, 2008: 305–7) recently added questions to Glaser's criteria that we summarize as: (1) How *applicable/useful* are the findings for policy and practice? (2) Do the findings inform *concepts* or themes rather than remain uninterpreted? (3) Are concepts situated in their *contexts* and thus allow the reader to understand and evaluate them? (4) Does the analysis demonstrate a *logical* flow of ideas or does it contain gaps? (5) Are the concepts given *depth* and *complexity* and show *variation* in findings through providing rich descriptive details and specifying the links between these concepts? (6) Does the study offer a *creative* contribution? (7) Have the researchers shown *sensitivity* towards their participants and data? (8) Have their *memos* successively gained depth and greater abstraction as the research proceeded? Charmaz's (2006) criteria further condense the above questions. Does the completed analysis fulfil the criteria of credibility, originality, resonance, and usefulness?

FURTHER READING

Charmaz, Kathy (2006) *Constructing Grounded Theory.* London: Sage.
Glaser, Barney G. (1978) *Theoretical Sensitivity.* Mill Valley, CA: Sociology Press.
Thornberg, Robert (2012) 'Informed grounded theory', *Scandinavian Journal of Educational Research*, 56 (3): 243–59.

REFERENCES

Anderson, Douglas R. (1987) *Creativity and the Philosophy of C.S. Peirce.* Dordrecht: Martinus Nijhoff.
Atkinson, Paul, Coffey, Amanda and Delamont, Sara (2003) *Key Themes in Qualitative Research.* Walnut Creek, CA: AltaMira Press.
Bryant, Antony (2002) 'Re-grounding grounded theory', *Journal of Information Technology Theory and Application*, 4 (1): 25–42.
Bryant, Antony and Charmaz, Kathy (2007a) 'Grounded theory in historical perspective: An epistemological account', in Antony Bryant and Kathy Charmaz, K. (eds.), *The SAGE Handbook of Grounded Theory.* Los Angeles: Sage. pp. 31–57.
Bryant, Antony and Charmaz, Kathy (2007b) 'Introduction: Grounded theory research: Methods and practices', in Antony Bryant and Kathy Charmaz (eds.), *The SAGE Handbook of Grounded Theory.* Los Angeles: Sage. pp. 1–28.
Burton, Robert ([1638] 2007) *The Anatomy of Melancholy: Vol. 1.* Teddington: Echo Library.
Charmaz, Kathy (1995) 'Between positivism and postmodernism: Implications for methods', *Studies in Symbolic Interaction*, 17: 43–72.
Charmaz, Kathy (1999) 'Stories of suffering: Subjects' tales and research narratives', *Qualitative Health Research*, 9: 369–82.
Charmaz, Kathy (2000) 'Grounded theory: Objectivist and constructivist methods', in Norman K. Denzin and Yvonna S. Lincoln (eds.), *Handbook of Qualitative Research*, 2nd edition. Thousand Oaks, CA: Sage. pp. 509–35.

Charmaz, Kathy (2003) 'Grounded theory', in Jonathan A. Smith (ed.), *Qualitative Psychology: A Practical Guide to Research Methods*. London: Sage. pp. 81–110.

Charmaz, Kathy (2006) *Constructing Grounded Theory*. London: Sage.

Charmaz, Kathy (2009) 'Shifting the grounds: Constructivist grounded theory methods', in Janice M. Morse et al. (eds.), *Developing Grounded Theory: The Second Generation*. Walnut Creek: Left Coast Press. pp. 127–54.

Charmaz, Kathy (2010) 'Studying the experience of chronic illness through grounded theory,' in Graham Scambler and Sasha Scambler (eds.), *Assaults on the Lifeworld: New Directions in the Sociology of Chronic and Disabling Conditions*. London: Palgrave. pp. 8–36.

Clarke, Adele E. (2003) 'Situational analyses: Grounded theory mapping after the postmodern turn', *Symbolic Interaction*, 26 (4): 553–76.

Clarke, Adele E. (2005) *Situational Analysis: Grounded Theory After the Postmodern Turn*. Thousand Oaks, CA: Sage.

Corbin, Juliet and Strauss, Anselm (2008) *Basics of Qualitative Research: Techniques and Procedures for Developing Grounded Theory*, 3rd edition. Los Angeles: Sage.

Dey, Ian (1993) *Qualitative Data Analysis*. London: Routledge.

Dunne, C. (2011) 'The place of literature review in grounded theory research', *International Journal of Social Research Methodology*, 14 (2): 111–24.

Glaser, Barney G. (1978) *Theoretical Sensitivity*. Mill Valley, CA: Sociology Press.

Glaser, Barney, G. (1992) *Basics of Grounded Theory Analysis*. Mill Valley, CA: Sociology Press.

Glaser, Barney G. (1998) *Doing Grounded Theory: Issues and Discussions*. Mill Valley, CA: Sociology Press.

Glaser, Barney G. (2001) *The Grounded Theory Perspective I: Conceptualization Contrasted with Description*. Mill Valley, CA: Sociology Press.

Glaser, Barney G. (2003) *The Grounded Theory Perspective II: Description's Remodeling of Grounded Theory Methodology*. Mill Valley, CA: Sociology Press.

Glaser, Barney G. (2005) *The Grounded Theory Perspective III: Theoretical Coding*. Mill Valley, CA: Sociology Press.

Glaser, Barney G. (2008) *Doing Quantitative Grounded Theory*. Mill Valley, CA: Sociology Press.

Glaser, Barney G. and Strauss, Anselm L. (1967) *The discovery of Grounded Theory*. Chicago: Aldine.

Goldkuhl, Göran and Cronholm, Stefan (2010) 'Adding theoretical grounding to grounded theory: Toward multi-grounded theory', *International Journal of Qualitative Methods*, 9 (2): 187–205.

Henwood, Karen and Pidgeon, Nick (2003) 'Grounded theory in psychological research', in Paul M. Camic et al. (eds.), *Qualitative Research in Psychology: Expanding Perspectives in Methodology and Design*. Washington, DC: American Psychological Association. pp. 131–55.

Holton, Judith A. (2007) 'The coding process and its challenges', in Antony Bryant and Kathy Charmaz (eds.), *The SAGE Handbook of Grounded Theory*. Los Angeles: Sage. pp. 265–89.

Kelle, Udo (1995) 'Theories as heuristic tools in qualitative research', in Ilja Maso et al. (eds.), *Openness in Research: The Tension between Self and Other*. Assen: van Gorcum. pp. 33–50.

Kelle, Udo (2005) '"Emergence" vs. "forcing" of empirical data? A crucial problem of "grounded theory" reconsidered', *Forum: Qualitative Social Research*, 6 (2), Art. 27: http://nbn-resolving.de/urn:nbn:de:0114-fqs0502275 (accessed 2 May 2013).

Lempert, Lora B. (2007) 'Asking questions of the data: Memo writing in the grounded theory tradition', in Antony Bryant and Kathy Charmaz (eds.), *The SAGE Handbook of Grounded Theory*. Los Angeles: Sage. pp. 245–64.

Mills, Jane, Bonner, Ann and Francis, Karen (2006) 'The development of constructivist grounded theory', *International Journal of Qualitative Methods*, 5 (1): 25–35.

Morse, Janice M., Stern, Phyllis N., Corbin, Juliet, Bowers, Barbara, Charmaz, Kathy and Clarke, Adele E. (2009) *Developing Grounded Theory: The Second Generation*. Walnut Creek: Left Coast Press.

Olesen, Virginia L. (2007) 'Feminist qualitative research and Grounded Theory', in Antony Bryant and Kathy Charmaz (eds.), *The SAGE Handbook of Grounded Theory*. Los Angeles: Sage. pp. 417–35.

Peirce, Charles S. (1960) *Collected Papers of Charles Sanders Peirce. Vol. I: Principles of Philosophy; Vol. II: Elements of Logic*, ed. A.W. Burks. Cambridge, MA: Harvard University Press.

Peirce, Charles S. (1979) *Collected Papers of Charles Sanders Peirce. Vol. VII: Science and Philosophy*, ed. A.W. Burks. Cambridge, MA: Harvard University Press.

Pidgeon, Nick and Henwood, Karen (1997) 'Grounded theory: Practical implementation', in John T. E. Richardson (ed.), *Handbook of Qualitative Research Methods for Psychology and the Social Sciences*. Leicester: The British Psychological Society. pp. 86–101.

Reichertz, Jo (2007) 'Abduction: The logic of discovery of grounded theory', in Antony Bryant and Kathy Charmaz (eds.), *The SAGE Handbook of Grounded Theory*. Los Angeles: Sage. pp. 214–28.

Schurz, Gerhard (2008) 'Patterns of abduction', *Synthese*, 164 (2): 201–34.
Strauss, Anselm (1987) *Qualitative Analysis for Social Scientists*. Cambridge: Cambridge University Press.
Strauss, Anselm and Corbin, Juliet (1990) *Basics of Qualitative Research*. Newbury Park, CA: Sage.
Strauss, Anselm and Corbin, Juliet (1998) *Basics of Qualitative Research*, 2nd edition. Thousand Oaks, CA: Sage.
Thornberg, Robert (2012) 'Informed grounded theory', *Scandinavian Journal of Educational Research*, 56 (3), 243–59.
Thornberg, Robert and Charmaz, Kathy (2012) 'Grounded theory', in Stephen D. Lapan et al. (eds.), *Qualitative Research: An Introduction to Methods and Designs*. San Francisco: Wiley/Jossey-Bass. pp. 41–67.
Thornberg, Robert, Halldin, Karolina, Bolmjsö, Natalie and Petersson, Annelie (2013) 'Victimising of school bullying: A grounded theory', *Research Papers in Education*, 28 (3): 309–329.
Walton, Douglas (2004) *Abductive Reasoning*. Tuscaloosa: The University of Alabama Press.

Qualitative Content Analysis

Margrit Schreier

WHAT IS QUALITATIVE CONTENT ANALYSIS?

Qualitative content analysis is a method for systematically describing the meaning of qualitative data (Mayring, 2000; Schreier, 2012). This is done by assigning successive parts of the material to the categories of a coding frame. This frame is at the heart of the method, and it contains all those aspects that feature in the description and interpretation (see Willig, Chapter 10, this volume) of the material. Three features characterize the method: qualitative content analysis reduces data, it is systematic, and it is flexible.

Unlike other qualitative methods for data analysis which open up (and sometimes add to) data, qualitative content analysis helps with reducing the amount of material. It requires the researcher to focus on selected aspects of meaning, namely those aspects that relate to the overall research question. There can be many such aspects – some coding frames contain well over 100 categories and subcategories – but ultimately the number of aspects is limited by the number of categories a researcher can handle. Also, when defining the categories, one will usually go beyond the specifics of any particular passage. Instead, the meaning of the passage will be taken to a higher level of abstraction, resulting in categories that apply to a number of concrete, slightly different passages. McDonald et al. (2009), for example, analysed the reports of people who had a spiritual experience in a wilderness setting. One participant wrote about seeing the sun set, a second wrote about the expanse of a glacier, and a third emphasized the sense of calm that she experienced in a fjord. When analysing these descriptions, the authors did not create separate categories for sunsets, glaciers and the calmness of fjords, but they created one overarching category of 'aesthetic experience' that covered all these descriptions and more. On the one hand, abstracting from the specifics of a given passage invariably results in the loss of concrete information. On the other hand, one gains a sense of how different parts of the material compare and relate to each other.

A second key feature of qualitative content analysis is that it is highly systematic. To start with, the method requires the examination of every single part of the material that is in any way relevant to the research question. In this way, the method counteracts the danger of looking at the material only through the lens of one's assumptions and expectations. The method is also systematic in that it requires a certain sequence of steps, regardless of the exact research question and material. As is often the case in qualitative research, this may be an iterative process, going through some of these steps repeatedly, modifying the coding frame in the process. But the steps and their sequence remain the same. The method is also systematic in that it requires coding (i.e. assigning segments of the material to the categories of the coding frame) to be carried out twice (double coding), at least for parts of the material. This is a test of the quality of the category definitions: they should be so clear and unambiguous that the second coding yields results that are very similar to those of the first coding (see in detail below).

A third key feature of qualitative content analysis – especially by comparison with the quantitative version (Krippendorff, 2004; Neuendorf, 2002) – is its flexibility. Qualitative content analysis typically combines varying portions of concept-driven and data-driven categories within any one coding frame. At the same time, a part of the categories should always be data-driven. This is to make sure that the categories in fact match the data – or, to put it differently, that the coding frame provides a valid description of the material. Qualitative content analysis is therefore flexible in that the coding frame should always be matched to the material.

WHAT ARE THE ORIGINS OF QUALITATIVE CONTENT ANALYSIS?

The Emergence of Qualitative Content Analysis

Qualitative content analysis developed out of the quantitative version of the method (on the history of content analysis, see Krippendorff, 2004: ch. 1; Schreier, 2012: ch. 1). This originated in the first half of the twentieth century, in the context of a broadening media landscape and a concomitant interest in media effects research, as well as the Second World War and the related interest of the US government in the analysis of propaganda issued in Nazi Germany.

In 1941, a conference on mass communication with a focus on content analysis was held in Chicago and was attended by all leading scholars in the field (Waples, 1942). In 1952 Berelson published what was to become the first leading textbook on quantitative content analysis. There he put forward his definition of the method which continues to be cited today: 'Content analysis is a research technique for the objective, systematic, and quantitative description of the manifest content of communication' (1952: 18).

With his definition of content analysis as quantitative and limited to the description of manifest communication content, Berelson had firmly established the method within the quantitative research tradition. But in the same year that Berelson published his textbook, his narrow definition of the method was contested by Kracauer (1952). Kracauer pointed out that meaning is often complex, holistic, context dependent, and that it is not necessarily apparent at first sight. He also argued against the practice prevalent in quantitative content analysis to equate the coding frequency of a given theme with its importance. On these grounds Kracauer advocated a different type of content analysis that does not limit itself to manifest content and frequency counts. Kracauer was therefore the first proponent of qualitative content analysis. His suggestions were later taken up by George (1959), who argued in favour of what he called 'non-frequency content analysis', and by Holsti (1969), who advocated a similar non-quantitative type of content analysis.

A Classic Example in Qualitative Content Analysis

A classic example from these early days of the method is Shannon's analysis (1954) of the newspaper cartoon *Little Orphan Annie*. The cartoon was originally intended for children, but soon attracted as much of an adult audience. Shannon was struck by how the editors of the paper used the cartoon as a vehicle for transporting conservative, middle-class American, anti-Roosevelt sentiment and values. Using qualitative content analysis, she examined these values in depth, focusing on five questions which she used for her main categories: (1) Who are Annie's friends and opponents, and who among the opponents is killed or injured? (2) What are the goals that Annie and her friends approve of and (3) how do the characters suggest to reach these goals? (4) Which symbols do Annie and her friends evaluate positively and (5) which symbols do they condemn?

Shannon and another coder answered these questions in writing, examining 104 weekly appearances of the comic strip over a period of two years (April 1948 to July 1950). Shannon then summarized the answers and in this way created her subcategories. The analysis shows that both the very poor (other orphans, for instance) and the very rich (whom Annie solicits to help the orphans) are Annie's most important friends, whereas Russian foreign agents and 'a gang of young hoodlums working the protection racket' (1954: 173) figure among her most notorious enemies. Her life goals include making a lot of money, being charitable, being a law-abiding citizen, making a good marriage, and raising a large family. To get there, making a large amount of money (i.e. money features both as an end and a means), the use of force and hard work are suggested. Orphans, work, honest merchants and smart businessmen figure among the symbols that Annie and her friends evaluate positively, whereas 'lazy mean people who are unwilling to work' (1954: 178), radicals, slave labour camps, the Soviet Union and Hitler, receive a negative evaluation. These findings are reported mostly in a narrative format, supplemented by coding frequencies and many examples from the cartoon strip.

Further Developments of Qualitative Content Analysis

Qualitative content analysis continued to be developed on the Continent, especially in Germany. Further developments include Ritsert's (1972) concept of an anti-ideological version of the method (in a similar tradition, Vorderer and Groeben, 1987), Rust's (1980) 'strict and qualitative' qualitative content analysis, and flexible content analysis (Rustemeyer, 1992). A major proponent of the method in Germany has been Mayring (2000; 2010), who developed several distinct versions of the method, notably summarizing and structural qualitative content analysis.

In English-speaking countries, especially in England and the United States, the situation has been different. As quantitative content analysis evolved methodologically, the method was increasingly applied to less manifest types of meaning – although the focus on presenting results in terms of coding frequencies was generally maintained. Because the quantitative had opened up towards qualitative versions of the method, many researchers argued that the distinction between a qualitative and a quantitative type of content analysis was only a matter of degree (Holsti, 1969; Krippendorff, 2004). Quantitative increasingly came to 'embrace' qualitative content analysis.

Because of this development, qualitative content analysis has not been well known as a method in its own right in most English-speaking countries until recently. Some qualitative researchers do not mention it at all in their textbooks (Gibbs, 2007; Mason, 2002), or else they present what is really quantitative content analysis (Berger, 2000; Bernard and Ryan, 2010). Others use the term 'qualitative content analysis' to refer to the full range of qualitative methods for data analysis, equating the method with other qualitative methods such as discourse or conversation analysis (Krippendorff, 2004). Yet other authors call the method by a different name, such as 'thematic coding' (Boyatzis, 1998) or 'qualitative media analysis' (Altheide, 1996). Descriptions of qualitative content analysis as a method in its own right started to appear in the Anglo-American literature only recently (e.g. Hsie and Shannon, 2005; Schreier, 2012).

This overview shows that there exist different versions of qualitative content analysis. The core ideas and steps in the version described here largely correspond to what Mayring (2010) has called structural, Hsie and Shannon (2005) conventional, Rustemeyer (1992) flexible (qualitative) content analysis, and what Boyatzis describes as thematic coding (1998).

HOW DOES QUALITATIVE CONTENT ANALYSIS RELATE TO OTHER METHODS?

Qualitative and Quantitative Content Analysis

There is no sharp dividing line between qualitative and quantitative content analysis (Groeben and Rustemeyer, 1994), and the two methods share many similarities. Both versions of the method are concerned with the systematic description of data through coding. To do so, they follow a predefined series of steps. In both cases this involves making use of a coding frame, generating category definitions, segmenting the material into coding units, and distinguishing between a pilot phase and a main phase of analysis. Quality criteria used in qualitative content analysis, notably consistency (to assess reliability) and validity (see Barbour, Chapter 34, this volume), are derived from the quantitative version of the method, although they are often applied less strictly. As in quantitative content analysis, presenting the findings of qualitative content analysis can involve frequency counts.

But despite these similarities, qualitative content analysis has specific features that set it apart as a method in its own right. Whereas the focus of quantitative content analysis continues to be on manifest meaning, qualitative content analysis is also applied to latent and more context-dependent meaning. Because latent meaning is harder to describe consensually, consistency as a quality criterion is handled less strictly in the qualitative version of the method. Quantitative content analysis is often used to test hypotheses, and, because of this, entire coding frames may be built in a concept-driven way, and the coding frame is always tried out on material that is different from the material used in the main study. The focus of qualitative content analysis is more often on providing a detailed description of the material under analysis. To provide a good fit with the material, the coding frame will at least in part be data-driven, and it should be built and tried out on the same material that is used in the main study. When it comes to presenting the findings, in quantitative content analysis the process of coding is only the starting point for a subsequent statistical analysis of the data. In fact, in the quantitative research tradition content analysis is usually considered a method for data *collection*. In the qualitative tradition, on the other hand, content analysis counts as a method for data *analysis*.

Qualitative Content Analysis and Other Qualitative Research Methods

Qualitative content analysis shares many features with other qualitative research methods, such as the concern with meaning and interpretation (see Willig, Chapter 10, this volume) of symbolic material, the importance of context in determining meaning, and the data-driven and partly iterative procedure. But the method also incorporates elements from the quantitative research tradition and in these respects it differs from other qualitative methods. Because the process of assigning units of meaning to the categories of the coding frame is termed 'coding' and because a 'coding frame' is at the heart of the method, qualitative content analysis is easily confused with (inductive) coding in particular (on coding, Gibbs, 2007; see also Thornberg and Charmaz, Chapter 11, this volume). But whereas inductive coding allows for assigning any number of codes to a piece of text, qualitative content analysis is more restrictive here (see below on the requirements of unidimensionality and mutual exclusiveness for coding frames). In inductive coding, code development and application go hand in hand, whereas they have to be performed separately and consecutively in qualitative content analysis, and the coding frame can no longer be changed during the main analysis phase. Unlike coding, qualitative content analysis requires a step of segmentation, a pilot coding and a subsequent evaluation of the coding frame in terms of reliability and validity (see Barbour, Chapter 34, this volume).

HOW TO DO QUALITATIVE CONTENT ANALYSIS?

Data Preparation

Qualitative content analysis is divided into a series of steps which are summarized in Box 12.1. Usually, no special data preparation is necessary. If transcripts are used, there is no need for a detailed description of paralinguistic features, especially if the focus is on the themes mentioned in the material. But because qualitative content analysis is concerned with describing meaning in context, relevant context should always be made available in or with the material. Transcripts should be complete, including the questions asked by the interviewer, not leaving out anything that may seem 'unimportant' while transcribing (see Kowal and O'Connell, Chapter 5, this volume).

Box 12.1   Steps in Qualitative Content Analysis

1. Deciding on a research question.
2. Selecting material.
3. Building a coding frame.
4. Segmentation.
5. Trial coding.
6. Evaluating and modifying the coding frame.
7. Main analysis.
8. Presenting and interpreting the findings.

Building a Coding Frame

Building a coding frame consists of the following steps: selecting material; structuring and generating categories; defining categories; revising and expanding the frame. Before going through these steps one by one, the idea of a coding frame will be described in more detail. Descriptions of these steps can, for example, be found in Boyatzis (1998), Mayring (2010), Rustemeyer (1992), and Schreier (2012).

The Coding Frame

The coding frame is at the heart of the method. It consists of at least one main category and at least two subcategories. Main categories are those aspects of the material about which the researcher would like more information, and subcategories specify what is said in the material with respect to these main categories.

In a recent study about prioritizing in health care (Diederich and Schreier, 2009), we conducted interviews where we presented our participants with a number of scenarios. One of these scenarios described the case of Terri Schiavo, a woman who had been in a coma vigil for 15 years, when it was decided in 2005 to discontinue intravenous feeding. Aspects that we wanted to know more about included participants' opinions about turning off the machines that were keeping Terri Schiavo alive and their reasons for considering this course of action to be justified or not. For the main category *Opinion*, we generated the following subcategories: *morally justified, long overdue, morally wrong, refusal to take any decision, unclear, miscellaneous*. Subcategories for the main category *reasons in favour of turning off the machines* included: *unnecessary prolongation of suffering, high costs, long duration of comatose state, agreement by the relatives*, and several others.

Coding frames can vary in complexity, consisting of any number of main categories and hierarchical levels, with subcategories containing additional sub-subcategories (cf. Schreier, 2012: ch. 4). In practice, however, more than three hierarchical levels can be difficult to handle.

Coding frames should meet a number of requirements. To start with, main categories should cover one aspect of the material only (requirement of *unidimensionality*). This is why we created separate main categories for *opinion* and *reasons* in the above study. But there can of course be many such main categories, that is the requirement of unidimensionality applies to any one main category – which should cover one concept only – but not to the entire coding frame, which can and usually will be multi-dimensional.

Second, subcategories within one main category should be created so that they are mutually exclusive (requirement of *mutual exclusiveness*). The reasons for this are partly conceptual (there would be little point in classifying a participant as considering the decision in the case of Terri Schiavo to have been both justified and unjustified) and partly practical (Schreier, 2012: ch. 4). Again, it is important to see this requirement in the context of the entire coding frame. The requirement does not imply that any one unit can be coded only once – it implies that any unit can be coded *only once under one main category*. In our study, we routinely classified one and the same passage in terms of a participant's opinion about turning off the life support for Terri Schiavo, for example, and a reason for that opinion. The requirement also does not prevent the researcher from coding several subcategories under the same main category for the same person – it only prevents the researcher from doing so for the same unit of coding (units of coding are described in detail below). In other words, the same participant may well argue that it was wrong to turn off the life support for a number of reasons, for example both on moral and on legal grounds. And both reasons can be coded – but not for the same unit. Qualitative content analysis requires that the material is divided up ('segmented') in such a way that one segment is classified as, for example, 'moral grounds' and a second one as 'legal grounds'.

Finally, all relevant aspects of the material must be covered by a category (requirement of *exhaustiveness*). This is to make sure that all parts of the material are equally accounted for by the coding frame. In practice, the requirement is easy to meet by introducing *residual categories*. But there should not be too many of these and they should not be used too often, else the frame will not be sufficiently valid (see below).

Selecting Material

Qualitative research often involves large amounts of material. Because of this and to avoid 'cognitive overload', typically only a part of the material is used in building the coding frame. Therefore, the first step in building a frame is to select a suitable amount of material. The most important criterion here is to select the material so that it reflects the full diversity of data sources. If the data consist of interviews with different stakeholder groups, at least one interview from each group should be selected. If the material consists of newspaper articles from three different time periods, all three time periods should be represented in the selection.

But even if only part of the material is used, it is best to build the frame not in one step, trying to cover the material all at once. It is better to break the material down into smaller 'chunks' and to build the coding frame for one 'chunk' after another, for example according to source or (if interviews were used for data collection) according to topic. The two strategies can also be combined, and in fact this is what we did in our study on setting priorities in health care. We started out with the patients and what they had to say on one topic, such as the case of Terri Schiavo. We then moved on to what the physicians had to say about this case, including one group of participants after another. Once we had finalized the coding frame for this one topic, we moved on to another case vignette, again starting with the patients, and so on, until we had finalized a first version of the entire coding frame.

Structuring and Generating

Structuring and generating are the next steps in building the coding frame, where structuring refers to creating the main categories and generating to creating the subcategories for each main category. These steps can be carried out in a concept- or in a data-driven way. But it is not a good idea to generate all categories in a concept-driven way. A key objective of qualitative content analysis is to provide a good description of the material. Concept-driven categories alone, however, may leave part of this material unaccounted for. This is why concept-driven categories are usually combined with data-driven categories. One way to do this is to create main categories in a concept-driven way and to add subcategories in a data-driven way.

Working in a *concept-driven* way means basing the categories on previous knowledge: a theory, prior research, everyday knowledge, logic, or an interview guide (Schreier, 2012: ch. 5). In our study on setting priorities in health care, for example, we used our interview questions for generating main categories, such as: the participants' *opinion* on terminating Terri Schiavo's life support, their *reasons* why they considered this *justified* or *unjustified*, or *other information* they would have liked about the case before coming to a decision.

When working in a *data-driven* way, there are again several strategies to choose from (Schreier, 2012: ch. 6). The most important among these are *subsumption* and *progressive summarizing*; these strategies largely correspond to the structural (subsumption) and the summative (progressive summarizing) types of qualitative content analysis developed by Mayring (2010: section 5.2.4). Subsumption is a useful strategy for generating subcategories in a data-driven way once main categories have been decided upon. It involves examining one passage after another, going through the following steps:

1. Reading the material until a relevant concept is encountered.
2. Checking whether a subcategory that covers this concept has already been created.
3. If so, mentally 'subsuming' this under the respective subcategory.
4. If not, creating a new subcategory that covers this concept.
5. Continuing to read until the next relevant concept/passage is encountered.

This process is continued until a point of *saturation* is reached; that is, until no additional new concepts can be found.

Successive summarizing is a suitable strategy for developing entire coding frames in a data-driven way (Mayring, 2010: section 5.5.2). This involves paraphrasing relevant passages, deleting from these passages anything that appears superfluous, and summarizing similar paraphrases which are then turned into categories and subcategories.

Comparing and contrasting is another strategy for developing entire coding frames in a data-driven way. This is especially useful for comparing different sources (Boyatzis, 1998).

Defining

Once the structure of the coding frame has been developed, the next step is to define the categories. Category definitions consist of four parts: a category name, a description of what is meant by that name, positive examples, and decision rules.

Category names should provide concise descriptions of what a category refers to; they should be neither overly long nor overly short and cryptic. These are some examples of names that we used for subcategories referring to reasons why participants believed it was wrong to have turned off the machines that were keeping Terri Schiavo alive: *Reasons against: unethical/unjust procedure; playing God; criminal offence.*

Descriptions can consist of two parts: a definition and indicators. The definition is a mandatory part of the category description. It states what is meant by a given category and what features are characteristic of the category. It helps to think of definitions as instructions in a code book, telling the coders when a given category is applicable. A frequent mistake is to make definitions too narrow by limiting them to the instances of the category in the material that is used for building the coding frame. But of course the category should be more comprehensive than those specific instances and be applicable to the entire material. The following is our definition of the category *Reasons against: unethical/unjust procedure* (Winkelhage et al., 2008b: 81; my translation):

> This category applies if an interviewee argues that it was wrong on moral grounds to turn off the machines that were keeping Terri Schiavo alive. The category applies whenever an interviewee expresses the view that turning off the machines is unethical and/or constitutes a violation of a moral rule or principle, for instance the principle of justice. It is not relevant which moral principle or rule the interviewee considers to have been violated. The interviewee's exact reasoning why s/he considers turning off the machines to be in violation of a moral rule or unethical is also not relevant.

Indicators are signs that point to the presence of a phenomenon, something by which to recognize a phenomenon. They can be specific words, or they can be descriptions of the ways in which the presence of a phenomenon manifests itself in the data. Indicators of the above category might include words such as *unethical, immoral, morally wrong* or *unfair.*

Because category definitions are by necessity somewhat abstract, it is helpful to illustrate them by providing examples from the material. Ideally, these should be typical examples of the category, but hypothetical examples may also be used. One or two examples are perfectly enough – otherwise, the coding frame quickly becomes too large and therefore difficult to handle. The following is the example we used to illustrate the category *Reasons against: unethical/unjust procedure* (Winkelhage et al., 2008a: 81; my translation):

> I would say that it is an ethical thing really. And that a society, like American society which relies on – well, finding one's way in society, acting appropriately, liking sports, being dynamic, all that sort of thing. And being old, fragile, sick, disabled, all this is marginal. ... So it has something to do with ethics, with the ethics of a society. And because of this I would say – Well, I believe that this was a very unfortunate decision. (ID–110: 59)

To make sure that subcategories within one main category are indeed mutually exclusive, decision rules may be needed. Unlike the category name, description and examples which are a necessary part of category definitions, decision rules are optional and are needed only where subcategories may overlap and where coders may therefore be uncertain which category to use. In these cases, decision rules tell the coders which of the two categories to use. They should specify what is not to be included in a category and which category to use instead. We used the following decision rule to differentiate between *Reasons against: unethical/unjust procedure* and the closely related subcategory *Reasons against: manner of death* (Winkelhage et al., 2008b: 81; my translation).

> If it is not primarily turning off the machines as such which the participant considers to be unethical, but Terri Schiavo's manner of death (such as: starving or dying of thirst), the present category does not apply. In this case, the category 'manner of death' should be used.

Extensive definitions, including a name, description, example, and decision rules if needed, should be generated for all subcategories in the coding frame. With main categories, a brief description of the scope of the category is usually enough.

Revising and Expanding

Once all categories have been generated and defined, it is time to take a step back, look at the structure of the coding frame once again, and 'tidy up' any loose ends. If subcategories are very similar, it might be best to collapse them. Some subcategories may be much more comprehensive than others and might be better conceptualized as main categories. These and other considerations may lead to a revision of the structure of the frame.

If the coding frame has so far been based on part of the data only, the frame should in a next step be expanded to include the next part. Each expansion involves going through all the previous steps once again, checking whether any additional main categories (structuring) and any new subcategories (generating) are required and defining any new subcategories. These steps are repeated as many times as there are different sources or parts of the material that have not yet been covered.

Segmentation

Coding consistency, that is applying categories to the entire material in a consistent manner, is an important quality criterion in qualitative content analysis. It is assessed by comparing two rounds of coding that are carried out either by two independent coders or by one coder at two points in time. But comparing two rounds of coding only makes sense if the codes are applied to identical parts of the material each time. Because of this, the material has to be segmented into units before any coding is done.

Segmentation involves dividing the material into units in such a way that each unit fits into exactly one (sub)category of the coding frame. These coding units are those parts of the material that can be interpreted in a meaningful way with respect to the subcategories, and their size can vary from an entire book to a single word. This definition shows that segmentation is in fact closely related to developing the coding frame and meeting the requirement of mutual exclusiveness. The size of segments or units should be chosen so as to match the definition of the categories.

Dividing the material into units of coding requires a criterion that specifies where one unit ends and another one begins. There are two such types of criteria: formal and thematic (Rustemeyer, 1992). Formal criteria draw on the inherent structure of the material. They are formal units such as words, sentences or paragraphs in a legal text. Formal units make segmentation easy because they are usually very obvious. However, unless the category definitions match the internal structure of the material, formal criteria may not result in meaningful units. Especially in qualitative research, a thematic criterion will often be more useful. This involves looking for topic changes, and one unit essentially corresponds to a theme. What constitutes a theme will vary with the coding frame and main categories. Thematic criteria are much less clear cut than formal criteria, but they often provide a better fit with the coding frame.

In our study on prioritizing in health care, we used a thematic criterion for segmentation (Winkelhage et al., 2008a), as in the following example where the focus is on reasons and considerations raised by the interviewee concerning the case of Terri Schiavo:

> [Of course this is – it's a complete borderline issue, and of course you can never tell whether someone might not wake up again after 20 years or so.] [This is not, it is not just about the costs, but, well] … [You have to, and this always applies where medical issues are concerned: Have another very close look at the medical parameters. This is a very decisive factor.]

When dividing the material into segments, units of coding should be numbered consecutively per source. If a formal criterion is used, segmentation can be done in parallel with the coding. If a thematic criterion is used, segmentation should precede coding. This can be done by one person, but if two coders will be working on the material, it is useful to do part of the segmentation process together.

The Pilot Phase

In the pilot phase, the coding frame is tried out on part of the material. This is crucial for recognizing and modifying any shortcomings in the frame before the main analysis is carried out. The pilot phase consists of the following steps: selecting material; the trial coding; evaluating and modifying the coding frame.

Selecting and Preparing Material

Material for the pilot phase should again be selected so as to cover all types of data and data sources in the material. In addition, the material should also be selected so that the majority of categories in the coding frame can be applied during the trial coding. In our study on prioritizing in health care, for example, we included interviews with participants who approved and who did not approve of turning off the machines that were keeping Terri Schiavo alive. This material is then segmented into coding units, as described above.

The Trial Coding

The next step, the trial coding, is at the heart of the pilot phase. The categories from the coding frame are applied to the material during two rounds of coding, following the same procedure that will be used during the main coding. This can be done by two coders working independently of each other or else by one person coding and recoding the material within approximately 10 to 14 days.

Frames that consist of more than 40 categories should be divided into parts that are applied consecutively, else coders are likely to make mistakes. An obvious way to do this is to divide the frame by main categories, that is to start out by applying all subcategories for this one main category, then move on to the next main category, and so on. All codings should be entered into a coding sheet, where the coding units are the rows and the main categories are the columns. The subcategory to which each unit of coding is assigned is entered into the cells.

Evaluating and Modifying the Coding Frame

Evaluating the coding frame involves examining the results of the trial coding in terms of consistency and validity (see Barbour, Chapter 34, this volume).

If the definitions of subcategories are clear and straightforward and if the subcategories are mutually exclusive, units of coding will usually be assigned to the same subcategories during both rounds of coding. In other words, the higher the consistency between the two rounds of coding, the higher the quality of the coding frame. This is why it is important to identify those units of coding that were assigned to different subcategories during the two rounds. If the coding was done by two coders, it is helpful to have them sit down together and discuss their reasons for assigning a coding unit to different subcategories. It can also be helpful to quantify the degree of coding consistency by calculating a coefficient of agreement (Neuendorf, 2002: ch. 2; Schreier, 2012: ch. 9). Usually this examination of inconsistencies will show which subcategories were difficult to use and which subcategories were used interchangeably, pointing to overlaps between categories. The definitions of such subcategories should be revised, and decision rules should be added where needed.

The second criterion for evaluating coding frames is validity, that is the extent to which the categories adequately describe the material and the concepts that are part of the research question. For all data-driven parts of the frame, the distribution of coding frequencies across the subcategories for a main category is indicative of validity. In particular, the coding frame does not adequately describe the material wherever coding frequencies are high for residual categories. In this case, additional subcategories to capture these aspects should be created. For all concept-driven parts of the coding frame, ideally an expert on the research topic should assess the frame.

If only few changes are made to the frame following the trial coding, the frame can now be used for the main analysis. Otherwise, it may be best to run a second trial coding before moving on to the next step.

The Main Analysis Phase

The main analysis phase is where *all* material is coded. It is important to keep in mind that the coding frame can no longer be modified at this stage. Therefore it is crucial that the frame is sufficiently reliable and valid before entering this phase.

A first step in the main analysis is to divide the remaining part of the material into coding units. In a next step, the material is coded by assigning these units to the categories in the coding frame. Because the frame has already been evaluated and revised, it is now no longer necessary to double-code each unit. The exact amount of material to be double-coded at this stage depends on the results of the pilot phase. The lower the coding consistency and the validity of the first version of the frame, and the more changes were made as a result of the pilot coding, the more the material should be double-coded during the main analysis phase. If only few changes were made following the pilot coding, double-coding approximately one-third of the material during the main analysis is sufficient. This, however, is only a rule of thumb.

The results of the main coding should again be entered into a coding sheet. The final meaning of a unit is obvious for those parts of the material that were coded only once and for those that were double-coded and where the two rounds of coding agree. Any coding inconsistencies need to be discussed and resolved. Researchers who are working on their own should try to keep track of their reasons for interpreting the unit differently each time and arrive at a final meaning in this way. If an inconsistency cannot be resolved, it can be useful to bring in a third person who is also familiar with the research.

In a final step of the main analysis phase, the results of coding should be prepared so that they are suitable for answering the research question. This is necessary whenever the units of coding are smaller than the cases specified in the research question. In this case, the coding has to be transformed from the level of the unit of coding to the level of the case. This is done by creating a new data matrix where the columns continue to correspond to categories, but the rows now represent cases. In our study about prioritizing in health care, one of our concerns was with comparing the reasons why members of different stakeholder groups (patients, physicians, politicians, etc.) believed that it was or was not a good decision to turn off the machines that were keeping Terri Schiavo alive. We therefore had to create a new data matrix where each row no longer corresponded to a unit of coding, but to an interviewee.

Presenting the Findings

With qualitative content analysis, the coding frame itself can be the main result (this was the case with our study on setting priorities in health care, see Winkelhage et al., 2008b; for another example, see Heil, 2011). In this case, presenting the findings involves presenting the frame and illustrating it through quotes. This can be done through continuous text or through text matrices, that is tables that contain text instead of or in addition to numbers. Text matrices are very flexible and especially useful for contrasting different sources or illustrating selected cases (Miles and Huberman, 1994). The findings can also serve as a starting point for further data exploration, examining the results of qualitative content analysis for patterns and co-occurrences of selected categories. This involves moving beyond the individual units of coding and categories to the *relations* between the categories (Gibbs, 2007; Miles and Huberman, 1994).

All the above are essentially qualitative ways of presenting the findings of qualitative content analysis. Alternatively, findings can also be presented in quantitative style. This typically involves reporting coding frequencies, percentages or inferential statistics such as chi-square analysis. Inferential statistics are especially useful for comparing different sources, provided that there are enough cases (for an example see Odag, 2008; see also Denzin, Chapter 39, and Morse and Maddox, Chapter 36, this volume).

APPLICATIONS AND PERSPECTIVES

Applications

Qualitative content analysis is suitable for a wide range of materials, visual or verbal, self-generated (by conducting interviews or focus groups etc.) or sampled from available sources (websites, newspapers, magazines, blogs, letters, etc.). Because of this inherent flexibility, the method has been applied across a wide range of disciplines, branching out from its early usage in communication studies. These include, but are not limited to, research in education (Kapustka et al., 2009), psychology (McDonald et al., 2009), sociology (Finn et al., 2011), political science

(Heil, 2011), the empirical study of literature (Odag, 2008), and research in health-related fields (Diederich and Schreier, 2009).

But of course there are limits to the applicability of qualitative content analysis. The focus of this method is on description. This implies that the material is taken 'for granted'; the method is, so to speak, ontologically and epistemologically 'naive'. Therefore, if a researcher is concerned with doing a critical analysis, discourse analysis (see Willig, Chapter 23, this volume) would be a better method to use (Van Dijk, 1997a; 1997b). With its focus on description, qualitative content analysis is also not suitable for theory building (here grounded theory would be the better choice: Corbin and Strauss, 2008; see Thornberg and Charmaz, Chapter 11, this volume). Furthermore, qualitative content analysis is a method that *reduces* data, making use of categories that abstract from individual passages. If the data are to be opened up instead, some type of coding would again be a better option (Gibbs, 2007). Qualitative content analysis also reduces data by forcing the researcher to assign each coding unit to one subcategory only (within one main category; of course one coding unit can be classified under several main categories). Where the researcher is concerned with exploring multiplicity of meaning and how different meanings relate to each other, a method like semiotics would be the better choice (Chandler, 2007).

Perspectives

On the one hand qualitative content analysis is flexible, concerning the material to which it is applied, but on the other hand the idea of the coding unit works best when applied to textual material. It is much more difficult to segment visual material (see Banks, Chapter 27, this volume) or online material (see Marotzki et al., Chapter 31, this volume) with a hypertext structure where units may range across different websites. This difficulty is unfortunate in a time and age where multimodality is ever increasing in importance (Kress and Van Leeuwen, 2002). It is therefore crucial to develop the method so as to facilitate its application to material other than texts.

Today, qualitative data analysis increasingly makes use of software (Lewins and Silver, 2007). However, the majority of the programs currently on the market do not seamlessly fit the requirements of qualitative content analysis (Schreier, 2012: ch. 12). Several programs have been developed for conducting content analysis – but this refers to *quantitative* content analysis, and the programs are not suitable for the qualitative version of the method. Qualitative software (see Gibbs, Chapter 19, this volume), on the other hand, was often developed with grounded theory (see Thornberg and Charmaz, Chapter 11, this volume) in mind. And while it can easily be adapted to qualitative content analysis, this type of software does not equally support all steps of the method. Software that supports qualitative content analysis in particular is still under development. Bringing computer-aided qualitative data analysis and qualitative content analysis together by developing flexible software that supports all steps of the method is the next step ahead.

FURTHER READING

Groeben, Norbert and Rustemeyer, Ruth (1994) 'On the integration of quantitative and qualitative methodological paradigms (based on the example of content analysis)', in Inger Borg and Peter Mohler (eds), *Trends and Perspectives in Empirical Social Research*. Berlin: DeGruyter. pp. 308–26.

Mayring, Philipp (2000) 'Qualitative content analysis' [28 paragraphs], *Forum Qualitative Sozialforschung/ Forum: Qualitative Social Research*, 1 (2), Art. 20: http://nbn-resolving.de/urn:nbn:de:0114-fqs0002204 (accessed 2 May 2013).

Schreier, Margrit (2012) *Qualitative Content Analysis in Practice*. London: Sage.

REFERENCES

Altheide, David (1996) *Qualitative Media Analysis*. Thousand Oaks, CA: Sage.

Berelson, Bernard (1952) *Content Analysis in Communication Research*. Glencoe, IL: Free Press.

Berger, Arthur A. (2000) 'Content analysis', in Arthur Berger (ed.), *Media and Communications Research Methods*. Thousand Oaks: Sage. pp. 173–85.

Bernard, Russell H. and Ryan, Gery W. (2010) 'Content analysis', in Russell Bernard and Gery Ryan (eds), *Analyzing Qualitative Data. Systematic Approaches*. Los Angeles: Sage. pp. 287–310.

Boyatzis, Richard E. (1998) *Transforming Qualitative Information: Thematic Analysis and Code Development*. Thousand Oaks, CA: Sage.

Chandler, Daniel (2007) *Semiotics: The Basics*. New York: Routledge (1st edition, 2002).

Corbin, Juliet and Strauss, Anselm (2008) *Basics of Qualitative Research: Techniques and Procedures for Developing Grounded Theory*. Thousand Oaks, CA: Sage (1st edition, 1990).

Diederich, Adele and Schreier, Margrit (2009) 'Kriterien der Priorisierung aus gesellschaftlicher Sicht', *Zeitschrift für Ärztliche Fortbildung und Qualitätssicherung*, 103: 111–16.

Finn, James, Mukhtar, Vera, Kennedy, David, Kendig, Hal, Bohle, Philip and Rawlings-Way, Olivia (2011) 'Financial planning for retirement village living: A qualitative exploration', *Journal of Housing for the Elderly*, 25 (2): 217–42.

George, Alexander L. (1959) 'Quantitative and qualitative approaches to content analysis', in Ithiel de Sola Pool (ed.), *Trends in Content Analysis*. Urbana: University of Illinois Press. pp. 1–32.

Gibbs, Graham (2007) *Analyzing Qualitative Data*. London: Sage.

Groeben, Norbert and Rustemeyer, Ruth (1994) 'On the integration of quantitative and qualitative methodological paradigms (based on the example of content analysis)', in Inger Borg and Peter Mohler (eds), *Trends and Perspectives in Empirical Social Research*. Berlin: DeGruyter. pp. 308–26.

Heil, Simone (2011) *Young Ambassadors*. Baden-Baden: Nomos.

Holsti, Ole R. (1969) *Content Analysis for the Social Sciences and the Humanities*. Reading, MA: Addison-Wesley.

Hsie, Hsiu-Fang and Shannon, Sarah E. (2005) 'Three approaches to qualitative content analysis', *Qualitative Health Research*, 15: 1277–88.

Kapustka, Katherine A., Howell, Penny, Clayton, Christine D. and Thomas, Shelley (2009) 'Social justice in teacher education: A qualitative content analysis of NCATE conceptual frameworks', *Equity and Excellence in Education*, 42 (4): 489–505.

Kracauer, Siegfried (1952) 'The challenge of qualitative content analysis', *Public Opinion Quarterly*, Winter: 631–42.

Kress, Gunther R. and Van Leeuwen, Theo (2002) *Multimodal Discourse: The Modes and Media of Contemporary Communication*. London: Edward Arnold.

Krippendorff, Klaus (2004) *Content Analysis: An Introduction to Its Methodology*. Thousand Oaks, CA: Sage (1st edition, 1980).

Lewins, Ann and Silver, Christina (2007) *Using Software in Qualitative Research: A Step-by-Step Guide*. London: Sage.

Mason, Jennifer (2002) *Qualitative Researching*. London: Sage.

Mayring, Philipp (2000) 'Qualitative content analysis' [28 paragraphs], *Forum Qualitative Sozialforschung/ Forum: Qualitative Social Research*, 1 (2), Art. 20: http://nbn-resolving.de/urn:nbn:de:0114-fqs0002204 (accessed 2 May 2013).

Mayring, Philipp (2010) *Qualitative Inhaltsanalyse: Grundlagen und Techniken*. Weinheim: Beltz (1st edition, 1983).

McDonald, Matthew M., Wearing, Stephen, and Ponting, Jess (2009) 'The nature of peak experience in wilderness', *The Humanistic Psychologist*, 37: 370–85.

Miles, Matthew B. and Huberman, A. Michael (1994) *Qualitative Data Analysis: An Expanded Sourcebook*. Thousand Oaks, CA: Sage (1st edition, 1984).

Neuendorf, Kimberly A. (2002) *The Content Analysis Guidebook*. Thousand Oaks, CA: Sage.

Odag, Özen (2008) 'Of men who read romance and women who read adventure stories ... An empirical reception study of the emotional engagement of men and women while reading narrative texts', in Jan Auracher and Willie van Peer (eds), *New Beginnings in Literary Studies*. Newcastle: Cambridge Scholars Publishing. pp. 308–329.

Ritsert, Jürgen (1972) *Inhaltsanalyse und Ideologiekritik. Ein Versuch über kritische Sozialforschung*. Frankfurt: Athenäum.

Rust, Holger (1980) *Struktur und Bedeutung*. Berlin: Verlag Volker Spiess.

Rustemeyer, Ruth (1992) *Praktisch-methodische Schritte der Inhaltsanalyse*. Münster: Aschendorff.

Schreier, Margrit (2012) *Qualitative Content Analysis in Practice*. London: Sage.

Shannon, Lyle W. (1954) 'The opinions of the little orphan Annie and her friends', *Public Opinion Quarterly*, 18: 169–79.

Van Dijk, Teun (ed.) (1997a) *Discourse as Structure and Process*. London: Sage.

Van Dijk, Teun (ed.) (1997b) *Discourse as Social Interaction*. London: Sage.

Vorderer, Peter and Groeben, Norbert (eds) (1987) *Textanalyse als Kognitionskritik? Möglichkeiten und Grenzen ideologiekritischer Inhaltsanalyse*. Tübingen: Narr.

Waples, Douglas (ed.) (1942) *Print, Radio, and Film in a Democracy*. Chicago: University of Chicago Press.

Winkelhage, Jeannette, Winkel, Susanne, Schreier, Margrit, Heil, Simone, Lietz, Petra and Diederich, Adele (2008a) 'Qualitative Inhaltsanalyse: Entwicklung eines Kategoriensystems zur Analyse von Stakeholder-Interviews zu Prioritäten in der medizinischen Versorgung' [Electronic Version], *FOR655*, 15: www.priorisierung-in-der-medizin.de (accessed 17 March 2012).

Winkelhage, Jeannette, Winkel, Susanne, Schreier, Margrit, Heil, Simone, Lietz, Petra and Diederich, Adele (2008b) *Anhang zu FOR Working Paper No. 15* [Electronic Version], *FOR655*, 16: www.priorisierung-in-der-medizin.de (accessed 18 March 2012).

Phenomenology as a Research Method

Thomas S. Eberle

Phenomenology is a philosophy that called for an analysis of 'the things themselves'. It has developed new methods of analysis and produced findings that proved very seminal for the methodology of the social sciences. The phenomenological method is not just a method of data interpretation; phenomenological analysis begins before empirical data are even constituted. It is therefore inevitable to describe phenomenology at a much more fundamental level than as a mere strategy of data analysis. As phenomenology has greatly contributed to the methodology of qualitative research, the aim of this chapter is to elucidate several crucial aspects: phenomenology as an epistemology; as a protosociological foundation to the methodology of the social sciences; as a sociological paradigm; and as an empirical research procedure. Hopefully, I will succeed in providing a solid overview of the complex relationship between phenomenology and qualitative empirical research and clarifying some common misunderstandings.

In pursuing this goal I will first delineate the origin of phenomenology, what it means to analyse 'the things themselves' and how the phenomenological life-world analysis was used for providing a philosophical foundation of the methodology of the social sciences. Then I describe two basic versions of how to conceive of the relationship between phenomenology and the social sciences. The first makes a strict distinction between phenomenology and sociology and proclaims the phenomenological analysis of the life-world as a protosociology. The second attempts to merge or synthesize phenomenology and sociology and sees phenomenological sociology as a new paradigm that replaces the positivist paradigm and radically renews empirical research. The first prevails in German sociology, the second in US sociology – a constellation full of misunderstandings. After some basic clarifications I describe three new developments that use phenomenology as a strategy of empirical research.

THE CALL OF PHENOMENOLOGY: TURNING TO THE THINGS THEMSELVES!

The notion *phenomenon* is often equated with 'appearance' or 'experience', and the term *phenomenology* is often used in a loose and superficial way, even by social scientists: namely, as a mere description of the 'appearances' or 'experiences' of something. *Phenomenology*, however, is also a philosophy that claims to be a 'rigorous science' with an 'autonomous philosophical method'. It was founded at the beginning of the twentieth century by Edmund Husserl (1859–1938) and became a broad *Phenomenological Movement* that Herbert Spiegelberg (1982) described in its many ramifications.

Husserl studied philosophy, mathematics, physics and astronomy in Germany. After his long research on numbers, calculations and logics he developed the idea that philosophical analysis should turn to *'the things themselves'*. The next question was: What are 'the things themselves?' How to perceive and conceive of them? This was the birth of phenomenology, the 'science' of phenomena. Scrutinizing 'the things themselves' obviously requires an *epistemological framework*. Following Descartes, Husserl ([1928] 2012; [1939] 1973) started his analyses with the subjective consciousness: it is the locus of cognition with the best evidence. There is no cognition without consciousness. While Descartes inferred from the *ego cogito* to the *ergo sum*, Husserl pointed out that a crucial part was missing: ego cogito *cogitatum*. 'Ego cogito' cannot happen as an act per se but is always bound to the *cogitatum*, namely to something that is (re)cognized. Husserl theorized this aspect with the concept 'intentionality' that he borrowed from his teacher, Franz Brentano: subjective consciousness is always a 'consciousness *of something*'. If I perceive, think, feel, imagine – I always perceive something, think of something, feel something, imagine something. The ensemble of 'ego cogito cogitatum' is the phenomenon.

For analytical purposes, Husserl distinguished between the *noesis* and the *noema* of a phenomenon: the *noesis* consists in the acts of consciousness, the *noema* in the properties of the cogitatum. If I perceive, for instance, a bird in my garden I can observe it with great attention and see it fairly clearly; if I glimpse it only hastily, my perception of that bird remains rather blurred and vague. My different kinds of attention obviously constitute a different phenomenon – in each case a bird but once with clear and once with only vague contours. The *noema* consists in the properties of the perceived. The bird is not an elephant, and if it has a red belly it does not have a blue belly, and if it is an old bird it is not a young bird. Whether I notice any of these noematic aspects depends on my noetic attention. Therefore both aspects, the noesis and the noema, constitute the phenomenon. *A phenomenon is always a noetic–noematic unity* and includes acts of consciousness as well as properties of their 'object'. Husserl attempts thereby to overcome the *aporia* that empiricism and rationalism have produced by separating the cognizing subject and the objective world.

Husserl developed several methods to pursue a phenomenological analysis. All of them are descriptive and egological, that is a phenomenologist investigates the phenomena in his or her own subjective consciousness:

1. A famous and popular one is the *method of 'free imaginative variation'* or of *'eidetic variation'*. It aims at finding the essence of phenomena, their *eidos*. One imagines, for example, if a cube is still a cube when it is made of wood, plastic, glass or steel, or if it has different colours or a different size. One finds that the *eidos* of a cube is independent of colours or material or size, but if the proportions of the sides are changed or if the angles are not rectangular, it is no longer a cube. Obviously, the *eidos (essence)* of a cube is that it has six equal sides and that all angles are rectangular. The basic idea is to find the *eidos*, the platonic *idea*, the invariant properties that are universal. In the context of a book on empirical research it is noteworthy that eidetic variations are not bound to empirical observation but are

infinite: one can imagine whatever is logically possible even if it does not exist.
2. A closely related method aiming at the same goal to reveal the *eidos* of things is the *epoché* or *'eidetic reduction'*, the 'bracketing' of the assumptions of the natural attitude that we regularly rely upon in everyday life. It reduces iteratively the beliefs, the theoretical and pre-theoretical presuppositions, hypotheses and elements of knowledge which are usually involved in the constitution of a phenomenon. Elucidating all these presuppositions helps to clear the way from the particulars to the universal 'pure' essences.
3. A further method is the *transcendental reduction* that Husserl also calls the *phenomenological reduction*. In addition to the eidetic *epoché* it brackets also the existence of things in order to scrutinize exclusively the 'whatness' of phenomena – no matter if they refer to the 'real' world or to fantasy and fiction – and to analyse the transcendental subjectivity in which the pure phenomena are constituted. This was the turn of phenomenology to a transcendental philosophy, *in search for a prioris* like Kant.

These methods are said to produce *apodictic* findings that need no intersubjective validation. Husserl recommended elucidating the *eidos* of concrete phenomena but himself preferred to focus his constitutive analyses rather on the universal and invariant eidetic properties of *all* phenomena. In other words, he dispelled with the noema and restricted his analyses to the noesis, to the basic constitutive achievements of consciousness. Husserl provided many lucid insights on *how we constitute the sense of phenomena*. The core is *apperception*: what is actually perceived? Phenomena are constituted with an outer horizon – against a 'background', within a 'context' – but they have also an inner horizon which is constituted by *appresentation*: we perceive not only what is perceivable but 'appresent' also aspects that are not perceivable (e.g. we see a 'house' although we just perceive its front side). Phenomena are constituted in passive syntheses and include sensuous apperception as well as meaning. A crucial difference to many other, especially linguistic approaches is that phenomenology analyses meaning constitution on a *pre-predicative level*. Subjective experience is always more than and different from what is formulated in language. It is therefore crucial to start analysis at the pre-predicative level of subjective experience and not just at its representations on the *predicative level of language* (for an illustration of such a 'reflective analysis' see Embree, 2011).

Three aspects of phenomenology are common to all strands: description as method, the claim for apriority, and the claim to serve as the foundation of all other sciences. The concept of the 'life-world' that has become so common in modern sociology was coined by Husserl ([1936/54], 1970). He argued that the crisis of modern sciences – he meant, as always, the natural sciences – was caused by the fact that they had taken their idealizations and abstractions, their mathematical and geometrical formulae for bare truth, and forgotten that they originated in the life-world. The phenomenological life-world analysis will therefore allow for solving this crisis and elucidate the workings of scientific methods.

MUNDANE PHENOMENOLOGY: CARVING OUT THE MEANINGFUL STRUCTURES OF THE LIFE-WORLD

Alfred Schutz was the key figure who introduced phenomenology into sociology. His basic idea is that the methodology of the social sciences has two pillars: first, the logics of scientific explanation; and, second, a constitutive analysis of the social world. The second is much more crucial. Schutz therefore contrasted Carnap's *The Logical Structure of the World* ([1928] 1967) with his own book *The Meaningful Structure of the Social World (Der sinnhafte Aufbau der sozialen Welt)* – which is not recognizable anymore in the English translation of the book title, *The Phenomenology of the Social World*, (Schutz, [1932], 1967). As the social world is meaningfully constituted in everyday life *before* any scientific research begins, the social sciences have to take this fact systematically into account.

Phenomenology proved to be seminal for analysing the constitution of sense in social reality. Schutz opposed a 'picture book phenomenology' that attempted to describe the *eidos* of concrete social phenomena (e.g. of a family, a state, a community), and he endorsed Husserl's search for universal, invariant formal structures of the life-world. He advocated a *mundane phenomenology* that does not bracket the existence of things but posited that Husserl's findings in the transcendental reduction are also valid in the mundane sphere. Mundane phenomenology analyses the natural attitude and accepts the *socio-cultural a priori*: an actor's subjective stock of knowledge with its typifications and systems of relevances are *socially derived*.

As Max Weber ([1922], 1978) stipulated that *sociology has to understand (verstehen) the subjective sense of social actions*, Schutz investigated carefully what Weber had overlooked: that the modes of givenness of social actions – and therefore their meanings – are different to the actor him- or herself (S^1), to an observer in everyday life (S^2) and to a social scientist (S^3). While the actor perceives his actions in the context of his biographically determined stock of knowledge at hand and knows about his experiences, his plans and systems of relevances, the observer in everyday life can only perceive observable behaviour and has no direct access to the subjective sense of the other's actions. The *alter ego* is only understandable by means of *appresentative systems*: by indications, marks, signs and symbols. Schutz disapproves of Max Scheler's concept of empathy: we can never empathize in the sense that we feel what the other is feeling. *We can only understand the other on the basis of our own subjective experiences*, of our own feelings, of our own reasoning. The other's experiences and subjective constructions are not directly available but only with the help of appresentative systems (for phenomenologists, it is utterly disturbing that some other qualitative approaches do not recognize and acknowledge this basic difference and treat interview data or narrations as direct representations of another person's 'experience').

Schutz (1962: 207–59) postulated, like William James (1907), that *we live in multiple realities*: we live in different provinces of meaning, not only in everyday life but also in fantasy and imagination (reading a novel, watching a movie, daydreaming) or we are dreaming when sleeping. The world of everyday life as the realm of pragmatic actions is the paramount reality because we experience it as shared with others. According to Schutz, the theoretical attitude of social scientists also constitutes a different province of meaning as scientists orient to a different stock of knowledge – the one of the discipline and past research – and to a different system of relevance (research question, methodical and theoretical concerns) than actors in everyday life. The (interpreted) subjective sense of an other's actions is therefore constituted differently in the perspective of a scientific observer, compared with the observer in everyday life who is guided by pragmatic interests and not by scrutiny. In addition, the sense will differ if scientists research past actions (as historians do), present actions (as sociologists do) or future actions (as futorologists do). And it will differ, if we analyse our own subjective experience or rely on empirical data like audio and video recordings or on narratives or even mere indications and clues.

The 'structures of the life-world' that Schutz elucidates are rich and detailed (cf. Schutz and Luckmann, 1973; 1989). Are they indeed universal and invariant? Schutz claims they are the same for all human beings in this world. The social world is structured in space and time in relation to the experiencing subject: there are those I personally know, and there are contemporaries, predecessors and successors. And every ('normal') actor on earth has a subjective, biographically determined stock of knowledge at hand; uses (linguistic and pre-linguistic) typifications and is guided by systems of relevances; orients in time and space; and relies on systems of appresentation in order to understand others or relate to multiple realities. Such universal formal structures can be phenomenologically described and represent a philosophical anthropology, while the concrete contents of stocks of knowledge, of typifications and systems of relevances, of temporal and spatial orientation, and so on, are historically and culturally contingent and therefore research objects of empirical sciences.

PHENOMENOLOGY AS PROTOSOCIOLOGY: SOLVING THE MEASUREMENT PROBLEM?

Phenomenological Life-World Analysis as Protosociology

The Structures of the Life-World (Schutz and Luckmann, 1973; 1989) represents a systematic account of Schutz's work; it also carries the distinct signature of Thomas Luckmann and therefore was published in co-authorship. Schutz's original intention to provide a philosophical foundation of the methodology of the social sciences remained the same throughout his life. Luckmann confirmed this aim but omitted Schutz's final chapter on methodology (which corresponds to Schutz, 1962: 3–47). With his famous *postulate of adequacy*, Schutz demanded that the second-order constructions of the scientist have to be consistent with the first-order constructions of the actor in everyday life. As the phenomenological constitutive analysis elucidated the formal properties and structures of the life-world, this implies that the scientific constructions have to be consistent with the described *structures of the life-world*. Schutz also claimed that scientific models should fulfil the *postulate of subjective interpretation*; that is, that they refer to the subjective consciousness of an actor and his stock of knowledge with its typifications and systems of relevances. In addition, he discerned that *rationality* on the level of scientific constructs has quite a different character than the rationalities of everyday life (cf. Eberle, 2010) – a point that became crucial in Harold Garfinkel's (1967) ethnomethodology.

Luckmann (1973; 1979) interprets the analysis of the structures of the life-world as a *protosociology* that works as a foundation to 'sociology'. He distinguished the two concisely: *either you do phenomenology or you do sociology*:

1. Phenomenology is a philosophy. It analyses phenomena of subjective consciousness. Its perspective is egological and its method proceeds reflexively. Its goal is to describe the universal structures of subjective orientation in the life-world.
2. Sociology is a science. It analyses phenomena of the social world. Its perspective is cosmological and its method proceeds inductively. Its goal is to explain the general properties of the objective world.

Luckmann contends that the universal and invariant structures of the life-world represent a protosociology in the sense of a *mathesis universalis*, a formal matrix that provides a solution to the problem of measurement in the social sciences. They serve as a *tertium comparationis*, that is they allow for translating propositions that are formulated as empirical observations in a certain language into a proper formal language. In Luckmann's view, Schutz has succeeded in providing the scope of this protosociological matrix; the details of it may be scrutinized and modified by further phenomenological analyses.

Luckmann's concise distinction between phenomenology and sociology was very influential in German sociology. It implies that there is no such thing as a 'phenomenological sociology', and in the context of the present book it *implies that phenomenology is inapt as a strategy of data analysis* in the usual sense of 'empirical data': it has an egological, not a cosmological, perspective. We will see later that US sociology took quite a different direction in this respect.

Pragmatic Life-World Theory as Social Anthropology

As Ilja Srubar (1988; 2005) has convincingly shown, there is more to Schutz than a phenomenological analysis of the intentional processes in the subjective consciousness. Schutz's life-world analysis has not only a *subjective* but also a *pragmatic pole*. The life-world is not only perceived and experienced in subjective consciousness, but also constituted by pragmatic social actions. Srubar

(1988) detects this 'pragmatic turn' already in Schutz's early writings and postulates that Schutz complemented Husserl's *paradigm of perception* by a *paradigm of action*: a human being is not only *ego cogitans* but also *ego agens*. The pragmatic life-world theory encompasses both the subjective as well as the pragmatic pole, and the two are related to each other. Schutz realized that his mundane, pragmatic theory of the life-world was a legitimate counterpart of transcendental phenomenology and emphasized the *primacy of the pragma*: it is sociality that founds subjectivity, not the other way around (Srubar, 1988: 266). The interaction in a we-relationship represents the heart of mundane sociality, and thinking is derived from communication (similar to George H. Mead).

In accordance with Luckmann, Srubar considers Schutz's pragmatic life-world theory as a philosophical anthropology and as such as a *basic formal matrix* and a *tertium comparationis* that allows for comparing different cultures. Schutz's theory of constitution describes the human reality as an interlinking of life-worlds with a multiplicity of perspectives and manifold realms of meaning, and it systematically takes into account the variability of cultural worlds and of different life-forms. Srubar (2005) shows why and how the pragmatic life-world theory has more potential to facilitate *adequate* cultural comparisons, than have concepts that evolved in a specific scientific discourse.

The Relationship Between Protosociology and Empirical Research

Luckmann's clear-cut methodological distinction between phenomenology and sociology also served strategic purposes. He attempted to prevent sociologists from immersing exclusively in an exegesis of Schutz's work; they should rather engage in empirical research of concrete social settings. Luckmann proclaimed a *close relationship between phenomenology and sociology*. A well-known example for a sociological theory that is clearly compatible with Schutz's protosociology is Berger and Luckmann's (1966) *The Social Construction of Reality*. It consists of three parts: (1) the foundations of knowledge in everyday life; (2) society as objective reality; and (3) society as subjective reality. In the first part they present some key results of Schutz's phenomenological life-world analysis and characterize them explicitly as 'philosophical prolegomena' that are 'presociological' and 'not scientific' (1966: 20). But they treat them as an apt 'starting point for sociological analysis' (ibid.). In line with these protosociological considerations, they design a sociology of knowledge that consists of two perspectives. In 'society as objective reality' they analyse the processes of institutionalization and legitimation; in 'society as subjective reality', the processes of internalization and the evolvement of identity. Many failed to recognize this basic logical structure. Luckmann specified later that the term '*constitution*' should refer to the acts in subjective consciousness, while the term '*construction*' should be used for (empirically observable) social processes. In line with this, most German sociologists who base their research on Schutz's phenomenological protosociology label themselves not as 'phenomenological sociologists' but as 'sociologists of knowledge' (in the German Sociological Association there exists a section with this label).

The Constitution of Empirical Data

A protosociological perspective on empirical data differs significantly from methodological strategies and practices of data analysis and interpretation. Phenomenology provides an epistemological framework and has proved seminal for elucidating how sense and meaning are constituted in subjective consciousness and how they are constructed in everyday interaction and in scientific observations and interpretations. The life-world analysis of Schutz represents a *suitable epistemological framework for (qualitative and quantitative) social research* in general. If we carefully analyse our 'lived experience' (the phenomena we perceive, feel, imagine or think of) as well as our 'experiences' (the sense-connexions we constitute of our past 'lived experiences') we immediately become aware of how rich and complex meaning constitution is, how many facets we notice when considering the mode of givenness with all our senses, and how reductive we are when talking about them. The social sciences are text sciences, tied to linguistic constructions, and until recently they have vastly overlooked the importance of visual data (see Banks, Chapter 27, this volume), of soundscapes (see Maeder, Chapter 29, this volume), of smells and odours, or of haptic experiences. Based on our subjective experience we know that linguistic descriptions often cannot catch a phenomenon properly, and we all know how selectively we proceed in communication. Meaning and sense are constituted on a pre-predicative level, and all predications are a different kind of act. In spite of our non-linguistic bodily sensations and our non-verbal behavioural expressions, many social scientists reduce reality to linguistic representations. And although it is evident that we have direct access only to our own experiences, many qualitative researchers claim to talk about 'the experiences of others' when collecting and interpreting autobiographical narrations or interview data. Phenomenology helps to clarify what happens when we constitute empirical data by our practices of recollection, analysis and interpretation. Phenomenologists are always aware that they interpret on the basis of their own subjective experiences, and that a linguistic representation never really catches what was experienced. However, we can ponder systematically how much we can understand of the other's experiences on the basis of our own.

Based on Schutz's life-world analysis, Cicourel (1964) and Garfinkel (1967) pointed out that the methodology of the social sciences has not sufficiently recognized and dealt with the *interpretive procedures* (see Willig, Chapter 10, this volume) that are employed in research. These are crucial for the constitution of data but usually remain hidden and unexplicated in the research reports. Cicourel analysed the relevant methods of data collection and analysis, elucidated their hidden assumptions and their implicit practices of common-sense reasoning, and argued that half of the applied methods in empirical research remains in the dark, which heavily affects the possibility of intersubjective verification. As the social world is pre-interpreted, the involved common-sense operations must be methodically reflected, too, in quantitative as well as in qualitative research.

In the late 1970s, Luckmann supervised a similar research project. As social reality is transient and passes by inevitably and irrevocably, the basic question is how it can be registered and conserved. In order to judge the objectivity and intersubjectivity of scientific propositions, empirical research requires that data are objectified. Traditionally, data consist of texts: of ethnographic descriptions (see Gubrium and Holstein, Chapter 3, this volume), interview transcriptions (see Roulston, Chapter 20, and Kowal and O'Connell, Chapter 5, this volume), proceedings of events, and so on. Then they often get further encoded into certain categories or transformed into numbers. Many researchers have, however, overlooked that the constitution of such basic textual data actually transforms experienced or observed events into another mode of givenness, namely into their textual representation. Bergmann (1985) suggested distinguishing between a 'recording conservation' (see Toerien, Chapter 22, this volume) and a 'reconstructing conservation'. The first consists in pure registration that can be done by audio and video equipment and does not include any interpretation of what is registered; the second transforms recorded data into transcripts (see Kowal and O'Connell, Chapter 5, this volume), interprets them and usually makes use of reconstructive genres. Recent methodological reflections argue that even 'recording conservation' implies a construction in many respects, by the (corporate) actor who produced the material and enacted the 'camera action' (Reichertz and Englert, 2011) as well as by the specific qualities of the employed technology, that is its 'technological co-constructive elements' (see Knoblauch et al., Chapter 30, this volume). Gross (1981), who worked in Luckmann's data constitution project, questions the researcher's increasing belief that audio- and video-recorded data picture a thematic event in the best available form – in fact these data treat from the outset as irrelevant what they do not present, like haptic touches, odours and smells, the energies that could be felt by the participants, the perspectives that were not taken, etc.

Triangulation

Luckmann acknowledges the problem of epistemological reflexivity (see May and Perry, Chapter 8, this volume). Phenomenological analysis, too, cannot avoid using language for its descriptions and cannot strip itself completely from a specific colloquial language. Even if the method of phenomenological reduction allows the systematic stripping of cognition from the historically and culturally specific elements, how can we be sure that we have reached that plane of universal and invariant insights? To solve this problem, Hubert Knoblauch suggests – in line with Luckmann – a triangulation of three different methods. The phenomenological method is 'to be corrected and complemented by two other methods: (a) the "cosmological" methods of the sciences studying the human body, on the one hand, and (b) the sciences studying the variety of human culture and social structure, on the other' (Knoblauch, 2011: 140f.). If such a triangulation is accepted, Luckmann's dualistic methodological distinction between phenomenology and science still holds, but the sciences then are included in the foundational project, at least for correction and complementarity. (For a 'parallel action' of protosociological and sociological analysis, see Dreher, 2009.)

PHENOMENOLOGICAL SOCIOLOGY: A NEW APPROACH TO EMPIRICAL RESEARCH

The distinction between phenomenology (as a protosociology) and sociology is well established in German sociology, due to the eminent intellectual influence of Luckmann. In US sociology and other countries, however, the label 'phenomenological sociology' has widely spread. What is phenomenological sociology, and how does it proceed?

Phenomenological Sociology as a New Sociological Paradigm

The most influential representative of such a program was George Psathas (1973; 1989). He presents 'phenomenological sociology' as a 'new paradigm' that does not approach social reality with preconceived notions – as did the prevailing structural functionalism at the time – but investigates the social reality-as-it-is-experienced by the members of society. Phenomenological sociology is seen as a kind of 'synthesis' of phenomenology and sociology and a promising alternative to positivist sociology. It offers a fresh, open and innovative approach that encourages suspension of the natural attitude, seeing the phenomena-as-they-are, and avoiding preconceived sociological concepts as well as the established recipes and formulae of research procedures. Psathas (1989: xii) sees the goal of his research as 'the understanding, description and analysis of the life-world as experienced by those who live it'. This does not imply accepting 'the statements respondents make as the literal and sufficient explanations of their conduct, beliefs, values, or knowledge' (1973: 16). More sophisticated methods are needed as they were developed by Husserl, Schutz and Garfinkel.

Gregory Bird (2009) is right in stating that much of what was said about phenomenological sociology at that time was strategic: the goal was to get it included in the discipline of sociology. But there are also some clear-cut differences in content compared with Luckmann's version (Eberle, 2012b): First, Schutz's findings are not interpreted as a systematic whole or even as a protosociological *mathesis universalis*; Schutz is rather considered to have paved the way for a new way of doing sociological research. Second, there is no need to separate protosociology from sociology as every sociological paradigm implies philosophical premises; phenomenological sociology is a sociology that operates with different premises than positivist sociology. Third, no distinction is made between egological, reflexive and cosmological, inductive procedures; phenomenological sociology investigates not the researcher's subjective perspective but rather how other people experience their life-world. How come?

Ethnomethodology's Program

Phenomenological sociology in the United States is strongly influenced by ethnomethodology. It was Garfinkel who inspired many young sociologists to read Husserl, Schutz and Gurvitsch (and later Merleau-Ponty) in order to devise a new paradigm of sociological research (Psathas, 2004). Garfinkel gave the phenomenological life-world analysis from the outset *a sociological twist*:

1. He confronted Parsons' structural functionalism in a careful analysis with Schutz's phenomenological studies and interpreted the latter as an alternative approach to explain the problem of social order (Garfinkel, 1952). Schutz's conception of the actor, in contrast to Parsons' norm-guided role-player, does not make the actor a 'judgmental dope'. Garfinkel (1967) showed by his incongruity (or breaching) experiments that the social order does not break down when norms get violated but only when people do not manage to make sense of the situation. Therefore he explains social order not by normative but by constitutive rules and by sense-making.
2. This view implied a methodological reorientation. Ethnomethodology investigates sense-making not egologically in the subjective consciousness but in empirical settings that are intersubjectively available. Not the constitutive acts of consciousness are the topic of study but the empirically observable accounting practices whereby actors make sense recognizable.
3. Garfinkel (2002; [1948] 2006) does not treat Schutz's structures of the life-world as validated insights but seeks new answers himself. He uses Schutz's and other phenomenologists' analyses only as inspiration, calls for 'misreading' them (by which he meant an 'alternate' reading) and starts a new kind of research from scratch. The basic question, however, remains the same: asking for the how, the know-how, and investigating the constitution of social phenomena.

How does ethnomethodology proceed? Garfinkel (1967) was very creative and employed *many different methods of data collection*. He tape-recorded the deliberations of jurors; he interviewed the transsexual person 'Agnes'; he asked students to transcribe everyday conversations and fill in all the implicit knowledge the participants were referring to; or he asked them to make incongruity experiments, that is to breach social expectations by behaving strangely, and take notes of the others' reactions (e.g. acting like a guest at home and observing the other family members' consternation; negotiating prices at the supermarket; asking for clarification of ordinary expressions in conversations that nobody would ask; and so on). *How he analysed these different sorts of data* remained, however, vastly in the dark. Much more crucial was indeed the alternative perspective of his questioning and framing. How are jurors recognizable as 'jurors'? What practices did Agnes employ for 'doing gender' for making evident that she was a natural woman? How do members manage the indexicality of expressions in everyday conversation? How do people make sense when elements of the 'natural attitude' are breached?

It is important to distinguish two procedures here:

1. Insofar as ethnomethodologists reflect on the givenness of empirically observed, social phenomena and scrutinize what is seen by systematically bracketing their worldviews, assumptions and specific intentionalities, they proceed phenomenologically. A phenomenological analysis can also be done collectively. When observing the same social phenomena, they start with their subjective 'lived experience' and bracket their subjective assumptions step by step.
2. Insofar as ethnomethodologists only investigate how the members of a setting orient and interact, they have an observer's perspective and can only

analyse what is observable. Many have converted to conversation analysis and adopted the practice to accept only audio-visual data for analysis. If they restrict analysis to Harvey Sacks' dictum (1974) 'Can we find order? How can we provide for that order?', they only capture the subjective perspective of actors insofar as it is observable – and all the rest is excluded from analysis.

Is ethnomethodology still a phenomenological approach? Psathas (1989: 79–98) explicitly affirms that. Most ethnomethodologists nowadays, however, acknowledge just the historical importance of Schutz for ethnomethodology and assert that they have moved beyond. In our context we can state that Garfinkel obviously builds upon the pragmatic pole of Schutz's life-world analysis and is interested in the noema of phenomena. While the question 'What can I know?' makes us consider the noesis, the question 'Why do we see something as something?' leads to the noema, to the meaningful actions that constitute the social world. In this respect, Garfinkel's question 'What makes jurors "jurors"?' or 'What makes Agnes a woman?' is therefore a genuine phenomenological question that focuses on the noema. On the other hand, ethnomethodology moved away from phenomenology. Garfinkel stripped it from anthropological premises, dispensed with the notion of 'subjective consciousness' and considers 'members' as being produced by self-organizing social settings. He replaced the 'subjective perspective' by an observer's perspective. (cf. Eberle, 2012a).

Ethnomethodology investigates the common-sense reasoning, the practices of making sense, the members' ethnomethods whereby a social setting is produced and the accounting practices that make it identifiable, reportable and intelligible. Of course, ethnomethodology faces the trap of epistemological reflexivity, too. To what extent is the explication of members' ethnomethods dependent on the ethnomethods of sense-making that are used in ethnomethodological research? In fact, the theoretical status of 'ethnomethods' remained unclarified. While the early Garfinkel spoke of 'eidetic' and 'invariant' 'formal properties', he later became more and more interested in the details of situations and emphasized the 'haecceitas' of the social, its 'just-thisness', which means that the social only exists as something individual and unique. In the context of his *Ethnomethodological Studies of Work* (Garfinkel, 1986) he formulated the *unique adequacy requirement* as an ideal. Ethnomethodologists must be competent practitioners of the social phenomena they study. In order to study the working practices of lawyers and mathematicians, his students had to study law and mathematics, not just ethnomethodology. Consequently, his concept of *adequate description* that ethnomethodology is striving for became more and more restrictive: a description is adequate if it successfully serves as an *instruction*. Garfinkel reduced the presupposed intersubjectivity of ethnomethods (or sense-making practices) more and more, and ultimately one can remember Schutz's insight that understanding the subjective sense of another's actions is only possible as an approximation.

A Recent Example of Phenomenological Sociology: The New Orleans Sniper

In her recent study on *The New Orleans Sniper: A Phenomenological Case Study of Constituting the Other*, Frances Waksler (2010) demonstrates how phenomenological sociology (in Psathas's sense) analyses data. The researched event happened in 1973 when a sniper in New Orleans shot 16 people, 7 of whom died, before he was eventually shot dead by the police. But the shooting went on the next day as there presumably existed a second sniper; seven more policemen were wounded but the second sniper was never found. Waksler ponders the thrilling *research question of 'how the second sniper was first constituted and later unconstituted'* (2010: 3). The case is particularly interesting as the existence of the second sniper was problematic and ambiguous. For this reason 'the work of constituting the other becomes evident' (3). Waksler draws on Husserl's phenomenological analyses of the constitution of the other in the transcendental sphere and shows that they 'can be directly applied to a particular instance of a problematic other and can illuminate the intricate processes whereby the Other is constituted' (3). Like Psathas, she uses phenomenological insights to interpret people's actions sociologically: '*how* people, with their general procedures and resources, use them to constitute an other in a specific situation' (3). In other words, she uses Husserl's insights where applicable, but, unlike Husserl, she investigates the givenness of the other not egologically in the sphere of transcendental reduction, but as a social process that can be reconstructed on the basis of empirical data. The question is how *others* constitute – and later unconstitute – the other, namely the second sniper. This question is a genuine sociological one but inspired by phenomenology.

The findings are intriguing (cf. Eberle 2013a). On the basis of newspaper reports and interviews of participants Waksler demonstrates the power of first assumptions; the mundane reasoning about what one ordinary or even extraordinary person is capable of doing and what indicates the participation of a second sniper; which signs of another sniper were perceived and how they were interpreted (what was seen, what was heard, which turn-taking took place, which leavings were found that provided evidence of a second person involved; which speculations and conspiracy theories were formulated to provide ways to deal with the events as a meaningful whole; how the possibility of an escape of the second sniper was assessed; the prevailing use of either/or explanations; and the procedures of legitimizing evidence). The reported evidence was contradictory – even the persons who were in direct interaction with the (first) sniper described him differently and some of them did not recognize him on the photo of the person shot by the police. While the police were convinced there was a second sniper, they changed their assessment over time, based on the collected evidence, and arrived at the conclusion that there was only one sniper as a second one could not have escaped from the site; the wounded police officers during the shootings on the next day were obviously victims of police ricochets.

What is the *strategy of data analysis* in this case? Waksler collects and documents all those pieces from newspaper reports, TV reports and interviews that seem relevant in regard to her research question and reconstructs the assumptions in regard to the existence of a second sniper on the basis of these data. Husserl's analyses of intersubjectivity are used to make the different kinds of assumptions visible and demonstrable in her data.

PHENOMENOLOGY AS AN EMPIRICAL RESEARCH PROCEDURE

Ethnomethodology and US phenomenological sociology adopt an observer's strategy and deal with members' subjective perspective only insofar as it is, first, relevant for their research question and, second, inasmuch it can be reconstructed on the basis of observational data (e.g. audio–video recordings and reports). On the one hand, ethnomethodologists have greatly contributed to refining the strategies of empirical data analysis, in particular by their attention to detail and their emphasis on and high standards of 'adequate description'. This is undoubtedly a result of their phenomenological training and awareness.

On the other hand, much is lost of what can be accessed in a *subjective perspective*: the 'lived experience' in its multimodality and intersensuousness on a pre-predicative level, before it is formulated on the predicative level of language, and its embodiment as well as its embeddedness in the sense-connexions of past experiences. In the following section I will ponder *how phenomenology could serve as an empirical research procedure*. Schutz actually wrote some fine analyses of concrete social phenomena, like the stranger, the homecomer or the well-informed citizen (Schutz, 1964). He was not familiar with the methods of empirical research but rather with the method of free imagination and homunculi construction, which was common in the social sciences at the time. Based on his own experiences he carefully analysed the 'typical' experiences of a stranger (a European immigrant in the United States), of a homecomer (a soldier after the war) and of a well-informed, 'participating citizen' (which he was – see Barber, 2004). In these 'applied' analyses Schutz demonstrated how useful his 'structures of the life-world' actually are for investigating concrete social phenomena. At the same time he further developed his 'structures' in the context of these concrete studies. Nowadays we expect, however, a closer connection of such analyses to empirical data.

The *empirical research building on Schutz's analyses of the life-world* has become rich and well differentiated. On the one hand, they mark the enormous difference between today's social scientific research and the role models that Schutz oriented to. On the other hand, they both mirror the variety of empirical approaches to the social world that strive for adequacy. Let me choose and present *three new developments on how phenomenological analysis can directly contribute to empirical research.*

The Phenomenological Analysis of Small Social Life-Worlds

Phenomenological analysis can be applied not only in order to find the universal, invariant formal structures of the life-world, but also to research specific socio-cultural life-worlds. The German researchers Ronald Hitzler and Anne Honer have developed a research approach, which they call – in line with Luckmann's distinction between phenomenology and sociology – *life-world analytic ethnography*. In the course of fieldwork, data are collected on the one hand by participant observation, interviews in the field, analysis of artefacts and documents, and then get hermeneutically interpreted, much like other ethnographic approaches do. On the other hand – and this is specific about this approach – the *subjective experience of the researcher* in the field is used explicitly and reflexively as an '*instrument*' *of data generation and collection*. The researchers thus rely not only on participant observation for their data collection, but also on what they call, with a different emphasis, *observing participation* in a field-specific role, and analyse their experiences phenomenologically. For example, a certain experience of well-being during a techno rave is researched not only through observation of and interviews with other participants, but also through a systematic phenomenological analysis of their own personal experiences as co-participants. The basic idea is that the *genuine form of an experience* is lost, once it is brought into an objectified form, for example by narrating and transcribing and subsequently interpreting it. As a researcher, one should therefore use the *immediate access* to one's own subjective experience (e.g. the multimodal sensations of a rave) to conduct a methodologically controlled, phenomenological analysis of the experienced (i.e. of the researcher's experiences and their correlates) through systematic reductions (or bracketings – Hitzler and Eberle, 2004). In contrast to other ethnographic approaches, 'the native's point of view' is not understood indirectly, but is complemented by an 'existential view from the inside' (Honer, 2004). This way phenomenological researchers explore 'small social life-worlds' as suggested by Benita Luckmann (1970), such as fitness studios, techno raves, religious happenings, and so on, and phenomenological and ethnographic analyses mutually inform each other.

The *difference between a phenomenological view and an observer's perspective* is blatantly clear if you cannot assume that the other perceives the world like you. How much can we grasp of a blind man's subjective orientation in an observer's perspective? Just by watching him or by asking him? Siegfried Saerberg (2006) demonstrates in a fine analysis how much a phenomenological training helps in analysing his spatial orientation as a blind man. Based on self-observation, experiments and interviews he describes the specific style of lived experience, notably the specific style of the multimodal, intersensory perception of the blind. Most illuminating are his analytical descriptions of how he orients himself in space: how he interprets every kind of noise and sound; how he attends to the 'basic sound' of a space in order to guess its topological structure; how he notices smells and what he recognizes by touching things, in particular by using his stick; how he identifies and recognizes objects; how he avoids bumping into things; and so on. In an observer's perspective we could only record and analyse the sequence of behaviours but infer little about the subjective acts of orientation. That would not suffice if we were interested, for instance, in improving interactions between the sighted and the blind. For such a project we cannot dispense with the subjective orientation of the blind.

How does such a phenomenological analysis proceed? This is not easy to describe. Phenomenological analysis starts before empirical data are constituted. The researcher starts analysis with his or her own lived experience. What do I see, hear, touch, smell and taste? Which phenomena do I perceive and how is their meaning or sense constituted? What is their mode of givenness: spatially, temporally, in terms of typicality and relevance? Are they distinct or vague, general or concrete, anonymous or personal, strange or familiar? Which connotations are activated by my biographically determined, subjective stock of knowledge at hand? Which assumptions are involved when constituting the phenomena of my life-world? What happens if they are bracketed and reduced step by step?

If we perceive not just objects but other human beings, our assumptions and intentionalities are more complex. Hitzler (2012) did extensive research with a PVS (Persistent Vegetative State) patient. The staff of the special-care home treated its patients with dignity – that means as human beings, as social persons; they even addressed them with their academic titles if they had one. This is the ethnographic aspect. In a phenomenological perspective, one proceeds with the systematic bracketing of one's assumptions, intentionalities and worldviews – which causes a basic doubt. What can I actually perceive? Is this PVS patient still a human being, a subject, an alter ego, a person that *is* and as well *has* a body? Is 'it' still a 'he' or a 'she' and a 'member' of society? Is there really an encounter, an interaction, a communication with this patient taking place? All the usual categories that we normally use in the natural attitude of everyday life – and which are used by the special-care home's staff – become suddenly questionable and are suspended step by step. The patient and the patient's movements are observed and scrutinized meticulously, sometimes audio-visually recorded, and each bodily movement is carefully analysed if it was a communicative reaction – a turn-in-interaction – or just a coinciding, accidental muscular spasm. Such a procedure reveals all the assumptions with which a researcher usually operates when doing observation and paves the way to get hold of the eidetic structure of a phenomenon. And it provides a foil that also manifests the assumptions of the special-care home's staff whose actions are ethnographically observed.

Phenomenological Hermeneutics

Phenomenology analyses a subject's own experiences. But it can also help to better understand an alter ego (cf. Nasu, 2005). In order to avoid any confusion between a phenomenological analysis of one's own subjective experiences and of analysing the experiences of an *alter ego*, I call the latter approach *phenomenological hermeneutics* (see Wernet, Chapter 16, this volume). The experiences of others are always understood on the basis of a subject's own experiences. They are inaccessible to the researcher and thus require communication – that means we operate on the basis of data on a predicative level. A phenomenological perspective, however, may help to elucidate deeper layers of sense-connexions of the other's experiences. In our recent collaborative research with a patient who suffered a cerebral hemorrhage, we tried carefully to reconstruct how the patient gradually regained sense-connexions after awakening from an artificial coma of

2–3 weeks (Eberle and Rebitzke, 2012; Eberle, 2013b). Our data consist of audio recordings, diary entries by researcher as well as patient, field observations and interviews. In an observer's perspective it was recognizable that the patient was at times confused and disoriented during the first weeks after awakening from the coma. And it could be observed that the patient read the newspaper every morning after entering the rehabilitation clinic. But it could not be observed what she explained later: that she only saw letters and words but could not make sense of them. She displayed – or made accountable – a practice of reading but actually did not understand anything, and she felt so humiliated by her lack of capabilities that she consciously tried to deceive others about her actual mental state (and often successfully did).

While patients with dementia or Alzheimer's are usually not capable of describing their subjective experiences and how they orient in their specific life-world, patients with a stroke or cerebral hemorrhage sometimes fully recover and can retrospectively analyse what they experienced over time. This happened in our case and so we could tap the most important resource: the experiences of the patient. We tried to reconstruct her experiences retrospectively in *collaborative narrative interviews*. We started with her recollections of specific situations and experiences and recorded and transcribed them. Based on my own experiences I attempted carefully to understand how she experienced her life-world at the time. And based on Schutz's analysis of the life-world I asked questions that aimed at further clarification.

She told me, for instance, that when she came home for a Sunday visit for the first time after the incident, 'everything was empty, without contents, without meanings' and that she felt hugely overstrained. Analysing her narrations in a phenomenological perspective, I asked her step by step if she recognized her living room, the sofa, the closet, the table and chairs, the plants, and so on, and we gradually recognized that in fact she did – that these things actually had meanings and were not without content at the time. Eventually we detected that she meant that they had *no meaning to her*; that she was able to identify all the pieces of furniture but that she did not sense any personal relation to them anymore. She missed any sort of *familiarity* with these surroundings. Thus there *was* content, there *was* meaning and the space was *not* empty, but she did not feel familiar with her home anymore, she felt like a stranger. When she entered her kitchen she felt completely overwhelmed: she could not remember what was in which cabinet, she could not figure out how one would go about cooking, how properly to organize a sequence of actions, and so on. Before, in the clinic, she had been convinced that she was healed and could return home – but now she suddenly realized that she was not (yet) able to manage her life on her own and accomplish the usual everyday affairs.

Another example of this research was the long way to regaining her sense of smell. She could no longer identify odours, aromas and smells. As soon as she smelled several different odours at the same time, she ran away because the stink was sickening. Neither doctors nor therapists knew how to deal with the problem, and so she – a professional therapist herself – developed a therapy on her own: only exposing her to one odour, aroma or smell at a time; trying to identify them (smelling different spices, for instance) one by one and trying to remember each smell; and finally beginning to combine two of them, later three. Step by step she regained her olfactory sense and finally started to enjoy eating again. In a phenomenological perspective, I could participate in the whole procedure, smelling and attempting to identify the same spices, and so on. Based on my own subjective experience of smells I could certainly understand much more adequately what she was talking about. The phenomenological perspective has clearly helped to go beyond her narrations and analyse what she experienced on a deeper, more adequate level.

Ethnophenomenology

The German sociologists Hubert Knoblauch and Bernt Schnettler developed an approach, which they call *ethnophenomenology*. In their research on near-death experiences (Knoblauch et al., 1999) as well as in their research on visions (Knoblauch and Schnettler, 2001), both researchers realized that the egological analysis of phenomenologists remains tied to their specific biographic situation: 'Mundane phenomenology can only describe one's own experiences. Therefore, phenomenologists cannot make any analytic statements regarding the constitution of transcendental experiences that the phenomenologists themselves did not have' (Schnettler, 2008: 145; my translation). During their research they detected that ordinary people, although philosophical laypersons, are quite able to reflect on their own modes of extraordinary experiences.

The analogy to ethnomethodology is obvious. Ethnophenomenology describes the research approach as well as its subject matter. But in contrast to ethnomethodology, it is not methodologically produced, observable, ordinary communicative acts but rather non-observable, extraordinary subjective experiences of actors that are empirically explored. In his study of visionary experiences Schnettler (2004) showed on the basis of interview data that passages with ethnophenomenological descriptions of *form* differed clearly from the descriptions of the *content* of the experiences – in fact, the contents of what was witnessed were often of secondary importance in comparison with the extraordinary *mode* of those experiences. Finally, he was able to elicit a number of recurring features of an ethnophenomenology of visions of the future. Knoblauch and Schnettler carefully differentiate between the different reference levels of mundane phenomenology and ethnophenomenology. Mundane phenomenology aims at establishing a protosociological *general theory* with a *universal* relevance by describing *general* forms of human experience. Ethnophenomenology reconstructs *sociologically* and *empirically* the communicatively conveyed descriptions of extraordinary experiences (e.g. of near-death experiences) by everyday people in a certain historical epoch, and it transforms their generalizations into theoretical notions of a 'medium range' (Schnettler, 2008: 142).

While *phenomenological hermeneutics* attempts collaboratively to explicate deeper layers of sense-connexions of another person's experiences, *ethnophenomenology* goes beyond and tries to explore types of extraordinary experiences that the phenomenological researcher never had. Both approaches are based on communication and rely on narrative data – unlike the first approach where the researcher pursues a phenomenological analysis of his or her own subjective experiences in the field.

LIMITS OF PHENOMENOLOGY AND FUTURE PROSPECTS

Phenomenology is basically an *epistemological endeavour*. It starts analysis with the embodied lived experience that is accessible in the subjective consciousness on a pre-predicative level. Phenomenological analysis begins before empirical data are constituted and makes evident that all empirical data are already reductions: audiotapes, video recordings (see Knoblauch et al., Chapter 30, this volume), narrations (see Esin et al., Chapter 14, this volume), interview data (see Roulston, Chapter 20, this volume), transcripts (see Kowal and O'Connell, Chapter 5, this volume), field notes (see Marvasti, Chapter 24, this volume), and so on. Phenomenological analysis therefore takes place in the here-and-now of lived experience, not on the basis of recorded data. Of course, the findings of phenomenological analyses get finally objectified and communicated in language, too. Phenomenology also produces data, in that sense, but is aware that these data have already transformed the character of the original experience. A basic concern of phenomenology is to avoid inadequate

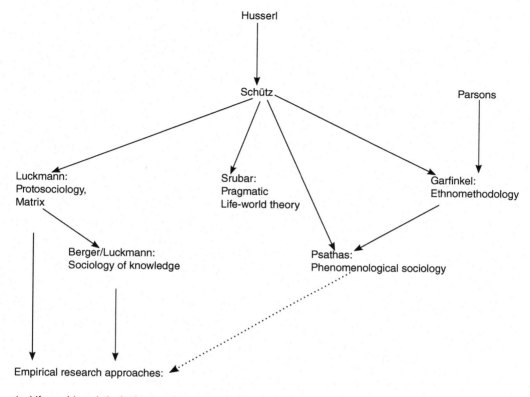

Figure 13.1 Major perspectives of phenomenological sociology

epistemological and methodological interpretations, like, for example, equating people's narrations with 'their experience'.

This chapter has attempted to clarify the basic difference such as interpreting phenomenological life-world analysis as a protosociology (the German version) as opposed to interpreting it as empirical phenomenological sociology (the US version). It emphasized the difference between a phenomenological analysis of the subjective perspective and a hermeneutical analysis of another person's perspective. It further reported on three new developments that use phenomenology as an empirical research procedure. Phenomenology intends to complement other empirical research approaches, not substitute them. Once its findings are objectified, they can be triangulated with different sorts of ethnographic data.

Of course, there are *limits of phenomenological analysis*. A phenomenological analysis proper can only be pursued in the state of wide-awakeness of an adult who is trained in phenomenology. It requires great sensitivity to analyse one's subjective experiences in their multimodality and intersensuousness. As the results are expressed in language, it also requires great skills in translating experiences into linguistic descriptions. Many realities remain inaccessible as the experience of phenomenologists is limited: if they have not had 'near-death' experiences or epiphanies, they are not able to describe that on their own. Other forms of research, like ethnography or ethnophenomenology, may provide valuable information.

What are the *future prospects of phenomenology?* They look fairly promising. First, phenomenological analysis can be applied to *nearly any area of social research*. Second, after the subject was eliminated from theoretical approaches like Foucault's discourse analysis or Luhmann's systems theory, *we currently observe a return of the subject*. In our daily lives, we all experience the social world from our subjective perspective, and we know that what is observable of other's social actions and interactions is only the surface. The social sciences cannot reduce their analysis to what is observable only; they need to include the subjective experiences of actors as well as of researchers. There is no approach that analyses the subjective perspective as concisely as phenomenology.

FURTHER READING

Schutz, Alfred ([1944], 1964) 'The Stranger. An Essay in Social Psychology', in Alfred Schutz, *Collected Papers Vol. 2 – Studies in Social Theory* (ed. Arvid Brodersen). The Hague: Martinus Nijhoff. pp. 91–105.

Waksler, Frances Chaput (2010) *The New Orleans Sniper: A Phenomenological Case Study of Constituting the Other*. Boston: University Press of America.

Liberman, Kenneth (2004) *Dialectical Practice in Tibetan Philosophical Culture: An Ethnomethodological Inquiry into Formal Reasoning*. Lanham, MD: Rowman & Littlefield.

REFERENCES

Barber, Michael (2004) *The Participating Citizen: A Biography of Alfred Schutz*. Albany: State University of New York Press.

Berger, Peter L. and Luckmann, Thomas (1966) *The Social Construction of Reality: A Treatise in the Sociology of Knowledge*. Garden City, NY: Doubleday.

Bergmann, Jörg R. (1985) 'Flüchtigkeit und methodische Fixierung sozialer Wirklichkeit: Aufzeichnungen als Daten der interpretativen Soziologie', in Wolfgang Bonß and Heinz Hartmann (eds), *Entzauberte Wissenschaft (Sonderband 3 der Zeitschrift 'Soziale Welt')*. Göttingen: Schwarz. pp. 299–320.

Bird, Gregory (2009) 'What is phenomenological sociology again?', *Human Studies*, 32: 419–39.

Carnap, Rudolf ([1928], 1967) *The Logical Structure of the World: Pseudoproblems in Philosophy*. Berkeley: University of California Press.

Cicourel, Aaron V. (1964) *Method and Measurement in Sociology*. New York: Free Press.

Dreher, Jochen (2009) 'Phenomenology of friendship: Construction and constitution of an existential social relationship', *Human Studies*, 32 (4): 401–17.

Eberle, Thomas S. (2010) 'Phenomenological life-world analysis and the methodology of social science', *Human Studies*, 33 (2–3): 123–39.

Eberle, Thomas S. (2012a) 'Phenomenological life-world analysis and ethnomethodology's program', *Human Studies: Special Issue in Memory of Harold Garfinkel*, 35 (2): 279–304.

Eberle, Thomas S. (2012b) 'Phenomenology and sociology: Divergent interpretations of a complex relationship' in Hisashi Nasu and Frances Chaput Waksler (eds), *Interaction and Everyday Life: Phenomenological and Ethnomethodological Essays in Honor of George Psathas*. Lanham, MD: Lexington Books. pp. 151–67.

Eberle, Thomas S. (2013a) 'Phenomenological Sociology Reconsidered: On "The New Orleans Sniper"', *Human Studies* (2013) 26: 121–132.

Eberle, Thomas S. (2013b) 'Regaining sense-connexions after cerebral hemorrhage', *Schutzian Research*, 5: in Press.

Eberle, Thomas S. and Rebitzke Eberle, Verena (2012) 'Alles war ohne Inhalt, ohne Bedeutung. Der Umgang mit den Folgen einer Hirnblutung', in Norbert Schröer et al. (eds), *Lebenswelt und Ethnographie*. Essen: Oldib-Verlag. pp. 325–43.

Embree, Lester (2011) *Reflective Analysis*, 2nd edition. Bucharest: Zeta Books (1st edition, 2006).

Garfinkel, Harold (1952) 'The perception of the other'. Unpublished PhD dissertation, Harvard University.

Garfinkel, Harold (1967) *Studies in Ethnomethodology*. Englewood Cliffs, NJ: Prentice Hall.

Garfinkel, Harold (1986) *Ethnomethodological Studies of Work*. London: Routledge & Kegan Paul.

Garfinkel, Harold (2002) *Ethnomethodology's Program: Working out Durkheim's Aphorism*. Lanham, MD: Rowman & Littlefield.

Garfinkel, Harold ([1948] 2006) *Seeing Sociologically: The Routine Grounds of Social Action*. Lanham, MD: Rowman & Littlefield.

Gross, Peter (1981) 'Ist die Sozialwissenschaft eine Textwissenschaft?', in Peter Winkler (ed.),

Methoden der Analyse von Face-to-Face-Situationen. Stuttgart: Metzlersche Verlagsbuchhandlung. pp. 143–67.

Hitzler, Ronald (2012) 'Die rituelle Konstruktion der Person. Aspekte des Erlebens eines Menschen im sogenannten Wachkoma', *Forum: Qualitative Social Research*, 13 (3), Art. 12: www.qualitative-research.net/index.php/fqs/article/view/1878/3415 (accessed 16 September 2012).

Hitzler, Ronald and Eberle, Thomas S. (2004) 'Phenomenological life-world analysis', in Uwe Flick et al. (eds), *A Companion to Qualitative Research*. London: Sage. pp. 57–72.

Honer, Anne (2004) 'Life-world analysis in ethnography', in Uwe Flick et al. (eds), *A Companion to Qualitative Research*. London: Sage. pp.113–17.

Husserl, Edmund ([1936/54], 1970) *The Crisis of European Sciences and Transcendental Phenomenology*, trans. David Carr. Evanston, IL: Northwestern University Press.

Husserl, Edmund ([1939], 1973) *Experience and Judgment*, trans. James Spencer Churchill and Karl Ameriks. London: Routledge.

Husserl, Edmund ([1913], 1982) *Ideas Pertaining to a Pure Phenomenology and to a Phenomenological Philosophy – First Book: General Introduction to a Pure Phenomenology*, trans. Fred Kersten. The Hague: Nijhoff.

James, William (1907) *Principles of Psychology*. New York: Holt.

Knoblauch, Hubert (2011) 'Relativism, meaning and the new sociology of knowledge', in Richard Schantz and Markus Seidel (eds), *The Problem of Relativism in the Sociology of (Scientific) Knowledge*. Frankfurt: ontos. pp. 131–56.

Knoblauch, Hubert and Schnettler, Bernt (2001) 'Die kulturelle Sinnprovinz der Zukunftsvision und die Ethnophänomenologie', *Psychotherapie und Sozialwissenschaft. Zeitschrift für qualitative Forschung*, 3 (3): 182–203.

Knoblauch, Hubert, Schnettler, Bernt and Soeffner, Hans-Georg (1999) 'Die Sinnprovinz des Jenseits und die Kultivierung des Todes', in Hubert Knoblauch and Hans-Georg Soeffner (eds), *Todesnähe. Interdisziplinäre Beiträge zu einem außergewöhnlichen Phänomen*. Konstanz: UVK. pp. 271–92.

Luckmann, Benita (1970) 'The small life-worlds of modern man', *Social Research*, 37: 580–97.

Luckmann, Thomas (1973) 'Philosophy, science, and everyday life', in Maurice Natanson (ed.), *Phenomenology and the Social Sciences*. Evanston, IL: Northwestern University Press. pp. 145–85.

Luckmann, Thomas (1979) 'Phänomenologie und Soziologie', in Walter M. Sprondel and Richard Grathoff (eds), *Alfred Schütz und die Idee des Alltags in den Sozialwissenschaften*. Stuttgart: Ferdinand Enke. pp. 196–206.

Nasu, Hisashi (2005) 'How is the other approached and conceptualized in terms of Schutz's constitutive phenomenology of the natural attitude?', *Human Studies*, 28 (4): 385–96.

Psathas, George (ed.) (1973) *Phenomenological Sociology: Issues and Applications*. New York: Wiley.

Psathas, George (1989) *Phenomenology and Sociology: Theory and Research*. Boston: University Press of America.

Psathas, George (2004) 'Alfred Schutz's influence on American sociologists and sociology', *Human Studies*, 27 (1): 1–15.

Reichertz, Jo and Englert, Carina Jasmin (2011) *Einführung in die qualitative Videoanalyse*. Wiesbaden: VS Verlag für Sozialwissenschaften.

Sacks, Harvey (1984) 'Notes on methodology', in Maxwell J. Atkinson and John Heritage (eds), *Structures of Social Action*. Cambridge: Cambridge University Press. pp. 21–7.

Saerberg, Siegfried (2006) *'Geradeaus ist einfach immer geradeaus'. Eine lebensweltliche Ethnographie blinder Raumorientierung*. Konstanz: Universitätsverlag Konstanz.

Schnettler, Bernt (2004). *Zukunftsvisionen. Transzendenzerfahrung und Alltagswelt*. Konstanz: UVK.

Schnettler, Bernt (2008) 'Soziologie als Erfahrungswissenschaft. Überlegungen zum Verhältnis von Mundanphänomenologie und Ethnophänomenologie', in Jürgen Raab et al. (eds), *Phänomenologie und Soziologie. Positionen, Problemfelder, Analysen*. Wiesbaden: VS-Verlag. pp. 141–9.

Schutz, Alfred (1962) *Collected Papers Vol. 1 – The Problem of Social Reality*, ed. Maurice Natanson and Herman L. van Breda. The Hague: Martinus Nijhoff.

Schutz, Alfred (1964) *Collected Papers Vol. 2 – Studies in Social Theory*, ed. Arvid Brodersen. The Hague: Martinus Nijhoff.

Schutz, Alfred ([1932], 1967) *The Phenomenology of the Social World*, trans. George Walsh and Frederick Lehnert. Evanston, IL: Northwestern University Press.

Schutz, Alfred and Luckmann, Thomas (1973) *The Structures of the Life-World Vol. I*, trans. Richard M. Zaner and Tristram H. Engelhardt. Evanston, IL: Northwestern University Press.

Schutz, Alfred and Luckmann, Thomas (1989) *The Structures of the Life-World Vol. II*, trans. Richard Zaner and David J. Parent. Evanston, IL: Northwestern University Press.

Spiegelberg, Herbert (1982) *The Phenomenological Movement*. The Hague: Martinus Nijhoff.

Srubar, Ilja (1988) *Kosmion. Die Genese der pragmatischen Lebenswelttheorie von Alfred Schütz und ihr anthropologischer Hintergrund*. Frankfurt/M.: Suhrkamp.

Srubar, Ilja (2005) 'The pragmatic theory of the life world as a basis for intercultural comparison', in Martin Endress et al. (eds), *Explorations of the Life-World*. Dordrecht: Springer. pp. 235–66.

Waksler, Frances Chaput (2010) *The New Orleans Sniper: A Phenomenological Case Study of Constituting the Other*. Boston: University Press of America.

Weber, Max ([1922], 1978) *Economy and Society: An Outline of Interpretive Sociology*, ed. Guenther Roth and Claus Wittich. Berkeley: University of California Press.

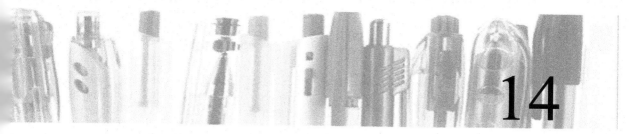

14

Narrative Analysis: The Constructionist Approach

Cigdem Esin, Mastoureh Fathi and Corinne Squire

Narrative analysis is an analytical method that accommodates a variety of approaches. Through these approaches, social researchers explore how people story their lives. This is also a process through which researchers understand the complexities of personal and social relations. Narrative analysis provides the researcher with useful tools to comprehend the diversity and the different levels involved in stories, rather than treating those stories simply as coherent, natural and unified entities (Andrews et al., 2004). It is this approach to narrative analysis, which we shall call the constructionist approach to narrative analysis, that we aim to explain in the chapter that follows.

Constructionism has a strong recent history within social sciences (Burr, 2003; Holstein and Gubrium, 2008; Sparkes and Smith, 2008). What we describe as a constructionist approach is very often adopted, in many of its features, by contemporary narrative researchers. The approach is distinct, first, as Holstein and Gubrium (2008) suggest, because of its critical take on naturalism, and in consequence its

attention to the diversity, contradictions and failures of meaning, research participants' own generations of meaning, and to the mutual constitution of meanings between participants, researchers, the research context and the wider context – where 'context' refers to many different levels and complex relations of power. However, the constructionist approach has also a great deal in common with narrative frameworks that rely on analyses of social positioning, or performance, or some variety of complexity theory.

In this chapter, we start by providing a brief overview of the contemporary place of narrative research, and summarizing the epistemological arguments involved with a constructionist view of narratives and narrative analysis. We examine the place of audience, the positioning of subjects within narratives, and the significance of power relations in stories, from within the constructionist perspective. We then proceed to describe, via examples, three analytical sites in which multiple, interconnected elements in the construction of narratives might be examined. The chapter ends with a brief discussion on the range and limitations of the constructionist approach to narrative analysis.

THE DEVELOPMENT OF NARRATIVE RESEARCH

Squire et al. (2008: 3–12) describe the development of narrative research within different theoretical and epistemological traditions, and at different historical times. Across these sizeable differences, researchers most often work with narratives because they want to address narratives' different and sometimes contradictory layers of meaning, to put them in dialogue with each other, and to understand how narratives operate dialogically between the personal and the surrounding social worlds that produce, consume, silence and contest them.

The use of narrative methods and analysis in social science research has proliferated since the 1980s. The narrative turn in social sciences (see Czarniawska, 2004) opened up an interdisciplinary space in which researchers used narratives as a tool to analyse participants' experiences of a wide range of social issues such as social inequalities, migration, gender relations, health and illness. Research in the fields of sociology (Bell, 1999; Riessman, 1993; 2002; Somers and Gibson, 1994), psychology (Bruner, 1990; Mishler, 1986; Rosenwald and Ochberg, 1992), history (White, 1984) and anthropology (Mattingly, 1998) all helped constitute this narrative turn. Such researchers criticize methods that treat research respondents only as sources of information, rather than also paying attention to the ways these respondents construct and express their understandings of social reality.

Recent work in the field of narrative research tries to bring together humanist and posthumanist academic traditions (Squire et al. 2008: 3–4), often in the direction of a modified critical humanism, informed by for instance psychoanalysis (Rustin, 2001) or Foucault (Plummer, 2001). Alternatively, such work abdicates the task of theoretical reconciliation in the service of other theoretical goals, for instance, the conceptualization of narrative incoherence (Hyvarinen et al., 2010) or time (Freeman, 2010); or in order to examine the human functioning of narratives (Herman, 2004); or in order to pursue political thinking about narratives (Andrews, 2007; Polletta, 2006), or to adopt a pragmatist position (Squire, 2007).

Narrative analysis, whatever its theoretical and methodological orientation, whether it is addressing biographical life stories, or dealing with the linguistic or discursive structure of stories, or describing various levels of positioning performed by narratives, tends to focus on participants' self-generated meanings. Even narrative analysis which is primarily interested in the linguistics of stories, for instance, tends now to address the contexts of telling and hearing as well (De Fina and Georgakopoulou, 2012: 18).

THEORETICAL BACKGROUND ASSUMPTIONS OF CONSTRUCTIONIST NARRATIVE ANALYSIS

What Is Constructionist Narrative Analysis?

The constructionist approach to narrative analysis may focus on the linguistic minutiae of the co-construction of a story between speaker and listener, but usually it also takes into account the broader social construction of that story within interpersonal, social and cultural relations.

This approach is placed within socially oriented narrative research, one of the two forms of narrative research. Socially oriented narrative research differentiates from individually oriented forms which draw on the assumptions that narratives are expressions of individuals' internal states (Squire et al., 2008: 5). The narrative constructionist approach is not really interested in internal states that can be separated off from the narratives themselves. It is interested in the states produced socially by the narratives; the narratives themselves are, in such accounts, social phenomena.

These characteristics mean that the constructionist approach also differs from cognitively based approaches to narrative. Such approaches argue that particular cognitive records gain their linguistic expression, directly or indirectly, in stories – as Labov (Patterson, 2008: 23) thought happened with the 'event stories' we tell of striking events. In these approaches, the stories are useful but in the end secondary servants of internal states – here, of thinking, rather than feeling. The narrative constructionist approach, by contrast, is more concerned with stories as social events and/or social functions.

In our application of the constructionist approach, we extend Riessman's (2008) dialogic narrative analysis model of stories as co-constructed in various contexts: interactional, historical, institutional and discursive (2008: 105).

In this model, narrative constructionism operates at different and connected levels. At one level, such constructionism takes in the interactional co-constructions that operate between stories *within* any one text, including, perhaps, between stories of different kinds, and even perhaps between conscious and preconscious or unconscious stories (Hollway and Jefferson, 2004). The power relations that are played out within stories (Phoenix, 2008) are also considered as part of co-construction processes. By addressing stories as co-constructed, or dialogically constructed (Bakhtin, 1981), this constructionist approach stresses the constantly changing elements in the construction of narratives rather than reading them as finished products of particular circumstances that may change over time.

The Constructing Effects of Audiences on Stories

Whether it is individually or socially oriented, narrative analysis is interested in the role of audience in the constitution and understanding of narratives, albeit to varying degrees. Although individually oriented approaches focus on analysing narratives as told by individual narrators, they usually acknowledge the role of the listener in shaping the structure of narratives. However, it is within more socially oriented forms of narrative analysis that the role of audience is strongest, and it is integral to constructionist approaches.

The meanings of narratives are constructed not only in relation to the audience's meaning-making at the time, location and social context within which the story is first told, but also by many differently positioned audiences. Audiences include future readers who will interpret the words of a story within their own, perhaps radically different, frames of understanding (Bakhtin, 1981; see also Stanley, 1992). A story may also be retold for different audiences, or told for several different audiences at the same time.

All these different aspects of the audienced construction of stories are also aspects of the audienced constitution of *subjectivities*. Subjects are performed into existence during and by their narrative telling. It is to this relationship between narrative and subjectivities that we now turn.

Positioning Within the Processes of Telling and Listening to Stories

Positioning is often included within descriptions of narrative analysis, as the part of the process that allows us to hear the multiplicity and complexity of the narrative voices that make meaning (Davies and Harré, 1990).

Narrative researchers who take a constructionist approach pay attention to the 'positioning' of two kinds of subjects – the tellers and the listeners, their personal, social, cultural and political worlds, and how these worlds come together and interact within the narrative process. As Davies and Harré (1990: 46) point out, tellers draw upon both cultural and personal resources in constructing their stories. This makes narratives a kind of conversation between and across the personal and cultural resources of both narrator(s) and audience(s).

However, such narrative 'conversations' are not simply rational and value-free exchanges between subjects and subject positions; they are alliances, conflicts and negotiations, and they are not conducted entirely according to the laws of reason or even of individual affect. Having once taken up a particular position as their own, a person inevitably sees the world from the vantage point of that position and in terms of the particular images, metaphors, storylines and concepts which are made relevant within the particular discursive practices in which they are positioned and by their own lived histories (Davies and Harré, 1990: 46, 51). Storytellers and listeners do not move freely between subject positions; they are invested in and by them.

In addition, while telling stories, individuals do not speak from a single position. As they draw on available storylines, public discourses and others' stories, storytellers' positions continuously change in relation to what discursive resources they deploy. Moreover, while the notions of 'positioning' and 'subject position' might suggest that people are choosing subjects, as indeed we mostly think of ourselves as doing, the constructionist account of narrative asks us to understand ourselves as chosen, as much as choosing.

Power Relations in the Analysis of Narratives

Power relations are frequently invoked as a constituent of narratives in the constructionist narrative analysis. Analysing 'context' is, indeed, one way to describe analysing power relations that shape the research practice on different levels. For researchers who take a constructionist approach, this interest in power relations is even more significant; for in this approach, power is usually understood in a Foucauldian way (Foucault, 1998; 2001), as widely dispersed, and held everywhere, in different forms. Power is multiple, mobile and contestable, always relational, and inheres within language itself.

When taking a constructionist approach to narratives, we would therefore want to examine how a set of power relations operates in the construction of narratives. A constructionist narrative analysis would put relations of research under scrutiny. At the same time, it would examine how the narrative is an effect of specific historical, social, cultural, political and economic discourses, rather than being natural and unquestionable (Tamboukou, 2008: 103). Addressing power relations within the constructionist analysis of narratives is critical, in order to see the points at which power works to reproduce or produce some narratives as dominant while marginalizing others (Tamboukou, 2003; 2008).

Narrative researchers' own positioning within power relations, and the power relations operating between them, the participants, the data and its interpretation, also have to be taken into account in a constructionist analysis. Researchers working within this tradition have to analyse their own personal, social and cultural positioning(s), as well as their methodological and theoretical frameworks. From this analysis there can emerge a creative approach to the 'story' of the research itself that is perhaps more likely to be critical and qualified about what that story is doing than would be the case with researchers simply telling stories of data (see for instance Taylor, 2012 and Walkerdine, 1986).

CONSTRUCTIONIST NARRATIVE ANALYSIS IN PRACTICE

We turn now to the procedures through which a constructionist narrative analysis might proceed, using as an example some data from a recent empirical study. However, we need to start with a few qualifications.

Narrative analysis rarely provides strict guidelines for researchers that tell them where to look for stories, how to identify them, how to obtain them, or what aspects of them they should investigate (see Chase, 2011, for a detailed review of multiple approaches in the field of narrative research). Even within a single approach to narrative analysis, there is no single way to implement it. Many researchers combine different narrative-analytic approaches, for instance taking a constructionist approach but also looking at particular thematic narratives; or they combine different qualitative approaches, for example following content analysis with narrative analysis (Simons et al., 2008). The aim is, therefore, as full as possible an understanding of stories' constituting elements (Elliott, 2005; Squire, 2008).

A practical start to narrative analysis using the constructionist approach is to think about the steps that will be taken within the analysis. It is difficult to predefine these steps. However, a constructionist approach will generally concentrate on the story as the analytical unit and explore how different levels of context – processes of research and broader socio-cultural and historical contexts – generate stories and are responded to by them. Similar to other qualitative analysis methods, there are decisions to be made. Researchers need to clarify the analytical approach to be used in their research and how they are going to select narratives to be analysed. Even though the constructionist narrative analysis aims to explore multiple constituent elements of narratives on various levels, it is practical to select narrative segments and focus on these segments as the micro units of analysis.

The focus of analysis within the constructionist approach is to address a couple of questions that help the analyst to examine constituents of stories in specific contexts. In the sections that follow, we will describe how some of these questions could be addressed in analysis. The outline below considers the analysis within and between three sites of narrative constructions: (a) the research process, (b) the interview context, and (c) historical and cultural contexts. For these are three main sites in which several elements interconnect in the configuration of narratives. Narrative researchers may use these sites as a starting point to build up their own analytical path.

It is also practical for researchers to consider addressing particular questions while working on their analysis. We include questions and examples of analysis in each section, in order to demonstrate an application of constructionist narrative analysis in current research.

The Research Process

One way to begin constructionist narrative analysis is to consider the research process as one contextual level and to look at elements of language, sociality and power within the research situation, and the broader determinants of those elements within the analysis.

In what follows, we look at four elements that operate on and in constructionist narrative analysis: transcription (see Kowal and O'Connell, Chapter 5, this volume), where narrative research involves spoken material; translation, where narrative research is carried out across languages, as is increasingly the case; the researcher's own processes of analysis and writing (see Denzin, Chapter 39, this volume); and ethical considerations as part of research relations (see Mertens, Chapter 35, this volume).

Analysis of Transcription

As Riessman (2002) reminds us, it is misleading to focus only on the transcripts that have been constructed from the interviews (see Roulston, Chapter 20, this volume) while conducting narrative analysis. Much that is important about interviews themselves, and about the research situation, is not in the transcripts. However, transcription of interviews remains integral to a great deal of narrative research. From a narrative constructionist perspective, it is one part of analysis. The choices of what to include, and how to structure and present the transcribed text, 'have serious implications for how a reader will understand the narrative' (Riessman, 1993: 12).

Transcription is often carried out in multiple rounds. Riessman (1993: 56) advises beginning with a 'rough transcription'. This is a first draft of the entire interview and includes all the words and other main features of the conversation such as crying, laughing and pauses, however these are defined. The interview can be re-transcribed to add the shorter pauses, false starts, emphases and non-verbal utterances such as 'uhm'. There is no possibility of reaching an 'end' to this kind of data collection; tone, pitch, aspiration and many other characteristics of voice could also be included; levels of detail could be perpetually increased and checked. This is why decisions about what to transcribe, and at what level, are also decisions about analysis, and need to be discussed within research reports.

Questions to be addressed:

- *What decisions were involved in the transcription process?*
- *How have these decisions constructed the narratives to be analysed?*

Narrative researchers also make field notes about the interview situation and interactions, usually directly after interview, so that they are able to include relevant details in transcriptions (see Frost, 2009, for a clearly described implementation). Again, this is not a simple process; field notes of such kinds are never complete. Some researchers use additional materials such as video records, in order to aid or expand transcriptions. Field notes may also raise ethical issues, since they may contain material and lead to analyses that were not foreseen during the original planning for voice- and text-based narrative research and analysis (see Kowal and O'Connell, Chapter 5, this volume).

Analysis of Translation

Researchers who work across languages, or between different versions of the same language, should consider translation as another layer in the construction of stories.

'Constructing a transcript from a translated interview involves difficult interpretative decisions' (Riessman, 2008: 42). In translating stories, the researchers play an active role, not limited to their knowledge of the two languages, but including their understanding of the full lived and spoken contexts of those two languages (see Temple, 2005).

Both Fathi and Esin carried out interviews in languages other than English and produced theses and publications in English. They found that although parts of the stories are indeed 'lost in translation', new meanings also emerge within translated materials, which can help the analysis of narrative constructions. A translator–researcher, like any other speaker or writer, does not play an invisible or disinterested role. Concerns about who the future readers of their translations are, are always at the back of their minds. And despite the positive possibilities that translation presents, it must be acknowledged that some nuances of one language may never be adequately translated into another. Accounts of such translation issues need, therefore, to be incorporated into reports of research, which involves more than one language.

Question to be addressed:

- *To what extent does telling a story in one language and translating it into another affect aspects of the story such as its sequencing, its characters, and the meanings it has within a particular language-specific context?*

See, for an example, Box 14.1.

Box 14.1 Excerpt from Fathi's (2011) Research with Iranian Doctors Living in London

I translated the word 'khanoom' initially as 'woman' when referring to women doctors. But after re-reading the data and thinking of the links between the context and how the word is used in Farsi, I realised that 'lady' carries a specific meaning, referring to the upper middle class position of female doctors. Although the same word, 'khanoom', translates to both 'woman' and 'lady' in English, I decided that I had to use the word 'lady' when referring to doctors to keep the classed load of the word 'khanoom' when used with the word doctor. The term 'lady doctor' conveys the specialness of this role in a way that 'woman doctor' does not.

Analysis of Research Positioning

The analysis of the power relations that shape the research and how they affect the narratives obtained is another element to be included into constructionist narrative analysis. This can be initiated by examining how researchers are positioned within the research.

Chase's (2005: 664–6) typology of the three voices that narrative researchers use in the interpretive process might be useful to demonstrate the ways in which the analysts' voices could be positioned in the analysis. The first voice is *the researcher's authoritative voice* through which researchers separate their own interpretation from the narrators' voice by making clear that, as researchers, they have a different interest in the narratives under analysis (2005: 664). The second voice is the *researcher's supportive voice* which is used by researchers to make narrators' voices more heard within the analysis; often this involves presenting it with minimum intervention (2005: 665). The third voice is *the researcher's interactive voice*, through which researchers examine the complex interaction between voices of narrators and their own in research processes. Narrative researchers are able to put subject positions under detailed scrutiny through this strategy (2005: 666).

Questions to be addressed:

- *How do researchers position themselves within the context of their research*
  - *in their interaction with participants and audiences?*
  - *in relation to the cultural, social and political contexts that shape their research?*
- *How do these positioning(s) affect the co-construction of narratives?*

The following excerpt from Fathi's work (see Box 14.2) is an example where the positioning of both the researcher and the participants, in their interaction with each other and in relation to broader cultural and political contexts of the research, affected the story.

Box 14.2 Example

F: Where do you feel you belong to, to here or to Iran?

Roxana: I don't know. My heart beats for Iran. A lot. I mean I am so worried about Iran all the time, it is like, I really like it. But I never like to live there.

F: Have you been to Iran since you have come here?

Roxana: Yes, I have been to Iran. Especially these last incidents which happened, I am very upset for Iran.

Above, Roxana (not her real name) is referring to the events after the 2009 presidential elections in Iran. She does not explicitly say this – she simply mentions 'these last incidents which happened', but as an Iranian, conducting the interview in 2009, Fathi realised what she was talking about. Again, at the beginning, when Roxana responds to Fathi's question about belonging with, 'my heart beats for Iran' – a strong but generalized worry – and at the end, when she is 'upset for Iran', again for unspecified reasons, she is talking specifically to someone who she knows is Iranian, who is herself not in Iran, and who she thinks will understand. To analyse such a narrative, it is obviously necessary to define, at the start, who is listening to it. In this case, it is indeed an Iranian woman, like the Iranian women participants; but Fathi is also positioned by them as having a particular interest in the current state of Iran by virtue of her research topic.

It should be noted that a constructionist approach will often take such analysis further than we have done here, to examine researchers' disciplinary and institutional positioning, educational history, funding, publication and conference plans. All of these play a part in how the research participants are addressed, and how the research materials are elicited, recorded, analysed and reported.

Ethical Considerations

Because narrative research focuses on people's lives and selves, ethical considerations have particular importance in this kind of research and become part of a constructionist analysis of research positioning. As with other research practices, participants are assured that personal identifiers will be removed or changed from the written data and presentations of analysis. Sharing the transcripts, analysis and publications with research participants is a common practice in narrative studies, which enables researchers to expand the limits of co-constructed interpretive process (see Mertens, Chapter 35, this volume).

What, though, does a constructionist approach say, specifically, about the ethics of narrative research? First, it sees explicit considerations of ethical issues as particularly useful for research audiences, not because such considerations legitimate the research, but because they make the particularities of research decisions highly visible. Second, such considerations will often, within a constructionist approach, go beyond ethical nostrums, for instance about what 'consent' is, when it should be obtained and what for, or what is a sensitive topic or a vulnerable subject, to understand such categories in positioned and relational ways (Hydén, 2008).

The constructionist approach considers research ethics as constituted by the particular circumstances of each research project – that is, the relationship between the teller and the listener; the institutional context; the broader cultural and historical context. Obtaining institutional 'consent' may not adequately address the ambiguous and ongoing relations that participants have with the research, or the differential responses they may have to the research process and the research outcomes. When working with personal narratives, it is difficult to work with fixed definitions of confidential, secure, private or sensitive. Confidentiality and anonymity may be such high priorities as to be met for some research participants; for others, extremely 'difficult' topics may be readily engaged with in a non-judgemental research context which they will never have to revisit.

Question to be addressed:

- *How do ethical decisions in the research process affect the co-construction of narratives?*

In her research on the sexual stories of young Turkish women, Esin found that participants often welcomed the opportunity to talk about sexual experiences, which are highly private and confidential in many cultural contexts, to a stranger who was a researcher, promising to listen to these stories confidentially and without judging the teller. In Squire's (2007) research with South Africans living with HIV, refusing anonymity was part of some interviewees' personal and political self-positioning as accepting, campaigning HIV citizens, working against the mainstream governmental silencing of the condition. However, other interviewees were so concerned about confidentiality within this non-disclosing, pathologizing context, that they signed consent forms with pretend names or deliberately illegible scrawls.

The Interview as a Context

Interviews (see Roulston, Chapter 20, this volume) are processes of construction in which respondents constitute worlds of meaning and make sense of their experiences (Mishler, 1986: 118). But the interview partnerships shape how the stories are told and heard. Therefore, they must be integrated into the analysis process. Interviewing as a context is a rich source for narrative analysis, although what, exactly, is to be analysed is sometimes difficult to define. This difficulty is compounded when we address narratives as co-constructed within interviews. The material of the interviews – spoken words, paralinguistic communications, other sounds, and non-verbal communications – has multiple meanings that are multiplied again by the changing interactions between research participant and researcher.

Respondents' agreement to cooperate with interviewers does not necessarily mean that cooperation is limited to their responses to what they are asked. Rather, the interview is constituted over a complex interaction between responses (Mishler, 1986: 54–5). This process turns into collaborative meaning-making rather than simply the imposition or reception of the interviewer's or interviewee's framework of meanings (see for instance Phoenix, 2008). A constructionist narrative analysis thus needs to explore the negotiation of meanings within the micro context of interviews.

Questions to be addressed:

- *What do interviewers and interviewees say to each other in the interviews?*
- *How does the interaction between interviewer and interviewee shape the co-construction narratives?*

In the example in Box 14.3, Fathi explores how interview negotiations influence the way in which the research participants made sense of the concept of class in myriad ways. Meanings of class constituted in the interviews were not only responses to questions, but also responses given to the researcher's responses.

Box 14.3 Example

In an interview with Giti (not her real name), the research participant at one point asserts the importance of migrants' 'integration'. As we see in the extract below, she first associates integration with paid work, specifically, professional work – an association with a particular class characteristic. However, one can then see how this story of class and identity develops in different directions through the exchanges between interviewer and interviewee.

> G: ... you see lots of Iranians who have professional jobs. They have lots of good ones. Who are INTEGRATED in the society.
>
> F: hmm, yes. So do you see any relationships between education and integration and the sense of shame?
>
> G: I think it is very important. Integration. The problem with the English society is that the migrants are not integrated. There was a good talk in London, I don't know whether you were aware of it, there was a woman who came from Canada and was talking about migrants in different societies. She was saying that England is a country where people are not integrated. For example an Indian family. They have been here for generations, but they still talk Indian. Or they live in Banglatown. This is the problem of the society in here. So it is worse for them rather than for me who is freer in the society, or (our) kids in society (who) are like other kids.
>
> F: Hmm, if you have children in future, would you like them to speak Farsi or English?
>
> G: Hmm, Farsi. Well of course they should know English but yes, Farsi they should speak.

(Continued)

(Continued)

> F: And do you think because he (a child) is speaking Farsi he should feel ashamed?
>
> G: I have heard it from other friends who do not want the children to be different from other kids. But I think it depends on us if we teach the person it is good for him to speak to a mother language. It is a good culture. I think it depends on us and how much we can teach him and how intelligent the child will be.
>
> **Excerpt from the Analysis**
>
> First, Fathi follows up Giti's association between education and integration – and the idea of shame, which Giti has previously talked about. Giti, however, in the position of the interviewee, has the power not to follow the interviewer down that path, and indeed she does not. She departs from the researcher's class focus towards a more universalist one, thus implicitly opposing Fathi's suggestion, and her own previous implication that integration might be a class issue, and leaving aside the topic of shame. Instead, Giti tells an exemplifying story of a 'woman who came from Canada' and gave a talk in London. The authority of a woman who gives 'talks' legitimates Giti's perspective, as does the woman's internationalism. Giti also asks Fathi if she were aware of the talk, a question that allies Giti herself with academic knowledge, and with Fathi herself. Through the story that Giti then tells, integration becomes a universally prized property, and England a nation that, regardless of class, fails this standard. Giti gives an example of that failure which perhaps would not have been given to all researchers – Fathi, she knows, is herself an Iranian living in the UK.
>
> Fathi responds to Giti's new positioning of integration as a moral right of the young, including the Iranian young, by asking about children and language, and bringing this issue back to Giti herself: 'would you like your children to speak Farsi or English?' Giti now sounds like another person entirely to the one who last spoke. Educationally, 'of course' they should speak English, she says, returning to the professionalized, classed notion of integration she advocated at the start – but they must at the same time speak Farsi.
>
> Following up on the possibilities above, we turn now to examining how a constructionist approach might look at narratives such as Giti's and Fathi's in terms of narrative positioning other than those operating between narrator, researcher and audience, and in relation to cultural and historical narrative contexts.

Historical and Cultural Contexts

Narrative researchers who take a constructionist approach also emphasize that these processes are tied to and make sense within specific historical and cultural contexts. Stories are drawn from a repertoire of available narrative resources – although these become personalized (Atkinson et al., 2003: 117). Somers (1994) calls such resources public narratives; Malson (2004) calls them 'meta narratives'; Esin (2009) refers to them as 'macro narratives'. These are 'narratives attached to cultural and institutional formations larger than the single individual' (Somers, 1994: 619). While constituting their narratives, individuals use public narratives available within specific cultural and historical contexts. These narratives may also function as a tool to facilitate the co-construction between the tellers and reader/hearers of stories. Here, though, we examine them more simply, in terms of their effects on a story, rather than on story co-construction.

Questions to be addressed:

- *How is the narrative linked to macro/meta/public narratives available within the historical and cultural context of research?*
- *How does the narrative reiterate or counter these macro/meta/public narratives?*

For example, in Esin's (2009) research about sexual narratives on narratives of educated young women and their mothers in Turkey, the analysis focuses on understanding how modernist discourses available within this historically specific context operated to construct participants' personal narratives of sexuality. Part of the aim was to trace modernist political and cultural grand narratives surrounding gender and sexuality in the stories within the interviews, in order to elucidate the ways in which individual narratives reiterate and/or contest these macro narratives.

As the excerpt in Box 14.4 demonstrates, these ways could be identified through participants' references to and more implicit positioning in relation to modernist narratives of lifestyles, families and relationships. These narratives were closely linked to the sexual regulations for women, and the sexual regulation of women, in contemporary Turkey. The interview from which this extract is taken was conducted in Turkish. It was transcribed and translated into English by Esin herself. The excerpt is taken from Zuhal's (not her real name) long opening narrative. The ellipses at the beginning and end of the excerpt are used to indicate that Esin chose this particular passage for analysis but that it is actually part of a longer response to the opening question posed by the researcher, 'Could you please tell me about yourself?'

Box 14.4   Example

Zuhal: […] My mum, I can say that she was an intellectual housewife. She was never conservative. That's what I observed during the time I lived at home. My parents had four children. I'm one of them, the third daughter … My dad didn't plan to leave an inheritance to us. Instead he wanted all of us to be educated well. Education was indisputable. Although I was the third daughter and accepted to the university in my third year, I was still sent to courses when they had financial problems. Not only me, but all my sisters and my brother were given the same opportunity. Daddy had only a cheap flat bought by the debt when he died. I can say that he spent all his money on our education. All of us are university graduates. (err) I'm proud of it […].

Analysis

Zuhal was very careful in positioning herself within the interview context. At different points in the interview, she indicated that she was very conscious of giving an interview for a research project in a UK university, and that she was telling her stories to shed light on the lifestyle of a modern Turkish woman. I read Zuhal's references from a critical perspective on the construction of women's identities within the modernisation project. This perspective is informed by my reading of the feminist literature on the socio-cultural narratives of gender relations and regulations in contemporary Turkey.

Zuhal shapes her narrative through the dominant storylines of the specific modernist gender regime in Turkey. Beginning with a description of her mother as an 'intellectual housewife' who was 'never conservative', Zuhal makes her own position explicit as one of the modernised women who can also analyse the modernisation, or lack of it, of others. She presents her mother as an 'intellectual mother', using the modernist discourse that makes parenting a part of modern gender roles for both women and men – but still preserving her as a 'mother' and 'housewife', so reiterating the dominant narrative that constitutes women primarily as mothers and wives who are responsible for the reproduction of modernist values and lifestyles. The same dominant discourse operates to construct modern fathers in a different way from mothers, by shifting the image of the masculine father into one who is an engaged parent who cares for his children by giving them equal opportunities for education. Zuhal's description of her father fits seamlessly with this new image of masculinity constructed in the modernisation discourse.

CONCLUSION: LIMITS AND RANGE OF THE CONSTRUCTIONIST APPROACH

Working with a narrative constructionist approach does not mean that researchers can explain everything about narratives by parsing their social and cultural constituents, however complexly. It is possible for constructionist narrative analysis to adopt a variety of positions about narrative truth, truths or persuasiveness that allow for personal and political beliefs and actions. We think of the constructionist approach as a very useful way of thinking about and through narrative analysis, with its strong attention to language, process and change, to different levels of social phenomena, and to the co-construction of phenomena.

Yet, as in every approach to data analysis, the constructionist approach to narrative analysis has some limitations. The approach focuses on contextual interrelations in the construction of narratives. It does not deal with specific self-contained stories – for instance, stories about salient events, or key moments. Neither does it treat life stories as holistic accounts, and so it is quite different from what is often thought to be characteristically 'narrative' research, based on a few cases, or complete interviews. It does not, necessarily, consider stories' relations to reality.

Thus this approach is not suitable for researchers who are interested primarily in the direct relation between narratives and phenomena beyond them. The approach is also not focused principally on agency, though it is often interested in the effects of narratives and the ways in which they instantiate, enact and impact on subjectivities. Nor does it separate out 'ethics' from the analysis of other contextual elements. Ethical considerations are rather being treated as part of the broader pattern of power relations sustaining research.

Researchers who work within the constructionist approach to narrative analysis may have varying research interests and concerns in relation to the sociality and fluidity of narratives, such as how broader cultural narratives are exemplified and resisted in personal narratives (Plummer, 2001; Squire, 2007), how personal narratives are constructed through interaction and the performance of identities in common cultural spaces (Phoenix, 2008; Riessman, 2008); and how the political and cultural contexts of research shape the understanding of stories by researchers (Andrews, 2007; Riessman, 2002).

However, as we have discussed in this chapter, the constructionist approach to narratives has some common and, we would argue, useful features. It focuses on narratives as socially constructed by the interplay between interpersonal, social and cultural relations, rather than analysing them as a representation of reality, or as a representation with a single meaning. Within the constructionist approach, too, the unit of analysis is not only the story itself as it is told and/or written, but also how it is told and makes sense to both tellers and listeners/readers, including the researchers and the research audience. Elucidating these elements and coming to a provisional interpretive ending is what characterizes such analysis.

FURTHER READING

Andrews, Molly, Squire, Corinne and Tamboukou, Maria (eds) (2008) *Doing Narrative Research*. London: Sage.

Holstein, James and Gubrium, Jaber (eds) (2012) *Varieties of Narrative Analysis*. Thousand Oaks, CA: Sage.

Josselson, Ruthellen, Lieblich, Amia and McAdams, Dan (2003) *Up Close and Personal: The Teaching and Learning of Narrative Research*. Washington, DC: American Psychological Association.

REFERENCES

Andrews, Molly (2007) *Shaping History: Narratives of Political Change*. Cambridge: Cambridge University Press.

Andrews, Molly, Day Sclater, Shelley, Squire, Corinne and Tamboukou, Maria (2004). 'Narrative research', in Clive Seale et al. (eds), *Qualitative Research Practice*. London: Sage. pp. 97–112.

Atkinson, Paul, Coffey, Amanda and Delamont, Sara (2003) *Key Themes in Qualitative Research*. Oxford: AltaMira Press.

Bakhtin, Mikhail (1981) *The Dialogic Imagination*, ed. M. Holquist. Austin: University of Texas Press.

Bell, Susan (1999) 'Narratives and lives: Women's health politics and the diagnosis of cancer for DES daughters', *Narrative Inquiry*, 9: 347–89.

Bruner, Jerome (1990) *Acts of Meaning*. Cambridge, MA: Harvard University Press.

Burr, Vivien (2003) *Social Constructionism*. London: Sage.

Chase, Susan E. (2005) 'Narrative inquiry: Multiple lenses, approaches, voices', in Norman K. Denzin and Yvonna S. Lincoln (eds) *Handbook of Qualitative Research*, 3rd edition. Thousand Oaks, CA: Sage. pp. 651–79.

Chase, Susan E. (2011) 'Narrative inquiry: Still a field in the making', in Norman K. Denzin and Yvonna S. Lincoln (eds), *Handbook of Qualitative Research*, 4th edition. Thousand Oaks, CA: Sage. pp. 421–34.

Czarniawska, Barbara (2004) *Narratives in Social Science Research*. London: Sage.

Davies, Bronwyn and Harré, Rom (1990) 'Positioning: The discursive construction of selves', *Journal for the Theory of Social Behaviour*, 20: 43–63.

De Fina, Anna and Georgakopoulou, Alexandra (2011) *Analyzing Narratives: Discourse and Sociolinguistic Perspectives*. Cambridge: Cambridge University Press.

Elliott, Jane (2005) *Using Narrative in Social Research: Qualitative and Quantitative Approaches*. London: Sage.

Esin, Cigdem (2009) 'Construction of sexuality in the narratives of well-educated women in Turkey', PhD thesis, University of East London.

Fathi, Mastoureh (2011) 'Classed pathways: narratives of Iranian women migrants', PhD thesis, University of East London.

Foucault, Michel (1998) *The History of Sexuality 1 – The Will to Kno*wledge. London: Penguin.

Foucault, Michel (2001) 'The subject and the power', in James D. Faubion (ed.), *Power: Essential Works of Foucault (1954–1984)*. London: Allen Lane/The Penguin Press. pp. 326–48.

Freeman, Mark (2010) *Hindsight*. New York: Oxford University Press.

Frost, Noleigh (2009) '"Do you know what I mean?" The use of a pluralistic narrative analysis approach in the interpretation of an interview', *Qualitative Research*, 9 (1): 9–29.

Herman, David (2004) *Story Logic*. Lincoln: University of Nebraska Press.

Hollway, Wendy and Jefferson, Tony (2004) 'Narrative, discourse and the unconscious', in Molly Andrews et al. (eds), *The Uses of Narrative*. New Brunswick, NJ: Transaction. pp. 139–149.

Holstein, James and Gubrium, Jaber (eds) (2008) *Handbook of Constructionist Research*. New York: Guilford Press.

Hydén, Margareta (2008) 'Narrating sensitive topics', in Molly Andrews et al. (eds), *Doing Narrative Research*. London: Sage. pp. 121–36.

Hyvarinen, Matti, Hyden, Lars-Christer, Saarenheimo, Marja and Tamboukou, Maria (eds.) (2010) *Beyond Narrative Coherence*. Amsterdam: John Benjamins.

Malson, Helen (2004) 'Fiction(ising)', in Molly Andrews et al. (eds), *The Uses of Narrative*. New Brunswick, NJ: Transaction. pp. 150–63.

Mattingly, Cheryl (1998) *Healing Dramas and Clinical Plots: The Narrative Structure of Experience*. Cambridge: Cambridge University Press.

Mishler, Elliot (1986) *Research Interviewing: Context and Narrative*. Cambridge, MA: Harvard University Press.

Patterson, Wendy (2008) 'Narratives of events: Labovian narrative analysis and its limitations', in Molly Andrews et al. (eds), *Doing Narrative Research*. London: Sage. pp. 22–40.

Phoenix, Anne (2008) 'Analyzing narrative contexts', in Molly Andrews et al. (eds), *Doing Narrative Research*. London: Sage. pp. 64–77.

Plummer, Kenneth (2001) *Documents of Life 2*. London: Sage.

Polletta, Francesca (2006) *It was like a Fever: Storytelling in Protest and Politics*. London: University of Chicago Press.

Riessman, Catherine K. (1993) *Narrative Analysis*. London: Sage.

Riessman, Catherine K. (2002) 'Analysis of personal narratives', in Jaber F. Gubrium and James A. Holstein (eds), *Handbook of Interview Research*. Thousand Oaks, CA: Sage. pp. 695–710.

Riessman, Catherine K. (2005) 'Narrative analysis', in Nancy Kelly et al. (eds), *Narrative, Memory and Everyday Life*. Huddersfield: University of Huddersfield Press. pp. 1–7.

Riessman, Catherine K. (2008) *Narrative Methods for the Human Sciences*. Thousand Oaks, CA: Sage.

Rosenwald, George C. and Ochberg, Richard L. (1992) 'Introduction: Life stories, cultural politics, and self-understanding', in George C. Rosenwald and Richard L. Ochberg (eds), *Storied Lives: The Cultural Politics of Self-understanding*. New Haven, CT: Yale University Press. pp. 1–18.

Rustin, Michael (2001) *Reason and Unreason*. London: Athlone Press.

Simons, Lucy, Lachlean, Judith and Squire, Corinne (2008) 'Shifting the focus: Sequential methods of analysis with qualitative data', *Qualitative Health Research*, 18: 120–32.

Somers, Margaret R. (1994) 'The narrative constitution of identity: A relational and network approach', *Theory and Society*, 23: 605–49.

Somers, Margaret and Gibson, Gloria (1994) 'Reclaiming the epistemological "Other": Narrative and the social constitution of identity', in Craig Calhoun (ed.), *Social Theory and the Politics of identity*. Oxford: Blackwell. pp. 37–99.

Sparkes, Andrew C. and Smith, Brett (2008) 'Narrative constructionist inquiry', in James Holstein and Jaber Gubrium (eds), *Handbook of Constructionist Research*. New York: Guilford Press. pp. 295–314.

Squire, Corinne (2007) *HIV in South Africa: Talking about the Big Thing*. London: Routledge.

Squire, Corinne (2008) 'Experience-centred and culturally oriented approaches to narrative', in Molly Andrews et al. (eds), *Doing Narrative Research*. London: Sage. pp. 41–63.

Squire, Corinne, Andrews, Molly and Tamboukou, Maria (2008) 'Introduction: What is narrative research?', in Molly Andrews et al. (eds), *Doing Narrative Research*. London: Sage. pp. 1–21.

Stanley, Liz (1992) *The Auto/Biographical I: Theory and Practice of Feminist Auto/Biography*. Manchester: Manchester University Press.

Tamboukou, Maria (2003) *Women, Education, and the Self: A Foucauldian Perspective*. New York: Palgrave Macmillan.

Tamboukou, Maria (2008) 'A Foucauldian approach to narratives', in Molly Andrews et al. (eds), *Doing Narrative Research*. London: Sage. pp. 102–20.

Taylor, Stephanie (2012) '"One participant said …": The implications of quotations from biographical talk', *Qualitative Research*, 12 (4): 388–401.

Temple, Bogusia (2005) 'Nice and tidy: translation and representation', *Sociological Research Online*, 10 (2): www.socresonline.org.uk/10/2/temple.html (accessed 3 May 2013).

Walkerdine, Valerie (1986) 'Video replay: families, films and fantasy', in Victor et al. (eds) *Formations of Fantasy*. London: Methuen.

White, Hayden (1984) 'The question of narrative in contemporary historical theory', *History and Theory*, 23 (1): 1–33.

15

Documentary Method

Ralf Bohnsack

As a method for analysing qualitative data the documentary method first was worked out in the 1980s (Bohnsack, 1983; 1989) being inspired theoretically by Karl Mannheim and ethnomethodology.

In the 1920s, with his draft of the 'documentary method of interpretation', Karl Mannheim presented the first comprehensive argument for a particular approach to observation in the social sciences, which even today is able to meet the requirements of epistemological reasoning (see Mannheim, 1952a). However, Mannheim's works which are especially relevant for the documentary method and the methodology and epistemology of social sciences in general (Mannheim, 1952a; 1982) have not yet been adopted on a larger scale.

In the 1950s and 1960s, Harold Garfinkel, the originator of ethnomethodology, was able to bring the documentary method back into social scientific discourse. He understood it as a method which 'is prominent in and characteristic of both social-scientific and daily-life procedures for deciding sensibility and warrant' (Garfinkel, 1961: 57). For Garfinkel as well as for Mannheim, the documentary method was significant as a methodological concept in the context of discourse concerning the epistemological substantiation of the social sciences. Neither Mannheim nor Garfinkel conceived it as a method for practical empirical inquiry: 'Whether its widespread use is necessary to sociological inquiry is an open question' (Garfinkel, 1961: 58 n10).

Whereas it was an open question for Garfinkel whether the documentary method could direct practical empirical inquiry, we began to develop the documentary method in the 1980s, both as a methodology for qualitative research and as a method for practical empirical inquiry (Bohnsack, 1989; 2010a). Originally, it was used in the context of group discussions and the analysis of talk, but soon it was adopted for the interpretation of a great variety of texts, especially biographical interviews, but also for semi-structured interviews (see Roulston, Chapter 20, this volume), the interpretation of field notes from participant observation (see Marvasti, Chapter 24, this volume), and, as of 2001, for the interpretation of pictures (see Banks, Chapter 27, this volume), and in video analysis (see Knoblauch et al., Chapter 30, this volume).

The fields of research based on the documentary method are widespread: starting with research about youth, peer groups and juvenile delinquency, the main fields today cover: evaluation, education in schools, media reception analysis, organizations and their cultures (among others: hospitals, welfare organizations, the police, schools, firms), social work, medical work, migration, childhood, biography and human development, life-long education, educational and sociological aspects of religion, and entrepreneurship.[1]

SOCIAL SCIENTIFIC OBSERVATION AND THE GENETIC ATTITUDE OF ANALYSIS

The methodology of observation developed by Mannheim in the 1920s is still relevant today. It is essentially based upon a specific stance or analytical approach: the 'genetic' or 'socio-genetic' attitude (Mannheim, 1982: 80ff.). When taking such an analytical approach, questions concerning the normative rightness or the validity of utterances and depictions, which are taken for granted by the persons who are the subjects of research, are 'put in brackets' (1982: 61). When 'bracketing the validity aspect' (1982: 88) of objectivistic pre-conceptions, we are able to turn from the question of *what* cultural and social facts *are* all about to the question of *how* they are *accomplished* or *generated*, that is to questions concerning the social processes of the coming about of what is taken for granted as cultural and social facts: 'In this respect it is not the content, the "What" of objective meaning that is of preponderant importance, but the fact and mode of its existence – the "That" and the "How"' (Mannheim, 1952a: 67).

This analytic stance, which has been characterized by Mannheim as the (socio-)genetic attitude, is one of the main components of the documentary method. Thus Mannheim anticipated and partly influenced what today belongs to the core of constructivism. The 'world itself' or 'reality', that is the 'What', remains unobservable. Merely the processes of the accomplishment or construction of 'world' and 'reality', that is the 'How', are observable. When characterizing the analytic attitude of the scientific observer, Niklas Luhmann (1990: 95) has formulated: 'The questions of *What* are transformed into questions of *How*.'

SOCIOLOGY OF KNOWLEDGE, ETHNOMETHODOLOGY, SOCIAL PHENOMENOLOGY AND DOCUMENTARY METHOD

The type of constructivism we find in ethnomethodology (see Eberle, Chapter 13, this volume) has been essentially influenced by Mannheim. For Garfinkel (1967: vii), the fundamental phenomenon under observation is 'the objective reality of social facts as an ongoing accomplishment of the concerted activities of daily life'.

In addition to Mannheim's sociology of knowledge, one of the other roots of ethnomethodology can be found in the social phenomenology of Alfred Schutz (see Eberle, Chapter 13, this volume). His model of social action (Schutz, 1962; 1967) can be seen as the most advanced development of Max Weber's postulate of the interpretation of subjective meaning (1978). According to Schutz, the ability to act is based in the construction of types of subjective 'preconceived projects' in the sense of 'in-order-to motives' (Schutz, 1962: 19; 1967: 86ff.), to which action is oriented. In-order-to motives are strictly utilitarian projects of action.

The interpretation of subjective meaning, and thus the ascription of motives, is the basis of our constructions and typifications in everyday life, of the so-called 'constructs of the first degree' (Schutz, 1962: 6). Schutz thus has given us valuable insights into the architecture of our *common-sense theorizing* and its analytic attitude, and into the architecture and thus also into our *methods of observation and construction in common sense*. But he can hardly give us – as I will explain more comprehensively later on – insights *into* our everyday practice, which extend beyond this theorizing *about* our practice.

Schutz (1962: 27) already saw some other limitations of this model of the reconstruction of subjective meaning: 'There is a mere chance ... that the observer in daily life can grasp the subjective meaning of the actor's act. This chance increases with the degree of anonymity and standardization of the observed behavior' (1962: 27); that means – as we may add – with the degree of institutionalization and the role-character of the behaviour. Whereas Schutz pointed out these limitations of the model of subjective meaning for the area of standardized or institutionalized behaviour, this is not true for the qualitative researchers in his tradition (for instance, for the so-called hermeneutic sociology of knowledge in Germany – see Soeffner, 2004).

This leads to severe methodological problems, because actors' subjective intentions cannot be observed by the interpreter. The interpretation thus depends on introspection. As Pierre Bourdieu (1972: 166) has put it: 'if it has no other instruments of recognition at its disposal than, according to a term of Husserl, the "intentional empathy into the other", even the most "comprehensive" interpretation risks becoming not much more than a very perfect form of ethnocentrism.'[2]

Thus the interpretation of the subjective meaning may provide more information about the *interpreter's* frame of relevance than about the relevancies of those who are the *objects* of these interpretations or observations. The intentions and motives of the actors are not observable, but rather the ascription of motives by the observers, the processes of constructing motives. These constructivist criticisms have been voiced by ethnomethodologists (see McHugh, 1970). Thus processes of the interpretation and definition of reality which underlie the construction of motives and consequential decisions, especially in bureaucratic organizations and federal agencies of control such as the police (Cicourel, 1968), the administration of justice (Garfinkel, 1967b; Emerson, 1969; McHugh, 1970) and social work (Zimmermann, 1969), became the objects of ethnomethodological observations. The construction of motives, biographies and also milieus, for example of the 'criminal', 'the mentally ill' (Smith, 1978), the 'transsexual' (Garfinkel, 1967a: ch. 5), could be reconstructed, as well as similar constructions in the practice of social scientific research (see Garfinkel, 1967a: ch. 6; Cicourel, 1964). It could be shown that even scientific research was bound up with the logic of common-sense interpretation.

Social phenomenology, however, while allowing us precise reconstructions of our common-sense *theorizing*, does not question its architecture and the methods it implies, and thus remains descriptive and uncritical towards common sense. The question of if and where there is a difference between the analytic attitude of everyday life and scientific interpretation has not really been answered by Schutz or the social scientists and researchers in his tradition.[3] This is true, for instance, for the so-called sociology of knowledge in the understanding of Peter Berger and Thomas Luckmann (1966; see Eberle, Chapter 13, this volume).

In contrast, different methodological positions such as Bourdieu's sociology of culture and knowledge, constructivism in the sense of Luhmann's modern systems theory, and also Mannheim's sociology of knowledge are convergent in that a scientific approach to observation may not limit itself to describing common-sense theories. Rather it must be able to define the difference between common sense and a social scientific approach to analysis and methodology. Thus scientific observation must be able to define its methodology and to realize in practical research the 'rupture with the presuppositions of lay and scholarly common sense' (Bourdieu, 1992: 247). This is an essential component of the analytical approach which – using a term of Luhmann (1990: 86) – we may call 'observation of the second order'.

Very early on, ethnomethodology took the first steps in the direction of observations of the second order, following the (socio-)genetic attitude in the tradition of Mannheim. Ethnomethodology may be understood as a successful 'critique of methods' in the broadest sense of the word. However, ethnomethodology has remained only 'half' of a sociology of knowledge, because it has not answered the question of how, after all, it can be possible to find *adequate* access to an unknown and foreign milieu-specific (and biographical) reality. In contrast, the central idea of the documentary method in the understanding of Mannheim and his sociology of knowledge was to find adequate access to unknown social worlds and milieus, or, as Mannheim (1982: 204) called it, to their 'spaces of conjunctive experience'.[4] For this reason, we decided to go back to the roots in the works of Mannheim and his understanding of the documentary method.

Mannheim not only has shown us the way to gain access to an understanding of the internal logic of unknown milieus, but his sociology of knowledge is so complex as to integrate the approach or paradigm of social phenomenology (as we can see retrospectively). This is possible because social phenomenology is a genuinely *reconstructive* approach as well. In the understanding of Mannheim's sociology of knowledge, however, there are two quite different areas, spheres or layers of knowledge, which must be *reconstructed*. Both of these layers of knowledge constitute a *structure of 'duality'* in our everyday life, 'a duality in which individuals bear themselves, in relation to concepts as well as realities' (Mannheim, 1982: 265). The two spheres are the '*communicative*' and the '*conjunctive*' knowledge or experience.

COMMUNICATIVE AND CONJUNCTIVE KNOWLEDGE

As an example, we may take a look at the concept or reality of the 'family'. Relatively independent from our belonging to different milieus and even cultures, we are familiar with the reality of the family on a general or *communicative* level. This concerns the family as an institution, that is the institutionalized or role-guided action, which, among other things, comprises the generalized knowledge about the role-relations between parents and children, knowledge about the legal and the religious tradition of the family in our culture, but also – as a further component – our *theories about* the family, our theoretical and legitimatory knowledge concerning the family. This *communicative knowledge* corresponds to the level of knowledge, which Schutz (1962: 72) has characterized as its 'anonymity and standardization'. This is one aspect of the 'constructs of the first degree' in his sense (1962: 6). We can find the architecture and logic of these constructs also in our *theorizing* in everyday life, in our *common-sense theories*.

Schutz's social phenomenology with its 'constructs of the second degree' (1962: 6) thus may be understood as a precise and profound reconstruction of Mannheim's understanding of communicative knowledge.

Returning to our example of the family, we can differentiate communicative knowledge as knowledge *about* the family from the knowledge which results from our existence *within* the family, within its everyday practice. This is the implicit or tacit knowledge and experience, which we share with other members of the family because of our shared biographies and our 'collective memory' (Halbwachs, 1980). In this respect, the family is a 'conjunctive space of experience'. The *conjunctive knowledge* serves as an orientation for our practical action and – in the case of our example – our practice and existence in the family.

A-THEORETICAL, IMPLICIT AND INCORPORATED KNOWLEDGE

In contrast to social phenomenology, Mannheim's sociology of knowledge gives access not only to the reconstruction of theoretical knowledge, but also to the reconstruction of conjunctive knowledge as implicit or tacit knowledge which guides our practical action. For this reason, we also call it the 'praxeological sociology of knowledge'.

Mannheim (1982: 67ff.) has illustrated the character of this specific knowledge by referring to the example of how a knot comes about. The knowledge that enables me to tie a knot is *a-theoretical* knowledge, as Mannheim has called it. The practical action is performed intuitively and pre-reflexively. In the genetic analytical approach (Mannheim, 1982: 80), *understanding* the phenomenon of a knot is realized by virtue of imagining the sequence of movements, the practical action and manual skills 'as the resultants of which the knot appears before us' (1982: 68). In the sense of Martin Heidegger (2010: 68), this is the existential level of the 'pre-thematic being': 'This being is not the object of a theoretical "world" cognition, it is what is used, produced, and so on', whereas the 'theoretical "world"-cognition' characterizes the level of *communicative knowledge*.

It seems to be highly complicated, if not even impossible, to explain this process of accomplishment, this generic principle, theoretically or in theoretical concepts in an adequate way. It is much easier to explain the accomplishment of tying a knot with a *picture* that is an illustration or representation of the actual practical process of accomplishing the 'knot-tying'. Pictures or images seem to be predestined as media for understanding a-theoretical or tacit knowledge.

As long as I have to use my *imagination* to bring to mind the process of tying a knot in its entirety, including the necessary movements – that is, through the medium of mental images or material pictures – I have not yet fully incorporated and automated the process of tying. In the case of pictorial or mental imagination, the habitus or the frame of orientation (see Bohnsack, 1989) of the actor is the product of a modus operandi based on *implicit* knowledge. When reconstructing this implicit knowledge, empirical analysis deals with the interpretation (see Willig, Chapter 10, this volume) of metaphorical representations that mean narrations (see Esin et al., Chapter 14, this volume) and depictions of their own practical actions by the actors themselves. The objects of reconstruction are the *mental images* of the actors, which are implicated in their narrations, depictions and conversations (see Toerien, Chapter 22, this volume).

The *frame of orientation* that enables us to tie a knot may also be the product of *incorporated* – so to speak: *automated* – practical action. In this case, the orientation or *habitus* is accessible in a methodically controlled way by direct observation of the performance of interaction or talk and by the representation of bodily movements in the medium of *material pictures*, that is photographs (see Banks, Chapter 27, this volume) or videographs (see Knoblauch et al., Chapter 30, this volume).

In the framework of the documentary method, we use the term *a-theoretical* knowledge as a general term, including the *incorporated* knowledge, which we acquire in a valid way through the medium of material pictures, as also the *implicit* or *metaphoric* knowledge, which we acquire through the medium of mental images as we can find them in narrations and descriptions – that is to say, in texts.

As a synonym for 'frame of *orientation*', we also use the term *habitus* (Bohnsack, 2010c). There is a comprehensive correspondence between the genetic interpretation and the 'generative grammar' of the habitus in the understanding of Bourdieu on the one hand and the genetic attitude and the understanding of practical action and conjunctive knowledge in the documentary method on the other. Whereas Bourdieu, however, in his analysis is seeking the genesis of habitus and class primarily in the medium of *distinction*, our analysis according to the documentary method tries to understand the genesis of the habitus and the constitution of classes (respectively milieus) primarily in the medium of *conjunction* and *habitual concordance* (Bohnsack et al., 2002; Bohnsack and Nohl, 2003; Bohnsack, 2010c).

UNDERSTANDING AND INTERPRETATION

Individuals sharing common a-theoretical knowledge and experiences, and thus a habitus, are connected by the elementary form of sociality, which we call 'conjunctive knowledge' or 'conjunctive experience'. They *understand* each other immediately. This is what Mannheim has called 'understanding' as apposed to '*interpretation*': 'we shall take mere understanding to mean ... the spiritual, pre-reflexive grasping of formations, and we shall take interpretation to mean the theoretically reflective explication of what is understood' (1982: 243). Social phenomenology can give us a definition of interpretation, but is not able to differentiate it from the more fundamental understanding (*Verstehen*). Phenomenological analysis (see Eberle, Chapter 13, this volume) starts from a model of mutual interpretation between individuals who are strangers to each other. Thus, intersubjectivity must be established in a complicated process of taking the other's perspective – based upon the idealizing of assumptions: the idealization of the 'reciprocity of perspectives' and the idealization of the 'reciprocity of motives' (Schutz, 1962: 11 and 23). This is an adequate description of the *communicative* level of interaction, the level of institutionalized and role-oriented action, but not of the area of *conjunctive understanding* as immediate understanding.

Not only tangible groups like families, friendships or peer groups are constituted on the basis of spaces of conjunctive experience and conjunctive understanding. As Mannheim has shown in his essay about the *formation of generations* in society, generations are also constituted by commonalities in the 'stratification of experience' (1952b: 297). Such commonalities in the stratification of experience result from existential involvement in a common practice of historical events, especially but not only in periods of radical development, change and crisis. For example, the experience of the period of reconstruction in Germany after the Second World War in (synchronization with) a specific phase of the development (life cycle) of the individual (here, childhood) has been seen as an explanation for the constitution of a specific generational conjunctive space of experience: the generation of 1968.

The members of this generation share a conjunctive space of experience, which results from being involved in a specific everyday practice. This does not imply any direct communication or interaction with each other. Thus their experiences are not identical but they are *identical in structure*. The same may be true for milieu-specific or gender-specific spaces of conjunctive experience or those involving commonalities of experience resulting from life-cycle transitions (for instance, from education in school to vocational training). In our empirical analysis with the documentary method, we thus differentiate between milieu-, gender-, generation- and development-specific spaces of conjunctive experiences, among others. In empirical analysis, each single case (based on, for example, an interview with an individual or a discussion with a group) can be differentiated by the interpretation of different spaces of experiences, which we also call *types* (see below).

PRAXEOLOGICAL SOCIOLOGY OF KNOWLEDGE, PRACTICAL HERMENEUTICS AND INTERPRETIVISM

Conjunctive knowledge is acquired by experience in everyday practice, by lived experiences with the 'modus operandi' as the 'generic formula' of practical action in the understanding of Bourdieu and his 'theory of practice'. In a certain analogy to Bourdieu (and partly influenced by him), Thomas Schwandt (2002) has drawn attention to the problem that the current understanding of research in social sciences is committed to a concept of knowledge (and intelligence) which is not able to meet the requirements of understanding practices in everyday life and our practical relation to the world. Schwandt has named the theoretical approach and modus of social research to meet such requirements 'practical hermeneutics' (2002: 47).

Nonetheless, Schwandt has not worked out the resulting consequences for the practice of empirical research. However, we can make a direct connection between practical hermeneutics in the sense of Schwandt and the documentary method with its long tradition of practical research and Mannheim's sociology of knowledge as its theoretical background, which we have called the praxeological sociology of knowledge.

Schwandt's position is somewhat different from the mainstream of qualitative research in the United States, where we can identify a tendency to restrict research to the dimension of communicative (explicit and theoretical) knowledge. This mainstream is overwhelmingly orientated to the *interpretive paradigm*, as can be seen when reading for example the *Handbook of Qualitative Research*, edited by Norman K. Denzin and Yvonna S. Lincoln (1994). 'Constructivism' is more or less used here as a synonym for 'interpretivism' (among others: Guba and Lincoln, 1989; Greene, 1994). That means the interpretive, definitional and theoretical production of reality as we have seen in social phenomenology (see, for a more detailed critique, Bohnsack, 2009), which is different from the production or generation of the world in everyday practice.

THE FUNDAMENTAL CONSTITUTION OF MEANING IN PRACTICE AND INTERACTION

The production of the world in everyday practice is the fundamental dimension of reality, which is primordial in relation to the dimension of attributing subjective meanings, communicative intentions and motives. Here we also agree with Anthony Giddens (1976: 89). Above all George Herbert Mead (1934: 186f.) has pointed out 'the temporal and logical pre-existence of the social process to the self-conscious individual that arises in it. The conversation of gestures is a part of the social process which is going on.' The fundamental structure of meaning which is constituted by the pre-reflexive social process and the conversation of gestures, and which merely has a residual character in Mead's work, corresponds to Mannheim's category of the space of conjunctive experience.

The meaning of a single utterance or action is determined by its relation to the context of the other utterances and actions which sequentially take place. In the case of the interpretation of texts, the relation between actions or utterances on one hand and their context on the other hand is a *sequential* relation, a relation between utterances or gestures and the succeeding ones. In this way, the utterances or gestures mutually impart their significance to each other – which may be understood thoroughly in the sense of Mead (1934). In the case of the interpretation of *pictures* (see Banks, Chapter 27, this volume), this relation is not a sequential but a *simultaneous* one – a relation between the single *elements* of a picture and the *whole* picture and its overall context (see below; Bohnsack, 2010b; 2011). In both cases, the ethnomethodologists have called the relation between context and a single utterance or single element *reflexive* (Garfinkel, 1961; 1967a: 7f.). It is this reflexive character by which talk and pictures are constituted as a *self-referential system* – as we can call it in terms of modern system theory.

When the meaning of an utterance or action is determined by the reaction of the other participants, respectively by a sequence of reaction and re-reactions, the interpretation of the relation of an (empirically observed) utterance to an (empirically observed) reaction opens up access to the constituted *implicit meaning* or the *implicit rule*. The reconstruction of this rule is achieved by searching for possible alternatives to the observed reaction, which are equally meaningful. These equally meaningful and thus *functionally equivalent* reactions form a class, which adheres to the same rule. Thus a rule, which was until now unknown to the interpreter (but available to those being observed as implicit knowledge), can be generated and brought to explication. This method of generating knowledge and rules corresponds to the logical form of 'abduction' in the understanding of Charles S. Peirce (1934; see also Reichertz, Chapter 9, and Thornberg and Charmaz, Chapter 11, this volume).

Searching for *functionally equivalent* or – as we call it – *homologous* reactions always presupposes a (counter-)horizon of comparison (consisting of reactions not belonging to the rule) which remains implicit for the moment. This is the 'blind spot' of interpretation, as Luhmann (1990: 85) has called it. The interpretation thus depends on the existential (everyday) experiences of the interpreter, on the 'existential bonds' or 'standpoint bonds' in the understanding of Mannheim (1936: 239).[5]

In a methodological perspective, the selectivity of our understanding or interpretation, which is a result of our existential bonds, is constituted by the selectivity of the intuitive *horizons of comparison* which are stored in our everyday knowledge, and which are constitutive for the interpretation which we also call *reflecting interpretation* (see below). The more those *intuitive* horizons of comparison are replaced or substituted by *empirical* and *explicit* ones, that means by *empirical cases of comparison*, the more our interpretations and typifications can be controlled methodically. Thus *comparative analysis* is one of the central components of the documentary method.[6] Methodically or empirically controlled comparative analysis also opens up a certain chance for the self-reflection of my existential and standpoint bonds and thus helps me to get an idea of my 'blind spot'.

The main task of the documentary method is thus the explication of the hitherto implicit knowledge of those being observed. This is connected with some basic epistemological assumptions or implications: the goal of research is to gain access to knowledge which is at the disposal of the actors and not knowledge which only the social scientific observers have privileged access to, as is typical for objectivistic approaches.[7] The latter implies a 'hierarchization of knowing better', as Luhmann (1990: 510) has called it. There is no epistemological foundation for such a demand for privileged access in the sense of a higher rationality. In the understanding of the documentary method, the social scientific interpreters thus do not presume or presuppose that they know *more* than the actors in the field, but rather that the actors themselves *do not really know exactly what they know all about*. The explication of the implicit knowledge of those being observed is not the result of a higher, but of *another* rationality, of a *change in the analytic attitude* as characterized above.

WORKING STEPS OF THE DOCUMENTARY METHOD IN PRACTICAL RESEARCH

The working steps outlined here were first worked out in our research about adolescence developments in different milieus on the basis of group discussions with peer groups from different educational backgrounds, age and gender in a small town and villages in Northern Bavaria. The working steps among others were then used in a triangulation of group discussions (see Barbour, Chapter 21, this volume), biographical interviews (see Roulston, Chapter 20, this volume) and field notes from participant observation (see Marvasti, Chapter 24, this volume) in our research about hooligans and members of rock bands (e.g. Bohnsack, 1997) and in another large research project about young people of Turkish origin (e.g. Bohnsack and Nohl, 2003). Later on the working steps were transferred to the interpretations of pictures and videos (see below).

Constitutive for the documentary method is the differentiation between the *communicative* or explicit, literal and immanent meaning and the *conjunctive* or implicit and documentary meaning. In our practical research, this differentiation leads to two consecutive steps of interpretation: the *formulating interpretation* and the *reflecting interpretation*.

Formulating Interpretation

The explicit meaning – what participants have 'literally' said – is *formulated* [8] by the researcher. The basic structure of formulating interpretation is the decoding and formulation of the *topical structure* of a text. We reconstruct the topical order by differentiating paramount topics (PT), subordinated topics (ST), sub-subordinated topics (SST), etc.

Reflecting Interpretation

The transition from the immanent (explicit) to the documentary meaning is, as already explained, the transition from asking *what* to asking *how*. Accordingly, *what* has been said, depicted or discussed and *what* has become the topic of discourse is to be separated from *how* – that means, in which framework – the topic is dealt with. This *framework of orientation*, which we also call *habitus*, is the central subject of documentary interpretation. As already explained above, comparative analysis is, from the outset, of central importance for the reflective interpretation. The framework of orientation of a specific case takes shape and can be examined in an empirically controlled manner only in comparison with the framework of other cases: individuals or groups. We must ask: How, that is in which (different) framework of orientations, is the same topic dealt with by other groups or by other individuals?

Whereas the reconstruction of the *topical order* is the basic scaffold for the formulating interpretation, the reconstruction of the so-called *organization of discourse* is the basic scaffold for the reflecting interpretation of *talk and group discussions* (e.g. Bohnsack, 2004; 2010c). The reconstruction of the *genres of texts* is here only of marginal importance but of central importance for the interpretation of all sorts of single *interviews* (Nohl, 2010).

We mainly differentiate between two genres of texts: narrations and descriptions on the one hand and theorizing (or arguing) texts on the other. The practical, implicit or a-theoretical knowledge, that is the frame of orientation or habitus, which is guiding *practical action*, is represented in (preferably, detailed) narrations and descriptions. We can differentiate them from those (arguing) genres of texts which represent the theorizing about practical action of those under research.

For the *analysis of talk and group discussions*, the so-called organization of discourse is of much more importance than the genres of texts. Different modes of discourse organization can be distinguished representing fundamental manners of sociality and of interactional references among individuals: mutually increasing and promoting each other (parallelizing mode), diametrically being against each other and talking at cross-purposes (oppositional mode), systematically roping the other, but also a mode of seeming to be against each other, in which the participants actually encourage each other to present more and more appropriate depictions (antithetical mode). The reconstruction of the mode of discourse organization can tell us if and by how much the participants share a conjunctive space or experience and thus collective (milieu-specific) orientations.

In the next step, the reflecting interpretation and typification will be demonstrated with the example of a short transcript (see Box 15.1) of a group discussion from a research project about young people of Turkish origin.

Example for Formulating and Reflecting Interpretation

Box 15.1   Transcript⁹

1. Dm: Yes, ask a couple of questions, yeah you also
2. Y2:   ⌊Perhaps what you do
3.   at home in the family
4. Hm: ⌊sleeping;
5. Dm: ⌊We're like at our place anyway, well I can only
6.   like speak for myself now; at my place it's like (.) for example even
7.   if I'm not home much like, (.) I'm always thinking about the family, y'know. It's
8.   not like I'd say (.) oh, man, what a shitty family or this that's that's
9.   none of my business or something. Like with some of the Germans it's that way because
10.   they come from another culture but (.) me, like when I come from work
11.   then I go home for dinner, my mother has already made dinner
12.   and then I watch a little TV, (1) then she's talking and this and that
13.   and this; then I'm listening and then like I go out onto the street again; hanging around.
14.   then like I come home at around ten or so, (.) then she's talking
15.   again like I mean then we have a little conversation and then (.) like I go
16.   to bed again. But like you run errands weekends like
17.   go shopping and if you like have something official and like something like that (3) you don't
18.   like talk that much about pleasure or like fun or anything, only what's necessary you just
19.   get it done (4).
20. Am: ⌊It's like so totally different what happens at home like for example,
21.   I mean (.) you're totally different at home than you are like outside
22.   because you have to
23. Dm: ⌊Yeah
24. ?m: ⌊Mhm
25. Fm: ⌊Outside.
26. Dm: ⌊Yeah at home they have like no
27.   idea; like they think our son is going outside for a little bit
28. Am: ⌊yeah
29. Dm: getting a little fresh air and like he's coming like (.) uh eating rice

30.	Am:	⌊(laughs)
31.	Dm:	standing at the table again, I mean really, they think like
32.	?m:	⌊(laughs)
33.	Dm:	they they I mean like they're so old-fashioned in thinking.

Box 15.2 Formulating Interpretation

1–4   PT: Searching for a topic

1   ST: Asking for asking a question

Dm asks for questions while directly addressing Y2 (conductor of the discussion)

2–4   ST: Activities at home

Y2 initiates the topic of activities at home which is immediately answered by Hm with 'sleeping'

5–10   PT: Attitude towards the family

5–8   ST: Continuous mental presence of the family

For Dm the family is continuously present – not so much in the sense of a physical but of a mental presence. His statement is restricted to his own person ('for myself')

8–10   ST: Disregard of the family

The continuous presence of the family is differentiated from an attitude of abusing the family and indifference to it as it is attributed to the Germans because of their different cultural background

10–26   PT: Activities at home

10–17   ST: Run of the day at home

After work Dm comes home having his dinner prepared by his mother and watching a little bit of TV. His mother is talking and Dm listening. Finally he goes out into the street again without a clear plan of activities. After his return in the evening he goes to bed after a little bit of conversation with his mother

17–20   ST: Tasks and topics of talk in the family

Dm has tasks in the family out from home (shopping at the weekend or visiting administrative agencies). These are the only topics of talk in the family whereas pleasure and fun are mostly excluded.

21–26   ST: The strong difference between the behaviour at home and outside

As to Am as well as Dm and Fm the activities and their behaviour at home are quite different from outside

27–35   ST: The total lack of knowledge of the family concerning their sons

At home they are totally ignorant about the activities of their sons outside. They are concerned with the internal familiar affairs of supply ('eating rice'). They have the old-fashioned way of thinking

Reflecting Interpretation

01–03 Joint initiation of a question by Dm and Y2

The interviewer (Y2) reacts to a directive utterance from Dm, appropriating it in a cooperative way by 'contracting' his demand and her utterance syntactically so that we understand a complete question: 'I'd like to know what you do at home.'

04 Proposition[10] by Hm

In Hm's utterance, the following frame of orientation is documented. First it is expressed that the relation to the family is hardly communicative and in this respect distant. (It can, however, not yet be clarified if this is primarily due to recreation needs or to a social demarcation. For this we need the interpretation of the further development of the discourse.) Second, the reaction is kept as short as possible, documenting only very little willingness to give information to the interviewers about this sphere of life.

05–19 Differentiation of the proposition (05–10) and elaboration of this differentiation in the mode of description (10–19) by Dm

Through Dm's reaction to Hm's proposition, its conjunctive, that is group or milieu-specific, meaning becomes increasingly precise: the distance to the family is grounded in a social demarcation, but not in a lack of respect (08: 'fucking family' is not his attitude) and also not in indifference or carelessness towards the family (07: Dm is 'always thinking' about it). Because this is insinuated to 'some Germans' (09), there is also an expression of demarcation against them.

With his description (10–19), which is somehow a reaction to his own proposition, the demarcation toward the family is contextualized by Dm in an interaction scenario, and thus made more precise. This documents, respectively reveals, that:

- the communication with his mother is one-sided;
- neither the utterances nor other activities of the participants have a (reciprocal) reference to each other, rather they stand unrelated next to each other (e.g. 'then she's talking ... then I'm listening', 12–13);
- only urgent pragmatic business is negotiated and not more comprehensive orientations and interests.

20–33 Connecting propositions by Am and Dm

The lack of reference and reciprocity of the perspectives of the parents and the children (i.e. sons) to each other is now specified and made more precise in a way which shows its connection to a strict separation of two different spheres: the *inner sphere* ('at home'; 20, 21, 26) and the *outer sphere* ('outside'; 21, 25). This separation of spheres is based upon different modes of existence or identities ('you're totally different at home'; 21). The genesis of the separation of spheres must – according to the orientations of the young men – be sought in the minds of the older generation (33).

Reflecting Interpretation and Case-Internal Comparative Analysis

The reflecting interpretation begins with the *explication* of the (implicit) frame of orientation – here, the separation of spheres – within a single passage (here, with the topic 'at home'). In the next step of interpretation, the case-internal reflecting interpretation, we look – in a comparative analysis – at passages dealing with other topics (e.g. the relationship to the German girlfriend or to the police) in the same group discussion and then also in interviews with single members of the same group. This determines if the same orientation of the separation of spheres is evident here in a *homologous way*. Moreover, we look at this homologous pattern not only on the level of the *propositions* of the young people, but also on the *performative* level, that is in certain demarcation from the interviewers as members of the outer sphere, as indicated in our example in the beginning of the transcript.

Typification and Comparative Analysis between Cases

As soon as we have worked out – in the next step – a common frame of orientation by comparing *different cases*, we call it a type. The first level of typification is – using a term of Mannheim (1982: 78ff.) – 'the *meaning-genetic*' typification. Here we reconstruct the generic principle, the modus operandi of the frame of orientation or the habitus.

Socio-genetic typification

At this second level of typification, we are looking for the genesis of the generic principle (of the separation of spheres). Socio-genetic typification tries to answer the question of what the orientation or habitus *is typical for*. Saying that an orientation is 'typically rural' means that the genesis of the orientation can be found in the *rural space of experience*. The reconstruction of the socio-genesis may be understood as the identification of relevant spaces of experience, respectively as 'trying to penetrate into the existential background of an experiential space' (Mannheim, 1982: 248), that is into the background of socialization and biographical development. For our example, it could be determined that the socio-genesis of the separation of spheres can be found in the traditional mode of *respect for parents* (especially the father), among others. This respect requires keeping problems and complications in the outer (public) sphere outside of the internal sphere, that is the communication in family and the ethnic community. Thus differences between the two spheres, which have their origin in the migration history of the family, are increased, and their negotiation is forestalled. In addition to group discussions, biographical interviews can also give us deeper insights into socio-genesis (see Bohnsack and Nohl, 2003; Bohnsack et al., 2002).

The Multi-dimensionality of Typification

While analysing the socio-genesis of the orientation of the separation of spheres, we can already assume that the orientation is typical for the space of experience of migration. This must be further validated by comparative analysis, not just with autochthonous young people (from Germany, but also from Turkey, where we conducted group discussions with young people from Ankara). Beyond that, it was necessary to examine the importance of other spaces of experience and their relation to the space of experience of migration. By including peer groups of different gender, age and educational backgrounds in our sampling, we tried to determine if and how the orientation of the separation of spheres (typical for migration) can be identified even when being overlaid by other spaces of experience, respectively other types. We reconstructed whether the migration-specific space of experience, as our *basic type*, can still be identified on a general level throughout variations and modifications of gender, milieu and age-specific (referring to adolescent development) types. Thus we ended up with a whole *typology* (see Figure 15.1).

The level of validity and generalizability of a single type depends on how precisely it can be differentiated from other possible types. It depends on how manifold, that is multi-dimensional, the single case can be found within a whole typology.[11] With our typification procedure based on the documentary method we can take into account

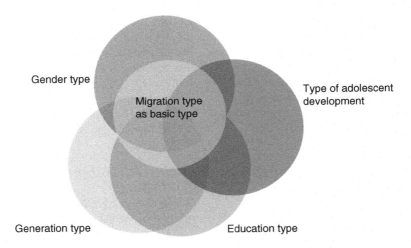

Figure 15.1 Example of a typology

that a case under research – a group or an individual – does not belong to only one, but always to different types and spaces of experience overlying and modifying each other.

RECENT DEVELOPMENTS: THE INTERPRETATION OF PICTURES AND VIDEOS

One of the characteristic features and achievements of the documentary method is giving access to implicit, tacit or a-theoretical knowledge. As the knowledge mediated to us by a picture is per se implicit knowledge, the documentary method seems to be predestined for the interpretation of pictures. During the last 10 years, remarkable progress has been made in the documentary interpretation of pictures. There has been broad research about photos (family, advertising, etc.), children's drawings, cartoons, posters, as well as videos and films.[12]

In a very early stage of its development, in the 1920s, Erwin Panofsky, the most famous historian of the arts, had already adopted the documentary method for the interpretation of pictures. Panofsky was a contemporary and (as far as forced emigration is concerned) companion in misfortune of Karl Mannheim. At the centre of Panofsky's works we find the epoch-making differentiation between the *iconographic* and the *iconological* meaning. This corresponds to the differentiation of the immanent (communicative) and the documentary (conjunctive) meaning in the understanding of Mannheim, as Panofsky himself had pointed out, calling the iconological meaning also 'documentary meaning' (Panofsky, 1932: 115). The object of iconological or documentary interpretation is the 'habitus'. As is generally known, Bourdieu adopted this concept from Panofsky (see Bourdieu, 1977).

Because of these correspondences, we can transfer our working steps of the formulating and reflecting interpretation to the analysis of pictures on a general level. However, we must put our iconographic pre-knowledge as language-bound and textual knowledge into brackets much more radically than in text interpretation in order to gain access to the peculiarity and internal logic of the picture (as it has been theoretically postulated for instance by Roland Barthes and Michel Foucault). Analogous to the interpretation of texts, the reconstruction of the *formal structure*, of the formal composition (see above), can show us the way to the deeper semantics of the picture and its internal logic (see Mitchell, 1994). Here we can build upon reflections in the history of arts concerning the importance of formal aesthetics, which go beyond Panofsky. Especially relevant are the works of Max Imdahl (1996). Gaining an *empirical* access to the internal logic of the picture (still as well as moving) and treating it as a self-referential system by bracketing language-bound and textual pre-knowledge and by giving specific attention to the formal structure of the picture can be seen as the singular achievement of the documentary interpretation of pictures and videos.

OPEN QUESTIONS

The central domain of the documentary method is the analysis of milieu-specific orientations and understandings in the sense of the *conjunctive* spaces of experience, which we can find in society as well as within organizations. We differentiate conjunctive from *communicative* orientations and knowledge, as we can find them in the media and in public communication and which are the central domain of discourse analysis (in the tradition of Foucault – see Willig, Chapter 23, this volume) and especially cultural studies (see Winter, Chapter 17, this volume). Different from media reception analysis, which belongs to the centre of the domain of the documentary method (e.g. Geimer, 2010), media analysis itself is a new field and (with the exception for example of the analysis of advertising photos and a television show; Bohnsack, 2011) it is still an open question how successful the method will be in this area.

NOTES

1. An anthology (Bohnsack et al., 2010) provides an overview in English including 11 examples of research with the documentary method on the basis of group discussions, interviews and the interpretation of pictures and videos. There are also anthologies containing examples of research with the documentary method in Portuguese (Weller and Pfaff, 2010) and in Polish (Krzychała, 2004).
2. My own translation from the French original (Bourdieu, 1972), because the English translation (Bourdieu, 1977) does not include this chapter.
3. Schutz (1962: 26) tried to define the analytic attitude of the scientific observer by his '"disinterestedness" or detachment'. That means that on the level of action 'his motives are not interlocked with those of the observed person or persons' (1962: 26). Such a detachment from the interests of *action* in everyday life, however, can tell us nothing about the interests of *interpretation*. These interests of the scientific observer, and thus his construction of motives, depend on his social standpoint, his 'standpoint bonds' (*Standortgebundenheit*) in the term of Mannheim or, as it is also translated, by his 'social determination of knowledge' (Mannheim, 1936: 239).
4. Different from the English translation in Mannheim (1982: 204), where we can find the formulation 'conjunctive experiential space', I prefer to translate the German term *konjunktiver Erfahrungsraum* (Mannheim, 1980: 227) as 'space of conjunctive experience'.
5. The German term *Seinsverbundenheit* (Mannheim, 1952: 227) also has been translated as *the social determination of knowledge* (Mannheim, 1936: 239). This formulation does not seem to impart adequately the particularity of Mannheim's sociology of knowledge.
6. Concerning comparative analysis and also theoretical sampling, we also owe much to grounded theory in its original version (Glaser and Strauss, 1967). The concept of generating theory in grounded theory, however, does not reach the level of multi-dimensionality in generating types as seen in the documentary method.
7. A prominent representative for an objectivistic approach in qualitative methods in Germany is 'objective hermeneutics' in the tradition of the Frankfurt School (see Wernet, Chapter 16, this volume). As opposed to implicit knowledge as the object of the documentary method, the 'latent structure of meaning' as the object of objective hermeneutics has its place *beyond* the knowledge of those under research and thus is only available to the researcher (see also Bohnsack, 2010a: ch. 4).
8. With the term 'formulating interpretation' I follow Harold Garfinkel and Harvey Sacks (1970: 350ff.) with their reconstruction of the practices of 'formulating'.
9. For the rules of transcription see the appendix to Bohnsack et al. (2010).
10. A depiction wherein an orientation is documented is called a 'proposition'. This term goes back to Garfinkel (1961).
11. Multi-dimensional typologies have to date been realized in more than 40 studies: complex research projects, dissertations and second dissertations.
12. See, among others, Bohnsack (2011) and, in English, Bohnsack (2010b), Nentwig-Gesemann (2006), Wagner-Willi (2006), Baltruschat (2010) and Philipps (2012).

FURTHER READING

Bohnsack, Ralf (2004) 'Group discussions and focus groups', in Uwe Flick et al. (eds), *A Companion to Qualitative Research*. London: Sage. pp. 214–20.

Bohnsack, Ralf, Pfaff, Nicolle and Weller Wivian (eds) (2010) *Qualitative Analysis and Documentary Method in International Educational Research*. Opladen & Farmington Hills: Barbara Budrich (also as e-book free of charge: www.budrich-verlag.de/pages/details.php?ID=334).

Mannheim, Karl (1952a) 'On the interpretation of "Weltanschauung"', in Karl Mannheim, *Essays on the Sociology of Knowledge*. New York: Oxford University Press. pp. 33–83.

REFERENCES

Baltruschat, Astrid (2010) 'The interpretation of films based on the documentary method', in Ralf Bohnsack et al. (eds), *Qualitative Analysis and Documentary Method in International Educational Research*. Opladen and Farmington Hills: Barbara Budrich. pp. 311–42.

Berger, Peter and Luckmann, Thomas (1966) *The Social Construction of Reality*. Garden City, NY: Anchor.

Bohnsack, Ralf (1983) *Alltagsinterpretation und soziologische Rekonstruktion*. Opladen: Westdeutscher Verlag.

Bohnsack, Ralf (1989) *Generation, Milieu und Geschlecht. Ergebnisse aus Gruppendiskussionen mit Jugendlichen*. Opladen: Leske & Budrich.

Bohnsack, Ralf (1997) 'Youth violence and the "episodical community of fate": A case analysis of hooligan groups in Berlin', *Sociologicus*, 46 (2): 160–74.

Bohnsack, Ralf (2004) 'Group discussion and focus groups', in Uwe Flick et al. (eds), *A Companion to Qualitative Research*. London: Sage. pp. 214–221.

Bohnsack, Ralf (2009) 'Qualitative Evaluationsforschung und dokumentarische Methode', in Ralf Bohnsack and Iris Nentwig-Gesemann (eds), *Dokumentarische Evaluationsforschung. Theoretische Grundlagen und Beispiele aus der Praxis*. Opladen and Farmington Hills: Verlag Barbara Budrich. pp. 23–62.

Bohnsack, Ralf (2010a) *Rekonstruktive Sozialforschung. Einführung in qualitative Methoden*, 8th edition. Opladen and Farmington Hills: Barbara Budrich (1st edition,1991).

Bohnsack, Ralf (2010b) 'The interpretation of pictures and the documentary method', in Ralf Bohnsack et al. (eds), *Qualitative Analysis and Documentary Method in International Educational Research*. Opladen and Farmington Hills: Barbara Budrich. pp. 267–92 (also in *Forum: Qualitative Social Research*, 9 (3), 2008. URL: http://nbn-resolving.de/urn:nbn:de:0114-fqs0803276).

Bohnsack, Ralf (2010c) 'Documentary method and group discussions', in Ralf Bohnsack et al. (eds), *Qualitative Analysis and Documentary Method in International Educational Research*. Opladen and Farmington Hills: Barbara Budrich. pp. 99–124.

Bohnsack, Ralf (2011) *Qualitative Bild- und Videointerpretation. Die Dokumentarische Methode*, 2nd edition. Opladen and Farmington Hills: Barbara Budrich (1st edition, 2009).

Bohnsack, Ralf and Nohl, Arnd-Michael (2003) 'Youth culture as practical innovation: Turkish-German youth, time out and actionisms of breakdance', *European Journal of Cultural Studies*, 6 (3): 367–86.

Bohnsack, Ralf, Loos, Peter and Przyborski, Aglaja (2002) '"Male honor". Towards an understanding of the construction of gender relations among youths of Turkish origin', in Helga Kotthoff and Bettina Baron (eds), *Gender in Interaction*. Amsterdam: John Benjamins. pp.175–207.

Bohnsack, Ralf, Pfaff, Nicolle and Weller, Wivian (eds) (2010) *Qualitative Analysis and Documentary Method in International Educational Research*. Opladen and Farmington Hills: Barbara Budrich (www.budrich-verlag.de/pages/details.php?ID=334).

Bourdieu, Pierre (1972) *Esquisse d'une Théorie de la Pratique précédé de Trois Études d'Ethnologie Kabyle*. Genève: Librairie Droiz.

Bourdieu, Pierre (1977) *Outline of a Theory of Practice*. Cambridge: Cambridge University Press.

Bourdieu, Pierre (1992) 'The practice of reflexive sociology (The Paris workshop)', in Pierre Bourdieu and Loïc J.D. Wacquant (eds), *An Invitation to Reflexive Sociology*. Cambridge: Polity Press. pp. 217–60.

Cicourel, Aaron Victor (1964) *Method and Measurement in Sociology*. Glencoe, IL: Free Press.

Cicourel, Aaron Victor (1968) *The Social Organization of Juvenile Justice*. London: Heinemann.

Denzin, Norman K. and Lincoln, Yvonna (eds) (1994) *Handbook of Qualitative Research*. Thousand Oaks, CA: Sage.

Emerson, Robert M. (1969) *Judging Delinquents*. Chicago: University of Chicago Press.

Garfinkel, Harold (1961) 'Aspects of common-sense knowledge of social structures', *Transactions of the Fourth World Congress of Sociology*, Vol. IV: 51–65.

Garfinkel, Harold (1967a) *Studies in Ethnomethodology*. Englewood Cliffs, NJ: Prentice Hall.

Garfinkel, Harold (1967b) 'Conditions of successful degradation ceremonies', in J.G. Manis and B.N. Meltzer (eds), *Symbolic Interaction*. Boston, MA: Allyn & Bacon. pp. 205–12.

Garfinkel, Harold and Sacks, Harvey (1970) 'On formal structures of practical actions', in John C. McKinney and Edward A. Tyriakian (eds), *Theoretical Sociology*. New York: Meredith Corporation. pp. 337–66.

Geimer, Alexander (2010) 'Cultural practices of the reception and appropriation of films from the standpoint of a praxeological sociology of knowledge', in Ralf Bohnsack et al. (eds), *Qualitative Analysis and Documentary Method in International Educational Research*. Opladen and Farmington Hills: Barbara Budrich. pp. 293–309.

Giddens, Anthony (1976) *New Rules of Sociological Method: A Positive Critiques of Interpretative Sociologies*. London: Hutchinson.

Glaser, Barney G. and Strauss, Anselm (1967) *The Discovery of Grounded Theory: Strategies for Qualitative Research*. Chicago: University of Chicago Press.

Greene, Jennifer C. (1994) 'Qualitative program evaluation: Practice and program', in Norman K. Denzin and Yvonna S. Lincoln (eds), *Handbook of Qualitative Research*. Thousand Oaks, CA: Sage. pp. 530–44.

Guba, Egon G. and Lincoln, Yvonna S. (1989) *Fourth Generation Evaluation*. Newbury Park, CA: Sage.

Halbwachs, Maurice (1980) *The Collective Memory*. New York: Harper.

Heidegger, Martin (2010) *Being and Time*. Albany, NJ: State University of New York Press.

Imdahl, Max (1996) *Giotto – Arenafresken. Ikonographie – Ikonologie – Ikonik*. München: Fink.

Krzychała, Sławomir (2004) *Społeczne przestrzenie doświadczenia – metoda interpretacji dokumentarnej*. Wrocław: Wydawnictwo Naukowe.

Luhmann, Niklas (1990) *Die Wissenschaft der Gesellschaft*. Frankfurt a.M.: Suhrkamp.

Mannheim, Karl (1936) 'The sociology of knowledge', in Karl Mannheim, *Ideology and Utopia: An Introduction to the Sociology of Knowledge*. London: Routledge & Kegan Paul. pp. 237–80.

Mannheim, Karl (1952a) 'On the interpretation of "Weltanschauung"', in Karl Mannheim, *Essays on the Sociology of Knowledge*. New York: Oxford University Press. pp. 33–83.

Mannheim, Karl (1952b) 'The problem of generation', in Karl Mannheim, *Essays on the Sociology of Knowledge*. New York: Oxford University Press. pp. 267–320.

Mannheim, Karl (1980) *Strukturen des Denkens*. Frankfurt a.M: Suhrkamp.

Mannheim, Karl (1982) *Structures of Thinking*. London: Routledge & Kegan Paul.

McHugh, Peter (1970) 'A common sense conception of deviance', in Jack D. Douglas (ed.), *Deviance and Respectability*. New York: Basic Books. pp. 61–88.

Mead, George Herbert (1934) *Mind, Self, and Society*. Chicago: University of Chicago Press.

Mitchell, William John Thomas (1994) *Picture Theory: Essays on Verbal and Visual Representation*. Chicago: University of Chicago Press.

Nentwig-Gesemann, Iris (2006) 'The ritual culture of learning in the context of family vacation: a qualitative analysis of vacation pictures', in Tobias Werler and Christoph Wulf (eds), *Hidden Dimensions of Education: Rhetoric, rituals and anthropology*. Münster: Waxmann. pp. 135–48.

Nohl, Arnd-Michael (2010) 'The documentary interpretation of narrative interviews', in Ralf Bohnsack et al. (eds), *Qualitative Analysis and Documentary Method in International Educational Research*. Opladen & Farmington Hills: Barbara Budrich. pp. 195–218.

Panofsky, Erwin (1932) 'Zum Problem der Beschreibung und Inhaltsdeutung', *Logos*, 21: 103–19.

Peirce, Charles S. (1934) *Collected Papers*, vol. 5. Cambridge, MA: Harvard University Press.

Philipps, Axel (2012) 'Visual protest material as empirical data', *Visual Communication*, 11 (1): 3-21.

Schutz, Alfred (1962) *Collected Papers, Vol. I: The Problem of Social Reality*. The Hague: Nijhoff.

Schutz, Alfred (1967) *The Phenomenology of the Social World*. London: Heinemann.

Schwandt, Thomas A. (2002) *Evaluation Practice Reconsidered*. New York: Peter Lang.

Smith, Dorothy E. (1978) '"K is mentally ill": The anatomy of a factual account', *Sociology*, 12: 23–53.

Soeffner, H.G. (2004) 'Social science hermeneutics', in Uwe Flick et al (eds), *A Companion to Qualitative Research*. London: Sage. pp. 95–100.

Wagner-Willi, Monika (2006) 'On the multidimensional analysis of video-data: Documentary interpretation of interaction in schools', in Hubert Knoblauch et al. (eds), *Video Analysis: Methodology and Methods: Qualitative Audiovisual Data Analysis in Sociology*. Frankfurt a.M.: Peter Lang. pp. 143–53.

Weber, Max (1978) *Economy and Society: An Outline of Interpretive Sociology*, vol. 1. San Francisco: University of California Press.

Weber, Max (2002) *The Protestant Ethic and the "Spirit" of Capitalism and other Writings*. New York: Penguin.

Weller, Wivian and Pfaff, Nicolle (2010) *Methodologias da pesquisa qualitativa em Educação. Teoria e Prática*. Petrópolis: Vozes.

Zimmermann, Don H. (1969) 'Recordkeeping and the intake process in a public welfare agency', in Stanton Wheeler (ed.), *On Record: Files and Dossiers in American Life*. New York: Russell Sage Foundation. pp. 319–54.

Hermeneutics and Objective Hermeneutics

Andreas Wernet

HERMENEUTICS – FROM EXEGESIS TO DIALOGUE

Hermeneutics as the art of understanding has its origin in the problem of exegesis. And as the basic point of reference of exegesis is the text, hermeneutics initially is *textual exegesis* (Ricoeur, 2004 [1969]). It deals with the question of the 'true meaning' of texts. This strong textual orientation clearly accounts to the fact that the authors of antique and sacred, religious texts (to mention the historically most important objects of exegesis) are not in reach. They cannot be questioned whether the interpretation of their texts (see Willig, Chapter 10, this volume) corresponds to their intentions (Baumann, 1978).

This scriptual orientation finally comes to an end with the hermeneutic conceptions of Schleiermacher and Dilthey. Their interest is not a philological one, but a philosophic interest in the question of understanding as such. For Dilthey, the distinction between the natural sciences and the '*Geisteswissenschaften*' is built upon the aim of 'understanding' in the field of human affairs in contrast to the search for 'explanations' of natural phenomena. Hermeneutics no longer only deals with the narrow topic of textual understanding but widens to the question of understanding as a fundamental principle of human action and everyday life encounters.

Philosophical hermeneutics seeks to formulate a theoretical concept of understanding as a basic principle of the constitution of the human world and as a necessity of scientific investigation of this world (Grondin, 1994). The idea of the one and only adequate interpretation is rejected in favour of a notion of understanding that emphasizes the role of tradition, prejudice and different subjective horizons (Freeman, 2008). The hermeneutical approach is a biased one. The process of interpretation therefore involves a 'self-examination' of the interpreter. Interpretation is no longer seen as the result of a distanced view of a scientific interpreter that leads to an unbiased understanding, but as a dialogue, in which different perspectives meet.

It is the encounter, the 'hermeneutic experience', which leads to a fusion of horizons (Gadamer, 2011 [1960]).

It should be quite clear that philosophical hermeneutics, despite its important contributions to a theory of understanding and interpretation, does not provide methods of interpretation in the narrower sense of data analysis in qualitative empirical research. The several approaches of qualitative research that refer to hermeneutics rather stand in close relationship to phenomenology and sociology of knowledge (Soeffner, 2004; Alfred Schutz and Karl Mannheim are the most important theorists in these fields – see Eberle, Chapter 13, and Bohnsack, Chapter 15, this volume). Nevertheless the qualitative paradigms of phenomenology, interpretivism and social constructionism (as three of the 'five qualitative approaches to inquiry' suggested by Cresswell, 2007) more or less refer to certain concepts of philosophical hermeneutics, for example the hermeneutic circle, the importance of fore-conceptions or the significance of subjective experience.

OBJECTIVE HERMENEUTICS

In the field of these hermeneutically influenced research approaches, objective hermeneutics plays a specific role. It takes up the older tradition of textual hermeneutics in a radical reference to the *text* as the object of data analysis. There is no method in the field of qualitative research that is bound so strictly to the text as the central point of reference of hermeneutic inquiry.

The method of objective hermeneutics was developed in the 1970s by the German sociologist Ulrich Oevermann. To give a first insight into the central features of this method it is helpful to bring to mind the research context in which objective hermeneutics was developed. This was a research project concerned with the interaction process in families based on participating observance of families and audio records of family interaction. The aim of this project was to study the 'natural' interaction of family members. But the research setting confronted the researchers with the fact that a naturalistic approach to family interaction has to fail, because the presence of researchers deeply influences the reality they are studying. This experience of the sheer impossibility of grasping family interaction in an authentic way contrasted with the experience that audio recording of interaction nevertheless preserved the particular characteristics of a concrete family interaction. This led to a basic theoretical and methodological concept: in its varying interactions a family is still identifiable. There must be a structure operating beyond the strategies of 'impression management' (Goffman, 1959), which does not allow a family to hide its identity. And this structure can be disclosed by a detailed study of records of interaction. This was the starting point of conceptualizing qualitative empiric research as a reconstruction of the meaning of texts. Over the years objective hermeneutics has developed into a highly influential method of qualitative data analysis with a wide range of research contributions in nearly every thematic field.[1]

SOME GENERAL REMARKS ON BASIC METHODOLOGICAL ISSUES

The basic theoretical orientation of objective hermeneutics is based on structuralistic theory. The psychology of Jean Piaget, the ethnology of Claude Lévi-Strauss and the grammar theory of Noam Chomsky are central theoretical references. Their interest in social reality as based on meaning is focused neither on description nor on the subjective experiences or intentions of actors. In accordance with this approach the main interest of objective hermeneutics in meaning (in the sense of 'structure of meaning') is to reveal the *latent* meaning of utterances and its relation to the intentions (manifest meaning) of actors. This difference between manifest and latent meaning, similar to the difference between manifest and latent functions, formulated by Robert K. Merton (Merton, 1968) and to the difference between the manifest topic of a dream and its latent idea (Freud, 2001a [1900]; 2001b [1900–1]; 2001c [1915–16]), is of great importance for the methodological point of view of objective hermeneutics. In order to guard against misunderstandings, the aim of objective hermeneutics is not just to reveal the latent meaning of an actor's speech; it is to reconstruct the relations between the manifest intentions and the latent meaning of utterances (Oevermann, 1987: 438). The social object of this method is not the meaning of action, lying beyond an actor's consciousness and his or her intentions, but the differences, tensions and even contradictions between intentions and the latent meaning of action.

Objective hermeneutics stands in the German tradition of sociology of language (Gerhardt, 1988: 34). The world (of meaning) is represented by texts.[2] The empirical fundament of the reconstruction of latent meaning structures is a *fixed text as a precise record of interaction*. As Oevermann argues, there is no other access to meaning than through symbolic representation (Oevermann, 1986). Meaning only occurs in its symbolic form. And a method of reconstruction of meaning therefore has to rely on texts. To claim validity (see Barbour, Chapter 34, this volume), the interpretation process needs a fixed record as a basis of scientific dispute.

These few remarks help to understand the characterization of this method as 'objective'. It points out to the principle claim of validity. It does not mean that objective hermeneutics suggests that its interpretations achieve absolute or final truth or a non-biased viewpoint. It only means that it highly values the possibility of controlling interpretations by the scientific community.[3] Without a fixed record, this control is impossible. The designation of the method as hermeneutic points less to the scientific conception of understanding but more to the conception of a method of understanding as a method of analysing texts (see the introductory paragraph). The difference between manifest and latent meaning follows up the claim of classic hermeneutics to understand 'the utterer better than he understands himself' (Schleiermacher – see Smith, 2007: 4).

Finally we want to point out that Oevermann characterizes his method as a method to reconstruct case-structures (*Fallstrukturrekonstruktion*). The term 'case' – in general dependent on the methodological background in which it is embedded (Ragin and Becker, 1992: 4) – is used in objective hermeneutics in a special manner. The notion of 'case' is rooted in the structural concept that a particular phenomenon (the case)[4] cannot be seen as an isolated event, but as a variation of a general structure. This model can be divided into two further assumptions: (1) A case is not only an expression of a subjective or individual social constellation, but also an expression of general structures. (2) These general structures cannot be studied as such. They do not appear beyond or outside of cases. The empirical path to generality leads through the study of the particular case. Therefore, the reconstruction of the structure of a case allows two directions of generalization. First, a case appears as a token of a type. It represents a special and insofar typical disposition for solving a certain problem. Second, this special and typical solution is only one way of reacting to a general problem. To give an example, according to Parsons the basic problem of the modern, nuclear family interaction lies in the dissolution of the family of origin and its replacement by a foundation of new, nuclear families ('the process of selfliquidation of each particular nuclear family' – Parsons, 1964: 74). Every family has to handle this process of dissolution and foundation. And every family is an outcome of this process. But every family has to find its own way to solve this problem. In examining families, we can formulate types of solutions of this problem (e.g. the centripetal and centrifugal mode of detachment; Stierlin, 1977) in the same manner, as we can formulate an empirical-based general theory of dissolution and foundation of families.

RULES

(Inter)action is based on social rules. Social action emerges in line with these rules, and the interpretation of the meaning of action is only possible by recourse to our knowledge of rules. The rule concept constitutes a link between object and method. On the one hand it concerns the constitution of social action; on the other hand it represents the key issue of the methodically guided reconstruction of social action.

The concept of rule differs from the concept of convention as well as from the concept of knowledge. Whereas conventions define social action as conforming (resp. deviant), rules define the horizon of action alternatives and the *meaning* of these alternatives. As a simple example, the modalities of greeting can be seen as conventions that define in which situations it is adequate or not to greet one another. When boarding an airliner, we know that it is expected to greet (or to greet back) the members of the crew awaiting the passengers. And we know that it is unusual to greet all the passengers we meet. Behind these conventions there are operating rules that define the social consequences of greeting or not greeting. In a situation in which greeting is expected, not greeting may be a deviation; but it may also be a meaningful action that shows the other – that ego is not interested in social exchange. The possibility to do so and the fact that this action has specific consequences are only given by rules of action.

This example also shows that conventions and rules stand in different relation to knowledge. Conventions belong to common knowledge and to our expectations of everyday life. Rules generate action by 'tacit knowledge'. They are not consciously applied by actors. Like linguistic rules – as with Chomsky's concept of linguistic competence – rules in general enable the actor to create meaningful action.

A very interesting implication of this concept concerns the question of validity. How can we identify rules and how can we know whether the identified rules are operating? Oevermann points out that rules according to the competence concept can only be examined and reconstructed by relying on them and by presuming their prevalence. According to Oevermann, this applies to the following types of rules: (1) the universal and language-specific rules of linguistics; (2) the rules of communicative or illocutionary competence (universal pragmatics); and (3) the universal rules of cognitive and moral competence (Oevermann et al., 1979: 387). These types of rules can be considered universal insofar as their validity is ineluctable. Criticism of the material content of these rules must always utilize its validity beforehand. For instance, I can only criticize the adequacy of a linguistic judgement utilizing the validity of linguistic rules.

In addition there are several types of rules with restricted scope and extent: rules that apply only in specific social classes or milieus and rules that change in time (Oevermann, 1986: 22ff.). Because the validity of interpretation depends on the validity of rules, we have to prove the validity of the rules that the analysis is based on. In the process of interpretation, on some occasions there may remain an uncertainty in this question (see Willig, Chapter 10, this volume). It is important to accept that and to be frank about this uncertainty rather than to hide it.

In order to avoid these uncertainties the privileged type of rule drawn upon by the methodical controls of objective hermeneutics are the ineluctable rules we draw on as competent members of society. The objective hermeneutics method aims at basing the interpretation on these rules. The practical interpretative procedures make use of our rule competence.

In this context, special attention is paid to the fact that the validity of an interpretation does not rely on knowledge about or familiarity with the object of research. If, for example, an objective hermeneutic analysis has to interpret a promise, the main interpretative operation will not consist of activating our everyday life experiences – perhaps that promises are often not serious – but to explicate the rule-based implications of a promise, for example the supposition of fulfillment. The rule competence enabling us to specify clearly 'what a promise is' provides the basis for the establishment of validity in textual interpretation.

The rule concept is of great importance for defending the methodological and epistemological capability of interpretation. Because the interpreter shares the same rules as the object of examination, it is possible to understand the meaning of action. To do so, it is not necessary to reconstruct the operating rules themselves. We do not need grammar theory to understand a sentence and to differentiate between linguistically correct or wrong sentences. In the reconstruction of a case structure we rely on rules and we formulate social theories along with the case, not theories of rules.

STRUCTURE AND HABITUS

Rules do not determine action; they only determine the realm of possible actions. They do not tell the actor what to do; they only constitute a frame of reference to the actor's decisions. These decisions are not a function of the underlying and ineluctable rules but a function of the autonomy of the actor (Oevermann, 1991, uses the term 'autonomy of life-practice'). This autonomy constitutes the subjectivity of action. Without this 'freedom', social action could only be understood as a rule-determined and insofar fixed reality. Processes of change and of subjective variation could not be explained. On the other hand, subjectivity is not the result of sheer contingency. Subjectivity emerges as a structured process of action. We can say that the autonomy of the subject is limited not only by the rule-generated possibilities, but also by its own, self-generated structure. This structure can be conceived of as the identity of the subject or the identity of the case. This identity is formed by the iteration of decision-making by acting in the same way. The reproduction of a case structure seen as its identity can be studied by the fact that in a new situation the subject tends to decide or to act in a similar way. To describe this phenomenon Bourdieu has suggested the term 'habitus'. He conceived habitus as the 'modus operandi' of a case (dependent on different perspectives on social structure; Bourdieu, 1984 [1979]; see Bohnsack, Chapter 15, this volume).

We refer here to the concept of habitus and 'modus operandi' to point out that this process of the reproduction of a structure is itself a creative process, which cannot be appropriately understood as a reproduction of the same behaviour. It is not the simple repetition of the same action as with mere habits. The shape (*Gestalt*) of action that reproduces a certain structure shows unlimited variations. Therefore the recognition of processes of reproduction of a case structure requires a procedure of reconstruction.

HOW TO DO OBJECTIVE HERMENEUTICS TEXT INTERPRETATION

After having outlined the basic methodological assumptions of objective hermeneutics above, the following paragraphs will be concerned with the methodical procedures of text analysis and with the principles that the interpretation has to follow.

The basic tool of objective hermeneutics interpretation is the "thought experiment" to formulate different stories, that is different contexts, in which the text to interpret could occur as a well-formed utterance. This procedure helps to reveal the latent implications of an utterance – its objective meaning structure. As an example of this first step of analysis Maiwald considers the utterance A: 'Where have you been?' (2005: 8). Maiwald comes to the following conclusion: 'it implies that the recipient should have been there or at least the speaker should have known that the recipient was not where he should have been, and, in general, that the speaker claims to have a right to know' (2005: 8). If we imagine an answer of the recipient, like B: 'Why do you want to know?', the importance of the foregoing analysis seems to be quite clear. Now we can see that the interaction deals with the question of the *relationship* between A and B. B's counter-question doubts that A has the right to ask where B has been. Only if we push forward the interpretation to the level of the objective meaning structure can we reveal the dynamics of the relationship that lie behind the simple game of question and counter-question.

This basic procedure of the reconstruction of meaning in detail is based on the principles of interpretation that I will outline in the following. These principles are (I) to exclude the context, (II) to take the literal meaning of a text seriously, (III) sequentiality, and (IV) extensivity.

Exclude the Context

The methodical principle to exclude the context before a text is interpreted may seem surprising at first. Why should a method which claims to understand texts not make use of the context? Does the con-text, as the word itself suggests, not add relevant information to the text? Is it not sometimes even necessary to know in which context an action or a speech act has taken place to understand its meaning?

These are some of the objections that the first principle of objective hermeneutics text interpretations frequently evokes. To a certain extent they are based on a misunderstanding, as the context of a text is not completely excluded in an interpretation. As a matter of fact objective hermeneutics even systematically contextualizes its interpretations. What the principle to exclude the context in interpretations demands, though, is to interpret a sequence separately without its context *before* taking into account the kind of situation in which a sentence was uttered. The contextualization follows the context-free interpretation of a text.

This methodical proceeding helps to differentiate analytically between the meaning of a text as such and its meaning in a certain context. This is important as it forces the interpreter systematically to contrast a latent and a manifest level of meaning in every text sequence. Following the principle to exclude the context before starting to interpret a text makes sure, for example, that ambiguous meanings of expressions that are overlooked in everyday conversations because the context of an utterance is taken into account are exposed in an interpretation.

To give an example, imagine a couple sitting at the kitchen table eating pudding and the woman saying to her husband: 'You can take some more if you like.'[5]

From the context it is quite clear what the woman wants to say and even if the sentence sounds a bit odd there hardly seems to be a great demand for an in-depth analysis of her utterance. A context-free interpretation, though, can show that the exact words the woman uses in the example to tell her husband he can take some more imply that she is treating her husband as a child who cannot express his own wishes.

The methodical operation by which this can be revealed is to formulate contexts in which the utterance 'You can take some more if you like' could be said absolutely naturally. This would be the case in the following situation. A young boy visiting a friend's house for the first time after school has finished his meal and shyly looks at the dishes obviously still hungry. His friend's mother says, 'You can take some more if you like.'

In the next step in context-free interpretations one has to make sure that every other situation in which a speech act could occur naturally would be structurally similar to the concrete example that one has formulated so far. If this is the case then one tries to identify the essential characteristics of the type of situation connected to a speech act.

In the case of the speech act 'You can take some more if you like' mainly two conditions have to be met in order for the speech act to be appropriate: a person saying 'You can take some more if you like' (a) has to be sure that whoever is addressed actually wants some more. The speech act *is not giving information*, it is, rather, *interpreting someone's behaviour as an expression of an unuttered wish*. In order for such an interpretation of someone's behaviour not to be inadequate (b) there have to be specific reasons why the person addressed does not dare to express their wish for more themselves. In the example above the mother for instance has reason to assume that the boy is too shy to ask for more because he is at someone else's house for the first time.

From this context-free interpretation it becomes clear now that the woman in the above formulated example telling her husband that he can take some more is actually insinuating that her husband, like a child, would like some more but dare not ask. And as she is talking to a grown-up man and there are no specific reasons why her husband might not dare to ask for more, she is further implying that he is not able to express his wishes in a grown-up manner. So, to summarize, she is infantilizing her husband.

The example should illustrate that beyond the obvious meaning of a text sequence a text also has a latent level of meaning, which is revealed only if one analyses a text context-free before taking into account its context. The differentiation between a context-free meaning of a text sequence and its meaning in a specific situation enables interpreters to detect a latent level of meaning which would be overlooked if a text were explained through the context.

The essential operation that objective hermeneutics uses to arrive at the latent level of meaning is to sketch out contexts in which the text sequences one is about to analyse could appear naturally as a well-formed utterance. It is important here to note that the formulation of contexts should take absolutely no notice of the contexts in which the speech acts were actually spoken. On the contrary, it is absolutely vital only to consider whether, in the diverse contexts one has tried to creatively sketch out, a speech act could occur naturally or not. If one tries to look for contexts close to the factual context of a text there is a great risk that the latent meaning structure of a text sequence is overlooked.

Our example shows quite clearly that a scientific interpretation does not necessarily conform to the self-understanding of the actors. We may assume that the woman in our example would not agree with the thesis of her 'infantilizing her husband'. This is a simple implication of the concept of latent meaning. The dynamic of infantilizing, reconstructed in only one utterance, is not in the consciousness of the actor. The outcomes of an interpretation can therefore be rather disturbing for the actors.

Take the Literal Meaning of a Text Seriously

Just like the exclusion of the context, the second principle of objective hermeneutics interpretations – to take seriously the literal meaning of a text – forces an interpreter to concentrate strictly on the text in interpretations. While the exclusion of the context serves to eliminate attempts to clarify the meaning of a text by using context information, the obligation to focus on the literal meaning of a text demands from an interpreter not to clarify the text itself by smoothing out expressions that seem to suggest that a person wanted to say something different from what they actually said.

The most prominent interpretative approach which is based on the principle of taking seriously the literal meaning of a text is the 'parapraxis' ('Freudian slip'). Here, the tension between what somebody intentionally wanted to say and the literal meaning of what was actually said is quite obvious. If, for example, an assistant wants to toast his boss by saying '*Ich fordere Sie auf, auf das Wohl unseres Chefs* anzustoßen' (Let us *drink a toast* to the health of our boss), but he says actually '*Ich fordere Sie auf, auf das Wohl unseres Chefs* aufzustoßen' (Let us *burp* to the health of our boss) (Freud, 2001c [1915–16]: 32), the mistake is obvious to everyone as well as the rough meaning of the mistake. The positive and complimentary action (an*stoßen* = *to drink a toast*) is substituted by a negative and discourteous action (auf*stoßen* = *to burp*). The slip of the tongue of the assistant shows an ambivalent attitude towards his boss; a tension between acknowledgement and disregard.

The example of parapraxis helps one to understand the difference between scientific and everyday interpretation. It seems to be quite clear that the everyday attitude is not interested in the literal meaning. If not completely disregarded, the literal meaning is treated like a joke and the potential serious implications of the utterance are neutralized by laughter. But the laughter itself shows that the disinterest is not a function of cognition – if there were no idea of the literal meaning, there would be no reason to laugh – but a function of the pragmatic of everyday social exchange.

The scientific interest in the literal meaning is in sharp contrast to the action attitude of social exchange. The researcher becomes a 'disinterested observer' (Schutz, 1971: 36ff.). This change of perspective is of crucial importance for objective hermeneutics text analysis. The difficulty is not located on the level of knowledge or cognition. It lies in the ability to look at interaction in a different way, to find and to allow such interpretations that everyday or common-sense attitudes would consider inadequate.

Objective hermeneutics interpretations basically focus on what was said and not on what somebody might have wanted to say. This also applies to text sequences in which there does not appear to be such a great gap between the latent and the manifest meaning of an utterance as in parapraxes. Metaphorically speaking, objective hermeneutics treats every text sequence which shows a difference between intention and literal expression as a Freudian slip by never trying to normalize expressions to make them more familiar and therefore easier to interpret. Instead an interpretation always has to be grounded in the literal meaning of a text.

Of course the principle to take seriously the literal meaning of a text is not relevant all the time. Very often the literal meaning of a text does not raise the question whether a person wanted to say something different or not. If a chairperson opens a meeting by saying 'I would like to welcome everybody to this meeting', there is no difference between intention and speech. Only if the chairperson opens the session by saying 'I would like to close the meeting' (yet another famous example of a Freudian slip; Freud, 2001c [1915–16]: 34) does the question of the meaning of this difference occur. When this question arises the second principle of objective hermeneutics interpretation becomes important. It reminds the interpreter to stick to the meaning of the text instead of focusing on what someone might have wanted to say intentionally. Only if this is done can a latent and a manifest level of meaning be systematically differentiated and used in case reconstructions, so the main aim of objective hermeneutics interpretations, the reconstruction of the 'latent meaning structures' in texts, can be achieved.

There is another reason why interpretations should strictly be based on the literal meaning of a text. It makes sure that interpretations are done in accordance with a fundamental scientific standard: only the text provides a solid database in which interpretations can be criticized and controlled by others while the accuracy of assumptions about what someone possibly wanted to say cannot be checked.

Focusing on the literal meaning of a text therefore solves a problem the interpretative methods that rely on subjective impressions about the meaning of texts are confronted with. While subjective reactions are not always absolutely comprehensible the literal meaning of a text is determined by grammatical rules und the rules of speech acts. This is one reason for the 'objective' character of objective hermeneutics interpretations.

That of course does not mean to say that the intuitive impressions people have when reading texts are without value. Without intuition no interpretation and no discovery would be possible. What objective hermeneutics merely claims is that only when an interpretation can be unfolded stringently from a database, which is the same for everyone, can an interpretation be said to be intersubjectively comprehensible.

Sequentiality

In the praxis of text interpretation the principle of sequentiality merely demands the text to be analysed line by line (Flick, 2006: 335). The principle of sequentiality is deeply rooted in the methodology of objective hermeneutics. It marks a great difference to qualitative research methods, which search through texts for certain recurring elements.

The main argument according to the constitutive theory of objective hermeneutics for the necessity to interpret a text sequentially is that structures generally unfold in a process of reproduction. In a certain sense objective hermeneutics does not distinguish between structures and processes but claims that structures only exist in the form of their process of reproduction.

Now this process is sequential by nature because the reproduction of a structure occurs in time as a constant choice of options, which are opened up by social rules. At every moment in every situation structures are confronted with possible alternatives of action. It is impossible in the social world not to make choices. The specific characteristic of a specific structure lies in the pattern of its choices.

The term 'sequentiality' therefore does not refer to a mere chronological order of sequences. It points out that structures in the social world are in a constant process of having to choose actions from given alternatives which then again open up new alternatives from which again one has to be chosen and so on.

Oevermann uses the example of greetings again to illustrate the sequential nature of social behaviour (see above). Imagine someone greeting another person on the street with a friendly 'hello'. The person greeted has exactly two possibilities: they can either say 'hello' as well or say nothing at all. The second option cannot be seen as a refusal of a choice but it is the choice to express that one is not interested in an interaction with the greeting person. Neutral social behaviour is thus impossible.

The sequentiality of greeting situations can be generalized. At every moment, even when someone is not interacting with another person, choices have to be made as to how a situation should continue and whatever choice someone makes has a certain meaning determined by social rules. In this ongoing process structures reproduce themselves by a certain systematic of the choices they make.

From this pivotal idea of an identity between structures and their sequential process of reproduction the methodical principle to interpret texts sequentially can be easily inferred. The sequentiality of interpretations simply follows the sequential process of the reproduction of structures by a line-by-line analysis. The reproduction of a structure cannot show itself in an isolated text sequence. It is instead necessary to follow the choices 'producing' a text. Only if a systematic in a series of choices is identified can one say that a structure was successfully reconstructed.

The principle of sequentiality has pragmatic implications for doing interpretations that need to be sketched out.

First, it raises the question of where to start an interpretation. This question can be answered easily. Although Oevermann recommends commencing at the beginning of a protocol, it is possible to start interpreting a text at whatever sequence one likes. What the principle of sequentiality merely demands is that wherever one starts with an interpretation one has to continue the interpretation with whatever sequence follows. Only then can a full cycle of reproduction be reconstructed.

It is strictly not allowed to 'jump' in the text in order to verify hypotheses, because this would contain the risk of looking only for those sequences that fit one's hypotheses. Especially if an interpretation comes across sequences that are difficult to interpret because their meaning is hard to reconstruct, the principle of sequentiality has to be followed. While avoiding sequences that cannot be smoothly integrated in an interpretation can easily lead to self-fulfilling interpretations, a stubborn sequential interpretation forces the interpreter to ground an interpretation in the text.

To follow the sequential order of texts is, according to experience, especially difficult for interpreters who are not familiar with objective hermeneutics. It may be very tempting to take a look how a text continues or what was said before the sequence one is currently interpreting.

Just like the other principles explained above, the principle of sequentiality forces the interpreter to follow the dynamic of the text itself instead of explaining certain features of texts by referring to other parts of the text or knowledge about the context.

Another pragmatic consequence of the principle of sequentiality is that it makes it necessary to consider how to relate interpretations of following text sequences to each other. In objective hermeneutics the results of interpretations of preceding sequences form what is called the 'inner context' of interpretations. While knowledge about the 'outside' context first has to be strictly excluded, the 'inner context' of interpretations always has to be taken into account. The reason is of course that a meaning of a single text sequence has to be considered as a part of the reproduction process of a structure, which means that it needs to be seen in its sequential position.

Extensivity

The principle of extensivity is probably the most striking characteristic of objective hermeneutics interpretations for someone who is not familiar with the method. Hypotheses about the structure of a case are formulated on small text segments which are analysed in extreme detail. The interpretation goes into depth more than into breadth. Therefore in most research contexts it is impossible to analyse the entire text (the *whole* interview, the *whole* interaction, etc.). This approach frequently provokes the following two objections: (1) As interpretations focus only on small parts of texts it is criticized that objective hermeneutics does not do justice to its database. This objection implies that an interpretation of a text should consider the text as a whole. (2) The meticulous and in-depth analysis even of expressions that seem to be of secondary importance is often confronted with the criticism that objective hermeneutics disproportionally attaches importance to negligible parts of texts instead of concentrating on statements that are seemingly more important in a text with regard to their content.

Concerning the first objection, the theoretical justification of objective hermeneutics for analysing small text segments extensively instead of interpreting whole texts is grounded in the idea that small fragments of a text always also represent something general of social reality. This idea conforms to the concept of 'totality' which points to the fact that isolated phenomena do not exist in social reality because every utterance is generated by a case structure. So the principle of extensivity is based on the assumption that every segment of a text is characterized by the dialectic of particularity and generality. The particular features of a case structure can be identified as such only against the background of general social phenomena. Even seemingly insignificant text segments point to a social reality beyond the text.

The methodology of objective hermeneutics picks up on this dialectic of particularity and generality by claiming that one cannot act 'outside' of the social world with its rules that attach meaning to every social act. It is, in other words, impossible to act meaninglessly. The meaning of every particular social act protocolled in a text sequence is determined by general social rules.

Insofar as objective hermeneutics is interested not only in the particularity of cases, but also in something general about social reality that expresses itself through the particularity of cases – and there is no other way to capture general social reality than in the form of particular cases – then it is true to say that the particular structure of a case can be reconstructed in every part of a protocol. Because, if interpretations are not restricted to reconstructing the particular meaning of utterances in their specific situations but aim at reaching out for the general structural patterns that are present on the latent level of meaning in every text sequence, then, at least in principle, it does not matter where one starts with an interpretation. Just as the 'habitus' of a person is not limited to certain activities but is a 'modus operandi' that shows itself in every activity the person is engaged in, so does a structure expresses itself in every text segment. This does not mean of course that in practice there are no prominent text segments to start an interpretation. But wherever one starts with an interpretation one can rely on the fact that it is always the same structure underlying the text.

The second objection concerning the principle of extensivity, that the in-depth analysis of even the seemingly most insignificant text fragments is an unnecessary and uneconomic approach, can be answered with two different arguments.

The first argument corresponds to the importance the text is given through the principle to take seriously the literal meaning as a means to establish a database that allows interpretations that are intersubjectively comprehensible. An interpreter who ignores certain text fragments because of their apparent insignificance will damage his database. In contrast, when every part of a text is included in an interpretation the interpreter has little chance of deforming the meaning of a text by projecting his or her pre-established beliefs about a case. So just like the other principles explained above, the principle of extensivity tries to make sure that interpretations are grounded in the text itself and not in subjective conceptions about a case. Pragmatically this demands that it is forbidden to skip words or even paralinguistic elements, but that one takes one's time to analyze every element of a text patiently. According to experience it can be very costly to rush over seemingly insignificant parts of texts because they can change the meaning of a text sequence dramatically.

This leads us to the second argument justifying the principle of extensivity. While in everyday conversations it is necessary to pay particular attention to the most important information someone is providing with an utterance, an interpretation that is concerned with latent meaning structures has to disengage itself from this everyday perspective. Now to focus on seemingly insignificant elements of a text means to analyse meaningful elements that are not under the conscious control of a speaker. Normally, excluding the case of a Freudian slip, a speaker is fully aware of what the main statement is that he or she wants to make with an utterance. In contrast it is impossible for speakers to overlook the meaningful implications of the more unremarkable parts of their expressions. Consequently, the latent level of meaning can often be more easily detected in the parts of a text that gain the least attention in everyday conversations. By claiming that every text element is worth analysing, objective hermeneutics therefore systematically accentuates the level of latent meaning in a text.

LIMITATIONS

As we have seen, objective hermeneutics is a pronounced method of text interpretation (see more generally Willig, Chapter 10, this volume). In principle it can be applied to any inquiry focusing on records of interactions as a database. And since in nearly all qualitative research records of interaction are used as data, there is a high potential of methodical combinations in which objective hermeneutics can be used as an additional research instrument.

As a method specializing in text interpretation, objective hermeneutics has not developed a method of fieldwork and of collecting data. Every new research project has to find its own strategy of gaining access to the field and to the data. Objective hermeneutics does not provide methodical rules that instruct inexperienced colleagues on how to organize fieldwork and to collect data. This lack of rules and techniques of research organization is due to the concept of an open, non-standardized process of research, which has to be newly adjusted for every research question.[6] Even such simple questions like 'how many cases should I examine?', 'how many sequences should be considered?', etc., cannot be answered in general. From the standpoint of an inexperienced researcher planning a research project this lack will, of course, be considered as a deficiency. The researcher will therefore need to get advice from more experienced researchers, look for cooperation in a research group or inform him- or herself by reading empirical studies that are similar to his or her own research interest.

Another limitation concerns the strong bias on language analysis. There is no doubt that Oevermann claims the fundamental possibility to analyse any type of record of action: pictures, photographs, videos, etc. Since meaning structures find their expression in every form of symbolic representation, language is only one type of representation among others. This assumption implies that there is no research context in the field of reconstruction of meaning that necessitates extralinguistic data. The reconstruction of a case structure is always possible in restricting it to its linguistic articulation. Even if we follow this methodological position, we can claim that the analysis of extralinguistic data could be at least helpful. Although many researchers in objective hermeneutics have analysed such data (especially photographs and pictures), there is not yet a clear instruction or guidance on 'how to do' so. The principles of interpretation outlined in this chapter cannot be applied one-to-one to extralinguistic analysis. It is an important desideratum of further methodical development. Especially, the application of objective hermeneutics for the analysis of videos needs to be methodically developed because video protocols currently play a vital role in the discovery of new fields and approaches in qualitative inquiry.

Finally we want to stress the special character of insights generated by objective hermeneutics. We pointed out that objective hermeneutics is not interested in the description of social reality. We should keep in mind that inquiries that aim at collecting social facts or producing inside descriptions of social contexts cannot benefit from objective hermeneutics. The mere gathering of information about social reality is not the concern of this method.

Objective hermeneutics is not limited to special objects or topics of research. It can be applied to any formation of the social world. It is also not bound in a strict sense to sociology. It can be applied in historical, psychological, educational (and so on) contexts of research as well. The limitation of this method does not lie in the object. It lies in the questions that this method poses, in the answers it can give and the theoretical constructs that can be derived from the empirical analysis. As mentioned above, a special interest and capacity of objective hermeneutics lies in the reconstruction of tensions and contradictions of manifest and latent meaning. This may be seen as a limitation of the method. If, for example, we are interested in the topics that families talk about and if we only want to note and to collect these topics, or if we are only interested in the contents of professional ethics, objective hermeneutics is obviously the wrong method. Only if we are interested in latent dimensions of family interaction or if we are interested in unconscious motives of professional work and its tacit ethics is objective hermeneutics a suitable empirical method.

ACKNOWLEDGEMENTS

The author thanks Uwe Flick, Florian Grawan, Kai-Olaf Maiwald, Thomas Wenzl and the two anonymous reviewers for comments.

NOTES

1. The website of AG Objektive Hermeneutik (http://www.agoh.de/cms/) gives an insight into the various fields of inquiry of objective hermeneutics.
2. *The World as Text* (*Die Welt als Text*) is the title of a prominent book in German on the method of objective hermeneutics, edited by Detlef Garz and Klaus Kraimer in 1994 (Suhrkamp).
3. In clear contrast to the concept of group consensus, as is often associated with hermeneutics (see e.g. Willis, 2007: 302).
4. This means that the question 'What is the case?' cannot be answered by merely pointing at concrete subjects. By way of illustration see Silverman (2005: 126).
5. I thank Thomas Wenzl for suggesting this example.
6. According to Oevermann, the praxis of interpretation is an 'art' (*Kunstlehre* – Reichertz, 2004).

FURTHER READING

Maiwald, Kai-Olaf (2005) 'Competence and praxis: sequential analysis in German sociology' [46 paragraphs], *Forum Qualitative Sozialforschung/Forum: Qualitative Social Research* [Online Journal], 6 (3), Art. 31. Available at: www.qualitative-research.net/fqs-texte/3-05/05-3-31-e.htm (accessed 7 May 2013).

Reichertz, Jo (2004) 'Objective hermeneutics and hermeneutic sociology of knowledge', in Uwe Flick et al. (eds), *A Companion to Qualitative Research*. London: Sage. pp. 290–95.

Wernet, Andreas (2009) *Einführung in die Interpretationstechnik der Objektiven Hermeneutik*, 3rd edition. Wiesbaden: VS Verlag für Sozialwissenschaften.

REFERENCES

Baumann, Zygmunt (1978) *Hermeneutics and Social Science: Approaches to Understanding.* London: Hutchinson.

Bourdieu, Pierre (1984 [1979]) *Distinction: A Social Critique of the Judgment of Taste.* London: Routledge & Kegan Paul.

Creswell, John W. (2007) *Qualitative Inquiry & Research Design: Choosing Among Five Approaches*, 2nd edition. Thousand Oaks, CA: Sage.

Flick, Uwe (2006) *An Introduction to Qualitative Research*, 3rd Edition. London: Sage.

Freeman, Melissa (2008) 'Hermeneutic traditions', in Lisa Given (ed.), *The Sage Encyclopedia of Qualitative Research Methods.* Los Angeles: Sage. pp. 385–8.

Freud, Sigmund (2001a [1900]) 'The interpretation of dreams (first part)', in Sigmund Freud, *The Standard Edition of the Complete Psychological Works of Sigmund Freud*, vol. 4. London: Vintage.

Freud, Sigmund (2001b [1900–1]) 'The interpretation of dreams (Second Part)', in Sigmund Freud, *The Standard Edition of the Complete Psychological Works of Sigmund Freud*, vol. 5. London: Vintage.

Freud, Sigmund (2001c [1915–16]) 'Introductory lectures on psycho-analysis (Parts 1 and 2)', in Sigmund Freud, *The Standard Edition of the Complete Psychological Works of Sigmund Freud*, vol. 15. London: Vintage.

Gadamer, Hans-Georg (2011 [1960]) *Truth and Method*, 2nd rev. edition. London: Continuum.

Gerhardt, Uta (1988) 'Qualitative sociology in the Federal Republic of Germany', *Qualitative Sociology*, 11: 29–43.

Goffman, Erving (1959) *The Presentation of Self in Everyday Life.* New York: Doubleday.

Grondin, Jean (1994) *Introduction to Philosophical Hermeneutics.* New Haven, CT: Yale University Press (originally published in German in 1991).

Maiwald, Kai-Olaf (2005) 'Competence and praxis: Sequential analysis in German sociology' [46 paragraphs]. *Forum Qualitative Sozialforschung/Forum: Qualitative Social Research* [Online Journal], 6 (3), Art. 31. Available at: www.qualitative-research.net/fqs-texte/3-05/05-3-31-e.htm (accessed 7 May 2013).

Merton, Robert K. (1968) *Social Theory and Social Structure*, enlarged edition. New York: Free Press.

Oevermann, Ulrich (1986) 'Kontroversen über sinnverstehende Soziologie. Einige wiederkehrende Probleme und Mißverständnisse in der Rezeption der "objektiven Hermeneutik"', in Stefan Aufenanger and Michael Lenssen (eds), *Handlung und Sinnstruktur: Bedeutung und Anwendung der objektiven Hermeneutik.* München: Kindt-Verlag. pp. 19–83.

Oevermann, Ulrich (with Tilman Allert, Elisabeth Konau and Jürgen Krambeck) (1987) 'Structures of meaning and objective hermeneutics', in Meja Volker et al. (eds), *Modern German Sociology*, European Perspectives. New York: Columbia University Press. pp. 436–47.

Oevermann, Ulrich (1991) 'Genetischer Strukturalismus und das sozialwissenschaftliche Problem der Erklärung der Entstehung des Neuen', in Stefan Müller-Doohm (ed.), *Jenseits der Utopie: Theoriekritik der Gegenwart.* Frankfurt/M.: Suhrkamp. pp. 267–336.

Oevermann, Ulrich, Allert, Tilman, Konau, Elisabeth and Krambeck, Jürgen (1979) 'Die Methodologie einer "objektiven Hermeneutik" und ihre allgemeine forschungslogische Bedeutung in den Sozialwissenschaften', in Hans-Georg Soeffner (ed.), *Interpretative Verfahren in den Sozial- und Textwissenschaften.* Stuttgart: Metzler-Verlag. pp. 352–434.

Parsons, Talcott (1964) 'The incest taboo in relation to social structure and the socialization of the child', in Talcott Parsons, *Social Structure and Personality.* Glencoe, IL: Free Press. pp. 57–77 (originally published in *The British Journal of Sociology* in 1954).

Ragin, Charles C. and Becker, Howard S. (eds) (1992) *What is a Case? Exploring the Foundations of Social Inquiry.* Cambridge: Cambridge University Press.

Reichertz, Jo (2004) 'Objective hermeneutics and hermeneutic sociology of knowledge', in Uwe Flick et al. (eds), *A Companion to Qualitative Research.* London: Sage. pp. 290–5.

Ricoeur, Paul (2004 [1969]) 'Existence and hermeneutics', in Paul Ricoeur, *The Conflict of Interpretations: Essays in Hermeneutics.* London: Continuum. pp. 3–26.

Schutz, Alfred (1971) 'Common-sense and scientific interpretation of human action', in Alfred Schutz, *Collected Papers I: The Problem of Social Reality.* The Hague: Nijhoff. pp. 1–47.

Silverman, David (2005) *Doing Qualitative Research*, 2nd edition. London: Sage.

Smith, Jonathan A. (2007) 'Hermeneutics, human sciences and health: Linking theory and practice', *International Journal of Qualitative Studies on Health and Well-being*, 2: 3–11.

Soeffner, Hans-Georg (2004) 'Social scientific hermeneutics', in Uwe Flick et al. (eds), *A Companion to Qualitative Research.* London: Sage. pp. 95–100.

Stierlin, Helm (1977) *Psychoanalysis and Family Therapy: Selected Papers.* New York: Aronson.

Willis, Jerry W. (2007) *Foundations of Qualitative Research: Interpretative and Critical Approaches.* Thousand Oaks, CA: Sage.

Cultural Studies

Rainer Winter

I understand my contribution to this volume as part of a necessary 'renewal of Cultural Studies' (Smith, 2011). Sometimes, cultural studies has been criticized that it is not a formalized approach with a distinct set of methods (cf. Cruz, 2012: 257). Against this, I will show that there is common ground in the practice of qualitative research in cultural studies. There are a range of theories, perspectives and methods that are used and combined in order to reach a particular goal. We generate different forms of qualitative data that will be analysed to understand the particular conjuncture of the present. This is the background of putting research questions, answering them and producing useful knowledge. It is time to intensify debates on critical methodologies, qualitative methods and analysing data.

THE CONJUNCTURAL ANALYSIS OF CULTURE AND POWER

The transdisciplinary approach of cultural studies that usually connects different disciplinary perspectives from the humanities and social sciences applies itself to the analysis of lived experiences, social practices and cultural representations, which are considered in their network-like or intertextual links, from the viewpoints of power, difference and human agency. From early on cultural studies has been shaped by an interest in equality, democracy and emancipation (see Williams, 1961). It does not analyse an isolated practice or event but is driven by the attempt to radically contextualize cultural processes (Grossberg, 2010). Every practice is connected to other practices. An assemblage of practices is part of a conjuncture, an intersection of discourses, practices, technologies of power and everyday life (Grossberg, 2010: 25). Conjunctures and contexts are changing. Cultural studies is reacting to these changes. It is a committed and engaged intellectual–political practice that attempts to describe the complexity, contradictions and relational character of cultural processes. It wants to produce (politically) useful knowledge to understand the problems and questions of a conjuncture. It is hoping to help people to struggle against and to transform power structures in order to realize radical democratic relations.

Its approach to culture regards this not as a subsystem or a field but rather it penetrates and structures every aspect of social life and of subjectivity. In this perspective culture therefore does not belong to a single individual nor does it distinguish them, rather it is the medium by which shared meanings, rituals, social communities and identities are produced. The researcher is located 'inside culture' (Couldry, 2000) and has to consider the complex, contradictory and many-layered context of reality in the global era of the twenty-first century. The knowledge produced by cultural studies ought to increase the reflexivity of those acting in everyday life, which is formed by power relationships and structured by a discursive order of representation, and reveal to them the possibility for changing restrictive and repressive living conditions.

Theories can help to explore and illuminate contexts but they are not enough. Understanding a conjuncture is only possible by a transdisciplinary approach. This orientation can lead to complex theoretical work based on different approaches that carefully describe and analyse discourses and practices (cf. Grossberg, 2005). It can also include qualitative–empirical research. Since its beginnings in Birmingham cultural studies used and developed qualitative methods (cf. Willis, 1977; 1978). The central characteristic of qualitative data analysis in the context of cultural studies is the theoretical and empirical examination of the relationship between experiences, practices and cultural texts in a specific context. The researcher has to construct or reconstruct this context.

Regarding the research in cultural studies we can differentiate between verbal and visual data. Verbal data are mainly produced by qualitative interviews (see Roulston, Chapter 20, this volume), group discussions (see Barbour, Chapter 21, this volume) or narrations (see Esin et al., Chapter 14, this volume), visual data (see Banks, Chapter 27, and Knoblauch et al., Chapter 30, this volume) and by analysing and interpreting media texts (photographs, films, soap operas, etc.). The tripartite focus of cultural studies on experiences, practices and texts brings various methodological orientations for data analysis with it and their mutual connections have dominated the approach since its beginnings. Its singularity and creativity touches on mutual endorsement and enrichment but also on causes of friction, which result from different theoretical and methodological options and are used productively (Saukko, 2003; Johnson et al., 2004).

For example, the qualitative empirical research of media reception (see Hodgetts and Chamberlain, Chapter 26, this volume) and appropriation has a phenomenological–hermeneutical (see Eberle, Chapter 13, and Wernet, Chapter 16, this volume) focus on the one hand, because it deals with cultural experiences mainly in the form of verbal data in order to understand the 'lived realities' of experiences and practices in different social contexts. As I carried out my ethnographic study on the reception of horror movies, for example, which lasted several years, I realized that this practice was embedded in different contexts and varied considerably (Winter, 2010; 1999). Together with my research group I combined various methods: participant observation (see Marvasti, Chapter 24, this volume), narrative as well as biographical interviews (see Roulston, Chapter 20, this volume), group discussions (see Barbour, Chapter 21, this volume), analysis of films (see Mikos, Chapter 28, this volume) and newspapers (see Hodgetts and Chamberlain, Chapter 26, this volume) and the use of field notes as well as field diaries. To contextualize the different forms of reception practices it was necessary to examine the lifestyles, the social activities along with the relationships of the media audience within their own circles. A particular media culture was formed by this audience's use and appropriation of the media or of a specific genre within it. It became clear that a (international) social world of horror fans existed. This ethnographic approach in the tradition of cultural studies and symbolic interactionism filled a gap that existed in many studies in this field. The problem arose when researchers began with a particular text and, therefore, concentrated principally on the text–audience–interaction specific to the text or genre in question. During my ethnographic field study I tried to reach a 'thick description' (Geertz, 1973) of this fan culture. This ethnography of the horror fans' social world mainly based on the analysis of verbal data has made it clear how different and varied the experiences and practices of fans could be. Therefore, they develop in a distinct social world in whose construction they are actively involved, relating techniques of emotion management to the context of the social world. Their experiences, emotional involvement as well as their operation network (e.g. fan clubs) were clear signs that there existed a 'neo-tribe', which is an aesthetic and affective community, as Michel Maffesoli (1995) suggested. This theory set out that the everyday routine of postmodern life ('conjuncture') could be distinguished through the expression of a multitude of local rationalism and contrasting values.

The analysis of social and political contexts in which texts are received and appropriated has to have a realistic character, for example in the description of the situational settings in which media reception is carried out or in the grasping of the increasingly global network of media flows. The analysis of media texts (visual data) is often based on structural or post-structural approaches. The logic of a film or a TV series can be deduced by revealing the cultural values which are hidden in the binary logic of texts, by examining discursive frameworks which structure media realities or by disclosing the intertextual relationships which are between media texts and which emphasize the mediatized character of our knowledge and of our experience of reality.

Cultural studies is characterized by focusing its analysis on tensions, contradictions and conflicts that arise in the process of production and analysis of data and by generating at times surprising insights on the connection between different perspectives. The 'bricolage' of the research process, the triangulation of various methods and theories depending on the question being researched, demonstrates that this research tradition has broken with the positivistic agenda. The aim of this research is apparently to produce hypotheses or theories about what 'really' takes place in the world and then to find out through methodically produced and controlled analysis of (hard) data if this is 'real'. Cultural studies shows that research questions, methods and interests are characterized by social, political and historical contexts. In the research, reality cannot be analysed 'objectively' but rather research is part of the reality that it (co-)generates and (co-)constructs socially. Because the researcher's methodologies and writing styles do not reflect reality it is reasonable that different methods will produce and present different data and perspectives on reality as well. Therefore the particularity of perspectives becomes clear and their different constructions of reality are taken into account. The knowledge gained is always localized socially and politically so the researcher is also required to question critically the discourses and positions that characterize his or her own thinking. Nevertheless, the aim is to understand the complexity of contextual relations.

Considered epistemologically, cultural studies champions an anti-objectivistic view of knowledge like pragmatism or social constructionism. It is always directed at particular contexts, which are shaped locally and historically (Grossberg, 2010). Its knowledge objects do not exist independently from the research but rather they are (co-)created by it and are considered as contingent, theoretical object constructions. The confession of 'partiality' is defined by Donna Haraway (2004), who describes thus the limits of research through temporal, physical and social factors, as well as the motivation caused by ideologies, interests and desires and also the positioning within power structures. This concession distinguishes this approach, which does not strive for 'objectivity' in the classic sense but rather for dialogue, reflexivity and self-understanding. Thus, since the beginnings of cultural studies in adult education in the UK, students were inspired to reflect on their own living conditions, their social background and their personal development, and to bring these reflections to their research in order to explain in this way their own social position and their relationship to the research object (Winter, 2004).

The confession of the approach's positionality, of the situation and localization of knowledge does not mean, however, that cultural studies proceeds in a reductionist way, nor that it gives up on demands for rigorous research and systematic knowledge. On the contrary, according to the research questions, theoretical approaches and methods of various disciplines are combined in order to construct research objects in multifaceted and sophisticated ways: 'the task for cultural studies, from the beginning, was precisely to develop methods to do things that have never been done before' (Turner, 2012: 53). In the ideal case cultural practices and representations are then analysed from multiple perspectives in the dialogue of different approaches and methods (Kellner, 2009). This reveals and bypasses the necessary limit of single methodological or disciplinary approaches. Cultural studies demands that there is joint reflection on the design of research and in the presentation of research results and that other methods or even a combination of them are possible, but also that transgressions are desired (Johnson et al., 2004: 42) in order to attain different perspectives on generating and analysing data. But there is no 'how to do?' list of separate steps or any other strictly formalized procedure available in the field of cultural studies. The radical contextuality of the approach demands a careful (re)construction of the particular context by using suitable methods that generate qualitative data to understand it.

In the process of research, the realization of reflexivity (see May and Perry, Chapter 8, this volume) is essential. In this way, for example, it can be made clear how the researcher's spatial and temporal localization plays a part in the research. Even the dialogue with the others intensifies the desired reflexivity. Thus cultural studies' newer approaches have performed a 'performance turn' (Denzin, 2003). They recognize that culture is 'performed' in contradictions and conflicts when they research and write about it. 'Reflexive performance' and (auto) ethnography are the focus of the latest qualitative research.

THE PERSPECTIVE OF RESISTANCE

From its beginnings in the context of the New Left in the UK, cultural studies has examined the power structures of society and the possibilities of their transformation. Resistance has become a basic concept in cultural studies which is defined following Antonio Gramsci's analysis of hegemony (Gramsci, 1971), his reflections on popular culture and, above all, by Michel Foucault's analytics of modern power (Foucault, 1977; 1979). Despite massive criticism, resistance still occupies a very important role in the analysis of lived experiences and practices. That it is still of such significance demonstrates that cultural studies considers cultural and media processes in the context of social and cultural inequality as well as considering it part of the structures of power. Also, its perspective is always that of the underclass, subjugated or marginalized, which registers and analyses suffering from society and grief in the world but at the same time would also like to reveal the possibility of utopia and social transformation (Kellner, 1995).

Thus it is no surprise that resistance became the central category of this critically interventionist theory and research practice in the 1980s and 1990s. It was precisely in the everyday use of cultural and media texts, in their reception and in their (productive) appropriation that the characteristics and traces of rebellious practices and creative '*Eigensinn*' (ability to create your own sense) were found. Media texts were read differently from how they were intended and used for the articulation of their own perspective by the readers (Winter, 2001). Therefore the question came to the fore as to how far reaching this resistance against power could be and what significance it should be given in the context of the present. Did the resistance (only) have a symbolic nature or did it also have a 'real' effect? Methodologically, of course, it proved difficult to grasp the creative and resistive elements of everyday experience because these were already always informed and structured by discourses of the ruling elites. Often, the analysis of the polyphonic character of media texts could give insight into possible subversive readings that opposed the readings in accordance with the dominant ideologies.

In early research into resistance, which does not really show a uniform tradition ensuing from a programme, a central aspect of cultural studies already became clear: its (radical) contextualism (Grossberg, 2009; 2010). Resistant practices could only be understood when the context in which they happened and which they (jointly) set up, was (re)constructed. Thus, Paul Willis could show in his, now classic, ethnographic study *Learning to Labour* (1977) how the 'lads', working-class boys, created a living and rebellious counter culture, which disapproved of the middle-class norms of school and subversively circumvented it. Their creative practices rejected the boredom and alienation of educational socialization, but did not lead to a transformation of 'real' power structures, because, of course, nothing else was left for the badly educated 'lads' than to accept manual jobs after school. Thus their protest, which they subjectively experienced as freedom, was actively involved in the reproduction of social inequality. Willis came to this conclusion by doing ethnographic work on a local school (participant observation) and analysing interviews and discussions with the 'lads'. He studied their point of view and how they resisted. As a second step, he developed a sociological theory of the social reproduction of inequality and applied it to his own ethnographic findings.

In her now equally famous study, *Reading the Romance* (1984), which was arranged multi-dimensionally by using a combination of methods and which links historical reflection to narrative analysis of novels and to empirical research of the reader's perspective (verbal data), Janice Radway concluded that the reception of romance novels, at first independent of their content, could have an essentially positive significance for women. She felt that the regular and enthusiastic reading, the losing of oneself in reading, helped women in particular to distance themselves from social obligations and everyday relationships and created a space for themselves among the domestic noise of everyday life where otherwise they were expected to be exclusively for the family to which they were expected to link their self-realization. Furthermore, Radway could show by text analysis how in romance novels female sensitivities could be upgraded and played off against those of the patriarchal order. The apparently harmless practice of the reading of relatively standardized romances proved to be unruly and led to the formation of a vibrant, resistant subculture. Admittedly, Radway concluded that the real patriarchal structures, which penetrated family and social relationships, were not transformed. Resistance could even help strengthen them.

The analysis of resistance within cultural studies is concerned with the practices of subordinate groups and everyday experiences, which are at first sight trivial and insignificant. These are examined in their unique character, particularly for how they resist the real structures of power. Even if, in cultural studies' interpretation, ideologies and the hegemonic culture convey the subjects' relationship with the world, they know these structures most closely by means of their practical knowledge that is the necessary prerequisite for their resistance. As a rule, however, this resistance remains in the imagination and is in vain.

Methodologically the everyday experiences and practices are taken seriously. For example, qualitative interviews and group discussions are conducted and analysed. Admittedly, the researcher contextualizes the verbal data and therefore actually determines their meaning by applying the analytics of power in the work of Foucault, Gramsci's theory of hegemony or other approaches, which deal with the relationship of culture and power. In this context the criticism has often been expressed that the researchers' theoretically based views stand in the way of their self-reflexivity. Therefore, they cannot recognize, for example, how the 'real' power structures, which they analyse, only gain a notional shape because of their own theoretical presuppositions (Marcus and Fischer, 1986: 81ff.). Both Willis and Radway were criticized for allowing their theoretical presuppositions to lead to the development of blind spots, though admittedly this could be said of all empirical research. In more recent ethnographic discussion, there are sometimes slightly exaggerated critiques that the researchers learn more about their own theoretical perspective than about the people being examined. Above all, this criticism was aimed at John Fiske (1989), considered the most important representative of the resistance paradigm. For many, his analysis exploring the possibilities of agency in the *'Lebenswelt'* ('lifeworld') had too optimistic conclusions.

In his analysis of the popular in the present (Fiske, 1989), he drew closely on Foucault's (1977) distinction between power and resistance. 'Resistance' can arise in specific historic situations in the relationship of discursive structures, cultural practices and subjective experiences. Following Michel de Certeau (1984), Fiske conceived the postmodern everyday life as a continuous battle between the strategies of the 'strong' and the guerrilla tactics of the 'weak'. In the use of resources, which makes the system available in, for example, the form of media texts and other consumer objects, the everyday agents try to define their living conditions and express their interests by themselves. Therefore, he was interested not only in the process of appropriation, which contributed to social reproduction, but in the secret and hidden consumption, which according to de Certeau (1984) is a fabrication, a production of meanings and enjoyment. These are used by the consumers to make their own issues clearer and can (perhaps) contribute to gradual cultural and social transformation (Winter, 2001).

In his work, Fiske critically deconstructed popular texts from the video performances of Madonna via *Die Hard* (1992) to *Married... With Children* (1987–97) with the aim of revealing their potential for plural meanings, which was differently realized by the viewers appropriate to their particular social and historical situation. He revealed the inconsistencies, the incompleteness, the contradictory structure or the polyphony of media texts by structuralist (e.g. structural analysis of narrative codes) and post-structuralist methods (e.g. the analysis of style), and he worked out how closely popular texts were related to the particular reality of the postmodern conjuncture and how they articulated social difference by articulating different ideologies. As my own studies showed (Winter, 2010; 1999), the reception and appropriation of texts examined by participant observation and analysing of interviews became social practices, which were contextually anchored and in which the texts were not predefined as objects with determined meanings but rather were only produced on the basis of social experiences. In combining different methods and forms of data analysis Fiske (1994a) successfully revealed the situational uniqueness and significance of cultural practices, which took place in a particular place at a particular time. Especially, his later work (Fiske, 1993; 1994b) is a good example of radical contextualism and the attempt to determine the conjuncture of the United States in the 1990s.

As with Radway and Willis, the question was asked of Fiske what significance beyond the immediate context these symbolic battles could have. An obvious criticism stated that resistive media consumption, as Fiske (1992) revealed in his famous and strongly disputed study of Madonna, remains ineffective because it does not change the patriarchal power structure. To argue in this way means, however, ignoring that on the one hand Fiske did not claim this. On the other hand, for him it was more about taking seriously the significance of being a Madonna fan, the subjective perspective of the fans, and – particularly in his later work – about working out the uniqueness of cultural experiences and practices in specific contexts, without at all claiming generalizations or immediate transformations of power structures. Admittedly, Fiske too did not escape the criticism that as a researcher he pretended to understand the significance of the practices of the examined better than the examined themselves.

Later works have tried to escape this dilemma, by considering phenomena from different viewpoints, by analysing different forms of data, and in this way the methodological tools ought to become more sensitive to the experience of the other (Saukko, 2003: 55ff.). For example, biographical interviews and narrations are used to understand the cultural situation of research partners (see Winter, 2010). Popular cultural phenomena are analysed from as many points of view as possible (Morris, 1998) in order to be able to reveal the different forms of symbolic struggle with dominant meaning structures and also to reveal discrepancies and conflicts resulting from those struggles. Many doubt that these unruly or resistant practices have wider reaching systemic consequences. Thus, it has to examine whatever specific effects a particular local resistance can have and how this influences other experiences, events and practices in different areas of social life (Winter, 2001). Furthermore, experiences, practices and discourses are analysed in multiple local contexts with the result that different forms of subordination and resistance can be revealed (Saukko, 2003: 40ff.). Within cultural studies the analysis of subversive media consumption plays a further role even when the optimistic hopes linked to it are no longer at the centre of the reflection.

In the current discussions of cultural studies, a variety of topics are considered, from media spectacles (Kellner, 2012) and cultural industries (Hesmondhalgh, 2007) via sport (Giardina and Newman, 2011) to indigenous voices (Denzin et al., 2008). As a rule, questions develop in local contexts; particular 'objects' are chosen for analysis that produce knowledge of a particular situation from a particular perspective. Nevertheless, the central aim is to construct the different contexts and to understand the particular conjuncture and its problems and conflicts (Grossberg, 2010). Due to historical and geographical contingencies, which influence cultural practices and contexts across the world, there is a variety of cultural studies traditions formed nationally or regionally, in which, however, culture is not on a level with language, nor is it treated as the 'essence' of a nation or a region but rather it is understood as an open, frequently embattled, polyphonic and relational process (Frow and Morris, 2003: 498).

PERSPECTIVES OF TEXTUAL AND CONTEXTUAL ANALYSIS

Cultural studies strives to analyse cultural processes from as many perspectives as possible in order to reveal frames and discourses which structure these, our research strategies and also our understanding of everyday life. 'Mapping the field' (Johnson et al., 2004: 31) is an important step in all cultural studies research. The researchers have to become familiar with the particular theoretical frameworks or approaches relevant to their research topic. Their orientation is transdisciplinary. They appropriate theories and methods from different disciplines to construct the particular context and its problems. Over the course of this process the researchers must figure out their commitments, interests and concepts that are shaped historically, politically and socially.

A central methodological characteristic of data analysis in cultural studies is that it examines cultural texts not as discrete entities but in their contextual setting. It is interested in how texts and discourse are articulated with social, historical or political contexts. From the beginning, it has rejected the traditionally Marxist view that culture can be understood primarily in the framework of a dominant ideology. Above all, Stuart Hall's famous 'Encoding and decoding' model (Hall, 1980) emphasizes in the production and reception of news programmes that there is a struggle for the meaning of the presented events. Media texts become the place of debate between different social groups who wish to assert their own interpretations and views of the world.

Thus, semiotic and structural analysis of qualitative data played an important role. Signs were defined as polysemous with a range of different foci; the link between signifier and signified was primarily, in the perspective of cultural studies, politically motivated. Media texts, as shown for example in the well-known study of James Bond (Bennett and Woollacott, 1987), were analysed in their intertextual setting in order to overcome the often formalistic character of semiotic and narrative analysis, which is aimed at primary texts. Instead the authors analyse 'the social organization of the relations between texts within specific conditions of reading' (1987: 45). The social contexts of reading frame the meaning of texts. By considering textual and social contexts, the analysis of popular texts gained depth and complexity because their social meaning is analysed in the context of complex social and cultural powers. For example, Douglas Kellner examines in *Cinema Wars* (2010) how popular Hollywood movies articulate the right-wing discourses of the Bush–Cheney era, its militarism and racism. He can also show that there are movies criticizing this system. In addition, Henry Giroux (2002) deconstructs the politics of representation in Hollywood movies by critically analysing the discourses and images of race, gender, class and sexuality.

The studies on visual media data illustrate that, on the one hand, close reading techniques are transferred from the field of literary criticism to TV series and shows. In contrast to research on the effect of the media, the analysis of the cultural meaning of media texts was considered centrally. From the start, however, these were not regarded as isolated, discrete entities, but rather in their inter- and contextual relations. The *radical contextualism* of cultural studies (Grossberg, 2009) assumes that the meaning of texts and practices can only be determined in relation to more complex social and cultural power relationships.

Therefore the focus becomes the semiotic 'surroundings' of research objects and the relationships between media and other spatial and temporal contexts of social life (Frow and Morris, 2003: 501). This is because, for example, media texts on the coverage of scandals are placed in the context of the contemporary US media culture of spectacles (Kellner, 2012). Cultural texts are linked in a type of network to cultural and social practices, which they have initiated or modified.

One essential insight coming from research in cultural studies is that interpretations always vary and that there are always several possible uses for each text. As John Frow and Meaghan Morris (2003: 506) write: 'Structures are always structures-in-use and that uses cannot be contained in advance.' Therefore there is no 'right' or 'true' reading of media texts from the perspective of cultural studies. Media texts are not monologic, they are not completed entities, but rather they are a complex constellation of signs and meanings with the result that they are interpreted and understood differently, even contradictorily in each social context. Their social (further) existence is an open and incomplete process. Against this background, the readings by researchers must also be qualified and they must be considered in their contextual bonds.

Thus Janice Radway in her already mentioned *Reading the Romance* (1984) contrasted the interpretations of readers trained in literary criticism with those of fans of the genre. Her aim was to research as comprehensively as possible the experiences and practices of women who deal with this popular genre. Therefore, she combined the analysis of literary texts with the analysis of quantitative and qualitative data (generated by surveys, group discussions, interviews). In addition she introduced psychoanalytical and feminist theoretical positions to the discussion. The deliberate dialogue between theories and methods helped her to overcome the limits of a purely textual analysis and tellingly to show how texts can be construed and experienced differently in interpretative communities.

As far as the analysis of media texts has been concerned, at first structuralist interpretative strategies dominated within cultural studies. Above all Roland Barthes' *Mythologies* (1972), and the narratological analysis by Vladimir Propp, Umberto Eco and Gérard Genette, supplied the methodical basis for the analysis of popular texts. Thus the structural analysis of social ideologies and contexts are placed in context. Genre analysis as a contextualizing research strategy (Johnson et al., 2004: 163ff.) is directed at intertextuality because it examines how films, for example, repeat, vary or introduce new elements to the conventions of the genre. In addition, the cultural and political dimensions of a genre are examined by relating textual forms and reception practices to each other in context. The popularity of film genres is created together with the viewers, who delight in the predictable order of events and in the surprising variations that are incorporated in it. Popularity is bound to a time and a place as well as being situated in social and cultural contexts to which media texts refer and which they supply with stories. In everyday contexts, these stories can lead to personal narrations. An important question of research is by what means a genre remains interesting as it successfully keeps, changes or regains an audience.

One aim of cultural studies is to consider how texts are designed, for example for the context of production and the economic relationships linked to it. This is done in the context of broader cultural contexts and social power relationships. Therefore the tensions between text and context take centre stage. Media texts become moments of greater cultural formations.

Thus, in post-structuralist approaches, the polysemous potential contradictions and the possibility of diverse readings are worked out in social contexts. For this reason, Yvonne Tasker (1993) shows how action films (see Mikos, Chapter 28, this volume) do not simply reproduce dominant ideas of masculinity but also play with these categories and can even encourage a critical reading. In the framework of cultural studies texts are therefore contextualized and conventional divisions between text, experience and practice are discussed and often abolished.

To examine processes of political hegemony, approaches focus, for example, on 'close reading' of political speeches in order to reveal the connections between the popular and the dominant. Thus the analysis of small cultural units (as in the speeches of Bush and Blair on the war against terror) can give insights into complex strategic power relationships (Johnson et al., 2004: 170–86). A close reading of their speeches shows that both politicians use strong moral distinctions between good and evil. They make their Islamic enemies aliens and demons by rhetorical means. Media texts are read here in their contribution to the stabilization of power and the justification of military strategy.

However, this is only one of many approaches. A feature of cultural studies is its revelation of the 'partiality' of its approaches, which allows a dialogue with others about their construction of objects and readings to begin. As Donna Haraway writes: 'Objectivity turns out to be about particular and specific embodiment, and definitely not about the false vision promising transcendence of all limits and responsibility. The moral is simple: Only partial perspective promises objective view' (2004: 87). Therefore detailed analysis of data can show singular situational moments in the cultural production, circulation and reception of a popular genre in which complex cultural and also social debates are hidden and which contain the possibility of (transgressive) pleasure and of the construction of meaning. For example, Fiske (1994a) showed how the reception of *Married...With Children* enabled teenage viewers who attended a Catholic university to reflect on the relations with their absent parents. But this was only a particular small part of the cultural circulation of meanings and pleasures around the production and reception of this postmodern sitcom.

Very early on, the characteristics of postmodern media texts were also defined, borrowing from the archive of available media texts and understood primarily in the context of these circular references – and not as a reference to a 'primary reality' which is not structured by the media (Denzin, 1991). Thus a controversial film like *Natural Born Killers* (1994) deals self-reflexively and critically with media images as well as with our knowledge of serial killers presented by the media. However, not everyone has formed a postmodern sensibility and can understand the film as a parody of media violence. Cultural studies emphasizes therefore that every reading is contextually bound and has political character. The knowledge of texts and practices whose spatial and temporal characteristics have to be defined is always knowledge of a particular context. As research into popular culture shows, texts and practices exist in particular locations at particular times for particular people (Jenkins et al., 2002). Thus the significance of a media text can never be determined definitively. In the field of popular culture meanings multiply when consumers and researchers understand the texts in the context of their own social life and their cultural identity. In the framework of cultural studies, personal experiences of dealing with media texts are often the starting point for critical analysis (Johnson et al., 2004). Therefore it goes on to be about defining in a self-reflexive way the social basis of our interpretations and at the same time of the limits of these interpretations.

In cultural studies works, which are orientated in a post-structuralist way, genealogical and deconstructive analyses are also carried out (cf. Saukko, 2003: chs 6 and 7). Following Foucault (1977; 1979), genealogy can reveal how our perceptions, our ideas, our description of problems or our scientific truths have developed from historic contexts and specific social and political processes. Therefore the images we make of ourselves, our society and our history are never complete or independent. They remain linked to the social practices from which they have arisen. A genealogist tries to understand the media practices of our culture that we share with others and which have also made us what we are today.

Deconstruction makes a critical analysis of the logic of media texts possible (cf. Bowman, 2008). Therefore, for example, dichotomous oppositions are revealed and discussed. Behind these hide values, ideological presuppositions and cultural hierarchies. Furthermore, deconstructive readings reveal the essential uncertainty of the meaning of media texts, which are constituted by an unlimited play of differences and are receptive to diverse readings in different contexts. Therefore, deconstructive cultural studies also has an interventional character. Thus it deals with 'exposing the underlying "structural" preconceptions that organize texts and to reveal the conditions of freedom that they suppress' (Denzin, 1994: 196).

AUTOETHNOGRAPHY AND NEW FORMS OF ETHNOGRAPHY

In the analysis of reception and appropriation processes the ethnographic perspective is at the fore of cultural studies. However, at the same time, as a rule, this is not meant to be an extensive ethnographic piece of fieldwork in order to generate qualitative data as in sociology and anthropology, but rather (short-time) participant observation of cultural practices in modern and postmodern life. This should make an approach to the circulation of meaning possible and therefore access to cultural circulation (Johnson et al., 2004). Furthermore, the ethnographic perspective is often linked to autobiographical elements.

For example, Ien Ang (1985) in her study of *Dallas* (1978–91) has linked the analysis of female viewers' reactions to her own assessment of the series. Personal affinity to an object of research and sometimes even the very fact of being a fan as well as self-reflexion are important resources in the research process of cultural studies:

> My existence as a fan, my experiences, along with whatever other responses are available for describing the field of popular practices and their articulation to social and political positions are the raw material, the starting point of critical research. (Grossberg, 1988: 68)

As has already been mentioned, the criticism of the overly theoretical nature of research (into resistance), which indicates the theoretical view of the researchers more than the researched lived reality, leads within cultural studies to the discussion and development of new research strategies being more suitable for the examination of lived experience and reality. Important significance is given therefore to dialogue between the self of the researcher and the perspective of the other, the object of study (Lincoln and Denzin, 2003). The latter's world should not be described from outside but an interaction or meeting between different worlds should be performed, in which the perspective of the other should, as far as possible, be understood 'authentically' with their active contribution. Therefore the researchers must first figure out what is preventing them from understanding the world of the other, who, for example, watches horror films or listens to Gangsta rap. To be aware of one's own restricted frames of understanding demands sensitivity towards strange and radically different worlds of experience. For this reason researchers in cultural studies highlight the ethical duty as far as possible, to do justice to the world of the others. Dialogues between researchers and subjects should be possible. These should reduce prejudices and should overcome the limits of personal understanding. This should be a more just approach for the texture of the lived experience from the point of view of the participants.

Against this backdrop self-reflexivity is an important feature of this new form of ethnography. The researchers should reflect intensively about their own situation, their social and political obligations, as well as their theoretical presuppositions, in order to find easier access to the world of the subjects. However, self-reflexivity does not imply that a 'true' knowledge of the world is possible (Haraway, 2004). Rather it shows the limits of our worldview and even shows that different interpretations of our own world and that of the others are possible. In the forms of critical autoethnography, self-reflexivity contributes to researchers who examine which events and social discourses have defined their experiences (Bochner and Ellis, 2002). This process of reflection becomes complete by new forms of writing (Richardson, 2000). In a personal, literal and experimental way they show the aspects of the researcher's experience, which are not rational and which concern the (media) worlds of others.

Therefore, ethnographic practices in the framework of cultural studies also prove in the global media world of the twenty-first century to be a moral discourse (Denzin, 2010), which makes (problematic) life and media experiences available and can give insight into (new) forms of social and cultural inequality. In a further step, even existing power relationships in the everyday life should be questioned: 'Research that is more fully participatory will aim to use the research process itself to empower those who are being researched' (Johnson et al., 2004: 215).

Besides, it is important to capture the polyvocality of the field in ethnographic research. Lived experiences should be rendered by different voices in order to avoid a single voice standing for the 'truth' of an experience and in order to grasp appropriately the peculiarity of individual experiences (Saukko, 2003: 64ff.). Even in the presentation of research results it comes to an interaction between the voices of the others and the voices of the researchers. The consideration of autobiographical experiences also leads to experiments in the presentations of research results, which can even become a 'performance' of experiences and practices (Denzin, 2003; 2010). For example, in qualitative media research, this methodological reorientation is given important significance. On the one hand, dialogic relationships call on the researchers to challenge their own media experiences and practices, their preferences and aversions. On the other hand, informants who, for example, report on forms of problematic media consumption are taken seriously as subjects who have developed their own view. Furthermore, they are called to bring this to the presentation. The researchers do not take on the role of independent observers. They are more a supporting team mate. Like their research partners, their subjectivity is marked by media practices in modern societies, in particular by popular culture, and they should be clear about this in the research process:

> Popular culture matters ... precisely because its meanings, effects, consequences, and ideologies can't be nailed down. As consumers and as critics,

we struggle with this proliferation of meanings as we make sense of our own social lives and cultural identities. (Jenkins et al., 2002: 11)

As I have already shown, I have combined different methods in my own research on the reception and appropriation of horror movies in order to analyse the differential processes of the reception and appropriation, as well as to identify the meanings that the audiences ascribe to their own practices. Hereby, the viewers, in particular the fans of horror movies, could describe their lived realities as authentic as possible and be taken seriously as subjects in the research process. In journalistic or academic discourse, a negative representation of horror movie fans was predominant. They were usually depicted as obsessive lone wolfs, or as psychologically disturbed and vulnerable. Due to this reason, the aim of the survey was to describe their cultural practices from their very own perspective. I soon noticed that it was necessary to get oneself involved in horror movies to be able to do this research, in particular into the splatter film genre, where academic studies were widely non-existent. I wrote a diary about the primarily scaring and negative experiences I had watching these movies. I managed to watch the most important movies in this genre, which was not a pleasurable thing for me at all. But only after I had this basis of my own personal subjective experience could I start to understand the practices of the fans.

The first stage of the problem-centred interviews and group discussions was disappointing. I realized that the fans did not want to talk about intimate and tabooed experiences, because they perceived themselves as pure objects of the academic research. Furthermore, they believed that they would not gain insight into the study, and, moreover, that the study would be used against them, as had been the case in other surveys. It was tedious to gain their confidence and to build up a dialogical relation to them. Only when I started to talk about my own personal experiences with horror movies and discussed my attitude towards them did they open up to me. When this happened, some personal and even amicable relations were established between us in the course of time. I was now able to understand their cultural practices in the context of their own personal situation and biography.

To hold a reflexive attitude made it possible for me to reflect my presumptions and conceptions as well as to have an open mind about new experiences. A deeper understanding of the lived realities of the fans would not have been achievable without this. I even discussed the results of my survey in depth with them. They recognized their own point of view in the survey and were grateful for not having been exploited. During this ethnographic research, I realized that autoethnography is an essential component of empiric research. The engagement with one's own experiences can become a basis to the understanding of differentiated experiences and practices. Only the willingness to hold a dialogue can give access to the point of view of the other. Qualitative research involves subjects and therefore comprises moral commitment. Above all, the texture of lived realities has to do justice to the viewpoint of the people who are investigated.

Even in the new forms of ethnography, the critical analysis of social forms of injustice is central (Denzin, 2009; Niederer and Winter, 2010). These should be revealed, analysed from different perspectives and inspected for the possibility for change and for the increase of agency among those researched. Above all it is the aim of critical pedagogy in the field of cultural studies to contribute knowledge to this struggle and to improve the life of those affected by social injustice (cf. Kincheloe et al, 2011).

CONCLUSION

For a long time, there had been no explicit discussion of methodology and data analysis in cultural studies. Its practitioners rejected disciplinary boundaries and used and combined theories, perspectives and methods of different knowledge fields in order to enable transdisciplinary dialogues and collaborations between the humanities and the social sciences. In my contribution to this volume I have considered different methodological considerations and approaches. During the last decade a discussion on qualitative methods and methodologies has begun. This may be linked to the fact that the transdisciplinary direction of research is now itself formed as a type of discipline by some scholars (Couldry, 2000). However, cultural studies still remains true to its origins and seeks to link criticism of power to opportunities for intervention and democratic change. Cultural studies is always directed at the analysis and understanding of contexts. Therefore, it does not develop a general theory and the methods it applies depend on the respective questioning. The analysis of an individual cultural element contains its complex relationships to other cultural elements and social powers.

Cultural studies conducts qualitative research in the framework of comprehensive cultural and social analysis. Its theories and models are developed as an answer to the social problems and questions of specific contexts and conjunctures. Cultural studies is orientated both constructivistically, for example in the production of contexts, and critically in the analysis of the relationships with power. Stuart Hall defines its aim 'to enable people to understand what [was] going on, and especially to provide ways of thinking, strategies for survival, and resources for resistance' (Hall, 1990: 22).

FURTHER READING

Grossberg, Lawrence (2010) *Cultural Studies in the Future Tense*. Durham, NC: Duke University Press.
Johnson, Richard, Chambers, Deborah, Raghuram, Parvati and Tincknell, Estella (2004) *The Practice of Cultural Studies*. London: Sage.
Saukko, Paula (2003) *Doing Research in Cultural Studies: An Introduction to Classical and New Methodological Approaches*. London: Sage.

REFERENCES

Ang, Ien (1985) *Watching Dallas: Soap Opera and the Melodramatic Imagination*. London: Methuen.
Barthes, Roland (1972) *Mythologies*. London: Cape.
Bennett, Tony and Woollacott, Janet (1987) *Bond and Beyond: The Political Career of a Popular Hero*. London: Macmillan.
Bochner, Arthur P. and Ellis, Carolyn (eds) (2002) *Ethnographically Speaking: Autoethnography, Literature, and Aesthetics*. Walnut Creek, CA: Altamira Press.
Bowman, Paul (2008) *Deconstructing Popular Culture*. New York: Palgrave.
Certeau, Michel de (1984) *The Practice of Everyday Life*. Berkeley: University of California Press.
Couldry, Nick (2000) *Inside Culture: Re-imagining the Method in Cultural Studies*. London: Sage.
Cruz, John D. (2012) 'Cultural studies and social movements: A crucial nexus in the American case', *European Journal of Cultural Studies*, 15 (3): 254–301.
Denzin, Norman K. (1991) *Images of Postmodern Society: Social Theory and Contemporary Cinema*. London: Sage.
Denzin, Norman K. (1994) 'Postmodernism and deconstructionism', in David Dickens and Andrea Fontana (eds), *Postmodernism and Social Inquiry*. London: UCL Press. pp. 182–202.
Denzin, Norman K. (2003) *Performance Ethnography*. London: Sage.
Denzin, Norman K. (2009) *Qualitative Inquiry Under Fire: Toward a New Paradigm Dialogue*. Walnut Creek, CA: Left Coast Press.
Denzin, Norman K. (2010) *The Qualitative Manifesto: A Call to Arms*. Walnut Creek, CA: Left Coast Press.
Denzin, Norman K., Lincoln, Yvonna S. and Tuhiwai Smith, Linda (eds) (2008) *Handbook of Critical and Indigenous Methodologies*. London: Sage.
Fiske, John (1989) *Understanding Popular Culture*. London: Unwin Hyman.
Fiske, John (1992) 'British cultural studies and television', in Robert C. Allen (ed.), *Channels of Discourse, Reassembled*. Durham, NC: Duke. pp. 284–326.
Fiske, John (1993) *Power Plays – Power Works*. London: Verso.
Fiske, John (1994a) 'Audiencing: Cultural practice and cultural studies', in Norman K. Denzin and Yvonna S. Lincoln (eds), *Handbook of Qualitative Research*. London: Sage. pp. 189–98.
Fiske, John (1994b) *Media Matters: Everyday Culture and Political Change*. Minneapolis: University of Minnesota Press.
Foucault, Michel (1977) *Discipline and Punish: The Birth of the Prison*. London: Allen Lane.
Foucault, Michel (1979) *History of Sexuality: An Introduction*, vol. 1. London: Allen Lane.
Frow, John and Morris, Meaghan (2003) 'Cultural studies', in Norman K. Denzin and Yvonna S. Lincoln (eds), *The Landscape of Qualitative*

Research: Theories and Issues. London: Sage. pp. 489–539.
Geertz, Clifford (1973) *The Interpretation of Cultures*. London: Hutchinson.
Giardina, Michael D. and Newman, Joshua L. (2011) 'Cultural studies: Performative imperatives and bodily articulations', in Norman K. Denzin and Yvonna S. Lincoln (eds), *The SAGE Handbook of Qualitative Research*, 4th edition. London: Sage. pp. 179–94.
Giroux, Henry A. (2002) *Breaking in to the Movies: Film and the Culture of Politics*. Oxford: Blackwell.
Gramsci, Antonio (1971) *Selections from the Prison Notebooks of Antonio Gramsci*, ed. and trans. Q. Hoare und G. Smith Nowell. London: Lawrence and Wishart.
Grossberg, Lawrence (1988) *It's a Sin: Essays on Postmodernism, Politics and Culture*. Sydney: Power Publications.
Grossberg, Lawrence (2005) *Caught in the Crossfire: Kids, Politics and America's Future*. Boulder, CO: Paradigm.
Grossberg, Lawrence (2009) 'Cultural studies: What's in a name', in Rhonda Hammer and Douglas Kellner (eds), *Media and Cultural Studies: Critical Approaches*. New York: Peter Lang. pp. 25–48.
Grossberg, Lawrence (2010) *Cultural Studies in the Future Tense*. Durham, NC: Duke University Press.
Hall, Stuart (1980) 'Encoding and decoding', in Stuart Hall et al. (eds), *Culture, Media, Language*. London: Hutchinson. pp. 128–38.
Hall, Stuart (1990) 'The emergence of cultural studies and the crisis of humanities', *October*, 53: 11–23.
Haraway, Donna (2004) 'Situated knowledges: The science question in feminism and the privilege of partial perspective', in Sandra Harding (ed.), *The Feminist Standpoint Theory Reader*. New York: Routledge. pp. 81–102.
Hesmondhalgh, David (2007) *Cultural Industries: An Introduction*, 2nd edition. London: Sage.
Jenkins, Henry, McPherson, Tara and Shattuc, Jane (eds) (2002) *Hop on Pop: The Politics and Pleasure of Popular Culture*. Durham, NC: Duke University Press.
Johnson, Richard, Chambers, Deborah, Raghuram, Parvati and Tincknell, Estella (2004) *The Practice of Cultural Studies*. London: Sage.
Kellner, Douglas (1995) *Media Culture*. London: Routledge.
Kellner, Douglas (2009) 'Toward a critical and media cultural studies', in Rhonda Hammer and Douglas Kellner (eds), *Media and Cultural Studies: Critical Approaches*. New York. Peter Lang. pp. 5–24.
Kellner, Douglas (2010) *Cinema Wars: Hollywood Film and Politics in the Bush-Cheney Era*. Oxford: Wiley-Blackwell.
Kellner, Douglas (2012) *Time of the Spectacle*. Oxford: Wiley-Blackwell.
Kincheloe, Joe, McLaren, Peter and Steinberg, Shirley R. (2011) 'Critical pedagogy and qualitative research: Moving to the bricolage', in Norman K. Denzin and Yvonna S. Lincoln (eds), *The SAGE Handbook of Qualitative Research*, 4th edition. Los Angeles: Sage. pp. 163–78.
Lincoln, Yvonna S. and Denzin, Norman K. (eds) (2003) *Turning Points in Qualitative Research*. Walnut Creek, CA: Altamira Press.
Maffesoli, Michel (1995) *The Time of the Tribes: The Decline of Individualism in Mass Society*. London: Sage.
Marcus, George E. and Fischer, Michael M. (1986) *Anthropology as Cultural Critique: An Experimental Moment in the Human Sciences*. Chicago: University of Chicago Press.
Morris, Meaghan (1998) *Too Soon Too Late: History in Popular Culture*. Bloomington: Indiana University Press.
Niederer, Elisabeth and Winter, Rainer (2010) 'Poverty and social exclusion: The everyday life of the poor as the research field of a critical ethnography', in Norman K. Denzin and Michael D. Giardina (eds), *Qualitative Inquiry and Human Rights*. Walnut Creek, CA: Left Coast Press. pp. 205–17.
Radway, Janice A. (1984) *Reading the Romance: Women, Patriarchy, and Popular Literature*. London: Verso.
Richardson, Laurel (2000) 'Writing: A method of inquiry', in Norman K. Denzin and Yvonna S. Lincoln (eds), *Handbook of Qualitative Research*, 2nd edition. London: Sage. pp. 923–48.
Saukko, Paula (2003) *Doing Research in Cultural Studies: An Introduction to Classical and New Methodological Approaches*. London: Sage.
Smith, Paul (ed.) (2011) *The Renewal of Cultural Studies*. Philadelphia: Temple University Press.
Tasker, Yvonne (1993) *Spectacular Bodies: Gender, Genre and the Action Cinema*. London: Routledge.
Turner, Graeme (2012) *What's Become of Cultural Studies?* London: Sage.
Williams, Raymond (1961) *The Long Revolution*. New York: Columbia University Press.
Willis, Paul (1977) *Learning to Labour: How Working-Class Kids Get Working-Class Jobs*. Westmead: Saxon House.
Willis, Paul (1978) *Profane Culture*. London: Routledge & Kegan Paul.
Winter, Rainer (1999) 'The search for lost fear: The social world of the horror fan in terms of symbolic interactionism and cultural studies', in

Norman K. Denzin (ed.), *Cultural Studies: A Research Volume*, no. 4. Greenwich, CT: JAI Press. pp. 277–98.

Winter, Rainer (2001) *Die Kunst des Eigensinns: Cultural Studies als Kritik der Macht.* Weilerswist: Velbrück Wissenschaft.

Winter, Rainer (2004) 'Critical pedagogy', in George Ritzer (ed.), *Encyclopedia of Social Theory*, vol. 1. London: Sage. pp. 163–7.

Winter, Rainer (2010) *Der produktive Zuschauer. Medienaneignung als kultureller und ästhetischer Prozess*, 2nd enlarged edition. Köln: Herbert von Halem.

18

Netnographic Analysis: Understanding Culture through Social Media Data

Robert V. Kozinets, Pierre-Yann Dolbec, and Amanda Earley

In the past two decades, participation in online conversations has grown from a relatively marginal activity of hackers, geeks, and early cyberculture members to a mainstream activity recognized and supported by mainstream businesses and media. Starting from tiny numbers of enthusiasts, over a billion people now use social media to communicate, create, and share information, opinions, and insights. Online social spaces have become increasingly recognized as important fields for qualitative social scientific investigation because of the richness and openness of their multifarious cultural sites. At the same time, online data present unique challenges for researchers, as they are voluminous, optionally anonymous, and often difficult to categorize. This chapter introduces readers to netnography, a technique for the cultural analysis of social media and online community data. The purpose of this chapter is to discuss the distinctive cultural features of online, or social media, qualitative data and to overview, develop, and illustrate techniques for their rigorous analysis as they have been developed through the research approach of netnography.

OVERVIEW

Defining Netnography

Netnography is an established approach to qualitative research, whose name draws together the terms 'Internet' and 'ethnography' (see Kozinets, 2010). Netnography shares many of the characteristics of ethnography (see Gubrium and Holstein, Chapter 3, this volume), from which it has been adapted, in that it is a flexible approach that allows scholars to explore and explain rich, diverse, cultural worlds. Naturalistic in orientation, it approaches cultural phenomena in their local contexts, providing windows on naturally occurring behaviors. The output of a netnography can be descriptive as well as analytical and the method tends to generate rich, thick description through grounded interpretations (see Willig, Chapter 10, this volume), thereby providing a detailed representation of the lived online experience of cultural members. Netnography also emphasizes the role of the 'researcher-as-instrument' (Guba and Lincoln, 1981), and the immersion of the researcher into the computer-mediated context of study.

Netnography is also different from ethnography in many respects and thus requires a new set of skills (Kozinets, 2010). These differences emerge from the distinct nature of computer-mediated communications. The specificities of a rigorous and disciplined approach to netnography are organized around the entrée and data collection procedures, choices about field sites, decisions about the types of data to gather and analyse (see Marotzki et al., Chapter 31, this volume), the evaluation of the quality of netnographic research, and ethics, which we will review in the following paragraphs (Kozinets, 2002).

As netnography is a naturalistic method, its interpretations can be built from a combination of elicited and, more often, non-elicited data. These data emerge and are captured through the researcher's observation of and participation with people as they socialize online in regular environments and activities (Kozinets, 2010). Online cultural research is far less intrusive than traditional ethnography, as the online researchers can gather a vast amount of data without making their presence visible to culture members (Beaulieu, 2004; Kozinets, 2010). There are occasions where such non-participative activity (aka 'lurking') is appropriate; however, it tends not to be appropriate when the researcher is interested in the experience of participation in an online field site.

The field of social media offers several advantages rarely found in the traditional ethnographic field. First, researchers generally have access to vast amounts of data, archived through forums and search engines. These resources can provide an unprecedented amount of information on cultural members, values, and structures, allowing researchers to better choose their field sites and plan their entrée (Kozinets, 2010). Second, ethnographers that employ interview methods (see Roulston, Chapter 20, this volume) can transcend geographic and time limitations by using asynchronous communication technologies such as email to conduct interviews. Third, netnography can leverage the connective power of the Internet and the search and organizing capabilities of contemporary search engines to offer accessibility and openness to a vast variety of virtual voices (see Marotzki et al., Chapter 31, this volume).

Characteristics of Netnographic Field Data

The unique characteristics that distinguish netnographic data from face-to-face cultural data necessitate the ongoing development of new adaptations of ethnographic procedures. Some of the features we will briefly discuss in this chapter are: (1) increased field site accessibility; (2) increased communicative variety; (3) communication connectedness across multiple forms/fields; and (4) auto-archiving.

First, online fields offer dramatically increased fieldsite accessibility. The explosion in online social worlds offers participants a virtually (although not absolutely or uniformly) borderless environment where geographically dispersed members can meet and communicate. Because these social fields are accessible to anybody with an Internet connection, it has been argued that the position of 'ethnographer as sole and privileged witness [as found in ethnographies] may be more difficult to uphold as a subject position and authorial voice' in Internet-enabled social research (Beaulieu, 2004). On the Web and elsewhere, however, the difference between mere social observer and social scientist is clear. As Kozinets (2010: 113) elaborates, the difference is analogous to that between journalist and ethnographer – researchers adhere to the respected, legitimate, and rigorous methodological proscriptions of their field, and in the development of research answers and theories, as data are analysed and interpretive insights are structured and incorporated 'into a known and respected body of codified knowledge.'

The communicative variety of netnographic data refers to the many ways that researchers and community members relate across multiple online and mobile platforms, as well as through face-to-face interactions. Where once there were face-to-face meetings and conversations, supplemented by letters and phone calls, researchers now must also consider blogs, Twitter accounts, Facebook postings, Linkedin groups and meetings, and many other forms of social media meeting and communication. Moreover, the online interactions are themselves complex: they can happen both privately and publicly, both asynchronously and synchronously, over different time periods, and with numerous contributors (Ruhleder, 2000), as well as from a number of different site sources (e.g., corporate-owned forum or grassroots blog pages) and in different formats (e.g., textual, visual, audio).

Furthermore, there is added complexity in that these forms of communication are now often linked one to the other. Conversations are happening on multiple sites, between multiple community members, and recent technological advances make it possible to easily post and share content on multiple platforms. An entry might be cross-posted on a blog and a micro-blog, tagged in a geo-localized platform, shared on personal and professional social networks and social bookmarking services, talked about on independent and commercial-owned web forums, then re-blogged and ridiculed in an online video before ending up on national news. This marks a sharp contrast to both ethnographic work and earlier netnographic studies (e.g., Correll, 1995).

In order for a netnographer to understand the social circumstances of this activity, studying one manifestation of a particular message can often be insufficient. If a researcher attempted to mine, scrape, or download a descriptive posting on a web forum and thought that this posting 'told the whole story,' that researcher would be sadly mistaken. In order to gain a contextualized and nuanced cultural understanding of the social media phenomenon, the netnographer must be attuned to this multiform communicative connectedness, and be willing to follow multiple links to multiple sites and postings in order to gain a fuller and embedded understanding of the overlapping social worlds enacted through social media.

Finally, there is a constant and automatic saving, sorting, classifying, and archiving of all types of asynchronous – and much synchronous – media (e.g., a feed from the micro-blogging service Twitter) on the Internet, similar to having access to recordings of every public discourse, interaction, and social contact in a given real-world community (Kozinets, 2010). Archiving by search engines and specialized sites such as The Wayback Machine further this process. Again, this makes the Internet a very different site for ethnographic research compared to 'real'-life social interactions, and requires levels of procedural adaptation.

Challenges of Netnographic Fieldwork

In addition to these technical considerations, the structural characteristics of netnographic data present a number of interesting theoretical challenges. The first is ontological and concerns the somewhat false distinction between online and offline social 'worlds.' Because social worlds cut across complex networks of face-to-face and technologically mediated communications, the use of netnography, as with the use of any single method or focus, offers an incomplete view. Whereas before, community members would discuss face to face and over the phone, they are now supplementing their exchanges with online conversations on web forums and through emails (Wellman et al., 2001). Information search that happened offline is now radically altered and amplified by the Internet (Kayahara and Wellman, 2007). For example, the experience of preparing for childbirth might involve in-person conversations, doctor's visits, a baby shower, childbirthing classes, and other in-person activities.

However, if netnography offers only a partial view of many online–offline phenomena, the reverse is also true. That is, in the current environment – and increasingly in a rapidly computerized and mobile Internet world – many social activities cut across both online and offline worlds (Garcia et al., 2009; Kozinets, 2010; Miller and Slater, 2000). For example, adjusting to a new college might involve sharing information via email, reading student and university blogs, getting information from websites, participating in online communities, and joining conversations on social networks (DeAndrea et al., 2012). Because the Internet is part of our everyday life, ethnographies of aspects of contemporary society should carefully consider the importance of studying related online behaviors and the social worlds of social media (Garcia et al., 2009; Miller and Slater, 2000). 'Pure' netnographies, that is, netnography without an offline component, should be reserved for phenomena which are happening strictly in the online world, such as self-presentation on personal websites (Schau and Gilly, 2003) or online word of mouth (Kozinets et al., 2010).

Netnographic data also raise a number of epistemological and pragmatic questions. Because the Internet provides access to so much data, so easily, netnographers face the inherent challenge of data overload. Identification and classification of data can be challenging as the optional anonymity that the Web provides can lead to an absence of demographic markers. This seemingly convenient, easy, and anonymous datastream can also open a Pandora's box of ethical issues related to privacy, consent, and appropriate representation. Finally, although qualitative methods like netnography are contextually embedded, researchers often are drawn or directed to collect corroborating evidence in order to generalize findings or make them more transferable to diverse contexts (Kozinets, 2002). The next section begins the discussion of netnographic procedures developed to address these important challenges.

NETNOGRAPHIC PROCEDURES

Netnography is a relatively new method, and analysis techniques thus far have been developed in relation to analogous procedures in ethnography. Here, we provide explicit guidelines for adapting face-to-face data collection and analysis techniques to the new contingencies of computer-mediated cultural communications. We will work from five essential ethnographic considerations: (1) preparing for data collections and cultural entrée; (2) collecting and creating the data; (3) performing ethical research; (4) conducting an insightful and trustworthy analysis; and (5) representing the data analysis in a meaningful and appropriate manner. The section that follows will provide an illustration of how these procedures can be applied to actual social media data.

Netnographic Sites and Entrée

There are many different sites of culture on the Internet, and each one can be explored using the netnographic approach. Kozinets' list of the main types of netnographic field sites includes bulletin boards, chat rooms, playspaces (where videogame and other game play occurs), virtual worlds, lists and web-rings (a largely defunct form now replaced by blogrolls) (Kozinets, 2002), and blogs, wikis, audiovisual sites, social content aggregators, and social networking sites (Kozinets, 2010). It is crucial for researchers to be attuned to the format of different online field sites as it influences the 'types, forms and structures of online communication' found within it (Kozinets, 2010: 87), and the possible roles that can be assumed by users (e.g., being the reader of a blog, a follower of a Twitter poster, a member of a forum, or a friend on a social networking site).

Research questions addressed by netnographic studies may relate to a phenomenon that exists in both offline and online worlds; that can only be experienced virtually; or that concerns the very nature and structure of web-mediated communications. When choosing a field site to study, researchers should favor communities that (1) are more 'research question relevant'; (2) have a 'higher traffic of postings'; (3) have larger numbers of discrete message posters; (4) have more detailed or descriptively rich data; and (5) have more between-member interactions of the type required by the research question (Kozinets, 2002: 63). We suggest identifying research topics, or a set of research questions that will help in pinpointing relevant online sites; studying the sites and their participants to understand the social dynamics at play; and finding out if the community has been 'tapped out' (Kozinets, 2010: 79) by other researchers or 'turned off' by inconsiderate researchers in the past. Along the way, never assume you know more than the community about its own culture. Most importantly, pay attention to the kinds of social data that are available (textual, visual, audiovisual, graphic, and so on) and get prepared to collect and organize them.

Making a successful cultural entrée into these field sites and with their members requires understanding the data while collecting them, and, even more importantly, understanding and being sensitive to the needs and functioning of the social media community. Because netnography is attuned to the cultural realities of living, breathing communities of communicating people, netnographic research requires an initial and deepening cultural understanding of the community. As in any social settings, online gathering 'places' have particular histories, social structures, codes of etiquettes, particular ways of speaking, and unique rituals and identities. An entrée can make or break the interactions that will follow with a community; a researcher can be rejected if the researcher does not understand the customs of the community he or she is talking to (e.g., Kozinets, 2010: 77).

Given the abundance of 'intelligence' data available on the Web, researchers should conduct background research to ease the entrée. One example is 'lurking' – a form of online reconnaissance – to gain information on the community before making the entrée, an opinion shared by other researchers (e.g., Shoham, 2004). Lurking should only be the first step of a netnographic study, though: Beaulieu (2004) maintains that 'lurking' netnographers can miss parts of the phenomenon that are not publicly visible and Kozinets (2010) emphasizes the importance of engagement and participation in cultural worlds.

Once background research is complete and the various types of data and their approximate contents are identified and accommodated, active participation can move to the forefront. Participation in a netnography allows researchers to experience what it feels like to be a community member. Here it may be helpful to think of Walstrom's (2004) term 'participant experiencer,' offered as a counterpoint to the traditional but misleading ethnographic term 'participant observer.'

From the perspective of data collection, it is important for this participation to be captured in field notes, screen captures, recordings, and other permanent records. When performed well, online ethnographic participation enables enhanced cultural understanding, the confirmation of interpretation, and new opportunities to recast the research enterprise as collaboration rather than appropriation. Ideally, the researcher's participation should provide some benefit to the community, for example, by posting something that is useful and/or thought provoking and sharing it with a comment. Alternatively, a researcher could begin as a participant in a particular site and become a culture member before starting to study a particular community. As the introspective approach of 'auto-ethnography' (Hayano, 1979) morphs into 'auto-netnography' (Kozinets and Kedzior, 2009), pre-existing cultural membership can smooth entrée into an unnoticeable and much more personally complicated introspective event (e.g., Cherry, 1999).

UNDERSTANDING NETNOGRAPHIC DATA AND DATA COLLECTION

Three general types of data are available for collection in netnography: archival data, elicited data, and fieldnote data. Archival data comprise anything the researcher can gather from the Web that is not a product of his or her involvement to create or prompt the creation of data. These types of data can constitute a 'cultural baseline,' serving as a portrait of what the community was doing before the researcher made his or her incursion into that social media environment. From this point, the researcher seeks to deepen his or her knowledge of the cultural context (see Kozinets, 2010: 104). These types of so-called observational data can be difficult to find, depending upon the specificity of the topic, but once found are relatively straightforward to access, and can be gathered at a very low cost. Importantly, text (whether in text, image, or video format) also has context. Beyond the analysis of the text, researchers can also look at the way that a webpage and postings are formatted as a type of conversation between various users. They might analyse the pictures that people use to represent themselves, the way that they describe themselves, the various signs and signals that are used, and the interactions between these elements.

Numerous ways exist to record online data. The two most fundamental techniques are: (1) to copy and paste the content of a forum post, for example, into word processing software files such as a Microsoft Word document; and (2) to capture a screenshot of data using a program such as Windows 7's snipping tool or the Apple Grab utility. It is also possible to record in real time a researcher's visit to a particular website through programs such as Camtasia. It may be tempting for researchers to look into programs such as HTTrack Website Copier that allow the researcher to archive the full content of websites and forums, which seemingly provides an interesting alternative to copy–pasting text content, and/or screengrabbing pages. However, the temptation to 'mine' large amounts of data can overshadow real-time engagement with the cultural context. Although greatly facilitating data collection, automatic methods can thus can create a barrier to understanding. Such tools must be understood deeply and used judiciously in coordination with actual, real-time, engaged, confusing, all-too-human participation in the social media community; its conversations; its people; and its temporal unfolding. Archival data can be present in the form of text, such as messages exchanged on a forum; in visual forms, such as the layout and logos of websites, pictures of members of social networking sites, or images of avatars in online worlds; by way of audio, such as songs exchanged on forums; and through video, such as webcam conversations and user-generated videos.

Elicited data refer to content that is co-created by the researcher and members of the social media community through processes of social interaction. This includes the products of online interviewing, whether by asynchronous modes of communication (e.g., email, forums) or (quasi-)synchronous ones such as chat and video calling. Early literature on eliciting data through online channels raised concerns about how the medium itself can shape the interaction. In the now-classic work from the Dark Ages of netnographic inquiry, Markham (1998: 62–75) notes that textual online interviews (e.g., in chat rooms) limit the information that can be gathered from non-verbal cues. Moreover, as typing is usually significantly slower and more deliberate than text-based interviews, it could limit participant spontaneity (Catterall and Maclaran, 2002). At the same time, netnographers can use these structural characteristics to their advantage. Like conversations in the traditional, face-to-face field, the synchronous, real-time format of online chatting can provide the researcher with quick insight into a cultural phenomenon and can evolve into an informal interview. The deliberate nature of email exchange lends itself well to the goals of formal interviews, as it can enhance reflexivity, foster a sense of intimacy, and, if time is taken, deepen rapport (Kozinets, 2010; see McCracken, 1988, for methodological recommendations regarding offline interview methods). A high-bandwidth audiovisual interview can be offered, if the interviewer and interviewee possess a strong Internet connection, to simulate a face-to-face interview. As it restores access to participant body language, video chat provides a significant advantage over the well-established technique of telephone interviewing.

The third and final type of data associated with a netnographic research project are field note data, which are generated directly by the researcher for the purpose of research recording, reflection, and analysis. These data are not shared with the social media community, although they may contain captures of data such as texts, screenshots, moving images, and so on. In order to analyse the important transitions involved in cultural entrée and acculturation, netnographic researchers should begin recording reflective field notes as early in the research process as possible, ideally as soon as a project is initiated. These notes should continue through the search for a specific site, adding notes when experiencing the community, contacting and interacting with culture members, or even simply when thinking and reflecting about the research project. Field notes should document the journey of the netnographer from an outsider to an inside culture member. Although netnographers have many opportunities to automatically capture online images and actions, these actions are by no means a substitute for internal reflection, the capture of in-the-moment impressions and experiences, and the deep culture-bound introspective analysis that marks all strong anthropological and sociological ethnography.

With these three types of data in mind, along with the diversity of communication media they may involve, it is important to remember that *netnographic data collection is not simply one thing, but now offers a range and continuum of different offerings with different benefits, drawbacks, and concomitant tradeoffs*. This holds for almost every element of netnographic research. The online world has become enormously complex and variegated, and netnographic research approaches have followed suit.

ETHICS IN NETNOGRAPHY

Research ethics (see Mertens, Chapter 35, this volume) are a complex and difficult topic in netnographic exploration. As with all social inquiry, ethical netnographic practice is grounded in the principle of informed consent, and consideration of potential benefits and risks to individuals and communities. Since social media blend the public and private into a novel hybrid form, netnography demands new thinking and methodological innovation on issues of risk and privacy.

The online representation of identity is one factor that affects how we think about consent and the potential for harm, especially for elicited data. Some researchers approach the issue by requesting legal names and signed consent forms, or by combining online and offline methods. Although knowing a user's 'real-life' name and having access to more information about offline lives may enhance perceptions of netnography's credibility, this bears with it the same responsibility for protecting identities faced by ethnographers, interviewers, and all other social researchers who obtain data from human subjects.

For archived data, the researcher may approach web content as published content. Although information posted publicly on the Web is technically published, and subject to criticism and quotation with citation, netnographers should consider the ethical issues inherent in quoting directly from online sources (Bruckman, 2006; Kozinets, 2002). Although a web user is responsible for the consequences of publicly posting information on the Internet (either with an original name or a pseudonym), re-publication or citation in an academic publication may have unexpected consequences for the individual and/or the community. For example, it may be unsettling or injurious to the individual if the quote appears with the researcher's critical reading every time the individual's online alias is entered into a major search engine.

As such, when harm is likely, netnographers follow the ethnographic tradition of pseudonymization, protecting individuals' names – both legal and assumed. Many web users have valued pseudonymous identities that they have invested quite a deal of effort into creating and protecting, and netnographers should always be careful to treat these identities as if they were legal identities, creating further pseudonyms when human subjects need protection. Nevertheless, using real names may be appropriate in some cases. For example, an art historian using netnography may need to cite the blogs of famous art critics or artists.

From a legal perspective, three legitimate privacy concerns may arise in the course of such netnographic study. One is the use of online information found in 'semi-private' web spaces. Are all members of a particular online community bound by a Terms of Use agreement that defines the forum as a de facto private space? Do users have a reasonable expectation of privacy? Does the group stipulate other restrictions regarding how the content may be used? Generally, groups that anyone can join are still considered to be public, but the netnographer should be careful with any Terms of Use agreements that are 'signed' when signing up. The second privacy issue goes hand in hand with earlier discussions of anonymity, pseudonymity, and confidentiality. Whether or not a netnographer uses a poster's real name or 'real pseudonym' remains an ethical question, not a legal one, as the information is publicly published under that name. In addition to privacy laws, copyright laws may come into play when a researcher wants to publish a picture, quote, or other material. From an international level, this issue is so complex and dynamic that questions are best handled by experts (e.g., a university's lawyers advising about local copyright restrictions and fair use guidelines) on a case-by-case basis.

NETNOGRAPHY IN ACTION: A BRIEF ILLUSTRATION

In principle, the analysis of qualitative data yielded by a netnography will proceed in a fashion very similar to that of any other comparable type of qualitative data. As we mentioned earlier, netnography shares the inductive and iterative aspects of ethnography. Because of the nature of social media and online communications, netnography places the field site and research participants within easy access of the researcher. Thus the collection of data and their analysis are even more likely than they are with other methods to become blurred into a single ongoing process. Add to this the ubiquity and variety of search analytic engines and the convenience of qualitative data management software and coding programs (see Gibbs, Chapter 19, this volume), and we have the opportunity to automate many elements of the netnographic data collection and analysis. Although ethnography requires the researcher to become a finely tuned instrument (see Gubrium and Holstein, Chapter 3, this volume), the use of such software risks reducing the researcher to a mere button-pusher who finds the preprogrammed output of various web-mining and content analysis programs sufficient as either the outcome or primary basis of an interpretation. To avoid this, we advocate an 'old-fashioned,' hands-on approach to netnographic data analysis. Although netnography uses some of the most contemporary data available, and benefits from the most recent technological developments, this approach to data analysis grounds the researchers in the basics of inductive (see Reichertz, Chapter 9, this volume) and reflexive analysis (see May and Perry, Chapter 8, this volume).

We have four important prescriptions to guide researchers in conducting netnographic data analysis. The first core principle of quality netnography is that of "ethnographic siting" (see Gubrium and Holstein, Chapter 3, this volume). This means that netnographers should go site specific, initially at least, concentrating on a small number of postings or a very constrained data set in order to gain a deep cultural sense of 'what is going on' in that particular social space. From there, the analysis can broaden in scope as well as deepen. The second tenet of rigorous netnographic analysis is to undertake cultural analysis (see Winter, Chapter 17, this volume) while engaged as a participant in a manner appropriate to other cultural participants or community members. This is the rule of 'ethnographic engaging.' The third maxim is that of 'ethnographic communicating,' where communications are, at least initially, experienced, processed, and understood exactly as cultural members experience them. This means that they should be analysed and viewed in their natural 'real-text' format rather than experienced through the filters of some language processor or compressive software engine. The final recommended netnographic convention is to allow 'ethnographic timing' to unfold, such that messages and posts are experienced, read, interpreted, and analysed in real time, as they become available, rather than all at once.

As with ethnography, the purpose of netnographic data analysis is to organize the collected products of participation and observation into a rigorous, meaningful, and useful form of research output, such as an article, a report, a presentation, or even a book. The data will likely include various downloaded textual, graphical, photographic, audio, and audiovisual files, screen captures, online interview transcripts, and reflective field notes. In this section, we present coding and hermeneutic approaches to analysing these materials. As researchers who frequently work with textual data, we find a combination of these two approaches to be optimal, but other methods may be more appropriate for other types of netnographic data. For example, netnographers working in image or video-heavy field sites may want to reference the chapters of this handbook that explicate semiotic and visual studies approaches (see Banks, Chapter 27, and Knoblauch et al., Chapter 30, this volume).

Coding is a qualitative data analysis method commonly used by sociological researchers. Here, 'open coding' is arguably the most popular approach (Corbin and Strauss, 2008; see Thornberg and Charmaz, Chapter 11, this volume). Open coding begins when the researcher labels and categorizes data by 'emic,' field-level meanings, and then groups these categories into other abstract categories. The ultimate goal of open coding is to reach a theoretically relevant understanding of the phenomena of interest. Netnographers can organize many different types of data with the same codes. For example, a photograph, a scanned drawing, a blog entry, the format of a webpage, a few seconds of a YouTube video, the color of text in a posting, and the name of someone's avatar could possibly all be coded with the same term.

The 'grounded theory' that emerges from coding is tested as new data are collected and analysed; indeed, data may be collected specifically for that purpose. Because netnography allows such easy access to data, and often offers up large amounts of data, such cross-checking is facilitated in a rather unprecedented manner. Comparisons (see Palmberger and Gingrich, Chapter 7, this volume) look for convergence and divergence among the coded data and the categories. Generalizations try to explain the occurrences of the data and are used to construct new theories.

Simultaneous with such inevitably micro but effectively piecemeal approaches are more macro and holistic approaches that seek a kind of transcendent interpretation. As consumer researcher Susan Spiggle (1994: 497) describes them, these interpretations are like a type of decoding that 'occurs as a gestalt shift and represents a synthetic, holistic, and illuminating grasp of meaning.' Another way to conceptualize this form of insightful reading of texts is the notion of hermeneutics, where larger order conceptual readings are garnered from readings of the parts of the text in light of the text as a whole. In a netnography, this "text" can encompass particular sites; particular forms of social media; the Web or Internet itself; interview data about online interaction; the researcher's ongoing experience with online media; and a multitude of different types of communications such as email, blog posts, comments, ratings, photographs, and videos.

In netnography, coding (see Thornberg and Charmaz, Chapter 11, this volume) and hermeneutic interpretation (see Wernet, Chapter 16, this volume) may overlap in a variety of interesting ways. Rarely do hermeneutic insights simply burst into being like a light illuminating a dark room. Because netnographers must approach field sites as participants as well as observers, their interpretations of online communications and communities will emerge gradually, as they build up the cultural codes to make sense of virtual social spaces.

NETNOGRAPHIC ANALYSIS: UNDERSTANDING CULTURE THROUGH SOCIAL MEDIA DATA

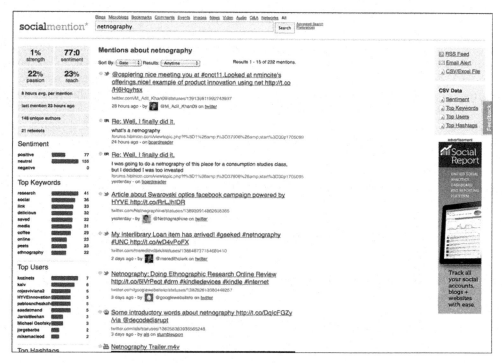

Figure 18.1 Search using search term "netnography"

Source: socialmention.com website search using search term 'netnography', conducted April 2013

In order to demonstrate how coding and hermeneutic analysis can be utilized in netnographic data analysis, we offer a short example that involves both coding and hermeneutic interpretation. The 64-word sample text was drawn from a discussion about netnography on a LinkedIn group dedicated to netnography. It was located through a search of the term 'netnography' on a public, free (but ad-supported) semantic search engine named 'Social Mention' (which can be found at socialmention.com). The search engine looks for mentions of the word netnography across a range of domains on the Internet, including blogs, micro-blogs, bookmarks, comments, news stories, video and other forums and formats. The software attempts to recognize positive, neutral, and negative sentiments in the mention of netnography, and it also looks at the co-occurrence of the term and other terms. As Figure 18.1 shows, Social Mention classifies the term as having very little strength, but positive sentiment and reasonable passion.

Social Mention and other semantic search engines are very useful to netnographers because they can help to identify where to find particular mentions of topics or terms. In this case, the Social Mention output led us to a Twitter tweet, which had an embedded link that directed us to a discussion thread that was useful to develop as an example of netnographic data analysis. The post, written by a consultant and trainer from the UK, asked the following question:

> Does anybody do small scale, thick description Netnography using naturally formed communities on the net? I'm seeing a lot of stuff about Netnography that is getting hard to distinguish from social media listening. I want to know if people do research as observers / participant observers in naturally formed communities (not supported by brands) and if so, how you deal with the ethical issues?

Because of the space constraints of this chapter, we are prevented from entering into extreme detail; however, we can code a range of different topics from this posting. They include: research terms (small scale, thick description); method concerns (observers / participant observers, ethical issues); and distinctions for research and researchers (hard to distinguish, naturally formed). From these we can proceed to some higher order categories or theories, noting that some researchers are seeking to distinguish netnographies from other techniques such as 'social media listening' and that the terms 'naturally formed communities' may also be powerful and prevalent in setting up this distinction.

From these coding and higher order categorizations, our hermeneutic interpretation can build out a more general theory that attends to commercialization in the sphere of social media. It might see this posting as an authenticating strategy that seeks to establish the boundaries of authenticity and to link them in a notional space with morality, ethics, and particular research practices. The poster views organically developed communities as different in some sense from those which are cultivated by companies or brands, and simultaneously relates the use of 'small scale, thick description' ethnographic techniques to the study of these communities as a way to distinguish a particular kind of research and researcher as more authentic than others.

In this way, coding and hermeneutics are complementary techniques that can help to illumine various aspects of even short postings such as this one. Of course, such interpretations often require an insider's depth of knowledge, linguistic terms, and understanding, and such a deep understanding can only take place through prolonged engagement and immersion in a culture over a prolonged period of time.

There are a vast variety of different approaches we can take to analyse netnographic data. Another method that can be used to glean insights for analysis is to use word clouds. In Figure 18.2, we went to the Wikipedia entry on 'netnography,' which is the

Figure 18.2 Wikipedia.com entry on "netnography"

Source: output from wordle.com input of wikipedia.com entry on 'netnography', conducted April 2013

top listing on the Google search engine when we searched for that term. We selected the entire article, and then pasted it into the free word cloud generator 'Wordle' (available at wordle.com). The same method could of course be used to generate word clouds for entire postings, threads, or much larger sets of words. We can then proceed to analyse the output. The first author's name shows up as the largest word in the cloud, which perhaps suggests how closely the method is still associated with its pioneer and chief advocate (see also Kozinets, 2012). Other words that are large and significant (besides netnography) are communities, social, research, and consumer. The terms are still largely descriptive, which is to be expected in an encyclopedia entry such as Wikipedia, although the inclusion of the term 'communities' underscores the importance of the role of online community studies, and the use of consumer also indicates that the term is still largely associated with business schools and consumer research. It may be interesting to note some important words which do not appear prominently in the word cloud, such as marketing, business, method, digital, and anthropology. Obviously, these analyses are brief, rather superficial, and illustrative only. They invite considerably deeper exploration than our space constraint allows.

MOVING FORWARD

We conclude this chapter with a brief discussion of some of the challenges, strengths, and new directions that accompany the analysis of netnographic data. Many challenges have previously been identified in past literature on the topic, such as the anonymity of data; the difficulty of maintaining research ethics in a space that is both public and private; the nature of cyberculture; and its technological mediation of social communications (see, e.g., Kozinets, 2002; 2010; Langer and Beckman, 2005). We focus our closing comments on several overlapping areas: anonymity, legal issues, data overload, and the emergence of new social media forms.

Public perceptions about anonymity on the Internet have changed dramatically over the past decade or so, and with them netnography must also change. The Internet is now mainstream. Documentation mechanisms have emerged in many web forums, with the goal of verifying relevant parts of a person's identity, character, or behavior. Perhaps most importantly, increasingly, online interactions are no longer anonymous. Social networks like Facebook and LinkedIn strongly and successfully encourage people to use their real or legal names, often going so far as demanding it within Terms of Use agreements. These identities are further validated as users 'friend' others they know in real life, and activity in the physical world becomes fodder for conversation in the world of social networking. The integration of those websites with newspaper and magazine sites connects commentary to one's social network identity, furthering this trend. Portable technologies and services like Twitter allow advanced documentation of what is going on in 'real life.' There is a clear tension between the forces favoring anonymous interactions and the structures demanding or encouraging its decline. In short, the once more demarcated lines between offline and online identities are disappearing. However, the netnographer now must pay much more close attention to the limitations present when he or she has to conduct research on social networks such as Facebook that are governed by restrictive terms of use, and where social media community data are, in some sense, 'owned' by a corporation and bought, sold, and utilized mainly for its own private benefit.

Since social media present an overt risk of data overload, netnographic procedures suggest that careful sampling and analysis be used to cope with copious amounts of data. This is the netnographic edge, in which the 'researcher-as-instrument' demonstrates what a trained anthropologist can do that a sophisticated data-mining program cannot. To cope with overwhelming quantities of data, netnographers must clearly establish the boundaries of the phenomenon being studied. These boundaries should link the analysis, in an iterative and inductive manner, of the data collected with the research focus. As in any qualitative research project, the data collection should be rigorous and follow established methodological guidelines. Findings should be grounded and emerge from the data. Using a small data set does not equate to purposively sampling data to confirm a researcher's feeling of what is going on in the field site. If the researcher plans to analyse the data set by hand, Kozinets (2010) recommends limiting the amount of data to no more than 1000 double-spaced pages of text. If the researcher is using qualitative data analysis software, this amount can be increased to 5000 pages, but the analyst should proceed with caution and not lose sight of the social site's forest for the QDA's categorical trees (QDA: Qualitative Data Analysis – see Gibbs, Chapter 19, this volume).

Our advice is to think carefully about what kinds of data and how much data are necessary for a given project. Consider whether the project would be better served with more depth, analysing the comments and any linked content for a certain time period. It may also be instructive to think about the level of analysis and the boundaries of the community. Are you interested in comparing organizations or websites, or is your community defined by a particular group of users? How much data, and of what kind, are required to learn about the community of interest? Clear definitions of the community and strategies for collecting the necessary data should be established at the outset and reviewed regularly throughout the project, to ensure that the data are appropriate and not overwhelming (Kozinets, 2010). Throughout, be sure to start with the most promising areas of online content, in the event that even these amounts of data are overwhelming.

However, if you decide that your research project requires you to sample widely or broadly, and that large amounts of social media data are necessary, there are many useful tools to help address some of the organizational issues associated with data overload. Depending upon the project, software for automatically downloading web content may be helpful. For others, however, this may produce data that require a considerable quantity of manual cleaning. Regardless of the archiving method, keep in mind that online data often contain large quantities of noise, spam, or otherwise unusable material. Website searches often yield documents that are not relevant. Online community discussion boards frequently feature 'off-topic' discussion that may or may not be essential to your analysis. However, automated QDA software (often abbreviated to CAQDAS or Computer-Assisted or Aided Qualitative Data Analysis Systems or Software; see Lewins and Silver, 2007) such as ATLAS.ti or NVivo (see Gibbs, Chapter 19, this volume) offer assistance in coding, searching, classifying, and organizing large sets of qualitative data.

There are a range of different ways to judge the quality of a netnography as a tool for revealing insights from social media and online interactions. Kozinets (2010) follows the history of ethnography and its corresponding quality judgments and evaluations and suggests a pliable set of criteria that can be adapted to achieve many rhetorical research purposes. Some of these criteria contradict one another, indicating the need for a custom-made evaluative solution to be devised by the researcher, in the spirit of ethnographic research. The arrows in this evaluative quiver for judging the quality of a netnographic analysis are that the analysis is internally coherent; that it follows accepted procedures; that it recognizes relevant literature and approaches; that it follows from and links to the data; that the ideas provide new understandings; that a sensitizing connection is gained; that a believable sense of culture is presented; that the analysis is open to alternative interpretations; that the text inspires social action; and that the analysis accounts for the interaction of online and offline social interactions (see Kozinets, 2010, for more detail). These 10 criteria offer netnographic researchers a pragmatic 'toolkit' orientation for the evaluation of their data analysis.

In summary, the chapter offers various sets of advice that may lead the researcher to high-quality social media data analysis, and provides some 'best practices' advice for conducting netnographic studies and netnographic data analysis. At its core, netnographic data analysis is about maintaining the cultural quality of the social media phenomenon through the careful consideration of the researcher's own role and social intelligence throughout the process of online social scientific research.

FURTHER READING

Garcia, Angela Cora, Standlee, Alecea J., Bechkoff, Jennifer, and Cui, Yan (2009) 'Ethnographic approaches to the Internet and computer-mediated communication,' *Journal of Contemporary Ethnography*, 38 (1): 52–84.

Kozinets, Robert V. (2002) 'The field behind the screen: Using netnography for marketing research in online communities,' *Journal of Marketing Research*, 39: 61–72.

Kozinets, Robert V. (2010) *Netnography: Doing Ethnographic Research Online*. Thousand Oaks, CA: Sage.

REFERENCES

Beaulieu, Anne (2004) 'Mediating ethnography: Objectivity and the making of Ethnographies of the Internet,' *Social Epistemology*, 18 (2–3): 139–63.

Bruckman, Amy (2006) 'Teaching students to study online communities ethically,' *Journal of Information Ethics*, 15 (2): 82–98.

Catterall, Miriam and Maclaran, Pauline (2002) 'Researching consumers in virtual worlds: A cyberspace Odyssey,' *Journal of Consumer Behavior*, 1 (3): 228–38.

Cherny, Lynn (1999) *Conversation and Community: Chat in a Virtual World*. Chicago: University of Chicago Press.

Corbin, Juliet M. and Strauss, Anselm L. (2008) *Basics of Qualitative Research: Techniques and Procedures for Developing Grounded Theory*. Thousand Oaks, CA: Sage.

Correll, Shelly (1995) 'The ethnography of an electronic bar: The lesbian café,' *Journal of Contemporary Ethnography*, 24 (3): 270–98.

DeAndrea, David C., Ellison, Nicole B., LaRose, Robert, Steinfield, Charles, and Fiore, Andrew (2012) 'Serious social media: On the use of social media for improving students' adjustment to college,' *The Internet and Higher Education*, 15 (1), 15–23.

Garcia, Angela Cora, Standlee, Alecea J., Bechkoff, Jennifer, and Cui, Yan (2009) 'Ethnographic approaches to the Internet and computer-mediated communication,' *Journal of Contemporary Ethnography*, 38 (1): 52–84.

Guba, Egon G. and Lincoln, Yvonna S. (1981) *Effective Evaluation: Improving the usefulness of evaluation results through responsive and naturalistic approaches*. San Francisco: Jossey-Bass.

Hayano, David M. (1979) 'Auto-ethnography: Paradigms, problems, and prospects,' *Human Organization*, 38 (1): 99–104.

Kayahara, Jennifer and Wellman, Barry (2007) 'Searching for culture – high and low,' *Journal of Computer Mediated Communication*, 12 (4): 825–45.

Kozinets, Robert V. (2002) 'The field behind the screen: Using netnography for marketing research in online communities,' *Journal of Marketing Research*, 39: 61–72.

Kozinets, Robert V. (2010) *Netnography*. Thousand Oaks, CA: Sage.

Kozinets, Robert V. (2012), 'Marketing netnography: prom/ot(ulgat)ing a new research method,'*Methodological Innovations Online* (MIO), 1 (7): 37–45, online at: www.pbs.plym.ac.uk/mi/index.html (accessed May 8, 2013).

Kozinets, Robert V. and Kedzior, Richard (2009) 'I, avatar: Auto-netnographic research in virtual worlds,' in Michael Solomon and Natalie Wood (eds.), *Virtual Social Identity and Social Behavior*. Armonk, NY: M.E. Sharpe. pp. 3–19.

Kozinets, Robert V., de Valck, Kristine, Wojnicki, Andrea C., and Wilner, Sarah J. S. (2010) 'Networked narratives: Understanding word-of-mouth marketing in online communities,' *Journal of Marketing*, 74: 71–89.

Langer, Roy and Beckman, Suzanne C., (2005) 'Sensitive research topics: Netnography revisited,' *Qualitative Market Research: An International Journal*, 8 (2): 189–203.

Lewins, Ann and Christina, Silver (2007) *Using Software in Qualitative Research: A Step-by-Step Guide*. Los Angeles: Sage.

Markham, Annette (1998) *Life Online: Researching Real Experience in Virtual Space*. Walnut Creek, CA: Altamira.

McCracken, Grant (1988) *The Long Interview*. Thousand Oaks, CA: Sage.

Miller, Dame I and Slater, Don (2000) *The Internet: An Ethnographic Approach*. New York: Berg.

Ruhleder, Karen (2000) 'The virtual ethnographer: Fieldwork in distributed electronic environments,' *Field Methods*, 12 (1): 3–17.

Schau, Hope Jensen and Gilly, Mary C. (2003) 'We are what we post,' *Journal of Consumer Research*, 30 (3): 385–404.

Shoham, Aviv (2004) 'Flow experiences and image making: An online chat-room ethnography,' *Psychology and Marketing*, 21 (10): 855–82.

Spiggle, Susan (1994) 'Analysis and interpretation of qualitative data in consumer research,' *Journal of Consumer Research*, 21: 491–503.

Walstrom, Mary K. (2004) 'Ethics and engagement in communication scholarship: Analyzing public, online support groups as researcher/participant-experiencer,' in Elizabeth A. Buchanan (ed.), *Virtual Research Ethics: Issues and controversies*. Hershey, PA: Information Science Publishing. pp. 174–202.

Wellman, Barry, Quan Haase, Anabel, Witte, James, and Hampton, Keith (2001) 'Does Internet increase, decrease or supplement social capital?', *American Behavioral Scientist*, 45 (3): 436–55.

Using Software in Qualitative Analysis

Graham R. Gibbs

Computer software to assist with qualitative data analysis (QDA) has become established as an essential tool for many researchers in the last 20 years. One of the most commonly used acronyms for this software, CAQDAS, introduced by Fielding and Lee following a 1989 conference on the programs (Fielding and Lee, 1991), emphasizes that the software assists: Computer-Assisted Qualitative Data Analysis. However, the assistance given can be seen in different ways. For some, the use of software constitutes a separate kind of analysis to be considered alongside conversation analysis or grounded theory. *The SAGE Handbook of Qualitative Research* (Denzin and Lincoln, 2011b) lists 'computer assisted analysis' as a 'method of analysis' (table 1.1: 12) and comments that 'faced with large amounts of qualitative materials, the investigator seeks ways of managing and interpreting these documents, and here ... computer-assisted models of analysis may be of use' (Denzin and Lincoln, 2011a). Fielding finds this unsatisfactory because it suggests a coherence in the approaches taken by the software that underplays their differences and because it 'confuses a technical resource with an analytic approach' (2000: para. 6). One consequence is a kind of sidelining of such software as a special interest which, as Fielding notes, promotes a pattern of adoption where novices such as graduate students are more likely to use the software than established researchers. A similar point is made by Marshall in her literature survey of the impact of CAQDAS on qualitative sociology. She finds that novice users are apparently less concerned with the object (analysis) than with the tools they are using (Marshall, 2002). All too often this results in research proposals (at both student and research council levels), which imply that the analysis will be 'undertaken' using CAQDAS software. This is what MacMillan and Koenig (2004) refer to as the 'wow' factor, where the use of CAQDAS is seen as the method rather than treating the software as only an organizational support for a method. This chapter will argue that CAQDAS is not a distinct method or approach to analysis, that the software does not 'do' the analysis. On the contrary, a major function of the software is to help organize the analysis. In particular it is a way of managing the data and the analytic thoughts that are created in the analysis. The software no more 'does' the analysis than the word processor I am using now writes this chapter for me. Nevertheless, the use of technology is not neutral. Just as word processing has changed the way some people write, so CAQDAS has changed the way analysis is done and there is considerable debate about the extent to which the software has affected practice.

DEVELOPMENT OF CAQDAS

There is no doubt that the idea of code and retrieve as a form of analysis had a central influence on the development of CAQDAS. It was the development of the personal computer in the early 1980s that made clear the possibilities for supporting qualitative analysis. Breakthroughs came with the development of the Macintosh computer and then the publication of Windows for the PC, which presented much more accessible interfaces to users. The first programs focused on code and retrieve functions by implementing simple ways in which the researcher could attach codes or tags to sections of text and then undertake retrievals of all the text similarly coded, or in more complex cases text that had been coded that matched a (usually) Boolean combination of codes. (Such combinations are discussed later in the section 'Development of the analysis'.) Some software addressed additional issues such as the incorporation of memo writing, supporting the analysis of audio and video, the analysis of narratives or the undertaking of case-based analysis and hypothesis testing. Even though many programs have 'fallen by the wayside' over the last few decades, many survive: at least 25 are still on sale or freely available and their persistence suggests they are serving a variety of analytic niches.

Many of those producing software were themselves academics undertaking their own data analysis and their close ties with and their understanding of the research needs of the social science community from which they came meant that early adopters felt confident that, once bugs were ironed out, the programs would have the capability to assist in the analysis of qualitative data (Mangabeira et al., 2004: 176). The first developments were in the United States but were followed very rapidly by programs written in Germany, the Netherlands, Australia and the UK. In the UK at least, this period coincided with a growth in the use of qualitative methods (Fielding and Lee, 1996). But the most significant factor promoting dissemination in the UK must be the activities of the CAQDAS Networking Project at the University of Surrey, funded for over 15 years by the UK Economic and Social Research Council to promote the use of software and train researchers to use it. Over 6000 postgraduates and researchers have been trained on courses run at the Project.

Despite the early beginnings, the adoption of CAQDAS in academia has only taken off since 2000. A bibliographic search of all social science journal papers using any of a range of qualitative methods and using CAQDAS (Figure 19.1) shows the increasing number of papers mentioning CAQDAS from 1983 to 2011.

Set against this upward trend is the fact that of the recent papers using thematic approaches such as grounded theory, qualitative content analysis and framework analysis, only around 2.5% mentioned using CAQDAS. This low level of use is found outside academia too. In a recent survey of UK companies that undertook market research, only 9% said they usually used special computer software for the analysis of qualitative data and only 2 out of 153 who replied used it regularly (Rettie et al., 2008). Ereaut (2002) suggests that one reason for

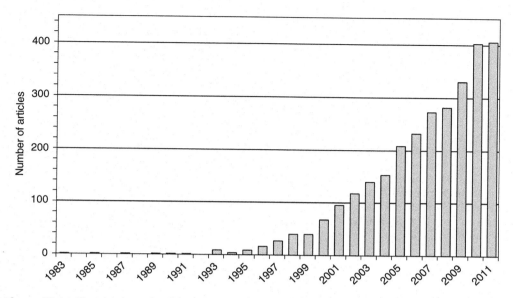

Figure 19.1 The number of refereed papers published using qualitative methods that used CAQDAS, 1983–2011

Source: Original to author

this low take-up is that the use of software is seen as undermining the essentially humanistic approach of qualitative research. In market research, qualitative research is seen as the opposite of quantitative research – an approach that emphasizes the insight of human understanding in the analysis and especially the interpretation of highly experienced human experts. In contrast, in academic social research the use of CAQDAS is seen in a positive light, showing that one is using the best possible approach to ensure the work is of high quality, reliable and exhaustive (Ereaut, 2002).

Of course, the low percentage of academics apparently using CAQDAS may simply reflect a decision not to mention the software they used (just as they did not mention the word processor they used). If, as I am suggesting, CAQDAS is not a method but rather a way of managing the analytic process, then its use may not be of key relevance to the reporting of the data analysis methods. On the other hand, where its use, for example to manage large-scale teamwork, has affected the analysis, then readers need to know.

SELECTING THE PROGRAM

Most of the software now available provides a common core of functions to support the thematic coding of data and for the comparison of themes across cases. Thus these programs provide good support for analytic approaches that use these ideas, such as grounded theory (Charmaz, 2006; Glaser and Strauss, 1967; see Thornberg and Charmaz, Chapter 11, this volume), interpretive phenomenological analysis (IPA; Smith et al., 2009), template analysis (King, 2012), framework analysis (Ritchie and Lewis, 2003), qualitative content analysis (Mayring, 2000; see Schreier, Chapter 12, this volume) and general thematic approaches. This core of software functions includes:

- The construction, modification and maintenance of code lists.
- The use of these to code documents (usually by selecting data with the mouse and then applying a code to them and usually with some visual way of showing what has been coded).
- Retrievals (at its simplest the retrieval of all materials coded the same way, but also including more complex retrievals of material coded by several codes – in Boolean combinations).

- Ways of dealing with case-based data (often quantitative variables or attributes).
- Writing memos and linking them with other elements in the project.
- Sophisticated text searches (which may also include concordance and word list features).
- A range of diagrams and charts (in many cases with their elements linked back to items in the project).
- The ability to deal with a range of documents including digitized media documents such as images, audio and video. Several programs now have much improved interfaces for applying coding to these media using rectangular subsets of the image or sections of the timeline (in the case of video and audio).

One of the questions most often asked of the CAQDAS Networking Project is 'what software should I use for my project?' In truth, for any project that is undertaking straightforward coding and thematic analysis, just about any of the popular CAQDAS programs will do the job: Atlas.ti, MAXQDA, NVivo, HyperRESEARCH, QDA Miner, Qualrus. Of course, if the research requires additional features, then an examination of the software must be made. Fortunately, most software companies have informative websites and they allow the download of a trial version of the software so these features can be checked. Nevertheless, frequently the choice comes down to other factors: what is available; what support and expertise are there; what can be afforded? For many researchers undertaking doctorates or working in collaborative projects, the decision about software will be made for them. It is what the university or project is already using. But this is not necessarily a bad thing, as it may mean that help and expertise are available. One point to bear in mind is that learning how to use the software is not the same as learning about how to undertake analysis using a specific method such as grounded theory (Charmaz, 2006; Glaser and Strauss, 1967; see Thornberg and Charmaz, Chapter 11, this volume), IPA (Smith et al., 2009) or qualitative content analysis (Mayring, 2000; see Schreier, Chapter 12, this volume). It is best to have a clear idea of how the analytic approach should be undertaken before learning the technical skills needed to use a new piece of software.

A recent attempt to generate more information about the strengths and weaknesses of the software was the Kwalon Experiment, named after The Netherlands Association for Qualitative Research, the body from which the exercise originated, which was run in collaboration with the CAQDAS Networking Project, based in the UK, *FQS*, an international journal, based in Germany, and Kwalitatief Sterk, based in Belgium (Evers et al., 2010). Researchers from five different software teams (Atlas.ti, Cassandre (Lejeune, 2010), MAXQDA, NVivo, Transana) were given a common set of data to analyse. The data consisted of freely available data, collected from the Internet, of newspaper articles, websites and weblogs, video and audio files. There was a broad variety of geographical origin, actors involved and file formats. The comparison was not in terms of how good an analysis could be done with the software as it was recognized that the quality of analysis still depends largely on the researcher. Each software team reported on its experience, and this highlighted the strengths and occasionally the weaknesses of each program in dealing with particular kinds of data. All dealt well with the core kinds of documents, word-processed transcripts, audio recordings, images. But there were differences in dealing with the range of video formats, with documents in pdf format and material taken from the Internet. In the end, for most users the choice should be based on whether the software has the tools or functions needed, or which is found to be the most convivial/easy to use.

Some programs offer things that lie outside the mainstream. One issue is price. Most programs are expensive – 10 times or more the price of a mobile app. But Weft, Open Code, AnSWR and TAMS Analyzer (and some others) are free, though often come at the price of limited support/updating and some programs may not run on new operating systems. Transana has specialized in dealing with video and has some of the best facilities for this (and is cheap). But other programs (such as Atlas.ti, NVivo and MAXQDA) also now have ways of dealing with video. HyperRESEARCH is currently the only software that comes in a Macintosh version, but Macintosh versions of Atlas.ti, NVivo and MAXQDA have been announced. All the others run under some version of Windows, though they can be run on Macintosh computers using Boot Camp or on Mac OS X using virtualization software. Dedoose and Saturate are new approaches to analysis in that they work through the web browser and data are stored 'in the cloud' – that is, on rented Internet servers – rather than on the local PC. This means that the software will run on any operating system, even some tablet computers, but some feel this may compromise the security of the data. Access to data is encrypted to a high degree (in a similar way to secure transactions using credit cards) and the software companies claim this is as secure, if not more so, than data stored on local university PCs or in institutional storage areas. It remains to be seen whether research ethics panels will be convinced that data stored this way are properly curated.

The use of CAQDAS makes most sense when most, if not all, of the source files being used are in digital form. Most commonly this means having transcriptions of interviews, focus groups and field notes as word-processed files. Most of the popular programs can also import images in a variety of common formats as well as audio and video files, and they provide ways of viewing and coding such media.

ANALYSIS USING CAQDAS

CAQDAS software is essentially a database that holds source data, such as transcripts (including ethnographic notes), video, audio, memos and any other documents that are available in electronic form, and then supports the annotation, coding, sorting and other manipulations of them and keeps a record of all this activity. The one key advantage that most researchers using the software claim is that the programs help them to keep everything neat and tidy and make it easy to find the material they need later in the analysis. In order to keep a clear mind and not become overwhelmed by the sheer amount of data and analytic writings, the analyst needs to be organized. The bigger the project and the more researchers who are involved, the more sensible it is to use software to support the analysis.

What follows is an attempt to highlight the main issues and functions that need to be thought about as a project is analysed with the help of CAQDAS. Read the instructions and help files and watch the online video lessons that many of the program's publishers have now produced. At least knowing what the software can do means it is possible to use the help files to see exactly how to do it.

Setting up a New Project

The best advice when starting with new software is to spend a bit of time 'playing' with it using some real data; be prepared to throw everything away and start over again. Prepare all the sources, documents (see Coffey, Chapter 25, this volume), video (see Knoblauch et al., Chapter 30, this volume), etc., so that they can be imported into the program. For information about transcription, see the chapter by Kowal and O'Connell (Chapter 5, this volume). The programs can accept transcripts in a variety of file formats. Atlas.ti, MAXQDA, NVivo and QDA Miner can import pdf too and these programs now do quite a good job in keeping all the layout information intact so that both text and images can be coded. Word-processed files may use formatting such as colour, fonts, bold, italic, underline, indents, etc., and all are preserved on import. (Although check this, as some of the more basic programs can only accept plain text.) There are, however, some aspects of formatting that are not preserved on import, such as footnotes, tables of contents, bibliographies. But usually the textual content is imported in some way even if the formatting is not preserved.

Dealing with video (see Knoblauch et al., Chapter 30, this volume), audio (see Maeder, Chapter 29, this volume) and images (see Banks, Chapter 27, this volume) can be more complicated. Video camera manufacturers use different codecs in their cameras: that is, different ways of storing and compressing the digital signal. Often the recording will need to be processed through an editing suite to get a file that is usable, but this is fairly normal. Audio is relatively simpler. Most people use digital recorders, so simply choose standard formats like WAV for uncompressed, high-quality but rather large files, or MP3 for compressed files. Most software can import both these formats. In the case of images there is a range of formats, but most CAQDAS programs can handle the common ones. Ensure that files are saved in the appropriate format from the image editing or scanning software.

At this stage it is important to think about where the project files and all the associated source files will be stored and how to ensure they are safe and secure. Some programs (such as NVivo) will store all the materials in a single file that includes all the source files along with the coding attribute data etc. Others (such as Atlas.ti) store the source material separately from the project file. Because video files can be very large (hundreds of megabytes) even NVivo needs to store them separately from the project file. Once a project is started it is not an easy matter to move externally stored files from one folder to another, so keep all this material together in one folder (which can have subfolders) on the hard disk. Make sure the work is safe. Do not keep just a single copy on the hard disk of one computer (or, even worse, on one memory stick). If this breaks down or gets stolen, all the work will be lost. So make backups and keep copies on other machines in other places. Most universities now have a form of secure storage on campus that can be accessed from machines with the right password and which is backed up on a regular basis. So use this if possible for keeping one of the copies. It may also be necessary to keep the data private, especially if they are of a sensitive or confidential nature. Password-protected computers and even password access to the project can help here. Keeping data secure and confidential are key ethical issues. See Mertens (Chapter 35, this volume) on ethics for the other issues that all qualitative researchers need to consider.

A less technical issue to think about when setting up a project is what the cases are. This is particularly important if some quantitative, perhaps biographical, data will be used in the analysis. For example, if the cases are people the data might be their age, gender, education or work experience; or if the cases are places the data might be population, crime rate, state; or if events they might be date, duration, size, type, etc. These will depend on the research question and in complex studies there may be several different case types. Several CAQDAS programs can import quantitative data in spreadsheets (or sometimes in SPSS format). These allow the use of variables or attributes alongside coding in the analysis. Thus it is possible, for example, to narrow down a retrieval to just those cases that match a certain variable value – such as, they are female. Such variable data have to be attached to cases, which in the simplest case might just be represented by a document (the interview with that person, for instance). But some software allows a range of sources or even parts of sources to represent a case (all the interviews, sections of group discussions, and video that represent one person, for example) that can be combined into one case. If biographical or other quantitative case data are needed in the project then it is best to decide on the cases when the project is first set up. Things to resolve are the names of the cases (these are used in the variable data files) and whether such variable data will be imported (e.g. from a related quantitative survey). A good idea here is to use informative case name abbreviations that include some of the key descriptions relevant to the study, such as F23MC8 to mean family 23, male child aged 8, or Josie_FPhysio to mean Josie (a pseudonym), female physiotherapist. Normally it is best to introduce case data early in the analysis, but attributes or variables can be added after the project has been set up, either from data collected in the field or on the basis of the analysis of the qualitative data as a way of classifying the cases (see Miles and Huberman, 1994: 102–9).

It makes sense to import into the project a substantial number of the sources before starting analysis. However, depending on the analytical approach, they may not all be needed at the start. For example, when following an IPA or template analysis approach it is common to start the analysis and the coding on the basis of just a small number of documents or cases. And, of course, if the design uses theoretical sampling (see Thornberg and Charmaz, Chapter 11, this volume) the analysis must be started on the early cases in order to identify which further ones are needed for the sample.

Coding

Once some sources (documents, video, etc.) have been entered into the project, most researchers want to start analysis and the core analytic procedure that the software supports is coding (see Thornberg and Charmaz, Chapter 11, and Schreier, Chapter 12, this volume). Usually this is done as a way of indicating all the content (text, images, video, etc.) that is relevant to some identified theme. At its simplest, coding enables researchers quickly to retrieve and collect together all the text and other data that they have associated with some thematic idea so that they can be examined together and different cases can be compared.

There has been a long-lasting debate about the role of coding in QDA and *a fortiori* in CAQDAS. Some writers, such as Coffey and Atkinson (1996), suggest that coding is just a matter of data management. It may be part of the analysis process but should not be thought of as a substitute for analysis, which they see as an interpretative process. Others say it is more than that. Tesch (1990) argues that coding is not merely the random division of text into smaller units, but requires skilled perception and artful transformation, and for Richards and Richards (1994: 148) coding is 'a theorising process'. It involves the expedient retrieval of categories, theory building and the pragmatics of breaking down or dissecting one's data into manageable and meaningful analytical units (Bong, 2002: 31). King, in describing his template analysis, goes even further and considers the development of the coding template as a key part of the analysis (2012).

However, whichever view the analyst may take on this issue, the software remains agnostic. For the programs, coding is simply a process of attaching a name or tag to a passage of text, or an area of an image, or a section of a video or audio recording. The software does not care about the analyst's motivation for this act of tagging and it certainly does not understand any interpretation given to it. The intention may be to use the code to represent a deeply thought-through, cross-case, thematic idea, or may just be used to highlight some text as a reminder to come back to it later. A similar distinction is made by Seidel and Kelle (1995) for whom codes are differentiated in two basic ways: they can act as 'objective, transparent representations of facts'; or they are heuristic tools to enable further investigation and discovery. In the latter case, codes are used simply as a way of marking the source without the implications that thematic coding brings with it. Thus the coding of some passage or timeslice can be used simply as a way of highlighting the text or video as an *aide mémoire* (Weaver and Atkinson, 1994). Of course the text can be highlighted in other ways using italics, bold, colour, etc., but using coding to do this is advantageous because it is easy to find all the text highlighted that way by a simple retrieval. Moreover, because it is done electronically it is very easy to delete such coding when there is no further need for it. The point to recognize is that coding in a CAQDAS program can be used in a variety of ways and for a variety of purposes, and researchers are free to use it any way they want, to use several different ways in the same project and to change and delete coding as they wish.

All the CAQDAS programs make a fundamental distinction between the data sources (text, audio, video, image) that can be coded and the list of codes with which they are coded. Usually the data will be shown in a different window or pane on the screen from the pane or window showing the list of codes. This division goes deeper in the software design, though, because there is a range of different things the programs can do with data sources, especially textual data. Apart from coding, one of the most important of these is searching for words or phrases (similar to that found in word processors). Alongside this there is a range of things the programs support that are to do with codes. This includes, at its most basic, retrieval (showing all the text that has been coded at that code), but also includes more complex retrievals or queries that allow the user to retrieve source material to meet a combination of criteria that include coding by a combination of codes and in documents or cases that have certain attributes.

The discussion of coding in qualitative analysis has been dominated by the grounded theory approach. This is an essentially inductive approach that starts from a *tabula rasa*. The idea is to put aside any pre-existing theory or understanding of the data and use coding to allow new ideas, themes and theories to emerge. Following this advice, researchers using CAQDAS would start reading the text (or listening to the audio or watching the video) and code the sections of data as they come to them, interpreting what they see or hear and developing new codes with which to code them. In this process, which is often referred to as open coding, the coding frame, or list of codes, is built up, inductively, by interpreting the data. The software makes it easy to do this both by having simple ways of creating new codes once the text to be coded has been selected and by having clear ways of reusing these codes when further instances are found later in the data. In the software the actual process of coding usually consists of selecting the text to be coded with the mouse cursor and then assigning it to a code. This latter step can be achieved in a number of different ways. Often it is a matter of dragging the selected data (text, image, etc.) to the code name (or vice versa in some software), or choosing a code name and clicking on a code button or, using the right mouse button, the pop-up menu to select a dialog box that enables the user to choose the code(s) to be used. In the past, when using pen and paper transcripts, analysts would indicate the passage they were coding by drawing a line or a bracket in the left or right margin of the page. Several of the programs mimic this by showing a coding bracket or coding stripe with a code name to the left or right of the text being coded. For most users, this gives a very strong visual cue as to what they have coded and how they have coded it,

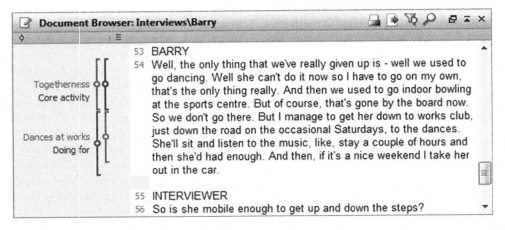

Figure 19.2 Document showing coding brackets in MAXQDA

Source: Original to author

which is both reassuring (see how much I have done!) and analytically useful (e.g. when looking for co-occurring codes or consecutive coding – see Figure 19.2).

But such inductive coding is not the only way to proceed. For a variety of good reasons many research projects already have a set of codes before any analysis is started. Sometimes the analytic approach actually recommends this, as is the case with template analysis. But it is also the case that many research projects are addressing a set of predetermined issues that can constitute an initial, a priori coding scheme. Typically this is because the bidding process has obliged them to do so, and perhaps even specify this in the grant application documents, or because the project is of an applied or policy-based nature where the issues and themes are well established. Another source of a priori coding schemes is what a review of the literature in the field indicates are key issues, themes and interpretations. Such ideas are often represented in the interview schedule used in interview-based research, so these schedules are another source of initial coding ideas. More grounded sources of codes are both the hunches that researchers have because of their familiarity with the field they are researching and the ideas that they have generated or thought of during the field research or the interviews.

Working with the Codes

Although for some writers coding is simply a form of data management and has no analytic implications on its own, many researchers have found that thinking about the codes, writing about them (e.g. writing memos about them) and manipulating them is a central part of the analytic process they go through in order to extract a coherent and novel understanding from their data. The software includes a variety of tools for the manipulation of codes that supports this kind of thinking.

Most programs have ways of attaching definitions and, in many cases, memos to codes. The latter thus supports the grounded theory practice of writing 'analytic memos'. At its simplest this keeps a record of the definition of the codes and any deliberations about their implications and importance. Such analytic thinking along with inspection of the coded data following a retrieval may indicate that there is a need to make some changes to the codes themselves or to the data they code. So the programs have tools to support such changes. Retrieval, in order to inspect all the data coded the same way, is usually just a matter of selecting a code, double clicking on it or activating it using the pop-up menu. This supports two analytic activities. First, it enables a check that the theme identified makes sense, is well evidenced by the sources that have been coded and the coding has been done consistently. It is thus a way of checking the quality of the analysis. Second, the researcher can begin to look for patterns within the data sources coded to the same theme. For example, the results across different cases can be compared to see whether there are differences in what has been coded between groups of cases – perhaps all the older cases talk about this thematic issue in a different way from the younger ones. In this way it is possible to build up a more sophisticated account of what is happening among the cases in the study.

In addition, the programs have ways to rename codes and to combine them or even divide them into two or more new codes (and to separate the data coded at each new code). In the software this is achieved by cutting and pasting the codes or by dragging and dropping them. The data they code move with them so that if one code is merged with another, the data each one codes are merged together so that the merged code codes all the data that both original codes coded.

Coding Crisis

Researchers using an inductive, grounded approach often find they have created a very large number of rather descriptive codes. Gilbert refers to this as 'a coding trap' where endless and often needless codes are assigned to the data (2002: 220). Others refer to the dangers of 'data fragmentation' and 'decontextualisation' that may follow such overcoding (Ereaut, 2002; Welsh, 2002). Having so many codes is not necessarily a bad thing. It may simply reflect the heterogeneity of the data and the complexity of the analysis. However, it can be a barrier to further analytic work and especially to developing a clear understanding and explanation of the data.

To deal with this researchers often find that they move away from the CAQDAS program for a while. One reason why some researchers like to do this is that they are attempting to rethink the analysis. Moving away from the existing project stops it interfering with the rethink. One way to do this is to print out all the codes (possibly with definitions and even short samples of the coded text), cut them up, one code to a piece of paper, and then try to rearrange them. This can help to see connections and arrangements that are currently hidden by the arrangement of the codes. Alternatively such details might be cut and pasted into a spreadsheet with rows for each code and columns for things like definitions and examples and for other thoughts about the code. In both cases, look to rearrange and sort the codes or possibly re-express them, and also look for patterns and categories among them.

However, CAQDAS programs do also offer a range of functions to help with the problem. One common approach is to create a hierarchy or tree of codes. The logic of this is that lower level codes are in some way types, cases or examples of the codes under which they are arranged. Lewins and Silver suggest there are three ways this is done in the software: functional, organizational and cosmetic (2007: 93). MAXQDA, for instance, has a functional hierarchy so that codes can be arranged into top-level codes and subcodes and sub-subcodes. Activating a top-level code (e.g. for a retrieval) automatically activates all its subcodes. NVivo has organizational hierarchies of codes (which the program calls 'nodes') that can be arranged into a tree, but there is no automatic inheritance of the data coded by the subcodes when doing a retrieval. Atlas.ti has no hierarchical arrangement of codes but they can be given names that cosmetically mimic such an arrangement or they can be arranged into families, that is collections of codes. Many programs also have a way of representing the coding in diagrammatic or network forms. This allows not only hierarchical arrangements to be portrayed, but also other kinds of relationships to be represented. Of course this can be done in other software or even with pen and paper, but the great advantage of doing it in the CAQDAS program is that the connection between each code and the data it codes is preserved and usually the researcher can undertake quick retrievals from items in the charts and diagrams. Rearranging the coding scheme and combining codes can be assisted and directed by one very simple activity, which is to use the information about how many times and in how many documents a code has been used. Codes used only once or in one case are candidates for combination with other codes or for rearranging into subcodes in a hierarchy.

Such rearrangements allow a variety of analytic ideas to be captured. For example, Corbin and Strauss (2008) in discussing grounded theory suggest that codes can have dimensions. That is, when participants do something, they may do this in a variety of ways, or when they adopt a particular strategy this may be one of a range of strategies for achieving the same outcomes. Reorganizing codes this way (along with renaming, combining and dividing codes) is also a way in which the analyst may begin to identify key or core themes or categories in the data. These may be higher level codes in the hierarchy or even entirely new codes that combine coding in new ways.

DEVELOPMENT OF THE ANALYSIS: RETRIEVAL AND SEARCHING

CAQDAS programs support two kinds of searching: searching for text, also called lexical searching, and searching for codes. Both can be used as ways of advancing the analytic process. In some programs a query tool is used to do one or both of these searches.

Lexical searching is rather like the word searching facility in a word processor, only more powerful. The CAQDAS program can search for a number of different terms (perhaps synonyms) at the same time, search for word roots (and find all the words with different endings), and some programs can even do 'fuzzy searches', that is a search for words spelt like the terms being used or with similar meanings. Lexical searching can help the analysis in a number of ways. First, it can be used as a way of becoming familiar with the text, for example a search for terms that are connected with the theoretical hunches in the research and then allow inspection of the passages where the terms are found in the original documents. This might produce new ideas or candidates for new codes. Second, such searching can be used as a way of looking for passages similar to those already coded. These will contain terms, words or phrases that might occur elsewhere and indicate similar topic matter. Put these terms and other-related terms into the text search tool to find all the further occurrences. Of course, this will not necessarily find all relevant passages but it can complement a reading of the documents. Third, the approach can be used as a way of checking the validity (see Barbour, Chapter 34, this volume) of the analysis and in particular to check for the occurrence of negative cases – that is, instances that are inconsistent with current explanations in the analysis. These cases may have been missed because they were not expected in the context in which they appear. But if they use the same terms or words as other instances then lexical searching will find them. Of course, the approach is not infallible. Relevant passages of text might just not use the terms being searched for and so will not be found. In the end it is still necessary to read the text and inspect the other sources in a comprehensive way.

Searching for codes, or rather the data they code, is another key way of extending the analysis. At its simplest this amounts to a retrieval on one code. It is quite common, even in published work, for researchers just to summarize the major thematic codes in the report on their study, having done such retrievals. This expresses what they have found and, naturally, tends to be quite descriptive. Sometimes that is interesting, but as Seale notes, all too often what is produced is 'an impressionistic and anecdotal reporting of data' that, at its worst, highlights data that are dramatic but unrepresentative (2001: 657). Qualitative studies can go a lot further and offer accounts of the patterns of the occurrence of such themes and, perhaps, suggest causes or explanations for those patterns. In CAQDAS programs it is searching for coded data and searching in cases having certain attributes (often combined with a search for codes) that support this type of investigation. In this case what is compared in the search is the actual data coded at or linked to the code or attribute. Thus, in the simplest case, in a search for one code *or* another the search will find all the text coded at either code, if any (including that coded at both codes, if any).

Searching (or running queries as many programs refer to the activity) with such combinations of codes is divided into two kinds, Boolean and proximity. Boolean searches combine codes using logical terms like 'and', 'or' and 'not'. Proximity searches rely on the coded data being near, after or perhaps overlapping some other coded data. Commonly used proximity searches are 'followed by' (also referred to as 'sequence' or 'preceding') and 'near' (also referred to as 'co-occurrence'). Boolean searches are most useful in examining hypotheses or ideas about the data and rely on consistent and accurate coding, whereas proximity searches can be used more speculatively and to explore the data, often at an early stage of coding.

For example, in a study of the rehabilitation services available to men and women in prison to help them after their release, it would be interesting to compare what respondents said about different kinds of courses: courses focused on family life such as home finances and parenting, courses focused on work skills such as job application or basic literacy, and courses focused on academic areas such as distance learning qualifications. Assuming there were codes in the project for each course type and the data had been comprehensively coded, then retrievals on each code in turn would be a first step to analysing what prisoners thought about the courses. However, other hypotheses and ideas might be investigated; for example, that there were differences in men's and women's attitudes to the courses or that reactions to the courses varied with the educational background of the prisoners. Assuming the project has variable data on the gender and educational level of prisoners (the cases in the study), then a search for, say, the code 'work skills course' along with the attribute 'case is female' would retrieve what the women said about work skills courses and this could then be compared with what the men said. This could be repeated for other course types and for cases with different educational levels.

Such thinking about the data, their constant comparison and the close inspection of passages, language, events and actions is a key part of moving the analysis forward. In an influential paper Agar (1991) suggested that qualitative researchers using CAQDAS should use the left brain more, by which he meant being able to synthesize and explore the patterns in the data using diagrams, charts, colour and visual representations of their data and their analytic thinking. These suggestions were taken up first by Atlas.ti, which now has a particularly well-integrated modelling function where diagrams can be created, with elements representing codes, quotations (passages of text or parts of images) and memos in the project linked with lines indicating a range of different relationships. Several other programs such as NVivo and MAXQDA now offer similar charting features and have extended them to include representations such as word clouds, cluster analyses and frequency tables. Many researchers find this ability to think visually a liberating way of developing models about their results.

AN EXAMPLE OF CAQDAS USE

The Coping study is a large-scale, cross-country study of the effect of the imprisonment of parents on their children and in particular is concerned with what affects the resilience of the children to deal with the situation (http://coping-project.eu/). The study of children, prisoners and carers in four countries (Germany, Romania, Sweden and the UK) had several stages, the first of which was a large quantitative survey of the families involved. The second stage, on which I worked, involved in-depth interviews with a subsample of the families in the survey – a total of 343 interviews. NVivo was used to support the qualitative analysis of this interview data, all of which were transcribed. As the researchers undertaking the coding were not necessarily those who undertook the specific interviews, interviewers also wrote short reports on each interview that were stored in the NVivo project as memos attached to the interview documents. These reports contained summaries of the key points that the interviewers thought had come out of the interviews, their impressions of the interview (particularly important in the case of some of the younger children) and suggestions for coding and/or analysis.

Initially, an a priori coding framework was used. This was developed in large part from the themes addressed in the interview schedule that had been used and also reflected the researchers' prior familiarity with the literature. Major codes used were: Resilience, Stability, Honesty/disclosure, Family relationships, School, Friendships, Interests/sports/hobbies, Bullying, Achievements, Prisoner–child contact, Significant past events, Services and support, Health and well-being, and Experience of the criminal justice system. Many of these also had subcodes. The researchers ensured that they coded exhaustively, taking particular care to code passages to as many different codes as applied. So typically passages were coded to two, three or more codes.

Teams in the four countries started coding with this framework, but at regular team meetings to discuss the coding, several changes were suggested. Some of these were new inductive coding ideas, often suggested by one researcher. The ideas were discussed and either accepted as new codes to be used by all (which meant that other researchers had to reread their data to incorporate the new code and its coding) or incorporated into existing codes (in which case the data already coded were merged with the respective existing code). Revised coding frames in the NVivo project were shared across all four countries. In some cases the new codes were added as top-level codes in the hierarchy. One particular example of this was the introduction of two new codes to indicate positive experiences, outcomes, feelings, etc., and negative ones. This meant that the researchers could use a Boolean combination of two codes in the query tool to retrieve, say, all the positive outcomes to do with Honesty/disclosure (and contrast it with the negative outcomes of Honesty/disclosure). The first stage of the analysis consisted of taking all the text about key major themes, for example School, and identifying the issues and patterns of experience faced by the children by using a combination of Boolean queries along with simple inspection of the overlapping coding using the coding stripes. It became clear that a positive outcome in school was associated with the school having in place systems for dealing with the bullying and stigma which children of prisoners experienced, and that the ability of children, carers and professionals to express their emotional experiences was a key aspect of this.

A subset of data from the quantitative survey (selected variables and selected cases) was imported into the project and used to create attributes (such as age and gender) for all the cases in the study. Among the attributes introduced was a scale, the Strengths and Difficulties Questionnaire (SDQ) score, that was a measure of the individual's mental health (Goodman, 1997). Honesty and complete disclosure (or at least disclosure appropriate to the age of the child) was identified as a major issue in promoting the resilience of the children. By using these SDQ attributes in Boolean queries it was possible to determine in more detail the kind of disclosure (and what other intervening experiences) promoted the development of good resilience in the children.

ANALYTIC APPROACHES SUPPORTED

Thematic Analysis

There are significant differences in the degree of use of the software by those adopting different approaches to qualitative analysis. Without question, given the central role of coding in most programs, analytic approaches using this, including grounded theory, framework analysis, thematic analysis, IPA, template analysis and qualitative content analysis, are served best by the software. In general, approaches to analysis that are concerned with the development of themes and with analysing data across cases are well supported by the software's functions. Many programs now support a very wide range of types of data to which this coding can be applied. So projects using video, audio, images and documents in the form of pdfs (e.g. projects concerned with analysing the printed media) should all consider using CAQDAS.

Discourse Analysis

Approaches that are more ideographic or are more concerned with how language is used and do not use cross-case, thematic analysis are less well served by the software and its functions. This includes discourse analysis (see Willig, Chapter 23, this volume), conversation analysis (see Toerien, Chapter 22, this volume) and narrative analysis (see Esin et al., Chapter 14, this volume). Some have argued that the software is of little use at all in such analysis. For example, after a detailed investigation, MacMillan (2005) concludes that as there are no universal procedures in discourse analysis, the software cannot offer functions to support any such procedures and is therefore of very limited use in discourse analysis. On the other hand, Silver and Fielding (2008), while admitting the reluctance of discourse analysts to use CAQDAS, suggest that the increased power of search and retrieve tools in the programs means they should look again. They point to the data management functions of the software, 'the storage and accessibility of data and interpretation' (2008: 343) and suggest that the ability of the software to isolate passages of text (e.g. the procedure of specifying quotations in Atlas.ti) and annotate them will be useful for discourse analysts. In addition, they propose that the text searching and data-mining tools that are now built into many programs will be of use in an exploratory way. For example, the Keyword in Context (KWIC) search in programs like MAXQDA enables the researcher to search for terms quickly and see their use in context – just the kind of recontextualization that MacMillan complains CAQDAS programs prohibit.

As I suggested earlier, the software is indifferent as to how it is used. It is the human analyst who has to work out the method of analysis and use the software as a tool for his or her needs. This is shown convincingly by Ryan (2009) in her description of how she used NVivo to assist with her discourse analysis. She used coding and linking to identify and retrieve examples of various kinds of discursive activity such as a range of types of positioning. Having identified appropriate passages she then used the linking of documents, discussions and drawings to produce what she calls 'multimodal pastiches' in a critical discourse analysis of the data. As she concludes, 'the benefits of quick retrieval, efficient linking of data and creating illustrative models, do not preclude contextualised and rigorous qualitative inquiry' (2009: 158).

Mixed Methods

One of the biggest recent developments in CAQDAS programs has been their ability to hold quantitative data about cases and to use these data in retrievals and queries along with the coding. This clearly makes the software of interest to researchers engaged in mixed methods research – a growing approach to research (Tashakkori and Teddlie, 2010; see Morse and Maddox, Chapter 36, this volume). The most common situation here is a project design in which there is a large-scale quantitative survey from which a smaller subsample is selected for further qualitative investigation, for example by interview. In this case the appropriate subset of the data from the survey (selecting only the relevant cases and only the variables required) can be imported into the CAQDAS project and linked with the appropriate case files. Another mixed methods design is where some of the qualitative data are used to create descriptive variables (Bazeley, 2006; Miles and Huberman, 1994: 102–9). In this case the qualitative data are interpreted and applied to cases to classify or even rank them. Such information can then be incorporated into the project as variable or attribute data for further investigations.

Teamworking

Another situation where CAQDAS programs are proving particularly useful is research involving teams of researchers (see Cornish et al., Chapter 6, this volume). These may involve teams of qualitative researchers, perhaps covering different geographical areas, or, as just discussed, mixed methods designs with qualitative and quantitative research being used.

Several programs now support teamworking by allowing, for example, the merging of projects so that the work done by several different researchers can be combined and/or compared. Some programs have server versions that allow multiple users to access the project data at the same time. When there are several researchers, then it is useful to set up different users' accounts and user details for each one so that it is possible to see what work in the project each researcher has done. The work of different researchers can be identified by reference to their registration in the project if the software supports that, or by using specifically titled codes, memos, annotations, etc. This means it is possible to check on the coding work done by different researchers on the same data as a check on inter-coder reliability (Armstrong et al., 1997; Bourdon, 2000; Hesse-Biber and Dupuis, 2000; Morse, 1997; Ryan and Bernard, 2003; Welsh, 2002; see Barbour, Chapter 34, this volume). In some research, often that using broadly defined, a priori coding schemes that are not altered during the analysis, this can be done on all the coding to ensure that it is done in a consistent way throughout the project. In other cases, the comparisons of coding and code construction can be used as a discussion point in teams. By discussing differences in coding and code construction between researchers, the team will be able to come to a more consistent use of the thematic ideas and produce more reliable research, but also, crucially, the team will be able to identify deeper and less obvious differences in the interpretations that may point to richer interpretations of the data.

DEBATES ABOUT CAQDAS

For a long time now there have been researchers who have remained suspicious of CAQDAS. Some feel it alienates them from their data by creating an apparent distance between them and their participants. However, while early versions of the software made it relatively difficult to see the wider context from which retrieved data came, current programs either show retrievals directly in context or make it easy and rapid to display. Others have suggested that the software's design owes too much to grounded theory and that its use will thus enforce certain analytic strategies (Coffey et al., 1996; Lonkila, 1995). But as Kelle (2004) has noted, the coding, indexing, cross-referencing and comparison techniques of the CAQDAS programs are simply different version of the 'age-old' techniques of data management used implicitly in social science research. The same might be said for the often-expressed criticism that software use is associated with a superficial and descriptive analysis of the data. There is nothing in the software that either demands or encourages this. In fact, if anything, the software makes it transparent or more visible when analysis is so limited (Johnston, 2006).

In fact, transparency is one of the advantages of using CAQDAS. Software-assisted analysis means that all the analytic work can be kept organized and together, and with some planning it is possible to keep a good record of how the analysis has developed and (if the methods of identifying researchers discussed above are used) who has done it. Analytic thinking is thus rendered transparent, although, it has to be said, very few research reports or journal papers take advantage of this to discuss the development of their theoretical conclusions and outcomes. Moreover, far from imposing an analytic method, the use of software actually makes the analysis more flexible. Researchers using just paper and pen are reluctant to modify their coding schemes and find it very time consuming to undertake anything other than very simple retrievals based on their coding. Software makes the restructuring and reorganization of the coding scheme possible without starting from scratch (although it may still involve a lot of work) and especially if variable or attribute data are included in the database, all kinds of complex retrievals are relatively quick to perform. The software does not require certain kinds of analysis or particular analytic activities; it is simply a tool that can be used any way the researcher wants.

But, if that is the case, does it mean that CAQDAS use has had no impact on actual analytic methods? While, as I suggested at the start, CAQDAS is not itself an analytic method, I think its use has, and will continue to have, an impact on how analysis is undertaken. First, it has made it easier to deal with large and often mixed (qualitative and quantitative) data sets. For example, market researchers surveyed by Rettie et al. said of CAQDAS 'that it helps when handling a large volume of data, that it helps when handling complex data, that it makes the analysis more scientific and that it makes the analysis more systematic' (2008: 81). Some commentators had worried that in-depth, careful analysis may be lost to a shallower type of exploration of larger and larger data sets, just because it had become more possible. However, as Fielding and Lee (1996) have argued, it is not the availability of CAQDAS packages that has led to large projects but rather that researchers who are undertaking large projects seek out the software. The size of the project, they suggested, is more likely to be determined by methodological stance or by the sponsor. In fact, Fielding and Lee provide some evidence that, on average, data sets and samples in qualitative projects have not been getting larger.

Second, many programs now include a range of functions that offer various quantitative measures and statistics. These include a range of word search (and phrase search) functions and statistics (such as cluster analysis) and tables of coding frequency and amount. While I suspect these are not much used at the moment, they do offer ways of undertaking mixed methods research that goes beyond the simple combination of qualitative and quantitative analysis. Given the growing popularity of mixed methods, the use of these analytic methods seems set to grow.

Third, and I believe this is a pointer to the future, CAQDAS programs are now offering mechanisms for dealing with a wide range of digital data beyond the images, audio and video already mentioned. This includes, for example, geo-tagging data in the project (as done by Atlas.ti), linking the data with an external geographic information system (Fielding, 2012; Fielding and Cisneros-Puebla, 2009), importation of pdfs (long awaited by media researchers) and making accessible a range of web sources such as blogs, discussion groups, Facebook and Twitter (see Marotzki et al., Chapter 31, this volume). As more of our social life happens on the Internet or at least is mediated by it, so there will be a growing need to use appropriate software to investigate it.

RESOURCES

The CAQDAS Networking Project provides practical support, training and information in the use of a range of software programs designed to assist qualitative data analysis and has links to all the manufacturers' websites (caqdas.soc.surrey.ac.uk).

Manufacturers' videos are mainly on YouTube. There are links to these on OnlineQDA (onlineqda.hud.ac.uk).

FURTHER READING

Note that some of the books mentioned here cover older software versions. However, their advice and much of the detailed instructions will still apply to the most recent versions.

The first text is written by two experts from the CAQDAS Networking Project, which covers in detail the three most popular programs, namely NVivo, MAXQDA and Atlas.ti, as well as some discussion of other programs. There is good advice on how to choose the software and how to set up and use it in a project. A new edition, covering the latest versions of the software is due out soon.

The second text focuses on the issues around the ways that a research design will influence and be influenced by the use of software. In particular it contains sage advice about things to consider when first setting up data in a new computer project.

The third text works through all the stages of undertaking an analysis using one program, NVivo. There are detailed instructions on how to use the software at each step of the research.

The last text does the same for Atlas.ti and is particularly strong on the use of the network explorer in the program.

Lewins, Ann and Silver, Christina (2007) *Using Software in Qualitative Research: A Step-by-Step Guide*. London: Sage.

di Gregorio, Silvana and Davidson, Judith (2008) *Qualitative Research Design for Software Users*. Maidenhead: Open University Press/McGraw-Hill.

Bazeley, Pat (2007) *Qualitative Data Analysis with NVivo*. London: Sage.

Friese, Susanne (2013) *Qualitative Data Analysis with ATLAS.ti*. London: Sage.

REFERENCES

Agar, Michael (1991) 'The Right Brain Strikes Back', in Nigel Fielding & Ray M. Lee (eds.), *Using Computers in Qualitative Research*, London: Sage. pp. 181–194.

Armstrong, David, Gosling, Ann, Weinman, Josh and Martaeu, Theresa (1997) 'The place of inter-rater reliability in qualitative research: An empirical study', *Sociology*, 31 (3): 597–606.

Bazeley, Pat (2006) 'The contribution of computer software to integrating qualitative and quantitative data and analyses', *Research in the Schools*, 13 (1): 64–74.

Bong, Sharon A. (2002) 'Debunking myths in qualitative data analysis', *Forum Qualitative Sozialforschung/Forum: Qualitative Social Research*, 3 (2): www.qualitative-research.net/index.php/fqs/article/viewArticle/849 (accessed 8 May 2013).

Bourdon, Sylvain. (2000) 'Inter-coder reliability verification using QSR NUD*IST', Paper presented at the Strategies in Qualitative Research Conference on Issues and Results from Analysis Using QSR NVivo and QSR NUD*IST, The Institute of Education, University of London, London, UK.

Charmaz, Kathy (2006) *Constructing Grounded Theory: A Practical Guide Through Qualitative Analysis*. London: Sage.

Coffey, Amanda and Atkinson, Paul (1996) *Making Sense of Qualitative Data Analysis: Complementary Research Strategies*. London: Sage.

Coffey, Amanda, Holbrook, Beverley and Atkinson, Paul (1996) 'Qualitative data analysis: technologies and representations', *Sociological Research Online*, 1 (1).

Corbin, Juliet M. and Strauss, Anselm L. (2008) *Basics of Qualitative Research: Techniques and Procedures for Developing Grounded Theory*, 3rd edition. Thousand Oaks, CA: Sage.

Denzin, Norman K. and Lincoln, Yvonna S. (2011a) 'Introduction: The discipline and practice of qualitative research', in Norman K. Denzin and Yvonna S. Lincoln (eds), *The SAGE Handbook of Qualitative Research*, 4th edition. Los Angeles: Sage. pp. 1–19.

Denzin, Norman K, and Lincoln, Yvonna S (eds) (2011b) *The SAGE Handbook of Qualitative Research*, 4th edition. Los Angeles: Sage.

Ereaut, Gill. (2002) *Analysis and Interpretation in Qualitative Market Research*, vol. 4. London: Sage.

Evers, Jeanine C., Silver, Christina, Mruck, Katja and Peeters, Bart (2010) 'Introduction to the KWALON experiment: Discussions on qualitative data analysis software by developers and users', *Forum Qualitative Sozialforschung/Forum: Qualitative Social Research*, 12 (1): www.qualitative-research.net/index.php/fqs/article/viewArticle/1637 (accessed 8 May 2013).

Fielding, Nigel G. (2000) 'The shared fate of two innovations in qualitative methodology: The relationship of qualitative software and secondary analysis of archived qualitative data', *Forum Qualitative Sozialforschung/Forum: Qualitative Social Research*, 1 (3): www.qualitative-research.net/index.php/fqs/article/viewArticle/1039 (accessed 8 May 2013).

Fielding, Nigel G. (2012) 'Triangulation and mixed methods designs: Data integration with new research technologies', *Journal of Mixed Methods Research*, 6 (2): 124–36.

Fielding, Nigel G. and Cisneros-Puebla, César A. (2009) 'CAQDAS-GIS convergence: Toward a new integrated mixed method research practice?', *Journal of Mixed Methods Research*, 3 (4): 349–70.

Fielding, Nigel G. and Lee, Raymond M. (eds) (1991) *Using Computers in Qualitative Research*, 2nd edition. Newbury Park, CA: Sage.

Fielding, Nigel G. and Lee, Raymond M. (1996) 'Diffusion of a methodological innovation: CAQDAS in the UK', *Current Sociology*, 44: 242–58.

Gilbert, Linda S. (2002) 'Going the distance: "Closeness" in qualitative data analysis software', *International Journal of Social Research Methodology*, 3 (5): 215–28.

Glaser, Barney G. and Strauss, Anselm L. (1967) *The Discovery of Grounded Theory: Strategies for Qualitative Research*. Chicago: Aldine.

Goodman, Robert (1997) 'The strengths and difficulties questionnaire: A research note', *Journal of Child Psychology and Psychiatry*, 38: 581–6.

Hesse-Biber, Sharlene and Dupuis, Paul (2000) 'Testing hypotheses on qualitative data: The use of HyperRESEARCH computer-assisted software', *Social Science Computer Review*, 18 (3): 320–8.

Johnston, Lynne H. (2006) 'Software and method: Reflections on teaching and using QSR NVivo in doctoral research', *International Journal of Social Research Methodology*, 9 (5): 379–91.

Kelle, Udo (2004) 'Computer-assisted qualitative data analysis', in Clive F. Seale et al. (eds), *Qualitative Research Practice*. London: Sage. pp. 473–89.

King, Nigel (2012) 'Doing template analysis', in Gillian Symon and Catherine Cassell (eds), *Qualitative Organizational Research: Core Methods and Current Challenges*. London: Sage. pp. 426–50.

Lejeune, Christophe (2010) 'From normal business to financial crisis ... and back again. An illustration of the benefits of Cassandre for qualitative analysis', *Forum Qualitative Sozialforschung/Forum: Qualitative Social Research*, 12 (1): www.qualitative-research.net/index.php/fqs/article/viewArticle/1513 (accessed 8 May 2013).

Lewins, Ann and Silver, Christina (2007) *Using Software in Qualitative Research: A Step-by-Step Guide*. London: Sage.

Lonkila, Marrku (1995) 'Grounded theory as an emerging paradigm for computer-assisted qualitative data analysis', in Udo Kelle (ed.), *Computer-aided Qualitative Data Analysis: Theory, Methods and Practice*. London: Sage. pp. 41–51.

MacMillan, Katie (2005) 'More than just coding: Evaluating CAQDAS in a discourse analysis of news texts', *Forum Qualitative Sozialforschung/Forum: Qualitative Social Research*, 6 (3), Art. 25: www.qualitative-research.net/index.php/fqs/article/viewArticle/28 (accessed 8 May 2013).

MacMillan, Katie and Koenig, Thomas (2004) 'The wow factor: Preconceptions and expectations for data analysis software in qualitative research', *Social Science Computer Review*, 22 (2): 179–86.

Mangabeira, Wilma C., Lee, Raymond M. and Fielding, Nigel G. (2004) 'Computers and qualitative research: Adoption, use and representation', *Social Science Computer Review*, 22 (2): 167–78.

Marshall, Helen. (2002) 'Alchemists, housekeepers or artisans? Approaches to computer assisted qualitative data analysis systems', Paper presented at the International Sociological Association, Brisbane, Australia (ISA).

Mayring, Philipp (2000) 'Qualitative content analysis [28 paragraphs]', *Forum Qualitative Sozialforschung/Forum: Qualitative Social Research*, 1 (2): www.qualitative-research.net/index.php/fqs/article/viewArticle/1089 (accessed 8 May 2013).

Miles, Matthew B. and Huberman, A. Michael (1994) *Qualitative Data Analysis: A Sourcebook of New Methods*, 2nd edition. Beverly Hills, CA: Sage.

Morse, Janice M. (1997) '"Perfectly healthy, but dead" – The myth of inter-rater reliability', *Qualitative Health Research*, 7 (4): 445–7.

Rettie, Ruth, Robinson, Helen, Radke, Anja and Ye, Xiajiao (2008) 'CAQDAS: A supplementary tool for qualitative market research', *Qualitative Market Research: An International Journal*, 11 (1): 76–88.

Richards, Lyn and Richards, Thomas J. (1994) 'From filing cabinet to computer', in Alan Bryman and Richard G. Burgess (eds), *Analyzing Qualitative Data*. London: Routledge. pp. 146–72.

Ritchie, Jane and Lewis, Jane (eds) (2003) *Qualitative Research Practice: A Guide for Social Science Students and Researchers*. London: Sage.

Ryan, Gery W. and Bernard, H. Russell (2003) 'Techniques to identify themes', *Field Methods*, 15 (1): 85–109.

Ryan, Mary (2009) 'Making visible the coding process: Using qualitative data software in a post-structural study', *Issues in Educational Research*, 19 (2): 142–61.

Seale, Clive F. (2001) 'Computer-assisted analysis of qualitative interview data', in Jaber F. Gubrium and James A. Holstein (eds), *Handbook of Interview Research: Context and Method*. Thousand Oaks, CA: Sage. pp. 651–70.

Seidel, John V. and Kelle, Udo (1995) 'Different functions of coding in the analysis of textual data', in Uso Kelle (ed.), *Computer-aided Qualitative Data Analysis: Theory, Methods and Practice*. London: Sage. pp. 52–61.

Silver, Christina and Fielding, Nigel (2008) 'Using computer packages in qualitative research', in Carla Willig and Wendy Stainton-Rogers (eds), *The SAGE Handbook of Qualitative Research in Psychology*. Los Angeles: Sage. pp. 334–51.

Smith, Jonathan A., Flowers, Paul and Larkin, Michael (2009) *Interpretative Phenomenological Analysis: Theory, Method and Research*. London: Sage.

Tashakkori, Abbas and Teddlie, Charles (eds) (2010) *The SAGE Handbook of Mixed Methods in Social and Behavioral Research*, 2nd edition. Los Angeles: Sage.

Tesch, Renata (1990) *Qualitative Research – Analysis Types and Software Tools*. London: Falmer Press.

Weaver, Anna and Atkinson, Paul (1994) *Microcomputing and Qualitative Data Analysis*. Aldershot: Avebury.

Welsh, Elaine (2002) 'Dealing with data: Using NVivo in the qualitative data analysis process', *Forum Qualitative Sozialforschung/Forum: Qualitative Social Research*, 3 (2): www.qualitative-research.net/index.php/fqs/article/viewArticle/865 (accessed 8 May 2013).

PART IV

Types of Data and their Analysis

After approaches to the data and their backgrounds were the focus in the earlier parts of the handbook, in Part IV the approach is taken from the other side. In the 12 chapters, specific *types of data* are the starting point for outlining the specific challenges they produce for qualitative data analysis. Data coming from the application of specific methods of data collection such as interviews (see Roulston, Chapter 20), focus groups (see Barbour, Chapter 21) and observation (see Marvasti, Chapter 24) will be discussed, as well those coming from documenting specific practices such as conversations (see Toerien, Chapter 22) or discourses (see Willig, Chapter 23).

Various kinds of documents (see Coffey, Chapter 25), and media such as news media (see Hodgetts and Chamberlain, Chapter 26) or sounds (see Maeder, Chapter 29), are discussed for their challenges to qualitative analysis. A number of chapters are devoted to visual data such as images (see Banks, Chapter 27), films (see Mikos, Chapter 28) and video data (see Knoblauch et al., Chapter 30), complemented by a chapter on virtual data (see Marotzki et al., Chapter 31).

Guideline questions as an orientation for writing chapters were the following: How did these kinds of data become an issue for qualitative data analysis? What are the theoretical and epistemological backgrounds of working with these data? What are specific challenges of working with these data? How can these data be prepared and elaborated for analysis? How does one proceed (maybe step by step?) in analysing these kinds of data? What is a recent example of using these types of data in a qualitative study? What are the limits of using these kinds of data? What are the new developments and perspectives in this context?

Reading the chapters in Part IV should help to answer questions like the following ones for a study and its method(s): What are the specific characteristics of these types of qualitative data? How can data analysis in qualitative research be planned for these specific types of data? How can these data be prepared for analysis – specific needs in transcribing or elaborating the data? What are the steps in applying the selected method for analysing these types of data? What characterizes good (and bad) example(s) of analysing these types of data? What are the main stumbling blocks in analysing these types of data? What are the criteria of good practice in analysing these types of qualitative data? What are the specific ethical issues in analysing these forms of data?

In answering questions like the ones just mentioned, the chapters in this part are meant to contribute to developing data-sensitive ways of analysing empirical material in qualitative studies and thus to further develop the methodological toolkit for qualitative data analysis.

Analysing Interviews

Kathryn Roulston

> ... you have to pay attention to the whole process of how that data is brought forth in your analysis. ... I think it [the interview] just provides such a rich understanding of human nature and human experience. (Melissa Freeman, interview, March 21, 2007)

> I think it's [the interview] probably ... the most powerful qualitative research technique, certainly most used in most studies. (Sharan Merriam, interview, April 3, 2007).

These two researchers' comments about qualitative interviewing reflect common understandings of the ubiquity and value of interview data for understanding the social world. But another qualitative researcher points to the complexity involved in the use of interview data:

> you can't assume that a person's words are a transparent window. They're more like the smoky, veiled, dirty window that you're trying to see through. (Judith Preissle, interview, June 26, 2007)

For researchers to go beyond the metaphor of interviews as transparent windows to each other's 'thinking, and souls and hearts and minds' in ways suggested by Judith Preissle, by what processes are interview data transformed into findings?

Social researchers are held accountable for how research is conducted and the processes of data analysis and representation of findings. Qualitative researchers' studies encompass a broad array of intellectual projects from those that seek to represent peoples' lived experiences, perceptions, opinions, and beliefs, to those that aim to contribute to social justice work, to projects that trouble our understandings of topics. Thus, approaches to the design and conduct of qualitative interviews and data analysis are diverse. In discussing the analysis of interview data, I work from four assumptions about qualitative interviews:

1. Analysis of interview data is theoretically informed.
2. There are many forms of 'qualitative interview.'
3. There is no one right way to analyse qualitative interview data.
4. The criteria for assessment of quality differ in relation to various communities of practice.

I begin by examining theoretical conceptualizations of qualitative interviews. Second, I discuss steps that researchers take in preparing interview data for analysis. Third, I explore theoretical and methodological influences on the analysis of interview data and the practical phases involved in analysis. Fourth, I outline challenges in working with interview data. Next, I discuss quality in relation to the analysis and representation of interview data, before concluding with a review of current issues in relation to analysing interview data.

THEORETICAL BACKDROPS TO WORKING WITH INTERVIEW DATA

Elsewhere I have characterized interview research as encompassing a full spectrum of work (Roulston, 2010a) including:

- neo-positivist inquiries in which researchers assume a unitary human subject in which the interviewer aims to collect factual reports about participants' subjective states, experiences, and observations about social worlds (e.g., Holme and Rangel, 2012);
- romantic portrayals in which researchers account for their subject positions in relation to participants, and work to accomplish genuine rapport with participants in which to elicit confessional reports of lived experiences from which to fashion in-depth descriptions (e.g., Johnson-Bailey, 2001);
- constructionist work that views research interviews as socially situated events in which *how accounts are co-constructed* by interviewers and interviewees may be either the focus of analysis, or of equal importance to topical analyses (e.g., Roulston, 2006);
- dialogic explorations of topics by speakers in which interviewers and interviewees argue, debate, and transform their understandings of topics via research conversations (e.g., Wolgemuth and Donohue, 2006);
- postmodern representations in which parties to interviews are viewed as performing fragmented, non-unitary selves, data from which may be reconstructed and/or deconstructed using creative analytic practices and arts-informed approaches to analysis and representation (e.g., Berbary, 2011); and
- decolonizing methodologies that aim to pursue social justice agendas while avoiding the injustices and objectifications of human subjects that have occurred via scientific inquiries (e.g., Bartlett et al., 2007).

Researchers generate interview data that align with their research purposes. For example, if a researcher aims to generate factual information concerning a research topic, then thought is given to whether or not multiple sources of data might be helpful in order to verify participants' interview reports. If narrative approaches to analysis are intended (see Esin et al., Chapter 14, this volume), researchers conduct interviews in ways that encourage participants to tell stories about the phenomenon of interest. Researchers working from a decolonizing perspective pay deliberate attention to how the design, conduct, and use of interviews contribute to social justice agendas.

Along with a proliferation of approaches to qualitative inquiry that constitutes a backdrop for considering how to analyse interview data, there is also a substantial body of historical literature that informs contemporary interview practice (Lee, 2008; 2011; Platt, 2012). Since neither the terms 'qualitative research' nor 'qualitative interviews' refer to unitary phenomena, in order to analyse interview data, researchers must carefully consider the following questions:

- What are the theoretical assumptions upon which a research project is based?
- What are the analytic possibilities and representational strategies implied?

The strategies used by qualitative researchers to analyse interview data may look quite different depending on answers to these questions. Below I focus on the analytic phase of a study, although data analysis begins in the process of asking questions of interviewees and interpreting answers.

PREPARING DATA FOR ANALYSIS

As argued above, in order to prepare data for analysis, researchers must align the theoretical assumptions about interviewing with the kind of research design and interview methods used to generate data. In cases where the substantive content or topic of talk is the focus of analysis, data are usually transcribed (see Kowal and O'Connell, Chapter 5, this volume) to include words spoken. Researchers commonly punctuate transcriptions in order to transform spoken utterances to a written text. Transcriptions frequently omit utterances that are seen not to contribute to the topics of talk (e.g., 'um,' 'uh,' 'yeah,' and so forth). In my own practice, I have found it helpful to include these sorts of utterances in initial transcriptions. In cases in which data are analysed for topical content, to respect participants who are frequently reluctant to have the stumbles and slips that take place in everyday interaction included in representations of findings, I edit transcripts for reports with an emphasis on readability for particular audiences, letting readers know how transcripts have been edited, for example:

> Excerpts have been edited for clarity. Words such as 'you know,' 'um,' and 'like' have been deleted, and word repetitions have been removed and replaced with …. Words added for clarification are noted by use of square brackets [ ]. Stressed words are noted by underlining (e.g., <u>very</u>).

Consideration might also be given to how particular ways of talking (e.g., dialect) are represented in transcriptions, and whether or not these contribute to unfavorable stereotypes of specific groups (e.g., Oliver et al., 2005). For researchers pursuing social justice agendas, this is an important consideration that needs to be considered prior to gaining informed consent from participants.

Transcription practices that focus only on the topic of talk invariably omit features of talk that have important implications for how talk is understood. During face-to-face communication, speakers make meaning by attending to both the context and delivery of utterances (e.g., jokes, sarcasm). For example, whispered accounts and frequent pauses may indicate that a topic is sensitive; lengthy pauses prior to answering a question could indicate potential disagreement. By indicating features of delivery and attending to the contexts in which interview data are co-constructed by speakers, researchers may enrich representations of findings. Thus, researchers consider what descriptive information needs to be included in the transcription in order to indicate relevant features of how talk transpired. For example, in an interview that I conducted with a first-year resident in a family care residency concerning a training program, the following exchange occurred:

Excerpt 1
IE: Interviewee
IR: Interviewer

IE: So this is the computer that HeartMath is on. [Looking at computer monitor in room in which interview was taking place.]
IR: I believe so, yes. Yes.
IE: ((chuckle)) See, that's news to me. ((laughter))
IR: OK. Yeah, yeah. So, so that's …
IE: Where the hell is this magical HeartMath machine? Oh, here it is, OK. Good to know.

The topical content of this interaction as delivering commentary about having received insufficient information concerning the training program also functions as a complaint. Here, the inclusion of descriptions of non-verbal behaviors (laughter) and action (looking at an object in the interview context) supports this interpretation of the interaction.

Approaches to data analysis such as conversation analysis (CA – see Toerien, Chapter 22, this volume), various forms of discourse analysis (see Willig, Chapter 23, this volume) and some variations of narrative analysis (see Esin et al., Chapter 14, this volume) make use of additional transcription conventions to portray other features of interaction, such as overlapping talk, pauses, re-starts, sighs, and laughter. For example, Excerpt 2 below shows the application of transcription conventions

Table 20.1 Transcription conventions drawn from conversation analysis

Symbol/notation	Action indicated
(.)	A micro-pause between utterances
(3.0)	Pause timed in seconds
sure	Underlined words indicate emphasis
=	Indicates "latched" utterances, or no pause between turns
[	Square brackets indicate overlapping utterances
u::m	Colon indicates elongated utterance
w-	Word begun, but cut off
.hhh	In-breath

drawn from CA (see Table 20.1) applied to interview data.

There are numerous features of talk-in-interaction that may be notated in addition to the conventions listed in Table 20.1 (see, e.g., Liddicoat, 2007).

Excerpt 2 (June 2008, 22:10–24:05)

```
1. IR    u::m what are your beliefs about the use of say mind body spirituality
2.       u:m approaches to (.) uh patient care with underserved and minority
3.       populations
4.       (3.0)
5. IE    .hhh (.) w- I don't I'm not sure what you [mean by this question because I
6. IR                                              [uh huh           uh huh
7. IE    don't like to separate out people=
8. IR    =uh huh uh huh=
```

At line 4, a three-second pause occurs prior to the interviewee's answer, indicating potential disagreement with the assumptions encompassed by the interview question. Disagreement did occur over a lengthy sequence (not shown here), in which the IE provided a lengthy rationale explaining why the premise on which the interview question was based was not relevant to her conceptualization of her clinical practice. By transcribing sequences of interview interaction in detail, it is possible to examine how speakers accomplish mutual understanding, and manage disagreement and interactional problems. Nevertheless, researchers may not have time and funds to transcribe a whole data set in the ways demonstrated in Excerpt 2.

Whereas some research reports include interview excerpts in the language of delivery with translations (e.g., Dorner, 2012), others do not (e.g., Hecht, 1998). Interviews conducted in languages other than the language of presentation involve further decision-making. Researchers let readers know the language in which the interview was conducted, at what point the analysis was undertaken, and consider how translation impacts the overall presentation of findings. For example, in a recent study conducted by Seon Joo Kim (2011), in which she conducted and analysed interviews in her native language, Korean, and then translated findings into English as the language of representation, she grappled with representing meanings via translation. On completion of her study, Kim commented (personal communication, October 23, 2011):

> My concern was how to convey the original meanings of the cultural and contextual nuances of the interviewee's important accounts. I frequently had to make decisions about cultural meanings and what language and words would appropriately convey the translation of Korean into English. As an attempt to clarify my translation, I invited the assistance of a Korean-American graduate student, who speaks more proficient Korean than English. We discussed some Korean words that contain cultural nuances. For example, the word *ya-in*—(*ya* means a wild field and *in* means human/person/people)—denotes the meaning of a free and wild person who has no interest in worldly or political issues. The discussion led us to two possible translations: 'I think I was more of a wild guy than a usual professor' and 'I guess I was something more of the wild and free, than a professor.' The final decision, with support from a native speaker of English, who has had many experiences as a writing tutor, 'I guess I was more of a free-spirited man.' The word *ya-in*, which I interpreted as a representation of the participant's identity, was conveyed in English as 'a free-spirited man.'

Consideration of translations as demonstrated here show some of the decision-making involved in analysing and representing data when interviews have been conducted in a language other than the language of representation.

To sum up, there are no 'right' ways to transcribe and/or translate interview data, but the choices made in the processes of transcription and/or translation allow certain kinds of analytic questions to be asked. Similarly, some researchers choose to transcribe interviews selectively, whereas others transcribe entire interview corpora. In the former case, this might be done in large studies in which analysis focuses on answers to specific interview questions. In smaller studies, my own preference is to transcribe all interviews conducted, even if talk deviates from research topics. I have found it beneficial to ask how such deviations occurred, and to consider the role that these kinds of accounts play in participants' discussion of research topics.

Other transcription practices have been developed for particular forms of data analysis (see Chapter 3 in this volume for further information). For more on translation see Bogusia Temple and Alys Young (2004).

THEORETICAL AND METHODOLOGICAL INFLUENCES ON THE ANALYSIS OF INTERVIEWS

In broad terms, analysing interview data includes the phases of (1) data reduction; (2) data reorganization; and (3) data representation. There is a good deal of variation among researchers as to how these phases are described and enacted. For example, Matthew Miles, Michael Huberman and Johnny Saldaña (1994; 2013) refer to the process of data analysis as including phases of 'data reduction' or 'condensation,' 'data display,' and 'conclusion drawing and verification,' and emphasize the importance of using visual displays to interpret and represent data (e.g., matrices, charts, graphs, networks etc.). Steinar Kvale (2007: 104) describes the process of analysing interviews for topical content as involving 'meaning coding,' 'meaning condensation,' and 'meaning interpretation.' Approaches to research that have substantially influenced how interview data are commonly analysed and interpreted include hermeneutics and phenomenology, and grounded theory, ethnographic, and narrative methods.

Hermeneutic Influences

In that all qualitative research involves interpretation of texts (see Willig, Chapter 10, this volume), qualitative inquiry involves hermeneutics (see Wernet, Chapter 16, and Eberle, Chapter 13, this volume), or 'the understanding of understanding itself' (Soeffner, 2004: 95). Jo Reichertz (2004: 293) argues that an essential feature of sociological hermeneutics is that the researcher 'who wishes to understand his or her observation must also observe his or her own action of "understanding".' Melissa Freeman proposes that hermeneutics has influenced qualitative inquiry in three ways: 'how both participants' experiences and the interpretive process are mediated by language'; the 'conceptualization of the research process as holistic in nature'; and 'the re-conceptualization of research as "cross-cultural dialogue"' (2008: 388).

Of the many approaches to hermeneutic inquiry, Rosemary Anderson's (Wertz et al., 2011: 250–6) intuitive inquiry integrates intuitive and imaginative understandings in the research process. This approach entails five cycles of interpretation, reflecting the influence of Martin Heidegger's hermeneutic circle. Cycles include the researcher's focus on the phenomenon of interest, reflection on his or her "pre-understandings" of the topic, data collection and presentation, and an iterative process in which the researcher considers emergent findings in light of pre-understandings, and contextualizes findings within the relevant literature. Intuitive inquiry highlights the creative leaps entailed in interpreting data, the iterative process involved in reviewing the literature, reflecting on data and making assertions, and reviewing and revising prior understandings of topics. Another approach is that of objective hermeneutics (see Wernet, Chapter 16, this volume), which entails sequential and detailed analysis encompassing examination of contexts, and multiple levels of interpretation. Further information on objective hermeneutics may be found in Reichertz (2004); Stefan Titscher et al. (2000), and Wernet (Chapter 16 in this volume).

Phenomenological Influences

Qualitative research is based on fundamental assumptions of phenomenology (see Eberle, Chapter 13, this volume), in that research examines the life world as experienced by humans. Among numerous approaches to phenomenological thought, Alfred Schutz's systematic account of the phenomenological foundations of the life world (Schutz, 1967; Schutz and Luckmann, 1973; 1989) has been particularly influential, building 'a bridge between phenomenology and social science' through explicating the 'unity of the social world' (Webb, 1992: 290–4).

Yet, while some qualitative research identifies as 'phenomenological' because it studies human experience, 'phenomenological' is sometimes used as a synonym for 'qualitative' – as compared to experimental methods used in natural sciences research. In contrast to this broad application of 'phenomenological' ideas, other research is specifically informed by various strands of phenomenological philosophy (e.g., transcendental or hermeneutic phenomenology).

Approaches to phenomenological analysis outlined by scholars (Moustakas, 1994; Vagle, 2010; van Manen, 1990) indicate commonalities in how findings from analysis of interview data are generated. Phenomenologists place importance on (1) 'bracketing' (Gearing, 2004) assumptions and prior conceptualizations about a phenomenon of interest in order to remain open to what is in the data; (2) spending time reflecting on data and what they mean – moving from parts to the whole to the parts in a recursive fashion (i.e., the hermeneutic circle); (3) reducing data in order to discern the 'horizons' of meaning, 'invariant' properties, or 'meaning units' of a particular lived experience (e.g., trauma, grief, etc.); and (4) constructing findings through writing and rewriting.

It is possible to see how phenomenological research has informed general practices used in analysing qualitative interviews through identification of one's prior assumptions about topics, attention to ongoing reflection, and engagement in an iterative process of sense-making that involves writing, rewriting, and revisiting data. For more information on phenomenology in qualitative analysis, see Eberle (Chapter 13, this volume).

Grounded Theory Influences

Barney Glaser and Anselm Strauss's book, *The Discovery of Grounded Theory* (1967), has been enormously influential in how qualitative researchers analyse interview data. Interestingly, Glaser and Strauss did not specifically refer to the analysis of interview data (1967: 17–18), commenting: 'We believe that *each form of data is useful for both verification and generation of theory*, whatever the primacy of emphasis' (emphasis in original). In practice, many of the analytic strategies described by Glaser and Strauss have been taken up by qualitative researchers, whether or not the research purpose involves the development of grounded theory. In particular, the description of the 'constant comparative' method has been widely used by researchers to analyse interviews, documents, and field notes from participant observations (e.g., Lofland et al., 2006). In the constant comparative method researchers begin by open coding of transcripts. This is a process of associating a conceptual label with a section of transcript that conveys an idea about the topical features of the talk. Many grounded theorists have elaborated on the processes that researchers use to code and interpret interview transcripts. Memo writing (Lempert, 2007) is a process of writing about initial code labels that is used to conceptualize the 'properties' and 'dimensions' of codes and aid in theoretical development. As Juliet Corbin notes (Corbin and Strauss, 2008), some researchers end their analysis at 'thematic descriptions,' while others go on to integrate the concepts into an overarching 'core category' or 'theory' (see also Bryant and Charmaz, 2007, and Thornberg and Charmaz, Chapter 11, this volume).

Ethnographic Influences

While foregrounding the value of observing participants in specific contexts and recording field notes, ethnographers also make use of informal and formal interviews (Lofland et al., 2006; Spradley, 1979). Because of the anthropological influences in ethnographic work that focus on describing and interpreting culture, the generation and analysis of ethnographic interview data take place in conjunction with the collection and/or generation and analysis of other data (e.g., field notes, documents, and artifacts). However, the ethnographic focus on uncovering native language use is an influence often found in interview research that is not ethnographic.

An interest in how language is used by participants is apparent in 'institutional ethnography' – a method developed by Dorothy Smith that combines an interest in developing a 'sociology for women' that examines women's everyday experiences through ethnographic research, as well as how women's experiences are organized within 'ruling relations' (DeVault and Gross, 2007; Smith, 2005). Smith sees the interview as a 'moment in a social relation, a sequence of coordinated action that organizes the dialogue between informant and researcher as a step or moment in a sequence that hooks back into the institutions of academic, professional, and related specialized discourses' (2005: 136). Thus, while ethnographers might examine cultures and contexts, there is also an emphasis on examining how people use language in the setting of interest and in dialogue with the researcher (see Gubrium and Holstein, Chapter 3, this volume).

Narrative Influences

Research interviews involve both participants telling stories and researchers representing the stories of participants. Narrative inquiry (see Esin et al., Chapter 14, this volume), as a family of approaches, includes research that focuses specifically on stories. Donald Polkinghorne (1995) has conceptualized narrative inquiry as involving either 'paradigmatic' or 'narrative' cognition. In paradigmatic work, researchers analyse narrative data, including interviews, in order to generate themes that represent patterns observable across a data set. The constant comparative approach described earlier is an example of a paradigmatic approach to the analysis of narrative data.

Researchers also compare the structural features of talk. For example, one well-known approach draws on a model of narrative storytelling developed by William Labov and Joshua Waletzky (1997). Labov examined the structural features of stories collected from people in the United States using prompts about near-death experiences, and developed a model for the organization of clauses in these stories. Analysis of structural features of talk showed that stories included similar elements: (1) an *Orientation* in which details of who, when, where, and what are mentioned; (2) a *Complication*, in which a complicating event is described; (3) an *Evaluation*, in which the narrator assesses his or her response to the event; (4) the *Resolution* in which the question of 'What happened?' is answered; and (5) a *Coda* in which the story is concluded. A key element to locate in stories is that of the 'evaluation' – since these clauses provide clues as to what the narrator took the event to mean and what the speaker wants the audience to understand as the point of the story. Although this structural approach to examining narratives has been critiqued as overlooking non-Western modes of storytelling, the narrative approach of examining structural aspects of participants' stories is useful. This is because, whether or not interviewers seek stories, interviewees frequently frame their answers as stories. For example, in an interview that I conducted, I formulated the interviewee's talk in a way that misrepresented the participant's views. At the time, instead of immediately disagreeing, he inserted a lengthy story marked by an evaluation clause that functioned to disagree with my formulation: 'and the original point I was making' (Roulston, 2001: 296).

There are numerous other ways to analyse interview data from a narrative approach (see Esin et al., Chapter 14, this volume). Two common ways in which narrative approaches have informed the analysis of interview data include: (1) the examination of storytelling by participants (e.g., structural and performative features of storytelling); and (2) the use of the idea of 'narrative cognition' in representing findings in terms of participants' unique stories, which may or may not be used in conjunction with thematic presentations of data.

Among numerous theoretical and methodological influences, analytic approaches to interview data have been influenced by hermeneutics, phenomenology, grounded theory, ethnography, and narrative inquiry, and there is overlap between procedures used to analyse interview data. Across these various approaches three phases in the analytic process are discernible: (1) data reduction or 'meaning condensation' (Kvale, 2007); (2) data reorganization; and (3) interpretation and representation. In the next section, I review processes entailed in each of these phases.

ANALYSING AND REPRESENTING INTERVIEW DATA: PRACTICAL STEPS

Reducing Data to Locate and Examine Phenomena of Interest

One challenge faced by qualitative researchers is that of reducing data sets in order to interpret and distill the 'essence' or meaning of participants' descriptions. In grounded theory approaches, gaining an understanding of the main ideas is accomplished by applying codes to transcripts that are opened up conceptually via extensive reflection and memo writing. In phenomenological traditions, researchers reduce data by eliminating repetitive statements and data irrelevant to the phenomenon being examined. For narrative researchers aiming to represent participants' stories, interviews are edited to represent the central ideas discussed. Similarly, the data reduction phase for an ethnographer is guided by the purpose of research – if a research purpose is to examine culture, coding might focus on native language use or identifying participants' interpretations of symbolic features of a particular setting. This search for the phenomenon of interest is theoretically driven – that is, theoretical perspectives and research purposes govern what analysts look for in data. Yet, qualitative analysis emphasizes the importance of remaining open to what is in the data, rather than simply applying concepts imported from the literature.

Reorganizing, Classifying, and Categorizing Data

In this phase of analysis researchers generate assertions about topics by reassembling and reorganizing the data, codes, categories, or stories. Findings might be assembled through sorting and comparing data, codes, and categories, and considering the links between these via memo writing. By developing the codes through an iterative process involving reading, focused coding, reflection, writing, and rereading, researchers make connections between ideas, collapse codes into larger ideas (variously called themes or categories), and begin to develop assertions concerning the phenomenon of interest. Although researchers may vary in their theoretical approach, what is common in this phase of analysis is that researchers discern the key concepts concerning the topic of study, reflect on prior understandings and initial assertions, and search iteratively through the data set to check, recheck, and revise preliminary ideas about the topic of study. An important step in this phase is to search for data that might discount preliminary assertions. Some researchers make use of tables, diagrams, and charts to represent initial understandings and developing interpretations (e.g., Miles and Huberman, 1994; Miles, Huberman & Saldaña, 2014; Spradley, 1979).

Interpreting and Writing up Findings

In this phase, researchers consider assertions and propositions in light of prior research and theory in order to develop arguments. Researchers develop stories that convey the main ideas developed in data analysis and present data excerpts or stories to support assertions (see Denzin, Chapter 39, this volume). Qualitative researchers use a wide range of methods to represent data, including themes supported by direct quotations from interview transcripts; descriptions and models of processes that may include diagrams and visual representations of key concepts; and narratives that represent participants' experiences and perspectives. Researchers commonly construct stories as first- or third-person accounts. A growing body of work draws on the arts to use poetry, fiction, theater, readers' theater and performance texts to represent findings to audiences (Cahnmann-Taylor and Siegesmund, 2008; Kouritzin et al., 2009).

The generation of themes via coding (see Thornberg and Charmaz, Chapter 11, this volume) and categorization (see Schreier, Chapter 12, this volume) is arguably the most common analytic approach taken by qualitative researchers using interviews (e.g., Kvale and Brinkmann, 2009; Rubin and Rubin, 2005). Coding practices described in the methodological literature (e.g., Bernard and Ryan, 2010; Braun and Clarke, 2006; Miles and Huberman, 1994; Saldaña, 2013) draw extensively on strategies detailed by Glaser and Strauss (1967), while making few distinctions between interview data and other data sources (e.g., documentary data, memoirs, field notes of observations).

In recent years, post-structural researchers have questioned the reliance on coding and categorization to interpret qualitative data. Elizabeth St. Pierre argues that coding data is a way of sorting and counting data, but it is not necessarily 'analysis,' and may not produce significant or theorized stories (2011: 621–2). St. Pierre deconstructs the concepts of data, data collection, and data analysis, arguing for analysis through writing and thinking. Rather than generating themes via coding and categorization of data, researchers working from decolonizing and post-structural perspectives question if this is indeed possible. There are a growing number of publications that explore ways to analyse data and represent findings to create new meanings and do research differently (e.g., Bhattacharya, 2009; Jackson and Mazzei, 2012; Kaufmann, 2011).

CHALLENGES OF ANALYSING INTERVIEW DATA

In my research and teaching, I have noticed stumbling blocks that routinely occur in relation to analysing interview data. These include managing data, forcing data into preconceived categories, discovering methodological problems in data generation, and anxiety about using the 'right' method 'correctly.' I discuss these in turn.

Data Management and Reduction

Managing large amounts of data and locating, naming, and retrieving files that include hard copies, electronic copies, and audio files presents challenges. To keep track of data, researchers need to systematically label, store, and password-protect data files. Increasingly, this means keeping track of electronic, rather than hard, copies of transcripts in ways that allow for rapid retrieval. Transcripts should include the date and details of the interview and interview context and pseudonyms used to represent participants. Researchers need to keep an inventory of information about interviews (e.g., an interview code to identify transcripts, name of transcriber, date of interview and transcription, whether or not a copy of the transcript has been shared with the participant, progress concerning data analysis, and so forth). Backup copies should be made of all files. Computer-Assisted Qualitative Data Analysis Software (CAQDAS) packages may assist with storing, locating, analysing, and retrieving data and information about a project (see Gibbs, Chapter 19, this volume).

A related challenge is that of reducing or condensing data. Given that one hour-long interview may generate a 20-page transcript, interview projects may generate hundreds of pages of data. An analyst's task is to reduce and interpret the data in order to present findings in articles, books, and dissertations that are limited in size. Researchers begin by selecting and applying an approach to data analysis that fits with their assumptions about knowledge production. During the reduction and/or coding phase, the analyst must become well acquainted with the data set as a whole in order to select appropriate examples to support assertions.

Forcing Data to Fit Preconceived Hypotheses

Many methodologists warn against the dangers of 'forcing data' to fit preconceived hypotheses. This problem is one of sifting through data sets to locate data to support one's preconceptions about findings. As analysts develop interpretations of data, a useful strategy is to review the data to search for negative cases and discrepant data that would disprove or complicate findings. The phenomenological concept of 'bracketing' one's assumptions is also helpful. By identifying one's preconceptions throughout a project, researchers become sensitive to how prior understandings inform analysis.

Much has been written about reflexivity in research (Finlay and Gough, 2003; see May and Perry, Chapter 8, this volume), and how researchers can identify their subjectivities in relation to their projects and project participants, although feminist researchers have warned against the use of subjectivity statements as an indicator of reflexivity (e.g., Harding, 2007). A reflexive research practice does not end with the conclusion of interviews, but continues throughout the analysis process and writing up of research findings. Novice researchers might also benefit from participating in data analysis groups in which researchers with different levels of expertise discuss analytic decision-making and data interpretation.

Methodological Issues

Periodically, I have heard researchers say that they conducted interviews that could not be used, and accounts of interview failures may be found in the methodological literature. If researchers are focused on generating in-depth stories about specific lived experiences, and have failed to generate data that include these kinds of descriptions, then methodological analysis of what went awry is helpful. Thus, any interview, whether it has been poorly conducted or involved a reluctant participant, provides data about something – although data generated may not relate to the researcher's initial analytic focus.

For example, in a project in which I served as a research assistant some years ago, the following exchange occurred between me and two indigenous youths who were taking part in a collaborative project involving a university and a school system in Australia.

Excerpt 3
IR: Interviewer
S1: Student 1
S2: Student 2

IR: I just wondered firstly what are some of the things that you enjoyed about the whole project that you've been involved in since you've been coming over here.
S1: I dunno.
IR: Anything?
S1: You get to look at the pictures on the internet and make your own web pages. It's fun.
IR: Yep.
S2: The same.

In this interaction, the data generated are topically thin, and rather than providing an opinion, S2 merely agrees with S1. This interaction was characteristic of this interview as a whole, suggesting that the methods for generating data were inadequate. In-depth methodological analysis of these sorts of interactions during the data collection phase of this project could have been enormously helpful in guiding the development of the research design. For example, collaborative approaches in which young people were engaged as researchers might have been used, or interviews by the researcher or the indigenous liaison for the project might have focused on students talking about the products that they had designed in the project rather than answering questions. Alas, this did not occur, which speaks to the importance of ongoing analysis during the life of a project.

Other approaches to dealing with methodological issues that routinely occur in qualitative research studies include conducting pilot interviews in which interview methods are explored to assess the potential of interview data to respond to research questions, and being flexible within the overall life of a project to amend processes to deal with issues identified in data analysis (Roulston, 2011).

Using the 'Right' Method of Analysis in the 'Correct' Way

Novice researchers often experience anxiety about whether they have applied an analytic procedure 'correctly.' For researchers experimenting with an approach for the first time, it is useful to reflect that all researchers began with a first project. Researchers learn from practice, reviewing the substantive and theoretical literature, and reading others' accounts of practice. For qualitative analysts, analysis of interview data is never really complete, since data may always be subject to analysis from a different theoretical perspective, or may focus on different aspects. Thus any analysis is a partial representation of the data set. This partiality and ambiguity may be experienced as deeply disturbing by researchers pursuing a definitive conclusion. Yet, these facets of qualitative analysis may also be liberating – in that no single interpretation is taken as representing an all-encompassing portrayal of a phenomenon. Since researchers must withstand the scrutiny of others in order to have their work deemed credible, the actions of continued reflection, demonstrations of a reflexive practice, and participation in collaborative data analysis with other researchers are practical ways to 'keep going' (Wolcott, 2009), in an effort to 'not get it all wrong' (Wolcott, 1994: 347).

JUDGING QUALITY

Given paradigm proliferation (Lather, 2006), there are no generic ways to judge the quality (see Barbour, Chapter 34, this volume) of the analysis and interpretation (see Willig, Chapter 10, this volume) of interview data (Freeman et al., 2007). Rather, as discussed earlier, the criteria for assessing quality must be considered in relation to various theoretical conceptualizations of interviews (Roulston, 2010b) and disciplinary conventions. To use Stephen Toulmin's (Toulmin et al., 1984) terminology concerning the construction of arguments, in assessing the quality of research reports, readers examine *claims* or assertions, *grounds* or foundations upon which an argument is constructed, *warrants* for assertions, and *backing* for the argument presented. As Toulmin argues, the specifics of how arguments are constructed differ both in and across fields. Therefore, researchers must attend to the conventions of various communities of practice, and craft research reports for specific audiences.

In recent years, there has been a resurgence in criticism of interview research that adds to well-worn critiques associated with positivist conceptions of research (e.g., difficulties in comparing interview data because of interviewer bias; reliability of interviewees' accounts as accurate portrayals of events). For example, Jonathan Potter and Alexa Hepburn (2012: 556) discuss eight challenges of interview research in terms of two key ideas. The first of these attends to *how interview studies are reported* and the second relates to *what kinds of assertions* might be made from interview data in relation to the social world. Potter and Hepburn's interests in discursive psychology and conversation analysis merge in these recommendations through their attention to detail in relation to adequate reporting of interview contexts and interview interaction, and how topics of research interest in the social sciences are talked into being by speakers. Specifically, Potter and Hepburn (2012: 556) argue that researchers should provide more detailed information concerning the interview context and the co-construction of interview data:

1. Improving the transparency of the interview set-up.
2. More fully displaying the active role of the interviewer.
3. Using representational forms that show the interactional production of interviews.
4. Tying analytic observations to specific interview elements.

The second set of challenges described by Potter and Hepburn focuses specifically on the analysis of interview data. They argue that interview researchers must attend to:

1. How interviews are flooded with social science categories, assumptions, and research agendas.
2. The varying footing of interviewer and interviewee.
3. The orientations to stake and interest on the part of the interviewer and interviewee.
4. The way cognitive, individualist assumptions about human actors are presupposed.

Although these challenges to interview research are significant, recent methodological work indicates that interview researchers have made considerable progress in generating rich and complex understandings of interview data in ways that do take into account interview contexts and the researcher's work in the generation of data. This work is theoretically diverse and demonstrates new directions in the analysis and representation of interview data (Mallozzi, 2009; Miller, 2011; Talmy, 2010; Watson, 2006).

CONCLUSIONS

Current work concerning the analysis of interview data suggests four trends to consider:

1. The idea that interview data are co-constructed (rather than collected) has had considerable impact in the field of qualitative inquiry. Researchers are called upon to account for the contexts in which interview data are generated in relation to specific interviewers, as well as how the co-constructed nature of interview data might be represented in reports.
2. Paradigm proliferation has resulted in numerous innovations in the theorization of research interviews, interview strategies, and methods of analysis and representation. Researchers must apply interviews as a research method in theoretically coherent ways, as well as ensuring that analyses and representation are rigorous and meaningful to the audiences to whom they speak.
3. Technological innovation continues apace, and researchers who take advantage of new modes of communication must account for the prompts that form the focus of questions and answers in analyses. The foci of analyses of new types of interviews need not be constrained to attending to verbal discussions of beliefs, opinions, recollected events, and experiences, but might also entail attending to how think-aloud protocols are activated by interviewers and interviewees, how dialogues around objects, images, and artifacts take place, and how text-based conversations generated via computer-mediated communication unfold.
4. Higher education and research in the twenty-first century involves research that crosses borders. Cross-cultural researchers need to account for the implications of decision-making concerning translation in the analytic process.

The popularity of interviews to generate information about the social world is unlikely to abate. Therefore, researchers analysing interview data need to be aware of current methodological work on interviewing, rather than relying on everyday understandings of how interviews work. Interview analysis is complex work informed by researchers in multiple disciplines working from diverse perspectives. Although there is no right way to analyse interviews, researchers can forward qualitative research by doing informed, thorough, and rigorous analysis situated in particular theoretical traditions.

ACKNOWLEDGEMENTS

Thanks to Kathleen deMarrais, Seon Joo Kim, the anonymous reviewers, and Uwe Flick, who provided comments on earlier versions of this manuscript.

FURTHER READING

Faircloth, Christopher A. (2012) "After the interview: What is left at the end", in Jaber F. Gubrium et al. (eds.), *The SAGE Handbook of Interview Research: The Complexity of the Craft*, 2nd edition. Los Angeles: Sage. pp. 269–77 (1st edition, 2002).
Rapley, Tim (2012) "The (extra)ordinary practices of qualitative interviewing", in Jaber F. Gubrium et al. (eds.), *The SAGE Handbook of Interview Research: The Complexity of the Craft*, 2nd edition. Los Angeles: Sage. pp. 541–54 (1st edition, 2002).
Talmy, Stephen and Richards, Keith (eds.) (2010) *Qualitative Interview Analysis in Applied Linguistics: Discursive perspectives*. Special Issue of *Applied Linguistics*, 32 (1).

REFERENCES

Bartlett, Judith G., Iwasaki, Yoshitaka, Gottlieb, Benjamin, Hall, Darlene, and Mannell, Roger (2007) "Framework for Aboriginal-guided decolonizing research involving Métis and First Nations persons with diabetes," *Social Science & Medicine*, 65 (11): 2371–82.

Berbary, Lisbeth A. (2011) "Poststructural writerly representation: Screenplay as creative analytic practice," *Qualitative Inquiry*, 17 (2): 186–96.

Bernard, H. Russell and Ryan, Gerry W. (2010) *Analyzing Qualitative Data: Systematic Approaches*. Thousand Oaks, CA: Sage.

Bhattacharya, Kakali (2009) "Negotiating shuttling between transnational experiences: A de/colonizing approach to performance ethnography," *Qualitative Inquiry*, 15 (6): 1061–83.

Braun, Virginia and Clarke, Victoria (2006) "Using thematic analysis in psychology," *Qualitative Research in Psychology*, 3 (2): 77–101.

Bryant, Antony and Charmaz, Kathy (eds.) (2007) *The Sage Handbook of Grounded Theory*. Thousand Oaks, CA: Sage.

Cahnmann-Taylor, Melisa and Siegesmund, Richard (eds.) (2008) *Arts-based Research in Education: Foundations for Practice*. New York: Routledge.

Corbin, Juliet and Strauss, Anselm (2008) *Basics of Qualitative Research*, 3rd edition. Los Angeles: Sage (1st edition, 1990).

DeVault, Marjorie L. and Gross, Glenda (2007) "Feminist interviewing: Experience, talk, and knowledge," in Sharlene Nagy Hesse-Biber (ed.), *Handbook of Feminist Research: Theory and Praxis*. Thousand Oaks, CA: Sage. pp. 173–98.

Dorner, Lisa M. (2012) "The life course and sensemaking: Immigrant families' journeys toward understanding educational policies and choosing bilingual programs," *American Educational Research Journal*, 49 (3): 461–86.

Finlay, Linda and Gough, Brendan (eds.) (2003) *Reflexivity: A Practical Guide for Researchers in Health and Social Sciences*. Oxford: Blackwell Science.

Freeman, Melissa (2008) "Hermeneutics," in Lisa M. Given (ed.), *The SAGE Encyclopedia of Qualitative Research Methods*, vol.1. Los Angeles: Sage. pp. 385–88.

Freeman, Melissa, deMarrais, Kathleen, Preissle, Judith, Roulston, Kathryn, and St. Pierre, Elizabeth A. (2007) "Standards of evidence in qualitative research: An incitement to discourse," *Educational Researcher*, 36 (1): 25–32.

Gearing, Robin Edward (2004) "Bracketing in research: A typology," *Qualitative Health Research*, 14 (10): 1429–52.

Glaser, Barney G. and Strauss, Anselm L. (1967), *The Discovery of Grounded Theory: Strategies for Qualitative Research*. New York: Aldine de Gruyter.

Harding, Sandra (2007) "Feminist standpoints," in Sharlene Nagy Hesse-Biber (ed.), *Handbook of Feminist Research: Theory and Praxis*. Thousand Oaks, CA: Sage. pp. 45–70.

Hecht, Tobias (1998) *At Home in the Street: Street Children of Northeast Brazil*. Cambridge: Cambridge University Press.

Holme, Jennifer Jellison and Rangel, Virginia Snodgrass (2012) "Putting school reform in its place: Social geography, organizational social capital, and school performance," *American Educational Research Journal*, 49 (2): 257–83.

Jackson, Alecia Y. and Mazzei, Lisa A. (2012) *Thinking with Theory in Qualitative Research: Viewing Data Across Multiple Perspectives*. New York: Routledge.

Johnson-Bailey, Juanita (2001) *Sistahs in College: Making a Way Out of No Way*. Malabar, FL: Krieger.

Kaufmann, Jodi (2011) "Poststructural analysis: Analyzing empirical matter for new meanings," *Qualitative Inquiry*, 17 (2): 148–54.

Kim, Seon Joo (2011) "Voices in career transitions: A qualitative study to understand Korean adults' career construction in post-retirement," PhD dissertation, University of Georgia.

Kouritzin, Sandra G., Piquemal, Nathalie A., and Norman, Renee (eds.) (2009) *Qualitative Research: Challenging the Orthodoxies in Standard Academic Discourse(s)*. New York: Routledge.

Kvale, Steinar (2007). *Doing Interviews*. Thousand Oaks, CA: Sage.

Kvale, Steinar and Brinkmann, Svend (2009) *InterViews: Learning the Craft of Qualitative Research Interviewing*, 2nd edition. Thousand Oaks, CA: Sage (1st edition, 1996).

Labov, William and Waletzky, Joshua (1997) "Narrative analysis: Oral versions of personal experience," *Journal of Narrative and Life History*, 7 (1–4): 3–38.

Lather, Patti A. (2006) "Paradigm proliferation as a good thing to think with: Teaching research in education as a wild profusion," *International Journal of Qualitative Studies in Education*, 19 (1): 35–57.

Lee, Raymond (2008) "David Riesman and the sociology of the interview," *Sociological Quarterly*, 49 (2): 285–307.

Lee, Raymond (2011) "'The most important technique …': Carl Rogers, Hawthorne, and the rise and fall of nondirective interviewing in sociology," *Journal of the History of the Behavioral Sciences*, 47 (2): 123–46.

Lempert, Lora Bex (2007) "Asking questions of the data: Memo writing in the grounded theory tradition," in Antony Bryant and Kathy Charmaz (eds.),

The Sage Handbook of Grounded Theory. Los Angeles: Sage. pp. 245–64.

Liddicoat, Anthony J. (2007) An Introduction to Conversation Analysis. London: Continuum.

Lofland, John, Lofland, Lynn, Snow, David A., and Anderson, Leon (2006) Analyzing Social Settings: A Guide to Qualitative Observation and Analysis, 4th edition. Belmont, CA: Thomson, Wadsworth.

Mallozzi, Christine A. (2009) "Voicing the interview: A researcher's exploration on a platform of empathy," Qualitative Inquiry, 15 (6): 1042–60.

Miles, Matthew B. and Huberman, A. Michael (1994) Qualitative Data Analysis: An Expanded Sourcebook, 2nd edition. Thousand Oaks, CA: Sage.

Miles, Matthew B., Huberman, A. Michael, and Saldaña, Johnny (2013) Qualitative Data Analysis: A Methods Sourcebook, 3rd edition. Los Angeles, CA: Sage.

Miller, Elizabeth R. (2011) "Indeterminacy and interview research: Co-constructing ambiguity and clarity in interviews with an adult immigrant learner of English," Applied Linguistics, 32 (1): 43–59.

Moustakas, Clark (1994) Phenomenological Research Methods. Thousand Oaks, CA: Sage.

Oliver, Daniel G., Serovich, Julianne M., and Mason, Tina L. (2005) "Constraints and opportunities with interview transcription: Towards reflection in qualitative research," Social Forces, 84 (2): 1273–89.

Platt, Jennifer (2012) "The history of the interview", in Jaber F. Gubrium et al. (eds.), The SAGE Handbook of Interview Research: The Complexity of the Craft, 2nd edition. Los Angeles: Sage. pp. 9–26 (1st edition, 2002).

Polkinghorne, Donald E. (1995) "Narrative configuration in qualitative analysis," International Journal of Qualitative Studies in Education, 8 (1): 5–23.

Potter, Jonathan and Hepburn, Alexa (2012) "Eight challenges for interview researchers," in Jaber F. Gubrium et al. (eds.), The SAGE Handbook of Interview Research: The Complexity of the Craft, 2nd edition. Los Angeles: Sage. pp. 555–70 (1st edition, 2002).

Reichertz, Jo (2004) "Objective hermeneutics and hermeneutic sociology of knowledge," in Uwe Flick et al. (eds.), A Companion to Qualitative Research. London: Sage. pp. 290–5.

Roulston, Kathryn (2001), "Data analysis and 'theorizing as ideology'," Qualitative Research, 1 (3): L279–302.

Roulston, Kathryn (2006) "Close encounters of the 'CA' kind: A review of literature analysing talk in research interviews," Qualitative Research, 6 (4), 515–34.

Roulston, Kathryn (2010a) Reflective Interviewing: A Guide to Theory and Practice. London: Sage.

Roulston, Kathryn (2010b) "Considering quality in qualitative interviewing," Qualitative Research, 10 (2): 199–228.

Roulston, Kathryn (2011) "Dealing with challenges in doing interview research," International Journal of Qualitative Methods, 10 (4): http://ejournals.library.ualberta.ca/index.php/IJQM/article/view/8305/9359 (accessed May 8, 2013).

Rubin, Herbert J. and Rubin, Irene S. (2005) Qualitative Interviewing: The Art of Hearing Data, 2nd edition. Thousand Oaks, CA: Sage.

Saldaña, Johnny (2013) The Coding Manual for Qualitative Researchers, 2nd edition. Los Angeles: Sage.

Schutz, Alfred (1967) The Phenomenology of the Social World, trans. George Walsh and Frederick Lehnert. Evanston, IL: Northwestern University Press.

Schutz, Alfred and Luckmann, Thomas (1973) The Structures of the Life-World, trans. Richard M. Zaner and H. Tristram Engelhardt Jr., vol. 1. Evanston, IL: Northwestern University Press.

Schutz, Alfred and Luckmann, Thomas (1989) The Structures of the Life-World, trans. Richard M. Zaner and David J. Parent, vol. 2. Evanston, IL: Northwestern University Press.

Smith, Dorothy E. (2005) Institutional Ethnography: A Sociology for People. Lanham, MD: AltaMira Press.

Soeffner, Hans-Georg (2004) "Social scientific hermeneutics," in Uwe Flick et al. (eds.), A Companion to Qualitative Research. London: Sage. pp. 95–100.

Spradley, James (1979) The Ethnographic Interview. Belmont, CA: Wadsworth.

St. Pierre, Elizabeth Adams (2011) "Post qualitative research: The critique and the coming after," in Norman K. Denzin and Yvonna S. Lincoln (eds.), The SAGE Handbook of Qualitative Research, 4th edition. Los Angeles: Sage. pp. 611–25.

Talmy, Steven (2010) "Qualitative interviews in applied linguistics: From research instrument to social practice," Annual Review of Applied Linguistics, 30: 128–48.

Temple, Bogusia and Young, Alys (2004) "Qualitative research and translation dilemmas," Qualitative Research, 4 (2): 161–78.

Titscher, Stefan, Meyer, Michael, and Vetter, Eva (2000) Methods of Text and Discourse Analysis. London: Sage.

Toulmin, Stephen, Rieke, Richard, and Janik, Allan (1984) An Introduction to Reasoning, 2nd edition. New York: Macmillan.

Vagle, Mark D. (2010) "Re-framing Schon's call for a phenomenology of practice: A post-intentional approach," Reflective Practice, 11 (3): 393–407.

Van Manen, Max (1990) *Research Lived Experience: Human Science for an Action Sensitive Pedagogy*. London, Ontario: The Althouse Press, The University of Western Ontario.

Watson, Cate (2006) "Unreliable narrators? 'Inconsistency' (and some inconstancy) in interviews," *Qualitative Research*, 6 (3): 367–84.

Webb, Rodman B. (1992) "The life and work of Alfred Schutz: A conversation with Maurice Natanson," *International Journal of Qualitative Studies in Education*, 5 (4): 283–94.

Wertz, Frederick J., Charmaz, Kathy, McMullen, Linda M., Josselson, Ruthellen, Anderson, Rosemarie, and McSpadden, Emalinda (2011) *Five Ways of Doing Qualitative Analysis: Phenomenological Psychology, Grounded Theory, Discourse Analysis, Narrative Research, and Intuitive Inquiry*. New York: Guilford Press.

Wolcott, Harry F. (1994) *Transforming Qualitative Data: Description, Analysis, and Interpretation*. Thousand Oaks, CA: Sage.

Wolcott, Harry F. (2009) *Writing Up Qualitative Research*. Los Angeles: Sage.

Wolgemuth, Jennifer R. and Donohue, Richard (2006) "Toward an inquiry of discomfort," *Qualitative Inquiry*, 12 (5): 1022–39.

Analysing Focus Groups

Rosaline S. Barbour

As focus group usage has become more widespread, this has sparked sometimes heated debates about the best approach to analysing focus group data. Historically, although focus groups were used in some other contexts, marketing research certainly pioneered the application of this method and has been influential in terms of providing advice on setting up and running such discussion sessions. The marketing tradition, however, has had considerably less to say about analysing focus group data, due, perhaps, to its focus – on gauging the likely success of specific products or advertising campaigns – and, therefore, on producing answers. Focus groups have enjoyed a particularly enthusiastic reception by the health services research community, but here, too, guidance on analysis has been scant.

There is no 'one-size-fits-all' approach to analysing focus group data. This is because approaches to analysis and research aims are inextricably linked. Research utilising focus groups can usefully be envisaged as forming a continuum – with practical or applied projects at one end and studies which address disciplinary or theoretical concerns at the other end.

The approach to analysis and the degree of sophistication possible are largely determined by the overarching aims of the research and the format and structure of the original focus group discussions – for example, the extent to which the moderator leads the discussion or intervenes; the number and specificity of questions asked; and the content and manner in which any stimulus materials are used. This depends, ultimately, on the epistemological and ontological assumptions underpinning the research. This is the first topic to be addressed in this chapter, which will then outline the initial steps in making sense of focus group data, before presenting further analytic resources. A case is made for employing a composite approach, which blurs the distinction between applied and more theoretical orientations in focus group research, and it is argued that being open to a range of analytic strategies can confer benefits for all types of projects. Finally, the potential benefits and challenges of new developments are considered.

EPISTEMOLOGICAL AND ONTOLOGICAL UNDERPINNINGS

As Kidd and Parshall (2000) observed, focus groups have been 'relatively agnostic' in that they have not been firmly associated with any one qualitative paradigm. While this has led to an unusually rich and stimulating variety of applications in a wide range of research contexts, this has, inevitably, also led to some confusion – especially in terms of selecting which pieces of advice to follow when embarking on analysing focus group data. This permissive appropriation of focus groups masks important epistemological and ontological differences, which impact on how projects are designed, how data are generated and, most importantly, how they are analysed. The different disciplines that have espoused focus groups as a method have, inevitably, each put their own 'spin' on this, since they have used this approach to interrogate further their own disciplinary and theoretical concerns building on their own distinctive set of techniques and procedures.

It is not especially helpful, then, to take a simplistic view that differentiates between realist and constructivist usages. In effect, the picture is much more complex and focus group research is carried out across a continuum that ranges from realist to constructivist approaches. Given the additional constraints of funding requirements and the need for many focus group researchers to produce findings that are of relevance also to practice situations, many projects are located somewhere in the middle of this continuum and approach analysis of data drawing on 'critical realism' (Bhaskar, 1989) or 'subtle realism' (Hammersley, 1992). This stance acknowledges the need to address practical concerns in presenting findings, but also allows for development of more theoretical explanations. Maxwell (2011) has more recently argued that it is possible – indeed, perhaps, preferable – to marry a relativist epistemology with a realist ontology (see Maxwell and Chmiel, Chapter 2, this volume).

Focus group researchers, as individuals, however, are likely to lean towards one or other end of the 'realist–constructivist' continuum, by virtue of their disciplinary training, and this can make for challenging, but potentially invigorating, discussion in multidisciplinary teams charged with analysing focus group data. Whether or not these differences are openly acknowledged, such orientations fundamentally impact on the research process, influencing assumptions about what counts as data, and how they should be analysed and presented.

Some commentators (e.g. Wilkinson, 1998) have been critical of the tendency to report focus group findings using quotes from individuals, to the exclusion of longer exchanges between participants. These longer excerpts, it is claimed, showcase the capacity of focus groups to elicit rich interactional data, as participants go about co-producing explanations (Barbour, 2007). Morgan, however, advocates taking a pragmatic approach to this vexed issue, arguing that the choice of which focus group excerpt to use is 'obvious when one quote makes (a particular) point more forcefully' (2010: 719). Quotes from individuals have their advantages in terms of their shortness and efficiency and we should not, perhaps, be too precious about the use to which individual comments are put.

One of the reasons for the emphasis on individuals' comments, however, is the underlying idea that focus groups provide a more efficient means of collecting the views of individuals than do other methods. Some researchers certainly employ focus groups as a 'back door' to obtaining survey-type data relating to attitudes (Barbour, 2007). This involves certain problematic assumptions regarding the measurability of attitudes and the capacity of focus groups to capture these effectively through recording, as immutable opinions, statements that have been made in a specific context and setting. Such usages overlook the way in which views are debated, defended and sometimes modified, in what is a much more fluid presentation of ideas. However, acknowledging that attitudes are 'performed' rather than being 'preformed' (Puchta and Potter, 2004) need not mean that we should focus exclusively on the interaction and performance to the neglect of the content. Morgan recently made the helpful observation: 'saying that the interaction in focus groups produces the data is not the same as saying that the interaction itself is the data' (2010: 721). As Morgan points out, it is entirely fitting that research espousing different goals should involve differing levels of analysis.

At the more applied end of the spectrum are those health services research endeavours, which have used focus groups for a variety of purposes, such as understanding the low uptake of screening programmes or resistance to health promotion or condition-specific treatment plans. Thus, researchers working in this context are, understandably, more interested in examining the content of focus group discussions. Researchers working at this end of the focus group continuum are likely to emphasise outputs, such as the development of appropriate health promotion materials (often for disadvantaged or marginalised groups with specific cultural needs, e.g. Vincent et al., 2006). Action research applications may not involve publication, since such work (according to commentators such as Hilsen, 2006) should be judged on its achievements rather than its methodological sophistication or findings. Occasionally researchers enlist participants as co-analysts, providing them with training, as did Makosky Daley et al. (2010) when carrying out a project with American Indians in Kansas and Missouri.

At the other end of the spectrum is focus group research that is more overtly framed to address theoretical or disciplinary concerns. Here the focus is on form and process, rather than content or outputs. In this iteration, focus groups are prized for their capacity to illuminate empirically a theoretical construct, such as Bourdieu's (1999) notion of 'habitus' (dispositions or lenses through which people view the world – see Bohnsack, Chapter 15, this volume), singled out by several sociologists (e.g. Callaghan, 2005) as being especially amenable to illumination via focus groups, since they allow researchers to access the process through which participants simultaneously manage their individual identities and make a collective representation to the researcher.

'Conversation analysis' (CA – see Toerien, Chapter 22, this volume) is based on the assertion that 'ordinary talk, mundane talk, the kind of everyday chat we have with one another is fundamental to understanding all kinds of more specialised interaction' (Puchta and Potter, 2004: 9). Focusing on form and process, conversation analysis studies the regularities and conventions that underpin talk and pays particular attention to the sequencing of conversations and the impact that this has on the content of discussions and, crucially, what these exchanges allow participants to achieve. Closely related to conversation analysis, but originating from different disciplinary concerns, is 'discourse analysis' (DA), which also focuses on 'the action orientation of talk' (Willig, 2003: 163; see Willig, Chapter 23, this volume). With regard to such approaches, resources – that is, what counts as data – can be 'words, categories ... or "interpretative repertoires"' (Hepburn and Potter, 2004: 168).

Exponents of CA/DA approaches have sometimes been criticized for their overriding attention to detail. Criticism also includes the lack of attention paid to the broader context in which interactions are played out, resulting in a neglect of issues such as power, and social or political structures, as Rapley (2007) acknowledges. However, this is not a foregone conclusion, since some studies employ CA or DA methods to address such issues. Willig outlines the approach of 'Foucauldian discourse analysis' which, she argues, allows for the study of discourse as a mechanism for enacting, reproducing or challenging "wider social processes of legitimation and power"' (2003: 171; see Willig, Chapter 23, this volume).

Whereas CA has mainly relied on naturally occurring interaction (with a significant body of work relating to doctor–patient consultations), some researchers (e.g. Myers and Macnaghten, 1999; Macnaghten and Myers, 2004) have argued that focus group transcripts (see Kowal and O'Connell, Chapter 5, this volume) can also be analysed as text. In effect, the distinction between naturally occurring and researcher-convened groups is not especially helpful. If sufficient preparatory work is carried out by researchers – in terms of focusing the discussion (through careful development of topic guides and selection of stimulus materials) – the moderator can, in the event, take a 'back seat' – more akin to that of a traditional ethnographer – as discussion unfolds (Barbour, 2007).

The outline provided here, however, suggests an overly neat typology, whereas, in practice, there are many similarities and even some 'hybrid' projects. One point of convergence between realist and constructivist approaches is the emphasis on the internal/alternative logic that informs the views/perspectives/accounts of respondents or groups. Such ideas will, undoubtedly, be expressed by researchers adhering to various disciplinary contexts through the use of different language (as is suggested by the range of terms used here).

Projects may simultaneously serve realist and constructivist agendas. For example, Angus et al. (2007) convened focus groups to explore the everyday production of health and cardiovascular risk, drawing explicitly on Bourdieu's theoretical construct of 'habitus'. Nevertheless, this work allowed them to address issues of relevance to service providers, including providing insights into the interaction of person, place, social and material circumstances in shaping beliefs and behaviour.

There is also the possibility of different levels of analysis within the one study, drawing on the same data set, as is illustrated by Matoesian and Coldren's (2002) linguistically nuanced CA-informed analysis of focus group data which were also subjected to thematic analysis. Matoesian and Coldren describe the process involved in formulating their analysis for the evaluation report, and translating this into public policy, as 'domesticating' their findings (2002: 471). It is, therefore, possible to present findings in a variety of formats for different audiences (and such possibilities are enhanced by the broader scope afforded by interdisciplinary research teams). Several studies relating to environmental issues also bridge this gap, addressing contentious political issues and seeking to elicit public responses (Waterton and Wynn, 1999, on views of the nuclear industry; Macnaghten, 2001, on animal experimentation; Collier and Scott, 2010, on industrialized peat extraction) while simultaneously employing some of the tools developed for CA or DA approaches.

INITIAL STEPS IN MAKING SENSE OF FOCUS GROUP DATA

Most of the general advice on analysing qualitative data also pertains to focus groups, although there are some additional challenges and concerns. Some relate to specific focus group usages. Since 'conversation analysis' concentrates on fine-grained analysis of turn-taking, pauses, overlaps of speech, and pauses, it requires that transcriptions be produced according to a specific set of criteria (the Jeffersonian transcription system – see Rapley, 2007: 52–63; also see Kowal and O'Connell, Chapter 5, this volume). This system relies on the use of standardized notation to denote specific, and very detailed, aspects of talk. It allows researchers to take account of such features as the length of silences; the location of micro-pauses; rises and falls in volume (denoted, respectively, by the use of CAPITALS and degree signs); overlaps in participants' talk; faster or slower segments of speech; and even features such as 'sound-stretching' and 'in-breaths' (Rapley, 2007: 60).

Some focus group researchers (e.g. Matoesian and Coldren, 2002) have videotaped discussions in order to ensure that they capture non-verbal communication in addition to talk. They argue: 'an exclusive focus on topic talk ignores the function of the body as it intersects with speech in the conceptualisation of socially embodied action' (Matoesian and Coldren, 2002: 484). However, even when the purpose of producing transcripts is simply to engage in content or thematic analysis, attention to such details can still pay dividends, as participants' emphases, tones of voice, facial expressions or gestures can fundamentally alter interpretations of specific statements. The vocabulary of stage directions, borrowed from the theatre, may, on occasion, be more helpful than the standard language employed by methods texts (Barbour, 2008) and field notes are invaluable resources. Interestingly, Matoesian and Coldren, while not overtly adopting a CA approach, have combined many of its features, alongside usage of colourful and extremely detailed descriptions of body language – including terms such as 'lateral head jerk' and 'open palms recoil' (2002: 474).

Producing summaries of discussions, as is routinely done in marketing research, although not a bad starting point, is generally insufficient on its own for analysis of focus groups carried out in a more academic context. A further complication in terms of seeking to summarize complex discussions is that, as Waterton and Wynn (1999) point out, many groups do not reach a consensus. In order to make meaningful comparisons between the content covered in focus groups, however, it is necessary to have information regarding the individuals who have participated. Focus group researchers differ to the extent to which they collect demographic information (such as age or occupation) – with relevant characteristics dependent on the research topic. Usages which rely on snowball sampling (drawing on participants' own networks; see Rapley, Chapter 4, this volume) may not involve recording of such details. Short questionnaires can be extremely helpful in such situations, allowing detailed information to be captured without breaking the flow of discussion or using up valuable discussion time (Barbour, 2007). It is an increasingly common research practice for the principal investigator (i.e. the most senior grant-holder) not to be involved in generating data, although he or she is usually involved in analysis and writing up. In such cases, the additional information possessed by moderators is a valuable resource, leading some commentators to advocate interviewing moderators (Traulsen et al., 2004), or, at least, to involve them actively as members of the team carrying out data analysis (Barbour, 2007).

One of the hallmarks of qualitative research is its capacity to capture and illuminate context (Barbour, 2008). As pieces of social interaction, focus groups are especially sensitive to and reflective of context. The location of focus group sessions and the associations this has for the group and individuals involved are likely to have an important impact on the discussions. In addition, the composition of the group also influences what is and is not said. It is essential that such information is drawn upon throughout the process of analysis.

Sometimes variation in responses to moderators' questions can alert researchers to important differences between groups. Heikklä (2011) presents findings from a focus group study with Swedish-speaking Finns (themselves a minority) and has analysed these discussions in order to explore the relevance of social class position in relation to their talk about good and bad taste. Heikklä characterizes three clear-cut categories of response to the question 'What do you think good taste is?' These were: (1) astonishment at the difficulty of addressing this question (followed by engagement with the topic); (2) posing of a further question requesting clarification; and, finally, (3) a silence or making a joke. She found that initial responses to the moderator's question broadly prefigured the orientations of the different groups as expressed in the discussion following on from this question, with the first response characterizing the perceptions of upper class groups; the second those of middle-status groups; and the third that of low-status groups. Paying retrospective attention to this sort of patterning can prove to be a valuable aid to analysis.

Heikklä's (2011) work also provides an example of the value of making comparisons between groups. Of course the potential to do this is determined by the attention paid to sampling in formulating the study design. In this case the researchers had convened groups comprising Swedish-speaking Finns with different social class positions (low, middle and high) since they were keen to explore the influence of background on ideas about taste. This suggests a broadly sociological orientation, highlighting the importance of disciplinary assumptions in shaping research designs. Heikklä found that discussion in the low-status groups consisted entirely of examples (generally of bad taste) and moral judgements, whereas, in the high-status groups, discussion flowed more freely, probably due to the upper/upper middle classes' established cultural repertoire, which allowed them to talk more analytically. Of course, researchers' own cultural repertoire and language also frame the way in which they phrase questions and interpret responses. We are sometimes alerted to potentially fruitful lines to pursue in analysis through paying attention to our own reactions to comments that jar with our own understandings and expectations.

The moderator can also play a significant role in shaping data, since participants may react differently to moderators who are or are not perceived to share their own characteristics (and assumed values). This is not an argument for matching moderators and participants; rather a reminder that useful insights may be gleaned by comparing the responses to moderators of differing age, gender, race or ethnicity – among other characteristics – that either pertain to moderators or that are attributed to them by participants (Kitzinger and Barbour, 1999).

The setting where focus groups are carried out can also be a resource for comparison. Green and Hart (1999) used focus groups to study how children's knowledge about accident risks is produced in local contexts. Reflecting on this experience, they highlight the markedly contrasting nature of stories told by children in the classroom (where formal safety messages were emphasised) and in the playground (where risk-taking experiences were recounted – sometimes very dramatically).

The neat – and sometimes overly simplistic – sampling categories (see Rapley, Chapter 4, this volume) we imagine when writing our research proposals are often revealed to be less straightforward once we begin to do our fieldwork.

When planning a study about carer involvement in drug services, a colleague (Orr et al., 2012) decided to hold separate focus groups with carers of drug users, health care professionals and policy-makers, anticipating that there would be important differences in their perceptions. However, on several occasions she discovered that individuals recruited to her health care professionals' groups were also carers of problem drug users, and that some people taking part in carers' groups were also employed within the health or social services sector. Such individuals were frequently an enormous analytic resource, since they were able to comment from more than one perspective and also encouraged other participants in the focus group, who did not have the benefit of these dual identities, to reflect more deeply on the issues being discussed. Further opportunities for comparison can, thus, arise fortuitously and it is important to be alert to such unanticipated bonuses.

FURTHER ANALYTIC RESOURCES

Identification of patterning in data is key to developing explanatory frameworks – that is, paying attention to who says what in which context (Barbour, 2008). Especially important here is critical examination of apparent contradictions or exceptions (as in the approach termed 'analytic induction'). Our explanations can be refined through detailed and systematic analysis of 'confirming' or 'disconfirming' excerpts, taking additional features (e.g. participants' characteristics or focus group settings) into account. For an illustration of the approach of 'analytic induction' in building an explanation from focus group data see Frankland and Bloor (1999) who systematically looked for exceptions in interrogating, building up and continuously modifying their understanding of how peer pressure operated in relation to adolescents' smoking behaviour. As Flick explains, 'analytic induction' is 'a way to take the exceptions as a point of reference rather than the average and normal in the material' and allows researchers to 'further elaborate models' (2007: 32).

Despite the enormous popularity of 'grounded theory' (see Thornberg and Charmaz, Chapter 11, this volume) as an approach to analysing qualitative data, one of the most under-exploited aspects of Glaser and Strauss's (1967) approach is the notion of returning to the field to generate further data in order to explore emergent and partial hypotheses. It is not necessary to have a grandiose theoretical framework to interrogate, as this can involve little more than a 'hunch'. Hussey et al. (2004) decided to go back into the field to explore whether – as their initial data on doctors' views about issuing sickness certificates suggested – there were important variations in concerns on the part of general practitioners (family physicians) occupying different employment statuses (as locums, registrars and principals). This led these authors to convene another three focus groups which also utilized, as stimulus material, some quotes from earlier focus groups, which allowed emergent hypotheses to be interrogated. A similar approach was employed by Murdoch et al. (2010) who shared data with participants as they sought to develop their analyses.

Although it can be a useful starting point, categorizing individuals in terms of the views they espouse is unlikely to convey the whole story, due to the nuanced and contingent nature of views and perceptions. A detailed examination of the contradictions and shades of meaning conveyed, however, may well go some way towards uncovering the patterns that govern responses – always acknowledging, of course, that such schema are imperfect, provisional, and subject to revision and reformulation as our analyses proceed. A particularly useful resource for analysis is afforded by any tensions and dilemmas reflected in focus group discussions – either as differences of opinion between participants (Farnsworth and Boon, 2010) or as difficulties that are acknowledged and which participants attempt to address collectively. It is not only focus group researchers who 'worry away' at such conceptual puzzles – focus group participants may also charge themselves with this task – and may even 'problematize' our questions and language.

Heikklä (2011), for example, found that some focus group participants found it difficult to define good taste, but spoke at length about bad taste. Paying attention to such 'backhanded' or circuitous ways of discussing specific topics is likely to be fruitful. Silences can also be a valuable resource for further interrogation by the researcher – either by drawing these to the attention of participants and seeking clarification or by subjecting these to detailed analysis. Poland and Pedersen (1998) highlight the potential of what they term 'silences of familiarity', which may escape the attention of the uncritical or unwittingly complicit researcher, but which may, nevertheless, be key to understanding the interaction. Moderators may possess – or may acquire along the way – valuable 'insider' knowledge of the unspoken rules governing behaviour, such as conversational turn-taking. For example, when carrying out focus groups with Pacific North West Indian people, Strickland (1999) noted that elders were always allocated the final words in any discussion, but never contributed until that point was reached.

In analysing focus group data researchers should seek to maintain a critical or sceptical focus with regard to what focus group participants say, bearing in mind the potential provided by this setting for self-presentation, offering what Brannen and Pattman (2005) refer to as a 'site of performativity'. It is important to guard against the dangers of taking participants' comments too literally. An example is provided by a recently completed study. This was a health services research project located at the applied end of the research spectrum, which was carried out to inform development of a weight-loss intervention package for women following childbirth. In their discussions women interrogated the 'ideal' of weight loss and were often critical of received health promotion 'wisdom'.

One of the groups, for example, engaged in a lengthy and jointly constructed explanation as to why the weather had a big impact on their ability to address weight management. What is achieved in such exchanges is relatively complex, in that the women, themselves, are aware of the justificatory nature of their talk, which is often punctuated by admissions. This was the case with the following excerpt coded under our '*in-vivo*' (see Thornberg and Charmaz, Chapter 11, this volume) code of 'heavy bones' – that is, a code derived from the ideas of those being researched (Kelle, 1997):

Excerpt 1

Jen   ... Your actual weight I don't think is as important as what clothes are fitting. Because some people can be heavier than others due to **heavy bones** or, you know. And people often ... even when I went to Weightwatchers the lady used to say to me, I can't believe you actually weigh that, because I must be quite heavy inside. Because you're obviously fitting into a size 12 *(US size 10, European size 40)* pair of trousers but you can be a lot heavier than another size 12.

Sally   Hazel was speaking about that the other day as well. Because I was saying, if I never ate for like five years I would never be eight stone *(US 112 pounds; European 44.8 kilos)*.

Jen   No, well that's it. You're kind of built either ...

Sally   I've just ... I've never been that, I don't think since ... I can't remember ever being, like, that size.

Jen   No, neither can I.

Sally   I obviously was at one point as a child. But as a grown up person ...

...

Jen   I was like, "What?" I knew I was a bit heavier, but I wouldn't have said ... I didn't feel like I was particularly unfit. So I feel it's how you ... what clothes you fit into rather than your actual weight. Some people are bigger boned than others.

(Post-partum Weight Management Study – Focus Group 4)

(Transcriber's description in *italics*; Researcher's emphasis in **bold**.)

(The ellipsis '...' in a block of text denotes a short pause or speech tailing off and '...' between lines indicates that some text has been omitted from the quote in the interests of brevity.)

DIVERSE INSIGHTS: THE CASE FOR A COMPOSITE APPROACH?

Halkier (2010) makes a case for employing a range of tools, derived, variously, from the work of Goffman (1981), conversation analysis (see Toerien, Chapter 22, this volume), discourse psychology (see Willig, Chapter 23, this volume) and positioning theory, and merges this assembly of approaches in which she calls 'a practice-theoretical perspective' or, perhaps more illuminatingly, a 'moderate social constructivist view'. She provides a helpful – but not overly prescriptive – set of suggestions with regard to how to go about analysing focus group data. Essentially, this paves the way for analyses that combine a focus on topic, form and structure of talk.

The reference to Goffman reflects the importance of the performative aspects of interaction, with focus groups viewed as a stage where participants tell, negotiate and reformulate their 'self-narratives'. According to this formulation, focus group participants are engaged not just in presenting their own narratives, but in supporting or challenging others' narratives, forging, testing and occasionally repairing relationships along the way, and, sometimes, in co-constructing accounts.

According to Halkier's approach, it is possible to see how participants draw on strategies – frequently those identified in CA approaches – in order to strengthen the claims that they are making in discussions. Halkier demonstrates how '*positioning analysis*' can alert the researcher to the stance that particular focus group participants are affecting, which, of course, aids in interpreting the comments made and the effect that is desired. Halkier also points out that focus group members may also seek to position others in the group, through overt challenges that question their self-presentations. The following excerpt from our focus group study of women's perspectives on post-partum weight loss shows three women negotiating around the first speaker's self-presentation:

Excerpt 2

Veronica	I think the way I seem to have lost weight is because, not what I'm eating, but trying to educate myself to think about healthy eating because ... My kids don't get chocolate. Well, they get lots of crisps and biscuits because Daddy eats them.
Helen	See crisps and biscuits are just as bad as chocolate.
Eileen	But kids run around and burn it off, you know ... 'can I go out to play, yeah?' ... 'bye'. Three hours later they come in.
Helen	But if it's not in your cupboard, you're not going to eat it.
Veronica	Yeah, yeah, if I don't eat it, they don't tend to get it. I go for the healthy things and I think that's how I've lost weight ... apart from running after them!

(Focus Group 3)

Veronica starts by sharing her experience of trying to put into practice what she has learnt about healthy eating. Helen, however, is quick to point out the flaw in this approach, while Eileen comes in to defend Veronica. Undeterred, Helen reiterates her point about restricting availability of food that is deemed unhealthy. Veronica chooses not to react to Helen's further challenge and returns to her initial topic of how she has achieved some modest success with regard to healthy eating and weight loss. Eileen then joins in to locate the issue within the context of busy family life and this idea is echoed by others:

Excerpt 3

Veronica	I think if the mums are provided with, say, an idea of what's healthy and what isn't ... and then again who wants to sit and read healthy when they've got kids?
Nan	On a Friday night after baby's gone to bed sometimes you <u>need</u> that little bit of chocolate cake, or that naughty bag of crisps [*voices overlap*]
Eileen	You've got to have something.
Nan	All the diet groups say that you shouldn't ever deprive yourself or go hungry.
Nan	Have you tried that Skinny Cow chocolate fudge brownie ice cream by Ben and Jerry's? And it was wicked, I felt naughty eating it, but it tasted so good [*voices overlap*] ...
Eileen	Oh, I <u>love</u> [*voices overlap*] ...

(Focus Group 3 – Underlining denotes emphasis in the original.)

Another strategy highlighted by Halkier (2010) – that of '*category entitlement*' – involves making an appeal based on personal experience and knowledge in order to authenticate a specific comment or perspective. This is what the women in these excerpts are appealing to when they invoke the demands of parenting and domestic responsibilities in justifying their disregard of dietary and dieting advice. Veronica can be seen starting to make claims about the impact of knowledge, which she then, in the next breath, goes on to question, appealing to the demands of child-rearing.

As Halkier's examples (provided in her paper) show, language selection is far from accidental and such strategies tend to involve the use of particular linguistic appeals, such as using the term 'you' to appeal to shared views and experiences. Again, this usage can be seen in the previous excerpts, conveying solidarity and shared assumptions.

Halkier (2010) also recommends that we analyse our focus group transcripts by looking for instances of strategies such as *'factist characterised descriptions and evaluations'*, whereby personal opinions are presented as 'shared by most people' or as 'common knowledge' (as with Veronica's initial utterance in Excerpt 3).

Another group in the same study expanded their critique to challenge the accuracy of the Body Mass Index (BMI) charts routinely used by health professionals to determine target weights:

Excerpt 4

Debbie   It was because the target weight they had that, that was 'overweight' and the target weight that I <u>am</u> is classified as 'obese'.

Kim   That's like me when I got it done. It said that I was obese and I looked at myself and thought 'eh? that can't be'.

Laura   Yeah, I'd be quite happy to be 'overweight' in their categories. [*She laughs*]

Debbie   The target weight for my height was about nine and a half stone *(US 133 pounds, European 53.2 kilos)* and I just thought, 'Do you know what? There's no way that I'm going to get down to there so they can **stick it where the sun don't shine!**'

Laura   Mine was something like seven and a half stone *(US 105 pounds, European 42 kilos)* and I was like no way, I was maybe that when I was at school. Sorry …

Debbie   **It's extremely unrealistic the actual BMI, it just was not achievable** … yeah, it just seemed so unachievable that it didn't matter, like ideally I'd like to be about ten and a half *(US 147 pounds, European 58.8 kilos)* maybe eleven stone *(US 154 pounds, European 61.6 kilos)*, and to even be that and still be told you're obese …

(*Focus Group 1* – Researcher's emphasis in **bold**; Underlining denotes emphasis in the original.)

At first glance this looks like just another challenge to received wisdom. However, what is striking about this example is the shift in register from Debbie's vernacular 'they can stick it where the sun don't shine!' to her 'It's extremely unrealistic …' and all in the space of a few lines. Interestingly, here she appears to be invoking a 'factist' style to challenge received wisdom – seeking to 'have it both ways', in fact.

These excerpts show the women employing all of the strategies outlined by Halkier (2010), ranging from *'factist'* displays of knowledge, with these being set up only to be brought into question by *'positioning'* strategies, with *'category entitlement'* being invoked through the power of personal experience (of various types).

As outlined earlier, discussions about weight management could be subversive in focus, with women making wry references to 'cheating', focusing on the fruit content in high-calorie foods, or confessing to piling 'portion plates' (designed to aid portion control) as high as possible (thereby subverting their purpose). Sometimes the women appear to be vying with each other, telling funny stories (and the talk is punctuated by shared laughter):

Excerpt 5

Nan   You see, I'm really evil because my cheese sits in the fridge and I've got written on it, 'Nan's diet cheese', so as my husband doesn't like strong cheese, he likes, like, double Gloucester and all these cheeses. I like cheese that you [*voices overlap*] and I write, like, 'Diet cheese', but inside it's like seriously strong stuff, and he thinks it's diet so he never touches it … [*Several snorts and laughter from other participants*] I just put 'Diet' on something even though it's not, he goes, 'Oh, that's my wife's diet stuff, I'd better not touch it', and I get it. [*Prolonged laughter*] Oh, I come from an Italian family – I'm not stupid … I let him think I am.

Alison   Yeah, they've got to think you're a little bit stupid.

[Nods from some of the others.]

(Focus Group 3)

The shared laughter here affirms common experiences in relation to struggles with weight and dieting and also acknowledges complicity in 'managing' male partners.

The following excerpt, produced in response to the moderator's question about how best to approach the topic of weight loss, provides a clue with regard to interpreting the comments about BMI made earlier in this group and in other focus group discussions, including the 'they can stick it where the sun don't shine' comment. Here the exchange resembles a comedy improvisation 'riff' as the women build on each other's comments to humorous effect:

Excerpt 6

Rose	Okay. So thinking about just to round off, I think we've just about got through all of our questions here. What advice would you give to us really in terms of developing a weight management intervention?
Nan	Tread gently.
Eileen	Very gently.
Veronica	Don't be pushy.
Nan	Or patronizing.
Nan	Because we <u>know</u> we're overweight but we just don't need you telling us we are, we've got mirrors in the house as well. [*Several affirmative head shakes*]
Eileen	And we're not dense.
Nan	We know what vegetables and fruit are, we know we should eat them, but at the end of the day a KitKat *(UK manufactured branded chocolate wafer bar)* is easier to get through than an orange. Orange is like 'aarg!' but a KitKat – done; gone. [*Laughter*]
Nan	A lot of it is more time management – the convenience of it … If you've got a KitKat you think, 'Well, I <u>should</u> have that lovely fresh healthy orange, but, bugger it, I haven't got time, and it gets sticky … wash my hands …' the KitKat – done … Yeah, peel it, and wash your hands, and change your top …
All	Yeah. [*Accompanied by nods and smiles*]
Nan	And then you get hacked off about it and think, you know, I still fancy eating a KitKat [*Several nods and laughter*]
Veronica	I think you can get orange KitKats now too [*Voices overlap amidst lots of laughter*]

(Focus Group 3)

A sense of anger and hurt pervades these discussions with overweight women who consider themselves a beleaguered minority in a world that emphasizes a narrow vision of attractiveness to which they do not conform. The hilarity produced in this discussion echoes Jefferson's (1984) observations about the important role of laughter in talk about 'troubles' and the analysis might well benefit from paying more detailed attention to how laughter is ordered and structured – as Jefferson suggests.

The analytic strategies recommended by Halkier (2010) can certainly produce useful insights into the intent and effect of conversational gambits and exchanges and, ultimately, what is attempted or achieved by participants in the course of a focus group exchange. It has been extremely helpful in looking beneath the surface of the 'plucky' talk produced by the women in the post-partum weight management study focus groups. Whether or not it is necessary to label strategies in the ways suggested by Halkier (2010) in order for our analyses to derive benefit is another matter. There is much to recommend in terms of paying attention to such strategies, where this helps to explain analytically troublesome or potentially rich exchanges, although one might stop short of routinely documenting and interrogating all instances that occur throughout focus group discussions. As Halkier, herself, concedes, 'just like pure content analysis of focus group data is relatively uninteresting, and does not take the specific methodological strengths of this kind of data seriously, likewise pure interaction form analysis is a methodological dead-end for most social scientific uses of focus groups' (2010: 86). Ultimately, the choice for the data analyst will be governed by the aims of the research and the audience for whom the analysis is to be produced.

NEW DEVELOPMENTS AND PERSPECTIVES

New developments – particularly those afforded by the Internet – bring tantalizing new possibilities, but also new challenges, in terms of both generating and analysing focus group data. Online discussion forums (see Marotzki et al., Chapter 31, this volume) are often considered to be in the public domain and thus are likely to be seen as providing ready-transcribed data. Since such forums have an existence independent of the research being carried out, they are also attractive to those who are concerned about the effect of the moderator on the data generated. 'Harvesting' such ready-made data, however, brings its own challenges – in addition to ethical issues – including lack of researcher control over selection of participants, or even access to demographic information which might be useful in analysis. Although asynchronous formats (with a delay between successive 'postings') potentially allow the moderator to ask questions or seek clarification, synchronous (i.e. real-time) discussions do not afford such opportunities. Commentators such as Stewart and Williams (2005) highlight the need for focus group researchers to develop new techniques in response to such challenges, including exploiting the analytic potential of 'emoticons' (symbols as used in texting, e.g. :-) to denote a happy face) (Fox et al., 2007).

Seale et al. also point out that text produced via online forums is 'grammatically and lexically less dense than written language and is often unedited, with numerous contradictions of words and uncorrected typing or punctuation oddities that contribute to the style of this mode of communication in informal context' (2010: 596). This raises several problems with regard to interpretation.

The internet, however, also offers some new approaches to analysing these new forms of data. Computerized data analysis software packages such as NVivo (see Gibbs, Chapter 19, this volume) offer the possibility of counting word frequency and it is possible to customize such searches. A feature of Web 2.0 websites and blogs (see Marotzki et al., Chapter 31, this volume) is what is termed 'tag clouds', which is an approach borrowed from the visual design field and which allows for a visual depiction (utilizing different font sizes and colours) of the relative frequency of selected terms and concepts. Although this makes for arresting graphic displays it is more difficult to make analytical use of these. Social networking sites, such as Facebook, also provide their own network analysis tools, but, similarly, this has produced complex diagrams which, so far, have proved somewhat resistant to incorporation into in-depth analysis. While such tools can aid in establishing broad patterns, a more nuanced analysis of complex texts is still likely to demand yet more sophisticated methods to allow for extrapolation between visual display and explanatory frameworks.

Interestingly, new applications in marketing research have also been focusing on how to capture and use information relating to word frequencies in analysis of focus group data. Reviewing these developments, Schmidt (2010) argues that commercial software can identify 'rule based webs' – of associations between words. Seale et al. (2010) have simultaneously been exploring the potential of keyword analysis for online data. Their approach, of 'keyword analysis', relies on the comparative analysis of two texts, but they acknowledge that this can capture a wealth of information that may, in the event, be largely irrelevant for the research question being addressed. They argue that, ultimately, a qualitative judgement has to be made with regard to choosing the keywords that 'best bring out the characteristics of a particular text' (Seale et al., 2010: 598). There are likely to be significant challenges in terms of utilizing such methods to explore ironic or strategic use of words, imagery and metaphors. While it is important to keep a weather eye on new developments, the original focus of the research and the disciplinary and theoretical persuasion of the researcher or research team remain the key to deciding what does and does not work. There is still no substitute for thoughtful research design, and imaginative, but attentive and thorough analysis.

FURTHER READING

Barbour, Rosaline (2007) *Doing Focus Groups*. London: Sage.
Frankland, Jane and Bloor, Michael (1999) 'Some issues arising in the systematic analysis of focus group materials', in Rosaline S. Barbour and Jenny Kitzinger (eds), *Developing Focus Group Research: Politics, Theory and Practice*. London: Sage. pp.144–55.
Macnaghten, Phil and Myers, Greg (2004) 'Focus groups', in Clive Seale et al. (eds), *Qualitative Research Practice*. London: Sage. pp. 65–79.

REFERENCES

Angus, Jan, Rukholm, Ellen, St. Onge, Renée, Michel, Isabelle, Nolan, Robert P., Lapum, Jennifer and Evans, Sarah (2007) 'Habitus, stress and the body: The everyday production of health and cardiovascular risk', *Qualitative Health Research*, 17: 1088–1102.
Barbour, Rosaline (2007) *Doing Focus Groups*. London: Sage.
Barbour, Rosaline (2008, (2nd edition in press)) *Introducing Qualitative Research: A Student Guide to the Craft of Qualitative Research*. London: Sage.
Bhaskar, Roy (1989) *Reclaiming Reality*. London: Verso.
Bourdieu, Pierre (1999) *Culture of a Theory of Practice*. Cambridge: Cambridge University Press.
Brannen, Julia and Pattman, Rob (2005) 'Work-family matters in the workplace: The use of focus groups in a study of a UK social services department', *Qualitative Research*, 5 (4): 523–42.
Callaghan, Gill (2005) 'Accessing habitus: Relating structure and agency through focus group research', *Sociological Research Online*, 10 (3): (accessed 9 May 2013).
Collier, Marcus J. and Scott, Mark (2010) 'Focus group discourses in a mined landscape', *Land Use Policy*, 27: 304–12.

Farnsworth, John and Boon, Bronwyn (2010) 'Analysing group dynamics within the focus group', *Qualitative Research*, 10 (5): 605–24.
Flick, Uwe (2007) *Managing the Quality of Qualitative Research*. London: Sage.
Fox, Fiona E., Morris, Marianne and Rumsey, Nichola (2007) 'Doing synchronous online focus groups with young people: Methodological reflections', *Qualitative Health Research*, 17: 539–47.
Frankland, Jane and Bloor, Michael (1999) 'Some issues arising in the systematic analysis of focus group materials', in Rosaline S. Barbour and Jenny Kitzinger (eds), *Developing Focus Group Research: Politics, Theory and Practice*. London: Sage. pp.144–55.
Glaser, Barney and Strauss, Anselm (1967) *The Discovery of Grounded Theory*. Chicago: Aldine.
Goffman, Erving (1981) *Forms of Talk*. Oxford: Basil Blackwell.
Green, Judith and Hart, Laura (1999) 'The impact of context on data', in Rosaline S. Barbour and Jenny Kitzinger (eds), *Developing Focus Group Research: Politics, Theory and Practice*. London: Sage. pp.21–35.
Halkier, Bente (2010) 'Focus groups as social enactments: Integrating interaction and content in the analysis of focus group data', *Qualitative Research*, 10 (1): 71–89.
Hammersley, Martyn (1992) *What's Wrong with Ethnography? Methodological Explorations*. London: Routledge.
Heikklä, Riie (2011) 'Maters of taste? Conceptions of good and bad taste in focus groups with Swedish-speaking Finns', *European Journal of Cultural Studies*, 14 (1): 41–61.
Hepburn, Alexa and Potter, Jonathan (2004) 'Discourse analytic practice', in Clive Seale et al. (eds), *Qualitative Research Practice*. London: Sage. pp. 180–96.
Hilsen, Anne Inge (2006) 'And they shall be known by their deeds: Ethics and politics in action research', *Action Research*, 4 (1): 23–36.
Hussey, Susan, Hoddinott, Pat, Wilson, Phillip, Dowell, Jon and Barbour, Rosaline (2004) 'The sickness certification system in the UK: Qualitative study of views of general practitioners in Scotland', *British Medical Journal*, 328: 88–92.
Jefferson, Gail (1984) 'On the organization of laughter in talk about troubles', in J. Maxwell Atkinson and John Heritage (eds), *Structures of Social Action: Studies in Conversation Analysis*. Cambridge: Cambridge University Press. pp. 346–69.
Kelle, Udo (1997) 'Theory building in qualitative research and computer programs for the management of textual data', *Sociological Research Online*, 2 (1): (accessed 9 May 2013).

Kidd, Pamela S. and Parshall, Mark B. (2000) 'Getting the focus and the group: Enhancing analytical rigour in focus group research', *Qualitative Health Research*, 9 (3): 293–308.

Kitzinger, Jenny and Barbour, Rosaline S. (1999) 'Introduction: The challenge and promise of focus groups', in Rosaline S. Barbour and Jenny Kitzinger (eds), *Developing Focus Group Research: Politics, Theory and Practice*. London: Sage. pp. 1–20.

Macnaghten, Phil (2001) *Animal Futures: Public Attitudes and Sensibilities Towards Animals and Biotechnology in Contemporary Britain*. London: Agriculture and Environment Biotechnology Commission.

Macnaghten, Phil and Myers, Greg (2004) 'Focus groups', in Clive Seale et al. (eds), *Qualitative Research Practice*. London: Sage. pp. 65–79.

Makosky Daley, C., James, Aimee S., Ulrey, Ezekiel, Joseph, Stephanie, Talawyma, Angelina, Choi, Won S., Greiner, K. Allen and Coe, M. Kathryn (2010) 'Using focus groups in community-based participatory research: Challenges and resolutions', *Qualitative Health Research*, 20 (5): 697–706.

Matoesian, Gregory M. and Coldren, James R. (2002) 'Language and bodily conduct in focus group evaluations of legal policy', *Discourse and Society*, 13 (4): 469–93.

Maxwell, Joseph A. (2011) *A Realist Approach for Qualitative Research*. Thousand Oaks, CA: Sage.

Morgan, David. L. (2010) 'Reconsidering the role of interaction in analysing and reporting focus groups', *Qualitative Health Research*, 20 (5): 718–22.

Murdoch, Jamie, Poland, Fiona and Salter, Charlotte (2010) 'Analysing interactional contexts in a data-sharing focus group', *Qualitative Health Research*, 20 (5): 582–94.

Myers, Greg and Macnaghten, Phil (1999) 'Can focus groups be analysed as talk?', in Rosaline S. Barbour and Jenny Kitzinger (eds), *Developing Focus Group Research: Politics, Theory and Practice*. London: Sage. pp. 173–85.

Orr, Linda C., Barbour, Rosaline S. and Elliott, Lawrie (2012) 'Carer involvement with drug services: A qualitative study', *Health Expectations*, DOI: 10.1111/hex. 12033.

Poland, Blake and Pederson, Ann (1998) 'Reading between the lines: Interpreting silences in qualitative research', *Qualitative Inquiry*, 4 (2): 293–312.

Puchta, Claudia and Potter, Jonathan (2004) *Focus Group Practice*. London: Sage.

Rapley, Tim (2007) *Doing Conversation, Discourse and Document Analysis*. London: Sage.

Schmidt, Marcus (2010) 'Quantification of transcripts from depth interviews, open-ended responses and focus groups', *International Journal of Market Research*, 52 (4): 483–509.

Seale, Clive, Charteris-Black, Jonathan, MacFarlane, Aidan and McPherson, Ann (2010) 'Interviews and internet forums: A comparison of two sources of qualitative data', *Qualitative Health Research*, 20 (5): 595–606.

Stewart, Kate and Williams, Matthew (2005) 'Researching online populations: The use of online focus groups for social research', *Qualitative Research*, 5 (4): 395–416.

Strickland, C. June (1999) 'Conducting focus groups cross-culturally: Experiences with Pacific Northwest Indian people', *Public Health Nursing*, 16 (3): 190–7.

Traulsen, Janine Morgell, Almarsdóttir, Anna Birna and Björnsdóttir, Ingunn (2004) 'Interviewing the moderator: An ancillary method to focus groups', *Qualitative Health Research*, 14 (5): 714–25.

Vincent, Deborah, Clark, Lauren, Zimmer, Lorena Marquez and Sanchez, Jessica (2006) 'Using focus groups to develop a culturally competent diabetes self-management programme for Mexican Americans', *The Diabetes Educator*, 32: 89–97.

Waterton, Claire and Wynne, Brian (1999) 'Can focus groups access community views?', in Rosaline S. Barbour and Jenny Kitzinger (eds), *Developing Focus Group Research: Politics, Theory and Practice*. London: Sage. pp. 127–43.

Wilkinson, Sue (1998) 'Focus group methodology: A review', *International Journal of Social Research Methodology*, 1 (3): 181–203.

Willig, Carla (2003) 'Discourse analysis', in Jonathan A. Smith (ed.), *Qualitative Psychology: A Practical Guide to Research Methods*. London: Sage. pp. 159–83.

22

Conversations and Conversation Analysis

Merran Toerien

Conversation analysis (CA) is more than a methodology. It has become a paradigm in its own right, spanning multiple disciplines, including sociology, psychology and linguistics (Heritage, 2009). Its focus is 'talk-in-interaction', a term used to denote language *in use* by two or more people *interacting* with each other. This includes non-vocal aspects (like head movements, eye gaze and gesture) as well as interactions that do not use speech, such as British Sign Language (Schegloff, 2006). This focus reflects the recognition that talk-in-interaction is uniquely human and central to human social life (Sidnell, 2010). It is the primary means by which we manage and negotiate our mutual roles, identities and relationships with one another (Drew, 2005). Likewise, the 'big issues' of interest to social scientists are managed through various kinds of interaction. As Schegloff (1996a: 4) argues:

> Conversational interaction may ... be thought of as a form of social organization through which the work of the constitutive institutions of societies gets done ... such as the economy, the polity, the family, socialization, etc. It is, so to speak, sociological bedrock.

CA is distinctive for focusing on this 'bedrock' in its own right; for studying how, on the one hand, talk-in-interaction works and, on the other, the work that is done through talk-in-interaction. This has necessitated the study of real (recorded) interactions. Although I will touch on some theoretical underpinnings, the chapter is largely dedicated to illustrating the analysis of these kinds of data. I will conclude by considering the limits of this approach as well as some new directions within CA.

CA'S STARTING POINT: NATURALLY OCCURRING, RECORDED INTERACTIONS

Starting with the data is especially apt for CA because access to specific kinds of data sparked its development. Harvey Sacks, who – together with Emanuel Schegloff and Gail

Jefferson – founded CA in the early 1960s, was a Fellow at the Center for the Scientific Study of Suicide in Los Angeles. Consequently, he had access to recorded calls to the Suicide Prevention Center. Today, when mobile phones act as video recorders and we routinely hear that our calls 'may be recorded for training purposes', it is difficult to appreciate how significant those recordings were. Then, as Schegloff describes in his introduction to Sacks's (1995: xvii) *Lectures on Conversation*, Sacks was in the habit of jotting down fragments of talk in a notebook. This reflected his search for a way to study precisely how 'ordinary activities get done'. When he came across the suicide prevention recordings, he realized they were a tremendous resource because:

> I could study it again and again. And also, consequentially, others could look at what I had studied, and make of it what they could, if they wanted to be able to disagree with me. (Sacks, 1995: 622)

Two features of this dataset were profoundly significant for CA's development (see Kitzinger and Toerien, 2009):

1. *The data were naturally occurring*, allowing Sacks to study the phenomenon of interest first hand. The contrast is with data generated for research purposes, such as interviews with people who have called a suicide helpline. These would reveal a great deal about callers' *accounts of* the service, but not the *actual practices* occurring within the calls themselves. This methodological shift remains innovative. Even today, interviews and focus groups tend to be the method of choice for qualitative research. Yet researcher-generated data pose some well-recognized difficulties, including the recognition that people, unavoidably, put a 'slant' on events when reporting them. This makes it difficult to theorize the relationship between *talk about* a phenomenon and the phenomenon itself (see Kelle, Chapter 38, this volume). CA avoids this gap by recording the latter (Kitzinger, 2004). This is often taken to mean that CA cannot be used to study interview or focus data. It can. However, conversation analysts treat the data in a distinctive way (see Wilkinson, 2006). The fundamental shift is from thinking of talk as a proxy for, or conduit to, some other event or experience (described in the talk), to thinking about talk as the object of study *in its own right*.

2. *The data were recorded*, allowing Sacks to study the *precise details* of the interaction. No matter how carefully you take field notes, it is impossible to write down every detail of a conversation in real time. Coding events during observations fails to solve this problem since, again, the details are irretrievably lost. Equally, no matter when you interview someone, they could never remember precisely what was said. This loss of detail matters because there is substantial evidence that the details matter to interactants. For example, in primary care consultations, Heritage et al. (2007) have shown that one word can make a difference. They compared two question forms used to elicit patients' additional concerns (other than their main reason for the visit): 'is there ANYthing else' versus 'is there SOMEthing else you want to address today?' In response to 'anything', patients were no more likely to express their additional concerns (as recorded in a pre-consultation questionnaire) than if the question *was not asked at all*. In contrast, the use of 'something' eliminated 78% of unvoiced concerns compared with no question (odds ratio = 0.154, $p = 0.001$). The only difference was the change from 'any-' to 'something'.

Similarly, in ordinary conversation, even a tiny pause can be consequential. For example, Levinson (1983) has shown how the silence at line 2 in Extract 1 (shown by the dot inside parentheses; see the Appendix below) is treated by R as indicating a likely rejection of his proposal (at line 1). The evidence lies in line 3: instead of waiting for C to respond, R produces another bit of talk, which conveys an expectation that C may have some difficulty with the proposal. On the basis of only a 'micro-pause' (line 2), R has shifted from proposing a plan ('coming here on the way') to offering C a candidate reason for rejecting that plan (that C will not have 'enough time'). C endorses this at line 4.

Extract 1 [from Levinson, 1983: 335]

```
1   R:  What about coming here on the way
2           (.)
3   R:  Or doesn't that give you enough time?
4   C:  Well no I'm supervising here.
```

How this might be inferred from a micropause is beyond the scope of this chapter. The point is that *the details matter*. They matter for the participants in any interaction and so, if we are serious about analysing how human social life is managed through talk, we – as analysts – cannot afford to lose them.

SOME THEORETICAL UNDERPINNINGS

The data-driven origins of CA reflect a substantive theoretical position on the nature of talk: that talk, rather than being primarily about conveying *meaning* from one person's head to another's, is fundamentally about performing *social actions* (see Drew, 2005; Schegloff, 1996b). For example, we make offers, requests, apologies; we accept or decline invitations, agree or disagree with assessments, argue and find subtle ways to shift blame away from ourselves; we tease, exaggerate and so on. To talk is always *to do* something. This view of talk has profound implications for analysis. Rather than focusing primarily on topic – as one might do in a standard thematic analysis – our starting point is to ask: *what* is being *done* in the talk, and *how*?

These questions hint at the influence of Goffman and Garfinkel on the development of CA – 'two giants of American social theory' with whom Sacks and Schegloff had significant contact during the 1960s (Heritage, 2009: 301). From Goffman, as Heritage notes, came the idea that 'talk-in-interaction is a fundamental social domain that can be studied as an institutional entity in its own right' (2009: 302). From Garfinkel came the idea that 'the practices and procedures with which parties produce and recognize talk are talk's "ethnomethods"' (2009: 302–3; see Eberle, Chapter 13, this volume). In other words, for conversation analysts, talk-in-interaction is neither purely idiosyncratic nor haphazard. On the contrary, it must be a site of exceptional order – otherwise, it would be impossible to achieve mutual understanding (Schegloff, 2006). The primary goal of CA is, then, to describe and explicate those orderly mechanisms (or 'ethnomethods') that make mutual understanding possible (Atkinson and Heritage, 1984); or, to use Goffman's (1983) terminology, to describe and explicate the 'interaction order'.

This goal rests on a realist stance towards qualitative data analysis. Sacks (1995) conceptualized the enterprise as being akin to the natural sciences. He wanted to find a way for sociology to be an 'actual science', capable of handling the 'details of actual events' (1995: 621). This does not mean that CA is incompatible with the view that our realities are socially constructed. Indeed, it has been used to develop powerful arguments around how particular realities are (re-)produced and maintained through talk (e.g. Kitzinger, 2005; Whitehead, 2009). However, as a methodology, CA is to the 'interaction order' as anatomy is to the human body; rather than seeking to interpret what lies beneath an interaction (in the psychology or cognition of an individual), CA aims to produce cumulative findings about the structures of interaction and how they work.

AN IMPORTANT DISTINCTION: 'ORDINARY' VERSUS 'INSTITUTIONAL' TALK

Sacks's data set consisted of calls to a formal organization. CA has since been applied to numerous workplace settings (see Antaki, 2011; Drew and Heritage, 1992; Heritage and Clayman, 2010), gaining particular respect as a method for investigating doctor–patient interaction (Drew et al., 2001; Heritage and Maynard, 2006). Nevertheless, studies of 'ordinary' conversation – talk-in-interaction that is *not* directed towards some institutional goal (like diagnosing a patient, cross-examining a witness or teaching a class) – are viewed as *foundational* in CA.

This is because ordinary conversation is 'the most fundamental form of talk-in-interaction, the form from which all others derive' (Drew, 2005: 74). Not only does ordinary conversation pre-date more specialized forms of interaction historically, it does so in our personal development; we are largely socialized through ordinary conversation. Moreover, as Heritage (1984: 239) emphasizes, ordinary conversation is richer than its institutional counterparts, which involve a reduction and specialization of the wider 'range of conversational practices available for use'. Thus, while 'applied CA' is a burgeoning field, it is crucial that studies of ordinary conversation continue – both in order to understand what Schegloff (1998: 535) calls 'the primordial site of sociality and social life', and to develop a better basis for applying CA to workplace problems.

PREPARING DATA

CA has a distinctive approach to transcribing interactions, known as Jeffersonian notation after Gail Jefferson (see Kowal and O'Connell, Chapter 5, this volume). There is debate over how much detail should, and can, be captured in a transcript – and, indeed, in the analysis itself (for a useful overview, see www-staff.lboro.ac.uk/~ssjap/transcription/transcription.htm). CA transcripts usually show everything that was said – including cut-off words, little sounds and laughter particles – and make some attempt to show how it was said, using a range of conventions (see the Appendix). These are not as well established for non-vocal aspects, which is still a developing area of CA study (e.g. Goodwin, 1979; Heath et al., 2010; Lerner, 2002; Mondada, 2007). Increasingly, however, video recordings are seen as the gold standard for work on face-to-face interaction, since otherwise one misses not only the non-vocal aspects but an adequate understanding of what is happening during any silences on the recording.

Some conversation analysts use standard word processing packages for transcription. Others use data management programs, such as Transana, CLAN, ELAN, or Praat. There is not space here to consider their comparative merits. However, the main advantage of specialist packages is their added functionality, including tools to time pauses, organize and annotate data, and link recordings with transcripts. (For further advice see www.paultenhave.nl/Transcription.html and for further information about data collection see ten Have (2007)).

When working on funded research, I sometimes pay for basic transcripts. These allow me to trawl through my data set – while listening to the recordings – in search of phenomena of relevance to the study. I then re-transcribe relevant sections using Jeffersonian notation. This can be a satisfactory compromise, depending on your aims. However, it is crucial not to rely on basic transcripts when conducting the analysis proper – you need transcripts that show at least, in my view, every word (including cut-offs), the timing of talk (i.e. overlaps and pauses), and whether turns at talk are produced with rising or falling intonation. If you are using video, it is also crucial at least to note what happens during silences (e.g. a nod, a smile, etc.).

KEY ANALYTIC STAGES

In this section I will distil what is a messier, iterative process into four broad stages. Although I will skim over important points dealt with in longer introductions (e.g. Hutchby and Wooffitt, 2008; Sidnell, 2010; ten Have, 2007), these stages capture the fundamental approach. They highlight the *systematic* nature of doing CA; that – although single-case analyses can be appropriate (e.g. Schegloff, 1987; Toerien and Kitzinger, 2007; Whalen et al., 1988) – the goal is typically to identify *practices/mechanisms/structures* evident across *a collection* of cases. The four stages (see Drew, 2003), reflecting this goal, are:

1. Collection-building.
2. Individual case analysis.
3. Pattern-identification.
4. Accounting for or evaluating your patterns.

To provide a taste of what it is like to do CA, I will illustrate these through discussion of two studies – of ordinary and institutional talk-in-interaction. The first, conducted by my colleague at York, Traci Curl (now Walker), focused on the social action of *offering* in the classic corpora of telephone calls collected by conversation analysts across 40 years of research (Curl, 2006). As part of a study of affiliation in everyday interaction funded by the UK's Economic and Social Research Council (ESRC), Curl's aim was to describe how offering gets done and explain any patterns in interactional terms. The second, which I conducted in collaboration with colleagues Paul Drew, Annie Irvine and Roy Sainsbury (all at York), entailed examining over 200 recordings we had made of 'work-focused interviews', which are part of the UK's programme for administering unemployment benefits and helping people into work (Drew et al., 2010). These interviews, conducted by personal advisers in the government-funded organization Jobcentre Plus, vary depending on the benefit being claimed. For clarity, I will draw only on interviews with lone parents who, to receive benefit, had to attend periodic work-focused interviews, which included consideration of how they might prepare for future work. Funded by the UK's Department for Work and Pensions (DWP), our goal was to examine such interviews, with a view to producing effective practice guidelines.

These two studies represent opposite ends of the basic–applied spectrum. I hope to give a sense of the value of each within CA, and of how the stages I describe apply to both.

Analytic Stage 1: Collection-Building

Collections play a central role in CA (Drew, 2003: 148). They are what their name suggests: instances, collected together by the researcher, of an interactional phenomenon. What you collect depends on the purpose of your research; but in broad terms, you are likely to be collecting:

- a social action (e.g. offering) or specialized activity (e.g. advisers asking claimants for their job goals); or

- a technical feature of talk-in-interaction (e.g. how people produce collaborative turns at talk or the patterns associated with agreement and disagreement).

Collection-building is part of the analytic process – not just a preliminary step. This is because the question of what counts as an instance is analytically crucial. For example, in building her collection of offers, Curl was constantly having to decide what to include – to figure out what an offer looks like in real interaction. This was key to developing her analysis of how offers are designed. In the Jobcentre study, our collections were more clear cut because – like most institutional interactions – the interviews were partially structured by the organization (Heritage, 1997). We were, therefore, guided by this structure. However, as with any CA study, we identified this structure *inductively* (see Reichertz, Chapter 9, this volume) – from our data – rather than from organizational protocols. For example, it was clear from how they managed the interviews that advisers were expected to provide information to lone parents about the available support; all cases of them doing so were included in a collection.

When collection-building, it is crucial to be systematic (not selective): all available *candidate cases* of your focal action/activity/practice/structure should be included, even those about which you are uncertain. Analysis should begin with clear instances but your final account must be able to deal with the 'fuzzier' cases too – and any anomalies (Peräkylä, 2011; Schegloff, 1968). Although, in your write-up, you will show (mainly) your clearest cases, it is important to demonstrate that your findings are derived from the systematic study of a larger collection.

Analytic Stage 2: Individual Case Analysis

Quite how to set about analysing your cases depends on what you are trying to find out. However, two fundamental principles are likely to be relevant:

- turn design; and
- sequence organization.

As Drew (2012) puts it in a chapter devoted to the first of these: 'Turn design refers to how a speaker constructs a turn at talk – what is selected or what goes into "building" a turn to do the action it is designed to do, in such a way as to be understood as doing that action' (for more on what constitutes a 'turn at talk' see Sacks et al., 1974). Turn design goes hand in hand with the principle that talk is action. For example, we might select specific words to convey that we are making an offer rather than another action. If we want to understand what action is being performed, we must consider the design of the turn; if we know what action is being done, we must analyse how it was done. Ask yourself: what is it about this turn that makes me hear it as doing the action I think it is doing? Try to describe, as precisely as possible, exactly how the turn is designed. You might consider word choice, format (e.g. is it done as an interrogative or a declarative?), intonation and whether the action is done straightforwardly or is somehow disguised or mitigated. For an introduction to identifying actions in talk, see Sidnell (2010).

In addition to focusing on the design of individual turns, CA considers the 'sequential' relationship *between turns*. As Schegloff (2007) shows in his primer on sequence organization, turns at talk are not haphazard, but have a structure. They are organized into sequences. Most basically, a sequence consists of an initiating and responsive turn – such as a greeting and return greeting; a question and answer; a request and its granting or denial. A sequence is, then, *a course of action* implemented through talk (rather than just a single action in one turn). So, if we are analysing an offer, we should look also at what happens next. How is the offer responded to? All the questions we have asked about the design of the offer we can ask about its response.

The sequential relationship between two turns is crucial because *linked turns* are the basic building blocks of meaningful interaction; when a speaker responds to a turn, the speaker is displaying an understanding of what kind of action he or she takes the prior speaker to have performed (Heritage, 1984). This makes linked turns a powerful analytic resource. For example, if the recipient of a turn responds with an acceptance and appreciation, we have a basis for arguing that the recipient was treating the prior turn as an offer – not just that we, as analysts, saw it that way. This is referred to as the 'participant's orientation', and reflects another core principle: that the analyst should explicate what the *participants* were doing in the talk, as opposed to our own interpretation, perhaps overlaid with our intellectual or political preoccupations (Schegloff, 1997). Of course recipients (like analysts) can be wrong. Perhaps the first speaker did not mean to be doing an offer after all. Like the analyst, the first speaker can inspect the responsive turn to see whether the recipient has understood his or her turn in the way it was meant. If so, the interaction can move forward. If not, there are mechanisms in talk for the first speaker to 'repair' such misunderstandings (see Hayashi et al., 2013; Schegloff, 1992a).

There is not space to develop this discussion further. However, I hope the key points are clear: that individual case analysis includes both careful examination of the *design of individual turns at talk* and of *the relationship between turns*. When building collections, then, it is important to include the relevant sequence, not just the single turn.

Analytic Stage 3: Pattern-Identification

Stages 2 and 3 are closely intertwined. As you carry out your case analyses, you should also note comparative features. The goal is to identify *patterns* in your collection. Again, precisely what you will be looking for will depend on your aims. However, *variations in turn design* are likely to be important in many studies. Curl's (2006) research provides a good example. She found three main formats for doing offering. For brevity, we will consider two:

- a '*do you want me to X*' construction, such as: 'd'you want me=b:ring the: chai:rs' (2006: 1266); and
- an announcement of the offered assistance, which matches a previously identified trouble – such as 'I:ll take her in: Sunday' (2006: 1271) as a response to the prior speaker's difficulty in getting her daughter to the bus depot.

Crucially, Curl (2006) showed that these formats are not used randomly; there is a clear pattern across her collection. The 'do you want' format is *only* used (in Curl's collection of around 50 offers) for problems *educed* from talk that took place earlier in the conversation – meaning that the problem may have been latent in the conversation, but was not treated as a problem in need of remedy in the talk immediately preceding the offer. For offers in response to such overtly expressed problems, the second format (above) is used. There is, then, a clear relationship between turn design and the sequential location of offers. This is a powerful example of what I mean by pattern-identification. When identifying patterns, the interrelated concepts of *action* (e.g. an offer), *turn design* (e.g. one of the above two formats) and *sequence* (e.g. where in the interaction the formats occur) are fundamental to the analytic process.

Pattern-identification is equally important in studies of institutional interaction. In our Jobcentre cases we found a striking difference in how advisers informed claimants about the 'back-to-work' support available: typically, advisers simply provided the information; in some cases, however, they went on – after delivering the information – to ask the claimant directly whether he or she wanted additional support. Extracts 2 and 3 illustrate this contrast. In Extract 2, the adviser treats the activity as one of information provision *only*. This is made explicit by the adviser at lines 3–8. In Extract 3, the adviser goes on to produce another social action: a kind of offer to the claimant. So here we have not so much a difference in design of the same action, but an entirely different approach to performing the same institutional activity.

Extract 2; lone parent interview 092

```
01    PA:     .hhh Eh:m (0.3) your other op:tion (.) i:s: that you are
02            eligible for trainin::g (0.4) through our (0.3) training
03            providers … so (0.4) it's en:ti:rely up to you really you know
04            (.) which way you want to go … you can leave it until the
05            time's right and just start looking for jobs you know i- if if
06            that's your decision [but .hhh all I'm here for is: you
07    Cla:                         [Yeah
08    PA:     [know to give you the (yeah) (0.4) the advice
09    Cla:    [To advise yeah
```

Extract 3; lone parent interview 172

```
((Earlier information provision not shown due to space constraints))
01    PA:     Ha- how- how would you feel at this moment in time
02            ((claimant name)) me sort of helping you find [(.) the
03    (Cla):                                                [(Mm)
04    PA:     right type of job to match your circumstances now by you
05            being put on my caseload
06    Cla:    Well I d- I- [I do
07    PA:                  [Would you=
08    Cla:    =Yeah=
09    PA:     =Would you like that
10    Cla:    Yeah
```

The analytic process moves, then, between individual cases and cross-case comparisons in an effort to identify patterns in a collection. Once we have done so, we need to make sense of these in some way. This is typically the hardest part.

Analytic Stage 4: Accounting for or Evaluating Patterns

This final stage involves 'trying to identify the contingency which the pattern [you have identified] systematically handles, or to which it offers a solution' (Drew, 2003: 153). Drew acknowledges that it is hard to say how to look for such an account but that 'very often, this will involve ... consider[ing] *where and how the object or pattern in question arose*' (2003: 153). Curl's (2006) study again provides a good example. You will recall that she identified three formats for doing offers. She then needed to go one step further: to explain why the three formats are not interchangeable. Why should it matter so much which format is used that speakers will shift from one to another if they figure they have picked the wrong one?

Curl (2006) shows that the formats differ on a core dimension: whether they foreground the speaker (the one making the offer) or the recipient (the one who would benefit). By selecting from among the formats, Curl argues, 'offerers can display themselves as independent actors, choosing to assist; or they can make offers which expose the implicit desires of others' (2006: 1277). This distinction really matters when an offer has been generated within the current interaction. If a speaker produces an offer using the 'do you want' format, they foreground the other's desires. Thus, using this format immediately after someone has announced a trouble implies that the other was 'fishing' for the offer – that it is only being made because the other expressed a need. Avoiding this format is a way of claiming that the offerer is acting independently; the other's need is not overtly exposed. By going beyond describing her data, Curl explained what is at stake, *interactionally*, for participants using the formats she identified.

In our Jobcentre study, we were tasked with identifying effective practice in work-focused interviews. Our final analytic step was, therefore, less about explaining the patterns we saw and more about evaluating them in relation to what was expected of advisers (Toerien et al., 2011). Our measure of effectiveness was the *interactional consequences*, within the interview, of what advisers did. Extract 4 provides an example. It shows the pattern illustrated in Extracts 2 and 3: the distinction between an 'information-only' approach (to talking about available support) and the addition of an offer for the claimant to take up that support. In Extract 4, one adviser uses both approaches in the same interview.

From lines 1–29 it looks like she is going to provide information only (note the similarity between lines 20–21 in Extract 4 and lines 3–4 in Extract 2). However, she returns to the matter of additional support, this time offering the claimant the chance to take it up: 'd'you want to actually join us and see us regularly' (lines 30–32). As it turns out, this claimant declines the offer – as she is entitled to do. Of significance, for our evaluation, is how the two approaches create very different 'slots' for what the claimant can properly do next. As the turns in bold show, 'informings' by the adviser can be properly receipted just with minimal acknowledgements like 'yeah' and 'mm' (Heritage and Sefi, 1992). By contrast, an offer makes relevant something more: an acceptance or declination (see line 33).

Extract 4; lone parent initial interview (ID 031)

```
01   PA:    What we do sometimes if y- if you're looking for work and
02          you're ready for work you can join: our caseload. hh so:
03          you can see us regularly or you [can keep in touch with
04   Cla:                                   [Yeah
05   PA:    us by phone (.) (    ) advisor by phone [to kind
06   Cla:                                           [Yeah
07   PA:    of .hhh you know .hh [we'll look for work for you:
08   Cla:                        [Yeah
09          (.)
10   Cla:   M[m
11   PA:    [You'll look for work for yourself obviously but we'll
12          look for work for you and we'll let you know if we find
```

```
13            out about any[thing you might be
14   Cla:                [Yeah
15   PA:      interested s[o you: can do that
16   Cla:                 [Okay
17   PA:      .hhh
18   Cla:     Yeah
19            (.)
20   PA:      If you choose not to do that that's fine it's enti:rely
21            up to you
22   Cla:     Yeah=
23   PA:      =But (0.2) you know (.) obviously (0.4) you know (.)
24            we're here

((a little later …))

30   PA:      And it- (.) I don- what do you want to do: d'y- would
31            (0.2) d'you want to actually join us and see us
32            regu[larly or
33   Cla:         [I would like to look f:- (0.6) on my own hh.
34   PA:      That's [fi:ne
35   Cla:            [Is that okay [((laughs))
36   PA:                           [Absolutely there's no compunction
37            at all
```

The 'information-only' approach runs, then, a clear risk for advisers: missed opportunities to sign claimants up to a support programme. Because it relies on claimants taking the initiative to get in touch in the future, even those who might respond positively to an offer of further support may never participate for reasons such as forgetting what is on offer, anxiety about contacting Jobcentre Plus, lack of motivation, etc. By contrast, an explicit offer gives them a slot to sign up right away. In this sense, the second approach is more effective because it *opens up* such an opportunity in the immediate interaction. In our sample, lone parents only ever joined an adviser's caseload during the interview if such an offer was made; none of the lone parents responded to an adviser's 'information-only' approach by asking, there and then, to be signed up. We do not have appropriate data to evaluate what happened after the interviews but will return to this issue in our discussion of 'new developments'. The point is that we – like Curl (2006) – went beyond describing the pattern we observed. In Curl's case, she sought to explain that pattern; in ours, we described the interactional consequences of the two advisory practices as part of our wider evaluation of effectiveness. In both studies this final stage addressed the 'so what?' question about our findings.

LIMITS OF STUDYING RECORDED INTERACTIONS

I have emphasized what I take to be a central advantage of CA: its focus on what happens in real interactions. As is often true, this is also a limitation: there are questions that cannot be answered by direct observation. Notably, CA cannot access speakers' intentions or emotions and is deliberately agnostic on such matters because it understands talk *as social action* rather than as a conduit to some underlying state. For example, we know that speakers typically do not 'just say no' in response to actions like invitations and requests. Instead, they tend to delay, mitigate and/or account for their declination (Pomerantz, 1984) – hence the joke about 'I'm washing my hair' as a response to being asked out by someone you do not like. Although the poverty of this account makes it funny, the point is accurate: there can be a significant disconnect between the *procedures* by which we perform an action (giving an inability account for declining an invitation) and how we *feel* (we do not want to go). This is not a problem if you are aiming to understand how people decline invitations – something CA can address. It is if you want to know how it felt to do so or what, in psychological terms, motivated the declination – things that CA cannot address.

For some, this focus on the interaction is unproductively limited. For example, other researchers working on effectiveness in work-focused interviews regularly asked us about the impact of adviser training, experience, working environment, location and so forth. To some extent, these questions missed the point of using CA: that it gave direct access to the immediate interactional consequences of different adviser strategies (the unit of analysis is the interactional practice, not the adviser or location). Such questions may, however, be usefully addressed in mixed methods studies (see Morse and Maddox, Chapter 36, this volume) which combine CA with quantitative approaches. More troubling is the charge that, in focusing only on recorded interactions, CA cannot address society's 'big issues'. Debate has centred on the study of inequalities (especially gender). Some have argued cogently in CA's favour (e.g. Kitzinger, 2000; 2008; Speer and Stokoe, 2011; Wilkinson and Kitzinger, 2006) on the basis that, since talk-in-interaction is at the heart of almost any social process, to study talk is to study how our world – with all its inequalities – is (re-)produced.

However, there are at least two difficulties. The first is practical: how to obtain relevant data. The second is conceptual: how to ground the claim that gender (or any demographic factor) is *relevant* in a specific interaction. Given that anybody may be categorized in multiple ways (e.g. as South African, an adult, a researcher, etc.), what gives us the warrant to say that somebody is *speaking as* a woman or man (Schegloff, 1992b)? One solution is to rely on the concept of 'participant orientations' – to treat as gendered only talk in which participants make gender overtly relevant. Studies have shown, however, both that non-gendered terms can be used to index gender and that gendered terms can be used in ways that, while making gender available, do not make gender relevant; for example, 'grown man' may be used to emphasize someone's adult status rather than gender (Stockill and Kitzinger, 2007; also see Kitzinger, 2007). Moreover, as Kitzinger (2000) argues, it would be 'unbearably limiting' if one could only explore inequalities when participants overtly oriented to them: 'Indeed it is *precisely the fact that sexist, heterosexist and racist assumptions are routinely incorporated into everyday conversations* without anyone noticing or responding to them that way which is of interest' (Kitzinger, 2000: 171; emphasis in original). Drawing on some of Sacks's analysis, Kitzinger argues that it *is* possible to address such interests 'without violating the precepts of CA' (ibid.). There is not space to explore these debates further, but see Speer and Stokoe (2011) for a detailed overview, and Stokoe (2006) for a discussion of how membership categorization analysis (MCA), which is rooted in Sacks's work, may be a useful tool alongside CA.

The take-home message here is twofold. First, the data you collect will impose limits on the questions you can answer. As with any method, it is vital to be sure there is a comfortable fit between the two. Second, CA demands a level of empirical rigour that can make it difficult to follow a predetermined path. For example, I began my PhD – an analysis of the norm for women's hair removal – with an interest in the social construction of gender (Toerien and Wilkinson, 2003). When I shifted from interviewing women to recording salon hair removal sessions I found it hard to retain this focus; in the salon, gender was seldom made overtly relevant. My analysis thus shifted to hair removal as work (Toerien and Kitzinger, 2007). For some, this is constricting; for others, it is a 'voyage of discovery'.

NEW DEVELOPMENTS

In this final section I will touch on two significant developments within CA: cross-linguistic studies and epistemic domains. Then, since we started with CA's focus on recorded interactions, I will end by discussing the combination of CA and quantitative approaches, which depend on other kinds of data.

Students often ask whether CA's foundational findings – based mainly on American or British English – are universal. Because these findings are used as an analytic resource, researchers working on other languages need to know whether they can legitimately do the same. A team at the Max Planck Institute for Psycholinguistics in Nijmegen has been working on this ambitious question. Thus far, their findings indicate greater universality of interactional structures (such as the turn-taking system) than the anthropological literature would have predicted. This points, as Stivers et al. argue, 'to a single shared infrastructure for language use with likely ethological foundations' (2009: 10587). This work, together with the growing use of CA to study languages other than English, offers both a corrective to CA's Anglo-bias and the promise of a better understanding of being human.

The concept of 'epistemic domains' derives predominantly from a series of studies by Heritage and Raymond (e.g. 2005; Raymond and Heritage, 2006) and is fast attaining the status of a key concept in CA. Essentially, the focus is on what a speaker knows and is entitled to know relative to the recipient. Although this is an inherently relational matter, open to manipulation and challenge, a person's epistemic *status* is typically treated as largely agreed upon with respect to specific domains (Heritage, 2012a). For example, individuals are generally treated as knowing more about their 'relatives, friends, pets, jobs and hobbies than others' (2012a: 6), while socially sanctioned 'experts' are generally treated as knowing more about their field than 'amateurs'. The epistemic *stance* we display through our turn design may – but need not – align with this typical status. For example, when talking about a medical diagnosis with my physician, I may or may not treat myself as less knowledgeable than him or her. Although I cannot do justice to it here, the significance of this line of analysis should not be underestimated. Heritage is starting to show that epistemic asymmetries are central to the construction of social action (2012a) and to the machinery that drives sequences in interaction (2012b) – both of which underpin much of the conversation analytic enterprise.

Finally, you may have been puzzled by my use of a *statistical* finding as evidence that the details of talk matter. This reflects a trend towards combining CA with quantitative methods (see Morse and Maddox, Chapter 36, this volume) – a significant shift given the fear that coding may result in 'the truly interactional properties of the object being overlooked' (Drew, 2005: 99). So why the shift? The answer lies in the nature of the research question. As Heritage (1999) argues, most applied CA is underpinned by a distributional, quantitative logic – an interest in the association between interactional practices and some other aspect of the social world. Examples include whether doctors prescribe medically unnecessary antibiotics (Stivers, 2007) and patients report being satisfied with their consultation (Robinson and Heritage, 2006). Such studies require the collection of both recorded consultations and extra-interactional data – for example, questionnaire responses, demographic information, and knowledge about prescribing guidelines. In our Jobcentre study, the link between advisory practices and whether lone parents take up support programmes at some point after the work-focused interview could have been explored in a similar way had we had access to the requisite data.

A word of caution: such studies depend on robust CA findings for their success (Heritage, 1999). To code one's data meaningfully for statistical analysis requires a nuanced understanding of how interaction works; without this, one risks lumping together practices that are interactionally distinct. It is also worth reiterating the need for basic CA research to flourish alongside its applied counterpart. As Heritage puts it:

> There continues to be an unquestionably compelling need for the fundamental research that renews the analytical base of CA. ... Nonetheless, part of the claim of any framework worth its salt is that it can sustain 'applied' research of various kinds ... just as an architect can shift from a vertical to a horizontal view of a building, so ... it seems to be possible to shift from basic CA to 'applied' analysis and back again. (1999: 73)

APPENDIX: TRANSCRIPTION GLOSSARY (SEE ATKINSON AND HERITAGE, 1984; JEFFERSON, 2004)

Some aspects of the relative timing of utterances

[ ] square brackets	Overlapping talk
= equals sign	No discernible interval between turns
(0.5) time in parentheses	Intervals within or between talk (measured in tenths of a second)
(.) period in parentheses	Discernible interval within or between talk but too short to measure (less than two-tenths of a second)

Some characteristics of speech delivery

Punctuation symbols are designed to capture intonation, not grammar, and are used to describe intonation at the end of a word/sound, at the end of a sentence or at some other shorter unit:

. period	Closing intonation
, comma	Slightly rising intonation (a little hitch up on the end of the word)
? question mark	Fully rising intonation
- dash	Abrupt cut off of sound
: colon	Extension of preceding sound – the more colons, the greater the extension
here underlining	Emphasized relative to surrounding talk
HERE upper case	Louder relative to surrounding talk
hhh.	Audible outbreath (number of h's indicates length)
.hhh	Audible inbreath (number of h's indicates length)
(h)	Audible aspirations in speech (e.g. laughter particles)
Hah hah or huh huh etc.	Beats of laughter
( ) empty single brackets or words enclosed in single brackets	Transcriber unable to hear words or uncertain of hearing
((word)) words enclosed in double brackets	Transcriber's comments

ACKNOWLEDGEMENTS

I'd like to thank Paul Drew for all I've learnt from teaching CA alongside him for the past three years. This chapter reflects the development of my thinking over that time. I'm also very grateful for the funding I've received through my RCUK fellowship and the DWP.

Many thanks also to Uwe Flick and two anonymous reviewers for their helpful comments on an earlier draft of this chapter.

FURTHER READING

Although it is impossible to learn to do CA by reading one chapter, I hope I have given you enough of a taste of this highly specialized approach for you to decide whether to pursue it further. If so, you may like to start with the following:

Sidnell, Jack (2010) *Conversation Analysis: An Introduction*. Oxford: Wiley-Blackwell.

Drew, Paul (2005) 'Conversation analysis', in Kristine L. Fitch and Robert E. Sanders (eds), *Handbook of Language and Social Interaction*. Mahwah, NJ: Lawrence Erlbaum. pp. 71–101.

Heritage, John (1997) 'Conversation analysis and institutional talk: Analysing data', in David Silverman (ed.), *Qualitative Research: Theory, Method and Practice*. London: Sage. pp. 161–82.

REFERENCES

Antaki, Charles (ed.) (2011) *Applied Conversation Analysis: Intervention and Change in Institutional Talk*. Basingstoke: Palgrave Macmillan.

Atkinson, J. Maxwell and Heritage, John (eds) (1984) *Structures of Social Action: Studies in Conversation Analysis*. Cambridge: Cambridge University Press.

Curl, Traci (2006) 'Offers of assistance: Constraints on syntactic design', *Journal of Pragmatics*, 38: 1257–80.

Drew, Paul (2003) 'Conversation analysis', in Jonathan Smith (ed.), *Qualitative Psychology: A Practical Guide to Research Methods*. London, Sage. pp. 132–58.

Drew, Paul (2005) 'Conversation analysis', in Kristine L. Fitch and Robert E. Sanders (eds), *Handbook of Language and Social Interaction*. Mahwah, NJ: Lawrence Erlbaum. pp. 71–101.

Drew, Paul (2012) 'Turn design', in Jack Sidnell and Tanya Stivers (eds), *The Handbook of Conversation Analysis*. Oxford: Wiley-Blackwell. pp. 131–49.

Drew, Paul and Heritage, John (1992) *Talk at Work: Interaction in Institutional Settings*. Cambridge: Cambridge University Press.

Drew, Paul, Chatwin, John and Collins, Sarah (2001) 'Conversation analysis: A method for research into interactions between patients and health-care professionals', *Health Expectations*, 4 (1): 58–70.

Drew, Paul, Toerien, Merran, Irvine, Annie and Sainsbury, Roy (2010) 'A study of language and communication between advisers and claimants in work focused interviews', *Department for Work and Pensions Research Report 633*.

Goffman, Erving (1983) 'The interaction order', *American Sociological Review*, 48: 1–17.

Goodwin, Charles (1979) 'The interactive construction of a sentence in natural conversation', in George Psathas (ed.), *Everyday Language: Studies in Ethnomethodology*. New York: Irvington. pp. 97–121.

Hayashi, Makoto, Raymond, Geoffrey and Sidnell, Jack (eds) (2013) *Conversational Repair and Human Understanding*. Cambridge: Cambridge University Press.

Heath, Christian, Hindmarsh, Jon and Luff, Paul (2010) *Video in Qualitative Research*. London: Sage.

Heritage, John (1984) 'Conversation analysis', in John Heritage, *Garfinkel and Ethnomethodology*. Cambridge: Polity Press. pp. 233–80.

Heritage, John (1997) 'Conversation analysis and institutional talk: Analysing data', in David Silverman (ed.), *Qualitative Research: Theory, Method and Practice*. London: Sage. pp. 161–82.

Heritage, John (1999) 'CA at century's end: Practices of talk-in-interaction, their distributions and their outcomes', *Research on Language and Social Interaction*, 32: 69–76.

Heritage, John (2009) 'Conversation analysis as social theory', in Bryan S. Turner (ed.), *The New Blackwell Companion to Social Theory*. Oxford: Wiley-Blackwell.

Heritage, John (2012a) 'Epistemics in action: Action formation and territories of knowledge', *Research on Language and Social Interaction*, 45: 1–29.

Heritage, John (2012b) 'The epistemic engine: Sequence organization and territories of knowledge', *Research on Language and Social Interaction*, 45: 30–52.

Heritage, John and Clayman, Steven (2010) *Talk in Action: Interactions, Identities and Institutions*. Chichester: Wiley-Blackwell.

Heritage, John and Maynard, Douglas W. (2006) *Communication in Medical Care: Interaction between Primary Care Physicians and Patients*. Cambridge: Cambridge University Press.

Heritage, John and Raymond, Geoffrey (2005) 'The terms of agreement: Indexing epistemic authority and subordination in talk-in-interaction', *Social Psychology Quarterly*, 68: 15–38.

Heritage, John and Sefi, Sue (1992) 'Dilemmas of advice: Aspects of the delivery and reception of advice in interactions between health visitors and first time mothers', in Paul Drew and John Heritage (eds), *Talk at Work: Interaction in Institutional Settings*. Cambridge: Cambridge University Press. pp. 359–419.

Heritage, John, Robinson, Jeffrey D., Elliott, Marc N., Beckett, Megan and Wilkes, Michael (2007) 'Reducing patients' unmet concerns in primary care: The difference one word can make', *Journal of General Internal Medicine*, 22: 1429–33.

Hutchby, Ian and Wooffitt, Robin (2008) *Conversation Analysis: Principles, Practices and Applications*, 2nd edition. Cambridge: Polity Press.

Jefferson, Gail (2004) 'Glossary of transcript symbols with an introduction', in Gene H. Lerner (ed.), *Conversation Analysis: Studies from the First Generation*. Philadelphia: John Benjamins. pp. 13–23.

Kitzinger, Celia (2000) 'Doing feminist conversation analysis', *Feminism & Psychology*, 10: 163–93.

Kitzinger, Celia (2004) 'Feminist approaches', in Clive Seale et al. (eds), *Qualitative Research Practice*. London: Sage. pp. 125–40.

Kitzinger, Celia (2005) '"Speaking as a heterosexual": (How) does sexuality matter for talk-in-interaction?', *Research on Language and Social Interaction*, 38: 221–65.

Kitzinger, Celia (2007) 'Is "woman" always relevantly gendered?', *Gender and Language*, 1: 39–49.

Kitzinger, Celia (2008) 'Developing feminist conversation analysis: A response to Wowk', *Human Studies*, 31: 179–208.

Kitzinger, Celia and Toerien, Merran (2009) 'The turn of talk', *Association of Qualitative Research In-depth paper*. Available at: www.aqr.org.uk/indepth/summer2009/ (accessed 9 May 2013).

Lerner, Gene H. (2002) 'Turn-sharing: The choral co-production of talk in interaction', in Cecilia E. Ford et al. (eds), *The Language of Turn and Sequence*. Oxford: Oxford University Press. pp. 225–56.

Levinson, Stephen C. (1983) *Pragmatics*. Cambridge: Cambridge University Press.

Mondada, Lorenza (2007) 'Multimodal resources for turn-taking: Pointing and the emergence of possible next speakers', *Discourse Studies*, 9 (2): 195–226.

Peräkylä, Anssi (2011) 'Validity in research on naturally occurring social interaction', in David Silverman (ed.), *Qualitative Research*, 3rd edition. London: Sage. pp. 365–82.

Pomerantz, Anita (1984) 'Agreeing and disagreeing with assessments: Some features of preferred/dispreferred turn shapes', in J. Maxwell Atkinson and John Heritage (eds), *Structures of Social Action: Studies in Conversation Analysis*. Cambridge: Cambridge University Press. pp. 57–101.

Raymond, Geoffrey and Heritage, John (2006) 'The epistemics of social relations: Owning grandchildren', *Language in Society*, 35 (5): 677–705.

Robinson, Jeffrey D. and Heritage, John (2006) 'Physicians' opening questions and patients' satisfaction', *Patient Education and Counseling*, 60: 279–85.

Sacks, Harvey (1995) *Lectures on Conversation*, ed. Gail Jefferson, with Introduction by Emanuel A. Schegloff. Malden, MA: Blackwell.

Sacks, Harvey, Schegloff, Emanuel A. and Jefferson, Gail (1974) 'A simplest systematics of turn-taking for conversation', *Language*, 50: 696–735.

Schegloff, Emanuel A. (1968) 'Sequencing in conversational openings', *American Anthropologist*, 70: 1075–95.

Schegloff, Emanuel A. (1987) 'Analyzing single episodes of interaction: An exercise in conversation analysis', *Social Psychology Quarterly*, 50: 101–14.

Schegloff, Emanuel A. (1992a) 'Repair after next turn: The last structurally provided defense of intersubjectivity in conversation', *American Journal of Sociology*, 97: 1295–1345.

Schegloff, Emanuel A. (1992b) 'In another context', in Alessandro Duranti and Charles Goodwin (eds), *Rethinking Context: Language as an Interactive Phenomenon*. Cambridge: Cambridge University Press. pp. 193–227.

Schegloff, Emanuel A. (1996a) 'Issues of relevance for discourse analysis: Contingency in action, interaction and co-participant context', in Eduard H. Hovy and Donia R. Scott (eds), *Computational and Conversational Discourse: Burning issues – an Interdisciplinary Account*. Heidelberg: Springer. pp. 3–38.

Schegloff, Emanuel A. (1996b) 'Confirming allusions: Toward an empirical account of action', *American Journal of Sociology*, 104: 161–216.

Schegloff, Emanuel A. (1997) 'Whose text? Whose context?', *Discourse & Society*, 8: 165–87.

Schegloff, Emanuel A. (1998) 'Body torque', *Social Research*, 65: 535–96.

Schegloff, Emanuel A. (2006) 'Interaction: The infrastructure for social institutions, the natural ecological niche for language, and the arena in which culture is enacted', in Nicholas J. Enfield and Stephen C. Levinson (eds), *Roots of Human Sociality: Culture, Cognition and Interaction*. London: Berg. pp. 70–96.

Schegloff, Emanuel A. (2007) *Sequence Organisation in Interaction: A Primer in Conversation Analysis*, vol. 1. Cambridge: Cambridge University Press.

Sidnell, Jack (2010) *Conversation Analysis: An Introduction*. Oxford: Wiley-Blackwell.

Speer, Susan A. and Stokoe, Elizabeth (2011) *Conversation and Gender*. Cambridge: Cambridge University Press.

Stivers, Tanya (2007) *Prescribing Under Pressure: Parent–Physician Conversations and Antibiotics*. New York: Oxford University Press.

Stivers, Tanya, Enfield, N.J., Brown, Penelope, Englert, Christina, Hayashi, Makoto, Heinemann, Trine, Hoymann, Gertie, Rossano, Federico, de Ruiter, Jan Peter, Yoon, Kyung-Eun and Levinson, Stephen C. (2009) 'Universals and cultural variation in turn-taking in conversation', *Proceedings of the National Academy of Sciences*, 106 (26): 10587–592.

Stockill, Clare and Kitzinger, Celia (2007) 'Gendered "people": How linguistically non-gendered terms can have gendered interactional relevance', *Feminism & Psychology*, 17 (2): 224–36.

Stokoe, Elizabeth (2006) 'On ethnomethodology, feminism, and the analysis of categorical reference to gender in talk-in-interaction', *The Sociological Review*, 54: 467–94.

ten Have, Paul (2007) *Doing Conversation Analysis: A Practical Guide*, 2nd edition. London: Sage.

Toerien, Merran and Kitzinger, Celia (2007) 'Emotional labour in action: Navigating multiple involvements in the beauty salon', *Sociology*, 41 (4): 645–62.

Toerien, Merran and Wilkinson, Sue (2003) 'Gender and body hair: Constructing the feminine woman', *Women's Studies International Forum*, 26 (4): 333–44.

Toerien, Merran, Irvine, Annie, Drew, Paul and Sainsbury, Roy (2011) 'Should mandatory Jobseeker interviews be personalised? The politics of using conversation analysis to make effective practice recommendations', in Charles Antaki (ed.), *Applied Conversation Analysis: Intervention and Change in Institutional Talk*. Basingstoke: Palgrave Macmillan. pp. 140–60.

Whalen, Jack, Zimmerman, Don H. and Whalen, Marilyn R. (1988) 'When words fail: A single case analysis', *Social Problems*, 35 (4): 335–62.

Whitehead, Kevin (2009) '"Categorizing the categorizer": The management of racial common sense in interaction', *Social Psychology Quarterly*, 72 (4): 325–42.

Wilkinson, Sue (2006) 'Analysing interaction in focus groups', in Paul Drew et al. (eds), *Talk and Interaction in Social Research Methods*. London: Sage. pp. 72–93.

Wilkinson, Sue and Kitzinger, Celia (2006) 'Conversation analysis, gender and sexuality', in Ann Weatherall et al. (eds.), *Language, Discourse and Social Psychology*. Palgrave Macmillan. pp. 206–30.

23

Discourses and Discourse Analysis

Carla Willig

Discourse analysis is concerned with the ways in which language constructs and mediates social and psychological realities. Discourse analysts foreground the constructive and performative properties of language, paying particular attention to the effects of our choice of words to express or describe something. Discourse analysis involves the careful examination of talk and texts in order to trace the ways in which discourses bring into being the objects and subjects of which they speak. Discourse analysis is based on the premise that the words we choose to speak about something, and the way in which they are spoken or written, shape the sense that can be made of the world and our experience of it. Discourse analysts are acutely conscious of the power of discourse, and they consider our social and experiential worlds to be the product of our discursive construction of them.

A discourse analytic approach challenges the idea that the accounts people provide of their thoughts, feelings and experiences are comparable to a mirror image of what is going on inside of them, in their hearts and minds. Such an approach is the intellectual product of what is often referred to as 'the turn to language', itself a consequence of a philosophical reappraisal of the role of language in human interaction and experience. This reappraisal involved considering the social effects of language, its action orientation and its constitutive power. Ludwig Wittgenstein (1953) and John Austin (1962) are perhaps the most well-known early proponents of this perspective on language. Wittgenstein's (1953) argument that the meaning of words is constituted by their function in particular 'language games' and Austin's (1962) assertion that speech is a form of action and that we 'do things with words' have been enormously influential within this context.

A discourse analytic approach to qualitative research adopts what Forrester (1996: 32) describes as the 'language-dominant view of language'. According to this view, language and thought are inextricably bound up with one another because language produces 'versions and visions of reality as codes and conventions embedded within particular cultural contexts' (Forrester, 1996: 33). From this point of view, language is organized into discourses which are culturally specific and whose availability depends upon social, historical and cultural contexts. Discourses may be defined as 'sets of statements that construct objects and an array of subject positions' (Parker, 1994: 245). Discourses make available particular interpretative repertoires, which provide us with 'a lexicon or register of terms and metaphors', which can be 'drawn upon to characterise and evaluate actions and events' in particular ways (Potter and Wetherell, 1987: 138). Discourse analysis is concerned with understanding these processes of discursive construction and their social consequences.

VARIETIES OF DISCURSIVE ANALYSIS

A concern with the role of discourse can be identified across a wide range of disciplines within the social and human sciences (e.g. sociology, philosophy, cultural studies, linguistics, social psychology), and as a result a variety of approaches to the analysis of discourse have emerged. Although all of them emphasize the importance of processes of discursive construction in the organization and management of social life, they differ in the emphasis they place on different aspects and dimensions of these processes. For example, some discourse analysts are particularly concerned with the ways in which institutional discourses are implicated in the maintenance of power relations within a society, for example by obscuring or mystifying power inequalities (e.g. Wodak, 1996; Fairclough, 1995), thus taking a 'critical' approach to the analysis of discourse. Others are more interested in the micro-level processes associated with the use of discourse in relatively mundane, everyday conversations (e.g. Schegloff, 1968; Drew and Heritage, 1992) and their role in creating and maintaining the social worlds that speakers inhabit; this approach is referred to as 'conversation analysis' (see Toerien, Chapter 22, this volume). Another approach, perhaps best described as 'socio-linguistic', involves the close examination of the 'language behaviour' of different social groups in order to understand the differences between them and their implications for social (and power) relations (e.g. Labov, 1966; Tannen, 1990). Yet another way of studying the role of discourse involves the examination of cultural representations (see Winter, Chapter 17, this volume), for example in the media (see Hodgetts and Chamberlain, Chapter 26, this volume), and the ways in which they make available and thus perpetuate shared meanings. Here, the focus is upon 'the production and circulation of meaning through language' (Hall, 1997:1) and its role in the production of 'culture'. There is also narrative analysis (see Esin et al., Chapter 14, this volume) which is concerned with the structure, content and function of the stories people tell about their experiences, in terms of both their social impact and their psychological effects (e.g. Riessman, 1993; Mishler, 1995). There are many ways in which researchers have addressed questions about the role of discourse in social life, and in this chapter we are going to examine in more detail only one of these. However, Wodak (1996: ch. 1) provides a helpful historical overview of a range of perspectives on the study of discourse.

APPROACH ADOPTED IN THIS CHAPTER

The approach to discourse analysis adopted in this chapter is informed by a concern with the availability of discourses and interpretative repertoires to individuals when they speak about their experiences. As such, the approach adopted here can be located within the social psychological tradition of discourse analysis as it was developed within the UK over the last 25 years or so (e.g. Potter and Wetherell, 1987; Parker, 1992). The type of discourse analysis described in the remainder of this chapter seeks to generate insights about how speakers draw on available discursive resources in order to construct particular versions of their experiences. It is also interested in the action orientation of the deployment of discursive resources within a particular context; for example, we may want to understand what may be achieved, socially and/or interpersonally, by describing something in a particular way. Thus, the analytic method described here is influenced by a Foucauldian approach to discourse analysis as well as by ideas drawn from conversation analysis and ethnomethodology as they are incorporated into their analytic approach by discursive psychologists (see Willig, 2008a: chs 6 and 7, for accounts of Foucauldian discourse analysis and discursive psychology, respectively; see also Wetherell, 1998, for an account of how to integrate the two).

ANALYTIC APPROACH

Approaching data from a discursive perspective means focusing on language. The purpose of a discursive analysis is to gain a better understanding of how the use of language (that is to say, the choice of words, grammatical constructions and various rhetorical strategies) is implicated in the construction of particular versions of events. Discourse analytic research is very much concerned with the effects of discourse, with what discourse can do and, as a result, discursive research is primarily interested in discourse itself rather than in the individuals who use it and whose speech or writing constitutes the data to be analysed. In other words, the research questions which drive discourse analytic research are about the (social, institutional, psychological) effects of discourse, and not about the thoughts and feelings within the individual speakers which may give rise to the words they utter. A discursive analysis always starts with discourse. Discourse analysts can go on to ask questions about how discourses may construct subjectivities, and this is a particular concern of Foucauldian versions of discourse analysis; however, here subjectivity is conceptualized as the product of internalized discursive constructions and positionings, never as an entity that pre-exits the use of discourse.

Any text constitutes suitable data for discourse analysis. Indeed, Parker advises that 'we consider all tissues of meaning as texts', including 'speech, writing, non-verbal behaviour, Braille, Morse code, semaphore, runes, advertisements, fashion systems, stained glass, architecture, tarot cards and bus tickets' (1992: 7). In *Critical Textwork* Parker presents discursive analyses of a wide range of 'symbolic systems that are not usually thought of as textual' (1999: 1) including material from visual media and physical settings such as cities and gardens. Hall (1997) reminds us that the signs and symbols, which constitute language as a representational system (see Winter, Chapter 17, this volume), include more than words; they can take the form of sounds (see Maeder, Chapter 29, this volume), images (see Banks, Chapter 27, this volume), musical notes or objects. This means that discourse analysis can be conducted on 'texts' in the widest sense. Some examples of such research can be found in Hall (1997) and Reavey (2011). Non-linguistic texts are particularly suitable for analyses, which are concerned with the production of cultures and social identities (e.g. Edwards, 2011; Gill, 2011). Versions of discourse analysis which are particularly concerned with how speakers deploy discursive resources within specific conversational contexts, however, require data which capture the to and fro of discursive engagement between speakers. Potter and Hepburn (2005) argue that ideally data for discursive analysis should consist of naturally occurring conversations, rather than written narrative accounts or semi-structured interviews (see Roulston, Chapter 20, this volume). Transcription conventions (see Kowal and O'Connell, Chapter 5, this volume) for preparing data for discourse analysis also vary depending on the approach taken. Foucauldian versions of discourse analysis, for example, require less detailed transcription of the various non-linguistic features of speech than does discursive research inspired by conversation analysis. The analysis presented in the second part of this chapter draws on both Foucauldian and discursive psychology strategies for analysis using an extract from a semi-structured interview. The nature and quality of the data are suitable for the analytic approach adopted as they provide evidence of a range of discursive resources deployed as well as their strategic deployment within the context of the research interview.

Once a suitable text for analysis has been obtained, discourse analysis proceeds by working through the text line by line. Although there are a number of step-by-step guides to discourse analysis (e.g. Parker, 1992; Kendall and Wickham, 1999; Langdridge, 2004; Willig, 2008a), it is important to bear in mind that discourse analysis is not so much a recipe as a perspective from which to approach a text. It is a perspective on language which allows the researcher to produce a particular kind of reading of a text, a reading which foregrounds the constructive and performative properties of language. As Potter and Wetherell put it:

> There is no analytic method ... there is a broad theoretical framework which focuses attention on the constructive and functional dimensions of discourse, coupled with the reader's skills in identifying significant patterns of consistency and variation. (1987: 169)

One way of generating a discursive reading is to approach the data with a set of questions in mind, and to interrogate each line of text as well as the text as a whole with the help of these questions. Helpful questions with which to approach a text include the following (see also Holt, 2011):

- What sorts of assumptions (about the world, about people) appear to underpin what is being said and how it is being said?
- Could what is being said have been said differently without fundamentally changing the meaning of what is being said? If so, how?
- What kind of discursive resources are being used to construct meaning here?
- What may be the potential consequences of the discourses that are used for those who are positioned by them, in terms of both their subjective experience and their ability to act in the world?
- How do speakers use the discursive resources that are available to them?
- What may be gained and what may be lost as a result of such deployments?

It is important to bear in mind that when analysing interview transcripts, a discursive analysis requires that as much attention is paid to the interviewer's contribution to the conversation as to the interviewee's. This is because the interviewer's questions and comments constitute the discursive context within which the interviewee's contributions are made and to which they will inevitably orient themselves.

EPISTEMOLOGICAL ORIENTATION

The epistemological position associated with discourse analytic research is social constructionism (see Esin et al., Chapter 14, this volume). Here, the researcher adopts a relativist position whereby the data are of interest not because they inform the researcher about 'how things really are' (e.g. what people are really thinking or feeling, or what happened in a particular social context), but rather because they tell the researcher something about how people construct meaning around events using the discursive resources that are available to them. The researcher is not concerned with the truth value of what participants are telling him or her; rather, the aim of the research is to generate an understanding of what people are doing when they talk about something in a particular way. In other words, the aim of the research is to gain a better understanding of the social dimension of participants' meaning-making activities.

Here, the type of knowledge sought is not knowledge about the world itself or knowledge about how things are experienced by research participants, but rather knowledge about the process by which such 'knowledge' is constructed in the first place. Such an approach to research is based upon the assumption that all human experience is mediated by language and that all social and psychological phenomena are discursively constructed in one way or another. The discourse analytic researcher is interested in how socially available ways of talking about the phenomenon of interest are deployed and what the consequences of this may be (see Willig, 2012a, for a discussion of the epistemological bases of different qualitative approaches; also see Willig, Chapter 10, this volume).

LIMITATIONS OF DISCOURSE ANALYSIS

Discourse analytic research focuses on the role of language in the construction of social and psychological phenomena. It is concerned with the effects of discourse rather than with human experience as such, and it constitutes a profoundly non-cognitive form of social psychology. Discourse analytic research has been criticized for privileging discourse over 'the person' and for failing to theorize subjectivity (e.g. Langdridge, 2004; Burr, 2002; Butt and Langdridge, 2003; Nightingale and Cromby, 1999) including our sense of self, intentionality, self-awareness and autobiographical memory. While discourse analysts have argued that speculation about mental entities is not relevant to discourse analytic research (e.g. Potter and Wetherell, 1987), it could be argued that the concern of discourse analysis with action orientation does beg the question of why it may be that particular individuals or groups of people pursue particular discursive objectives. In other words, while discourse analysis is very good at generating insights into how speakers deploy discursive resources and with what effects, it is not very good at telling us what motivates them to do so. It has been argued that 'discursive psychology brackets, and yet relies upon, a notion of motivation or desire, which it is incapable of theorising' (Willig, 2008a: 107). Another criticism of discourse analytic research concerns its claim that the analysis draws on nothing outside of the text itself. However, it could be argued that it is impossible to make sense of what is going on in a text without importing ideas and concepts from outside of it. For example, the very assumptions about the role and function of language, which underpin discourse analytic research, are themselves brought to the text from outside of it (see Willig, 2012b, for a more detailed discussion of these issues; also see Willig, Chapter 10, this volume).

From an ethical standpoint (see Mertens, Chapter 35, this volume), one could question the acceptability of analysing research participants' accounts through a discursive lens when their accounts were provided in good faith with the participants, assuming that the interviewer was genuinely interested in the nature of their experiences rather than in how they deployed discursive resources. It could be argued that for ethical reasons certain types of accounts, such as those which are concerned with suffering and distress and which were provided by participants who believed that the interviewer was genuinely interested in the experiential aspects of their account (rather than the discursive ones), should not be subjected to discursive analysis (see also Willig, 2004).

The Foucauldian approach to discourse analysis does attempt to address some of these limitations. Here, research participants are not simply seen as strategic users of discourse but rather as historical subjects who are themselves constructed through and positioned within discourse. From this point of view, discourse is directly implicated in the process by which 'human beings are made subjects' (Foucault, 1982: 208). The argument here is that the availability and uptake of subject positions in discourse give rise to different kinds of selves and to possibilities of subjective experience. However, there are still unanswered questions about the extent to which subjectivity can be theorized on the basis of discourse practices alone, and what may be the role of other factors and structures in this process.

WORKED EXAMPLE

The data from which this example is drawn were originally collected as part of a phenomenological study of the experience of taking part in extreme sport (Willig, 2005; 2008b). Extracts from one of the participants' transcribed interviews will be used here in order to illustrate what is involved in a discursive analysis (see Willig, 2012b, for an extended version of this analysis). In the interview extract the participant, whom we shall call Anna, is asked to describe an occasion on which she took part in a form of extreme sport. In her response to this question Anna produces a lengthy account of not one but two such occasions. In her account she describes an initial white-water rafting expedition which did not satisfy her desire for an 'adrenaline rush' and which was followed by a second trip which did deliver the desired 'rush'. Although the data had not been collected specifically for the purpose of discursive analysis, it was felt that the nature and quality of the data were suitable for the discourse analytic approach described in this chapter. The data are rich in evidence of a range of discursive constructions of the participant's experience, and the research interview constituted enough of a conversation between the interviewer and the participant to elicit clear evidence of a variety of action orientations.

In order to protect the participant's identity, all identifying details have been either changed or removed from all quotations used.

Process of Analysis

The process of analysis of the data involved careful reading and rereading of the transcript. This reading was done with an awareness that the focus of the analysis was the text itself; this meant that this was not a reading 'for gist' but rather a reading which was concerned with the properties of the language used in the account. The questions listed on p. 344 were used to guide the initial encounter with the text.

The second phase of the analysis involved a line-by-line analysis of the transcript. Here, analytic notes were written in the margins of the text in order to capture systematically what was talked about (construction), how it was talked about (discursive strategies) and with what consequences (action orientation). These notes were then reviewed and after a process of cross-referencing and integration of analytic observations, a discursive reading of the extract was produced. In what follows two analytic observations are presented and discussed in order to provide some illustration of what is involved in a discursive analysis and what kinds of insights can be generated on the basis of it. We will be focusing on Anna's use of a discourse of addiction to frame her engagement with extreme sport and her deployment of dualistic constructions of self in her account.

Discourse of Addiction

In Anna's account of her engagement with extreme sport activities she positions herself as an active seeker of 'thrill and excitement', somebody who goes to great lengths in order to generate a sufficiently powerful 'rush'. With reference to her decision to repeat the white-water rafting expedition in order to access a more intense experience, she says, 'even though it had cost me a fortune, but I was gonna do it again'. In her narrative we can identify repeated constructions of herself as someone who is strongly drawn to experiences which provide her with an 'adrenaline rush'; in fact, she explains that her attraction is so strong that her ability to resist this 'urge' is compromised. Having described the second white-water rafting trip as involving a complete loss of control over the raft and as being 'probably the most terrifying thing I've ever done in my life', Anna concludes that she 'had to love' the experience ('I just loved it. I had to'). In her construction of herself as someone who is so powerfully attracted to courting danger that this disables any cautionary impulse within her, Anna uses a series of extreme case formulations (Pomerantz, 1986):

So I went down with pedals, steering ourselves down and it was probably the *most* terrifying thing I've *ever* done in my *whole* life (laughs) I *actually thought I was going to die* but we went down, we were *completely* out of control the *whole* way and one of the guys *very nearly drowned* (laughs) ...

Extreme case formulations (italicized in the quote above) are formulations which take claims or evaluations to their extremes; in this way, they provide an effective warrant for the speaker's actions and thus legitimize them. In our case, Anna's claim (that she is irresistibly drawn to extreme sport) is supported by the extreme nature of the risks and dangers she exposes herself to and which she evokes very powerfully with the help of the extreme case formulations deployed in the quote. The compulsive dimension of Anna's relationship with extreme sport is affirmed at the end of the extract when she concludes, 'I need to do these things. It's something I just have to do.'

In her construction of herself as irresistibly drawn to extreme sport and her frequent references to the impact of the extreme sport experience on her physiology (e.g. when she talks about the 'adrenaline rush', her 'frayed nerves', the 'buzz', the 'huge amounts of energy' generated, and the observation that 'your heart's going a million miles per hour'), Anna invokes a discourse of addiction. 'Addiction' as an explanatory construct attributes the compulsion to engage in a behaviour to its powerfully rewarding physiological effects which in turn have a positive impact on mood thus leading to the desire to repeat the behaviour. Anna's use of a discourse of addiction is particularly evident in her description of the pleasurable after-effects of an episode of extreme sport:

The feeling, the rush that you get is just so, it takes a good day to come down, at least for me it does. Even longer, actually, 'cos I'm just thinking of when I first went on a big hike that lasted over a week and for about a month and a half after the walk, I was just bouncing off the walls. I just had such a great time. This made everything in my body was just going, I just loved it. My sister thought I was completely nuts when I got back because I just couldn't sit still. So when I finish things like this it's just (intake of breath) you know.

The terminology used by Anna in this extract (her references to 'the rush', 'coming off it' and 'coming down') is identical to that used to describe drug users' experiences. These commonalities confirm that Anna does indeed position herself within a discourse of drug addiction when she talks about her experiences of extreme sport.

In addition, Anna's incomplete sentence ('It's just ...') followed by a sharp intake of breath emphasizes the embodied quality of her experience, constructing it as something which cannot be adequately captured in words. Again, here we can see parallels with the way in which drug addiction is constructed: that is, as something which is seen as irrational and overwhelming and which neither the addict nor those close to the addict can make sense of; Anna 'just loves it' while her sister thought 'she was completely nuts'.

Positioning herself within a discourse of addiction allows Anna to offer a vivid and captivating account of her high-risk activities without having to justify her risk-taking in a way that appeals to rational considerations. Through drawing on a discourse of addiction Anna is able to talk openly about her extreme sport activities without having to take responsibility for choosing to engage in such dangerous pursuits, as her engagement with extreme sport is constructed as a compulsion rather than a choice. Within a context which invites accountability (after all, she is being interviewed about her extreme sport activities) the deployment of a discourse of addiction serves to disclaim responsibility for taking part in a potentially socially undesirable activity and to ward off potential criticism.

Dualism

Anna's account of her engagement with extreme sport is shot through with dualistic constructions of the self. Here, the self is constructed as being composed of distinct and separate parts, which do not necessarily communicate with one another. For example, a dualistic construction of the self, which constructs the material body (with its powerful urges and desires) as being in conflict with the moral self (which attempts to overrule the material body), is part and parcel of a discourse of addiction. Another way of constructing the self dualistically involves invoking conscious and unconscious parts of the self which do not have direct access to one another. Such a construction emerges when Anna is asked to reflect on her motives for taking part in extreme sport. In her reply she takes up the position of an outside observer of herself. She constructs a dualism between herself as the observer and herself as the object of her observations. In this way, she disavows an insider perspective and finds herself speculating about her motives in much the same way that somebody else may speculate. For example, in the following quote Anna disclaims any knowledge of why she does what she does:

> Actually, it's funny when you think about it 'cos I don't know what makes me do that. When I went bungee-jumping and I was standing there, I was the first person to go and I didn't see anyone jump before me and I didn't know, I hadn't even seen it on TV, I'd never seen anyone bungee-jump before. And standing on the edge of this platform and the guy just said, I'm gonna count down from 10 and then you just jump, alright? And then he counted down and I just jumped and I can't tell you what made me jump. I don't know what went through my head. It was sort of not an option. I was there, I made myself get to the edge of the platform and I just was gone …

Here, a dualistic construction of the self allows Anna to disclaim knowledge of her motives. Something other than her conscious self ('I don't know *what made me* do that'; 'I can't tell you *what made me* jump'; 'I don't know *what went through my head*') is responsible for her decision to jump and this means that Anna is unable to account for her actions. A little later, she goes on to develop a hypothesis about her motives for giving up sky-diving:

> Yeah, but I'm just thinking, it's interesting 'cos I wonder if the events, the sports that I've done I've always got that faith in somebody else? I'm just wondering, maybe when I stopped doing things like my sky-diving, when it's just me. I have to rely on myself. I don't have that much confidence in myself to keep on going. You know, when you get to a stage, 'cos when I started sky-diving I was doing (partnered jumps) … so I was completely relying on somebody else to hook me up to the plane and everything. But when it got to the stage where I could jump on my own, I just stopped going. I mean there were a lot of reasons for that but I just wonder …

Again, although she identifies a possible motive ('I don't have that much confidence in myself to keep on going'), Anna presents this as a hypothesis which she has arrived at through observation and reflection rather than as an insight based on direct self-knowledge ('It's interesting 'cos I wonder …'; 'I'm just wondering, maybe …'; 'I mean there were a lot of reasons for that but I just wonder …'). Anna constructs her insights as the product of a dualistic scrutiny of herself as an object of interest, thus creating a gap between herself as a conscious agent and her motivations for taking part in extreme sport activities. Again, as was the case in relation to the deployment of a discourse of addiction, Anna's use of dualistic discourse allows her to distance herself from her engagement with extreme sport and to disclaim responsibility for her actions and their consequences.

Reflections on the Analysis

A discursive analysis of Anna's interview extract has generated some insights into her use of discursive resources (such as the discourse of addiction and dualistic constructions of self) and their implication in the construction of a particular version of her engagement with extreme sport. The question of what Anna was doing when she constructed her experience of extreme sport in the way she did was also addressed. It was suggested that by positioning herself within a discourse of addiction and by drawing on dualistic constructions of self, Anna was able to disclaim responsibility for taking part in leisure activities which are considered to be extremely dangerous and which relatively few people engage in. However, in order to better understand the action orientation of Anna's deployment of discursive resources, we need to consider the discursive context within which Anna was positioned when she spoke about her relationship with extreme sport. Taking a closer look at the interviewer's style of questioning, we can see that the questions put to Anna constructed extreme sport as an experience which is composed of distinct elements (thoughts, feelings, sensations) which can be described and understood, and they positioned the interviewee as a self-aware, reflective subject who is willing and able to scrutinize herself. For example, Anna was invited to 'describe one occasion when you took part in a form of extreme sport' and a little later she was asked, 'So if we look at it in terms of just before you did it and then during it and after … can you remember how you felt …?' On occasion the style of questioning seems to imply that the purpose of the interview was to subject the interviewee's experiences to something akin to almost scientific scrutiny, for example when Anna is invited to dissect the feelings she has during a particular episode of extreme sport ('So the feelings during it were like a mixture of excitement and fear? Or how would you describe it?'). This style of questioning places Anna at the centre of events; the questions construct Anna as an active agent in the narrative as they are concerned with what she did and what she felt (rather than, say, what happened to her or what other people did). Anna responded to this by providing an account which served to distance her from full responsibility for her actions. If we accept that the style of questioning, and indeed the entire interview situation itself, positioned Anna as having to account for her engagement with extreme sport (an activity which is not universally approved of as it carries serious risks to the life and health of the practitioner), it should come as no surprise that she deployed discursive devices and rhetorical strategies that would help her manage her own stake in the conversation. It follows that from a discursive point of view, our analysis of Anna's account tells us more about the type of situation she found herself in (i.e. an interview in which she was invited to account for her extreme sport practices) than about Anna herself or about the experience of extreme sport.

In addition, the analysis tells us something about the discursive resources which are culturally available to Anna and which can be used to construct 'extreme sport'. For example, we discovered that the same discourse (a discourse of addiction) can be used to frame extreme sport and drug use. We also observed that a dualist discourse was invoked in the construction of pleasure (e.g. when Anna attributes her love of extreme sport to unconscious forces). Such observations resonate with a construction of the body as the primary site for pleasure and enjoyment, and the assumption that rational thought interferes with feeling good. This is reflected in the strict separation between 'work' and 'leisure' characteristic of late capitalist cultures where 'leisure' is increasingly associated with physical gratification (eating, drinking, the use of recreational drugs, sex) and where the purpose of leisure activities is to help the individual to 'switch off' (from work, from worry, from responsibility). It would be interesting to develop this analysis by examining wider social discourses and cultural practices in order to better understand how such a mind–body separation functions, how it arose historically and how it is maintained through various institutional practices.

Another avenue that could be pursued in a Foucauldian-style discourse analysis involves asking questions about how the discursive positionings adopted by Anna in her construction of her engagement with extreme sport may shape her actual experience of herself. By positioning herself within a discourse of addiction, Anna accepts that there are powerful forces at work within her over which she has little or no control. This could be experienced as disempowering; as a result it may be difficult for Anna to stop engaging in extreme sport should she wish to do so (see Eiser, 1984; Gillies and Willig, 1997). Similarly, positioning oneself within a dualist discourse may discourage attempts to integrate experiences which seem to originate in different parts of the self, leading to an increasingly fragmented sense of self.

Appraisal of the Discursive Reading

In the worked example presented in this chapter, discourse analysis was used in order to better understand how a research participant constructs her experiences of extreme sport through language within the context of a research interview, how this positions her and what may be some of the consequences of these constructions and positionings. The analysis has generated insights into the interviewee's use of rhetorical devices and the discourses available to her which she could draw on to construct a particular version of the extreme sport experience. It was acknowledged that a discursive analysis does not allow us to answer questions about why Anna engages in extreme sport, the role of her personality within this or the nature of her motivations. Furthermore, it has little to say about the nature or meaning of the experience of extreme sport as such. Within the context of a discursive analysis questions about the inner world of research participants, their motivations, desires and intentions are suspended; instead the researcher is concerned with how discursive resources are used within particular contexts in order to construct meaning, and what happens as a result of that, interpersonally, socially and in some cases (e.g. Foucauldian analysis) also in terms of the production and availability of particular subjectivities. Some of the limitations and ethical challenges associated with such an exclusive focus on language have been discussed earlier in this chapter (see p. 345). In the final section we will identify some attempts at widening the focus of discourse analytic work, for example by advocating 'binocularity' in order to 'thicken' a discursive analysis (e.g. Frosh and Young, 2008) or by being more openly interpretative (e.g. Bell, 2011).

RECENT DEVELOPMENTS AND OUTLOOK

As seems to be the case with most qualitative research methods, discourse analysis continues to evolve into increasingly distinctive versions or varieties. Like grounded theory methodology, discourse analysis now encompasses a wide range of approaches with quite different priorities and emphases (see e.g. Glynos, et al., 2009; Wetherell et al., 2001). These reflect disciplinary differences as well as wider theoretical and also political commitments on the part of discourse analysts. For example, in a recent review of developments in discourse analysis in social psychology, Parker (2011) argues that while early discursive work in social psychology was critical of psychology as a discipline, seeking to deconstruct and critically appraise the processes which give rise to the 'psy-complex' itself (cf. Rose, 1985), the currently dominant version of 'discursive psychology' has become incorporated into the discipline as it offers an alternative (this time, 'discursive') account of what motivates and shapes human behaviour. Its preoccupation with the spoken word and its lack of interest in anything that might be happening at the level of emotion or cognition have also meant that this version of discursive psychology is associated with a relatively narrow, almost behaviouristic focus (see Corcoran, 2009, and Billig, 2012, for examples of critical appraisals of some of the assumptions underpinning discursive psychology).

In recent years discourse analysts have become increasingly concerned with the relationship between discourse and subjectivity. While earlier Foucauldian discourse analytic work had already engaged with questions about the ways in which available discourses may shape subjectivities, this work was still based on the assumption that subjectivity is very much a product of discursive structures and processes (e.g. Henriques et al., 1984). In other words, it was concerned with the consequences of discourse, its products and productions, and its power to make us who we are.

More recently, questions have been asked about what underlying psychic structures and processes may lead speakers to invest in and commit themselves to the discourses and positionings they deploy when they talk about their experiences. Here, the psychological subject is seen as not (just) a product of discourse practices but as something which both shapes and is shaped by them (see e.g. Frosh, 2010, for a detailed account of such a perspective). Research informed by such a psychosocial approach combines a discursive analysis of participants' accounts with a further reading which attempts to make sense of their discursive actions by developing hypotheses about their deeper motivations and emotional investments (e.g. see Frosh and Young, 2008). Much of this work draws on theoretical resources from psychoanalysis in order to accomplish this.

Another recent development in the field of discourse studies has been to reconnect discourse analytic research with hermeneutics (see Wernet, Chapter 16, this volume), and to embrace and explicate much more openly the process of interpretation (see Willig, Chapter 10, this volume) that is involved in discourse analysis (e.g. Bell, 2011; see also Willig, 2012b). Here, the argument is that discourse analysis – that is to say, the textual analysis of data involving a line-by-line scrutiny of the linguistic, structural and functional characteristics of the discursive material – is really only one part of a wider project which could be referred to as 'discourse interpretation' (Bell, 2011: 520). This is because the analysis of discourse forms part of a wider reading of a text within its social and historical context, and this reading is informed by the researcher's own perspective, the assumptions they bring to the analysis, and their theoretical and personal orientation. The interaction between the researcher and the text generates a new understanding which is based upon the researcher's critical reflection upon both their own and the text's claims and assumptions. Bell argues that a purely descriptive approach to discursive work which produces only a 'structural description of textual features' (2011: 520) is ultimately irrelevant; however, it could be argued that a purely descriptive analysis is not only irrelevant but also impossible as even the identification of particular textual features requires a commitment to an interpretative lens that attributes a particular significance to such textual features (see Willig, 2012b: ch. 7).

To conclude, it is clear that different versions of discourse analysis are based on different conceptualizations – of human agency, of subjectivity and of the primacy of language (or otherwise), and this means that they address quite different research questions. It is, therefore, important that researchers who consider using a discursive approach as a method of data analysis are clear about the question(s) they are asking of their data and the kinds of insights they seek to gain from the analysis. This will enable them to select the type of discourse analysis which best suits the aims of their study.

FURTHER READING

Gill, Rosalind (2000) 'Discourse analysis', in Martin W. Bauer and George D. Gaskell (eds), *Qualitative Researching with Text, Image and Sound: A Practical Handbook*. London: Sage. pp. 172–90.

Hepburn, Alexa and Wiggins, Sally (eds) (2007) *Discursive Research in Practice: New Approaches to Psychology and Interaction*. Cambridge: Cambridge University Press.

Wetherell, Margaret, Taylor, Stephanie and Yates, Simeon J. (eds) (2001) *Discourse Theory and Practice: A Reader*. London: Sage.

REFERENCES

Austin, John L. (1962) *How to Do Things with Words: The William James Lectures*. Oxford: Clarendon Press.

Bell, Allan (2011) 'Re-constructing Babel: Discourse analysis, hermeneutics and the interpretive arc', *Discourse Studies*, 13 (5): 519–68.

Billig, Michael (2012) 'Undisciplined beginnings, academic success, and discursive psychology', *British Journal of Social Psychology*, November. DOI: 10.1111/j.2044-8309.2011.02086.x.

Burr, Vivian (2002) *The Person in Social Psychology*. Hove: Psychology Press.

Butt, Trevor and Langdridge, Darren (2003) 'The construction of self: The public reach into the private sphere', *Sociology*, 37 (3): 477–94.
Corcoran, Tim (2009) 'Second nature', *British Journal of Social Psychology*, 48: 375–388. DOI: 10.1348/014466605X82341.
Drew, Paul and Heritage, John (eds) (1992) *Talk at Work: Interactions in Institutional Settings*. Cambridge: Cambridge University Press.
Edwards, Tim (2011) *Fashion in Focus: Concepts, Practices and Politics*. London: Routledge.
Eiser, J. Richard (1984) 'Addiction as attribution: Cognitive processes in giving up smoking', in J. Richard Eiser (ed.), *Social Psychology and Behaviour Medicine*. Chichester: Wiley. pp. 281–302.
Fairclough, Norman (1995) *Critical Discourse Analysis: The Critical Study of Language*. London: Longman.
Forrester, Michael A. (1996) *Psychology of Language: A Critical Introduction*. London: Sage.
Foucault, Michel (1982) 'The subject and power: An afterword', in Hubert Dreyfus and Paul Rabinow (eds), *Michel Foucault: Beyond Structuralism and Hermeneutics*. Chicago: University of Chicago Press. pp. 208–26.
Frosh, Stephen (2010) *Psychoanalysis Outside the Clinic: Interventions in Psychosocial Studies*. Basingstoke: Palgrave Macmillan.
Frosh, Stephen and Young, Lisa Saville (2008) 'Psychoanalytic approaches to qualitative psychology', in Carla Willig and Wendy Stainton-Rogers (eds), *The SAGE Handbook of Qualitative Research in Psychology*. London: Sage. pp. 109–26.
Gill, Rosalind (2011) 'Bend it like Beckham: The challenge of reading and visual culture', in Paula Reavey (ed.), *Visual Methods in Psychology. Using and Interpreting Images in Qualitative Research*. Hove: Psychology Press. pp. 29–42.
Gillies, Val and Willig, Carla (1997) '"You get the nicotine and that in your blood": Constructions of addiction and control in women's accounts of cigarette smoking', *Journal of Community and Applied Social Psychology*, 7: 285–301.
Glynos, Jason, Howarth, David, Norval, Aletta and Speed, Ewen (2009) 'Discourse analysis: Varieties and methods', ESRC National Centre for Research Methods Review paper, August, NCRM/014.
Hall, Stuart (1997) 'Introduction', in Stuart Hall (ed.), *Representation: Cultural Representation and Signifying Practices*. London: Sage. pp. 1–11.
Henriques, Julian, Hollway, Wendy, Urwin, Cathy, Couze, Venn and Walkerdine, Valerie (1984) *Changing the Subject: Psychology, Social Regulation and Subjectivity*. London: Methuen.
Holt, Amanda (2011) 'Discourse analysis approaches', in Noraig Frost (ed.), *Qualitative Research Methods in Psychology: Combining Core Approaches*. Maidenhead: McGraw-Hill/Open University Press. pp. 66–91.
Kendall, Gavin and Wickham, Gary (1999) *Using Foucault's Methods*. London: Sage.
Labov, William (1966) *The Social Stratification of English in New York City*. New York: Center for Applied Linguistics.
Langdridge, Darren (2004) *Introduction to Research Methods and Data Analysis in Psychology*. Harlow: Pearson Education.
Mishler, Elliott, G. (1995) 'Models of narrative analysis: A typology', *Journal of Narrative and Life History*, 5 (2): 87–123.
Nightingale, David and Cromby, John (1999) *Social Constructionist Psychology: A Critical Analysis of Theory and Practice*. Buckingham: Open University Press.
Parker, Ian (1992) *Discourse Dynamics: Critical Analysis for Social and Individual Psychology*. London: Routledge.
Parker, Ian (1994) 'Reflexive research and the grounding of analysis: Social psychology and the psy-complex', *Journal of Community and Applied Social Psychology*, 4 (4): 239–52.
Parker, Ian (1999) *Critical Textwork: An Introduction to Varieties of Discourse Analysis*. Buckingham: Open University Press.
Parker, Ian (2011) 'Discursive social psychology now', *British Journal of Social Psychology*, July: 1–7. DOI: 10.1111/j.2044-8309.2011.02046.x.
Pomerantz, Anita (1986) 'Extreme case formulations: A new way of legitimating claims', in G. Button et al. (eds), *Human Studies* (Special Issue: Interaction and Language Use), 9: 219–30.
Potter, Jonathan and Hepburn, Alexa (2005) 'Qualitative interviews in psychology: Problems and possibilities', *Qualitative Research in Psychology*, 2: 38–55.
Potter, Jonathan and Wetherell, Margaret (1987) *Discourse and Social Psychology: Beyond Attitudes and Behaviour*. London: Sage.
Reavey, Paula (2011) *Visual Methods in Psychology. Using and Interpreting Images in Qualitative Research*. Hove: Psychology Press.
Riessman, Catherine, K. (1993) *Narrative Analysis*. London: Sage.
Rose, Nikolas (1985) *Governing the Soul: The Shaping of the Private Self*. London: Free Association Books.

Schegloff, Emanuel, A. (1968) 'Sequencing in conversational openings', *American Anthropologist*, 70: 1075–95.

Tannen, Deborah (1990) *You Just Don't Understand: Women and Men in Conversation*. New York: William Morrow.

Wetherell, Margaret (1998) 'Positioning and interpretative repertoires: Conversation analysis and post-structuralism in dialogue', *Discourse and Society*, 9 (3): 387–413.

Wetherell, Margaret, Taylor, Stephanie and Yates, Simeon J. (2001) *Discourse as Data: A Guide for Analysis*. London: Sage.

Willig, Carla (2004) 'Discourse analysis and health psychology', in Michael Murray (ed.), *Critical Health Psychology*. Basingstoke: Palgrave Macmillan. pp. 155–70.

Willig, Carla (2005) 'A phenomenological investigation of the experience of taking part in extreme sport', MA thesis, Regent's College, London.

Willig, Carla (2008a) *Introducing Qualitative Research in Psychology*, 2nd edition. Maidenhead: McGraw-Hill/Open University Press.

Willig, Carla (2008b) 'A phenomenological investigation of the experience of taking part in extreme sport', *Journal of Health Psychology*, 13 (5): 690–702.

Willig, Carla (2012a) 'Perspectives on the epistemological bases for qualitative research', in H. Cooper (ed.), *The Handbook of Research Methods in Psychology*. Washington, DC: American Psychological Association. pp. 5–21.

Willig, Carla (2012b) *Qualitative Analysis and Interpretation in Psychology*. Maidenhead: McGraw-Hill/Open University Press.

Wittgenstein, Ludwig (1953) *Philosophical Investigations*. Malden: Blackwell.

Wodak, Ruth (1996) *Disorders of Discourse*. Harlow: Addison Wesley Longman.

24

Analysing Observations

Amir B. Marvasti

Observation is the foundation of science. Specifically, to the extent that empirical evidence is used to test theories or advance knowledge, observation is the backbone of all scientific research. Observational methods emerged alongside scientific methods; in fact, the two are often used interchangeably. The history of observational methods parallels the history of sciences as a whole. Lorraine Daston and Elizabeth Lunbeck nicely describe the overall importance of observations in the introduction to their edited book *Histories of Scientific Observation*:

> Observation is the most pervasive and fundamental practice of all modern sciences, both natural and human. It is also among the most refined and variegated. Observation educates the senses, calibrates judgment, picks out objects of scientific inquiry, and forges "thought collectives." Its instruments include not only the naked senses, but also tools such as the telescope and the microscope, the questionnaire, the photographic plate, the glassed-in beehive, the Geiger counter, and a myriad of other ingenious inventions designed to make the invisible visible, the evanescent permanent, and the abstract concrete. Where is society? How blue is the sky? Which ways do X-rays scatter? Over the course of centuries, scientific observers have devised ways to answer these and many other riddles. (2011: 1)

While a full treatment of the history and nature of 'scientific observation' is beyond the scope of this chapter, two things are worth noting here. First, it took centuries for what we now consider 'scientific observation' to be separated from wisdom, experience, intuition, feeling, and divine knowledge. Second, 'scientific observation' could refer to a wide array of data collected in the course of empirical research. In the social sciences, this means observations can be based on surveys, in-depth interviews (see Roulston, Chapter 20, this volume), focus groups (see Barbour, Chapter 21, this volume), and participant observation, to name a few examples. For the purpose of this chapter, I especially focus on the analysis of ethnographic observations (whether they are heard or seen in the field).

I begin the chapter with a general description of ethnography (see Gubrium and Holstein, Chapter 3, this volume), with an emphasis on making sense of the observer–observed relationship as a type of 'provisional analysis' (Becker, 1958: 653) in its own right. I then offer three strategies (descriptive, inductive, and constructionist) for the analysis of observational data using examples from my own ethnographic research on homelessness and other sources. I end the chapter with a brief discussion of strategies for evaluating and representing analysis of observations.

OBSERVER–OBSERVED RELATIONSHIPS IN THE FIELD

Ethnographic techniques of observation have a long and well-established history in the social sciences, particularly in the fields of anthropology and sociology. Ethnography (literally translated 'writing about culture') essentially involves a researcher observing and recording human behavior in a particular setting (often referred to as 'the field'). The strength of this approach, compared to closed-ended surveys or experimental designs is that it allows the researcher to directly observe the many nuances and contingencies of human behavior as they become manifest in a 'natural' setting (i.e., the field). Of course, what the researchers actually see or hear in the field and how they interpret it are both filtered through the researchers' orientation toward the object of the observations. In other words, the researchers' substantive focus and analysis are mediated by the way they relate to the object of analysis.

Quite likely no other tradition of data collection has engendered more theorizing (or hand-wringing) about the relationship between the observer and the observed than ethnographic research. This is evidenced by the numerous volumes written on the topic (see, for example, *Emotions in the Field* (Davies and Spencer, 2010), *Others Knowing Others*, (Fowler and Hardesty, 1994), *Observers Observed* (Stocking, 1983)). More than two decades ago, James Clifford cogently framed the emerging analytical problem as an 'impossible attempt':

> Anthropological fieldwork has been represented as both the scientific 'laboratory' and a personal 'rite of passage.' The two metaphors capture nicely the discipline's impossible attempt to fuse objective and subjective practices. Until recently, this impossibility was masked by marginalizing the intersubjective foundations of fieldwork, by excluding them from serious ethnographic texts, relegating them to prefaces, memoirs, anecdotes, confessions, and so forth. Lately, this set of disciplinary rules is giving way. ... Much of our knowledge about other cultures must now be seen as contingent, the problematic outcome of intersubjective dialogue, translation, and projection. This poses fundamental problems for any science that moves predominantly from the particular to the general, that can make use of personal truths only as examples of typical phenomena or as exceptions to collective patterns. (1986: 109)

In the 20 years or so since, ethnographers have tried to solve the riddle of the 'impossible attempt' by more systematically exploring the reflexive relationship between the researcher self and the observed other (see May and Perry, Chapter 8, this volume). As a whole, new approaches to writing and analysing field observations are more inclined to acknowledge the presence of the observer. Amanda Coffey's *The Ethnographic Self* nicely underlines this shift:

> In writing, remembering, and representing our fieldwork experiences we are involved in processes of self representation and identity construction. In considering and exploring the intimate relations between the field, significant others and the private self we are able to understand the process of field work as practical, intellectual and emotional accomplishment (1999: 1; see also 'The relational self and its stories' in Gubrium and Holstein, 2008: 243–5).

Thus in this chapter I emphasize that the act of observing is done from a certain analytic position toward the object. To illustrate this point, consider, for example, the different ways people observe the objects in an art museum. Years ago I visited a museum of modern art with my elderly father. We were looking at some abstract paintings, and my father asked, 'Is this art?' I replied, 'Yes. In fact, these paintings were done by *famous* artists and are very *expensive*,' hoping to reorient my father's view of the painting toward the dimensions of fame and value. My father, however, remained unconvinced: 'A child could do this. I don't see it.' My point is that how we see something involves a certain orientation that in turn shapes the meaning we attribute to the object. This means that the interpretation and related analysis of observations is foreshadowed by the researcher's orientation toward, or relationship with, that which is being observed. In the next section, I offer three ways of conceptualizing the observer–observed relationship in the context of ethnographic research (for a similar treatment of interviewer–interviewee duality see Gubrium and Holstein, 2002).

Roles

In my view, the most salient conceptualization of the observer–observed interconnection is found in Patricia and Peter Adler's *Membership Roles in Field Research* (1987; see also Gold, 1958). The authors begin with the assumption that a researcher's position in the field reflects a combination of personal choices, theoretical orientation, and structural necessities (1987: 52–3). From there, the Adlers discuss three possible roles in the field, corresponding to the continuum of complete observer to complete participant. The first of these is 'peripheral membership,' which implies marginal involvement in what is being observed. By contrast, the second type of field role, 'active membership,' involves:

> far more profound *effects on the researcher's self* than are generated by peripheral membership involvement. In functioning as a member, researchers get swept up into many of the same experiences as members. While this has the distinct advantage of adding their own selves as data to the research, both as a cross-check against the accounts of others and as a deepened awareness of how members actually think and feel, it propels researchers through various changes. (1987: 64)

With the third category of membership, 'complete participant,' the goal is to achieve a sort of unconditional belonging in the world of the other, further closing the gap between the observed and the observer:

> The complete membership role entails the greatest commitment on the part of the researcher. Rather than experiencing more participatory involvement, complete-member-researchers ... immerse themselves fully in the group as 'natives.' They and their subjects relate to each other as status equals, dedicated to sharing in a common set of experiences, feelings, and goals. (1987: 67)

The complete participant is an observer whose viewpoint is presumably the same as those being studied. In this context, the observer's claims to insider knowledge become as valid as any other member in the field. The three categories of membership are useful as general guides, but, as the Adlers note, these roles are difficult to distinguish from one another in practice as they 'shift and evolve' in the field (1987:14).

A corollary to this discussion is the matter of 'covert' and 'overt' observer roles. The issue here is whether the observed is aware that his or her conduct is being recorded for the purpose of analysis. There are at least two facets to this debate. First, some believe that if people know they are being watched, they will change their conduct, so a covert role would provide more objective observations. Second, and perhaps more important in the era of institutional review boards (IRBs), is the ethics of doing research (see Mertens, Chapter 35, this volume) without obtaining informed consent (see Calvey, 2008), and this is where 'covert' research faces the greatest opposition. For example, the British Association of Sociology has taken the position that:

covert methods violate the principles of informed consent and may invade the privacy of those being studied. Participants or non-participant observation in non-public spaces or experimental manipulation of research participants without their knowledge should be resorted to only where it is impossible to use other methods to obtain essential data. (Cited in Calvey, 2008: 907)

However, as David Calvey points out, while there are good ethical reasons not to spy on people, covert research is not without its justifications:

> Covert research is part of a somewhat submerged tradition that needs to be recovered for future usage in its own right rather than being treated correctively as teaching material for cases of 'failed or bad ethics'. … Moreover, research in this mould is a tradition that has significantly shaped, often in controversial ways, debates about the research relationship. My deep concern is that, in the present context of governance, we develop forms of 'methodological hypochondria'. This is not a belligerent stance nor a heroic portrayal of the covert researcher as, quite clearly, covert research is not appropriate for certain sensitive topics. … For me, covert research has a potentially creative and imaginative part to play and a voice to be heard in the sociological community. (2008: 914)

Rapport

Rapport can be viewed as having greater understanding of and entrance into the world of the other. Thus building and maintaining rapport is a key component of observational research. One of the earliest references to the significance of rapport can be found in Harriet Martineau's *How to Observe Morals and Manners* (originally published in 1838, and arguably the first how-to book on qualitative research):

> Unless a traveller interprets by his sympathies what he sees, he cannot but misunderstand the greater part of that which comes under his observation. He will not be admitted with freedom into the retirements of domestic life; the instructive commentary on all the facts of life, discourse, will be of a slight and superficial character. People will talk to him of the things they care least about, instead of seeking his sympathy about the affairs which are deepest in their hearts. He will be amused with public spectacles, and informed of historical and chronological facts; but he will not be invited to weddings and christenings; he will hear no love-tales; domestic sorrows will be kept as secrets from him; the old folks will not pour out their stores to him, nor the children bring him their prattle. (1838: 43)

In her own eloquent and pre-disciplinary-jargon language, Martineau highlights the intricate links between 'sympathy,' rapport, and quality of observations. She makes it clear that without a sufficiently close relationship with the people being observed, the observer at most is afforded a superficial glance of the other's world.

Contemporary field researchers employ a variety of strategies to establish rapport with their respondents. Self-disclosure (sharing with respondents relevant details of one's own life) is arguably the easiest way to build rapport. In fact, it is not uncommon for research participants to make direct inquiries about the background and interests of the observer. The following excerpt from Leigh Berger's ethnography of a synagogue illustrates this process:

> Rabbi Levinson smiles warmly at me, his gray beard crinkling and his dark eyes lighting up behind his glasses. 'Let me ask you a question. Do you come from a religious family?'
>
> 'Not exactly. My parents are not religious at all. But my grandparents were. They kept kosher and my grandfather walked to synagogue,' I reply. 'I think their belief is one reason I've always been drawn to try and understand faith,' I confess.
>
> He nods. 'Yes. My grandfather was a religious man as well. He is one reason why I love religion so much. You were close with your grandparents?'
>
> 'Very.' I smile with warmth of family memories. (2001: 512)

On the other hand, some ethnographers question the value of rapport and assert that it is possible to get too close to the world of the other (i.e., 'go native'). Accordingly, an unreflective affinity with research participants biases the analysis. In this context, analytical detachment is valued over empathic understanding. Such seemingly diametrical positions on the significance of rapport in observational research serve to underline the assertion that the observer's method of relating to the observed involves analytical standpoints corresponding to whether the observations are to be treated as objective facts or collaborative and subjective constructions. While the first two positions discussed thus far (roles and rapport) remain somewhat faithful to the notion of capturing an external, objective world, the next mode of observation concerns itself almost entirely with the subjective self.

Observing the Researcher Self

With this model of conceptualizing the observer–observed dichotomy, the researcher self takes center stage. Here the gap between the observer and the observed is dissolved altogether by allowing the two to become one and the same, as in this example from Carol Ronai's story of her life with an abusive father and a mentally retarded mother:

> My father, Frank Gross (no lie, pronounced 'Grass') Rambo, had a police record as a child molester, a rapist, and an exhibitionist. He was also violent. Even though we were on public assistance, our lives were much calmer during the time he was in prison. Her beating me [referring to her mother] was an enormous betrayal. Yes, I needed to be disciplined, but this was not a spanking. This was the kind of beating Frank dished out. (1996: 121)

What is referred to as 'autoethnography,' particularly 'evocative or emotional autoethnography' (Ellis, 1997; see also Ellis, 1991), turns the observer's attention inward and treats self-reflection as empirical observation in its own right:

> Autoethnography is an autobiographical genre of writing and research that displays multiple layers of consciousness, connecting the personal to the cultural. Back and forth autoethnographers gaze, first through an ethnographic wide-angle lens, focusing outward on social and cultural aspects of their personal experience; then, they look inward exposing a vulnerable self. (Ellis and Bochner, 2000: 739)

Norman Denzin (1997) has noted that the approach has the added advantage of addressing the problems surrounding how to best represent human experience. In his words, 'bypass the representational problem by invoking an epistemology of emotion, moving the reader to feel the feelings of the other' (1997: 228, cited in Anderson, 2006: 377). However, critics have voiced concern that too much emphasis on the observer self amounts to narcissism and erodes the scientific validity of the data (its connection with the empirical world), which presumably exists outside the self-reflexive observer's head.

One attempt to reign in the excesses of autoethnography is to counter it with the more traditional self-observational methods. So, for example, as an alternative to 'evocative autoethnography' Leon Anderson offers 'analytic autoethnography,' which in his words 'does contribute to a spiraling refinement, elaboration, extension, and revision of theoretical understanding' (2006: 388). Anderson goes on to argue, 'autoethnographic inquiry, which has been advocated primarily in recent years as a radically non-traditional, poststructuralist form of research, actually fits well with traditional symbolic interactionist ethnography' (2006: 391).

Another solution to unchecked analysis of the researcher self is something called 'systematic self-observation' (Rodriguez and Ryave, 2002), which involves training informants to methodically observe and record their own experiences in the field. Accordingly, '[systematic self-observation] generates data that are written in informants' own words and marked with their unique personal sensibilities, voices, perspectives, experiences, and points of view' (2002: 10). Presumably, this method allows the more systematic observer, the researcher, not the research participant, to maintain some sense of analytic detachment from the recorded observations.

So far in this chapter we have reviewed the significance of the researcher's position relative to those under study as a type of ongoing 'provisional analysis' (Becker, 1958: 653) that informs how observations are collected in the field. The remainder of the chapter considers the more explicit and finite task of making sense of recorded observations.

ANALYSIS OF OBSERVATIONS

In this section, I review methods of analysing observations building on the previous discussion about observer–observed relationships. My focus here is how observations are transformed from loosely connected records of encounters between the researcher self and the other into documented analysis.

Description as Analysis

In the social sciences (with the exception of subfields such as visual anthropology) all observations either begin as written texts (e.g., newspapers and other mass media texts – see Hodgetts and Chamberlain, Chapter 26, this volume) or are transformed from the visual and audible to the written text (e.g., recorded field notes or transcribed interviews; see Kowal and O'Connell, Chapter 5, and Roulston, Chapter, 20, this volume). Consequently, the simplest way to represent observations is to only describe them – write them down as you see them.

Among qualitative researchers, ethnographers in particular, observations from the field (eyewitness accounts of places and behaviors) are typically used to describe the setting, or to provide a social context for what people say in the field about themselves and others. The most elaborate ethnographic descriptions are generally in sections where the authors attempt to convey the ambiance of the setting where the observations were collected. The following excerpt is from my own ethnography of a homeless shelter:

> Only a few blocks away from downtown, placed between a funeral home and a fire station, the pastel green Abbot House building was surrounded by a six-foot wall and chain-link fences. The occasional sound of a fire truck siren rushing to an emergency combined with the smell of burning flesh from the funeral home's crematorium completed the gloomy picture of poverty amid the modern urban landscape. The across-the-street convenience store displayed a flashing neon sign advertising beer to the presumably vulnerable residents of the shelter, and the nearby city park provided a suitable location for the consumption of recently purchased alcohol, thanks to generous contributions from university students, who during their weekend escapades in the downtown entertainment district were either too drunk or too scared to snub a street person. (Marvasti, 2002: 619)

As this excerpt shows, the description of the setting sets up the stage for the forthcoming empirical documentation and is to some degree analytical in its own right. Indeed, labeling this kind of writing as purely 'descriptive' is somewhat misleading as it is based on a false duality between raw observation and refined analysis. As Robert Emerson notes:

> What is included or excluded ... is not determined randomly; rather, the process of looking and reporting are guided by the observer's implicit or explicit concepts that make some details more important and relevant than others. Thus, what is selected for observation and recording reflects the working theories or conceptual assumptions employed, however implicitly, by the ethnographer. To insist on a sharp polarity between description and analysis is thus misleading; description is necessarily analytic. (1988: 20; see also Geertz's discussion of 'thick description,' 1988)

This implies that to some extent there is no such thing as 'raw data.' To illustrate this point further, let us consider the most evidentiary of all recorded observations, the film (see Mikos, Chapter 28, this volume). We are all familiar with the saying 'a picture is worth a thousand words,' presumably because a photographic image is a flawless mode of recording an object of interest. In the earlier part of the twentieth century visual anthropologists did just that as they earnestly tried to record on film their field observations in such classics as Robert Flaherty's 1922 silent documentary *Nanook of the*

North. However, in recent decades the authenticity of the photographic representation of the field (along with other claims about capturing reality 'in the raw,' pure, or pristine form) has come under assault. Consider the following sarcastic characterization of the visual anthropologists' claims to realism:

> There is a tribe, known as ethnographic filmmakers, who believe they are invisible. They enter a room where a feast is being celebrated, or the sick cured, or the dead mourned, and, though weighted down with odd machines, entangled with wires, imagine they are unnoticed – or, at most, merely glanced at, quickly ignored, later forgotten. Outsiders know little of them, for their homes are hidden in the partially uncharted rainforests of the Documentary. Like other Documentarians they survive by hunting and gathering information. Unlike others of the filmic groups, most prefer to consume it raw. ... Their handicrafts are rarely traded, and are used almost exclusively among themselves. Produced in great quantities, the excess must be stored in large archives. (Weinberger, 1994: 3–4, cited in Grimshaw, 2001: 1)

The point is that the observer is always implicated in the act of observing and recording, no matter how refined, or analytically pure, the technique of observation and recording.

Inductive Analysis

What I have in mind here is analysis that moves from the specific to the general, where the general would represent a concrete and objective finding that is logically and empirically backed by the analysis. The best-known strategy for inductive analysis of qualitative observations is 'grounded theory' (see Thornberg and Charmaz, Chapter 11, this volume; see also Athens, 2010, and Charmaz, 2008) where specific field observations gradually lead the researcher to generalized 'plausible relationships proposed among concepts and sets of concepts' (Strauss and Corbin, 1994: 278). The following excerpt from Elijah Anderson's ethnography provides a poignant example of how a seemingly trivial observation (i.e., the fact that some African Americans prominently wear their institutional identification cards even outside their workplace) is inductively connected with a larger theoretical argument about the continuing struggle for civil rights:

> The common identification card associates its holder with a firm, a corporation, a school, a union, or some other institution of substance and influence. Such a card, particularly from a prominent establishment, puts the police and others on notice that the youth is 'somebody,' thus creating an important distinction between a black man who can claim a connection with the wider society and one who is summarily judged as 'deviant.' Although blacks who are established in the middle class might take such cards for granted, many lower-class blacks, who continue to find it necessary to campaign for civil rights denied them because of skin color, believe that carrying an identification card brings them better treatment than is meted out to their less fortunate brothers and sisters. (1997: 145–6)

For another illustration of how one can go from specific observation to broader theoretical premise, I will use an example from my ethnography of a homeless shelter in which I linked a set of observations about a bathroom with a larger argument about how homelessness is deviant in part because it involves the unauthorized use of space. Basically, after many complaints about homeless clients relieving themselves in the parking lot of the shelter, it was decided an outside bathroom would remedy the problem. And it did. However, the bathroom was also used for less authorized purposes. For example, it afforded some the privacy they needed for injecting themselves with drugs away from the prying eyes of undercover police officers ('narcs'). Others used it for sexual rendezvous. Finally, on occasion it was used as a makeshift barbershop. All of this, of course, was the cause of some aggravation for the shelter staff who only wanted the space to be used for its official purpose. These observations were consistent with the theory that an important part of the public outcry about homelessness is about the unauthorized use of public spaces by people who do not have their own private spaces (Ruddick, 1996; Wright, 1997).

Another way of thinking about inductive analysis (moving from the particular to the general) is the transformation of general observations into specific measurements, or 'enumeration' (Goetz and LeCompte, 1981: 54). Ideally, this type of counting of observations would be done using precise questions or surveillance regimens that could produce exact and easily quantifiable response categories. Where that is not possible in the field (as in the case of covert observations), the researcher would have to attend to measurable features of the field using a less regimented and more inductive process. So, for example, in my research on homelessness, I could begin with the observation that many older homeless clients appear to be intoxicated. From there I could move on to a more systematic observation and recording of the clients' age. Along with that, I could develop a profile or a checklist for the appearance of alcoholism (e.g., smell of alcohol, especially if present during the morning hours). The next step in the analysis would then be to establish a correlation between the signs of alcoholism and age among the homeless. Note that my conclusions, given the non-random nature of my sample and the lack of control variables, would at best constitute a sort of 'quasi-statistical support' (Becker, 1958: 656).

This does not imply that numbers and measurements are otherwise useless to field researchers. Indeed, even the most qualitatively oriented among us still speak of sample size (i.e., how many people or things were observed) in presenting our findings.

However, in purely measurement-oriented analysis, observations are *only* meaningful to the extent that they can be used to count *something*. Indeed, one way of establishing the legitimacy of qualitative research is to suggest it can be used as a basis for developing more rigorous concepts and quantifiable measures later down the road. Once observations are transformed into quantified measures, the rest of the analysis is really about applying descriptive or inferential statistics to a data set.

CONSTRUCTIONIST ANALYSIS

In this type of analysis, rather than isolating, or inducing, an objective finding or fact, the goal is to uncover meaning-making processes that people in the field use to make sense of their world. Instead of mining the data for general and enduring concepts or patterns, constructionist analyses highlight particular and contextually meaningful processes. Unlike the descriptive analysis with its emphasis on a realistic depiction of the field, constructionist analysis is concerned with how participants create their social worlds using spoken and written words (whether these words are solicited through interviews or naturally occurring in the field). For example, consider the following excerpt from my observations at a homeless shelter. In this excerpt, Tim, a client, is about to end an intake interview with his social worker.

Social Worker: All right. Can you think of anything else?

Tim: I think that's probably got it.

Social Worker: Okay.

Tim: That's got me fixed up. Not unless you got any million-dollar checks?

Social Worker: Um, let me check my drawers here. [They both laugh.]

Tim: Okay, remember when we were talking about, you know, what was it, World War, World War I and II veterans? [They were] supposed to have some allies in Burma, you know. Uh, Burma, and Algiers, all different kinds of places, you know, where they, and they – you know, army people, military people are funny, you know, about money. Where it's at, who gets it and everything, you know. Who's acceptable, you know. They may not like someone because he may be a toughie. May not be any good. They say, "No, you ain't gonna get, no money. We don't like you." And so you'll never get no money. ...

Social Worker: So what are you saying? You didn't get your money when you got out of the service?

Tim: No. Uh, I didn't get no million if I supposed to get one. I didn't get one. ...

Social Worker: Well, think about it, Tim. If they gave you a million dollars when you got discharged from the service, then everyone would join the service.

Tim: Right, uh-huh.

Social Worker: And they're not, so I don't – there may be some kind of separation pay. But it's not as much as a million bucks.

Tim: Uh-huh. [Pause] Well, that should do me, hon.

Social Worker: Okay.

Tim: Thanks much.

Social Worker: Okay. Well, as long as you keep cooperating and so forth while you're here, we'll have you through the weekend.

Tim: Okay. I thank you so much, dear. (Marvasti, 2002: 643–5)

I analysed this exchange using a constructionist narrative paradigm (Gubrium and Holstein, 2009) and focused on the way the social worker skillfully edits Tim's off-topic remarks. She does not necessarily engage his flights of fancy about a 'million-dollar check' or delve into whether he has a legitimate claim as a disabled veteran. Instead, the social worker narratively makes the nonsense sensible by coaxing the client back to what is most relevant for his stay at the shelter: 'cooperating and so forth.' I compared this extract to others to suggest that who receives help at a homeless shelter (i.e., 'service worthiness'; Spencer, 1994) is in part decided by how the staff edit client stories, and, in turn, how the clients respond to this sort of narrative intervention.

It would be an interesting exercise to apply the different analytical strategies discussed in this book (e.g., narrative analysis, see Esin et al., Chapter 14; conversation analysis reports, see Toerien, Chapter 22; discourse analysis, see Willig, Chapter 23; and so on) to this data extract. Suffice it to say that the analysis of the observation in part depends on what the researcher chooses to focus on as the more revealing or the most relevant feature of the observation. In a sense, different analysts might see different things in the same bit of data (discourse, conversation, narrative). Note also that, depending on one's analytical framework, the observation might be completely useless. An experimental behaviorist, for example, will have no use for this exchange since there are no controls or clearly identifiable cause-and-effect variables to be analysed. Similarly, a conversation analyst might find such data less than useful, or just plain sloppy, because it lacks detailed transcriptions (e.g., special notations indicating the length of pauses in the conversation).

Looking at analysis and observing as interrelated components also sheds light on the question: What is the object of observation? The answer depends on what matters for the purpose at hand. The object of observation should not be confused with the taken-for-granted topic of analysis. Rather, what an observation represents is decided by one's disciplinary orientation and related methods and theories.

CONCLUSION

In this chapter, I approached the topic of analysing observations with an emphasis on the following questions:

- How does the observer–observed relationship influence what we see?
- How does one analyse observations from field research?

In addressing these questions, I followed the premise that analysis of observations cannot be separated from the interactional and theoretical framework within which observations are seen and known. In the words of Amanda Coffey and Paul Atkinson:

> The process of analysis should not be seen as a distinct stage of research; rather, it is a reflexive activity that should inform data collection, writing, further data collection, and so forth. Analysis is not, then, the last phase of the research process. It should be seen as part of the research design and of the data collection. The research process, of which analysis is one aspect, is a cyclical one. (1996: 6)

The three types of analyses and observer–observed relationships discussed here fall on a theoretical 'subjective–objective continuum' (Goetz and LeCompte, 1981: 54) that ranges from an emphasis on external qualities (describing the empirical facts as they *really* are) to constructive practices (understanding how facts are made meaningful by the people in the field). At the same time, it is possible to see the descriptive, inductive, and constructionist approaches as overlapping orientations toward making sense of observations in general. Indeed, any research manuscript based on observational techniques invariably includes a *description* of the setting before proceeding to the rigor of analysis. Similarly, as Kathy Charmaz (2008) has demonstrated, it is entirely possible for inductions gleaned from grounded theory to point to constructive practices. Therefore, the quality of the analysis should not be judged solely on the researcher's unrelenting adherence to this or that particular technique, which happens to be in vogue at the time. Rather, in my view, 'good' analysis evinces the complementary qualities of the craft and science of research.

I have in mind here what Harry Wolcott describes as being 'intellectually rigorous without succumbing to the rigor mortis of oversystematization' (1994: 176). In the same vein, the eminent symbolic interactionist, Herbert Blumer, once cautioned sociologists against the overuse of concepts and 'the tendency to manufacture them with reckless abandon' (1969: 169). Blumer went on to say, 'I suspect that this steady production of new concepts arises from the effort to pose as scientific and to be judged as profound and learned' (1969: 169). Research findings (the product of analysis) should flow from the empirical observations and make sense. If the reader cannot understand how the researcher began with a particular set of observations and arrived at the findings, then the analysis has failed; and it means that in all likelihood the researcher could have written the findings with or without the actual observations from the field. As Blumer puts it:

> As I see it, most improper usage of the concept in science comes when the concept is set apart from the world of experience, when it is divorced from the perception from which it has arisen and into which it ordinarily ties. Detached from the experience which brought it into existence, it is almost certain to become indefinite and metaphysical. (1969: 168)

To avoid this problem, I favor what Gubrium and Holstein call 'cultivated tentativeness' and 'troubled curiosity' (see Gubrium and Holstein, Chapter 3, this volume). This means that fieldworkers should not succumb to ready-made answers to questions posed by their empirical observations. Instead, they should be open to 'analytic inspiration' (see Gubrium and Holstein, Chapter 3, this volume) see their observations from multiple perspectives and resist the temptation to impose taken-for-granted concepts on what they observe in the field. However, it is important not to confuse 'analytic inspiration' with an anything-goes, sloppy view of ethnographic research. As Gubrium and Holstein put it, 'Analytic inspiration isn't license for procedural recklessness' (see Gubrium and Holstein, Chapter 3: p. 47, this volume).

In short, 'bad analysis' can be characterized as research that either lacks rigor and focus, or so rigidly adheres to methods that it artificially forces observations into predetermined categories. By comparison, 'good' analysis is both rigorous and flexible; it is guided by a healthy mix of 'analytic inspiration' and empiricism written for and directed at a particular audience (Silverman, 2005: 327).

The business of sharing one's analysis with an audience invariably brings us into the realm of representational strategies. Analysis is rhetorical to the degree that the researcher has to convince readers that his or her observations correspond to the empirical observations at hand. Fortunately, there is a vast body of literature on writing qualitative research (see, for example, Clifford and Marcus, 1986; Hesse-Biber and Leavy, 2008; Marvasti, 2008; Wolcott, 2008; see also Denzin, Chapter 39, this volume). Relatedly, researchers like Laurel Richardson (2002) are at the forefront of a movement to create new aesthetics of writing and analysis. In her words, 'Poetic representation ... is a practical and powerful, indeed transforming, method for understanding the social, altering the self, and invigorating the research community that claims knowledge of our lives' (2002: 888). Such alternative practices aim to transcend the limitations of traditional science by turning to poetic forms and away from the more purely analytical text. In essence, such approaches try to create what the English poet, William Wordsworth, called 'a heart that watches and receives':

> Our meddling intellect
> Misshapes the beauteous form of things:–
> We murder to dissect.
> Enough of science and art;
> Close these barren leaves.
> Come forth, and bring with you a heart
> That watches and receives.
> (Excerpt from William Wordsworth's *The Tables Turned*, cited in Manly, 1907: 330)

However, it is important to keep a vigilant and critical eye on these practices as well, since no genre of representing social observations is inherently authentic (Marvasti and Faircloth, 2002). Indeed, it is exceedingly difficult to assume any 'heart' can simply 'watch and receive' with no ulterior motives. Another English poet, John Keats, once wrote: 'Beauty is truth, truth beauty, – that is all / Ye know on earth, and all ye need to know' (*Ode on a Grecian Urn*, cited in Strachan, 2003: 156). It may be that the fusion of beauty and truth remains the fugitive goal of qualitative methods and analysis.

FURTHER READING

The readings listed below offer three somewhat different perspectives on transforming observations. Becker approaches data analysis as a process that moves in different stages (i.e., from 'provisional analyses' to 'final comprehensive analyses'). Goetz and LeCompte catalogue as contrasting pairs the many ways of conceptualizing analysis of observational data (e.g., 'enumerative' vs. 'constructive' and 'subjective' vs. 'objective'). Finally, Charmaz outlines strategies for incorporating both constructionist and objectivist concerns into a single analytical framework.

Becker, Howard (1958) 'Problems of inference and proof in participant observation,' *American Sociological Review*, 23: 652–60.
Goetz, Judith P. and LeCompte, Margaret D. (1981) 'Ethnographic research and the problem of data reduction,' *Anthropology & Education Quarterly*, 12: 51–70.
Charmaz, Kathy (2008) 'Constructionism and the grounded theory method,' in Jaber F. Gubrium and James Holstein (eds.), *Handbook of Constructionist Research*. New York: Guilford Press. pp. 397–412.

REFERENCES

Adler, Patricia, and Adler, Peter (1987) *Membership Roles in Field Research*. Newbury Park, CA: Sage.
Anderson, Elijah (1997) 'The police and the black male,' in Patricia A. Adler and Peter Adler (eds.), *Constructions of Deviance: Social Power, Context, & Interaction*, 2nd edition. Belmont, CA: Wadsworth. pp. 142–52.

Anderson, Leon (2006) 'Analytic autoethnography,' *Journal of Contemporary Ethnography*, 35 (4): 373–95.

Athens, Lonnie (2010) 'Naturalistic inquiry in theory and practice,' *Journal of Contemporary Ethnography*, 39: 87–125.

Becker, Howard (1958) 'Problems of inference and proof in participant observation,' *American Sociological Review*, 23: 652–60.

Berger, Leigh (2001) 'Inside out: Narrative autoethnography as a path toward rapport,' *Qualitative Inquiry*, 7 (4): 504–18.

Blumer, Herbert (1969) *Symbolic Interactionism: Perspective and Method*. Berkeley: University of California Press.

Calvey, David (2008) 'The art and politics of covert research: Doing "situated ethics" in the field,' *Sociology*, 42: 905–18.

Charmaz, Kathy (2008) 'Constructionism and the grounded theory method,' in Jaber F. Gubrium and James Holstein (eds.), *Handbook of Constructionist Research*. New York: Guilford Press. pp. 397–412.

Clifford, James (1986) 'On ethnographic allegory,' in Clifford James and George Marcus (eds.), *Writing Culture: The Poetics and Politics of Ethnography*. Berkeley: University of California Press. pp. 98–121.

Clifford, James and Marcus, George E. (eds.) (1986) *Writing Culture: The Poetics and Politics of Ethnography*. Berkeley: University of California Press.

Coffey, Amanda (1999) *The Ethnographic Self: Fieldwork and the Representation of Identity*. London: Sage.

Coffey, Amanda and Atkinson, Paul (1996) *Making Sense of Qualitative Data: Complementary Research Strategies*. London: Sage.

Daston, Lorraine and Lunbeck, Elizabeth (2011) 'Introduction: Observation observed,' in Lorraine Daston and Elizabeth Lunbeck (eds.), *Histories of Scientific Observation*. Chicago: University of Chicago Press. pp. 1–9.

Davies, James and Spencer, Dimitrina (eds.) (2010) *Emotions in the Field – The Psychology and Anthropology of Fieldwork Experience*. Stanford, CA: Stanford University Press.

Denzin, Norman K. (1997) *Interpretive Ethnography: Ethnographic Practices for the Twenty-First Century*. Newbury Park, CA: Sage.

Ellis, Carolyn (1991) 'Sociological introspection and emotional experience,' *Symbolic Interaction*, 14: 23–50.

Ellis, Carolyn (1997) 'Evocative autoethnography: Writing emotionally about our lives,' in William G. Tierney and Yvonna S. Lincoln (eds.), *Representation and the Text: Re-Framing the Narrative Voice*. Albany: State University of New York Press. pp. 115–42.

Ellis, Carolyn and Bochner, Arthur P. (2000) 'Autoethnography, personal narrative, reflexivity: Researcher as subject,' in Norman K. Denzin and Yvonna Lincoln (eds.), *Handbook of Qualitative Research*, 2nd edition. Thousand Oaks, CA: Sage. pp. 733–68.

Emerson, Robert (1988) *Contemporary Field Research: A Collection of Readings*. Prospect Heights, IL: Waveland Press.

Fowler, Don D. and Hardesty, Donald . L. (eds.) (1994) *Others Knowing Others: Perspectives on Ethnographic Careers*. Washington: Smithsonian Institution Press.

Geertz, Clifford (1988) 'Thick description: Toward an interpretive theory of culture,' in Robert Emerson (ed.), *Contemporary Field Research: A Collection of Readings*. Prospect Heights, IL: Waveland Press. pp. 37–59.

Goetz, Judith P. and LeCompte, Margaret D. (1981) 'Ethnographic research and the problem of data reduction,' *Anthropology & Education Quarterly*, 12: 51–70.

Gold, Raymond (1958) 'Roles in sociological field observation,' *Social Forces*, 36: 217–223.

Grimshaw, Anna (2001) *The Ethnographer's Eye: Ways of Seeing in Modern Anthropology*. New York: Cambridge University Press.

Gubrium, Jaber F. and Holstein, James A. (2002) 'From the individual interview to interview society,' in Jaber F. Gubrium and James A. Holstein (eds.), *Handbook of Interview Research: Context and Method*. Thousand Oaks, CA: Sage. pp. 3–32.

Gubrium, Jaber F. and Holstein, James A. (2008) 'Narrative ethnography,' in Sharlene Hesse-Biber and Patricia Leavy (eds.), *Handbook of Emergent Methods*. New York: Guilford Press. pp. 241–64.

Gubrium, Jaber F. and Holstein, James A. (2009) *Analyzing Narrative Reality*. Thousand Oaks, CA: Sage.

Hesse-Biber, Nagy, Sharlene, and Leavy, Patricia (eds.) (2008) *Handbook of Emergent Methods*. New York: Guilford Press.

Manly, John Matthews (1907) *English Poetry: 1170–1892*. Boston, MA: Ginn.

Martineau, Harriet (1838) *How to Observe Morals and Manners*. London: Charles Knight.

Marvasti, Amir (2002) 'Constructing the service-worthy homeless through narrative editing,' *Journal of Contemporary Ethnography*, 31 (5): 615–51.

Marvasti, Amir (2008) 'Writing and presenting social research,' in Pertti Alasuutari et al. (eds.), *The SAGE Handbook of Social Research Methods*. London: Sage. pp. 602–16.

Marvasti, Amir and Faircloth, Christopher (2002) 'Writing the exotic, the authentic, and the moral: Romanticism as discursive resource for ethnographic text,' *Qualitative Inquiry*, 8 (6): 760–84.

Richardson, Laurel (2002) 'Poetic representation of interviews,' in Jaber F. Gubrium and James A. Holstein (eds.), *Handbook of Interview Research: Context and Method*. Thousand Oaks, CA: Sage. pp. 877–91.

Rodriguez, Neolie and Ryave, Alan (2002) *Systematic Self-Observation*. Thousand Oaks, CA: Sage.

Ronai, Carol R. (1996) 'My mother is mentally retarded,' in Carolyn Ellis and Arthur Bochner (eds.), *Composing Ethnography*. Newbury Park, CA: Altamira Press. pp. 109–31.

Ruddick, Susan M (1996) *Young and Homeless in Hollywood: Mapping Social Identities*. New York: Routledge.

Silverman, David (2005) *Doing Qualitative Research: A Practical Guide*, 2nd edition. London: Sage.

Spencer, J. William (1994) 'Homeless in River City: Client work in human service encounters,' in James A. Holstein and Gale Miller (eds.), *Perspective on Social Problems*, vol. 6). Greenwich, CT: JAI Press. pp. 29–46.

Stocking, George W. (1983) *Observers Observed: Essays on Ethnographic Fieldwork*. Madison: University of Wisconsin Press.

Strachan, John (2003) *The Poems of John Keats: A Sourcebook*. New York: Routledge.

Strauss, Anselm and Corbin, Juliet (1994) 'Grounded theory methodology: An overview,' in Norman K. Denzin and Yvonna S. Lincoln (eds.), *Handbook of Qualitative Research*. Thousand Oaks, CA: Sage. pp. 273–85.

Weinberger, Eliot (1994) 'The camera people,' in Lucien Taylor (ed.), *Visualizing Theory: Selected Essays from V.A.R., 1990–1994*. New York: Routledge.

Wolcott, Harry F. (1994) *Transforming Qualitative Data: Description, Analysis, and Interpretation*. Thousand Oaks, CA: Sage.

Wolcott, Harry F. (2008) *Writing Up Qualitative Research*, 3rd edition. Thousand Oaks, CA: Sage.

Wright, Talmadge (1997) *Out of Place: Homeless Mobilizations, Subcities, and Contested Landscapes*. Albany: State University of New York Press.

25

Analysing Documents

Amanda Coffey

Most qualitative research takes place in settings that are 'documented' in various ways. That is to say, many social settings are self-documenting and there is considerable methodological potential to study the documentary realities of social worlds. What can be included as a 'document' in social research covers a potentially broad spectrum of materials, both textual and otherwise. There are, of course, 'official' records of various kinds – organizational and 'state' documents designed as records of action and activity (such as large data sets and public records). There are also everyday documents of organizations and lives – notes, memoranda, case records, email threads and so forth; semi-public or routine documents that are at the heart of everyday social practice. There are also private papers of various kinds that we can also treat as documentary data or evidence – for example, diaries, testimony, letters and cards. But we can go further than that in defining what might count as a document for social research purposes – maps, photographs (see Banks, Chapter 27, this volume), newspaper reports (see Hodgetts and Chamberlain, Chapter 26, this volume), autobiographies, novels, advertisements and paintings can all be considered documents that tell of settings, organizations, times and lives. In contemporary times, documentary materials also now encompass a wide range of technological, digital and social media – for example, email conversations (see Marotzki et al., Chapter 31, and Kozinets et al., Chapter 18, this volume), SMS text messaging, websites, social networking sites and hypermedia. All kinds of documents are routinely written, produced, read, consumed, stored, circulated and used in everyday social life and practice. Indeed, documents can be thought of as the 'physical traces' of social settings (Webb et al., 2000); as data or evidence of the ways in which individuals, groups, social settings, institutions and organizations represent and account for themselves. Documents provide a mechanism and vehicle for understanding and making sense of social and organization practices or, as May describes, 'documents, read as the sedimentations of social practices, have the potential to inform and structure the decisions which people make on a daily and longer-term basis: they also constitute particular readings of social events' (2001: 176).

Qualitative researchers have not always recognized the analytical potential of studying written documents and textual recordings as research data; indeed in many qualitative accounts of social settings there is often little or no mention of the documentary realities of those settings. Of course, documentary research has a long history within social science more generally. Many early sociological thinkers (including for example Marx, Weber and Durkheim) gathered and analysed documents as part of their empirical and theoretical practice, as did many later scholars of social science (such as Foucault and Bourdieu). In this chapter I argue that qualitative research can be enriched by a careful and critical attention to the gathering and analysis of documents, of various kinds, in various modes and through various media. This might usefully include a close reading of documents themselves, but also include developing an understanding of the ways in which documents are authored, produced, used and consumed. Thus this chapter explores the potential of documents as social research data, and considers some of the methodological and technical aspects of analysing documents as a way of understanding social practice.

DEFINING DOCUMENTARY DATA

Documents are pervasive in organizational and social life – consider, for example, a typical or ideal-type organization, such as a private business, a public sector organization, a school, hospital, car manufacturer, university or accountancy firm. It is hard to imagine such a modern kind of social organization without recourse to its routine documentation – administrators, managers, accountants, lawyers, civil servants, managers and practitioners are all, routinely and extensively, involved in the production and consumption of everyday documents and texts as part of their daily work. If we wish to understand how organizations and social settings operate and how people work with/in them, then it makes sense to consider social actors' various activities as authors and audiences of documents. And, of course, there are differing levels of formality and informality in the production and intention of such documents, which can include official brochures, records and minutes, but also other physical traces such as email threads and conversations. Textual records also embody individual actions, interactions and encounters within social settings. 'People-processing professions' for example, such as medicine, nursing, teaching or social work, routinely compile documents of professional–client interactions (case notes, medical records, care plans, school reports). These written records can be used to inform future action, and are themselves drawn upon in the more formal recording (and documentary) mechanisms of official statistics, performance indicators, efficiency league tables and similar constructs.

Qualitative explorations of a range of social settings have included some attention to the production and consumption of such documentary data. Examples include studies that have incorporated analyses of school reports (Woods, 1979), medical records (Rees, 1981), classifications of causes of death (Prior, 1985), coroners' records (Fincham et al., 2011) and health visitors' case records (Dingwall, 1977). Indeed there are many research questions and settings that arguably cannot be investigated adequately without reference to the production and use of documentary materials. For example, it would be impossible to study the everyday work and occupational culture of a profession such as actuaries without addressing the construction and interpretation of documentary artefacts such as the life-table (Prior and Bloor, 1993); and difficult to understand the modern university and higher education more generally without studying their documentary realities – for example, prospectuses, committee minutes, accounts of research performance and student feedback are all part of the ways in which universities 'do' their work (Atkinson and Coffey, 2010). As Bloomfield and Vurdabakis (1994) point out, textual communicative practices are a vital way in which organizations constitute 'reality' and the forms of knowledge appropriate to it. But as I have noted above, formal organizational documents form only part of the documentary reality in which and through which organizations, social settings and lives are represented, lived and told.

Like organizations and other social settings, individual and collective lives are also marked by, with and through documents of various kinds. Alongside organizational and professional records of lives, for example as told through medical notes or school reports, are a myriad of other kinds of 'life document'. Thus documents and their analyses can also be utilized to understand personal lives and experiences, and to place biography within and in relation to social context. As Plummer reminds us:

> the world is crammed full of human, personal documents. People keep diaries, send letters, make quilts, dash off memos, compose auto/biographies, construct web sites, scrawl graffiti, publish their memoirs, write letters, compose CVs, leave suicide notes, film video diaries, inscribe memorials on tombstones, shoot films, paint pictures, make tapes and try to record their personal dreams. ... They are all in the broadest sense 'documents of life'. (2001: 17)

Plummer contends that social science should treat such life documents seriously both as resources for understanding complex social life and as topics of analysis in their own right. Just as organizations and social settings have documentary realities so, too, do individuals, families and other social groups. Thus paying analytic attention to documents can shed light on the intimate and the personal as well as the public, organizational and corporate.

It is also helpful to make a distinction between documents that are 'found' in the process of social research (documents that exist prior to, and not because of, the research) and documents that are 'made' as part of the research (produced explicitly for the research to hand). So, for example, during social research we might gather together documents that pre-exist in a setting, that are there 'anyway' as part of the everyday order of the setting, but we might also ask participants to keep a diary or paint a picture or construct a webpage as part of the research process itself. This distinction between unsolicited and solicited documents (Scott, 1990) is useful in helping to explore the social context and circumstances of documentary production. Such a distinction, however, should not distract us from recognizing the characteristics (and therefore the analytic potential) of all documents as constituting social science data or evidence.

Documents, then, are literary, textual or visual devices that enable information to be shared and 'stories' to be presented. Thus, all documents are, in that sense, artefacts that are created for a particular purpose, crafted according to social convention to serve a function of sorts. It is this social production (and indeed consumption) of documents that gives them analytical affordance. At the same time it means that we need to be quite clear about what documents can and cannot be used for in social research. Documents are 'social facts', in that they are produced, shared and used in socially organized ways. They are versions of reality, scripted according to various kinds of convention, with a particular purpose in mind. This is equally true of the most public of record or the most private of diary. Documents construct particular kinds of representations using particular kinds of textual (and often, too, non-textual) convention. Documents should not be seen as replacements for other kinds of data. We cannot, for instance, learn through written records alone how an organization actually operates day by day. Similarly, we cannot treat documents – however official or otherwise – as firm evidence of what they report. This observation has been made repeatedly about data from official sources, such as statistics on crime, suicide, health, death and educational outcomes (Cicourel and Kitsuse, 1963; Sudnow, 1968; Atkinson, 1978; Roberts, 2003; Maguire, 1994; Macdonald, 2008; Scourfield et al., 2012). This understanding means we should always be reflexive in how we treat documents as social data.

The recognition of the existence of documents as social facts (or constructs) alerts us to the necessity to treat them seriously in social research (Prior, 2008). Documents can tell us a lot about a social setting or an individual life. However, we have to approach the analysis of documents for what they are and for what they are used to accomplish. This means paying attention to the knowledge that documents 'contain' about a setting, but also examining their role and place in settings, the cultural values attached to them, their distinctive types and forms. The analysis of such documentary evidence can form an important part of broader ethnographic studies of everyday life; documentary analysis may also be employed as the main method for qualitative research in its own right (Prior, 2003). In either event it is important to establish a methodological framework for documentary analysis. In the remainder of this chapter I outline some strategies for approaching the qualitative analysis of documents. This is certainly not intended as a comprehensive review of all analytical strategies or approaches (see Silverman, 2006; Prior, 2011), nor a technical manual of prescriptive techniques. Rather I introduce approaches to the systematic analysis of documentary data and discuss some contexts of their use.

ANALYTICAL STRATEGIES

A useful starting position for the analysis of documents in social research is that documents are socially defined, produced and consumed. Thus in looking at documents analytically, we need to examine the *processes of production and consumption* – be they technical, linguistic or conceptual – as well as the content contained *within* documents. In that sense we might think of documents as resources (i.e. as information repositories, telling us *about* a setting, an organization, an event, or a person), but also as artefacts for exploration in their own right. A document in and of itself can tell us something about the social setting. If we understand documents as accomplishments, as products with purpose, then it naturally follows that analysis should seek to locate documents within their social as well as textual context. Documents then are resources to be 'mined' but also topics to be studied.

In keeping with most other kinds of qualitative data analysis it is entirely possible and appropriate to undertake a thematic analysis of documentary data. Following on from the analytical conventions of content analysis (see Schreier, Chapter 12, this volume) or 'code-and-retrieve' (Seidel and Kelle, 1995; see Gibbs, Chapter 19, this volume), documents can be read in terms of their content meaning. Practical strategies for this kind of analysis can vary from almost quantitative measures (counting instances, for example) through to the kinds of thematic analysis supported by Straussian approaches to coding and grounded theorising (Strauss, 1987; Strauss and Corbin, 1990; also see Thornberg and Charmaz, Chapter 11, this volume). Thus we can approach documents in terms of the frequency of words, phrases or other elements or characteristics. We can index and code data to identify key themes and thus generate theoretical categories and identify patterns. It is not my intention here to provide detailed instruction in or critique of thematic or content analysis. There are good overviews in this volume and elsewhere on such approaches. Suffice to say that such approaches to the analysis of documents focus on the product (the document as information resource or vessel), and not on the processes of production per se. For many researchers who use documents in social research this approach to analysis may be entirely appropriate, particularly if documents are being used primarily to provide background information or context. However, for our purposes in this chapter I want to argue that the analytical potential of documents as social data is in also understanding the circumstances of production and the receiving (reading) of the document as an artefact of the setting under study. Thus it is important that we bring to bear analytical strategies that enable the meaning-making of documents to be subjected to critical scrutiny – analytical approaches that recognize documents themselves as ways in which social actors make sense of social worlds. Hence we also need to be concerned with intended meanings (and thus with the authorship and function of documents) and received meanings (recognizing the importance of readership and audience, and the ways in which documents are interpreted by intended and unintended audiences). Documents, as social artefacts, have narrative structures and are imbued with cultural ways of telling (see Esin et al., Chapter 14, and Winter, Chapter 17, this volume). They draw upon and conform to various genres, in terms of style, structure and language. They employ visual signs, literary devices and other symbols to present and display meaning. Documents are also rarely, if ever, produced and read in isolation from other documents. In adopting this more semiotic approach to documents we can explore relationships and meanings within a text and in relation to other texts. It is helpful here to distinguish between what documents 'look like' (i.e. language and form), what they 'do' (i.e. purpose or function) and how they are related (i.e. intertextuality between documents).

Language and Form

Documentary constructions of social reality – documents – depend upon particular uses of language and form. Documents will constitute and conform to particular *genres* with specific styles and conventions. These are often marked by quite distinctive use of language and structure. Documents may use specialized language (which might be referred to as a *linguistic register*) associated with particular domains of everyday life, and will draw on culturally recognized ways of telling (what we might refer to as *narrative structures* – see Esin et al., Chapter 14, this volume). Occupations, for example, often have distinctive language (with specialized vocabularies and narrative forms), as do particular kinds of organization or cultural activity. We can therefore learn a lot about such settings by paying particular attention to these structures, registers and forms. We can often recognize what *sort* of document we are looking at simply from its distinctive use of language or the way in which it is presented. We can, for example, recognize a theatre review, or a university prospectus, or a personal diary entry from their characteristic styles – both linguistically and stylistically. At an elementary level we can recognize that 'official' or public reports are crafted in language that differs from everyday, spoken, language use (see Toerien, Chapter 22, this volume). Similarly we can distinguish between the register and form we might use to draw up a shopping list and the register and form we might use in an obituary or other similar kind of semi-public announcement. Indeed, culturally understood registers and narrative forms are precisely the kinds of devices that are used to construct, and make distinctive or special, modes of documentary representation.

In approaching the analysis of documents in this way, it is helpful to adopt an interpretative standpoint (see Willig, Chapter 10, this volume). The initial task is to pay close attention to the question of *how* documents are constructed as distinctive kinds of artefacts or productions. It is therefore appropriate to pay close attention to the textual organization of documents, and the semiotic and narrative qualities of the materials within the documents. Important analytic questions in this context are: What kind of reality is the document creating? How is the document accomplishing that task? In undertaking such analyses we can draw on a repertoire of analytical techniques and resources – drawn for example from formal approaches to the study of language and structure – such as narrative analysis (see Esin et al., Chapter 14, this volume), discourse analysis (see Willig, Chapter 23, this volume) and semiotics. For our purposes here it is most appropriate to outline some of the general features of such approaches in terms of their specific application to documentary sense-making. When we look at a document, therefore, we can ask questions about the role and use of language as well as other discursive practices. Many documents will display a distinctive *register*: that is, a distinctive and specialized use of language associated with a particular context or *domain*. It might be associated with a particular group, occupation, activity or organization, or with a distinctive kind of intellectual field, or an esoteric pursuit. It implies a general feature of language in social life: distinctive uses of language (written and spoken) are associated with, and are constitutive of, specific social contexts. Thus in developing an interpretative understanding of documents as topics to be studied, we are interested in language, words and phrases, and also in the systems of convention that guide the ordering and structure of the text. Hence we are interested in the ways in which the messages (the meanings or social realities) are produced and articulated by an author or authors to an audience (or audiences). The look and feel of a document can thus tell us something about the social setting or social practice under consideration.

Studying the Function of Documents

As well as analysing the form and content of documents it may also be useful to consider the ways in which documents function and have function. That is, we can explore the ways in which documents are *used* and have use in everyday life and social context. We might usefully make a distinction here between intended and received messages or functions. What purpose is the document intended to serve by the author or authors, and how is the document read, understood and used by audiences or readers? As well as asking analytical questions in relation to 'how' the document is 'constructed', it is therefore also appropriate to ask how documents 'function' in everyday activities and thus how they help to construct everyday realities in their procurement and usage. In other words, what is the document doing?

A way of approaching this kind of question is to think in terms of what the linguistic philosopher John L. Austin described as speech acts. This refers to the fact that language does not merely describe events or states of affairs. It also creates or performs them. When you make a promise or utter a threat, you are not using language to describe something else; you are using the language to accomplish the act itself. In just the same way documents can be seen not (just) as describing an event, organization, emotion or state of affairs, but also as helping to create them (see Toerien, Chapter 22, this volume). In doing so documents deploy discursive or rhetorical devices – to create plausible accounts and to construct believable versions of reality; in other words, documents *persuade*. Rhetoric in this context is not being referred to in a negative way, nor does it imply wrongdoing. Rather it is an acknowledgement that a document can be conceptualized as an act of persuasion – and as such, and in line with any other act of persuasion, depends on rhetorical devices to describe, explain and justify. Moreover, the social actors who write documents and the social actors who read (and evaluate) them bring to bear their knowledge – often tacit – of the conventions that go into their production and reception. Writers develop and display a working knowledge of the register(s) of their own professions, or organizational setting or cultural activity or intimate life. Readers, too, bring to bear a repertoire of conventional understanding to interpret and make sense of documents. Indeed, the phrase 'making sense' is especially apposite when we think of the ways in which documents are interpreted and come to be understood. Making sense is a socially organized activity of interpreting documents. This suggests that the interpretation of documents is an active process. Thus documentary sources do not transparently describe or reveal goings on or states of affairs. They help to construct and display them; and that construction requires the active *participation* of readers as well as writers. Reading documents and making sense of their contents requires readers to bring their own assumptions and understandings to bear. The culturally competent reader will 'know' how to use documentary sources to create the organizational reality they purport to describe. Knowledgeable readers will know something of the cultural features of the organization or cultural setting, and thus will be well placed to use what Mannheim called – appropriately – the 'documentary method' (see Bohnsack, Chapter 15, this volume). That is, the text is used to furnish indications or provide physical traces of what the reader interprets or understands as the social reality. Thus readers will read into the text what might reasonably be assumed to be the case, given a shared stock of tacit knowledge about this organization or social setting or intimate life and how they typically function. Typical cases are interpreted in terms of their typical manifestations, and their typical rhetorical representations. Thus documentary realities are built, consolidated and confirmed.

This focus on the functions of documents can be usefully developed and illustrated by exploring the ways in which documents do various kinds of 'work'. Consider for example what a school or university prospectus is setting out to achieve, or a social work case report, school report or suicide note. We might usefully use terms such as 'to persuade', 'to validate', 'to justify'. A classic example of this is Garfinkel's seminal commentary on the analysis of clinical hospital records (Garfinkel, 1967; also see Eberle, Chapter 13, and Bohnsack, Chapter 15, this volume). Garfinkel's actual starting point was the use made of clinical records by social researchers, who appeared to be able to make practical use of clinical records as data in order to make sense of how hospital clinics work. Garfinkel argued that the researchers were only able to make sense of those records by 'reading into' them what they had already come to understand about clinics as particular kinds of organization. The clinical records themselves were messy documents, but culturally competent readers of these records – for example, clinicians, administrators or indeed researchers – were able to *make* sense of them by bringing to bear prior assumptions and cultural understandings. In this way documents can be seen to presuppose a community of readers and writers who share a common stock of knowledge and taken-for-granted assumptions. The analysis of documents can therefore examine those cultural and organizational features that are implicitly invoked when records and documents are produced and used. In invoking the documentary method in this context we are returning again to an earlier claim – whereby everyday social actors use a generally understood methodology to interpret documents as 'physical traces'. In this sense documents are signs or symbols through which social actors infer underlying patterns or states of affairs, and to which social actors add and embellish with their common-sense knowledge.

Intertextuality and Authority

Documents do not construct domains of documentary reality as individual, separate activities. Documents refer – however tangentially – to other realities and domains. Moreover, documents refer and are connected to *other* documents. This is especially the case for particular kinds of organizational settings and their systems of accountability via documentation, though can be just as applicable to other kinds of social or cultural settings. The analysis of documents and documentary reality must, therefore, look beyond individual texts as artefacts, and also ask how (and in what ways) they are related. That is, we can recognize that, like any system of symbols and signs, documents often make sense because they have relationships with and to other documents. Thus we can pay attention to the *intertextuality* of documents: that is, their relational qualities and what these can reveal about the setting under investigation. The concept of audit is useful here. If we consider the basic mechanics of audit, then it starts to become quite easy to grasp the point and significance of systematic relations between documents. One of the root metaphors of an audit is that of the *audit trail*. Conventionally defined audits, for example of firms and organizations, carried out by accountants or auditors, place great emphasis on the *audit trail*. Audit trails trace each document and statement presented in organizational accounts to other documents contained in the audit file (the preparation of papers for an audit). There is an assumption that references can and should be made to other documents; indeed it is through these references and trails that decisions, accounts and everyday practices are documented and justified. An auditor's task is to establish the extent of these relationships and intertextualities, in order to account for and make sense of the process and practice of the organization. These relationships between documents are usually based on elementary – but significant – principles. They include the principles of sequence and hierarchy, which form part of the constitutive machinery whereby organizations produce and reproduce themselves. From a general analytic perspective, therefore, we can see that documentary realities do not rely on particular documents mirroring and reflecting a social reality. Rather, we can think of a semi-autonomous domain of documentary reality, in which documents reflect and refer to other documents.

We can analyse such documentary realities in various ways. The term 'intertextuality' derives from contemporary literary criticism and is used, in that context, to refer to that fact that literary texts (such as novels) are rarely free-standing pieces, nor do they just or only refer to a fictional world. Literary texts, in their very nature, refer to other texts, albeit sometimes implicitly. This can include other texts of the same genre, or other kinds of textual product (such as journalism or biography). Texts can therefore be analysed in terms of these intertextual relationships, tracing the dimensions of similarity, comparison, contrast and difference. We can examine, for example, how conventional formats are shared between texts, and thus how they construct a uniform style. We can note how texts are linked as sequences of documents, and seek to understand the nature and meaning of those sequences. We can also examine how relations between documents reveal temporality – documents can often provide a temporal sequence or structure to the organization or setting or life, though will not necessarily describe the passage of time as experienced as an everyday phenomenon by the individual actor(s) concerned. Documentary sources can hasten time, slow time, 'trouble' time and even *suppress* time – lifting events out of the flow of lived experience, and recording them in decontextualized language and formats of a documentary record. Intertextuality thus alerts us to the fact that documents are usually part of wider systems of distribution and exchange. Documents circulate through social networks and organizations, and in doing so help actively to construct those networks and organizations.

Documents move, flow and exchange because they can be used to decontextualize and recontextualize events. We can transform things, events, activities and lives by incorporating them into texts. By writing an event, activity or life in a documentary format, we translate them from the specific and the local, and make of them 'facts' and 'records' which take on an independent existence. Some texts become 'official', and can become 'proof' of events and roles. This is an argument that was made by Latour and Woolgar (1986) in relation to the production of scientific facts and findings through the production of scientific papers. Latour and Woolgar suggested that scientific 'facts', represented in documentary form, achieve an independence of their original site of production (e.g. the peopled and relational research group or laboratory), and take on an independent existence. In other words, the academic paper recounting or claiming the scientific discovery actually removes that discovery from the process of discovery (with the people, personalities, luck, judgement, risk and failure that might have been involved). A similar observation can be made about the routine circulation of minutes of meetings, which those of us who regularly attend meetings will know are only ever a partial and scripted version of events. The professional audit report of a business organization serves a similar purpose. The audit report *becomes* the documentary reality, superseding other files, records and memories.

One should also note here questions of authorship and readership in the analysis of documents and relations between documents. It is important to address authorship (whether actual or implied) and readership (again whether actual or implied) if one is to understand the system of production, exchange and consumption of documentary materials. Documents are usually 'recipient designed' (see Toerien, Chapter 22, this volume). That is, they are produced with readers in mind and will therefore reflect implicit assumptions about who will be the reader. This implied reader does not, of course, have to be an actual individual person. The implied recipient can correspond to what George Herbert Mead referred to as the 'generalized other'. Indeed it is a basic tenet of interactionist social analysis that social actors monitor and shape their actions in the light of generalized others' imputed responses and evaluations. When a document is created it is often in the light of the kind of readership expected or being written for. And as analysts of documents we need to be attuned to addressing this. Equally, while it is self-evident that a person or a group must actually author documents (since they do not write themselves), that does not always imply a social recognition of 'authorship'. Indeed, it is part of the facticity of many documents (particularly but not exclusively 'official' documents) that they are not identifiably the work of an individual author. Anonymity itself can be part of the production of documentary reality. For example, while there may be an implied 'ownership' of a document – such as the originating administrator or department – official materials usually do not have visible social actors expressing opinions. It is important therefore to inspect texts for indications of authorship, or its absence. In that sense, too, we can look for how documents claim whatever *authority* may be attributed to them. In simple terms 'texts must be studied as socially situated products' (Scott, 1990: 34), with socially situated authors and readers.

AN EXEMPLAR – DOCUMENTARY ANALYSIS IN PRACTICE

This chapter has argued that, in analysing documents as social research data, we should be mindful, not only of what the documents might contain in terms of information or content, but also of how they are structured and the functions to which they are (or might be) put. Moreover, I have noted that documents are rarely present in isolation from other documents, and explorations of relationships between documents can be analytically fruitful. In this section I turn to an exemplar that draws on a multifaceted approach to the analysis of documents in social research. A recent example of the qualitative analysis of documents in social research is the work of Scourfield and colleagues on suicide and the sociological autopsy (see Scourfield et al., 2012; Fincham et al., 2011). This choice of exemplar is apposite of course, as official records (documents) of suicide were used by Durkheim in what is still heralded as a watershed development within sociology (Durkheim, 2002 [1897]). Drawing on 100 suicide case files from a UK coroner's office, Scourfield and his colleagues set out to develop a sociological approach to the study of suicide, examining individual suicidal lives in their broader social context, and with recourse to the social construction of knowledge. The project focused on the myriad of documents contained in the coroner's files, thus drawing on a rich diversity of documentary data, including: 'forms filled out by coroner; scribbles by the coroner on file wallets; police statements from witnesses and significant others; forensic pathology reports; medical letters and reports, especially psychiatric ones; suicide notes; mobile phone records; photographs of corpses; letters to the coroner and newspaper clippings' (Scourfield et al., 2012: 467). Aside from noting the important role of the coroner's office in putting together or constructing these interrelated files of evidence, Scourfield and his colleagues also reveal the ways in which these documentary artefacts can be analysed as sites for the creation of identity; 'we are concerned with relationships: how they extend into documents and how they constitute different kinds of persons and identities, during someone's lifetime and beyond' (Fincham et al., 2011: 65). The project explored the ways in which documents as 'evidence' are constructed by parties to the suicidal life (and death), by those living and those now dead, and the ways in which documentary data can be used to explore how knowledge about suicide is constructed by professionals, families and publics.

In terms of our interest here in the analysis of documents in qualitative research practice, this project is an excellent exemplar in a number of important ways. First, as highlighted above, the project demonstrates some of the sheer richness and diversity of documentary possibilities for social research, drawing as it does on many different kinds of documentary artefact, all present within a single file. Second, the project demonstrates the ways in which documents can be analysed in terms of thematic content, to reveal patterns, sequences and absences. The project was unusual in that it sought to draw on a qualitative thematic analysis of whole cases (rather than extracts), which also enabled the generation of quantitative analyses that went beyond the individual case. Code-and-retrieve was used to analyse across as well as within different genres of documents, as well as providing some quantification of the qualitative data. Third, the project focuses particular attention on the form and structure of documents and the analytical possibilities of understanding such characteristics and qualities between and across different kinds of documents. For example, the project examined official and professional reports of the living person (e.g. as patient or client) and the dead person (as body or corpse). The project also examined witness statements:

> [S]uch statements were not verbatim records of the interview. Rather the events recounted in them had been consecutively ordered and the narrative itself had been shaped by the need to be concise and to the point. In order to achieve this aim, the statements were drafted first by a police officer using institutional conventions of language and content. These documents' hybrid production process and the need to fulfil institutional and legal requirements, lent the accounts a shared appearance. (Fincham et al., 2011: 76)

These contrast sharply to individual suicide notes – which 'vary greatly in their form and content', are the only documents written by the deceased in the file, and the only documents 'produced before the deceased died' (Fincham et al., 2011: 80–1). Moreover, this project reveals the ways in which documents can be analysed in terms of the functions, intended or otherwise, that documents can perform. For example, they reveal the ways in which documents justify decisions or verdicts, display professional hierarchies or exercise agency (in this case, after death).

The coroner's file on the suicidal life and death, and the analyses of multiple cases, also allow for a sociological understanding of intertextuality in practice. The diversity of documents, and the exploration of their pre- and post-death production, provide an opportunity to explore the relationships between and within documents – within and across cases. In doing so the project provides ways of looking at the complex documentary realities of suicidal lives and action, and the ways in which these realities are imbued with socially situated meaning and authorship. And in doing so the project articulated and worked with the opportunities heralded by documentary analysis, as well as noting some of the limitations of seeking to understand social worlds through documents. As the authors note, 'we accept that evidence about suicide, including documents in coroners' files, is produced under specific circumstances which affect how it should be read, but maintain that such evidence aims to establish something about an externally verifiable social world' (Fincham et al., 2011: 52–3). In the final section of this chapter I elaborate a little further on some of the challenges of documentary analysis, as well as looking towards further development in this area.

THE LIMITATIONS OF, AND NEW POSSIBILITIES FOR WORKING WITH DOCUMENTS

Working with documents in social research means paying careful attention to the ways in which documents are classified and conceptualized. What counts as a document, and what meaning we attach to a document, is a complex and multifaceted task. There are various ways in which we might usefully classify documents for social research purposes, and such classifications help to distinguish between kinds of documents, provide opportunities for thinking across documents and enable us to recognize some of the possible limitations of documents. For example, Scott (1990) makes the distinction between primary, secondary and tertiary documents, and in some contexts this might be useful. Primary documents are materials produced by those experiencing events or settings first hand, secondary documents are constructed as a representation of an event (by others), and tertiary documents include such things as catalogues, references and the grey literature. Another useful classification might be private and public documents – distinguishing aspects of the intended purpose and function of documents, though not necessarily accessibility for social research. And, as noted earlier, we can also think about the ways in which documents exist regardless of a particular research project, or are constructed as part of a research project. Such classifications might tell us very little about the authority and authenticity of documents, nor their accessibility for the social researcher. But they do alert us to the ways in which authority and authenticity are claimed in documentary form. In all cases what is key to the analysis of documents for social research is that documents do not necessarily consist of descriptions of the social world that can be used directly as evidence of that social world. All documentary accounts are just that – a constructed account rather than necessarily an 'accurate' portrayal of complex social reality. Documents construct their own kinds of reality – of people, places, organizations and other social settings. It is therefore important that we approach documents as texts and as representative of the practical accomplishments involved in their production. That is, documents are resources and topics for investigation – and produced according to conventions that are themselves part of a documentary reality. Thus it is important that we ask appropriate questions about documents and what they can and cannot reveal about the social world. Rather than ask whether a document offers a 'true' account, or whether it can be used as 'valid' evidence about a research setting, it is more fruitful to ask questions about the form and function of documents themselves. We should also examine documents for their formal properties. As noted in this chapter, it is important to consider the ways in which documents tell and persuade, and there is analytical affordance in exploring the linguistic registers and rhetorical features of texts as documents of persuasion. In doing so we need to think about documents in relation to their production (authorship) and their consumption (readership), but one should note that in textual terms these are not necessarily just coterminous with the particular individual social actors who write and read. We need to pay close attention to the implied readers, and to the implied claims of, in some cases anonymous, authorship. The analysis of documents requires considerable reflexivity (see May and Perry, Chapter 8, this volume) on the part of the researcher, both in relation to understanding the possibilities and limitations of documents as artefacts and representations of social life, and in the selection (see Rapley, Chapter 4, this volume) of documents for analysis. As we know, documents do not refer transparently to the social world. Their referential value is often in their *intertextuality* – their relation to other documents or texts. Indeed in many settings and in relation to many events we can identify semi-autonomous domains of texts and documents that refer primarily to one another. A dense network of cross-referencing and shared textual formats can create powerful documentary realities. Indeed some of the limitations of working with documents – the often complex and hidden relations between documents, the selectivity of documentary accounts, the prescriptive and often formulaic structure of documents, the functional purposes to which many kinds of documents are put (intentionally and unintentionally) – are also the same characteristics of documents that make them such a rich source of data for sustained and creative analysis.

A limitation of this chapter has been that I have primarily focused, albeit often implicitly, on the analysis of written texts – documents of words. The approaches I have suggested for analysis – thinking about documents as resources (or repositories of information), as structures (with narrative form and convention), with purpose and function, and in relation to other documents – are equally applicable to other kinds of documents or material artefacts. Thus it is important to acknowledge that the analysis of documents can be developed beyond the confines of the written text. Indeed, as was noted at the beginning of this chapter, documents, as physical traces of social settings, can be thought of in much broader terms, offering considerable potential for innovative research practice. Documents can and do incorporate visual materials that construct and present the social world in pictures as well as words. The analysis of visual materials, including photographs (see Banks, Chapter 27, this volume), moving images (see Mikos, Chapter 28, this volume), maps, drawings and other art practices, is a growing field of scholarly activity within qualitative social science, and there are now both established and increasingly innovative methods for visual analysis. Moreover, in the contemporary digital age, there is considerable scope for developing our understandings of social worlds and social life through scholarly analysis of new and emergent forms of documents. Information technology has created new possibilities for communication and representation, allowing us to think about documentary realities in ever expansive ways. For example, the Internet and World Wide Web, electronic communication, SMS text messaging and social networking sites have broadened the scope and genres of documents potentially available for analysis (see Kozinets et al., Chapter 18, and Marotzki et al., Chapter 31, this volume). And it is increasingly the case that such documents can be seen both as multimodal (encompassing for example text, sound (see Maeder, Chapter 29, this volume) and pictures (see Banks, Chapter 27, this volume) and as dynamic or fluid – that is, documents can be thought of, not as static or fixed representations, but as increasingly shifting and changing. Digital technologies create new possibilities too for authorship, readership and connections between documents, and indeed serve to disrupt some of the documentary distinctions – for example, what counts as public or private, primary or secondary, is complicated by virtual social worlds, working with different 'realities' of time and space. In that sense documents and the documentary realities they create are likely to become more rather than less important to the accomplishment and understanding of everyday life and to social research.

FURTHER READING

Fincham, Benjamin, Langer, Suzanne, Scourfield, Jonathan and Shiner, Michael (2011) *Understanding Suicide: A Sociological Autopsy*. Basingstoke: Palgrave Macmillan.
Plummer, Ken (2001) *Documents of Life 2*. London: Sage.
Prior, Lindsay (2011) *Using Documents and Records in Social Research*. London: Sage.

REFERENCES

Atkinson, J. Maxwell (1978) *Discovering Suicide: Studies in the Social Organization of Sudden Death*. London: Macmillan.
Atkinson, Paul and Coffey, Amanda (2010) 'Analysing documentary realities', in David Silverman (ed.), *Qualitative Research: Theory, Method and Practice*. London: Sage. pp. 56–77.
Bloomfield, Brian P. and Vurdabakis, Theo (1994) 'Re-presenting technology: IT consultancy reports as textual reality constructions', *Sociology*, 28(2): 455–78.
Cicourel, Aaron and Kitsuse, John (1963) *The Educational Decision-Makers*. New York: Bobbs-Merrill.
Dingwall, Robert (1977) *The Social Organization of Health Visitor Training*. London: Croom Helm.
Durkheim, Emile (2002 [1897]) *Suicide: A Study in Sociology*. London: Routledge.
Fincham, Benjamin, Langer, Suzanne, Scourfield, Jonathan and Shiner, Michael (2011) *Understanding Suicide: A Sociological Autopsy*. Basingstoke: Palgrave Macmillan.
Garfinkel, Harold (1967) *Studies in Ethnomethodology*. Englewood Cliffs, NJ: Prentice Hall.
Latour, Bruno and Woolgar, Steve (1986) *Laboratory Life*. Princeton, NJ: Princeton University Press.
Macdonald, Keith (2008) 'Using documents', in Nigel Gilbert (ed.), *Researching Social Life*. London: Sage. pp. 194–210.
Maguire, Michael (1994) 'Crime statistics, patterns and trends', in Michael Maguire et al. (eds), *Oxford Handbook of Criminology*. Oxford: Oxford University Press. pp. 322–75.

May, Tim (2001) *Social Research: Issues, Methods and Process*. Buckingham: Open University Press.
Plummer, Ken (2001) *Documents of Life 2*. London: Sage.
Prior, Lindsay (1985) 'Making sense of mortality', *Sociology of Health and Illness*, 7(2): 167–90.
Prior, Lindsay (2003) *Using Documents in Social Research*. London; Sage.
Prior, Lindsay (2008) 'Documents and action', in Pertti Alastuutari et al. (eds), *The SAGE Handbook of Social Research Methods*. London: Sage. pp. 479–92.
Prior, Lindsay (ed.) (2011) *Using Documents and Records in Social Research*. London: Sage.
Prior, Lindsay and Bloor, Mick (1993) 'Why people die: social representations of death and its causes', *Science as Culture*, 3 (3): 346–74.
Rees, Colin (1981) 'Records and hospital routine', in Paul Atkinson and Christian Heath (eds), *Medical Work: Realities and Routines*. Farnborough: Gower. pp. 55–70.
Roberts, Gareth (2003) *Review of Research Assessment*. Bristol: Higher Education Funding Council for England.
Scott, John (1990) *A Matter of Record*. Cambridge: Polity Press.
Scourfield, Jonathan, Fincham, Ben, Langer, Suzanne and Shiner, Michael (2012) 'Sociological autopsy: An integrated approach to the study of suicide in men', *Social Science & Medicine*, 74: 466–73.
Seidel, John and Kelle, Udo (1995) 'Different functions of coding in the analysis of textual data', in Udo Kelle (ed.), *Computer-aided Qualitative Data Analysis: Theory, Method and Practice*. London: Sage. pp. 52–62.
Silverman, David (2006) *Interpreting Qualitative Data*, 3rd edition. London: Sage.
Strauss, Anselm L. (1987) *Qualitative Analysis for Social Scientists,* Cambridge: Cambridge University Press.
Strauss, Anselm and Corbin, Juliet (1990) *Basics of Qualitative Research: Grounded Theory Procedures and Techniques*, 2nd edition. Thousand Oaks, CA: Sage.
Sudnow, David (1968) *Passing On*. Englewood Cliffs, NJ: Prentice Hall.
Webb, Eugene, Campbell, Donald, Schwartz, Richard and Sechrest, Lee (2000) *Unobtrusive Measures: Nonreactive research in the Social Sciences*, revised edition (1st edition, 1966). Thousand Oaks, CA: Sage.
Woods, Peter (1979) *The Divided School*. London: Routledge & Kegan Paul.

26

Analysing News Media

Darrin Hodgetts and Kerry Chamberlain

Daily life is often punctuated with mediated experiences: communications via telephone, email or chat rooms, and engagements with television, radio, magazines, newspapers, websites, libraries, digital games, billboards, packaging and advertising (Deuze, 2011; Silverstone, 2007). People use media for such things as communicating with others, maintaining social networks, accessing information, staying informed, sustaining a sense of self and place, and sourcing entertainment. Combined, media technologies create a nexus, from within which people can engage with events in society, and navigate the pleasures and dilemmas of everyday life (Chamberlain and Hodgetts, 2008; Ostertag, 2010). Media can foster a sense of certainty and belonging, and provide opportunities to reformulate social relations. It is 'through these various media that our relations with others, both neighbours and strangers, are facilitated or, indeed, denied. Relations are created and sustained. Prejudices likewise' (Silverstone and Georgiou, 2005: 434).

Rather than simply 'impacting' on people in everyday life, media devices and content are absorbed into social life and become part of the dynamics of daily practice (Chamberlain and Hodgetts, 2008; Deuze, 2011). Many of the activities people engaged in before the introduction of various contemporary media technologies, such as catching up with friends, continue via Skype, social networking sites, email and mobile phones (Silverstone, 2007; see Marotzki et al., Chapter 31, this volume). Scholars have gone as far as to propose that media are central to the organization of society today (Curran and Seaton, 2003), and that 'media cannot be conceived of as separate from us, to the extent that we live *in* media, rather than *with* media' (Deuze, 2011: 143).

Because media are central to daily life, social scientists have often explored the role of media in sustaining or undermining intergroup relations, political structures and social policies (Hodgetts et al., 2010). As exemplified by analyses focusing on social inequalities, media can encourage understanding and support as well as ignorance, discrimination and domination (Silverstone and Georgiou, 2005; Wasburn and Wasburn, 2011). This is particularly apparent in news media analysis. Documenting whose perspectives are privileged and whose views are restrained in news reports reveals much about wider power relations in a society (Couldry and Curran, 2002). Such symbolic power – the power to name and define a group or issue – is often linked to economic and social privilege, and enables dominant group assumptions to impact on the lives of minority groups. However, in examining symbolic power, we should be careful not to regard media power as being overly deterministic by asserting media to be an overdetermining influence on our understandings of social life and practices (Chamberlain and Hodgetts, 2008). After all, media can be equally used to increase participation in civic life and to support efforts for social inclusion. Stigmatizing and discriminatory media practices can be resisted, refused and challenged through, for instance, media advocacy (Carroll and Hackett, 2006; Hodgetts et al., 2008). Such activism requires an analysis of media to ensure effectiveness (Carroll and Hackett, 2006).

Media are situated within a range of societal practices. Therefore, to understand the influence and functions of media, analyses need to link specific texts (e.g. news items) to the socio-political contexts and practices within which these are produced and embedded. This chapter focuses on issues of symbolic power and the complex social influences embedded within media in society today and suggests how qualitative media analyses can be conducted with that in view. Often, when tackling such issues, scholars report on trends in coverage from the position of a detached observer. In this chapter, we take a critical social science approach to media analysis, focusing on the broader societal processes within which both media and researchers are enmeshed. As Flyvbjerg notes, social science is 'a practical, intellectual activity aimed at clarifying the problems, risks, and possibilities we face as humans and societies, and at contributing a social and political praxis' (2001: 4). Our intent is not to review the range of approaches – semiotic, psychoanalytic or even neo-formalist – to analysing media texts (Berger, 2011). Rather, we explore media texts in the contexts of production and reception, and with a view to changing processes of mediated exclusion and symbolic power.

This chapter presents a practical guide to media analysis, exemplified through a focus on print news media and the topic of homelessness, but outlining principles of qualitative media analysis which are applicable to all media forms. The first section charts our shift in focus, out from media content analysis as a dominant approach to news analysis towards the role of media in society and intergroup relations. The second section offers a broader conceptual outline for understanding and analysing the role of news media depictions, focusing on marginalized groups. The third section provides a worked example of our analysis process, which includes efforts to bring the broader perspective into action. The chapter is completed with some concluding comments.

TEXTUAL CAPTURE AND THE LIMITS OF CONTENT ANALYSIS

It has been established for some time that news does not simply 'select' and 'report' on topics from the outside world. News 'constructs' events and relationships between groups of people. In doing so, news reports call 'attention to some aspects of reality while obscuring other elements' (Entman, 1993: 55). Research into news representations is crucial for revealing aspects of media power, particularly in terms of how stories frame social issues and societal groups (cf. Berger, 2011; Dreher, 2010). News analysis can answer questions about how controversies surrounding issues of public concern are played out, who are identified as key stakeholders, and how their positions within the controversy are constructed. News analysis can also establish what issues and stakeholders are ignored, and provide information about alternative representations that can be developed.

Content analysis (see Schreier, Chapter 12, this volume) is a prominent methodology used extensively to study news representations. The focus is typically on identifying and, in its quantitative guise, enumerating key features of a body of news items, such as sources, positive or negative orientation, settings and ideologies (Krippendorff and Bock, 2008). Researchers often take samples from particular periods of time, and this approach is more suited to ongoing issues such as homelessness, which evolve over months or years (Hodgetts et al., 2005; Schneider et al., 2010). Analysis involves the development and use of specific coding frames to categorize key features of news reports. Analytic steps include: (1) formulating a testable research question; (2) establishing what items will be analysed; (3) defining mutually exclusive variables central to the analysis; (4) piloting and refining the coding frame; (5) coding the data; and (6) interpreting the findings and writing the report. Quantitative content analysis is promoted as a systematic and replicable strategy for compressing the mass of media data, and for analysing news items to give an overall account of trends in coverage and particular features that warrant further in-depth analysis.

Quantitative content analysis can be used to conduct more in-depth analysis. For example, it could be used to unravel how news images reproduce social relations central to the lives of homeless people (Schneider et al., 2010). The predominant way in which homeless people are characterized in news items contributes to public understandings of homelessness, and affects the way homeless people are treated (Greenberg et al., 2006; Hodgetts et al., 2006). With such issues in mind, we have interrogated news characterizations of homeless people (Hodgetts et al., 2005; Schneider et al., 2010) and have shown that UK television and Canadian print news provide symbolic spaces for homeless and housed people to meet. News items often reproduce the social distance distinction between 'us' (domiciled majority) and 'them' (homeless minority). The latter are often positioned as 'strangers' living unhealthy lifestyles when compared with 'us', the housed audience members (Hodgetts et al., 2011). Despite being ever present in news landscapes, homeless people are rarely given opportunities to frame their own experiences, relationships or public images (Hodgetts et al., 2005). The symbolic space created by news items is textured from a domiciled perspective and this, in turn, textures the physical environment in which homeless people dwell. These processes reveal how news can simultaneously contribute to a social climate that advances punitive measures to displace vagrants, and one that ensures tolerance and social inclusion of homeless people (Hodgetts et al., 2011). Such analyses are crucial in that, as Silverstone writes, 'We need to know about each other in a way that can only involve a constant critical engagement with our media's representation of the other' (2007: 334).

There are, however, significant limitations inherent in quantitative content analyses of news texts. First, such analyses are frequently conducted and used as if the meaning of news items is located primarily in the items themselves, and transmitted uncritically to audiences. But such content analysis cannot tell us definitively what audiences make of news items or what meanings they take way from such texts (Hall, 1997). Audience research demonstrates that the meaning of media content does not simply reside in the text being consumed, and is often constructed differently by different viewers (Hodgetts et al., 2006). News items therefore do not hold, contain or convey a single set of meanings. These cultural objects (see Winter, Chapter 17, this volume) are subject to reinterpretation by people 'reading' and using them in their daily lives. Another limitation is that, while news content analyses enable us to document trends in news representations offered to audiences and issues of symbolic power, scholars often fail to consider solutions to the problems they identify and fail to offer alternative and more equitable depictions (Dreher, 2010).

These limitations do not render content analyses superfluous. Rather, they invoke the need for researchers to document and justify their interpretations, and to outline how they arrived at an interpretation and why it is useful. The limitations also alert us to the complexities of mass communication, and the need to consider broader production and reception processes within which news items are produced and used (see next section). Scholars are also reaching out beyond the limitations in text-focused news analysis methods by engaging with news production processes and the responses of groups being depicted in the news. Such researchers are working to shape and encourage the uptake of alternative and more positive representations that reflect the experiences of symbolically and materially marginalized groups, such as homeless people (Carroll and Hackett, 2006; Hodgetts et al., 2008). From this line of reasoning, media activism is positioned as being central to media analysis in invoking strategies for challenging discriminatory news portrayals and symbolic power (Curran and Couldry, 2002; Dreher, 2010). This chapter illustrates such media analysis and advocacy strategies through an example from our research with homeless people.

Our analytical example invokes a broader social science agenda (Flyvbjerg, 2001). If we are to ensure the inclusion of homeless people as citizens, we must develop ways to manage social distancing processes occurring, in part, through news reporting (Hodgetts et al., 2011). Collaborations between journalists and social scientists, which are informed by the experiences of homeless people, can provide a starting point for addressing these issues of distance and estrangement, and in promoting more inclusive news media practices (Hodgetts et al., 2008). Some readers may be pessimistic about the potential for more equitable and less disempowering representations of homeless people in the news. Such pessimism is often associated with the perception of news production as a closed system. This assumption can:

> blind analysts to the complexities of journalism's communicative architecture as well as its democratizing possibilities. Simply put, there is more going on in the communication of news than the manipulation of news agendas by powerful strategic interests or the circulation of powerful semiotic codes and agendas. (Cottle and Rai, 2006: 164)

Efforts to ensure that prejudices do not dominate news depictions of homeless people require a reconceptualization of news production. Briefly, negative news characterizations of homeless people do exist, but they are not fixed or absolute. This means there is potential for negative depictions to be contested in a manner that opens up the potential for the inclusion of diversity in perspectives and voices (Carroll and Hackett, 2006).

MEDIA ANALYSIS FOCUSED ON THE CIRCUIT OF MASS COMMUNICATION

It is important that researchers conceptualize news outlets as socio-politically embedded institutions and as active participants in social processes, rather than as detached observers and reporters of events (Meijer, 2010). This requires us to move beyond the treatment of media products as just another 'text' to be analysed. We need to keep in mind the broader societal processes and relationships shaping both the production of news items and how these items are circulated within and understood by different groups in society. Our orientation to analysis can be described as *text-in-context*. News items are already situated in social relations and cultural practices that lie beyond the text. These items can be explored as metonymic cultural artefacts of broader societal processes that involve powerful groups pushing particular meanings, and the people being depicted as those who often resist these meanings (Hodgetts et al., 2006; 2008). It is these broader processes that are reflected in, but lie beyond, the frame of news texts that are the target of media analysis.

We therefore recommend a focus on the 'circuit of mass communication' (Miller et al., 1998). This implicates news media in circulating and reframing understandings of social issues such as homelessness and how it is 'managed'. To understand how homelessness is communicated ideally requires an engagement with the social construction of homelessness at all three levels of mass communication: production, representation and reception. First, organizational and professional practices shape what issues get covered, the 'angle' taken in covering these issues, the sources drawn upon, and whether coverage enhances or detracts from public deliberations. Further, various stakeholder groups, including government representatives, media advocacy groups and researchers, often influence the scope and shape of coverage. Second, an analysis of the resulting news items provides a means for revealing which perspectives are promoted and which are neglected in the news. However, the social processes through which public understandings of homelessness are negotiated by audiences cannot be gauged by analyses solely at the production and textual levels. So, third, researchers need to explore how people experiencing homelessness come to understand their situations, in part, through their engagements with media representations of homelessness. Scholars can do this by engaging with this particular audience.

The process of mass communication outlined above is not necessarily linear or sequential. The levels of the circuit overlap in dynamic ways. We need to embed the concept of the circuit of mass communication in the context of the role of contemporary media in everyday life. For example, traditional audiences or receivers of news messages are now recognized as 'prosumers' who not only consume, but also produce and circulate media content (Napoli, 2010). This orientation involves a shift in focus from news texts to what people do with these in everyday life (Couldry, 2004). 'Prosumer' practices also highlight the need for researchers to consider the overlaps across news and other media forms. Moe (2010) invokes the older notion of the 'pamphleteer' to draw comparisons between the emergence of print and digital technologies in the production of news content. Moe sees a return, through the use of digital technologies such as blogs, to an idealized image of the pamphleteer or contemporary 'citizen journalist' (Meijer, 2010) who produces, reconsiders, repackages and redistributes news content. Such practices do not render the traditional concept of mass communication redundant. Rather, they render our engagements with it more complex (Moe, 2010; Napoli, 2010), and require us to approach the levels of production, text and audience as parts of an integrated and dynamic circuit in society.

The *text-in-context* approach to news analysis that we advocate, focused on the circuit of mass communication, explores how stories emerge across production processes, play out in specific news items, and are negotiated by audience members (Barnett et al., 2007). Key questions for such analyses include:

- How do journalists gather information for their reports?
- How are the efforts of media advocates, such as community service providers and researchers, interpreted by journalists and responded to in the production of news?
- What depictions of the issue are circulated to the public?
- What depictions are missing?
- What do 'ordinary' people and those experiencing the issue think of the resulting reports?
- What actions to address the issue are encouraged and warranted by coverage?

In answering such questions, materials from all three levels of the circuit of mass communication (i.e. production, representation and reception) can be explored as specific sites within which the issue is rendered meaningful and contested.

AN ANALYTIC EXAMPLE

Despite the regular appearance of articles using qualitative media analyses, there are few guides on how to produce such analyses. Most authors discuss theoretical assumptions about the role of media in society (as we have done above) and the nature of the texts under examination (e.g., Berger, 2011). In outlining our analytic strategy, we emphasize that analysis involves organizing, describing and interpreting both what is there and what lies beyond media content, to situate it within dynamic societal processes. Flyvbjerg makes a relevant point here: 'The rules of a ritual are not a ritual, a grammar is not a language, the rules of chess are not chess, and traditions are not actual social behaviour' (2001: 43). In the same way, the theory and procedures for analysing media are not media analysis. There is no one right way to analyse media. There are, however, strategies in the analytic sense-making process. We offer a series of steps, as a guide to core elements that make up a qualitative media analysis. Outlining these steps enables us to articulate the dynamic and creative nature of analysis, as a craft skill. You may skip, reorder or spend less time on some steps we outline, or even develop steps of your own. The point is to develop a way of rigorously examining and interpreting mediated processes. The steps we propose are also reasonably common in qualitative analysis. We have added a focus on the circuit of mass communication and action processes, and we emphasize the value of writing as an interpretative practice. In producing this analytic guide, we are also very aware that the roles of journalists and social scientists overlap in many ways, given that people from both professions often work to understand and report on social events from within society (Hodgetts, 2012).

We discuss these analytic steps below, exemplifying each with our process of producing an analysis of a mediated controversy. This controversy was over attempts to have homeless people banned from a public library (Hodgetts et al., 2008). We emphasize how the three interrelated levels of the circuit of mass communication can be shaped through various forms of action, including collaborations with journalists to broaden their understandings of homelessness (Hodgetts, 2012), and working with stakeholders to examine the role of media in public constructions of homelessness. Publication of results can also have unanticipated implications for policy development and civic processes in other locales. In our case, our New-Zealand-based article (Hodgetts et al., 2008) that provides the basis for our worked example was used in the United States in a legal challenge to oppose attempts to exclude homeless library patrons in Minnesota.

The particular idea for the journal article about the library emerged when we were engaged in a large multifaceted project on homelessness with a focus on processes of inclusion and exclusion of homeless people in public places (Hodgetts et al., 2010; 2011). During this research a local newspaper in one of the cities where we were working published an item in which a city councillor raised concerns about the appropriateness of homeless men being present in a city library ('Guards sought to police library', *Waikato Times*, 19 May 2007). The item promoted the exclusion of homeless men by emphasizing the deviancy of these men and the danger they allegedly posed for housed citizens. We responded by brokering a dialogue between a local journalist, a group of homeless men, leading social agency staff, and other stakeholders. Through the ensuing conversation an alternative portrayal of homeless men was created that presented the library as a central place for them to take time out to read, to reflect on their situation, and to engage in positive interactions with housed people. Emphasis was placed on the importance of relationships enacted within the library, where positive interactions between homeless men, library staff and other patrons supported a sense of belonging, respite and refuge among the homeless men. This alternative account bridged the 'us' and 'them' framing, typical of homelessness in news coverage (Schneider et al., 2010). This dialogue resulted in a two-page feature article ('Shelf life: Shelter for the day', *Waikato Times*, 2 June 2007) which foregrounded the positive functions of libraries in homeless men's lives, and challenged previous accounts advocating the exclusion of 'the homeless' from this public space. The feature article included comments by domiciled library patrons who were more compassionate towards the homeless men, and it also raised the importance of the everyday interactions with library staff and patrons for engaging homeless men in civic life. Calls to exclude these men from the library were subsequently dropped.

We obtained data from multiple sources: direct observations (see Marvasti, Chapter 24, this volume); field notes of interactions with journalists, librarians, homeless people, and members of the domiciled public; photo-elicitations (see Banks, Chapter 27, this volume) with homeless men; interviews (see Roulston, Chapter 20, this volume) with multiple stakeholders; and news items. We next outline the analytic steps taken in this project to present and exemplify our media analysis process.

Step 1: Identify the Topic and Scope of Data Required

Research topics can arise from a range of sources, including observations of media content and practices, previous research, theoretical arguments and discussions with colleagues, or any combination of these. Controversies played out in the news media can be a particularly informative site for topic development. Once a topic has been established, the research aims and questions can be identified, although these remain open to clarification and refinement as the research progresses. Next is consideration of what materials are needed to address the research aims, and how these are to be accessed and compiled. To address issues regarding the role of media in everyday life we need to move beyond texts to engage audiences and beyond audiences, keeping the components of the circuit of mass communication in view. Materials may be drawn from a wide variety of sources, including your own efforts to record and collate media items, clipping services, and archives. Other qualitative data collection methods, including observations (see Marvasti, Chapter 24, this volume), interviews (see Roulston, Chapter 20, this volume), focus groups (see Barbour, Chapter 21, this volume), media diaries, mapping and photo-elicitation techniques (see Banks, Chapter 27, this volume) may also be used. Note that the scope of material to be included for analysis may extend as you uncover new information and reconsider directions. From the beginning of the research it is important to keep a research log, recording research activities, reflections on research processes, analytic ideas and insights, and emerging themes and storylines. This log should be considered as part of your data set.

The topic of our media analysis arose when, without prompting, two homeless participants in the larger research project alerted us to the existence of a newspaper controversy around their presence in the local public library. This controversy was manifest in two contrasting news items, the newspaper article mentioned above and a sardonic column written in response to the article ('Taking a stab at library loitering', *Waikato Times*, 19 May 2007). These items both appeared in the same issue of the local newspaper, and both had been pinned up on a noticeboard in the men's night shelter, a site for our research. Our interest in this topic was piqued for two reasons: first, by the strong interest of our homeless participants in the controversy and their request for some action on this front; and, second, by our knowledge of the capacity for news media to reflect on their own processes, evident in the interplay between the two items (Cottle and Rai, 2006). From our initial review of the newspaper items we realized that opinion was divided between those supporting the call to have homeless men removed from the library and those opposed to this proposition.

We recognized that this divergence of opinion provided an opportunity for action, and this led us to develop our aim – to explore the controversy and to work with stakeholders (journalists, homeless men, librarians and domiciled library patrons) to produce alternative, more positive, portrayals of homeless men in the media.

A crucial question at this point was what material we needed to understand the controversy, and to promote alternative media portrayals. The local newspaper provided a primary focus for data sourcing and a key target for intervention. Given the tendency of journalists to talk *about* rather than *to* homeless people, it was necessary to establish the legitimacy of the claims made in the newspaper. This led us to interview librarians, homeless men and domiciled library patrons. Despite the fear-mongering promoted in the article, concerns about the presence of homeless men were not widely shared. Several informed us that the man depicted in the photograph in the news item was actually not homeless. We spent time in the library making direct observations to learn more about the function of this public space. We also gathered literature on the civic function of libraries and media advocacy. In addition, we returned to the data gathered in the larger project, because it contained images and accounts of the function of the library in the everyday lives of our homeless participants. We included all these materials in the media analysis data set.

Our discussions with the librarians also alerted us to the fact that the national professional association for librarians had picked up on the controversy and had polled their members in an Internet poll. This situation reflects how different media forms are interlinked in a media nexus in which deliberations on social issues occur (Deuze, 2011; Silverstone, 2007).

We also engaged with the journalist who produced the initial negative news item, and drew on insights from our engagements with key stakeholders and literature on homeless depictions, news production and media advocacy. Our interaction with the journalist resulted in the production of two further news items containing more positive depictions of homeless men and their library use. These, in turn, became part of our overall data for analysis. This reflects how, as social scientists, we are all inevitably part of the world we study, and can become more engaged with the issues we analyse.

Step 2: Gridding and Plotting as Strategies for De-familiarizing Mediated Accounts

People consume media all the time and often take its communicative architecture for granted. This means we can read texts as a whole and miss the subtleties of form and content. Qualitative researchers need strategies for breaking texts open and getting inside specific empirical objects and to gain an overview of the data set. We used simple grids to establish the range of items, orientate us to what the news items were promoting, key sources, relationships being promoted, library uses, and types of characterizations of homeless people (see, for example, Table 26.1). The use of such grids is not an attempt to quantify the data. Gridding is an analytic strategy for breaking down the data, de-familiarizing items and exploring emerging patterns. It can enable you to reorientate yourself to what is and is not in each item and to raise questions for further analysis across items. Grids provide an initial strategy for producing timelines for the publication of news items, mind mappings of reader responses, the introduction of opposing views and sources. Grids also provide a basis for establishing an initial understanding of the evolving story, in that news stories are rarely contained within a single item, and develop over time across multiple items (Barnett et al., 2007).

The example grid in Table 26.1 highlights key differences between the initial article relying on the views of the city councillor and the feature article that draws on a broader range of sources. This distinction

Table 26.1 Example of a media analysis grid

Item type and title	Date	Sources speaking or not	Library civic or restricted space	Homeless/housed relations	Homeless men Pos./Neg.	Primary focus
General news	May 19 2007	Homeless no rights to speak	Library as restricted space only for 'productive' citizens	Distant and contested with emphasis on displacement of homeless	Negative, though some points of scepticism from council staff	Public concerns about the presence of homeless men
Weekend feature	June 2 2007	Homeless right to speak	Library as lively civic space for all	Close and personal, emphasizing tolerance and inclusion	Positive across a range of sources and converging perspectives	Homeless men's appropriate uses of the library

Note: This grid is for illustrative purposes and the rows and columns can be extended to allow for other patterns. It is also narrative rather than numerical in focus.

was communicated in different photographs across the news items. In the first article, a person roughly dressed and mistakenly identified as being homeless is depicted misusing the library as a place to sleep. In the feature article homeless men are depicted around the library looking through shelves and reading. These men actually speak in the feature article and are presented with agency and as people who use the library for its intended purposes. We began to note links between such images and the broader context of relations between homeless and housed life worlds (see step 5).

Information on the production of the texts, audience responses and the broader societal processes at play provides further material that can be used to bring into question what is present in news items, what is not there, and why this may be so. Grids can be used for production data like interviews with journalists and press releases, as well as audience data like participant photographs and discussions (see Table 26.2). A collection of such grids focused on different data forms provides a basis for highlighting and exploring issues of symbolic power and in particular who speaks, depictions of relations between homeless and housed people, and the construction of the library as civic or exclusionary space.

Table 26.2 Example of a homeless participant grid

Participant	Library uses	Examples inclusion/ exclusion	Reflections on first article	People interacted with	Photo of library	Media and uses
Phil	Reading, time out, watching documentaries as part of self-education	Reactions to his presence in public spaces and his being forced to move on Librarians as primary supports	Discriminatory and unjust	Librarians, other homeless men and housed patrons	Two showing the building from outside but no people	Range of library based media including newspaper, books, internet, documentaries
Luke	Maintaining links to lifelong interests such as writing poetry and reading	Librarians as primary supports	Silly politicking	Librarians and housed patrons	Two, one showing building from outside and one depicting librarian friend who posed for the shot	Books, radio, magazines, newspapers and Internet

Particularly pertinent at this point of the analysis is the creation of a plot synopsis that follows the trajectory of the news story. Such synopses are important for communicating the trajectory of news coverage and the juxtaposing and weaving together of various sources of information into the overall story. The synopsis is initially descriptive in terms of key developments, introduction of news sources and changes in focus. Once the media synopsis is complete it can be used in its own right or, as was the case for us, other data such as interviews and participant photographs can also be summarized and included. Initially, the synopsis for our analysis was 11 pages long and had to be edited down at the completion of our analysis for inclusion in the article (see step 4).

The key point of this step is to use grids, plot synopses and other strategies to gain an overview of the data set and to establish initial insights into what is going on within and across particular items and to establish points of contrast across the data set. This can be a playful and creative process, and grids and other devices need to be developed to reflect your research aims. You can lay them out in a table as a kind of shorthand index to the data that orientates you to particular features of analytic interest. Emerging patterns and ideas should be noted in your research log as they will become useful during latter steps in the analysis progresses.

Step 3: Identifying Key Themes, Coding, Selecting and Checking for Discrepancies

This step involves coding through inductive and deductive processes across all sources that have been included. Deductive themes can be generated from the research aims and existing literature, while inductive themes can be generated from the data and the gridding process. These issues then need to be refined and selected: codes may be better combined into larger themes or broken into sub-themes and categories. As a pre-emptive move to step 4, there will be a process of selecting the themes felt to be most central for addressing the research aims. In some cases one might change the research aims at this point to better reflect the scope of the data. You need to be open to this possibility. Another consideration during coding is what examples will be used at each of the three levels of the circuit of mass communication and how these will be ordered and related. This step also involves checking for discrepancies within the data (e.g. across news items), and between different levels.

During this step we took all the materials relating to a particular theme and placed these together and then considered if the theme was coherent in its own right and distinct from other themes. You may integrate some themes at this point or split others into sub-themes. We explored relationships between themes and across cases more specifically at this point and began integrating these. Comparing the news items' construction with the accounts of librarians, members of the public and homeless men according to specific themes enabled us to establish points of contrast and to deconstruct the news items as contrasting representations of homeless men and their use of the library (see step 4). Here we established the functions of the library in the lives of homeless men, drawing on their accounts and those of the librarians to capture what was missing from the first news item. For example, we found that the theme of the library as an inclusive space articulated by homeless men and librarians was also in accord with the views of the housed patrons interviewed. In contrast to the image promoted by the city councillor in the first newspaper item, the housed library patrons did not perceive homeless men as nuisances, as threats, or as disruptive.

We identified a range of themes from the characterization of homeless men across the news items, the librarian association website and stakeholder accounts and photographs. Key related themes included the mediation of homeless and housed relations, estrangement, media use, the library as a contested civic space, and the classic form of social media. We then began to consider links between these themes. For example, item 1 positioned homeless men as strangers, whereas the other items questioned this portrayal and positioned them as members of the public. We also identified public safety versus the rights of homeless men as a key dualism, along with the library as a civic space within which the politics of inclusion and exclusion were played out. Subsequently, we coded for the interrelated nature of media, including news items, the library, books and documentaries, which informed our understanding of the functions of media in homeless men's everyday lives. This was important because different media combine to make up a nexus in everyday life. When analysing news, other media come into play. We then coded for how media are clustered in the lives of homeless men and were evident in the photographs (see Banks, Chapter 27, this volume) taken (in the photo-elicitation exercise within the larger project) and accounts these men provide (see Thornberg and Charmaz, Chapter 11, this volume, for further discussion of coding procedures).

Step 4: Ordering Themes, Linking and Constructing a New Analytic Story

This is the step where we attempt to combine and order the elements of the analysis into a logical progression of ideas, which tells an analytic story that responds to the research aims. This researcher story differs from that provided by the plot synopsis developed in step 2. The plot synopsis focused on describing the structure and progression of the news story and related events. The analytic story may not necessarily follow the chronology of the news controversy, and will be more aligned with the logic of combining key themes identified by the researchers as central to the analysis. A shorter version of the synopsis that includes the news trajectory and other action-orientated activities we engaged in around it is provided in our overview of the library case in the paragraph just prior to step 1. Such paragraphs provide a useful introduction to the analysis and provide a context for themes identified for further analysis and placed into the new context of your interpretation (see step 5). In sum, this step involves establishing a logic for sequencing key themes according to an overall narrative of the analysis. Here, we are not just describing what is in the data, but rather communicating what the data mean and show about the social processes within which media are embedded.

We drew from across the whole data set to illustrate links between the imagined library in the first news item and the library experienced by staff and homeless and housed patrons. We clustered our notes from the research log according to emergent themes and our research questions. During this step it is important to think about the sequencing of themes and how these contribute to a larger interpretation and argument about the topic of interest. Several possible structures and clusters of themes were noted in the research log and we played with different combinations as we attempted to write the analysis (see step 5). The analysis was eventually structured into four sections, each containing several interrelated themes. Section 1 explored a newspaper-based call to exclude homeless men from the library, and considered the associated texturing of library spaces and the politics of inclusion associated with media deliberations. Section 2 went beyond the news report to focus on the general views of homeless men, librarians and housed library patrons regarding the presence of homeless people in the public library. We considered social practices surrounding library use, within the context of other spaces frequented by homeless people. Section 3 paid particular attention to homeless men's efforts at cultivating a sense of belonging, support and self through their library use that could transcend their present circumstances and enable an imagining of possible housed futures. Section 4 documented our efforts to challenge news narratives that seek to exclude homeless people from the library and to promote more inclusive stories based on the lived experiences of people involved in the local setting.

Step 5: Overall Interpretation and Writing

Elements of this step are embedded throughout the analytic process, reflecting the dynamic nature of analysis and the somewhat artificial separation of the previous steps. Interpretation (see Willig, Chapter 10, this volume) occurs with each step. The core idea here is about weaving theory into the account and producing a coherent argument about what is going on. Here we work more to link with the literature and to produce an overall interpretation of the phenomenon under study. The focus is on how themes work in concert and contribute to broader understandings of the societal processes under investigation and the role of media in these processes. Without doing this step we would produce an analysis that describes rather than interprets the data. This is the stage at which we go further to integrate insights from the literature throughout the manuscript and to make clear what is being contributed to current knowledge. Writing (see Denzin, Chapter 39, this volume) and publishing are also a form of action in that they can inform the actions of other civic-orientated scholars, as noted earlier with the use of our article in Minnesota.

Central to this stage is what the various media sources and our research participants are trying to convey and how this relates to existing knowledge and theory. Theory and concepts relating to symbolic power, the mediapolis, civic journalism, and public characterizations of homeless were drawn upon and woven into the emerging narrative that we wanted to tell. We noted links in the research log between the literature and key themes in the analysis. We also strived to move out beyond the rich description produced from previous steps and to annotate links to specific academic sources. A goal here is to develop key themes, arrange and interpret these, and link them back to the existing empirical and theoretical work as well as considering the conditions of life for people in such circumstance. This step invokes a process of drafting, redrafting and going back to previous steps to fill gaps and refine arguments.

A particular conceptual issue became central to the overall interpretation and structure of this article. This was the overlap between the representational space created by news media and the material space of the library as welcoming for homeless men, but with their inclusion being under threat as the overarching frame for our analysis. We drew on the various sources identified in step 1 and refined through the other analytic steps to articulate the potential for news media to represent homeless men in ways that emphasize citizenship and social inclusion. This analysis revealed the potential for news media to function as a symbolic site for negotiating the use of public spaces by homeless people. This linked to a key issue in previous research around 'us' and 'them' distinctions in news coverage, and the texturing and policing of public spaces that can be challenged through media advocacy. We wanted to show that media analysis and action can be used to reduce the social distance between groups by shifting media characterizations from depicting homeless men as strangers to showing homeless men as community members.

CONCLUSION

Media analyses are important because the public often expect local media to provide a space for public deliberation, and to foster a general sense of connection and cohesion, as well as ensuring voice or inclusion from marginalized groups (Meijer, 2010). Such analyses can identify who exercises symbolic power in relation to the construction of disadvantaged people, how this power is accessed and negotiated in media framings, and how we can challenge and change such framings. Analysis enables us to understand potential implications of media framing for mediated and face-to-face interactions in society (Hodgetts et al., 2008). Effective media analysis relies on a sound understanding of news production processes, the intricacies of news items and audience practices (Barnett et al., 2007). It also requires us to be familiar with the societal context in which news reports are enmeshed. This involves seeing media as being embedded in the social practices that make up daily life, rather than as external influences that come from outside daily life to do things to people (Hodgetts et al., 2010).

When they arise, controversies involving the media can be used as case studies to explore the role of the media in society. Social scientists can respond to these events with a view to addressing issues such as social exclusion in which news media are often implicated. Incorporating responsive media advocacy work reflects an approach to research where the emphasis is on adapting to events as they arise – and adjusting to the messiness of social life during the research process. For us, research and action are part of a dynamic whole. Media analysis informs and provides the focus for an action-oriented social science that matters (Flyvbjerg, 2001) in a media-saturated society.

The incident explored in this chapter demonstrates that even when a welcoming and inclusive library environment is achieved, it is fragile and subject to disruption due to the tradition of distancing homeless people from the domiciled majority in news reports and public spaces (Hodgetts et al., 2011). Nonetheless, challenges to homeless people's patronage of public spaces in news coverage should not be seen solely as a negative process. Such controversies can profile the plight of homeless people and open a space for critiquing exclusionary practices and building coalitions to support the inclusion of homeless citizens. Despite the often narrow and reactionary focus of news, there are opportunities to extend and add depth to news-based public discussions on homelessness. This involves framing and supplying information that meets journalists' needs and work constraints while staying faithful to the hopes and aspirations of the marginalized and minority groups. Such actions work with the capacity of news media to pause and reflect on the ways in which events have been covered or people have been characterized (Hodgetts et al., 2007). Journalists can be receptive to suggestions from scholars for expanding coverage of controversial issues if they are approached as colleagues engaged in similar pursuits to social scientists.

FURTHER READING

Chamberlain, Kerry and Hodgetts, Darrin (2008) 'Social psychology and media: Critical considerations', *Social and Personality Psychology Compass*, 2, 1–17.

Hodgetts, Darrin, Stolte, Ottilie, Chamberlain, Kerry, Radley, Alan, Nikora, Linda, Nabalarua, Eci and Groot, Shiloh (2008) 'A trip to the library: Homelessness and social inclusion', *Social and Cultural Geography*, 9: 933–53.

Silverstone, Roger (2007) *Media and Morality: On the Rise of the Mediapolis*. Cambridge: Polity Press.

REFERENCES

Barnett, Alison, Hodgetts, Darrin, Nikora, Linda, Chamberlain, Kerry and Karapu, Rolinda (2007) 'Child poverty, news media framing and the symbolic disempowerment of families in need', *Journal of Community and Applied Social Psychology*, 17 (4): 296–312.

Berger, Arthur A. (2011) *Media Analysis Techniques*, 4th edition. London: Sage.

Carroll, William and Hackett, Robert (2006) 'Democratic media activism through the lens of social movement theory', *Media, Culture and Society*, 28 (1): 83–104.

Chamberlain, Kerry and Hodgetts, Darrin (2008) 'Social psychology and media: Critical considerations', *Social and Personality Psychology Compass*, 2 (3): 1–17.

Cottle, Simon and Rai, Mugdha (2006) 'Between display and deliberation: Analyzing TV news as communicative architecture', *Media, Culture and Society*, 28 (2): 163–89.

Couldry, Nick (2004) 'Theorising media as practice', *Social Semiotics*, 14 (2): 115–32.

Couldry, Nick and Curran, James (2002) *Contesting Media Power: Alternative Media in a Networked World*. Lanham, MD: Rowman and Littlefield.

Curran, James and Seaton, Jean (2003) *Power Without Responsibility*. London: Routledge.

Deuze, Mark (2011) 'Media life', *Media Culture and Society*, 33 (1): 137–48.

Dreher, Tanja (2010) 'Speaking up or being heard? Community media interventions and the politics of listening', *Media Culture and Society*, 32 (1): 85–103.

Entman, Robert (1993) 'Framing: Toward clarification of a fragmented paradigm', *Journal of Communication*, 4 3(4): 51–8.

Flyvbjerg, Bent (2001) *Making Social Science Matter: Why Social Inquiry Fails and How it can Succeed Again*. Cambridge: Cambridge University Press.

Greenberg, Josh, May, Tim and Elliott, Charlene (2006) 'Homelessness and media activism in the voluntary sector: A case study', *The Philanthropist*, 20 (2): 131–51.

Hall, Stuart (1997) *Representation: Cultural Representation and Signifying Practices*. Buckingham: Open University Press.

Hodgetts, Darrin (2012) 'Civic journalism meets civic social science: Foregrounding social determinants in health coverage', *Comunicação e Sociedade*, Numero especial: *23-38*

Hodgetts, Darrin, Cullen, Andrea and Radley, Alan (2005) 'Television characterizations of homeless people in the United Kingdom', *Analyses of Social Issues and Public Policy*, 5 (1): 29–48.

Hodgetts, Darrin, Radley, Alan and Cullen, Andrea (2006) 'Life in the shadow of the media: Images of street homelessness in London', *European Journal of Cultural Studies*, 9 (4): 517–36.

Hodgetts, Darrin, Chamberlain, Kerry, Scammell, Margaret, Nikora, Linda and Karapu, Rolinda (2007) 'Constructing health news: Media production and the possibilities for a civic-oriented journalism', *Health: An Interdisciplinary Journal for the Social Study of Health, Illness and Medicine*, 12 (1): 43–66.

Hodgetts, Darrin, Stolte, Ottilie, Chamberlain, Kerry, Radley, Alan, Nikora, Linda, Nabalarua, Eci and Groot, Shiloh (2008) 'A trip to the library: Homelessness and social inclusion', *Social and Cultural Geography*, 9 (8): 933–53.

Hodgetts, Darrin, Drew, Neil, Sonn, Chris, Stolte, Ottilie, Nikora, Linda and Curtis, Cate (2010) *Social Psychology and Everyday Life*. Basingstoke: Palgrave Macmillan.

Hodgetts, Darrin, Stolte, Ottilie, Radley, Aalan, Groot, Shiloh, Chamberlain, Kerry and Leggatt-Cook, Chez (2011) '"Near and far": Social distancing in domiciled characterizations of homeless people', *Urban Studies*, 48 (8): 1739–53.

Krippendorff, Klaus and Bock, Mary A. (2008) *The Content Analysis Reader*. Thousand Oaks, CA: Sage.

Meijer, Irene (2010) 'Democratizing journalism? Realizing the citizen's agenda for local news media', *Journalism Studies*, 11 (3): 327–42.

Miller, David, Kitzinger, Jenny, Williams, Kevin and Beharrell, Peter (1998) *The Circuit of Mass Communication*. London: Sage.

Moe, Hallvard (2010) 'Everyone a pamphleteer? Reconsidering comparisons of mediated public participation in the print age and the digital era', *Media, Culture and Society*, 32 (4): 691–700.

Napoli, Philip (2010) 'Revisiting "mass communication" and the "work" of the audience in the new media environment', *Media, Culture and Society*, 32 (3): 505–16.

Ostertag, Stephen (2010) 'Establishing news confidence: A qualitative study of how people use the news media to know the news world', *Media, Culture and Society*, 32 (4): 597–614.

Schneider, Barbara, Chamberlain, Kerry and Hodgetts, Darrin (2010) 'Representations of homelessness in four Canadian newspapers: Regulation, control and social order', *Journal of Sociology and Social Welfare*, 37 (4): 147–71.

Silverstone, Roger (2007) *Media and Morality: On the Rise of the Mediapolis*. Cambridge: Polity Press.

Silverstone, Roger and Georgiou, Myria (2005) 'Editorial introduction: Media and minorities in multicultural Europe', *Journal of Ethnic and Migration Studies*, 31 (3): 433–41.

Wasburn, Philo and Wasburn, Mara (2011) 'Media coverage of women in politics: The curious case of Sarah Palin', *Media Culture Society*, 33 (7): 1027–41.

27

Analysing Images

Marcus Banks

INTRODUCTION: WHY IMAGES?

The very ubiquity of anthropogenic images in society is simultaneously an opportunity and a problem. Their ubiquity is justification for treating them as qualitative data items, produced by and in the context of social relations, and at the same time that ubiquity seemingly renders singling certain images out for analytical consideration as arbitrary and capricious: of all the tens of thousands of images in circulation in society, why select this subset and not that subset? Yet it is the dual nature of images – to be and to represent – that renders this sociological action possible. Images are produced by human subjects in the context of, or in response to, human social action. They therefore exist independently of their creators, although they retain affective and agentive ties to them. At the same time images are representations: they are pictures of (other) things, and in that sense remain tied iconically or indexically to that which they represent.

In this chapter I consider a number of ways in which social scientists have approached the study of images in order to gain insight into social processes. Two other chapters in this volume ('Analysis of Film' – see Mikos, Chapter 28; and 'Video Analysis and Videography' – see Knoblauch et al., Chapter 30) deal with particular visual media forms, some of which are associated with specific forms of social analysis (e.g. the use of video recording in discourse analysis – see Willig, Chapter 23, this volume) and other kinds of ethnomethodological analysis (see e.g. Heath et al., 2010; also see Eberle, Chapter 13, this volume); meanwhile, the chapter 'Analysing News Media', which deals with newspapers (see Hodgetts and Chamberlain, Chapter 26, this volume), engages with a medium which is increasingly dominated by images: photographs, strip cartoons, basic tables and other graphical elements.[1] In this chapter, by contrast, I aim to provide some more general discussion about image analysis in the context of social research, considering all kinds of images (paintings, photographs, film, videotape, drawings, diagrams and others) but with a particular emphasis on still photography.

There are many methodological guides to image analysis in libraries, bookshops and online;[2] in this chapter I cannot hope to do any more than touch on a wide number of issues or methodologies, but I do aim to draw out the main threads. Equally, different academic disciplines within the social sciences have developed their own distinctive visual methodologies[3] and while I aim to give even coverage I have my own disciplinary bias towards anthropology.

Returning to the idea of image ubiquity, does the sheer volume of images circulating in society, and the large number of social science disciplines that might be interested in image analysis, mean that there can be no generalizable forms of image analysis (see Maxwell and Chmiel, Chapter 37, this volume)? And how distinctive are these analytical methodologies anyway – can visual analysis reveal results that are not available to any other form of sociological analysis? As will be shown below, while there are certainly methodologies that are matched quite closely to certain disciplinary interests (conversation analysis, see Toerien, Chapter 22, this volume; and frame-by-frame video notation, for example, see Goodwin, 2001), there are others that are quite open and scalable, and that can be applied in a very wide variety of contexts (social semiotic 'readings' of photographs, for example; note how Goffman's and Williamson's works on advertising are still cited today – Goffman, 1979; Williamson, 1978).

With regard to methodological distinctiveness, it is true that in some cases it is not always possible to be certain that the analysis of images has yielded sociological insight that would not be accessible by any other means. If this were quantifiably demonstrable then one might argue that the image analysis was redundant. However, by its very nature it is impossible to subject qualitative analysis to such metrical assessments: in the laboratory of life there are no non- or extra-human contexts to act as a control. What can be asserted is an intellectual goodness of fit, a series of skilled judgements that assert a method is fit for its context. Such an idea is commonplace within the humanities (see e.g. Prendergast et al., 2009), and has an enduring life within qualitative social science (e.g. Geertz's highly visual metaphorical and extremely enduring promulgation of Gilbert Ryle's philosophical attention paid to the distinction between an involuntary muscular movement around the eye, 'a twitch', and the self-conscious but culturally specifically eyelid movement, 'a wink' (1973: 5)).

FOUND OR MADE? WAYS OF SEEING

This chapter is largely concerned with visual analysis – the methodologies by which images are 'read'. It is, however, worth spending some time considering where images come from, and in particular what analytical significance if any should be given to the producer of the image and the context of image production.

Ethnomethodologists, (see Eberle, Chapter 13, this volume) for example, and others concerned with extending discourse analysis (see Willig, Chapter 23, this volume) and conversation analysis (see Toerien, Chapter 22, this volume) beyond spoken utterances ('talk') and into gesture and proxemics, have taken to creating video recordings to gather data for analysis (see Heath et al., 2010, for a recent overview), but they aim to make such recordings as neutral or 'transparent' as possible. The emphasis is entirely on creating the least mediated transcription (see Kowal and O'Connell, Chapter 5, this volume) of what is known in film studies (see Mikos, Chapter 28, this volume) as the pro-filmic event: the action in front of the camera. This is a relatively recent development (as befits a relatively recent discipline). In contrast, anthropology is unusual among the older social sciences in having a long and sustained tradition of image production, in the form of ethnographic film and photography. While these films and photographs were largely taken for purposes of documentation, especially in the early decades of the twentieth century – acting as Latourian immutable mobiles which enabled anthropologists to transmit and store information about far-flung places and people (Latour, 1987: 226–7) – in some instances, such as the anthropometric photography of Thomas Henry Huxley, the act of image creation was part of a process of analysis (see Marien, 2002: 153). By first selecting photographic subjects and then placing them (often naked or semi-naked) in front of a gridded background, or next to a measuring stick, researchers such as Lamprey were performing a visual analytical task (Lamprey, 1869). Few social scientists would have much time for Lamprey's endeavours today, but that is not the point: he created images to analyse, but in doing so he performed the first steps towards that analysis (see also Edwards, 1990).

Several decades later, the pioneering (in many ways) social scientists Gregory Bateson and Margaret Mead deployed photography and film in a fashion that was explicitly in service of and dictated by a specific theoretical agenda. In their ethnographic fieldwork on the island of Bali, Indonesia, they sought to capture the 'character' of Balinese society in images, arguing that by using film and photography 'the wholeness of each piece of behaviour was preserved', something which also allowed for visual cross-referencing (Bateson and Mead, 1942: xii). While a large number of photographs were published, with analysis (Bateson and Mead, 1942), the film footage they produced took rather longer to edit and disseminate. Some of the photographs raise an important ethical issue: Bateson, the photographer, sometimes used an angular viewfinder on the camera, such that when the photographer appeared to be pointing in one direction, he was actually capturing an image at right angles (Bateson and Mead, 1942: 49).[4] Such deception would be considered unethical today – see Box 27.1 – but Bateson considered the ends to justify the means. Of the films, only one has really become well known (*Trance and Dance in Bali*, 1952) and even then it did not have the impact that Mead might have wished (Ginsburg, 2003: 3). Again, as with Lamprey, scholars today might have problems with Bateson and Mead's approach, but the point again is that they had an analytical approach.[5]

In contrast again, cultural studies and disciplines such as cultural geography use largely 'found' images – that is, images produced by the society or social group (typically the analyst's own) that is under study. For example, cultural geographer Gillian Rose's magnificently detailed and very wide-ranging student textbook on visual methodologies, now in its third edition (Rose, 2012), is almost entirely concerned with the analysis of 'public' images in circulation in Euro-American society; only one chapter (of thirteen) is given over to image-making on the part of the analyst.

The kinds of images that social scientists subject to visual analysis are not therefore easily divided into those created by the analyst to collect 'data' (however defined) versus those created by society or a group within society, which are treated by the analyst *as* 'data' (however defined). Rather, the images that social scientists subject to analysis all carry different kinds of intentionality in their production, an intentionality which needs to be taken into account in most if not all forms of subsequent analysis.[6] This is most certainly relevant when issues of image 'meaning' are taken into account. For example, Ryle's 'wink', as a self-conscious visual gesture of complicity, only carries meaning within societies where 'the wink' is already established as such a gesture. This therefore raises questions concerning the degree to which all people see in the same way. Here I am not concerned with the (neuro-)physiology of vision, or with the more technical aspects of the psychology of vision, but with the ways in which vision is socially embedded, or is treated as a social skill. In some societies that anthropologists have investigated vision is not a socially privileged sense, and therefore not privileged as a source of metaphor (e.g. for understanding).[7] Euro-American society by contrast is often characterized by social scientists as ocularcentric (e.g. Jay, 1993), privileging vision – and the objects of vision – above all other channels of perceptual experience. While this is probably a correct assessment it is important to realize that the ubiquity of images in Euro-American society, and the importance placed upon them, is not a given but a social construction; iconoclastic movements have existed before and may again. More particularly, despite the ubiquity of CCTV surveillance, the ability to look at other people and to record that 'looking' is not a right, far less a 'natural' mode of social praxis.

The art historians John Berger and Michael Baxandall simultaneously introduced the related concepts of 'ways of seeing' (Berger, 1972) and 'the period eye' (Baxandall, 1972) to social science discourse about vision, in the former case highlighting the political significance of apparently 'neutral' representational practices, and in the latter using the tools of the social historian to recreate the viewing experience of viewers far removed in time. In both cases, the situatedness of visual practice was emphasized; whatever neuro-physiological processes are involved in visual perception, the brain can only interpret the images it receives through the filter of 'culture'. Baxandall's idea of the 'period eye' was taken up, for example, by anthropologist Jeremy Coote as the 'cultural eye': a way of seeing that allows visual parallels to be drawn by viewers as they encounter the visible world, and novel items within the world, but in a way which is culturally specific (Coote, 1992).

Social scientists have also been concerned with the study of visual enskillment, or the ways in which particular ways of seeing are inculcated, developed and transmitted. The conversation analyst Charles Goodwin has termed this 'professional vision': 'a socially situated, historically constituted body of practices through which the objects of knowledge which animate the discourse of a profession are constructed and shaped' (Goodwin, 1994: 606). Professional vision is not merely about perception, or even necessarily about visual acuity (though there are studies of professionals, such as radiographers, who do indeed need to develop quite technical visual skills – see the various essays in Edwards et al., 2010 and in Grasseni, 2007), but is certainly about visual practices in context. Grasseni, for example, examines the ways in which Alpine farmers are having to learn to 're-see' their environment as a result of the increasing penetration of the market and the commodification of their goods (Grasseni, 2009).

Box 27.1 'A Note on Image Ethics'

I noted above that Gregory Bateson, during his investigation into Balinese 'character' with Margaret Mead in the 1930s, used an angular viewfinder on his camera, one which misleadingly pointed at 90 degrees to the angle of the lens, to aid in taking surreptitious photographs of Balinese people. Why did he do this? Certain activities, particularly being observed eating, were considered shameful by the Balinese villagers that Bateson and Mead studied and they would perhaps not have permitted Bateson to photograph them; not that this really mattered, as Bateson also notes that 'we never asked to take pictures, but just took them as a matter of routine' (Bateson and Mead, 1942: 49). This apparently rather cavalier attitude towards visual research ethics might need to be reconsidered in the twenty-first century: for example, while some psychological experiments depend for their outcome on the deception

(Continued)

> *(Continued)*
>
> of participants (who might otherwise seek to foreguess the 'correct' answer sought by the researcher), this deception is always carefully managed and planned.
>
> While most ethical concerns arising out of image-based research stem from the making of images, the discussion in this chapter is largely confined to image analysis, rather than image capture or image dissemination. Images taken from the public domain, or those private images (perhaps family photographs) subjected to analysis in the researcher's office but not distributed more widely, or published, should not trigger any particular ethical questions.
>
> Where researchers do create their own images as a step in generating data for analysis, in ethnomethodological work for example, the by now well-established conventions for obtaining informed consent from research subjects and ensuring data security can be employed with only minor modifications to take account of the specifically visual nature of the material generated (see e.g., the discussion in Heath et al., 2010: 26–32). Equally, the ethical concerns that are raised when a researcher works with children, or with vulnerable categories of person, remain the same for visual research as for any other kind of research.
>
> Nonetheless, all image analysts – even if they do not work directly with human subjects but only with pre-existing images – should familiarize themselves with the range of ethical issues that can be raised by image-based research. For example, certain cultural groups, including some Aboriginal Australian groups, have prohibitions on who is and who is not allowed to see photographs of the recently deceased. There is a useful and detailed summary of various perspectives in Wiles et al. (2012).

LOOKING AT PICTURES

Above I have stressed the methodological importance of considering image creation (and creators) as a step in image analysis, and noted that in at least one social science tradition (anthropology) image creation can or could itself be considered an analytical act. However, I appreciate that most images that social scientists are concerned with are either created by the investigator as an apparently methodologically neutral mode of data generation (e.g. for conversation analysis – see Toerien, Chapter 22, this volume) or, more commonly, 'found' images, those created by 'society'.

The apparently a-sociological, indeed, perhaps, asocial, character of images created by social researchers through visual recording technologies in pursuit of 'data' for sociological analysis is an issue that needs further exploration, but for the moment let us consider the analysis of images not created by the researcher. That is, images created by society – or a section of society – that are subsequently considered by social researchers to provide insight into that society or section of society. The dichotomy that I am setting up here between social researchers as image creators (e.g. in anthropology) and image analysts (e.g. in cultural geography) is, of course, mediated by the category of image facilitators: social researchers who derive sociological insight from encouraging research subjects to create images for analysis. I will return to this aspect of social research at the end of the chapter.

In the meantime, let us consider different methodological strategies for image analysis. Rose (2012), for example, discusses five sociological modalities: 'compositional interpretation' (i.e. a detailed study of the various elements within the image frame), content analysis, semiotic analysis, psychoanalytical analysis and discourse analysis. I tend to see 'compositional interpretation' as a subset of semiotic analysis, and one prone to what I refer to (undoubtedly unfairly) as the 'art historical' problem (see below). Rose then also goes on to consider empirical approaches to the study of audiences and strategies by which images may be created 'in the field' for sociological research. In addition to the fact that, as Rose herself notes, some of the 'in the office' approaches, as outlined by authors who advocate and develop these perspectives, can be terminologically daunting (2012: 145), I find this division of research strategies into those that take place in or are relevant to 'the office' and those for 'the field' rather artificial and thus problematic. Images created by the researcher 'in the field' may not be amenable to the same analytical strategies as those 'found' in the field. For example, there is little point in a researcher subjecting photographs that she has taken herself in the field to content analysis, which is generally understood to uncover unconscious cultural skewing in image form and composition, unless she is seeking to uncover her own unconscious biases. Equally, so-called participatory visual research strategies, whereby the researcher creates images in consultation with the research subjects, are hard to classify in terms of intentionality and agental direction. Participatory visual research projects are almost always predicated on breaking down the perceived barrier between researcher and researched in terms of the creation of the *object* of research.

Although I personally favour a more eclectic and less 'labelled' approach to visual research, I appreciate that the literature on visual research methodologies does not on the whole support this (see Rose, 2012). Of the various formal approaches, the two most common are probably content analysis and semiotic analysis. Both are interpreted fairly widely; indeed, 'semiotic analysis' could be a label applied to more or less any investigation concerned with the 'meaning' of an image. As it is, in the work of Kress and van Leeuwen (1996), van Leeuwen and Jewitt (2001) and others, the aim is generally to uncover latent meaning (connotative meaning in Barthes' terms (1977: 32–51)) in publically circulating images, often advertising images. Kress and van Leeuwen (1996) are concerned in particular with combinations and sequences of images, which can be considered akin to statements in a communicative utterance. For an anthropologist, or an historian, there is always a suspicion (see Willig, Chapter 10, this volume) that the latent meanings uncovered are too culturally (or historically) specific to be fully understood, without a very thorough investigation into the cultural or historical context more widely. More particularly, without empirical investigation, one can never know how readers/viewers actually respond to the images presented to them.

With regard to content analysis (see Schreier, Chapter 12, this volume), a very clear 'how to' example is provided by Philip Bell, taking as his main example the cover images of an Australian women's magazine: two sets of 20 cover images (all but one showing a single woman in close-up or medium close-up) roughly 20 years apart are selected as the sample, with a research question seeking to investigate how the magazine's 'image' has changed over the years (Bell, 2001). Bell then combines this with a social semiotic approach derived from the work of van Leeuven and others. The approach relies on coding (in this case two (hypothetical) coders are trained to identify features of the image content – women's hair colour, for example – and to assign a code) and fairly simple quantitative analysis (e.g. chi-squared tests). Bell concludes that the significance of the findings is only as strong as the precision of the research questions asked (Bell, 2001: 34).

As Jewitt and Oyama (2001: 154) note, strategies such as content analysis and, especially, semiotic analysis are essentially descriptive in intent, strategies to produce data. Those data then need to be analysed within a theoretical frame. There are, of course, many theoretically strong traditions within social science research and it is unsurprising that most of them have, at one time or another, been trained upon the analysis of images. For example, Berger's *Ways of*

Seeing (originally a BBC television series and accompanying book) introduced the British viewing public not simply to critical art history but to *Marxist* art history in a dramatic and still highly influential way (Berger, 1972).[8] Meanwhile, Mulvey's (1975) article on 'the gaze' stands as a landmark of both feminist and psychoanalytical approaches to the study of mainstream cinema. More recently, Jean Baudrillard's (in)famous claim that the First Gulf War of 1990–1 'did not take place' is a classic – if now rather dated – example of postmodernist deconstruction. His argument, crudely stated, is that in a world of simulacra rather than mere representation, the images of rocket attacks and tracer gunfire in a far-off place seen by viewers in Europe and the United States on their television screens each evening could not be meaningfully distinguished from the video games they played (Baudrillard, 1995).

Rather than dwell on any one of these conjunctions of theoretical position and image analysis in any further detail (all are extensively discussed by Rose (2012), Pink (2007a), and the numerous other visual methodological texts available, such as Pink (2012)), in the second half of this chapter I wish to discuss a number of cases and the visual methodological strategies adopted to address them.[9]

CASE STUDY: VISUAL METHODS IN ANTHROPOLOGY

As I noted above, the use of visual methods in my own discipline of anthropology is as old as the discipline itself. Through the second half of the nineteenth century still photography was allied to various anthropological and quasi-anthropological projects to map and explore differences between peoples of the world. In the twentieth century, up to the Second World War, film joined photography to document the lives of those peoples in greater richness and complexity. What method there was, however, in the use of these visual media was relatively straightforward, unproblematic and lacking in sophistication. The camera was generally assumed to be a transparent recording medium and what discussion there was about its use was generally limited to technical matters: how to set up the squared grid and measuring bars to ensure comparability in anthropometric photography, for example. The 'method' therefore was simply to create a permanent record, a document, of that which the anthropologist or other observer could see for themselves: reality showed itself, the camera captured it. There are exceptions of course (see Figure 27.1).

This image was taken by the Cambridge anthropologist Alfred Haddon on the island of Mabuiag in 1898, one of the islands in the Torres Strait, between northern Australia and New Guinea. The image is one of a sequence Haddon (or possibly his colleague, Anthony Wilkin) took as a young man from the island acted out the myth of Kwoiam, the culture hero of the western Torres Strait Islands. The Kwoiam cult had been abandoned after Christian missionaries arrived a decade or so earlier, but Haddon had learned about it from his informants and he undertook what in his own words he called 'a pilgrimage' to visit and photograph all the sites on the island associated with Kwoiam, whose body and actions had marked the landscape in a variety of ways. This is the final shot in the sequence: Kwoiam's death, in which he bows his head to the inevitable after being captured by a head-hunting party. Thus on one of if not the earliest professional anthropological expedition we find the camera employed to document what the anthropologist – and the locals – could not actually see: a myth.[10]

After the First World War, however, at least in the English-speaking world, visual methods went into something of a decline. Associated primarily with the increasingly outmoded ethnological project of documenting material culture processes for museum collections, images were reduced in serious anthropological writing to mere illustrations, capable of giving an impressionistic flavour to a written account of political process or kinship organization, but incapable of yielding any data in their

Figure 27.1

own right. There were exceptions, but they were few and far between.

It was really only with the rise of interpretative anthropology from the 1960s onwards that visual research, and consequently the use of visual methods, began to become more popular. As anthropologists came increasingly to realize that more attention had to be paid to the ways in which those they studied construct their life worlds, so strictly observational methods (such as counting and measuring) and deductive methods (such as filtering linguistic utterances or ritual performances for unconscious meaning) were revealed as inadequate. Methods in which informants took a greater part in contributing to the uncovering and creation of meaning came more to the forefront, as did methods which situated the ethnographer as a social person rather than an a-social outsider: the so-called reflexive anthropology movement. Visual methodologies accommodated happily to both these agendas. Through a re-examination of historical anthropological photography, contemporary visual anthropologists came to realize just how subjective earlier forms of 'documentary' photography had been, while projects in which media of visual production, such as video cameras and disposable stills cameras, were handed over to research subjects to allow them to document themselves generated direct insight into ethnosociological understandings.

Today, although the nineteenth-century project of using the camera to collect 'data' and 'evidence' still retains utility and value as a method (e.g. using video to document the movement of participants in a ritual for subsequent kinaesthetic analysis), a battery of further techniques has been developed. In photo-elicitation, for example, the use of images in formal and informal interview settings can ground the discussion in substantive detail, while the multivocality of images can prompt informants to discuss matters of which the ethnographer was not even aware. Ethnographic studies of photographic or video practice reveal an insight into local aesthetic systems (the well-documented studio photography of India and West Africa, for example) as well as providing historic grounding for colonial processes of material consumption and appropriation. Studies of, and encouragement given to, forms of so-called indigenous media inside or outside participatory community development projects allow informants to become more engaged with the anthropological research process, again revealing insights into social organization and ethnic or community mobilization that might otherwise have been missed.

QUANTIFIABLE EVIDENCE

For all the successes that visual anthropologists have claimed with their methods, some fundamental questions remain unaddressed and unanswered, and it is to these that I wish to devote the rest of this chapter. First, throughout the social sciences (perhaps less so in anthropology) there is often felt to be an impasse in reconciling the quantitative methods deployed by more positivistic forms of sociology and allied disciplines, and the qualitative methods favoured by most anthropologists. This is perhaps most acutely felt when the matter of what constitutes 'data' is considered: discrete isolable quanta of information that can be distinguished one from another, extracted from context, and held up for comparative analysis. While qualitative researchers frequently fudge this issue, by making spurious use of quantitative terms – for example, referring to 'many people I spoke to …', 'most cases of marriage …' or, worst of all, 'the symbolic weight of exchange in society X is greater than in our own' (Davis, 1992: 79) – this is clearly unsatisfactory. Yet for the findings to be convincing to other social researchers, some form of robustness in methodology must be apparent.

While these doubts and concerns can be raised with regard to all forms of qualitative research, visual research methodology is particularly prone to such accusations: the 'art history problem', as I (undoubtedly unfairly) refer to it, in which the subjective opinions of elderly white men pronouncing on pictorial composition, fineness of line and other attributes of fine art (all, in themselves, measurable) are then used as the basis for completely unverifiable and unquantifiable claims of 'greatness' and 'genius'.

To narrow the range of discussion I wish in what follows to consider two aspects by which the robustness of visual methods could be considered: on the one hand, taking up one of my opening remarks, are there any visual research projects that have uncovered 'data' simply unavailable by any other means? And, on the other hand, what are the limitations of visual research? It is only by delineating areas where the methods cannot reveal anything or be shown to work that we can have greater confidence about the areas where they do seem to be of value. First, though, a word on quantification, an area where visual methodology would seem least applicable.

It is, of course, perfectly possible to combine visual and quantitative methods. A psychologist for example can administer a Rorschach ink-blot test to a sample of n subjects, and code the variations in their answers very easily. The method has to be visual (there is no point in the psychologist attempting to describe the shape of the ink blot verbally), and yet the results can be coded: X per cent of subjects saw an image of their father, Y per cent saw an image of a dog, and so forth.

A rather more detailed, real-world and illuminating example is provided by the statistician and graphic designer Edward Tufte. In his *Visual Explanations* (1997), Tufte retells the famous story of Dr John Snow and the London cholera outbreak of 1854. During September 1854 over 600 people died from cholera, the vast majority of them within a small area of central London; it was the worst outbreak of modern times. Snow, a physician who had investigated earlier cholera outbreaks, was on the scene quickly and attempted to derive a theory of disease transmission by examining information about the deaths. For the history of medical science, this was Snow's great breakthrough: he did not subscribe to the then popular idea that cholera was transmitted, even caused, by foul air or vapours, but suspected that the infectious agent was water-borne. From Tufte's point of view, Snow's great breakthrough was to use a form of visual analysis – mapping – to pinpoint the exact water source responsible.[11]

As Tufte shows, there are ways of presenting the mortality data visually that are apparently revealing but are in fact merely descriptive, not explanatory (1997: 29). For example, plotting deaths by day, and cumulative deaths over the month, as curves on a graph most certainly says something about the rate of cholera transmission, but nothing at all about cause or indeed the cure. Snow's insight was to combine iconic and symbolic visual representations (the graphs are symbolic alone), by placing symbols representing deaths (at any time) onto a map of the area (a map is iconic, it 'looks like' the thing it represents).

Combined with the hypothesis that the infectious agent was possibly water-borne as opposed to air-borne in the form of noxious 'vapours' or 'miasma' (an hypothesis not verified until some 30 years later with the discovery and isolation of the bacterium by Robert Koch in Germany in the 1880s), the mapped evidence clearly pointed to a particular water pump in what was then Broad Street (now Broadwick Street) as the source. Confirmatory evidence also came from that which was not seen: for example, the densely crowded and almost certainly unsanitary workhouse north of the pump had far fewer cases than might be expected for the simple reason that it had its own independent water supply. There is obviously far more to be said about Snow's work and the importance of visual analysis combined with other methods, but the case is clean and neat as it stands: the visual representation of quantifiable data yields a result which supports an hypothesis that can then be further tested.[12]

MAKING VISIBLE

The story of John Snow and his visual analysis of the 1854 cholera outbreak is (rightly) well known, but it was stimulated by a very clear and urgent concern about infection; one could surmise that given the concern, a wide variety of technologies, analyses and other forms of intervention could be – and were – applied in order to address the problem. Yet in a more disinterested context, away from the applied public health intervention, can it be shown that visual analysis yields results that might not be obtainable by other means?

In the mid-1970s the American anthropologist Paul Stoller began conducting field research in Niger as part of a doctoral research project into how symbolic forms in Songhay society are used in the arena of local politics. From his semi-autobiographical account (*The Taste of Ethnographic Things*, 1989) we learn that from the outset he was aware that some symbols were straightforwardly visual and amenable to the most banal visual method of all: simply looking (e.g. nobles, the top stratum of the three-part division of society into nobles, former slaves and foreigners, dress in white, signifying that they do not cultivate the soil but pay others to do so, and carry canes, a symbol of chiefly authority (1989: 57)). Stoller, however, claims more substantial insight as a result of his desire to 'see' in the way the Songhay do.

In the course of an exercise to map residences and agricultural landholdings onto the geography of the small town of Mehanna he noted a correspondence of topographical space and social hierarchy, such that the fields of the nobles were clustered along the so-called 'Noble' road, while those of their former slave clients were adjacent to them. The fields of more recently arrived merchants and other migrants were more outlying.

Similarly, the residence compounds of the nobles were clustered around the main Friday mosque in the heart of the town – the most sacred space in Songhay society – and those of their former slave clients were again adjacent to them, while those of the foreigners and merchants were most distant from this sacred centre. While the inhabitants of Mehanna might not have been consciously aware of this topographical replication of social hierarchy, as Stoller notes, their daily walks from compound to field, from field to market, would become part of the fabric of life, through which intellectual knowledge of the social system becomes embodied knowledge. Of course, Stoller is not the first to note a correspondence between topographic or physical space and social or cosmological space, as he himself admits. Nor for that matter can the method employed be seen as particularly distinctive or extraordinary; while certainly visual – at least in part – it is only slightly less banal than observing the symbolic statement made by the colour of the nobles' clothing.

Stoller, however, goes further than this. He is troubled by some exceptions to his otherwise neat and also static mapping exercise: two merchants had bought fields directly adjacent to the landholdings of the nobles, one former slave had moved his compound from the 'traditional' area to the merchants' residence area, and the wealthiest merchant in the town had moved his compound to the very outskirts of the town – the area normally inhabited by the very poorest of foreigners (Stoller gives no time frame for these moves). One response he could have taken was simply to treat these exceptions as noise in the system, exceptions that prove the rule, and then to move on. Instead, Stoller sees these as wilful acts, ones of which their perpetrators are aware. In so doing he introduces two crucial elements to his analysis. The first is to introduce the idea of process, that things change, and that 'traditional' society does not remain locked in some timeless ethnographic present.

Although Stoller does not comment upon this, this is one of the axiomatic and distinctive features of visual media, and the methods that deploy them: photographs, within a very short space of time, speak eloquently of their temporal fixity, or rather their inexorable temporal journey from their point of origin to the present (a fact that many people find disturbing when they look at photographs of themselves or loved ones from years before – Berger, 1980: 56); film, in a quite different manner, also speaks of process, of movement and of change, simply by its linear unfolding and the manifest disjunction between 'real' time and 'screen' time. The second element Stoller introduces by taking these noise-in-the-system examples is self-awareness on the part of the actors themselves. Briefly, Stoller claims that the introduction of money to Songhay society in the colonial period has gradually led to an effective shift of political power from the nobles to the merchants. The merchants, many of whom are also foreigners, are – Stoller claims – aware of this and aware of the symbolic value of their actions. Consequently, some are asserting this new econo-political order by colonizing powerful topographical places, while others are simply rejecting the existing cosmological–topographical–political order by reconfiguring space entirely – establishing a residence on the outskirts of the town. In like fashion, at least one former slave client of the nobles has cast in his spatial lot with the merchants. According to Stoller, the merchants and former slaves can 'see' (literally and metaphorically) the changing political order or indeed are actively constituting it topographically and hence visually, while the nobles are 'blinded' by tradition and cannot 'see' what is going on.

It is of course impossible to know whether Stoller would have reached this conclusion in any other way, but it is telling that by using visual analysis he brings into the foreground something that could not be seen, just as almost a century earlier Haddon had used a camera to bring the Torres Strait culture hero Kwoiam from a state of invisibility to visibility. However, such strategies, employed by Stoller and Haddon to render the invisible

visible, are not infallible. Returning to Dr John Snow and the 1854 London cholera outbreak, Tufte shows how Snow's visual mapping exercise, combined with his hypothesis about the water-borne mode of transmission, pointed him clearly to the Broad Street pump – and the exclusion of other pumps in the areas – as the source of infection. Tufte, however, also refers to the work of a mathematician, Mark Monmonier. Taking the same data Snow had available to him, Monmonier (1991) redraws the map of the central London area, aggregating the deaths in clusters by neighbourhood. Depending on the definition of neighbourhood boundaries, the death clusters aggregate differently, to the point where some distributions have no obvious visual association with the Broad Street pump at all. In this albeit rather contrived case, the visual method can conceal what it is supposed to reveal (see Tufte, 1997: 35).

CONCLUSION

For all its apparent strength, visual analysis in the social sciences is often passed over by social scientists, or treated as a superficial mode of analysis, lacking robustness. One cause of this is perhaps that some reported projects appear to treat visual methods and visual analyses as an exclusive end in themselves, yielding reports (in the form of films, photographic essays, websites, or simply heavily illustrated texts) that lack any great sociological insight or innovation, or where the insight is actually derived from other forms of analysis and merely confirmed or simply illustrated by the visual evidence. Another cause lies in the problem of images themselves: visual information, visual data, visual results, are simply too messy, too rich, too particular to be reduced to abstraction and linear theorization.

Rather than apologize for this, or to attempt to deny it, some visual researchers are honest about it and see the apparent limitations of visual methodologies as synonymous with the limits of human self-knowledge itself. Let me return one final time to the Torres Strait. The irony of Haddon's photograph of Kwoiam is that it is an image of something doubly invisible. Invisible first, because as a result of Christian conversion the Kwoiam cult had been all but extinguished a decade earlier and thus in both a literal but also a metaphorical sense the Torres Strait Islanders had not 'seen' Kwoiam for many years. Invisible second, because of course no one – living or dead, Christian or pre-Christian – had or has ever literally 'seen' Kwoiam: he is an idea, not a 'thing'.

Haddon's poignant photographic representation of Kwoiam's death therefore returns us to the tension with which I opened this chapter: that between the ontological and the representational dimensions of the visual image in sociological research and analysis. To Haddon – we assume – a young man enacted/play-acted/pretended to be Kwoiam, but what did it mean to the Mabuiag islanders?[13] The thing we wish to see sociologically – and to present to others – is both present and not present in the images we seek to analyse. The challenge is to craft a form of analysis and subsequent representation that is epistemologically open to the simultaneity of presence and absence.

NOTES

1. In their study of the 'grammar' of visual design, Kress and van Leeuwen make an illuminating if rather exaggerated contrast between the front pages of the *Sun* (a UK tabloid newspaper) and the *Frankfurter Allgemeine* (a German broadsheet), both from August 1995; in the former case the visual images 'displace' language in an attempt to appeal to a particular readership (Kress and van Leeuwen, 1996: 28–30).
2. In addition to the Heath et al. volume already mentioned (2010) the most recent and most wide-ranging text on visual analysis is probably Rose (2012), a volume that is accompanied by a very full and useful 'companion website'. Other book-length works on visual analysis include the collection of essays in van Leeuwen and Jewitt (2001), while Hamilton (2006) and Evans and Hall (1999) are col-

lections of essays which discuss the theoretical underpinnings to much visual research and analysis (a strength also of Rose, 2012). Works which discuss the use and creation of images in the research process, as well as their subsequent analysis, include Banks (2007), Mitchell (2011) and Pink (2007a).
3. Most works on visual methods tend to aim for fairly broad-spectrum coverage of the social sciences. The essays in Prosser (1998) cover specific disciplinary perspectives such as education studies; the essays in Reavey (2011) showcase the latest use of visual methods in psychological research, while those in Azzarito and Kirk (2013) promise to be the first to bring 'the visual turn' in the social sciences to bear on the sociology of sport and physical education. Meanwhile Pink (2007b) is a collection of essays on the use of visual methodologies in applied social research; see also Woodhouse (2012) for a recent overview of visual methodologies in nursing health care research.
4. An illustration from the 1931 Leica catalogue shows how this is effected; see Leitz Leica (1931: 8).
5. The production of *Trance and Dance in Bali* was part-funded by the (US) 'Committee for Dementia Praecox' (an earlier name for schizophrenia), because Mead and Bateson were exploring the hypothesis that 'Balinese character' was inherently pathological; see Henley (2013).
6. Sometimes, however, intentionality can only ever be inferred. As well as a category of genuinely 'found' images (see e.g. *Found* magazine (foundmagazine.com)), all historical images come with a greater or lesser amount of supporting contextual documentation.
7. Typically such societies are those that inhabit densely forested environments, such as the Amazon rainforest, where sound carries far better than light; the Suyá people, of the Mato Grosso in Brazil, for example, place great emphasis on sound and hearing (Seeger, 1987).
8. The importance of Berger's contribution has to be seen against the earlier success of the highly influential – and very 'establishment' – 1969 BBC television series *Civilization*, a conservative, Christian and Eurocentric recounting of the Western art historical tradition.
9. Much of the material that follows was originally developed as a presentation given to the German Anthropological Association; some of the examples were then subsequently used in Banks (2007).
10. Edwards (1997) discusses the Torres Strait photographs in some detail.
11. In recent years GIS (Geographic Information Systems) have been used extensively in archaeology in relation to visual analysis; for example, Llobera (2006) is one of several archaeologists who uses GIS to substantiate analyses of viewsheds or visualscapes – the visual structure of a landscape and how it would have been perceived by those who lived there in the past.
12. With ever-increasing computer processing power and data storage, online data visualization – innovative ways of graphing, tabulating and otherwise visually representing data – is a booming field; see Hage and Harary (1991) for an early example from my own field; see also Wheeldon and Åhlberg (2012) for a recent overview of visualization techniques such as mind mapping in social science more generally.
13. Margaret Mead reported that she discussed the Balinese films with the villagers (1995: 8). It is unclear if Haddon did, though he did remain in contact with key informants for many years afterwards.

FURTHER READING

Evans, Jessica and Hall, Stuart (eds) (1999) *Visual Culture: The Reader*. London: Sage.
Pink, Sarah (ed.) (2012) *Advances in Visual Methodology*. London: Sage.
Rose, Gillian (2012) *Visual Methodologies: An Introduction to Researching with Visual Materials*, 3rd edition. London: Sage.

REFERENCES

Azzarito, Laua and Kirk, David (eds) (2013) *Pedagogies, Physical Culture and Visual Methods*. London: Routledge.
Banks, Marcus (2007) *Using Visual Data in Qualitative Research*. London: Sage.
Barthes, Roland (1977) *Image–Music–Text*. London: Fontana.
Bateson, Gregory and Mead, Margaret (1942) *Balinese Character: A Photographic Analysis*. New York: New York Academy of Sciences.
Baudrillard, Jean (1995) *The Gulf War Did Not Take Place*. Bloomington: Indiana University Press.
Baxandall, Michael (1972) *Painting and Experience in Fifteenth Century Italy: A Primer in the Social History of Pictorial Style*. Oxford: Clarendon Press.
Bell, Philip (2001) 'Content analysis of visual images', in Theo van Leeuwen, and Carey Jewitt (eds), *Handbook of Visual Analysis*. London: Sage. pp. 10–34.
Berger, John (1972) *Ways of Seeing*. London: British Broadcasting Corporation.
Berger, John (1980) *About Looking*. London: Writers' and Readers' Publishing Co-Op.
Coote, Jeremy (1992) 'Marvels of everyday vision: The anthropology of aesthetics and the cattle-keeping Nilotes', in Jeremy Coote and Anthony Shelton (eds), *Anthropology, Art and Aesthetics*. Oxford: Clarendon Press, pp. 245–73.
Davis, John (1992) *Exchange*. Buckingham: Open University Press.

Edwards, Elizabeth (1990) 'Photographic "types": The pursuit of method', *Visual Anthropology*, 3(2–3): 235–58.

Edwards, Elizabeth (1997) 'Making histories: The Torres Strait expedition of 1898', *Pacific Studies*, 20 (4): 13–34.

Edwards, Jeanette, Harvey, Penelope and Wade, Peter (eds) (2010) *Technologized Images, Technologized Bodies*. Oxford: Berghahn.

Evans, Jessica and Hall, Stuart (eds) (1999) *Visual Culture: The Reader*. London: Sage.

Geertz, Clifford (1973) 'Thick description: Toward an interpretive theory of culture', in Clifford Geertz, *The Interpretation of Cultures: Selected Essays*. New York: Basic Books. pp. 3–30.

Ginsburg, Faye (2003) '"Now watch this very carefully . . .". The ironies and afterlife of Margaret Mead's visual anthropology', *The Scholar and Feminist Online*, 1 (2): http://sfonline.barnard.edu/mead/ginsburg.htm (accessed 28 June 2013).

Goffman, Erving (1979) *Gender Advertisements*. London: Macmillan.

Goodwin, Charles (1994) 'Professional vision', *American Anthropologist*, 96 (3): 606–33.

Goodwin, Charles (2001) 'Practices of seeing: Visual analysis. An ethnomethodological approach', in Theo van Leeuwen, and Cary Jewitt (eds), *Handbook of Visual Analysis*. London: Sage. pp. 157–82.

Grasseni, Cristina (ed.) (2007) *Skilled Visions: Between Apprenticeship and Standards*. Oxford: Berghahn.

Grasseni, Cristina (2009) *Developing Skill, Developing Vision: Practices of Locality at the Foot of the Alps*. Oxford: Berghahn.

Hage, Per and Harary, Frank (1991) *Exchange in Oceania: A Graph Theoretic Analysis*. Oxford: Clarendon Press.

Hamilton, Peter (ed.) (2006) *Visual Research Methods*, 4 vols. London: Sage.

Heath, Christian, Hindmarsh, Jon and Luff, Paul (2010) *Video Analysis and Qualitative Research*. London: Sage.

Henley, Paul (2013) 'Trouble in paradise: Recovering the films of Margaret Mead and Gregory Bateson', *Visual Anthropology*, 26 (2): 75–108.

Jay, Martin (1993) *Downcast Eyes: The Denigration of Vision in Twentieth-Century French Thought*. Berkeley: University of California Press.

Jewitt, Carey and Oyama, Rumiko (2001) 'Visual meaning: A social semiotic approach', in Theo van Leeuwen and Carey Jewitt (eds), *Handbook of Visual Analysis*. London: Sage. pp. 134–56.

Kress, Gunther and van Leeuwen, Theo (1996) *Reading Images: The Grammar of Visual Design*. London: Routledge.

Lamprey, John (1869) 'On the method of measuring the human form, for the use of students in ethnology', *Journal of the Ethnological Society*, 1: 84–5.

Latour, Bruno (1987) *Science in Action*. Cambridge, MA: Harvard University Press.

Leitz Leica (1931) *Leica Camera. Catalogue for 1931*. Available at http://books.google.co.uk/books?id=PKph_E1NCFAC&printsec=frontcover&dq=Leica+camera+catalogue+1931&hl=en&sa=X&ei=S6f1T7HjJuyV0QXf-6C4Bw&ved=0CEQQ6AEwAA#v=onepage&q&f=false> (accessed 13 May 2013).

Llobera, Marcos (2006) 'What you see is what you get? Viewscapes, visual Genesis and hierarchy', in Thomas Evans and Patrick Daly (eds), *Digital Archaeology: Bridging Method and Theory*. London: Routledge. pp. 148–67.

Marien, Mary W. (2002) *Photography: A Cultural History*. London: Laurence King.

Mead, Margaret (1995) 'Visual anthropology in a discipline of words', in Paul Hockings (ed.), *Principles of Visual Anthropology*. Berlin: Mouton de Gruyter. pp. 3–11.

Mitchell, Claudia (2011) *Doing Visual Research*. London: Sage.

Monmonier, Mark (1991) *How to Lie with Maps*. Chicago: University of Chicago Press.

Mulvey, Laura (1975) 'Visual pleasure and narrative cinema', *Screen*, 16 (3): 6–18.

Pink, Sarah (2007a) *Doing Visual Ethnography*. London: Sage.

Pink, Sarah (ed.) (2007b) *Visual Interventions: Applied Visual Anthropology*. Oxford: Berghahn.

Pink, Sarah (ed.) (2012) *Advances in Visual Methodology*. London: Sage.

Prendergast, Monica, Leggo, Carl and Samishima, Pauline (eds) (2009) *Poetic Inquiry: Vibrant Voices in the Social Sciences*. Rotterdam: Sense.

Prosser, Jon (ed.) (1998) *Image-based Research: A Sourcebook for Qualitative Researchers*. London: Falmer Press.

Reavey, Paula (ed.) (2011) *Visual Methods in Psychology*. London: Routledge.

Rose, Gillian (2012) *Visual Methodologies: An Introduction to Researching with Visual Materials*, 3rd edition. London: Sage.

Seeger, Anthony (1987) *Why Suyá Sing: A Musical Anthropology of an Amazonian People*. Cambridge: Cambridge University Press.

Stoller, Paul (1989) *The Taste of Ethnographic Things: The Senses in Anthropology*. Philadelphia: University of Pennsylvania Press.

Tufte, Edward (1997) *Visual Explanations: Images and Quantities, Evidence and Narrative*. Cheshire, CT: Graphics Press.

Van Leeuwen, Theo and Jewitt, Cary (eds) (2001) *Handbook of Visual Analysis*. London: Sage.

Wheeldon, Johannes and Åhlberg, Mauri (2012) *Visualizing Social Science Research: Maps, Methods, and Meaning*. Thousand Oaks, CA: Sage.

Wiles, Rose, Coffey, Amanda, Robison, Judy and Prosser, Jon (2012) 'Ethical regulation and visual methods: Making visual research impossible or developing good practice?', *Sociological Research Online*, 17 (1), 8.

Williamson, Judith (1978) *Decoding Advertisements: Ideology and Meaning in Advertising*. London: Boyars.

Woodhouse, Jan (2012) 'The use of visual methodology in nursing', *Nurse Researcher*, 19 (3): 20–5.

28

Analysis of Film

Lothar Mikos

Analysing films is becoming increasingly important in a mediatized society. As media of communication, films are embedded in the circumstances by which society communicates and interacts. Movies are part of discursive and social practices. They reflect the conditions and structures of society and of individual life:

> I will tell you something about movies. They aren't just entertainment; they are powerful ways to see into the workings of our minds and hearts. With movies, we can get a better sense of what we are doing here, why we are doing it, and what in the world we need to do to bring about the changes we seek. (Teays, 2012: XI)

Movies have to be understood essentially as media of communication. Therefore the analysis of films should be a systematic investigation of the structures of film texts, their conditions of production and reception, and the societal contexts. This approach differentiates academic analysis from the everyday, which tends to proceed unsystematically and refers to a film as a whole but does not investigate its individual components. In addition, everyday discussions often look at films and television programmes for their content. That process allows them a subjective meaning. However, academic study should not seek subjective meaning but produce knowledge, which is objective and can be verified intersubjectively. The purpose of this chapter is to provide the theoretical apparatus and the methodological tools for investigating films systematically.

That means recognizing how every media representation is a subjective construction, which is selected from a myriad of possible representations and which is also determined by particular interests. In addition, this involves realizing that films and television programmes always aim at an audience, sometimes an unspecified one, and sometimes a precisely defined one in the shape of a special target group. With films the processes of co-deliberation have to be performed in three ways: first with regard to the intentions, on the part of producers or institutions (e.g. television broadcasters,

Hollywood studio system), which underpin the media products; second – referring to the structure of films – with regard to the functions that the individual components have in relation to the whole film; and, third, with regard to what function these components have for the audience. This last aspect relates to how what this chapter sets out as the basics of film analysis are based on an understanding of film and television as communications media. In this sense, films come about in their audience's minds first of all. That is because films have to be seen before they can begin communicating. So analysis aims to observe how the structures of films function in the framework of the communication processes they are bound up in. Therefore, we are concerned with grounding film analysis in communication and cultural studies. That is what separates the film analysis presented here from other kinds of film analysis in film or literature studies. By film analysis I mean the analysis of moving images, including television.

What follows in this chapter is not intended to analyse 'film language' but to look instead at the means a film employs to communicate with viewers. This process means that the use of content, acting, dramaturgy, narrative and aesthetics plays just as much a role as the contexts that the filmic structures and viewers are bound up in. During analysis, filmic structures are liable to investigation in three ways: first as regards the coherence of a film in terms of content and narrative; second as regards the creative means directed for viewers' attention and perception; and third as regards the communicative process and its contexts, because the meaning of a film does not arise until viewers take notice of it. The 'meaningfulness' of films does not exist as a quasi-objective, factual entity; it is produced only when viewers watch or academics analyse them. Films have to be regarded as meaningful symbolic material, which is significant only in the framework of meaningful discourse.

Amid all that, we have to bear in mind that communication between audiovisual works and viewers is not just a question of making meaning. James B. Twitchell (1992: 203) has also pointed this out with his critical comments on television: that engagement with this medium has concentrated above all on content but not on television as an experience. This is also true of film.

FILM AS COMMUNICATION

Film analysis has to begin by acknowledging that the objects under investigation (moving images) enter into communication with their viewers. That happens in two ways: on the one hand, viewers respectively watch or receive images (in the sense of absorbing them); on the other hand, they respectively use or appropriate them. In my opinion, it is important to establish this differentiation between reception and appropriation, because that makes it then analytically possible to separate the concrete interaction between a film and its viewers from further appropriation of the film, for example in a conversation with friends and acquaintances. Reception means actually engaging with films. In it, the structures of film texts integrate with the allocation of meaning as well as the experience of them by the viewer. In reception, the active recipient creates the so-called received text, which, to a certain extent, denotes the concrete meaning of the 'original text'. The received text is the film that the viewer has seen, and it is one enriched by the meanings allocated to it and by the way it structures experience. It is the result of the interaction between film texts and viewers. By contrast, appropriation means the transfer of the received text into the everyday discourse of common experience and into viewers' sociocultural praxis. A film can be the object of further interactions and activities when it, for instance, serves to prompt a discussion during lunch. People use films to shape their own identities as well as their social relations. The difference between reception and appropriation is analytic in nature, and, as viewer activities, the two cannot be separated empirically. Why, then, are reception and appropriation important for analysing films?

To answer this question, we have to be quite clear what films are about. In a film the perspectives of production and reception meet in a particular way. The task of analysis is to find out exactly how this happens. From the perspective of reception aesthetics, analysis provides an understanding not only of the media contents as communication offerings, but also of the entire symbolic material of films – that is, of narration and dramaturgy, as well as of the creative means for attracting the viewers' attention. In this context, film texts are to be understood as pointers to reception and appropriation. The texts contain pointers to what viewers are supposed to do, and that is how they pre-structure those activities. It is not the medium that is the message, but its role in social use. Film – and television too – can therefore be regarded as social practice (see Turner, 2006). That does not mean that film and television texts determine the viewers' reception of them. All they do is make offers, which viewers can use by engaging with the text in question. John Fiske (1987: 95–9) does not talk about texts either, but about their 'textuality' or about 'producerly' texts. What this means is that film and television texts seek completion by their viewers; that is, they only come about in the act of reception and appropriation. Understanding them like this also means that films and television programmes do not contain any complete meanings, which, for instance, scholars can uncover 'objectively' in an analysis; instead, they only develop their semantic and symbolic potential through active viewers, that is they can only have potential meanings: they form a 'semiotic resource' (Fiske, 1987). A text is, like a film, able to favour several meanings, yet it can also set boundaries and therefore limit its own potential.

Film texts can only make offers, and stage possible ways of reading themselves, to pre-structure what viewers then do. However, there is one thing texts cannot do: they cannot determine meanings. They function as agents in the social circulation of meanings and pleasures, and they can only deploy their potential for meaning where they are integrated in social and cultural relations. Films only work in the social context of their usage. There, and nowhere else, is where their power to create structure is brought to bear. According to Fiske, it is where the social and textual determinations intersect that viewers appropriate popular texts like films, which also indicates how texts always exist in the field of social debate. As regards analysis, this means that the structure of films needs to be related to the activities of reception and appropriation. Nevertheless, in doing this, we have to note that the structuring power of film texts is greater in reception than in appropriation, as it is here that the socio-cultural contexts that viewers belong to are more influential. Therefore, it is the activity of reception that occupies the foreground in the following reflections; appropriation is included in our observations only where it seems relevant.

Fundamentally, film and television texts are aimed at an audience. For that reason, they are open to knowledge, emotions, affects, practical meaning and their recipients' social communication. It follows that four sorts of activity can be differentiated as playing a role in reception and appropriation: (1) cognitive activities; (2) emotional and affective activities; (3) habitual and ritual activities; and (4) social-communicative activities. All of them basically connect with two modi operandi, which define how we deal with film texts: understanding and experiencing film and television. So analysis is above all concerned with setting out these processes of understanding and experience. What is meant by 'understanding film' is the tackling of an audiovisual product to investigate how it is constituted as a meaningful text bound up in the cultural circulation of production and reception. This kind of analysis is strongly related to the concept of reception aesthetics (see the summary in Storey, 1999: 64–7). A film text is an instruction manual for the performance of meaning. Therefore it is possible to find the implied viewer in the textual structure of films. The main task of the analysis is to investigate systematically how the viewer is constructed by a film.

From the perspective of reception aesthetics, the object of film analysis is the textual structure of films, because they pre-structure what people do in perceiving and appropriating them. All forms of representation and all systems of signs used by audiovisual media are up for investigation, in terms of both the framework of the structure of texts and the framework of their function in audiences' cognitive, affective and emotional, social-communicative, routine and ritual activities. In this sense, the analysis always has to have an eye to possible and actual perception and appropriation. Also, attention must be paid to covering the cultural and social contexts of film and television texts as well as the viewers' activities connected, at all levels, with perceiving and appropriating them:

> We cannot fully comprehend what a text is all about until we investigate how texts address their readers or viewers, and how readers, viewed singly or as a group, interpret texts and integrate them into the everyday doings in their lives, that is: until we analyse how texts circulate in a particular social space and extend their effect. (Casetti, 2001: 156)

Analysis of film does not simply exist for itself, but always has a cognitive purpose bound up with it. An analysis can serve various purposes: through a quite pragmatic analysis of the structures of a particular film, it can explain its success with a certain target group (e.g. the role of genre hybridity in the *The Lord of the Rings* trilogy); it can develop theoretical reflections on the role of gender in a particular genre (e.g. the role of the femmes fatales in film noir or the identity construction of female action heroes, such as the bride in *Kill Bill*); it can serve structural considerations in montage theory (e.g. the constructive montage in Hong Kong action movies); and it can also serve to confirm or refute theoretical assumptions about film and television by means of concrete case studies (e.g. the meaning of reality TV in *The Truman Show*).

These examples suffice to show that analysing film is a complex undertaking. On the one hand, it is always linked to theoretical insights about movies; on the other, it usually arises from a particular perspective. For example, it makes a difference whether a film like *Pulp Fiction* is analysed from the perspective of feminist film studies, or whether the film is the object of an analysis within the framework of a scriptwriting workshop, which is demonstrating narrative and dramaturgical structures. This latter example also shows that analyses usually exist in an applied context, which does not have to be exclusively academic.

Beyond that, each analysis, which is not just investigating individual aspects of films, has to take theories from various disciplines into account according to its cognitive purpose. In this sense, analysing film is necessarily both interdisciplinary and transdisciplinary: interdisciplinary, because it brings together theoretical assumptions from various disciplines; transdisciplinary, because it can contribute to transforming the boundaries between disciplines through the interplay of analysis and theory. There is no one true path for analysis (see also Salt, 1992: 27). It appropriates various theoretical assumptions from differing disciplines and various methods, which orientate themselves according to the cognitive purpose. Analysing film and television is not independent of the contexts because it favours specific theoretical aspects, serves a specific social practice or frames some research tendencies. Therefore an analysis of *Brokeback Mountain* referring to queer theory (Etherington-Wright and Doughty, 2011: 181–98) will lead to different findings from an analysis of the same film referring to montage theory.

Every analysis of film and television is, then, bound up with academic discourses and it is also bound up in the discursive contexts of the respective disciplines which it cites and exploits to endow its object with perspective. Yet, precisely what is the actual object when analysing film?

In the framework of the theoretical categorization of films as media of communication, the analysis of film can only take concrete films as its object to investigate their textual structure with an eye to their interaction with viewers. This can involve a corpus of films, which is investigated as to its common traits or differing structures. On the other hand, at the centre of all this there may be nothing more than a single scene from an auteur film or a fantasy blockbuster, which provides the example for demonstrating textual structures or a specific viewpoint. Individual film images are not the object of analysis, because film is a moving image medium. The sequence of individual images that constitute the essence of film in their chronological, linear succession forms the core of analysis. Individual images can certainly play a role here, but they should always be seen in the context of the images before and after them. The object of a concrete analysis can be, for example, individual scenes or sequences in a film, typical scenes from a sample of genre films, typical opening sequences from auteur films, complete films or a group of films. The last of these can be assembled according to various criteria, for example all of a director's films or all science fiction movies between 1960 and 1990. Determining an object for a concrete analysis coincides closely with the cognitive purpose.

THE COGNITIVE PURPOSE OF FILM ANALYSIS

If we can assume that analysis generally concerns how the structural function of film texts is significant for reception, then the concrete cognitive purpose can be said to focus on the five following levels:

- Content and representation
- Narration and dramaturgy
- Characters and actors
- Aesthetics and configuration
- Contexts.

Every film can be investigated on these levels. In doing so, analysis can confine itself to a single level, but it can take several layers into account as well. Each level relates to the others; for example, *contexts* affect the level of *narration and dramaturgy*, the level of *aesthetics and configuration* plays an important role in the level of *content and representation*, and the level of *characters and actors* is linked closely to the level of *narration and dramaturgy*.

The above-named levels can be investigated in the analysis of both fictional and documentary films. Both kinds of films have a content, they represent real or possible worlds, they tell stories that are fashioned as dramas, characters and actors do things in them, they are crafted and shaped aesthetically, and, finally, they exist in textual, cultural, social and societal contexts. In this way, for example, it is not only fictional films telling stories invented by scriptwriters that are narrative; so are documentary films. The following briefly sets out the general cognitive purposes which are linked to the above-named five levels.

Content and Representation

The first level for analysing films is closely bound up with establishing meaning. As a general principle, we can assume that films have content and they represent a social world. Yet, what exactly is the content and how, precisely, does representation function?

As a first step, we can generally confirm that everything said and shown represents content. On a general level, we could say that the content of a film consists of some characters acting in social environments. On a more concrete level, the topics dealt with in spoken and visual items can be understood as content. All the same, the content of a film is, in the sense described above, not interesting. Instead, what is interesting in the analysis of film is how content is presented and, by that, how it contributes to the production of meaning and the social construction of societal reality. The content to be expressed is united with the format for representing it. Only in this form can it become an element in communication with audiences or spectators.

Here, we basically have to assume that everything the camera shows is important and significant. If film and television texts are open towards what viewers know, towards emotions, social communication and their practical appreciation, then at the core of analysis is how these texts contribute to the 'meaningful construction of a social world' (Schütz, 1962), and do so, in fact, with respect to the structural role of the media in societal communication as well as the concrete role of individual media and media contents in constituting subjects and forming identity in concrete viewers and viewer groups.

Representation means 'the production of meaning through language' (Hall, 1997: 28). It is not an impersonal process. Rather, there are individuals active in producing meaning. So representation is more precisely 'the process by which members of a culture use language to produce meaning' (Hall, 1997: 61). In this case, every sort of sign system counts as language, and that includes media such as films too. Signs are used, which are 'organised into languages of different kinds to communicate meaningfully with others' (Hall, 1997: 28). As far as film and television goes, these are images, sounds, writing, language, graphics and music (see also Hartley, 1994: 265). The signs can stand for objects in the so-called real world, but they can also stand for abstract ideas and fantasy worlds.

According to Hall, there are two systems of representation: the system of signs, in which articulation happens; and the system of mental concepts, which 'classify and organise the world into meaningful categories' (1997: 28). Reality does not exist outside of representation. In this sense, the cognitive activities that film texts are open towards can be seen as mental systems of representation. Films can be regarded as systems of signs, which represent real worlds and abstract ideas stemming from societal reality, or possible worlds, as recounted in stories. As systems of signs, they relate to 'historical, cultural and social change. Representations are, therefore, a site of struggle about meaning' (Taylor and Willis, 1999: 40). However, in analysing film and television, it is not just a question of what is shown, but, above all, of how it is shown.

At this point, it becomes clear which theoretical relations are significant for analysing content and representation. For media systems of representation, this is semiotics on the one hand and, on the other, discourse theory; for mental systems of representation, it is cognitive theory of film, psychology of film, and pragmatic theory of film and television.

Analysing content and representation in films has a particular status. It is important for understanding the processes governing the meaningful construction of the social world, because subjects position themselves in society that way. As representations, film texts correspond to societal structures, through which relations of dominance and power also become manifest in texts. This is where film texts' ideological components lie. And at the same time, they relate to what individuals in society know, which is what decides their positions in it (cf. Berger and Luckmann, 1971).

As the texts are, however, simultaneously open towards viewers' activities, they play an important role in identity and subjectivity. On this basis, people reflect 'their experiences and their place in the world' (Grossberg et al., 1998: 227). In the framework of understanding films as media of communication, the reception and appropriation of film texts become a societal praxis, in which the texts are produced on the basis of social experience, by viewers dealing meaningfully with them in their daily routines and everyday world. That grounds the relevance of the analysis of film, which engages with, for example, the representation of women, the use of ethnic stereotypes or the role of childhood. Therefore, it is possible to do research on ethics through movies (cf. Teays, 2012).

Narration and Dramaturgy

The second level on which films can be analysed is indeed closely bound up with the first, but is not identical with it, because, with the second level, it actually is a matter of the way social worlds represent both societal reality and possible worlds springing from the imagination. What should we, however, understand by the term *narration and dramaturgy* in relation to films?

To formulate it succinctly, we can say that narration, or recounting, consists of causally weaving situations, actors and activities into a story, whereas dramaturgy is the way this story is constructed appropriately to the medium, in order to make it take shape in the viewers' heads – and in their innards too. More precisely, we can first understand storytelling as a form of communicative messaging, which differs from other forms, for example from description or argumentation (cf. Chatman, 1990: 6–21). It is the result of a communicative action: of storytelling. The person carrying out this activity is the storyteller, who directs the story to receivers, the audience. A story always comes about through the storytellers' positioning and perspectives, and through their viewpoint on what is being told or the story, against the background of addressing the audience. Fundamentally, we can understand storytelling as a communicative activity in everyday life. Storytellers can use various forms of media for storytelling; they can use, for example, language, writing, film, television or hypertext. In doing that, films use various strategies for storytelling, which include viewers. Narration (see Esin et al., Chapter 14, this volume) is a process that needs to be interpreted by spectators (cf. Bordwell, 1990: xi). The interpretive action of the spectator becomes very obvious in so-called 'puzzle films', referring to a film 'that rejects classical storytelling techniques and replaces them with complex storytelling' (Buckland, 2009: 1).

The nature of a story as a process already points to its temporal dimension, which is constituted as a duality: on the one hand, how long it takes to show a film, and on the other how long the story takes, or, more precisely put, the story's narrated time (see on this Chatman, 1990: 9). In this sense, we differentiate between the narrative time – for example, the 100 minutes of a feature film – and the narrated time – for example, the five days in which the story of a film happens.

At the same time, we have to distinguish between what films and television programmes show (plot or subject) and the narrated story (or tale), which only comes about in the viewers' heads (cf. Bordwell, 1990: 48–53). The story produces a diegetic world, which appears as both possible and consistent in itself. It is created in the narrated story, both with the content and with representation, which relates to the social world outside of films.

Film texts are usually stories. This applies not only to fictional texts, but also to documentary ones. Most forms of entertainment are structured around stories. They are one of the 'fundamental sources of pleasure' in the media (Casey et al., 2002: 138). All narratives have storytelling in common. A narrative can be designated a 'sequence of situations, in which events are realised and persons do things in specific surroundings' (Casetti and di Chio, 1994: 165; see also Berger, 1997: 4–11). In analysis, what needs setting out are the situations and events, which are linked to each other as well as to the persons and to the surroundings these persons are active in. Narratives employ certain storytelling strategies to draw audiences into stories. Storytelling strategies are, therefore, always linked to activities by viewers, who have also acquired some narrative knowledge in the course of their media socialization. This narrative knowledge includes typical plot structures and episodes, typical actors' roles, typical narrative conventions and typical staging. Spectators have some knowledge about the typical staging of horror effects, for example. Film adaptations of novels are a special case. Readers may already know the characters and the main plot of a certain story. The readers of the novel *The Lord of the Rings* already know the story of Middle Earth when they watch the films (cf. Mikos et al., 2008: 115). Narrative forms and strategies make it clear that stories do not simply offer a succession of events and plots, but that they are shaped dramaturgically.

Films have constructed their own structures of storytelling and of dramaturgy, which diverge partially from the literary and theatrical structures of storytelling. At base, dramaturgy reaches back to the way a story is constituted dramatically. The visual storytelling in temporal sequence is the fundamental principle of dramaturgy in film. It, therefore, relates in the first place clearly to what a film shows on the big screen. Yet there is, in fact, more behind this. At the core of dramaturgy there are conflicts that permit figures to become active and drive the plot. Dramaturgy has, therefore, the task of arranging the sequence of events in which persons are active in such a way that certain cognitive and emotional activities are stimulated in viewers. Knowledge accumulates, and feelings arise. How a story is shaped makes it, for instance, exciting, comical or threatening. The analysis of film has, then, to demonstrate how the sequences of events are structured. This is because it is the only way to show how film texts pre-structure what viewers do in receiving them and how they make the stories come about in their heads. The dramaturgical structuring of stories determines the way information reaches audiences and how they process this information cognitively and emotionally (cf. Elsaesser and Buckland, 2002: 37).

In analysing narration and dramaturgy, several theoretical relations are significant. Even though narrative theories from literary and linguistic studies can be applied to films only narrowly, they do play a not unimportant role all the same. More important are the treatises on narrative theory stemming from cognitive film theory and its environment (cf. Bordwell, 1990; 2006; Branigan, 1992; Buckland, 2009; Chatman, 1990; 1993; as well as what is set out in Elsaesser and Buckland, 2002: 168–94) that engage fundamentally with narration and in doing so relate explicitly to films and other popular media (cf. Berger, 1997), which approach the topic with recourse to work on literary studies and film theory, or which devote themselves to narration in the environment of digital media.

Analysing narration and dramaturgy is important, because it forms the basis for the stories in the viewers' heads and regulates their cognitive and emotional attitude to the screen. The cognitive purpose of any analysis can then, for example, focus on how tension is generated in a thriller, how the zone of empathy is built up in a melodrama, how comedy arises, or how the conflict between protagonists and antagonists is built up and resolved. In general, it is possible to tell the same story (the relationship of a couple) in different ways: as comedy, as tragedy or as horror. If dramaturgy structures the sequence of events in a narrative, and narrative can be seen as a linkage of situations in which persons act, then it becomes clear how closely narration and dramaturgy in film texts are bound up with the characters and people active in them.

Characters and Actors

In films people play an important role, in the most literal sense of the word. It is only in nature and animal films that they become a marginal phenomenon, if they do appear at all. In feature films they have an essential function in advancing the plot. Analysing the persons, characters and figures in audiovisual media production is significant for two reasons: on the one hand, the persons who appear are important for advancing the plot and they function in the dramaturgy and in the narrative structure of film texts, because the story being told is often presented from the perspective of one of the characters; on the other hand, how viewers perceive the persons depends on the meanings and concepts of self, person and identity circulating in society and the everyday world. Society determines, among other things, its concepts of identity and roles with and through film figures. In this sense, characters and actors have a crucial function in the framework of representation for positioning viewers as subjects and forming their identity.

We have to make a fundamental distinction between figures and characters who appear in fictional film texts, and actors who undertake specific functions in media roles, such as a candidate or host, or who appear in documentary films. Staging figures and actors is fundamentally open towards what viewers know, towards their emotions, their cultural appropriation and their practical appreciation. The cultural concepts from everyday life, which play a role in the perception of human beings as persons, are also significant for the perception of figures and actors in film texts. What criteria and characteristics affect the perception of human beings as persons? This formulation already contains a criterion: in the case of persons, it is clearly a question of human beings. But that on its own is not enough, because artificial humans, aliens, cyborgs and robots appearing in films are also perceived and identified as persons.

For any being to be perceived as human, it has to have an individual human body, which remains consistent through time and space – unless it changes due to biological, chemical or technical processes, which the film also explains. Furthermore, it has to be a being which can itself perceive things, has feelings and intentional states like convictions or wishes and is capable of self-recognition. Additionally, it has to use and understand a natural language and it has to be able to act individually and interpret its own self. Finally, it has to possess potentially characteristic qualities and consistent traits (cf. Smith, 1995: 21). To perceive this being as a person, further criteria are necessary: it has to have a name, a gender and an age, a background and a nationality. All these make a person different from others, and people are identifiable precisely through this difference from others. This difference also becomes conspicuous in some of the general criteria for human beings, for instance in their differing characteristics and, not least, in their differing bodies.

Common knowledge about social types, personality profiles, lifestyles and so on provides the patterns, which contribute to the interpretation of figures and actors, and how they fit into everyday contexts of reference. David Bordwell (1992: 188–93) demonstrated how schemata of persons and roles, as they relate to characters advancing the plot in films, are a vital element of cognition and understanding. The cast of film texts always relate to the respective notions of the self and identity, to knowledge about how social roles and persons are typified, and to how that knowledge circulates in the framework of specific cultural contexts within everyday circumstances.

If we proceed from an understanding of films and television as media of communication, then a decisive aspect of analysing them is the fact that figures and actors are significant not only for cognition and understanding, but precisely for the emotional processes of reception and appropriation too. That requires employing aspects of both cognitive film theories and psychological, psychoanalytical, sociological and social–psychological theories of reception.

It is above all figures and actors that determine how close viewers are to the happenings on the large screen – or how distant they are from them. In *The Truman Show*, for example, the camera follows the main character Truman and places the viewers into his perspective. Every spectator has to follow the story through the perspective of Truman. So analysis has to demonstrate which of the invitations from film texts to make connections pre-structure this relationship between figures or actors respectively, and the viewers. This is because all the connections that viewers build up with film characters and television actors play a crucial role in forming identity, and they are also significant in governing the closeness or distance of fan behaviour too and in the social-communicative construction of film stars.

Aesthetics and Configuration

The fascination of films rests above all on the fact that they concern media of moving images. Individual images are configured in a specific way and assembled into a continuous stream. The stories arising in the viewers' heads also rest on what people know about the ways films represent things and configure images, something closely linked to what people know about narratives. In this context, film studies talk about the discourse of films (cf. Chatman, 1993: 146–61; Tolson, 1996: 41–3) or about style (cf. Belton, 2009: 41; Bordwell and Thompson, 2010: 143–4). The specific filmic means of representation bind viewers, through the process of receiving a film, into what is happening on the big screen. They guide viewers, above all emotionally, through the story, transport them into particular moods, and steer their attention to individual aspects of the film image without their always being aware of it. In this way, viewers are bound up into the perspectives of story and representation. In the framework of an analysis, that then means demonstrating precisely these aspects and relating them through filmic ways of depiction to what viewers know, in order to contribute to making this process recognizable. How things are configured can also become central to analysing contents and representation, narration and dramaturgy, as well as figures and actors. The reason is that the formal and stylistic means of configuring moving pictures positions the viewer vis-à-vis with what is happening on the screen, and this constitutes the quality of films as experience.

How images are configured rests on conventions of presentation. This means that they are learnable and that knowing about them becomes routine, a part of making meaning practically. In the course of receiving a film, processes unfold with respect to ways of presentation that can be preconscious and partially unconscious. Analysis can make these processes recognizable, yet this does not mean that they become recognizable in the concrete situation where viewers are doing the reception. Anyone using what they already know to engage with a film will carry on being steered emotionally by what is happening, yet they will subsequently be able to say more exactly why the film has exercised a particular fascination. Ways of presenting and configuring things in films serve above all to inculcate certain moods in viewers. That is why comedies, for example, play in bright, generous spaces, while characters in psycho-thrillers have to move through poky, dark ones.

At the same time, the means of configuring things arouses viewers' expectations regarding future events. Conventions in presenting and configuring are based on the way they are frequently applied in films and how the viewers' learning experiences are bound up with them.

If, for example, in a scene from a film a woman running down a street appears and is sometimes looking back, seems harassed and is clearly being followed, the camera first shows her obliquely from behind, then from the side. When she looks back, the camera follows her gaze. Finally, the camera shows her viewpoint looking ahead, and viewers see what she sees as she runs towards the corner of a house. Now they expect that someone she does not expect will appear round the corner. If the woman has been previously set up as a figure for viewers to identify with, they will feel fear at this point because they are empathizing with her. The tense expectation generated by the way the scene is represented transports viewers into a state of psycho-physiological excitement, or, to put it another way, they fall under the film's influence, it enthrals them. A 'good' film makes viewers become active cognitively and emotionally. It is true that it also grants them an occasional breather, but by the end it gives them the feeling that they have contributed something to the experience of the film. In that process, the way that the film configures things can also lead to excessive demands and consequently to exhaustion. *The Dark Night Rises*, the *Lord of the Rings* trilogy, the *X-Men* films and

Natural Born Killers can serve as examples here. The last of these films works with harsh colours, rapid cutting, numerous special effects and loud music, and in doing so it reaches the limits of what people are able to take in.

Declaring that films consist of moving pictures is not exactly correct, as they consist, in fact, of single static images, which viewers perceive as moving. Every individual film image not only depicts something and displays it, but is configured in a quite specific way. That applies not only to invented, fictional stories but to the reality as depicted. Every reproduction of reality presents only a segment of it and is formed by technology and the possibilities for display specific to the media. In this way, social complexity is reduced to the amount that the media can convey, but individual film images also reduce the complexity of what is depicted down to what can be depicted; a residue remains, which is both invisible and inherent in every image. Then again, this invisible element can become, if not unconditionally visible, at least perceptible through the specific ways of configuring it. This is what stage sets have aimed at in the theatre, and it is what the production design of films still aims at.

Since sound film was invented, we have been able to add sounds, noises, speech and music to the images. The camera itself can add its bit to the production design by its range of shots and of movements. How individual images are arranged is not unimportant for the general impression of a film, and for a television programme; how the editing of the images organizes the individual images from the cameras is no minor matter either. Yet even if the media do reduce the complexity of the real world, film images are in themselves still notably complex. We can talk about the 'visual richness' (Chatman, 1990: 39) of the images. Because film images are so complex, viewers receiving them are forced to scan them for the information important to their activities. Doing that is, however, not a question of picking out individual pieces of information and regarding those as relevant; what viewers do instead is relate the various aspects of the image to each other (cf. Ellis, 1992: 54). This endows the individual configurative measures with a particular significance, because they guide the viewers' attention. In addition, they have a narrative function, as they support the plot. They serve viewers with indications that contribute to the understanding of a film's narrative and they can arouse expectations about what happens next. That is why they are indispensable for the story in the viewers' minds.

In analysing the formal, stylistic means, we have to look at images both individually and in their mutual interactions. The latter then become clear, when the individual elements are set out in their narrative function. With that, the following aspects of a film shift into the focus of analysis: camera, production design, light, sound, music, special effects, montage and editing, respectively. Apart from editing, all elements belong to what film studies also call *mise-en-scène*. Generally speaking, *mise-en-scène* includes all elements which are introduced into the scene. It is not only the elements per se that are important in that process, but how they relate to each other (cf. Belton, 2009: 43–4) as well as to content and representation, narration and dramaturgy, figures and actors. As the means used to configure images interact, they stimulate viewers' activities and tie them into the process of understanding and experiencing film and television.

The conventional means of depiction and configuration, also called filmic or televisual codes, steer viewers' attention and have a considerable hand in producing meaning. In this sense, they can be understood as the aesthetic techniques of film and television, which become concrete as viewers perceive film texts through their senses. That is why cognitive purpose focused on these formal, aesthetic techniques can be very fruitful. In this way, we can, for example, use analysis to demonstrate the role of the camera in developing the emotional bond between a character and the viewer, or to investigate the significance of montage for building up dramatic tension.

Contexts

Film texts only acquire meaning through interacting with their viewers. This interaction does not exist in an extra-social space, but happens in contexts: in historical, economic, juridical, technical, cultural and social–societal contexts. In analysing films, five contexts have a central function in viewers' production of meaning and they relate to the textual, media-related and cultural–social levels of film and television texts:

- Categories and genres
- Intertextuality
- Discourse
- The everyday life world
- Production and market.

These contexts are significant for analysis in two respects: on the one hand, they play an important role in the above-named levels of analysis (content and representation, narration and dramaturgy, characters and actors, aesthetics and configuration) by having concrete effects on film texts; on the other hand, the production of meaning does not happen independently of them. Depending on the respective context, viewers can produce various meanings around the same film. That is because texts are always contextually articulated and have contradictory, unstable and debatable meanings.

The insights meant to be gained from analysing film can aim at one of the five named levels – contents and representation, narration and dramaturgy, characters and actors, aesthetics and configuration, and contexts. However, all of the levels and contexts are empirically indivisible and mutually determine each other in the concrete communication of film texts with their spectators. Their interaction shows the complexity of film communication. Yet it is important for analysis to separate the individual levels and contexts, so that it can accordingly demonstrate their respective contributions to the success (or otherwise) of communication. By analysing the textual structure of films it is possible to explain why some films are very successful and others not.

STEPS OF ANALYSIS

There are three main challenges for an analysis of film, which relate to (1) the volatility of moving images, (2) the general infinity of analysis, and (3) the lack of a universal method of analysis. Therefore, to undertake an analysis it is necessary to operationalize the methods of analysis in a way which takes account of the conditions of the research and the cognitive purpose. We can differentiate 14 steps that guide the analytic research (cf. Mikos, 2008: 82–95):

1. Development of a general cognitive purpose
2. Watching the visual material
3. Theoretical and historical reflection
4. Development of a concrete cognitive purpose
5. Development of questioning
6. Sampling of the material for analysis
7. Fixing of analytic tools
8. Collection of data
9. Description of data collection
10. Analysis of data – Inventory of the film components
11. Interpretation and contextualization of analysed data
12. Evaluation I – Assessment of the analysed and interpreted data
13. Evaluation II – Assessment of the results with the regard to the cognitive purpose and the operationalization
14. Presentation of the results.

Steps 1–6 are important to reduce the general infinity and define more precisely the scope of the film analysis. The analytic tools are important for fixing the volatility of moving images. This is the point at which to decide whether to use a DVD player for analysis or to produce a transcript of the films in question. Steps 1–8 are the preparatory work for the analysis. Steps 9–13 represent the main analytic work. In the end there should be a presentation, whether an essay, a paper at a conference or a book.

Let me give an example of an analysis. Let us say that the general cognitive purpose is an interest in the representation of society in science fiction movies. The next step is to watch as many science fiction movies as possible and read articles and books about the genre (e.g. Kaveney, 2005; Telotte, 2001), which contribute to Step 3 (theoretical and historical reflection). At the next stage we have to develop a concrete cognitive purpose, for example whether there has been a change in the representation of society and extraterrestrial intelligence between the 1950s and 1960s, when the Cold War plays a dominant role, and the beginning of the twenty-first century. At the next step we develop concrete questions like: How does the camera position aliens and humans? Does this have an effect on how we perceive them? How are aliens staged emotionally and by what kinds of staging and narration is this supported? What kind of discourse about aliens and human society is presented in the films? The next important step (6) is the sampling of the material for analysis. In this case it is necessary to analyse the films of every period, let us say the 1950s/1960s, the 1970s/1980s, the 1990s/2000s. We could choose three films from every defined period; for example, *Forbidden Planet*, *Them* and *Plan 9 from Outer Space* from the first period; *Close Encounters of the Third Kind*, *E.T. The Extraterrestrial* and *Alien* from the second period; and *Mars Attacks*, *Independence Day* and *I, Robot* from the third period. For the next two steps we have to decide whether to use a DVD player or legally download the films in question, and if necessary write a protocol of some important sequences and scenes. Before we start the analysis we should describe our data material: a brief description of the content of the films, and a brief description of the characters and of the aesthetic tools. Now the concrete analysis can begin. We have to look intensely at the films' components and relate them to each other. For each film we can analyse the intimacy–distance relationship of humans and aliens, how it is staged by camera position and movement, and how the cutting and music support the emotional elements of this relationship. The next step is the interpretation and contextualization of the analysed data. Here we need to enrich our results with theoretical and historical insights. For example, in the later movies the staging is in general more emotional than in those of the 1950s and 1960s. One interpretation of these data could be that a change in the structure of societies took place and emotions came to play a more important role in identity construction. The last three steps of the analysis are the assessment of the analysis and the results, after which a paper can be prepared, 'The changing nature of human relations to aliens: An analysis of the emotional staging of aliens in science fiction films', for presentation at an international conference.

SUMMARY

The most important tasks of a film analysis are the development of a concrete cognitive purpose, the development of concrete questions and the operationalization of the analysis. Otherwise, there is no possibility of dealing with the generally infinite scope of film analysis. The theoretical background of any film analysis is the insight that film is a medium of communication. A film gets its meaning through its circulation in the discourse of audiences; it is a sociological event. The film's reception and appropriation by the spectators bring it to life. Producers and directors are, on the one hand, bound to public discourses, therefore their films are connected to these discourses. On the other hand, they want to obtain revenues from selling films to audiences, or they want to get an artistic reputation from showing the film. Every single element of a film, whether it is a camera angle, the acting of the stars, the editing or the sound, is addressed to audiences and single spectators. With regard to reception, aesthetic film analysis has to investigate the spectator (the audience) in the film text. There are several cognitive purposes that can guide an analysis: (1) content and representation, (2) narration and dramaturgy, (3) characters and actors, (4) aesthetics and configuration, and (5) contexts. In the context of sociology or political science, the main cognitive purpose of film analysis is the level of representation, because movies are part of the representational structure of societies. But it is also important to examine the level of aesthetics and configuration, because the way a story is told puts the spectator in a specific position in relation to a film text and to its representation. Doing film analysis in this way makes a contribution to the analysis of the meaning of movies in the communication and discourse structure of societies.

FURTHER READING

Bordwell, David and Thompson, Kristin (2010) *Film Art: An Introduction*, 9th edition. New York: McGraw-Hill.
Plantinga, Carl (2009) *Moving Viewers: American Film and the Spectator's Experience*. Berkeley: University of California Press.
Teays, Wanda (2012) *Seeing the Light: Exploring Ethics through Movies*. Malden, MA: Wiley-Blackwell.

REFERENCES

Belton, John (2009) *American Cinema/American Culture*, 3rd edition. New York: McGraw-Hill.
Berger, Arthur Asa (1997) *Narratives in Popular Culture, Media, and Everyday Life*. Thousand Oaks, CA: Sage.
Berger, Peter L. and Luckmann, Thomas (1971) *The Social Construction of Reality: Treatise in the Sociology of Knowledge*. London: Penguin.
Bordwell, David (1990) *Narration in the Fiction Film*, 3rd printing. London: Routledge.
Bordwell, David (1992) 'Cognition and comprehension: Viewing and forgetting in "Mildred Pierce"', *Journal of Dramatic Theory and Criticism*, VI (2): 183–98.
Bordwell, David (2006) *The Way Hollywood Tell it: Story and Style in Modern Movies*. Berkeley: University of California Press.
Bordwell, David and Thompson, Kristin (2010) *Film Art: An Introduction*, 9th edition. New York: McGraw-Hill.
Branigan, Edward (1992) *Narrative Comprehension and Film*. London: Routledge.
Buckland, Warren (ed.) (2009) *Puzzle Films: Complex Storytelling in Contemporary Cinema*. Malden, MA: Wiley-Blackwell.
Casetti, Francesco (2001) 'Filmgenres, Verständigungsvorgänge und kommunikativer Vertrag', *Montage/AV*, 10 (2): 155–73.
Casetti, Francesco and di Chio, Federico (1994) *Analisi del Film*, 6th printing. Milano: Bompiani.
Casey, Bernadette, Casey, Neil, Calvert, Ben, French, Liam and Lewis, Justin (2002) *Television Studies: The Key Concepts*. London: Routledge.
Chatman, Seymour (1990) *Coming to Terms: The Rhetoric of Narrative in Fiction and Film*. Ithaca, NY: Cornell University Press.
Chatman, Seymour (1993) *Story and Discourse: Narrative Structure in Fiction and Film*, 6th printing. Ithaca, NY: Cornell University Press.
Ellis, John (1992) *Visible Fictions: Cinema, Television, Video*, rev. edition. London: Routledge.
Elsaesser, Thomas and Buckland, Warren (2002) *Studying Contemporary American Film: A Guide to Movie Analysis*. London: Arnold.
Etherington-Wright, Christine and Doughty, Ruth (2011) *Understanding Film Theory*. Basingstoke: Palgrave Macmillan.
Fiske, John (1987) *Television Culture*. London: Methuen.
Grossberg, Lawrence, Wartella, Ellen and Whitney, D. Charles (1998) *Media Making: Mass Media in a Popular Culture*. Thousand Oaks, CA: Sage.
Hall, Stuart (1997) 'The work of representation', in Stuart Hall (ed.), *Representation: Cultural Representations and Signifying Practices*. London: Sage. pp. 13–74.
Hartley, John (1994) 'Representation', in Tim O'Sullivan et al. (eds), *Key Concepts in Communication and Cultural Studies*. London: Routledge. pp. 265–6.
Kaveney, Ron (2005) *From Alien to the Matrix: Reading Science Fiction Film*. London: I.B. Tauris.
Mikos, Lothar (2008) *Film- und Fernsehanalyse (Film and Television Analysis)*, 2nd rev. edition. Konstanz: UVK.
Mikos, Lothar, Eichner, Susanne, Prommer, Elizabeth and Wedel, Michael (2008) 'Involvement in "The Lord of the Rings": Audience strategies and orientation', in Martin Barker and Ernest Mathijs (eds), *Watching the Lord of the Rings: Tolkien's World Audiences*. New York: Peter Lang. pp. 111–29.
Salt, Barry (1992) *Film Style and Technology: History and Analysis*, 2nd edition. London: Starword.
Schütz, Alfred (1962) *Collected Papers. Volume 1: The Problem of Social Reality*, ed. Maurice Natanson. The Hague: Nijhoff.

Smith, Murray (1995) *Engaging Characters: Fiction, Emotion, and the Cinema*. Oxford: Oxford University Press.

Storey, John (1999) *Cultural Consumption and Everyday Life*. London: Arnold.

Taylor, Lisa and Willis, Andrew (1999) *Media Studies: Texts, Institutions and Audiences*. Oxford: Blackwell.

Teays, Wanda (2012) *Seeing the Light: Exploring Ethics through Movies*. Malden, MA: Wiley-Blackwell.

Telotte, J.P. (2001) *Science Fiction Film*. Cambridge: Cambridge University Press.

Tolson, Andrew (1996) *Mediations: Text and Discourse in Media Studies*. London: Arnold.

Turner, Graeme (2006) *Film as Social Practice*, 4th edition. London: Routledge.

Twitchell, James B. (1992) *Carnival Culture: The Trashing of Taste in America*. New York: Columbia University Press.

29
Analysing Sounds

Christoph Maeder

Whenever society happens there is sound. When people are talking, making music, being called by church bells, driving cars, using computers, or making love, they produce sounds and acoustic effects. At the same time they become embedded into a sonic environment, which ultimately transcends the single actors. Larger social structures like families, schools, hospitals, shopping centers, factories, harbors, airports, train stations, and finally villages and even whole cities constantly generate acoustic environments that people live in. This fact of a ubiquitous acoustic sphere simultaneously being produced by social action and surrounding that social action as a context has largely been ignored by qualitative research. Obviously there are some domains, like conversation analysis (Silverman, 1998; also see Toerien, Chapter 22, this volume) or the ethnography (see Gubrium and Holstein, Chapter 3, this volume) of communication (Keating, 2001) that bring into focus a particular aspect of the acoustic world, namely, speech. In their ethnographical study of the workplace, Karine Lan Hing Ting and Barbara Pentimalli (2009) refer to noise as an important and functional resource used by hearing, or overhearing, non-linguistic acoustics like noisy typing on the keyboard, the snapping of fingers, the clapping of hands, etc. They argue that becoming a member of the workforce in a call center is based on the capacity to recognize and interpret significant sounds of this kind within an environment, which is acoustically demanding due to the general noise level of such operations. But these acoustically aware approaches restrict their interest to sound as language and as a form of communication. In this realm the amount of literature is vast, and highly sophisticated methods for research are accessible. The same holds true for music, where ethnomusicology, starting from the oral tradition of music like folk songs passed on without the use of notation (McLucas, 2011) and going up to a 'Global Music Theory' (Hijleh, 2012), covers the field.[1] But if we take the acoustic environment, sonic effects, auditory cultures, and sound practice as topics each in their own right, the outlook changes. By mainly considering the non-linguistic and non-musical aspects of sound in society, we are challenged by a whole new field of study (Vannini et al., 2010). And this becomes even more apparent when we try to blend sound analysis with qualitative research.

Before I turn to the practice and the methods in what might turn out to become qualitative sound research, I introduce the development of some perceivable strands of research on sound: sound ecology, sonic experience, and sound culture. My purpose is to explain selected important concepts that might be new, or that might need some elucidation for those who are not familiar with the field of what today is only loosely captured in the term 'sound studies.'

THE DEVELOPMENT OF SOUND STUDIES

Sound studies are obviously not yet a consolidated and fully established field of qualitative research in the social sciences. And there are knowing voices suggesting that sound studies may stay an emerging field for ever: 'Perhaps sound study is doomed to a position on the margins of various fields of scholarship, whispering unobtrusively in the background while the main action occurs elsewhere' (Hilmes, 2005: 249). At least a geographical and linguistic spread of sound studies is observable. For a long time it seemed that sound studies were only systematically available in English and French. But a German branch has now emerged around the University of Arts in Berlin (see Schulze, 2008). However, research on the audio-sphere, the acoustic environment, the soundscape and even sound culture as we know it today remains an often confusing composition of different disciplines and perspectives. Those involved neither share a common method or theory, nor systematically take notice of each other. For instance, studies in architecture (Blesser and Salter, 2007; Hedfors, 2008), cultural anthropology (Hammou, 2011), art (LaBelle, 2006), philosophy (Ihde, 2007), history (Sterne, 2003; Szendy, 2008), film and cinema science (Altman, 1992), sociology (Attali, 1985), and others have made important and valuable contributions to the undertaking of making sound in society a researchable matter. But the topics, theories, focuses, and objects that are studied vary widely. And the boundaries between these endeavors are often blurred and rather fuzzy.

In order to identify key streams in the research on sound, I propose to arrange the existing sound studies, which have a potential for qualitative research into three bundles:

(a) sound ecology and acoustic communication;
(b) sonic experience and sonic effects; and
(c) auditory culture and sound culture studies.

This yields an incomplete grid, of course, which omits some disciplines, and the classification cannot encompass all there is on sound and acoustics. But it does at least make some methodological sense, as we will see later on in the text. To a certain degree it funnels together what is being analysed. Exponents of bundle (a) try to analyse the sound itself, whereas proponents of (c) take on more of the context and practices in and out of which sounds emerge and which sounds in turn also create. And the mainly French approach of (b), with its idea of the sonic effect as a core concept, stands somewhere in the middle of (a) and (c). It does not offer a clear-cut and systematic link between the two, but nevertheless incorporates some ideas from each side.

Sound Ecology and Acoustic Communication

The work to make sound a topic in its own right in the social sciences goes back to Murray R. Schafer's 'World Soundscape Project' in the 1970s.[2] The essence of this research is published in Schafer's (1994) book *Soundscape*. Originally published in

English in 1977, the book was not translated into French until 1991, and was only translated into German in 2010. The initial project at the Simon Fraser University in Vancouver not only created a place where sound studies could be pursued at university level for presumably the first time, but also triggered the development of what is known today as the field of 'acoustic communication' (Truax, 2001), where, as well as the features of acoustic communication, the impact of technology on acoustic design by means of electro-acoustics is singled out as a dominant issue for research. Looking back, it is fair to say that everything to do with sound studies has been initiated, or at least has profited, in one way or another, from the groundbreaking work of Schafer and his group. In retrospect this approach can be labeled 'sound ecology,' because it looks at the phenomena of sounds in society in an encompassing and holistic way.

The key concept introduced by these studies is the term soundscape, by analogy to landscape:

> The soundscape is any acoustic field of study. We may speak of a musical composition as a soundscape, or a radio program as a soundscape or an acoustic environment as a soundscape. We can isolate an acoustic environment as a field of study just as we can study the characteristics of a given landscape. ... A soundscape consists of events heard not objects seen. (Schafer, 1994: 7f.)

Soundscapes as willfully extracted aspects of the human senses feature some special properties: Schafer (1994: 9) distinguishes keynote sounds, signals and soundmarks. Keynote sounds are the anchor or fundamental tone in a soundscape. They do not have to be listened to consciously, and they might even be overheard. As an example one might think of the keynote sounds of a shopping mall. There we are immersed in a complex blend of sounds composed of electronically distributed music, voices, footsteps, etc., which we do not analytically separate but take as the keynote of the situation. In an analogy to ethnomethodology (see Eberle, Chapter 13, this volume), where some quite complex features of understanding in everyday life go as 'seen but unnoticed' (Garfinkel, 1967: 38–75), we can refer to the mundane keynote as the heard but unnoticed features of everyday life. And the keynote sounds of a given place are the background of a soundscape against which the signals can be perceived. Signals are foreground phenomena and they must be listened to consciously. Sound signals may be organized into quite elaborate codes, permitting messages to be transmitted to those who can understand them. Signals in the form of functional sounds are abundant in modern society. Think of all the sirens, warning bells, software sounds, elevator jingles, cashier rings, etc., to which we are exposed as functional sounds in everyday life. Some of these signals can turn out to become soundmarks:

> The term soundmark is derived from landmark and refers to a community sound which is unique or possesses qualities which make it specially regarded or noticed by the people in that community. Once a soundmark has been identified, it deserves to be protected, for soundmarks make the acoustic life of the community unique. (Schafer, 1994: 10)

Soundscapes can, furthermore, be split into lo-fi and hi-fi environments by looking at the signal-to-noise ratio. In sound studies a hi-fi environment is one in which sounds may be heard and perceived clearly by a listener, while a lo-fi environment has overcrowded and masked signals, and lacks clarity.

Besides the soundscape and its particular features, Schafer also developed an almost completely encompassing taxonomy of the first natural soundscape up to the post-industrial one. The two big changes for human lives and living, in this perspective, have been the introduction of the engine during the process of the Industrial Revolution and the mastery of electro-acoustics (radio, sound recording, the telephone, etc.). Since the olden days of the pre-industrial society, natural and rural soundscapes are receding for more and more of us and are being replaced by artificial, engineered acoustic environments. These changes are sometimes regarded as unfavorable, and hence demand what is nowadays called acoustic ecology and noise reduction (Wrightson, 2000).[3]

The combined work of Schafer and his colleagues points toward an innovative and promising, though not easily applicable, perspective for qualitative research: innovative because they turn our attention to the acoustic dimension of society beyond mere communication; and promising because they have introduced new concepts like the soundscape for the observation of our physical and social environment.[4] But the endeavor remains very challenging due to its multidisciplinary way of thinking about the sonic sphere, and because some 'non-compatible' theorems of social theory are used.

Sonic Experience and Sonic Effects

Another approach, which judges that the soundscape is too wide and imprecise to let the researcher work at the scale of everyday practice and at the scale of urban spaces at the same time (Augoyard and Torgue, 2006: 7), has developed in France. At the National School of Architecture of Grenoble the philosopher, urban planner and musicologist Jean-François Augoyard founded the 'Centre de recherche sur l'espace sonore et l'environnement urbain' (CRESSON) in 1979. He and his co-workers focused on the effects of sound on listeners and hearers. They developed the concept of the 'sonic effect' in order to describe and analyse the experience of everyday sounds in architectural and urban contexts. In their pivotal publication, *Sonic Experience: A Guide to Everyday Sounds*, Augoyard and Torgue defined 66 such effects and grouped them into 16 effects, which they defined as 'basic ... always existing in concrete space or in the listening process ... effects that directly participate in the nature of the urban environment or in the cultural processes' (2006: 15). An example given for such an effect is 'Metamorphosis: A perceptive effect describing the unstable and changing relations between elements of a sound ensemble ... the relation between elements that compose the sound environment, defined as addition and superimposition of multiple sources heard simultaneously' (2006: 73). As an example for metamorphosis the reader might think of being in a soccer stadium during a game. There, all kinds of sounds (natural voices, electronically amplified voices, sounds of engines, and many more) mix in a continuous and complex way. For the hearer this blends into the sonic properties of this particular happening, which oscillate around different perceivable acoustic sources and finally blend into the joint and specific outcome that defines the acoustic dimension of the game. Because the sonic effect is seen as a multidisciplinary object by the authors themselves, the major effects are discussed in relation to the domains of:

- Psychology and physiology of perception
- Physical and applied acoustics
- Architecture and urbanism
- Sociology and everyday culture
- Musical and electro-acoustic aesthetics
- Textual and media expressions.

But even given such a clear structure, the sonic effect in this tradition should be understood as a paradigm rather than as a strictly defined concept of cause and effect. As the authors write:

> Halfway between the universal and the singular, simultaneously model and guide, it allows a general discourse about sounds. ... Rather than defining things in a closed way, it opens the field to a new class of phenomena by giving some indication of their nature and their status. Finally, it characterizes the modal or instrumental dimensions of sound. (Augoyard and Torgue, 2006: 9)

Put in a nutshell, the sonic effect bridges the gap between sound ecology (i.e., the concept of the soundscape as acoustic sensations that are just there and observable) and the phenomenology of sound as something linked to individual experience and social practice.

But since these authors present the concept of sound effect as a complex array following its own logic, the link is somewhat obscure and incomplete.

The human ear as a sensory organ has some remarkable properties and capacities. Since there is no 'ear lid,' sounds once in the air must be heard. And this holds true over the 360 degrees around the receiving subjects. Our ears are permanently screening the acoustic environment, even when we would prefer them not to operate in such a manner. Think of yourself alone in a mountain hut where the wooden beams creak and crack in the wind. The effect of such a situation frightens us, and has been named 'the uncivilized ear' ('l'oreille primitive') by Pierre Schaeffer (1982). The fact that we are hearing nearly all the time makes it necessary to adapt our ears continuously to the acoustic environment. The adjustment of hearing sounds 'in' and 'out' consists of two parallel processes or effects (Augoyard and Torgue, 2006: 123f.). The processes are at the center of auditory perception and enable metamorphosis as described earlier. They are called synecdoche and asyndeton. The synecdoche effect is the aptitude to extract one specific audible element through selection. Selective listening is a fundamental competence in everyday practice and is complementary but antithetic to asyndeton, the selective deletion or 'overhearing' of sounds. These two effects of perceptive organization are the basis of any meaningful interpretation of the acoustic environment, because 'they make it possible to create a gap between the physical sound of reference and the object of listening. In this sense, they are at the basis of the idea of sonic effect itself' (Augoyard and Torgue, 2006: 174). The culture to which someone belongs thus has a central function in shaping the way they hear, evaluate, and valorize sounds and their capacity to do this. Schaeffer therefore introduced the term 'l'objet sonore' in France, as early as the late 1940s (Schaeffer, 1982, quoted in Schafer, 1994: 129), defining it as something from the audio-sphere which is chosen and experienced by one person but might be irrelevant for others. If we perceive the sonic environment as just a physical phenomenon, which can be recorded and displayed as waveforms, we obviously miss what sounds can and do mean to people, and how actors create social order by the use of sounds. This has already been clearly formulated in the acoustic communication approach:

> Whether an environmental sound has a meaning or not (i.e., whether it is 'just' a noise) depends entirely on its context and how it is understood. The 'sound object' (an environmental sound isolated on tape from its context) cannot mean anything except itself as an aural sensation. (Truax, 2001: 53)

Auditory Culture and Sound Culture Studies

New instrumental capacities have radically transformed the auditory world, and still do so. One such capacity is the electrical amplification and reproduction of sound by electromagnetic audio technologies. This makes it possible nowadays for sound – which was once attached to a discernible and original source – to flow everywhere. As a consequence, the hearing subject has to shape his or her 'acoustic territories' and even 'acoustic identity' (LaBelle, 2010) accordingly. Looked at in this way, the meaning of sounds in everyday life and sound-related practices become the cornerstones of auditory and sound culture studies (see Winter, Chapter 17, this volume). Whereas the auditory culture approach (see, e.g., Cox and Warner, 2004) focuses more or less on the consumption of and listening to music, sound culture studies do have a wider angle. An illuminative example of such an approach toward soundscapes, sound experience, and society is given by Michael Bull (2003). A social practice, the use of a car, is analysed with regard to the meanings that can be attached to the artifact, and it becomes comprehensible how 'the historical turning point between "dwelling on the road" and "dwelling in the car" can be located in a very specific technological development: the placing of a radio within the automobile' (Bull, 2003: 360). The car becomes an acoustic sanctuary where you can listen to what you want, as loud as you like, and even sing along with it. And nobody will hear this, except, obviously, the driver.[5] This privatized and exclusive acoustic situation in the car becomes a symbol of personal freedom shaped by technology and even infuses sense into the time spent in the car. But – and this is the critical part of the analysis – the individual is still embedded in, and controlled by, larger social structures, and might overestimate his or her individuality and freedom 'by sound' in the car. A further example of this kind is Bull's study on portable electronics, namely the iPod (Bull, 2007). I consider the *Auditory Culture Reader* of Bull and Back (2003) a major step forward for qualitative methods in the study of sounds in society. But the book is still structured to cover the acoustic social sphere of sounds in an encompassing way, similar to the sound ecology approach, because it is divided into 'Thinking about Sound,' 'Histories of Sound,' 'Anthropologies of Sound,' 'Sounds in the City,' and 'Living and Thinking with Music.' Given the year of publication and the pioneering character of the book, this should not be read as a criticism of the editors, but as a hint of where certain difficulties and challenges lie for the sound researcher. If we make the field too wide, it becomes difficult to develop a succinct approach.

A concise perspective has, however, been introduced in one of the latest efforts concerning sound and everyday life, where social places (the metro, the home, the sidewalk, the street, the shopping mall, the sky) as acoustic territories are systematically arranged as locales for acoustic practice:

> To map out the features of this auditory paradigm, I have sought to explore in greater detail the particular behavior or figures of sound. It is my view that sonic materiality operates as 'micro epistemologies,' with the echo, the vibration, the rhythmic, for instance, opening up to specific ways of knowing the world. Accordingly, I have traced each chapter by following a particular sonic figure. For instance, in exploring the underground I tune in to the specific ways in which subterranean spaces are conditioned and bring forward the echoic ... in this sense, the presentation of specific acoustic territories should not be exclusively read as places or sites but more as itineraries, as points of departure as well as arrival. As territories, I define them as movements between and among differing forces, full of multiplicity. (LaBelle, 2010: xxv)

Looked at in this way, the auditory life in, of, and as sound culture can be traced in the performative subtleties of everyday life. Such itineraries in acoustic territories imply a routinized knowledge of the competent actors who are interacting in and moving through the audio-sphere at the same time. Knowledge of this kind can be seen as a micro-epistemology of the mundane (see Eberle, Chapter 13, this volume) when it comes to the aural space: it allows society to function locally on proper acoustics and produces social phenomena transcending single social actions through embedding them into something bigger like a train system, a city, and so on. And such acoustic inserting includes the possibility of 'overhearing by others' (Goffman, 2010: 40) and of excluding someone from participation on the interactive level of society. Seen this way sounds and the acoustic environment resulting thereof function as a continuous indicator, a clue and a link from the micro-level of practice to the bigger levels of the social order. And this is happening in real time for the participants or hearers.

Last, but not least, there is the idea of sonic fieldwork and the creation of audio documentaries (Makagon and Neumann, 2009). It is correct to say that some of the most important archives of sound recordings have not come from scientists in the academy but from radio reporters, journalists, and other audiophiles (2009: 3–6, 9–14). The famous John Lomax Collection in the Library of Congress, which is available online today, is but one good example. The idea behind such collections was and still is to document and preserve the acoustic culture. The tokens in the collection do not follow any scientific logic or approach, but they represent what was remarkable for the collectors in those days. In this sense the collection is noteworthy in at least two ways: first, we can hear the historical sounds of a particular culture; and, second, we can discover what was considered a remarkable sound by those involved in recording. In the ever- and rapidly changing world we live in, audio documentaries can present and preserve the cultural richness and particularities of society in the audio-sphere.

ANALYSING SOUNDS: FROM SOUNDSCAPES TO SOUND CULTURE

Depending on the line of approach toward sound research taken by a scholar, he or she will use different data and varying concepts for the description and analysis of the relationship between social practice and the acoustic environment. As described in the previous part of this chapter, we can split the whole endeavor of sound studies, in an idealized manner, into those approaches that present sound and the corresponding analysis and those that focus on the sonic aspects of a social situation or social structures and embed them in everyday practice and culture.

The technology of digital sound recording available today makes it comparably easy to record sound. But suitable sound recording is quite challenging for many practical reasons. The practical aspects of sound recording or sonic documentation are interferences from wind, reverberations, echoes, distances, ephemerality of the sound objects, access problems, and many other disturbing factors. Wind, especially, is a constant source of trouble for the recording researcher. This is why high-level recording devices provide special windjammers. These are hairy hoods attached to the microphone lessening the sound of the wind. Anyone who seriously engages in sound recording in outside live settings will need a device like this. Echoes and reverberations are related to the topography of the space where the sound is recorded. There is no device which provides an easy cure to this except a good set of headphones plus test-driving with the recorder in 'pre-hearing mode.' This offers an opportunity to listen to the sound before it is stored on the recorder. While checking an acoustic environment in this mode, other nuisances like wind or strong foreground sounds overriding the targeted source will be heard. The recording system can then be configured accordingly. Basic digital recording is usually done on a device that can record formats (*.mp3, *.wma, *.wav, and others), which are suitable for storing and editing on the computer. Once recorded, elementary sound analysis concerned with the 'pure' aspects of sound can be applied: pitch, intensity, timbre, attack, duration, release, shape of the signal, etc., are the concepts used here (see Augoyard and Torgue, 2006: 17). The matter can become quite technical and even sophisticated for the enthusiast. But for the average researcher the standard options offered by widely available recorders from manufacturers like Olympus, Marantz, Tascam, or Sony are already demanding enough and are usually more than adequate. These recorders are also called 'pcm-recorders' or 'linear pcm recorders,' where pcm stands for pulse-code modulation. The term 'pcm' refers to a method for encoding analog audio data into a digital format. One important thing to note about the machinery involved is that the standard devices for dictation or voice recording are targeted at specific levels of the human voice. This equipment will not work for most sound studies, since important portions of the sound environment get cut out. Therefore sound recording regularly begins by reading the manuals for technical gadgets in order to get the desired recording. It makes a good deal of sense to test out the whole process of setting up the systems, defining and finding the acoustic object, recording and transferring the object to the computer, and working on it before a serious research involvement is at hand. For those who really intend to go into serious recording, Makagon and Neumann (2009: 73–81) provide a useful guide on taping, microphones, recorders, headphones, and editing software.

Besides handling hard- and software, there is another question to think about before fieldwork starts: How much and what kind of information besides the electromagnetic oscillation on the recorder is needed? There is no simple answer to that question, since even sound-only research designs can vary remarkably. But because a sound object without a context cannot make very much sense in social research, the framework for the recording and the perspective for the analysis should be defined beforehand, or at the latest during the fieldwork. Here the famous phrase 'the perceptual "something" is always in the middle of something else, it always forms a part of a "field"' by Merleau-Ponty (1962: 4) applies, and might stand as a reminder and a warning against a purely positivistic approach to collecting data. In this regard Bauer and Gaskell (2000) offer helpful concepts for analysing sounds (noise and music) as social data.

Classical soundscape research usually records whole acoustic surroundings or environments (as, for instance, the World Soundscape Project did in Vancouver: see the section on sound ecology) at selected times, and presents selected exemplars of the sound objects and soundscapes in a rather artistic way. These recordings are finally documented on a CD and/or the Web and refer to a certain body of related text. Indeed the Web might turn out to become the appropriate medium in the future for the presentation of sound studies, which operate with recorded specimens of sounds. Whereas photographic data can be displayed in printed matter, and even video data can to a certain degree be presented in a similar manner, sound and print do not coexist as well. So we need some procedures to make sound visible. There are different options available for the display of sound in such studies, where plots of intensity (or amplitude) against time, or frequency against amplitude, or time against frequency are the best known. Such displays allow a quick visual distinction between lo-fi and hi-fi environments. But, as we have learnt, humans hear differently from machines due to their capacity of selective listening. So: 'I want the reader to remain alert to the fact that all visual projections of sounds are arbitrary and fictitious' (Schafer, 1994: 127; italics in the original). In principle, sounds can be classified according to their physical quality (acoustics), the hearer's perception of their effects (sound effect), their function and meaning (semiotics and semantics), and their emotional qualities (aesthetics). Thus a soundscape cannot be understood or analysed by dividing it up into single parameters of, let us say, acoustics. Having a soundscape is like having a book compared to having just the letters of an alphabet and some rules of the grammar, to use an analogy from linguistics. Single-sound events such as, for instance, the barking of a dog, the ringing of a church bell, or the blast of a foghorn, but not complete soundscapes, might be described and analysed according to their physical and their referential aspects. The physical aspects in soundscape studies are (Schafer, 1994: 134–7): distance, intensity in decibels, distinctness of hearing (distinctly, moderate distinctly, indistinctly), texture of ambiance (hi-fi, lo-fi, natural, human, technological), occurrence (isolated, repeated, part of a larger context), and environmental factors (no reverberation, short reverberation, long reverberation, echo, drift, displacement). The referential aspects of functions and the meanings of sounds can only be organized arbitrarily according to their empirical occurrence. A model of such a catalogue is presented in the 'Tuning of the World' (Schafer, 1994: 137–9). Finally comes the mapping of whole soundscapes. For this purpose so-called 'sample sound notation systems,' the *isobel*, and the sound event map (Schafer, 1994: appendix I), have been developed. An *isobel* map shows the distribution of the acoustic intensity within a landscape along lines of equal intensity. The picture produced looks very similar to the one produced by ordinary contour lines on a geographic map but holds different information. A sound event map reproduces the sound events at a certain location over time. But even with these techniques, the fundamental problem of hearing versus seeing remains unsolved. All that visualization work can – at its best – do is to soften the fact that sounds have to be heard and cannot be seen. The fact still holds true today: there is no best way to visualize sounds and soundscapes in sound studies.

The empirical steps of an analysis in the tradition of the sonic experience as exemplified by the sound effects proposed by Augoyard and Torgue (2006) cannot be further elaborated here. The matrix of the 66 effects, disciplines, and categories of sonic effects form a three-dimensional array of remarkable complexity. This matrix is not intended as a manual or guideline, which has to be used in its entirety in each analysis. The 16 main effects described, or even a combination thereof, can be used for research in and on acoustic settings. But the variance of the internal construction of the effects and hence the corresponding empirical approach derived from them (sound and video recording, see Knoblauch et al., Chapter 30; interview, see Roulston, Chapter 20; and participant observation, see Marvasti, Chapter 24, this volume), plus their interrelatedness, make it necessary for the interested researcher to consult the list and then to consider what to register and to analyse.

If we finally leave the presentation and analysis of recorded sound and engage in participant observation, interviews, documents, and even movies or television broadcasts as data, we are approaching the level of sound practice and sound culture studies by means of ethnography. Here it is not primarily the sound itself which comes under scrutiny, but the social practices which produce or refer to sound, a soundscape, or an acoustic environment. A study worth reading in this realm is that by Panayotis Panopoulos (2003). He analyses the meanings and functions of animal bells with regard to gender, families, reputations, and economy in a pastoral culture. Although some romanticism of the kind of *à la recherche du temps perdu* in the study cannot be ignored, the text demonstrates in an exemplary and stunning way how sound, artifacts, and culture are interwoven phenomena.[6] One of the few sociological contributions using ethnography with a focus on sound is Daniel Lee's study on barbershop quartet singing (2005). He deals with the important question of the distinction between noise and music, and he shows how vocal noise can be turned into music in a complex way and only in a particular culturally embedded context. But sound practice can become even more complex than singing, which is already not simple. If we take the technosphere as a medium for sound production and reproduction, as Steve Wurtzler (1992) does in his study '"She sang live, but the microphone was turned off": The live, the recorded and the subject of representation,' we become aware of how intertwined culture and sound and the corresponding analysis can become. This brings us to the dark side of sounds, where sonic warfare (Goodman, 2010) is addressed. Sound can also be deployed to produce fear and dread. The sonic dimensions of conflict are old, and the militarization of sound has a long history from antiquity up to the torture of prisoners in Guantanamo Bay by very loud rock music. So it does not come as a surprise that sonic force and sonic power can be topics for sound research too. And finally we should not overlook the fact that when we turn our computers on we receive a sound logo. This is not only a functional sound, providing information on the status of the technical system, but also, as a logo, a symbolic part of our economies. So it is no longer a surprise that the German car maker Audi tunes not only the sound of the engine–which many other car makers do too – but also the sound of the doors and even the whole company by the use of a concept of sound as its own *Klangsprache* (= language of sounds).[7]

CONCLUDING REMARKS

Sound studies challenge qualitative research in different ways. First, the ear as an important human sense has largely been ignored in comparison to the eye. There has not yet been an effort to conceptualize an analytic apparatus comparable to that for vision (e.g., Knoblauch and Schnettler, 2009; also see Knoblauch et al., Chapter 30, this volume). Hence the field of sound studies remains rather exotic and unfamiliar to the qualitative researcher. Second, qualitative research has also largely ignored any theoretical study of the acoustic environment except speech or music. Thus it remains unclear if there will ever be qualitative research that takes the sonic environment into consideration and transcends the language-focused and visual-oriented mainstream of current qualitative social research. However, the sound culture studies might have opened a promising route: they showed how the tunes of the world are analytically transformed into the sounds in and of society.

NOTES

1. The publisher Ashgate devotes a special edition to the topic of ethnomusicology. See: www.ashgate.com/music (accessed 15 May 2013).
2. An informative description of the project and even some audio samples are available at the website: http://www.sfu.ca/~truax/wsp.html (accessed 15 May 2013).
3. See the website of the World Forum for Acoustic Ecology: http://wfae.proscenia.net/about/index.html (accessed 15 May 2013).
4. The concept of the soundscape appears to be very attractive, but it is also contested and often misunderstood (Kelman, 2010).
5. One of the reviewers of this text remarked, 'if you think loud car sound systems are limited to the inside of the car, you don't live in a big urban city, with "Boombox" culture!' This is certainly true, and I do not want to overstretch my argument. But the sound of 'Boomboxes' obviously exactly constitutes a particular urban space for those involved.
6. An inspiring impression of how anthropology approaches sounds was actually the program for a conference on 'Milieux Sonores (MILSON)' held in Paris in 2011. The link is: http://milson.fr/je2011/ (accessed 15 May 2013).
7. See https://www.audi-mediaservices.com/publish/ms/content/de/public/pressemitteilungen/2010/08/23/sound_satt__wie_klingt.standard.gid-oeffentlichkeit.html (accessed 15 May 2013).

FURTHER READING

Augoyard, Jean-Francois and Torgue, Henry (eds.) (2006) *Sonic Experience: A Guide to Everyday Sounds*. Montreal: McGill-Queen's University Press.
LaBelle, Brandon (2010) *Acoustic Territories: Sound Culture and Everyday Life*. London: Continuum.
Schafer, Murray R. (1994) *Soundscape: Our Sonic Environment and the Tuning of the World*. Rochester, VT: Destiny Books.

REFERENCES

Altman, Rick (ed.) (1992) *Sound Theory / Sound Practice*. New York: Routledge.
Attali, Jacques (1985) *Noise: Political Economy of Music*. Minneapolis: University of Minnesota Press.
Augoyard, Jean-Francois and Torgue, Henry (eds.) (2006) *Sonic Experience: A Guide to Everyday Sounds*. Montreal: McGill-Queen's University Press.
Bauer, Martin W. and Gaskell, George D. (eds.) (2000) *Qualitative Researching with Text, Image and Sound: A Practical Handbook for Social Research*. London: Sage.
Blesser, Barry and Salter, Linda-Ruth (2007) *Spaces Speak, Are You Listening? Experiencing Aural Architecture*. Cambridge, MA: The MIT Press.
Bull, Michael (2003) 'Soundscapes of the car. A critical study of automobile habitation,' in Michael Bull and Les Back (eds.), *The Auditory Culture Reader*. Oxford: Berg. pp. 357–74.
Bull, Michael (2007) *Sound Moves: IPod Culture and Urban Experience*. London: Routledge.
Bull, Michael and Back, Les (eds.) (2003) *The Auditory Culture Reader*. Oxford: Berg.
Cox, Christoph and Warner, Daniel (eds.) (2004) *Audio Culture: Readings in Modern Music*. New York: Continuum.
Garfinkel, Harold (1967) *Studies in Ethnomethodology*. Englewood Cliffs, NJ: Prentice Hall.
Goffman, Erving (2010) *Relations in Public: Microstudies of the Public Order*. New Brunswick, NJ: Transaction.
Goodman, Steve (2010) *Sonic Warfare: Sound, Affect, and the Ecology of Fear*. Cambridge, MA: The MIT Press.
Hammou, Karim (2011) *Pour une anthropologie des milieux sonores (Journées d'études MILSON)* ('For an anthropology of acoustic environments' (MILSON Conference)), Paris.
Hedfors, Per (2008) *Site Soundscapes: Landscape Architecture in the Light of Sound: Sonotope Design Strategies*. Saarbrücken: VDM Verlag.

Hijleh, Mark (2012) *Towards a Global Music Theory*. Farnham: Ashgate.

Hilmes, Michele (2005) 'Is there a field called sound culture studies? And does it matter?', *American Quarterly*, 57 (1): 249–59.

Ihde, Don (2007) *Listening and Voice: Phenomenologies of Sound*. New York: State University of New York Press.

Keating, Elizabeth (2001) 'The ethnography of communication,' in Paul Atkinson et al. (eds.), *Handbook of Ethnography*. London: Sage. pp. 285–301.

Kelman, Ari Y. (2010) 'Rethinking the soundscape: A critical genealogy of a key term in sound studies,' *The Senses and Society*, 5 (2):212–34.

Knoblauch, Hubert and Schnettler, Bernt (2009) *Video Analysis Methodology and Methods: Qualitative Audiovisual Data Analysis in Sociology*. Berlin: Peter Lang.

LaBelle, Brandon (2006) *Background Noise: Perspectives on Sound Art*. New York: Continuum.

LaBelle, Brandon (2010) *Acoustic Territories: Sound Culture and Everyday Life*. London: Continuum.

Lan Hing Ting, Karine and Pentimalli, Barbara (2009) 'Le "bruit" comme ressource pour la coopération et la coordination entre téléopérateurs dans les les centres d'appels,' *ethnographiques.org*. (9) 19: www.ethnographiques.org.

Lee, Daniel B. (2005) 'Making music out of noise: Barbershop quartet singing and society,' *Soziale Systeme*, 11 (2): 271–93.

Makagon, Daniel and Neumann, Mark (2009) 'Recording culture,' *Audio Documentary and the Ethnographic Experience*. Los Angeles: Sage.

McLucas, Anne Dhu (2011) *The Musical Ear: Oral Tradition in the USA*. Farnham: Ashgate.

Merleau-Ponty, Maurice (1962) *Phenomenology of Perception*. London: Routledge & Kegan Paul.

Panopoulos, Panayotis (2003) 'Bells as symbols: Sound and hearing in a Greek island village,' *The Journal of the Royal Anthropological Institute*, 9 (4): 639–56.

Schaeffer, Pierre (1982) 'L'oreille primitive,' *L'oreille oubliée*. Paris: Centre Pompidou.

Schafer, Murray R. (1994) *Soundscape: Our Sonic Environment and the Tuning of the World*. Rochester, VT: Destiny Books.

Schulze, Holger (ed.) (2008) *Sound Studies: Traditionen–Methoden–Desiderate: Eine Einführung*. Bielefeld: Transcript.

Silverman, David (1998) *Harvey Sacks – Social Science & Conversational Analysis*. Oxford: Oxford University Press.

Sterne, Jonathan (2003) *The Audible Past: Cultural Origins of Sound Reproduction*. Durham, NC: Duke University Press.

Szendy, Peter (2008) *Listen: A History of Our Ears*. New York: Fordham University Press.

Truax, Barry (2001) *Acoustic Communication*, 2nd edition. Westport, CT: Ablex.

Vannini, Phillip, Waskul, Dennis, Gotschalk, Simon, and Rambo, Carol (2010) 'Sound acts: Elocution, somatic work, and the performance of the sonic alignment,' *Journal of Contemporary Ethnography*, 39 (3): 328–53.

Wrightson, Kendall (2000) 'An introduction to acoustic ecology,' *The Journal of Acoustic Ecology*, 1 (1): 10–13.

Wurtzler, Steve (1992) '"She sang live, but the microphone was turned off": The live, the recorded and the subject of representation,' in Rick Altman (ed.), *Sound Theory/Sound Practice*. New York: Routledge. pp. 87–103.

30

Video Analysis and Videography

Hubert Knoblauch, René Tuma and
Bernt Schnettler

THE OMNIPRESENCE OF VIDEO IN EVERYDAY LIFE AND ITS APPLICATION TO QUALITATIVE RESEARCH

One of the major cultural changes with long-lasting effects on our way of life that can be witnessed in recent years is, indisputably, the *massive visualization* of our culture. Still and moving images are literally pervading our everyday and our professional life worlds; they are increasingly employed to operate in much of our communicative exchange and our knowledge production. They have invaded educational processes, and are even reshaping our self-representation. While visual studies have been focusing mainly on the role of 'images' (see Banks, Chapter 27, this volume) the cultural dynamics of video are still widely neglected. Video is a technology that allows the recording, storage and repeated viewing of visual and acoustic data. Developed on the basis of previous recording technologies including film (see Mikos, Chapter 28, this volume) and

audiotapes, it was particularly the combination of recording and replaying, as provided by the camcorder, and its *digitalization*, that opened up video technologies to a broad range of applications. Starting as a medium for 'time shifting' television (Zielinski, 2010 [1986]), the video has been combined with CCTV cameras for surveillance, and it has been introduced into teaching, occupational training and several other contexts, creating new fields of art, entertainment (Greenberg, 2008) and political communication.

Aside from its use in various professional fields, such as medicine, the arts or policing, video has been used in the social sciences for quite some time. In various disciplines, including sociology, anthropology, education and sports studies, various approaches to 'video analysis' have cropped up. Several methods for analysing video have been developed recently, some of which include the analysis of moving images from fields such as entertainment, television or arts.

In order to understand the concept of video analysis presented here, two types of methodological approaches have to be distinguished: 'standardized' versus 'interpretive' video analysis. *Standardized* video analysis is common in many research areas. In numerous fields, we find a strong tendency to sort, even automatize, data analysis (Mittenecker, 1987; Koch and Zumbach, 2002). In these approaches, the analytical procedure consists of the *coding* of video segments according to a pre-established coding scheme deduced from (more or less explicit) theoretical assumptions (see Schreier, Chapter 12, this volume). As a consequence, stretches of video-recorded interactions that vary in length from tens of seconds to several minutes are subsumed under prefixed categories, for example as 'supportive' or 'non-supportive', aggressive' or 'non-aggressive behaviour' or by counting speaker turns (Seidel, 2005). Often, the reasons for subsuming fragments of videos under theoretical codes are not explicated, so the process of data *interpretation* (see Willig, Chapter 10, this volume) remains implicit. Instead, the code may be habitualized and validated by tests on 'inter-coder reliability'; in recent years it has even been automatized by means of computer-supported analyses (Silver and Patashnick, 2011). Already by 2002 more than 40 computer programs (such as MotionPro or SimiMotion) for standardized analysis were available – most of them based on predefined categories (cf. Koch and Zumbach, 2002). Standardized methods are not restricted to experimental and quantitative studies of audiovisual conduct, as for example in social or educational psychology or in research on small-group interaction. They can be found also in approaches that claim to proceed according to a qualitative methodology, as in some of the works cited above.

In sharp contrast, *interpretive* video analysis follows a different methodological premise: it assumes that the actions recorded are guided by meanings that must be understood by the actors themselves. It is only on the basis of the meanings of actions to the actors involved, that is, 'first order constructs', that researchers pursue their questions and create their 'second order constructs' (Schutz, 1962; also see Eberle, Chapter 13, and Bohnsack, Chapter 15, this volume). The methodology suggested here accounts for both the process of understanding and the ways in which researchers arrive at their constructs.

Consequently, the methodology referred to here as 'video analysis' is not a general, but a rather specific method, not suited for every type of video recording. Video technology can surely be used for taping every audiovisual phenomenon. Our particular approach to video analysis, however, refers primarily to video recordings of *social interactions*. Social interaction involves any action performed by someone who is motivated by, oriented to and coordinated with others, irrespective of whether these 'others' are other participants, animals, artefacts, or whatever. This notion of 'social interaction', thus circumscribes a broad range of different forms of interaction, of which human interaction with humans is only one – although perhaps the most important – type. It also includes human interaction with machines, animals and objects, technically mediated interactions, interaction with oneself and even interactions with invisible actors, for example spirits or gods or other 'supernatural' entities, insofar as they are addressed by human actors and if they become observable in ritual interaction.

SORTS OF VIDEO DATA AND TYPES OF VIDEO ANALYSIS

Given the enormous variety of videos, the way in which they are analysed does not depend exclusively on the methodology applied to the footage. It is determined even more by the conditions of production – the practices by which videos are being recorded, made accessible and handled by the researchers. We should stress that, in any case, video results from certain activities and interventions carried out by the researchers, so the recordings cannot be considered as mere 'material' in the sense of a 'natural discovery'. Video recordings have to be considered as 'data', because the researchers actively construct them. More precisely, it should be recognized that different kinds of research activities lead to different types of data, to which we refer as 'data sorts'. With regard to video, data sorts can be distinguished along the following lines (Knoblauch et al., 2006a: 13ff.):

(1) 'Native' video data: There is one form of video analysis that draws on videos which have been recorded – and produced in a more or less professional way – by actors other than researchers, for example private tapes made available to the researchers, video clips uploaded on YouTube or 'video diaries' triggered by the researchers (Pink, 2007). A huge variety of this kind of 'native' video exists. From the very beginning of popular video technology and the invention of the camcorder, there have been two major ways of dealing with this type of material for research purposes. Both are related to the two different functions that camcorders combine: the apparatus provides (a) an audiovisual *recording* technology for events taking place in the common environment of actors; and it also offers a device for (b) *viewing* these recordings. Accordingly, some researchers use video produced by actors, in some cases by invitation to produce video for research purposes and in other cases drawn from a more or less publicly available collection from DVDs, television or the Internet. A number of approaches refer to this kind of 'media data' as video analysis (Raab, 2008; Bohnsack, 2009; Reichertz and Englert, 2010).

(2) Video data induced by researchers: By contrast, there are videos which are recorded by the scientists themselves during the research process. Here, we are concerned with these latter sorts of data. Among the category of researcher-induced video data, there are two main types: 'experimental' and 'natural' video documents. (a) On the one hand, videos record *situations created by researchers*. For example, video data produced in an experiment in which standardized interviews were documented by four cameras installed in a linguistic laboratory setting (Luckmann, 2006). (b) On the other hand and opposed to settings created by the researchers, video analysis of the kind we will concentrate on focuses on settings as they are created by the actors under study. These are referred to as *natural settings* in the sense of 'naturally occurring' social situations, whose existence does not depend on a purposeful research design. We may add that this does not exclude the study of experiments, if experiments themselves are the subject matter (and not the method), as in some recent studies conducted in the field of social science and technology studies. The notion of 'natural setting' does not imply naive naturalism. It gives credit to the researchers' attempt to record situations, which are neither triggered nor created by them but by the subjects under study. This approach is guided by a methodological principle that takes us as near as possible to the situations of social interactions as the very subject matter of social sciences. The analysis of video recorded by the researchers themselves, in the field, is referred to here as 'videography': that is, when video is used as an instrument for collecting and analysing social interaction in natural settings.

In general terms, *reactivity* is a serious methodological problem. It is a particular challenge for any social research interested in the natural situation. While some situations of interactions are hardly affected by recordings, in others the camera may, to a greater or lesser extent, modify the situation under scrutiny. Consequently, the interfering effects of researchers and their technology in natural situations are, indeed, serious methodological issues for video analytical studies (Lomax and Casey, 1998; cf. Laurier and Philo, 2006). More precisely, audiovisual recording and analysis of 'natural' social interactions require the researchers to go 'where the action' is. Researchers conducting this type of video analysis regularly enter particular fields in ways that resemble ethnography (see Gubrium and Holstein, Chapter 3, this volume). Therefore, interpretive video analysis of the natural situation is embedded in a specific variant of field research called 'focused ethnography' (Knoblauch, 2005). Therefore, we will refine our notion of video analysis by referring to it more specifically as *videography*, in order to stress the relevance of its ethnographic contextualization. This denomination prevents confusion with quantitative, standardized and experimental forms of video analysis.

Recording 'natural' data, however, does not imply that the video records of social interactions are simply 'registering conservations', as Bergmann (1985) suggests with respect to audio recordings. Rather than being mere material outcomes, these video recordings as data are co-produced by the researchers as human actors. The product, however, depends greatly on the employed technology's specific qualities and thus entails 'technological co-constructive elements'. The camera contributes to data construction by transforming a certain 'picture detail' of auditory and visual processes into a two-dimensional recording with stereo sound. Recently, 3D video and surround sound have become technically available and might bring some additional advantages in future video recording technologies.

The machine, although providing a technological framework, does not operate on its own. Given the virtues of video recording technology, to which we will turn below, researchers intentionally select a certain field, a focus within the field and a certain kind of camera action. There are many things researchers have to consider in producing recordings, from gaining access to choosing the right camera position and angle. Typically, camera action focuses on the participants in social interactions, including everybody visibly and audibly 'aware' of and attentive to an ongoing interaction. In videography, the camera may be following the subjective eye of the researcher (Mohn, 2006); it may try to track the course of an ongoing action or centre on the dominant actors (Schubert, 2006); or, in cases of spatially stable settings, it takes the role of a fixed observer seemingly only 'registering' the course of the social interaction. Like multi-sited ethnography (Marcus, 1995), videography can also record interaction across different spaces, for example the coordination of action between an airport tower with other activities going on in ground operations elsewhere in the airport, as described in the 'workplace project' (Goodwin and Goodwin, 1996). Videography is characterized by the fact that the researchers themselves are recording the video 'in the field' and then using these audiovisual tapes for their analyses. Thereby, researchers can account, explicitly and methodically, for the ways and processes of data production and its circumstances.

HISTORY OF INTERPRETIVE VIDEO ANALYSIS OF SOCIAL INTERACTION

The analysis of social interaction with audio-visual data in natural settings has a substantial tradition. Although much of the history of 'visual sociology' focuses on photography, film was used very early on for the analysis of human conduct. Famous examples are A.C. Haddon, Baldwin Spencer or Robert Flaherty, who since the turn of the twentieth century used film to analyse human conduct. Obviously, footage is highly useful, because it opened up new possibilities for analysing human conduct. Anthropology produced an unprecedented collection of film data, although it was mainly employed to document particular social worlds, rather than analyse them. In the 1930s, Arnold Gesell (1935) published a book on 'cinema analysis' as a 'method for behaviour study' in which he used frame-by-frame analysis. Some years later, Gregory Bateson and Margaret Mead (1942) conducted their famous visual analysis of Balinese dance. Later Bateson and the so-called 'Palo Alto group' used film to study interaction between family members. The team also initiated the famous project on the 'History of the interview', in which the various modes of interaction were captured for the very first time (Bateson, 1958). Footage was used to focus on non-verbal behaviour (Ekman and Friesen, 1969) resulting in a series of studies conducted by films that tried to capture behaviour in a more encompassing and meaningful way. Birdwhistell (1952) analysed the interplay between non-verbal and verbal behaviour in minute detail, coining the notion of 'kinesics'. Scheflen (1965) analysed the role of posture for the structuring of psychotherapeutic encounters.

While these analyses were performed on the basis of film, the situation changed substantially with the introduction, miniaturization and technical sophistication of video recording technology. As early as the late 1970s, Luckmann and Gross (1977) started a project which used video to develop a multimodal annotation system for interactions modelled on a musical score. Since the 1970s, video analysis based on the sociological approaches of ethnomethodology (see Eberle, Chapter 13, this volume) and conversation analysis (see Toerien, Chapter 22, this volume) became more common. As conversation analysis had been supported by the invention of the portable audio recorder, the introduction of the camcorder helped to extend that. Thus, Goodwin (1981) analysed verbal interaction to show how visual aspects, particularly gaze, help to bestow order. Erickson and Shultz (1982) employed video for the studies of four school counsellors in their interview interaction with pupils. Heath has undertaken video studies since the 1970s, targeting complex social situations, namely medical encounters (Heath, 1986).

Methodological reflection began in the 1980s (Erickson, 1982; Heath, 1997; Lomax and Casey, 1998) and is now documented in the first edited volumes (Knoblauch et al., 2006b; Kissmann, 2009) and the first introductory book in English (Heath et al., 2010), along with collections for particular fields of application like the learning sciences (Goldman et al., 2007).

ANALYSING AUDIOVISUAL DATA OF SOCIAL INTERACTION

As a methodological approach in qualitative research, videography is especially useful for studying communication and interaction in its contexts. Video provides a distinctive form of data with particular qualities for research in the social sciences. No other recording technology is able to allow for such a richness of detail on aspects and 'modalities' of communication which become available for inspection retrospectively. In addition to language and speech, gesture and facial expression as well as body movements, the spatial relation of bodies and objects, and their movements, are accessible for scrutiny. There are various ways of approaching these aspects. Whereas within linguistics and gesture studies researchers tend to divide these aspects into different modalities, videographers typically go for a more holistic approach and use video recordings as a device to study social interaction (Mondada, 2007) and to conceive ongoing interactive coordination of communicative modalities and objects in space and time as 'orchestration' (Schnettler, 2006). The reconstruction of its core elements and their particular interplay is one of the most important aims of interpretive video analysis.

Compared with other forms of participatory observation, video recordings are characterized by two features already highlighted by Grimshaw: 'The two principal advantages of SIR [Sound-Image Data Records] are Density and Permanence. Other records may have one or the other of these attributes; no other has both' (1982: 122). Density refers to the complex quality of video technology data to register observations in a social situation. Density means that minute aspects (the perceptual features of certain things, the exact course of certain events), which might have passed unnoticed by the actors or the observer in the situation, become accessible in the recorded data. Density, of course, only holds for those audiovisual aspects focused on in the situation. They are represented in a perspective co-constructed by the camera. Similar to photography and despite their constructed character, audiovisual representations carry a mimetic character, which can be understood as 'representing' aspects of a situation. Density can be exploited by freezing images and by enlarging or highlighting certain parts of single audiovisual frames or sequences – a feature that has been substantially simplified with the digitalization of video.

Concerning its permanence, a recording 'turns motion into data'. Video is, like film, a *temporal* medium – a medium that records in stretches of time. As a result, video recordings preserve the structural temporal ordering of the ongoing activity. Thus, the processual character of social interactions becomes accessible for scrutiny. This is the most important advantage of video compared with photography. Permanence is accounted for by the very possibility of replaying the video as often as desired. In fact, the advantage of video recordings over film is the ease with which video can be repeated and thence evidence can be reproduced with the data. Expressed in standardized methodological diction, this feature would be referred to as 'validity'. Without adopting this terminology, it is obvious that reproducibility is one of these data's major benefits for social research.

Moreover, the temporality of audiovisual data is exploited by the use of slow or fast motion, that is the technical manipulation of the temporality of what has been recorded. Thus, in their famous studies on emotions, Ekman and Friesen (1969) used slow motion in order to identify different facial expression. Similarly, in another early video study of social interaction, Goodwin (1986) applied slow motion to analyse the coordination of gaze and speech. Slow motion and replay are also employed for audio data, particularly in the production of transcripts. In this regard, video can be called a *social microscope* able to examine the minutiae of ongoing social interaction and the ways in which they contribute to the social construction of reality.

In addition to the temporal order and the form of movement, video also conserves those features of situational arrangements that remain permanent throughout the course of interaction. Static artefacts, equipment, accessories, spatial organization, colour, texture and the atmosphere of the immediate environment in which the interaction is taking place are depicted, at least partly conserved in two-dimensional representations and thus can later be reconstructed from the video, including its symbolic meaning.

However, modalities such as smell, temperature and the 'emotional atmosphere' cannot be captured with video, although they may be decisive for understanding the situation under scrutiny. One should be aware that video is, on the one hand, reductive with respect to the numerous aspects, perspectives and modalities of social situations, and, on the other hand, constructive in that it provides a specific frame, perspective and audiovisual format.

Both essential qualities of video as data sorts – its density and its temporality in permanence – are accounted for in video analysis methodology. Below, we will turn to its temporal feature that is addressed by the notion of *sequentiality*. Put succinctly, sequentiality is the major resource for interpreting social interaction with respect to its temporality as represented on the audiovisual records. Therefore, sequential analysis is the main methodological procedure applied to videos of social interaction.

SEQUENTIAL ANALYSIS

Sequential analysis (see Wernet, Chapter 16, and Toerien, Chapter 22, this volume) is directly linked to the technical potential of video technology and the practices related to it. The fact that recordings of social interactions can be repeated and recurrently observed (in stills, slow or fast motion) parallels an essential feature of action and interaction as stressed by some major theories of social action. Action is, as Schutz (1962) and Mead (1938) pointed out, essentially a temporal structure – and interaction depends basically on the coordination of actions. The video data's temporal structure helps to access this temporality. Irrespective of whatever the camera may construct, there are few doubts that it helps to preserve the temporal order of the recorded actions and interactions, that is its sequentiality. While the tempo of the recording may be changing, the sequence of the course of action is maintained. It is this temporal order of the course of action we refer to as 'sequentiality'. This notion of sequentiality, however, is not restricted to the analysis of audiovisual data. It has already been suggested in the analysis of audio data from 'natural' conversations, particularly by conversation analysis (Sacks, 1972; Sacks et al., 1974; Have,

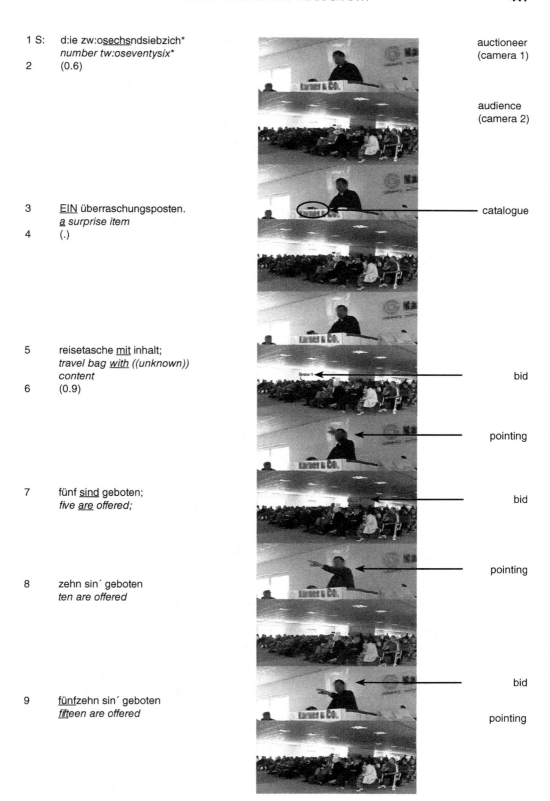

Figure 30.1 Audio-visual moves in auctioneer-audience interaction

1999; also see Toerien, Chapter 22, this volume). Sequentiality may be best understood by a classical empirical example in which Schegloff (1968) studied openings of telephone calls to a 'disaster centre'. After his first examination of the acoustic data, Schegloff had assumed that there must be a 'distribution rule of first utterances', that is the answerer speaks first. Then, however, he was confronted with the following deviant case to this rule:

#9 (Police makes call)

Receiver is lifted, and there is a one second pause

Police: Hello

Other: American Red Cross

Police: Hello, this is Police Headquarters ... er, Officer Stratton

This example seems to disconfirm Schegloff's rule, because of the one-second pause after the call has been dispatched. The one called does not talk first. Instead, the caller starts with 'hello'. However, the fact that the caller is talking first is not really a violation of that rule. Rather, the pause left by the person called is taken as a kind of answer to which the 'hello' in the second turn replies. And this 'hello' not only is a greeting, but also accounts for the lack of response. To be more correct, it can be seen as motivated by the phone ringing, which 'acts' like a summons and turns the 'hello' as an answer into a second turn. The general insight from this example is that actions are rendered meaningful in the context of other actions, and that this context is constituted by the sequence of this action. Sequentiality is based on the temporality of action and interaction. Conversely it is this temporal order of action that constitutes a decisive resource by which actions are rendered meaningful. Thus, sequentiality is a crucial device for sense-making in a double sense: first, it allows the actors themselves to show their own understanding of the ongoing course of interaction; and, second, it also enables observers to make inferences as to what exactly these actors are doing.

Sequentiality is linked to a further methodological principle derived from ethnomethodology: *reflexivity*. Reflexivity (see May and Perry, Chapter 8, this volume) refers to the assumption that actors not only act, but (in the way they are acting and coordinating with others temporally) 'indicate', 'frame' or 'contextualize' what they do while they are acting. When asking a question, for example, actors not only perform an action – by the way they act and its temporal order – but also show if and how the given answer could be read as an answer to the question.

The combination of sequentiality and reflexivity facilitates the validation of interpretations. Following Schegloff (1992), it is the sequential embedding in prior and later turns that can be considered as a decisive reason for the relevance of the next turn. Because of its reflexivity, each next turn entails the actor's interpretation of prior turns in the light of the subsequent one. Sequential analysis always follows a prospective order, so that turns are only interpreted before focusing on the next turn. Based on this 'rule of prospective analysis', the interpretation of a negation as a contradiction, for example, can be validated or falsified in the next, third move – if it does not contain an argumentative extension or the continuation of a contradiction (Knoblauch, 1991).

Sequential analysis has proven its methodological power in the analysis of audio-recorded conversation. If we raise the question of how it applies to other data different to verbal interaction, Schegloff's example cited above provides a valuable hint, for one 'turn' in the sequence he analysed is not actually constituted by a 'speech act'. It is not even direct human action but rather a technologically mediated action – the phone ringing. Thus, the 'unit' to be considered can be a non-linguistic event if it triggers another action, such as a bodily move or a sound. That telephone rings fulfil this function of a 'turn' is not surprising since acoustically coordinated action depends on the temporal ordering of sound. How do we address visual turns or 'moves'?[1] In order to illustrate how moves can be analysed sequentially, it may be useful to look at an example from our own research.[2] The video fragment in Figure 30.1 is taken from an auction at a point where the auctioneer is offering a new item to the audience. Because he does not say what it contains, he describes it as a 'surprise'. He starts by identifying its number in the catalogue.

Steven, the auctioneer, starts (lines 1–2) with a number that, for the moment, seems to be opaque, and also his description of a 'surprise' object (line 3) remains unintelligible if we look at the text only. By turning our attention to his visual conduct, we can see that he is looking at the desk (line 2). Our ethnographic knowledge of the situation tells us that there is one common document available in the auction – the catalogue – including all objects on offer. Therefore, actors and observers may infer that he is reading the catalogue. In fact, we can identify a number of actors in the audience looking at their copy of the document resting on their knees. In this case, the visual conduct not only accompanies turn-taking (line 1), but rather allows us to specify what the speaker refers to while speaking – a specification that is made visible by his glance and the pause (line 2). The verbal interaction consists of a dual unit separated by a short pause (lines 3–5). The first part is pronounced upwards, announcing the 'surprise', whereas the second part prosodically falls down so as to finish the turn and open the floor for the next turn. This is called a 'transition relevance place' (Sacks et al., 1974). As opposed to the analysis of audiotapes only, we need not depend only on prosodical knowledge of how the speaker raises his voice, for the interpretation is supported sequentially: the speaker (while pronouncing 'a surprise item') raises his head and looks at the audience. What appears as a pause in the verbal transcript is a move if we look at the video: immediately after the transition point a number of people in the audience raise their hands. As with the telephone ringing, the raising of the head can be understood as the speaker opening the floor for the audience. The 'reaction' of the audience, on the other hand, can be considered as a reflexive interpretation of the action by the speaker.

As indicated above, there is a way of validating this interpretation. In the next move, the speaker points with his arm towards certain actors in the audience who are raising their hands. In this move he 'interprets' their action by identifying it with a number: 'Five are offered' is the response that takes raising the hand as the performance of a bid, literally meaning 'I want to buy this item and I offer 5 euros'. We do not want to delve into more intricate questions, such as how prices are set and negotiated in such settings (Heath and Luff, 2007). Rather, we should note that the turn following the speaker's initiation is purely a visual turn or 'move' (looking up, raising the hand), and that it is produced as such by the next move of the speaker identifying it as a bid verbally and hinting in a certain direction.

The visuality of this move is underlined if we acknowledge that none of these sequences could have been detected from an analysis of the verbal interaction. Only careful study of the video allows the researcher to identify the sequential unfolding of the interaction and the moves that constitute it. One may argue that understanding audiovisually recorded sequences could be accomplished without the transcript, but experience proves that the written transcript is a very helpful tool for identifying the sequence of audiovisual action. If there are no verbal utterances, other temporal actions – such as gazing – relevant for interpretation may need to be transcribed into more detail. As Goodwin puts it:

> Rather than wandering onto field sites as disinterested observers, attempting the impossible task of trying to catalogue everything in the setting, we can use the visible orientation of the participants as a spotlight to show us just those features of context that we have to come to terms with if we are to adequately describe the organization of their action. (2000a: 1508f.)

It will be necessary to answer detailed questions like: Do actors look at the screen before they push a button? Does a phone ring before person A walks away? Does person B point at the slide after she said X or when she says Y?

THE DENSE VISUAL CONTEXT, ETHNOGRAPHIC KNOWLEDGE AND SAMPLING STRATEGIES

The outstanding quality of video data is their capacity to record ongoing, sequential processes. However, video data are 'dense' in a further sense. They also capture those aspects of the situation that remain unchanged over time. Thus, video recordings also represent *permanent* visual elements, including material objects and artefacts, bodily configurations and built spaces, furniture, walls, buildings, instruments, clothes, spectacles or hairstyle. These elements constitute the aforementioned 'density' of audiovisual records. How do we deal with these non-sequential aspects in video analysis?

There are different systematic approaches to address these enduring situational elements. One way has been suggested by Goodwin (2000b). He assumes that *semiotics* may be able to grasp these visual features. The elements are, then, taken as representing visual signs. On the basis of semiotics it is assumed that these signs form part of more encompassing sign systems from which the meaning of these signs can be derived (Kress, 2010). Thus, talk appears to be embedded in multiple sign systems, such as graphic codes, gestures and other features of the environment.

Another approach to the interpretation of these visually permanent elements is offered by *hermeneutics* (see Wernet, Chapter 16, this volume). Thus Soeffner (1996) suggests analysing videos decomposed in stills. On the basis of these 'frozen' visual representations, a group of culturally competent hermeneuticians produce various readings that are tested against the background of selected next stills. Step by step, certain readings of the situation represented visually or audiovisually are excluded so that the remaining reading is considered as validated.

While hermeneutics draws on general cultural knowledge, our way of handling the density of audiovisual data and permanent elements is *ethnography* (see Gubrium and Holstein, Chapter 3, this volume). As stated above, the collection of video data demands a certain degree of ethnographic fieldwork. On the background of general cultural knowledge which, if not present, needs to be acquired by conventional long-term ethnography, the videographer has to become familiar with the situation to such a degree as to be able to determine a relevant focus for recording the video. In addition, videographers are required to gain knowledge about the contextual elements that are represented on the video or even escape the focus of the video camera, yet are indispensable to understand what is going on. Thus, knowledge of the workings of instruments used, of the categories of actors, of the structure of space within the camera's focus or outside it, as well as of the events leading to the recording, is required in order to be able to later interpret and analyse audiovisual recordings. In some cases, this knowledge can be retrieved before or while recording; it can also be gained by subsequent processes, such as video elicitation, auto-confrontation, autoethnography (by the videographer) or video-based interviewing of the participants. In videography the analysis of permanent elements of the audiovisual recordings are not to be understood as visual analysis in the proper sense but, rather, as forms of protocols of the social interaction recorded and analysed. Depending on the kind of social interaction, understanding can draw on general everyday knowledge, yet regularly it demands more specific knowledge about the type of situation, the kind of actors and the context.

On these grounds, ethnographic data collection and sequential analysis are tightly intertwined in a way resembling the pattern described by Silverman (2007) as 'mapping the woods' and 'chopping up the trees'. While

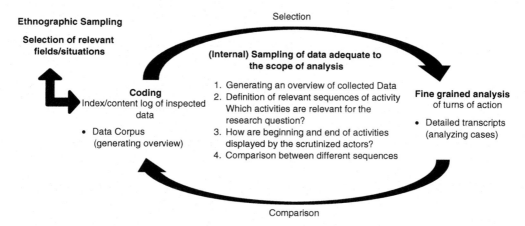

Figure 30.2 Process of analysis (from Knoblauch and Tuma, 2011)

'chopping up the trees' is represented by the fine-grained sequential analysis, 'mapping the woods' consists of the ethnographic fieldwork. This 'ethnographic sampling strategy' (see Rapley, Chapter 4, this volume) includes the selection of situations to be recorded as well as the selection of what is being recorded within these situations. Relevant situations are chosen due to their relevance in the field and to the theoretical research question and, of course, the selection of the recorded situation is based on characteristics of its typicality and relevance, and contrasted or compared with other situations. This selection already entails important assumptions that have consequences for the theoretical conclusions. Therefore, in order to determine a focus, selection of the empirical field is as important as the theoretical context.

Ethnographic sampling starts with questions of access to social situations, including legal and moral issues (Heath et al., 2010: 14ff.). As soon as access to a certain setting and situation is achieved, one has to decide on what exactly to record and potentially make subject to the time-consuming fine-grained analysis. Selection criteria, again, depend on the scientific question and on prior ethnographic observations in the field. For example, in studying work in an operating theatre, one may want to focus on the ways in which actors handle instruments with their hands and bodies, or one may want to focus on the use of space in the theatre. Then, work in similar theatres or in different settings may be compared with others that are selected by the ethnographic strategy. As mentioned above, seemingly simply technical selections such as the position of the camera or the microphones are as relevant to this selection as are theoretical considerations of what is relevant in the field and to the researcher. As Figure 30.2 shows, ethnographic sampling, and the sampling of video data for analysis, are iterative processes.

In a first step, the data recorded will be coded in a (digital) content logbook. A content log contains the temporal sequence of events, a rough transcription of activities, gestures and talk, reflections and coding of sequences according to the research topic. According to grounded theory (Glaser and Strauss, 1968), codes are developed within the course of the study (see Thornberg and Charmaz, Chapter 11, this volume), and 'emerge' from the material. As part of the internal sampling, coding consists of identifying fragments that can be subjected to a fine-grained sequential analysis. It is certainly useful to make exact transcripts of these fragments, at least with respect to the verbal modalities. We recommend that researchers should do the transcription on their own in order to attain familiarity with the data. There are a large number of more or less sophisticated transcription systems available, some of which are useful for transcribing video data (Heath et al., 2010: 70ff). The GAT-System (Selting et al., 2009) has proven to be a valuable reference (see Kowal and O'Connell, Chapter 5, this volume).

As Figure 30.2 illustrates, data collection, selection of fragments and sequential analysis are not consecutive phases of research, but follow an iterative research logic. Hence, the sample of data may be extended on the grounds of fine-grained analysis up to the point of saturation: that is, when no further insights are provided by new data.

Videography includes many different activities in the process ranging from fieldwork to fine-grained analysis of single utterances; they are organized around a research question sharpened step by step over the research process. However, we want to emphasize another aspect: in particular, the first approaches to fine-grained analysis, the definition of sequences and the 'selection of the scope' of the particular study should be done in the frame of group video *data sessions* (Heath et al., 2010: 156). The data session within a group is not just effective protection against misleading interpretations, but rather helps to 'break' with 'taken-for-granted' everyday interpretations of what is going on. Besides the fieldworkers, the group should also include members not familiar with the recorded situation. During the repeated step-by-step inspection of the recordings, 'ethnographic knowledge' will be explicated. This is a prerequisite for the interpretation of data, namely a basic understanding of what is going on. Sequential analysis done on this background is, then, made plausible by being based not on general assumptions, but on what can be shown in the video data.

NEW TENDENCIES AND THE LIMITS OF VIDEOGRAPHY

The dynamics of the field of interpretive video analysis prevent us from drawing premature conclusions. Therefore we close this chapter by discussing some pending issues and challenges. This kind of analysis, combining detailed observations with interpretation, is evidently not an automatic process. It rather includes specific activities of the researchers and the tools they use. Likewise, data sessions are not simple 'step-by-step proceedings' producing miraculous outcomes. They are a specific social form of interaction in and by which interpretations are elaborated. There are some approaches to reflect on how knowledge is generated in data sessions (Hindmarsh and Tutt, 2012; Tuma, 2012), which, as Knoblauch (2004) suggests, should be taken into consideration for the methodology of video analysis. Moreover, further technological innovations may prompt developments that focus more on the visual qualities of video data. With the ability to manipulate the visual, by drawing on the screen and easily comparing different instances visually, the ratio between sequential analysis and the analysis of other aspects of the data could change.

Videography is an approach that has shown its practical applicability in a number of fields, especially where focused interaction is occurring, as in educational settings, in workplaces, or even in religious rituals. But there are limits to its applicability due to the developments of mediatization that demand adaption of additional concepts: the character of ethnographic research changes if new media come into focus, because the field of research changes its shape. The specific possibilities offered by these new media are exploited both by researchers and by actors in a variety of fields. People make video recordings in nearly all spheres of social life; they produce all kinds of documentation and visual artefacts using the camera. Therefore, researchers are increasingly confronted with recordings of social interactions produced by actors on the scene that often are readily available. These video recordings can become part of a video-webnography or virtual ethnography (Domínguez et al., 2007; also see Kozinets et al., Chapter 18, this volume).

Digitalization also affects the analysis of video, for developments in analysis software may simplify transcribing, tagging and managing video data, without, however, replacing the necessity to interpret the data thoroughly. Newly developed visual technologies, finally, allow for new forms of post-processing data and representing final results of the analysis (Tuma, 2012) of social interaction. Established forms like printing selected transcripts including stills or frames taken from video recordings in social science articles do not exhaust the prospects of visual analysis. Experts from applied fields of 'vernacular' video analysis, for example in sports, already combine visual and spoken annotations to render their analysis intelligible to their audience. Interpretive video analysis in the social sciences might profit from these and other forms invented and conventionalized outside of social science, which, therefore, merit further study. Addressing these kinds of mediated video data may enhance the hermeneutic and semiotic aspects in video analysis and can become an integrated part of research processes studying mediated forms of audiovisual discourse (cf. Reichertz and Englert, 2010). Videography differs from the latter by the limits of both its data and its subject matter: it is the video analysis of social interaction in natural social settings.

NOTES

1. While the 'turn' in conversation analysis refers to stretches of verbal action, we use the term 'move' in order to indicate single identifiable 'units' of actions performed in various embodied communicative modalities, including verbal interaction. In this sense, the term differs slightly from its more 'strategic' meaning used by Goffman (1969).
2. We would like to thank Felix Degenhardt for his contribution of data. The video fragment is available at: http://www.as.tu-berlin.de/v-menue/videolabor/datenbeispiele/ (accessed 14 May 2013).

FURTHER READING

Goodwin, Charles (1994) 'Professional vision', *American Anthropologist*, 96 (3): 606–33.
Heath, Cristian, Hindmarsh, Jon and Luff, Paul (2010) *Video in Qualitative Research*. London: Sage.

Knoblauch, Hubert, Schnettler, Bernt, Soeffner, Hans-Georg and Raab, Jürgen (eds) (2006) *Video Analysis – Methodology and Methods. Qualitative Audiovisual Data Analysis in Sociology*. Frankfurt am Main: Lang.

REFERENCES

Bateson, Gregory (1958) 'Language and psychotherapy: Frieda Fromm-Reichmann's last project', *Psychiatry*, 21: 96–100.
Bateson, Gregory and Mead, Margaret (1942) *Balinese Character: A Photographic Analysis*. New York: New York Academy of Sciences.
Bergmann, Jörg (1985) 'Flüchtigkeit und methodische Fixierung sozialer Wirklichkeit', in Wolfgang Bonß and Heinz Hartmann (eds), *Entzauberte Wissenschaft (Soziale Welt, Sonderband 3)*. Göttingen: Schwartz. pp. 299–320.
Birdwhistell, Ray L. (1952) *Introduction to Kinesics: An Annotation System for the Analysis of Body Motion and Gesture*. Louisville, KY: University of Louisville.
Bohnsack, Ralf (2009) *Qualitative Bild- und Videointerpretation. Die dokumentarische Methode*. Stuttgart: UTB.
Domínguez, Daniel, Beaulieu, Anne, Estalella, Adolfo, Gómez, Edgar, Schnettler, Bernt and Read, Rosie (2007) 'Virtual ethnography', *Forum Qualitative Sozialforschung/Forum: Qualitative Social Research*, 8 (3).
Ekman, Paul and Friesen, Wallace (1969) 'A tool for the analysis of motion picture film or videotapes', *American Psychologist*, 24 (3): 240–3.
Erickson, Frederick (1982) 'Audiovisual recordings as primary data source', *Sociological Methods and Research*, 11 (2): 213–32.
Erickson, Frederick and Schultz, Jeffrey (1982) 'The counsellor as gatekeeper; Social interaction in interviews', in E. Hammel (ed.), *Language, Thought and Culture: Advances in the Study of Cognition*. New York: Academic Press. pp. 237–60.
Gesell, Arnold (1935) 'Cinemanalysis: A method of behavior study', *Journal of Genetic Psychology*, 47 (1): 3–16.
Glaser, Barney G. and Strauss, Anselm L. (1968) *The Discovery of Grounded Theory: Strategies for Qualitative Research*. London: Weidenfeld & Nicolson.
Goffman, Erving (1969) *Strategic Interaction*. Philadelphia: University of Pennsylvania Press.
Goldman, Ricki, Pea, Roy, Barron, Brigid and Denny, Sharon J. (2007) *Video Research in the Learning Sciences*. Mahwah, NJ: Lawrence Erlbaum.

Goodwin, Charles (1981) *Conversational Organization: Interaction Between Speakers and Hearers*. New York: Academic Press.

Goodwin, Charles (1986) 'Gestures as a resource for the organization of mutual orientation', *Semiotica*, 62 (1/2): 29–49.

Goodwin, Charles (2000a) 'Action and embodiment within situated human interaction', *Journal of Pragmatics*, 32: 1489–1522.

Goodwin, Charles (2000b) 'Practices of seeing: Visual analysis: An ethnomethodological approach', in Theo van Leeuwen and Carey Jewitt (eds), *Handbook of Visual Analysis*. London: Sage. pp. 157–82.

Goodwin, Charles and Goodwin, Marjarie Harness (1996) 'Seeing as situated activity: Formulating planes', in Yrjö Engeström and David Middleton (eds), *Cognition and Communication at Work*. Cambridge: Cambridge University Press. pp. 61–95.

Greenberg, Joshua M. (2008) *From Betamax to Blockbuster: Video Stores and the Invention of Movies on Video*. Cambridge, MA: MIT Press.

Grimshaw, Allen D. (1982) 'Sound-image data records for research on social interaction: Some questions answered', *Sociological Methods and Research*, 11 (2): 121–44.

Have, Paul ten (1999) *Doing Conversation Analysis: A Practical Guide*. London: Sage.

Heath, Christian (1986) *Body Movement and Speech in Medical Interaction*. Cambridge: Cambridge University Press.

Heath, Christian (1997) 'The analysis of activities in face to face interaction using video', in David Silverman (ed.), *Qualitative Research: Theory, Method, and Practice*. London: Sage. pp. 183–200.

Heath, Christian (2012) *The Dynamics of Auction*. Cambridge, MA: Cambridge University Press.

Heath, Christian and Luff, Paul (2007) 'Ordering competition: The international accomplishment of the sale of art and antiques at auction', *British Journal of Sociology*, 58 (1): 63–85.

Heath, Christian, Hindmarsh, Jon and Luff, Paul (2010) *Video in Qualitative Research*. London: Sage.

Hindmarsh, Jon and Tutt, Dylan (2012) 'Video in analytic practice', in Sarah Pink (ed.), *Advances in Visual Methodology*. Newbury Park, CA: Sage. pp. 57–73.

Kissmann, Ulrike Tikvah (ed.) (2009) *Video Interaction Analysis: Methods and Methodology*. Frankfurt am Main: Lang.

Knoblauch, Hubert (1991) 'Kommunikation im Kontext. John J. Gumperz und die interaktionale Soziolinguistik', *Zeitschrift für Soziologie*, 20 (6): 446–62.

Knoblauch, Hubert (2004) 'The future prospects of qualitative research', in Uwe Flick et al. (eds), *A Companion to Qualitative Research*. London: Sage. pp. 354–8.

Knoblauch, Hubert (2005) 'Focused ethnography', *Forum Qualitative Sozialforschung/Forum: Qualitative Social Research*, 6 (3): Art. 44. Available at: http://nbn-resolving.de/urn:nbn:de:0114-fqs0503440 (accessed 14 May 2013).

Knoblauch, Hubert and Tuma, René (2011) 'Videography: An interpretative approach to video-recorded micro-social interaction', in Eric Margolis and Luc Pauwels (eds), *The SAGE Handbook of Visual Research Methods*. Los Angeles: Sage. pp. 414–30.

Knoblauch, Hubert, Schnettler, Bernt and Raab, Jürgen (2006a) 'Video-analysis: Methodological aspects of interpretive audiovisual analysis in social research', in Hubert Knoblauch et al. (eds), *Video Analysis: Methodology and Methods*. Frankfurt am Main: Lang. pp. 9–26.

Knoblauch, Hubert, Schnettler, Bernt, Soeffner, Hans-Georg and Raab, Jürgen (eds) (2006b) *Video Analysis: Methodology and Methods. Qualitative Audiovisual Data Analysis in Sociology*. Frankfurt am Main: Lang.

Koch, Sabine C. and Zumbach, Jörg (2002) 'The use of video analysis software in behavior observation research: Interaction patterns of task-oriented small groups', *Forum Qualitative Sozialforschung/Forum: Qualitative Social Research*, 3 (2): Art. 18. http://nbn-resolving.de/urn:nbn:de:0114-fqs0202187 (accessed 14 May 2013).

Kress, Gunter (2010) *Multimodality: A Social Semiotics Approach to Contemporary Communication*. New York: Routledge.

Laurier, Eric and Philo, Chris (2006) 'Natural problems of naturalistic video data', in Hubert Knoblauch et al. (eds), *Video Analysis: Methodology and Methods*. Frankfurt am Main: Lang. pp. 183–92.

Lomax, Helen and Casey, Neil (1998) 'Recording social life: Reflexivity and video methodology', *Sociological Research Online*, 3 (2).

Luckmann, Thomas (2006) 'Some remarks on scores in multimodal sequential analysis', in Hubert Knoblauch et al. (eds), *Video Analysis: Methodology and Methods*. Frankfurt am Main: Lang. pp. 29–34.

Luckmann, Thomas and Gross, Peter (1977) 'Analyse unmittelbarer Kommunikation und Interaktion als Zugang zum Problem der Entstehung sozialwissenschaftlicher Daten', in Hans-Ulrich Bielefeld et al. (eds), *Soziolinguistik und Empirie. Beiträge zu Problemen der Corpusgewinnung und -auswertung*. Wiesbaden: Athenaum. pp. 198–207.

Marcus, George E. (1995) 'Ethnography in/of the world system: The emergence of multi-sited ethnography', *Annual Review of Anthropology*, 24: 95–117.

Mead, George Herbert (1938) *The Philosophy of the Act*, ed. Charles W. Morris with John M. Brewster, Albert M. Dunham and David Miller. Chicago: University of Chicago Press.

Mittenecker, Erich (1987) *Video in der Psychologie. Methoden und Anwendungsbeispiele in Forschung und Praxis*. Bern: Huber.

Mohn, Elisabeth (2006) 'Permanent work on gazes', in Hubert Knoblauch et al. (eds), *Video Analysis: Methodology and Methods*. Frankfurt am Main: Lang. pp. 173–81.

Mondada, Lorenza (2007) 'Multimodal resources for turn-taking: Pointing and the emergence of possible next speakers', *Discourse Studies*, 9 (2): 195–226.

Pink, Sarah (2007) *Doing Visual Ethnography: Images, Media and Representation in Research*, 2nd edition. London: Sage.

Raab, Jürgen (2008) *Visuelle Wissenssoziologie. Konzepte und Methoden*. Konstanz: UVK.

Reichertz, Jo and Englert, Carina J. (2010) *Einführung in die qualitative Videoanalyse. Eine hermeneutisch-wissenssoziologische Fallanalyse*. Wiesbaden: VS.

Sacks, Harvey (1972) 'An initial investigation of the usability of conversational data for doing sociology', in David Sudnow (ed.), *Studies in Social Interaction*. New York: Free Press. pp. 31–74.

Sacks, Harvey, Schegloff, Emanuel A. and Jefferson, Gail (1974) 'A simplest systematics for the organization of turn-taking for conversation', *Language*, 50 (4): 696–735.

Scheflen, Albert E. (1965) 'The significance of posture in communication systems', *Psychiatry*, 27: 316–31.

Schegloff, Emanuel (1968) 'Sequencing in conversational openings', *American Anthropologist*, 70: 1075–95.

Schegloff, Emanuel (1992) 'On talk and it institutional occasions', in Paul Drew and John Heritage (eds), *Talk at Work: Interaction in Institutional Settings*. Cambridge: Cambridge University Press. pp. 101–36.

Schnettler, Bernt (2006) 'Orchestrating bullet lists and commentaries: A video performance analysis of computer supported presentations', in Hubert Knoblauch et al. (eds), *Video Analysis: Methodology and Methods. Qualitative Audiovisual Data Analysis in Sociology*. Frankfurt am Main: Lang. pp. 155–68.

Schubert, Cornelius (2006) 'Video-analysis of practice and the practice of video-analysis', in Hubert Knoblauch et al. (eds), *Video Analysis: Methodology and Methods*. Frankfurt am Main: Lang. pp. 115–26.

Schutz, Alfred (1962) 'Common sense and scientific interpretation of human action', in *Collected Papers I: The Problem of Social Reality*, ed. Maurice Natanson. The Hague: Nijhoff. pp. 3–47.

Seidel, Tina (2005) *How to Run a Video Study: Technical Report of the IPN Video Study*. Münster: Waxmann.

Selting, Margret, Auer, Peter, Barth-Weingarten, Dagmar, Bergmann, Jörg, Bergmann, Pia, Birkner, Karin, Couper-Kuhlen, Elizabeth, Deppermann, Arnulf, Gilles, Peter, Günthner, Susanne, Hartung, Martin, Kern, Friederike, Mertzlufft, Christine, Meyer, Christian, Morek, Miriam, Oberzaucher, Frank, Peters, Jörg, Quasthoff, Uta, Schütte, Wilfried, Stukenbrock, Anja and Uhmann, Susanne (2009) 'Gesprächsanalytisches Transkriptionssystem 2 (GAT 2)', *Gesprächsforschung – Online-Zeitschrift zur verbalen Interaktion*, 10: 223–272 (www.gespraechsforschung-ozs.de).

Silver, Christina and Patashnick, Jennifer (2011) 'Finding fidelity: Advancing analysis using software', *Forum Qualitative Sozialforschung/Forum: Qualitative Social Research*, 12(1), Art. 37. Available at http://nbn-resolving.de/urn:nbn:de:0114-fqs1101372 (Accessed on 23 August, 2013).

Silverman, David (2007) *A Very Short, Fairly Interesting and Reasonably Cheap Book about Qualitative Research*. London: Sage.

Soeffner, Hans-Georg (1996) *The Order of Rituals: The Interpretation of Everyday Life*. New Brunswick, NJ: Transaction.

Tuma, René (2012) 'The (re)construction of human conduct: "Vernacular video analysis"', *Qualitative Sociology Review*, VIII (2), 152–63. Retrieved in August 2013 from http://www.qualitativesociologyreview.org/ENG/archive_eng.php

Zielinski, Siegfried (ed.) (2010 [1986]) *Zur Geschichte des Videorecorders. Neuausgabe des medienwissenschaftlichen Klassikers*. Potsdam:Polzer.

31

Analysing Virtual Data

Winfried Marotzki, Jens Holze and
Dan Verständig

In this chapter we will address the rather novel phenomenon of virtual data. We will start by introducing some concepts that are necessary for our considerations. By *virtual data* we mean all data that are generated in cyberspace and gathered for the purpose of scientific research. The term *cyberspace* describes the 'room' of social interaction and communication that is made possible by the Internet as the technical entity of networked computers and the World Wide Web as one service run on this infrastructure. A subclass of virtual data are *mobile data*, which are generated or edited on mobile phones, smartphones and other mobile devices. We will conclude the chapter with a consideration of types of mobile data that have become increasingly relevant.

Due to the rapid adoption of personal computing and the Internet during the last two decades, qualitative research finds itself with some new challenges. In cyberspace we are finding complex ways of social interaction which demand new or changed methods of data collection and analysis. Along with those developments we also saw the establishment of new kinds of mobile communication. Mobile telephony between any two places on earth was only the beginning, because other services like SMS (Short Message Service) and several stages of a mobile Internet have led to other innovative applications and, again, different ways of communication, which we will examine in this chapter.

Looking back at the historical evolution of research in cyberspace, one might argue that the discussion during the *first generation* of Internet studies mainly relied on a variety of predictions and assumptions about the effects of the Internet, without much empirical effort being made (see Wellman and Guilia, 1999; Wellman, 2004). Systematic collection of data, and a discussion about methods and methodologies based upon it, only started during the middle and late 1990s, when different disciplines tried to transfer established research approaches to the World Wide Web. The *second generation* of Internet studies mainly consisted of documentation of phenomena, spaces and structures in cyberspace: 'The second age was low-hanging fruit with analysts using standard social scientific methods – and some concepts – to document the nature of the internet' (Wellman, 2004: 127). At the same time, the Net was still treated as an isolated phenomenon, an assumption that was also brought forward by the 'citizens' themselves, as in the popular declaration of cyberspace independence that starts out like this:

> Governments of the Industrial World, you weary giants of flesh and steel, I come from Cyberspace, the new home of Mind. On behalf of the future, I ask you of the past to leave us alone. You are not welcome among us. You have no sovereignty where we gather. (Barlow, 1996)

For the current, *third generation* of Internet studies, it has become vital to work with different kinds of data collected from the Internet. Because of this, technical developments are of great importance to the researcher, as new technological possibilities may pose new challenges.

While for over a decade the Net was mainly represented in textual form, it started to change to a more graphical appearance with the emerging World Wide Web. Growing bandwidth and new technologies have dramatically transformed the Internet. Nowadays we come across a great variety of multimedia artefacts; written text is a secondary consideration when dealing with many online services like Flickr, YouTube, online radio and podcasts. We find an enormous set of audiovisual forms by which we can articulate ourselves, and, like anything in cyberspace, they tend to be linked to each other in complex configurations.

THEORETICAL APPROACHES

The Internet and computer-mediated communication (CMC) allow researchers to disconnect from local and temporal boundaries attached to face-to-face (F2F) communication and thus approach people who might not have been approachable prior to CMC. Mann and Stewart point out some examples like 'mothers at home with small children, shift workers, people with agoraphobia, computer addicts, people with disabilities' (2000: 17ff.). Additionally a researcher could contact participants who did not want to discuss the subject matter during a face-to-face session, but who *do* agree to discuss the material via CMC (Turkle, 1995). CMC can also have a safety function for both researcher and informant when it comes to censored or politically sensitive information.

Challenges arise from the fact that online research requires specific skills, as researchers are facing different circumstances in cyberspace than they would in the actual world. Using the Internet as an alternative way to access the field or as a form of communication technology might alter the outcome, but it can also enrich the research process due to its optionality. Online research offers a wide variety of proven methods, such as the online interview, online focus groups, or even several ethnographic approaches whose roots are in classical research methods but whose characteristics are novel today (see Mann and Stewart, 2000; also see Kozinets et al., Chapter 18, this volume). Specific methods will not be discussed at this point, but we want to point out that any transformation of established research methods must take the technological context into account. Questioning an informant via email poses different challenges to the researcher than a classic F2F interview, as in, for example, the asynchronicity of email, which might cause a greater distance to exist between both actors. There are also linguistic challenges for qualitative research. For example, gestures that can be recognized during an F2F interview are not observable in text-based chat, so users often take advantage of special expressions like emoticons. When evaluating and analysing data in the field, the researcher needs to consider that, apart from common phrases and emoticons, subcultural phenomena can also have a huge impact on the way users express themselves in a specific context.

The ways in which users generate data depends not only on the cultural context, but also on technological circumstances. In cyberspace, in addition to being anonymous, users often have the option to act and participate under pseudonyms, influencing online self-representation by choosing a specific nickname or alias. Role-playing and its implications for identity construction have been under discussion ever since virtual communities started to emerge; the discussion still persists today (see Rheingold, 1993; Turkle, 1995).

Further implications arise from the given data as well as access to the field. The researcher finds him- or herself among a high variety of given and generated data sets and a valid entrance point. To provide a better understanding regarding the different types of virtual data, some characteristics will be identified and discussed in the following sections.

Features of Virtual Data

If we look explicitly at data that are being generated by users in cyberspace, we typically can differentiate between static data and dynamic data. By *static data* we understand the kinds of data that (1) are not created by different users interacting with each other and (2) remain basically unchanged while they are continuously accessible. In this sense, many classic homepages can be considered collections of static data, since they tend to be available for long periods of time but are not usually altered through user interaction. By comparison we have *dynamic data* in situations of interaction, which means that they react to data generated by other users, as in a thread in a bulletin board discussion. If a user were to start a thread without referring to another discussion, and if the thread were not picked up by other users, it would not be considered dynamic. While the threads in bulletin boards may be relatively persistent, this persistence has vanished among today's social networking sites because of their continuous data streams; that persistence has been replaced with volatility.

When considering data quality, this differentiation is important, because it may cause different challenges to arise during the research process.

The difference can partly be traced back to the technical evolution of the Internet. Especially in the beginning of the digital age, it took greater effort to put data on the Internet than to retrieve data. To publish a website, a person needed webserver software and separate access to another computer (e.g. via file transfer protocol or 'FTP') connected to the Internet. The mere creation of a webpage required either knowledge of HTML or special software that took care of it. Even when the Internet was publicly available, only an elite were actually able to do that. It is for this reason that the World Wide Web during its first decade shaped an asymmetric relationship between the consumers and the producers of content, a relationship which could only be resolved very slowly. Even with free services like Geocities that took care of most of the technical effort and could be considered a mass phenomenon during their time, there still remained thresholds, like the ones we mentioned earlier, which a person had to overcome for active participation. To create dynamic content, one needed even further technical knowledge and production costs (e.g. connection to databases). During the last decade we have witnessed a shift to a so-called 'social' Web, which focuses even more on dynamic (i.e. interaction-generated) data, which is why we think it makes sense to talk about the two types of data, static and dynamic, in more detail.

Static Data

The early, text-based Internet consisted primarily of static content. On the one hand this meant that the relevance of content lasted for a longer period of time; on the other hand, the content could be kept available for years or even an indefinite time span (high persistency). Some very central data collections were migrated to newer technologies and actively cared for over generations by different people. Examples can be found in early Usenet, BBS or FTP servers that still exist today. Even the first Web-based services followed this pattern, which is evident from a glance at some of the bulletin boards or private homepages that still exist all over the Web (see Döring, 2002). The common pattern seems to have been that new content was added but old content remained basically untouched. Even when data were created through volatile forms of communication, they could be transformed into archives and thus become static. Monitoring changes on static websites seemed like a tedious task, but feeds and other automatically generated data fragments are much easier to analyse and can easily be sorted chronologically.

For scientific research, static data come with a long-term validity period and make it possible to do analysis over large time spans. Most of the time, static data are already sorted systematically, for example in a chronological format for easy navigation. Sometimes this happens on the level of the actual service, as on a web space service provider, for example; it can also be done by services like the 'Wayback Machine' offered by the non-profit organization Internet Archive (see www.archive.org/web/web.php). Snapshots have been taken since 1996 from a large portion of freely accessible websites, so that a person may be able to recreate a certain website's content and structure from various times in its past. These systematic approaches can also be found in the realm of computer science, where information retrieval or web archiving (Brügger, 2011) tackles the questions of systematic data collection. For scientific research, this means that extensive databases have already been created and you might not need to collect data yourself, though you may still need to filter and sort the data according to your specific research question in order to make most use of them. Approaches like information retrieval may also be helpful for qualitative social research because tools for data collection may be better realized as interdisciplinary efforts.

Dynamic Data

If we look at the historical and technical evolution, we can appreciate that the Internet has always been subject to a constant dynamic, which we can find both inside the infrastructure and in the ways it has been used socially. The development towards a social web reinforces this notion and at the same time allows us certain types of data. By 'dynamic data' we therefore mean data that users generate in interactive contexts when they react with their own data to the data of other users. In the case of communicational data, this would be information that has been picked up and republished while being changed in the process, as with 'retweets' on Twitter. The change can also come from contextualization. This does not imply that dynamic data are a novelty or a recent phenomenon, but rather that through the Internet's structural changes, which we are able to reconstruct, earlier frameworks and ways of utilization have been altered.

An important aspect comes with the archivability of data. Most of the time, data might be archived using additional tools and resources even when the service itself does not include this functionality, but we may also find huge streams of data that are volatile and of short-term availability. This shows the dynamic aspect's influence on data. An example can be found in the development of mobile devices. While we are able to reconstruct a diachronic perspective of bulletin boards, newsgroups, or blogs by means of a search function or an archive, social networking sites are an enormous challenge in this regard because of the relative volatility of data. This volatility results from a high interactivity that creates massive streams of data – as with Twitter, in which one tweet will 'chase' another. Data streams are very individual, because their composition depends on how many and which other users a person is following. But volatility also depends on the service's design and its technological framework. Particularly with mobile data we find that the central artefact on which data fragments are based can be very fleeting. As one example, the service Foursquare offers the ability for spontaneous local networks to arise based upon a common location and people's remarks about that particular place. By checking in at the same time to the same events or location, individuals' social networks might be extended for a limited period of time. The options for interaction are well defined: you can choose a place, post a comment, add a picture or photograph, and you may also send your check-in to other services. The latter is key to the current generation of dynamic data as described earlier. Based on the limits of a service or an application, the parameters of participation are changed. And while thematic communities are not a novelty, we do face new challenges as we have to identify new structural features with those new services. Other examples could include virtual game worlds. Especially in games like MMORPGs (Massively Multiplayer Online Role-Playing Games) we can find highly complex and yet volatile processes of communication, with different motivational aspects (see Yee, 2007).

PRACTICAL APPROACHES

The first examples of virtual communities on the Internet were created in the 1980s, long before Tim Berners-Lee developed the World Wide Web at CERN (Berners-Lee, 2000) and the Net was opened to broad public and commercial interests. The term *virtual community* was coined by Howard Rheingold (1993), who wrote about the early online community known as The WELL. The term started to grow into a universal concept for online communities in cyberspace. Because an important part of research in cyberspace focuses on the subject of communities, we will use them as examples here. The first generation of Internet studies, as we described, primarily tried to grasp those online phenomena and to describe the structures. However, many efforts back then relied on, as Wellman puts it, 'conjecture and anecdotal evidence' rather than on the systematic collection of data (2004: 124).

Using two specific types of online community, we are going to explain established research methods. The classic virtual communities have been around for about two decades and plenty of research has already been done on them. During the last decade, however, social networking sites seem to have become the dominant type of community on the Web.

Virtual Community Research

Qualitative research on community structures can be achieved through an ethnographic approach, which means having access to the type of community that is of interest. On the one hand, researchers can try to contact members of a community in real life (e.g. for further research, like classic offline interviews) and to collect data from them *outside* of cyberspace, but this would ignore the virtual environment and therefore would not deliver virtual data as defined in the beginning. On the other hand – and this will be our focus here – one can get data from media artefacts (e.g. layout and structures of websites or software platforms, collected communication and discussions, documentation, etc. – see Kozinets et al., Chapter 18, this volume). Apart from those structural elements, the researcher can use the means of communication available to interact with people directly.

To specify the different types of interesting data that could be found on community platforms, one would need a basic structure. Marotzki (2003) has developed a set of structural features of virtual communities, which were collected through a comparison of 40 online communities prior to Web 2.0 (Jörissen and Marotzki, 2009: 192ff.). Note that this is only one of several possible ways to structure online communities. The features consist of: (1) metaphor/infrastructure; (2) sociographic structures (system of rules); (3) communication structure; (4) information structure; (5) structure of self-presentation; (6) participatory structure; and (7) online–offline relations. This structure, which also demonstrates possible areas of research interest, helps us to get an impression of the types of data we could expect.

The first feature formerly was named *leading metaphors*, as many communities established real-world allegories that served as a template for the communities' structures and visual appearance, like the popular metaphor of the city (Dieberger, 1994). Those metaphors were no longer used after the end of the 1990s, which is why the term 'infrastructure' seems a better fit to describe the appearance and technical base of any given online community (Jörissen, 2007). It consists of the technical aspects, like the software that is used or a description of the functions of a platform. This also includes the community's layout and visual patterns, from which it may be possible to tell what the goals or general idea behind a community might be. If it is a website we are looking at, several basic forms could be identified (like wikis, blogs or bulletin boards, for example); outside of the Web, we usually have some kind of software to access the virtual space (as with Second Life or some online games), which may also follow certain standards in structure. The technical possibilities and functions of the infrastructure define the frame of reference for the following features.

The *sociographic structures* are considered to be a system of assigned social positions as well as special rights and duties within the community. This especially includes a set of rules, which may regulate access to the community and behaviour once a user is inside. Those sets may become quite complex and contain educational aspects, because they generally aim at rewarding desirable and sanctioning bad behaviour. There might be a sophisticated registration process, which could be analysed. We might be able to deduce the self-understanding of a community from these sorts of rules and processes.

The structure of *communication* describes all forms of communication that the members of a certain community may use, such as chats, boards or comment systems. From their technical parameters (e.g. asynchronicity/synchronicity or one-to-many/one-to-one/many-to-many) we get a rough framework, which is usually specified further through processes of social negotiation (e.g. rules). We can tap into this with methods of content or discourse analysis to get data from which we may be able to learn the effects of the forms of communication.

Like the previous feature, the *information* structure consists of all the aspects and ways through which information is presented in a community and to whom it is available. Some communities create large internal collections of links or texts, which grow continuously and can form very complex structures over time. Of course, apart from text, this can include pictures, sounds or videos, each of which requires different methods of analysis.

The structure of *self-presentation* asks about the ways in which individual members manage their identities. In communities, members usually encounter options for creating a profile or an identity card, and they submit information to it in an effort to present themselves to other members. The most basic example of this is choosing a nickname, but members may include additional information, pictures, or even a graphical avatar. Users decide whether or not to create a special online identity and how similar it is to their real-world identity. The Internet offers a way to reflect on oneself and to create a completely new self (see Boyd, 2007; Turkle, 1995; Marcus et al., 2006). Furthermore, users may have a private space online that they can share with a certain group of friends. Obviously, analysing all of this can be quite complex, and it may be complicated to reconstruct a whole identity. In the case of an analysis of graphical representations, for example, avatars might deliver interesting data (Jörissen and Marotzki, 2009).

The degree to which members might be able to participate in a community is subject to its *participation* structure. This is a central consideration when someone is offering the service, and so control may or may not be shared and decisions about the community might be made by one person or just a few people. There may also exist more democratic structures that offer rights of participation to any member; sometimes, a community's governing bodies are established through a process by which members choose privileged users to represent them. Those structures might be documented explicitly (e.g. in the rules or the terms of service), or they might be extracted from different roles that users might take in a community. Any discussion board, for example, might have a hierarchy of administrators, moderators, and registered and unregistered users, and each stratum may have different rights and functions to perform. If it is not otherwise available, we may get this kind of information through questionnaires, group discussions or interviews, depending on the research question. While certain roles might exist in different communities, their dedicated functions and qualitative character are usually bound to the specific community.

Depending on the aim of a community, there could be *relations between online and offline activities* of variable strength. There might be members' meetings, for example, or real-world events. Such things may be important if an online group was created from an already existing offline group and was designed to meet its specific needs. It is not uncommon for groups in communities to be created from the real-world proximity of their members. In the end there are always real people behind virtual communities, and their thinking and acting in the offline world may influence what they do online. In current research there seems to be an obvious and increasing trend to integrate online and offline aspects.

From these structural features, we can easily see that many kinds of virtual data could be gathered for any given research question. There might be a combination of more objective data, like written rules or technical structure (functional layout, visual style), with subjective data collected from informants. A triangulation of several methods of data collection and analysis will likely be necessary. Also, as mentioned previously, some kinds of data might not be collectable at all through certain established methods in cyberspace. There are special challenges inherited from the characteristics of CMC.

In many cases, access to the field for the researcher might be easy because the technical barriers are low (e.g. when there is only simple registration). So it might be quite easy to collect data from a given community. Yet researchers need to realize that they might operate in closed (non-public) or even private contexts. Thus they need to make sure to assess the character of a community prior to collecting and using data from there. In almost every case there are aspects of research ethics and law that may affect the researcher; we will elaborate on those at the end of the chapter.

With ongoing technical development and the evolution of the Internet, the options for creating virtual communities have changed as well. With the beginning of the so-called Web 2.0 we find more specialized and complex examples. Research has shown that communities online are no longer considered to be structures of only strong ties, but have grown to include weak ties and individual social networks. These changes are accompanied by a change in focus of many commercial services in cyberspace and might be considered a global mass phenomenon at the moment.

Social Network Platforms

After several kinds of virtual community spread across the Internet, new forms started to emerge that followed a rather different approach to community structure. Social networking sites are one of the main innovative phenomena brought forth by the social web or Web 2.0, and they have evolved continually since the beginning of the millennium. Along with new tools for online participation and collaboration, a massive growth in user numbers, and a relocation of complex applications from the PC to the Web (or the *cloud*), new web platforms have been built. They differ from classic virtual communities in that they are designed with a low threshold for obtaining membership and deal primarily with weak ties between individuals. Following Boyd and Ellison, social networking sites can be described as:

> web-based services that allow individuals to (1) construct a public or semi-public profile within a bounded system, (2) articulate a list of other users with whom they share a connection, and (3) view and traverse their list of connections and those made by others within the system. The nature and nomenclature of these connections may vary from site to site. (2007)

They emphasize that actual networking, which aims at establishing new connections with previous strangers, plays a minor role in those platforms and that the primary interest of users so far seems to be the representation and nurturing of existing contacts. Therefore communication is most likely to happen between people who already have a connection or who have already met in real life. Apart from this, the central idea consists of the creation and design of a personal profile, which connects to the identity management aspect in classic virtual communities. Despite these overlapping aspects, there are also new research methods available, which do provide researchers with different kinds of virtual data (see Kozinets et al., Chapter 18, this volume).

The first social networking site, SixDegrees, started in 1997, but the service was closed in 2000. Friendster was founded in 2002 and became the first social networking site to gain some popularity. During the last 10 years several large services have been developed, differing mainly because of a focus on certain technical features, on particular subjects, or on users from a shared geographical region. Twitter (http://twitter.com), for example, is a large micro-blogging platform through which you can exchange short messages of 140 characters or less with your social network (called your 'followers'). Last.fm (http://last.fm) is a Europe-based social networking site that focuses on the musical preferences of its users. Facebook (http://facebook.com) started out as a networking tool for students at Harvard University but gradually transformed into a worldwide meta-network for everybody. These few examples already show that every distinctive service can have very specific features even though they all serve the function of a digital social network.

To look into these new phenomena, researchers again can only rely very limitedly on established forms of data and methods to gather them. Many of the structural features mentioned earlier can also be found on social networking sites, but such sites lack the clear distinction and seclusiveness of a classic virtual community as well as the commonly visible strong ties between all members. But perhaps more obviously now than ever before, we are finding opportunities to apply the qualitative method of social network analysis – first used systematically in the 1950s (Barnes, 1954) – to describe social ties between individuals and the structures emerging from them. The method represents a 'shift from the individualism common in the social sciences toward a structural analysis' (Jones, 1999: 78). The method is based on the notion that researchers can make assumptions about a certain group, community or organization and its meaning for both the entity and the individuals involved by looking into the social relations that constitute the network. In cyberspace it is of course limited to digital ways of communication. Without explaining the method itself in detail (see Blank et al., 2008, Garton et al., 1999; Gaiser and Schreiner, 2009), it delivers a new kind of data, namely a network of social relationships that has gained new relevance because of the rise of social networking sites. We can differentiate between ego-centric and whole or organizational networks. With the former, of course, one has the ability to look at the emerging influences that a social network might have on any specific individual. Where the borders of a network should be drawn depends on the specific context and the research question at hand so that we have a very flexible approach. Social networking sites work especially well for social network analysis, if we want to look at the dynamic exchange of information or aspects of mutual support. Prior to social networking sites the only way to reconstruct a personal social network involved using questionnaires and interviews (see Roulston, Chapter 20, this volume), letting people write journals, or observation (see Marvasti, Chapter 24, this volume). Social networking sites by design make individuals' social networks visible, and the quality and strength of ties can be assessed from acts of communication or from labels that are attached to them (e.g. friends, family or fans). Furthermore, it is possible to identify special roles or actors in a social context, which can become the focus of ongoing qualitative research. Where an analysis based on structural features requires that a specific structure is actually present, network analysis is more open. Modern technical platforms, which only enforce very weak structures and leave specific possible uses to the actual users, may be easier to grasp with this approach. In another step, researchers may then take a closer look at online self-representation, means of communication, or rules.

Thus it seems evident to us that the theoretical framework and the method of social network analysis is a very relevant approach to analysing social networking sites, as they offer new ways to gather and evaluate virtual data on social relations. Especially when looking at method triangulation, there are new options and new potential views on virtual communities. But there are also some new problems. Collecting data from a very volatile source like Twitter might be a challenge due to the potentially huge amounts of data. A specification (e.g. using keywords or hashtags) might not serve the research question as communication threads might not be captured, a problem that stems from the data's dynamic nature as explained earlier. An automated way to collect data would be necessary when dealing with large data streams, yet flexible, case-by-case adjustments would also be needed. Such an analysis of dialogues seems to be problematic from a linguistic perspective at this point (Zappavigna, 2011).

Thoughts on Analysis

Based on the previous examples for research scenarios (virtual community research and social networking sites), virtual data can be classified into two groups. First, there are data which have already been generated and can be found and retrieved from the Internet. This includes, for example, archived conversations from newsgroups, online communities, or other kinds of Internet platforms such as online documents or friend lists. Second, a researcher or a researching group also can generate data by raising polls, conducting online interviews, or setting up a specific online service themselves, such as a wiki. Even if only textual data are the focus of epistemological interest, this may already result in a very complex set of interconnected data types and contextual shapes, which can be analysed within methods like discourse analysis, interview analysis or even a corpus analysis.

However, media artefacts such as images or videos can be evaluated separately with methods of image or film analysis, but connections between them always raise the questions of which data should be included, how to triangulate between different qualitative research methods, and how the whole sample should be structured. For example, when trying to get self-centred social networks from a video platform such as YouTube, additional information can be gathered by analysing the audiovisual articulation. This can be helpful for interpreting the relations between the users, and it goes far beyond looking for the nodes and relational positions inside a social network.

For research on social phenomena in an online group of players, as in a guild of MMORPGs, looking at the community and its structural elements as described earlier might be a key aspect. Therefore the researcher could systematically observe the 'naturalistic' behaviour of users (see Schroeder and Bailenson, 2008). Even an online ethnographic approach would need to consider using different media artefacts completely to understand subcultural dynamics and models of behaviour. Therefore it could be necessary to record in-game footage, while having players communicate and act together. It could also be very helpful to record their communication on a voice server. This could be realized, for example, with TeamSpeak, which is software that allows computer users to speak on a chat channel, just like a telephone conference call. This tool is designed for gamers and could provide additional help to researchers looking at gaming contexts, as they would use the same tools as the target group, thus perhaps increasing their social acceptability. Collecting online data such as in-game footage might require a huge amount of hard disk space, since the video material could be uncompressed. The kinds of data and evaluation method required by a researcher will greatly depend upon the individual epistemological interest.

Since data collected online are represented in digital form, they can in many cases be easily processed by a wide variety of specific software tools for qualitative research. Chapter 9 of *A Guide to Conducting Online Research* offers a general introduction to analysing online data (see Gaiser and Schreiner, 2009: 113ff.). There are several software applications, such as MAXQDA, NVivo or HyperRESEARCH (see Gibbs, Chapter 19, this volume), that are specifically designed for processing and coding text-based data with plenty of different tools. For reconstructing and visualizing social network relations, researchers can take advantage of tools such as InFlow. Several other tools can help with the basic tasks of data processing, but some challenges still persist. The problem of multimedia samples consisting of different media types will not be solved completely, because consideration of a coherent sample structure is required when interpreting the data. References to pictures, video or sound fragments inside a sample might not be easily included. Some methods will still require transcription or fragmentation of media artefacts to be integrated with other data. Thus working with multimodal data sets remains a sophisticated task despite the use of digital tools.

MOBILE DATA PLATFORMS

While for a long time the classic Internet was bound to stationary devices like the PC, we are now seeing the development of smaller, more mobile devices, particularly smartphones, which is leading to a new expansion of cyberspace. Currently we are able to carry much of the functionality of the Internet in our pockets at all times. Mobile data, therefore, are a new kind of structured virtual data found in new contexts and scenarios.

On a very basic level, the differences for mobile data come either from technical limitations or from the more flexible usage contexts. Mobile online services are mostly designed for a very specific purpose, and the form and kind of data are strictly pre-structured most of the time. Early mobile services like SMS (text messaging) could only transfer messages of a certain length because of technical limitations. The need for specifically formatted messages then was taken up by services like Twitter, which could technically offer much longer messages but keep the format and the limitations that came with them for convenient mobile communication. Strict enforcement of the 140-character limit has directly influenced usage. For example, URL-shortening services are offered to reduce the size of links, and even the style of language is heavily influenced by the limit (Boyd et al., 2010). Furthermore, social practices like retweeting, which means to share messages from others with all of one's followers, have been established because of the convenient data packages. Long postings to blogs cannot be done easily on mobile devices and do not fit well with mass distribution. Therefore, while technical access to the 'real' Internet over mobile devices might be available, services that specifically cater for mobile devices and special mobile applications (or apps) are much more popular. They may also use Web-based interfaces, but they do not necessarily have to deliver the same content that would be accessible via the Web.

Not only are user interfaces redesigned for mobile use, but mobile services usually only implement a set of functions that are actually relevant in mobile contexts. Ways of communication may be very different from the home PC or classic web services. Additionally, we also have platforms that perform only core functionality, which are then built upon by third-party services. Only through services like Twitpic has it become possible to share photos easily through Twitter; services like foodspotting (http://foodspotting.com) or Blip.fm (http://blip.fm) offer a thematic frame and try to combine users into sub-networks based on their common interests.

We will now look at some more examples of specific forms of mobile data.

Since the late 1990s, research has been carried out, for example, on the meaning and usage of mobile phones by young people (Lenhart and Madden, 2007). Numerous studies have attempted to show that mobile phones have drastically changed young people's habits of communication, and also that mobile phones are a big part of the processes of socialization and identity creation (Ling, 2004; 2007). Mobile services like SMS text messaging or messaging through Twitter are used by young people to uphold their social networks and to present themselves within their peer groups.

To capture these user habits, researchers have mostly used questionnaires or interviews, an example of the increasingly common practice of combining quantitative and qualitative methods (see Purwandari et al., 2011). Direct access to a set of exchanged messages could be quite problematic: for obvious legal and ethical reasons, mobile service providers cannot provide access to private data, although they might do their own research on their own data to optimize the services they offer. Other service providers (e.g. on the social web) might offer dedicated interfaces to create data collections and thereby encourage analysis. With the commercialization of many of these services, however, those options are fading again. One needs programming skills to be able to use those techniques in the first place. If we again take aspects of research ethics into account, it seems necessary for the researcher to have direct contact with each and every user. Only then is it possible to ask for adequate permission and also to get access to individual user strategies. Ethnographic observation might also be tricky because it may be hard for the researcher to access the actual real-life context of a virtual communication act (research on mediated rituals could be one example; see Ling, 2008). Also, the problem of the researcher's presence, which may influence and possibly change the outcome of the research, probably needs to be re-evaluated.

Structural features, like those we have examined in this chapter in regard to online communities and social networks, are also present in the mobile realm, but they might follow different rules (such as limitations on pre-structured data, as mentioned earlier). The infrastructure of mobile apps and services might follow some mobile-specific patterns. Additional sources of information (as in GPS location data, or photos and movies via integrated cameras) might be central artefacts in a communication act and therefore key to the construction of meaning. It is also clear that mere textual analysis may no longer be satisfactory in those cases as well: picture analysis may be an additional tool, but it will create new kinds of data. The researcher needs to be able to handle the data, which means that clever ways of reflected triangulation are necessary. Many recent studies have accessed the field through quantitative methods, and there seems to be room for exploring qualitative research in mobile contexts. But at the moment there are some barriers that keep hindering such efforts.

It is not yet certain whether *mobile* data really are going to be a category in themselves along with *virtual* data. It is possible that the process of merging the virtual stationary and the virtual mobile spaces is just another step towards the ubiquity of cyberspace. This could imply a change for the Internet, which simply integrates all the mobile aspects that were just mentioned. As the evolution of the Internet showed in the past, we may see strong paradigm shifts within only one generation of users. The Internet has changed many times and will probably continue to do so. For researchers this means that it is imperative to look very closely at the usage context of virtual data and to take it into account. This is, of course, true for social research in general, but it becomes more central in cases like the ones we have just described.

ETHICAL IMPLICATIONS

Online research does not bring up completely new problems or challenges; rather, it changes several parameters of issues that were previously known. Even if online data are accessible, the researcher needs to consider data collection legislation. Furthermore, a researcher has to consider that even if data are publicly accessible, users may not necessarily be aware of the fact that their information can easily be taken away. Also, interaction involves several aspects that need to be clear. For example, an online evaluation mostly takes place in public spaces, so other users are likewise witnesses. Even if there is no personal contact, it is appropriate to communicate the research interest and to specify the purposes of data collection.

The collected data should be accessible to participants; they should be able to know what data have been collected about themselves.

A direct citation from a newsgroup or discussion board, for example, can easily be back-traced, thanks to the power of modern search engines, even if the author is anonymized. As a result, users can find out further information about the cited person. It should be possible for a person to be comfortable with being connected with the data, but individuals may want to remain anonymous. A lack of data protection could deeply damage the trust between researcher and participant: 'Researchers need to consider the long-term implications of data protection issues at an early stage – they strike at the very heart of traditional qualitative research methodology' (Mann and Stewart, 2000: 41). Also, researchers need to consider the authenticity of data; therefore it often seems necessary not only to categorize the types of data, but also to identify important and relevant actors and their roles. As in classical qualitative research processes, the researcher needs to get a feel for what is happening and how data are being generated in the specific contexts. In each case, the researcher has to determine whether it would be useful or even essential to raise more information online and perhaps beyond cyberspace.

CONCLUSION

Virtual data and all of the subtypes of data, like mobile data, are becoming increasingly recognized, and not just in qualitative research. Current research on cyberspace is determined by two parallel lines of development. On the one hand we find a consolidation of the many types of data and research methods we have mentioned in this chapter into a separate discipline of Internet or Web studies. On the other hand, cyberspace, due to its ubiquity and interconnection with everyday life, can no longer be seen as a separate field, ignoring its dependence on real-world contexts (Wellman and Haythornthwaite, 2002; Wellman, 2004). Consequently, virtual data become increasingly important even to research projects that do not primarily focus on the Internet itself. It follows from this integration that new interfaces have to be created and that established methods need to incorporate virtual data into the research process. Discovery as well as explication of these distinct types of data often require individual as well as interdisciplinary strategies and thus pose new challenges to many research disciplines.

The recent evolution has shown that mobile data are becoming more and more important and that cyberspace is changing to become even more complex. This already influences research practicalities, such as, for example, when relevant data need to be identified and selected for further research from the numerous services and types of data. The advancing degree of complexity is illustrated not only by an ever-growing number of web services, but also by their increasingly complex interlinking, which could lead to a highly individualized and selective usage. It is certainly possible that well-known and common schemes, as were observed in the evolution towards the social web, will again be seen here. For researchers, the challenges emerge from the varieties of data and their particular specifics concerning services and formats. Consequently, the researcher needs to align methodical and methodological considerations with the socio-technological circumstances in the field.

FURTHER READING

Consalvo, Mia and Ess, Charles (eds) (2011) *The Handbook of Internet Studies*. Chichester: Wiley-Blackwell.

Gaiser, Ted J. and Schreiner, Anthony E. (2009) *A Guide to Conducting Online Research*. London: Sage.

Ling, Richard Seyler (2008) *New Tech, New Ties: How Mobile Communication Is Reshaping Social Cohesion*. Cambridge, MA: MIT Press.

REFERENCES

Barlow, John Perry (1996) *A Declaration of the Independence of Cyberspace*. San Francisco: Electronic Frontier Foundation.

Barnes, John A. (1954) 'Class and committees in a Norwegian island parish', *Human Relations*, 7 (February): 39–58.

Berners-Lee, Tim (2000) *Weaving the Web: The Past, Present and Future of the World Wide Web by its Inventor*. London: Texere.

Blank, Grant, Fielding, Nigel and Lee, Raymond (eds) (2008) *Handbook of Online Research Methods*. London: Sage.

Boyd, Danah (2007) *Why Youth (heart) Social Network Sites: The Role of Networked Publics in Teenage Social Life*. Cambridge, MA: MIT Press.

Boyd, Danah and Ellison, Nicole B. (2007) 'Social network sites: Definition, history, and scholarship', *Journal of Computer-Mediated Communication*, 13 (1), article 11. Available online at: http://jcmc.indiana.edu/vol13/issue1/boyd.ellison.html (accessed 23 July 2012).

Boyd, Danah, Golder, Scott and Lotan, Gilad (2010) 'Tweet tweet retweet: Conversational aspects of retweeting on twitter', Proceedings of HICSS-43, Kauai, HI, USA.

Brügger, Niels (2011) 'Web archiving – between past, present, and future', in Mia Consalvo and Charles Ess (eds), *The Handbook of Internet Studies*. Oxford: Wiley-Blackwell. pp. 24–42.

Dieberger, Andreas (1994) 'Navigation in textual virtual environments using a city metaphor', PhD dissertation, Technische Universität, Wien.

Döring, Nicola (2002) 'Personal home pages on the web: A review of research', *Journal of Computer-Mediated Communication*, 7 (3). Available online at: http://jcmc.indiana.edu/vol7/issue3/doering.html (accessed 23 July 2012).

Gaiser, Ted J. and Schreiner, Anthony E. (2009) *A Guide to Conducting Online Research*. London: Sage.

Garton, Laura, Haythornthwaite, Caroline and Wellman, Barry (1999) 'Studying on-line social networks', in Steve Jones (ed.), *Doing Internet Research: Critical Issues and Methods for Examining the Net*. Thousand Oaks, CA: Sage. pp. 75–106.

Jones, Steve (ed.) (1999) *Doing Internet Research: Critical Issues and Methods for Examining the Net*. Thousand Oaks, CA: Sage.

Jörissen, Benjamin (2007) 'Informelle Lernkulturen in Online-Communities. Mediale Rahmungen und rituelle Gestaltungsweisen', in *Lernkulturen im Umbruch*. Wiesbaden: VS-Verlag für Sozialwissenschaften. pp. 184–219.

Jörissen, Benjamin and Marotzki, Winfried (2009) *Medienbildung – Eine Einführung. Theorie–Methoden–Analysen*. Bad Heilbrunn: Klinkhardt.

Lenhart, Amanda and Madden, Mary (2007) *Teens, Privacy and Online Social Networks: How Teens Manage Their Online Identities and Personal*

Ling, Richard Seyler (2004) *The Mobile Connection: The Cell Phone's Impact on Society*. San Francisco: Morgan Kaufmann.

Ling, Richard Seyler (2007) 'Children, youth and mobile communication', *Journal of Children and Media*, 1 (1): 60–7. Available online at: www.richardling.com/papers/2007_Journal_of_child_and_media.pdf (accessed 23 July 2012).

Ling, Richard Seyler (2008) 'The mediation of ritual interaction via the mobile telephone', in James Katz (ed.), *Handbook of Mobile Communications Studies*. Cambridge, MA: MIT Press. pp. 165–76.

Mann, Chris and Stewart, Fiona (2000) *Internet Communication and Qualitative Research: A Handbook for Researching Online*. London: Sage.

Marcus, Bernd, Machilek, Franz and Schütz, Astrid (2006) 'Personality in cyberspace: Personal Web Sites as media for personality expressions and impressions', *Journal of Personality and Social Psychology*, 90 (6): 1014–31.

Marotzki, Winfried (2003) 'Online-Ethnographie – Wege und Ergebnisse zur Forschung im Kulturraum Internet', in Ben Bachmair et al. (eds), *Jahrbuch Medienpädagogik 3*. Opladen: Leske + Budrich, pp. 149–65.

Purwandari, Betty, Hall, Wendy and Wills, Gary B. (2011) 'Methodology for impact analysis of the mobile web in developing countries: A pilot study in Nairobi, Kenya', Paper presented at ACM WebSci 2011, Koblenz, Germany.

Rheingold, Howard (1993) *The Virtual Community: Homesteading on the Electronic Frontier*. Reading, MA: Addison-Wesley.

Schroeder, Ralph and Bailenson, Jeremy (2008) 'Research uses of multi-user virtual environments', in Raymond Lee et al. (eds), *The Handbook of Online Research Methods*. London: Sage. pp. 327–42.

Turkle, Sherry (1995) *Life on the Screen: Identity in the Age of the Internet*. New York: Simon and Schuster.

Wellman, Barry (2004) 'The three ages of Internet studies: Ten, five and zero years ago', *New Media and Society*, 6 (1): 123–9.

Wellman, Barry and Gulia, Milena (1999) 'Virtual communities as communities: Net surfers don't ride alone', in Barry Wellman (ed.), *Communities in Cyberspace*. New York: Routledge. pp. 331–6.

Wellman, Barry and Haythornthwaite, Caroline (2002) *The Internet in Everyday Life (Information Age Series)*. Maldon, MA. Wiley-Blackwell.

Yee, Nick (2007) 'Motivations for play in online games', *Cyberpsychology and Behavior*, 9: 772–5.

Zappavigna, M. (2011) 'Ambient affiliation: A linguistic perspective on Twitter', *New Media and Society*, 13 (5): 788–806.

PART V

Using and Assessing Qualitative Data Analysis

After illuminating qualitative data analysis from the two sides – starting from analytic approaches (Part III) or from specific types of data (Part IV) – we now focus again on the context of the data analysis. Part V covers *using and assessing* the *results* of qualitative data analysis in nine chapters. Using qualitative data analysis refers to several levels of use.

First, ways of practical use reaching from reanalyzing the data (see Wästerfors et al., Chapter 32) to using them in the context of meta-analysis (see Timulak, Chapter 33), then to integrating them in mixed methods designs (see Morse and Maddox, Chapter 36) and finally implementation of the results (see Murray, Chapter 40). Using the analysis and its results can refer to issues of generalization (see Maxwell and Chmiel, Chapter 37) and theorization (see Kelle, Chapter 38).

Using and assessing the results also refers to issues of quality of analysis (see Barbour, Chapter 34), to the ethics of using the data (see Mertens, Chapter 35) and to writing in and about analysis (see Denzin, Chapter 39).

Guideline questions as an orientation for writing the chapters were the following: What are the challenges of translating qualitative data analysis findings (into general statements, practices or theories)? What characterizes the history of this issue in qualitative research, and what is a good example of it? What are the theoretical backgrounds for this issue? What ways can be suggested for using (generalizing/implementing/theorizing) qualitative analysis in an ethically sound and reflexive way? How can the quality of analysis be maintained and how can one write about it? How can qualitative analyses be reused and what is the impact of intending to do so on the original analysis? What is a recent example of doing so? What are the limits and out-range of using qualitative data analysis for this purpose? What are the new developments and perspectives in this context?

Reading the chapters in Part V should help to answer questions like the following ones for a study and its method(s): How can findings be generalized or implemented? How can findings be made relevant? How can one arrive at theoretical insights on the basis of qualitative data analysis? How can one reflect ethics, quality and writing in and of the analysis?

In answering questions like these, the chapters in this part are meant to contribute to bringing the results of analysing qualitative data back into the world that was studied and beyond.

32

Reanalysis of Qualitative Data

David Wästerfors, Malin Åkerström
and Katarina Jacobsson

Reanalysis of qualitative data should be at the core of qualitative research. It facilitates dialogue, debate and progression in qualitative research, not only between various researchers and studies (Fielding and Fielding, 2008), but also between works from the same researcher at different times (Riessman, 2003; Roulston, 2001). Reanalysis slows down analysis to a point at which new findings, theories and methodologies can more easily crystallize. Using reanalysis, researchers may disentangle data from preceding perspectives and zeitgeists, make comparisons across time and cases, and frame data in a new way.

Many terms can be employed to describe what we want to discuss here. Instead of reanalysing we may talk about restudying, reinterpreting, re-examining, reviewing, reusing, recycling, or revisiting qualitative data, or in some cases simply repeating or continuing analysis. A generic term in research methodology is *secondary analysis*, which typically refers to a more distinct use of archived qualitative data by a second researcher (Corti, 2007; Corti and Thompson, 2004). Because we consider 'reanalysis' as one of the broadest terms of the area, including any second (or third, fourth, etc.) look at previously collected data, regardless of whether they are picked from archives or from other sources, we will primarily stick to this term, but we will also address secondary analysis. Studying archived qualitative data is the prime route to reanalysis for many researchers, but our intention here is to go beyond archive studies and include more subtle and scattered variants that have not yet been as articulated as the growing and promising strategy of secondary analysis (Corti, 2007; Corti and Thompson, 2004; Fielding and Fielding, 2008). Thus, reanalysis is suggested as an umbrella term, not as a substitute for secondary analysis.

Reanalysis is an option that needs to be cultivated rather than a clear-cut research design. As it is typically integrated in or tightly related to past projects, with their specific aims, data collections, perspectives and results, reanalysis can be described in processual, exemplifying and practical terms. Some examples in this chapter are taken from our own studies in order to draw on our knowledge of the respective contexts. For the sake of clarity, we summarize our discussions throughout the text by listing our most important points.

VARIATIONS AND SITUATIONS

Sources for Reanalysis

There are several variations of qualitative data reanalysis. A researcher may go back to data he or she generated previously, analyse them again, and build on, counter or find nuance in previous findings (Åkerström et al., 2004; Roulston, 2001). A researcher may employ others' data, for example borrowing from shared databases or archives (Fielding and Fielding, 2008), or combine such sources with data from his or her own files (Collins, 2004; 2008). A researcher may reuse data as they are already presented in published books and reports in the form of excerpts, quotations or retold experiences, or in their raw versions in the form of transcripts, notes, pictures or videos taken from researchers' shelves or computers.

Many researchers reuse pieces of old data from different research projects, not for the sake of arguing something in close relation to previous publications, but to free themselves from these publications and explore aspects hitherto unnoticed, scarcely explored, or left behind (Bloor and McIntosh, 1990; Riessman, 2003; Roulston, 2001). Methodological contributions in qualitative research often draw on the authors' or their colleagues' long-term stock of material to clarify principles or elaborate new arguments that are relatively liberated from the original research (e.g. Gubrium and Holstein, 1997; 2009; Ryen, 2004; Silverman, 1997). For example, Silverman (1997: 38–41, 101–6) reused data from his own studies of a paediatric clinic, as well as Carolyn D. Baker's data from interviews with teenagers that she had previously reanalysed (Baker, 1983), in order to discuss how to take field notes and capture 'membership work'. So even reanalysed data can be used again, especially to elaborate methodologies for reanalysis (Åkerström et al., 2004; Corti and Thompson, 2004).

Similar circumstances characterize the production of many theoretical works. Authors formulate general insights and findings from published articles or reports, sometimes adding previously unanalysed pieces of data. A strong anthropological tradition is to write several such works after finishing fieldwork (e.g. the works of Mary Douglas and Michael Herzfeld). Erving Goffman and Pierre Bourdieu worked within this tradition in sociology, as in *Frame Analysis* (Goffman, 1974) and *Distinction* (Bourdieu, 1984). Many sociologists return to classic scholars in order to get a handle on previously generated data scattered in published reports and articles, such as Sellerberg (1994) does with the help of Georg Simmel in *A Blend of Contradictions*.

What seems to unite all variations is suspended ambition to terminate analysis. The researcher conducting reanalysis is, for some reason, not entirely satisfied with the results thus far, but does not necessarily think (or is prone to question the idea) that new data are required to move forward.

Box 32.1 Various sources for reanalysis

1. The researcher's own data.
2. Other researchers' data, such as from archives or databases.
3. Other researchers' data in the form of published excerpts.
4. Combinations of the above.

Motives and Contexts for Reanalysis

The more specific motives and contexts for reanalysis vary. A researcher may feel somehow compelled to do it because the analysis thus far appears unsatisfactory, insufficient, inadequate or unfocused and requires new efforts as soon as an opportunity appears. The researcher may be asked or required to produce a new manuscript without having any practical possibility to gather new material. A research career may demand a new publication, and academic institutions and research networks benefit from it. Groups of researchers engaged in, for example, editing an anthology or a thematic journal issue often approach individual researchers to return to a set of qualitative data and contribute with new and publishable analyses. Sometimes the potential for reanalysis does not reveal itself until an invitation or pressure to do it occurs. Also hard to ignore is the quality of fun that reanalysis researchers demonstrate (e.g., Atkinson, 1992; Collins, 2004; 2008), because going back to old data does not have to be associated with 'oh, am I still not finished with this?', but with a delightful feeling of returning 'home' with fresh perspectives (Åkerström et al., 2004).

If qualitative data are archived, this itself may promote reanalysis, often called secondary analysis (Corti, 2007; Corti and Thompson, 2004). Hammersley (1997) points out that a function of archives is to facilitate the assessment of a particular study's validity (see Barbour, Chapter 34, this volume). He emphasizes the 'time-consuming business' reanalysis may involve and questioned whether data archives really can be used for that purpose, but examples of researchers approaching others' work, such as Rogers' (1992) critical reanalysis of Garfinkel's (1967) study of Agnes (argued against by Zimmerman, 1992), do suggest a strong interest in scrutinizing original data, especially to question an authority's argument and start a debate.

Experiences from the British archive *Qualidata* at the University of Essex show a growing interest in secondary analysis, not only to use previously collected data more effectively, but to further explore historical phenomena, perform comparative studies, and verify original studies (Corti, 2007; Corti and Thompson, 2004). Bishop (2009: 256) talks about a 'strong move toward data sharing' and that norms obstructing the reuse of qualitative data are changing. *Qualidata* started as a rescue operation for data from an expansion of British social research between the 1940s and 1970s (Corti, 2007). The demand for archived data from classic studies soon became significant; for example, Thompson's study of family life and work experience before 1918, Townsend's study of family life of old people between 1865 and 1955, and Blaxter's study on lone mothers between 1955 and 1966. Corti reports that the methods used in contemporary researchers' secondary analysis of these and other archived projects parallel those that are used in the secondary analysis of survey data: 'Over the last 5 years we have witnessed a new culture of the secondary use of qualitative data, which has been largely borne out of the UK data-sharing policy' (2007: 52).

If data are not stored and made available for future research, critique and debates can easily be blocked or curtailed. The Swedish sociologist Eva Kärfve (2000) questioned the results that indicated an extraordinary high proportion of a research population was suffering from 'DAMP', a Swedish neuropsychiatric diagnosis similar to ADHD. She requested access to the data collected by psychiatrist Christopher Gillberg but was denied such access. After several turns in a legal process, the material was eventually destroyed by Gillberg's colleagues so that Kärfve could not reanalyse it. Since that time the scientific debate regarding 'DAMP' has seemed difficult to complete despite the fact that Kärfve (2000) pointed out a range of methodological problems in the original study.

An interest in archived data can also be more straightforwardly incremental. When Fielding and Fielding (2008) revisited the original data on which Cohen and Taylor (1972) based their research on the long-term imprisonment of men in maximum security, they found that Cohen and Taylor had sidestepped prisoners' claims of rehabilitation and downplayed the researchers' own reformative impact. Cohen and Taylor were more interested in the prisoners' opposition and resistance, a theme consistent with the sociology of the late 1960s and the 'empowerment' orientation of the time. However, the Fieldings, freed from this zeitgeist, do not regard their new conceptualization as proof of Cohen and Taylor having been 'wrong', but as an alternative and complementary view of the archived prison data (Fielding and Fielding, 2008: 85). They benefited from Cohen's comments on their restudy in their article and thanked him for his positive response to their work.

One of the authors of this chapter used interviews with retired correctional officers conducted by a student in ethnology 10 years earlier and archived in the *Folk Life Archives* at the Division of Ethnology at Lund University in Sweden. The aim was to add new topics, as well as an historical dimension, to a study on quarrels in prison (Wästerfors, 2007). Though the archived interviews were originally intended to depict correctional officers' professional roles, their content (in terms of stories and examples from the everyday prison reality in the second half of the twentieth century) supplemented details and supported general tendencies in the rest of the study based on the author's recent interviews with inmates and prison staff. Nothing in this reanalysis of archived data disagreed with the first student's original conclusions (Arnedal, 1995). The archived data simply helped develop and substantiate an unfolding analysis of prison quarrels, on which the original study had not focused.

Indeed, takeovers of another researcher's data may generate not only theoretical contributions, but also methodological contributions. When Brekhus et al. (2005) reanalysed data in Humphreys' book *Tearoom Trade*, along with Humphreys' unpublished observational notes from the same project, they made a case for the need for 'thin descriptions'. Brekhus et al. (2005: 869) suggested that 'rich' data do not necessarily equal a thick description, but this depends as much on 'empirical purview and analytic need' as on the data themselves. When Humphreys' aim was to study the anonymous city life through hasty sexual encounters between men in the so-called tearooms, 'there was good analytic reason for thin description' (Brekhus et al., 2005: 869), even though he easily could have made the analysis richer considering the data he collected. Brekhus et al. use Humphrey's published and unpublished data not to object to his conclusions, but to reflect upon when qualitative researchers require a lot of empirical details: 'Our aim is to unpack and shed light on the operational meaning of *richness* or *thickness*' (2005: 863).

Box 32.2 Various motives and contexts for reanalysis

1. A lingering sense of not being done, or simply for the fun of it.
2. A request to produce a new text but not necessarily new data.
3. Validity assessments of past studies, often with the help of archived data.
4. To further explore historical phenomena and/or to do comparative studies.
5. Substantiating and developing current analyses or theories.
6. Making methodological contributions.

WHAT TO GAIN

Advancing Theory

Many researchers find reanalysis helpful when they want to uncover fundamental processes and general themes. For example, one of the authors of this chapter was helped by the use of ethnographies from other countries when writing about criminal lifestyles, drawing on data from Sweden (Åkerström, 1993). With the help of published data in these ethnographies, some skills and attractions among the investigated criminals could be derived from the demands and conditions of the criminal lifestyle per se rather than the specific culture or social conditions of, for instance, the Swedish welfare state. Without the comparison material, the interviewed criminals would have appeared much more 'local' or national and the theoretical points in the findings would have been harder to distinguish. A conventional literature review was not enough; she needed to tackle the data as directly as possible.

In another study originating from an investigation of informers in prison, the same researcher wanted to broaden the topic to the sociology of treachery (Åkerström, 1991). The way forward was to collect, read and analyse reports from studies of spies, war biographies, whistle-blowers, confessions, infidelity, children who tell tales, and so on, with as much sociological imagination as possible in order to identify generalities in the social forms and experiences of betrayal. This procedure in Georg Simmel's formal sociology or 'analogical theorizing' (Vaughan, 2004) aims to compare parallel activities, phenomena or experiences in various social settings in order to develop generalizable theoretical arguments (see Maxwell and Chmiel, Chapter 37, and Kelle, Chapter 38, this volume). Such a procedure would be almost insurmountable if previously collected data (others' and the researcher's own) were not reused. The point of producing formal sociology is to train one's gaze for similarities across cases, but to investigate personally all settings or phenomena in the treachery project would not be realistic. Sticking to the investigated informers in prison and adding data from others' reports, stories and studies seemed more productive.

Distance in time and lack of emotional proximity may stimulate scientific clarity in reanalysis projects. Atkinson (1992: 460) writes of being 'cold' when returning to one's own old data; that is, a feeling of being free from former emotional bonds. 'After some passages of time, the notes are alien in some respects', Atkinson (1992: 460) argues, but they 'can still evoke a lived experience'. This particular combination of familiarity and alienation seems to have helped him theorize the narrative flow and order of a medical setting formerly hidden in the fragmentation of his original notes.

Allowing sources and motives to vary in a reanalysis project can be crucial for advancing theory. It is – or should be – the quality of the analysis rather than the source of the data that ultimately matters (Silverman, 2007; 1997), and this is a strong argument for selecting more freely in relation to various sources according to a given motive. If the analytic quality is kept in focus there will be a better chance to advance theory. Collins argues along these lines when he accounted for reusing other sociologists' observations and data in his work on violence, including student reports, personal accounts and even media:

> Throughout I follow the rule to make my own interpretations of the data. This often means detaching them from the reporter's or the previous analyst's concern for what is important, and from their framework of understanding. One might say that sociology is to a large extent the art of reframing other people's observations. When the observations are those of previous sociologists and the reframing is strongly overlapping, we can speak of cumulative theoretical progress. (Collins, 2008: 32)

Economy

Parry and Mauthner (2004: 140) argue that there is a trend of viewing qualitative data as 'global commodities' that should be accessible through data archives, a trend stimulated by diminishing resources. Many types of qualitative material are time consuming to generate, particularly ethnographic fieldwork and its profound personal involvement. Indeed, there is an economy in reanalysis that does not need to be interpreted in cynical terms. Certainly, there ought to be time and resources for new fieldwork, but the time and resources already invested in previous fieldwork should be handled with care, especially those concerning hard-to-reach populations (Fielding and Fielding, 2008). Formal archives with digitized data undoubtedly provide the most economizing 'infrastructure' in this respect (Corti and Thompson, 2004), but informal archives, personal data collections, and published data in books and articles may also save a lot of work.

If we were to return to the treachery study (Åkerström, 1991), dismissing all published data in these studies of spies, war, whistle-blowers, confessions, infidelity, tell-tale children, etc., data that the researcher reused to compare with her own data on informers in prison, and instead ask for new projects, this would hardly be rational, at least not without seriously considering reusing the previous data. Reanalysis may pay respects to the findings of previous research, not by sanctifying these findings, but by carefully conceptualizing them differently.

Strengthening Qualitative Research

What, after all, distinguishes reanalysis of qualitative data from any other method of analysing qualitative data? Are the reframing processes and ideals in reanalysis commonplace in qualitative research in general? A reanalysis is special in every case, but basically it seems to draw on the same principles and traditions as any other analysis, aiming at, for example, 'non-obvious' sociology (Collins, 1992) or uncovering the irony in human conduct by applying new perspectives (Berger, 1991 [1963]: ch. 2). However, reanalysis typically accentuates such aims and traditions because they make them stronger and more distinct. When having a 'second look' (Baker, 1983) at data, we seem to demand more from ourselves.

Of course, a first analysis should be able to see 'around the corner', to challenge 'the implacable familiarity', or 'the common-sense models and expectations' regarding the data at issue (Schegloff, 1992/1998, I: lix). Being able to include new aspects and themes emerging during the fieldwork should be possible; 'the path of qualitative analysis is never linear' (Corti and Thompson, 2004: 334). For example, the original prison study that Fielding and Fielding (2008: 87) returned to should ideally have been conducted so that the prisoners' conversations about their pasts and family ties were taken into account. Cohen and Taylor should not have been so trapped in their efforts to study the prisoners' resistance that these things were overlooked.

However, this is easier said than done. An empirical project can be hard work, perhaps not leaving enough energy for major shifts in perspective. Silverman (1997: 39) writes that 'the rush to categorize is laudable'; there is not always time or energy to develop original interpretations. Few would doubt that Cohen and Taylor's (1972) original prison study was made better and more interesting with the help of Fielding and Fielding's (2008) secondary

---

Box 32.3   What is gained with reanalysis?

1. Data get relatively disentangled from former perspectives and theory can be advanced.
2. Time spent on new data collection is economized and more is made of the time already spent in the field.
3. Basic traditions and principles in qualitative research are strengthened.

analysis, but many would agree that all of this hardly could have been achieved from the very beginning. Surprising findings and fascinating sidetracks are more likely if analysis is performed more than once.

WHAT TO DO

What can researchers do to facilitate and encourage reanalysis? Readers of Harvey Sacks's collected lectures (Sacks, 1992/1998, I and II) are likely struck by his repeated reanalyses. The same dialogue or set of rejoinders are quoted again and again, making them into objects of successively more complex reasoning. Examples such as 'The baby cried. The mommy picked it up' are used so many times that one might get the impression of analytic mania. The quality of fun cannot be denied, nor the hard work, as Emanuel Schegloff pointed out in his introduction (Sacks, 1992/1998, I: lix).

Instead of hunting for new data or moving forward in the conversation or text he was dealing with at the time, Sacks often chose to return to the data he had already processed and discussed. By 'directly taking up particular occurrences, particular bits of tape and transcripts', he tried to free 'each next engagement with data from the past' (Sacks, 1992/1998, I: lix). Old ways of looking at conversation and interactions should be transcended, including his own, by relistening, rereading and reciting an 'old fragment of data' (Sacks, 1992/1998, I: lix).

Our most basic advice is found in Sacks's method. A body of material has to be identified and delimited, and at least fragments of it have to be reread, listened to or watched again (Åkerström et al., 2004; Roulston, 2001). Regardless of the kind of source or the specific relationship the researcher has with the data, he or she has to mobilize a new engagement that somehow frees itself from the past. The past still informs the analysis, and the analytic results should be communicated in relation to this past (e.g. an objection, a correction or an elaboration of previous knowledge), but the researcher should also try to be 'freshly open to what could be going on', as Schegloff put it (Sacks, 1992/1998, I: lix).

Reanalysis cannot be performed without direct contact with the data. Merely rereading conclusions, theoretical implications, overall results, summaries, or the like, does not help. Therefore, one important prerequisite is that data are kept in forms that allow such a new contact. Data should be stored and marked as carefully as possible and published as direct extracts; field notes should be saved in their original shape, transcripts should be as detailed as possible, and transcribed interactions should be possible to scrutinize again to improve the quality (Åkerström et al., 2004; Roulston, 2001). The availability of raw data and 'flat' descriptions is especially valuable (Corti and Thompson, 2004; Silverman, 1997).

It is not a coincidence that conversation analysis (see Toerien, Chapter 22, this volume) and its inbuilt reanalysis practice came about at a time when the tape recorder was starting to gain systematic use in the social sciences. The tape recorder allows researchers to go back to previously collected data on a countless number of occasions, allows the sharing of data in an uncomplicated way, allows the production of successively refined transcripts (see Kowal and O'Connell, Chapter 5, this volume) that can be reread repeatedly, and helps document significant matters that are impossible to catch as a note-taker: pauses, overlaps, inbreaths, etc. (Silverman, 1998). The tape recorder's rewind button was an important milestone.

When it comes to archived data, documenting the research process is particularly important for contextualizing the material for any second analyst, even though this cannot fully replace the experience of having been present (Corti, 2007; Corti and Thompson, 2004). Qualitative data are often kept on the researchers' computers or in boxes of personal papers, but 'there are few common descriptive standards, access to many collections is poor, and there are no integrated resource discovery tools' (Corti 2007: 39). Establishing more archives and inviting researchers to deposit their data would improve the infrastructure and quality of reanalysis. If a culture of sharing data is encouraged, scholars would not always prioritize new data collections or be reluctant to use others' data (Corti, 2007; Corti and Thompson, 2004).

After identifying and delimiting a body of material, other advice becomes relevant: create fruitful conditions for reorganizing the material and seeing it in alternative ways. Interesting reanalyses often include some kind of serendipity, that is to say some surprising and lucky discovery, and the trick is to make the research as capable as possible to achieve this. The researcher may actively look for new perspectives or theories to understand the data, but may also stumble over them, get trained in them, or be influenced in other ways. The researcher may get drawn into contemporary analytic trends or, alternatively, wish to resist such trends. Researchers may imitate or challenge colleagues and be inspired by the classics, fiction, other disciplines or forgotten works, among others. As long as the argument is clear and solid, and as long as the analysis is empirically grounded, an analyst need not hesitate to find impetus from any imaginable source.

In Collins' (2008) book on violence, his previously established framework of interaction ritual chains helped him reorganize previously documented data on violent situations in effective ways, making him see things as he would not have seen them without it. In Atkinson's (1992) case, an established interest in narratives helped him reorganize his old data from a medical setting in the form of extended stories, which freed him from his original idea of cutting extracts to illustrate themes or categories ('the [academic] culture of fragmentation', Atkinson, 1992: 470; also see Silverman, 1997: 39). In a study of transnational businessmen by one of the authors of this chapter (Wästerfors, 2008), the researcher's intensified interest in ethnomethodology (see Eberle, Chapter 13, this volume) helped him go back to a set of business accounts from Eastern Central Europe originally generated during his dissertation project, and to understand these accounts in terms of 'folk ethnography' within business activities. When Roulston (2001) revisited her data on music teachers, she left her old thematic analysis behind and embarked on a conversation analysis (see Toerien, Chapter 22, this volume) of interview data (see Roulston, Chapter 20, this volume), which enabled her not only to criticize her previous report and its representational view of language, but also to show the morally loaded nature of the teachers' cultural world. Inspired by ethnomethodological approaches to interview discussions, her original interviews could not be used to answer her original research questions, but they could show a lot of other and more delicate phenomena.

Readers of Harvey Sacks's collected lectures may be surprised by the fact that he often refers to social anthropologists; a closer guess would probably have been sociologists like Harold Garfinkel and Erving Goffman, who, of course, also influenced him a lot (see Silverman, 1998: 32–42). The lesson to learn is that specializing in a narrow body of literature probably works against the chances of serendipity. Rather, a broad and 'lustful'

Box 32.4 Ways to facilitate reanalysis

1. Identify a body of data to go over.
2. Be as open as possible to what might be going on in the material.
3. Create opportunities for conceptualizing the data in new ways; look for inspiration from multiple sources.
4. Store and mark data carefully to make future reanalysis possible; publish data as direct excerpts; encourage and improve data sharing through archives.

reading list helps, a list that does not necessarily respect conventional boundaries, as Silverman (1998: 42) pointed out: 'attempts to draw final boundaries between different approaches to social science serve to work against the very kind of lateral thinking that original minds like Sacks encourage'.

STUMBLING BLOCKS

One of the difficulties in reanalysis arises when we use others' data or data composed for purposes other than our own. We do not know everything about how, when, where or why the data were collected. Data are infused with specific circumstances and interests. If we use the media, for instance, they tend to publish breaking news, reports on what journalists deem to be scandalous behaviour, or reports on events that 'everybody' is considered to be interested in and talking about. The 'cumulative theoretical progress' that Collins (2008: 32) refers to may be built on ground we do not know very much about. Similar problems arise when other researchers' published data are reused. We know what the researcher explicitly states about the methods, settings and the researcher's role, among others, but any information on methodological details beyond what he or she chose to publish will be absent. However, communicating with the researcher personally may help (cf. Fielding and Fielding, 2008).

This problem, however, does not necessarily motivate any essentially different treatment from researchers' common cautiousness in how they treat, judge and use qualitative data. Analysts should always cultivate a cautious and reflexive attitude (see May and Perry, Chapter 8, this volume), asking themselves in what context the data was generated (how, when, where, by whom, etc.), so that we continuously consider the social circumstances of the particular instances at issue. The difference when reanalysing another researcher's collected data is that not only do we know relatively little about these circumstances, but that it may be hard to improve our knowledge. Fieldworkers use their personal insights and experiences from the field as tools initially to analyse and code data, but this may very well be 'indefinable' for others (Corti and Thompson, 2004). Also, when revisiting one's own data a loss of context may become evident, as field memories wane (Mauthner et al., 1998): 'The original context can never be truly reconstructed' (Corti and Thompson, 2004: 335).

First, this problem must be accounted for in publications so that readers are able to judge for themselves whether the reanalysis is still on solid ground. It is important not to conceal or gloss over the unavailability of the original context. Second, the fact that data are decontextualized can motivate a fresh perspective in relation to contexts previously taken for granted, making a virtue of necessity. For example, Collins (2008) reused media data originally created for the purpose of showing the drama of military violence (e.g. photos from war and riot situations) to scrutinize details, patterns and reported contexts to argue against this taken-for-granted interpretation, showing that violence typically is not that dramatic or all-encompassing as war reporters think. Similarly, Goffman's reuse of other researchers' and reporters' data typically aimed at subtle details in human face-to-face interactions that previous presentations had ignored. The context, in terms of an unfolding interaction, is thereby given much *more* significance than originally, albeit dressed in other forms and definitions.

A second obstacle to reanalysis has to do with the researcher. In the methodological literature one refers to saturation in terms of nothing new or unpredictable turning up when collecting data (Alasuutari, 1995; Glaser and Strauss, 1967; also see Thornberg and Charmaz, Chapter 11, this volume). In turning one's focus from the empirical field to a researcher reanalysing his or her own previously collected data, one may note how the researcher may also become 'saturated'. One's appetite for gaining more from a study that is completed, and from data that one has traversed over and over, may be lost in some cases. This problem has hardly anything to do with the data themselves, but is harboured in the researcher's emotions, energy, motivation or 'analytic appetite'. A way to overcome this challenge and start anew may simply be to let time elapse. Another way may be to turn to archived data or a colleague's data collection, thereby escaping the feelings attached to one's own material.

A third and related difficulty arises from cultural 'time norms' (Åkerström et al., 2004: 354). In many ways the new is celebrated; it is easier to get financing for new research projects and new data collections than for the reanalysis of old material: 'Few researchers either take the opportunity, or indeed are presented with an opportunity, to take more than one "stab" at a given project' (Roulston, 2001: 279). Colleagues often are more supportive, curious and respectful when you tell them about a major new effort. There is something visibly persuading and impressive in venturing onto untrodden fields, hiring new staff, constructing new ways of collecting data, and planning new field studies. New data gathering confirms the researcher's competence and ingenuity, and new proposals make us seem productive: 'Researchers' careers are made by discovering new things, not extracting the maximum from existing data' (Fielding and Fielding, 2008: 82). This means that a reanalyzing researcher may be sighed over in terms of 'being stuck in that old material', but once the article or book is written, the result might very well be a move forward in terms of new methodological, theoretical or analytical insights.

ETHICAL CONCERNS

To depart from an original plan and its ethical declarations may give rise to doubts regarding promises made to research subjects at the outset of the data collection. Yet, there are strong ethical arguments *for* reanalysis, which are often neglected when focusing solely on research subjects. In order to discuss this, we would like to share a case in which one of the authors of this chapter reanalysed data from two separate studies.

In the first study, the researcher interviewed prosecutors and police officers regarding cases of battered women (Jacobsson, 1997). Ten years later, the same researcher interviewed another collection of prosecutors and police officers about court cases of bribery. The researcher then became interested in something that had struck her in the first study: how the prosecutors talked during the interviews. For example, the prosecutors seldom stated personal beliefs, and, if they did, they quickly excused themselves for doing so. They strived to demonstrate objectivity by the very way they talked rather than, for instance, merely pointing to statistics, routines, rules, specific decisions or organizational principles. The prosecutors' choice of words, their firm corrections of the interviewer's questions and suggestions, their restricted methods of employing legal terms and phrases – all of these aspects indicated disciplined discursive behaviour.

When the second study was published and compared with the first one, the researcher realized that she had generated quite an extensive body of data on prosecutors' style of interview talk that, along with a new grant, made reanalysis possible. Now 'objectivity

---

Box 32.5 Difficulties in reanalysis projects

1. The original context of the data is wholly or partly unknown.
2. The researcher may lack further analytical appetite (personal saturation).
3. Time norms in the academic world.

talk' turned out to be a possible aspect to pinpoint and theorize, whether the prosecutors spoke about battered women or bribery or any other type of crime (Jacobsson, 2008).

An ethical problem (see Mertens, Chapter 35, this volume) in this case might be that the prosecutors were not informed about the third study's research questions, and that these questions could hardly be described as close enough to the original project so that their primary consent would be sufficient. One way of dealing with this problem would have been to contact the interviewees again to ask for their consent to reuse their old interview for a purpose other than what was originally stated, and to explain the scientific value. However, between 4 and 12 years had passed since the interviews were conducted. Some of the interviewees had retired or changed jobs, some of them would probably not even remember the interview. The researcher had initially avoided keeping records of the interviewees' names in order to preserve their anonymity; they all appeared difficult to reach.

What can be learned from this case? We are far from suggesting that it constitutes a serious flaw. Anonymity was still guaranteed and the linguistic details and focus in the eventually published data seemed quite innocent and mundane (Jacobsson, 2008). Yet, the third study retrospectively changed the terms and conditions upon which the agreements with the research subjects were based.

Bishop (2009) points out that researchers often make far-reaching promises to treat data with care and confidentiality. Sometimes researchers promise that data will only be used by the primary research team and only for the primary research purpose, and ethical review boards may request such promises. The result is written consent forms that go beyond what is ethically or legally necessary and basically make it impossible to reuse data. Our suggestion would be to include the eventuality of approaching the data with other research questions in the future, after the primary research has been carried out, on the form. A written consent form, as well as orally delivered promises, should not be too narrowly formulated, but open to possibilities to return to the data after the initial work is finished.

Consequently, our case of ethical queries when reanalysing prosecutors' talk can be seen in practical terms, as a consequence of incomplete consent forms during the original data collection. Basically, no consent form can ever be 'complete', particularly not regarding the 'informed' part ('informed consent'). Even in primary research it is impossible to state in advance all details about the research procedures, possible changes in purpose and possible outcomes; if this were doable there would be no reason to conduct research in the first place. Thus, in this respect, all consent is partial (Bishop, 2009). Social research is a search for new knowledge, including new methods to obtain it, and news cannot be foreseeable unless it ceases to be news: 'No one can actually provide full information about how research will be done, or no research could get done' (Bishop, 2009: 263).

VALUE OF REANALYSIS

Bishop (2009) convincingly argues that the debates surrounding data reuse and sharing are often narrowly focused on participants' rights. The research community and wider society make up two other parties to consider:

> To participants, researchers owe a duty to avoid or minimize harm, provide informed consent, and protect confidentiality. To the scholarly community, there is the responsibility to maintain professional standards of conduct with transparency and integrity. Finally, to the public at large, including funders, there is a duty to produce quality research of wider social value. (Bishop, 2009: 258)

Bishop's standpoint can be used to elaborate ethical and epistemological arguments for reanalysis. First, regarding participants, there are duties that must be considered in addition to protecting privacy (Bishop, 2009), such as to avoid unnecessary duplicative data collection and unnecessary intrusion. If data already exist to examine a new research question, repeating the investigation is hardly defensible. It is particularly important to make full use of previously collected material when it comes to small research populations (e.g. pregnant addicts, extreme elite groups) or hard-to-reach populations (e.g. prisoners, illegal migrants) in order to make sure that they are not 'over-researched' (Fielding and Fielding, 2008). Reanalysis may help the research community economize intrusion into populations and social worlds that otherwise are at risk of being put in the limelight and, consequently, marked as 'chronic' social problems. Without the option of reanalysis, researchers may end up reproducing categorizations of people that, in many respects, should be questioned or problematized.

Second, a widely accepted code within the research community is the strong expectation that researchers must not ignore or suppress findings, which is in line with Robert Merton's (1973) so-called CUDOS principles. Merton's first principle, communalism (he called this principle 'communism', but it was later renamed 'communalism'), stipulates that results must not be withheld from the research community and society at large. If a given body of data is deemed to harbour more significant findings than the first analysis was able to show, there is value in reanalysis. If the data are not considered in a new way, interesting results could be ignored or suppressed. Researchers may neglect an option to produce quality research of broader social value.

Third, the gathering of qualitative data is relatively time consuming and costly. To control expenses and avoid duplicating work efforts, researchers should seriously consider the possibility of spending more time exploring new analytic entries in the already available data than on simply collecting more. The intrinsic value of generating new data should be questioned in relation to (1) the data already at hand, and (2) a given research interest. Forcing researchers into new and grandiose data-collecting enterprises could easily turn ethically problematic if they have not been given sufficient time and resources to contemplate the already stored data. Such an approach seems difficult to defend to the public.

CONCLUSION

Qualitative data are generally so rich that they offer plenty of opportunities for reanalysis: 'The most trivial and matter-of-fact', as Sellerberg (1994: ix) noted, is reminiscent of the old Flemish proverb quoted by Georg Simmel: 'There is more within me.'

However, when it comes to methodology, perhaps there is not always more within reanalysis than any other analytic approach. The reflexive work requested by a reanalysis researcher resembles what we normally request from every researcher, such as the importance of taking context into account, as well as the researcher's invested emotions, the research community's norms, and the research subjects' and community's rights. A researcher conducting reanalysis has openly to account for and admit that he or she may sometimes use less than ideal data, that the original contexts are wholly or partially unknown, and account for the specific implications of the new analysis, but when all is said and done we have to conclude that this is more or less the case for all qualitative research. Ideal data do not exist and context cannot be fully described, regardless of whether the data are being analysed for the first, second or third time. Researchers can never 'settle down' in peace and do their analysis uninterrupted by epistemological, technical or ethical worries. In this and related ways, reanalysis is embedded in qualitative research and cannot be treated as a separate research design.

Even though the practice of reanalysing qualitative data clearly entails the idea of 'going back', there are interesting lessons to learn when moving forward. Several points we have tried to make in this chapter deal with how to secure the option of reanalysis in the future; that is, how to behave as researchers today in order to enable and simplify a retrospective project tomorrow. We should store and mark data carefully, possibly archive them jointly, and we should publish data in the form of direct excerpts from original transcripts. We should avoid writing research plans that are too narrow and purposes that are too precise, and we should include an option to reuse data when asking for consent and informing research subjects about ongoing projects.

It might even sound like we should be prepared for a new angle as we develop the 'old' (contemporary) one, but that would be a paradoxical recommendation. When we write that 'old' plan or proposal, it feels like a new one, not something that should be replaced or sidestepped later in a reanalysis. Typically, each project feels new and fresh, no matter how it appears later after we have read the latest book, talked to this colleague or informant, or come across that instance in recent fieldwork.

What we have tried to argue in this chapter is not that there is a completely different way of planning and carrying out qualitative research that permanently resolves all obstacles to reanalysing qualitative data. Rather, obstacles and incitements seem to be built into conventional research proceedings. Our argument is much simpler, and yet suggestive – that fine qualitative data never grow old. Keeping that notion in mind might be the best preparation of all.

FURTHER READING

Atkinson, Paul (1992) 'The ethnography of a medical setting: Reading, writing and rhetoric', *Qualitative Health Research*, 2 (4): 451–74.

Corti, Louise and Thompson, Paul (2004) 'Secondary analysis of archived data', in Clive Seale et al. (eds), *Qualitative Research Practice*. London: Sage. pp. 327–43.

Fielding, Nigel and Fielding, Jane (2008) 'Resistance and adaptation to criminal identity: Using secondary analysis to evaluate classic studies of crime and deviance', *Historical Social Research*, 33 (3): 75–93.

REFERENCES

Åkerström, Malin (1991) *Betrayal and Betrayers: The Sociology of Treachery*. New Brunswick, NJ: Transaction.

Åkerström, Malin (1993) *Crooks and Squares: Lifestyles of Thieves and Addicts in Comparison with Conventional People*. New Brunswick, NJ: Transaction.

Åkerström, Malin, Jacobsson, Katarina and Wästerfors, David (2004) 'Reanalysis of previously collected material', in Clive Seale et al. (eds), *Qualitative Research Practice*. London: Sage. pp. 344–57.

Alasuutari, Pertti (1995) *Researching Culture: Qualitative Method and Cultural Studies*. London: Sage.

Arnedal, Lotta (1995) *Kriminalvården – ett möjligt etnologiskt forskningsobjekt?* Magisteruppsats vid Etnologiska institutionen. Lund: Lund University.

Atkinson, Paul (1992) 'The ethnography of a medical setting: Reading, writing and rhetoric', *Qualitative Health Research*, 2 (4): 451–74.

Baker, Carolyn D. (1983) 'A "second look" at interviews with adolescents', *Journal of Youth and Adolescence*, 12 (6): 501–19.

Berger, Peter L. (1991 [1963]) *Invitation to Sociology: A Humanistic Perspective*. Harmondsworth: Penguin.

Bishop, Libby (2009) 'Ethical sharing and reuse of qualitative data', *Australian Journal of Social Issues*, 44 (3): 255–72.

Bloor, Michael and McIntosh, James (1990) 'Surveillance and concealment: A comparison of client resistance in therapeutic communities and health visiting', in Sarah Cunningham-Burley and Neil P. McKeganey (eds), *Readings in Medical Sociology*. London: Routledge. pp. 159–81.

Bourdieu, Pierre (1984) *Distinction: A Social Critique of the Judgement of Taste*. London: Routledge.

Brekhus, Wayne H., Galliher, John F. and Gubrium, Jaber F. (2005) 'The need for thin description', *Qualitative Inquiry*, 11 (6): 861–79.

Cohen, Stanley and Taylor, Laurie (1972) *Psychological Survival: The Effects of Long-Term Imprisonment*. London: Allen Lane.

Collins, Randall (1992) *Sociological Insight: An Introduction to Non-obvious Sociology*. New York: Oxford University Press.

Collins, Randall (2004) *Interaction Ritual Chains*. Princeton, NJ: Princeton University Press.

Collins, Randall (2008) *Violence: A Micro-sociological Theory*. Princeton, NJ: Princeton University Press.

Corti, Louise (2007) 'Re-using archived qualitative data – where, how, why?', *Archival Science*, 7 (1): 37–54.

Corti, Louise and Thompson, Paul (2004) 'Secondary analysis of archived data', in Clive Seale et al. (eds),

Qualitative Research Practice. London: Sage. pp. 327–43.

Fielding, Nigel and Fielding, Jane (2008) 'Resistance and adaptation to criminal identity: Using secondary analysis to evaluate classic studies of crime and deviance', *Historical Social Research*, 33 (3): 75–93.

Garfinkel, Harold (1967) *Studies in Ethnomethodology*. Englewood Cliffs, NJ: Prentice Hall.

Glaser, Barney G. and Strauss, Anselm L. (1967) *The Discovery of Grounded Theory: Strategies for Qualitative Research*. New York: Aldine de Gruyter.

Goffman, Erving (1974) *Frame Analysis: An Essay in the Organization of Experience*. Boston, MA: Northeastern University Press.

Gubrium, Jaber F. and Holstein, James A. (1997) *The New Language of Qualitative Method*. New York: Oxford University Press.

Gubrium, Jaber F. and Holstein, James A. (2009) *Analyzing Narrative Reality*. Los Angeles: Sage.

Hammersley, Martyn (1997) 'Qualitative data archiving: Some reflections on its prospects and problems', *Sociology*, 31 (1): 131–42.

Jacobsson, Katarina (1997) Den misshandlade kvinnan i den rättsliga processen (The battered woman in the legal process), in *Våld mot kvinnor* (*Violence against women*), BRÅ-rapport 1997:2. Stockholm: Brottsförebyggande rådet.

Jacobsson, Katarina (2008) '"We can't just do it any which way". Objectivity work among Swedish prosecutors', *Qualitative Sociology Review*, 4 (1):46–68.

Kärfve, Eva (2000) *Hjärnspöken. DAMP och hotet mot folkhälsan*. Eslöv: Brutus Östlings Bokförlag Symposion.

Mauthner, Natasha S., Parry, Odette and Backett-Milbrun, Kathryn (1998) 'The data are out there, or are they? Implications for archiving and revisiting qualitative data', *Sociology*, 32 (4): 733–45.

Merton, Robert (1973) *The Sociology of Science: Theoretical and Empirical Investigations*. Chicago: Chicago University Press.

Parry, Odette and Mauthner, S. Natasha (2004) 'Whose data are they anyway? Practical, legal and ethical issues in archiving qualitative research data', *Sociology*, 38 (1): 139–52.

Riessman, Catherine Kohler (2003) 'Performing identities in illness narrative: Masculinity and multiple sclerosis', *Qualitative Research*, 3 (1): 5–33.

Rogers, Mary F. (1992) 'They all were passing: Agnes, Garfinkel, and company', *Gender and Society*, 6 (June): 169–91.

Roulston, Kathryn (2001) 'Data analysis and "theorizing as ideology"', *Qualitative Research*, 1 (3): 279–302.

Ryen, Anne (2004) *Kvalitativ intervju. Från vetenskapsteori till fältstudier*. Malmö: Liber.

Sacks, Harvey (1992/1998) *Lectures on Conversation*, vols I and II. Oxford: Blackwell.

Schegloff, Emanuel (1992/1998) 'Introduction', in Harvey Sacks, *Lectures on Conversation*, vols I and II. Oxford: Blackwell. pp. ix–lxiv.

Sellerberg, Ann-Mari (1994) *A Blend of Contradictions: Georg Simmel in Theory and Practice*. New Brunswick, NJ: Transaction.

Silverman, David (1997) *Interpreting Qualitative Data: Methods for Analysing Talk, Text and Interaction*. London: Sage.

Silverman, David (1998) *Harvey Sacks: Social Science and Conversation Analysis*. New York: Oxford University Press.

Silverman, David (2007) *A Very Short, Fairly Interesting and Reasonably Cheap Book about Qualitative Research*. London: Sage.

Vaughan, Diane (2004) 'Theorizing disaster: Analogy, historical ethnography, and the Challenger accident', *Ethnography*, 5 (3): 315–47.

Wästerfors, David (2007) *Fängelsebråk. Interaktionistiska analyser av konflikter på anstalt*. Lund: Studentlitteratur.

Wästerfors, David (2008) 'Businessmen as folk ethnographers', *Ethnography*, 9 (2): 235–56.

Zimmerman, Don H. (1992) 'They were all doing gender, but they weren't all passing: Comment on Rogers', *Gender & Society*, 6 (2): 192–8.

Qualitative Meta-analysis

Ladislav Timulak

The number of qualitative research studies on a similar topic within the same field of study is growing. Traditional narrative reviews lack a systematic approach to the evaluation and synthesis of the research studies examining the same phenomenon/a. Several systematic approaches to the review, evaluation, analysis and synthesis of a group of studies investigating the same phenomenon/a have been proposed in recent years. These approaches use different, though in many aspects overlapping or similar, methodologies. They can be known under a variety of labels, such as qualitative meta-analysis, qualitative meta-synthesis, meta-ethnography, grounded formal theory, meta-study or meta-summary (cf. Thorne et al., 2004).

The most frequently used term, for what I refer to in this chapter as qualitative meta-analysis, is *qualitative meta-synthesis* (cf. Finfgeld, 2003; Jensen and Allen, 1996; Thorne et al., 2004). Authors preferring the term *meta-synthesis* argue that the meta-analytical procedure is, in the case of qualitative meta-analysis, more interpretive than aggregative (Finfgeld, 2003) and therefore the term *synthesis* is more appropriate. On the contrary, the argument for use of the term *qualitative meta-analysis* suggests using this term similarly as it is used in quantitative research (Timulak, 2009). Quantitative meta-analysis also aims at interpretation and inference, yet the activity of 'analysis' is stressed in the title.

Qualitative meta-analysis is a secondary analysis (see Wästersfors et al., Chapter 32, this volume) of the primary, original, studies addressing the same research questions. It has two main aims: (1) to provide a concise and comprehensive picture of findings across those studies; and (2) to examine and evaluate the impact of methodological influences in the original studies on their findings (Timulak, 2009). The ultimate goal is, as Schreiber et al. (1997: 314) put it, to review a group of studies '*for the purposes of discovering the essential elements and translating the results into an end product that transforms the original results into a new conceptualization*' (italics in original). This conceptualization should be, as Finfgeld (2003: 894) suggests, 'more substantive than those [conceptualizations] resulting from individual investigations'.

OUTLINE OF THE DEVELOPMENTAL AND THEORETICAL BACKGROUND OF THE APPROACH

The idea of qualitative meta-analysis was probably first proposed by Stern and Harris (1985; cf. Schreiber et al., 1997); however, the major impact on the field came from a work on meta-ethnography in education by Noblit and Hare (1988). Currently, there exist a variety of approaches to qualitative meta-analysis. Some, using Ponterotto's classification (2005), have more post-positivistic characteristics and tend rather to summarize findings of the original studies. Others have a more constructivist–interpretive approach and aim at interpreting the original studies and offering an overarching or a particular perspective presenting conceptualization. Therefore, it is important to note that the approach to conducting qualitative meta-analysis may vary across researchers and research teams, and that there is not one consensually agreed upon approach.

The variety and diversity in the approach to qualitative meta-analysis is also reflected in the fact that there exist various 'brand name' methods of conducting qualitative meta-analysis. Although it is probably true that each of the brand name approaches brings a unique set of skills and perspectives, which it emphasizes, and sees as defining, two meta-analyses using the same brand name approach may sometimes be more different than two meta-analyses using different brand name approaches.

Meta-ethnography

One of the first approaches to qualitative meta-analysis was the work of Noblit and Hare (1988) on *meta-ethnography*. The basic idea of meta-ethnography (see Gubrium and Holstein, Chapter 3, this volume), according to Noblit and Hare, is that of translating primary studies one into another and looking for similarities and dissimilarities in their findings. To accomplish this aim, they utilize three distinct approaches depending on the nature of primary studies.

Their first approach to meta-ethnography is called *reciprocal translations as synthesis*. It can be used for synthesizing similar studies. The basic idea of this approach is to translate findings of one study, as captured in the language of that primary study, into the language of other similar primary studies. Noblit and Hare (1988) describe how 'metaphors' of one study translate to other studies. Through this process of translation new metaphors can be generated that would capture findings present in meta-analysed studies.

The second approach to meta-ethnography that Noblit and Hare (1988) outline is that of *refutational synthesis*. According to them, it is necessary to apply this approach when the analysed primary studies are using interpretations (see Willig, Chapter 10, this volume) of data that are mutually refutational. In that case, according to Noblit and Hare, it is more meaningful to study what is responsible for this refutation. This means studying the conceptual rules ('ideology') of interpretation used in primary studies, the use of which may be responsible for mutually refutational conclusions. To demonstrate the use of refutational synthesis the authors present examples in which an ideological position or perspective taken (e.g. type of informants) may influence the interpretation of data. The final synthesis must then not only synthesize the primary findings through highlighting the complementarity of studies with each other, but also indicate points of departure between the studies and outline the reasons for this departure.

Finally, Noblit and Hare (1988) offer an approach to meta-ethnography that they call *lines-of-argument synthesis*. They find inspiration for this approach in grounded theory (Glaser and Strauss, 1967; also see Thornberg and Charmaz, Chapter 11, this volume). They see the usefulness of this method when there is a group of studies potentially contributing to a more comprehensive picture (the whole). Reciprocal translations are seen in the case of line-of-argument synthesis as a first step in the meta-ethnography that is then followed by clinical inference or grounded theorizing putting similarities and dissimilarities in the primary studies into a new context, providing a new interpretation, 'the whole' line of argument (Noblit and Hare, 1988: 64).

Noblit and Hare's (1988) meta-ethnographic approach was very important for the field of qualitative meta-analysis as many other authors (e.g., Beck, 2001; 2002; Paterson et al., 2001) refer to it as the source of inspiration. An interesting point in their approach is an assessment of whether the analysed studies are taking a comparable perspective on the subject of investigation and whether they could add to each other. It is especially interesting that in the case when studies are incompatible, the meta-analysis focuses on the reasons for this incompatibility. It resembles the quantitative meta-analytic strategy of looking at how methodological approaches in primary studies influence the effect sizes in them. Similarly interesting is the approach of translating the findings of one study into the framework of another study. This exercise seems to be an especially good interim step in analysing a larger group of studies. It allows for the illumination of similarities and dissimilarities between findings in primary studies.

Meta-study

Another approach to qualitative meta-analysis is that of *meta-study* summarized by Paterson et al. (2001) and influenced by other authors such as Zhao (1991) or Ritzer (1990). According to Patterson et al. (2001: 5), meta-study 'refers to investigations of the results and process of previous research'. It specifically consists of three components: meta-data analysis, meta-method, and meta-theory.

Meta-data analysis is an analysis of texts of primary studies. Once the data are determined (see more on this below where the description of meta-analytical procedures is provided), they are analysed using the analytic framework that would fit the research question. The researchers may draw on the whole variety of existing qualitative analysis strategies (e.g. grounded theory; see Thornberg and Charmaz, Chapter 11, this volume). The actual data analysis strategy may then depend on the type of available data in the original studies or particular preferences of the meta-analysts. In any case, the analysis is, according to Paterson et al., characterized by hermeneutic and dialectic processes that try to ensure that the analysis is truthful to the original studies, but also accessible to the reader of meta-data analysis.

The meta-method part of meta-study focuses on the methodological quality of primary studies as well as on how specific approaches applied in primary studies could have influenced the findings of those studies (Paterson et al., 2001). The meta-method aims at discovering underlying assumptions leading researchers to apply certain methodological approaches and interpret their role in shaping the whole area of research. The aspects of primary studies that are being appraised are: research questions, researchers and setting, sampling procedures, data collection and data analysis techniques.

The third component of meta-study is meta-theory (Paterson et al., 2001). The meta-theory aspect of meta-study explores the theoretical background leading to empirical investigations and interpretation of its socio-historical context as well as analysis of its assumptions. All three aspects of the meta-study method, namely meta-data analysis, meta-method and meta-theory, are synthesized in meta-synthesis (Paterson et al., 2001). Paterson et al. point to the fact that their meta-synthesis is broader than typical meta-synthesis of other authors who usually focus only on meta-data analysis. Meta-synthesis, in the case of Paterson et al., synthesizes insights from the three components of the meta-study method.

Overall, we can conclude that the meta-study approach to qualitative meta-analysis as developed by Paterson et al. (2001) represents a uniquely comprehensive contribution. It focuses not only on the secondary analysis of findings of primary studies and the impacts that original methodologies had on those findings, but also on theoretical frameworks that led to research questions and shaped the interpretation of findings in primary studies.

Metasummary

Another approach to qualitative meta-analysis represents *metasummary* (Sandelowski and Barroso, 2003). Sandelowski and Barroso use the term *metasummary* to distinguish their approach from the more mainstream term *meta-synthesis*. According to them, meta-synthesis normally offers interpretive synthesis, while their approach is not interpretative, but more descriptive, only providing summaries of the findings. Their approach consists of three steps: (1) extraction of findings from primary studies; (2) abstraction of those findings; and (3) calculation of effect sizes (the term borrowed from quantitative meta-analysis).

Extraction of findings is a process in which Sandelowski and Barroso focus on findings in primary studies that are pertinent to the research question of metasummary. The authors inspect primary studies for 'integrated discoveries, conclusions, judgments, or pronouncements researchers offered, regarding the events, experiences, or cases under investigation' (Sandelowski and Barroso, 2003: 228). Extracted findings are then abstracted to reduced thematic statements. Then they suggest calculating 'effect sizes' (See also Onwuegbuzie, 2003). They essentially recognize two types of effect size: *the frequency* effect size and *the intensity* effect size. The frequency effect size expresses a percentage of occurrences of a specific meta-analytic finding in all meta-analysed primary studies: for example, in how many primary studies that were meta-analysed does this finding occur? For instance, if an abstracted finding was present in 20 out of 100 meta-analysed studies, the frequency effect size would be 20%. The intensity effect size expresses the contribution of a particular study's findings to the overall number of findings (cf. Sandelowski and Barroso, 2003). It is again expressed as a percentage. For example, if one particular study contained 15 of the final 30 meta-analytic findings, the intensity effect size of this particular study would be 50%.

The metasummary approach of Sandelowski and Barroso (2003) makes an interesting contribution to the methodology of qualitative meta-analysis. It tries to resist the interpretive nature of other qualitative meta-analytical procedures, as is also expressed in its title (metasummary). The quantification of representativeness of findings from primary studies (the frequency effect size) or representation of specific primary studies in the overall metasummary (the intensity effect size) is also an interesting concept. The problem, however, may be in using this quantitative terminology, as it may not be that readily understood by the readers, since it is rather known in its quantitative connotations, which are diametrically different from how they are used by Sandelowski and Barroso. On the other hand, looking at the representativeness of the results of qualitative meta-analysis with regard to primary studies is certainly an important concept that can be utilized in qualitative meta-analysis.

Grounded Formal Theory

Grounded formal theory introduced by Kearney (1998) is another approach to qualitative meta-analysis. Kearney refers her work to the originators of the grounded theory approach to qualitative research, Glaser and Strauss (1967; also see Thornberg and Charmaz, Chapter 11, this volume). Kearney sees a parallel to qualitative meta-analysis in Glaser and Strauss's call for the development of formal theory on the basis of a 'substantive' theory. For them, substantive theory was directly based on the empirical investigation of a certain area, while formal theory was a more abstract elaboration of a substantive theory or theories. Glaser and Strauss outline two approaches as to how a formal theory is generated. One approach assumes that formal theory could be based on one substantive theory from which a more abstract pattern is elicited. The second approach assumes that the formal theory is based on the empirical investigations of multiple areas. The formal theory is then the abstraction of characteristics of the studied phenomenon or similar phenomena present in different contexts. For instance, one can study the process of dying in different contexts (e.g. at home, in hospital) and look at what they have in common (abstracted process).

According to Kearney (1998), grounded formal theory is a more abstract theory, which should be applicable to a broader context than 'substantive theories' developed in primary studies (Kearney, 1998; cf. Glaser and Strauss, 1967). To achieve this goal Kearney (1998) recommends applying known steps from the grounded theory tradition to analysing primary studies. For example, she recommends using theoretical sampling and saturation in selecting primary studies. This is quite a substantial digression from other meta-analytic approaches. It means that the researchers focus on studies that should contribute most to the building of a theory (starting with one study). They do not inspect all available studies once saturation is achieved, that is when new studies do not alter emerging meta-analytic results. She also recommends using constant comparative analysis of data (primary studies), open and theoretical coding, use of memos and finally the concept of *core category*.

Kearney (1998) likens grounded formal theory to a 'ready-to-wear' theory that should, due to the level of its abstraction, fit individuals across the contexts and populations. In evaluating her contribution one must acknowledge its originality in using theoretical sampling and saturation, epistemologically suitable qualitative concepts, as guiding principles for the selection of studies. Also, pointing to abstraction (essence) that would fit several contexts, as the main purpose of the grounded formal theory approach to qualitative meta-analysis, is very much in line with phenomenological influences in qualitative research.

Other Brand Name Qualitative Meta-analysis Methods

Several other methods of qualitative meta-analysis have been presented under different names. An example of another brand name approach is the *critical interpretive synthesis* method of Dixon-Woods et al. (2006). This method, though building on other qualitative meta-analysis methods such as the meta-ethnography of Noblit and Hare, contains some original steps. For instance, it claims to be an interpretive method that aspires to induct from the original studies and interpret them regardless of whether they are qualitative or quantitative in nature, with the aim of building conceptualizations and theories. It further contains a *critical* aspect similar to that in meta-study, which means that the whole body of reviewed literature and assumptions present in it are evaluated, reflected and integrated in the final synthesis.

Another brand name approach that can be found in the literature is the *thematic synthesis* of Thomas and Harden (2008). Their approach emphasizes the difference between describing the results of the original studies and analysing them. The analysis is then inferential and utilizes a particular interpretive framework posed by the meta-analysts. The product of this analysis is then captured in *analytical themes*. Thomas and Harden, among other procedures shared with other approaches, also stress the importance of examining the contribution of the individual studies to the final synthesis (similar for instance to Sandelowski and Barroso in their metasummary approach). For instance, they test how the final results would be influenced by the inclusion or exclusion of studies of different methodological quality.

A GENERIC DESCRIPTION OF QUALITATIVE META-ANALYTICAL PROCEDURES

Epistemological Issues

The epistemology embedded in qualitative research is often seen as post-positivistic, constructivist–interpretive and/or ideological (Ponterotto, 2005). The approaches to qualitative research oscillate between an understanding that gives voice to participants' disclosed or inferred subjectivity and an understanding that applies a particular researcher's theoretical understanding (for instance, a particular psychoanalytic theory in the case of psychotherapy investigations) that is being refined on the basis of complex observation and engagement with data (cf. Stiles, 2009).

Similarly, the meta-analysis can either try to summarize and give voice 'to the original studies' or keep its distance and provide a conceptualization of the original studies and their findings informed by a particular (theoretical) framework applied by the meta-analyst. The epistemological approaches to qualitative meta-analysis thus oscillate between: (1) a more dialogical and naturalistic approach in which the meta-analysts bring their theoretical background, acknowledge it, engage from it, refer to it, but ultimately want to see the original studies through the original studies' eyes and the eyes of the participants in them; and (2) more theoretically laden approaches that scrutinize the original studies more from the meta-analysts' perspective, although in a dialogical manner that allows for the incorporation of new, discrepant, unexpected findings. The meta-analyses are then either more descriptive or more interpretive (cf. Elliott and Timulak, 2005). Regardless of whether more descriptive or more interpretive, it is important that the epistemology of a given qualitative meta-analysis is reflected, owned by the meta-analysts and presented to the reader of the meta-analysis.

Research Question

Each meta-analysis is led by the particular question or questions it tries to answer (e.g. What are the clients' experiences of psychotherapy?). Such a question stems from a need to review a particular field of study in order to provide a comprehensive answer that goes beyond a single study. It typically covers all studies asking the same (or similar) research question and often includes also studies that do not directly pose this question, but are addressing it maybe indirectly. The research questions in qualitative meta-analysis may not be focusing only on findings present in the original studies, but also on methodological aspects of the original studies. For instance, we may be interested in how clients' experiences of psychotherapy are studied, what data collection procedures are applied, what samples are being selected, how the data are analysed, how they are presented, and how all of these aspects influence the findings and conclusions made.

The flexible nature of qualitative research in the case of qualitative meta-analysis may mean that the actual research questions are being adapted or developed as the review of the original studies in a particular area and its analysis progresses (see also Dixon-Woods et al., 2006). For instance, we may be interested in the clients' experiences of therapy, but then we may specifically discover that the findings in primary studies differentiate between significant experiences, processes leading to them, and in-session and out-of-session impacts. The research question may then be adapted, and more differentiated.

Selecting Original Studies

The selection of primary (original) studies for qualitative meta-analysis usually follows similar criteria as any systematic review or quantitative meta-analysis. Typically all studies pertinent to the research question(s) posed by the qualitative meta-analysts are considered. All the usual database searches are applied as well as searches of the references of already identified studies. Some authors (e.g. Sandelowski and Barroso, 2007; Thomas and Harden, 2008) caution that this process in the case of qualitative studies may not be that straightforward, as qualitative studies are often published in the format of books or book chapters that may not be readily available in some of the search databases.

The review of potentially relevant studies often poses further questions. For instance, should the studies that also involve non-qualitative (e.g. quantitative) elements be included (cf. Paterson et al., 2001)? Should qualitative studies utilizing different methodological approaches (e.g. discourse analysis, see Willig, Chapter 23, this volume, and grounded theory, see Thornberg and Charmaz, Chapter 11, this volume) be considered together or should the focus be narrowed or at least should such methodologically discrepant studies be analysed separately? All of those questions are legitimate; therefore, it is important that the meta-analysts are very transparent with their reasoning that leads to the final selection of considered studies.

While in general the meta-analysts try to scrutinize all available studies that meet the set inclusion criteria, the grounded formal theory approach of Kearney (1998) suggests analysing the studies on the merit of their potential contribution to the theory that is being built from the primary studies. In this case theoretical sampling (see Rapley, Chapter 4, this volume) serves as a guiding principle of studies selection. Further scrutiny of more studies may then be abandoned once saturation occurs. Saturation of findings is then a criterion for stability of findings (Thomas and Harden (2008) in the context of qualitative meta-analysis talk about 'conceptual saturation'). It may well be that this approach is more relevant for research areas with many studies. Indeed, while in some fields the meta-analyses are performed on as little as two studies (e.g. in the case of psychotherapy, see Jennings et al., 2008), in nursing it may go to over 100 studies (cf. Paterson et al., 2001), in which case using saturation as a criterion for capping the number needed to be analysed may be particularly useful. In any case, transparency of the meta-analysts' logical operations in selecting the studies for analysis and their justification is advisable.

One interesting observation visible in the published qualitative meta-analyses is that they often include the studies that the meta-analysts themselves were conducting (cf. Timulak, 2007). This is quite understandable as the meta-analysts are naturally interested in studies in the area of their primary research interest. However, one has to bear in mind in such instances that this may influence their approach not only to the selection of the studies, but also to their analysis, where such studies may carry more weight as they are more known to the meta-analysts. This fact therefore has to be reflected by the meta-analysts and transparently shared with the reader.

Appraisal of Primary Studies

The actual appraisal of primary studies is performed in several iterations. The very first one starts with the assessment of whether studies fulfil the criteria to be included in the meta-analysis. This may depend on quality criteria (e.g. utilization of credibility checks – see Barbour, Chapter 34, this volume) necessary for the inclusion of the study (Jensen and Allen, 1996). Including a broader set of pertinent studies (including the ones with many limitations) is sometimes more useful as it allows meta-analysis to be focused also on the overall status of the studied area, the one that also captures any possible methodological and theoretical trends and their potential limitations (cf. Sandelowski and Barroso, 2007).

After the studies are selected, methodological aspects of the primary studies, such as the theoretical framework used, the researchers' pre-conceptualizations, sampling (see Rapley, Chapter 4, this volume), data collection method, data analysis method, methods used to enhance the credibility and trustworthiness (see Barbour, Chapter 34, this volume) of the original studies, are assessed. Trends in how the findings are shaped by the methodological features of the studies and theoretical conceptualizations involved in them are then observed and recorded, and are later used for the final write-up of the meta-analysis (cf. Paterson et al., 2001).

Preparing Data

Once the primary studies are selected, they have to be read and inspected for the relevant data they offer. Naturally, the findings from the original studies are considered as data, but as the data can be considered also contextual information, or quotes from the original participants. Some of such data can sometimes be found also in the discussion sections of the original studies (Paterson et al., 2001; Sandelowski and Barroso, 2002; 2003). Some authors (e.g. McCormick et al., 2003) recommend even contacting the original authors to ask them for clarifications and/or original data sets that could be reanalysed.

When the data are being prepared several issues need to be considered. For instance, sometimes the findings from one project can be presented in several papers (cf. Finfgeld, 2003). Another typical issue has to do with the appraisal of the original studies and the quality of findings they provide. For instance, Thorne et al. (2002) warn that examples of the cited accounts in the original studies may not match the abstract descriptions provided by the original authors in the findings of the original studies. They also point to the fact that sometimes the original studies can be based on a few vocal participants that may not be particularly representative of the sample. Finally, they also stress that some original studies may be simplifying the complexity of participants' perspectives. Atkins et al. (2008) also point to the fact that the write-up (see Denzin, Chapter 39, this volume) of the original studies may lack the detail of contextual factors that could have shaped the findings of those studies.

Data Analysis

The steps highlighted so far contribute to data analysis. For instance, the identification of the data and the appraisal of the original studies are crucial for the analysis. The meta-analysts evaluate epistemological positions of the original studies and situate their own epistemological or theoretical position. They may decide to narrow the focus of the meta-analysis and analyse only epistemologically similar types of studies, or they may work with theoretically or epistemologically discrepant studies and provide a comprehensive picture that may highlight complementary, but also contradictory, findings. The meta-analysts may observe that, while in some methodological traditions (e.g. grounded theory, see Thornberg and Charmaz, Chapter 11, this volume) the meta-analysis is a natural part of analysis as the original researchers are trying to achieve a universal abstraction of social processes in some traditions (e.g. hermeneutic phenomenology, see Eberle, Chapter 13, this volume) that place the main emphasis on the uniqueness of the researcher and the researched, the qualitative meta-analysis does not appear as a natural option of furthering the original studies (Zimmer, 2006).

Several authors (see the section on methodological traditions in the qualitative meta-analysis) have proposed suggestions on how actually to conduct qualitative meta-analysis. Again the method will be informed by the epistemological and theoretical positions of the meta-analysts. What the variety of approaches to qualitative meta-analysis have in common is that they utilize a flexible analytical strategy, which is based on comparison, abstraction, observation of similarities and differences among the original studies, while trying to retain contextual influences and detail in the findings, such as rare findings (cf. Finfgeld, 2003; Thorne et al., 2004). The approaches to analysis then differ in their emphasis on interpretive or descriptive analytical processes, the levels of abstraction, the level of inclusion of theoretically diverse approaches, etc.

Here I present a *generic descriptive–interpretive approach* to the data analytic procedure involved in meta-analysis (cf. Timulak, 2009). This approach is informed by procedures described by Elliott and Timulak (2005) and by the consensual qualitative research method of Hill et al. (1997). It contains aspects of post-positivistic (as it puts a lot of emphasis on credibility checks – see Barbour, Chapter 34, this volume – and independent perspectives) as well as constructive–interpretive (as it gives voice to participants and is aware of the dialogical nature of research) research paradigms (see Ponterotto, 2005). Again variations of this approach may be more interpretive (see Willig, Chapter 10, this volume) or more descriptive.

The descriptive–interpretative approach to qualitative meta-analysis follows several steps when analysing data (see Timulak, 2009). Initially, after the studies are located, their methodological aspects assessed and the data for the analysis identified, a *conceptual framework* that helps to organize the data is formed by the meta-analysts. This conceptual framework usually follows a certain logic that allows breaking up data into manageable portions (domains). For instance, we can divide a complex phenomenon under meta-analytic inquiry, such as clients' experiences of therapy, into smaller areas such as helpful and unhelpful experiences of therapy. Or when we meta-analyse studies examining conflicts in the therapeutic relationship we can apply a chronological framework such as the relationship before the conflict, during the conflict and after the conflict.

The establishment of a conceptual framework is an emerging process. Although the meta-analysts apply a certain framework early on, they may adapt it, depending on what they observe in the analysed primary studies. Sometimes, a specific primary study may be using a framework that can be adopted by the meta-analysts on the basis of its effectiveness, comprehensiveness, informativeness, etc., and then applied to other studies in further analysis.

Once the data are assigned within the domains delineated by the established conceptual framework, they can be broken into *manageable units (meaning units)* within the domains. It is important that these units retain references to the original studies so their origin is easily traceable. The meaning units are then compared across the studies and clustered together according to similarities. The *abstracted wording (categorizations)* for clustered meaning units is then provided. This abstracted wording may be more descriptive or more interpretive, depending on the epistemological approach of the meta-analysts. The abstracted categories presented within a clear conceptual framework then represent the meta-analytic findings.

The meta-analysts' influence is present in the shaping of the conceptual framework as well as in the wording of the clustered meaning units. The meta-analysts' abstraction and conceptualization may either give voice to the participants in the original studies by trying to distil the essence of their experiences using their intentional frameworks, or be more interpretive and interpret the participants' experience through the stated meta-analysts' theoretical perspective. In any case, it is important that the meta-analysts are transparent about how they formulated the conceptual framework as well as how they approached the abstraction of clustered meaning units.

As qualitative research is often very wordy and provides extensive findings, the findings of qualitative meta-analysis often require *summarization* that enhances its readability (see e.g. Sandelowski and Barroso, 2007). To increase trustworthiness (Morrow, 2005) of the meta-analysis several credibility checks are recommended (see next section). Furthermore, a natural part of the data analysis involves inspection of how the original studies are represented in the final synthesis (see Sandelowski and Barroso, 2003) and how their methodological aspects influenced the final synthesis.

Credibility Checks

As with any other qualitative research, any qualitative meta-analysis needs to establish its trustworthiness (Morrow, 2005). A variety of credibility checks (Elliott et al., 1999) can be utilized for that purpose. Among them is the use of an independent auditor or auditors who can oversee all of the steps in the meta-analysis and offer their perspective and critical appraisal. Another option is to work in the team of meta-analysts, realize different steps of meta-analysis independently by each team member and consolidate synthesis through a consensual discussion (Atkins et al., 2008; Bondas and Hall, 2007). Another approach may be the use of independent raters who could be provided with the final results of the meta-analysis in the form of a categorical taxonomy and asked to assign all the data (the findings of the original studies) into the taxonomy (cf. Timulak, 2007).

Triangulation is another approach that can enhance trustworthiness of the meta-analysis. For instance, in some cases it is possible to compare the findings of qualitative meta-analysis with the findings from quantitative research and establish whether the meta-analytic findings are complementary or contradictory to the findings that were achieved through the use of different methodologies. Specific to qualitative meta-analysis is the option of having the final synthesis validated (commented on) by researchers from the primary studies (cf. McCormick et al., 2003; see also Barbour, Chapter 34, this volume).

Presentation of Findings

Qualitative meta-analysis, similarly to other forms of qualitative research, may be quite overwhelming with regard to the amount of findings and the detail that they may provide. Therefore, the meta-analysts often stand in front of a task that requires them to summarize the main features of their findings. The use of tables, figures and prototype examples is a good tool for accomplishing this (cf. Elliott and Timulak, 2005). The discussion section of the qualitative meta-analysis also offers a good space for theorizing and contextualizing the final synthesis with the emphasis on implications. Preparing an abbreviated account may require good editing skills and can also bring some disadvantages, such as loss of the context in which the original studies were conducted (Atkins et al., 2008). The simplification may thus increase readability at the expense of comprehensiveness and attention to detail (see Denzin, Chapter 39, this volume).

AN EXAMPLE OF QUALITATIVE META-ANALYSIS IN PSYCHOTHERAPY RESEARCH

As an illustrative example of the use of qualitative meta-analysis, we will have a look at the meta-analysis of outcomes of humanistic–experiential psychotherapies conducted by myself and my colleague Mary Creaner (Timulak and Creaner, 2010). In our study, we set out to discover how the clients perceive the impact of humanistic–experiential therapies. Our research question was: What outcomes/effects are reported by clients in qualitative studies investigating the outcome of humanistic–experiential therapies?

To localize the studies we searched the PsychInfo database using the following keyword terms entered into the database: (1) humanistic, therapy, qualitative, outcome; (2) experiential, therapy, qualitative, outcome; (3) client-centred, therapy, qualitative, outcome; (4) emotion-focused, therapy, qualitative, outcome. We then noticed that potential studies either asked the same question that led our meta-analysis or primarily assessed something else (e.g. quantitative outcomes) but also reported on qualitative outcomes of a humanistic–experiential therapy. We also noticed that the studies focused on a variety of outcomes/effects, some of which pertained to the actual experiences of therapy rather than outside the therapy changes; therefore, we limited our selection only to studies that focused on the latter. As we were inspecting the studies we noticed that some of them were actually case studies, so we extended our search to case studies. We also searched the references of all studies that met our inclusion criteria.

Our selection led to a shortlist of eight studies on individual therapy and one on couple therapy. The studies covered the perspectives of 106 clients with a variety of presenting issues, participating in a variety of experiential therapies (mainly emotion-focused or person-centred). We further appraised the studies with regard to several issues, such as theoretical orientation of the original researchers, that could serve as a basis for the interpretative framework they used; data collection method; sampling characteristics; the use of credibility checks; and so on.

The data collection method was typically a post-therapy interview (which could be administered also at a follow-up). The studies typically did not use the follow-up perspective. The clients were seen in outpatient settings and had conditions such as depression, anxiety, child abuse, veterans' problems, problems in interpersonal relationships, etc. The original studies typically analysed the clients' accounts without a particular theoretical framework, trying to be true to a common-sense understanding (face value) of the participants' description; however, as the researchers in the original studies were most typically of a humanistic–experiential allegiance, their reading of the participants' accounts could be informed by humanistic–experiential theories. The same was the case for the two meta-analysts. Nevertheless, the reported findings were more descriptive than interpretive, staying close to the meaning conveyed by the clients. Only one study used a more inferential analysis and provided a higher level of abstraction and meaning of the participants' accounts, although still staying within the humanistic–experiential framework.

The results and discussion sections of the original studies were first inspected by the first meta-analyst and all texts such as categories, descriptions or quotes relevant for the research question of the meta-analysis were selected. Then, the conceptual framework containing only one domain was created and named *Effects/outcomes of therapy*. However, on inspection of the studies it was clear that they contained two subdomains: *positive effects/outcomes* and *negative effects/outcomes*. All available data were then divided into manageable units (meaning units). Finally, the meaning units were compared with each other and clustered in a way that did not omit any data. An abbreviated description (also in the form of categories) was then prepared. Each step was first done by one of the meta-analysts and then carefully audited by the second meta-analyst.

The final results for positive outcomes/effects were conceptualized in the form of 11 meta-categories. These 11 meta-categories were further grouped into 3 main meta-categories: *Appreciating Experiences of Self* (Smoother and Healthier Emotional Experiencing, Appreciating Vulnerability, Experience of Self-compassion, Experience of Resilience, Feeling Empowered, Mastering Symptoms, Enjoying Change in Circumstances), *Appreciating Experiences of Self in Relationship with Others* (Feeling Supported, Enjoying Interpersonal Encounters), and *Changed View of Self and Others* (Self-insight and Self-awareness, Changed View of Others). Two to seven studies fed into each of the meta-categories. The final synthesis was also presented in the form of a table showing which primary studies' findings fed to which meta-categories and which meta-categories fed to the three main meta-categories.

The meta-analysts also offered a narrative account of each of the categories with an example of a quote from the original study supporting a particular category (e.g. the *Smoother and Healthier Emotional Experiencing* category was illustrated by a quote from Lipkin's study: 'one of the most surprising, most amazing things that would ever happen to a man ... I believe ... in the way I was feeling ... to ah suddenly come about and feel this way ... more free and easy, more lively, more light ... and to shake off this whole heaviness that seemed to be surrounding me and gripping'). Two studies included also negative outcomes/ effects such as feeling overwhelmed or afraid of changing and therefore being more emotionally restricted.

The findings of the meta-analysis were then discussed with regard to what is known from quantitative outcome research or qualitative outcome research on other than humanistic–experiential therapies (see Timulak and Creaner, 2010). For instance, it was pointed out that while many of the findings are shared by a variety of theoretical and paradigmatic approaches, to find *Appreciating Vulnerability* as an outcome of therapy was unexpected and unique, certainly contradicting the typical focus of psychotherapy on symptom removal. This finding, however, on reflection, was seen as 'fully compatible with experiential theoretical thinking that puts emphasis on authentic being ... [which] ... may not be free of suffering and pain' (Timulak and Creaner, 2010: 84). The discussion also covered methodological limitations of the original studies and the meta-analysis itself as well as recommendations for future studies (such as routinely probing for negative outcomes).

USE OF QUALITATIVE META-ANALYSIS

Many of the major methodologists in the area of qualitative meta-analysis come from nursing. The subjects that are being synthesized deal with the typical themes found in nursing research, such as experiences of various illnesses, injuries or natural developmental/physiological states such as motherhood, and the aspects of their treatment or caring for the concerned people (e.g. Barroso and Powel-Cope, 2000; Beck, 2001; 2002; Kearney, 2001). Qualitative meta-analyses can be found also in related fields such as public health (see for instance methodological papers in this area such as those by Atkins et al., 2008; Barnett-Page and Thomas, 2009; Thomas and Harden, 2008).

Qualitative meta-analysis originated in education (Noblit and Hare, 1988) and this tradition is visible in the present meta-analytic studies in this area (e.g. Téllez and Waxman, 2006; or the methodological paper of Suri and Clarke, 2009). Qualitative meta-analyses can also be found in the field of sociology (see Weed, 2008). Recently, meta-analyses have started to appear in the area of psychotherapy research (Hill et al., 2012; Jennings et al, 2008; Timulak, 2007; Timulak and Creaner, 2010).

LIMITATIONS OF QUALITATIVE META-ANALYSIS

Apart from the enthusiasm about the relatively new method of qualitative meta-analysis, there exists also significant criticism of, and scepticism about, the usefulness of this endeavour. The main criticism focuses on the fact that qualitative research is often attempting to capture local knowledge, a particularly situated constructed perspective, as opposed to an aspiration towards the definite generalizable view often searched for in a more traditional quantitative research. Therefore, the ambition to provide a more comprehensive picture or understanding of a certain phenomenon/a is somewhat contradictory to the nature of most qualitative research which cherishes more contextualized knowledge (cf. Paterson et al., 2001; Sandelowski and Barroso, 2007; Sandelowski et al., 1997; Walsh and Downe, 2004).

Another line of criticism points out that, despite the meta-analysts' claim to provide a synthesis of research, in fact it provides a particular synthesis coloured by an interpretive perspective of the meta-analysts. Therefore it is probably more precise to say that qualitative meta-analysis may not necessarily provide a definite final picture or understanding, but rather a unique, systematic, in-depth analysing portrait and its interpretation of a studied field (see also arguments in Walsh and Downe, 2004).

There are many other methodological issues involved in qualitative meta-analysis pointed out by different authors who have conducted meta-analysis and meta-synthesis of primary studies that I have not mentioned. Many of these issues have to do with the quality of the original studies and with the quality of their write-ups. The meta-analysts can work only with the data that are available to them and can only transparently point to the problems (if they are present) in the original studies.

NEW DEVELOPMENTS AND PERSPECTIVES

The number of qualitative meta-analyses and methodological papers devoted to the subject is growing. It is likely that with new experiences of conducting qualitative meta-analysis some procedures may become more standard and some may be used less. It is also possible that new problems may transpire as experience of conducting this type of analysis increases. Probably one of the central issues in the case of qualitative meta-analysis, similar to other methods of research synthesis, will be its relationship to policy-making (Atkins et al., 2008). The goal of meta-analysis is to provide a more comprehensive picture of a field of qualitative study. This more comprehensive picture aspires to have implications for theorizing, researching and especially for practical application. In that sense, the conclusions of a qualitative meta-analysis may become very important for the practice in the reviewed field. With experience of how some policies (e.g. NICE guidelines in the UK) may shape service delivery, I would caution that no meta-synthesis is seen as the definitive and ultimately authoritative state of the field. Qualitative meta-analysis as any other form of research review is dependent on the quality of the original research as well as the meta-analysts' theoretical and professional perspective.

FURTHER READING

To familiarize the reader further with qualitative meta-analytic review, I would suggest exploring the perspectives of researchers who conducted several meta-analyses and reflect on their own experiences as well as issues found in the literature in a book-length format. Two books that provide a comprehensive perspective on the use of qualitative meta-analysis are:

Paterson, Barbara L., Thorne, Sally E., Canam, Connie and Jillings, Carol (2001) *Meta-study of Qualitative Health Research: A Practical Guide to Meta-analysis and Meta-synthesis.* Thousands Oaks, CA: Sage.
Sandelowski, Margarete and Barroso, Julie (2007) *Handbook for Synthesizing Qualitative Research.* New York: Springer.

Another potential treat for the reader is the paper by Thorne et al. that provides reflections of five scholars who have significantly contributed to the development of qualitative meta-analysis:

Thorne, Sally, Jensen, Louise, Kearney, Margaret H., Noblit, George and Sandelowski, Margarete (2004) 'Qualitative metasynthesis: Reflection on methodological orientation and ideological agenda', *Qualitative Health Research*, 14: 1342–65.

REFERENCES

Atkins, Salla, Lewin, Simon, Smith, Helen, Engel, Mark, Fretheim, Atle and Volmink, Jimmy (2008) 'Conducting a meta-ethnography of qualitative literature: Lessons learnt', *BMC Medical Research Methodology*, 8: 21. DOI: 10.1186/1471-2288-8-21.
Barnett-Page, Elaine and Thomas, James (2009) 'Methods for the synthesis of qualitative research: A critical review,' *BMC Medical Research Methodology*, 9, 59. DOI: 10.1186/1471-2288-9-59.
Barroso, Julie and Powel-Cope, Gail M. (2000) 'Metasynthesis of qualitative research on living with HIV infection', *Qualitative Health Research*, 10: 340–53.
Beck, Cheryl. T. (2001) 'Caring within nursing education: A metasynthesis,' *Journal of Nursing Education*, 40: 101–9.

Beck, Cheryl T. (2002) 'Postpartum depression: A meta-synthesis,' *Qualitative Health Research*, 12: 453–72.

Bondas, Terese and Hall, Elisabeth O.C. (2007) 'Challenges in approaching metasynthesis research', *Qualitative Health Research*, 17: 113–21.

Dixon-Woods, Mary, Cavers, Debbie, Agarwal, Shona, Annandale, Ellen, Arthur, Antony, Harvey, Janet, Hsu, Ron, Katbamna, Savita, Olsen, Richard, Smith, Lucy, Riley, Richard and Sutton, Alex J. (2006) 'Conducting a critical interpretative synthesis of the literature on access to healthcare by vulnerable groups,' *BMC Medical Research Methodology*, 6: 35. DOI: 10.1186/1471-2288-6-35.

Elliott, Robert and Timulak, Ladislav (2005) 'Descriptive and interpretive approaches to qualitative research', in Jeremy Miles and Paul Gilbert (eds), *A Handbook of Research Methods in Clinical and Health Psychology*. Oxford: Oxford University Press. pp. 145–59.

Elliott, Robert, Fischer, Constance T. and Rennie, David L. (1999) 'Evolving guidelines for publication of qualitative research in psychology and related fields', *British Journal of Clinical Psychology*, 38: 215–29.

Finfgeld, Deborah L. (2003) 'Metasynthesis: The state of the art – so far', *Qualitative Health Research*, 13: 893–904.

Glaser, Barney G. and Strauss, Anselm (1967) *The Discovery of Grounded Theory: Strategies for Qualitative Research*. New York: Aldine.

Hill, Clara E., Thompson, Barbara J. and Nutt-Williams, Elizabeth (1997) 'A guide to conducting consensual qualitative research', *The Counseling Psychologist*, 25: 517–72.

Hill, Clara E., Knox, Sarah and Hess, Shirley A. (2012) 'Qualitative meta-analysis of consensual qualitative research studies', in Clara E. Hill (ed.), *Consensual Qualitative Research*. Washington, DC: American Psychological Association. pp. 159–72.

Jennings, Len, D'Rozario, Vilma, Goh, Michael, Sovereign, Ashley, Brogger, Megan and Skovholt, Thomas (2008) 'Psychotherapy expertise in Singapore: A qualitative investigation', *Psychotherapy Research*, 18, 508–22.

Jensen, Louise A. and Allen, Marion N. (1996) 'Metasynthesis of qualitative findings', *Qualitative Health Research*, 6: 553–60.

Kearney, Margaret (1998) 'Ready to wear: Discovering grounded formal theory', *Research in Nursing and Health*, 21: 179–86.

Kearney, Margaret H. (2001) 'Enduring love: A grounded formal theory of women's experience of domestic violence', *Research in Nursing and Health*, 24: 270–82.

McCormick, Janice, Rodney, Patricia and Varcoe, Colleen (2003) 'Reinterpretations across studies: An approach to meta-analysis', *Qualitative Health Research*, 13: 933–44.

Morrow, Susan L. (2005) 'Quality and trustworthiness in qualitative research in counselling psychology', *Journal of Counseling Psychology*, 52: 250–60.

Noblit, George W. and Hare, R. Dwight (1988) *Meta-ethnography: Synthesizing Qualitative Studies*. Newbury Park, CA: Sage.

Onwuegbuzie, Anthony J. (2003) 'Effect sizes in qualitative research: A prolegomenon', *Quality and Quantity*, 37: 393–409.

Paterson, Barbara L., Thorne, Sally E., Canam, Connie and Jillings, Carol (2001) *Meta-study of Qualitative Health Research: A Practical Guide to Meta-analysis and Meta-synthesis*. Thousands Oaks, CA: Sage.

Ponterotto, Joseph (2005) 'Qualitative research in counseling psychology: A primer on research paradigms and philosophy of science', *Journal of Counseling Psychology*, 52: 126–36.

Ritzer, George (1990) 'Metatheorizing in sociology', *Sociological Forum*, 5: 3–15.

Sandelowski, Margarete and Barroso, Julie (2002) 'Finding the findings in qualitative studies', *Journal of Nursing Scholarship*, 34: 213–19.

Sandelowski, Margarete and Barroso, Julie (2003) 'Creating metasummaries of qualitative findings', *Nursing Research*, 52: 226–33.

Sandelowski, Margarete and Barroso, Julie (eds) (2007) *Handbook for Synthesizing Qualitative Research*. New York: Springer.

Sandelowski, Margarete, Docherty, Sharon and Emden, Carolyn (1997) 'Focus on qualitative methods. Qualitative metasynthesis: Issues and techniques', *Research in Nursing and Health*, 20: 365–71.

Schreiber, Rita, Crooks, Dauna and Stern, Phyllis. N. (1997) 'Qualitative meta-analysis', in Janice M. Morse (ed.), *Completing a Qualitative Project: Details and dialogue*. Thousand Oaks, CA: Sage. pp. 311–26.

Stern, Phyllis N. and Harris, Chandice C. (1985) 'Women's health and the self-care paradox: A model to guide self-care readiness', *Health Care for Women International*, 6: 151–63.

Stiles, William B. (2009) 'Logical operations in theory-building case studies', *Pragmatic Case Studies in Psychotherapy*, 5 (3): 9–22.

Suri, Harsh and Clarke, David (2009) 'Advancements in research synthesis methods: From a methodologically inclusive perspective', *Review of Educational Research*, 79 (1): 395–430. DOI: 10.3102/0034654308326349.

Téllez, Kip and Waxman, Hersh C. (2006) 'A meta-synthesis of qualitative research on effective teaching practices for English language learners', in John M. Norris and Lourdes Ortega (eds), *Synthesizing Research on Language Learning and Teaching*. Philadelphia: John Benjamins. pp. 245–77.

Thomas, James and Harden, Angela (2008) 'Methods for the thematic synthesis of qualitative research in systematic reviews', *BMC Medical Research Methodology*, 8, 45. DOI: 10.1186/1471-2288-8-45.

Thorne, Sally, Paterson, Barbara, Acorn, Sonia, Canam, Connie, Joachim, Gloria and Jilling, Carol (2002) 'Chronic illness experience: Insights from a metastudy', *Qualitative Health Research*, 12: 437–52.

Thorne, Sally, Jensen, Louise, Kearney, Margaret H., Noblit, George and Sandelowski, Margarete (2004) 'Qualitative metasynthesis: Reflection on methodological orientation and ideological agenda', *Qualitative Health Research*, 14: 1342–65.

Timulak, Ladislav (2007) 'Identifying core categories of client identified impact of helpful events in psychotherapy – a qualitative meta-analysis', *Psychotherapy Research*, 17: 305–14.

Timulak, Ladislav (2009) 'Qualitative meta-analysis: A tool for reviewing qualitative research findings in psychotherapy', *Psychotherapy Research*, 19: 591–600.

Timulak, Ladislav and Creaner, Mary (2010) 'Qualitative meta-analysis of outcomes of person-centred/experiential therapies', in Mick Cooper et al. (eds), *Person-Centred and Experiential Psychotherapies Work*. Ross-on-Wye: PCCS Books. pp. 65–90.

Walsh, Denis and Downe, Soo (2005) 'Meta-synthesis method for qualitative research: A literature review', *Journal of Advanced Nursing*, 50: 204–11.

Weed, Mike (2008) 'A potential method for the interpretive synthesis of qualitative research: Issues in the development of "meta-interpretation"', *International Journal of Social Research Methodology*, 11 (1): 13–28. http://dx.doi.org/10.1080/13645570701401222.

Zhao, Shanyang (1991) 'Metatheory, metamethod, meta-data-analysis: What, why, and how?', *Sociological Perspectives*, 34: 377–90.

Zimmer, Lela (2006) 'Qualitative meta-synthesis: A question of dialoguing with texts', *Journal of Advanced Nursing*, 53: 311–18.

Quality of Data Analysis

Rosaline S. Barbour

INTRODUCTION

As Flick argues, 'discussions about the quality of qualitative research are located at the crossroads of internal needs and external challenges' (2007: 2). Calls for definitive criteria for measuring the quality of qualitative research reflect the growing acceptance of qualitative methods and the greater readiness of a wide range of journals to publish qualitative papers. Some researchers in disciplines which have previously privileged quantitative methods – including clinical specialties, psychology, education, social work, and geography – have started to engage with qualitative methods. Additionally, scholars in the field who have tended to focus on theoretical scholarship – such as cultural studies and political science – have also begun to rely more markedly on empirical work, which is frequently qualitative in nature.

In the UK health services research context, developments such as the Medical Research Council's Complex Interventions funding stream with a focus on process and recommendations for mixed methods approaches have also encouraged new constituencies of researchers to consider employing qualitative methods and to extend their literature reviews to include previously published work using this approach. Attempts to encompass qualitative studies in exercises such as the Cochrane Collaboration and the 'project' of systematic reviewing have led to calls for templates or checklists to assist in the critical appraisal of qualitative papers (see Murray, Chapter 40, this volume). Within the growing ranks of 'mixed methods' researchers (see Morse and Maddox, Chapter 36, this volume), too, there have been some interesting developments (discussed in more detail later in this chapter) which seek to break down the unhelpful – though frequently appealed to – dichotomy between quantitative and qualitative methods in order to take account of the benefits of both approaches in evaluating mixed methods outputs.

Wider social and political developments have also brought qualitative methods to the fore. Research assessment exercises – particularly in the UK and Australian context – have focused discussion on the evaluation of qualitative outputs. In the UK context, the impact agenda, as a component of the forthcoming Research Excellence Framework exercise, has further raised issues relating to judging quality, as research institutions are required to demonstrate how their work has benefited the economy, society, public policy, culture and quality of life.

Alongside such internal academic discussion, other developments – such as the Internet and associated portals such as YouTube/Facebook (see Marotzki et al., Chapter 31, this volume), and the arrival of open repositories of research publications – have also heightened awareness of work that was carried out within universities and research centres. It is now no longer only our quantitatively inclined academic peers to whom we are required to justify our methods and the quality of our analyses – we are now required to accomplish this on the wider stage. This means engaging in public debate, which has necessitated the acquisition of new skills in communicating with the media and rendering our research accessible to non- academic audiences. Such demands, of course, are not new for researchers engaged in action research (see Murray, Chapter 40, this volume) – particularly , particularly those projects at the most participative end of this spectrum, which may even involve participants as co-data analysts, and the rest of us have much to learn from exponents of such approaches.

Assumptions

Many doctoral theses contain a section that juxtaposes qualitative and quantitative approaches, contrasting positivist and interpretative paradigms. Such accounts tend to overemphasise the differences between the two traditions, often espousing what Hammersley (1995) has termed 'the creation myth' of qualitative research. This view valorises qualitative research as a refreshing new departure that overcame all the shortcomings of the positivist tradition. As qualitative researchers, however, we should know better than to accept at face value or to discount entirely such 'stories' as the 'creation myth' of qualitative research or quantitative versions which claim a monopoly over rigour. When views are as firmly espoused as this, however, there is generally a 'grain of truth' involved.

It is easy, as advocates of qualitative methods, to rail against classic criticisms of our analyses as subjective, impressionistic, or, in these days of evaluation on the popular front, 'simply stating the blindingly obvious'. Seale takes a more measured stance, arguing that 'Paradigm warfare, drawing on philosophical discussion to justify divisions between schools of research, potentially obscures the strengths of disfavoured research traditions' (1999: 31). Rather than simply shrugging off criticisms of qualitative analyses, as emanating from quarters where qualitative research is 'misunderstood', we should, perhaps, pay more attention to engaging constructively with potential shortcomings as we go about analysing and presenting our research, rather than retreating into a stance whereby we risk proclaiming that 'all qualitative research is good'. In our more reasonable moments, we could, perhaps, move beyond such protestations of 'standpoint methodology' and admit that 'some qualitative analyses are better than others'. While we probably all operate our own personal criteria for judging the quality of qualitative research, such potentially idiosyncratic 'tools' are unlikely to be of service either in convincing sceptics or, indeed, in providing guidelines for improving our own research practice.

Criteria and Checklists

Partly in response to this need to move beyond individual assessments and vague assessment criteria, the last 15 years have witnessed the development of a series of checklists or guidelines for evaluating qualitative research (e.g. Popay et al., 1998; Blaxter, 1996). Despite good intentions, this has proved an extremely difficult task. Overarching criteria for quality in qualitative data analysis remain elusive, in part due to the extremely broad range covered by qualitative approaches, which can encompass approaches with widely differing epistemological and ontological assumptions (Barbour, 1998). As Flick (2007) has observed, sometimes the only similarity between qualitative approaches is simply that they are 'not quantitative' in one way or another.

Some checklists have echoed quantitative criteria – including validity, reliability, replicability and generalizability (see Maxwell and Chmiel, Chapter 37, this volume) – while adopting a different language. Concepts such as 'member checking' or 'respondent validation', in effect, offer a qualitative variant of the quantitative criterion of 'inter-rater reliability'. A further complication is that, whatever the motivations of those who have sought to compile checklists, there may be a huge gap between intent and application. I have previously (Barbour, 2001) taken issue with the formulaic, strategic – and even cynical – use of such checklists by researchers. Statements regarding the use of 'purposive sampling' (see Rapley, Chapter 4, this volume) or 'grounded theory' (see Thornberg and Charmaz, Chapter 11, this volume) may be made, not with the intention of explaining how the research was carried out but, rather, in the hope that such claims will secure publication. Purposive sampling, in particular, is often invoked retrospectively by authors when describing the sample obtained, with little evidence of the sampling strategy having, at the outset, shaped the research design or, once data have been generated, having informed the comparative analysis carried out. When applied in a prescriptive manner, checklists can have the opposite of the desired effect and may end up driving not only how research gets written up but also how it is planned and carried out. Even more worryingly, appeals to checklists can afford a means whereby researchers can circumvent the need to pay attention to planning and process during the project, provided that standardised descriptions can be retrospectively appended. Thus checklists can, ultimately, function to the detriment of thoughtful or innovative research practice.

There have also been attempts to formulate not just new terms, but what Flick (2007) refers to as 'method-appropriate criteria'. An example is provided by Lincoln and Guba (1985) who offer as alternative criteria: trustworthiness; credibility; dependability; transferability; and confirmability. In practice, however, it has proved harder to pin down and operationalise such standards and definition remains essentially in the eye of the beholder. While these concepts may strike a chord with researchers already firmly committed to the qualitative cause, they are less likely to have resonance for those outside qualitative research or those who are new to this field. Rather than structure the discussion that follows around potentially confusing terms, which, themselves, are open to interpretation, I have, instead, opted to outline a number of issues which qualitative researchers are advised to consider in planning, carrying out, refining and presenting their analyses. Many of these, of course, echo the advice of others, including that of checklist authors.

HOW TO ADDRESS ISSUES OF QUALITY IN ANALYSING QUALITATIVE DATA

What follows is a series of hints regarding how best to ensure rigour in designing, carrying out, analysing and presenting qualitative research. This also serves as a guide to evaluating published work. Although it is roughly sequential in nature, due to the iterative nature of the qualitative research endeavour, it frequently jumps between discussion of research design and generating and analysing data, since anticipation and retrospective reflection are integral to this approach.

Processing Data

Although most researchers carry out their analysis using verbatim transcripts, this is not absolutely essential – unless, of course one is carrying out conversation analysis (see Toerien, Chapter 22, this volume), in which case a specific template (the Jeffersonian transcription system, see Puchta and Potter, 2004, for details; see also Kowal and O'Connell, Chapter 5, this volume) should be used, in order to denote a range of features of talk. As Gibbs (2007) points out, with the advent of digital recordings, it is possible to label segments, which can readily be retrieved. It is not the presence of verbatim transcripts that confers rigour (as some who invoke checklists hope) but, rather, the use that is made of this resource. There is little point in producing a verbatim transcript – itself a laborious and potentially expensive process – if only a superficial analysis is going to be carried out. What is important is the degree to which analysis is systematic and thorough. Utilization of verbatim transcripts does not prevent selective interpretations – often referred to as 'cherry-picking' – and a thoughtful analysis will draw on more than is contained in any written transcript: that is background information (about services, localities or, even, culture or subculture) or details of respondents' characteristics. Reification of verbatim transcripts can be an impediment to critical thinking (Barbour, 2001).

Initial Coding

Most qualitative analyses either explicitly mention 'grounded theory' (Glaser and Strauss, 1967; also see Thornberg and Charmaz, Chapter 11, this volume) or make a 'nod' in its direction, so pervasive is its influence on how we go about carrying out the business of analysing qualitative data. As Melia (1997) has observed, however, each researcher or research team is likely to develop their own pragmatic variant, depending on the precise conditions under which they are carrying out their studies – how much time and funding is available, what the original research question is, and for which audience their findings are intended. Again the term 'grounded theory' is often applied as a 'respectability' claim, which can involve little more than retrospectively badging a piece of work (Barbour, 2001). Bryman and Burgess (1994) describe such appeals as using the term as 'an approving bumper sticker'.

Returning to this topic in 2010, Melia reflects that 'grounded theory' is still frequently abused and Green and Thorogood point out that 'superficial thematic content analysis' is not the same thing (2004: 183). Of course, for some research projects, which are firmly located at the applied end of the spectrum, this is perfectly acceptable – there is no shame in such usage as applied projects need to use coding categories which are readily translatable back into practice. The problem is when there is an attempt to 'dress up' or elevate such endeavours by references to 'grounded theory'. In effect, this moves attention away from their real virtues – and, in all likelihood, the reason for doing the research in the first place.

One of the hallmarks of 'grounded theory' is its capacity to focus on members' categories – that is, terms or accounts routinely used by respondents or research participants – and to use these to build theoretical explanations. These have been termed *in vivo* codes, since they derive from the vocabulary and concepts invoked by respondents in research encounters (Kelle, 1997). Although such ideas may be common parlance for those being studied, it is obvious that these are likely to require some explanation when presented to another audience – particularly that of other academic researchers, who are likely not to share the particular experiences or circumstances that are the focus of the research in question. In practice, many data analysts still rely on *a priori* codes – that is, those concepts and categories which informed their own ideas about the research at the outset of the process – and which translate into somewhat unsurprising, unilluminating or 'pedestrian codes' (Barbour, 2008). This is the issue that Charmaz refers to as 'originality', asking 'are the categories fresh?' (2006: 182–3).

Paying Attention to Patterning

Although many qualitative analyses grind to a halt once a set of thematic codes has been developed and presented, this represents the very least of what such an analysis can help us to achieve. Charmaz (2006) also bemoans this missed potential. Analytically sophisticated analyses thrive on comparison and Glaser and Strauss's (1967) account of 'grounded theory' emphasises the importance of the 'constant comparative method'. This involves a laborious process of comparing and contrasting the frequency with which codes and categories occur in different transcripts. However, more than a simple frequency count is involved and it is important to document who is saying what and in what context. In order to achieve this it may be helpful to produce grids which allow us to see such patterns clearly. This is the approach advocated by Ritchie and Spencer (1994), which thereafter came to be referred to as 'framework analysis'. It is largely irrelevant whether the data analyst uses a computer package in order to produce such a diagram or whether this is delineated manually. Gibbs (2007) and Kelle (1997) – both pioneers in terms of developing and utilizing Computer-Assisted Qualitative Data Analysis (CAQDAS) packages – admit to employing a combination of facilities provided by such computerized packages (see Gibbs, Chapter 19, this volume) and the old-fashioned pencil and paper approach. What is important is the systematic and thorough approach followed – not the means of executing the exercise.

Constant comparison requires that the analyst pay particular attention to exceptions, or deviant cases. This is what is meant by the term 'analytic induction' and Frankland and Bloor (1999) provide an example of using this strategy in identifying exceptions, and using these to interrogate, build up and revise their explanatory framework. As Ritchie and Spencer (1994) point out, identifying patterning is the easy part of the process: what is infinitely more difficult, but potentially more rewarding, is seeking to explain such patterns.

An indicator of a thoughtful piece of work is the extent to which the original study design – and, in particular, the sampling strategy (see Rapley, Chapter 4, this volume) – is used as a resource. Although many published papers claim to have recruited a 'purposive' sample – and, indeed, provide exhaustive demographic details – fewer actually utilise such variations in order to interrogate their data, through exploring whether patterning maps onto sampling criteria. It is essential to use sampling in a *purposeful* manner, drawing on this as a resource in analysing the data generated (Barbour, 2001) – that is, there is a difference between strategic references to criteria and actually employing these to advantage. Although we can anticipate at the outset of our research many of the dimensions likely to impact on our respondents' perspectives, the process of qualitative data analysis is a fluid one and further criteria for comparison may suggest themselves along the way.

When carrying out a research project looking at mothers' views and experiences of taking folic acid in the run-up to and in the early stages of their most recent pregnancies (Barbour et al., 2012), we had somewhat naively assumed that, in convening focus groups, we could divide women into those who had taken folic acid and those who had not, using information elicited via a short questionnaire. However, once women engaged in discussion we realised that the picture was infinitely more complex, as some women who had taken folic acid had not followed standard guidance and may have taken folic acid for longer than the recommended period (up to 12 weeks' gestation), or may have taken it intermittently. In addition, some women suggested that folic acid might cause morning sickness, or, even, other problems during pregnancies and these beliefs also impacted on their folic-acid-taking behaviour. What we ended up with was a much more complex palette, allowing for many more comparisons than we had envisaged, and the unfolding of the sampling process, itself, provided valuable insights into women's ideas, priorities and behaviour.

As well as identifying differences in the perspectives of our respondents, paying attention to patterning in our data may also throw up surprising, but analytically promising similarities. This was the case with Orr's (2011) study of the views of carers (in the UK context this is a friend or family member who provides practical or emotional support or services), service providers and policy-makers regarding carer involvement in drug services. Previous research had documented the many areas of disagreement and tensions between these stakeholders, and Orr's study also identified such issues. However, the comparative study design (involving interviews – see Roulston, Chapter 20, this volume) and focus groups (see Barbour, Chapter 21, this volume) with members of all three groups highlighted many points of agreement, or commonalities, which allowed for the making of recommendations as to how to build on shared views and frustrations (Orr et al., 2012).

Explicating and Refining Codes

Rather than resting on their laurels once codes for organising and retrieving data have been developed, researchers should continue to interrogate and potentially refine these categories. One way of interrogating coding categories is through 'peer-debriefing' (Lincoln and Guba, 1985) whereby colleagues can be invited to take a critical look at the adequacy of codes. Close disciplinary colleagues, however, may share the same blind spots, whereas co-researchers on multi-disciplinary teams may subject ideas to a more exacting examination. Seale (1999) and Barbour (2008) both highlight the value of team meetings for interrogating and further developing coding frames.

I have already referred to the quantitative concept of 'inter-rater' reliability, which sometimes, unhelpfully, migrates to qualitative research practice and encourages teams simply to document the degree of agreement with regard to the assignment of coding categories. I have argued elsewhere (Barbour, 2001) that this is the very least of what can be achieved via team comparisons and discussions; what is infinitely more useful is to explore and build on such disagreements in order to develop more nuanced and useful categories. This involves not just a one-off exercise, but a continuous process of re-evaluation and revision throughout the duration of a research project.

The codes that we assign to data segments inevitably reflect our own disciplinary backgrounds, as was confirmed by the comparative exercise carried out by Armstrong et al. (1997), who asked researchers from different disciplinary backgrounds to analyse the same data. Armstrong et al. conclude that, although employing somewhat different language, analysts generally developed equivalent coding categories. Rather than viewing this as a challenge, this facility of interdisciplinary research teams can be a tremendous resource, as exploring even small labelling differences can be illuminating.

In assessing the quality of a thematic analysis it is important to consider the extent to which the researcher has interrogated *in vivo* codes, rather than simply taking them at face value and romanticizing respondents' accounts (Atkinson, 1997). Unless we are in the business of bearing witness to respondents' accounts – and qualitative research may not be the most effective vehicle for such endeavours – the role of the researcher is to provide an overview and to transcend the voices of individuals or groups (Barbour, 2008). Focus groups, in particular, afford us an opportunity to harness participants' insights, as we encourage them to 'problematise' issues and concepts alongside the researcher (Barbour, 2007).

Helpful though 'insiders' categories can be, researchers also have a responsibility to develop their coding categories further, reflecting on exactly what it is about *in vivo* codes that makes them so effective – for example, in terms of expressing experiences, thoughts or feelings. Attention to the language used and implicit references is key to developing a more nuanced interpretation. It is also worth exploring antonyms (words which mean the opposite) of those that initially suggest themselves as potential coding categories. This relates to C. Wright Mills' (1959) injunction to take a playful approach to our emergent theoretical categories, standing concepts on their heads, in order to exercise what he called 'the sociological imagination'. Strauss and Corbin (1990) also recommend comparing extremes during our analyses, terming this the 'flip flop technique'. Clearly it is difficult to convey the intricacies involved in such explication and refinement of coding categories – especially within strict word limits.

Much of the work in explicating and refining coding categories is carried out 'backstage' and is not always detailed in published accounts, with coding categories sometimes being presented as if they emerged intuitively rather than as a result of a lengthy and challenging process. However, an attentive reading of research outputs can help to establish the extent to which researchers and research teams have engaged in this difficult – but ultimately rewarding – conceptual work.

PRESENTING FINDINGS

The process of qualitative data analysis is very closely related to the craft of writing. Indeed, as Richardson attests: 'form and content are inseparable' (1994: 516). The words and phrases that we select convey much more than a literal reading might suggest. In this chapter, for example, I have chosen to use active headings of Processing Data; Paying Attention to Patterning; Explicating and Refining Codes; and Presenting Findings. This usage of the '…ing' form (a *gerund* according to the *New Oxford American Dictionary*, e-Book, 2008) is far from accidental. This form is described as denoting 'something that should or must be *done*' (*New Oxford American Dictionary*, e-Book, 2008) and was employed in order to convey the engagement of the researcher (or research team) throughout the whole process.

Rather than being the final step in the process, writing (see Denzin, Chapter 39, this volume) is something that is best carried out throughout a research project, whether in the form of notes on coding categories, fieldwork reflections, or successive drafts of report or thesis sections. Indeed, writing and conceptualization of the study begins with the research proposal, which anticipates and sets the scene for much of the analysis and discussion that follow.

As outlined earlier, sampling decisions, in particular, prefigure the comparative potential of our data sets and one criterion for judging the quality of the resulting report or journal article is the extent to which this capitalizes on the comparative potential inherent in the study design.

Suboptimal mining of data is another frequently encountered shortcoming of qualitative analyses. This relates not just to neglect of the potential for comparison, but can also involve the researcher in paying more attention to some respondents or settings than to others – that is, selective reporting. Of course some interviewees or focus group participants are likely to be more articulate or succinct than are others. This latter quality is, of course, attractive to writers aware of tight word limits. It is important not to fall into the trap of quoting from the same people all the time and providing 'identifiers' helps to guard against such overemphasis. This involves providing unique details – perhaps a pseudonym, and some demographic details, for example 'Sarah, 32 years old, lawyer' – to accompany quotes. Following this practice and showcasing a range of quotes also reassures the reader that researchers have taken their whole data set into account in formulating their explanations, rather than having strategically selected those examples that fit with the argument being advanced. In terms of making a compelling argument it is essential that the writer provide enough context for the reader to make a judgement as to whether, for example, the inferences made are logical (Huberman and Miles, 1998).

All of the above points relate to pulling together a convincing account and involve a combination of the more mechanical or prosaic aspects of writing (as suggested by the practical hints provided here) and the writer's command of language, literary structure and even rhetorical skills. In the hands of a gifted writer, form and content blend seamlessly to make for a compelling account and a degree of 'sleight-of-hand' is involved.

Although I have concentrated on thematic analysis, since this is the most common approach to qualitative data analysis, there are other approaches to processing data and presenting accounts. Narrative research (see Esin et al., Chapter 14, this volume), for example, in the absence of procedural guidelines, may rely even more on the skill of the writer in conveying a persuasive account, as do classical anthropology and some versions of ethnography (see Gubrium and Holstein, Chapter 3, this volume). So far I have discussed the assessment of quality in relation largely to 'process' criteria, but 'relevance' criteria (relating to resonance and usefulness of findings – see Murray, Chapter 40, this volume) and 'novelty' criteria (relating to originality) are equally important (Charmaz, 2006; Flick, 2007: 21). Maxwell (2011) offers a helpful framework for conceptualizing and evaluating studies, which distinguishes between the use of 'categorizing' and 'connecting' strategies (see Maxwell and Chmiel, Chapter 37, this volume). Underpinned by a constructivist approach, 'connecting' strategies allow for identification of the narrative *functions* of parts of respondents' stories, or framing of accounts, while acknowledging their 'situated relativity'. Maxwell (2011) does not see 'categorizing' and 'connecting' strategies as mutually exclusive, but suggests that they may be used sequentially, with the ordering depending, to a large extent, on the particular tradition or discipline within which the researcher is working. Indeed, Maxwell advocates a combined approach, cautioning that 'Exclusive emphasis on connecting strategies can prevent analysts from seeing alternative ways of framing and interpreting the text or situation in question' (2011: 117). An example is provided below of the use of 'connecting strategies' to build on initial thematic coding.

Connecting Strategies – An Example

In the course of supervision sessions (with Orr, 2011), we noted that a range of stories were being told – mainly by carers and front-line service providers – and decided that these stories merited further exploration in their own right. As Frank (1995) outlined, stories, or narratives, among other things, can explore the themes of restitution, chaos or quests, and it became clear that there were some common themes which suggested that these stories might have a particular function for those who were telling them. Carers, in particular, often ruefully recounted how they had been duped by their dishonest offspring, but the stories were not all concerned merely with sharing the problems encountered.

Some stories had a markedly different tone, telling about approaches to overcoming problems. One variant recounted how carers had 'faced up' to service providers and it is likely that at least part of such accounts had been embellished after the event – a feature not uncommon in the telling of 'getting even'-type stories.

The *in vivo* category (see Thornberg and Charmaz, Chapter 11, this volume) used to categorize further some of these 'prevailing over circumstances' stories was 'tough love' – a term used, on occasion, by both service providers and carers, to describe situations where carers had stopped bailing out drug users and had, instead, left them to suffer the consequences of their behaviour. As well as stories of abandoning drug users in this way, accounts included carers' active involvement in attempting to carry out detoxification at home (in response to the elusiveness of places on formal programmes).

Following the advice of Hepburn and Potter (2004), Orr attempted to maintain a sceptical stance on stories, and the *in vivo* code of 'tough love' was especially interesting in this respect. The term was also invoked by service providers (in a focus group with workers in social work services and non-government organisations):

Mike: But obviously the parent can be fed this line *(i.e. the dangers associated with withdrawal)* over a long period of time and has bought into it so we find a lot of the time we're actually saying to parents, well no, they're not going to die from opiate withdrawal. You maybe have to have a bit of tough love at some stage. I mean I don't believe people have to reach rock bottom to change ... but sometimes they need their safety net taken away a bit to actually feel the consequences of their use. Because if a granny is bailing them out all the time ...

Murray: ... it's just causing more problems [*general agreement around room*].

Mike: ... 'cos I've got a son and I'm not sure if I could say, 'Right you're on your own'. Do you know what I mean? So ...

Interestingly this was not the only group of professionals to imagine how they might, themselves, respond if placed in the situation of the carers with whom they worked. What is important about these comments, however, is that they prompted Orr to look again at carers' stories about 'tough love'. With fresh eyes she saw that a slightly different interpretation was possible and a rereading of the following data excerpt (from a focus group with a newly formed, carer-led family support group) was particularly illuminating in this respect:

Jane: I think we've learned how to live with ... I can only speak for me not the rest of you, I've learned how to get stronger through this group ... [*murmured assent from the others*] ... you know, with the tough love, and about enabling and things like that, and once I'd learnt this is what I'm doing ...'cause I'd been trying for years. Now I've made changes and they kicked off against it, they were angry and I've been called all the names you can call me and more. But I don't care, it's water off a duck's back now. You just look at them and think, 'If that's what you think of me, on you go, live your life without your mother'.

Ingrid: That's what I have to do ... she's got to go and she's no(t) wanting to ...

Hester: Because I've got a friend and her son got in about drugs and she asked him to leave and eh ... he got himself into a bit of mess. And she says, 'It's the hardest thing I've ever had to do'. And he came to the door one night and it was bucketing of rain and she just says, 'No, I'm sorry', and then she was getting phone calls about what a lousy mother she was and all the rest of it and she just put the phone down. But see that laddie, got himself sorted out and then said to his mum, 'Mum, I'm sorry for what I said because you did the right thing'.

This excerpt suggests that applying 'tough love' is more of a 'work in progress' for these carers. Crucially the success story recounted – and others in the same vein – related to *other* people, as do 'urban myths', for example. This highlights the support function of this newly formed carers' group, with 'tough love' stories serving the function of inspirational or motivational tales. What is important is not the 'veracity' of the story in question, but, rather, its 'authenticity' in terms of how well it works in terms of its intended purpose (which can also be judged in terms of its acceptability to others with whom the research respondent may be talking – either in the research encounter or beyond it).

Retracing and Presenting Analytical Trails

Altheide and Johnson (1998) recommend that, in writing up our qualitative analyses, we employ a process of 'reflexive accounting'. Although fieldwork diaries are an indispensable tool for carrying out writing up, these are not easy to condense and the material contained therein may not be very accessible to another reader – since this is not, of course, the primary intent of such documents. It can be difficult to convey the evolution of one's thinking, but it is, at least, important to acknowledge where there are contradictions or unsolved puzzles.

PhD students, in particular, often forget their eventual audience as they wrestle with the considerable demands of writing up complex pieces of work. Nevertheless, it is helpful to imagine this hypothetical reader, and how best to lead this person through the evolution of the project and the cumulative process involved in developing analyses. This helps guard against making unwarranted jumps in arguments. Providing an explanation of the process of refinement of coding categories can provide a useful window onto the evolution of our thinking and theorizing, but it is not sufficient merely to reproduce coding frames (with or without the aid of a specific CAQDAS; see Gibbs, Chapter 19, this volume) and leave the rest to the reader. What is important here is not so much the comprehensiveness of the description of codes, but, rather, providing an explication of how successive bouts of 'worrying away' at our data has yielded a more nuanced interpretation – that is, retracing our 'conceptual journey' (Barbour, 2008). Sometimes one well-chosen example will suffice, as the purpose is, after all, to reassure the reader that the process has been engaged in thoughtfully.

Silverman (1993) has emphasized the importance of counting in qualitative data analysis in order to guard against what he calls 'anecdotalism' or what I have termed 'cherry-picking'. Again, what is required is for the writer to provide reassurance that some form of counting (i.e. checking who is saying what, how often, how vehemently and in what context) has been carried out. It would be unhelpful – and rather tedious – to be confronted with accounts that tell us, 'four interviewees said this; seven said that'. I have elsewhere (Barbour, 2008) drawn an analogy with the rough working of proofs in algebra (as encountered in my far-off school days) where it is sufficient to show that such background work has been carried out rather than to reproduce this in detail. Here the role of the appendix comes into its own and here the thesis writer can lodge additional documentation, such as sampling templates or grids used to identify patterning in data analysis. This is more of a challenge in terms of writing for journals, where space is at a premium. Several journals do now allow supplementary materials to be lodged and an example of the use of this facility is provided by Hussey et al. (2004) who reproduced their coding framework and also included stimulus materials produced for their second round of focus groups. While this may reassure the writer eager to provide background information, it remains unclear whether such supplements actually fulfil a role as a useful resources for readers.

The effort put into this 'backstage' work can be demonstrated more succinctly, however, without the need to 'spell everything out'. To some extent this is a matter that defers to the personal taste of the author/s and the confidence that they have in the hypothetical reader. By this I mean that, with regard to some aspects of a qualitative study, the reader can be left to carry out supplementary 'detective work' if he or she wishes to pursue lines of argument that are not well developed in an article, but which are possible given the information presented. An example is provided again by Hussey et al. (2004), not this time in terms of the supplementary material lodged, but by the inclusion of more information in tables (regarding the geographical location of focus groups and their composition) than is actually mined in presenting the argument in this overview findings paper. When writing such papers (or producing concise findings for a funding body, for example) writers need to focus on key findings, but this does not necessarily preclude making some more complex points along the way – sometimes through the inclusion of such additional contextual detail. 'Identifiers' that provide information about individuals' characteristics (e.g. age, gender, length of experience, etc.) can also serve this function, whether or not the writer chooses to draw attention to the patterns thus suggested.

One way of dealing with the difficulties involved in explaining the construction of findings and analytical trails, of course, is to resort to the use of neat typologies or staged theories or explanations, which, effectively, write out complexity or contradictions. Sometimes reports of qualitative findings squeeze the data to fit a theory, or resort to the opposite strategy – that of oversimplifying a theoretical framework or partially presenting this so that it appears to describe, contain and account for all the data generated in a particular research project. Both approaches overlook the analytic potential of grey areas in between that are either not fully explained, or even ignored/brushed under the carpet in the interests of producing a tidy and under-theorized account.

These practices – and potential criticisms – extend to the use made of existing research literature, with lower quality qualitative studies frequently failing to embed a research project adequately in relation to other work or to place current findings within the context of those furnished by previous studies. While this may fleetingly make it look as if the study in question has produced novel insights, ultimately such practices lead to what Morse (2000) has termed 'theoretical congestion'. This involves researchers simply reproducing explanations or theoretical constructs, perhaps using new terms, but missing the opportunity to add incrementally to the knowledge base by comparing and contrasting findings with those of other researchers. Constant comparison (as Green, 1998, points out) does not relate only to analysing a specific dataset, but also should involve reviewing findings in the light of similarities and differences between the current study and earlier work. Such advice relates not just to the content of findings, but also potentially to identifying and capitalizing on conceptual parallels derived from other fields of study (or, even, from other disciplinary repertoires), which may, nevertheless, illuminate the concepts being explored. This is what Strauss and Corbin (1990) refer to when they talk about making 'far out comparisons'. Such 'far out comparisons' might include observations such as the similarities between gambling talk and the way in which couples weigh up the chances of success in deciding whether to pursue further cycles of fertility treatment. This can, in turn, allow for illuminating inferences to be drawn regarding their ideas and understandings of 'control' and 'lack of control', dealing simultaneously with the context of reproductive decision-making (where choice is emphasized and chance downplayed) and assisted reproduction (where chance becomes more apparent and options are severely constrained) (Barbour, 2011).

'Far out comparisons' can also lead to potentially fruitful alternative theoretical frameworks and such possibilities can be enhanced through working in an interdisciplinary way. A study of professionals' views and experiences of 'living wills' or 'advance directives' (Thompson et al., 2003) benefited from the inclusion of a philosopher/ethicist on the team, in addition to a general medical practitioner and myself as a medical sociologist. In particular, we were able to draw on the philosopher/ethicist's knowledge to refine our coding categories surrounding the concept of 'autonomy' (eventually arriving as a consensus code of 'conditional autonomy' – see Barbour, 2008, for a more detailed account). It is only through engaging in interrogating and refining theoretical constructs in this way that we can transcend descriptive accounts located within the confines of our own data set and disciplinary mindset and begin to aspire to achieving 'theoretical' – rather than 'statistical' – generalizability (see Maxwell and Chmiel, Chapter 37, this volume).

Theoretical Generalizability

PhD theses and published qualitative papers commonly include a section on limitations, where it is customary to emphasize the specificity of the context in which the research was carried out. Claims about generalizability are often confined to 'internal generalizability' – that is, the capacity of the typology, model or theoretical framework developed to explain adequately the processes observed within the research setting, group or institution studied. Or course, when carrying out research in an applied context, this is frequently the aspiration of the research project. However, Flick advocates that researchers also ask, 'Do your analytic categories suggest any generic processes?' (2007: 21). Even in an applied context, such a question may be worth posing – if not of immediate relevance for the research team and practitioners involved, it may be worth considering the transferability of the resulting model or recommendations for other related practice areas.

Consideration of the potential for 'theoretical generalizability' may relate to the usefulness of concepts and frameworks for a specific field of study. Unlike claims to 'statistical generalizability', which purport to provide a universal *answer*, the invoking of 'theoretical generalizability' can simply involve posing a general (but clearly articulated) *question* or tentative hypothesis.

When Bury (1982) published his findings from an interview study of patients with rheumatoid arthritis, he could not have anticipated the large number of subsequent studies (relating to a wider variety of chronic illnesses) which have subsequently drawn on and sought to revise and refine his original concept of 'biographical disruption'. What makes this such a good candidate for becoming part of the theoretical canon is the care with which Bury sought, first, to embed discussion of his findings within the existing theoretical literature on the sick role and interactionist studies of health and illness, and, second, to situate his new concept of 'biographical disruption' as an *example* of a 'critical situation'. Bury explained that his study was intended as a contribution to understanding 'the processes involved in the interaction between wider social structures and the experiences of ill-health', thereby underscoring its broader potential relevance (1982: 180). Continued engagement with the idea of 'biographical disruption' on the part of researchers in the sociology of health and illness (as evidenced by citations, further empirical papers utilizing the concept, and – in this day of the Internet – downloads) further testifies to the theoretical generalizability and transferability of the concept.

NEW DEVELOPMENTS AND CRITICAL REFLECTION

In seeking to provide a template for ensuring and evaluating quality in qualitative research there are, of course, many dangers of which to be wary. Many seminal papers or books which have had an enduring influence on qualitative research and professional practice in a variety of fields would not pass muster with regard to fulfilling all of these exacting criteria. I have written elsewhere (Barbour, 2001) of the danger that checklists might drive how research is reported and carried out rather than serving to encourage better practice. Concentrating on the items involved in such checklists and seeking to fulfil criteria in a mechanistic – even, sometimes, strategic – way can lead to 'technical essentialism' (Barbour, 2003). I have argued that there is even a 'grounded theory' variant of 'technical essentialism' whereby a set of procedures has become reified. This has frequently resulted in one specific reading of 'grounded theory' – as a fixed set of staged procedures – being religiously, but uncritically, applied (Barbour, 2003). Somewhat ironically, this has produced an effect that is exactly the opposite of the permissive approach to freeing up researchers' thinking that was the original intention of Glaser and Strauss's (1967) recommended approach (see Thornberg and Charmaz, Chapter 11, this volume).

Interestingly, some of the most interesting discussion regarding quality in qualitative research is emanating from the growing number of 'pragmatic' (Bergman, 2011) mixed methods researchers, or 'methodological connoisseurs' as they are described by Tashakkori and Teddlie (2010; see Morse and Maddox, Chapter 36, this volume). New developments, such as the 'validation framework' developed by Leech et al. (2010), afford promising new avenues for exploring this issue – despite the somewhat unfortunate terminology, which sounds as if it is privileging a quantitative approach. This framework covers items such as 'construct validation', 'inferential consistency', 'utilization/historical element' and 'consequential element', and echoes many of the points made here. Importantly it encompasses the literature review and contextualization of studies that other schema frequently overlook (Barbour and Barbour, 2003) – and which are key to developing 'theoretical generalizability'. In being designed to address issues of quality using parallel but sympathetic criteria, the approach favoured by Leech et al. eschews once and for all the unhelpful dichotomy between quantitative and qualitative approaches. Furthermore it is possible that evaluation of quantitative studies can ultimately be enhanced by incorporating questions that have previously been asked only in relation to qualitative research.

FURTHER READING

Flick, Uwe (2007) *Managing Quality in Qualitative Research*. London: Sage.
Melia, Kath (2010) 'Recognizing quality in qualitative research', in Ivy Bourgeault et al. (eds), *The SAGE Handbook of Qualitative Methods in Health Research*. London: Sage. pp. 559–74.
Seale, Clive (1999) *The Quality of Qualitative Research*. London: Sage.

REFERENCES

Altheide, David L. and Johnson, John M. (1998) 'Criteria for assessing interpretive validity in qualitative research', in Norman K. Denzin and Yvonna S. Lincoln (eds), *Collecting and Interpreting Qualitative Materials*. London: Sage. pp. 293–312.
Armstrong, David, Gosling, Ann, Weinman, John and Marteau, Theresa (1997) 'The place of inter-rater reliability in qualitative research: An empirical study', *Sociology*, 51: 597–606.
Atkinson, Paul A. (1997) 'Narrative turn or blind alley?', *Qualitative Health Research*, 7 (3): 325–44.
Barbour, Rosaline S. (1998) 'Mixing qualitative methods: Quality assurance or qualitative quagmire?', *Qualitative Health Research*, 8: 352–61.
Barbour, Rosaline S. (2001) 'Checklists for improving the rigour of qualitative research: A case of the tail wagging the dog?', *British Medical Journal*, 322: 1115–17.
Barbour, Rosaline S. (2003) 'The newfound credibility of qualitative research? Tales of technical essentialism and co-option', *Qualitative Health Research*, 13 (7): 1019–27.
Barbour, Rosaline S. (2007) *Analyzing Focus Groups*. London: Sage.
Barbour, Rosaline S. (2008) *Introducing Qualitative Research: A Student's Guide to the Craft of Doing Qualitative Research*. London: Sage (2nd edition in press).
Barbour, Rosaline S. (2011) 'The biographical turn and the "socialization" of medicine', *Medical Sociology Online*, 6 (1): 15–25. www.medicalsociologyonline.org
Barbour, Rosaline S. and Barbour, Michael (2003) 'Evaluating and synthesizing qualitative research: The need to develop a distinctive approach', *Journal of Evaluation in Clinical Practice*, 9 (2): 179–86.
Barbour, Rosaline S., MacLeod, Maureen, Mires, Gary and Anderson, Annie S. (2012) 'Uptake of folic acid supplements before and during pregnancy: Focus group analysis of women's views and experiences', *Journal of Human Nutrition and Dietetics*, 25 (2): 140–7.
Bergman, Manfred Max (2011) 'The politics, fashions and conventions of research methods', *Journal of Mixed Methods Research*, 5 (2): 99–102.
Blaxter, Mildred (1996) 'Criteria for the evaluation of qualitative research papers', *Medical Sociology News*, British Sociological Association Medical Sociology Group.
Bryman, Alan and Burgess, Raymond G. (eds) (1994) *Analyzing Qualitative Data*. London: Routledge.

Bury, Michael (1982) 'Chronic illness as biographical disruption', *Sociology of Health and Illness*, 4 (2): 167–82.
Charmaz, Kathy (2006) *Constructing Grounded Theory: A Practical Guide through Qualitative Analysis*. Thousand Oaks, CA: Sage.
Denzin, Norman K. and Lincoln, Yvonna S. (eds) (1994) *Handbook of Qualitative Research*. London: Sage.
Flick, Uwe (2007) *Managing Quality in Qualitative Research*. London: Sage.
Frank, Arthur. W. (1995) *The Wounded Story Teller*. Chicago: The University of Chicago Press.
Frankland, Jane and Bloor, Michael (1999) 'Some issues arising in the systematic analysis of focus group materials', in Rosalind S. Barbour and Janet Kitzinger (eds), *Developing Focus Group Research*. Thousand Oaks, CA : Sage. pp.144–55.
Gibbs, Graham (2007) *Analysing Qualitative Data*. London: Sage.
Glaser, Barney G. and Strauss, Anselm L. (1967) The *Discovery of Grounded Theories*. Chicago: Aldine.
Green, Judith (1998) 'Commentary: Grounded theory and the constant comparative method', *British Medical Journal*, 316: 1064–5.
Green, Judith and Thorogood, Nicki (2004) *Qualitative Methods for Health Research*. London: Sage.
Hammersley, Martyn (1995) *The Politics of Social Research*. London: Sage.
Hammersley, Martyn (2004) 'Teaching qualitative method: Craft, profession or bricolage?', in Clive Seale et al. (eds), *Qualitative Research Practice*. London: Sage. pp. 549–60.
Hepburn, Alexa and Potter, Jonathan (2004) 'Discourse analytic practice', in Clive Seale et al. (eds), *Qualitative Research Practice*. London: Sage. pp. 180–96.
Huberman, A. Michael and Miles, Matthew B. (1998) 'Data management and analysis methods', in Norman Denzin and Yvonna S. Lincoln (eds), *Collecting and Interpreting Qualitative Materials*. London: Sage. pp. 179–211.
Hussey, Susan, Hoddinott, Pat, Wilson, Phillip, Dowell, Jonathan and Barbour, Rosaline (2004) 'The sickness certification system in the UK: Qualitative study of views of general practitioners in Scotland', *British Medical Journal*, 328: 88–92.
Kelle, Udo (1997) 'Theory building in qualitative research and computer programs for the management of textual data', *Sociological Research Online*, 2 (1): (accessed 15 May 2013).
Leech, Nancy L., Dellinger, Amy B., Brannaghan, Kim B. and Tanaka, Hideyuki (2010) 'Evaluating mixed research studies: A mixed methods approach', *Journal of Mixed Methods Research*, 4 (1): 17–31.
Lincoln, Yvonna S. and Guba, Egon G. (1985) *Naturalistic Inquiry*. London: Sage.
Maxwell, Joseph A. (2011) *A Realist Approach for Qualitative Research*. Thousand Oaks, CA: Sage.
Melia, Kath M. (1997) 'Producing "plausible stories": Interviewing student nurses', in George Miller and Robert Dingwall (eds), *Context and Method in Qualitative Research*. London: Sage. pp. 26–36.
Morse, Janice M. (2000) 'Editorial: Theoretical congestion', *Qualitative Health Research*, 10 (6): 715–16.
Orr, Linda (2011) 'Carer involvement in drug services: A comparative study of the views of carers, service providers and policy makers', PhD thesis, University of Dundee.
Orr, Linda, Barbour, Rosaline S. and Elliott, Lawrence (2012) 'Carer involvement with drug services: A qualitative study', *Health Expectations*. DOI: 10.1111/hex.12033.
Popay, Jennie, Williams, Gareth and Rogers, Anne (1998) 'Rationale and standards for the systematic review of qualitative literature in health services research', *Qualitative Health Research*, 8: 341–51.
Puchta, Claudia and Potter, Jonathan (2004) *Focus Group Practice*. London: Sage.
Richardson, Laurel (1994) 'Writing: A method of inquiry', in Norman K. Denzin and Yvonna S. Lincoln (eds), *Handbook of Qualitative Research*. Thousand Oaks, CA: Sage. pp. 516–29.
Ritchie, Jane and Spencer, Liz (1994) 'Qualitative data analysis for applied policy research', in Alan Bryman and Robert G. Burgess (eds), *Analyzing Qualitative Data*. London: Routledge, pp. 173–94.
Seale, Clive (1999) *The Quality of Qualitative Research*. London: Sage.
Silverman, David (1993) *Interpreting Qualitative Data: Methods of Analyzing Talk, Text and Interaction*. London: Sage.
Strauss, Anselm L. and Corbin, Juliet (1990) *Basics of Qualitative Research: Grounded Theory Procedures and Techniques*. Thousand Oaks, CA: Sage.
Tashakkori, Abbas and Teddlie, Charles (2010) 'Putting the human back in "Human Research Methodology": The researchers in mixed methods research', *Journal of Mixed Methods Research*, 4 (4): 271–7.
Thompson, Trevor, Barbour, Rosaline S. and Schwartz, Lisa (2003) 'Advance directives in critical care decision making: A vignette study', *British Medical Journal*, 327: 1011–15.
Wright Mills, Charles (1959) *The Sociological Imagination*. London: Penguin.

35
Ethical Use of Qualitative Data and Findings

Donna M. Mertens

While qualitative researchers follow the same regulatory procedures for ethical review as all researchers, they situate themselves in consciously value-laden territory in which human relationships and critical self-reflection loom prominently. This positioning leads to the emergence of ethical dilemmas throughout the conduct of research with implications for the use of research that go beyond legal requirements or many professional standards for ethically responsible research. Ethics surrounding the use of qualitative research needs to take into consideration the rigor and ethical nature of the research activities that precede use, as well as those inherently connected with decisions about the use of the data and findings. There is an inherent connection between the quality (see Barbour, Chapter 34, this volume), analysis and interpretation (see Willig, Chapter 10, this volume) of the research data, and the use of the research, making it difficult to talk about use without reflecting on what precedes use. Hence, this chapter addresses issues associated with ethical use of qualitative research, with a retrospective look at implications for the entire research process.

What are the potential uses of qualitative data and findings? Answers to this question (see Murray, Chapter 40, this volume) depend on the purpose of the research and the philosophical positioning of the researcher. If qualitative researchers view the purpose of research as the creation of knowledge in a generic sense, then ethical obligations can be fulfilled by adhering to the ethical principles that are embodied in the policies set forth by institutional review boards and sharing the created knowledge through the traditional methods of academe: publications and presentations at professional conferences. However, qualitative researchers who situate themselves in the critical, post-structural school of thought (Christians, 2011; Cannella and Lincoln, 2011), feminists (Oleson, 2011), and those who align themselves with the transformative paradigm (Mertens, 2009; Mertens et al., 2011) conceptualize the purpose of research in terms of the researcher's ethical obligation to address issues of human rights and social justice. Mertens (2009; 2010) argues that qualitative researchers who hold transformative values have a responsibility to address issues of human rights, social justice, discrimination, and oppression. Denzin (2012: 85) describes the qualitative researcher's natural home as a critical, interpretive framework, thus supporting his endorsement of the ethical responsibility to use qualitative research for social change:

> The bricoleur is in the business of changing the world for social justice purposes. We must act as catalysts for social change. History, change, transformation belong to those who care, who remember, who struggle to re-remember, who turn history back against itself, who expose the cracks and contradictions in history itself (Smith, 2004: xvii). The goal is to provoke change, to create texts that play across gender and race, utopian texts that involve readers and audiences in this passion, moving them to action.
>
> Qualitative research scholars have an obligation to change the world, to engage in ethical work that makes a positive difference. We are challenged to confront the facts of injustice, to make the injustices of history visible and hence open to change and transformation. (Denzin, 2012: 85)

Qualitative researchers who work from a critical transformative stance challenge the sufficiency and even the appropriateness of ethics as defined by institutional review boards (Christians, 2011). Changing contexts of research such as the increased presence of marginalized voices and use of technology in research suggest that questions of representation, voice, and credibility are needed that go beyond the ethical principles associated with the typical institutional ethical reviews. No matter what the purpose, researchers need to give thought to the possible uses of their research from the beginning of the study throughout the entire process (Mertens and Wilson, 2012). Use can be considered as part of the dynamic of the research process, creating knowledge in partnership with stakeholders and providing opportunities for reflection at critical junctures in the research process in the form of written, oral, or signed (e.g., American Sign Language) reports, group discussions, Web-based dissemination, and other types of visual displays and performances.

In this chapter, the ethics of use are explored via the concepts of representation, voice, power and credibility, as well as in terms of use of qualitative research for social change with an emphasis on the involvement of community members or stakeholders in culturally responsive ways. As already alluded to in the introduction to this chapter, qualitative researchers are diverse in terms of the approaches they use and the assumptions that guide their work, hence the discussion of ethics that follows recognizes the heterogeneity within the qualitative communities.

ETHICS, REPRESENTATION, VOICE, POWER, AND CREDIBILITY

Qualitative researchers have long been cognizant of the challenges involved in terms of the representation of multiple socially constructed versions of reality and issues of whose voices are present in the findings and who has power to make interpretations of the data. Recommended practices to address these challenges include the use of member checks and triangulation to insure accuracy of data and to identify convergence and divergence in viewpoints (see Barbour, Chapter 34, this volume). Qualitative researchers who work within the action research traditions have emphasized the ongoing inclusion of member checks and triangulation as strategies to involve participants in the use of the qualitative data (Brydon-Miller et al., 2011; also see Murray, Chapter 40, this volume). Wertz et al. note a change in the conversation about use in qualitative research that presents the role of participants in a different light, one in which they play a more active role:

> Commentators, critics, and researchers themselves are increasingly calling on researchers to view participants as persons whose interests, methods of understanding, critical potential, and

outcomes are acknowledged and valued within science. Scientists are becoming increasingly sensitive to the political and ethical implications of the inequalities of power and privilege. Because the participant's role in research has become an important topic in contemporary research and has posed ambiguous and complex issues for research involving highly personal material, we [need to] explore and critically reflect on the variety and meanings of our research participant's responses to our analyses. (2011: 6–7)

If the research participant is an active agent in the decisions about use of the data and findings, this opens up new possibilities related to the ethical challenges associated with representation, voice, and credibility. Research participants share in-depth information about themselves. Researchers bring various theoretical lenses to the interpretation of the data. Suppose the researcher claims to have deeper insights into the participants' lives than the participants themselves have? Suppose a research participant who is described in unflattering terms objects to the way he or she is characterized. What are the opportunities for the participant to speak back to the researcher? What is the researcher's responsibility to be responsive to the participant's objections?

Issues about confidentiality also arise in the use of data. Suppose the researcher's description is so vivid and detailed that others who know the participant recognize who is being written/spoken about? What does that mean in terms of the promised confidentiality to the participant? What if the participant has the opportunity to examine the results of the analysis before they are made public? Even if the participants signed an informed consent agreement to be interviewed, do they have the option of withdrawing use of their data if they disagree with the interpretation and use? These questions raise ontological tensions in terms of whose reality is being privileged.

These tensions are illustrated in the following example of a qualitative research project in which five researchers agreed to analyse one participant's interview data (see Roulston, Chapter 20, this volume) using five different analytic approaches: phenomenological (see Eberle, Chapter 13, this volume), grounded theory (see Thornberg and Charmaz, Chapter 11, this volume), discourse analysis (see Willig, Chapter 23, this volume), narrative research (see Esin et al., Chapter 14, this volume), and intuitive inquiry (Wertz et al., 2011).

Example: Representation, Voice, Credibility

The five researchers used a single interview conducted as part of a class exercise on the topic of resilience in the face of trauma (Wertz et al., 2011). The researchers illustrated the effect of different analytic strategies applied to the same data for educative purposes. They encountered ethical challenges in the form of protecting the participant's privacy and well-being that surfaced during a presentation at a professional conference. When queried about the participant's reaction to their analyses, the panel members said that they had not shared their findings with the participant and therefore did not know how the participant viewed their descriptions of her. One panelist claimed that her interpretation (see Willig, Chapter 10, this volume) was credible because, following a presentation at another conference using the same data, she was approached by an audience member who recognized the participant based on the presentation. The panelist felt this was an indicator that her analysis was an accurate description of the participant. However, this also raised issues about the need for protecting the identity of the research participant and considering the participant's feelings about having the researcher's interpretation of her story made public.

Wertz et al. (2011) had followed the traditional practice of member checks (see Barbour, Chapter 34, this volume), that is, offering the participant a chance to read the transcript and eliminate anything that she felt was too personal. After the conference presentations, the researchers engaged in critical self-reflection and discussion about this question: Are research participants merely data sources or do they have the right to play an active role in their portrayal? The researchers decided to establish a relationship with the research participant to further explore the ethical issues that arose from their portrayals of her. They invited the participant to author a chapter in the book about the five analytic strategies in which she provided her reactions to the findings. This raised another set of ethical questions. Whose version of the portrayal of the participant should be given privilege? Where does the right of interpretation (see Willig, Chapter 10, this volume) rest? Wertz et al.'s struggle with these questions illustrates the tension when participants talk back to researchers. The researchers' solution was to add their reflections on the issues that arose from this process associated with 'power, privilege, ownership, interpretive authority, and validity in human scientific research' (2011: 10).

The research participant, Emalinda McSpadden, appreciated being asked to respond to their analyses and to waive her right to confidentiality in order to make a contribution to the research project. She wrote:

> I have noticed a dynamic that does not hold analyses directly accountable to those whose data have been analyzed, whether the results are quantitative or qualitative in nature. While qualitative methods seem to be more conscious of the participant on the whole, they nevertheless exhibit a lack of dialogue with the person or persons who provided the initial data, or at least no such dialogue is ever disseminated to the reader as a fundamental part of reporting the results. In terms of research ethics, I have always found this a problematic element in every methodology I've encountered to date: Namely, that the 'debriefing' process was not somehow a more explicit element of the research and findings themselves, but rather a mere procedural component of what constitutes the proper conduct of a scientist working with human subjects. (McSpadden, 2011: 340)

Based on the Oral History Association's (2009) ethical principles, Shopes (2011) provides insights into how to address these types of ethical challenges. These principles warn researchers not to make promises they cannot keep. Promises to avoid include: guaranteeing participants' control over the interpretation (see Willig, Chapter 10, this volume) and presentation (see Denzin, Chapter 39, this volume) of the interviews, hiding potentially damaging data, or revealing the identity of the participant. Oral historians' first ethical commitment is to truth and honesty, and when the situation warrants revelation of information and identity in the name of the greater good, this should be followed. This position is not unproblematic. The voices of marginalized communities are discussed later in this chapter; they call for the power to review, object to, and dismiss findings that they do not feel accurately represent their experiences.

The Right to Write Honestly

As illustrated in the Wertz et al. (2011) example, differences of opinion exist about who should have the final word regarding interpretation and use of the data. Ellis's (1986) work with a fishing village provides another twist to the ethical issues associated with honesty, complexity, and the right to write about others, especially if those others are people you live with or are friends with. Ellis collected data in a fishing village over nine years, never expecting that the village people would ever read what she wrote about them. However, another researcher did return to the village and read parts of her book to the people there. The result was:

> They were extremely hurt by what they heard. I had described them as smelling like fish and other things equally devastating. These people had become really good friends of mine. I loved them and cared for them, and what I said was very painful for them and also for me. I went back to the community and talked with them. Some people forgave me. Some people never did forgive me. (Ellis et al., 2008: 272)

Ellis (2009) continues to struggle with ethical issues connected with writing about people she lives among in an honest manner, inclusive of her own reactions to and interpretations of their words and behaviors. In a qualitative study of the mountain community in which she spends her summers, she writes about the racism, homophobia, and sexism that are entrenched in the culture shared by many of the people who have lived there for generations. She worries about the effect that writing about these topics will have on her relationships with her mountain neighbors. She wonders:

> Just how far do we take the idea of getting permission and approval for what we write? Do we need permission to write everything about anybody? Should I get permission from every character who appears in my writing, no matter how minimal? If we take this practice to the extreme, we won't be able to write honestly or critically about anything, including our own lives – especially our own lives. Don't I have the right to write about myself? (2009: 13)

She considers options, such as leaving out the problematic stories, but she rejects that in the name of honesty (Ellis, 2009). She also rejects the idea of presenting the stories in a camouflaged way to disguise identities. She does engage in extensive self-reflection (see May and Perry, Chapter 8, this volume) and discussion with her colleagues about the ethical issues she struggles with in writing (see Denzin, Chapter 39, this volume) about the mountain folk. She asks herself if she has an ethical obligation to bring the issues of prejudice and discrimination to the attention of the mountain people as part of relational ethics. She fears that if she showed her writings to these people then it would lead to a confrontation that would block progress toward having conversations about the topics. She says that if the mountain people were to read what she wrote about them, she is prepared to have conversations with them about prejudice. While not instigating such a direct confrontation, she looks upon the possibility of it as a way to talk across divides, find common ground in shared humanity, and be honest with herself about her research.

Ellis's quandary is in a way reflective of the quandaries that many writers, even those of fiction, find themselves in when portraying such persons. Recall that Thomas Wolfe's character, George Webber, concluded that 'you can't go home again' (1940: 306) when he tried to return to his small hometown after writing a novel in which the townspeople were easily recognizable, with all their faults, secrets, and idiosyncrasies.

Use of Data beyond Initial Purposes

Additional ethical challenges arise when qualitative data are used for secondary analyses (see Wästersfors et al., Chapter 32, and Timulak, Chapter 33, this volume) after the original study is completed. This may be done by the original researcher, or it might be another researcher who is using the previously collected data. The original researcher may reflect on the project and realize that substantial possibilities exist to analyse the data using a different theoretical lens that could yield heretofore unexpected insights into the phenomenon. In such cases, the researcher may no longer have contact with the original participants. This raises issues about the ethics of using data for purposes other than what was included in the initial informed consent process.

The focus of the previous sections is primarily on representation, voice, and credibility and their impact on the researcher–community relations. This provides a segue to the next section: What is the role of the use of qualitative data and findings in social change?

QUALITATIVE RESEARCH AS A TOOL FOR SOCIAL CHANGE

Qualitative researchers who accept that an appropriate use of their data and findings is as a tool for social change are likely to encounter issues of representation, voice, and credibility at a social and cultural level. In addition, challenges arise in terms of how to interact with communities to support the use of data and findings for the intended purposes. A number of strands in the qualitative (and mixed methods – see Morse and

Maddox, Chapter 36, this volume) communities address issues of relevance in terms of the use of research data and findings for the purpose of social change (see Murray, Chapter 40, this volume), especially as it relates to resistance against sexism, racism, ableism, audism (hearing people discriminating against deaf people), and other *isms* that are the basis for discrimination and oppression in society. Some of these strands include: transformative research (Mertens, 2009; 2010), action research (Reason and Bradbury, 2008; Brydon-Miller et al., 2011), feminist research (Brabeck and Brabeck, 2009; Olesen, 2011), queer theory research (Plummer, 2011; Dodd, 2009); disability and deaf rights research (Mertens et al., 2011; Harris et al., 2009); human rights researchers (Krog, 2011; Segone, 2009); critical theorists (Freeman, 2010; Cannella and Lincoln, 2011); as well as critical race theorists (Dillard and Okpalaoka, 2011; Madison, 2005; Thomas, 2009) and indigenous research (Chilisa, 2012; Cram, 2009; LaFrance and Crazy Bull, 2009). A thorough discussion of this body of literature is beyond the scope of this chapter. However, the breadth and depth of the attention given to this aspect of use support the need for qualitative researchers to engage in conscious critical reflection about how they address or do not address this potential use of their data and findings.

Representation, Voice, and Credibility on a Social Level

Members of marginalized communities, such as the indigenous and disability and deaf rights communities, direct researchers to rethink their roles and methodologies in order to be respectful of cultural expectations. Disability researchers coined the slogan 'Nothing about us without us' in response to research that did not include people with disabilities meaningfully in the research process and in the use of the findings (Charlton, 1998). Deaf rights researchers have developed terms of reference for the conduct of ethical research in their community that places the power in the hands of members of the community, rather than in the hands of the hearing outsiders (Harris et al., 2009).

Indigenous researchers have moved beyond calling for decolonizing research methods (Smith, 1999) to calling for a postcolonial, indigenous framework to guide researchers who work in their communities (Chilisa, 2012; LaFrance and Nichols, 2010). Maori researchers have developed an approach to research called the Kaupapa Maori that states that research be done 'by Māori, for Māori, with Māori' (Cram, 2009: 312). What these strands have in common is a challenge to Western ways of thinking at a very fundamental level in order to address the history of violations of human rights in these communities.

The philosophical assumptions that constitute the transformative paradigm provide one framework for systematically considering ethical considerations for the use of qualitative research for social change (Mertens, 2009; 2010). Building on the conceptual work of Guba and Lincoln (2005), the transformative paradigm is characterized by four philosophical assumptions related to the nature of ethics (axiology), reality (ontology), knowledge and the relationship between the researcher and that which would be known (epistemology), and systematic inquiry (methodology). The transformative paradigm provides a meta-physical umbrella that brings together commensurate theoretical lenses such as those described in the preceding paragraphs. It is applicable to people who experience discrimination and oppression on whatever basis, including, but not limited to, race/ethnicity, disability, deafness, immigrant status, political conflicts, sexual orientation, poverty, gender, age, religion, or the multitude of other characteristics that are associated with less access to social justice. The transformative paradigm includes the need for researchers to critically analyse relationships of power between themselves and their participants, as well as between the participants and the wider society in which they live.

As mentioned at the beginning of this chapter, the transformative axiological assumption is defined by a recognition that the purpose of research is to promote social justice and further human rights. The axiological assumption has a critical influence on the character of the other three assumptions because assumptions about the nature of reality, knowledge, and systematic inquiry need to be consistent with the ethical principles of human rights and social justice. Based on the transformative axiological assumption, researchers might ask themselves such questions as:

- How do my ethical principles reflect issues of culture and power differences?
- How can this research contribute to social justice and human rights?
- What do I need to do differently in terms of methodology in order to act in accordance with these principles?

In order to answer these questions, researchers need to investigate the cultural beliefs and norms in the communities in which they work. This includes knowing how to enter communities respectfully, identify the norms and beliefs, and distinguish between those norms and beliefs that support social justice and those that sustain an oppressive status quo. Cram (2009) in the Maori community, LaFrance and Crazy Bull (2009) in the American Indian community, and Battiste (2007) in the Canadian First Nations communities instruct researchers of the need to appear face to face to ask for permission to conduct research in these communities, and the expectation that the researchers will be honest about what they get out of the research (e.g., funding, publications) and what the tribe or clan gets out of the research. This needs to be done before there is an agreement to allow researchers to commence their work.

In addition, community members want researchers to focus on the strengths and resilience in their communities, not just on the problems, challenges, or deficits. They do not need another researcher coming into their communities to tell them that they have a high rate of alcoholism or that their children are not graduating from high school. They want researchers who will work with them, recognizing their strengths, and finding solutions to the problems that they have inherited from a legacy of discrimination and oppression. Researchers should be aware of the history of researchers coming into marginalized communities to take research data without providing anything in return. The voices of community members call for reciprocity; this is an important part of the transformative axiological assumption. Researchers need to work with communities to determine what the communities want and need, so there is hope of leaving the communities better off than they were before the research. At the same time, researchers have to honestly acknowledge the limitations of their work; they cannot make promises that they have no power to keep.

The transformative ontological assumption follows from the axiological assumption in that the nature of reality is viewed as multiple socially constructed realities, just as in the constructivist paradigm. However, the transformative paradigm holds that the versions of reality need to be critically interrogated in order to determine if they support the enhancement of social justice or sustain an oppressive status quo. In order to act upon this ontological assumption, researchers might ask the following questions:

- To what extent can the researcher identify cultural norms and beliefs within communities that are supportive of or deleterious to the pursuit of social justice and human rights?
- What are the consequences of identifying these versions of reality?
- How does this research contribute to the change in understandings of what is real?

Ellis's (2009) reflections on her neighbors' racist, homophobic, and sexist beliefs illustrate those norms and beliefs that are deleterious toward the pursuit of social justice and human rights. On the other hand, she also discusses the norms and beliefs that are positive, such as valuing family and friendship, self-sufficiency, and being a good neighbor.

Qualitative researchers need to give thought to these questions: Do we have a responsibility to try to change things when we bear witness to racism, ableism, audism, or sexism? How can we design, conduct, and use our research to facilitate the type of social change we desire? How can researchers address the use of their research once their hands have left the keyboard or their voices have faded away in a conference hall?

The transformative epistemological assumption explores the nature of knowledge and the relationship between the researchers and the participants. For researchers to act upon the assumptions presented thus far, they need to establish a relationship with the participants that is reflective of cultural respect and awareness of power differentials. They might begin with these questions:

- How can the researcher explicitly address power differentials and insure that the voices of the least powerful are accurately expressed and acted upon?
- What strategies can be used to establish a trusting relationship?

Researchers who are not working in their home communities or in their native language need to use strategies that are culturally appropriate to build trust. They need to acknowledge what they bring to the research context in terms of both their strengths and their limitations. This positioning allows researchers to work in a spirit of humility with community members who have a stronger understanding of the relevant cultural and social issues.

Other strategies might include the formation of teams of researchers (see Cornish et al., Chapter 6, this volume), including members of the community. If there is a need for capacity building in terms of research methods, then this can be provided by the more experienced researcher. This would address part of the need for reciprocity in the research process. Researchers can begin their relationships with the important community gatekeepers. If this relationship is developed appropriately, then the community leader can vouch for the researcher's credibility. Harris et al. (2009) make the point that members of the marginalized community should be accorded all the rights and privileges of those from the dominant group, and not be relegated to a research assistant role or as a token representative. With the emergence of strong indigenous researchers, there is a greater probability that the indigenous researchers will be better qualified to undertake the research than an outsider would be (Chilisa, 2012).

The transformative methodological assumption supports the use of methods that are appropriate within the context of the communities in which the research is conducted. In order to begin to understand the norms and beliefs of a community and the status of its members in terms of discrimination and oppression, transformative research needs to begin with qualitative moments of data collection. This can be combined with the use of quantitative methods as well. For example, beliefs about the transmission of HIV/AIDS can be learned through qualitative methods, while quantitative data about the occurrence of the disease in diverse populations can support the creation of useful knowledge. The use of mixed methods (see Morse and Maddox, Chapter 36, this volume) and the integration of the data from these methods can allow for the capture of the contextual complexity and provide for pluralistic avenues for appropriately engaging with diverse cultural groups. For sustainable social change to occur, it is often necessary to have a cyclical approach to the inquiry. Thus, researchers might ask these questions:

- How can a cyclical design be used to make use of interim findings throughout the study?
- How can the researchers engage with the full range of stakeholders to gather data that will enhance their understandings of the community?

- How can the data collection methods and feedback to the community be responsive to the needs of the different stakeholder groups?
- How can the methods be designed to enhance the use of the research for the purpose of enhancing social justice and furthering human rights?

The sharing of power at the methodological level is not without challenges. How much control should the researcher exert in order to maintain the integrity of the findings and their use? What happens when there is divisiveness within the community? How can the researcher respond to disagreements within the community about the meaning and use of the results? Should researchers be responsible only to their own consciences? Or, as Sullivan asks, should the researcher be a bit of a provocateur who 'recognizes inequality and injustices, possesses a shared sense of responsibility, and works humbly with the community to transform its situation' (2009: 77–8)?

Example: Transformative Research

Fierro (2006) conducted a study using mixed methods (see Morse and Maddox, Chapter 36, this volume) of the effects of a Welfare-to-Work program for parents who had lost custody of their children to the state (initially called non-custodial parents). The quantitative measures (demographics, employment barriers, education, staff surveys, and attendance records at job training) favored the measurements of outcomes. Via qualitative methods (ethnographic interviews, see Roulston, Chapter 20; observations, see Marvasti, Chapter 24; and focus groups, see Barbour, Chapter 21, this volume), the researcher explored the context within which participants lived and operated. On the basis of preliminary data analysis, the researcher used the results to change the label used to describe the participants from non-custodial parents to transitional custody parents. This change represents more than a simple language difference; it indicates that the parents do not currently have custody of their children, but by participating in the program they are in transition to regain custody. In sharing this shift of perspective with the program participants, the researcher proceeded to make visible the multiple challenges that these parents faced, often in the form of unsympathetic legal and welfare systems. During the focus groups, mothers met other mothers who were in similar circumstances, which engendered a sense of empowerment as they shared their struggles and strategies for success. The researcher began participating in a grassroots organization that advocates for parents to regain custody of their children and contributed to a policy report and film on the topic.

Members of marginalized communities have written that local control and review is an essential part of facilitating positive change and avoiding harm. For example, LaFrance and Crazy Bull (2009) describe the ethical review process implemented by an American Indian tribe and Cram (2009) describes a similar process initiated by Maori in New Zealand. Dodd (2009) recommends the use of a community advisory committee when conducting research with vulnerable populations such as the lesbian, gay, bisexual, transsexual, and queer communities. The Sign Language Community wants to know what is being said about them before it appears in print or is presented in a public forum (Harris et al., 2009). Even with these safeguards, research does not always yield the intended positive effect.

The Other Side of the Coin: Harmful Effects

Researchers may enter communities with the best of intentions, but there is no guarantee that their research will result in a positive experience for the participants or the type of social change that will bring about greater justice. Under some conditions, the research may actually result in harm. As Ellis et al. (2008) shared, the fisher folk were hurt by the knowledge of what she said about them; she also worries that the mountain folk will become angry with her for what she wrote about them (Ellis, 2009). Worse consequences have been associated with the conduct of research. For example, DeHaene et al. (2010) examined the effects of participating in research with refugees who had suffered trauma in the form of war and other forms of violence, ethnic cleansing, lawlessness, and persecution. The researchers chose the narrative method because they wanted to give voice to marginalized lives and enhance participants' personal well-being. However, they reported that the replaying of the traumatic experience through extensive interviewing increased the refugees' distress. The participants did have access to therapeutic support and were given referrals as part of the researcher–participant relationship. The researchers noted a fragile balance as participants made choices to participate or not and the reactivation of the refugees' feelings of being victims of coercive power.

In terms of implications of use of research that causes harm, the Presidential Commission for the Study of Bioethics Issues (2011) concluded that human subjects should not individually bear the costs of care required to treat harms resulting directly from that research. The Commission noted that promoting the effectiveness of community engagement had the potential to reduce the probability that harmful results would occur and to identify appropriate strategies to ameliorate the harmful effects. Almost all developed nations, except the United States, have developed guidelines to assure compensation for the care of human subjects harmed in the course of research. The Commission recommended that the United States undertake the development of such guidelines and to include in that process the need for respect for cultural differences that have implications for ethical conduct of research. The Commission wrote:

> Effective community engagement provides an additional layer of safeguards by providing the community with opportunities to thoroughly weigh and accept or reject the risks and benefits of research activities, discover possible implications of research that might have unintended consequences to the host community, and independently debate the effectiveness of research protections. Interactive and ongoing dialogue between communities and research teams allows for the integration of community norms, beliefs, customs, and cultural sensitivities into research activities. (2011: 12)

What is the ethical responsibility of the qualitative research community to provide input into the development of guidelines for effective community engagement with the goal of protecting diverse cultural groups? What is the ethical responsibility of the researcher when working in low-income communities to respond to the full range of the needs of the local community? If the researcher cannot provide reciprocity in the form of meeting community members' needs, should the researcher choose a different site for the research?

Community Involvement

Community involvement is a complex and challenging process. The United Nations agency responsible for AIDS research (UNAIDS) provides guidance for how to involve communities:

> through a transparent and meaningful participatory process which involves them in an early and sustained manner in the design, development, implementation, and distribution of results. ... Communities of people affected by research should conversely play an active, informed role in all aspects of its planning and conduct, as well as the dissemination of results. Achieving meaningful participation requires the acknowledgement of structural power imbalances between certain communities and researchers and/or research sponsors, and striving to overcome them. In practical terms, this means putting in place outreach and engagement measures to support participation. Special attention should be paid to the inclusion and empowerment of women for active involvement throughout the research process, as well as to the representation of populations at higher risk. (UNAIDS, 2007: 17–18)

This guidance is framed in relation to research related to HIV/AIDS; however, many of the issues discussed in the UNAIDS report have relevance for qualitative researchers more generally. For example, the definition of the relevant community can be a difficult process. Researchers can sometimes resolve this issue by discussing with the local authorities whether these are people in formal positions of authority or people who are recognized by the community as leaders in a less formal sense. In some circumstances, the definition of community needs to be broadened beyond the research participants to include advocates, media, human rights organizations, national institutions, and governments. Another complexity arises in the determination of who from these stakeholder groups will serve as their community's representative. Such decisions can be facilitated through appropriate consultation and negotiation to insure that the representatives are credible and legitimate in the eyes of their community members.

The UNAIDS report also provides useful guidance in terms of strategies for involvement of the various community members through formal meetings, educational materials, and support needed to insure meaningful participation:

> Formal community meetings need to be organized in a way that facilitates the active participation of those most affected by the research being proposed. The principal investigator and site research staff should work with representatives of affected communities to identify needs related to their participation, including logistical requirements such as transportation to the meeting site. Educational materials should be designed in an accessible format, using easy to understand language. Adequate consultation and full participation in the planning process will require more than formal community meetings, as such meetings may alienate some people or be inaccessible to others due to the timing or the format. The principal investigator and site research staff should make efforts to reach out to affected communities, meeting at community centers, workplaces, and other frequented locations. In both formal and informal consultations, the timing and length of the meetings should be convenient for community members, using approaches that facilitate two-way communication with two goals in mind: (1) to identify and understand community concerns and needs, as well as their knowledge and experience, and (2) to clearly describe the research being proposed, related benefits and risks, and other practical implications. (Tilousi, 2011: 19–20)

This type of involvement can yield improved outcomes in the form of developing the knowledge base needed to determine appropriate interventions and dissemination of the findings in ways that support social action.

QUALITY AND ETHICS OF USE

If a study's results are questionable on the basis of poor quality, then the use of that study's results is at best questionable and is potentially harmful. Criteria (see Barbour, Chapter 34, this volume) for quality or rigor in qualitative research were identified by Guba and Lincoln (1989) in terms of credibility, transferability, dependability, and confirmability. If researchers heed this advice, then they have a better chance of producing research that is viewed as believable and with the potential for application elsewhere. In 2009, Lincoln expanded this list in terms of facets of authenticity that have direct implications for how qualitative data are used:

1. Ontological authenticity refers to the mental or emotional awakening on the part of the inquirer and participants that occurs when a person recognizes feelings, attitudes, beliefs, values or other dispositions that were not previously expressed or understood as part of the outcomes of participating in the research.
2. Educative authenticity refers to the need to share the social constructions that emerged from all stakeholder groups. This type of authenticity is especially espoused by phenomenological and interpretivist researchers.
3. Catalytic authenticity refers to the stimulus to action based on the research findings. This implies that the research needs to be conducted in a way that stakeholders view the results as

having meaning for them and that they are presented in such a way that it engenders taking action to improve equity and justice in their lives or communities.
4. Tactical authenticity refers to the gaining of a sense of power by the stakeholders because they have learned that research can be used to speak truth to power. Stakeholders develop skills of advocacy for themselves or for their children so that they can have an impact on policies and programs that affect them. (Lincoln, 2009)

These criteria for rigor provide food for thought for the qualitative researcher. Does all qualitative research need to be designed in such a way that it stimulates increased knowledge, skills, and ability to become active agents for the participants? Is this too much to ask of qualitative researchers?

CONCLUSIONS

The ethical principles that guide qualitative researchers are complex because their work involves interactions with community members in ways that are more involved than they are with quantitative researchers (Mertens, 2012). Hence, issues of cultural respect and language are more salient and come with obligations on the part of the researcher to form relationships in appropriate ways. If qualitative researchers view their purpose as the creation of knowledge or even self-insight, then what are their ethical responsibilities in terms of representation, voice, and credibility? If qualitative researchers view their purpose as partnering with communities to further social justice and human rights, then what are their ethical responsibilities and what are the methodological implications of those responsibilities? The transformative paradigm presents a framework of philosophical assumptions that are rooted in human rights and social justice and is commensurate with feminist, critical, critical race, queer, indigenous, disability rights, and deaf rights theories.

The ethical principles that emerge from critical reflection on the challenges encountered in qualitative work do not provide simple answers. Rather, they call upon researchers to continuously reflect on how their relationships with members of the wider community of stakeholders can lead to accurate representations and the furtherance of social justice. Researchers have an ethical obligation to give serious consideration to what they are giving back to members of the communities in which they work. Reciprocity can take many forms; simply giving voice is a first step, but communities are demanding more of researchers. Researchers who work from a critical, transformative stance have an obligation to make visible power inequities and to do so in a way that stimulates action. They need to engage in those difficult conversations about shared rights to the results of the research and the implications of potential unintended harm coming from the research.

Ginsberg and Mertens (2009) explored the question of the researcher's ethical obligation to serve as an instrument of social change and found that it did not have a simple answer. The tensions inherent in the research community are apparent in this quotation:

> Some researchers place themselves squarely in the position of accepting this as a moral imperative. Others reject it for a variety of reasons: that it is outside the scope of the researchers' responsibility, that researchers cannot control the multitude of variables that facilitate or prevent social transformation, or that it is impossible to know the effects of one's research in advance. (2009: 596)

The community of qualitative researchers is heterogeneous; its members support the various possible answers. Even if we recognize the lack of control that researchers have over the larger systems in which they conduct their research, we have an obligation to critically reflect on the meaning of the ethics of use in terms of accurate representation and social change.

FURTHER READING

Chilisa, Bagele (2012) *Indigenous Research Methodologies*. Thousand Oaks, CA: Sage.
Mertens, Donna M. and Ginsberg, Pauline E. (eds.) (2009) *Handbook of Social Research Ethics*. Thousand Oaks, CA: Sage.
Nagata, Donna K., Kohn-Wood, Laura, and Suzuki, Lisa A. (eds.) (2012) *Qualitative Strategies for Ethnocultural Research*. Washington, DC: American Psychological Association.

REFERENCES

Battiste, Marie (2007) 'Research ethics for protecting indigenous knowledge and heritage: Institutional and research responsibilities,' in Norman K. Denzin and Michael D. Giardina (eds.), *Ethical Futures in Qualitative Research: Decolonizing the Politics of Knowledge*. Walnut Creek, CA: Left Coast Press. pp. 111–32.
Brabeck, Mary M. and Brabeck, Kalina M. (2009) 'Feminist perspectives on research ethics,' in Donna M. Mertens and Pauline G. Ginsberg, (eds.), *Handbook of Social Research Ethics*. Thousand Oaks, CA: Sage. pp. 39–53.
Brydon-Miller, Mary, Kral, Michael, Maguire, Patricia, Noffke, Susan, and Sabhlok, Anu (2011) 'Jazz and the banyan tree: Roots and riffs on participatory action research,' in Norman K. Denzin and Yvonna S. Lincoln (eds.), The *SAGE Handbook of Qualitative Research*, 4th edition. Thousand Oaks, CA: Sage. pp. 387–400.
Cannella, Gail S. and Lincoln, Yvonna S. (2011) 'Ethics, research regulations, and critical social science,' in Norman K. Denzin and Yvonna S. Lincoln (eds.), The *SAGE Handbook of Qualitative Research*, 4th edition. Thousand Oaks, CA: Sage. pp. 81–90.
Charlton, James I. (1998) *Nothing about Us without Us: Disability, Oppression and Empowerment*. Berkeley: University of California Press.
Chilisa, Bagele (2012) *Indigenous Research Methodologies*. Thousand Oaks, CA: Sage.
Christians, Clifford G. (2011) 'Ethics and politics in qualitative research,' in Norman K. Denzin and Yvonna S. Lincoln (eds.), The *SAGE Handbook of Qualitative Research*, 4th edition. Thousand Oaks, CA: Sage. pp. 61–80.
Cram, Fiona (2009) 'Maintaining indigenous voices,' in Donna M. Mertens and Pauline E. Ginsberg (eds.), *Handbook of Social Research Ethics*. Thousand Oaks, CA: Sage. pp. 308–22.
DeHaene, Lucia, Grietens, Hans, and Verschueren, Karine (2010) 'Holding harm: Narrative methods in mental health research on refugee trauma,' *Qualitative Health Research*, 20 (2): 1664–76.
Denzin, Norman K. (2012) 'Triangulation 2.0,' *Journal of Mixed Methods Research*, 6 (2): 80–8.
Dillard, Cynthia B. and Okpalaoka, Chinwe (2011) 'The sacred and spiritual nature of endarkened transnational feminist praxis in qualitative research,' in Norman K. Denzin and Yvonna S. Lincoln (eds.), The *SAGE Handbook of Qualitative Research*, 4th edition. Thousand Oaks, CA: Sage. pp. 147–62.
Dodd, Sarah-Jane (2009) 'LGBTQ: Protecting vulnerable subjects in all studies,' in Donna M. Mertens and Pauline E. Ginsberg (eds.), *Handbook of Social Research Ethics*. Thousand Oaks, CA: Sage. pp. 580–613.
Ellis, Carolyn (1986) *Fisher Folk: Two Communities on Chesapeake Bay*. Lexington: The University Press of Kentucky.
Ellis, Carolyn (2009) 'Telling tales on neighbors: Ethics in two voices,' *International Review of Qualitative Research*, 2 (1): 3–38.
Ellis, Carolyn, Bochner, Arthur, Denzin, Norman, Lincoln, Yvonna, Morse, Janice, Pelias, Ronald, and Richardson, Laurel (2008) 'Talking and thinking about qualitative research,' *Qualitative Inquiry*, 14 (2): 254–84.
Fierro, Rita (2006) 'African American agency in American agencies: A critical study of African American mothers with transitional custody,' Dissertation, Temple University, Philadelphia.
Freeman, Melissa (ed.) (2010) *Critical Social Theory and Evaluation Practice*. San Francisco: Jossey-Bass.
Ginsberg, Pauline E. and Mertens, Donna M. (2009) 'Frontiers in social research ethics: Fertile ground for evolution,' in Donna M. Mertens and Pauline E. Ginsberg (eds.), *Handbook of Social Research Ethics*. Thousand Oaks, CA: Sage. pp. 580–613.
Guba, Egon G. and Lincoln, Yvonna S. (1989) *Fourth Generation Evaluation*. Newbury Park, CA: Sage.
Guba, Egon G. and Lincoln, Yvonna S. (2005) 'Paradigmatic controversies, contradictions, and emerging confluences,' in Norman K. Denzin and Yvonna S. Lincoln (eds.), The *SAGE Handbook of Qualitative Research*, 3rd edition. Thousand Oaks, CA: Sage. pp. 191–215.
Harris, Rachelle, Holmes, Heidi, and Mertens, Donna M. (2009) 'Research ethics in sign language communities,' *Sign Language Studies*, 9 (2): 104–31.
Krog, Antjie (2011) 'In the name of human rights: I say (how) you (should) speak (before I listen),' in Norman K. Denzin and Yvonna S. Lincoln (eds.), The *SAGE*

Handbook of Qualitative Research, 4th edition. Thousand Oaks, CA: Sage. pp. 381–6.

LaFrance, Joan and Crazy Bull, Cheryl (2009) 'Researching ourselves back to life: Taking control of the research agenda in Indian country,' in Donna M. Mertens and Pauline E. Ginsberg (eds.), Handbook of Social Research Ethics. Thousand Oaks, CA: Sage. pp. 580–613.

LaFrance, Joan and Nichols, Richard (2010) 'Reframing evaluation: Defining an indigenous evaluation framework,' Canadian Journal of Program Evaluation, 23 (2): 13–31.

Lincoln, Yvonna S. (2009) 'Ethical practices in qualitative research,' in Donna M. Mertens and Pauline E. Ginsberg (eds.), Handbook of Social Research Ethics. Thousand Oaks, CA: Sage. pp. 580–613.

Madison, Soyini D. (2005) Critical Ethnography. Thousand Oaks, CA: Sage.

McSpadden, Emalinda (2011) 'The participant's response,' in Frederick J. Wertz et al. (eds.), Five Ways of Doing Qualitative Analysis. New York: Guilford Press. pp. 334–52.

Mertens, Donna M. (2009) Transformative Research and Evaluation. New York: Guilford Press.

Mertens, Donna M. (2010) Research and Evaluation in Education and Psychology: Integrating Diversity with Quantitative, Qualitative, and Mixed Methods, 3rd edition. Thousand Oaks, CA: Sage.

Mertens, Donna M. (2012) 'Ethics in qualitative research in education and the social sciences,' in Stephen D. Lapan et al. (eds.), Qualitative Research: An Introduction to Methods and Designs. San Francisco: Jossey-Bass. pp. 19–40.

Mertens, Donna M. and Wilson, Amy T. (2012) Program Evaluation Theory and Practice: A Comprehensive Guide. New York: Guilford Press.

Mertens, Donna M., Sullivan, Martin, and Stace, Hilary (2011) 'Disabilities communities: Transformative research for social justice,' in Norman K. Denzin and Yvonna S. Lincoln (eds.), The SAGE Handbook of Qualitative Research, 4th edition. Thousand Oaks, CA: Sage. pp. 227–42.

Olesen, Virginia (2011) 'Feminist qualitative research in the millennium's first decade: Developments, challenges, prospects,' in Norman K. Denzin and Yvonna S. Lincoln (eds.), The SAGE Handbook of Qualitative Research, 4th edition. Thousand Oaks, CA: Sage. pp. 129–46.

Plummer, Ken (2011) 'Critical humanism and queer theory: Living with the tensions: Postscript 2011 to living with the contradictions,' in Norman K. Denzin and Yvonna S. Lincoln (eds.), The SAGE Handbook of Qualitative Research, 4th edition. Thousand Oaks, CA: Sage. pp. 208–12.

Presidential Commission for the Study of Bioethical Issues (2011) Moral Science: Protecting participants in human subjects research. Washington, DC.

Reason, Peter and Bradbury, Hilary (eds.) (2008) The SAGE Handbook of Action Research: Participative Inquiry and Practice, 2nd edition. Thousand Oaks, CA: Sage.

Segone, Marco (ed.) (2009) Country Led Monitoring and Evaluation Systems. New York: UNICEF.

Shopes, Linda (2011) 'Oral history,' in Norman K. Denzin and Yvonna S. Lincoln (eds.), The SAGE Handbook of Qualitative Research, 4th edition. Thousand Oaks, CA: Sage. pp. 451–66.

Smith, Anna Deavere (2004) House Arrest and Piano. New York: Anchor.

Smith, Linda T. (1999) Decolonizing Methodologies: Research and Indigenous People. London: Zed Books.

Sullivan, Martin (2009) 'Philosophy, ethics and the disability community,' in Donna M. Mertens and Pauline G. Ginsberg (eds.), Handbook of Social Research Ethics. Thousand Oaks, CA: Sage. pp. 69–84.

Thomas, Veronica G. (2009) 'Critical race theory: Ethics and dimensions of diversity in research,' in Donna M. Mertens and Pauline G. Ginsberg (eds.), Handbook of Social Research Ethics. Thousand Oaks, CA: Sage. pp. 54–68.

Tilousi, Carletta (2011) Community Engagement – Needs, Models and U.S. Actions. Presentation to the Presidential Commission for the Study of Bioethical Issues, August 30, 2011: http://bioethics.gov/cms/node/319 (accessed May 15, 2013).

UNAIDS (2007) Ethical considerations in Biomedical HIV Prevention Trials. Geneva.

Wertz, Frederick J., Charmaz, Kathy, McMullen, Linda M., Josselson, Ruthellen, Anderson, Rosemarie, and McSpadden, Emalinda (2011) Five Ways of Doing Qualitative Analysis. New York: Guilford Press.

Wolfe, Thomas (1940) You Can't Go Home Again. New York: Harper.

36

Analytic Integration in Qualitatively Driven (QUAL) Mixed and Multiple Methods Designs

Janice M. Morse and Lory J. Maddox

INTRODUCING QUAL MIXED AND MULTIPLE METHODS DESIGNS

The primary reason researchers use a mixed or multiple methods design is to maximize benefits obtained from both qualitative and quantitative methods in the same project. Qualitative and quantitative methods each provide different types of data, and each access different aspects of the phenomenon under study, so that by integrating qualitative and quantitative findings, the study has increased scope, density, detail, and even increased validity.

However, the difficulty when utilizing both qualitative and quantitative methods within the same project is the analytic integration of the two types of data (textual and numerical), collected for different purposes and contributing different types of knowledge to the project. Data analysis and integration must occur in a form that provides transparency, increasing the credence and usability of the study as a whole.

Despite the emergence of mixed and multiple methods in the past two decades, there are discrepancies in the literature in the use of many terms, and clarification of these terms is essential. In this chapter, selected terms are defined in the Appendix.

DESIGN CONSIDERATIONS IN QUAL MIXED AND MULTIPLE METHODS PROJECTS

The first consideration when conducting a mixed or multiple methods study is to be clear about the differences between mixed or multiple methods. First, a mixed methods design is defined here as consisting of a core component that is a complete study in itself. This study, when finished, could stand alone, and could be published separately without the supplementary project. The core component is conducted using a standard qualitative method, such as ethnography (see Gubrium and Holstein, Chapter 3, this volume), grounded theory (see Thornberg and Charmaz,

Chapter 11, this volume), narrative inquiry (see Esin et al., Chapter 14, this volume), and phenomenology (see Eberle, Chapter 13, this volume); the findings are saturated, and the results solid. The supplementary project consists of an additional quantitative strategy that cannot stand alone. This component may consist of a single quantitative measure, or even a small survey, which serves to complement the qualitative core component, but is not publishable by itself.

On the other hand, multiple methods are two complete projects, one qualitative and one quantitative, and could both be publishable as separate studies. Here, the overall aim of the multiple methods study is addressed by the qualitative question that drives the project (i.e., is qualitatively driven). This gives the qualitative study 'priority' (Morgan, 1998) over the quantitative study, so that when the two studies are integrated in a third publication, the qualitative study forms the theoretical base of the publication, and the quantitative study expands the qualitative findings to inform 'how much, how many, how often,' and relationships between pertinent variables.

Theoretical Drive and Theoretical Thrust

Integral to mixed methods design is the theoretical drive. With qualitatively driven mixed methods design, the *aim* must be stated in a form fitting qualitative convention, that is, stated as inductive discovery with exploratory aims, rather than an aim that is deductive, declarative, or testing. In multiple methods the *theoretical thrust* has an overall aim that must also fit qualitative convention, although of course the quantitative supplementary project itself would have a quantitative secondary aim or question.

Sampling

With qualitatively driven mixed methods design, the sample of the quantitative supplement does not meet the requirements of quantitative sampling. The qualitative sample (see Rapley, Chapter 4, this volume) is too small and has been purposefully selected and, therefore, using this sample for the quantitative portion presents a threat to the validity of the quantitative supplement. Approaches to mitigate risks to validity include:

1. Use the core qualitative sample for the quan supplementary measurement, but compare the results to the external norms; that is, population scores usually available from the scale developers, or, if the scores are a frequently used measure, norms may be published in the literature.
2. Draw another sample. Researchers may draw another sample from the same population, according to the principles of quantitative inquiry (i.e., sample drawn from a clearly delimited population, randomly selected, and sample size determined by power calculation). This approach is most common in multiple methods design where studies that can stand alone are conducted.

Analysis of Results of Each Component

Analysis of the Core Component

In the core component of methods design, and in both projects of multiple methods design, there are no secrets or tricks in analysis. These are the easiest parts of analysis because there is no violation of the standard qualitative or quantitative design rules; all assumptions have been met, and analysis proceeds in a textbook fashion.

Analysis of Supplementary Components in Mixed Methods Design

The most challenging part of mixed methods research is in the conduct of the supplementary component. The goal of efficiency, when using a supplementary component, is a workaround for conducting a complete project (as in multiple methods design). It enables the researcher to obtain answers quickly and efficiently to additional questions that would otherwise be unobtainable. The tradeoff is that the researcher, using a smaller sample for the supplementary quantitative measures, must be confident and careful in the choice of measures.

Quantitative Supplementary Component

Selected quantitative measures, if used to directly evaluate some indicator in the qualitative sample, must have external norms in order to make sense of the results. For instance, blood pressures (or some other physiological measure) must be compared to population norms. The qualitative sample is likely to be too small to be discussed using descriptive statistics (i.e., group mean, standard deviation) but researchers can recognize if the sample measures are high or low or within a normal range. Similarly, psychometric measures may be used for external comparison if norms are available.

Another alternative is to draw a separate sample according to quantitative principles (adequate size, random selection) but of course this brings the mixed methods project dangerously close to multiple methods design, and therefore again loses the advantage of efficiency in using a mixed methods design.

Qualitative Supplementary Component

With a QUAL–*qual* mixed methods design the qualitative supplementary component consists of qualitative strategies that provide a different perspective from the qualitative method of the core component, but not enough data to be considered a complete method. Therefore, the supplementary component may consist of conversational analysis (see Toerien, Chapter 22, this volume), focus groups (see Barbour, Chapter 21, this volume), observations (see Marvasti, Chapter 24, this volume), document analysis (see Coffey, Chapter 25, this volume), interviews (see Roulston, Chapter 20, this volume), microanalysis, photographs (see Banks, Chapter 27, this volume), videos (see Knoblauch et al., Chapter 30, this volume), or new forms of media (see Marotzki et al., Chapter 31, this volume). Critical to this perspective is that these data provide the answers to sub-questions, to the level of *certainty*, but not to the level fo saturation (and replication), which is essential for the type of validity required for a qualitative core component.

Certainty

For consideration of the validity in the supplementary component, we introduce a new criterion (namely, that of certainty. *The criterion of certainty* is less 'solid' or valid than is saturation. In *saturation* the researcher collects data until the data repeat and no new data are obtained with continued sampling. Scoping (or sampling for variation) is important, and the researcher saturates the category by considering its entire variation and forms. With certainty, the scope of the question asked is usually much narrower and more specific, and the researcher collects data until he or she is confident that the question is answered accurately, and that the explanation or answer to the question is probably correct, makes sense, and fits the emerging theory. The explanation may be supported by indirect data (i.e., other indicators are consistent with the explanation) or by using shadowed data (Morse, 2001) (i.e., interviewee reports of what others do). Certainty is appropriate for answering reflexive questions that emerge during the course of the core component. Certainty enables researchers to defend their decisions. The level of certainty attained depends on the question, the purpose that data were collected, and the type of information that the supplementary component provides. Decisions based on certainty, however, are not as defensible as saturated decisions; they are not a replacement for a complete qualitative research study.

MODES OF ANALYTIC INTEGRATION IN QUAL DESIGNS

The key to mixed and multiple methods design is the integration of two or more data sets of different types and different findings related to the same topic or research aim. How this integration is attained depends on the purpose and design of the study (Bazeley and Kemp, 2012), and on the nature of the data. To date, researchers mainly analyse their results separately (which is appropriate), and then present the integration of these two sections, using the discussion section as the point of interface. We suggest that integration of findings occurring in the discussion section is inappropriate, as the integration is an *analytic process* that continues to expand the findings, and therefore should be given a separate section. This section, the *results narrative*, will be discussed at length later in this chapter.

Analytic integration may occur for several purposes: to transform qualitative data (i.e., 'quantitize'; Sandelowski et al., 2009) for quantitative analysis, to blend qualitative indicators to create a numerical variable, and to integrate both qualitative and quantitative results.

Data Transformation

Data transformation is conducted to create a numerical variable within the quantitative data set from qualitative data. In order for this conversion to occur, the qualitative data must fulfill certain requirements. The first is that the qualitative core sample must have N equal to the quantitative supplementary project; the second requirement is that all participants in the qualitative sample must have been asked the same interview question that will be transformed. For these reasons, the most common qualitative method used in mixed methods design is the semi-structured interview, as noted by Bryman (2006).

The methods of data transformation are commonly used and relatively standardized (see Bernard, 2000):

1. Working on one item at a time, content analyse a reasonable sample of the responses. Categories should be mutually exclusive, and do not allow too many categories.
2. Label and write definitions of the item and the categories in a code book, and assign a score (number) for each category. Include a score for 'No response,' 'other,' and 'more than one.'
3. Establish inter-rater reliability by coding an additional set of items.
4. Code all of the items, periodically rechecking the inter-rater reliability, and move the coded items into the quantitative data set as a new variable.

Blending

Blending is the combining of several sources of qualitative indices to develop an ordinal variable that is subsequently incorporated into the quantitative data component (Bazeley, 2009). Frequently, quantitative measures are required that are not easily 'measurable,' and qualitative indicators (from observation or interviews) are combined to create basic measures (such as present/absent; yes/no) or ordinal measures (some/more/most; one/two/three). These ordinal measures may be created from qualitative indicators, or combined with some quantitative variables such as age, ethnicity, gender, and socio-economic levels.

An example of a blended measure is in the development of a pain score for demented patients (Kayser-Jones et al., 2006). When exploring the pain management of hospice and non-hospice residents in nursing homes, Kayser-Jones et al. needed a quantified measure of pain. Because most of the residents were moderately to severely cognitively impaired, qualitative indicators were combined to create a nominal measure. A score was constructed using the following criteria: if able, residents' own assessment of pain (as none, mild, moderate, severe); researcher's observed pain behaviors and facial grimacing; review of medical records; family members' and nursing staff's assessment. From these indicators, a nominal pain 'scale' was created and moved into the quantitative data set.

POSITIONS FOR THE ANALYTIC INTEGRATION OF RESULTS

As mentioned earlier, in mixed and multiple methods designs, each component is first analysed separately using the analytic assumptions pertinent to that component. The qualitative core component is analysed using methods associated with the qualitative methods used. The mixed methods supplementary component is analysed according to the strategy used. If qualitative, the focus groups are analysed for themes; the interviews may be content or thematically analysed; and so forth. If quantitative strategies have been used, the researcher may use non-parametric statistics and/or compare scores to an external norm. The important point is that, apart from the exceptions listed above (blending or transforming data), data from each component are kept distinct and analysed separately.

Point of Interface

The position in the research design where the results from each component meet is the point of interface (Morse and Niehaus, 2009; Creswell et al., 2011). The point of interface may occur during the analysis when, for instance, textually transformed data are moved into the numerical data set as new variables. Most frequently, however, the point of interface occurs following the analysis of data from both (or all) components, and integration of results occurs in the results narrative section.

Results Narrative

Recall that mixed methods design is consistent throughout the core component. The theoretical drive determined by the aims, research questions, method, and results in this case are qualitative, and a complete method. Therefore, this component forms what we call the theoretical base in the results narrative section and the results from the supplementary component expand the qualitative narrative written as the core theoretical base. For instance, if the core component is grounded theory, it is in this results narrative section that the entire grounded theory is presented, with the supplementary findings providing appropriate detail.

Despite the fact that others have recommended that integration occurs in the discussion section, a review of mixed methods articles shows that when integration occurs in the discussion, it does not receive the attention it deserves. When integration is placed in the discussion section it is truncated, the components are often presented separately (i.e., integration does not occur), or adequate attention is not given to the integration – which is after all the purpose of mixed methods design. By completing the integration in the results narrative section the researcher has the space and attention of the reader to present rich, new, and expanded theory that includes additional quantitative or qualitative descriptors.

PATTERNS OF INTEGRATION

Examination of results sections of mixed methods articles revealed various patterns of integration, some with almost no integration at all, and others well integrated. Where integration occurs depends on the question, the purpose that the data were collected, and the type of information that the supplementary component provides. Bryman (2007) and Creswell et al.'s (2011) report for NIH (National Institutes of Health) recommend that the integration of mixed methods results be reported in the discussion section of the study. Some do not use the discussion section for this purpose; others present the results in the results section. As mentioned, there is a need to formalize a new section for the integration of results, the results narrative section. Presentation of results takes the following forms:

1. For QUAL–*quan* results: Results integrating QUAL–*quan* studies may be discussed as separate blocks of text, usually presenting the results

first from the core component followed by the results from the supplementary component.

2. *For QUAL–qual results:* When the supplementary component is qualitative, as in a QUAL–*qual* study, some researchers may keep the results separate and not integrated.
3. *In the results section:* Another style is to present the results in the results section according to the research questions asked. The researcher presents each research question (q1 ..., q2 ..., q3 ..., and so forth), providing the answer to each question, first using the analysis from the core project, followed by any pertinent information obtained from the supplementary project. Again, these results are not integrated.
4. *Integrate analysis according to the results pertaining to the topic of interest:* The fourth approach is to write the integrated findings according to the topic of interest to the researcher and pertinent to the study. If the researcher has used a theoretical framework, presentation of the findings follows that model. If, however, there is no theoretical framework, the researchers may describe the results in themes that follow first the main topic addressed by the question, followed by other topics of interest. Each component is kept separate from the other findings in its separate paragraph.

Rather, better merging of results is obtained by:

5. *Use the results narrative:* Using the results narrative section gives the researcher adequate space to present and highlight the findings in an integrated manner.
6. *Discussion:* The addition of a results narrative section now returns the discussion section to the original purpose of discussion. In this section, the researcher links the findings of the mixed methods study to other research, showing how the mixed methods study has added to the literature, and how the findings of other studies support or do not support the present study. The researcher also links the project to other literature, and discusses the implications and limitations of the study. This purpose of the discussion section is particularly important for the third (integrated) publication in a multiple methods research program.

While all of the above locations may be used for the presentation of the results, with varying degrees of integration, we recommend that the results narrative section be used. For qualitatively driven designs, the most appropriate mode of integration is described below.

Pattern of Integration of Results in the Results Narrative

With mixed methods design, the theoretical drive method forms the 'foundation' for the story. It is the major 'storyline' and data, or the analysis from the supplementary component, illustrate and add detail, depth, or *qual* or *quan* information to the findings.

This may be conceptualized as shown in Figure 36.1, representing manuscript pages on which the results narrative section is reported. For instance, the *quan* demographic information is used in the sample description; the results of the psychological test support the descriptions of the participants' behaviors; and the focus group data are used throughout the descriptions of the QUAL interview data.

Thus, in this way the results are appropriately integrated, with the use of each data type from each component used to support the other component. The researcher should, of course, check to ensure that the research question has been answered, and the aims of the study met.

DIAGRAMMING: MAINTAINING CONTROL OF DESIGN

The complexity of mixed and multiple methods designs often stymies researchers, as well as funders, and this confusion is reflected in the final reports and articles. Reviewers and readers have trouble tracing core and supplementary components, that is, where pieces of results were obtained from, how data were actually analysed, which data participant quotations were obtained, and so forth. In team research these problems are confounded, and the number of supplementary projects increases confusion and may become overwhelming. The lack of control in mixed methods design becomes a threat to validity, comprehension, and publication.

Why Diagram?

Diagramming quickly clarifies the nuances of the research design. Diagramming may be used:

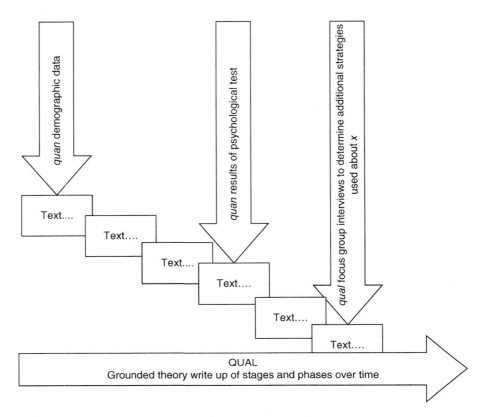

Figure 36.1 Hypothetical mixed-methods project QUAL + *quan* + *quan* + *qual*. (QUAL grounded theory of *x*. Supplementary component: *quan* chart demographic data about population, *quan* psychological test, and *qual* focus groups adding data from the supplementary component).

- for planning complex mixed methods projects, and making alternate choices among designs;
- to illustrate the design in the proposal, making complex designs clear to reviewers;
- as an audit trail to document decisions made in the research design during the conduct of the project – which is especially important when considering reflexivity (see Barry et al., 1999) and
- to illustrate the process and to explain the project in research reports and in publications. Diagrams therefore keep the research clear to the reviewers and to the readers.

The benefits of diagramming will be discussed in depth later in this chapter. Without the benefits of diagramming, the mixed and multiple methods research descriptions become entangled, and it is often not possible to reconstruct research designs in publications. Components become separated from other components, so that it is difficult to tell which piece of data came from which arm of the study, or even which sample belongs to which analysis. The cohesiveness of each component is confusing, so that it is difficult to ascertain whether results emerged from the core or supplementary component(s).

Diagramming clarifies and communicates research design making it less prone to interpretation errors. It keeps research on track, providing both a map and an audit trail throughout the research process.

Identifying core and supplementary component(s) clarifies the position of each component, and ensures that research questions are answered. Readers can easily track the research process from aims to result narrative when key points (samples, data sets, points of interfaces, outcomes, and results) are clearly presented in a well-constructed diagram.

Styles of Diagramming

The protocol and procedures for diagramming of mixed methods designs are poorly developed in texts and the literature. A review of articles in the *Journal of Mixed Methods Research* reveals a variety of approaches to diagramming research studies and reporting results which adds to confusion and a perception that mixed methods designs are difficult. Presently research designs are presented vertically or horizontally without regard to temporal sequencing, distinguishing core and supplementary component(s) including data selection, analysis and results, or consistent use of flowchart notation. Mixed methods researchers could benefit from a consistent use of diagramming and process flow notations to communicate complex research designs.

When diagramming, the main trick is to keep the questions being asked by each component associated with its methods and outcomes. Keep the pacing of supplementary components, the samples, data sets, points of interface, and outcomes organized. As such, in the proposal stage, diagrams illustrate to the reviewers how each component will be conducted – how it will be paced, sampled, what types of data will be collected and analysed, and the expected findings. This will show how the supplementary project will be conducted and the point of interface. It may even show what the final results will look like and extend to plans for dissemination.

To achieve this, we recommend the use of flowcharts as a visual representation of distinct processes, relationships, and dependencies among objects, including the utilization of standardized vertical diagrams, with a pathway for the core and each supplementary component, reading from top to bottom and left to right. Vertical orientations clearly depict project scope and distinguish between simultaneous and sequential study designs. Bringing bounded textual statements and ideas into a diagram as objects allows the researcher to use these objects as building blocks for the entire project. Generally, a researcher can manipulate objects more easily than text, which is an advantage when constructing, designing, and documenting a research project (Larkin and Hill, 1987).

Process flows should share the same level of detail and may be constructed at a macro level to represent a program of study. Additional diagrams can be used for an individual study or as subprocess critical to the successful completion of a research project. Diagrams should have a consistent level of detail embedded within each symbol so that research methods are easily traced. This approach to mapping research methods becomes even more useful as methods evolve from a single method to mixed methods or multiple methods designs. Visually representing research steps as objects with relationships, directionality, and dependencies in flowcharts allows researchers to envision a variety of approaches to their study. It is as though the researchers are positioned so they can see the entire research landscape before them.

Basic Flowcharting Symbols and Techniques

The use of standardized symbols is applicable to mixed methods flowchart conventions (International Organization for Standardization, ISO) used in information processing. Use of the ISO 1985 information processing symbols provides methodologists with a beginning toolkit to use when diagramming research studies. Conventions used with flowcharts recommend that the chart reads from top to bottom, which visually depicts distinctions between simultaneous

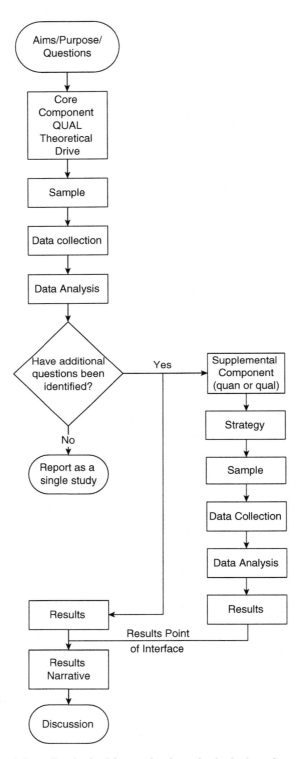

Figure 36.2 Sequential qualitatively driven mixed-methods design planned reflexively during the project (QUAL → *quan* or *qual*)

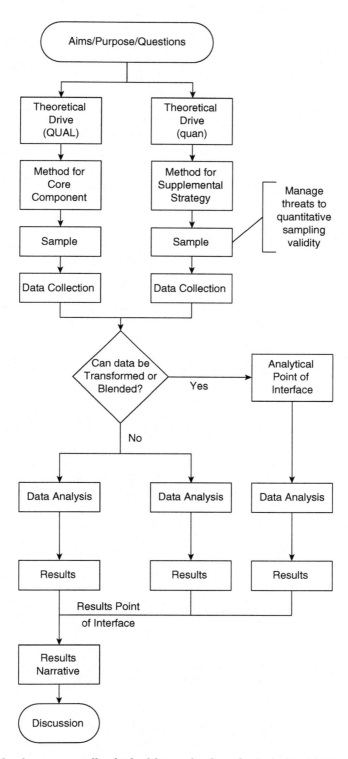

Figure 36.3 Simultaneous qualitatively driven mixed-methods design (QUAL → *quan*)

and sequential study designs. The beginning of the diagram is indicated with a rounded rectangle (which also may indicate the end); arrows indicate the direction, with a double-ended arrow indicating bi-directional; a diamond indicates a decision point, (which may split the process into two paths, such as, yes/no), and a circle visually represents how one study connects to another.

Examples of sequential and simultaneous diagrams are shown in Figures 36.2 and Figure 36.3. These two figures contain only basic information and can serve as templates for mixed methods research. Figure 36.2 shows the decision made to conduct the supplementary project reflexively, after the results were analysed for the QUAL core component.

The structure of simultaneous and sequential mixed methods designs are shown in Figures 36.2 and 36.3 respectively, and these figures are read from the top down. In these designs, as in all mixed and multiple methods designs, the qualitative data are analysed qualitatively and the quantitative data, quantitatively. The researcher must respect the assumptions and methods of each paradigm. The most difficult decisions for the researcher are in the selection of the sample. For the core component, the sample selection follows normal conventions: an adequate and appropriate, purposefully selected sample for a qualitative study, and an adequate, randomly selected sample from a delineated population for a quantitative sample. However, with a simultaneous core component, for the quantitatively driven QUAN + *qual*, the researcher *may* use some of the QUAN sample, *purposefully* selecting according to some criteria, or else select a separate sample. Errors are introduced if the researcher uses processes of randomization. For simultaneous QUAL + *quan* designs, the qualitative sample is not usually large enough for the quantitative component, and a separate random sample must be drawn from the same population. The exception, of course, is if non-parametric (small-sample) statistics are intended.

Other components of the mixed methods research process are shown in Figures 36.2 and 36.3. Each research pathway can be clearly indicated by arrows linking boxes and the stages in the research process: sample, methods, analysis, and results. Details about these steps may be placed in each box, so that the figure itself becomes an illustration of the proposed research, and the linking of pathways and the point of interfaces clearly marked. The point of interface (the point in the research process where the data or the results of the supplementary project meet those of the core project), can be clearly indicated.

Benefits of Flowcharting Research Projects

Facilitating Pre-study Planning

A study must be conceptualized from start to finish prior to conducting any research. Diagramming ideas generated during this armchair walkthrough externalizes ideas, but in qualitative inquiry, where reflexivity is important, this does not mean that the proposed procedures must be adhered to rigidly. Certainly one may choose text alone to convey the same ideas, but the advantage of externalizing the research study with diagramming and flowcharting is that one can visually represent the main objects of the study by symbols. Each symbol is easily manipulated and rearranged; researchers conceptualize various approaches to their research until they decide upon the most prudent plan to answer their study aims.

Object manipulation facilitates visual representation of study design, sequencing, identifying relationships between processes, and discrete start and endpoints to manage a research study. Stepping through a planned study in this manner allows the researcher to identify critical items required for completing the study. The researcher can then begin to evaluate risks associated with completing these critical phases. By identifying the probability of completion early in the pre-study design, the researcher can identify alternative processes to ensure completion of the study.

Good pre-study design can save researchers time, money, and heartache as they identify the most efficient path to answering their research questions.

Developing an Audit Trail

While pre-study design provides a theoretical map to answer the research question, documenting the actual steps involved in one's research project outlines the very real work involved in conducting research. Flowcharts maintained during the research project can serve as an audit trail to represent the actual steps taken during the research study. It is increasingly common for researchers to use flowcharts to depict subject recruitment and attrition. Maintaining flowcharts during a study documents sub-processes such as sampling, sample attrition, and data collection and analysis.

Because researchers have a theoretical map to achieve their research aims, researchers can document and compare theoretical and actual processes during the course of their study. Variations from the theoretical map provide early identification of potential risks or threats or the emergence of new reflexive questions to be included in the study. Early identification of variation from the theoretical map allows researchers time to integrate changes congruent with study aims. Documenting decisions and research steps as objects in a process flow diagram serves as an audit trail upon completing the study.

Communicating in Team Science

With the advent of multidisciplinary teams conducting much of the research study, clear communication of the aims, methods, and findings is imperative (see Cornish et al., Chapter 6, this volume). While diagramming a research study into distinct objects and directional processes may seem directive, it does facilitate communication within a large team. All team members can visualize the research study from beginning to end. Members are able to situate their work within the context of the entire team. Dependencies among team members are transparent when all members document their steps and contributions to the entire research study (Creswell and Plano Clark, 2011).

Despite the best theoretical map to accomplish the research aims, changes may occur during the course of research. A well-constructed process flow facilitates communication of these changes within the research team. As noted as a part of the audit trail, decisions are documented with a revised mapping to meet the study aims. All participants in the research team can visually see the impact of a change and how that may affect their respective work. Discussing and sharing these modifications within the team encourage participation from all members and can potentially identify additional barriers to completing the study. Diagrams serve as a guide for project management, keeping the team informed of the overall status of the study and changes that may influence research aims.

Enhancing Transparency of Design

Transparency of study methods is a critical requirement in research, whether qualitatively or quantitatively driven. Regardless of the paradigmatic approach, scientific research demands accountability, whether that implies a quantitative criterion of reliability or qualitative criteria of transferability.

To illustrate the value of diagramming for evaluating a design, we have prepared in Box 36.1 a summary of a research project published by Koppel et al. (2008). Fairly typically, this summary clearly presents information about the sample and causes of barcode errors. However, the study is not clear about the linkages between 'probable cause' and does not show the number of cases that falls into each cell in Table 3 in the article. We extended this analysis by diagramming the study in Figure 36.4 to illustrate its complexity, and to show how diagramming reveals problems in the interaction of the components. Diagramming the study reveals transparency, especially with complex studies, and this clarity enhances rigor (see Barbour, Chapter 34, this volume).

> **Box 36.1 Summary of Diagrammed Research**
>
> 'Workarounds to barcode medication administration systems: Their occurrences, causes, and threats to patient safety' (Koppel et al., 2008: 408). (See Figure 36.4.)
>
> The authors' aim was to 'develop a typology of clinicians' workarounds when using barcoded medication administration (BCMA) systems' and to identify the causes and consequences of each workaround. Procedures for drug administration include checking the patient's barcode with a hand-held device, and confirming with medical records that the right drug and dosage is being given to the right patient at the right time, by the right route. Despite these clear instructions errors occur and practices are circumvented. Drug administrations were studied at 5 hospitals, using the following methods:
>
> 1. Structured observations ($N = 62$) and shadowing 31 nurses at 2 hospitals.
> 2. Interviewing 21 nurses, 1 nursing administrator, and 2 barcode specialists, and 2 IT directors, 4 pharmacists, and 2 directors of clinical nursing at 5 hospitals.
> 3. Participating in meetings in which barcode administration was discussed.
> 4. Participating in 'one hospital's 'failure-mode-and-effects' analyses,' mapping causes and effects with an interdisciplinary team.
> 5. Analysing 1 month of overrides in barcode administration data records (workarounds).
>
> Data analysis: Of the 142,203 medication administrations, there were 6,035 overrides (or 4.2% of medication administrations). These were sorted according to the probable causes identified such as 'technology-related causes,' 'task-related causes,' 'organizational causes,' 'patient-related and environmental' in 31 categories. These were placed on a chart by 15 unauthorized steps, to identify 15 types of workarounds, with consequent errors in drug administration. The authors concluded that 'shortcomings in the design of barcode administration encourage workarounds.'
>
> Diagramming such a complex study shows the gaps in the authors' descriptions of method. The authors were clear about how each component of data produced their identification of the 'probable cause,' but Table 3, describing the linkages between causes and 'unauthorized process steps,' shows linkages, but not the number of cases that fall in each cell. Thus quantitative evidence was not fully displayed. (From author's abstract)

Organizing Data and Analysis by Theoretical Drive

To maintain rigor in sampling, data collection, data collection and analysis must be consistent with the theoretical drive, as determined by the research question. Diagrams visually represent and document consistent theoretical drive applied to sampling, data collection and analysis. Diagramming and sequencing data sampling, collection, and analysis as a process flow assist the researcher to keep data separate until a point of interface.

DISCUSSION

With the increased versatility of researchers' expertise in both qualitative and quantitative methods, and the rapidly developing insights in mixed and multiple methods designs, mixed methods studies, in particular, are becoming commonplace. Designs are becoming more complex, and reports and articles longer. But at the same time there are rapid gains in knowledge, and the receptivity of mixed methods research is increasing in funding and government agencies.

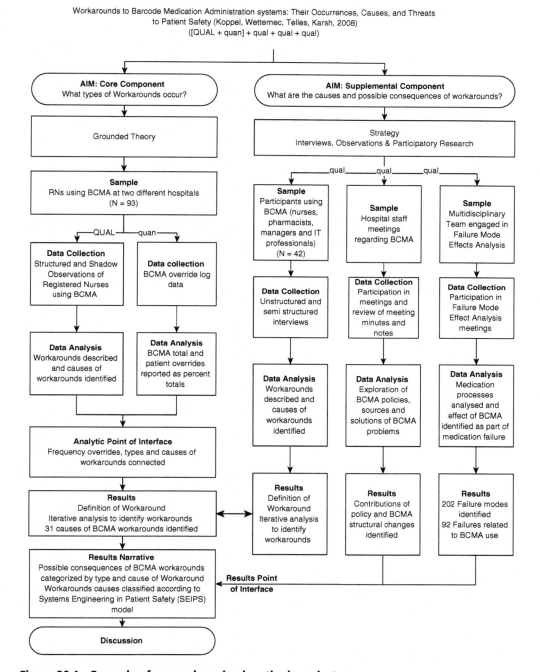

Figure 36.4   Example of a complex mixed methods project

The mixed methods technique of utilizing only a strategy to access answers to minor questions that do not warrant the conduct of an entire project is an especially strong and efficient part of mixed methods designs. But the use of a single data collection strategy introduces new standards. In this chapter, the introduction of *certainty*, as a concept more appropriate than saturation, is one such new standard. Here we have suggested criteria for the evaluation of certainty, as using the researcher's own judgment; once certainty is generally accepted, evaluation criteria must be extended for reviewer assessment.

This wave of new research designs requires the development of new ways to manage projects. The method of using diagrams is an important strategy which enhances the planning and conduct of research, as well as easing the evaluation, and the communication of how components are integrated.

Note that, although mixed and multiple methods designs are more comprehensive than a single method used alone, researchers may not be able to access information about all aspects of the phenomena. In other words, mixed and multiple methods will still have some limitations extending from research agendas and perspectives, and we are still far from reaching our goal of obtaining the ultimate answer when conducting research. Even using multiple methods leaves some areas open for further investigation or reveals tentative hypotheses or linkages to other concepts or phenomena extending from the present study. While in this chapter we have addressed only qualitatively driven designs, much of what we have written may also be applied to quantitatively driven designs.

APPENDIX: DEFINITIONS FOR MIXED AND MULTIPLE METHODS DESIGN

Core project: The primary (main) study in which the primary or core method is used to address the research question. This phase of the research is complete or scientifically rigorous and can therefore stand alone.

Supplementary project: In this phase of the research, one or more supplementary methodological strategies are used to obtain an enhanced description, understanding, or explanation of the phenomenon under investigation. This component of the project can either be conducted at the same time as the core component (simultaneous) or follow the core component (sequential). The supplementary component is incomplete in itself or lacks some aspect of scientific rigor, cannot stand alone, and is regarded as complementary to the core component.

Mixed methods design: A single complete study with a supplementary core strategy.

Multiple methods design: Two (or more) complete studies using different methods, and addressing the same *aim*, and a third study integrating the results of the first two.

Simultaneous design: Mixed methods design, indicated with a + (plus) sign, in which core and supplementary projects are generally designed and planned from the onset of the project. Sampling and data collection are conducted at the same time, which allows the researcher to have an *analytical point of interface*.

Sequential design: Mixed methods design, indicated with an → (arrow) sign, in which the core project is conducted with supplementary projects, commencing after sampling and data collection in the core project are complete. In sequential design, the researcher is constrained to a *results point of interface*.

QUAL: Upper case is used for the project representing the theoretical thrust of the research program; QUAL indicates a project with a qualitative theoretical thrust.

***quan*:** Lower case is used for the project representing the supplementary component in a mixed methods project; quan indicates a quantitative supplementary component.

Qualitatively driven: Indicates the theoretical, inductive, overall direction of the research project that guides the appropriate qualitative methodological core component.

Note: Definitions adapted from Morse et al. (2006) and Morse and Niehaus (2009).

FURTHER READING

Bazeley, Patricia and Kemp, Lynn (2012) 'Mosaics, triangles, and DNA: Metaphors for integrated analysis in mixed methods,' *Journal of Mixed Methods Research*, 6: 55–72. DOI: 10.1177/1558689811419514.

Crandell, Jamie, Voils, Corrine L., Chang, YunKyung, and Sandelowski, Margarete (2011) 'Bayesian data augmentation methods for the synthesis of qualitative and quantitative research findings,' *Quality and Quantity*, 45: 653–669. DOI 10 1117/s11135-010-9375-z.

Voils, Corrine S., Sandelowski, Margarete, Barroso, Julie, and Hasselblad, Victor (2008) 'Making sense of qualitative and quantitative findings in mixed research study synthesis,' *Field Methods*, 20: 3–25. DOI: 10.1177/1525822X07307463.

REFERENCES

Barry, Christine A., Britten, Nicky, Barbar, Nick, Bradley, Colin, and Stevenson, Fiona (1999) 'Using reflexivity to optimize teamwork in qualitative research,' *Qualitative Health Research*, 9 (1): 26–44.

Bazeley, Patricia (2009) 'Mixed methods data analysis,' in Sharon Andrew and Elizabeth Halcomb (eds.), *Mixed Methods Research for Nursing and the Health Sciences*. Chichester: Wiley. pp. 84–118.

Bazeley, Patricia and Kemp, Lynn. (2012) 'Mosaics, triangles, and DNA: Metaphors for integrated analysis in mixed methods,' *Journal of Mixed Methods Research*, 6: 55–72. DOI: 10.1177/1558689811419514.

Bernard, H. Russell (2000) *Social Research Methods: Qualitative and Quantitative Approaches*. Thousand Oaks, CA: Sage.

Bryman, Alan (2006) 'Integrating quantitative and qualitative research: How is it done?,' *Qualitative Research*, 6 (1): 97–113.

Bryman, Alan (2007) 'Barriers to integrating quantitative and qualitative research,' *Journal of Mixed Methods Research*, 1 (1): 8–22.

Creswell, John W. and Plano Clark, Vicki, I. (2011) *Designing and Conducting Mixed Methods Research*, 2nd edition. Thousand Oaks, CA: Sage.

Creswell, John W., Klassen, Ann Carol, Plano Clark, Vicki. L, and Clegg Smith, Katherine (2011) *Best Practices for Mixed Methods Research in the Health Sciences*. Washingon, DC: National Institutes of Health.

International Organization for Standardization (1985) *Information Processing* (ISO 5807): www.iso.org/iso/home.htm (accessed May 16, 2013).

Kayser-Jones, Jeanie S., Kris, Alison E., Miaskowski, Christine A., Lyons, William L., and Paul, Steven. M. (2006) 'Hospice care in nursing homes: Does it contribute to higher quality pain management?', *The Gerontologist*, 46 (3): 325–33. PMID: 16731871.

Koppel, Ross, Wetterneck, Tosha, Telles, Joel L., and Karsh, Ben-Tzion (2008) 'Workarounds to barcode medication administration systems: Their occurrences, causes, and threats to patient safety,' *Journal of the American Medical Information Association*, 15 (4): 408–23.

Larkin, Jill and Hill, Herbert (1987) 'Why a diagram is (sometimes) worth ten thousand words,' *Cognitive Science*, 11: 65–99.

Morgan, David L. (1998) 'Practical strategies for combining qualitative and quantitative methods: Applications to health research,' *Qualitative Health Research*, 3: 362–76.

Morse, Janice M. (2001) 'Using shadowed data (Editorial),' *Qualitative Health Research*, 11 (3): 291.

Morse, Janice M. and Niehaus, Linda (2009) *Mixed-Method Design: Principles and Procedures*. Walnut Creek. CA: Left Coast.

Morse, Janice M., Niehaus, Linda, Wolfe, Ruth, and Wilkins, Seanne (2006) 'The role of theoretical drive in maintaining validity in mixed-method research,' *Qualitative Research in Psychology*, 3 (4): 279–91.

Sandelowski, Margarete, Voils, Corrine I., and Knafl, George (2009) 'On quantizing,' *Journal of Mixed Methods Research*, 3: 208–22.

37

Generalization in and from Qualitative Analysis

Joseph A. Maxwell and Margaret Chmiel

Generalization, in research, refers to extending research results, conclusions, or other accounts that are based on a study of particular individuals, settings, times, or institutions, to other individuals, settings, times, or institutions than those directly studied (Polit and Beck, 2010). A widely accepted view, among both quantitative and qualitative researchers, is that there are two main types of, or strategies for, generalization in social research, typically (although not necessarily) associated with quantitative and qualitative research, respectively (Gobo, 2008: 195–6). Yin (2003: 32–3), addressing generalization in case study research, called these two strategies *statistical generalization* and *analytic generalization*; other terms for these (or similar) types include *enumerative induction* and *analytic induction* (Znaniecki, 1934) and *empirical generalization* and *theoretical generalization* (Hammersley, 2008: 36) or *theoretical inference* (Hammersley, 1992: 86ff.).

Yin described statistical generalization as occurring when 'an inference is made about a population (or universe) on the basis of empirical data collected about a sample' (2003: 32). This definition does not require that statistical methods be used, and the term is therefore somewhat misleading. For this reason, and because qualitative research rarely uses probability sampling (see Rapley, Chapter 4, this volume), we will use the term *empirical generalization* in the rest of this chapter; this seems to us to better capture what is most central to such generalization in qualitative research – that it relies on the descriptive *representativeness* of the sample (or set of participants or settings on which data are actually collected), in terms of the distribution of properties of individuals or groups, for the larger population to which the researcher wants to generalize.

Analytic generalization, in contrast, is that in which 'a previously developed theory is used as a template with which to compare the empirical results of the case study. If two or more cases are shown to support the same theory, replication may be claimed' (Yin, 2003: 32–3); Yin elsewhere described this strategy as 'generalizing to theory' (1984: 39;

see also Kelle, Chapter 38, this volume). Yin argued that this is the appropriate form of generalization for case study research, and that it is similar to the logic by which experiments are generalized.[1] This term has been adopted by some qualitative researchers to describe a sort of generalization that qualitative research can support (e.g., Schwandt, 1997: 2–3, 58), although dropping Yin's restriction to *prior* theory, since theories in qualitative research are often inductively developed (see Reichertz, Chapter 9; Thornberg and Charmaz, Chapter 11; and Kelle Chapter 38, this volume).

However, other qualitative researchers have proposed a third approach to generalization, in which the emphasis is not on the *generality* of the findings or interpretations so much as on their case-to-case *transferability*; this has become the usual term for this approach (Guba and Lincoln, 1989: 241–2; Jensen, 2008; Lincoln and Guba, 1985: 114–15; Schwandt, 1997: 57–60). Transferability does not require the discovery of the general conditions under which a finding or theory is valid; instead, it involves a transfer of knowledge from a study to a specific new situation. This shifts the responsibility for making generalizations from the researcher to the reader or potential user of the findings, and Misco (2007, cited by Polit and Beck, 2010) has called this 'reader generalizability.' Lincoln and Guba (1985; 1986; Guba and Lincoln, 1989) and Schofield (1990) identified some of the properties that a qualitative study must possess in order for such transferability to be possible, and Donmoyer (1990; 2008) developed a model for how transferability operates. Schwandt stated that Lincoln and Guba 'urge the investigator to provide sufficient details … so that readers can engage in reasonable but modest speculation about whether the findings are applicable to other cases' (1997: 58).

These three strategies for generalization in qualitative research – empirical generalization, analytic generalization, and case-to-case transfer – have been widely recognized (Firestone, 1993; Polit and Beck, 2010). However, these terms have often been interpreted in different ways. Polit and Beck argue that all of these models of generalization are idealized goals that are often not adequately supported by research publications, and that 'both quantitative and qualitative researchers uphold certain myths about adherence to the three models of generalization, and these myths hinder the likelihood that real opportunities for generalization will be pursued' (2010: 1451).

In what follows, we want to address an additional distinction among the types of generalization that are appropriate for qualitative research. Maxwell (1992) described this distinction as between *internal generalizability* and *external generalizability*. Internal generalizability refers to generalizing *within* the setting, institution, or case studied, to persons, events, times, and settings that were not directly observed (see Marvasti, Chapter 24, this volume), interviewed (see Roulston, Chapter 20, this volume), or otherwise represented in the data collected. For interview studies, this can also be seen as generalization to other aspects of the experiences, perspectives, actions, or relationships of the individuals interviewed than those that were addressed in the interview, that is, treating the individual as the 'case.' External generalizability, in contrast, refers to generalization beyond the case or cases specifically studied, to other persons or settings.

Brown-Saracino et al. (2008) made a similar distinction, between *lower-order generalizability* and *higher-order generalizability*. Lower-order generalizability is the generalizability of findings *within* the unit of analysis; higher-order generalizability is generalizability of findings across units of analysis of the same type (e.g., across similar organizations or neighborhoods). Mabry (2008), discussing generalization in case study research, likewise distinguished Ericksons's *petite generalizations* (Erickson, 1986), generalizations *within* a case, from Firestone's *case-to-population generalizations* (Firestone, 1993). We believe that this distinction has important implications for generalizing from qualitative data and for the ways in which qualitative data analysis can support such generalizations.

These two types of generalization overlap Hammersley's and Yin's distinctions, but only partly, because while the first type, internal generalization, often involves empirical generalization (is the sample or selection actually observed or interviewed *representative* of the case, setting, or group?), the second, making inferences to, or across, cases or populations *other than* those studied or sampled, also often follows an 'empirical' logic, of deciding to what extent the features of some target population *match* those of the participants or settings of the study – what Donald Campbell called 'proximal similarity' (Polit and Beck, 2010: 1453). Analytic or theoretical generalization is fundamentally different from this, since the 'generalization' is initially to theory, rather than to a population or a universe of cases (Polit and Beck, 2010: 1452).

The distinction between internal and external generalization is not an absolute or clear-cut distinction, and intermediate or ambiguous examples are common. Someone doing research on school principals in a particular school district, for example, is rarely able to observe every school or interview every principal, and whether generalizations beyond the schools or principals actually observed or interviewed are seen as internal or external depends on how the researcher defines the units or cases studied. However, it is important to be aware of how the times and places actually observed may differ from those that were not observed, or the ways in which interviewed individuals' beliefs and perspectives, as expressed in the interviews, may be atypical, or contextually variable in ways that the interview does not capture. The concept of internal generalizability is intended to highlight this potential variability, and to help researchers become aware of the risks of unreflectively extending their results and interpretations beyond what is justified by their data.

We see generalization in, and from, qualitative data analysis as central to generalization in qualitative research as a whole; the discussion of generalization (including transferability) in qualitative research has usually assumed that this pertains to generalization of the results or conclusions drawn from the analysis of the data. We will discuss internal and external generalization separately, identifying the implications of different approaches to generalization for each.

INTERNAL GENERALIZATION

Internal generalization is a key issue for qualitative data analysis. The validity of the results of such analyses, for the case, setting, or the collection of participants studied, depends on their internal generalizability to this case, setting, or collection of participants as a whole; for this reason, internal generalizability overlaps substantially with what are generally seen as validity issues[2] (see Barbour, Chapter 34, this volume). Sampling (selection, see Rapley, Chapter 4, this volume) is particularly relevant for internal generalizability. Miles and Huberman (1984) asked, 'Knowing, then, that one cannot study everyone everywhere doing everything, even within a single case, how does one limit the parameters of a study?' (1984: 36). They argued:

> Just *thinking* in sampling-frame terms is healthy methodological medicine. If you are talking with one kind of informant, you need to consider *why* this kind of informant is important, and, from there, which *other* people should be interviewed. This is a good, bias-controlling exercise.
>
> Remember that you are not only sampling *people*, but also *settings, events, and processes*. It is important to line up these parameters with the research questions as well, and to consider whether your choices are doing a representative, time-efficient job of answering them. The settings, events, or processes that come rapidly to mind at the start of the study may not be the most pertinent or data-rich ones. A systematic review can sharpen early and later choices. (1984: 41)

For example, if you are studying the patterns of interaction between a teacher and students in a single classroom, your account of that classroom as a whole is jeopardized if you have selectively focused on particular times, activities, or students and ignored others.[3]

This issue of representativeness is not only relevant to selection strategies, however; it also has important implications for data analysis. Representativeness, as a validity concern, pertains not simply (or even primarily) to the data sources used, or even to the data themselves, but to the conclusions, interpretations, or theories about the setting or participants that are drawn from the data (Brinberg and McGrath, 1985; Hammersley, 1992: 43–57; Maxwell, 2011; Shadish et al., 2002: 34). How these conclusions or interpretations are drawn is thus a key issue for internal generalizability.

An important aspect of internal generalizability is adequately understanding and representing the *diversity* in the phenomena of interest in the setting or group of people studied. Diversity is often underestimated in both quantitative and qualitative research (Maxwell, 1996; 2011). This can be the result of theoretical biases that emphasize similarities or common features at the expense of differences, or of methodological biases that obscure or neglect actual variation. We will address these two sources of bias in turn.

Theoretical biases toward uniformity are a threat to the internal generalizability of any analysis that assumes or is grounded in such theories. Postmodernism has been particularly critical of the imposition of such 'totalizing metanarratives' (Ayres, 2008; Olsson, 2008), and postmodernists have argued for more attention to diversity, seeing this as fundamental rather than superficial. For example, Rosenau identified as key characteristics of postmodernism its search for 'diversity rather than unity, difference rather than synthesis, complexity rather than simplification' (1992: 8). Wolf likewise saw diversity as central: 'The postmodernist goal is, I take it, to encourage the author to present a less tidy picture with more contradictory voices' (1992: 53).

In particular, the traditional definition of 'culture,' as those beliefs, values, and practices that are *shared* by members of a community, inherently marginalizes and obscures the actual diversity within cultures and communities. Many anthropologists have challenged this definition, and advocated instead for what has been called a 'distributive' concept of culture, one that recognizes the prevalence and importance of intracultural diversity (e.g., Atran and Medin, 2008; Hannerz, 1992; Wallace, 1970; for a more detailed review of this issue, see Maxwell, 2011). Hannerz warned that even postmodernism has tendencies toward ignoring or suppressing diversity:

> It is a problem of postmodernist thought that as it has emphasized diversity and been assertively doubtful toward master narratives, it has frequently been on the verge of becoming another all-encompassing formula for a macroanthropology of the replication of uniformity. (1992: 35)

In addition to such theoretical biases, both quantitative and qualitative methods contain methodological biases that tend to conceal the existence of diversity and make it more difficult to understand its nature and influence. These biases can undercut the value of an approach that has the theoretical potential to illuminate the extent and consequences of diversity. Thus, Strauss (1992) argued that Bourdieu's analysis of socialization in terms of 'habitus' (see Bohnsack, Chapter 15, this volume), the mental structures unconsciously created by individuals from the practices of everyday life, has exactly this problem:

> In Outline [*of a Theory of Practice*] he never analyzes the habitus of any particular individuals, but instead, like all too many social researchers, makes assumptions about the contents of the habitus of his Kabyle informants on the basis of social facts such as the organization of their households or the rhythms of their agricultural calendar. This leads him to ignore the potential for intracultural variation and change that is built into his theory of habitus formation and to stress instead the reproduction of hegemonic relations, at least for

'traditional' societies. In other words, although Bourdieu's theory takes us away from what I call 'fax' models of socialization, his own practice falls back into them. (Strauss, 1992: 9)

Such methodological biases include a lack of attention to selection issues, and emphasizing common features or themes and ignoring less prevalent ones (Maxwell, 2011: 64–5). For qualitative data analysis specifically, it is important to take account, not just of the intended selection strategy, but also of the *actual* selection of persons, settings, and times that the data represent, and the implications of this for the analysis, results, and interpretations. In addition, there is a strong and often unconscious tendency for researchers to notice supporting instances and ignore ones that do not fit their prior conclusions (Miles and Huberman, 1994: 263; Shweder, 1980).

A second issue for internal generalizability is understanding, and adequately theorizing (see Thornberg and Charmaz, Chapter 11, and Kelle, Chapter 38, this volume), the social and cultural processes that are operating in these settings or influencing these individuals. Arguments that an understanding of causal processes is a valid goal of qualitative research are increasingly common (Anderson and Scott, 2012; Donmoyer, 2012; Erickson, 1986; 2012; Hammersley, 2008: 80–4; Maxwell, 2004; 2011; 2012a), and this emphasis on processes, rather than variables, in understanding causality is supported by much recent work in philosophy (e.g., Little, 2010; Putnam, 1999; Salmon, 1998; see Maxwell, 2011, for a more extensive discussion) and in social science more generally (e.g., Lawson, 2003; Mohr, 1996; Pawson, 2006; Sayer, 2000: 114–18). The acceptance of causal processes, rather than causal laws, as fundamental to causal explanation entails that causal inference is legitimate in single cases (Miles and Huberman, 1994; Scriven, 2008), and thus that such inferences can be a matter of internal as well as external generalizability.

Interviewing (see Roulston, Chapter 20, this volume) poses some special problems for internal generalizability, because the researcher usually is in the presence of the person interviewed for only a brief period, and must necessarily draw inferences from what happened during that brief period to the rest of the informant's life, actions, and perspective. An account based on interviews may be valid as an account of the person's perspectives as expressed in that interview, but may miss other aspects of the person's perspectives that were not expressed in the interview, and can easily lead to false inferences about his or her perspectives or actions outside of that interview context.

In psychology, this lack of attention to context has been termed the *fundamental attribution error* (Nisbett, 2004) or *correspondence bias* (Gilbert and Malone, 1995). The term refers to the assumption that a person's behavior in some situation is a result of fundamental properties of the person, rather than features of the situation, and can thus be generalized to the person's behavior in other situations. This assumption has often been challenged in psychology (e.g., Nisbett, 2004), and has been central to the 'traits vs. states' debate in psychology. It has also been challenged by postmodern approaches to identity (Holstein and Gubrium, 1999; Rosenau, 1992) that deny the existence of a coherent, integrated self that is constant across situations, leading some researchers to completely reject the idea that interviewing is a way of accessing participants' understandings, and to treat it strictly as an interactional event (Olsson, 2008).

While we would not go this far in rejecting the generalizability of the results of interviews, it is undeniable that the interview is itself a social situation, and inherently involves a relationship between the interviewer and the informant. Understanding the nature of that situation and relationship, how it affects what takes place in the interview, and how the informant's expressed views could differ in other situations, is crucial to the analysis of accounts based on interviews (Briggs, 1986; Maxwell, 2012b; Mishler, 1986; Weiss, 1994).

STRATEGIES FOR INTERNAL GENERALIZATION IN QUALITATIVE DATA ANALYSIS

Qualitative researchers have many ways of assessing and improving internal generalizability, including systematic sampling (see Rapley, Chapter 4, this volume) or selection decisions (Miles and Huberman, 1994) – for example, stratified or maximum variation sampling (Morgan, 2008) – and asking participants themselves about the typicality of their views or of the situations you observed. For data analysis, a key strategy is paying specific attention to the diversity of views, behaviors, or contexts represented in the data you have collected, deliberately searching for variability and for data that do not fit prior expectations (Maxwell, 2011; 2012b). These data must be analysed in ways that retain these differences and attempt to understand their significance. Thorne and Darbyshire (2005: 1108, cited by Polit and Beck, 2010: 1453), discussing qualitative health research, identified a number of practices that interfere with valid generalization, including premature closure of analysis and imposing an artificial coherence on the data.

An additional strategy for supporting internal generalization, although one that is underutilized in qualitative research, is analysing the data to provide numerical results about the frequency and distribution of observations, or the number of instances of a particular type of event or statement (Maxwell, 2010; Seale, 1999). Becker called this strategy *quasi-statistics*, arguing that 'One of the greatest faults in most observational case studies has been their failure to make explicit the quasi-statistical basis of their conclusions' (1970: 81–2). This can be used to identify and accurately characterize the diversity in the case or setting you are studying.

Using numbers in this way is not 'statistical,' and does not make a study 'quantitative' in the usual meaning of this term (Maxwell, 2010); it simply makes explicit, and more precise, the implicitly numerical nature of claims such as that a particular activity, theme, or pattern is common, rare, or prevalent in the setting or interviews included in the study. The appropriate use of numbers not only allows you to test and support such claims, but also enables you to assess the *amount* of evidence in your data that bears on a particular conclusion or threat, such as how many discrepant instances exist and from how many different sources they were obtained. This strategy was used effectively in a classic participant–observation (see Marvasti, Chapter 24, this volume) study of medical students by Becker et al. (1961), which presented more than 50 tables and graphs of the amount and distribution of observational and interview data supporting their conclusions. In addition, numbers are important for identifying and communicating the *diversity* of actions and perspectives in the settings and populations you study (Heider, 1972; Sankoff, 1971; Zentella, 1990).

In addition, a goal of understanding specific, local, context-dependent processes has major implications for qualitative data analysis. The elucidation of such processes requires a different sort of analysis from the traditional coding and aggregation of data by coding categories (see Thornberg and Charmaz, Chapter 11, and Schreier, Chapter 12, this volume) that have been predominant in qualitative research. Abbott (1992) and Becker (1992; 2008) argued that narrative approaches to analysis (see Esin et al., Chapter 14, this volume) are far more useful for understanding processes than the traditional quantitative analysis of variables, and the same argument can be made for narrative analysis vs. coding. Coding inherently strips away both context and the sequencing of events, things that are intrinsic to process, leaving only the possibility of an aggregate understanding of the things coded. A discussion of how narrative and other sorts of connecting strategies for qualitative data analysis can be used for an understanding of process is beyond the scope of this chapter (see Maxwell and Miller, 2008, and Maxwell and Chmiel, Chapter 2, this volume, for such a discussion).

To summarize, internal generalizability is mainly concerned with the representativeness of the data and conclusions for the case, settings, or individuals studied, and relies primarily on empirical generalization, rather than analytic generalization or transfer. It thus depends significantly on sampling/selection issues; inadequate or unrepresentative selection can lead to flawed inferences about the case, setting, or individuals studied. These are problems that data analysis cannot by itself fully correct, although it can help you to identify such problems and provide ways to address them. However, other threats to internal generalizability, such as researcher bias or uniformist theoretical assumptions, can be addressed by data analysis strategies, including a deliberate search for data that are inconsistent with the emerging interpretation (see Willig, Chapter 10, this volume), the use of numbers to evaluate the actual variability and distribution of your data, and analyses appropriate for connecting data in ways that elucidate causal processes.

EXTERNAL GENERALIZATION

As noted above, external generalization in qualitative research is often assimilated, by quantitative researchers, to empirical generalization, and the imposition of quantitative views of generalization on qualitative research has frequently been criticized (e.g., Donmoyer, 1990; Guba and Lincoln, 1989). Bryman argued that:

> There are grounds for thinking that the 'problem' of case study generalization entails a misunderstanding of the aims of such research. In particular, the misconception arises from a tendency to approach a case study as if it were a sample of one drawn from a wider universe of such cases. (1988: 90)

However, the external generalizability of qualitative studies is normally either to theories (see Kelle, Chapter 38, this volume) (analytic generalization), or through the transferability of particular results or understandings to other cases, rather than to populations or universes (statistical generalization). For this reason, Bryman (1988: 50–4) and Yin (2003: 47–51) saw generalization in case study research as following a replication logic rather than a sampling logic, seeking to *test* the theory in other cases (similarly to multiple experiments) rather than to assess its representativeness for some larger population. Similarly, Donmoyer argued that 'good case studies employ theoretical constructs the way the historian of a particular revolution uses the construct of 'revolution' – to show not just its similarities to, but also its differences from, other revolutions' (1990: 196). Eisner described generalization as coming about in qualitative research via qualitative research's ability to 'bring about a set of observations or images' that can then facilitate 'the search and discovery processes when examining other situations' (1977: 270). That is, observations from qualitative studies are generalized in that they are used to create heuristics for other studies. He argued that in both quantitative and qualitative research, findings are used analogically or heuristically, but that the boundary conditions for developing an appropriate theory are seldom drawn.

For these reasons, the external generalizability of a qualitative study may depend on its *lack* of empirical or statistical generalizability, in the sense of being representative of a larger population. It may provide an account of a setting or population that is illuminating as an extreme case or 'ideal type,' one that highlights processes that are found in less visible form in many other cases. For example, Freidson's study of an innovative medical group practice (1975) made an important contribution to theory and policy precisely because this was a group for whom social controls on practice should have been most likely to be effective. The failure of such controls in this case not only highlights a social process that is likely to exist in other groups, but also provides a more persuasive argument for the unworkability of such controls than would a study of a 'representative' group. Similarly, Ruddin (2006) argued that studying an ideal case is a good way to falsify an existing generalization or theory. In such situations, the specific elements of the case produce knowledge that is itself general, namely, that the existing theory or knowledge is not a viable way to explain cases like this. In this case the general phenomena in question are best understood by seeking out a non-representative situation where we expect to find a particular effect. Here, the understanding of the general is attained by explicitly looking at an extreme.

Wievorka (1992) provided several instances of studies in which unrepresentative cases were particularly valuable in supporting or disconfirming general theories about some social phenomena. For example, in one study (Goldthorpe et al., 1968–1969), the researchers, in order to test the view that the working class were being assimilated into middle-class society, selected a case that would be highly favorable to this position: workers who were extremely affluent. The finding that these workers still retained a clear working-class identity provided more convincing refutation of this theory than a study of 'typical' workers would.

A detailed example of how generalization is possible despite a lack of empirical representativeness is given in Example 1.

Example 1

Becker (1990) provided an example of how a theory of the process by which prisoners' deprivations create a distinctive prison culture can be generalized from men's to women's prisons, despite the fact that the actual prison culture is quite different in the two cases. Studies of men's prisons found that prisoners created an elaborate culture separate from the formal administration of the prison, including a black market for cigarettes, drugs, and various services, a convict government that kept order, and a strict code of conduct that prevented prisoners from providing information about other prisoners to guards or officials. The researchers theorized that this culture was a response to the deprivations of prison life; deprived of autonomy, many goods and services, and sexual relations with women, they organized ways to provide a degree of autonomy, some of these goods, and prison-specific homosexual relations that did not threaten their male identities.

Other researchers then tried to apply this theory to women's prisons. However, they did not find the sort of culture that existed in men's prisons. There was no convict government, and not much of an underground market for anything; prisoners incessantly informed on other prisoners; and instead of the sorts of sexual relations found in the men's prisons, the women developed pseudo-families, in which some women acted as husbands and fathers of a group of wives and daughters. Becker argued that these differences did not invalidate the attempt to generalize the theory; it simply meant 'that the generalizations are not about how all prisons are the same, but about a process ... in which variations in conditions create variations in results' (1990: 240).

Deprivations shaped the prison culture in both cases, but the deprivations experienced by women were different than those experienced by men. Men primarily felt deprived of autonomy, while women, who by their own account had never had much autonomy to begin with, primarily felt deprived of protection. While the cultures of the two populations were different, those differences were explained by the general phenomenon of deprivation and the processes through which it influenced prison culture, in the context of the different deprivations felt by men and women. (Becker, 1990: 240–1)

Becker's focus on processes is consistent with the discussion of causal processes above, under internal generalization, and makes generalization from a single case an acceptable strategy, although by no means a straightforward and unproblematic one. Erickson argued that 'while certain causal processes may be at work in a local setting, the specific causal mechanisms in operation there may manifest differently in another setting, depending on the local social and cultural ecology of each' (2012: 687).

The theorizing of a causal process (see Kelle, Chapter 38, and Maxwell and Chmiel, Chapter 2, this volume), one that also elucidates the contextual influences on this process, can be the basis for some fairly specific ideas about the ways in which this process might apply to other situations and individuals. It can thus reconcile analytic or theoretical generalization and transferability, as two sides of the same coin: that 'transfer' can be, and often is, based on a theoretical understanding of the processes (including contextual influences) involved in a particular situation or outcome, an understanding that can then be applied to other situations. Eisner, in his presentation of an arts-based approach to qualitative inquiry, drew on learning theory to argue that 'I conflate generalization and transfer because transfer always requires more than the mechanical application of a set of skills, images, or ideas from one situation to another. ... Some features of the situations always differ. Hence transfer is a process that has generalizing features' (1998: 198).

STRATEGIES FOR EXTERNAL GENERALIZATION IN QUALITATIVE DATA ANALYSIS

There are a number of ways in which researchers can increase the credibility of the external generalizations they make from qualitative studies. First, qualitative studies often have what the statistician Judith Singer (personal communication) called *face generalizability*: there is no obvious reason *not* to believe that the results apply more generally to similar cases or settings. Hammersley (1992: 189–91) and Weiss (1994: 26–9) listed a number of features that lend plausibility to generalizations from case studies or non-random samples, including participants' own assessments of generalizability, the similarity of dynamics and constraints to other situations, the presumed depth or universality of the phenomenon studied, and corroboration from other studies. The logic of such generalization is empirical rather than analytic or transfer based, but it can nonetheless be a useful starting point for developing generalizations.

In addition, external generalization in qualitative research usually involves the development of a theory of *how* the results of a study came about, which goes beyond simple description. As Thomas (2010) argued, it may be better to think of how researchers develop knowledge not as induction (moving from individual incidents to an understanding of general phenomena), but as what Peirce described as *abduction* (see Reichertz, Chapter 9, and Thornberg and Charmaz, Chapter 11, this volume), the inference to the best explanation or interpretation (Shank, 2008). The answers to such 'how' questions involve an understanding of processes, which is not well served by coding/categorizing analysis strategies (see Maxwell and Chmiel, Chapter 2, this volume). This goal is better addressed by analysis methods that can elucidate the specific connections between events and among events and contexts, and allow the development of theories that can be applied to other settings and individuals that may or may not be superficially similar to those studied.

Thus, external generalization in qualitative research overlaps substantially with the development of theory, a topic that has been extensively discussed since Glaser and Strauss's creation of the concept of 'grounded theory' (1967; Anyon, 2009; Charmaz, 2006; Dressman, 2008; Glaser, 1978; Maxwell and Mittapalli, 2008 – see also Thornberg and Charmaz, Chapter 11, this volume). One particular strategy that is commonly invoked in qualitative research is 'theoretical saturation,' which Sandelowski described as when 'the properties and dimensions of the concepts and conceptual relations selected to render the target event are fully described and ... have captured its complexity and variation' (2008: 875). However, Sandelowski stated that theoretical saturation is often confused with data saturation, and Charmaz and Bryant argued that 'researchers often erroneously believe that they have achieved theoretical saturation when their data become repetitive. ... Most researchers assert saturation rather than provide evidence for it' (2008: 375).

Many of the analysis strategies described for internal generalization are also relevant for external generalization through theory development, including narrative and connecting approaches to analysis and the deliberate testing of theory by searching for discrepant data. In addition, it is important to develop and test *alternative* explanations for the results. One particular strategy that is rarely used explicitly in qualitative research, but is potentially useful for this, is what Scriven (1974) called the 'modus operandi method': developing alternative theories and then deliberately searching for 'clues' that could indicate which theory (or some combination of these) best explained the data. Maxwell (2011, Chapter 10) provides an ethnographic example of this strategy. Such a strategy would also be helpful in seeing whether the theory applied to other cases or situations than those studied. Similarly, Inglis argued for the value of *sociological forensics*, in which researchers think of studies of individual situations and cases as places 'to see clues that reveal the connection between macro level processes and structures and the micro level of action, meaning and emotion' (2010).

SUMMARY

In summary, there are analysis strategies that can be valuable in generalizing in and from qualitative data, but these differ somewhat between internal and external generalization. In addition, generalization cannot be guaranteed by mechanically applying a particular strategy as an algorithm or procedure. The effectiveness of any strategy depends on the specific theory and context involved, and, for external generalization, the particular cases or populations that are the targets of transfer or theoretical generalization.

NOTES

1. Statistical inference in experiments is almost always used to assess whether the observed effect was likely to be due to chance variation in *assignment*, not to make claims about the generalizability of the conclusions. Experimental studies rarely select participants or settings by using probability sampling, because participants are almost always volunteers, and statistical methods for generalizing the results to a larger population are therefore inappropriate (Bloom, 2008: 116).
2. Internal generalizability is analogous to what, in experimental research, is called *statistical conclusion validity*: the validity of inferences about a population (normally, inferences involving covariation of variables) that are based on sample data (Cook and Campbell, 1979: 37). Shadish et al. (2002) describe various threats to statistical conclusion validity, and strategies for dealing with these, some of which are relevant for qualitative research; the most important of these are discussed in this chapter.
3. The issues of sampling or selection in qualitative research, and its implications for generalization, are too complex to address in detail in a handbook on data analysis. Some qualitative researchers prefer the term *selection*, rather than sampling (e.g., LeCompte and Preissle, 1993: 69; Maxwell, 2012b; Stake, 1995), because, in quantitative research, samples are intended to be representative of a larger population (Morgan, 2008). The sort of sampling/selection done in qualitative research is usually what is called purposeful (Patton, 2001) or theoretical (Strauss, 1987) sampling (or selection), rather than random sampling or some other method of attaining statistical representativeness. Such selection can have a variety of purposes other than representativeness, including understanding the heterogeneity in the setting studied, or among the participants; selecting participants or settings that are critical for developing or testing the theory

employed; and selecting participants who are the most knowledgeable about, and/or most willing to discuss, the phenomena studied (Maxwell, 2012b: 97–9). For a more detailed discussion of these issues, see Gobo (2004; 2008) and Gomm et al. (2000).

FURTHER READING

Becker, Howard S. (1990) 'Generalizing from case studies,' in Elliot Eisner and Alan Peshkin (eds.), *Qualitative Inquiry in Education: The Continuing Debate*. New York: Teachers College Press. pp. 233–42.

Gobo, Giampietro (2008) 'Re-conceptualizing generalization: Old issues in a new frame,' in Pertti Alasuutari et al. (eds.), *The SAGE Handbook of Social Research Methods*. Thousand Oaks, CA: Sage. pp. 193–213.

Polit, Denise F. and Beck, Cheryl T. (2010) 'Generalization in quantitative and qualitative research: Myths and strategies,' *International Journal of Nursing Studies*, 47: 1451–58.

REFERENCES

Abbott, Andrew (1992) 'What do cases do? Some notes on activity in sociological analysis,' in Charles C. Ragin and Howard S. Becker (eds.), *What Is a Case? Exploring the Foundations of Social Inquiry*. Cambridge: Cambridge University Press. pp. 53–82.

Anderson, Gary L. and Scott, Janelle (2012) 'Toward an intersectional understanding of causality and social context,' *Qualitative Inquiry*, 18 (8): 674–85.

Anyon, Jean (2009) *Theory and Educational Research: Toward Critical Social Explanation*. New York: Routledge.

Atran, Scott and Medin, Douglas (2008) *The Native Mind and the Cultural Construction of Nature*. Cambridge, MA: MIT Press.

Ayres, Lioness (2008) 'Meta-narrative,' in Lisa M. Given (ed.), *The SAGE Encyclopedia of Qualitative Research Methods*. Thousand Oaks, CA: Sage. pp. 508–9.

Becker, Howard S. (1970) *Sociological Work: Method and Substance*. New Brunswick, NJ: Transaction.

Becker, Howard S. (1990) 'Generalizing from case studies,' in Elliot Eisner and Alan Peshkin (eds.), *Qualitative Inquiry in Education: The Continuing Debate*. New York: Teachers College Press. pp. 233–42.

Becker, Howard S. (1992) 'Cases, causes, conjunctures, stories, and imagery,' in Charles Ragin and Howard S. Becker (eds.), *What Is a Case?* Cambridge: Cambridge University Press. pp. 205–16.

Becker, Howard S. (2008) 'How to find out how to do qualitative research.' available at: http://home.earthlink.net/~hsbecker/articles/NSF.html (accessed February 8, 2011).

Becker, Howard S., Geer, Blanche, Hughes, Everett C., and Strauss, Anselm L. (1961) *Boys in White: Student Culture in Medical School*. Chicago: University of Chicago Press. Reprinted by Transaction Books, 1977.

Bloom, Howard S. (2008) 'The core analytics for randomized experiments in social research,' in Pertti Alasuutari et al. (eds.), *The SAGE Handbook of Social Research Methods*. Thousand Oaks, CA: Sage. pp. 115–33.

Briggs, Charles (1986) *Learning How to Ask*. Cambridge: Cambridge University Press.

Brinberg, David and McGrath, Joseph E. (1985) *Validity and the Research Process*. Newbury Park, CA: Sage.

Brown-Saracino, Japonica, Thurk, Jessica, and Fine, Gary Alan (2008) 'Beyond groups: Seven pillars of peopled ethnography in organizations and communities,' *Qualitative Research*, 8 (5): 547–67.

Bryman, Alan (1988) *Quantity and Quality in Social Research*. London: Unwin Hyman.

Charmaz, Kathy (2006) *Constructing Grounded Theory: A Practical Guide Through Qualitative Analysis*. Thousand Oaks, CA: Sage.

Charmaz, Kathy and Bryant, Antony (2008) 'Grounded theory,' in Lisa M. Given (ed.), *The SAGE Encyclopedia of Qualitative Research Methods*. Thousand Oaks, CA: Sage. pp. 374–7.

Cook, Thomas D. and Campbell, Donald T. (1979) *Quasi-experimentation: Design and Analysis Issues for Field Settings*. Boston, MA: Houghton-Mifflin.

Donmoyer, Robert (1990) 'Generalizability and the single-case study,' in Elliot W. Eisner and Alan Peshkin (eds.), *Qualitative Inquiry in Education: The Continuing Debate*. New York: Teachers College Press. pp.175–200.

Donmoyer, Robert (2008) 'Generalizability,' in Lisa Given (ed.), *The SAGE Encyclopedia of Qualitative Research Methods*. Thousand Oaks, CA: Sage. pp. 371–2.

Donmoyer, Robert (2012) 'Can qualitative researchers answer policymakers' what-works question?', *Qualitative Inquiry*, 18 (8): 662–73.

Dressman, Mark (2008) *Using Social Theory in Educational Research: A Practical Guide*. London: Routledge.

Eisner, Elliot (1997) 'The new frontier in qualitative research methodology,' *Qualitative Inquiry*, 3 (3): 259–73.

Eisner, Elliot (1998) *The Enlightened Eye: Qualitative Inquiry and the Enhancement of Educational Practice*. Upper Saddle River, NJ: Prentice Hall.

Erickson, Fred (1986) 'Qualitative methods,' in Merlin C. Wittrock (ed.), *Handbook of Research on Teaching*. New York: Macmillan.

Erickson, Fred (2012) 'Comments on causality in qualitative inquiry,' *Qualitative Inquiry*, 18 (8): 686–8.

Firestone, William A. (1993) 'Alternative arguments for generalizing from data as applied to qualitative research,' *Educational Researcher*, 22: 16–23.

Freidson, Eliot (1975) *Doctoring Together: A Study of Professional Social Control*. Chicago: University of Chicago Press.

Gilbert, Daniel T. and Malone, Patrick S. (1995) 'The correspondence bias,' *Psychological Bulletin*, 117: 21–38.

Glaser, Barney G. (1978) *Theoretical Sensitivity*. Mill Valley, CA: Sociology Press.

Glaser, Barney G. and Strauss, Anselm (1967) *The Discovery of Grounded Theory: Strategies for Qualitative Research*. Chicago: Aldine.

Gobo, Giampietro (2004) 'Sampling, representativeness, and generalizability,' in Clive Seale et al. (eds.), *Qualitative Research Practice*. London: Sage. pp. 435–56.

Gobo, Giampietro (2008) 'Re-conceptualizing generalization: Old issues in a new frame,' in Pertti Alasuutari et al. (eds.), *The SAGE Handbook of Social Research Methods*. Thousand Oaks, CA: Sage. pp. 193–213.

Goldthorpe, John H., Lockwood, David, Beckhofer, Frank, and Platt, Jennifer (1968–1969) *The Affluent Worker*, 3 vols. Cambridge: Cambridge University Press.

Gomm, Roger, Hammersley, Martyn, and Foster, Peter (eds.) (2000) *Case Study Method*. London: Sage.

Guba, Egon G. and Lincoln, Yvonna S. (1989) *Fourth Generation Evaluation*. Thousand Oaks, CA: Sage.

Hammersley, Martyn (1992) *What's Wrong with Ethnography? Methodological Explorations*. London: Routledge.

Hammersley, Martyn (2008) *Questioning Qualitative Inquiry Critical Essays*. London: Sage.

Hannerz, Ulf (1992) *Cultural Complexity: Studies in the Social Organization of Meaning*. New York: Columbia University Press.

Heider, Eleanor R. (1972) 'Probability, sampling, and ethnographic method: The case of Dani colour names,' *Man*, 7: 448–66.

Holstein, Jaber F. and Gubrium, James A. (1999) *The Self We Live By: Narrative Identity in a Postmodern World*. New York: Oxford University Press.

Inglis, Tom (2010) 'Sociological forensics: Illuminating the whole from the particular,' *Sociology*, 44 (3): 507–22.

Jensen, Devon (2008) 'Transferability,' in Lisa Given (ed.), *The SAGE Encyclopedia of Qualitative Research Methods*. Thousand Oaks, CA: Sage. p. 886.

Lawson, Tony (2003) *Reorienting Economics*. London: Routledge.

LeCompte, Margaret and Preissle, Judith (1993) *Ethnography and Qualitative Design in Educational Research*, 2nd edition. San Diego, CA: Academic Press.

Lincoln, Yvonna S. and Guba, Egon G. (1985) *Naturalistic Inquiry*. Thousand Oaks, CA: Sage.

Lincoln, Yvonna S. and Guba, Egon G. (1986) 'But is it rigorous? Trustworthiness and authenticity in naturalistic evaluation,' in David D. Williams (ed.), *Naturalistic Evaluation*. San Francisco: Jossey-Bass. pp. 73–84.

Little, Daniel (2010) *New Contributions to the Philosophy of History*. New York: Springer.

Mabry, Linda (2008) 'Case study in social research,' in Pertti Alasuutari et al. (eds.), *The SAGE Handbook of Social Research Methods*. Thousand Oaks, CA: Sage. pp. 214–27.

Maxwell, Joseph A. (1992) 'Understanding and validity in qualitative research,' *Harvard Educational Review*, 62: 279–300.

Maxwell, Joseph A. (1996) 'Diversity and methodology in a changing world,' *Pedagogía*, 30: 32–40.

Maxwell, Joseph A. (2004) 'Causal explanation, qualitative research, and scientific inquiry in education,' *Educational Researcher*, 33 (2): 3–11.

Maxwell, Joseph A. (2010) 'Using numbers in qualitative research,' *Qualitative Inquiry*, 16 (6): 475–82.

Maxwell, Joseph A. (2011) *A Realist Approach for Qualitative Research*. Thousand Oaks, CA: Sage.

Maxwell, Joseph A. (2012a) 'The importance of qualitative research for causal explanation in education,' *Qualitative Inquiry*, 18 (8): 649–55.

Maxwell, Joseph. A. (2012b) *Qualitative Research Design: An Interactive Approach*, 3rd edition. Thousand Oaks, CA: Sage.

Maxwell, Joseph A. and Miller, Barbara (2008) 'Categorizing and connecting strategies in qualitative data analysis,' in Patricia Leavy and Sharlene Hesse-Biber (eds.), *Handbook of Emergent Methods*. New York: Guilford Press. pp. 461–77.

Maxwell, Joseph A. and Mittapalli, Kavita (2008) 'Theory,' in Lisa Given (ed.), *The SAGE Encyclopedia of Qualitative Research Methods*. Thousand Oaks, CA: Sage. pp. 876–80.

Miles, Matthew B. and Huberman, A. Michael (1984) *Qualitative Data Analysis: A Sourcebook of New Methods*. Thousand Oaks, CA: Sage.

Miles, Matthew B. and Huberman, A. Michael (1994) *Qualitative Data Analysis: An Expanded Sourcebook*. Thousand Oaks, CA: Sage.

Misco, Thomas (2007) 'The frustrations of reader generalizability and grounded theory: Alternative considerations for transferability,' *Journal of Research Practice*, 3 (1): 1–11.

Mishler, Eliot G. (1986) *Research Interviewing: Context and Narrative*. Cambridge, MA: Harvard University Press.

Mohr, Lawrence B. (1996) *The Causes of Human Behavior: Implications for Theory and Method in the Social Sciences*. Ann Arbor: University of Michigan Press.

Morgan, David L. (2008) 'Sample,' in Lisa Given (ed.), *The SAGE Encyclopedia of Qualitative Research Methods*. Thousand Oaks, CA: Sage. pp. 797–8.

Nisbett, Robert (2004) *The Geography of Thought: How Westerners and Asians Think Differently ... and Why*. New York: Free Press.

Olsson, Michael R. (2008) 'Postmodernism,' in Lisa Given (ed.), *The SAGE Encyclopedia of Qualitative Research Methods*. Thousand Oaks, CA: Sage. pp. 655–9.

Patton, Michael Q. (2001) *Qualitative Research and Evaluation Methods*, 3rd edition. Thousand Oaks, CA: Sage.

Pawson, Ray (2006) *Evidence-based Policy: A Realist Perspective*. London: Sage.

Polit, Denise F. and Beck, Cheryl T. (2010) 'Generalization in quantitative and qualitative research: Myths and strategies,' *International Journal of Nursing Studies*, 47: 1451–8.

Putnam, Hilary (1999) *The Threefold Cord: Mind, Body, and World*. New York: Columbia University Press.

Rosenau, Pauline M. (1992) *Post-Modernism and the Social Sciences*. Princeton, NJ: Princeton University Press.

Ruddin, Lee P. (2006) 'You can generalize stupid! Social scientists, Bent Flyvbjerg, and case study methodology,' *Qualitative Inquiry*, 12 (4): 797–812.

Salmon, Wesley C. (1998) *Causality and Explanation*. New York: Oxford University Press.

Sandelowski, Margarete (2008) 'Theoretical saturation,' in Lisa Given (ed.), *The SAGE Encyclopedia of Qualitative Research Methods*. Thousand Oaks, CA: Sage. pp. 875–6.

Sankoff, Gillian (1971) 'Quantitative aspects of sharing and variability in a cognitive model,' *Ethnology*, 10: 389–408.

Sayer, Andrew (2000) *Realism and Social Science*. London: Sage.

Schofield, Janet W. (1990) 'Increasing the generalizability of qualitative research,' in Elliot W. Eisner and Alan Peshkin (eds.), *Qualitative Inquiry in Education: The Continuing Debate*. New York: Teachers College Press. pp. 201–32.

Schwandt, Thomas A. (1997) *The SAGE Dictionary of Qualitative Inquiry*. Thousand Oaks, CA: Sage.

Scriven, Michael (1974) 'Maximizing the power of causal investigations: The modus operandi method,' in W. James Popham (ed.), *Evaluation in Education – Current Perspectives*. Richmond, CA: McCutchan. Reprinted (1976) in G.V. Glass (ed.), *Evaluation Studies Review Annual 1*. Beverly Hills, CA: Sage. pp. 108–18.

Scriven, Michael (2008) 'A summative evaluation of RCT methodology: And an alternative approach to causal research,' *Journal of MultiDisciplinary Evaluation*, 5 (9): 11–24.

Seale, Clive (1999) *The Quality of Qualitative Research*. London: Sage.

Shadish, William R., Cook, Thomas D., and Campbell, Donald T. (2002) *Experimental and Quasi-experimental Designs for Generalized Causal Inference*. Boston, MA: Houghton Mifflin.

Shank, Gary (2008) 'Abduction,' in Lisa Given (ed.), *The SAGE Encyclopedia of Qualitative Research Methods*. Thousand Oaks, CA: Sage. pp. 1–2.

Shweder, Richard A. (ed.) (1980) *Fallible Judgment in Behavioral Research*. San Francisco: Jossey-Bass.

Stake, Robert (1995) *The Art of Case Study Research*. Thousand Oaks, CA: Sage.

Strauss, Anselm (1987) *Qualitative Analysis for Social Scientists*. Cambridge: Cambridge University Press.

Strauss, Claudia (1992) 'Models and motives,' in Roy G. D'Andrade and Claudia Strauss (eds.), *Human Motives and Cultural Models*. Cambridge, England: Cambridge University Press. pp. 1–20.

Thomas, Gary (2010) 'Doing case study: Abduction not induction, phronesis not theory,' *Qualitative Inquiry*, 16 (7): 575–82.

Thorne, Sally and Darbyshire, Philip (2005) 'Land mines in the field: A modest proposal for improving the craft of qualitative health research,' *Qualitative Health Research*, 15: 1105–13.

Wallace, Anthony F. C. (1970) *Culture and Personality*, 2nd edition. New York: Random House.

Weiss, Robert S. (1994) *Learning From Strangers: The Art and Method of Qualitative Interviewing*. New York: Free Press.

Wievorka, Michael (1992) 'Case studies: History or sociology?,' in Charles C. Ragin and Howard S. Becker (eds.), *What Is a Case?* Cambridge: Cambridge University Press. pp. 159–72.

Wolf, Margery (1992) *A Thrice-Told Tale: Feminism, Postmodernism, and Ethnographic Responsibility*. Stanford, CA: Stanford University Press.

Yin, Robert K. (1984) *Case Study Research: Design and Methods*. Thousand Oaks, CA: Sage.

Yin, Robert K. (2003) *Case Study Research: Design and Methods*, 3rd edition. Thousand Oaks, CA: Sage.

Zentella, Ana Celia (1990) 'Integrating quantitative and qualitative methods in the study of bilingual code switching,' in Edward H. Bendix (ed.), *The Uses of Linguistics. Annals of the New York Academy of Sciences*, vol. 583. pp. 75–92.

Znaniecki, Florian (1934) 'Analytic induction,' in Florian Znaniecki, *The Method of Sociology*. New York: Farrar and Rinehart.

38
Theorization from Data

Udo Kelle

How are theoretical statements and conclusions derived during qualitative analysis? How can researchers use qualitative data to develop new theories and to criticize, challenge or modify existing theories?

To discuss these questions I will proceed in four steps. In the first step the general problem of theory use in qualitative data analysis will be outlined: on the one hand qualitative researchers have to be careful not to force ready-made hypotheses on their data; on the other hand attempts to fully ignore or discard previous theoretical knowledge regularly fail in research practice. In the second step I will briefly describe prominent attempts developed in the history of qualitative research to reconcile the requirement for openness in research with the necessity to introduce previous theoretical knowledge in qualitative data analysis. In the third step theoretical foundations of theory building and theory testing will be explained – this covers the logic of theory building and the role of different types of previous theoretical knowledge in empirically grounded theory building (see Thornberg and Charmaz, Chapter 11, this volume). Drawing on examples from research practice different strategies of data-supported theorizing will be discussed in the fourth step: the generation of middle range theories from empirical data, the application of already existing theoretical concepts on qualitative data and the use of qualitative data for the criticism and modification of existing theories.

THEORIZING IN QUALITATIVE RESEARCH: THE CHALLENGES

The relation between theory and data in qualitative research is complex and contested: qualitative researchers who either want to apply theoretical knowledge on their data or try to transform qualitative findings into theoretical statements have to deal with two conflicting challenges:

1. Nowadays it is a generally accepted epistemological tenet that empirical research must always

refer to previous theoretical insights and already existing knowledge.
2. The qualitative tradition has always argued that in social life the meaning of social action and social structure is constantly changed and reinvented. Thus social researchers must be open to exploring previously unknown phenomena in their research field. Such an openness, however, may be hampered by the theoretical preconceptions researchers carry with them.

These two challenges have to be addressed simultaneously: qualitative theory building must apply a methodology of exploration and discovery and at the same time avoid naive inductivism (see also Reichertz, Chapter 9, this volume).

The Problems of Naive Inductivism

A simple and often assumed idea about empirical research is that one first collects all accessible data about facts in an open-minded way and then generalizes from them to general categories. This view can be traced back to the philosophy of early empiricism. In the seventeenth and eighteenth centuries empiricist philosophers, namely Francis Bacon and John Locke, developed the idea that all scientific theories had to be derived by generalizations from observables. According to Bacon, researchers must free their minds for that purpose from theoretical preconceptions and 'idols' before entering their research field. However, such an idea leads to unsolvable problems and antagonisms, as Immanuel Kant had shown in the eighteenth century: 'Naïve empiricism' or 'naïve inductivism' (Chalmers, 1999) of that kind was still popular among the early positivists but demonstrated its shortcomings in the debates of the 'Vienna Circle' in the 1930s. According to the logician Willard van Orman Quine, the idea that empirical data and observations are 'prior' to theoretical notions in the sense that they are not 'contaminated' by theory is one of the failed 'dogmas of empiricism' (Quine, 1951). Later on, the philosopher of science Norwood Hanson coined the term *theoryladenness of observation* to underline that all empirical observations are shaped by some prior knowledge (Hanson, 1965: 19). Nowadays, it is one of the most widely accepted insights of epistemology and cognitive psychology that 'there are and can be no sensations unimpregnated by expectations' (Lakatos, 1978: 15) and that the construction of theories cannot be based on data alone, but has to draw on already existing knowledge, since 'the world is always perceived through the "lenses" of some conceptual network or other and that such networks and the languages in which they are embedded may, for all we know, provide an ineliminable "tint" to what we perceive' (Laudan, 1977: 15).

The Need for a Methodology of Discovery

A hallmark of the qualitative tradition in social research has always been the emphasis on social process and on the flexible nature of the structures of society, which are constituted, stabilized and changed through actions and interactions of its members. For these processes the members' 'definition of the situation' is of utmost importance, as the early Chicago sociologist William Thomas had maintained (Thomas and Thomas, 1928: 572). Thus, social researchers must take into account the viewpoints of the actors in the domain under study in order to understand 'how he [sic] conceives his rôle in relation to other persons and the interpretations which he makes of the situations in which he lives' (Shaw, 1966 [1930]: 3f); social scientists have to put themselves 'in the position of the subject who tries to find his [sic] way in this world', keeping in mind 'that the environment by which he is influenced and to which he adapts himself is his world, not the objective world of science' (Thomas and Znaniecki, 1958 [1918]: 1846f.). This would make a case for not entering the field with too precise hypotheses but to stay open to the actors' 'definitions of the situations' which may widely differ from the researchers' expectations. Qualitative researchers, in other words, embark on a journey in which they hope to discover previously unknown attitudes, norms, beliefs, social rules and practices.

These two challenges seem to pose two contradictory or at least conflicting tasks on qualitative researchers. How can they be reconciled? How can one remain open for the discovery of new phenomena in the research field while accepting the necessity to draw on already existing knowledge at the same time?

In the history of qualitative research different proposals have been made to cope with these challenges, which will be discussed in the following section.

THE DEBATE ABOUT THEORY BUILDING AND THEORY TESTING IN THE QUALITATIVE RESEARCH TRADITION

In this section I will show how the two above-mentioned challenges have shaped the historical development of concepts for qualitative theory building: the shortcomings of methodological ideas of theory building of the early Chicago School inspired Glaser and Strauss's (1967) groundbreaking work *The Discovery of Grounded Theory*. In the subsequent evolution of what came to be known as 'grounded theory methodology' (GTM – see Thornberg and Charmaz, Chapter 11, this volume) both authors followed different paths to address the two challenges. The split between Glaser and Strauss not only led to the fact that competing approaches now claim the legacy of grounded theory, but also inspired the development of a variety of further proposals on how to reconcile the different challenges of theory building.

The Early Chicagoans and Theory Building

Empirical studies from the famous Chicago School at the beginning of the qualitative tradition in sociology (Bulmer, 1984; Deegan, 2001) often used and developed theory only marginally. Studies like 'The hobo' (Anderson, 1975 [1923]), 'The Gang' (Thrasher, 1973 [1927]) or 'The jack-roller' (Shaw, 1966 [1930]) were not conducted to develop theories but to provide a detailed description of an unknown and problem-ridden part of society. The rapid development of statistical research methods from the 1920s onwards inspired criticism of this kind of research: methodologists bemoaned that such studies lacked the formulation and examination of precise hypotheses and did not collect standardized data suitable for such purposes (e.g. Bain, 1929: 155; Lundberg, 1929: 169). At that time the hypothetico-deductive (HD) model was about to be established as the dominant research paradigm; thereby empirical research is understood as a testing of previously stated hypotheses. Florian Znaniecki's monograph *The Method of Sociology* (Znaniecki, 1934), the most influential methods course book in qualitatively oriented sociology departments (Cressey, 1971 [1953]) in the 1930s and 1940s, adopted this HD model for qualitative research. Znaniecki proposed a strategy named 'Analytic Induction' as the alternative to statistical methods, which was further elaborated in practical qualitative research by Donald Sutherland, Alfred Lindesmith and Donald Cressey. Thereby the research process starts with a tentative (causal) hypothesis developed from the first investigated case. This hypothesis is modified and refined with the help of further data or material. In this process the qualitative researcher has to look for 'crucial cases', which either confirm or refute the initial hypothesis. If such counter-evidence is found, the hypothesis has to be reformulated or the investigated phenomenon under study has to be redefined – 'this procedure of examining cases, re-defining the phenomenon and re-formulating the hypothesis is continued until a universal relationship is established, each negative case calling for a re-definition or a re-formulation' (Cressey, 1971 [1953]: 16).

Critics of this approach remarked that 'the function of theory in the determination of relevant variables and hypotheses as to the connections between them' remained unclear (Robinson, 1952: 494). However, researchers who had used and extensively reflected on the method, especially Alfred Lindesmith and Donald Cressey, had not only used the data for hypothesis generation but also drawn on previous theory. Lindesmith's sociological explanation of opiate addiction (1968 [1947]) as well as Cressey's theory about embezzlement (1971 [1953]), developed via analytical induction, were heavily influenced by symbolic interactionism: according to Lindesmith, drug abuse could only be adequately understood if the actors' changing constructions of their identities are taken into account. Analytic induction also had to wrestle with the second challenge of qualitative theory building: the requirement to formulate a causal hypothesis from the first case analysed could restrict the researchers' ability to stay open to the members' perspectives and seduce them into finishing hypothesis formation too early.

The Discovery of Grounded Theory

The monograph *The Discovery of Grounded Theory*, published in 1967 by Barney Glaser and Anselm Strauss, marked an important breakthrough. Similar to analytic induction, Glaser and Strauss conceptualized theory building as a process of stepwise refinement of empirically grounded theoretical statements, whereby empirical data were collected in a stepwise process (named 'theoretical sampling' – see Rapley, Chapter 4, this volume) which was guided by categories and hypotheses developed in the process. Other crucial elements of analytic induction were dropped, especially the idea to start empirical research with ready-made hypotheses. Theorizing was conceptualized as a stepwise construction of a set of connected statements: the researcher started by developing concepts from the data, and proceeded by deriving elaborated categories from these concepts which were related to each other to form theoretical propositions and hypotheses. Empirical data were not used to 'test' these hypotheses, but to increase their coherence and preciseness through 'constant comparisons' (Glaser and Strauss, 1967: 104f.).

Regarding the researchers' previous theoretical knowledge, Glaser and Strauss were ambiguous. *The Discovery of Grounded Theory* was meant as a critique of the 'overemphasis in current sociology on the verification of theory' (Glaser and Strauss, 1967: 1). The authors opted for an 'initial, systematic discovery of the theory from the data of social research' (1967: 3) whereby categories are empirically 'grounded', if they 'emerge' from the data. Since too much previous theoretical knowledge could lead to a 'forcing' of inappropriate categories, Glaser and Strauss recommended to 'literally ... ignore the literature of theory and fact on the area under study, in order to assure that the emergence of categories will not be contaminated' (1967: 37).

Bearing in mind the problem of 'theory-ladenness of observation' already mentioned, one would refer to the idea that researchers could approach reality 'as it is' (if they only free their minds from preconceived ideas) as naive inductivism – the construction of any theory has to draw on already existing stocks of knowledge. Also, qualitative researchers who investigate different environments cannot simply dismiss their cognitive schemes and conceptual lenses, for then they would not be able to observe or describe meaningful phenomena at all. This follows not just from epistemological arguments alone; research practice provides examples for it as well: attempts often made by novice researchers to abstain from theoretical preconceptions and merely let the data speak can lead to a 'drowning in the data' and to a proliferation of coding categories, along with numerous and endless team sessions, instead of producing good theories (Kelle, 2007: 196).

But Glaser and Strauss did not overlook this problem: 'Of course, the researcher does not approach reality as a tabula rasa. He must have a perspective that will help him see relevant data and abstract significant categories from his scrutiny of the data' (1967: 3). This competence to reflect upon empirical data in theoretical terms was named 'theoretical sensitivity', a faculty which builds up 'in the sociologist an armamentarium of categories and hypotheses. ... This theory that exists within a sociologist can be used in generating his specific theory' (1967: 46). But how can such an armamentarium be obtained? The authors only give a short hint on 'great man theorists', which have 'given us models and guidelines for generating theory' (1967: 11).

A much clearer image of the theorizing strategy that the authors themselves used can be obtained by looking at the empirical study that provided an important basis for their book. In the methodological appendix of their famous study *Awareness of Dying* both authors write: 'Shortly after Glaser and Strauss joined forces, they systematically worked out the concepts (and types) of death experiences and awareness contexts, and the paradigm for the study of awareness contexts. Thus, a concern with death expectations and awareness guided the preliminary data collection' (Glaser and Strauss, 1965: 287). Thus the theoretical concepts explaining the interactions between doctors, hospital staff and moribund patients did not solely 'emerge from the data': the idea that social interaction is structured by the actors' knowledge and expectations as well as by 'mutual awareness' of such knowledge and expectations is part and parcel of the symbolic interactionist theory tradition. 'Theoretical sensitivity' here means the ability to understand that the communication between dying hospital patients, nurses and doctors is a research field ideally suited for the application of such ideas. However, the concept of 'theoretical sensitivity' is barely elaborated in Glaser and Strauss's 1967 book.

Different Approaches towards the Grounding of Theory

This elaboration took place in later writings, which contained more extensive reflections on the role of previous theoretical knowledge in theory building, which led both authors in somewhat different directions.

Thereby Barney Glaser invented the terms 'theoretical coding' and 'theoretical codes' (Glaser, 1978; see also Thornberg and Charmaz, Chapter 11, this volume) – first 'substantive codes' (relating to the empirical substance of the research domain) are developed during 'open coding' and then theoretical codes are used to 'conceptualize how the substantive codes may relate to each other as hypotheses to be integrated into a theory' (Glaser, 1978: 72). Theoretical codes are terms useful for describing structures in the empirical (social) world: by coding certain events with the theoretical code 'cause' and others with the theoretical code 'consequence' or 'effect', the respective substantive codes are integrated into a *causal model*, for instance. Glaser presents an extended list of such theoretical codes stemming from different (sociological, philosophical or everyday) contexts loosely connected to each other to form 14 'coding families': the *degree family*, for instance, contains terms which relate to the degree of an attribute or property, like 'limit', 'range', 'extent', 'amount', etc., or the *cultural family* encompasses terms referring to *cultural phenomena* like 'social norms', 'social values', 'social beliefs', etc. But Glaser gives only limited advice on *how* such terms can be combined for theorizing from the data. One single coding family is often not sufficient for that purpose, as one can easily see if one attempts to employ the coding family *causal relations*: the concepts of cause and effect themselves cannot specify which types of events in a certain domain have to be regarded as causes and which ones are to be seen as effects – in principle all events which occur together can be regarded as cause and effect. To formulate a causal model at least one substantive (i.e. sociological, psychological, etc.) theoretical code must be applied to tell us which *types of events* could be considered as causes and effects. For theory building, *formal* or *logical concepts* (like 'causality') must be combined with *substantive concepts* (like 'social roles', 'identity', 'culture'). Unfortunately, Glaser's list of coding families lacks a differentiation between formal (= logical, epistemological) and substantial (= sociological, psychological, etc.) concepts, and his concept of theoretical coding does not clarify how formal and substantial concepts can be meaningfully linked to each other (for a more detailed discussion of this issue see Kelle, 2007: 199f.).

Strauss (partly together with Juliet Corbin) proposed a similar, but less complicated strategy of how previous theoretical knowledge can be integrated into qualitative analysis: a model of action derived from pragmatist and interactionist social theory (Corbin, 1991: 36; Strauss, 1990: 7), called the 'coding paradigm' (Strauss, 1987: 18f.; Strauss and Corbin, 1990: 99ff.), serves as the 'axis' of the core category and the developing theory. Employing Glaser's terminology one would regard the coding paradigm as an elaborated coding family guiding a particular form of theoretical coding (called 'axial coding' by Strauss, 1987: 32f.): the initial concepts developed from the data are structured according to (1) *phenomena* at which the actions and interactions of the actors are directed, (2) *causal conditions* which lead to their occurrence, (3) attributes of the *context*, (4) additional *intervening conditions*, (5) action and interactional strategies the actors use, and (6) their consequences.

Strauss's model of theory building was subjected to polemic attacks by Glaser who worried that the 'coding paradigm' would lead to the 'forcing' of the data (Glaser, 1992). Nevertheless, Glaser himself had broken with the inductivism of the 1967 book to a certain extent, by taking into account the use of previous theoretical knowledge via 'theoretical coding' which, however, requires extended training in social theory (Glaser, 1992: 28) and the ability to work with an unsystematic list of codes from various sociological and epistemological backgrounds. In contrast to this, Strauss's 'coding paradigm' is developed in the context of a particular tradition (pragmatism and symbolic interactionism) and can be traced back to Dewey's model of situated activity and reflexive agency which has its starting point in problematic situations (see also Corbin and Strauss, 2008: 2f.). This model is certainly compatible with different microsociological approaches (other than pragmatism or interactionism) that focus on individual action. However, researchers who wish to apply a different theoretical perspective on their data (general system theory, for instance), or even multiple perspectives (Thornberg, 2012: 250), may indeed feel that the use of the coding paradigm may lead to forcing the data to comply with a particular theoretical model.

Current Developments

The divide between 'Glaserian' and 'Straussian' GTM, as the two strands are often called in the current literature (Thornberg, 2012: 244), has persisted ever since. Regarding the role of previous theoretical knowledge for theorizing from the data, Glaser and his adherents, who claim to represent the original 'classical' grounded theory, still argue from an inductivist point of view: the basic purpose of empirical research should be 'to produce a clear, accurate understanding of what is' (Simmons, 2011: 18). That can only be obtained if researchers do not bring any 'preconceived questions or categories' (2011: 24) with them. Advocates of the Straussian approach normally acknowledge that 'theories, professional knowledge that we carry within our heads, inform our research in multiple ways' (Corbin and Strauss, 2008: 32), and that the researchers' theoretical sensitivity may increase with the theoretical background knowledge at hand. The use of concepts from the literature is thus encouraged, as long as they do not hamper the researchers' creativity. However, in the current edition of *Basics of Qualitative Research* (Corbin and Strauss, 2008) the notions of 'axial coding' and the 'coding paradigm' are put more into the background. Thereby Corbin expresses her concerns that by sticking to the coding paradigm too formally, researchers may 'rigidify' the analytic process (Corbin and Strauss, 2008: 90). The use of one particular coding paradigm seems indeed to be a certain risk – that the respective theoretical (microsociological) perspective may be used to 'force' data.

Over the past two decades further varieties of GTM have emerged, the most prominent among them being Kathy Charmaz's 'constructivist' GTM. Charmaz tries to strengthen and accentuate the interpretivist and constructivist elements in GTM (which was already pertinent for its first version in 1967): theories are not so much 'discovered' or 'emerging' from the data, but constructed by researchers through their 'past and present involvements and interactions with people, perspectives, and research practices' (Charmaz, 2006: 10). In other respects Charmaz is closer to the Glaserian approach – she draws extensively on the concept of coding families making use of the theoretical pluralism inherent in Glaser's idea.

Adherents of otherwise differing versions of GTM agree on not to 'dismiss extant theoretical and research literature nor apply it mechanically to empirical cases. … Instead these researchers use the literature as a possible source of inspiration, ideas, "aha!" experiences, creative associations, critical reflections, and multiple lenses' (Thornberg, 2012: 249). This supplementation of GTM techniques with explicit literature review can be named 'Informed GT' according to Thornberg. A further important development in GTM during the past few years has been the rediscovery of original ideas of the pragmatist philosopher Charles Sanders Peirce about the logic of scientific discovery. Peirce's concept of abduction (see Reichertz, Chapter 9, and Thornberg and Charmaz, Chapter 11, this volume) or retroduction (see section below) offers a way out of the difficulties and antinomies produced by the conflicting challenges of qualitative theorizing (not to force preconceived hypotheses on the data *and* to acknowledge the indispensability of theoretical background knowledge) towards a non-inductivist methodology of discovery.

THEORETICAL BACKGROUND

To clarify the relation between theory and data in qualitative research three questions have to be addressed: (1) What is a theory and what are its crucial elements? (2) How are theories and empirical data related to each other? (3) What different functions can theories perform in qualitative data analysis?

Theories and Their Crucial Elements

According to Hempel, 'Empirical science has two major objectives: to describe particular phenomena in the world of our experience and to establish general principles by means of which they can be explained and predicted' (1952: 1). Qualitative studies often do not claim to explain or predict events but try to give detailed descriptions of a social environment, its rules and practices as well as the orientations and interpretations of its members. Early studies from the Chicago School tradition can provide good examples for that: in 'The hobo', for instance, Nels Anderson attempts to describe structures, processes and events in a certain part of Chicago where migratory and casual workers met in the 1920s (Anderson, 1975 [1923]).

Following standard definitions, a theory consists of a connected set of statements, some of which can be directly linked to empirical phenomena. A theory can thus be compared with:

> a complex spatial network: its terms are represented by the knots, while the threads connecting the latter correspond, in part to the definitions and, in part, to the fundamental and derivative hypotheses included in the theory. The whole system floats, as it were, above the plane of observation and is anchored to it by rules of interpretation. These might be viewed as strings which are not part of the network but link certain points of the latter with specific places in the plane of observation. By virtue of those interpretative connections, the network can function as a scientific theory: From certain observational data, we may ascend, via an interpretive string, to some point in the theoretical network, thence proceed, via

definitions and hypotheses to other points, from which another interpretive string permits a descent to the plane of observation. (Hempel, 1952: 36)

Statements of a theory have to be logically connected with each other while the 'ascension' and 'descension' via the 'strings of interpretation' are related to two modes of logical inference, 'deduction' and 'induction' (see Reichertz, Chapter 9, this volume).

Linkages between Theory and Data

With deductive inferences one may descend from the theoretical level to the level of empirical observation: social researchers employing a theory of class conflict might thus deductively infer that certain events marking collective conflicts occur in the research field.

By making a deduction one draws a link from a general theoretical assumption to an empirical hypothesis: 'If A (a theoretical statement) is true then we would expect the empirical phenomenon C to happen.' This expectation that C would happen represents an 'empirical hypothesis' (in contrast to the 'theoretical hypothesis' A on the 'plane of theory').

By inductive inferences one 'ascends' to the level of theoretical statements by generalizing empirical observation statements: a social researcher frequently hearing from migratory workers about conflicts with police officers may come to the conclusion that migratory workers in general often have problems with law-enforcement agencies. However, such inductive generalization (taking the general form 'Since the observed objects of the class x have the attribute y, it is reasonable to assume that all x are y') is not theorizing from data. Theories are not merely *summaries*, but *explanations* of data. An inference which links an empirical observation to a theoretical explanation is neither a deduction nor an induction, but a third kind of logical inference described by the pragmatist philosopher Peirce under the name 'hypothesis' or 'abduction' (see also Reichertz, Chapter 9 this volume). In contemporary logic and philosophy of science the terms 'retroduction', 'retroductive inference' or 'inference to the best explanation' (Hanson, 1965; Lipton, 2004) are equally in use. Such inferences do not start with a theoretical statement as a premise (like a deductive inference), but with an empirical observation, for instance 'A migratory worker reports about trouble with the police.' So far it is similar to an induction. But instead of collecting further observation statements, as in an inductive inference, one draws on a general theoretical proposition which can explain the single observation, for example 'Members of deviant social groups are stigmatized by agencies of social control.' Contrary to an induction, this implies a statement about 'antecedent conditions' which shows that the theoretical explanation is applicable to the investigated case: 'Migratory workers are considered as members of a deviant social group.' A retroductive inference takes the following general form: 'We can explain the empirical phenomenon Y if we accept the theoretical statement "X leads to Y" and assume that X has happened.'

Contrary to deductive inferences in a retroduction the conclusion does not follow with necessity from premises: even if we accept the explanatory theoretical statement, it still begs the question whether a single migratory worker was stigmatized because he was regarded as a member of a deviant group or whether the trouble with the police occurred due to a real misdemeanour. A retroduction does not exclude alternative explanations; it only serves to find possible hypotheses explaining empirical findings – therefore Peirce also used the term 'hypothesis' to account for this kind of inference.

In the works of Peirce one can distinguish between two types of hypothetical inference depending on whether the explanatory theoretical statement is already at hand or not. If a researcher explains a phenomenon by subsuming it under already known theoretical concepts, Peirce has (especially in his later writings) used the term *induction by characters* or *qualitative induction*. In this way social researchers may identify certain events as instances of deviant behaviour, of stigmatization through institutions of social control, and so forth.

However, if a surprising event cannot be explained by previous theoretical knowledge, a second form of hypothetical reasoning comes into play called *abduction*:

> The surprising fact, C is observed.
> But if A were true, C would be a matter of course.
> Hence there is a reason to suspect that A is true.
> (Peirce, 1974: 5.189)

Abductions lead to possible explanations for surprising facts by generating new rules. Confronted with the event, 'we turn over our recollection of observed facts; we endeavor so to rearrange them, to view them in such new perspective that the unexpected experience shall no longer appear surprising' (Peirce, 1974: 7.36).

Although this is certainly a creative act which sometimes 'comes to us like a flash' (Peirce, 1974: 1903 5.182), the researcher's creativity is limited: abductions must lead to an explanation of the phenomenon and have to be related to previous knowledge – 'the different elements of the hypothesis were in our minds before' (Peirce, 1974: 1903, 5.181): new experiences are connected to previous knowledge so that (often long-standing, well-accepted) elements of that knowledge have to be abandoned and modified, so that they become consistent with the surprising observation.

Previous theoretical knowledge is needed in both types of hypothetical inference: it is either merely applied (through a qualitative induction) to a phenomenon or modified and transformed (through an abductive inference).

Dimensions and Types of Theoretical Knowledge

Such a use of previous theoretical knowledge is quite different from a strategy where definite hypotheses are deduced from general theories and tested. However, it also requires different types of theoretical propositions. To understand the function of theory in qualitative analysis, it is important to differentiate between four dimensions of theoretical knowledge: its *scope*, *source*, *degree of explicitness* and *empirical content*.

Scope

Sociological theories may relate to all social phenomena regardless of time and space, or they can refer to specific social events in a geographically and/or historically limited domain or to a limited class of social phenomena. The latter kind of theory often refers to a certain society, culture or a specific social group. The first type of theory, sometimes also called *grand theory*, can be found, for instance, in the works of classical sociologists like Durkheim, Parsons or Mead, or, to refer to current developments, in the *oeuvres* of Habermas, Luhmann, Coleman or Giddens, among others. Grand theory makes universal claims which should be applicable to all societies at all times in history. Durkheim's types of 'social integration' or Cooley's and Mead's concept of the 'self' can serve as good examples of that. In contrast, many theories in the social sciences are 'middle-range theories', lying 'between the minor but necessary working hypotheses that evolve in abundance during day-to-day research and the all-inclusive systematic efforts to develop a unified theory' (Merton, 1968: 39). Examples of middle-range theories are Weber's thesis about the relation between the Protestant ethic and capitalism (which refers to a certain period in European history) or Glaser and Strauss's model about interactions between patients, their relatives and hospital staff. Middle-range theories do not claim to explain social phenomena (e.g. the relation between economic success and religiosity or the interaction between patients and care workers) under all circumstances and in all societies, but can often be sensibly transferred to other domains – Weber's thesis could, for instance, be used to understand current Protestant movements in South America (Berger, 2010).

Source

Theories are not developed and used by academics alone. Actors in the research field normally utilize their own categories and hypotheses to understand and explain events in their life worlds. Such lay theories, which help to solve everyday problems, may contain highly speculative and abstract elements. Usually they form an amalgam of concepts from various sources – local and common-sense knowledge, passed orally within a particular culture, information coming from the media, ideas stemming from political and religious contexts, as well as scientific terms. Such knowledge is often highly relevant for the understanding of specific life worlds since it guides the perceptions, interpretations and actions of their members. If, for example, one investigates interactions between nurses and care home residents with dementia, one may find that the behaviour of care workers towards residents showing difficult behaviour is dependent on the care workers' theories about dementia. Such theories usually make up a more or less coherent blend of knowledge obtained through formal training, through the observation of fellow workers and through routines developed in processes of trial and error.

Degree of Explicitness

Some parts of the members' knowledge can be explicated by the respondents, other parts (especially those gained through practical experience) have to be reconstructed by observing or asking the members about their daily action and interaction routines. Similarly, social researchers usually can explicate only parts of their theoretical knowledge acquired during professional training. When sociologists make hypothetical inferences that certain events belong to certain general categories of social phenomena, they often have to draw on implicit knowledge. Usually such a spontaneous insight and its theoretical background can only be explicated afterwards.

Empirical Content

Theoretical terms and statements may have high or low empirical content. For HD research one would need precisely formulated propositions with high empirical content (or 'high falsifiability'). This may become clearer if one looks at statements like 'Young adults from a middle-class background (defined in terms of income and educational status of their parents) have better chances of attending university than young people from a working-class background.' Such a statement is empirically contentful to the extent that its different elements can be operationalized (for instance, by defining 'young adults' as 'men and women aged between 18 years and 25 years', by specifying 'educational status' by 'level of school leaving exam', and so on).

Theoretical definitions and categories from 'grand theories' – categories like 'identity', 'status', 'roles', 'systems', 'structure', and the like – usually lack empirical content: their broadness and abstractness make it difficult, if not impossible, directly to deduce empirically 'testable' propositions. As an example one could take the statement 'A social role defines the expected behaviour connected to a given social status.' An empirical test disproving this sentence is hard to imagine – a person who tries to find a counterexample (that means a social role not defining behaviour connected to a certain status) would even demonstrate thereby that they do not understand the meaning of this statement, which is not meant for being directly tested through empirical data but defines a particular category ('social role'). Each theory entails or at least refers to categories and assumptions of that kind, of which the most important represent the basic axioms (also called 'paradigmatic' assumptions) of theoretical traditions. However, to derive empirical statements from such basic categories or assumptions, 'bridge hypotheses' (Lindenberg, 1992; Kelle and Lüdemann,

1998) have to be added. Such bridge assumptions, which close the gap between abstract notions and empirical observations, normally refer to limited domains: taking our example ('social role'), bridge assumptions could, for instance, describe concrete expectations regarding a certain role in a specific organization.

TYPES OF THEORIZING FROM DATA

Theorizing from qualitative data means the understanding and explanation of phenomena through (qualitative inductive or abductive) hypothetical inferences. Thereby researchers must draw implicitly or explicitly on previous theoretical knowledge which may be derived either from grand theories (about universal social processes or structures) or from middle-range theories (about social phenomena in a limited domain). In the process of theorizing, the researchers' previous theoretical knowledge (containing concepts with limited empirical content) is integrated with members' knowledge ('lay theories') in order to construct empirically contentful categories and statements about the investigated domain.

Depending on the kind of theoretical knowledge used one can distinguish the following types of theorizing:

1. Using general theoretical concepts to develop grounded middle-range theories.
2. Using qualitative data to challenge theoretical concepts.
3. Transferring middle-range concepts to new research domains

Using General Theoretical Concepts to Develop Grounded Middle-Range Theories

Abstract concepts applicable to a broad range of social phenomena usually lack empirical content; this means that empirically testable statements cannot be directly deduced from such concepts without the help of bridge assumptions. However, if the goal is not hypothesis testing but empirically grounded hypothesis generation, a lack of empirical content is rather a strength than a weakness. A loss of empirical content may lead to a gain of flexibility so that such concepts can refer to many different phenomena and may serve as 'lenses' through which sociologically relevant data can be identified, or as heuristic concepts 'sensitizing' researchers for social phenomena. 'Sensitizing concepts' often necessarily 'lack precise reference and have no bench marks which allow a clean cut identification of a specific instance' (Blumer, 1954: 7). Take a category like 'social roles' as an example: the assertion that people in the field act in accordance with role expectations is not very informative by itself. The category is nevertheless sensitizing, since it helps to develop research questions: Are role expectations important for the research field? If so, which types of role expectations are prevalent? How do actors try to fulfil them? Do certain actors develop strategies to avoid fulfilment of the typical role expectations?

Even social researchers who merely wish to describe the investigated life world often refer incidentally to general concepts. Anderson, in his study of homeless men, for instance, commented on conflicts between different groups of 'hobos' in the following way: 'These antagonisms are evidence of a struggle of status. When a peddler denounces the beggars he is trying to justify himself' (1975 [1923]: 50).

Glaser and Strauss's (1965) study *Awareness of Dying* provides good examples of how general concepts can be used to develop middle-range categories from the data. In the resulting theory basic premises of symbolic interactionism described in an earlier book by Strauss, *Mirrors and Masks* (1959), can easily be identified: according to Strauss, interaction is a process in which actors mutually interpret their (assumed) expectations and at the same time may try to conceal these assumptions. This was obviously the 'paradigm for the study of awareness contexts (which) ... guided the preliminary data collection' (Glaser and Strauss, 1965: 287), since the research focused on the actors' mutual expectations and assumptions regarding their knowledge and their conjectures about a patient's impending death. Thus the resulting typology of 'awareness contexts' related to a theoretical paradigm as well as to the empirical data collected in the field.

Categories guiding such theorizing can remain implicit until a researcher comes across the concept best suited for the data through a hypothetical inference (which may be experienced as a sudden insight). This comes close to Glaserian 'theoretical coding', which is an ideal approach for an experienced researcher with an extended theoretical background knowledge. Others may prefer to explicate sensitizing categories before or during qualitative data analysis to form a definite paradigm. Thereby one is not restricted to the Straussian 'coding paradigm' – paradigms can be constructed and utilized according to theoretical pluralism (Thornberg, 2012: 250). For this purpose concepts coming from different traditions in social theory must be scrutinized to clarify their dimensions and elements. Once more we may take 'social role' as an example: roles denote the *expectancies* which are connected to a *social status* (which is a position in a *social hierarchy*) and which are enforced by *sanctions* and *gratifications*. These terms (or subcategories), put together, represent a fully fledged coding paradigm. Applying it means paying attention to incidents in the data which relate to social hierarchies and different positions in it as well as to the status connected to these positions. Which expectations do people in the field express regarding the behaviour of persons with a certain status? How are actors punished who fail to meet these expectations and how are those gratified who fulfil them?

Using Qualitative Data to Challenge Theoretical Concepts

Using theoretical statements and categories with limited empirical content is one important safeguard against the 'forcing' of theory on data, since such statements and categories may refer to a broad range of empirical phenomena. But how do we know whether a theoretical concept is broad enough to really capture phenomena in the field? Maybe it still has enough empirical content to exclude important incidents from consideration? This problem can only be addressed by carefully looking for data which do not fit into the categories of the initial theoretical framework. Such data can then serve as a challenge for the initial theory and lead to its adaptation and modification.

The following example may illustrate this. In an interview (see Roulston, Chapter 20, this volume) study, action strategies of people caring for a frail relative at home were investigated (Lüdecke, 2007). For a secondary analysis these data were analysed with an explicit coding paradigm based on decision theory (Coleman, 1990) focusing on the actors' decisions to take care of their spouses, parents or other relatives. These decisions were analysed with regard to the constraints and options of the situation, the actors' goals and intentions, and the consequences of the decisions in terms of their costs and benefits. However, the interview material soon demonstrated the limits of the underlying model of purposeful action: interview partners responded in a perplexed manner when asked about the reasons for their decision to look after their parent in need:

Interviewer:	Hm. Eh, you mentioned a while ago, it went without saying for you to take your mother to your house.
Interviewee:	Yes
Interviewer:	Can you explain that?
Interviewee:	Why?
Interviewer:	Why?

Interviewee: Yes, why. That's the way things were. My father ... he died aged 45. And my mother was in the same age. I was 18. My brother was 16. He was an apprentice. ... We had a small farm. ... We had two cows. And my mother was alone.

In this example (as well as in others we found in the data) no process of deliberate decision took place where costs and benefits of alternative options (to care or not to care for the ailing mother) were weighed against each other. Thus the (partly implicit) assumption underlying the selection of our initial theoretical frame (caregiving at home can principally be regarded as a process of choice) was heavily challenged and it became doubtful to what extent decision theory can account for the investigated social processes.

Heuristic theoretical frameworks pose further problems: sensitizing concepts which seemingly capture various different phenomena may still exclude alternative fruitful theoretical perspectives. This refers, for instance, to the Straussian coding paradigm, which represents an understanding of human action applicable to a wide array of social phenomena, and still may draw researchers towards a micro-sociological orientation they do not necessarily share. The paradigm one uses has to be consistent with one's theoretical orientations and simultaneously capable of covering relevant phenomena in the field. Even the advice to use only abstract categories with low empirical content may constrict and confuse inexperienced researchers, since not every theoretical concept can draw attention to relevant phenomena.

Transferring Middle-Range Concepts to New Research Domains

Often middle-range concepts for the description and explanation of behaviour in a limited domain are transferable to other fields. The category 'emotional labour', for instance, developed by Arlie Hochschild in her study about flight attendants (Hochschild, 1983), has been repeatedly and successfully transferred to the field of nursing, for example to the interactions between community nurses and patients in palliative care (Luker et al., 2000: 778). 'Emotional labour' clearly contains more empirical content than the terms 'role' or 'identity': emotional labour is not needed in every interaction and the assumption that certain professionals are providing emotional labour is thus a falsifiable statement. Often categories developed for a domain obviously remote to one's own field may prove rather fruitful on a second look. In her study about interactions between care home residents with dementia and care workers, Andrea Newerla (2012) employed the notion 'governmentality', a term coined by Foucault to describe organized practices that authorities in the rising modern states had invented to govern their subjects (Foucault, 1991). Newerla relates this term to the strategies that care workers use in daily routines to smoothly guide, control (and sometimes manipulate) residents with dementia and to avoid open conflicts thereby (Newerla, 2012). The category helps to develop a typology of action strategies employed by care workers to deal with residents under difficult working conditions.

Previous theoretical knowledge need not be restricted to abstract concepts from grand theories; it may also become sensible to use well-defined and empirically testable categories in theorizing from qualitative data. But regardless of whether researchers apply general theoretical categories with a large scope as sensitizing concepts, or whether they use categories with limited range and high empirical content, the purpose always is the construction of empirically contentful statements about the investigated domain. As the empirical content of the developing categories and theories increases, strategies of theory generation have to be supplemented by methods for provisional testing, including the systematic computer-assisted coding of the available data (Kelle,

1997) as well as the search for 'crucial cases' which may provide counter-evidence (sometimes also called 'Analytic Induction' – see above in this chapter, or Manning, 1991).

FURTHER READING

Corbin, Juliet and Strauss, Anselm (2008) *Basics of Qualitative Research: Techniques and Procedures for Developing Grounded Theory*, 3rd edition. Thousand Oaks, CA: Sage.
Hanson, Norwood Russell (1965) *Patterns of Discovery: An Inquiry into the Conceptual Foundations of Science*. Cambridge: Cambridge University Press.
Swedberg, Richard (2012) 'Theorizing in sociology and social science: Turning to the context of discovery', *Theory and Society*, 41 (1):1 –40.

REFERENCES

Anderson, Nels (1975 [1923]) *The Hobo: The Sociology of the Homeless Man*. Chicago: University of Chicago Press.
Bain, Read (1929) 'The validity of life histories and diaries', *Journal of Educational Sociology*, 3: 150–64.
Berger, Peter (2010) 'Max Weber is alive and well, and living in Guatemala: The protestant ethic today', *The Review of Faith & International Affairs*, 8 (4): 3–9.
Blumer, Herbert (1954) 'What is wrong with Social Theory?', *American Sociological Review*: 3–10.
Bulmer, Martin (1984) *The Chicago School of Sociology: Institutionalization, Diversity, and the Rise of Sociological Research*. Chicago: University of Chicago Press.
Chalmers, Alan F. (1999) *What Is This Thing Called Science?* Maidenhead: Open University Press.
Charmaz, Kathy (2006) *Constructing Grounded Theory: A Practical Guide through Qualitative Analysis*. London: Sage.
Coleman, James (1990) *Foundations of Social Theory*. Cambridge, MA: Belknap.
Corbin, Juliet (1991) 'Anselm Strauss: An intellectual biography', in David R. Maines (ed.), *Social Organization and Social Process: Essays in Honour of Anselm Strauss*. New York: Aldine de Gruyter. pp. 17–44.
Corbin, Juliet and Strauss, Anselm (2008) *Basics of Qualitative Research: Techniques and Procedures for Developing Grounded Theory*, 3rd edition. Thousand Oaks, CA: Sage.

Cressey, Donald R. (1971 [1953]) *Other People's Money: A Study in the Social Psychology of Embezzlement*. Belmont, CA: Wadsworth.
Deegan, Mary J. (2001) 'The Chicago school of ethnography', in Paul Atkinson et al. (eds), *Handbook of Ethnography*. London: Sage. pp. 11–25.
Foucault, Michel (1991) 'Governmentality', in Graham Burchell et al. (eds), *The Foucault Effect: Studies in Governmentality*. Chicago: University of Chicago Press. pp. 87–104.
Glaser, Barney (1978) *Theoretical Sensitivity: Advances in the Methodology of Grounded Theory*. Mill Valley, CA: Sociology Press.
Glaser, Barney (1992) *Emergence vs. Forcing: Basics of Grounded Theory Analysis*. Mill Valley, CA: Sociology Press.
Glaser, Barney and Strauss, Anselm (1965) *Awareness of Dying*. Chicago: Aldine.
Glaser, Barney and Strauss, Anselm (1967) *The Discovery of Grounded Theory: Strategies for Qualitative Research*. Chicago: Aldine.
Hanson, Norwood R. (1965) *Patterns of Discovery: An Inquiry into the Conceptual Foundations of Science*. Cambridge: Cambridge University Press.
Hempel, Carl G. (1952) *Fundamentals of Concept Formation in Empirical Science*. Chicago: University of Chicago Press.
Hochschild, Arlie (1983) *The Managed Heart: Commercialization of Human Feeling*. Berkeley: University of California Press.
Kelle, Udo (1997) 'Theory building in qualitative research and computer programs for the management of textual data', in *Sociological Research Online*, 2 (2): http://www.socresonline.org.uk/2/2/1/ (accessed 06-17-2013).
Kelle, Udo (2007) 'The development of categories – different approaches in grounded theory', in Antony Bryant and Kathy Charmaz (eds), *The SAGE Handbook of Grounded Theory*. London: Sage. pp. 191–213.
Kelle, Udo and Lüdemann, Christian (1998) 'Bridge assumptions in rational choice theory: Methodological problems and possible solutions', in Hans-Peter Blossfeld and Gerald Prein (eds), *Rational Choice Theory and Large-Scale Data Analysis*. Boulder, CO: Westview Press. pp. 112–25.
Lakatos, Imre (1978) *The Methodology of Scientific Research Programmes*. Cambridge: Cambridge University Press.
Laudan, Larry (1977) *Progress and its Problems: Towards a Theory of Scientific Growth*. London: Routledge & Kegan Paul.
Lindenberg, Siegwart (1992) 'The method of decreasing abstraction', in James S. Coleman and

Thomas J. Fararo (eds), *Rational Choice Theory: Advocacy and Critique*. Newbury Park, CA: Sage. pp. 3–20.

Lindesmith, Alfred R. (1968 [1947]) *Addiction and Opiates*. Chicago: Aldine.

Lipton, Peter (2004) *Inference to the Best Explanation*. London: Routledge.

Lüdecke, Daniel (2007) *Häusliche Pflegearrangements. Eine qualitative Studie protektiver und destabilisierender Faktoren*. Saarbrücken: VDM.

Luker, Karen A., Austin, Lynn, Caress, Ann and Hallett, Christine (2000) 'The importance of "knowing the patient": Community nurses' constructions of quality in providing palliative care', *Journal of Advanced Nursing*, 31 (4): 775–82.

Lundberg, George A. (1929) *Social Research: A Study in Methods of Gathering Data*. New York: Longmans, Green.

Manning, Peter (1991) 'Analytic induction', in Ken Plummer (ed.), *Symbolic Interactionism. Vol. 2: Contemporary Issues*. Brookfield, VT: Edward Elgar. pp. 401–30.

Merton, Robert (1968) *Social Theory and Social Structure*. New York: Free Press.

Newerla, Andrea (2012) 'Über das Regieren der Demenz. Wie sozialpolitische Rahmenbedingungen Handlungsstrategien professioneller Pflegekräfte in der Pflegepraxis von Menschen mit Demenz beeinflussen', PhD thesis, University of Marburg.

Peirce, Charles S. (1974) *Collected Papers*, ed. C. Hartshore et al. Cambridge, MA: The Belknap Press of Harvard University Press.

Quine, Willard van Orman (1951) 'Main trends in recent philosophy: Two dogmas of empiricism', *Philosophical Review*, 60: 20–43.

Robinson, William S. (1952) 'Rejoinder to comments on "The Logical Structure of Analytic Induction"', *American Sociological Review*, 17: 494.

Shaw, Clifford (1966 [1930]) *The Jack-roller: A Delinquent Boy's Own Story*. Chicago: University of Chicago Press.

Simmons, Odis E. (2011) 'Why classic Grounded Theory?', in Vivian B. Martin and Astrid Gynnild (eds), *Grounded Theory: The Philosophy, Method and Work of Barney Glaser*. Boca Raton, FL: Brown Walker. pp. 15–30.

Strauss, Anselm L. (1959) *Mirrors and Masks: The Search for Identity*. Glencoe, IL: Free Press.

Strauss, Anselm L. (1987) *Qualitative Analysis for Social Scientists*. Cambridge: Cambridge University Press.

Strauss, Anselm L. (1990) *Creating Sociological Awareness*. New Brunswick, NJ: Transaction.

Strauss, Anselm L. and Corbin, Juliet (1990) *Basics of Qualitative Research: Grounded Theory Procedures and Techniques*. Newbury Park, CA: Sage.

Thomas, William I. and Thomas, Dorothy S. (1928) *The Child in America: Behavior Problems and Programs*. New York: Knopf.

Thomas, William I. and Znaniecki, Florian (1958 [1918]) *The Polish Peasant in Europe and America*. New York: Dover.

Thornberg, Robert (2012) 'Informed grounded theory', *Scandinavian Journal of Educational Research*, 56 (3): 243–59.

Thrasher, Frederic M. (1973 [1927]) *The Gang: A Study of 1,313 Gangs in Chicago*. Chicago: University of Chicago Press.

Znaniecki, Florian (1934) *The Method of Sociology*. New York: Rinehart.

Writing and/as Analysis or Performing the World[1]

Norman K. Denzin

Once upon a time, the Lone Ethnographer rode off into

the subset in search of his 'native.' After undergoing a

series of trials, he encountered the object of his quest in

a distant land. There he underwent his rite of passage by

enduring the ultimate ordeal of 'fieldwork.' After collecting

'the data,' the Lone Ethnographer returned home and wrote a 'true' account of 'the culture.' (Rosaldo, 1989: 30)

I have been working to change the way I speak and write. (Hooks, 1990: 146)

Writing is not an innocent practice, it is a form of pedagogy, a way of making the world visible. Writing is simultaneously a method of discovery, a method of interpretation, and a method of analysis (Richardson and Lockridge, 2004: 1). In the interpretive social sciences there is only interpretation[2] (see Willig, Chapter 10, this volume). Nothing speaks for itself. Confronted with a mountain of impressions, documents, and field notes the qualitative researcher faces the difficult and challenging task of making sense of what has been learned. I call making sense of what has been learned the art of interpretation. This is also described as moving from the field, to the text, to the reader. The practice of this art allows the fieldworker-as-bricoleur (Levi-Strauss, 1962/1966: 17) to translate what has been learned into a body of textual work that represents these understandings to the reader.

These texts, borrowing from Van Maanen (2011), constitute tales from the field. They are performances; that is, they are stories we perform for one another (Diversi and Moreira, 2009; Wyatt et al., 2011). Performance-as-interpretation requires the telling of a story, or a narrative which states 'Things happen this way because,' or, 'This happened, after this happened, because this happened first' (Madison, 2012: 37). Interpreters as storytellers tell narrative tales with beginnings, middles, and ends (see Esin et al., Chapter 14, this volume). These tales always embody implicit and explicit theories of causality, where narrative or textual causality is presumed to map the actual goings on in the real world (Ricoeur, 1985: 4). How this complex art of interpretation, performance, and storytelling is practiced is the topic of this chapter.

The history of qualitative research in the social sciences reveals continual attempts to wrestle with this process and its methods (Flick, 2007; 2009; 2011; Wertz et al., 2011; Saldana, 2009; Saldana and Leavy, 2011). Today we have moved from writing thick descriptions of the world, to performances which put the world into motion. We have moved from a paradigm which says the world is a text to be read or analysed, to a paradigm which says the world is a performance. The performance model privileges experiential knowing, participatory epistemologies, intimacy, and involvement as forms of understanding. In this framework context replaces text, verbs replace nouns, structures become processes, analysis becomes interpretation and performance.

In this chapter I will review several of these methods, or traditions, paying special attention to those which have been employed in the most recent past, including the constructivist,[3] grounded theory (see Thornberg and Charmaz, Chapter 11, this volume), feminist, Marxist, cultural studies (see Winter, Chapter 17, this volume), arts-based (see Murray, Chapter 40, this volume), and post-structural perspectives (Wertz et al., 2011; Knowles and Cole, 2008; Finley, 2008; Pelias, 2008). Problems generic to this process will be examined. I will briefly allude to my own perspective called interpretive interactionism (Denzin, 2001), and conclude with predictions concerning where the art and politics of interpretation will be 10 years from now.

RIGHT AND LEFT POLE METHODOLOGIES

Eisenhart and Jurow (2011) reinforce the argument that the literature on doing (and teaching) qualitative analysis research continues to reflect 1980 paradigm disputes; namely, the battles between quantitative (positivist) and qualitative (non-positivist) researchers. They see two pedagogical camps, or two poles on a continuum, a right pole and a left pole. On the right pole are the traditionalists who view methods as objective tools. Traditionalists focus their teaching and interpretive activities on questions of design, technique, and analysis. This is **qi** in small letters (Eisenhart and Jurow, 2011).

As expected, the experimentalists are on the left pole; this is **QI** in big letters! Those on the left pole take a more 'avant-garde' activist view of method, analysis, and pedagogy. They adopt a subjective, interpretive approach to inquiry. They concentrate on method as praxis, or methods as tools for social action. Performance ethnographers, action researchers, and community organizers are all in the left pole group. They want to change the world by creating texts that move persons to action. They want texts that move from personal troubles to public institutions. They want to teach students how to do this.

There is a third pole: this is the space of social justice. Right and left pole methodologists can be united around social change issues. Traditional methodologists like left pole activists can teach students how to do ground-level social justice inquiry. This is inquiry that is indigenous, collaborative, and community based.

TEACHING TO THE LEFT POLE FOR BRICOLEURS

Eisenhart and Jurow (2011) observe that teaching to the left pole involves more than technique. It centers on postmodern epistemological, philosophical principles, including the politics of knowing, as well as issues surrounding objectivity (see Barbour, Chapter 34, this volume), performance, reflexivity (see May and Perry, Chapter 8, this volume), writing and the first-person voice, complicity with the other, ethics, values, and truth. In order to travel to the place of the experimental text, students obviously need instruction in a large literature that has traditionally not been regarded as central to methodology. This is qualitative research that is messy, performative, poetic, political, and reflexive.

There are three attitudes to be enacted, or goals to be pursued. First, teaching qualitative analysis skills is understood as critical pedagogy, as the practice of making the political and the ideological visible through the act of performance itself (Conquergood, 1998; Madison, 2012: 220). Second, teaching and qualitative analysis are performative acts. They are invitations for students to use their own experiences as vehicles for pushing push back against structures of racial, sexual, and class oppression, invitations to become agents in their own interpretive biographies.

Third, in order to realize the first two goals, students learn to write about and interpret their own lives; they become autoethnographers, authors of dramas about their own lives. This performance format presumes that all students can be taught to write performance texts, to think 'dramatistically' about their lives (Saldana, 2009: 33).

At the same time students on the left pole need instruction on the very topics that Hurworth (2007), or Preissle and Roulston (2009), discuss; that is, the right pole methodologies. Critical scholars need to, at some point in their careers, be deeply immersed in the methodological classics of their discipline. They need to know how to interview (see Roulston, Chapter 20, this volume), do fieldwork, work in archives, do participant observation (see Marvasti, Chapter 24, this volume), write autoethnography, do case studies, engage the various forms of PAR (see Murray, Chapter 40, this volume), do focus groups (see Barbour, Chapter 21, this volume), and do and write grounded theory (see Thornberg and Charmaz, Chapter 11, this volume), including constructing coding schemes, and doing theoretical saturation. As bricoleurs they need all of these methodologies and skills in their social action toolkit.

FROM FIELD, TO TEXT, TO READER

Moving from the field, to the text,[4] to performance, to the reader is a complex, reflexive process. The researcher creates a field text consisting of field notes and documents from the field. From this text is created a research text, notes, and interpretations based on the field text, what Plath (1990) calls field notes. The research text is then recreated as a working interpretive document. This working document contains the writer's initial attempts to make sense out of what has been learned, what Clandinin and Connelly (1994) term 'experiencing experience.' The writer next produces a quasi-public text, one that is shared with colleagues, whose comments and suggestions are sought. This statement is then transformed into a public document, which embodies the writers' self-understandings which are now inscribed in the experiences of those studied.[5] This statement, in turn, furnishes the context for the understandings that the reader brings to the experiences being described by the writer. Reading and writing, then, are central to interpretation, for as Geertz (1973: 18) argues, interpretation involves the construction of a reading of an event, by both the writer and the reader. Paraphrasing Geertz (1973: 18), 'A good interpretation takes us into the center of the experiences being described.'

Interpretation (see Willig, Chapter 10, this volume), like performance, is an art; it is not formulaic, or mechanical.[6] It can only be learned, like any form of storytelling, through doing. Indeed, as Laurel Richardson (1994) argues, writing is interpretation, or storytelling. Fieldworkers can neither make sense of nor understand what has been learned until they sit down and write the interpretive text, telling the story first to themselves and then to their significant others, and then to the public.

A situated, writing self structures this interaction that takes place between the writer, the text, and the reader. The writer-as-performer presents a particular and unique self in the text, a self that claims to have some authority over the subject matter that is being interpreted.

The writer-as-performer moves from textual ethnography to performative ethnography (Conquergood, 1998: 26; see Gubrium and Holstein, Chapter 3, this volume). This performance text can take several forms: a dramatic text, such as a poem or play; an ethnodrama in the form of a monologue or dialogue (Saldana, 2011); a performance autoethnography, or mystory (Spry, 2011); a collaborative, writing co-performance (Diversi and Moreia, 2009; Wyatt et al., 2011); an ethnography that uses historical texts and the voices from the past to tell its stories.

This version of the performance text is built around series of quotations, documents, and excerpts placed side by side (see Denzin, 2011). This format produces a de-centered narrative, a multi-voiced text with voices and speakers talking back and forth. This format allows the cracks and contradictions in history to be exposed.

INTERPRETATION AS STORYTELLING

The storytelling self that is presented is always one attached to an interpretive perspective, an 'espoused theory that gives the writer a public persona. Four major paradigms (positivist and post-positivist, constructivist, critical), and at least seven major perspectives (feminist, ethnic, indigenous, queer, border, post-colonial, post-human models) now structure qualitative writing (Lincoln et al., 2011: 106). The stories qualitative researchers tell one another come from one or another of these paradigms and perspectives.

These paradigms and perspectives serve several functions for the writer. They are masks which are hidden behind, put on, and taken off as writers write their particular storied and self-versions of a feminist, gay–lesbian, Afro-American, Hispanic, Marxist, constructionist, grounded theory (see Thornberg and Charmaz, Chapter 11, this volume), phenomenological (see Eberle, Chapter 13, this volume), or interactionist text. They give the writer a public identity. Each tradition has its own taken-for-granted and problematic writing style. These masks offer scenarios, which lead writers to impose a particular order on the world studied.

For example, if the paradigm is positivist or post-positivist, the writer will present a text which stresses variables, hypotheses, and propositions derived from a particular theory that sees the world in terms of causes and effects (see Lincoln et al., 2011).

WRITING ISSUES: SENSE-MAKING, REPRESENTATION, LEGITIMATION, DESIRE

Any discussion of how the researcher moves from the field to the performance text must address a host of issues or problems closely related to storytelling traditions. These issues group into four areas: sense-making, representation, legitimation, desire. They may be conceptualized as phases, each turning on a different issue, and each turning back on the other, as in Dilthey's (1976 [1900]) hermeneutic circle (see Wernet, Chapter 16, this volume). They interact with each other.

Sense-making

The first issue describes how the writer moves from and through field notes into the actual writing process (into the research and interpretive texts), making decisions about what will be written about, what will be included, and how it will be represented.

For example, Corbin and Strauss (2008) direct investigators to write memos, as well as theoretical, operational, and code notes concerning conceptual labels, paradigm features, emerging theoretical understandings, and visual representations of relationships between concepts and analytic terms (see Thornberg and Charmaz, Chapter 11, this volume). Richardson (2000) discusses other forms of anticipatory interpretive writing, including observation, methodological, theoretical, and personal notes that are kept in an ongoing journal.

Representation

The second area speaks to such topics as voice, audience, the Other, and the author's place in the reflexive texts that are produced. Representation turns on voice, and the use of pronouns, including first-person statements. Collins (1990: 202) describes her use of pronouns: 'I often use the pronoun 'our' instead of 'their' when referring to African-American women, a choice that embeds me in the group I am studying instead of distancing me from it.'

Frequently writers position themselves outside, yet alongside those Others who are written about, never making clear where they stand in these relationships which connect the Other to them. When 'Others' are not allowed to speak they remain 'an absent presence without voice' (hooks, 1990: 126.) There are major problems with this approach to 'Othering' and it has been extensively criticized (Fine, 1994). In such situations it is best to let others do their own talking. However, even when 'we' allow the 'Other' to speak, when we talk about, or for them, we are taking over their voice.

Legitimation

The third problem centers on matters of epistemology, including how a public text legitimates itself, or makes claims for its own authority. Criteria like reliability, validity (see Barbour, Chapter 34, this volume), and generalizablity (see Maxwell and Chmiel, Chapter 37, this volume) ground a text in a positivist epistemology. The postmodern sensibility doubts foundational arguments, which seek to anchor a text's authority in such terms. A more local, personal, and political turn is taken.

Desire

There is still a fourth problem, or phase in this project, given in the subtitle to Howard S. Becker's influential 2007 (orig. 1986) book (*Writing for Social Scientists: How to Start and Finish your Thesis, Book or Article*). This problem circles back on the first, making decisions about what will be written. But it goes deeper and refers to the writing practices that fieldworkers deploy: how one moves from a blank page (or screen) to a written text, one sentence after another, building an emergent, reflexive interpretation of the subject matter at hand. The topic, to borrow Barthes' (1975) phrase, is the pleasure of the text. Or, as Richardson (1994: 517) says, 'Can we create texts that are vital?'

A vital text is not boring. It grips the reader (and the writer). A vital text invites readers to engage the author's subject matter. The postmodern sensibility encourages writers to put themselves into their texts, to engage writing as a creative act of discovery and inquiry (Richardson, 1994: 517–18).

TWO MODELS OF THE WRITER

The foregoing discussion has separated, or isolated, four phases of writing. While analytically useful, this formulation conveys a sometimes heroic, Romantic picture of the writer and the text. It presumes a writer with the guts to tell it like it is, to put him- or herself on the line, so to speak. It presumes a socially situated (and isolated), unique writer who has the courage, and authenticity, to write a bold new text. This writer first experiences, feels, and thinks. Having had the experience, this bold writer then writes, deploying one or more narrative traditions in the story that is told.[7]

This model makes writing an expressive, and not a productive, process. It romanticizes the writer and his or her experiences. It distances experience from its expressions. Sense-making, interpretation, representation, and claims for legitimacy are all part of the same process. They can only be artificially separated.

Interpretation is a productive process, which sets forth the multiple meanings of an event, object, experience, or text. Interpretation is transformative. It illuminates, and throws light on experience. It brings out, and refines, as when butter is clarified, the meanings that can be sifted from a text, an object, or a slice of experience. So conceived, meaning is not in a text, nor does interpretation precede experience, or its representation. Meaning, interpretation, and representation are deeply intertwined in one another.

Raymond Carver, the short-story writer, describes it this way: writing is an 'act of discovery' (Carver, 1989: 25). The writer deals with moments of experience. The writer brings all of his or her powers, 'intelligence and literary skill' (1989: 27) to bear on these moments to show how 'things out there really are and how he [she] sees those things – like no one else sees them' (1989: 27). This is done 'through the use of clear and specific language; language that will bring to life the details that will light up the story for the reader ... the language must be accurately and precisely given' (1989: 27).

Experimental writing, Carver argues, is 'original. ... The real experimenters have to Make It New ... and in the process have to find things out for themselves ... writers want to carry news from their world to ours' (1989: 24). This means that 'absolutely everything is important' (1989: 38), including where the 'commas and periods [go]' (1989: 38). The writer invests experience with meaning, showing how everything has suddenly become clear. What was unclear before has 'just now become clear' (1989: 23). Such understandings emerge in moments of sudden awakening. The writer brings this sense of discovery and awakening to the reader.

Writing, then, relives and reinscribes experience, bringing newly discovered meanings to the reader. No cheap tricks, Carver (1989: 23) says, no gimmicks. Less is more, show, do not tell. Writing must bring news of the world to the reader. In writing the writer creates this world. He or she fills it with real and fictional people. Their problems and their crises are brought to life. Their lives gone out of control are vividly described. Their lives, suddenly illuminated with new meanings and new transformations of self, are depicted.

What is given in the text, what is written, is made up and fashioned out of memory and field notes. Writing of this order, writing which powerfully reinscribes and recreates experience, invests itself with its own power and authority. No one else but this writer could have brought this new corner of the world alive in this way for the reader.

The writer may use the following caveat (Denzin, 2011: 19):

This book is a product of my ethnographic imagination. Names, characters, places, events, and incidents are used fictitiously. Any resemblance to actual events, or locales or persons, living or dead is at least partially coincidental. The dialogue contained herein is intended as a stage play and should not be quoted or considered to be the actual words of the speakers unless contained in Quote marks. The opinions of the speakers are conjecture of the author.

REALISTIC WRITING STYLES

There are several styles of qualitative writing, several different ways of describing, inscribing, and interpreting reality. Each style creates the conditions for its own criticism. Some version of the realist tale, or style, however, predominates. The realist tale attempts to make the subject's world transparent, to bring it alive, to make it visible (Clough, 1992: 132). There are three prevailing realist styles.

Mainstream realist writing presents thick and thin descriptions of the worlds studied, giving accounts of events, persons, and experiences. These texts assume the author can give an objective accounting or portrayal, of the realities of a group or an individual. Such texts often utilize experience–distance concepts, like kinship structure, to explain a group's way of life. Mainstream realism leads to the production of analytic, interpretive texts, which are often single voiced.

Interpretive realism describes those texts where authors insert their personal interpretations into the life situations of the individuals studied. Geertz's (1973) study of the Balinese (which used thick description) frequently privileges Geertz's interpretations. For example, he states: 'In the cockfight, man and beast, good and evil, ego and id ... fuse in a bloody drama of hatred, cruelty, violence and death' (1973: 442). Here experience and its meanings are filtered through the researcher's, not the subject's, eyes.

In *descriptive realism* the writer attempts to stay out of the way and to allow the world being described to speak for itself. Of course this is impossible, for all writing is interpretative. However, the impulse is to tell a multi-voiced story.[8]

AN ANALYSIS OF INTERPRETIVE PRACTICES

A Summary

The art of interpretation produces understandings that are shaped by genre, narrative, stylistic, personal, cultural, and paradigmatic conventions. I turn next to a review of some of the major paradigms and perspectives that now structure qualitative research writing practices: positivist and post-positivist, constructivist, critical (Marxist, emancipatory), post-structuralist, including ethnic, feminist, and cultural studies and arts-based models. I select an exemplar from each tradition.

Grounded Theory as an Interpretive Style (Post-positivism)

The grounded theory perspective (see Thornberg and Charmaz, Chapter 11, this volume) reflects a naturalistic approach to ethnography and interpretation, stressing naturalistic observations, open-ended interviewing, the sensitizing use of concepts, and a grounded (inductive) approach to theorizing, which can be both formal and substantive (Charmaz, 2011; Bryant and Charmaz, 2010). Strauss and Corbin (1990) outline the criteria for judging a grounded theory study. They preface their discussion thusly: 'The usual canons of "good science" should be retained, but require redefinition in order to fit the realities of qualitative research.' These usual canons of good science (1990: 250) are: significance, theory–observation compatibility, generalizability, consistency, reproducibility, precision, and verification. They argue, for example, that if a similar set of conditions exist, and if the same theoretical perspective and the same rules for data gathering and analysis are followed, two researchers should be able to reproduce the same theoretical explanations of a given phenomenon.

Investigators should be able to provide information on the sample (including theoretical variations), core categories, key events and incidents, hypotheses, and the negative cases that emerged and were pursued during the research process. The empirical grounding of a study (its grounded theory) should be judged by the range, density, linkages between and systematic relatedness of its theoretical concepts, as well as the theory's specificity and generality. They urge that these criteria be followed so that readers can 'judge the credibility of [the] theory' (1990: 258).

The grounded theory perspective is perhaps the most widely used qualitative interpretive framework in the social sciences today.[9] Its appeals are broad, for it provides a set of clearly defined steps any researcher can follow. It answers to a need to attach the qualitative research project to the 'good science' model.

Constructivism as an Interpretive Style

The constructivist program of Lincoln, Guba, and others represents a break with the post-positivist tradition, while retaining (at one level) a commitment to the grounded theory approach of Strauss and associates.[10] A good constructionist interpretation (text) is based on purposive (theoretical) sampling (see Rapley, Chapter 4, this volume), a grounded theory, inductive data analysis (see Reichertz, Chapter 9, this volume), and idiographic (contextual) interpretations. The foundations for interpretations rest on triangulated empirical materials which are trustworthy.

Trustworthiness consists of four components: credibility, transferability, dependability, and confirmability. (These are the constructionist equivalents of internal and external validity, reliability, and objectivity (Lincoln and Guba, 1985: 300).)[11]

Trustworthy materials are subjected to the constant comparative method of analysis that grounded theory deploys, that is, comparing incidents applicable to categories, integrating categories and their properties, delimiting and writing the theory. These materials are then developed into a case report which is again subjected to a comprehensive member check, and an external audit. This done, the study is ready for public release (Lincoln and Guba, 1985: 381).

These constructionist interpretive strategies address many of the perceived problems in grounded theory, including the theory and value-laden nature of facts, ambiguities in incidence, and category analysis. The paradigm, while disavowing the ontology, epistemology, and methodologies of post-positivism (Guba, 1990a: 27; 1990b), sustains, at one level, Strauss's and Corbin's commitments to the canons of good science. Hence the enormous commitment to methods and procedures that will increase a text's credibility, transferability, dependability, and confirmability.

Critical Theory as an Interpretive Style

There are multiple critical theory and participatory action frameworks (see Cannella and Lincoln, 2011). All share a critical, realist ontology, a subjectivist epistemology, and a dialogic, transformative, ethnographic methodology (Guba, 1990a: 25).

There are two distinct traditions with the cultural studies, critical theory model (see Winter, Chapter 17, this volume). One school, following Freire (1982: 30), regards concrete reality, dialectically conceived, as the starting point for analysis which examines how people live their facts of life into existence. The other school reads social texts (popular literature, cinema, popular music) as empirical materials which articulate complex arguments about race, class, and gender in contemporary life. Some scholars merge the ethnographic and textual approaches, examining how cultural interpretations are acted on and given meaning in concrete local cultural communities. Such work moves back and forth between concrete ethnographic texts and the content, semiotic, and narrative analysis of systems of discourse, for example, a particular television show, or a film.

Critical inquiry is theory driven by neo- or post-Marxist and cultural studies models of the race, classed and gendered structures of contemporary societies. An emancipatory principle drives such research, which is committed to engaging oppressed groups in collective, democratic theorizing about their experiences of oppression. A constant focus is given to the material and cultural practices that create structures of oppression.

A critical text is judged by its ability to reflexively reveal these structures of oppression as they operate in the worlds of lived experience. A critical text thus creates a space for multiple voices to speak; those who are oppressed are asked to articulate their definitions of their situations. For some, critical theory must be testable, falsifiable, dialogical, and collaborative (Carspecken and Apple, 1992: 547–8). Others reject the more positivist features of this formulation. Smith (1992: 96), for example, evaluates a text by its ability to reveal the invisible structures of oppression in women's worlds.

Thus a good critical, emancipatory text is one which is multi-vocal, collaborative, naturalistically grounded in the worlds of lived experience, and organized by a critical, interpretive theory. These approaches, with their action criteria, politicize qualitative research. They foreground praxis, yet leave unclear the methodological side of the interpretive process that is so central to the grounded theory, and constructionist approaches.

Post-structural Interpretive Styles

I will discuss four post-structural interpretive styles: those connected to the standpoint and cultural studies perspectives (Olesen 2011; Lather, 2007), those articulated by women of color (Collins, 1990; 2000; hook, 1990), and my own approach, interpretive interactionism. Each of these perspectives is intimately connected to the critical and empancipatory styles of interpretation. Women of color first.

Style I: Women of Color

Collins (1990: 206–19; 2000: 257–71) offers four criteria of interpretation, which are contrasted to the positivist approaches to research. Derived from an Afrocentric standpoint, her criteria focus on the primacy of concrete lived experience, the use of dialogue in assessing knowledge claims, the ethic of caring, and the ethic of personal accountability.

Experience as a criterion of meaning directs attention to Black sisterhood, to the stories, narratives, and Bible principles embodied in Black church and community life. Concrete, Black feminine wisdom is contrasted to knowledge without wisdom, 'A heap see, but a few know' (Collins, 1990: 208; 1998; 2000). Wisdom is experiential, cultural, and shared in the Black feminine community. Dialogue, bell hooks argues, is humanizing speech. Black feminists assess knowledge claims through discourse, storytelling, connected dialogue in a group context. This emphasis on dialogue is directly translated into the Black feminist text. Zora Neale Hurston, for example, located herself inside the folktales she collected, and carried on extensive dialogues with them, thus creating a multi-vocal text (Collins, 1990: 214).

Dialogue extends to the ethic of caring, which suggests that 'personal expressiveness, emotions and empathy are central to the knowledge validation process' (Collins, 1990: 215). This ethic values individual uniqueness, the expression of emotionality in the text, and seeks writers who can create emotional texts which others can enter into. The ethic of personal accountability makes individuals accountable for their values and the political consequences of their actions.

These four criteria embody a 'self-defined Black women's standpoint using an Afrocentric epistemology' (Collins, 1991: 219–200; 27–271). They call into question much of what now passes for truth in methodological discourse. They articulate a set of criteria that stands in vivid contrast to those criteria contained in the grounded theory, constructionist, critical, and emancipatory traditions.

Style II: Post-structural Feminist Interpretive Styles

Olesen (2011) suggest that four interpretive themes structure qualitative feminist research: an emphasis on researcher and textual reflexivity, intersectionality, an action and praxis orientation, a troubling of traditional concepts like data and method, an attention to voice, difference, the affective, emotional components of research, and the ethics of inquiry.

Lather (1991; 2007), Olesen (2011), and others question the very nature of qualitative research, contending that traditional empirical research is embedded in regimes of power, that is, inquiry reproduces these structures. They do not seek a method, but look instead for strategies that question taken-for-granted terms like data, analysis, and interpretation. They deconstruct standard terms, including validity, reflexivity, voice, and science (St. Pierre, 2011).

Feminist research challenges narrative realism, and the traditional naturalistic ethnography, because there is now an 'uncertainty about what constitutes an adequate depiction of reality' (Lather, 1991: 91). Lather argues that the age of description has ended. We are, as we have always been, in the moment of inscription, the spaces of performance wherein writers create their own situated versions of the worlds studied. Accordingly the social text becomes a stage, or a site where power and knowledge are presented.

This means that we must explore alternative ways of presenting and authorizing our texts. Lather then turns (1993; 2007) to a discussion of five new forms of validity, different ways of authorizing a text. These new forms are called reflexive, ironic, neo-pragmatic, rhizomatic, and situated validity. Each enacts a multi-voiced, reflexive, open-ended, emotionally based text which is action, or praxis based.

For Lather, and others in this tradition, theory **is** interpretation. There is no break between empirical activity (gathering empirical materials, reading social texts) and theorizing. Theory **as** interpretation is always anchored in the texts that it purports to analyse. Conceptualizing theory-as-interpretation, or theory-as-criticism, means that the writer employs a style which immediately connects a theoretical term to its referent.

Style III: Interpretive Interactionism

I turn now to a brief exposition of another interpretive style, what I have elsewhere (Denzin, 1989; 1994; 2001; 2009; 2010; 2011) termed interpretive interactionism, and performance ethnography. Interpretive research begins and ends with the biography and the self of the researcher. The events and troubles that are written about are ones the writer has already experienced and witnessed firsthand. The task is to produce 'richly detailed' inscriptions and accounts of such experiences.

The focus of research is on those life experiences (epiphanies) that radically alter and shape the meanings persons give to themselves and their life projects. In epiphanies personal character is manifested and made apparent. By recording these experiences in detail, and by listening to the stories people tell about them, the researcher is able to illuminate the moments of crisis that occur in a person's life. Having had such experiences, the individual is often never quite the same again (examples of epiphanies are religious conversions, divorces, the experience of family violence, rape, incest, murders, the loss of a job).

Sartre's (1963: 85–166) progressive–regressive method of analysis organizes the interpretive process. The investigator situates a subject, or class of subjects, within a given historical moment. Progressively, the method looks forward to the conclusion of a set of acts or experiences undertaken by the subject. Regressively, the method works back in time to the historical, gender, class, race, cultural, biographical, and emotional conditions that moved the subject forward into the experience that is being studied.

Interpretive materials are evaluated by their ability to illuminate phenomenon as lived experience. Such materials should be based on thickly contextualized materials that are historical, relational, and processual. The core of these materials will be the personal experience stories that subjects tell one another. These stories should be connected to larger institutional, group, and cultural contexts, including written texts and other systems of discourse (cinema, music, folklore). The understandings that are put forth should engulf all that has been learned about the phenomenon. The moral biases that organize the research should be made evident to the reader. The competing models of truth and interpretation (rationality and emotionality) that operate in the subject's situations should be revealed. The stories that are presented to readers should be given in the language, feelings, emotions, and actions of those studied.[12]

Style IV: Performance and Arts-Based Inquiry

Performance ethnography is influenced by the arts-based tradition in qualitative research (Knowles and Cole, 2008). After Finley (2008), arts-based research engages a radical, ethical, political aesthetic, seeking artistic works – poetry, writing, dance, photography, drama, paintings, music – that empower people in their daily lives. Performance as a communicative act, as a way of knowing and as a form of interpretation, is basic to this project (Pelias, 2008: 185).

The focus is on embodied emotional experience, a poetics of performance that illuminates moments of epiphany in the culture (Finley, 2008: 72). These moments open up institutions for critical inspection and evaluation. Performance ethnography and interpretive interactionism are embedded in these radical aesthetic performative practices which help expose oppression and injustice in daily life.

CRITICISMS OF POST-STRUCTURALISM

Post-structural, postmodern, feminist, arts-based texts have been criticized because of their interpretive criteria. Critics complain that there is no way to evaluate such work because traditional, external standards of evaluation (internal, external validity, reliability, objectivity) are not followed. This means, so the argument goes, that there is no way to evaluate a good or bad post-structural, feminist text. Others argue that the feminist and post-structural text imposes an interpretive framework on the world, and does not allow subjects to speak. These criticisms come, of course, from the positivist and post-positivist traditions.

These criticisms are rejected on several grounds. First, they are seen as not reflecting an understanding of the new postmodern sensibility, which doubts and challenges any attempt to legitimate a text in terms of positivist or post-positivist criteria. Such criteria represent attempts to bring legitimacy and authority to the scientific project. Science, in its traditional forms, is the problem. Knowledge produced under the guise of objective science is too often used for purposes of social control (Clough, 1992: 134). The criteria of evaluation that post-structuralists employ answer to a different set of problems and to a different project. They seek a morally informed social criticism, a sacred version of science which is humane, caring, holistic, and action based.

Post-structuralists celebrate uncertainty, and attempt to construct texts that do not impose theoretical frameworks on the world. They seek to let the prose of the world speak for itself, mindful of all the difficulties involved in such a commitment. They, more than their post-positivist counterparts, are sensitive to voice, and multiple perspectives.

MULTIPLE INTERPRETIVE COMMUNITIES

They are many ways to move from the field to the text and to the performance, many ways to inscribe, describe, and perform experience. There are multiple interpretive communities that now circulate within the many terrains of qualitative research. These communities take different stances on the topics treated above, including the matters of writing, description, inscription, interpretation, understanding, representation, legitimation, textual desire, and the logic and politics of the text.

A simplistic approach to the multiple paradigm dialogues that are now occurring (Guba, 1990a) might use the old-fashioned distinctions between the humanists and the scientists, the tender and the tough minded, to borrow William James's (1978 [1908]: 10–13) terms. This is produced in Figure 39.1.

But critical analysis soon makes this pretty picture messy. On the surface, critical, emancipatory, feminist, interactional, post-structural, and postmodern researchers belong to the 'tender-minded interpretive community.' Following James, they are more intuitive, emotional, and open-ended in their interpretive work. Some are quite dogmatic about this. But many critical theorists write realist texts, are hardnosed empiricists, work within closed theoretical systems, and follow the canons of good science.

In the same vein, positivist, post-positivist, grounded theory, and constructivists appear to belong to the 'tough-minded interpretive community.' They are hardnosed empiricists, system builders, often pluralistic in their use of theory, and skeptical of non-systematic theory and empirical work. But there are feminists who use grounded theory

Two interpretive communities

Tender minded	Tough minded
Intuitive	Hardnosed empiricists
Emotional	Rational, cognitive
Open-ended texts	Closed texts, systems
Interpretation as art	Interpretation as method
Personal biases	Neutrality
Experimental texts	Traditional texts
Anti-realism	Realist texts
Anti-foundational	Foundational
Criticism	Substantive theory
Science-as-power	Good science canons
Multi-voiced texts	Single-voiced texts

Figure 39.1 Two interpretive communities

methods, and produce traditional-looking texts, based on foundational criteria. There are tough-minded constructivists who are anti-realist, anti-foundational, and who regard interpretation as more art than method.

So simplistic classifications do not work. Any given qualitative researcher-as-a-bricoleur can be more than one thing at the same time, be fitted into both the tender and the tough-minded categories. It is clear that in the current historical moment the concerns from each of James's two communities work alongside and inform one another. Accordingly, it can be argued that the following contradictory understandings operate in this broad field we have called qualitative research.

Interpretation is an art that cannot be formalized. Scholars are increasingly concerned with the logic of the text, especially the problems involved in presenting lived experience and the 'Other's' point of view. Many are preoccupied with the biases in the emotional stories they tell, and are drawn to experimental forms of writing, while some reject mainstream narrative realism. It is common for texts now to be grounded in anti-foundational systems of discourse (local knowledge, local emotions). These texts tell emancipatory stories, grounded in race, class, and gender. Personal experience is a major source of empirical material for many, as are cultural texts, and materials gathered via the ethnographic method. More than a few researchers expose their writerly selves in first-person accounts, and many are attempting to produce reader-friendly, multi-voiced texts that speak to the worlds of lived experience. It is becoming commonplace for qualitative researchers to become advocates of the moral communities they represent, while attempting to directly participate in social change.

At the same time there are those who remain committed to mainstream realism. They write texts which adhere to complex sets of methodological principles connected to post-positivist foundational systems of meaning ('good science'). Their texts are grounded in concrete empirical materials (case studies) and are inductively interpreted through the methods of grounded theory, or variations thereof. Existing theories, both substantive and formal, structure inquiry, which is organized in a rigorous, stepwise manner.

Finally, there are conflicting views, and disagreements on the very topic of interpretation itself. The immediate, local, personal, emotional biases of many lead them to tell stories that work outward from the self to society. These writers are writing to make sense of their own lives. Others write to make sense of 'another's' life. In the end it is a matter of storytelling and the stories we tell each other.

INTO THE FUTURE

Of course persons who do interpretations feel uncomfortable doing predictions. But where the field of interpretation, the art and politics of telling stories, will be in 10 years should be addressed. If the past predicts the future, and if the decade of the 1980s and the first half off the 1990s are to be taken seriously, then interpretation is moving more and more deeply into the regions of the postmodern sensibility. A new post-constructivist paradigm may emerge. This framework may attach itself to a new and less foundational post-positivism and a more expansive critical theory framework built on modified grounded theory principles.

Epistemologies of color will proliferate, building on Afrocentric Indigenous, Chicana, Native American, Asian, Third World and other group perspectives. More elaborated epistemologies of gender (and class) will appear, including queer theory, and feminisms of color. These interpretive communities will draw on their m group experiences as the basis of the texts they write and perform and they will seek texts that speak to the logic and cultures of these communities.

These race, ethnic, and gender-specific interpretive communities will fashion interpretive criteria out of their interactions with the post-positivist, constructivist, critical theory, and post-structural sensibilities. These criteria will be emic, existential, political, and emotional. They will push the personal to the forefront of the political, where the social text becomes the vehicle for the expression of politics.

This projected proliferation of interpretive communities does not mean that the field of qualitative research will splinter into warring factions, or into groups which cannot speak to one another. Underneath the complexities and contradictions that define this field rest three common commitments. The first reflects the belief that the world of human experience must be studied from the point of view of the historically and culturally situated individual. Second, qualitative researchers will persist in working outward from their own biographies to the worlds of experience that surround them. Third, scholars will continue to value and seek to produce works that speak clearly, and powerfully, about these worlds. To repeat Raymond Carver, the real experimenters will always be those who Make it New, who find things out for themselves, and who want to carry this News from their world to ours (Carver, 1989: 24).

And so the stories we tell one and perform for another will change and the criteria for reading stories will also change. And this is how it should be. The good stories are always told by those who have learned well the stories of the past, but are unable any longer to tell them. This is so because the stories from the past no longer speak to them nor to us.

NOTES

1. I thank Uwe Flick, and the other chapter readers, for their comments on earlier versions of this chapter.
2. A reader notes that texts are but one form of interpretation. Other interpretive forms include those connected to arts-based inquiry, including painting, dance, ethnodrama, poetry, video, music, and reader's theatre (see Finley, 2011: 444).
3. Here I deal with the constructivism of Guba and Lincoln (1989).
4. Rosaldo (1989: 8) argues that anthropological doctrine presents this as a three-step process, involving preparation, knowledge, and sensibility, but cautions that 'one should work to undermine the false comfort it can convey. At what point can people say that they have completed their learning or life experience?'
5. Mitch Allen and Yvonna Lincoln clarified these steps for me.

6. Yvonna Lincoln suggests that this may have been less the case in earlier historical moments, when realist tales were organized in terms of well-understood conventions.
7. I am deeply indebted to Meaghan Morris for her help in clarifying the meanings in this section.
8. Mainstream, interpretive, and descriptive realist stories may be supplemented by more traditional and experimental formats, including **confessional** ('The problems I encountered doing my study'), and **impressionistic** ('dramatic and vivid pictures from the field') tales of the field, as well as **personal memoirs** of the field experience, **narratives of the self, fiction texts, ethnographic dramas**, and **performance texts**.
9. The presence is greatest, perhaps, in education, the health sciences, and communication, but also in sociology, less so in anthropology. When one peels back the layers of discourse embedded in any of the numerous qualitative guides to interpretation and theory construction, the core features of the Strauss approach are presented, even when Strauss and associates are not directly named.
10. It argues that the facts for any theory are always interpreted and value laden, that no theory can ever be fully tested (or grounded), and an interactive relationship always exists between the observer and the observed. A dialectical, dialogic hermeneutic posture organizes inquiry which is based on thick descriptions of action and subjective experience in natural situations.
11. Specific strategies and criteria are attached to each of these components. Credibility is increased through prolonged field engagement, persistent observation, triangulation, peer debriefing, negative case analysis, referential analysis, and member checks (talking to people in the field). Thick description provides for transferability, while dependability can be enhanced through the use of overlapping methods, stepwise replications, and inquiry (dependability) audits (the use of well-informed subjects). Confirmability builds on audit trails (a 'residue of records stemming from inquiry,' 1985: 319), and involves the use of written field notes, memos, a field diary, process and personal notes, and a reflexive journal.
12. The five steps to interpretation (Denzin, 1989: 27) should be followed: deconstruction, capture, bracketing, construction, contextualization.

FURTHER READING

Finley, Susan (2011) 'Critical arts based inquiry: The pedagogy and practice of a radical ethical aesthetic,' in Norman K. Denzin and Yvonna S. Lincoln (eds.), *Handbook of Qualitative Research*, 4th edition. Thousand Oaks, CA: Sage. pp. 435–50.
Richardson, Laurel (2000) 'Writing: A method of inquiry,' in Norman K. Denzin and Yvonna S. Lincoln (eds.), *Handbook of Qualitative Research*, 2nd edition. Thousand Oaks, CA: Sage. pp. 923–48.

Wyatt, Jonathan, Gale, Ken, Gannon, Susanne, and Davies, Bronwyn (2011) *Deleuze & Collaborative Writing: An Immanent Plane of Composition*. New York: Peter Lang.

REFERENCES

Becker, Howard S. (1986) *Writing for Social Scientists: How to Start and Finish your Thesis, Book or Article* (2nd edition, 2007). Chicago: University of Chicago Press.
Bryant, Antony and Charmaz, Kathy (eds.) (2010) *The SAGE Handbook of Grounded Theory*. Thousand Oaks, CA: Sage.
Cannella, Gaile and Lincoln, Yvonna S. (2011) 'Ethics, research regulations, and critical social science,' in Norman K. Denzin and Yvonna S. Lincoln (eds.), *The SAGE Handbook of Qualitative Research*, 4th edition. Thousand Oaks, CA: Sage. pp. 81–90.
Carspecken, Phil Frances and Apple, Michael (1992) 'Critical research: Theory, methodology, and practice,' in Margaret D. LeCompte et al. (eds.), *The Handbook of Qualitative Research in Education*. New York: Academic Press. pp. 507–54.
Carver, Raymond (1989) *Fires*. New York: Vintage.
Charmaz, Kathy (2011) 'Grounded theory methods in social justice research,' in Norman K. Denzin and Yvonna S. Lincoln (eds.), *Handbook of Qualitative Research*, 4th edition. Thousand Oaks, CA: Sage. pp. 339–80.
Clandinin, D. Jean and Connelly, F. Michael (1994) 'Personal experience methods,' in Norman K. Denzin and Yvonna S. Lincoln (eds.), *Handbook of Qualitative Research*. Thousand Oaks, CA: Sage. pp. 413–27.
Clough, Patricia Ticineto (1992) *The End(s) of Ethnography*. Newbury Park, CA: Sage.
Collins, Patricia Hill (1990) *Black Feminist Thought*. New York: Routledge.
Collins, Patricia Hill (2000) *Black Feminist Thought, revised edition*. New York: Routledge.
Conquergood, Dwight (1998) 'Beyond the text: Toward a performative cultural politics,' in Sheron J. Dailey (ed.), *The Future of Performance Studies: Visions and Revisions*. Annadale, VA: National Communication Association. pp. 25–36.
Corbin, Juliet and Strauss, Anselm (2008) *Basics of Qualitative Research: Techniques and Procedures for Developing Grounded Theory*, 3rd edition. Thousand Oaks, CA: Sage.
Denzin, Norman K. (1989) *The Research Act*, 3rd edition. Englewood Cliffs, NJ: Prentice Hall.

Denzin, Norman K. (1994) 'The practices of interpretation,' in Norman K. Denzin and Yvonna S. Lincoln (eds.), *Handbook of Qualitative Research*. Thousand Oaks, CA: Sage. pp. 500–24.

Denzin, Norman K. (2001) *Interpretive Interactionism*, 2nd edition. Thousand Oaks, CA: Sage.

Denzin, Norman K. (2009) *Qualitative Inquiry Under Fire*. Walnut Creek, CA: Left Coast Press.

Denzin, Norman K. (2010) *The Qualitative Manifesto: A Call to Arms*. Walnut Creek, CA: Left Coast Press.

Denzin, Norman K. (2011) *Custer on Canvas: Representing Indians, Memory, and Violence in the New West*. Walnut Creek: Left Coast Press.

Dilthey, Wilhelm L. (l976 [1900]) *Selected Writings*. Cambridge: Cambridge University Press.

Diversi, Marscelo and Moreira, Claudio (2009) *Between Talk: Decolonizing Knowledge Production, Pedagogy and Praxis*. Walnut Creek, CA: Left Coast Press.

Eisenhart, Margaret and Jurow, A. Susan (2011) 'Teaching qualitative research,' in Norman K. Denzin and Yvonna Lincoln (eds.), *Handbook of Qualitative Research*, 4th edition. Thousand Oaks, CA: Sage. pp. 669–714.

Fine, Michelle (1994) 'Working the hyphen: Reinventing self and other in qualitative research,' in Norman K. Denzin and Yvonna S. Lincoln (eds.), *Handbook of Qualitative Research*. Thousand Oaks, CA: Sage. pp. 70–82.

Finley, Susan (2008) 'Arts-based research,' in J. Gary Knowles and Ardra L. Cole (eds.), *Handbook of the Arts in Qualitative Research*. Thousand Oaks, CA: Sage. pp. 71–82.

Finley, Susan (2011) 'Critical arts based inquiry: The pedagogy and practice of a radical ethical aesthetic,' in Norman K. Denzin and Yvonna S. Lincoln (eds.), *Handbook of Qualitative Research*, 4th edition. Thousand Oaks, CA: Sage. pp. 435–50.

Flick, Uwe (ed.) (2007) *The SAGE Qualitative Research Kit*, 8 vols. London: Sage.

Flick, Uwe (2009) *An Introduction to Qualitative Research*, 4th edition. Thousand Oaks, CA: Sage.

Flick, Uwe (2011) 'Mixing methods, triangulation, and integrated research: Challenges for qualitative research in a world crisis,' in Norman K. Denzin and Michael D. Giardina (eds.), *Qualitative Inquiry and Global Crises*. Walnut Creek, CA: Left Coast Press. pp. 132–52.

Freire, Paulo (1982) *Pedagogy of the Oppressed*. New York: Continuum.

Geertz, Clifford (1973) *Interpreting Cultures*. New York: Basic Books.

Guba, Egon G. (1990a) 'The alternative paradigm dialog,' in Egon C. Guba (ed.), *The Paradigm Dialog*. Newbury Park, CA: Sage. pp. 17–30.

Guba, Egon G. (1990b) 'Carrying on the dialog,' in Egon C. Guba (ed.), *The Paradigm Dialog*. Newbury Park, CA: Sage. pp. 368–78.

hooks, bell (1990) *Yearning: Race, Gender, and Cultural Politics*. Boston, MA: South End Press.

Hurworth, Rosalind E. (2007) *Teaching Qualitative Research: Cases and Issues*. Rotterdam: Sense.

James, William (l978 [1908]) *Pragmatism and the Meaning of Truth*. Cambridge, MA: Harvard University Press.

Knowles, J. Gary and Cole, Ardra L. (eds.) (2008) *Handbook of the Arts in Qualitative Research*. Thousand Oaks, CA: Sage.

Lather, Patti (1991) *Getting Smart*. New York: Routledge.

Lather, Patti (1993) 'Fertile obsession: Validity after poststructuralism,' *Sociological Quarterly*, 35: 673–93.

Lather, Patti (2007) *Getting Lost: Feminist Efforts Toward a Double(d) Science*. Albany: State University of New York Press.

Levi-Strauss, Claude (l962/l966) *The Savage Mind*. Chicago: University of Chicago Press.

Lincoln, Yvonna S. and Guba, Egon G. (1985) *Naturalistic Inquiry*. Beverly Hills, CA: Sage.

Lincoln, Yvonna S., Lynham, Susan A., and Guba, Egon G. (2011) 'Paradigmatic controversies, contradictions, and emerging confluences, revisited,' in Norman K. Denzin and Yvonna S. Lincoln (eds.), *Handbook of Qualitative Research*, 4th edition. Thousand Oaks, CA: Sage. pp. 97–128.

Madison, D. Soyini (2012) *Critical Ethnography: Method, Ethics and Performance*. Thousand Oaks, CA: Sage.

Olesen, Virginia (2011) 'Feminist qualitative research in the Millennium's first decade,' in Norman K. Denzin and Yvonna S. Lincoln (eds.), *Handbook of Qualitative Research*, 4th edition. Thousand Oaks, CA: Sage. pp. 129–46.

Pelias, Ronald J. (2008) 'Performative inquiry: Embodiment and its challenges,' in J. Gary Knowles and Ardra L. Cole (eds.), *Handbook of the Arts in Qualitative Research*. Thousand Oaks, CA: Sage. pp. 185–94.

Plath, David (1990) 'Fieldnotes, filed Notes, and the conferring of Note,' in Robert Sanjek (ed.), *Fieldnotes*. Albany: State University of New York Press. pp. 37l–84.

Preissle, Judith and Roulston, Kathryn (2009) 'Trends in teaching qualitative research: A 30-year perspective,' in Mark Garner et al. (eds.), *Teaching Research Methods in The Social Sciences*. Farnham: Ashgate. pp.13–22.

Richardson, Laurel (1994) 'Writing: A method of inquiry,' in Norman K. Denzin and Yvonna S. Lincoln (eds.), *Handbook of Qualitative Research*. Thousand Oaks, CA: Sage. pp. 516–29.

Richardson, Laurel (2000) 'Writing: A method of inquiry,' in Norman K. Denzin and Yvonna S. Lincoln (eds.), *Handbook of Qualitative Research*, 2nd edition. Thousand Oaks, CA: Sage. pp. 923–48.

Richardson, Laurel and Lockridge, Ernest (2004) *Travels with Ernest: Crossing the Literary/Sociological Divide*. Walnut Creek, CA: AltaMira Press.

Ricoeur, Paul (1979) 'The model of the text: Meaningful action considered as a text,' in Paul Rabinow and William M. Sullivan (eds.), *Interpretive Social Science: A Reader*. Berkeley: University of California Press. pp. 73–101.

Rosaldo, Renato (1989) *Culture & Truth*. Boston, MA: Beacon.

Saldana, Johnny (2009) *The Coding Manual for Qualitative Researchers*. Thousand Oaks, CA: Sage.

Saldana, Johnny (2011) *Ethotheatre: Research from Play to Stage*. Walnut Creek, CA: Left Coast Press.

Saldana, Johnny and Leavy, Patricia (2011) *Fundamentals of Qualitative Research: Understanding Qualitative Research*. New York: Oxford University Press.

Sartre, Jean-Paul (1963) *Search for a Method*. New York: Knopf.

Smith, Dorothy (1992) 'Sociology from women's perspective: A reaffirmation,' *Sociological Theory*, 10: 88–97.

Spry, Tami (2011) *Body, Paper, Stage: Writing and Performing Autoethnography*. Walnut Creek, CA: Left Coast Press.

St. Pierre, Elizabeth Adams (2011) 'Post qualitative research: The critique and the coming after,' in Norman K. Denzin and Yvonna S. Lincoln (eds.), *Handbook of Qualitative Research*, 4th edition. Thousand Oaks, CA: Sage. pp. 611–26.

Strauss, Anselm and Corbin, Juliet (1990) *Basics of Qualitative Research*. Newbury Park, CA: Sage.

Van Maanen, John (2011) *Tales of the Field: On Writing Ethnography*, 2nd edition. Chicago: University of Chicago Press.

Wertz, Frederick J., Charmaz, Kathy, McMullen, Linda M., Josselson, Ruthellen, Anderson, Rosemarie, and McSpadden, Emalinda (2011) *Five Ways of Doing Qualitative Analysis: Phenomenological Psychology, Grounded Theory, Discourse Analysis, Narrative Research, and Intuitive Inquiry*. New York: Guilford Press.

Wyatt, Jonathan, Gale, Ken, Gannon, Susanne, and Davies, Bronwyn (2011) *Deleuze & Collaborative Writing: An Immanent Plane of Composition*. New York: Peter Lang.

Implementation: Putting Analyses into Practice

Michael Murray

AIMS

At the core of qualitative research has been a desire by its practitioners to contribute to the improvement in the quality of people's lives. In this sense, it breaks down the traditional dichotomy between pure and applied research which has pervaded much social science research. In contemporary qualitative research there has been considerable work to improve the rigour of the approach so as to develop a sophisticated understanding of aspects of everyday life, but in doing so the desire to contribute to personal and social transformation has been somewhat underplayed. The aim of this chapter is to consider how we can reforge that connection between research and practice and to consider ways of increasing the impact of qualitative research.

Murphy and Dingwall (2003) identified three reasons why qualitative research has often been dismissed by policy-makers: (1) it is not scientific, (2) it is indistinguishable from journalism, and (3) it has an underlying agenda. It was because of these criticisms that policy-makers have often preferred quantitative research with its assurances of objectivity and impartiality. In their attempts to address such criticism some qualitative researchers have tried to mimic the standards of quantitative research. This can be the case with forms of content analysis (see Schreier, Chapter 12, this volume) of interview transcripts (see Roulston, Chapter 20, this volume), which have often sought uniformity in data analysis. However, this handbook has detailed how qualitative research has developed its own standards of rigour (see Barbour, Chapter 34, this volume) which are based less upon a positivist approach to science which seeks uniformity and more on detailing the processes underlying different interpretations of our world. The earlier dismissal of its being like journalism has been addressed by the increased theorization of the data analysis going beyond earlier concern with description to more sophisticated interpretation. As regards an underlying agenda, this is somewhat more contentious since the aim of all good research is to raise questions about the nature of reality and to offer new insights into ways of living.

This chapter aims to further challenge these criticisms of qualitative research as being of limited value to policy-makers and other stakeholders, and instead considers how qualitative research has historically been concerned with critiquing the status quo and developing ways of enhancing quality of life. It will begin by reflecting on some of the earlier aims of qualitative research as collaborative (see Cornish et al., Chapter 6, this volume) emancipatory practice and how this potential has been reduced with the rise of expert-driven, evidence-based practice. While the original form often sought actively to involve the participants in the research process as a means of engaging them in a joint process of investigation and of challenge to various forms of oppression, the latter has sought to develop new standards of research defined by objective experts. In particular, there is a need to consider the potential 'pathway to impact' throughout the research rather than as an add-on at the end. How this is done will depend upon a range of factors, not least the various research participants and collaborators, the subject of research and the potential audience.

Historically, various traditions both within and outside social science have influenced the growing interest in qualitative methods. This chapter will briefly consider three of these traditions, namely oral history, feminism and action research, which have a common desire to link research with social change. Although much qualitative research does not explicitly draw on these traditions, it does implicitly integrate some of their principles through involving participants actively in the research process, reflecting on the purpose and nature of the research and connecting with various stakeholders throughout the investigation. Attention to these principles will further increase the impact of qualitative research. Furthermore, while a range of theories inform much qualitative research, this chapter draws on narrative and social representation theory which are particularly useful in framing interpretations. The chapter briefly considers the relevance of these theories and then a number of empirical examples to illustrate them. Finally, the chapter considers some limitations and opportunities in using qualitative research to effect personal and social change.

SHORT HISTORY

Quantitative research has traditionally adopted a 'god's eye' approach designed to produce objective evidence about social and psychological processes (Putnam, 1981). Conversely, qualitative research is based upon the researchers developing relationships with the research participants in which both shape the research outcome. These relationships open up the potential for change being a conscious part of the research process and not just a consequence of the research outcome. Such connectedness was evident in some of the earlier versions of qualitative research. Here I consider initially the influence of oral history and of feminism, which were both concerned with the emancipatory potential of research. The use of qualitative methods in both of these approaches was deliberately aimed at bridging the academic and non-academic worlds of theory and practice. This approach has been particularly self-conscious within action research which I consider subsequently.

Oral history is a form of historical research, sometimes described as a movement, which aimed to introduce the perspective of the ordinary person into discussions about history. In particular, it was concerned with working-class struggles and attempts to promote solidarity and to challenge various forms of injustice and so was informed by Marxist and other radical traditions. As Selbin noted: 'Traditionally, history has been constructed from above, composed by the victorious, orchestrated by the powerful, played and performed for the population. There is another history, rooted in people's perception of how the world around them continues to unfold and of their place in that process' (2010: 9). This approach led to the rise of local oral history groups whose members aimed to collect and systematize the experiences of their peers and in doing so write a 'history from below'. (Thompson, 2000)

The enthusiasm for this approach has waned somewhat but its basic philosophy still informs the original desire of qualitative researchers who have been particularly concerned with exploring the lives of the disenfranchised and marginalized (see Cox et al., 2008). At the centre of this oral history making was the recounting of personal and collective stories of struggle with which the audience could identify and sympathize. Modern qualitative research often loses this concern for understanding personal and collective experiences of adversity and resistance. Further, the sense of personal agency is often discarded. Mishler discussed how, in the coding of qualitative research transcripts, the person often ended up on the cutting room floor. As he said:

> the relative absence of narratives in reports of interview studies is an artefact of standard procedures for conducting, describing and analysing interviews: interviewers interrupt respondents' answers and thereby suppress expression of their stories; when they appear, stories go unrecorded because they are viewed as irrelevant to the specific aims of specific questions; and stories that make it through these barriers are discarded as stages of coding and analysis. (1986: 106)

Similarly, Willis has argued:

> The problem with many empirical data, empirically presented, is that they can be flat and uninteresting, a documentary of detail which does not connect with urgent issues. On the other hand the 'big ideas' are empty of people, feeling and experience. (2000: xi)

In deepening the link between research and practice qualitative researchers can consider how they can maintain that sense of personal agency, as was the case with oral history, while retaining an awareness of structural factors and of the role of language in constructing our reality. This attention to the connection between agency and context has been particularly the case with narrative research (e.g. Hammack, 2012), which is considered later.

Another important influence on the growth of qualitative methods has been feminism, with its demands that other voices be heard in scientific research. Similar to oral history, feminism had a radical agenda pushing research beyond describing the world to developing ways of changing it. In particular, feminist researchers have not only researched women's experiences of such issues as sexuality and motherhood, but also been actively involved in campaigns for the rights of women and of other oppressed groups.

In reviewing the contribution of feminism to qualitative research Ussher identified five main features:

> the centrality of the critical analysis of gender relationships in research and theory; the focus on the detrimental impact of patriarchal power and control in both academic theory and professional practice; an appreciation of the moral and political dimensions of research; the view that women are worthy of study in their own right; and the recognition of the need for social change to improve the lives of women. (1999: 99)

In developing qualitative methods feminist researchers were keen to infuse their work with an action or change orientation located within an awareness of women's position in society.

Ussher continued: 'The goal of feminist research could be described as the establishment of collaborative and non-exploitative relationships in research, to place the researcher in the field of study so as to avoid objectification, and to conduct research which is transformative' (1999: 99). Admittedly, this is not restricted to qualitative research but in view of the concern with hearing the voice of women many feminists have preferred this approach. In particular, feminists were keen to expose and challenge the pervasiveness of inequitable power relations in everyday social life.

A particular influential approach within feminist research has been that of standpoint theory developed by Sandra Harding. This theory argues that it is necessary to view the world 'through our participants' eyes' (Harding, 1991) if the researcher is to grasp the experience of women. However, this approach goes further and argues that the research process itself can be used as a means of empowering the women participants. For them, qualitative research could take the form of consciousness raising by which the women participants became more aware of the various social forces constraining their advancement and how they could work together to initiate social transformation (e.g., Kearney, 2006).

A common theme of both oral history and feminist research has been a concern to involve the research participants actively in the research process. Such a concern has been central to action research. Greenwood and Levin in their standard textbook note that action research 'centers on doing "with" rather than doing "for" stakeholders and credits local stakeholders with the richness of experience and reflective possibilities that long experience living in complex situations brings with it' (2007: 1). In a recent commentary, Levin and Greenwood (2011) argue that such an approach provides an opportunity for reinventing the social sciences not as some supposed dispassionate discipline but rather one that is socially committed and engaged. This passionate commitment to forms of social action is one articulated by Reason and Bradbury in the introduction to their *Handbook of Action Research*:

> action research is a participatory, democratic process concerned with developing practical knowing in the pursuit of worthwhile human purposes, grounded in a participatory worldview that we believe is emerging at this historical moment. It seeks to bring together action and reflection, theory and practice, in participation with others, in pursuit of practical solutions to issues of pressing concern to people, and more generally the flourishing of individual personas and their communities. (2001: 1)

Of particular note in their definition is the importance of reflection in action research. Together the researchers and participants reflect on the research (see May and Perry, Chapter 8, this volume) and how it can contribute to various forms of action. Thus action research becomes more a process of mutual learning rather than the imposition of an agenda by the outside researcher.

Various versions of action research have evolved particularly in education (e.g. Atweh et al., 1998) and in nursing (e.g. Holter and Schwartz-Barcott, 2008). It is seen as a method which can ensure the involvement of the research participants in the research process and greater sensitivity to the context such that research findings can be more easily integrated into practice.

Participatory action research (PAR) developed out of the work of Latin American social scientists who were keen that their research should both reflect the interests of study participants and that through the research they could initiate action contributing to some form of positive change. Emerging in Latin America at the time of intense political strife, PAR and its developers not only were very conscious of the broader political context, but also had the desire to position their research within that context and to work with their study participants to challenge various forms of social oppression.

One of the most influential theorists within this tradition was Paulo Freire (1974) who developed a form of critical literacy theory. This theory viewed literacy not simply as the ability to read but to critique the broader social world and your position in it. He contrasted the traditional form of literacy education which he considered a form of banking, whereby the educator deposited objective knowledge in the minds of the students, with more critical literacy in which the educator and the student worked together to reflect on their circumstances and the potential for change. This transformative process he termed *concientizacion*, or critical consciousness raising.

Contemporary forms of participatory research may place less emphasis on formal political power and instead integrate ideas from feminist and Foucauldian thought on the role of power in everyday relationships. This includes awareness of the power of the academic researcher in shaping the research process and calls for greater reflexivity in the research process (see May and Perry, Chapter 8, this volume). It also means involving various stakeholders in the research process from the outset and challenging internal power differentials.

Although qualitative research has developed from many other traditions, the connections with oral history, feminism and action research highlight the importance of active engagement of the research participants which has now become an accepted part of other traditions. Further, rather than qualitative research being considered as separate from practice, it can explore how one can inform the other. Finally, these traditions emphasize the importance of taking into consideration the broader context within which research and practice operate and so break down the classic individualism of much quantitative research and enable qualitative methods to develop a more social and relational human science. Sampson (2003) in his discussion of such a science refers to Levinas's ethical imperative to be responsible for others, which provides qualitative research with a moral dynamism often lacking in quantitative research. Similarly, Anne Inga Hilsen in her commentary on the ethical dimensions of action research refers to the relational ideas of the Danish philosopher Knud Logstrup who argues, in Hilsen's words, that 'we are not only necessary to each other; we constitute each other's life-worlds, or, as he quotes Martin Luther, "we are each other's daily bread"' (2006: 26).

THEORETICAL BACKGROUNDS

A range of theoretical traditions inform contemporary qualitative research (see Maxwell and Chmiel, Chapter 2, this volume). We are concerned not with the internal quality (see Barbour, Chapter 34, this volume) of the research but more on how can we maximize its impact. To that extent we explore two particular traditions. One is more concerned with the character of the research participants and how their 'voice' can be more effectively heard. The second is concerned with the broader world of meanings within which the research is conducted.

Narrative research and in particular life story research (see Esrin et al., Chapter 14, this volume) places the whole person at the centre of inquiry as a social and historical being who connects with the social context. In understanding the person's story the researcher gives life to something which may appear abstract to the policy-maker. In their study of lay juries in the British health service, Barnett et al. (2006) noted how resistant lay people were to evidence that was presented in an impersonal manner. Rather they were keen to know who was presenting the evidence. They sought additional personal information which could provide a level of real-life feeling to more impersonal accounts. This illustrates how qualitative researchers can increase the impact of their work by drawing attention to the personal stories behind their analyses.

In their study of the impact of life stories on sexual policy-making, Frost and Ouellette (2011) considered the case of Laurel Hester. Laurel was a New Jersey police detective who was diagnosed with terminal cancer. The local council denied her the right to transfer her pension to her long-term, same-sex partner. Laurel publicly defended her right and attracted widespread publicity. When she won the right other jurisdictions accepted that pensions could be transferred to same-sex partners and finally the state legislature enacted that right in legislation. This case has implications for narrative research in the sense that it illustrates the power of a single story, widely told, on social policy. Stories provide an opportunity for the listener to go behind the research and to explore connections with their own lives.

The link between narrative research (see Esin et al., Chapter 14, this volume) and narrative practice provides an opportunity to explore narrative further as a theoretical framework for change. While much of narrative research has been concerned with the stories told about past events, we can also consider narrative in its subjunctive sense to develop new opportunities. Polletta has noted the power of narrative to convince others of the legitimacy of an argument. As she noted:

> Most recent theorizing about narrative has attested to its value for disadvantaged groups. Personal stories chip away at the wall of public indifference, scholars argue. Stories elicit sympathy on the part of the powerful and sometimes mobilize official action against social wrongs. Where authorities are unyielding, storytelling sustains groups as they fight for reform, helping them build new collective identities, link current actions to heroic pasts and glorious futures, and restyle setbacks as way stations to victory. (2006: 2–3)

This future narrative orientation can also be used in more clinical settings as a way of involving clients in the process of change. It has been established that not only do narrative interventions promote more emotional reactions in clients, but they are more likely to build their confidence for change (e.g. McQueen and Kreuter, 2010). There is also evidence from cancer screening programmes that narrative interventions are an effective way of reducing perceived barriers to health care (Dillard et al., 2010).

Through participating in collaborative research the participants can develop a new narrative orientation. Williams et al. (2003) reported a study in which they considered the use of narrative as a framework for promoting collective action. In this study a group of women shared their own individual stories of exclusion and identified commonalities in their experiences. Through this collective experience they began to explore collective ways of challenging oppression, some of which brought them into conflict with family members. However, their group solidarity provided them with the support necessary to persist with challenge and illustrate in action the power of the new resistant narrative.

In developing ways to increase impact qualitative researchers need to consider the popular knowledge context within which they work. One theory which is particularly important here is social representation theory, which is concerned with the shared understandings of a particular group or community (Moscovici, 2000). These social representations shape our understandings of social reality and our social relations. Research which is concerned with change must take these social representations into consideration.

Jodelet deliberately links social representation theory with action research in her comments:

> Researchers deal with the study of SRs not only as a toolbox to understand their reality, but also as a path of action upon it, thus illustrating Lewin's principle (1963): 'No action without research; no research without action.' (2012: 79)

She further develops this argument:

> all social intervention whose objective is social transformation depends on groups' potentialities among which figures their proper knowledge. All intervention focused on change of social reality implies an emphasis on popular knowledge, the necessity of taking into account in the interaction between the researchers and the social groups. Also appears the importance of working on lay forms of knowledge, in terms of consciousness-raising and formulation of new necessities and identities. (2012: 79)

Her argument is akin to that of Freire with its emphasis on consciousness raising. To have an impact, qualitative researchers need to develop an understanding of how others view the world. This is increasingly important in our multicultural world where different social representations held by different groups often clash. Certain social representations have greater power than others because of the availability of resources, particularly the media in Western society, and other forms of communication associated with other social institutions, for example science, religion.

In developing their argument qualitative researchers need to be aware of this context.

For example, the power of science in Western society with its emphasis upon measurement and experimentation can lead to qualitative research being portrayed in a negative light, especially in the popular media. Jovchelovitch terms this process that of legitimation:

> Legitimation relates to the positioning of knowers in the social fabric and the resources they hold, material and symbolic, to have their knowledge recognised. In other words, it is a process that relates to the power of different systems of knowing. (2008: 27)

Thus qualitative researchers need to harness particular resources to challenge particular dominant social representations of science and to gain legitimacy for alternative forms of knowledge production. They need to be aware of how different forms of knowledge are viewed and explore ways of conveying the legitimacy of their approach.

WAYS OF GENERALIZING

Many contemporary qualitative researchers focus on the potential of their research to contribute to personal and social change. This argument has been developed by Barreras and Massey (2013), who introduce the concept of impact validity to describe 'the extent to which research has the *potential* to play an effective role in some form of social and political change or is useful for advocacy or activism'. In developing their projects the researchers are concerned about how their impact can be maximized outside of academia both during and after the research.

Qualitative researchers continue to work in a society which is dominated by demands for scientific evidence. Thus the qualitative researcher has to convince the other of the value of their findings and the consequent need for certain changes. One problem faced by qualitative research concerns its generalizability (see Maxwell and Chmiel, Chapter 37, this volume) or transferability from one setting to another. Here, in particular, it has been found wanting by many policy-makers who have been strongly influenced by the standards of evidence-based science – what Denzin (2011) has called the elephant in the room. Instead Denzin argues that we should reflect upon the purpose of our research and set our own standards:

> there is more than one version of disciplined, rigorous inquiry – counter-science, little science, unruly science, practical science – and such inquiry need not go by the name of science. We must have a model of disciplined, rigorous, thoughtful, reflective inquiry. (2011: 653)

This means engaging with but not being pressurized by the standards of positivist inquiry. One of the foremost of these standard debates has been around generalizability, which has been based largely on statistical arguments around sample size. Realizing that they cannot satisfy positivist standards in terms of sample size, qualitative researchers are concerned about theoretical generalizability.

Mishler reflected on this debate in his early work. He noted that 'the critical issue is not the determination of one singular and absolute "truth" but the assessment of the relative plausibility of an interpretation compared with other specific and potentially plausible alternative interpretations' (1986: 112). The argument has to be plausible not just to the researcher but to the audience. Thus in developing his or her interpretation the researcher has to justify clearly why researchers argue in a certain way with reference to a particular theoretical framework. Thus the researcher may engage with the research from a different theoretical background in developing his or her criticism. In literary criticism this approach is accepted on the grounds that there is no one single truth but multiple interpretations based upon different theoretical traditions. Within qualitative research this acceptance of different interpretations is conditioned by a desire to move beyond understanding to developing impact.

Several researchers have recently argued that pragmatism offers a solution to the epistemological challenge of accommodating contrasting interpretations. Pragmatism considers knowledge as a tool for action such that interpretation which enhances the capacity for positive change is favoured by the researcher (Cornish and Gillespie, 2006). Keleman (2013) has taken this argument further by exploring how the researcher can involve the community in developing actionable knowledge using a range of methods such as storytelling, drama and community action.

Over the past 20 years a major challenge facing qualitative researchers has been the rise of evidence-based practice. This was an exciting development which tackled many of the vested interests within policy-making and instead argued for an approach based upon objective scientific evidence. However, the equation of supposed quantitative objectivity with science in this new approach initially placed qualitative researchers at a disadvantage. This disadvantage has been challenged in two ways, first by critiquing the nature of science and, second, by critiquing the role of evidence in decision-making.

The evidence-based approach has been particularly influential within health care where it was clear that various vested interests had traditionally influenced resource allocation. The accumulation of evidence from randomised controlled trials (RCTs) on the efficacy of drugs and other interventions helped to highlight which ones were appropriate to prescribe. This has led to the development of the Cochrane database of such evidence for a wide range of interventions. However, there are a number of criticisms of such trials including the ignorance of variability in efficacy, the neglect of context, the relative disregard of processes, etc. These criticisms provided an opportunity for qualitative researchers to introduce their work to contextualize the evidence base. Qualitative research can now be submitted to the database and included in systematic reviews of interventions (Hannes, 2011).

This is a major initiative and an opportunity for qualitative researchers to have a broader impact in the health field. However, there is a tension in that researchers attempting to have their research included on this database may attempt to ensure its acceptability to more quantitative researchers. In combining with quantitative research there is also the danger of mixing epistemological assumptions and sliding into the positivist camp. There has been the development of several nuanced procedures to address these concerns through the identification of certain sensitive quality criteria. The Critical Appraisal Skills Program (CASP) tool (Public Health Resource Unit, 2006) is one example of such a procedure. This tool assesses research quality on the basis of 10 criteria: clear statement of project aims; appropriateness of qualitative methodology; appropriateness of research design; appropriate recruitment strategy; clarity of data collection; details of the relationship between researcher and study participants; ethical issues; details of data analysis; clarity of findings; and value of the research. While these criteria do not need to be used as a blueprint for quality, they can still be a useful guide to ensure that qualitative researchers are aware of factors that can improve the broader acceptability and impact of their work.

In a recent review of qualitative research on pain Newton et al. (2012) highlight the value of the CASP criteria. They note that qualitative research has gained widespread acceptance such that there is now less need to argue for its legitimacy but rather to focus on the details of the particular approach adopted. One concern they noted was the lack of reference to reflexivity, which has not historically been considered by more positivist researchers. This clear positioning of the researcher in the research report introduces the issue of values and standpoint which were highlighted by oral history and feminist researchers.

The search for qualitative evidence can also be criticized as being akin to the traditional one-way direction assumed within classical knowledge transfer models. These models rest upon the assumption that the 'other' has little knowledge to contribute to the process. The alternative knowledge exchange model is more participatory in its assumptions as is the more recent knowledge sharing approach (Wang and Noe, 2010). The various government research councils have been keen to expand knowledge exchange. In the UK this move has been coloured by the debate about the impact of research which may be difficult to demonstrate for many researchers, especially in the short term. The UK research councils provide a useful guide to exploring different forms of impact (www.rcuk.ac.uk/kei/Pages/home.aspx).

In addition, it is important to be aware that decision-making in health care and elsewhere is not based solely upon research evidence but on a variety of other factors. While qualitative research can be included as evidence, the acceptability of such research depends upon the reader. It is here that the qualitative researcher can be at a disadvantage as the reader may still apply standard quantitative criteria to judge qualitative work (see e.g. Lewin et al., 2009). Further, it is not just the perceived scientific status of research which is important, but its perceived relevance to a particular situation. As Burton and Chapman (2004) emphasize, the reader tries to connect the 'evidence' from research with his or her local knowledge of the situation and decide on the extent of match. Thus once again the qualitative researcher has to connect with that local knowledge if he or she is to have an impact.

QUALITATIVE RESEARCH AND CREATIVE ARTS

The previous sections have considered some historical and theoretical ideas about increasing the impact of qualitative research. This section further develops these ideas through more detailed consideration of two research projects which have incorporated some of these ideas. Both of these projects were concerned with researching the character of dominant social representations of ageing and ways of challenging these representations through artistic interventions.

It is well established that older people often report social isolation and loneliness. The Call-Me project was designed to increase our understanding of the process of growing older in a disadvantaged urban neighbourhood. It was also designed to explore the processes involved in developing and the value of participating in local social activities (Murray et al., 2013; Middling et al., 2011). From the outset the project was participatory with both the older people and a range of community stakeholders including city council officials and housing regeneration officers. The project was designed to enhance the confidence of the older people through both the activities they developed and the publicity generated around these activities, which attracted media attention and the attention of policy-makers. This broader impact was expanded through workshops with various stakeholders in which the main project findings were further discussed.

The participatory nature of this study illustrates the various opportunities to involve the study participants in increasing its impact. In many ways, the project design was similar to that developed by Caroline Wang and her colleagues (e.g. Wang et al., 2004) in their photovoice method (see Banks, Chapter 27, this volume). The photovoice method involves engaging participants in critiquing their community through the process of taking and exhibiting photographs of the community. These photographs then become the focus of an exhibition which provides an opportunity for the participants to expose the deficiencies in their living conditions and the need for additional resources. Thus the research participants become active advocates for change.

In the Call-Me project the artwork developed by the older residents was displayed in the community as part of an exhibition to which other community residents and various stakeholders were invited. This provided the opportunity for the project participants to both showcase their work and argue for additional resources (Murray and Crummett, 2010). This advocacy on the part of the participants was supplemented by the researchers in their workshops with the stakeholders.

Although practically the project was underpinned by ideas from PAR, it was also influenced by concepts from narrative and social representation theory. In the interviews and focus group discussions (see Barbour, Chapter 21, this volume) with the older participants, they shared their narrative accounts of living in a disadvantaged community and the perceived social representation of their community by outsiders as being not only disadvantaged but of limited talent. Through participating in the arts and other projects the older people were able to gain confidence and to challenge this negative social representation. Through this collective action the older participants were able to demonstrate to others their capacity. Thus the research moved from understanding the experience of growing older to involving older people in a challenge to the dominant negative social representation of ageing and of a disadvantaged community.

In this study detailed life story interviews (see Roulston, Chapter 20, this volume) were also conducted with a sample of key stakeholders who were involved in a range of community development activities. In the analysis of the structure and content of these interviews the emotional connection between the community workers and the residents was identified as being central to their work (Murray, 2013). They were passionately engaged in a project to address issues of social injustice and provide opportunities for disadvantaged people. They offered a vision of a better world and worked to engage people with that vision. In his description of stories of change, Selbin noted that people are often 'asked to rise above their present, often dreary circumstances and imagine a new future, to set out a new vision to which they can aspire and yet which somehow is made to seem within reach, even if there are at times substantial demands for self-abnegation and sacrifice' (2010: 30). The narrative of the community development worker was also infused with examples of disappointment and setbacks. To overcome the emotional load of such setbacks the workers required a broader values commitment to the importance of their work – it was not just a job but part of a broader movement for social justice.

Although focusing on the role of the community development worker, the findings of this subsidiary project can be applied to the qualitative researcher. It illustrates the importance of emotional commitment to the research and an acceptance that research findings may not connect with a particular audience because they challenge certain established views. A longer view of the potential impact of research is necessary.

Another study of social representations of ageing used a local theatre as a means of both collecting and disseminating ideas from the research. The New Vic theatre in the Potteries district of the English Midlands has a historic reputation for active engagement with the local community. This theatre was established by Peter Cheeseman in the 1960s and had a remit to represent and engage local residents (Elvgren, 1974). Over a period of 50 years it developed a substantial reputation for its theatrical productions, which took up local issues and encouraged local discussion. In many ways Cheeseman was developing many of the ideas of oral history as performance (Watt, 2009). The actors interviewed local residents about their everyday experiences and from this material developed documentary dramas about local issues designed to raise awareness of those issues and promote further discussion. The Ages and Stages project (Bernard et al., 2013) explored not only the character of social representations of ageing, but how they were challenged in a particular theatrical context.

The project developed over three strands. The first explored the substantial archival material which Cheeseman had developed over the years and which provides a veritable treasure trove of audiovisual material of all sorts about life in the local area. The second strand was a series of extensive individual and group interviews with audience members, volunteers, theatre employees and actors, and those who were sources for the original documentaries. The third strand brought these two strands together in the development of a new performance about the project, and about growing old.

Frequently in the interviews there was discussion about the growing social isolation that can come with ageing. The theatre provided an opportunity to combat the supposed inevitability of such isolation both as an audience member and as a volunteer. A dominant image of ageing is one of loss. As people grow old their children often move away from the family home and they lose connections with work colleagues. When one partner in a couple dies the experience of loss of social contacts is accentuated. The theatre provided an opportunity to resist this social isolation. Also, the many social roles which people have in terms of the family and work can fade as they grow older. The theatre can provide a new sense of purpose. Finally, there was mention of the mental decline which is often considered another consequence of ageing. The older people were aware of this public image and sought ways to combat this — involvement in the theatre even as an audience member was such an opportunity.

Through participation in the theatre the older participants deliberately challenged the negative social representation of ageing as a period of decline and social exclusion. This was done in an everyday manner through attending as an audience member or in a more active manner through becoming a volunteer at the theatre. The project team was keen to take this challenge to a higher level through the development of a theatrical performance. A play was developed in collaboration with some of the study participants, some members of a youth theatre group and some professional actors. This play was developed in a workshop fashion led by the theatre director of education using material from the interviews. It was designed both to describe the process of growing old and to ask questions of the audience. Subsequently the play was performed to a wide range of audiences including young people and residents of nursing homes.

At the centre of this project was a reflection (see May and Perry, Chapter 8, this volume) on ways of increasing the impact of qualitative research findings. The original theatre used the material from interviews with local residents to develop a corpus of knowledge about local issues which were used to develop 'docu-dramas' about those issues. The performance of these docu-dramas then provided a means of promoting greater discussion about those issues which generated considerable media interest evidenced in the archival material. In the research project the experience of growing older detailed in the many interviews was then transformed into a play, the performance of which in different venues promoted widespread discussion.

Both of these projects illustrate how the impact of qualitative research is not just a process of dissemination but rather one of active and often emotional engagement with different communities of interest. By involving participants in the research process they can become the agents of change themselves.

OPPORTUNITIES AND LIMITS

While qualitative research can provide an opportunity to develop an understanding of human experience, it is often not sufficient to convince others of the need for change. As we noted earlier, the dominance of positivist science can lead to the disparagement of qualitative research. It is for this reason that many qualitative researchers have embraced mixed methods (see Morse and Maddox, Chapter 36, this volume). By combining qualitative with quantitative research it has been argued that it is possible to benefit from the strengths of both. There are various concerns about the naive adoption of this approach which can potentially reduce the critical edge of qualitative research. To protect against such slippage Steinitz and Mishler (2001) have argued for the central importance of values in qualitative research to ensure that the critical potential of qualitative research remains central. In addition, reference to mixed methods frequently overlooks the potential of combining different qualitative methods. Thus, rather than relying upon interviews, which is by far the most common qualitative method, researchers should consider other methods including group discussions, written and video diaries, ethnography (see Gubrium and Holstein, Chapter 3, this volume), performative research (e.g. Gray and Sinding, 2002), etc.

Similarly, the qualitative researcher needs to seize the many opportunities provided by new technology. We have already detailed the benefits of using the creative arts to expand impact. To this innovation can be added the use of social media, websites, blogs, graphic novels and multimedia as ways of reaching out to different audiences (see Marotzki et al., Chapter 31, this volume). Involvement of the research participants in the design and operation of these methods can further enhance their potential.

Another challenge faced by all researchers is the cultural and historical specificity of research findings. Within qualitative research this awareness of context is central. By considering how the actor engages with the context, the qualitative researcher avoids the traditional reification of human action in quantitative research. For example, in exploring smoking behaviour quantitative researchers have sought to identify the individual personality attributes and attitudes which predicted such behaviour. Murray et al. (1988) in their qualitative study of smoking among young adults detailed how they deliberately used smoking as a means of engaging with their social world. Smoking was an important tool for managing one's position in a particular social setting, for example initiating social relationships, signalling to others as regards your mood, marking time, etc.

The findings of a research project are not sufficient in themselves to promote change. They need to convince the other of the validity of the argument and of the need for some form of change. If the project is participatory then the research participants become aware of the conflicting social representations and the obstacles to change. For wider impact there is a need for qualitative researchers to explore various partnerships. Steinitz and Mishler (2001) explored the potential of partnerships with oppressed groups in society. Other partnerships can be with various stakeholders who have a role to play in providing services to particular groups in society. Finally, policy-makers should not be considered a group apart but also as potential collaborators in research. Policy-makers are members of society prone to a range of competing interests and are looking for solutions to pressing social problems. Qualitative researchers can connect with policy-makers through providing a conduit for the voices of excluded citizens. They can actively engage policy-makers throughout the project but maintain the potential to criticize and expose inadequacies in social policy. Without the potential to critique, qualitative researchers risk being co-opted by more established interests.

NEW DEVELOPMENTS AND PERSPECTIVES

Qualitative research has garnered widespread respect in the scientific community. However, the widespread acceptance of positivist science means that qualitative researchers are often placed in a defensive position when presenting their work to policy-makers. In trying to expand their impact, qualitative researchers need to explore new approaches to engaging both with the public and with policy-makers. I have introduced some of these in this chapter but it is necessary to return to some of the original points to develop perspectives.

Research is an active engagement with the social world. It is not simply the collecting of data but rather the development of a practical understanding of the world through a dialectical process. This practical understanding is informed by our theoretical imagination as Willis argues:

> ethnography needs a theoretical imagination which it will not find, 'there', descriptively in the field. Equally, I believe that the theoretical imaginings of the social sciences are always best shaped in close tension with observational data. (2000: iix)

Here, Willis is emphasizing the importance of the theoretical imagination which constructs an understanding of the world in interaction with the data. You are not imposing a pattern on the world, neither are you collecting patterns. As Willis continues:

> Imagination is thereby forced to see the world in a grain of sand, the human social genome in a single cell. ... They should not be self-referenced imaginings but grounded imaginings. (2000: iix)

In looking to explore the potential to transfer the interpretation to another setting, these grounded imaginings need to consider what is the nature of that new setting and what are the problems facing it. In many ways all qualitative research projects are case studies which need to connect with the setting within which they are conducted.

The past generation has seen major social issues confronting society and policy-makers. Qualitative research can contribute substantially to understanding these issues. Some questions can encourage further reflection:

1. What is the contribution of a particular qualitative research project to practice? There is a need for ongoing critical engagement with the social world and acceptance of the moral responsibility of the researcher to contribute to beneficial change.
2. How are the research participants involved in the research? Qualitative researchers need to reflect upon the ways research participants and others are involved in setting the particular research agenda and in all aspects of the research process.
3. Who is setting the bigger research agenda? In this time of intense competition for research funds qualitative researchers need to reflect upon the broader assumptions behind particular research trajectories which are promoted by funding agencies.
4. What do you get out of the research? There is an ongoing need for personal reflection of your role in the research process.

In terms of perspectives qualitative research has come a long way since its recent rebirth. It is now accepted as a central approach within social science. It has evolved as a challenge to the dominant quantitative approaches. However, in the future there will remain the ongoing resistance from those who want definite answers which seem to be more easily provided by quantitative researchers. While qualitative researchers can continue to refine their tools of data collection and analysis, the extent to which they can translate their findings will remain crucial to their success.

In addition, a focus on method to the neglect of theory can become a form of fetishism (Moscovici, 1972). There remains the challenge of connecting method with theory and with practice. The importance of this praxis orientation is evident in Lewin's frequently quoted comment that progress in cooperation between applied and theoretical psychology 'can be accomplished ... if the theorist does not look toward applied problems with highbrow aversion or the fear of social problems, and if the applied psychologist realizes that there is nothing so practical as a good theory' (1951: 169).

FURTHER READING

Smith, Linda Tuhiwai (1999) *Decolonizing Methodologies. Research and Indigenous Peoples.* London: Zed Books.

A critique of many of the assumptions underlying social science research and of its theoretical and practical linkages with colonization.

Cox, Pat, Gesisen, Thomas and Green, Roger (eds) (2008) *Qualitative Research and Social Change. European Contexts.* London: Palgrave.

Collection of articles linking qualitative research with social change.

Whitehead, Jack and McNiff, Jean (2006) *Action Research: Living Theory.* London: Sage.

Detailed account of how to do action research.

REFERENCES

Atweh, Bill, Kemmis, Stephen and Weeks, Patricia (eds) (1998) *Action Research in Practice: Partnership for Social Justice in Education.* London: Routledge.

Barnett, Elizabeth, Davies, Celia and Wetherell, Margaret (2006) *Citizens at the Centre: Deliberative Participation in Healthcare Decisions.* London: Policy Press.

Barreras, Ricardo E. and Massey, Sean G. (eds) (2013) 'Impact validity as a framework for advocacy-based research [special issue]. *Journal of Social Issues,* 69(4).

Bernard, Mim, Ricketts, Michelle, Amigoni, David, Munro, Lucy, Murray, Michael, and Rezzano, Jill (2013). 'Ages and stages; the place of theatre in representations and recollections of ageing', *NDA Findings 15,* Available at http://www.newdynamics.group.shef.ac.uk/assets/files/FINAL%20NDA%20Findings%2015%20(2).pdf

Burton, Mark and Chapman, Melanie, J. (2004) 'Problems of evidence based practice in community based services', *Journal of Intellectual Disabilities,* 8: 56–70.

Cornish, Flora and Gillespie, Alex (2006) 'A pragmatist approach to the problem of knowledge in health psychology', *Journal of Health Psychology,* 14: 800–809.

Cox, Pat, Geisen, Thomas and Green, Roger (eds) (2008) *Qualitative Research and Social Change: European Contexts.* London: Palgrave.

Denzin, Norman, K. (2011) 'The politics of evidence', in Norman K. Denzin and Yvonna, S. Lincoln (eds), *The SAGE Handbook of Qualitative Research,* 4th edition. Thousand Oaks, CA: Sage. pp. 645–57.

Dillard, Amanda J., Fagerlin, Angela, Dal Cin, Sonya, Zikmund-Fisher, Brian J. and Ubel, Peter A. (2010) 'Narratives that address affective forecasting errors reduce perceived barriers to colorectal cancer screening', *Social Science & Medicine,* 71: 45–52.

Elvgren, Gilette, A. (1974) 'Documentary theatre at Stoke-on-Trent', *Educational Theatre Journal,* 26: 86–98.

Freire, Paulo (1974) *Pedagogy of the Oppressed.* New York: Continuum.

Frost, David M. and Ouellette, Suzanne C. (2011) 'A search for meaning: Recognising the potential of narrative research in social policy-making efforts', *Sexuality Research and Social Policy,* 8: 151–61.

Gray, Ross, and Sinding, Christina (2002). *Standing Ovation. Performing Social Science Research about Cancer.* Walnut Creek, CA: AltaMira.

Greenwood, Davydd and Levin, Morten (2007) *Introduction to Action Research.* London: Sage.

Hammack, Phillip L. (2012) 'Narrative and the politics of meaning', *Narrative Inquiry,* 21: 311–18.

Hannes, Karin (2011) 'Critical appraisal of qualitative research', Chapter 4 in J. Noyes et al. (eds), *Supplementary Guidance for Inclusion of Qualitative Research in Cochrane Systematic Reviews of Interventions.* Version 1 (updated August 2011) Cochrane Collaboration Qualitative Methods Group, 2011. Available from: http://cqrmg.cochrane.org/supplemental-handbook-guidance.

Harding, Sandra G. (1991) *Whose Science? Whose Knowledge? Thinking from Women's Lives.* Milton Keynes: Open University Press.

Hilsen, Anne I. (2006) 'And they shall be known by their deeds: Ethics and politics in action research', *Action Research,* 4: 23–36.

Holter, Inger M. and Schwartz-Barcott, Donna (2008) 'Action research: What is it? How has it been used and how can it be used in nursing?', *Journal of Advanced Nursing,* 18: 298–304.

Jodelet, Denise (2012) 'Interconnections between social representations and intervention', in Annamaria Silvana de Rosa (ed.), *Social Representations in the 'Social Arena'.* London: Routledge. pp. 77–88.

Jovchelovitch, Sandra (2008) 'Reflections on the diversity of knowledge: power and dialogue in representational fields', in Toshio Sugiman et al. (eds), *Meaning in Action: Constructions, Narratives, and Representations.* New York: Springer. pp. 23–36.

Kearney, Anne, J. (2006). 'Increasing our understanding of breast self-examination: women talk about cancer, the health care system, and being women'. *Qualitative Health Research,* 16: 802–20.

Kelemen, Mihaela (2013). Bridging the gap between academic theory and community practice. AHRC Connected Communities. Available at www.ahrc.ac.uk

Levin, Morten and Greenwood, Davydd (2011) 'Revitalising universities and reinvesting the social sciences', in Norman K. Denzin and Yvonna S. Lincoln (eds), *The SAGE Handbook of Qualitative Research,* 4th edition. Thousand Oaks, CA: Sage. pp. 27–42.

Lewin, Kurt (1951) 'Problems of research in social psychology', in Dorwin Cartwright (ed.), *Field*

Theory in Social Science: Selected Theoretical Papers. New York: Harper & Row. pp. 155–69.

Lewin, Simon, Glenton, Claire and Oxman, Andrew D. (2009) 'Use of qualitative methods alongside randomised controlled trials of complex healthcare interventions: Methodological study', *British Medical Journal*, 339: b3496.

McQueen, Amy and Kreuter, Matthew W. (2010) 'Measuring the effects of cancer survivor stories on cognitive and affective outcomes: A structural equation analysis', *Patient Education and Counselling*, 81: 15–21.

Middling, Sharon, Bailey, Jan, Maslin-Prothero, Sian and Scharf, Thomas (2011) 'Gardening and the social engagement of older people', *Working with Older People*, 15: 112–20.

Mishler, Elliot G. (1986) *Research Interviewing: Context and Narrative.* Cambridge, MA: Harvard University Press.

Moscovici, Serge (1972) 'Society and theory in social psychology', in Joachim Israel and Henri Tajfel (eds), *The Context of Social Psychology: A Critical Assessment.* London: Academic Press. pp. 17–68.

Moscovici, Serge (2000) *Social Representations: Explorations in Social Psychology.* Cambridge: Polity Press.

Murphy, Elizabeth and Dingwall, Robert (2003) *Qualitative Methods and Health Policy Research.* Hawthorne, NY: Walter de Gruyter.

Murray, Michael (2013) *Community narratives and community change.* Paper presented at Department of Psychology, Twente University, NL.

Murray, Michael and Crummett, Amanda (2010) '"I don't think they knew we could do these sorts of things": Social representations of community and participation in community arts by older people', *Journal of Health Psychology*, 15: 777–85.

Murray, Michael, Jarrett, Linda, Swan, Anthony V. and Rumun, Richard (1988) *Smoking among Young Adults.* Aldershot: Avebury.

Murray, Michael, Scharf, Thomas, Maslin-Prothero, Sian, Beech, Roger, and Ziegler, Friederike (2013) 'Call-Me: Promoting independence and social engagement among older people in disadvantaged communities', *NDA Findings 18.* Available at http://www.newdynamics.group.shef.ac.uk/assets/files/NDA%20Findings_18.pdf

Newton, Benjamin J., Rothlingova, Zuzana, Gutteridge, Robin, LeMarchand, Karen and Raphael, Jon H. (2012) 'No room for reflexivity? Critical reflections following a systematic review of qualitative research', *Journal of Health Psychology*, 17: 866–85.

Polletta, Francesca (2006) *It was Like a Fever: Storytelling in Protest and Politics.* Chicago: University of Chicago Press.

Public Health Research Unit (2006) *Critical Appraisal Skills Programme: Making sense of evidence about clinical effectiveness.* Available at: www.casp-uk.net/wp-content/uploads/2011/11/CASP_Qualitative_Appraisal_Checklist_14oct10.pdf (accessed 17 May 2013).

Putnam, Hilary (1981) *Reason, Truth and History.* Cambridge: Cambridge University Press.

Reason, Peter and Bradbury, Hilary (2001) 'Introduction: Inquiry and participation in search of a world worthy of human aspiration', in Peter Reason and Hilary Bradbury (eds), *Handbook of Action Research: Participatory Inquiry and Practice.* London: Sage. pp.1–14.

Sampson, Edward, E. (2003) 'Unconditional kindness to strangers: Human sociality and the foundation for an ethical psychology', *Theory & Psychology*, 13: 147–75.

Selbin, Eric (2010) *Revolution, Rebellion, Resistance: The Power of Story.* London: Zed Books.

Steinitz, Vicky and Mishler, Elliot (2001) 'Reclaiming SPSSI's radical promise: A critical look at JSI's "Impact of welfare reform" issue', *Analyses of Social Issues and Public Policy*, 1: 163–75.

Thompson, Paul (2000) *The Voice of the Past: Oral History*, 3rd edition. Oxford: Oxford University Press.

Ussher, Jane, M. (1999) 'Feminist approaches to qualitative health research', in Michael Murray and Kerry Chamberlain (eds), *Qualitative Health Psychology: Theories and Methods.* London: Sage. pp. 98–110.

Wang, Caroline C., Morrel-Samuels, Susan, Hutchinson, Peter M., Bell, Lee and Pestronk, Robert M. (2004) 'Flint photovoice: Community-building among youths, adults and policy-makers', *American Journal of Public Health*, 94: 911–13.

Wang, Sheng and Noe, Raymond A. (2010) 'Knowledge sharing: A review and directions for future research', *Human Resource Management Review*, 20: 115–31.

Watt, David (2009) 'Local knowledge, memories, and community: From oral history to performance', in Susan C. Haedicke et al. (eds), *Political Performances: Theory and Practice.* Amsterdam: Editions Rodopi. pp. 189–210.

Williams, Lewis, Labonte, Ronald and O'Brien, Mike (2003) 'Empowering social action through narratives of identity and culture', *Health Promotion International*, 18: 33–40.

Willis, Paul (2000) *The Ethnographic Imagination.* Cambridge: Polity Press.

Author Index

Abbott, Andrew D., 30, 545
Abu-Lughod, Lila, 36, 37, 38, 40, 47
Adler, Patricia, 356
Adler, Peter, 356
Agar, Michael, 288
Åhlberg, Mauri, 406n
Åkerström, Malin, 468, 469, 471, 472, 473, 476
Akkerman, Sanne, 80, 81, 87, 88, 89
Alasuutari, Pertti, 7, 9, 475
Albrow, Martin, 109
Aliseda, Atocha, 126
Allen, Marion N., 481, 487
Allen, Mitch, 581n
Altheide, David, 172, 505
Altman, Rick, 425
Anderson, Douglas R., 127, 161
Anderson, Elijah, 360
Anderson, Gary L., 544
Anderson, Leon, 358
Anderson, Nels, 556, 560
Anderson, Rosemary, 302
Andrews, Molly, 203, 204, 214
Ang, Ien, 256
Angus, Jan, 316
Antaki, Charles, 329
Anyon, Jean, 21, 548
Apple, Michael, 576
Arcidiacono, Francesco, 80, 88, 90
Argyris, Chris, 22
Aristotle, 100, 104, 123
Armstrong, David, 291, 501
Arnedal, Lotta, 470
Arthur, Sue, 103
Athens, Lonnie, 360
Atkins, Salla, 488, 490, 492, 493
Atkinson, J. Maxwell, 72, 74, 329, 370
Atkinson, Paul, 23, 24, 25, 27, 29, 30, 31, 55, 83, 162, 212, 283, 363, 369, 469, 471, 474, 501
Atran, Scott, 543
Attali, Jacques, 425
Atweh, Bill, 588
Aufenager, Stefan, 65
Augoyard, Jean-Francois, 427, 428, 430, 432
Austin, John L., 340, 372
Ayim, Maryann, 127
Ayres, Lioness, 26, 543
Azzarito, Laua, 406n

Back, Les, 429
Bacon, Francis, 555
Bailenson, Jeremy, 459
Bain, Read, 556

Baker, Carolyn D., 468, 472
Bakhtin, Mikhail, 205
Baltruschat, Astrid, 231n
Bamberg, Michael, 37
Banerji, Riddhi, 83
Banks, Marcus, 13, 16, 104, 105, 181, 190, 218, 221, 223, 248, 270, 282, 343, 367, 378, 386, 390, 406n, 435, 526, 593
Barber, Michael, 195, 508
Barbour, Rosaline S., 7, 10, 11, 13, 16, 61, 82, 112, 114, 115, 116, 155, 167, 173, 174, 179, 195, 224, 236, 248, 287, 291, 295, 308, 314, 316, 317, 318, 354, 465, 469, 487, 488, 489, 490, 498, 499, 500, 501, 505, 506, 507, 508, 510, 511, 512, 518, 520, 526, 528, 535, 542, 570, 573, 585, 589, 594
Barker, Judith C., 36
Barlow, John Perry, 451
Barnes, John A., 457
Barnett, Alison, 384, 387, 392
Barnett, Elizabeth, 589
Barnett-Page, Elaine, 492
Barone, Thomas, 26
Barreras, Ricardo E., 591
Barroso, Julie, 484, 485, 487, 488, 489, 492
Barry, Christine A., 83, 85, 530
Barthes, Roland, 23, 230, 254, 399, 573
Barth-Weingarten, Dagmar, 65, 74, 75
Bartlett, Judith, 298
Bartunek, Jean M., 80, 83
Bastos, Ana Cecilia S., 86–7
Bateson, Gregory, 396, 397, 406n, 438
Battiste, Marie, 516
Baudrillard, Jean, 400
Bauer, Martin W., 80, 81, 82, 431
Baumann, Zygmunt, 234
Baxandall, Michael, 397
Bazeley, Patricia, 31, 290, 527
Beatty, Warren, 67, 69
Beaulieu, Anne, 263, 266
Beck, Cheryl T., 483, 492, 540, 541, 542, 545
Beck, Ulrich, 98, 111, 120
Becker, Howard S., 83, 89, 236, 355, 359, 361, 545, 547, 548, 573
Beck-Gernsheim, Elisabeth, 120
Beckman, Suzanne, C., 273
Bell, Allan, 350, 351
Bell, Philip, 399
Bell, Susan, 204
Belton, John, 418, 419
Benaquisto, Lucia, 30
Ben-Ari, Adital, 80
Bender, Amy, 80

AUTHOR INDEX

Bengry-Howell, Andrew, 145
Benington, John, 80, 82, 84, 86, 89, 90
Bennett, Tony, 254
Berbary, Lisbeth A., 298
Berelson, Bernard, 171
Berger, Arthur A., 172, 381, 385, 404, 406n, 415, 416
Berger, John, 397, 399–400
Berger, Leigh, 357
Berger, Peter L., 124, 189, 219, 414, 472, 563
Bergmann, Jörg R., 190, 437
Bergmann, Manfred Max, 508
Bernard, H. Russell, 24, 172, 291, 305, 527
Bernard, Mim, 594
Berners-Lee, Tim, 454
Bernez, Norine, 71
Bhaskar, Roy, 314
Bhattacharya, Kakali, 306
Bidlo, Oliver, 125
Biklen, San K., 24
Billig, Michael, 350
Bird, Gregory, 191
Birdwhistell, Ray L., 438
Bishop, Libby, 469, 477
Blank, Grant, 457
Blaxter, Mildred, 469, 497
Blesser, Barry, 425
Bloom, Howard S., 549n
Bloomfield, Brian P., 369
Bloor, Michael, 318, 500
Bloor, Mick, 368, 468
Blumer, Herbert, 6, 35, 36, 154, 363, 564
Bochner, Arthur P., 257, 358
Bock, Mary A., 382
Boeije, Hennie, 94
Bogdan, Robert, 24
Bohnsack, Ralf, 11, 16, 217, 221, 223, 224, 225, 229, 231, 234, 238, 315, 373, 436, 437, 543
Bondas, Terese, 490
Bong, Sharon A., 283
Boon, Bronwyn, 319
Bordwell, David, 415, 416, 417, 418
Bourdieu, Pierre, 111, 112, 113, 219, 221, 222, 230, 231n, 238, 315, 316, 368, 468, 543
Bourdon, Sylvain, 291
Bowen, John Richard, 100
Bowman, Paul, 256
Boyatzis, Richard E., 147, 172, 173, 174, 176
Boyd, Danah, 455, 457, 459
Brabeck, Kalina M., 515
Bradbury, Hilary, 515, 588
Braebeck, Mary M., 515
Branigan, Edward, 416
Brannen, Julia, 319
Braun, Virginia, 147, 305
Brekhus, Wayne, H., 470
Brentano, Franz, 185
Briggs, Charles, 544
Brinberg, David, 543

Brinkmann, Svend, 305
Brown-Saracino, Japonica, 541
Bruckman, Amy, 268
Brügger, Niels, 453
Bruner, Jerome, 23, 204
Bryant, Antony, 32n, 125, 153, 154, 303, 549, 575
Brydon-Miller, Mary, 511, 515
Bryman, Alan, 97, 499, 527, 528, 546
Buckland, Warren, 415, 416
Bull, Michael, 428, 429
Bull, Peter, 67
Bulmer, Martin, 556
Burgess, Raymond G., 499
Burr, Vivien, 203, 345
Burton, Mark, 593
Burton, Robert, 163
Bury, Michael, 507
Butt, Trevor, 345

Cabell, Kenneth, 87
Cahnmann-Taylor, Melisa, 305
Calvey, David, 356, 357
Campbell, Donald T., 542, 549n
Cannella, Gail S., 510, 515, 576
Caracelli, Valerie, 31n
Carnap, Rudolf, 186
Carroll, William, 381, 383
Carspecken, Phil Frances, 576
Carver, Raymond, 574, 581
Casetti, Francesco, 415
Casey, Bernadette, 415
Casey, Neil, 437, 439
Castells, Manuel, 112
Catterall, Miriam, 267
Certeau, Michel de, 252
Cerwonka, Allaine, 37, 48n
Chafe, Wallace, 65, 66, 67, 72, 74
Chalmers, Alan F., 555
Chamberlain, Kerry, 248, 342, 359, 367, 380, 381, 394
Chandler, Daniel, 181
Chapman, Melanie J., 593
Charlton, James I., 515
Charmaz, Kathy, 7, 10, 11, 12, 16, 24, 25, 30, 32n, 35, 37, 49, 81, 84, 125, 130, 144, 153, 154, 155, 156, 157, 158, 159, 160, 162, 163, 167, 173, 181, 224, 270, 279, 280, 283, 303, 305, 319, 320, 360, 363, 364, 370, 390, 445, 475, 482, 483, 484, 487, 488, 498, 499, 500, 503, 508, 512, 524, 528, 541, 544, 545, 548, 549, 554, 556, 560, 570, 571, 572, 575
Chase, Susan E., 206, 209
Chatman, Seymour, 415, 416, 418, 419
Chauviré, Christiane, 130, 131
Cheeseman, Peter, 594
Chen, Kuang-Hsing, 98
Cherny, Lynn, 266
Chiari, Isabella, 69, 70
Chilisa, Bagele, 515, 517

Chmiel, Margaret, 12, 15, 17, 19, 42, 51, 53, 62, 127, 146, 314, 395, 465, 471, 498, 503, 506, 545, 548, 573, 589, 591
Chomsky, Noam, 234, 237
Christians, Clifford G., 510, 511
Cicourel, Aaron V., 190, 219, 370
Cisneros-Puebla, César A., 292
Clandinin, D. Jean, 571
Clarke, Adele E., 153, 154, 162
Clarke, David, 492
Clarke, Victoria, 147, 305
Clayman, Steven, 329
Clifford, James, 35, 355, 364
Clinton, Bill, 67, 73, 74
Clinton, Hillary, 73
Clough, Patricia Ticineto, 574, 579
Coffey, Amanda, 10, 13, 16, 23, 24, 25, 27, 29, 30, 31, 116, 155, 281, 283, 291, 295, 355, 363, 369, 526
Cohen, Stanley, 470, 472
Coldren, James R., 316
Cole, Ardra L., 570, 578
Coleman, James, 562, 565
Collier, David, 100
Collier, Marcus, 316
Collins, Patricia Hill, 573, 577
Collins, Randall, 469, 471, 472, 475
Connelly, F. Michael, 571
Conquergood, Dwight, 571, 572
Cook, Judith, 112
Cook, Thomas D., 549n
Cooper, Mick, 89
Coote, Jeremy, 397
Corbin, Juliet, 7, 24, 25, 30, 31n, 58, 145, 153, 154, 155, 160, 162, 163, 167, 181, 270, 286, 303, 360, 370, 502, 506, 559, 560, 572, 575, 576
Corcoran, Tim, 350
Cornish, Flora, 15, 16, 19, 80, 81, 83, 90, 290, 517, 535, 586, 592
Correll, Shelly, 264
Corti, Louise, 467, 468, 469, 472, 473, 474, 475
Cottle, Simon, 386
Couldry, Nick, 248, 259, 381, 383, 384
Couper-Kuhlen, Elizabeth, 65, 74, 75
Cox, Christoph, 428
Cox, Pat, 587
Craik, Fergus I.M., 23
Cram, Fiona, 515, 516, 518
Crawley, Jim, 143
Crazy Bull, Cheryl, 515, 516, 518
Creaner, Mary, 490, 492
Cressey, Donald R., 556, 557
Creswell, John W., 235, 528, 535
Cromby, John, 345
Cronholm, Stefan, 153, 162
Crossley, Michelle, 147
Crummett, Amanda, 593
Cruz, John D., 247

Curl, Traci, 331, 332, 333, 334, 335
Curran, James, 380, 381, 383
Czarniawska, Barbara, 204

Darbyshire, Philip, 545
Daston, Lorraine, 354
Davidson, Judith, 14
Davies, Bronwyn, 205, 206
Davies, James, 355
Davis, John, 402
De Fina, Anna, 204
DeAndrea, David C., 265
Deegan, Mary J., 556
DeHaene, Lucia, 519
Denzin, Norman K., 6, 7, 8, 10, 12, 17, 115, 180, 223, 250, 255, 256, 257, 258, 277, 305, 358, 364, 391, 488, 490, 502, 511, 513, 514, 570, 572, 574, 578, 582n, 591
Dere, Ekrem, 23
Derrida, Jacques, 141
Descartes, René, 185
Deuze, Mark, 380, 387
DeVault, Marjorie L., 303
DeWalt, Billie R., 82, 83
DeWalt, Kathleen Musante, 82, 83
Dewey, John, 154, 559
Dey, Ian, 23–4, 27, 29, 31n, 163
di Chio, Federico, 415
di Gregorio, Silvana, 14
Dieberger, Andreas, 455
Diederich, Adele, 174, 181
Dillard, Amanda J., 590
Dillard, Cynthia B., 515
Dilthey, Wilhelm, 137, 140, 234, 572
Dingwall, Robert, 52, 368, 585
Dittmar, Norbert, 67
Diversi, Marscelo, 569, 572
Dixon-Woods, Mary, 485, 486
Dodd, Sarah-Jane, 515, 518
Domínguez, Daniel, 446
Donmoyer, Robert, 541, 544, 546
Donohue, Richard, 298
Döring, Nicola, 453
Dorner, Lisa M., 300
Doucet, Andrea, 113, 114
Doughty, Ruth, 412
Douglas, Mary, 468
Downe, Soo, 492, 493
Draucker, Claire B., 54
Dreher, Jochen, 191
Dreher, Tanja, 381, 383
Dresing, Thorsten, 64, 68–9
Dressman, Mark, 21, 548
Drew, Paul, 327, 329, 330, 331, 332, 334, 337, 338, 342
Du Bois, John W., 68, 75
DuBow, Fred, 100
Dunne, C., 162

Dupois, Paul, 291
Durkheim, Emile, 95, 368, 375, 562

Eastwood, Clint, 73
Eatough, Virginia, 143
Eberle, Thomas S., 7, 9, 11, 16, 110, 125, 126, 143, 188, 191, 193, 194, 195, 197, 218, 219, 222, 234, 248, 301, 302, 329, 394, 395, 426, 429, 436, 439, 474, 488, 512, 525, 572
Eco, Umberto, 134n, 254
Edwards, Derek, 143
Edwards, Elizabeth, 396, 406n
Edwards, Jane A., 71, 76
Edwards, Jeanette, 397
Edwards, Tim, 343
Eggan, Fred, 96
Ehlich, Konrad, 71, 72, 74, 75
Eisenhart, Margaret, 570
Eiser, J. Richard, 349
Eisner, Elliot, 546
Ekman, Paul, 438, 440
Elliott, Heather, 114
Elliott, Jane, 207
Elliott, Robert, 486, 489, 490
Ellis, Carolyn, 257, 358, 513, 514, 516–17, 518–19
Ellis, John, 419
Ellison, Nicole B., 457
Elsaesser, Thomas, 416
Elvgren, Gilette A., 594
Ember, Carol R., 97
Embree, Lester, 186
Emerson, Peter, 147
Emerson, Robert M., 43, 56, 219, 359
England, Kim, 114
Englert, Carina J., 437
Englert, Carina Jasmin, 190
Enosh, Guy, 80
Entman, Robert, 381
Ereaut, Gill, 278–9, 286
Erickson, Frederick, 22, 28, 30, 439, 541, 544, 548
Erickson, Ken, 87
Erzberger, Christian, 65
Esin, Cigdem, 16, 24, 27, 28, 37, 146, 198, 208, 210, 212, 213, 221, 289, 298, 300, 303, 304, 342, 344, 362, 371, 372, 415, 503, 512, 525, 545, 569, 589
Etherington-Wright, Christine, 412
Etzioni, Amitai, 100
Evans, Jessica, 405–6n
Evers, Jeanine C., 14, 280
Ezzy, Douglas, 24

Faircloth, Christopher, 364
Fairclough, Norman, 144, 342
Fanshel, David, 24
Farnsworth, John, 319
Fathi, Mastoureh, 208, 209, 211, 212
Fay, Brian, 119
Fetterman, David M., 25

Fielding, Jane, 467, 470, 472–3, 475, 476, 478
Fielding, Nigel G., 277, 278, 290, 292, 467, 470, 472–3, 475, 476, 478
Fierro, Rita, 518
Fincham, Benjamin, 368, 375, 376, 377
Fine, Michelle, 573
Finfgeld, Deborah L., 481, 482, 488
Finlay, Linda, 143, 306
Finley, Susan, 570, 578, 579, 581n
Finn, James, 180
Firestone, William A., 541
Fischer, Michael M., 252
Fiske, John, 252–3, 255, 411
Flaherty, Robert, 359–60, 438
Flick, Uwe, 6, 8, 9, 11, 12, 14, 23, 65, 96, 99, 102, 125, 241, 318, 496, 498, 503, 507, 570, 581n
Flinders, David J., 21
Flowers, Paul, 142
Flyvbjerg, Bent, 381, 383, 385, 392
Fonow, Mary, 112
Forrester, Michael A., 340, 342
Foster, Helen E., 51
Foucault, Michel, 143–4, 200, 204, 206, 230, 231, 250, 251, 252, 256, 343, 345, 349, 350, 368, 566
Fowler, Don D., 355
Fox, Fiona E., 324
Fox, Richard G., 95, 96, 97
Fox, Robert, 69
Frank, Arthur W., 503
Frankland, Jane, 318, 500
Freeman, Mark, 204
Freeman, Melissa, 234, 297, 302, 308, 515
Frege, Gottlob, 123
Freidson, Eliot, 546
Freire, Paulo, 576, 588, 590
Freud, Sigmund, 236, 240, 241
Friese, Susanne, 14
Friesen, Wallace, 438, 440
Frosh, Stephen, 141, 147, 351
Frost, David M., 589
Frost, Nollaig, 64, 68, 80, 81, 208
Frow, John, 253, 254

Gadamer, Hans-Georg, 140, 141, 235
Gaiser, Ted J., 457, 459
Garcia, Angela Cora, 265
Garfinkel, Harold, 6, 7, 44, 110, 188, 190, 191, 192, 193, 217, 218, 219, 223, 231n, 329, 373, 426, 469, 474
Garton, Laura, 457
Garz, Detlef, 245n
Gaskell, George D., 80, 81, 82, 431
Gearing, Robin Edward, 302
Gee, James P., 24, 27–8
Geer, Blanche, 83
Geertz, Clifford, 7, 249, 359, 395, 571, 574, 575
Gehlen, Arnold, 124
Geimer, Alexander, 231

Genette, Gérard, 254
Georgakopoulou, Alexandra, 204
George, Alexander L., 171
Georgiou, Myria, 380, 381
Gerhardt, Uta, 236
Gesell, Arnold, 438
Ghosh, Riddhi, 81, 83
Giardina, Michael D., 253
Gibbons, Michael, 112
Gibbs, Graham R., 4, 7, 8, 14, 15, 16, 30, 88, 103, 172, 173, 180, 181, 269, 274, 306, 324, 370, 499, 500, 505
Gibson, Gloria, 204
Giddens, Anthony, 111, 223, 562
Gilbert, Andrew, 119
Gilbert, Daniel T., 544
Gilbert, Linda S., 285–6
Gill, Rosalind, 343
Gillam, Lynn, 120
Gillberg, Christopher, 469
Gillespie, Alex, 80, 81, 83, 592
Gillies, Val, 349
Gilligan, Carol, 114
Gilly, Mary C., 265
Gingrich, Andre, 16, 19, 24, 94, 95, 96, 97, 98, 99, 101, 103, 104, 105, 270
Ginsberg, Faye, 396
Ginsberg, Pauline E., 521
Giroux, Henry A., 254
Glaser, Barney G., 4, 7, 8, 12, 31n, 35, 36, 48n, 58, 60, 96, 145, 153, 154, 155, 156, 157, 158, 159, 160, 161, 162, 163, 167, 231n, 279, 280, 303, 305, 319, 445, 475, 482, 484, 485, 499, 500, 508, 548, 556, 557, 558, 558–9, 562, 564–5
Glynos, Jason, 350
Gobo, Giampietro, 9, 49, 50, 54, 540, 550n
Goetz, Judith P., 361, 363, 364
Goffman, Erving, 43, 235, 320, 329, 395, 429, 447n, 468, 474, 475
Gold, Raymond, 356
Goldkuhl, Göran, 153, 162
Goldman, Ricki, 439
Goldthorpe, John H., 547
Gomm, Roger, 550n
Goodman, Robert, 289
Goodman, Steve, 432
Goodwin, Charles, 330, 395, 397, 438, 439, 440, 443, 444
Goodwin, Marjorie Harness, 438
Gough, Brendan, 306
Gouldner, Alvin W., 110
Gramsci, Antonio, 250, 251
Grant, Jan, 143
Grasseni, Cristina, 397
Gray, Ross, 596
Green, Judith, 318, 499, 506
Greenberg, Josh, 382, 435
Greene, Jennifer C., 31n, 223

Greenwood, Davydd, 588
Griffin, Christine, 145
Grimshaw, Allen D., 439
Grimshaw, Anna, 360
Groeben, Norbert, 172, 173
Grondin, Jean, 234
Gross, Glenda, 303
Gross, Peter, 190, 438
Grossberg, Lawrence, 247, 248, 249, 251, 253, 254, 414
Grossen, Michele, 84
Guba, Egon G., 24, 49, 52, 223, 263, 498, 501, 515, 520, 541, 546, 575, 576, 579, 581n
Gubrium, Jaber F., 10, 15, 19, 28, 37, 39, 40, 45, 47, 111, 125, 145, 190, 203, 262, 269, 303, 355, 356, 362, 363, 424, 437, 444, 468, 482, 503, 524, 544, 572, 596
Guilia, Milena, 450
Guillemin, Marilys, 120
Gumperz, John J., 71
Gurvitsch, George, 192

Habermas, Jürgen, 562
Hackett, Robert, 381, 383
Haddon, Alfred, 400, 404, 405, 438
Hage, Per, 406n
Halbwachs, Maurice, 220
Halkier, Bente, 320–2, 323
Hall, Elisabeth O.C., 490
Hall, John R., 109
Hall, Peter, 112
Hall, Stuart, 253, 259, 342, 343, 382, 405–6n, 414
Hall, Wend A., 80, 81, 84, 85, 87–8, 90, 259
Hamilton, Peter, 405–6n
Hammack, Phillip L., 587
Hammersley, Martyn, 52, 53, 55, 83, 314, 469, 497, 540, 542, 543, 544, 548
Hammou, Karim, 425
Hannerz, Ulf, 543
Hannes, Karin, 592
Hanson, Norwood R., 555, 561
Harary, Frank, 406n
Haraway, Donna, 249, 255, 257
Harden, Angela, 485, 487, 492
Hardesty, Donald L., 355
Harding, Jamie, 96
Harding, Sandra, 111, 306, 588
Hare, R. Dwight, 482, 483, 492
Harré, Rom, 205, 206
Harris, Chandice C., 482
Harris, Rochelle, 515, 517, 518
Harris, Roy, 64, 65
Hart, Laura, 318
Hartley, Jean, 80, 82, 84, 86, 89, 90
Hartley, John, 414
Hartsock, Nancy C.M., 110
Hartung, Martin, 76
Harvey, David, 98

Hayano, David M., 266
Hayashi, Makoto, 332
Haythornthwaite, Caroline, 461
Heath, Christian, 110, 330, 394, 395, 398, 405n, 438, 439, 443, 445, 446
Hecht, Tobias, 300
Hechter, Michael, 21
Hedfors, Per, 425
Heidegger, Martin, 140, 141, 221, 302
Heider, Eleanor R., 545
Heikklä, Riie, 317–18, 319
Heil, Simone, 180, 181
Heinze, Thomas, 12
Hempel, Carl G., 560, 561
Henley, Paul, 406n
Henriques, Julian, 350
Henwood, Karen, 160, 163
Hepburn, Alexa, 308, 315, 343, 504
Heritage, John C., 43, 72, 74, 327, 328, 329, 330, 331, 332, 334, 337, 342
Herman, David, 204
Herzfeld, Michael, 468
Hesmondhalgh, David, 253
Hesse-Biber, Sharlene, 291, 364
Hester, Laurel, 589
Hijleh, Mark, 424
Hill, Clara E., 489, 492
Hill, Herbert, 531
Hilmes, Michele, 425
Hilsen, Anne Inge, 315, 589
Hindmarsh, Jon, 110, 446
Hitzler, Ronald, 195, 196
Hochschild, Arlie, 566
Hodgetts, Darrin, 248, 342, 359, 367, 380, 381, 382, 383, 384, 385, 392, 394
Hollway, Wendy, 114, 142, 143, 205
Holme, Jennifer Jellison, 298
Holmes, Dave, 116
Holstein, James A., 10, 15, 19, 28, 37, 39, 40, 42, 45, 47, 111, 125, 145, 190, 203, 262, 269, 303, 355, 356, 362, 363, 424, 437, 444, 468, 482, 503, 524, 544, 572, 596
Holsti, Ole R., 171, 172
Holt, Amanda, 344
Holter, Inger M, 588
Holton, Judith A., 159
Holy, Ladislav, 96, 97
Honer, Anne, 195
Hooks, Bell, 573, 577
Horne, Christine, 21
Hosking, Diane M., 119
Houser, Nathan, 127
Hsie, Hsiu-Fang, 172, 173
Hsiung, Ping-Chun, 9
Huberman, A. Michael, 24, 28, 29, 31, 31n, 57, 180, 283, 290, 301, 305, 503, 542, 544, 545
Hughes, Everett, C., 35, 154
Hume, David, 22

Humphreys, Laud, 470
Hurston, Zora Neale, 577
Hurworth, Rosalind E., 571
Husserl, Edmund, 140, 185–6, 187, 189, 191, 192, 194, 219
Hussey, Susan, 319, 505
Huston, John, 71
Hutchby, Ian, 330
Huxley, Thomas Henry, 395
Hydén, Margareta, 210
Hyvarinen, Matti, 204

Ihde, Don, 425
Imdahl, Max, 231
Inglis, Tom, 549
Ionesco, Eugene, 128
Irvin, John, 69
Irvine, Annie, 331

Jackson, Alecia Yl., 306
Jackson, Kristi, 31
Jacobsson, Katarina, 476, 477
Jakobson, Roman, 22, 23, 30
James, William, 80, 127, 187, 579
Jay, Martin, 397
Jefferson, Gail, 74, 323, 327–8, 330
Jefferson, Tony, 142, 143, 205
Jenkins, Henry, 256, 258
Jenks, Christopher J., 66, 76
Jennings, Len, 487, 492
Jensen, Devon, 541
Jensen, Louise A., 481, 487
Jewitt, Carey, 399
Jodelet, Denise, 590
Johnson, John M., 505
Johnson, Richard, 248, 250, 253, 254, 256, 257
Johnson-Bailey, Juanita, 298
Johnston, Lynne H., 291
Jones, Steve, 457
Jörissen, Benjamin, 454, 455
Josselson, Ruthellen, 81
Jovchelovitch, Sandra 591
Jurow, A. Susan, 570

Kaelble, Hartmut, 96
Kagan, Carolyn, 84, 146
Kant, Immanuel, 186
Kaplan, Abraham, 22
Kapustka, Katherine A., 180
Kärfve, Eva, 469
Kaufmann, Jodi, 306
Kaveney, Ron, 421
Kayahara, Jennifer, 264
Kayser-Jones, Jeanie S., 527
Kearney, Anne J., 588
Kearney, Margaret, 484, 485, 487, 492
Keating, Elizabeth, 424
Keats, John, 364

Kedzior, Richard, 266
Kelemen, Mihaela, 592
Kelle, Udo, 17, 65, 133, 162, 163, 283, 291, 320, 328, 370, 471, 499, 500, 541, 544, 546, 548, 557, 559, 563–4, 566
Kellner, Douglas, 250, 253, 254
Kelman, Ari Y., 433n
Kemp, Lynn, 527
Kendall, Gavin, 144, 344
Kidd, Pamela, S., 314
Kim, Seon Joo, 301
Kincheloe, Joe, 258
King, Nigel, 279, 283
Kirk, David, 406n
Kissmann, Ulrike Tikvah, 439
Kitsuse, John I., 42, 370
Kitzinger, Celia, 328, 329, 330, 336
Kitzinger, Jenny, 318
Knoblauch, Hubert, 9, 13, 16, 110, 117, 118, 190, 191, 198, 218, 221, 248, 270, 282, 295, 394, 432, 433, 437, 439, 442, *445*, 446, 526
Knoll, Eva-Maria, 98
Knowles, J. Gary, 570, 578
Koch, Robert, 403
Koch, Sabine C., 436
Koelen, Maria, 80, 84
Koenig, Thomas, 277
Koppel, Ross, 535, 536
Kouritzin, Sandra G., 305
Kowal, Sabine, 12, 15, 19, 65, 67, 68, 69, 70, 71, 72, 73, 74, 116, 174, 190, 198, 207, 208, 281, 299, 315, 316, 330, 343, 359, 395, 446, 473, 499
Kozinets, Robert V., 13, 16, 262, 263, 264, 265, 266, 267, 268, 273, 274, 367, 378, 446, 451, 457
Kracauer, Siegfried, 171
Kraimer, Klaus, 245n
Kreff, Fernand, 98
Kress, Gunther R., 181, 399, 405n, 444
Kreuter, Matthew W., 590
Kreuz, Roger J., 66, 76–7
Krippendorff, Klaus, 171, 172, 382
Krog, Antijie, 515
Kruijff, Geert-Jan, 126
Krzychala, Slawomir, 231n
Kvale, Steinar, 301, 304, 305

LaBelle, Brandon, 425, 428
Labov, William, 24, 205, 304, 342
LaFrance, Joan, 515, 516, 518
Laitin, David D., 100
Lakatos, Imre, 555
Lakoff, George, 31n
Lamerichs, Joyce, 80, 84
Lampert, Martin D., 76
Lamprey, John, 396
Lan Hing Ting, Karine, 424
Langdridge, Darren, 137, 142, 344, 345
Langer, Antje, 64

Langer, Roy, 273
Lapadat, J.C., 67
Larkin, Jill, 531
Larrabee, Mary J., 110
Lash, Scott, 111
Lather, Patti A., 308, 577, 578
Latour, Bruno, 374–5, 396
Laudan, Larry, 555
Laurier, Eric, 437
Lawson, Tony, 544
Lazarsfeld, Paul F., 153–4
Leavy, Patricia, 364, 570
LeCompte, Margaret D., 361, 363, 364, 549n
Lee, Daniel B., 432
Lee, Raymond M., 277, 278, 292, 298
Leech, Nancy L., 508
Leibniz, Gottfried Wilhelm, 127
Lejeune, Christophe, 280
Lempert, Lora Bex, 163, 303
Lenhart, Amanda, 460
Lerner, Gene H., 330
Levin, Morten, 588
Levinas, Emanuel 589
Levinson, Stephen C., 328, 329
Lévi-Strauss, Claude, 23, 234, 569
Lewin, Kurt, 597
Lewin, Simon, 593
Lewins, Ann, 181, 274, 286
Lewis, Jane, 95, 102, 279
Liddicoat, Anthony J., 300
Lieblich, Amia, 27, 28
Lijphart, Arend, 99
Lincoln, Yvonna S., 6, 7, 8, 24, 52, 223, 257, 263, 277, 498, 501, 510, 515, 520, 521, 541, 546, 572, 575, 576, 581n, 582n
Linde, Charlotte, 24, 28
Lindenberg, Siegwart, 563
Lindesmith, Alfred R., 556, 557
Ling, Richard Seyler, 460
Lingard, Lorelei, 80, 81, 82, 83, 86, 87, 88, 89–90
Linsay, Anne C., 67
Lipton, Peter, 561
Little, Daniel, 544
Llobera, Marcos, 406n
Locke, John, 555
Lockridge, Ernest, 569
Lofland, John, 303
Logstrup, Knud, 589
Lomas, Peter, 141
Lomax, Helen, 437, 439
Lonkila, Marrku, 291
Lopez, Kay A., 143
Louis, Meryl Reis, 80, 83
Lu, Chi-Jung, 81
Luckmann, Benita, 195
Luckmann, Thomas, 124, 187, 188, 189, 190, 191, 195, 200, 219, 302, 414, 437, 438
Lüdecke, Daniel, 565

Lüdemann, Christian, 563–4
Luff, Paul, 443
Luhmann, Niklas, 218, 219, 224, 562
Luker, Karen A., 566
Lunbeck, Elizabeth, 354
Lundberg, George A., 556
Luther, Martin, 589
Lynch, Michael, 113
Lyons, John, 22

Mabry, Linda, 541
Macdonald, Keith, 370
Maclaren, Pauline, 267
MacMillan, Katie, 277, 289, 290
Macnaghten, Phil, 315, 316
MacWhinney, Brian, 68, 76
Madden, Mary, 460
Maddox, Lory J., 11, 17, 180, 290, 336, 337, 465, 496, 508, 515, 517, 518, 595
Madison, Soyini D., 515, 569, 571
Maeder, Christoph, 13, 16, 190, 282, 295, 343, 378
Maffesoli, Michel, 249
Magnani, Lorenzo, 130
Maguire, Michael, 370
Mahoney, James, 101
Maiwald, Kai-Olaf, 238
Makagon, Daniel, 429, 430–1
Makosky, Daley C., 315
Malinowski, Bronislaw, 6
Malkki, Liisa H., 37, 48n
Mallozzi, Christine A., 309
Malone, Patrick S., 544
Malson, Helen, 212
Mangabeira, Wilma C., 278
Manly, John Matthews, 364
Mann, Chris, 451, 461
Mannheim, Karl, 16, 217, 218, 219, 220, 221, 222, 223, 224, 229, 230, 231n, 234, 373
Manning, Peter K., 21, 567
Marcus, Bernd, 455
Marcus, George E., 35, 252, 364, 438
Marien, Mary W., 396
Markham, Annette 267
Marková, Ivana, 80, 82
Marotzki, Winfried, 13, 16, 181, 263, 292, 295, 324, 367, 378, 380, 454, 455, 497, 526, 596
Marshall, Helen, 277
Martineau, Harriet, 357
Marvasti, Amir B., 10, 16, 41, 83, 155, 198, 217, 224, 248, 295, 359, 362, 364, 386, 432, 458, 518, 526, 541, 545, 571
Marvin, Simon, 114
Marx, Karl, 95, 368
Mason, Jennifer, 172
Massey, Sean G., 591
Matoesian, Gregory M., 316
Mattingly, Cheryl, 204

Mauthner, Natasha S., 113, 114, 471–2, 475
Maxwell, Joseph A., 12, 15, 17, 19, 21, 22, 25, 26, 28, 30, 31n, 42, 51, 53, 62, 127, 146, 314, 395, 465, 471, 498, 503, 506, 541, 543, 544, 545, 548, 549, 549n, 550n, 573, 589, 591
May, Tim, 16, 35, 83, 95, 99, 109, 111, 112, 115, 118, 120, 145, 155, 191, 250, 269, 306, 355, 367–8, 378, 442, 475, 514, 530, 570, 588, 589, 595
Mayer, Kate, 67
Maynard, Douglas W., 329
Mayring, Phillip, 12, 170, 172, 173, 174, 176, 279, 280
Mazzei, Lisa A., 306
McCabe, Janet, 116
McCormick, Janice, 488, 490
McCracken, Grant, 267
McDonald, Matthew M., 170, 180
McGrath, Joseph E., 543
McHugh, Peter, 219
McIntosh, James, 468
McLucas, Anne Dhu, 424
McMillan, James H., 25
McMullen, Linda M., 12
McQueen, Amy, 590
McSpadden, Emalinda, 513
Mead, George H., 109, 189, 223, 375, 440, 562
Mead, Margaret, 396, 397, 406n, 438
Medin, Douglas, 543
Meijer, Irene, 383, 384, 391
Melia, Kath, 499
Merleau-Ponty, Maurice, 192, 431
Merriam, Sharan, 26, 297
Mertens, Donna M., 9, 15, 16–17, 114, 141, 210, 268, 282, 345, 356, 477, 478, 510, 511, 515, 521
Merton, Robert K., 153–4, 236, 562
Mey, Günter, 113, 118
Meyer, Michael, 144
Michel, Jean-Baptiste, 64
Middling, Sharon, 593
Mikos, Lothar, 13, 16, 248, 254, 295, 359, 378, 394, 395, 416, 420, 435
Miles, Matthew B., 24, 28, 29, 31, 31n, 57, 180, 283, 290, 301, 305, 503, 542, 544, 545
Mill, John Stuart, 100
Miller, Barbara, 545
Miller, Barbara A., 22, 30
Miller, Dame I., 265
Miller, David, 384
Miller, Elizabeth R., 309
Mills, Geoffrey, E., 21
Mills, Jane, 154
Misco, Thomas, 541
Mishler, Elliot, 25, 28, 204, 210, 211, 342, 544, 587, 591, 596
Mitchell, Claudia, 406n
Mitchell, J. Clyde, 49, 53
Mitchell, William John Thomas, 231

Mittapalli, Kavita, 21, 548
Mittenecker, Erich, 436
Mitteness, Linda S., 36
Moe, Hallvard, 384
Mohn, Elisabeth, 438
Mohr, Lawrence B., 544
Mondada, Lorenza, 330, 439
Monmonier, Mark, 405
Moran-Ellis, Jo, 79
Moreira, Claudio, 569, 572
Moretti, Franco, 29
Morgan, David L., 314, 315, 525, 545, 549n
Morris, Meaghan, 253, 254, 582n
Morrow, Susan L., 489, 490
Morse, Janice M., 11, 17, 154, 180, 290, 291, 336, 337, 465, 496, 506, 508, 514–15, 517, 518, 526, 528, 595
Moscovici, Serge, 590, 597
Moustakas, Clark E., 110, 302
Mruck, Katja, 113, 118
Muller Mirza, Nathalie, 80, 88, 89
Mulvey, Laura, 400
Murdoch, Jamie, 319
Murdock, George Peter, 96
Murphy, Elizabeth, 55, 59, 585
Murray, Michael, 15, 17, 62, 84, 115, 117, 146, 465, 496, 497, 503, 510, 511, 515, 570, 571, 593, 594
Myers, Greg, 315

Napoli, Philip, 384
Nasu, Hisashi, 196
Nazroo, James, 103
Needham, Rodney, 100
Nentwig-Gesemann, Iris, 231n
Neuendorf, Kimberly A., 171, 179
Neumann, Mark, 429, 430–1
Newerla, Andrea, 566
Newman, Joshua L., 253
Newton, Benjamin J., 592
Nichols, Richard, 515
Niederer, Elizabeth, 258
Niehaus, Linda, 528
Niewöhner, Jörg, 96
Nightingale, David, 345
Nisbett, Robert, 544
Noblit, George W., 482, 483, 492
Noe, Raymond A., 593
Nohl, Arnd-Michael, 221, 224, 225, 229
Nubiola, Jaime, 126

Ochberg, Richard L., 204
Ochs, Elinor, 74
O'Connell, Daniel C., 12, 15, 19, 65, 67, 68, 69, 70, 71, 72, 73, 74, 116, 174, 198, 207, 208, 281, 299, 315, 316, 330, 343, 359, 395, 446, 473, 499
Odag, Özen, 180, 181

Oevermann, Ulrich, 235, 236, 237, 238, 242, 244–5, 245n
Okpalaoka, Chinwe, 515
Olesen, Virginia L., 154, 510, 515, 577
Oliver, Daniel G., 299
Olsson, Michael R., 543, 544
Onwuegbuzie, Anthony J., 484
Orr, Linda, 318, 501, 503
Ostertag, Stephen, 380
Ouellette, Suzanne C., 589
Outhwaite, William, 110
Oyama, Rumiko, 399
Øyen, Else, 99

Paavola, Sami, 124
Padilla, Raymond V., 31
Palmberger, Monika, 16, 19, 24, 102, 270
Panofsky, Erwin, 230, 231
Panopoulos, Panayotis, 432
Pape, Helmut, 127
Park, Robert, 154
Parker, Ian, 143, 342, 343, 344, 350
Parry, Odette, 471–2
Parshall, Mark B., 314
Parsons, Talcott, 192, 236, 562
Patashnick, Jennifer, 436
Paterson, Barbara L., 483, 484, 487, 488, 492
Patterson, Wendy, 205
Pattman, Rob, 319
Patton, Michael Quinn, 26, 49, 50, 53, 54, 55, 56, 549n
Pawson, Ray, 544
Pederson, Ann, 319
Peez, Georg, 65
Pehl, Thorsten, 64, 68–9
Peirce, Charles Sanders, 123, 124, 125, 126, 130, 131, 133, 134n, 154, 161, 224, 548, 560, 561–2
Pelias, Ronald J., 570, 578
Penn, Arthur, 67, 69
Pentimalli, Barbara, 424
Peräkylä, Anssi, 331
Perry, Beth, 16, 35, 83, 109, 111, 112, 115, 118, 145, 155, 191, 250, 269, 306, 355, 378, 442, 475, 514, 530, 570, 588, 589, 595
Pfaff, Nicolle, 231n
Philipps, Axel, 231n
Phillips, David, 102
Philo, Chris, 437
Phoenix, Anne, 205, 211, 214
Piaget, Jean, 234
Piazza, Alberto, 29
Pidgeon, Nick, 160, 163
Pillow, Wanda S., 117
Pink, Sarah, 400, 406n, 437
Plano Clark, Vicki I., 535
Plath, David, 571
Platt, Jennifer, 298
Plichtová, Jana, 80, 82

Plummer, Kenneth, 204, 214, 369, 515
Pluut, Bettine, 119
Poland, Blake, 319
Polit, Denise F., 540, 541, 542, 545
Polkinghorne, Donald E., 303
Polletta, Francesca, 204, 590
Pomerantz, Anita, 335, 346
Pontecorvo, Clotilde, 80, 90
Ponterotto, Joseph, 482, 486, 489
Popay, Jennie, 497
Popper, Karl R., 125, 131, 138
Potter, Jonathan, 21, 143, 308, 314, 315, 342, 343, 344, 345, 499, 504
Powel-Cope, Gail M., 492
Preissle, Judith, 297, 549n, 571
Prendergast, Monica, 395
Prior, Lindsay, 368, 370
Propp, Vladimir, 254
Prosser, Jon, 406n
Psaltis, Charis, 89
Psathas, George, 191, 192, 193, 194
Puchta, Claudia, 314, 315, 499
Purwandari, Betty, 460
Putnam, Hilary, 544, 586

Quine, Willard van Orman, 555
Quinn, Naomi, 94

Raab, Jürgen, 437
Rabinovich, Elaine P., 87
Radway, Janice A., 251, 252, 254
Ragin, Charles C., 57, 95, 236
Rai, Mugdha, 386
Rangel, Virginia Snodgrass, 298
Rapley, Tim, 10, 12, 19, 156, 315, 316, 317, 378, 445, 487, 498, 500, 525, 540, 542, 545, 557, 575
Raymond, Geoffrey, 337
Reason, Peter, 515, 588
Reavey, Paula, 343, 406n
Rebitzke Eberle, Verena, 197
Rebstein, Bernd, 9
Rees, Colin, 368
Reichenbach, Hans, 125
Reichertz, Jo, 8, 12, 16, 19, 125, 126, 134n, 161, 190, 224, 269, 302, 331, 437, 541, 548, 555, 560, 561, 575
Rettie, Ruth, 278, 291
Rheingold, Howard, 452, 454
Richards, Lyn, 31, 283
Richards, Thomas J., 283
Richardson, Beth, 83
Richardson, Laurel, 257, 364, 502, 569, 571, 572, 573
Ricoeur, Paul, 81, 137, 138, 139, 140, 141, 234, 570
Riesman, David, 87
Riessman, Catherine K., 24, 68, 204, 205, 207, 208, 214, 342, 467, 468
Riordan, Monica A., 66, 76–7

Ritchie, Jane, 279, 500
Ritsert, Jürgen, 172
Ritzer, George, 483
Roberts, Gareth, 370
Robinson, Jeffrey D., 337
Robinson, William S., 556
Robson, J. M., 100
Rodriguez, Neolie, 358
Rogers, Mary F., 469
Rogers-Dillon, Robin H., 80
Röhnsch, Gundula, 9
Roman, Leslie G. 576
Ronai, Carol R., 358
Rorty, Richard, 80
Ros, Jenny., 84
Rosaldo, Renato, 581n
Rose, Gillian, 396, 398, 399, 400, 406n
Rose, Jack, 72
Rose, Nikolas, 350
Rosenau, Pauline M., 543, 544
Rosenwald, George C., 204
Roulston, Kathryn, 10, 13, 16, 23, 64, 114, 116, 155, 190, 198, 207, 210, 217, 224, 248, 263, 295, 298, 304, 307, 308, 343, 354, 359, 386, 432, 458, 467, 468, 473, 474, 476, 501, 512, 518, 526, 528, 541, 544, 565, 571, 585, 594
Rubin, Herbert J., 305
Rubin, Irene S., 305
Ruddick, Susan M., 360
Ruddin, Lee P., 547
Rueschemeyer, Dietrich, 101
Ruhleder, Karen, 264
Russell, Bernard H., 147
Russell, Bertrand, 130
Rust, Holger, 172
Rustemeyer, Ruth, 172, 173, 174, 178
Rustin, Michael, 204
Ryan, Gery W., 24, 81, 147, 172, 291, 305
Ryan, Joanna, 114
Ryan, Mary, 290
Ryave, Alan, 358
Ryen, Anne, 9, 468
Ryle, Gilbert, 395

Sacks, Harvey, 193, 231n, 327, 328, 329, 332, 336, 440, 443, 473, 474, 475
Saerberg, Siegfried, 195
Sainsbury, Roy, 331
Saldaña, Johnny, 301, 305, 570, 571, 572
Salmon, Wesley C., 544
Salt, Barry, 412
Salter, Linda-Ruth, 425
Sampson, Edward E., 589
Sandelowski, Margarete, 49, 54, 61, 484, 485, 487, 488, 489, 492, 527, 549
Sankoff, Gillian, 545
Santaella, Lucia, 130
Sartre, Jean-Paul, 578

Saukko, Paula, 248, 253, 256, 257
Saussure, Ferdinand de, 22, 23
Sayer, Andrew, 31n, 544
Schaeffer, Pierre, 428
Schafer, Murray R., 425, 426, 427, 428, 431
Schau, Hope Jensen, 265
Scheff, Thomas J., 42
Scheffer, Thomas, 95, 96
Scheflen, Albert E., 438
Schegloff, Emanuel A., 71, 74, 327, 328, 329, 330, 331, 332, 336, 342, 442, 472, 473
Scheler, Max, 187
Schiavo, Terri, 174, 175, 176, 178, 179, 180
Schleiermacher, Friedrich, 137, 140, 234, 236
Schmidt, Lawrence K., 136, 137, 140
Schmidt, Marcus, 324
Schmidt, Thomas, 64–5, 76
Schneider, Barbara, 382, 386
Schnettler, Bernt, 9, 198, 433, 439
Schoen, Donald A., 22
Schofield, Janet W., 541
Schreiber, Rita, 481, 482
Schreier, Margrit, 9, 11, 12, 170, 171, 172, 174, 175, 176, 179, 181, 279, 280, 283, 305, 370, 382, 399, 436, 528, 545, 585
Schreiner, Anthony E., 457, 459
Schriewer, Jürgen, 94, 96
Schroeder, Ralph, 459
Schröer, Norbert, 125
Schubert, Cornelius, 438
Schulman, Stuart W., 81
Schultz, Jeffrey, 439
Schulze, Holger, 425
Schumacher, Sally, 25
Schurz, Gerhard, 161
Schütz, Alfred, 8, 110, 127, 186, 187, 188, 189, 190, 191, 192, 193, 194, 218, 220, 222, 231n, 235, 241, 302, 414, 436, 440
Schütze, Fritz, 8
Schwandt, Thomas A., 222, 223, 541
Schwartz-Barcott, Dorina, 588
Schweisfurth, Michele, 102
Scott, Janelle, 544
Scott, John, 369, 375, 377
Scott, Mark, 316
Scourfield, Jonathan, 370, 375, 376
Scriven, Michael, 544, 549
Seale, Clive F., 287, 324, 497, 501, 545
Seaton, Jean, 380
Seeger, Anthony, 406n
Sefi, Sue, 334
Segone, Marco, 515
Seidel, John V., 283, 370
Seidel, Tina, 436
Seidman, Irving E., 23, 27, 29
Selbin, Eric, 594
Sellerberg, Ann-Mari, 468, 478
Sellers, Lisa, 45, 46
Selting, Margret, 65, 74, 446
Shadish, William R., 543, 549n
Shank, Gary, 548
Shannon, Lyle W., 171, 172
Shannon, Sarah E., 172, 173
Shavelson, Melville, 72
Shaw, Clifford, 556
Shepard, Lorrie A., 26
Shettleworth, Sara, 23
Shoham, Aviv, 266
Shopes, Linda, 513
Shukla, Anuprita, 83
Shulman, Stuart W., 82
Shweder, Richard 544
Sidnell, Jack, 327, 330, 332
Siegesmund, Richard, 305
Silver, Christina, 181, 274, 286, 290, 436
Silverman, David, 53, 59, 125, 245n, 364, 370, 424, 444, 468, 471, 472, 473, 474, 475, 505
Silverstone, Roger, 380, 381, 382, 387
Simmel, Georg, 468, 471, 478
Simmons, Odis E., 559
Simons, Lucy, 206–7
Sinding, Christina, 596
Singer, Judith, 548
Slater, Don, 265
Sliep, Yvonne, 119
Smith, Anna Deavere, 511, 515
Smith, Brett, 146, 147, 203
Smith, Dorothy E., 110, 111, 219, 303, 576
Smith, Hans-Georg, 303
Smith, Jonathan A., 81, 143, 236, 279
Smith, Louis, 23
Smith, Mary Lee, 26
Smith, Murray, 417
Smith, Paul, 247
Snow, Catherine, 68
Snow, John, 402, 403, 405
Soeffner, Hans-Georg, 219, 235, 302, 444
Somers, Margaret R., 204, 212
Sontag, Susan, 136
Sparkes, Andrew C., 146, 147, 203
Speer, Susan A., 336
Spencer, Baldwin, 438
Spencer, Dimitrina, 355
Spencer, J. William, 362
Spencer, Liz, 500
Spiegel, Sam, 71
Spiegelberg, Herbert, 185
Spiggle, Susan, 270
Spradley, John, 303, 305
Spry, Tami, 572
Squire, Corinne, 204, 207, 210, 214
Srubar, Ilja, 188–9
St. Pierre, Elizabeth Adams, 305–6, 577
Stake, Robert, 549n
Stanley, Liz, 205
Steiner-Khamsi, Gita, 102

Steinitz, Vicky, 596
Stern, Phyllis N., 482
Sterne, Jonathan, 425
Stewart, Fiona, 451, 461
Stewart, Kate, 324
Stierlin, Helm, 236
Stiles, William B., 486
Stivers, Tanya, 337
Stockill, Clare, 336
Stocking, George W., 355
Stokoe, Elizabeth, 336
Stoller, Paul, 403, 404
Storey, John, 411
Strachan, John, 364
Strauss, Anselm L., 7, 8, 22, 24, 25, 29, 30, 31n, 35, 36, 48n, 58, 96, 126, 145, 153, 154, 155, 158, 160, 162, 163, 167, 181, 231n, 270, 279, 280, 286, 303, 305, 319, 360, 370, 445, 475, 482, 484, 485, 499, 500, 502, 506, 508, 548, 549n, 556, 557, 558, 559, 560, 562, 564–5, 572, 575, 576
Strauss, Claudia, 94, 543
Strickland, C. June, 319
Strong, Phil, 59
Stull, Donald, 87
Sudnow, David, 370
Sullivan, Martin, 518
Suri, Harsh, 492
Sutherland, Donald, 556
Szendy, Peter, 425

Talmy, Steven, 309
Tamboukou, Maria, 206
Tannen, Deborah, 342
Tartas, Valerie, 80, 88, 89
Tashakkori, Abbas, 290, 508
Tasker, Yvonne, 255
Taylor, Laurie, 470, 472
Taylor, Lisa, 414
Taylor, Stephanie, 206
te Molder, Hedwig, 80, 84
Teays, Wanda, 414
Teddlie, Charles, 290, 508
Téllez, Kip, 492
Telotte, J.P., 421
Temple, Bogusia, 208, 301
ten Have, Paul, 27, 67, 74, 110, 330, 440
Tesch, Renata, 24, 283
Teune, Henry, 95, 99, 102
Theo, Jewitt, Cary, 405n
Thomas, Dorothy S., 555
Thomas, Gary, 548
Thomas, James, 485, 487, 492
Thomas, Veronica G., 515
Thomas, William I., 555
Thompson, Kristin, 418
Thompson, Paul, 467, 468, 469, 472, 473, 474, 475
Thompson, Trevor, 506

Thornberg, Robert, 7, 10, 11, 12, 16, 24, 25, 30, 35, 37, 81, 84, 130, 144, 153, 154, 157, 158, 159, 160, 161, 162, 163, 164–5, 173, 181, 224, 270, 279, 280, 283, 303, 305, 319, 320, 360, 370, 390, 445, 475, 482, 483, 484, 487, 488, 498, 499, 503, 508, 512, 524, 528, 541, 544, 545, 548, 548–9, 554, 556, 559, 560, 565, 571, 572, 575
Thorne, Sally, 481, 488, 545
Thorogood, Nicki, 499
Thrasher, Frederick M., 556
Tilley, Nick, 544
Tilley, Susan A., 67, 69
Tilly, Charles, 95
Tilousi, Carletta, 520
Timulak, Ladislav, 15, 16, 465, 486, 487, 489, 490, 492
Titscher, Stefan, 302
Toerien, Merran, 10, 11, 13, 16, 27, 46, 74, 110, 155, 190, 221, 289, 315, 320, 328, 330, 334, 336, 342, 362, 371, 372, 395, 398, 424, 439, 440, 474, 499, 526
Tolson, Andrew, 418
Tomasello, Michael, 124
Torgue, Henry, 427, 428, 430, 432
Toulmin, Stephen, 308
Townsend, Peter, 469
Traulsen, Janine Morgell, 317
Truax, Barry, 426, 428
Tufte, Edward, 402, 403, 405
Tulving, Endel, 23
Tuma, René, *445*, 446
Turkle, Sherry, 451, 452, 455
Turner, Graeme, 250, 411
Tutt, Dylan, 446
Twitchell, James B., 410

Urban, Greg, 97
Ussher, Jane, 587

Vagle, Mark D., 302
van den Hoonaard, Deborah K., 24
van den Hoonaard, Will C., 24
Van Dijk, Teun, 181
Van Leeuwen, Theo, 181, 399, 405n
Van Maanen, John, 302, 569
Vannini, Philip, 425
Vaughan, Diane, 471
Vauss, David de, 100
Vertovec, Steven, 98, 99
Vincent, Deborah, 315
Vorderer, Peter, 172
Vurdabakis, Theo, 369
Vygotsky, Lev, 124

Wacquant, Loïc, 83, 111
Wagner, Johannes, 76
Wagner-Willi, Monika, 231n

Waksler, Frances Chaput, 193, 194
Waletzky, Joshua, 304
Walker, Anne D., 68
Walkerdine, Valerie, 206
Wallace, Anthony F.C., 543
Walsh, Denis, 492, 493
Walstrom, Mary K., 266
Walton, Douglas, 161
Wang, Caroline M., 593
Wang, Sheng, 593
Waples, Douglas, 171
Ward Schofield, Janet, 49, 52
Warner, Daniel, 428
Wasburn, Mara, 381
Wasburn, Philo, 381
Wästerfors, David, 15, 16, 465, 470, 474, 481, 514
Waterton, Claire, 316, 317
Watson, Cate, 309
Watson, Jean, 87
Watt, David, 594
Waxman, Hersh C., 492
Weaver, Anna, 283
Webb, Eugene, 367
Webb, Rodman B., 302
Weber, Max, 8, 95, 109, 110, 187, 218, 368, 562–3
Weed, Mike, 492
Weinberger, Eliot, 360
Weiss, Robert S., 26, 544, 548
Weitzman, Eben A., 31
Weller, Vivian, 231n
Wellman, Barry, 264, 450, 451, 454, 461
Welsh, Elaine, 286, 291
Wernet, Andreas, 8, 10, 11, 12, 81, 111, 137, 138, 196, 248, 270, 301, 302, 351, 440, 444, 572
Wertz, Frederick J., 302, 511, 512, 513, 570
West, Candace, 45
Wetherell, Margaret, 342, 343, 344, 345, 350
Whalen, Jack, 330
Wheeldon, Johannes, 406n
White, H., 204
Whitehead, Kevin, 329
Wickham, Gary, 144, 344
Wievorka, Michael, 547
Wiggins, Sally, 143
Wiles, Rose, 398
Wilkin, Anthony, 400
Wilkinson, Sue, 314, 328, 336
Williams, Lewis, 590
Williams, Malcolm, 49, 52
Williams, Matthew, 324
Williams, Raymond, 247

Williamson, Judith, 395
Willig, Carla, 11, 12, 13, 16, 19, 21, 28, 74, 80, 81, 111, 137, 143, 170, 173, 181, 190, 221, 231, 234, 237, 262, 301, 308, 315, 320, 343, 344, 345, 346, 349, 351, 362, 371, 372, 391, 394, 395, 399, 436, 487, 489, 510, 512, 513, 569, 571
Willis, Andrew, 414
Willis, Danny G., 143
Willis, Jerry W., 245n
Willis, Paul, 248, 251, 252, 587, 597
Wilson, Amy T., 511
Winkelhage, Jeannette, 177, 178, 180
Winter, Rainer, 13, 231, 248, 250, 252, 253, 258, 269, 342, 343, 371, 382, 428, 570, 576
Wittgenstein, Ludwig, 100, 154, 340
Wodak, Ruth, 144, 342
Wolcott, Harry F., 36, 308, 363, 364
Wolf, Margery, 543
Wolfe, Thomas, 514
Wolgemuth, Jennifer R., 298
Woodhouse, Jan, 406n
Woods, Peter, 368
Wooffitt, Robin, 330
Woolf, John, 71
Woolgar, Steve, 374–5
Woollacott, Janet, 254
Wordsworth, William, 364
Wörner, Kai, 64–5, 76
Wright, Talmadge, 360
Wright Mills, Charles, 502
Wrightson, Kendall, 427
Wurtzler, Steve, 432
Wyatt, Jonathan, 569, 572
Wynne, Brian, 111, 316, 317

Yee, Nick, 454
Yengoyan, Aram A., 96, 99
Yin, Robert K., 26, 52, 540, 541, 542, 546
Young, Alys, 301
Young, Lisa Saville, 351

Zappavigna, Michele, 458
Zeman, Jay J., 124
Zentella, Ana Celia, 545
Zhao, Shanyang, 483
Ziegler, Friederike, 594
Zielinski, Siegfried, 435
Zimmer, Lela, 488
Zimmermann, Don H., 219, 469
Zittoun, Tania, 83, 84
Znaniecki, Florian, 540, 555, 556
Zumbach, Jörg, 436

Subject Index

Page references to Figures or Tables will be in *italics*, whereas those relating to Notes will contain the letter 'n' following the number.

a priori coding, 285, 288
abduction, 131, 134n, 548, 562
   abductive turn, 124–5
   in grounded theory, 161–3
   offside rule, soccer, 132–3
   as reasoning habit, 126–7
academic research projects (2002–7), 114–15
acoustic communication, and sound ecology, 425–7
acoustic territories/identity, 428, 429
action research, 146, 315, 511, 588
active membership, 356
aesthetics and configuration, film analysis, 418–20, 422
African Americans, 360
African Queen (film), 71
agreement, method of, 100
AHRC (Arts and Humanities Research Council), 118
alter ego, 187, 196
Alzheimer's disease, 197
American Indian community, 516
analogical theorizing, 471
analytic auto-ethnography, 358
analytic generalization, 540, 546
analytic induction, 318, 500, 540
analytic inspiration, 363, 364
analytic strategies, 16, 28
analytical generalization, 52
analytical inspiration, in ethnographic fieldwork, 35–48
   bed-and-body work, 41, 42
   Egyptian Bedouin life, feminist interpretation, 36, 37, 38
   field notes, 42, 43
   inspiration and method, 47–8
   Murray Manor nursing home, 39, 40, 41, 42
   museum view of culture, 37–8
   and qualitative research, 35–6
   rhetoric, 47
   value of, 37
   ways of seeing, 36
   see also ethnography/ethnographic fieldwork
analytical trails, retracing and presenting, 505–6
anecdotalism, 505
anonymity, 210, 219, 477
anthropology
   European, 124
   image analysis, 395–6
   interpretative, 401
   legacy of comparison in, 96–7
   premises, 123–4

anthropology *cont.*
   social, pragmatic life-world theory as, 188–9
   visual methods in, 360, 398, 400–2
   writing, 581n
anthropometric photography, 396
anxiety, 126
apodictic findings, 186
apperception, 186
Apple Grab utility, 267
'applied' research, 84
appresentation, 186, 187
appropriation, film analysis, 410–11, 412, 421
archival data/archivability of data, 266, 453–4, 473–4
art history, 400
Arts and Humanities Research Council (AHRC), 118
arts-based inquiry, and performance, 578–9
associative (similarity-based) relations, 23
asyndeton effect, 428
a-theoretical knowledge, 221
ATLAS.ti program (CAQDAS), 8, 14, 280, 281, 282, 286, 292
audio documentaries, 429
audit trails, 374, 535
Auditory Culture Reader (Bull and Back), 429
authoritative voice, researcher, 209
authority, and intertextuality, 373–5
auto-ethnography, 256–8, 266, 358, 571
autonomy 238, 506
Awareness of Dying (Glaser and Strauss), 558, 564
axial coding, 30, 31–2n, 559

'bad analysis,' 364
Bali, Indonesia, 396, 397–8, 406n
Basics of Qualitative Research, The (Corbin and Strauss), 559
Basque Country, national revivals and violence, 100
bed-and-body work, 41, 42
beliefs, 127
bias, 66, 308
biblical hermeneutics, 137
binary comparison, 101
Black women, writing styles, 577
Blend of Contradictions, A (Simmel), 468
blending, 527
blurred genres, 7
Body Mass Index (BMI), 322
Bonnie and Clyde (film), 69

Boolean searching, 278, 279, 287, 289
bracketing, 302
brain, 127, 129
'bricolage,' research process, 249
bridge hypotheses, 563–4
British Association of Sociology, 356–7
British Sign Language, 327
Brokeback Mountain (film), 412
Brussels Conference on Neo-nationalism, 105

Call-Me project, 593–4
Camtasia program, 267
Canadian First Nations communities, 516
capitalism, 562
CAQDAS (Computer-Assisted Qualitative Data Analysis), 14–15, 88, 274, 277
   coding, 283–5
   coding crisis, 285–6
   debates, 291–2
   development, 278–9
   example of use, 288–9
   impact on qualitative sociology, 277
   importing of data, 282, 283
   interviews, 306
   low take-up, 278–9
   method, seen as, 277–8
   new project, establishing, 281–3
   programs, 8, 14, 280, 281, 282, 283–4, 286, 287, 288, 290, 292, 324, 459
   quality of data analysis, 500, 505
   retrieval and searching, 285, 286–8
   teamworking, 290–1
   use of, 281–8
   working with codes, 285
   see also software
CAQDAS Networking Project, University of Surrey, 278, 280, 292
case studies/case analysis, 26, 331–2
case-to-case population generalizations, 541
case-to-case transferability, 541
casing, 57
Cassandre (program), 280
CAT (software package), 82
Catalonia, national revivals and violence, 100
categorizing strategies, 22, 24–5, 305
   abstracted wording, 489
   decontextualisation dangers, 26
   integrating with connecting strategies, 29–30
causality, 31n, 558, 559, 570
CCTV cameras, 435
Centre for Sustainable Urban and Regional Futures (SURF), University of Salford, 113, 114, 115, 118, 119
certainty criterion, mixed methods, 526
'cherry-picking,' 499, 505
Chicago Conference (on mass communication), 1941, 171
Chicago School, 6, 556–7, 560

cholera outbreak, London (1854), 402–3, 405
cinema analysis, 438
Cinema Wars (Kellner), 254
circuit of mass communication, 383–4
CIRCUS (Collaborative Interdisciplinary Research Connecting Urban Society), 118–19
citizen journalism, 384
Civilization (BBC television series), 400, 406n
cloud computing, 281, 457
CMC (computer-mediated communication), 451, 456
Cochrane Collaboration, 496, 592
coding, 16
   axial, 30, 31–2n, 559
   CAQDAS (Computer-Assisted Qualitative Data Analysis), 283–5
   as categorizing strategy, 22
   crisis, 285–6
   data sources versus list of codes, in CAQDAS programs, 283–4
   encoding/coding model (Hall), 253
   explicating and refining codes, 501–2
   filmic/televisual codes, 419
   focused, 158–9
   generalization, 545
   Glaser's coding families, *160*
   grounded theory, 156–61
   hierarchy/tree of codes, 286
   inductive, 173, 285, 289
   initial, 156–8, 499
   inter-coder reliability, 81–2
   and interviews, 305
   netnographic analysis, 270
   news media, 389
   open, 270, 284
   a priori, 285, 288
   sampling strategies, 58
   similarity/contiguity distinction, 23
   theoretical, 159–61, 558
   versus transcription, 67
   units of, 175
   video segments, 436
   working with codes, 285
coding categories
   categorizing strategies, 24–5
   types, 25–6
   working with, 26–7
coding frame
   building, 173, 174–8
   categories, 170
   category names, 176
   cognitive overload, avoiding, 175
   concept-driven way, working in, 176
   consistency of coding, 178, 179
   data-driven, 173, 176
   defining, 176–7
   descriptions, 176–7
   double-coding, 171, 179, 180

coding frame *cont.*
    evaluating and modifying coding, 174, 179
    exhaustiveness requirement, 175
    material selection/preparation, 175, 178–9
    matrices, creating, 180
    mutual exclusiveness requirement, 173, 175
    pilot phase, 178–9
    revising and expanding, 177–8
    segmentation, 171, 178
    structuring and generating, 176
    trial coding, 179
    unidimensionality requirement, 173, 175
    validity requirement, 179
    see also content analysis, qualitative
coding paradigm, 559
coding trap, 285–6
cognition, paradigmatic or narrative, 303
cognitive psychology, 21
Cold War, 98
collaborative analysis, 79–93
    challenges, 87–9
    defined, 79
    difference in collaboration, 80
    epistemological frame, 80–1
    identity challenges, 87–9
    iterative process (Hall), 84–7
    methodological benefits, 80, 90
        inter-coder reliability, 81–2
        perspective-transcending knowledge, 82–3
        reflexivity, 83–4
        rich local understandings, incorporating, 82
        useful knowledge, 84
    models of team organization, 86–7
    open debate, challenges to, 89–90
    perspectivism, 80–1, 90
collaborative construction, documenting, 42–7
Collaborative Interdisciplinary Research Connecting Urban Society (CIRCUS), 118–19
collection-building, conversation analysis, 331
common-sense theorizing, 218, 219, 220
communalism, 478
communication
    acoustic, and sound ecology, 425–7
    computer-mediated, 451, 456
    ethnographic, 269–70
    face-to-face, 299, 451
    films as media of, 409, 410–13
    gaps, between communities, 84
    'good' and 'bad,' 83–4
    mass communication, media analysis focused on, 383–4
    non-verbal, 316, 327, 330
    oral and written, disparity between, 64
    sound as, 424
    team science, 535
communication structures, 454, 455
communicative (explicit) knowledge/experience, 220, 221, 222, 223, 225, 231

community involvement, 519–20
community research, virtual, 454–6
comparative practices, 94–107
    binary comparison, 101
    constant comparative method, 96
    criteria, 104
    dependent methodologies, 103
    dimensions, 94–6, 102
    distant comparison (case study), 101–2
    documentary method, 224
    education, 102
    ethnographic fieldwork, 94, 97, 102
    fluid forms, 106
    implicit and explicit comparison, 94–5
    legacy of comparison in anthropology, 96–7
    methodological choices, 99–103
    migration and new diversities in global cities, 98–9
    national revivals and violence, 100
    neo-nationalism, qualitative comparison in data analysis, 104, 105–6
    new interest, in globalization context, 98
    particularism, 95, 96, 97
    political science, 99, 100
    qualitative comparison, 95
    regional comparison, 101
    thick comparison approaches, 95
    typification and comparative analysis between cases, 229–30
    units and procedures of analysis, 103–4
    universalism, 95, 97
    variable-oriented approaches, 97, 104
complete participant, 356
component/integrated distinction, in design, 31n
compositional interpretation, 398–9
computer-mediated communication (CMC), 451, 456
computers, and qualitative data analysis, 30–1
    see also CAQDAS (Computer-Assisted Qualitative Data Analysis); Internet; software; virtual data
confessional writing format, 582n
confidentiality, 210, 512, 513
configuration, film, 418–20, 422
conjunctive (implicit) knowledge/experience, 220, 222, 225, 231
connecting strategies, 22, 24
    displays as, 29–30
    integrating with categorizing strategies, 29–30
    quality of data analysis, 503–4
    theory of qualitative data analysis, 27–9
consciousness, 129, 136
    subjective, 193
consciousness raising, 588, 590
consent issues, 210, 512
conservation, recording versus reconstructing, 190
constant comparative method, 96
constructionist analysis, 361–2

constructionist narrative analysis, 298
  versus cognitively based approaches to narrative, 205
  constructing effects of audiences on stories, 205
  definition, 204–5
  ethical issues, 210
  example of Iranian doctors living in London, 208, 209, 211–12
  example of South Africans living with HIV, 210
  historical and cultural contexts, 212–13
  levels operating on, 205
  limits and range of constructionist approach, 214
  meta narratives, 212
  positioning within processes of telling/listening to stories, 205–6
  power relations, 206
  in practice, 206–13
  research positioning, 209–10
  research process, 207
  sexual narratives, 213
  subjectivities, constitution, 205
  theoretical background assumptions, 204–6
  transcription, 207–8
  translation, 208
  value to researcher, 203, 214
  voice of researcher, 209
  see also narrative analysis
constructivism, as interpretive style, 575–6
content analysis, qualitative, 170–83
  anti-ideological version, 172
  applications, 180–1
  classic example, 171–2
  coding compared, 173–4
  coding frame, building, 170, 174–8
  and data analysis, 173
  data preparation, 174
  defined, 170–1
  emergence, 171
  in English-speaking countries, 172
  film, 413–14
  findings, presenting, 180
  flexibility of, 170, 171, 180
  further developments, 172–3
  image analysis, 398, 399
  limits, 181, 381–3
  main analysis phase, 173, 179–80
  material, reducing amount of, 170
  news media, 381–3
  non-frequency, 171
  origins, 171–3
  other qualitative research methods compared to, 173–4
  perspectives, 181
  procedures involved, 174–80
  and quantitative content analysis, 173, 181
  statistical techniques, 180
  strict and qualitative, 172

content analysis, qualitative *cont.*
  as systematic, 170, 171
  terminology, 172–3
  see also news media
contexts
  comparative practices, 98
  constructionist narrative analysis, 210–13
  context-free interpretation, 239–40
  cultural studies, 253–6
  data analysis, 19–20
  film analysis, 420
  images, 395
  interviews, 210–12
  radical contextualism, 252, 254
  sampling strategies, 50
  specificity of research findings, 596
  text interpretation, 253–6
contextualization thesis, 112
contiguity/similarity distinction, 22–3, 31
  relations in qualitative data analysis, 23–4
convenience sampling, 55
conventions, and rules, 237
conversations/conversation analysis (CA)
  accounting for/evaluating patterns, 333–5
  applied, 330, 337
  collection-building, 331
  cross-linguistic studies, 336
  data preparation, 330
  and discourse analysis, 342
  epistemic domains, 336, 337
  focus groups, 315, 316, 320
  foundational findings, 330, 336–7
  individual case analysis, 331–2
  and interviews, 300
  Jobcentre Plus study (UK), 331, 333, 334, 335, 337
  key analytic stages, 330–5
  limits of studying recorded interactions, 335–6
  lone parent interview, 333, 334–5
  naturally occurring, recorded interactions, 327–9
  new developments/perspectives, 336–7
  'ordinary' versus 'institutional' talk, 329–30
  pattern-identification, 332–3
  pauses, 328
  and reanalysis, 473
  speech delivery characteristics, 338
  talk-in-interaction, 74, 329
  theory, 329
  timing of utterances, 338
  transcription, 330, 338
  transcripts, 330
  turn in, 447n
  see also discourse analysis; narrative analysis
co-research, 86, 89
corpora, spoken language, 65, 76
  German, 68
correspondence bias, 544
counter-culture, 251

counter-transference, 143
courtroom proceedings, 43
covert and overt observer roles, 356–7
'creation myth,' qualitative research, 497
creative arts, 593–5
credibility
  ethical issues, 512, 515–18
  meta-analysis, 490
  on social level, 515–18
CRESSON, 427
criminal lifestyles, ethnographic study, 471, 472–3
Critical Appraisal Skills Program (CASP) tool, 592
critical inquiry, 576
critical interpretative synthesis, 485
critical literacy theory, 588
critical realism, 314
Critical Textwork (Parker), 343
critical theory, as interpretive style, 576
cross-linguistic studies, 336
CUDOS principles, 478
cultivated tentativeness, 363
'cultural eye,' 397
cultural relativism, 96
cultural studies, 247–61, 396
  auto-ethnography/new forms of ethnography, 256–8
  conjunctural analysis of culture and power, 247–50
  data analysis, 253
  ethnographic approach, 248, 256–8
  horror films, 248–9
  origins, 248
  partiality, 249, 255
  popular culture, 257–8
  reflexivity/self-reflexivity, 248, 250, 251, 256, 257
  resistance perspective, 250–3
  romance novels, 251, 254
  sound culture, 428–30
  textual and contextual analysis perspectives, 253–6
culture
  as narrative, seeing, 37–9
  and power, conjunctural analysis, 247–50
  traditional definition, 543
cumulative theoretical progress, 475
cyberspace, 450, 451, 454

Dallas, 256
'DAMP' (Swedish neuropsychiatric diagnosis), 469
Dark Night Rises, The (film), 418
data
  archival/archivability of, 266, 453–4, 473–4
    categorizing, 305
    classifying, 305
    documentary, defining, 368–70
    dynamic, 453–4
    elicited, 10–11, 266, 267
    empirical, constitution of, 189–91

archival/archivability of *cont.*
  field note *see* field notes
  forcing to fit preconceived hypotheses, 306
  fragmentation, 286
  linkages with theory, 561–2
  linking, 24
  management of, 306
  multiple types, 11–12
  naturally occurring, 328
  new types of data/phenomena as challenges, 13
  observational, 267
  processing of, 498–9
  reduction of, 302, 304–5, 306
  reorganizing, 305
  semiotic and structural analysis, 253–4
  static, 452–3
  suboptimal mining, 502
  theorization from, 554–68
  transformation, 527
  types, 16, 295–6
  use of beyond initial purposes, 514
  verbal, 248, 249
  video, 436–8
  virtual *see* virtual data
  visual, 248
  see also data analysis; data collection; data preparation; qualitative data analysis (QDA)
data analysis
  basics, 19–20
  concepts, 19–20
  and content analysis, 173
  contexts, 19–20
  cultural studies, 253
  ethnical issues, 15
  existing phenomena, analyzing, 10–11
  field, 3–18
  formalization and intuition, tension between, 12–13
  German-speaking areas, 8–9
  historical developments, 6–9
  implementation, call for, 15
  interviews, 304–6
  major approaches, 11
  meta-analysis, 488–9
  meta-data analysis, 483
  methods, 15–17
  and phenomenology, 184, 194
  and qualitative research, 3
  quality *see* quality of data analysis
  reanalysis/meta-analysis of results, 15
  reflexive approach, 114
    see also reflexivity
  relevance and evidence, call for, 15
  role in research process, 9–10
  technical developments, 14–15
  using "right" analysis method in "correct" way, 307–8
  visualization of a textualized field, 13–14
  see also qualitative data analysis (QDA)

data collection, 142
 ethnography/ethnographic fieldwork, 36, 47
 ethnomethodology, 192
 image analysis, 396, 401
 meta-analysis, qualitative, 491
 mixed and multiple methods research, 537
 netnographic analysis, 266–8
data preparation
 content analysis, qualitative, 174
 conversation analysis, 330
 meta-analysis, 488
data streams, 453
deconstruction, 256
deduction, 124–6
 offside rule, soccer, 132
 subsumption, 127, 176
 truth, 127–8
dementia, 197
democracy, defined, 82
Department of Work and Pensions (DWP), UK, 331
description, 67
 adequate, 193
 as analysis, 359–60
 coding frame, building, 176–7
 thick, 249, 271, 570
descriptive realism, 575, 582n
desire, 573
deviance theory, 42
diagramming, 529–36
 flowcharting symbols and techniques, 531–4, *532–3*
 audit trail, developing, 535
 benefits, 534–6
 conventions, 531–2
 object manipulation, 534–5
 pre-study planning, facilitating, 534–5
 team science, communicating in, 535
 transparency of design, enhancing, 535
 reasons for, 529–31
 styles, 531
 see also mixed and multiple methods research
dialect, 299
Die Hard (film), 252
difference, indirect method of, 100
digital sound recording, 430
digitalization, 446–7
disability research, 515
discourse analysis, 80, 143–4, 340–53
 addiction discourse, 346–7
 analysis process, 346
 analytic approach, 343–4
 approach adopted, 342–3
 and conversation analysis, 342
 definition of 'discourses,' 342
 discursive reading, appraisal of, 350
 dualism/dualistic construction of self, 347–8
 epistemological orientation, 344–5

discourse analysis *cont.*
 ethical issues, 345
 Foucauldian approach, 143–4, 343, 345, 349, 350
 and grounded theory, 350
 and image analysis, 398
 interpretation, 143–4, 342, 351
 and interviews, 300
 and language, 345
 limitations, 345
 and narrative analysis, 342
 recent developments/outlook, 350–1
 reflections, 348–50
 social psychological tradition, 342, 345
 software, 289–90
 subjectivity and discourse, 350
 transcription, 343, 344
 varieties of discursive analysis, 342
 worked example, 346–50
 see also conversations/conversation analysis (CA)
discourse interpretation, 351
discourse transcription (DT), 68, 75, 76
Discovery of Grounded Theory, The (Glaser and Strauss), 48n, 303, 556, 557–8
disinterestedness of scientific observer, 231n
displays, as categorizing and connecting strategies, 29–30
distant reading, 29
Distinction (Bourdieu), 468
distributive culture, 543
District Attorneys (DAs), 43, 44, 46
diversity, institutional, 88
documentary meaning, 230
documentary method, 116, 217–33, 373
 anthologies, 231n
 common-sense theorizing, 218, 219, 220
 comparative analysis, 224
 ethnomethodology, 217, 219–20
 formulating interpretation *see* formulating interpretation
 frame of orientation, 221, 225, 228
 genetic attitude of analysis, 218
 incorporated knowledge, 221
 interpretation/interpretivism, 219, 222, 223
 meaning, fundamental constitution in practice and interaction, 223–4
 open questions, 231
 organization of discourse, 225
 practical hermeneutics, 222
 praxeological sociology of knowledge, 223
 reflecting interpretation *see* reflecting interpretation
 social phenomenology, 219
 social scientific observation, 218
 sociology of knowledge, 218
 a-theoretical knowledge, 221
 typification and comparative analysis between cases, 229–30

documentary method *cont.*
  typology, example, *230*
  understanding, 110, 187, 222
  working steps in practical research, 224–30
  see also communicative (explicit) knowledge/
    experience; conjunctive (implicit) knowledge/
    experience
documentary photography, 401
documents
  analyzing, 367–79
    strategies, 370–5
  as artefacts, 369, 371, 378
  authenticity, 377
  authority, 373–5, 377
  defining documentary data, 368–70
  exemplar, 375–7
  function, 372–3
  and information technology, 378
  intertextuality, 373–5, 378
  language and form, 371–2
  limitations/new possibilities, 377–9
  primary, secondary and tertiary, 377
  private and public, 377
  production and consumption of documentary data,
    368–9, 370
  as social facts, 369, 370
  solicited and unsolicited, 369
'dogmas of empiricism,' 555
double hermeneutic, 111
doubt, 126, 133
dramaturgy, film, 413, 415–16
dualism/dualistic construction of self, 347–8
duplicative data, 477
duration, pause, 73
dynamic data, 452, 453–4

ear, 428, 432–3
Economic and Social Research Council (ESRC), UK
  CAQDAS Networking Project,
    University of Surrey, 278
  conversation analysis, 331
  Science in Society programme, 114, 115
education, comparative, 102
Egyptian Bedouin life, feminist interpretation,
  36, 37, 38
eidetic reduction, 186
eidetic variations (Husserl), 185–6
eidos (essence), 185, 186
Eigensinn (ability to create own sense), 250
electro-acoustics, 426
electromagnetic oscillation, sound recorders, 431
elicited data, 10–11, 266, 267
emblematic sampling, 54
emic categories, 25
emotions, 166, 358
Emotions in the Field (Davies), 355
'empathic' interpretation, 138–9, 142, 143,
  145, 147

empathy, 187, 219
emphasis, 72
empirical generalization, 52, 53, 540
empirical research
  abduction, deduction and induction, 124, 126
  constitution of empirical data, 189–91
  phenomenological sociology as new approach to,
    191–4
  phenomenology as empirical research procedure,
    184, 188, 194–8, 195
  and protosociology, 189
encryption of data, 281
endogenous reflexivity, 111
Engineering and Physical Sciences Research Council
  (EPSRC), 118
enlightenment, 136
enumeration, 361
enumerative generalization, 540
episodic memory, 23
episodic nature of human conduct, 110
epistemic domains, 336, 337
epistemic permeability, 112
epistemology/epistemological issues, 16, 100
  collaborative analysis, 80–1
  colour, 581
  and constructionism, 203
  discourse analysis, 344–5
  emotion, 358
  focus groups, 314–16
  genuine epistemology, 111
  meta-analysis, 486
  naive inductivism, 555
  netnographic analysis, 265
  and phenomenology, 184, 185, 198
  reflexivity, 191
  see also knowledge
EPSRC (Engineering and Physical Sciences Research
  Council), 118
ESRC (Economic and Social Research Council)
  see Economic and Social Research Council
    (ESRC), UK
ethical issues, 15, 510–23
  community involvement, 519–20
  complexity of principles, 521
  confidentiality, 210, 512, 513
  consent, 210, 512
  constructionist narrative analysis, 210
  credibility, 512, 515–18
  deception, 396
  discourse analysis, 345
  ethics, 512
  example, 512–13
  harmful effects, 268–9, 518–19, 519, 520
  image analysis, 396, 397–8
  interpretation, 141–2
  netnographic analysis, 268–9
  norms and beliefs, 516
  power, 512

ethical issues *cont.*
   qualitative research as tool for social change, 514–20
   quality and ethics of use, 520–1
   reanalysis of qualitative data, 476–7
   representation, 512, 515–18
   rigor, criteria for, 521
   transformative assumptions, 515, 516, 517
   use of data beyond initial purposes, 514
   virtual data, 461
   voice, 512, 515–18
   writing honestly, 513–14
ethnographic communication, 269–70
Ethnographic Self, The (Coffey), 355
ethnography/ethnographic fieldwork
   analytical inspiration, 35–48
   auto-ethnography, 256–8, 266, 358
   Bali, Indonesia, 396, 397–8, 406n
   collaborative construction, documenting, 42–7
   comparative practices, 94, 97, 102
   and cultural studies, 248, 256–8
   culture as narrative, seeing, 37–9
   empirical grounding of, questioning, 35
   focused ethnography, 437
   inspiration and method, 47–8
   institutional ethnography, 111, 303
   interpretation, 145–6
   interviews, influence on, 303
   meta-ethnography, 482–3
   multi-sited, 438
   and netnographic analysis, 262, 263, 264, 269–70, 274
   new forms, 256–8
   observations, 354
   participant observation, 37
   procedure, moving beyond, 36–7
   sampling strategies, 445
   social worlds, discovering, 39–42
   sound culture, 432
   theoretical base, 145
   video analysis, 444–5
   virtual, 446
Ethnomethodological Studies of Work (Garfinkel), 193
ethnomethodology, 110, 192–3, 439
   documentary method, 217, 219–20
   ethnomethods, 329
   versus ethnophenomenology, 198
ethnomethods, 193
ethnomusicology, 424, 433n
ethnophenomenology, 198
Euro-American society, as ocular-centric, 397
evidence, quantifiable, 402–3
evidence-based practice, 592–3
exegesis, 234
EXMARaLDA system, 65, 76

experience
   lived/subjective, 186, 187, 189–90, 192, 194, 248, 256
   reflexivity, 113–20
   sonic, 427–8
   stratification of, 222
experimentalists, 570
extensivity, 243–4
external generalization, 541, 542, 546–8
   strategies, in qualitative data analysis, 548–9
extreme case formulations, 346, 347, 349
extreme/deviant case sampling, 54
eye dialect, 71–2

face generalizability, 548
Facebook, 273
face-to-face (F2F) communication, 299, 451
facial expression, 439
faith, hermeneutics of, 81
falsifiability, 563
fan clubs, 249
feminism
   film studies, 412
   post-structural interpretive styles, 577–8
   and qualitative research, 586–8, 589
   reflexivity, 110–11
fiction texts, 582n
field, the, 355–9, 399
field notes, 31, 217, 248
   ethnographic fieldwork, 41, 42, 43, 44–5
   netnographic analysis, 266, 267–8
field of data analysis
   aims of qualitative data analysis, 5–6
   definition of qualitative data analysis, 5–6
   historical developments, 6–9
   proliferation of qualitative research, 4–5
   theoretical backgrounds and basic methodological approaches, 6
fieldworker-as-bricoleur, 569
file transfer protocol (FTP), 452
film analysis, 409–23
   aesthetics and configuration, 418–20, 422
   appropriation by spectators, 410–11, 412, 421
   characters and actors, 416–17
   cognitive activities, 411
   cognitive purpose, 413–20
   communication, film as, 410–13
   content and representation, 413–14
   contexts, 420
   and emotions, 411, 418
   habitual and ritual activities, 411
   as interdisciplinary and transdisciplinary, 412
   meaning in film, 410, 411
   media of communication, films as, 409, 410–13
   narration and dramaturgy, 413, 415–16
   novels, adaptations of, 415–16
   plot versus tale, 415
   reception by spectators, 410–11, 412, 421

film analysis *cont.*
  social-communicative activities, 411
  steps, 420–1
  storytelling techniques, 415
  tasks, 421
  texts, 411, 415–16
filmic/televisual codes, 419
flowcharting symbols and techniques, 531–4, 532–3
  audit trail, developing, 535
  benefits, 534–6
  conventions, 531–2
  object manipulation, 534–5
  pre-study planning, facilitating, 534–5
  team science, communicating in, 535
  transparency of design, enhancing, 535
focus groups, 116, 313–26
  as 'agnostic,' 314
  analytic resources, 318–20
  comparisons, 317–18
  composite approach, case for, 320–4
  conversation analysis, 315, 316, 320
  epistemological and ontological issues, 314–16
  grounded theory, 319
  making sense of data, initial steps, 316–18
  moderator, role, 318
  new developments/perspectives, 324–5
  non-verbal communication, 316
  positioning analysis, 320–1, 322
  quality of data analysis, 501
  realist and constructivist usages, 314, 316
  sampling strategies, 318
focused coding, 158–9
focused ethnography, 437
folic acid supplementation, 500–1
Folk Life Archives (Division of Ethnology, Lund University Sweden), 470
football, offside rule, 131–3
formal sociology, 471
formulating interpretation, 226–7, 231n
  example, 227
  topical order, 225
Foucaldian discourse analysis, 143–4, 343, 345, 349, 350
  see also discourse analysis
Foursquare, 454
FQS (international journal), 280
fragmentation of data, 286
Frame Analysis (Goffman), 468
frame of orientation, 221, 225, 228
framework analysis, 500
Frankfurt School, 231n
FTP (file transfer protocol), 452
functional categories, 28
functional equivalence, 223, 224
fundamental attribution error, 544

gaze, the, 400
Geisteswissenschaften, and natural sciences, 234
generalization/generalizability
  analytic generalization, 540, 546
  analytic induction, 540
  analytical generalization, 52
  case-to-case population generalizations, 541
  coding, 545
  definitions, 540
  empirical generalization, 52, 53, 540
  enumerative generalization, 540
  example, 547
  external, 541, 542, 547–9
  face generalizability, 548
  generalization in and from qualitative analysis, 540–53
  generalized other, 375
  grounded theory, 548
  induction, 128
  internal, 541, 542–6, 549
  interviews, 544
  lower- and higher-order generalizability, 541
  moderate, 52
  narrative analysis, 545
  petite generalizations, 541
  pragmatism, 591–2
  processes, 548
  qualitative approaches, 52–3
  quality of data analysis, 507
  reader generalizability, 541
  representativeness, 51, 540, 542, 543, 546, 547
  sampling strategies, 50–3, 62, 549–50n
  statistical generalization, 540
  theoretical biases toward uniformity, 543
  theoretical generalization, 507, 540
  transferability, 52, 541
  ways of generalizing, 591–3
genetic attitude of analysis, 218
genres
  blurred, 7
  genre analysis as contextualizing research strategy, 255
  sampling strategies, 50
Geographic Information Systems (GIS), 406n
German Anthropological Association, 406n
German sociology, 184, 191, 219, 236
Gesprächsanalytisches Transkriptionssystem 2 (*GAT 2*), 65, 74–5, 76
Gestalt (shape), 238
gestures, 439
global cities, new diversities in, 98–9
global commodities, 471–2
Globaldivercities, 98
globalization, 98–9
grand narratives, 7
grand theories, 96, 562
graphics programs, 31
Graphs, Maps and Trees (Moretti and Piazza), 29

Greater Manchester
  Centre for Sustainable Urban and Regional Futures (SURF), University of Salford, 113, 114, 115, 118, 119
  Innovation Investment Fund (IIF), 115–18
  Local Interaction Platform, 119
gridding and plotting, news media, 387–9
grounded theory, 30, 36–7, 84, 153–69, 231n, 270
  abduction in, 161–3
  aim of conducting, 154–5
  background, 153–4
  coding, 156–61
  data gathering/theoretical sampling, 155–6
  different approaches towards grounding of theory, 558–9
  and discourse analysis, 350
  discovery, 557–8
  focus groups, 319
  formal, 484–5
  generalization, 548
  internal victimizing, *164*
  interpretation, 144–5
  as interpretive style, 575
  interviews, influence on, 303
  memorandum writing and sorting, 163–5
    example, 165–6
  quality in research, 167
  quality of data analysis, 499, 500, 507
  sampling strategies, 51, 58
  software, 280, 284
  theory building, 557–8
grounded theory methodology (GTM), 556, 560
group consensus, 245n
guesswork, 126, 127
Gulf War (1990), 400

habitual concordance, 221
habitus, 238, 315, 543
  documentary method, 221, 225, 229, 230
ha-ha laughter, 73
Handbook of Action Research (Reason and Bradbury), 588
handicraft production, 31
harmful effects, 518–19
health service, lay juries, 589
hearing, sense of, 428
hegemony theory, 251, 255
hermeneutic circle, 140, 302
hermeneutics, 137, 234–46
  biblical, 137
  double hermeneutic, 111
  of faith, 81
  habitus, 238
  interviews, influence on, 301–2
  legal, 137
  methodological issues, basic, 235–6
  objective, 231n, 235
  phenomenological, 196–7, 198

hermeneutics *cont.*
  philological, 137
  philosophical, 234, 235
  practical, 222
  rules, 237–8
  structure, 238
  of suspicion, 81
  universal, 137
  see also interpretation
HIAT (*Halbinterpretative Arbeitstranskriptionen*) acronym, 71, 75, 76
hierarchization of knowing better, 224
higher-order generalizability, 541
historical developments, data analysis, 6–9
Histories of Scientific Observation (Daston and Lunbeck), 354
'History of the interview' project, 438
HIV/AIDS
  beliefs concerning transmission, 517
  UNAIDS (UN agency responsible for AIDS research), 519–20
holistic versus categorical approaches, 27
Hollywood movies, 254
homologous reactions, 224, 229
horror films, 248–9
Houseboat (film), 72
How to Observe Morals and Manners (Martineau), 357
HRAF (Human Relations Area Files), 96
HTML, 452
HTTrack Website Copier, 267
Human Relations Area Files (HRAF), 96
humanist/post-humanist academic traditions, 204
hyperlinks, 27
HyperRESEARCH program (CAQDAS), 280, 459
hypertext programs, 31
hypothesis testing, 130–1, 134n, 173, 278, 556, 557
hypothetical inferences, 563
hypothetico-deductive (HD) model, 556, 563

iconoclastic movements, 397
iconographic and iconological meaning, 230
ideal types (Weber), 109
IIF (Innovation Investment Fund), Manchester, 115–18
image analysis, 394–408
  anthropology, 395–6
    visual methods in, 360, 398, 400–2
  case study, 400–2
  configuration of images, 418
  contexts, 395
  data collection, 396, 401
  ethical issues, 396, 397–8
  'found' images, 396
  intentionality, 396, 406n
  online data visualization, 406n
  passing over by social scientists, 405
  photography, 394, 396, 401
  pictures, looking at, 398–400

image analysis *cont.*
   quantifiable evidence, 402–3
   reasons for, 394–5
   ubiquity of images, 394, 395, 397
   and video, 435
   visible, making, 403–5
   ways of seeing, 395–8
implementation, 585–99
   aims, 585–6
   data analysis, 15
   generalization methods, 591–3
   new developments/perspectives, 596–7
   opportunities and limits, 595–6
   qualitative research and creative arts, 593–5
   theoretical backgrounds, 589–91
implicit knowledge, 221
   see also conjunctive (implicit) knowledge/experience
impression management, 235
impressionistic writing format, 582n
incorporated knowledge, 221
in-depth interviews, 103
indigenous media, 402
indigenous researchers, 515, 517
induction, 124–6
   by characters, 562
   comparative practices, 100
   offside rule, soccer, 132
   qualitative, 128–30, 562
   quantitative, 128–30
inductive analysis, 360–1
inductive coding, 173, 285, 289
inferences, 53, 130, 134n
information structures, 454, 455
informed consent, 210, 512
Innovation Investment Fund (IIF), Manchester, 115–18
in-order-to-motives, 218
insider/outsider perspective, 83, 86
Inspiration (graphics program), 31
Institute of Innovation Research, University of Manchester, 116
institutional ethnography, 111, 303
institutional review boards (IRBs), 356
institutionalized behaviour, 219
intensity sampling, 54
interactive voice, researcher, 209
inter-coder reliability, 81–2
inter-group relations, 88
internal generalization, 541, 542–4, 549
   strategies, in qualitative data analysis, 545–6
International Organization for Standardization (ISO), 531
International Phonetic Alphabet (IPA), 72
Internet
   generations of studies, 450–1
   and netnographic analysis, 262, 265
Internet Archive (non-profit organization), 453

interpretation
   action research, 146
   approaches to, 137
   as an art, 571
   context-free, 239–40
   as dialogue, 234
   discourse analysis, 143–4, 342, 351
   documentary method, 222
   'empathic,' 138–9, 142, 143, 145, 147
   ethical challenges, 141–2
   ethnography, 145–6
   formulating, 225, 226–7, 231n
   grounded theory, 144–5
   interpreter's frame of reference, 219
   interpretive strategies, analysis, 575–9
   interview data, 305–6
   meta-ethnography, 482
   methodological and epistemological capability, 238
   models of writer, 573–4
   multiple interpretive communities, 579–81
   narrative analysis, 146–7
   news media, 391
   origins, 136–7
   performance as, 569
   phenomenological research, 143
   pictures and videos, 230–1
   post-structural interpretive styles, 577–9
   process of, 137
   psychoanalytic case study, 142–3
   reflecting, 225, 226–7, 228–9
   relationship between 'suspicion' and 'empathy,' 139–41
   as storytelling, 572
   'suspicious,' 137–8, 142, 145, 147
   thematic analysis, 147
   theory-driven, 138, 578
   versus understanding, 222
   validity, 237
   see also hermeneutics
interpretive interactionism, 570, 578
interpretive paradigm, 223
interpretive realism, 574–5
interpretive styles
   constructivism as, 575–6
   critical theory as, 576
   criticisms, 579
   grounded theory as, 575
   post-structural, 577–9
interpretivism, 223
inter-rater reliability, 501
intertextuality, 255, 373–5
interviews, 116, 297–312
   analysis challenges, 306–8
   analyzing and presenting of data, 304–6
   bias of interviewer, 308
   biographical, 253
   as contexts, 210–12
   contiguity, 22

interviews *cont.*
  data management and reduction, 306
  in-depth, 103
  documentation levels, 12
  episodic, 11, 23
  ethnographic influences, 303
  expert, 11–12
  face-to-face, 299, 451
  generalization, 544
  grounded theory influences, 303
  hermeneutic influences, 301–2
  'History of the interview' project, 438
  interpreting/writing up findings, 305–6
  life story, 594
  methodological issues, 307
  narrative influences, 303–4
  phenomenological hermeneutics, 197
  phenomenological influences, 302
  pilot, 307
  preparation of data for analysis, 299–301
  pseudonyms, 306
  quality, judging, 308–9
  reducing data to locate/examine phenomena of interest, 304–5
  reorganizing, classifying and categorizing data, 305
  semi-structured, 217, 527
  theoretical and methodological influences on analysis, 301–4
  theoretical approaches, 298
  transcription, 64
  translation, 301
  work-focused, 331
  see also narrative analysis; transcription
introverting, 166
IPA (International Phonetic Alphabet), 72
IRBs (institutional review boards), 356
ISO (International Organization for Standardization), 531
isobel map, 431
iterative collaborative analysis process (Hall), 84–7

Jeffersonian Transcript Notation, 74, 76, 330
JIA (juvenile idiopathic arthritis), sampling strategies, 50–8
John Lomax Collection, Library of Congress, 429
jottings, 43, 44–5
Journal of Mixed Methods Research, 531
justification, logic of, 125
juvenile idiopathic arthritis (JIA), sampling strategies, 50–8

keynote sounds, 426
Keyword in Context (KWIC), 290
Kill Bill (film), 412
kinesics, 438
Klangsprache (language of sounds), 432

knowledge
  anti-objectivistic view, 249
  common-sense, 563
  communicative (explicit), 220, 221, 222, 223, 225, 231
  conjunctive (implicit), 220, 222, 225, 231
  discourse analysis, 344–5
  distinctive, in qualitative research, 113
  human feeling for, 124
  implicit, 221
  incorporated, 221
  perspective-transcending, 82–3
  praxeological sociology of, 220, 223
  prior, 140
  social determination, 231n
  sociology of, 124, 218, 223
  a-theoretical, 221
  theoretical *see* theoretical knowledge
  useful, 84
  see also epistemology/epistemological issues
knowledge workers, 112
Kwalitatief Sterk, 280
KWALON experiment, 14
Kwalon Experiment, 280
Kwoiam, myth of, 400, 404, 405

landscape, 426
language
  discourse analysis, 345
  focus groups, 321–2
  and form, 371–2
  language-dominant view of, 340
  predicative level, 186
  sociology of, 236
  sound as, 424
  see also corpora, spoken language
laughter, 73–4
lay theories, 564
leading metaphors, 455
Learning to Labour (Willis), 250
legal hermeneutics, 137
Leitz, Leica, 406n
lexical searching, 286
life-cycle transitions, 222
life-world
  agency in, 252
  concept, 186
  meaningful structures, 186–8
  pragmatic life-world theory as social anthropology, 188–9
  protosociology, phenomenological life-world analysis as, 188
  reflexivity, 110
  small social life-worlds in phenomenological analysis, 195–6
  see also phenomenology
lines-of-argument synthesis, 482–3
linguistic register, 371

SUBJECT INDEX

linked turns, 332
linking of data, 24
listening, selective, 428
literacy theory, critical, 588
literary texts, 374
literary transcription, 69, 71
Little Orphan Annie (newspaper cartoon), 171–2
lived experience, 189–90, 192, 194, 248, 256
Local Interaction Platforms, 119
logic of research, three-stage, 130–1
logical reasoning, 123, 125, 130
  see also abduction; deduction; induction
Logical Structure of the World, The (Carnap), 186
"logic-in-use," 22
loose team research, 86
Lord of the Rings film trilogy, 412, 416, 418
loudness, 72
lower-order generalizability, 541
lurking, 263, 266

Mabuiag island (Torres Straits), 400
Macintosh computer, 278, 281
macro narratives, 212
Madonna (singer), 252
mainstream realism, 574, 580, 582n
Manchester, England *see* Greater Manchester
Maori community, 515, 516
maps, 28
Married . With Children (film), 252, 255
mass communication, circuit of, 383–4
Massively Multiplayer Online Role-Playing Games (MMORPGs), 454, 458
mathesis universalis, 188, 191
matrices (tables), 28, 29
Max Planck Institute for Psycholinguistics, 337
Max Planck Institute for the Study of Religious and Ethnic Diversity, 98
maximum variation sampling, 51
MAXQDA program (CAQDAS), 8, 280, 281, 286, 288, 290, 292, 459
  coding brackets, *284*
meaning
  abduction, 130
  in film, 410, 411
  fundamental constitution in practice and interaction, 223–4
  iconographic and iconological, 230
  image analysis, 396
  implicit, 223
  imposition by ruling elites, 141
  interpretation, 136
  latent, 399
  life-world, meaningful structures, 186–8
  making sense, 51–5, 316–18, 372–3
  manifest and latent, 235–6
  observations, 356
  and phenomenology, 190
  post-positivist foundational systems of, 580

meaning *cont.*
  reflexivity, 110
  self-generated meanings, in narrative analysis, 204, 205
  sense-making, 572
  subjective, 218, 219
  see also interpretation; phenomenology
Meaningful Structure of the Social World, The (Schutz), 186
measurement-oriented analysis, 361
media research, 76, 248–9
  see also news media
mediated accounts, gridding and plotting strategies, 387–9
Medical Research Council, Complex Interventions funding stream, 496
Mehanna (Niger town), 403, 404
member checks, 511, 512
membership categorization analysis (MCA), 336
Membership Roles in Field Research (Adler), 356
memoirs, 582n
memory, 23
memos, 24, 31
  example, 165–6
  software, 278
  writing and sorting, 163–5
meta narratives, 212
meta-analysis, qualitative, 15, 481–95
  credibility checks, 490
  data analysis, 488–9
  data preparation, 488
  defined, 481–2
  developmental and theoretical background, 482–5
  epistemological issues, 486
  grounded formal theory, 484–5
  limitations, 492–3
  new developments/perspectives, 493
  other qualitative meta-analysis methods (brand name), 485
  presentation of findings, 490
  primary studies, appraisal, 487–8
  procedures, generic description, 486–90
  psychotherapy research, example of qualitative meta-analysis in, 490–2
  research question, 486
  selection of original studies, 486–7
  use of, 492
meta-data analysis, 483
meta-ethnography, 482–3
meta-method, 483
metanarratives, 96
metaphor, 454, 455, 482
meta-study, 483–4
metasummary, 484, 485
meta-synthesis, 481, 483, 484
meta-theory, 483
Method of Sociology, The (Znaniecki), 556
method-appropriate criteria, 498

microethnographic approaches, 22
Microsoft Word, 267
middle-range theories
　examples, 562
　general theoretical concepts, using to develop, 564–5
　transferring to new research domains, 566–7
migration, 98–9
mind, 127
Mirrors and Masks (Strauss), 564
MISTRA (Swedish Foundation for Strategic Environmental Research), 119
Mistra – Urban Futures (M-UF), 119
mixed and multiple methods research, 11, 508, 518
　analysis of core components, 525
　analysis of supplementary components, 525–6
　blending, 527
　certainty, 526
　complex mixed-method project, *537*
　core project, 538
　data collection, 537
　data transformation, 527
　definitions, 538–9
　design considerations, 524–6
　diagramming, 529–36
　ethical issues, 514–15
　flowcharting symbols and techniques, 531–4, *532–3*
　　audit trail, developing, 535
　　benefits, 534–6
　　conventions, 531–2
　　object manipulation, 534–5
　　pre-study planning, facilitating, 534–5
　　team science, communicating in, 535
　　transparency of design, enhancing, 535
　hypothetical mixed-methods project, *530*
　integration patterns, 528–9
　meaning of 'qualitatively driven,' 538–9
　mixed methods design, 538
　modes of analytic integration in qualitatively driven designs, 526–7
　multiple methods design, 538
　point of interface, 528
　positions for analytic integration of results, 527–8
　qualitative supplementary component, 526
　qualitatively driven designs, analytic integration, 524–38
　quantitative supplementary component, 526
　reasons for, 524
　results narrative, 528, 529
　sampling strategies, 525
　sequential qualitatively driven design planned reflexively during project, *532*, 534, 538
　simultaneous qualitatively driven design, *533*, 534, 538
　software, 290
　supplementary project, 538
　theoretical drive and thrust, 525, 536
　transparency of design, 535

MMORPGs (Massively Multiplayer Online Role-Playing Games), 454, 458
mobile data, 450
mobile data platforms, 459–61
mobile phones, 328
modernist phase, qualitative research, 6–7
modus operandi method, 238, 549
Month at the Lake, A (film), 69
mortality data, 403
motives, 218
multi-dimensionality, typification, 229–30
multimodal pastiches, 290
multiple realities, 187
Murray Manor nursing home, 39, 40, 41, 42
music, 424, 432
Mythologies (Barthes), 254

naive inductivism, problems, 555
Nanook of the North (silent documentary), 359–60
narrative analysis, 203–16
　categories, working with, 26–7
　combined approaches, 206
　connecting strategies, 22, 27
　culture as narrative, seeing, 37–9
　development of narrative research, 204
　and discourse analysis, 342
　film, 415–16
　generalization, 545
　guidelines for researchers, 206
　holistic versus categorical approaches, 27
　interpretation, 146–7
　interviews, 210–12, 300, 303–4
　macro narratives, 212
　research and practice, 589–90
　stories, common elements, 304
　theories, narratives replacing, 7
　see also constructionist narrative analysis
narrative structures, 371
National School of Architecture, Grenoble, 427
nationalism, 100
Natural Born Killers (film), 255, 419
natural sciences, and *Geisteswissenschaften*, 234
neo-nationalism, qualitative comparison in data analysis, 104, 105–6
neo-positivist inquiries, 298
Net, the *see* Internet
Netherlands Association for Qualitative Research, 280
netnographic analysis, 262–76
　auto-archiving, 263
　auto-ethnography, 266
　auto-netnography, 266
　challenges of netnographic fieldwork, 264–5
　characteristics of netnographic field data, 263–4
　coding, 270
　communication connectedness, 263, 264
　communicative variety, 263–4
　data collection and types, 266–8
　defining netnography, 262–3

netnographic analysis *cont.*
  epistemological issues, 265
  ethical issues, 268–9
  and ethnography, 262, 263, 264, 269–70, 274
  field site accessibility, 263
  future perspectives, 273–5
  illustration, 269–73
  and Internet, 262, 265
  limits, 264
  and lurking, 263, 266
  as naturalistic method, 263
  procedures, 265–6
  pure netnographies, 265
  sites and entrée, 265–6
  and social media, 262, 263, 273–4
  Wikipedia entry, 272–3
networks (figures), 28, 29
New Left, UK, 250
New Orleans Sniper: A Phenomenological Case Study of Constituting the Other (Waksler), 193–4
New Oxford American Dictionary, 502
New Vic theatre, English Midlands, 594–5
news media, 380–93
  analytic example, 385–91
  coding, 389
  content analysis, limits, 381–3
  and daily life, 380–1
  discrepancies, checking for, 389
  homeless people, study of, 382, 383, 386, 387, *388*, 389, 390, 392
  identifying topic/scope of data required, 386–7
  and journalists, 383, 384, 385, 386, 387, 388, 392
  key themes, identifying, selecting or ordering, 389–90
  mass communication, media analysis focused on, 383–4
  mediated accounts, gridding and plotting strategies, 387–9
  new analytic story, linking and constructing, 390–1
  overall interpretation and writing, 391
  societal practices, 381
  text-in-context, 383, 384
  textual capture, 381–3
nodes, 286
noetic–noematic unity, phenomenon as, 185
noise, 424, 432
non-verbal communication, 316, 327, 330, 439
notations/notation systems
  Jeffersonian Transcript Notation, 74, 76, 330
  transcription, 67, 74–5
novels, film adaptations, 415–16
NVivo program (CAQDAS), 280, 281, 282, 286, 288, 289, 292, 324, 459

objective hermeneutics, 231n, 235
  application, 245
  case-structures, 236
  interviews, 302
  limitations, 244–5
  method, 235, 243
  text as object of data analysis, 235
  text interpretation, 238–44
    exclusion of content, 239–40
    extensivity, 243–4
    literal meaning, taking seriously, 240–1
    sequentiality, 241–3
  see also hermeneutics
objectivity, 476–7
observational data, 267
observations, 354–66
  analysis, 359–61
  analytical problem, as 'impossible attempt,' 355
  constructionist analysis, 361–2
  covert and overt observer roles, 356–7
  description, as analysis, 359–60
  ethnographic techniques, 354
  field, the, 355–9
  inductive, 360–1
  observer–observed relationships, 355–9, 363
  rapport, 357–8
  researcher self, 358–9
  roles, 356–7
  scientific, 354
  theoryladenness of observation, 555, 557
observer–observed relationships, 355–9, 363
Observers Observed (Stocking), 355
offside rule, soccer, 131–3
online–offline relations, 455, 456
ontology, 140, 512, 516
  focus groups, 314–16
open coding, 270, 284
open debate, challenges to, 89–90
open questions, 231
opportunistic sampling, 55
oral history, 586–7, 588, 589, 594
Oral History Association, 513
orchestration, 439
organization of discourse, 225
organizational categories, 25
originality, 499
orthography, standard, 66, 68, 70–1
Other, The, 573, 580
Others Knowing Others (Fowler and Hardesty), 355
overlaid laughter, 73–4

pain management research, 527
'Palo Alto' group, 438
paradigms
  alternative, 7
  paradigmatic relations, 23
  proliferation, 308, 309
paralinguistic transcription, 66, 67, 73–4

paramount topics (PT), 225
parapraxis, 240–1
partiality, cultural studies, 249, 255
participant experience, 266
participant observation, 37, 83, 103, 217, 439
    cultural studies, 252, 256
participant orientations, 336
participatory action research (PAR), 588, 594
participatory structures, 454–5, 456
participatory visual research, 399
particularism, 95, 96, 97
password protection, 282, 306
pattern-identification, conversation analysis, 332–3
pause duration, transcription, 73
pdf formats, 281, 292
'peer-debriefing,' 501
pem-recorders/linear pem recorders, 430
'people-processing professions,' 368
perception, 124, 127, 186, 189
performance
    and arts-based inquiry, 578–9
    and oral history, 594–5
    performance turn, cultural studies, 250
    performance-as-interpretation, 569
    texts, 582n
    writer-as-performer, 571, 572
'period eye,' 397
peripheral membership, 356
Persistent Vegetative State (PVS), 196
person–environmental fit model, 39
perspectivism, 80–1, 90
petites perceptions, 127
phenomenological hermeneutics, 196–7, 198
Phenomenological Movement, 185
phenomenological sociology
    as new approach to empirical research, 191–4
    New Orleans sniper example (1973), 193–4
    as new sociological paradigm, 191–2
phenomenology, 184–202
    analysis methods (Husserl), 185–6
    and data analysis, 184, 194
    as empirical research procedure, 184, 188, 194–8, 195
    and epistemology, 184, 185, 198
    ethnophenomenology, 198
    future prospects, 200
    hermeneutics, phenomenological, 196–7
    interviews, influence on, 302
    life-world, meaningful structures, 186–8
    limits, 198–9
    mundane, 186–8, 198
    noetic–noematic unity, phenomenon as, 185
    notion of, 185
    versus observer's perspective, 195–6
    origins, 184, 185–6
    phenomenological research, 143
    as a philosophy, 188
    as protosociology, 188–91

phenomenology *cont.*
    small social life-worlds in phenomenological analysis, 195–6
    social, 219
    and sociology, 184, 188, 189
    'things themselves,' analysis of, 184, 185–6
Phenomenology of the Social World (Schutz), 186
phenomenon, notion of, 185
philological hermeneutics, 137
philosophical hermeneutics, 234, 235
phonetic transcription, 72
photo-elicitation, 401
photography, 394, 396, 401
    video compared, 439–40
pictures
    image analysis, 398–400
    interpretation, 230–1
pitch, 72
point of interface, 528
political science, comparative practices, 99, 100
popular culture, 257–8
Port Royal School, 123
portraits, 26
positioning analysis, 320–1, 322
postmodernism, 7, 249, 252, 298, 543
post-mythic consciousness, 136
post-positivism, 575, 580
post-structuralism, 255, 305, 577–9
    criticisms, 579
postulate of adequacy (Schutz), 188
power
    constructionist narrative analysis, power relations, 206
    and culture, conjunctural analysis, 247–50
    ethical issues, 512
    news media, 381
    reflexivity, 114
    and resistance, 252
    sharing at methodological level, 518
pragmatism/pragmatic research, 64–5, 249, 591–2
    pragmatic life-world theory as social anthropology, 188–9
praxeological sociology of knowledge, 220, 223
preconceived hypotheses, forcing data to fit, 306
predisposition, theoretical, 126
pre-knowledge, 230
presentation of findings, 490, 502–7
Presidential Commission for the Study of Bioethics Issues, 519
pre-study planning, 534–5
pre-understanding, 302
prison research, 471, 472–3, 547
problem-solving, 124
professional vision, 397
profiles, 23, 27
project evaluation, formative (2008–10), 115–18
promises, avoiding, 513
propositions, 231n

SUBJECT INDEX

prosodic transcription, 66, 72–3
Protestant ethic, 562
protosociology
   and empirical research, 189
   phenomenological life-world analysis as, 188
   phenomenology as, 188–91
provisional analysis, 355, 359
proximal similarity, 542
pseudonyms, 306
psychoanalytic case study, 142–3
psychoanalytical analysis, 398
psycholinguistic research, 68
psychotherapy research, example of qualitative meta-analysis in, 490–2
Pulp Fiction (film), 412
purposive/purposeful sampling, 51, 54, 56, 62n, 498, 500

QDA Miner program (CAQDAS), 280, 281
Qualidata (British archive), 469
qualitative content analysis *see* content analysis, qualitative
qualitative data analysis (QDA)
   aims, 5–6
   basics, 19
   and computers, 30–1, 277
      see also software
   concepts, 15, 16, 19
   content versus formal aspects, 6
   contexts, 15, 19
   defined, 5–6
   frameworks, 15
   qualitative data analysis 2.0, 13–15
   relations in, 23–4
   theory *see* theory of qualitative data analysis
Qualitative Data Analysis (QDA) program, 4, 274
qualitative research
   combining with quantitative research, 595–6
   'creation myth,' 497
   and creative arts, 593–5
   dismissal by policy-makers, reasons for, 585–6
   and feminism, 586–8, 589
   and hermeneutics, 235
   history, in social sciences, 570
   internationalization of, 8
   as non-sequential, 36
   and oral history, 586–7, 588, 589
   paradigm disputes, 570
   potential uses of data and findings, 510–11
   proliferation of, 4–5
   qualitative social research, 125
   reanalysis of qualitative data, 472–3
   semiotic and structural analysis of data, 253–4
   short history, 586–9
   stages, historical, 6–7, *8*
   tacit assumptions of major methods, 8
   theory building/testing debate in tradition of, 556–60

qualitative research *cont.*
   as tool for social change, 514–20
   video, application to, 435–6
quality of data analysis, 496–509
   addressing of issues in analyzing, 498–507
   analytical trails, retracing and presenting, 505–6
   assumptions, 497
   CAQDAS (Computer-Assisted Qualitative Data Analysis), 500, 505
   connecting strategies, 503–4
   criteria and checklists, 497–8
   ethical issues, 520–1
   explicating and refining codes, 501–2
   focus groups, 501
   grounded theory, 499, 500, 507
   initial coding, 499
   judging, 308–9
   new developments/critical reflection, 507–8
   patterning, 500–1
   presentation of findings, 502–7
   processing of data, 498–9
   thematic analysis, 499, 501, 503
   theoretical generalization, 507, 540
Qualrus program (CAQDAS), 280
quantitative induction, 128, 129
quantitative research, 36
   abduction, 126
   combining with qualitative research, 595–6
   content analysis, 173, 181
   image analysis, 399
   induction, 128–30
   mixed and multiple methods design, 526
   sampling strategies, 50
   transcription, 65
quasi-statistics, 545
queer theory, 412
quota sampling, 54

radical contextualism, 252, 254
random sampling, 50
rapport, 357–8
rationality, 188
reader generalizability, 541
Reading the Romance (Radway), 251, 254
reanalysis of qualitative data, 15, 467–80
   benefits
      advancing theory, 471
      economy, 471–2
      strengthening qualitative research, 472–3
   and conversation analysis, 473
   cultivation of, 467–8
   difficulties, 475, 476
   direct contact with data, 473
   distinguished from other qualitative methods, 472
   ethical issues, 476–7
   facilitation, 474
   motives and contexts, 469–70
   prison study (Sweden), 471, 472–3

reanalysis of qualitative data *cont.*
   research steps, 473–5
   sources, 468
   stumbling blocks, 475–6
   value of, 477–8
reasoning habits, 124
received text, 410
reception, film analysis, 410–11, 412, 421
recorded interactions
   limits of studying, 335–6
   naturally occurring, 327–9
referential reflexivity, 111–12
reflecting interpretation, 224, 225, 226–7
   case-internal comparative analysis, 228–9
   example, 228
reflexive modernization, 111
reflexivity, 16, 83–4, 109–22, 223, 306
   academic research projects (2002–7), 114–15
   consequences and issues, 111–13
   cultural studies, 248, 250, 251, 256, 257
   designing reflexive processes and projects (from 2009), 118–20
   endogenous, 111
   epistemological, 191
   experiences and insights, 113–20
   feminist perspective, 110–11
   formative project evaluation (2008–10), 115–18
   history and content, 109–11
   multiple reflexivities, 113, 117
   referential, 111–12
   reflexive accounting, 505
   relational nature of in qualitative research, 116
   self-reflexivity, 251, 256, 257
   video analysis, 442
refutational synthesis, 482
regional comparison, 101
relativism, 112
representation
   crisis of, 7
   ethical issues, 512, 515–18
   film analysis, 413–14
   reflexivity, 117
   on social level, 515–18
   systems of, 414
   writing, 573
representativeness, 51, 540, 542, 543, 546, 547
Research Councils, 118
research ethics *see* ethical issues
Research Excellence Framework, 497
research process, 9–10, 207, 249, 588
researcher self, observing, 358–9
"researcher-as-instrument," role of, 263
resistance perspective, cultural studies, 250–3
   power and resistance, 252
retrieval, 285, 286–8, 453
retroduction, 134n, 561
Retrofitting the City project, 118
rhetoric, 47, 372

Rhinoceros (Ionesco), 128
roles, 356–7
romance novels, 251, 254
Rorschach ink blot test, 402
rules, hermeneutics, 237–8

SAGE Handbook of Qualitative Research (Denzin and Lincoln), 277
sample sound notation systems, 431
sampling strategies, 49–63
   'atypical' cases, 62
   challenging assumptions, 57–9
   context of case, 50
   convenience sampling, 55
   emblematic sampling, 54
   ethnographic, 445
   'eureka moments,' 59, 60
   exploring phenomenon in no particular order, 55
   exploring phenomenon through somebody else's order, 55–7
   extreme/deviant case sampling, 54
   focus groups, 318
   generalization, 50–3, 62, 549–50n
   genres, 50
   ideas, building, 57–9
   information-rich cases, 50, 56–7
   initial round of sampling, 53–5
   intensity sampling, 54
   maximum variation sampling, 51
   mixed and multiple methods design, 525
   opportunistic sampling, 55
   others, presenting data to, 60–2
   phenomena, making sense of, 51–5
   practical solutions, finding, 59–60
   public accounts, 51
   purposive/purposeful, 51, 54, 56, 62n, 498, 500
   quota sampling, 54
   random sampling, 50
   representativeness, 51, 540
   significance of sampling, 49
   snowball sampling, 54
   theoretical sampling, 10, 58–9, 283
   typicality, 53–4, 59, 61
   video, 445–6
sampling-in-action, 62
saturation, 475, 526, 549
Science in Society programme (ESRC), 114, 115
scientific observation, 354
scientism, 112
searching, in software, 286–8
Second Life, 455
segmentation, 24, 178
self-disclosure, 357
self-inhibiting, 166
self-isolation, 165–6
self-presentation structures, 454, 455–6
self-protection, 165
self-referential systems, 223

self-reflexivity, 251, 256, 257
semantic memory, 23
semiotic analysis, 253–4, 398, 399
semi-structured interviews, 217, 527
sequentiality, 241–3
  conversation analysis, 332, 333
  video, sequential analysis, 440, *441*, 442–4
sex workers, community mobilization, 83
sexual policy-making, impact of life stories, 589
SIDA (Swedish International Development Cooperation Agency), 119
sign language, 327
Sign Language Community, 518
signals, 426
signs, 253–4, 343
similarity/contiguity distinction, 22–3, 31
  relations in qualitative data analysis, 23–4
Simon Fraser University, Vancouver, 425
simulacre, 400
SIR (Sound-Image, Data Records), 439
SixDegrees (social networking site), 457
SMS (Short Message Service), 450, 459, 460
snowball sampling, 54
social anthropology, pragmatic life-world theory as, 188–9
Social Construction of Reality, The (Berger and Luckmann), 189
social interaction
  audiovisual data, analyzing, 439–40
  interpretive video analysis, 436, 438–9
social media/social networking sites
  and netnographic analysis, 262, 263, 273–4
  virtual data, 453, 457, 458, 459
Social Mention (search engine), 271
social phenomenology, 219
social representation theory, 590, 594
social science
  comparative practices, 96
  and constructionism, 203
  documentary method, 218
  and everyday theorizing, 110
  narrative turn in, 204
  news media, 381, 383
social shielding, 166
social status, and open debate, 89, 90
'social' Web, 452
socio-genetic attitude, 218, 220
socio-genetic typification, 229
sociographic structures, 454, 455
sociological imagination, 502
sociology
  formal, 471
  German, 184, 191, 219, 236
  of knowledge, 124, 218, 223
  'non-obvious,' 472
  phenomenological, as new approach to empirical research, 191–4
  and phenomenology, 184, 188, 189

sociology *cont.*
  praxeological sociology of knowledge, 223
  as a science, 188
  visual, 438
  see also protosociology
socio-scientific research, 125
software, 277–94
  analysis, using CAQDAS, 281–8
  analytic approaches supported, 289–91
  Boolean searching, 278, 279, 287, 289
  core functions, 279–80
  discourse analysis, 289–90
  file formats, 282
  in Germany, 8
  grounded theory, 280, 284
  mixed methods, 290
  pdf formats, 281, 292
  program selection, 279–81
  teamworking, 290–1
  thematic analysis, 289
  "theory-building" programs, 31
  video analysis, 436
  see also CAQDAS (Computer-Assisted Qualitative Data Analysis)
Songhay society, symbolic forms, 403, 404
sonic effects, 427–8
Sonic Experience: A Guide to Everyday Sounds (Augoyard and Torgue), 427
sonic fieldwork, 429
sonic warfare, 432
sound, 424–34
  analysis, 430–2
  auditory culture and sound culture studies, 428–30, 432
  as communication, 424
  ecology and acoustic communication, 425–7
  as language, 424
  loudness, 72
  pitch, 72
  sonic experience/effects, 427–8
  sound studies, 432, 433
  development of, 425–30
sound culture studies, 428–30, 432
sound film, 419
sound recording, 430, 431
soundmarks, 426
Soundscape (Schafer), 425
soundscapes, 426, 431, 433n
spatial differentiation, 8
specificity of research findings, 596
speech acts, 239–40, 372
SPSS software, 14
standard orthography, 66, 68, 70–1
standpoint theory, 231n, 497, 588
stanzas, 24
static data, 452–3
statistical conclusion validity, 549n
statistical generalization, 540

statistical inference, in experiments, 549n
statistical techniques, qualitative content analysis, 180
storytelling
    interpretation as, 572
    techniques, in film analysis, 415
Straussian coding paradigm, 566
Strengths and Difficulties Questionnaire (SDQ), 289
stress, 72
structuralist linguistics, 22–3
Structures of the Life-World, The (Schutz and Luckmann), 188
subcategories, 30
subjective experience, 186, 187, 192, 194
subordinated topics (ST), 225
substantive categories, 25, 28
substantive theories, 485
sub-subordinated topics (SSTs), 225
subsumption, 127, 176
subtle realism, 314
suicide, 375–7
Suicide Prevention Center, Los Angeles, 328
summarization, 489
supportive voice, researcher, 209
suprasegmental notation signs, 74
SURF (Centre for Sustainable Urban and Regional Futures), University of Salford, 113, 114, 115, 118, 119
surprise, 126, 133
survey-type data, 314
suspicion, hermeneutics of, 81
'suspicious' interpretation, 137–8, 142, 145, 147
Swedish Foundation for Strategic Environmental Research (MISTRA), 119
Swedish International Development Cooperation Agency (SIDA), 119
syllogisms, 123
synecdoche effect, 428
syntagmatic (contiguity-based) relations, 23
synthesis
    lines-of-argument, 482–3
    meta-synthesis, 481, 483, 484
    reciprocal translations as, 482
    refutational, 482
    thematic, 485
systematic self-observation, 358
systems theory, 219

talk-in-interaction, 74, 329
Taste of Ethnographic Things, The (Stoller), 403
Teamroom Trade (Humphreys), 470
teamworking, 86, 290–1
technical essentialism, 507
teleological accounts, twentieth century, 120
tertium comparationis, 104, 188, 189
text interpretation, 238–44
    exclusion of content, 239–40
    film texts, 411, 415–16
    literal meaning, taking seriously, 240–1
    textual and contextual analysis perspectives, 253–6

text-in-context, 383, 384
textual exegesis, 234
The WELL (online community), 454
thematic synthesis, 485
themes/thematic analysis, 23, 26, 27, 147, 289, 305
    news media, analyzing, 389–90
    quality of data analysis, 499, 501, 503
    superficial thematic content analysis, 499
theoretical categories, 25–6
theoretical coding, 159–61, 558
theoretical congestion, 506
theoretical generalization, 507, 540
theoretical imagination, 597
theoretical inference, 53, 540
theoretical knowledge
    dimensions and types, 562–4
    empirical content, 563–4
    explicitness, degree of, 563
    scope, 562–3
    source, 563
theoretical sampling, 10, 58–9, 283
theoretical sensitivity, 558
theories
    crucial elements, 560–1
    definition of 'theory,' 21–2
    facts, 582n
    grand, 96, 562
    interpretation, 138, 578
    lay, 564
    linkages with data, 561–2
    meta-theory, 483
    middle-range *see* middle-range theories
    narratives replacing, 7
    standpoint, 231n, 497, 588
    see also theoretical categories; theoretical coding; theoretical congestion; theoretical generalization; theoretical imagination; theoretical inference; theoretical knowledge; theoretical sampling; theoretical sensitivity; theorization from data; theory of qualitative data analysis
theorization from data, 554–68
    challenges, 554–6
    Chicago School and theory building, 556–7
    crucial elements of theories, 560–1
    current developments, 559–60
    dimensions and types of theoretical knowledge, 562–4
    grounded theory, discovery, 557–8
    linkages between theory and data, 561–2
    middle-range theories
        general theoretical concepts, using to develop, 564–5
        transferring to new research domains, 566–7
    naive inductivism, 555
    need for methodology of discovery, 555–6
    theoretical background, 560–4
    theory building/testing debate in qualitative research tradition, 556–60

theorization from data *cont.*
 types of theorizing, 564–7
 use of qualitative data to challenge theoretical concepts, 565–6
theory of qualitative data analysis, 21–34
 categorizing strategies, 24–5
 coding categories, types, 25–6
 connecting strategies, 27–8
 definition of 'good' theory, 133
 displays as categorizing and connecting strategies, 28–9
 and sampling strategies, 58–9
 similarity and contiguity, 22–3
 working with categories, 26–7
 see also theorization from data
"theory-building" programs, 31
"theory-in-use," 22
theoryladenness of observation, 555, 557
thick description, 249, 271, 570
Third Man, The (film), 73
time norms, cultural, 476
time–space compression, 98
Torres Straits Islands, 400, 404, 405, 406n
traditional period, qualitative research, 6
traditionalists, 570
training, transcribers, 70
Trance and Dance in Bali (film), 396, 406n
Transana (data management program), 280–1, 330
transcendental reduction, 186
transcription, 64–78, 147
 appropriate use, 65
 coding, 67
 conversation analysis, 330, 338
 court transcripts, 68
 defined, 66–7
 deletions and additions, 68
 description, 67
 discourse analysis, 343, 344
  discourse transcription (DT), 68, 75, 76
 duration, 73
 heterogeneity of purposes served by, 64
 HIAT acronym, 71, 75, 76
 interviews, 64, 299, 300
 Jeffersonian Transcript Notation, 74, 76
 loudness, 72
 minimal transcript, 75
 narrative analysis, 207–8
 new technologies/perspectives, 76
 non-linguistic activity, 67
 notation/notation systems, 67, 74–5
 pitch, 72
 punctuation of, 299
 research results, 68–70
 standard orthography, 66, 68, 70–1
 terminology, 66–70
 transcribers and transcript users, 68, 70
 transcript, 67, 174
 transcription systems, 68
 turn-taking, transcribing, 66, 75–6

transcription *cont.*
 as universally indispensible step in research, 65–6
 verbatim transcripts, 498, 499
 vocal behaviour components, 70–4
 see also interviews
transferability, generalization, 52, 541
transference, 143
transformative assumptions, ethical issues, 515, 516, 517
translation, narrative analysis, 208
transparency, 291, 535
Treatise of Human Nature, A (Hume), 22
triangulation, 11–12, 191, 490, 511
troubled curiosity, 363
Truman Show, The (TV series), 412, 417
truth, 141
 deductive reasoning, 127–8
turn design, 332, 333, 337
Twitter, 273, 453, 457, 458, 459
typicality, sampling strategies, 53–4, 59, 61
typification, 218, 229–30
typologies, *230*, 231n

UNAIDS (UN agency responsible for AIDS research), 519–20
understanding, 110, 187, 222, 234
unitizing, 24
universal hermeneutics, 137
universalism, 95, 97
universities, as engines of growth or knowledge factories, 112
University of Arts, Berlin, 425
University of Manchester, Institute of Innovation Research, 116
University of Salford, Centre for Sustainable Urban and Regional Futures (SURF), 113, 114, 115, 118, 119
Urban Futures Arena, 119

validity, 179, 237, 549n
verbal data, 249
 visual distinguished, 248
verbal transcription, 66, 70–2
verbatim transcripts, 498, 499
verstehen (understanding), 110, 187, 222
video/videography, 435–49
 analysis process, *445*, 446
 application to qualitative research, 435–6
 audiovisual data of social interaction, analyzing, 439–40
 audio-visual discourse compared to videography, 447
 computer software, 282
 data, video recordings as, 436–8
 data sessions, 446
 dense visual content, 439, 444

video/videography *cont.*
  digitalization, 446–7
  ethnography, 444–5
  interpretation, 230–1
  interpretative analysis, 436, 438–9
  limits of videography, 446–7
  'native' video data, 437–8
  new tendencies, 446–7
  omnipresence in everyday life, 435
  permanence, 440
  photography compared, 439–40
  reactivity problem, 437
  researchers, video data induced by, 437
  sampling strategies, 445–6
  sequential analysis, 440, *441*, 442–4
  social interaction, interpretative analysis, 436, 438–9
  sorts of data, 436–8
  standardized analysis, 436
  as temporal medium, 439–40
  3D video and surround sound, 438
  types of analysis, 436–8
  video-webnography, 446
Vienna Circle, 555
violence, 474
virtual community, 454–6
virtual data, 450–66
  analysis issues, 458–9
  community research, virtual, 454–6
  cyberspace, 450, 451, 454
  defined, 450
  dynamic, 452, 453–4
  ethical issues, 461
  features, 452
  first generation of Internet studies, 450
  mobile data platforms, 459–61
  practical analytic approaches, 454–9
  second generation of Internet studies, 450–1
  social network platforms, 456–8
  static, 452–3
  theoretical approaches, 451–4
  third generation of Internet studies, 451
virtual ethnography, 446
visual anthropology, 360, 400–2
visual data, verbal distinguished, 248
visual enskillment, 397
Visual Explanations (Tufte), 402–3
visual sociology, 438
vocal behaviour components
  eye dialect, 71–2
  literary transcription, 69, 71
  paralinguistic transcription, 66, 67, 73–4

vocal behaviour components *cont.*
  phonetic transcription, 72
  prosodic transcription, 66, 72–3
  standard orthography, 66, 68, 70–1
  verbal, 66, 70–2
voice, 512, 515–18, 589
  researcher, 209

waveforms, 428
Wayback Machine, 264, 453
Ways of Seeing (Berger), 399–400
Web 2.0, 456
windjammers, 430
Windows for the PC, 278
  Windows 7, 267
Wordle (free word cloud generator), 273
word-processing, 282
World as Text, The (reader in German), 245n
World Forum for Acoustic Ecology, 433n
World Soundscape Project, Vancouver, 425, 431
World Wide Web (WWW), 452
writing, 569–84
  descriptive realism, 575, 582n
  desire, 573
  ethical issues, 513–14
  experimental, 574, 582n
  as form of pedagogy, 569, 570
  future perspectives, 581
  interpretation as storytelling, 572
  interpretive realism, 574–5
  interpretive strategies, analysis, 575–9
  legitimation, 573
  mainstream realist, 574, 580, 582n
  models of writer, 573–4
  moving from field, to text, to reader, 571–2
  multiple interpretive communities, 579–81
  news media, 391
  poles on a continuum, 570–1
  process of, 7
  realistic styles, 574–5
  representation, 573
  right and left pole methodologies, 570
  sense-making, 572
  social justice, 570
  teaching to left pole for bricoleurs, 570–1
  writer-as-performer, 571, 572
Writing for Social Scientists (Becker), 573
Writing Women's Worlds: Bedouin Stories (Abu-Lughod), 38

X-Men films, 418–19

YouTube, 292, 458